# Edmunds.com
# 2005
# New Cars
# & Trucks
# Buyer's Guide

where smart car buyers start®

# Table of Contents

## Edmunds.com New Cars & Trucks Buyer's Guide

2005 Annual, Volume C3801
ISBN: 0-87759-686-7  ISSN: 1541-8502

Library of Congress Catalog Card No: 71-80100

Copyright ©2005 Edmunds.com, Inc.
Further copyright information on page 4

## Contents

### All-New for 2005 Vehicle Pages

### 2005 Model Year Vehicles

# Table of Contents

**Publisher**
Peter Steinlauf

**President**
Jeremy Anwyl

**Chief Operating Officer**
Avi Steinlauf

**Vice President, Consumer Services**
Matthew Kumin

**Editorial Director**
Kevin Smith

**Editor in Chief**
Karl Brauer

**Managing Editor**
Donna DeRosa

**Senior Road Test Editor**
Ed Hellwig

**Manager of Vehicle Testing**
Kelly Toepke

**Senior Editor, Content & Syndication**
Erin Riches

**Senior Consumer Advice Editor**
Phil Reed

**Photography Editor**
Scott Jacobs

**Road Test Editors**
John DiPietro, Brian Moody, Dan Kahn

**New Vehicle Reviews Editor**
Jeff Bryan

**Content Editor**
Warren Clarke

**Production Editor**
Caroline Pardilla

**Vice President, Data Analysis and
Operations**
Jane Liu, Ph.D.

**Director, Automotive Research**
Allyson Colgrove

**Manager, New Vehicle Data**
Ken Brown

**Photographic Data Specialist**
Matt Landish

**Data Editors, New Vehicles**
Armando Espinoza, Dianne Hassan, Artis
Houston, KJ Jones, Casey Jordan, Wandi
Kunene, Larry London, Henry Roland,
David Sun, Rex Tokeshi-Torres

**Programmer, Book Automation**
John Song

**Director, Creative Services**
Guy Schackman

**Design Manager, Creative Services**
Justin Nowlen

**Book Designer and Master Layout**
Jeff Zugale

**Production Artists**
Sara Flemming, Nadia Potiyenok

**Printed in USA**

# Welcome to the
# 2005 New Cars and Trucks Buyer's Guide

Ever since we published our first automotive pricing guide in 1966, the name Edmunds has been associated with timely, accurate and unbiased new and used vehicle information. Whether it was advice on getting the best deal when buying a vehicle, a complete breakdown of new car and truck pricing or a straightforward, consumer-friendly explanation of terms like "incentive" and "holdback," Edmunds has been helping car shoppers for 38 years.

In 1994 Edmunds took a monumental step forward by offering all this valuable content to Internet users…for free! As the first automotive pricing company to go on-line, we introduced buyers to the concept of "information transparency," which essentially means giving consumers access to all the same pricing information used by automotive dealers and manufacturers. No one could match the quality of our on-line content offering in 1994, and over a decade later, Edmunds.com continues to be an information pioneer in the automotive industry.

## How does this affect the book?

But how has the electronic age affected our stalwart print publications? Is there room in this world of high-speed Internet access and "information on demand" for a buyer's guide constructed from paper and ink?

The answer (in case you haven't guessed from the book you hold in your hands) is yes. But to make a buyer's guide that works in the 21st century, we have focused on a print publication's advantages over electronic media. Specifically, our new book offers long-term reference material rather than short-term data that is out of date before the book ever reaches store shelves. While a specific car or truck might have several small price changes in a 12-month period, the basic range of pricing for any given model stays consistent. Additionally, a vehicle's interior design, exterior styling, safety features and driving impressions remain consistent throughout a given model year.

## How does this book serve today's car or truck buyer?

Whether you're just starting your search for a new vehicle or you consider yourself ready to take the new car plunge, you'll find valuable information on the following pages. At Edmunds.com we understand that knowledge is power, and too often car buyers feel powerless once they get on a dealer lot. To remedy this, we've compiled everything you'll need to know about the 2005 model year cars and trucks for sale in the U.S., and we've broken this information down into easy-to-understand sections. They include:

## In-Depth Model Reviews (page 156)

We've created an in-depth vehicle "Review" for nearly every 2005 model sold in the United States with a base price under $100,000. This includes every car, truck, SUV, minivan and full-size van available. The reviews are broken down into key sections that include "Body Styles, Trim Levels and Options," "Powertrains and Performance," "Safety," "Interior Design" and "Driving Impressions." This makes it easy to zero in on the specific vehicle aspects you really care about without having to read the entire review. Each review page also features charts with drivetrain specifications and basic pricing information.

### All-New Models for 2005 (page 62)

To assist buyers interested in the latest models, we've created a special "All New for 2005" section of the book. Here you'll find a thorough discussion of all-new or completely redesigned vehicles for 2005. These all-new models are covered in the regular "Reviews" section as well, but by giving them additional coverage and grouping them together, we make it easy for you to quickly learn about the latest cars and trucks to hit the market.

### 10 Steps to Finding/Buying/Leasing Your New Car (page 10)

Buying this book is a great first step on the path to acquiring your new vehicle, but finding the car or truck that's right for you, and ensuring you get that vehicle at a fair price, can be a daunting process. To help you through it, we've created a simple, straightforward "10 Steps" series. These 10-step tutorials, written by a former car salesman, will guide you through the process of assessing your vehicle needs, locating the exact model you want and (perhaps most importantly) getting a fair deal, regardless of whether you're buying or leasing.

### Comparison Charts (page 446)

You can't accurately research a specific model without also learning about its competition. Nothing is worse than buying a car only to learn (after your purchase) that a competing vehicle would have served your needs far better. Using our comparison charts will quickly give you basic information on every model within a given vehicle type and market segment. After studying these charts you can confidently focus on the model, or models, that appeal to you. Included in these charts is a listing of each model's "Pros" and "Cons," plus basic pricing and drivetrain information. We've even identified our "Most Wanted" and "Top Rated" picks on each chart to let you know which models we feel are the best choices in a specific segment. These charts are a tremendous resource when starting your search, or later in the process when you just want to confirm that the vehicle you've settled on is really the one you want.

### Future Vehicles (page 565)

While the focus of this book is 2005 cars and trucks, we've added a new section called "Future Vehicles" that showcases some of the exciting models hitting the market in 2006 and beyond. Much of this information is preliminary, and therefore speculative in nature. However, just knowing that a specific model is being redesigned, or that an all-new vehicle is only a year away, can be helpful. Who knows — maybe you'll even see something that convinces you to stick with your current ride for another 12 months.

### And Much More...

In addition to the features already discussed, you'll find a chart showing warranty coverage and customer assistance numbers for each manufacturer. There's also a section devoted to our "Most Wanted" vehicles for 2005 that showcases which cars and trucks we'd park in our own garage, given the opportunity. The "Generations" articles on our cover models (the all-new Ford Mustang and Toyota Tacoma) give you a complete historical analysis on both of these popular vehicles. Finally, the latest safety and crash test data is provided and addresses an issue that should be high on every shopper's priority list when buying a new vehicle.

## Don't Forget Our Web Site

There's no denying that the Edmunds.com New Cars and Trucks Buyer's Guide is a powerful tool in your quest to find the right car at the right price. But shopping for a car or truck without using the Internet is like gambling in Vegas with your life savings. Sure, everything might work out in the end, but do you really want to take that kind of risk? The truth is that most car shoppers (over 80 percent) utilize the Internet as part of their car-buying research. If you're already part of that majority, consider this book a travel-size version of Edmunds.com. Use it to do basic vehicle research and as an easy reference guide (especially the "10 Steps" section) when navigating the often treacherous waters that make up the new-car buying process.

When it comes down to crunch time and you're prepared to commit to a new vehicle purchase, do yourself a favor and visit our Web site at Edmunds.com. Once there, you'll find all the latest pricing and incentive information, including a powerful pricing tool called True Market Value that can actually tell you what other people are paying for a specific model based on color, options and region within the United States. You'll also find easy-to-use financing tools to help you calculate your monthly payments, an on-line automotive community of over half a million consumers who are discussing just about any and every automotive topic and more vehicle reviews than you can shake a driving glove at.

The Internet has undeniably changed the way we shop for cars, but after 39 years our buying guide's mission remains the same: To inform and entertain consumers, striving to give them the benefit of our vehicular knowledge, our insight into the automotive industry, our experiences of owning and driving vehicles and the lessons we've learned about buying and selling automobiles. We exist for the consumer, and write to that audience. Everything we publish is designed to make our readers better-educated car and truck buyers, owners and sellers.

**Karl Brauer**
Editor in Chief
Edmunds.com

## Feedback from our Web site users:

**E-mail from: Russ E.**
You have created one of the very best Web sites on the Internet!!! Easy to navigate, wealth of information. A pleasure to use. Cannot say enough positive things. Content is A+ but even with so much information you can find things and move around with ease! Simply a GREAT JOB. You help consumers everyday save money and make good auto choices!!!

**E-mail from: Madeline P.**
I want to thank you for being my research tool in buying a car. I have been using your information for over six years. I can walk into dealerships with confidence that the information that you give and the advice you have given are excellent.

**E-mail from: Steven**
I happened on your site via Google and what a site it is! It is possibly one of the top 10 sites I've come across in my 10 years on the Internet. EXCELLENT job. It's comprehensive and everything is intuitive and at the tip of your fingers. Very well done!

# How to Use This Book

Our new design makes it easy for you to quickly compare factual information about vehicles you are researching. Refer to this diagram to learn about the useful features of *Edmunds.com New Cars & Trucks Buyer's Guide.*

## The Header

The top of the page is designed to help you find the car you're looking for quickly and easily:

**Make** – Vehicle manufacturer

**Model** – Vehicle model name

**Type** – Refers to vehicle size and body style

## The Sidebar

Along the outside edge of each detail page, the Sidebar presents the important factual details about the vehicle, along with a text summary of our thoughts:

**Pricing** – These figures represent the range of Manufacturers Suggested Retail Prices (MSRPs) from the least expensive model trim to the most expensive, or "premium," trim. This price range does not include the cost of any options.

**Destination Charge** – This figure represents the fixed destination charge that the manufacturer has added to the MSRP for a given model. This charge remains the same regardless of trim level or added options.

**Most Wanted** – An icon that identifies our favorite model within a vehicle segment.

**Top Rated** – This icon means the vehicle scored the best when put through our comprehensive evaluation process.

**Ratings Chart** – Consumer ratings come from our Web site visitors, while Editors' ratings are assigned by the Edmunds.com editorial staff. Both of these ratings can range from 1 to 10, with 10 being the best possible rating.

**What Edmunds.com says** – A one- or two- sentence summation of how we feel about a given model.

**Pros** – What we consider to be a model's most appealing characteristics.

**Cons** – What we consider to be a model's least appealing characteristics.

**What's New** – A detailed description of what changed on a model for the current (2005) model year.

**Specifications Chart** – Contains engine size and transmission information, with "A" representing an automatic transmission and "M" representing a manual transmission. An "A/M" symbol means both transmission types can be mated to a particular engine. This chart also includes peak horsepower and torque figures and, when available, fuel mileage information.

**Body Styles Chart** – The Body Styles chart lists the various body styles (sedan, coupe and convertible, for example) available within a model range and the associated price ranges for each style.

## The Overview

Here you'll find our editors' in-depth analysis of each car, separated into a number of targeted sections:

**Body Styles, Trim Levels and Options** – A detailed description of the available body styles, trim levels, standard equipment and major options.

**Powertrains and Performance** – Describes the various engines and transmissions offered within the model line. Horsepower, torque and fuel mileage are discussed here.

**Safety** – Standard and optional safety equipment is described here. If a vehicle has been crash tested by either the National Highway Traffic Safety Administration (NHTSA) or the Insurance Institute for Highway Safety (IIHS) the results of those test(s) will also be listed here.

**Interior Design and Special Features** – An overall examination of a vehicle's interior design is provided here. Special or unique features are described here as well. For SUVs, vans and wagons, you'll often find cargo capacity specs.

**Driving Impressions** – This is where we discuss how a vehicle feels from behind the steering wheel. These descriptions can focus on performance, comfort, utility or any other characteristics that are related to the type of vehicle being discussed.

## Vehicle Detail Page Key

**Award Icons**
- Editors' Most Wanted
- Editors' Top Rated

**Make**

**Model**

**MSRP Price Range**

**Destination Charge**

**Ratings Chart**
- Consumer Rating
- Editors' Rating

**Summary Text**
- What Edmunds.com Says
- Pros & Cons
- What's New for 2005

**Specifications Chart**
- Engine & Transmission Choices
- Peak Horsepower
- Peak Torque
- EPA Mileage Estimates

**Body Styles Chart**
- Body Styles
- MSRP Range by style

**Vehicle Type**

**Photo**

**Overview**
- Introduction (All-New section only)
- Body Styles, Trim Levels and Options
- Powertrains and Performance
- Safety
- Interior Design and Special Features
- Driving Impressions

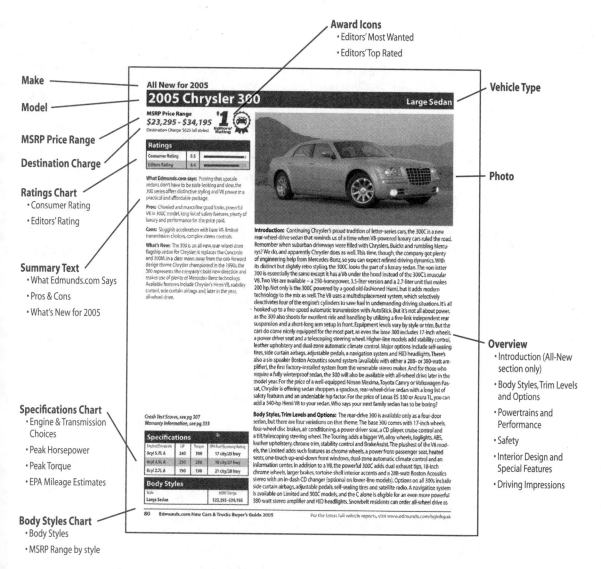

## All-New for 2005

The section of All-New for 2005 vehicles contains even more information spread across two pages per vehicle. There is an expanded Introduction in the Overview section, three more photos showing an interior, engine and rear 3/4 view of the vehicle, and a handy Competitive Vehicles box in the right sidebar listing up to four different comparable models from other manufacturers, along with their MSRP price range for quick comparison.

# 10 Steps to Finding the Right Car for You

## Introduction

"Do I want to buy or lease my next car?" "What is the right vehicle for me?" "How can I save money and get a good deal?" We have created three 10-Step sections to help answer these questions and guide you through this sometimes overwhelming process. If you are undecided about what car you want, read "10 Steps to Finding the Right Car for You." Then you can read either the buying or leasing 10 Steps to actually make a deal on your car. As you read, if you find words you don't understand, consult our glossary at the end of this section.

## 10 Steps to Finding the Right Car for You

The following steps are devoted to helping you price, locate and test-drive the car, truck or van that is best for you.

### 1. What kind of car do you need?

If you examine your needs, you will quickly discover what the right car is for you. Take a moment to think about what you use your car for. How many people do you need to transport? What kind of driving do you most often do? How long is your commute, and is it important that your next vehicle get good gas mileage?

In too many cases, people choose a car because it has an eye-catching style or is a trendy favorite. If you go in this direction, you may either break your budget or have to go car shopping again soon. Let your needs, not your wants, drive your decision.

Here are a few other questions to keep in mind when you begin your car-buying process:

- Do you want a manual or automatic transmission?
- Do you really need four-wheel drive? Or all-wheel drive?
- What safety features do you want?
- Do you require a lot of cargo-carrying capacity? Will you be doing any towing?
- Will the car fit in your garage or parking area?

### 2. How much can you afford?

Regardless of whether you decide to buy or lease your next car, establishing a realistic monthly payment that will fit into your budget is a crucial first step. How much should this be?

A rule of thumb is that your total monthly car payments—whether you own one car or more than one—shouldn't exceed 20 percent of your monthly take-home pay.

The Edmunds.com Web site has a variety of calculators to help you estimate what your monthly payment will be based on purchase price, down payment, interest rate and length of loan. Take the time to run the numbers now, before you go car shopping, and put this information into your car-buying folder. It will not only show you what you can afford, it will also help you control the numbers when you negotiate with a car salesman.

# 10 Steps to Finding the Right Car for You

## 3. Should you lease or buy your next car?

A lease requires little or no money up front and offers lower monthly payments. But when the lease ends, you are left without a car and need to replace it.

Buying a car is more expensive initially and the monthly payments are higher. But at the end of the loan, you will own a car you can still drive, or sell if you desire.

Other key factors that differentiate leasing and buying include:

### Advantages of Leasing:

- You can drive a better car for less money
- You can drive a new car every few years
- No trade-in hassles at the end of the lease

### Advantages of Buying:

- When interest rates are low, it makes more financial sense to own a car rather than lease it
- No mileage penalty
- Increased flexibility—you can sell the car whenever you want

## 4. Have you considered all vehicles in that class?

Today's new car (and truck) market is filled with great products. Most shoppers have difficulty keeping up with all of the vehicles manufacturers introduce and the changes they make to their older vehicles, so it's important to do your research. Use this printed guide and the Edmunds.com Web site to research all your choices before you hit the showrooms.

## 5. Have you considered all of the costs of ownership?

Here is an often overlooked fact of car ownership: one car might be cheaper to buy, but more expensive to own. Why? Even if two cars cost about the same to buy, one can depreciate at a different rate or cost significantly more to insure or maintain. Before you commit to one car, you should estimate the long-term ownership costs of the vehicle you are considering. These include depreciation, insurance, maintenance and fuel costs. The Edmunds.com Web site has a feature called True Cost to Own (TCO), which presents this information in an easy-to-read table. Many so-called "invisible costs" are revealed here. If you take these figures to heart and make the smart decision up front, you will have saved hundreds of dollars over that five-year period which you can apply toward the purchase of your next car.

## 6. Research options.

Car buyers have been trained to visit their local dealer lots to find the car they want. In the Internet age, this is a wasted motion since you can quickly cover more ground by shopping on-line or by using the **Edmunds.com New Cars & Truck Buyer's Guide.** Car dealers are waking up to this new breed of shopper and have created the Internet department, which is a separate department within a dealership dedicated to the educated buyer who already knows what he wants and what he's willing to pay. The only things you have to do in person are test-drive the car and sign the contract. And in some cases, you can have the car "delivered" to you by the salesperson.

Edmunds.com is your link to the automotive world. Through our printed buying guides and comprehensive Web site, you can not only educate yourself about cars, but also find local dealers, check interest rates for buying or leasing and calculate your exact monthly payment. Before even heading out the door, try to answer any question you may have via this guide or the Edmunds.com site. Remember, you don't want to go to the dealership until you're really ready.

### 7. Scheduling an appointment for a test-drive.

It's a good idea to make your initial contact with a dealership by phone before going there in person. This can give you some sense of the business atmosphere you will be dealing with throughout the buying or leasing process. Additionally, if you can establish a rapport with a specific salesperson, it can bolster your confidence when you arrive on the lot. With the salesperson on the phone, try to find out if the car you're looking for—in the right color and trim level—is actually on the lot.

We recommend initiating contact with the dealership through the Internet department. You can do this with an e-mail message or over the telephone. Tell the Internet salesperson that you want to set up a test-drive—but that you won't be buying right away. However, assure them that you will buy there if you decide to purchase this particular make and model, and if they can offer the vehicle at a price you feel is fair.

Keep in mind that if you deal with the standard salesperson, he or she will try to start the negotiations at a high price with the expectation of being negotiated down. However, the Internet manager will often quote you a "rock-bottom" price as soon as negotiations begin. Obviously, a few minutes taken to set up an appointment with the Internet manager can save you both time and money.

### 8. How to test-drive a car.

The goal of a test-drive is to experience—as closely as possible—the same type of driving conditions the car will be used for after purchase. If you commute, do your best to simulate your daily drive, be it stop-and-go traffic or freeway driving (likely both if you live in an urban area). If you frequently go into the mountains, try to find some steep grades to climb. Drive over bumps, take tight corners at aggressive (but not dangerous) speeds and test the brakes in a safe location, such as a deserted parking lot. Get in and out of the car several times and be sure to sit in the backseat, especially if you plan on carrying passengers. In short, ask yourself what it will be like to live with this car for a number of years.

While you are evaluating the car, don't be distracted by the salesperson's pitch. Don't drive with the radio on—you can evaluate that later. A new car is a big investment; make sure you spend enough time really looking at it. And then, consider one last thing: your intuition. If you are uneasy about this car, follow your instincts. A vehicle purchase decision is too important (and expensive) to undertake without total confidence.

# 10 Steps to Finding the Right Car for You

## 9. After the test-drive.

After the test-drive, you will need to leave the car lot. Why? Because you will probably need to drive other types of cars at other dealerships. It's a good idea to do all of your test driving in one morning or afternoon. Driving the cars back to back will help you uncover even minor differences, which will lead to a more educated purchase decision.

So, how do you get out of the clutches of the salesperson? Just remind them you still have other cars to drive and you can't make a decision yet. Most good salespeople will respect that. If they don't, you probably shouldn't be coming back to make a deal with them anyway.

## 10. Getting ready for the buying cycle.

At this point you should have considered all the cars in the class that interest you. You should have a good idea what you can afford. You should have test-driven your top choices. You should also know if you want to buy or lease your next car.

Now it's time to narrow down your choices to one car and make a deal. If you plan on leasing, read the "10 Steps to Leasing a New Car." If you are going to buy your next car, read "10 Steps to Buying a New Car." In either case, take a moment to congratulate yourself. You have done your homework to find the right car for you. Now you can move forward with confidence.

## 10 Steps to Buying a New Car

The following steps will tell you how to locate, price and negotiate to buy the car you want. Remember to consult our glossary if you find words here you don't understand.

### 1. Starting out.

These steps will help you to find the exact car you want, and at a price that is fair to both you and the dealer. In the previous steps, you did plenty of research to find the best car for your needs, and you got a good idea of what you should expect to pay for it. Now you need to narrow the research even more. You will soon be finding the exact car you want to buy—with the options you have chosen—and you will be setting a target price to pay. If you have done your homework, this will be a fairly easy process with no unexpected surprises. Buying a car is a big investment, but it can be exciting and rewarding, especially if you feel like you got the right car at a fair price.

### 2. Using incentives and rebates.

Today's new-car market is crowded and competitive. Many new cars are offered for sale with attractive incentives to make you choose a particular model. In most cases, the cars with the best incentives are those that aren't selling very well on their own.

An incentive is anything that gives you an added reason to buy a particular car. Often, however, it comes in the form of a cash rebate or low-interest financing. A car might be selling for $22,000 but the manufacturer is offering $3,000 in customer cash for a final price of $19,000. In another example, a $22,000 car financed for five years at six percent would have a monthly payment of about $550. But with zero-percent financing, the payment is roughly $480. That's a huge savings to you.

Check the Edmunds.com Web site for the latest incentives. You can also watch for TV and newspaper promotions but, remember, the incentives don't apply to all models and are not offered in all regions of the country. Furthermore, your credit must be very good to get the low-interest financing. And finally, keep in mind that there are some hidden incentives paid directly to dealers to push certain cars. Edmunds.com tracks many of these as well, and posts them on the Web site.

Research what incentives are offered for the car you want to buy. Write down this information and keep it in your car-buying folder as you move to the next step.

### 3. Pricing the car.

Car salesmen will usually point to a car's "sticker price" as the correct amount to pay. However, the price the dealership is willing to sell a car for is often well below the sticker price. How do you know what to pay? Edmunds.com has created a valuable tool for car buyers called True Market Value (TMV) pricing. Based on actual sales figures, TMV is the average price buyers are paying (also known as the "transaction price") for a specific model of car in your area. The TMV figures, found on Edmunds.com, are adjusted for many factors including mileage, condition, options, geographic region and color.

# 10 Steps to Buying a New Car

To calculate TMV, begin by looking up the car you want to buy on Edmunds.com. Follow the prompts to arrive at a final TMV price for the exact car you are buying. Keep in mind that this price includes the destination charge, which is levied by all manufacturers. (However, the invoice price might vary in certain regions where advertising costs and other fees are included. Edmunds recommends paying the fees listed on the invoice, but questioning any advertising fees that appear on the purchase contract.)

Now it's time to factor in the incentives you researched and wrote down in the previous step. Take the final TMV price and deduct the amount of the cash rebate. In other words, you create your best deal based on TMV, and then lower it by whatever the rebate is. If you are going to use low-interest financing, calculate your final buying price, then use the payment calculator on Edmunds.com to find your monthly payment.

Write down these figures—the TMV, the customer cash incentives and the monthly payment—and carry them with you for reference as you continue the car-buying process.

## 4. Finding the exact car you want to buy.

You should now have a very specific idea of the car you want to buy. This means you know the make, model, trim level, options and color. The more flexible you can be about these specifics, the wider the range of the cars you'll find available for sale. Ultimately, the ability to consider several versions of the same model can give you additional bargaining power. For example, a shopper might be very firm about the make, model and trim level, but could accept a variety of options and colors. If you're a shopper who definitely wants hard-to-find options and a specific color, it will be more difficult to make a great deal. Why? You have no leverage as a negotiator. You have to pay the dealer's price or try to locate another identical vehicle. Obviously, if you do find the exact car you're looking for, there's no need to volunteer this information to the dealership during the negotiation process.

In any case, locate the exact car you want by searching online dealer inventories or sending e-mails to the Internet managers of dealers in your area. Using Edmunds.com, you can simultaneously solicit quotes from multiple dealers. In many cases, you will have to follow up with a phone call. Say something like: "I'm looking for a 2003 Matsura Accell. I'm not too fussy about the color but I don't want black or white. I want ABS and side airbags. What do you have on your lot?" Often the salesperson will have to check his inventory and call you back. After a few phone calls you will have a good idea of how widely available the car is. If there are several dealerships offering the same car, you will be in a better position to make a good deal.

As you make phone calls and exchange e-mails, take careful notes. You should record information about each car you locate, including the color options, and the dealership name. This will save time as you continue through the shopping process.

## 5. Test-driving the car salesman.

As you call dealerships to locate the exact car you want to buy, you can also test-drive the dealership's salesman. In other words, you can determine if this is a person you want to do business with. It's a good idea to consider this issue ahead of time, before you get to the deal-making phase of the process.

The first way to evaluate a good salesperson is to ask yourself if you feel comfortable dealing with them. Are they impatient and pushy? Or are they relaxed and open? If you asked them about a specific car's availability, did they respond to your needs? Or did they try to steer you toward another car simply because they have too many of that model in stock? Do they return your phone calls? Do they answer your questions in a straightforward manner? Or are they evasive and confusing?

By considering these issues you should have a sense of whether or not you want to buy from this salesperson. If you feel comfortable with the individual when researching by phone, and if the dealership does indeed have the car you're interested in, set up a time to test-drive the car, preferably when the dealership will not be very busy, such as a weekday morning. Before heading to the car lot, review all your notes and make sure you bring your car-buying folder. This might include your checkbook, registration and proof of insurance. Keep in mind that you're bringing these items so you'll be ready to buy a car if you get a fair deal. Don't feel obligated to purchase a car simply because you have all the necessary paperwork with you.

### 6. If you are trading in your old car...

If you are trading in your old car to a dealer, you will probably not get as much money toward the price of a new car as you would have if you'd sold it yourself to a private party. However, trading in offers some advantages. You can solve all of your car-buying problems in one visit to the dealer. You can unload a hard-to-sell car with no newspaper ads, DMV lines or tire-kicking buyers involved. In some states, you will even pay less sales tax on a deal that involves a trade-in.

Begin the process by looking up your car's trade-in value on Edmunds.com. After you plug in all of the vehicle's information (mileage, options and colors), you will get a specific trade-in price. This will often be slightly different from the offers you get once you are on the car lot. At a dealership the value assigned to your trade-in varies based on the time of the month, the dealer's specific inventory and the used car manager's mood, but at least TMV will give you a rough idea of what your trade-in is worth.

If it's important to you to get the maximum value for your trade-in, you should visit several dealerships and solicit bids. Tell the salesperson that the sale of a new car will be contingent on the amount he or she will give you for your trade-in. Also, tell them you are visiting several dealerships. With a little legwork, you may be able to boost the price you get for your old car by several hundred dollars or more. Remember, the extra effort you spend in getting competitive bids is far less than what it would take to advertise, show and sell the car yourself.

### 7. Negotiating for your lowest price.

Many buyers like to handle the question of price before they even go to the dealer. Internet salespeople are willing to discuss price over the phone—even by e-mail. This wasn't the case a few years ago when the salesperson wanted you in his office before he would get down to brass tacks and talk price.

It's quite possible that, in your calls to various Internet departments, the selling price of the car has already come up. Often Internet salespeople will volunteer the selling price of their cars since they know this is the make-or-break factor in most buyers' decision-making process. If the price they've quoted is at or below Edmunds.com's TMV, then you are already in the right range to buy the car. If you want to try to improve the deal, you have a few options.

# 10 Steps to Buying a New Car

Everyone has their own idea of what makes a good deal, but most people just want to know they got a fair price. Here, TMV will be your best guide. If you want to try for a rock-bottom price, start by getting bids from three local dealers. Follow this up by taking the lowest price, calling the two other dealerships and saying, "I've been offered this car at this price. If you beat it I'll buy it from you." They almost certainly will. However, keep in mind that you can't play this game forever. Eventually, they will give you a take-it-or-leave-it price.

Also, be warned that if you ask dealers to cut their profit, they might try to take it back somewhere else. Remember, a good deal isn't just the lowest selling price. It's the lowest total out-the-door cost on a car that meets your needs.

## 8. Closing the deal.

If you feel good about the price you have been quoted, it's time to take a look at the big picture. Many buyers focus on the cost of the car and ignore the related expenses. Besides the cost, you will have to pay sales tax and various fees that vary from state to state.

The simplest way to estimate total cost is to ask the salesperson to fax you a worksheet and in-voice before you go to the dealership. This way, you'll be able to review the figures in a relaxed environment. Compare the numbers from the dealership to those you have calculated and the TMV prices on Edmunds.com.

In some areas of the country, dealers have costs that don't show up on Edmunds.com. This means the invoice prices of the cars you are researching won't exactly match the TMV prices. As we mentioned before, any additional charges listed on the *invoice* are usually non-nego-tiable. However, look for charges the dealer has written into the *contract* such as "D&H" or "Administrative Costs." If these fees seem bogus or redundant and the dealer can't explain them, you should ask to have them removed, or go to another dealership.

## 9. Reviewing and signing the paperwork.

At the dealership, you will be presented with the contract for your new car and a dizzying array of forms to sign. This might be done by the Internet salesperson you have been dealing with, or it could be done in a separate office by the finance and insurance (F&I) manager. If this happens, the F&I manager might try to sell you additional items such as extended service contracts, fabric protection or an anti-theft device. In most cases, we recommend turning down these extras.

If you have already seen a worksheet for the deal you've made, the contract should be a formality. Make sure the numbers match the worksheet and no additional charges or fees have been inserted. You will also be asked to sign various forms that register your new car and transfer ownership of your trade-in. Understand what you are signing and what it means. Ask questions if you don't understand, and don't ever feel like you have to hurry. Buying a car is a serious commitment and it's the F&I manager's job to ensure you are comfortable with every document involved. Remember, once you have signed, there is no going back.

## 10. Inspecting and taking possession of your new car.

Most dealerships detail the car and provide a full tank of gas. You will have one more chance to inspect the car before you take possession of it. Make sure you walk around the car and look for scratches in the paint and wheels or dents and dings on the body. If you are paying for floor mats make sure they are included. If anything is missing, or if any work needs to be done, ask for a "Due Bill" that puts it in writing. You will then be able to come back and get the work done later.

As you drive away inhaling that new-car smell, there is only one more thing to do: enjoy your new car.

# 10 Steps to Leasing a New Car

The following steps will tell you how to locate, price and negotiate to lease the car you want. Remember to consult our glossary if you find words here you don't understand.

## 1. How leasing works.

Leasing a car is just like renting a car—but for a longer time period. Unlike buying, you never actually own the car and you have to give it back at the end of the lease. Leasing became popular in the 1990s because cars became too expensive to buy for many people. Leasing allows a person to drive a brand-new car and make lower monthly payments, thus making the "new car experience" more accessible to a greater number of people. Finally, leasing can offer tax breaks for certain occupations.

In an earlier section, we talked about the pros and cons of leasing. It might be a good idea to review those points now. Remember that, while leasing may not save you money in the long run, it might fit more easily into your budget on a monthly basis. Also keep in mind that some people find leasing to be confusing since many of the terms are different. We'll do our best to quickly and clearly explain the process in the following steps.

## 2. Checking incentives and special lease deals.

Car manufacturers commonly offer lease specials. This is a good way to shop for a leased car because it can save you additional money on top of the lower monthly payments you make when leasing versus buying. However, the specials might have hidden costs that make the offer not as beneficial as it appears. You should always check to see if the promised monthly payment includes sales tax and fees. Also, does the advertised lease require a large down payment (sometimes called a "cap reduction payment" or "cap cost reduction"), bank fees and a security deposit? What about the annual mileage limit? These are questions you want answered long before you close a lease deal.

Edmunds.com compiles and regularly updates a list of lease specials. Check the "Incentives and Rebates" section of the site to see what is being offered in any given month. Be sure to confirm the specific make, model and geographic region that the incentive applies to.

## 3. How long should your lease be?

Cars are usually leased for two, three, four or five years. However, the three-year lease is the best choice for most people. The majority of carmakers offer three-year warranties. If your lease is for three years, you will always be under warranty without paying extra for an extended service contract. Furthermore, a car really begins to show its age at about three years—right at the time the lease is expiring. Remember, one of the reasons for leasing is to drive a new, or nearly new, vehicle on a constant basis. Why would you lease for five years and be forced to deal with extended warranty fees and higher maintenance costs? If these items don't bother you, you should seriously consider buying the car.

Of course, everyone wants a low lease payment, and extending the length of the lease will drop the monthly cost. But extending the lease means you're investing more and more money into a vehicle that's not even yours. It's better to shop aggressively for a competitive lease deal and keep the length of the contract to three years.

### 4. Estimating your lease payments.

A lease payment is calculated from many different numbers and can be difficult to understand. However, you should attempt to estimate your own lease payment before you go shopping to avoid overpaying. In the old days (like, five years ago), this meant an hour or two with a calculator. Now, the process has been streamlined by the Internet.

Visit Edmunds.com and click on the link to our "Site Directory" on the upper right of the page. Then click on "Calculators." This suite of calculators allows you to generate your own lease payments based on purchase price, lease length, interest rate and more. You can even use the same figures to create a side-by-side comparison to see what it would cost to buy the car. When you are done, print out the results and keep them with you in your car-buying folder as you continue shopping.

### 5. Finding the exact car to lease.

If you followed the "10 Steps to Finding the Right Car for You," it should be obvious which car you want to lease. This means you know the make, model, trim level, options and color. The more flexible you can be, the better the lease deal you will be able to make. For example, a shopper might be very firm about the make, model and trim level, but could accept a variety of options and colors. If another shopper definitely wants hard-to-find options and a specific color, it will be harder to make a great deal. Why? You have no leverage as a negotiator. You have to pay the dealer's lease rate or try to locate another identical vehicle. Obviously, if you do find the exact car you're looking for, there's no need to volunteer this information to the dealership during negotiations.

As you make phone calls and exchange e-mails with the dealership's Internet manager, take careful notes. You should record information about each car you locate, including the color options, and the dealership name. This will save time as you continue through the shopping process.

### 6. Test-driving the car salesman.

As you call dealerships to locate the exact car you want to lease, you can also test-drive the dealership's salesman. In other words, you can determine if this is a person you want to do business with. It's a good idea to consider this issue ahead of time, before you get to the deal-making phase of the process.

The first way to evaluate a good salesperson is to ask yourself if you feel comfortable dealing with them. Are they impatient and pushy? Or are they relaxed and open? If you asked them about a specific car's availability, did they respond to your needs? Or did they try to steer you toward another car simply because they have too many of that model in stock? Do they return your phone calls? Do they answer your questions in a straightforward manner? Or are they evasive and confusing?

By considering these issues, you should have a sense of whether or not you want to lease from this salesperson. If you feel comfortable with the individual when researching by phone, and if the dealership does indeed have the car you're interested in, set up a time to test-drive the car, preferably when the dealership will not be very busy, such as a weekday morning. Before heading to the car lot, review all your notes and make sure you bring your car-buying folder. This might include your checkbook, registration and proof of insurance. Keep in mind that you're bringing these items so you'll be ready to lease a car if you get a fair deal. Don't feel obligated to sign a lease simply because you have all the necessary paperwork with you.

## 7. The final test-drive.

When you arrive on the lot you will want to take a careful look at the car you are considering. You should also drive the car one more time. You might have driven several other cars during the "10 Steps to Finding the Right Car for You" phase, and need to refresh your memory. If you specified several options—such as side airbags or ABS—check the window sticker to make sure they are on the car you are leasing.

If everything checks out, it's time to make a deal for your lowest lease payment.

## 8. How to negotiate a lease payment.

Negotiations can be handled several ways. If the car is widely available, you can call local dealerships and solicit bids. Take the lowest bidder and call the other dealers. Can they beat that price? If not, you are at rock bottom.

If the car is harder to find, and you are on the lot, you can still refer to the lease payments you calculated at home. If the lease quote from your salesperson matches your estimate, you're probably getting a fair deal, but make sure the numbers and terms match your calculations. Check the down payment (we recommend a zero down payment), the term of the loan, the monthly payment and the annual mileage allowance.

In the past, Edmunds.com recommended that the best way to negotiate a lease was to begin by negotiating for the lowest selling price for the car. Once that was set, you would get the salesperson to draw up a lease payment. The thinking was, if the salesperson knew you were leasing, he would focus on the monthly payment while ignoring the negotiated price. But the reality is that if you're happy with the down payment, monthly payment and mileage allowance, the purchase price of the vehicle is probably right. Keep in mind, however, that if you end up wanting to buy the vehicle at the end of the lease, the original price listed on the lease contract will affect the purchase price at the end of the lease.

Whichever method you choose, it is a good idea to ask the salesperson to fax you a worksheet, detailing all the costs before you go to the dealership. This will allow you to review the figures in a relaxed environment. Compare the numbers to those you have calculated and the TMV prices on Edmunds.com.

## 9. Reviewing and signing the paperwork.

At the dealership, you will be presented with the lease contract for your new car and a dizzying array of forms to sign. This might be done by the Internet salesperson you have been dealing with, or it could be done in a separate office by the finance and insurance (F&I) manager. If this happens, the F&I manager might try to sell you additional items such as extended service contracts, fabric protection or an anti-theft device. In most cases, we recommend turning down these extras.

If you have already seen a worksheet for the deal you've made, the contract should be a formality. Make sure the numbers match the worksheet and that no additional charges or fees have been inserted. You will also be asked to sign various forms that register the new car and transfer ownership of your trade-in. Understand what you are signing and what it means. Ask questions if you don't understand, and don't ever feel like you have to hurry. Leasing a car is a serious commitment and it's the F&I manager's job to ensure you are comfortable with every document involved. Remember, once you have signed there is no going back.

Most lease cars are based on the owner driving 12,000 miles a year. If you drive farther than this, you are charged from 10 to 15 cents for each mile over the limit at the end of the lease. If you think you are going to drive farther than the allowed mileage, you may be able to buy extra miles up front. Usually, you can buy extra miles at five cents per mile and have this rolled into your lease payment. This pay-as-you-go approach prevents any unpleasant surprises at the end of the lease.

One last thing, check to make sure the contract you are buying includes "gap insurance," which is recommended when leasing and will cover you if the vehicle is involved in an accident and the insured value is below the car's market value. If this coverage isn't included in the lease, you can easily buy it from your own insurance agent.

### 10. Successfully managing your leased vehicle.

As you drive your leased vehicle, you need to remember that the car will have to be returned in good condition. Have all the scheduled maintenance performed at an authorized dealer and keep your eye on the odometer to avoid exceeding the mileage limit.

When the time approaches to end the lease, you will have several alternatives. You can renew the lease contract on the car or turn it back in and lease a new vehicle. You can buy the car for the amount stated in your contract and continue driving it. You can turn the lease car back in and buy, rather than lease, another car. Whatever you decide to do, take the time to consider each avenue carefully. Check current market values of the cars that interest you and shop for lease deals from manufacturers. Making the effort to research your decision will save you money and ensure that you wind up driving the right vehicle.

# How the Dealer Works the Numbers

By Philip Reed

To help you get the best deal when you buy your next car, you should understand how the salespeople will "work the numbers" on a four-square worksheet as they negotiate. The worksheet helps the salespeople view the total profit to the dealership while reviewing the separate elements of the deal.

As the name suggests, the sheet is divided into four large squares:

- **Trade-in:** How much the dealership will credit you for your trade-in. This figure is credited toward your purchase of a new vehicle. Dealers would like you to put 1/3 down. However, this figure is negotiable and can certainly be less than 1/3 the price of the car.

- **Purchase price of the dealer's car:** This is the price of the car. Often a dealer will write the price of the car, then write "plus fees," indicating that, on top of the cost of the car, you will pay sales tax, title and licensing fees.

- **Down payment:** How much cash are you are willing to pay up front? Down payments made using a credit card are also considered "cash up front."

- **Monthly payments:** How high a monthly payment are you willing to make? Car salespeople try to get the customer to focus on this figure since it most directly affects a person's budget.

As you can see, these four separate pieces are interconnected. If, for example, a customer is concerned about receiving the full value of her trade-in, the dealer will inflate the amount of the trade-in and then raise the monthly payment on the new car. Now the customer is satisfied, but the dealer is still making the same total amount of profit.

## Avoid Being Trapped by the Four-square

First of all, try to keep the deal as simple as possible. Consider selling your old car rather than trading it in. With a little effort, you could save a lot of money. Or secure outside financing before you go to the dealership. Taking these advance steps will allow you to negotiate the price of the car only rather than playing the monthly payment game.

If you want to trade in your current vehicle and become a monthly payment buyer (sometimes dealers can offer attractively low interest rates), work the numbers yourself before you go to the dealership. Decide what your maximum down payment and monthly payment should be. Then, decide on your lowest figure for the trade-in. Look at the Edmunds.com TMV® to find out what a fair selling price for the car should be. Now, write all these figures down so that you can control the whole deal to limit your expenses in the same way the dealer tries to maximize his profit.

This four-square worksheet was used in an actual negotiation for a van at a Los Angeles-area dealership. You can see the progress of the deal by reviewing the numbers written in the different boxes.

# 4-Square Basics

The four-square worksheet. The top section is for your name, address and phone number. The next section is for information about the car you are buying and the car you're trading in. The boxes below are used to negotiate the four main elements of the deal (clockwise from top left): credit for your trade-in, the purchase price of the new car, your down payment and your monthly payment (if you're financing).

|  |  |  |
|---|---|---|
| | | DATE _____ |
| | | SOURCE _____ |
| NAME | SALESPERSON | MGR |
| ADDRESS | | PHONE H ( ) W ( ) |

| MILEAGE | | V.I.N. | | | LIC. NO. |
|---|---|---|---|---|---|
| STOCK NO. | NEW ☐ USED ☐ DEMO ☐ | YEAR | MAKE | BODY STYLE | TAB. NO |
| | | | | | YR. EXP |

**TRADE-IN INFORMATION**

| YEAR | MAKE | CYL. | BODY STYLE | SALE PRICE | | |
|---|---|---|---|---|---|---|
| | | | | | | |

| MILEAGE | LIC. NO. | ADDITIONAL ACCESSORIES | | |
|---|---|---|---|---|

_____ PAYMENTS OF $_____
NUMBER

## 1/3 CASH DOWN
$ _____

## MONTHLY PAYMENTS
$ _____

**Many car buyers don't understand what dealer holdback is, what it is used for and what its role is, if any, in the deal-making process. Let's try to clear up some of the confusion.**

Dealer holdback is a percentage of either the MSRP or invoice price of a new vehicle (depending on the manufacturer) that is repaid to the dealer by the manufacturer. The holdback is designed to supplement the dealer's cash flow and indirectly reduce "variable sales expenses" (code words for sales commissions) by artificially elevating the dealership's paper cost.

Contrary to what some consumer think, the holdback itself can't really be used as a bargaining chip. However, knowing about it might help you get a better deal on a new car. How? Well, first here's a little background:

Dealerships must have an inventory on hand so that consumers can browse and ultimately select a vehicle. Dealerships must pay for this inventory when it is obtained from the manufacturer, and the amount it pays is the price reflected on the invoice from the manufacturer to the dealer, the so-called "invoice price."

Now the twist: with the introduction of holdbacks some years ago, most manufacturers inflated the invoice prices for every vehicle by a predetermined amount (2-3% of MSRP is typical). The dealer pays that inflated amount when it buys the car from the manufacturer. But later, at predetermined times (usually quarterly), the manufacturer reimburses the dealer for that excess amount. This is the "holdback," so named because funds are "held back" by the manufacturer and released only some time after the vehicle is invoiced to the dealership.

Why the sleight-of-hand you might ask? Because holdbacks can benefit dealers in three ways:

1. Dealerships borrow money to finance cars based on an invoiced amount that includes the holdback. So the higher the invoiced amount, the more the dealership can borrow from its lender.

2. Inflating the dealership's "cost" can have the effect of increasing profit, since sales personnel are paid commissions based on the "gross profit" of each sale. Holdbacks have the effect of lowering the gross profit and thus the sales commissions.

3. Holdbacks enable dealerships to advertise "invoice price" sales and sell their vehicles at or near invoice and still make hundreds of dollars on the transaction.

This holdback amount is "invisible" to the consumer because it does not appear as an itemized fee on the window sticker. For example, let's say you're interested in a Chevrolet with a Manufacturer's Suggested Retail Price (MSRP) of $20,500, including optional equipment and a $500 destination charge. Let's also say that dealer invoice on this hypothetical Chevy is $18,000. The cost of the car includes a dealer holdback that, in the case of all Chevy vehicles, amounts to 3% of the MSRP, or $600. (Note that the $500 destination charge should not be included when computing the holdback.) So, on this particular Chevy, the true dealer cost is actually $17,400. Even if the dealer sells you the car for the invoice price, which is unlikely, he would still be making as much as $600 on the deal (when his quarterly check from GM arrives).

Dealer holdback allows dealers to advertise attractive sales. Often, ads promise that your new car will cost you just "$1 over/under invoice!"

Almost all dealerships consider holdback money "sacred" and are unwilling to share any portion of it with the consumer. Don't push the issue. Your best strategy is to avoid mentioning the holdback during negotiations. Mention holdback only if the dealer gives you some song-and-dance about not making any money on the proposed deal when you know that isn't true.

However, there are many other holdback-types of dealer credits, such as flooring assistance, wholesale credits, advertising credits, etc. In addition, the dealer stands to reap further benefits if there is "dealer cash" being offered by the manufacturer on the car you are considering. In many instances you can learn about dealer cash in our Incentives and Rebates section. However, unless you know all of these other fees (and who does?), establishing the dealer's true cost can be frustratingly elusive. It's for this reason that Edmunds.com has established True Market Value pricing that accurately reflects "what others are paying" by taking into account all of these fees. The Edmunds.com True Market Value Price is the "bottom line" and what you really need to know in order to negotiate a fair deal. Check it out at: http://www.edmunds.com/tmv/new/.

In summary, holdback is nice to know, but is just one small piece of a complex puzzle.

Domestic manufacturers (Ford, General Motors and the Chrysler half of DaimlerChrysler) generally offer dealers a holdback equaling 3% of the total sticker price ( MSRP) of the car. Foreign manufacturers (Honda, Toyota, Volkswagen etc.) provide varying holdback amounts that are equal to a percentage of total MSRP, base MSRP, total invoice or base invoice, as indicated in the list below.

When calculating holdback, use the following guidelines.

If a holdback is calculated from the:

- Total MSRP: consumers must include the MSRP price of all options before figuring the holdback.

- Base MSRP: consumers must figure the holdback before adding desired options.

- Total Invoice: consumers must include the invoice price of all options before figuring the holdback.

- Base Invoice: consumers must figure the holdback before adding desired options.

# Dealer Holdback

| Make | Dealer Holdback |
| --- | --- |
| Acura | 3% of the Base MSRP |
| Audi | No holdback |
| BMW | No holdback |
| Buick | 3% of the Total MSRP |
| Cadillac | 3% of the Total MSRP |
| Chevrolet | 3% of the Total MSRP |
| Chrysler | 3% of the Total MSRP |
| Daewoo | No holdback—one-price sales. |
| Dodge | 3% of the Total MSRP |
| Ford | 3% of the Total MSRP + additional 1.25% rebate of Total Invoice to Blue Oval dealers |
| GMC | 3% of the Total MSRP |
| Honda | 3% of the Base MSRP |
| HUMMER | 3% of the Total MSRP |
| Hyundai | 2% of the Total Invoice |
| Infiniti | 1% of the Base MSRP (holdback) + 2% of the Base Invoice |
| Isuzu | 3% of the Total MSRP |
| Jaguar | No holdback |
| Jeep | 3% of the Total MSRP |
| Kia | 3% of the Base invoice |
| Land Rover | No holdback |
| Lexus | 2% of the Base MSRP |
| Lincoln | 2% of the Total MSRP + additional 2.5% rebate of Total Invoice to Certified Dealers |
| Mazda | 2% of the Base MSRP |
| Mercedes-Benz | 3% of the Total MSRP |
| Mercury | 3% of the Total MSRP |
| MINI | No holdback |
| Mitsubishi | 2% of the Base MSRP |
| Nissan | 2% + 1% of the Total invoice (holdback + floor planning allowance) |
| Oldsmobile | 3% of the Total MSRP |
| Plymouth | 3% of the Total MSRP |
| Pontiac | 3% of the Total MSRP |
| Porsche | No holdback |
| Saab | 2.2% of the Base MSRP |
| Saturn | 3% of the Total MSRP. But with one-price sales, this is a moot point. The customer pays MSRP. |
| Scion | No Holdback |
| Subaru | 3% of the Total MSRP (Amount may differ in Northeastern U.S.) |
| Suzuki | 3% of the Base MSRP (holdback) + an additional 1% (floor planning allowance) |
| Toyota | 2% of the Base MSRP (Amount may differ in Southern U.S.) |
| Volkswagen | 2% of the Base MSRP |
| Volvo | 1% of the Base MSRP |

## Glossary for Car-buying and Leasing

**Add-ons:** Items that the dealer installs after the car is delivered from the factory. These are generally high-profit items such as entertainment systems, wood paneling or chrome wheels. Usually, the prices for these things are listed on a second sticker in the car's window.

**Allowable Mileage:** This is the number of miles you are allowed to drive over the term of the lease, per year. Most leasing companies allow 12,000 miles a year. If the allowable miles are exceeded, you typically must pay between 12 and 15 cents per mile.

**APR:** This stands for Annual Percentage Rate. This is related to, but slightly different than, the interest rate. This is the interest rate multiplied by the number of periods in the year. If an interest rate is 4 percent quarterly, the APR would be 16 percent. The APR supposedly makes it easier to compare different loans because it always translates the loan to a yearly figure. But some experts caution against putting too much stock into the APR, because hidden fees can raise or lower this figure.

**Asking Price:** This is the price at which negotiations start. It is what the dealer or seller hopes to get for the car.

**Balance:** The balance of the loan is the amount remaining to be paid. Each time you make a payment, the balance is reduced.

**Capitalized Cost:** Often called the cap cost, this is basically the negotiated price of the car to be leased and all the options. This becomes one of several figures used in calculating a monthly lease payment.

**Closer:** An experienced salesman or sales manager at a dealership who is brought in late in negotiations. The closer is used either to persuade hesitant buyers to commit or to try to sweeten the price for the dealership.

**Credit:** This word is loosely used in a number of ways. In the financial world, it means the ability to borrow money. If someone says, "She has strong credit," it means a lending institution would gladly lend her money. A company might be given a "line of credit."

**Credit Report:** A document that comprehensively details an individual's credit payment history. Also included is information such as one's name, current and previous addresses and social security number.

**Credit Score:** A reckoning of an individual's creditworthiness based on an analysis of the data reflected in his or her credit report. This number provides potential lenders with the means to evaluate credit risk quickly and in a relatively objective manner.

**Demo:** This refers to one of two things: either a test-drive, or a car that has been used as a "demonstration" model for the dealership.

**Depreciation:** This is the amount by which property (in this case, a vehicle) loses its value over time. In leasing, depreciation is the difference between the new car's cost and the value of the car at the end of the lease (plus tax, interest and various leasing fees).

**DMV Fees:** When buying a car at a dealership, you have to register it and pay for license plates before you can drive it away. These various fees are referred to as DMV (Department of Motor Vehicles) fees. These costs might also be called "title and license fees." These fees are a percentage of the purchase price of the car and will slowly decrease as the car ages and loses value.

# Glossary for Car-buying and Leasing

**Down Payment:** When someone buys a car and finances it through the dealership, they often want to make a cash payment — called a down payment — to reduce the amount of the loan. For example, if you are buying a $20,000 car, and make a $3,000 down payment, the loan will be for $17,000. At Edmunds.com we recommend a 20 percent down payment when buying a vehicle.

**Drive-off Fees:** This is the amount of money you pay to begin the lease. Typically, this includes various DMV and leasing fees such as a security deposit. Some people, who want to reduce the amount of their monthly payments, will also make a "cap reduction payment." This is like making a down payment on a traditional auto loan. However, most experts recommend that you ask for zero drive-off fees when arranging a lease. This is because, if the car is totaled in an accident in the first few months of the lease, your insurance company would repay the car loan but you would lose all of your drive-off fees.

**Early Termination:** This means you want to get out of the lease contract before all your payments have been made. After 24 months of a three-year lease, for example, you might decide you no longer can afford the car, or you are sick of it. So you decide you want to terminate the lease. This is very costly since leasing companies typically require you to pay a huge penalty. However, some new companies have sprung up on the Internet to help people transfer their leases to someone who wants to step into a short-term lease at lower payments.

**Equity:** This is the difference between what the car is worth and what you owe on it. In other words, the car is worth $10,000 but you still have $6,000 left to pay on the loan. You have $4,000 worth of equity in the car. If this is a negative number, then you are "upside down" in the car.

**Excess Wear and Tear:** Most lease contracts have a clause which states that the person leasing the car is responsible for the cost of "excess wear and tear" to the vehicle when it is returned. When cars are used, they will eventually show signs that someone has been in them. What is considered excessive? Check your contract for specifics. But keep in mind that it is important to have the car washed and detailed before you return it. This can go a long way toward avoiding having your security deposit revoked or extra charges levied by the leasing company.

**Finance:** If a car is "financed," it means you are borrowing money—either as a loan or a lease—to pay for it as you drive it. Instead of financing a car, you could buy it outright with cash. When you buy a car with cash, it immediately becomes yours. When you finance the car, the bank owns it, and holds the title, until you've made the last payment.

**Finance and Insurance Office:** Often referred to as the "F&I office." When you buy a car at a dealership, you negotiate with the salesman. Once a deal is reached, you are escorted into the finance and insurance office where the contracts are drawn up and signed.

**Four-Square Work Sheet:** A standard form, used at many dealerships, to help the salesman keep track of the four elements of a deal as he negotiates with the customer. The squares allow him to jot down offers and counteroffers for the trade-in, the price of the car, the down payment and monthly payments.

**Gap Insurance:** If your leased car is stolen or totaled in an accident, there might be a gap between what your insurance company will pay you for the loss and the amount you now must pay to the leasing company. If you take out gap insurance (it is included in some lease contracts), this will cover you for the loss.

**Holdback:** This is a percentage (usually 2 or 3 percent of the invoice or sticker price) that the dealer is paid by the manufacturer after the car is sold. This is another incentive for the dealer

# Glossary for Car-buying and Leasing

to quickly sell the car, because the holdback diminishes the longer the vehicle sits on the lot. Although you can't easily use the holdback in negotiating, knowing about it might help you get a lower price.

**Incentive:** An incentive is a general term for anything that motivates a customer to buy a car. The most common incentives are customer cash rebates and low-interest financing. However, hidden dealer rebates are sometimes available.

**Interest Rate:** When money is borrowed, the lending institution, often a bank, charges a small fee for this service. Interest rates are charged as a percent of the amount loaned.

**Invoice:** This is roughly what the dealer paid for the car. If you are getting a car for $200 over invoice, then it is assumed the dealer is making only $200 profit. However, other factors enter into the equation such as hidden dealer rebates and holdbacks.

**Lease:** If you lease something, such as a car, you don't actually own it. You pay a monthly fee to use the car. At the end of the lease, you return the car and owe nothing more (assuming it is returned in good condition and with the agreed-upon mileage).

**Lending Institution:** Any company that loans money is a lending institution. It's sometimes thought that only banks loan money, but this isn't true. Auto loans can be arranged by credit unions, banks or the auto manufacturer itself.

**Lessee:** This is the person who has leased the vehicle.

**Lessor:** The lessor is the party who is leasing the car to you. Even though the dealership is arranging the lease, the lessor is often a bank or the financial arm of a car manufacturer.

**Money Factor:** Also called a lease factor or even a lease fee, this is the interest rate you are being charged. It is expressed as a multiplier that can be used to calculate your monthly payments. For example, 7.9 percent interest, when expressed as a money factor, is 0.0033. To convert a money factor to an interest rate, multiply by 2,400. To convert an interest rate to a money factor, divide by 2,400. (Always use 2,400 regardless of the length of the loan.)

**MSRP:** Also called "sticker price" (or even the "Monroney sticker") this stands for Manufacturer's Suggested Retail Price. The MSRP is what a dealer would like you to pay for the car. Most cars are sold below MSRP. Many dealers will try to base their leases on MSRP or above. However, you can negotiate a lower price to base the lease on.

**Payoff Amount:** Sometimes called the "buyout amount," this is the amount of money you have to pay to own a car you are financing or leasing. In the case of leasing, the payoff amount might be different from the residual value because of a refunded security deposit.

**Rebate:** See "Incentive."

**Residual Value:** This is the leasing company's prediction of what the car will be worth at the end of the lease. The residual value is also important because it affects your monthly payment. The higher the residual, the lower your monthly payments.

**Sales Tax:** When someone buys an item, they are charged a percentage of the purchase as state sales tax. The actual percentage varies widely from one state to the next and, often, within the state. The sales tax is often made up of a state tax and a local tax. These two are

# Glossary for Car-buying and Leasing

combined for one grand total. On small items, the sales tax doesn't seem significant. But when purchasing a car, it can be a large factor that affects the total cost of ownership.

In a lease, a portion of every monthly lease payment is paid for sales tax. However, you pay tax only on the amount of the car's value you are using. In other words, rather than paying 8 percent sales tax on a $20,000 car, you pay 8 percent of the $8,000 the car declines in value as you drive it. People who hate paying taxes love this part of leasing.

**Security Deposit:** The security deposit for a lease is usually equal to one monthly payment. However, multiple security deposits can be made to reduce the interest rate charged.

**Sticker Price:** See "MSRP."

**Subsidized or Subvented Lease:** To make leases more attractive to consumers, manufacturers sometimes subsidize or subvent the leases. This means that they are either offering very low interest rates or they are inflating the residual value of the vehicle. Both tactics have the effect of lowering the monthly payment for the consumer.

**Term:** This is the length of the loan, usually stated in months. Common terms for car loans and leases are 36, 48 or 60 months.

**Title:** Also called the "pink slip," the title is a legal document providing specific information about the vehicle and stating who owns it. If you borrow money from a bank to get a car, the title will be held by the bank until you make all the agreed-upon payments.

**Title and License Fees:** See "DMV Fees."

**Wholesale Value:** This is the price at which cars are bought by dealerships so they can resell them and make a profit.

Edmunds.com solicits e-mail queries from consumers who visit our Web site at http://www.edmunds.com. Below are some commonly asked questions regarding new cars and the buying process, answered by Consumer Advice Editor Philip Reed.

### How much over invoice should I pay?

This will vary from one car to the next. Use Edmunds.com True Market Value® (TMV) as your guide. On our Web site, look up the car you want to buy and see how much over invoice the TMV figure is. Now, you can use that as a benchmark when purchasing that car.

Sometimes, when you get to the car lot, you decide to buy a car that is configured differently than what you specified on the Web. However, if you've used TMV to confirm that this particular model sells for $300 over invoice, for example, this information can serve as a guide to calculate the fair price on a different car within the model line.

### Do I have to pay dealer advertising fees?

This has been the source of much aggravation for both consumers and dealers. Furthermore, since these fees are regional, it's hard to keep track of them. Here is a simple rule to resolve this issue: If the advertising fee is listed on the dealer invoice, pay it. If, however, there are advertising fees written into the dealer's contract, you might be able to challenge them. If the dealer will not remove the advertising fees they are charging, try another dealership. Or, press for a better price somewhere else in the deal.

### Should I tell the dealer I have a trade-in or try to negotiate the best purchase price for the car I want to buy first?

If you are trading in a vehicle, the deal is going to become more complicated. The risk you run is that the true amount you are getting for your trade-in will become obscured and may not be fully credited to the price of your new car. Therefore, it's a good idea to treat these issues — the purchase price of the car you want to buy and the value of your trade-in — separately. Negotiate a purchase price for the car you want to buy. Then, ask for the "actual cash value" of your trade-in. Now you know two of the figures the deal will be based on.

### What's the difference between the destination price and the delivery and handling fee?

A destination fee is listed on the car's invoice and is passed along to you, the buyer. This is a legitimate part of buying any car. A delivery and handling fee is charged by some dealers in addition to the destination charge. This is easy to spot since it is written into the dealer's own contract, rather than being listed on the invoice. We feel this is a redundant charge to the consumer and an attempt for the dealer to increase profit.

### Is sales tax on my car calculated before or after the price is adjusted for incentives/rebates?

Sales tax laws are set by the state and each state is a little different. You should ask about this ahead of time so you know what to budget for. Also, keep in mind that there may be other local taxes from the city and county — not to mention the DMV fees. If you are considering crossing state lines to save tax money, think again — you often pay tax based on where you live, not where you buy the car.

### Who is the Internet manager and why do I want to buy a car from him or her?

In the late 1990s consumers began to get a lot of car-buying information on the Internet. Recognizing that some car shoppers were becoming better informed about the fair market value of new cars, dealerships created the "Internet department." Internet managers operate from a different perspective compared to other car salespeople. If you ask the typical car salesperson for a price on a car, they will either be evasive or tell you to pay MSRP. The Internet manager knows that you are well-informed and will usually quote a very-close-to-final figure. Furthermore, the attitude of most Internet salespeople is kinder and gentler. As you can tell, we think the Internet department is the best place to shop at a dealership.

### What should my monthly car payment be?

A rule of thumb is that your monthly car payment shouldn't exceed 20 percent of your monthly take-home pay. If you own two vehicles and make payments on both, the total should not exceed 20 percent of your monthly net income. The Edmunds.com Web site has a variety of calculators to help you estimate what your monthly payment should be. Take the time to run the numbers before you go car shopping. It will not only show you what you can afford, it will also help you control the numbers when you negotiate with a car salesman.

### What is a "blast fax" and how can it save me time and money?

A "blast fax" is a one-page letter faxed to fleet or Internet managers describing the car you want to buy. It is an easy way to simultaneously solicit quotes from multiple dealers. You can achieve the same effect on Edmunds.com by requesting prices via e-mail from dealers. The only advantage to the blast fax is that a physical, personalized letter arrives in the dealership. This might receive more attention from the Internet manager.

The blast fax letter should describe the year, make, model and trim level of the car you want to buy. It should list your favorite colors and the options you want. Keep in mind that the more specific you are in your requests, the harder it will be to find just the right car. Include a fax or telephone number for responses. Once you get a quote you like, have the invoice faxed to you along with a "worksheet" which lists all the prices, tax and fees.

### What are some of the typical dealer add-ons that I should be wary of?

If you go to a car lot and find a second sticker in the car window, next to the factory-generated window sticker, the dealership has installed extras. This can be anything from pin striping to a CD changer. If you want the CD changer, that's fine, but prepare to pay dearly for it. Dealers often mark these add-ons up substantially. In most cases, you are better off buying these accessories directly from an aftermarket supplier.

Additionally, some dealerships install alarms and include the cost in the contract without telling the prospective buyer. This is an ugly $800 surprise when it comes time to sign the papers. They are hoping you just sign and swallow the added expense. We recommend you find a dealership that doesn't practice this approach to profit-taking.

Keep this guiding principle in mind: the purchase price of the car isn't the only area the dealer can make a profit on a new car. Don't become fixated on just the price during your negotiation — look at the deal as a whole to confirm it's a fair one.

## Why won't the dealer give me the full value of my trade-in?

The less you accept for the trade-in, the more room the dealer has to make a profit when he sells it. Furthermore, the dealer will spend money washing, detailing, smogging and possibly repairing your car before it goes up for sale, so he has to factor these expenses into his trade-in offer.

If the car doesn't sell, the dealer will have to sell it for wholesale price at an auction. If the dealer paid you wholesale price when you traded in the car and then spent money refurbishing your car, he wouldn't make the money back in the event that the trade-in went to auction. Regardless of the condition of your car, the dealer will anticipate taking the car to auction, and will leave room to make money in that event. In most cases, your best bet is to sell your car on your own to a private party.

## Who sets the residual value for a lease?

Over the last few years, American Leasing Guide (ALG) (www.alg.com) has cornered the market on setting residual values that most lenders follow. However, the final control over the residual value lies with the financing institution that is handling the lease for the dealership. Residual values have, in recent years, been found to be overly optimistic (too high) causing the manufacturers to lose money when the lease car is returned. A car's residual value is affected by a variety of factors such as vehicle popularity, availability, time of year and the economy. When shopping for a good lease, it is important to query different financial institutions for the highest residual rate and the lowest interest rate. This combination will help give you a low monthly lease payment.

## When is the best time to purchase a car from a dealer?

There's as much advice about when to visit a dealer as there are days in a year. Some say that Mondays are good because business is slower than on the weekend. Some say holidays are good for the same reason; nobody will be there and the sales team will be hungry for a sale. Others advise to go when it's raining or snowing; after all, who wants to look at a car and get wet? Then there's the advice that the end of the month is the best time because the dealership needs to make its "quota" of car sales and will be more willing to cut a deal.

Our advice is not to buy a car until you're ready. By then you have had time to do your research for the lowest interest rate and the current incentives and rebates. This is a much better way to approach car shopping than trying to outguess market factors, which might not be significant anyway.

## How soon after a price increase does Edmunds.com modify its data?

This depends on how soon our sources are notified. Sometimes, it's a matter of days; other times, it can take longer. Rest assured that we painstakingly attempt to maintain the most up-to-date pricing available. If a dealer disputes the accuracy of our pricing, ask him to prove it by showing you the invoice so you can compare. If prices have indeed increased, the amount will not be substantial; the new figures should easily be within a few percentage points of those published in this guide or on our Web site.

Also, keep in mind that the dealer's invoice in your section of the country may have additional charges we don't track. The most notable example of this is the advertising fee. If it is on the invoice, it is a legitimate dealer cost. If it is written into the contract, the dealer may be trying to increase profit.

## When should a car be considered used?

Technically, a vehicle is used if it has been titled through the DMV. However, some dealers rack up thousands of miles on a new car without titling it. In these cases, the definition of a used car should be any car used for extensive demonstration or personal use by dealership staff members. The only miles a new car should have on the odometer when purchased are those put on during test drives by prospective buyers. (Some dealerships use "demos," or demonstration cars, for test drives and later sell these cars at a discount.) A car might also rack up a few hundred miles from a "dealer trade" because they had to drive the car from out of the area. Also, "program cars" are used by a factory representative and then sold at a discount when they have about 10,000 miles on them.

If the new car you're considering has more than 300 miles on the odometer, you should question how the car accumulated them, and request a discount for the excessive mileage. We think a discount amounting to a dime a mile is a fair charge for wear and tear inflicted by the dealership. A car should not be considered used if it is a brand-new vehicle leftover from a previous model year. However, it should be discounted because many manufacturers offer dealers incentives designed to help the dealer clear out old stock.

# How A Hybrid Works

As the national average price of unleaded fuel spills over $2 a gallon and rises toward the $3 mark, many Americans are swimming toward the hybrid vehicle life raft. They have good reason to — the fuel cost savings of a hybrid versus a conventional vehicle are dramatic.

A comparison between the regular Ford Escape and the Ford Escape Hybrid is very compelling. Ford has released city mileage estimates between 32-37 mpg for the Escape Hybrid. Comparing two-wheel-drive versions, that's an 85-percent improvement over the 19 mpg city rating for the conventional V6-powered Ford Escape.

Considering their miserly fuel-sipping nature, it's no wonder that hybrids took the top three spots on our Top 10 Most Fuel-Efficient Cars list.

Capable of pulling down 32-37 mpg in city driving, the Escape Hybrid blends the practicality of an SUV with the fuel economy of a compact car.

In addition to the Escape Hybrid's remarkable fuel economy, it represents an important expansion in hybrid vehicle offerings — it's the first sport-utility hybrid. Until it appeared, consumers could choose from the two-seater Honda Insight hatchback (the first hybrid ever offered in the U.S.), the compact Honda Civic Hybrid sedan and the midsize Toyota Prius four-door hatchback. Although the Prius offers plenty of passenger and cargo room and makes a fine family car in its own right, the Escape has advantages like optional all-wheel drive for buyers who live in harsh climates, extra cargo capacity and a commuter-friendly high seating position.

Another major benefit of hybrid vehicles is their low environmental impact. Because they are propelled partially by electric motors and their small gasoline engines are so efficient, they produce very little emissions. Most hybrid vehicles qualify as Super Ultra Low Emission Vehicles (SULEV) under California Air Resources Board standards, meaning they produce 90-percent fewer smog-forming emissions than the average 2003 model year vehicle. In addition, many hybrids meet the Partial Zero Emission Vehicle (PZEV) standard, because they produce no evaporative emissions and carry a fully transferable 15-year/150,000-mile warranty for their emissions-control equipment.

So, the benefits of hybrids are obvious, but it still leaves the question: What exactly is a hybrid?

## Side by Side: Gasoline Power and Electric Power in Perfect Harmony

Though the basic principles of hybrid operation are the same — that is, an electric motor is used to assist a gasoline engine to reduce fuel consumption and emissions — there are two types of hybrids.

The first type can propel itself using only the electric motor at very low speeds. The electric motor also has the ability to kick and help out the gasoline engine when more power is needed, such as when passing or climbing a steep grade. The Toyota Prius and the Ford Escape Hybrid fall into this category.

The second-generation Prius is a bona fide midsize car perfect for families who like the idea of getting 50 miles to the gallon.

The second type uses the electric motor only to assist the gasoline engine when it needs extra boost, again during brisk acceleration or when going up a hill. The Honda Insight and Civic Hybrid fall into the second category.

To illustrate the difference, when a Toyota Prius accelerates from a standstill, the electric motor gets the vehicle rolling and continues to drive it up to around 25 mph before the gasoline engine automatically starts up. Under hard acceleration from a stop, the gas engine starts immediately to provide maximum power. The electric motor and the gas engine also work in tandem when driving conditions demand more power, such as while climbing a hill or passing other vehicles. Because the electric motor is used so much at low speeds, the Prius and Escape get better mileage in the city than they do on the highway.

In the case of the Honda Insight and Civic Hybrid, the electric motor assists the gas engine only when driving conditions demand more power, such as during hard acceleration from a stop, while climbing a hill or passing other vehicles. As with normal, gas-powered cars, these hybrids get better fuel economy while cruising on the highway, as that is when the gas engine is least taxed.

And that's where the differences end.

Both types of hybrids draw power from their batteries when the electric motor is used, which, of course, depletes battery power. A hybrid does not need to be plugged in to a power source to recharge, however. That's the beauty of hybrids — they recharge themselves.

The Civic Hybrid sedan looks, feels and drives like other Civics, but it's more fuel efficient than the rest.

## The Battery Pack and Regenerative Braking

The Ford Escape Hybrid, Honda Insight and Civic Hybrid and Toyota Prius utilize sealed nickel metal hydride (NiMH) batteries, the same battery technology used in cell phones and note-book computers. The Prius system is composed of 38 modules containing 228 individual cells (each the size of batteries commonly used in flashlights) for a combined total power rating of 273.6 volts. The Honda vehicles utilize 120 cells, with a total power rating of 144 volts. Ford employs 250 cells to provide the Escape Hybrid a total of 330 volts.

An onboard CPU monitors the electrical system, and when the vehicle is coasting downhill or its brakes are applied, the system reverses its polarity, turning the electric-assist motor into a generator. At this point, the forward momentum and braking of the vehicle are converted from mechanical energy into electrical energy and sent to the battery pack for storage. This is known as regenerative braking.

## Mechanical Innovations, Engine Refinements and Advanced Technology

Hybrid vehicles incorporate the latest automotive innovations and engine refinements, many advanced technologies, many developed by auto racing engineers. All are engineered to increase performance, reduce emissions and maximize fuel efficiency. Some are exclusive to specific makes, others are common in all hybrids. They include:

**Aerodynamics/Lower Drag Coefficient:** Seeking sleeker profiles, hybrid engineers often resort to unconventional design features to maximize airflow. For example, the Honda Insight has an ultralow drag coefficient of 0.25 due to its sleek profile and odd-looking covered rear wheels. Even the Toyota Prius, which looks fairly normal to the untrained eye, has a drag coef-ficient of just 0.29 because every effort was made to make it as slippery as possible. Because a vehicle with less drag requires less power (and fuel) to move, all manufacturers try to reduce drag wherever possible.

**Auto Shut-off:** To conserve fuel, all hybrids shut down the gasoline-powered engine during stops. Called an idle-stop feature, this not only saves fuel and reduces emissions, but cuts electrical consumption as well. Similar to a golf cart, the electric motor restarts the gasoline engine when the driver presses the accelerator pedal again. This is a fairly seamless operation, with virtually no delay or loss of performance noticeable to the driver.

**Carbonized Connecting Rods:** Toughens the rod's surface so it resists cracking and reduces rod weight by 25 percent. Reduced weight means better performance because the engine does not have so much mass to push around.

**Continuously Variable Transmission (CVT):** A new kind of automatic transmission (that has actually been around for more than 100 years, but only recently began appearing in cars), the CVT has no gears, friction plates, hydraulic fluids or torque converter. Instead, it uses a simple belt-and-pulley design, which enables it to closely match the transmission ratios with the optimum rpm range of the engine for better power delivery and increased fuel efficiency. Used mostly in light industrial applications, recent advancements in materials and microprocessor technology have made CVTs more suitable for automobiles.

**Cylinder Idling System:** The Honda Civic Hybrid uses this system to reduce engine drag and allow the electric motor to reclaim as much energy as possible during the regenerative braking process. A traditional gasoline engine provides resistance (or "engine braking") during coasting by the pumping action of its cylinders. This robs the electric motor of energy it could otherwise use to charge the batteries. Engine drag can be avoided by engaging the clutch in cars with a manual transmission or putting the vehicle in neutral with a CVT. Effectively, Honda's Cylinder Idling System does this for you by closing the intake and exhaust valves on up to three of the four cylinders, which allows the pistons to move freely within the cylinders, thereby reducing engine drag and maximizing the amount of energy the electric motor is able to reclaim.

**Integrated Exhaust Manifold:** Built directly into the cylinder head to reduce weight and optimize exhaust flow, thereby improving performance and fuel efficiency.

**Low-Friction Pistons:** Through a special forging process called shot-peening, further reduces cylinder sidewall friction, again improving engine efficiency.

**Offset Cylinder Bores:** Improves engine efficiency by reducing the side thrust friction of the pistons as they move within the cylinder.

**Space-Age Materials:** The use of advanced materials — such as magnesium, aluminum alloys and plastic resins — reduces weight throughout the vehicle. Weight reduction translates into higher fuel economy, lower emissions and more efficient performance.

**Variable Valve Timing:** The engine valves are calibrated to stay open longer at higher speeds and close more quickly at lower speeds to maximize combustion efficiency, thereby improving performance and fuel economy, as well as reducing emissions.

## What's Next?

With all their advanced technology, exceptional fuel economy and low emissions, hybrid vehicles are often referred to as the cars of the future. Certainly, with all the new hybrid models coming out and others under development, the technology will be a major part of the automobile landscape for years to come — or at least until somebody figures out fuel cell technology or some other solution to rising gas prices, depleting fossil fuel reserves and accumulating emissions.

For more information on hybrids, check out our Special Report: Hot Hybrids. To read about real-life experiences with hybrids, refer to our road tests on the Ford Escape Hybrid, Honda Civic Hybrid and Insight and Toyota Prius.

| | | | | | |
|---|---|---|---|---|---|
| 4A | 4-speed automatic | HVAC | heating, ventilation and air conditioning | TMV® | Edmunds.com's True Market Value® |
| 5A | 5-speed automatic | I-4 | inline four-cylinder engine | TOD | torque on demand |
| 6A | 6-speed automatic | I-5 | inline five-cylinder engine | ULEV | ultralow emission vehicle |
| 2dr | 2-door | I-6 | inline six-cylinder engine | V6 | V-type six-cylinder engine |
| 4dr | 4-door | i-VTEC | intelligent variable valve timing and lift electronic control | V8 | V-type eight-cylinder engine |
| 5M | 5-speed manual | | | V10 | V-type 10-cylinder engine |
| 6M | 6-speed manual | L | liter | V12 | V-type 12-cylinder engine |
| 8V | 8-valve | LB | longbed | VSC | vehicle skid control |
| 12V | 12-valve | lb(s). | pound(s) | VTEC | variable valve timing and lift electronic control |
| 16V | 16-valve | lb-ft | pound-feet (measurement of torque) | | |
| 24V | 24-valve | | | VVT-i | variable valve timing, intelligence |
| 2WD | two-wheel drive | LCD | liquid crystal display | Wgn. | wagon |
| 4WD | four-wheel drive | LED | light emitting diode | X-Cab | extended cab |
| A | automatic | LEV | low emission vehicle | | |
| ABS | antilock braking system | M | manual | | |
| A/C | air conditioning | mm | millimeter | | |
| ALR | automatic locking retractor | mpg | miles per gallon | | |
| Amp | ampere | mph | miles per hour | | |
| ASR | automatic slip regulation | MPI | multi-port injection | | |
| AT | automatic | MSRP | manufacturer's suggested retail price | | |
| Auto | automatic | | | | |
| AWD | all-wheel drive | N/A | not available OR not applicable | | |
| CC | cubic centimeter | NHTSA | National Highway and Traffic Safety Administration | | |
| CD | compact disc | | | | |
| CFC | chloroflourocarbon | NLEV | National Low Emission Vehicle | | |
| Conv. | convertible | NVH | noise, vibration and harshness | | |
| Cpe | coupe | OD | overdrive | | |
| Cu. Ft. | cubic foot (feet) | OHC | overhead cam | | |
| Cyl. | cylinder | OHV | overhead valve | | |
| DOHC | dual-overhead cam | Opt. | option OR optional | | |
| DRL | daytime running light(s) | Pass. | passenger | | |
| DSC | dynamic stability control | Pkg. | package | | |
| DVD | digital video disc | Reg. | regular | | |
| EDL | electronic differential lock | rpm | revolutions per minute | | |
| EFI | electronic fuel injection | RWD | rear-wheel drive | | |
| EPA | Environmental Protection Agency | SAE | Society of Automotive Engineers | | |
| ETR | electronically tuned radio | SB | shortbed | | |
| Ext. | extended (wheelbase or truck cab) | Sdn | sedan | | |
| | | SFI | sequential fuel injection | | |
| FWD | front-wheel drive | SLA | short/long arm (suspension design) | | |
| Gal. | gallon(s) | | | | |
| GAWR | gross axle weight rating | SMPI | sequential multi-port injection | | |
| GVW | gross vehicle weight | SOHC | single-overhead cam | | |
| GVWR | gross vehicle weight rating | SPI | sequential port injection | | |
| GPS | global positioning satellite | Std. | standard | | |
| Hbk. | hatchback | SULEV | super ultralow emission vehicle | | |
| HD | heavy-duty | SUV | sport-utility vehicle | | |
| hp | horsepower | TDI | turbocharged direct injection | | |
| HUD | head-up display | | | | |

2005 Editors' Most Wanted

by the Editors at Edmunds.com

## Most Significant Vehicle of the Year

### Winner: Chrysler 300

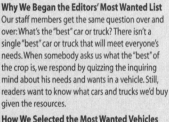
It's been all too long since a new American sedan created anything more than an apathetic yawn from consumers. Between relentless Japanese competition and America's seemingly endless obsession with trucks and SUVs, the idea that a domestic four-door could be the "it" car of the year seemed laughable. Then along came Chrysler's new 300 sedan, a car so unabashedly nontraditional in both its style and its substance that it makes the competition look hopelessly bland in comparison.

Chrysler veered from the usual route of designing a car that would appeal to the broadest swath of the general public and instead went for a look that's original at best and polarizing at worst. Like it or not, there's no denying that it has a presence on the road that no Camry or Taurus could ever hope to duplicate. Backing up its sinister looks is the performance of a rear-wheel-drive chassis and a suspension design shared with some of its more expensive Mercedes cousins. And not only does the outrageous exterior look good, it surrounds a cavernous, well-trimmed interior that's as spacious as any sedan on the road.

Built to straddle the lines between upscale family car and entry-level luxury sport sedan, the 300 offers both a base V6 (190 horsepower) and a midlevel V6 (250 hp), depending on your budget. As surprisingly adept as these V6s are at getting the big sedan up to speed, it's the top-of-the-line Hemi-engined 300C that gives the car its star power. With 340 horses running through a five-speed automatic transmission, the 300C is in a class of its own. And if that's not enough, you can always step up to the high-performance SRT-8 version that packs a 425-hp Hemi under the hood along with larger wheels and a lowered stance.

Chrysler took a chance when it decided on such a radical design for the 300 and the results speak for themselves. Along with an award like Most Significant of the Year, the 300 will also serve to garner the respect of car buyers who always yearned for something a little different but couldn't justify something exotic to fulfill their wishes. The 300 not only gives them something to aspire to, it gave fans of the American sedan something to be proud of—a most significant feat indeed.

### Honorable Mention: Ford Mustang

Redesigning a legend is never easy. Sticking with an old-school look might not be enough to attract new customers while taking too many steps forward threatens to alienate the legions of fans who worship the original. Ford looks to have successfully straddled the line between retro influences and modern design with the 2005 Mustang as it's both visually appealing and physically potent. With more power under the hood, a simple yet effective suspension and an interior that will impress young and old alike, this Mustang is a winner.

### Honorable Mention: Subaru Legacy

After years of toiling in relative obscurity, Subaru's top-of-the-line model finally has the kind of refinement, performance and comfort to land it in the heart of the entry-level luxury segment. It still has all the capability of its predecessors thanks to standard all-wheel drive and plenty of ground clearance, but with two powerful engine options and an upscale interior it feels more like a luxurious sport sedan than just an all-weather "winter car." If you haven't driven a Subaru lately, the Legacy will surprise you.

### Honorable Mention: Lotus Elise

The temptation of the Elise is nothing new to European drivers, but after waiting several long years American drivers finally get to taste the thrills of the Lotus design philosophy. Weighing in at just 2,000 pounds, the Elise offers a power-to-weight ratio that makes this 190-horsepower two-seater as fast as any high-dollar exotic. And not only is it fast, it can rip the corners off a racetrack like few other street-legal cars on the market. Its interior is sparse and there's not much room for luggage, but if you want to have the most fun possible for the least amount of money the Lotus has no equal.

## Sedan Under $15,000

### Winner: Mazda 3

A year after its introduction, the sharp-looking Mazda 3 has become the fastest-selling nameplate in the Mazda lineup and not without good reason: The 3 is a thrill behind the wheel thanks to a precisely tuned suspension, quick steering and strong brakes. Throw in two of the most powerful engines in its class and it's easy to see why we're big fans of this four-door sedan and four-door hatchback duo. But the 3 is about more than just performance, as it features a stylish interior that proves both functional and comfortable as well. For the money, you would be hard-pressed to find a better economy sedan or four-door hatchback on the market.

### Honorable Mention: Honda Civic

Years into its life cycle, the Civic sedan continues to outperform an ever-improving array of economy cars. Honda's long-standing reputation for exceptional build quality and reliability has always made it a smart choice among savvy consumers. But there's more to it than that. The Civic also gives buyers refined handling characteristics and a thoughtfully designed interior with the roomiest backseat in the segment. Although it's not the fastest, the biggest or the cheapest, the Civic always feels like one of the most competent vehicles in this price range regardless of whether you choose a sensible LX or a fuel-sipping Hybrid.

# Sedan Under $25,000

### Winner: Chrysler 300

Chrysler has introduced numerous all-new vehicles during the past couple of years, but none have hit with quite the same enthusiastic approval as the Chrysler 300. With its unique styling and optional 340-horsepower V8 Hemi engine, the 300 disposes of the notion that a family sedan can't be exciting. Its distinctive exterior look complements its unique interior treatment that's traditional in nature but upscale in appearance and feel. With base models starting in the low $20Ks, the 300 competes head-on with the Accord and Camry, but it's the top-of-the-line V8-powered 300C that really makes our mouths water. Where else can you get rear-wheel drive, over 300 hp and an interior that can swallow four adults with room to spare? While the competition tries to figure that one out, we'll be content behind the wheel of this ground-breaking sedan from Chrysler.

### Honorable Mention: Mazda 6

Mazda has admitted the 626 was a poor attempt at trying to beat the Accord and Camry at their own game. Plus, if we're being honest, the 626 had absolutely zero "zoom-zoom." The Mazda 6 (which replaced both the Millenia and 626) is all about the "zoom-zoom." We love the 6's willing and free-revving 220-hp V6 and find the handling to be fun, sporty and confident without sacrificing everyday civility. Many editors praise the 6's good looks and refined power-train but lament the somewhat cramped rear seat and questionable interior materials quality. Still, we can't resist the sheer fun-to-drive factor or the attractive design elements—the Mazda 6 is a truly sporty car cloaked in a sedan's body.

# Sedan under $35,000

### Winner: BMW 3 Series

In the case of BMW's utterly charming 3 Series, you get what you pay for. It's pricier than much of the competition, but with its handsome good looks and world-class performance, this winning sedan feels like a bargain. Its cabin is a study in luxurious understatement—pared-down elegance executed with the finest materials money can buy. And on the road, the 3 Series offers hours of nonstop entertainment, thanks to best-in-show handling and a selection of silky-smooth engines. A pleasure to look at and a dream to experience, the 3 Series stands tall as the most seductive car in its class.

### Honorable Mention: Acura TL

It's easy to see why we love the Acura TL; this ultracapable sedan offers lots of bang for the buck. It's good-looking enough to be a head-turner on the road. It comes armed with as much luxury as any snooty German, with supple leather, a stylish cabin and acres of soft-touch surfaces. It's a blast to drive, thanks to its muscular 270-horsepower V6. And best of all, it's got a long, long list of standard features; included in its goodie bag are leather upholstery, heated seats, satellite radio and a power sunroof. Endlessly appealing, the TL distinguishes itself by offering a compelling mix of value and luxury.

# Sedan under $45,000

### Winner: Cadillac STS

Never much of a threat to the dominance of its German counterparts, the redesigned STS now has all the tools necessary to compete on the world stage. The switch to rear-wheel drive, along with a stronger, stiffer and lighter chassis, gives the STS the feel of a much smaller, more agile sedan. And whether you stick with the standard 255-hp V6 or go for the top-of-the-line 320-hp V8, the STS delivers more than enough power to have some fun. Gadgets galore are offered in the cabin with everything from active cruise control to a 15-speaker Bose 5.1 audio system, but unlike some of its competitors, the STS integrates its high-tech hardware without resorting to overly complicated controls. Couple such attention to detail with a high level of style, comfort and performance and it's easy to see why the STS is a sedan that satisfies on all fronts.

### Honorable Mention: Audi A6

A full redesign for 2005 gave the A6 a new look and more powerful engines, yet it still manages to maintain the kind of subtle sophistication that has drawn us to it year after year. Settle into its plush cabin and it has all the elements of the true luxury sedan—high-quality materials, a crisp design and the latest technology. A new, highly advanced V6 injects the base A6 with more power than ever before while the top-line V8 delivers 335 horses to the ground via a standard all-wheel-drive system. Some might find it stark in comparison to the STS, but for those who like the Germans' sense of style the A6 is a midsize luxury sedan at the top of its game.

# Sedan Over $45,000

### Winner: Audi A8

With cosmetic changes to the grille, headlights and roofline for 2005, this handsome sedan further refines its striking yet subtle styling. The A8 may not have the name cachet of its German peers, but it matches or beats them in just about every meaningful category. With its polished demeanor, spacious and luxurious cabin and capable road manners, the A8 leaves little to be desired. And at a price tag thousands less than its chief rivals, we would strongly suggest visiting the dealer of the four rings before putting down your money on one of its more well-known competitors.

### Honorable Mention: Mercedes-Benz E-Class

It doesn't sit at the top of Mercedes' lineup, but that doesn't mean the E-Class is any less deserving of attention from serious sedan buyers. From the new E320 diesel all the way up to the AMG-tuned E55, the E-Class offers a combination of performance, comfort and style that makes it every bit as enticing as the top-of-the-line S-Class. Its status as one of Mercedes' newest sedans assures that it includes all the latest technological features and a long list of advanced safety equipment, but the E-Class is about more than just features and numbers. This is a car that exemplifies our idea of what a modern luxury sedan should look and feel like. From its exquisitely detailed cabin to its unshakable stability at speed, the E-Class delivers the kind of driving experience you would expect from a car in this price range.

# Wagon Under $15,000

### Winner: Scion xB

An amazing example of space efficiency, the small but boxy Scion xB accommodates four adults with ease. Handling is not the phone-booth-on-wheels experience its mini-truck styling suggests—in fact, it's amazingly buttoned down and responsive for such a tall vehicle. Add to that a generous standard features list (including a Pioneer CD sound system, air conditioning, power everything, ABS and stability control) along with a long list of accessories that allows owners to customize their vehicles, and it's easy to see why the xB is scoring big with younger buyers. And when you consider Toyota's long-standing reliability reputation, it's clear you don't have to be young and hip to like the xB.

### Honorable Mention: Suzuki Forenza

In spite of its low profile in the economy car segment, the Forenza has plenty to offer for the money. Like its sedan companion introduced last year, the new-for-2005 wagon version comes with a long list of standard equipment and has a tastefully styled cabin with comfortable seating and solid build and materials quality. And because it's a wagon, prospective buyers can look forward to 61.8 cubic feet of cargo space with the rear seats folded. The driving experience is certainly acceptable for this class, with adequate power, a smooth ride and capable handling. Other wagons may offer more features, but very few can put all the essentials together for such a low price.

# Wagon Under $25,000

### Winner: Dodge Magnum

Move over, Moms, this is a wagon that will get Dads fired up about driving carpool. With retro styling that crosses a family hauler with a '50s chop top, the Magnum is rapidly becoming a design icon. A low-slung roof and dark tinted windows give it a look unlike any other wagon. The Magnum is also the first Dodge vehicle to take advantage of the Daimler part of parent company DaimlerChrysler. By using a suspension setup similar in design to that of upper-class Mercedes sedans, the Magnum is able to deliver ride and handling qualities that rival many sedans, let alone other wagons. Add in an optional Hemi-powered V8 engine, and over 70 feet of cargo space, and we say leave the SUV in the garage.

### Honorable Mention: Subaru Legacy

For several years now, Subaru has been enjoying recognition for its active lifestyle Outback wagon, and has recently received numerous accolades for its sporty Impreza WRX models. Lost in the shadows, however, was the dependable yet unexciting Subaru Legacy. Finally the Legacy comes into its own, with the availability of both a normally aspirated six-cylinder engine and a turbocharged four-cylinder as well. The Legacy's interior has also been upgraded to offer the same sporty appeal as a German sedan. Now, as both a sleek and well-performing station wagon, the Legacy proves that family transportation needn't be wood-paneled and boring.

# Wagon Under $35,000

### Winner: Audi A4 Avant

There's a lot to be said for Audi's gorgeous wagon. Its sculpted lines are the ultimate in laid-back elegance, commanding attention without being the least bit showy. Its razor-sharp handling keeps you gurgling with bliss on the open road. And you'll fall in love with its cabin; slip inside and you'll find yourself swaddled in a cocoon of modern opulence, where materials are first-rate, build quality is beyond reproach and aesthetics are sleek and engaging. Topping it all off is the fact that the Avant is a few grand cheaper than its stiffest competition. Some believe wagons to be stodgy and dull. The luscious Avant illustrates just how wrong these assumptions can be.

### Honorable Mention: Volvo V70

Given its role as family hauler, one trait that most no doubt value above all others in their wagon is safety. With features like whiplash-reducing headrests and head curtain airbags, this is one area in which the V70 shines—hardly a surprise since it is, after all, a Volvo. Of course, the V70 offers lots more to win you over, like wonderfully comfortable accommodations, loads of room relative to the competition and more performance than you'd likely expect from a wagon. And don't forget its muscular exterior, miles removed from that of the boxy Volvos of yesteryear. If you need family transportation, you need to take a second look at the thoroughly competent V70.

# Wagon Over $35,000

### Winner: Mercedes-Benz E-Class Wagon

E-Class wagons feature a sleek and dignified design inside and out, a pleasing blend of ride and handling and optional all-wheel drive. Available with either a capable V6 or a downright vigorous V8, the E-Class wagon makes an excellent touring car. As a family hauler, safety is a concern and shoppers won't be disappointed. In IIHS frontal offset crash testing, it was named a "Best Pick" in its class. Despite our minor quips of a confusing control layout and electronically controlled brakes that lack a progressive feel, its combination of excellent driving dynamics, numerous safety and luxury features and high style make the E-Class one of our favorites.

### Honorable Mention: Audi allroad

It may have lost some of its rugged looks, but Audi's sport wagon still has enough of what we like to make it attractive. Devised as an alternative to bulky SUVs, the allroad combines the practicality of a wagon with the all-weather prowess of an SUV. The recent addition of optional V8 power gives it the kind of punch that few other wagons can match. Inside, it's all Audi as the allroad's interior is covered from head to toe in top-quality materials that will make you forget you're driving such a practical vehicle. If you need a wagon but don't want something too traditional, the allroad is the answer.

## Coupe Under $15,000

### Winner: Honda Civic

Versatile, refined and environmentally friendly, today's Civic coupe has broad appeal. If you're pinching pennies, there's the Value Package and LX coupes, which give you access to all the basics. If you want a full load of amenities and a more powerful engine, there's the EX coupe. If fuel economy is most important to you, the HX coupe has a leaner-burning engine that allows it to get up to 44 mpg. And if you're looking for a little performance from your Civic, not to mention extra cargo space, you'll want to look at the Si hatchback. Whether you're a seasoned commuter or a budget-minded enthusiast (with plans for aftermarket upgrades), there's something to please just about everyone.

### Honorable Mention: Ford Focus

Although the Focus can't match the refinement and bulletproof reliability outlook of its Honda peer, there are plenty of reasons to buy one anyway. Chief among these are its excellent driving dynamics, as the Focus manages to deliver the smooth, comfortable ride that wins favor with commuters, along with the responsive handling in corners that makes it a perfect starting point for young driving enthusiasts. Inside, the car offers roomy accommodations for its passengers, simple controls and a great stock audio system. And around back, the three-door hatchback body style opens up plenty of cargo space for hauling groceries or moving back to the dorms.

## Coupe Under $25,000

### Winner: Ford Mustang

There's a certain amount of risk involved in reinventing a legend, and Ford undoubtedly weighed its options carefully before bringing the all-new Mustang to the market just after celebrating its 40th anniversary. Luckily, what arrived on the scene for 2005 is a Mustang that does its heritage proud. Filled with old-school influences, like a dual-hooded dash with aluminum accent panels and numerous mechanical improvements that advance the coupe's handling characteristics, the Mustang, with its capable 4.0-liter V6 or 300-horsepower, 4.6-liter V8 engine, continues to shine as an audacious thoroughbred.

### Honorable Mention: Volkswagen Golf

With nimble handling and brisk performance, the Rabbit GTI was an instant hit with driving enthusiasts when it was introduced back in 1983. Twenty years later, the Golf and GTI are still providing thrifty thrills for drivers with their precise handling and spirited acceleration. Whether you're driving the 180-horsepower, turbocharged 1.8-liter inline four or the 24-valve, 2.8-liter VR6, you can get your kicks with an automatic or six-speed manual transmission. There is a wide range of trim levels to choose from in both the Golf and GTI models, but what really puts the Golf near the top of our list is its hatchback design and unmatched utility wrapped around an entertaining driver's machine.

# Coupe Under $35,000

### Winner: BMW 3 Series

Its sharp exterior will draw your eye, but all it takes is a few minutes behind the wheel to see that this coupe's beauty is more than skin-deep. Its handling is superb and the steering almost begs you to push it hard through every turn. And none of this comes at the expense of ride comfort which, for the most part, is forgiving enough to guarantee hours of comfortable cruising. Thrill-seekers in need of an added rush will want to sign up for the line's high-performance M3, which delivers even more excitement thanks to a 333-horsepower engine and ultraresponsive suspension. For all this and more, the stunning 3 Series easily zooms to the head of the pack.

### Honorable Mention: Mazda RX-8

This curvy little coupe offers your standard bevy of sports-car thrills, teamed with a surprising degree of practicality. Its rotary engine packs up to 238 horsepower, delivered with remarkable smoothness. Grins won't be in short supply when you're behind the wheel; the RX-8 feels at one with the road, with ample steering feedback and loads of grip through the twisties. Best of all, the Mazda's nifty cruiser boasts more in terms of day-to-day livability than the competition, with seating for four and handling that's reasonably commuter-friendly. Fun to drive and more versatile than you'd probably imagine, the RX-8 is a standout in its class.

# Coupe Under $45,000

### Winner: Chevrolet Corvette

The sixth-generation Corvette made its debut this year with an all-new body style, retooled suspension and an even larger version of its tried-and-true small-block V8. Available as either a coupe or convertible, the C6 uses the same underlying structure as its predecessor, the C5, to bring the Corvette into the 21st century. Ride and handling is more consistent on this latest edition of Chevy's iconic sports car than it has been in years' past, sacrificing none of the car's characteristic high performance. At the heart of the C6 is the LS2 V8 that produces a remarkable 400 horsepower and 400 pound-feet of torque. With that much power on tap, the C6 is able to keep up with just about any of the world's most exotic sports cars. Available options include three different suspension packages, Magnetic Ride Control, plus a Z51 package with upgraded brakes. Regardless of how it's equipped, this is undoubtedly one of the best Corvettes ever.

### Honorable Mention: Mercedes-Benz CLK-Class

The CLK just barely squeaks into this category but that doesn't mean it's any less deserving of praise. Unlike the Corvette, the CLK offers a more spacious and refined coupe experience. This is a car that not only looks good, it feels good. You could drive it everyday to work and then take off for a weekend getaway without hesitation. Although the base V6 offers just 215 hp, those who prefer more potent power plants can upgrade the CLK with a choice of two serious V8s—a 302-hp, 5.0-liter version or an AMG-tuned 5.4-liter good for 362 hp. No matter what engine is under the hood, the CLK delivers an excellent balance of everyday comfort mixed with plenty of capability in the turns. The cabin is nothing to complain about either as its clean design and top-quality materials make it feel the way a luxury coupe should.

# Coupe Over $45,000

### Winner: Mercedes-Benz CL-Class

The Mercedes-Benz CL is an uncompromising coupe that earns its praise with every trip behind the wheel. It's an artful blend of performance, technology and classic luxury that will impress even the most spoiled car buyer. Although available in several power iterations ranging from the base 302-horsepower CL500 to an asphalt-smoking 604-hp CL65, the choice of engine is virtually the only option as every CL comes fully loaded. This flagship coupe offers so much more than any competitor that it's in a segment virtually unto itself.

### Honorable Mention: BMW 6 Series

The 6 Series coupe is back after a 14-year hiatus from the BMW lineup. It's a phenomenal work of engineering that combines such highly advanced features as Active Steering, Active Roll Stabilization, Active Cruise Control and an optional Sequential Manual Gearbox along with progressive German styling. As a complete package, the 6 Series is refined beyond reproach, but its insistence on endless technological gadgetry keeps it from toppling the aging but still sensational CL.

# Convertible Under $25,000

### Winner: Mazda MX-5 Miata

With the addition of the hot Mazdaspeed version, the Miata is better than ever. With 178 turbo-charged ponies under the hood, the Mazdaspeed Miata is the high-powered MX-5 enthusiasts have been waiting for. A retuned suspension, larger wheels and tires and a unique interior further sweeten the deal that this affordable roadster offers. But even those who don't need the added performance of the turbocharged model will still find the standard versions every bit as enjoyable. With just enough modern conveniences to keep it comfortable, the Miata is still the classic convertible that made it a hit over a decade ago. You can drop the top without ever leaving your seat and there's just enough space in the trunk for a weekend's worth of cargo. When it comes to affordable convertibles, it's hard to go wrong with Mazda's Miata.

### Honorable Mention: Mini Cooper Convertible

Get ready for a dose of Mini mania all over again as the Cooper is finally available in convertible form. We've loved this fun-to-drive economy car since the day it rolled onto American shores, but the introduction of the convertible model has us checking it out all over again. Sporting virtually the same lines as the standard coupe, the convertible gives up little in the way of style or performance. Offered in both standard and supercharged Cooper S trim, the Mini convertible has a power-operated top that folds away in seconds to deliver the kind of fun that only a Mini can. There's still seating for four and cargo space is expectedly tight, but if you're looking for wind-in-your-hair fun on a budget, it's hard to top a topless Cooper.

# Convertible Under $35,000

### Winner: BMW Z4

There were some people who felt this "flame surfaced" design was going just too far. We disagreed. Or was it because, when we got behind the wheel, the superb German-car feeling distorted our sense of vision? Whatever the reason, this roadster grabbed our attention with its refinement, exhilarating handling dynamics and superb engines. Slightly longer than its predecessor, the Z3, the body is stiffer and lighter while retaining rigidity. Handling is even sharper than before, and the new electrically assisted steering rack delivers solid road feel. For power, the Z4 lets you choose between a 184-horsepower, 2.5-liter straight six or a 225-hp, 3.0-liter straight six. Whatever way you set it up, you'll find the Z4 provides the most fun you can have with the top down and an empty road ahead of you.

### Honorable Mention: Nissan 350Z

This roadster rarely has to play second fiddle to anything, but this time it came up just short of the Z4 for top honors. With 287 horsepower under the hood, there are more than enough ponies to take on die-hard sports cars let alone cruise with the top down on warm summer nights. Regardless of how you drive it, however, the Z roadster is bound to please. Its sharp-edged looks get noticed at every turn while the precise handling and quick steering always keep it pointed right where you want it to go. And go it does, as this drop top will go from zero to 60 in just over 6 seconds. So whether you want the power and performance of a true sports car or the carefree feeling of a convertible, the 350Z roadster gives you both.

# Convertible Under $45,000

### Winner: Audi A4

We've always loved the style of the A4 sedan, yet Audi somehow managed to improve upon those lines with the A4 convertible. And not only does it look good standing still, it feels good behind the wheel. From the well-sorted suspension to the dead-on steering, this is a convertible that can be driven fast or slow with gratifying results every time. With a range that extends from the base 1.8 turbo four-cylinder all the way up to the V8-powered S4, there's a model for the enthusiast right down to the weekend cruiser. Regardless of how fast you're going, this Audi's interior will delight as it's bathed in high-quality materials from head to toe. Usable rear seats and a sizable trunk keep it practical while stability control and rollover protection keep it safe. If you're looking for a stylish, luxurious and fun-to-drive drop top, the A4 has few equals.

### Honorable Mention: Lotus Elise

Unlike the A4 that blends luxury and performance into its topless package, the fact that the Elise can lose its top is almost an afterthought. This car is designed for one thing and one thing only—performance. Its combination of an ultralightweight chassis, free-revving four-cylinder and stiff suspension result in a raw track car that can run circles around exotics that cost three times as much. But unlike thrown-together kit cars, this track star uses reliable Toyota power and years of Lotus construction expertise to keep it in one piece. Amenities are few, but that's the idea. If you want seat heaters and a good stereo, this isn't the convertible for you. If you're looking for one of the most incredibly unfiltered driving experiences this side of $50K, however, the Elise has no equal.

# Convertible Over $45,000

### Winner: Mercedes-Benz SL-Class

In years past, a sports car had to sacrifice comfort in the name of speed, while a touring car gave up breakneck acceleration in order to achieve opulence. Thanks to the joys of modern technology, the line between the two has been dissolved. After a 50-year odyssey, the Mercedes SL-Class has reached legendary status, and for good reason. The latest version features razor-sharp handling, an incredibly refined interior and even a retractable hardtop so sunny days and chilly nights can be enjoyed with equal aplomb. Power choices range from a 302-horsepower V8 all the way up to a wicked twin-turbocharged V12, and a bevy of cutting-edge safety equipment comes standard in case things get out of hand. A car with this many positive traits comes with a high price tag, and it is well worth it in our book.

### Honorable Mention: BMW 6 Series

BMW has a worldwide reputation for building refined and comfortable cars packed with technology and style. The new 645Ci convertible is no exception, thanks to a glorious 4.4-liter, 325-horsepower, V8 engine and stunning looks that elicit love-it or hate-it responses wherever it goes. No matter what you think of the car's lines, there's no arguing with the technology that lies beneath. Three different six-speed transmissions are available, including a manual, automatic and even a Sequential Manual Gearbox for the dedicated driving enthusiast. A combination of composite and aluminum materials keeps the big drop top relatively light. Heated seats, DVD navigation and a killer sound system come standard, while options include active suspension and active cruise control. Overall, the new 6 Series is one heck of a driving machine.

# Compact Truck

### Winner: Dodge Dakota

The brawny Dodge Dakota is all new for 2005, and improvements across the board make it a strong choice among compact pickups. A hydroformed frame provides eight times more rigidity than the previous design, and all-new suspension combined with rack and pinion steering lends the platform a nimble, carlike feel. A highly refined V6 and two V8s offer plenty of power, and an optional first-in-class all-wheel-drive system provides surefooted traction in just about any situation. The spacious cabins are comfortable, especially in crew cab form, and the varying degrees of features and options allow you to tailor the price and capabilities to your needs. It all adds up to a refined and well-thought-out compact truck that drives like a car and can haul loads like a full-size pickup.

### Honorable Mention: Toyota Tacoma

With 18 different variations available and Toyota's legendary reputation for quality backing things up, the all-new Tacoma is a great choice for compact truck buyers. A revised suspension makes it a solid performer on and off the beaten path, and a variety of special packages like the PreRunner and TRD model are available for true off-road aficionados. A 2.7-liter four-cylinder provides power in base 4x2 models, while higher-end versions get a powerful new 4.0-liter, 245-horsepower V6. Offering more room in every direction, a slick interior design and several unique new features, the Tacoma has just about everything you could possibly want in a compact truck

# Large Truck

### Winner: Nissan Titan

After being named our Most Significant Vehicle of the Year for 2004, the Titan is back and relatively unchanged for 2005. The powerful 5.6-liter Endurance V8 is still the only engine available and it delivers a notable balance of smooth around-town operation and impressive towing capacity. Four doors are standard on both extended and crew cab models, and the Titan's interior is spacious and functional with ample storage and plenty of passenger room. Trim levels are broken down into XE, SE and LE levels, with the top rung of the ladder offering luxury-car level amenities, including power leather seats, adjustable pedals and a Rockford-Fosgate stereo system. Notable options like a sunroof, spray-in bedliner, adjustable tie-downs and even a DVD-navigation system make this a full-size truck that's hard to ignore.

### Honorable Mention: Dodge Ram 1500/2500/3500

Still the king of big-truck attitude, the Ram can handle the diverse duties of comfortable daily driver and capable workhorse with equal aplomb. Big-rig styling and a spacious interior have been Dodge hallmarks since this version was introduced in 1999, yet nimble handling and a comfortable ride make the Ram truly standout from the pack. The 3.7 V6 and 4.7 V8 are now available with either six-speed manual or five-speed automatic transmissions, and the 5.7 Hemi is optional for those who crave extra power. New options for 2005 include a power sunroof and satellite radio, and the 500-hp SRT-10 is now available as a quad cab. Offering a wide array of positive features with few compromises, it's easy to see why the Ram is consistently at the top of our shortlist.

# SUV Under $25,000

### Winner: Chevrolet Equinox

Midsize in dimensions but compact in price, the attractive Equinox is one car-based SUV that families will want to put on their shopping lists. Its greatest asset is its roomy and comfortable interior, which offers a fair amount of supple materials along with tasteful aluminum accents. The front and rear seats are equally accommodating, thanks to the backseat's 8 inches of fore/aft travel and reclining back cushions. A standard V6 provides ample power in just about any situation while returning respectable mileage. And the softly tuned suspension delivers a smooth ride that's perfect for long road trips. Best of all, the Equinox comes with a starting price in the low-$20Ks.

### Honorable Mention: Ford Escape/Mazda Tribute

There's a lot to like about the Ford Escape/Mazda Tribute duo. Thanks to a spacious interior and a stylish exterior, these are practical vehicles you'll be proud to call your own. On pavement, they handle like cars with little body roll and responsive steering. While not as rugged as some of the competition, they manage to hold their own off-road as well. With a choice of both four- and six-cylinder engines, acceleration ranges from adequate to spirited. Escape buyers have another option this year, as a hybrid model pairs a four-cylinder with an electric motor, resulting in V6-like acceleration and fuel mileage in the 20s. Whichever model you choose, you'll be getting an enjoyable compact SUV.

# SUV Under $35,000

### Winner: Toyota 4Runner

Looks don't lie when it comes to the 4Runner. Its rugged visage suggests that this bruiser packs a mean punch off-road, and indeed it does—if you're seeking a vehicle capable of serving up all-terrain excitement, rest assured that this brawny beast has you covered. This versatility doesn't come at the expense of on-road handling; when rubber meets pavement, the 4Runner goes about its business with minimum fuss, delivering a smooth ride and tight handling. The cherry on top? Roomy quarters, and a competitive list of creature comforts and standard equipment. A winner in almost any environment, the 4Runner is an SUV for those seeking the best of both worlds.

### Honorable Mention: Ford Explorer/Mercury Mountaineer

It's hard not to warm up to the Explorer/Mountaineer; these appealing twins deliver much of what people want in an SUV. Each offers a spacious cabin that boasts a versatile layout and seating for seven. You'll feel safe coming and going thanks to crash test scores that prove these vehicles hold their own in a crunch. And the duo offers as much fun as you'll have behind the wheel of an SUV; handling is pleasant thanks to a rear independent suspension system that keeps jostling to a minimum and tires firmly planted on rough road. It's no wonder the Explorer has long been a sales success; the Explorer/Mountaineer satisfies on most every level.

# SUV Under $45,000

### Winner: Volkswagen Touareg

Volkswagen waited awhile before hopping on the SUV bandwagon, but when it finally got on-board it did it in a very big way. The highly refined and well-engineered Touareg offers a near perfect blend of nimble handling, supple ride quality, luxury-carlike amenities, stellar towing capacity and off-road ability that far exceeds anything most suburbanites will ever require. A 240-horse V6 is standard, while a 310-horse V8 and ultrahigh-tech V10 TDI turbodiesel are both optional. Unfortunately, the gasoline motors aren't exactly the most fuel-efficient in their class, and the miserly yet powerful TDI isn't available in certain states due to emissions standards. However, the five-passenger Touareg is one of safest SUVs on the road today and it offers a superior driving experience that is truly a credit to the breed.

### Honorable Mention: Cadillac SRX

Cadillac is the hottest brand at GM these days, and for good reason. Aggressive styling, powerful engines and rear-wheel drive are giving the marque an all-new image, and the SRX is a shining example of this new philosophy. The crossover SUV rides on a version of the CTS platform, meaning balanced handling comes standard. Power plants include a 260-horse V6 or 320-horse Northstar V8, and options like all-wheel drive and magnetic ride control ensure proper traction in any situation. The comfortable interior is loaded with leather and wood trim, and goodies like a panoramic sunroof, DVD-entertainment system and satellite radio are available for those who enjoy the finer things in life. Overall, Cadillac's first shot at a crossover SUV is a real winner.

# SUV Over $45,000

### Winner: Land Rover Range Rover

The company's heritage lies in the rocky hills of Wales, but the Range Rover has a vein of German design excellence in its pedigree. Despite Land Rover's record of mediocre reliability, this stylish British wunderkind's remarkable capability and exceptional comfort is the result of extensive efforts by BMW's engineers. Their labor has produced one of the most desirable luxury sport-utes around. Though built for the bush, Rovers are bought for bragging rights and thus more likely to be found in Beverly Hills than Botswana. Regardless of its image, we love the fact that we can climb a boulder while enjoying a fat-free soy milk latte.

### Honorable Mention: Toyota Land Cruiser/Lexus LX 470

For nearly 50 years, versions of the Land Cruiser have been sold in the U.S. The model has evolved from the hardy 1958 original to the luxury all-terrain family-hauling sport-ute we drive today. The adept Land Cruiser/LX 470 is able to tackle the most challenging terrain without breaking a sweat. What's more, this ability doesn't hamper the SUV's level of control and ease of operation on the asphalt. Just because they're ruggedly capable doesn't make them any less luxurious as each one comes loaded with creature comforts galore. Its extensive history of outstanding durability and reliability has created a quasi-cult of loyal customers, and we can see why.

# Minivan

### Winner: Honda Odyssey

Creating the ultimate minivan requires more than just offering a roomy and comfortable box-on-wheels. Today's minivans must have abundant power, uncompromised utility and the latest in creature comforts, and the newly redesigned Honda Odyssey doesn't miss a trick. It offers plenty of power from its 250-horsepower V6 engine, coupled with an all-new cylinder deactivation system that improves mileage without sacrificing a single pony. A new body structure increases the Odyssey's overall crash-worthiness over its predecessor, plus Honda added a rear camera and side airbag canopies that span all three rows. Combine performance with improved safety and a nine-inch DVD rear entertainment system with unparalleled sound quality, and you've got a vehicle your family will want to spend time in.

### Honorable Mention: Toyota Sienna

Revamped in 2004, the Toyota Sienna spent a triumphant year on top, finally surpassing the Honda Odyssey prior to its 2005 redesign. While the Odyssey may have reclaimed the lead, the Sienna still offers enough mechanical and feature content to make it a close runner-up. With a standard split-folding third-row seat, side door windows that roll down, A/C power outlets and available eight-passenger seating, plus optional adaptive cruise control, three-zone climate control and a JBL audio system, the Sienna may no longer be the most attractive package in the minivan market, but its interior luxury still verifies its status as the Lexus of minivans.

# Exotic

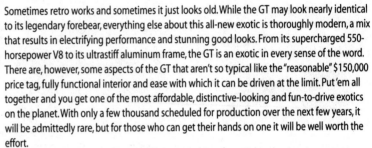

### Winner: Ford GT

Sometimes retro works and sometimes it just looks old. While the GT may look nearly identical to its legendary forebear, everything else about this all-new exotic is thoroughly modern, a mix that results in electrifying performance and stunning good looks. From its supercharged 550-horsepower V8 to its ultrastiff aluminum frame, the GT is an exotic in every sense of the word. There are, however, some aspects of the GT that aren't so typical like the "reasonable" $150,000 price tag, fully functional interior and ease with which it can be driven at the limit. Put 'em all together and you get one of the most affordable, distinctive-looking and fun-to-drive exotics on the planet. With only a few thousand scheduled for production over the next few years, it will be admittedly rare, but for those who can get their hands on one it will be well worth the effort.

### Honorable Mention: Bentley Continental GT

Who would have thought that Bentley would still be making cars at all in the 21st century, let alone a coupe as visually stunning and mechanically mouth-watering as the Continental GT? History aside, the newest member of the Bentley family not only offers the expected level of British charm and exotic exclusivity, it also delivers those goods with a surprisingly reasonable price tag ($150,000). Consider that the average Ferrari goes for well over $200K and the GT is an obvious bargain. With 550 hp, standard all-wheel drive and a shape that's every bit as eye-catching as a red Maranello, the GT can hold its own with the world's fastest despite its more genteel demeanor. If that's your style, this is your car.

# 2005 Ford Mustang

**Not merely a retro reskinning, the newest Mustang improves its performance in all areas and offers V8 enthusiasts a tempting price tag.**

## Looking Back While Galloping Forward

**By John DiPietro**
**Photos courtesy of Ford Motor Company**

After reacting like Pavlov's dog every time we saw the '05 Mustang prototype at the car shows and the production version in pictures, we were beside ourselves. What a looker this car is —they could sell a million of them if they just gave last year's car these new threads. Still, we were hoping that there would be more to Ford's latest pony than head-turning retro looks. The day of reckoning came when we got to spend a full day with the 2005 Mustang, both on the road and the track, and let's just say that we weren't disappointed.

As far as exterior design goes, not since the 1970 Fastback has there been a Mustang that's been so right. Like the latest Thunderbird, the designers managed to pay homage to a classic style without having the end result looking like a caricature of the original. The canted nose with its big grille and round headlights recalls the '67 to '69 Mustangs, while the side sculpting, fastback roofline and taillights recall those ponies of the 1965 vintage. Even the triangular side windows are reminiscent of what Carol Shelby did when he made the 1965 Mustang "2 + 2" (a.k.a. the Fastback) into his Shelby GT 350.

Unlike the similarly retro-styled Thunderbird, whose cabin borrows its dash and console from its Lincoln LS cousin, the Mustang's interior is unique and matches the exterior design theme. Look at the instrument panel and it's obvious that the old-school influences are there—a dual-hooded dash with (optional) aluminum accent panels pays obvious (and tasteful) homage to the 1967-'68 Mustang, as do the big speedo and tach, circular air vents and plump, round steering wheel hub. Changeable backlighting illuminates the nostalgic instruments—a modern touch that's intriguing but a little gimmicky for a pony car.

The materials and features aspects of the interior were not overlooked, either. The door panels and release handles are now more substantial in look and feel, and one-touch up-and-down power windows add a bit of unexpected convenience. The climate control setup is the tried-and-true three-knob design, which is fine with us—if it ain't broke, ya don't need to fix it.

We're also glad to report that the sorry ergonomics of previous Mustangs, such as the "sitting on an ottoman" seating position and gorilla's-reach gearshifter location have been exorcised

The classic three-bar taillights and a simulated gas cap in the center of the rear panel are a few more timeless styling cues from the 'Stang's early days.

for 2005. With the new car, you sit more in rather than on the seats. Although they're generally quite comfortable (as we discovered on a rather lengthy ride back from the track—yes, we took a wrong turn), we still think more aggressive lateral bolstering is in order.

Although the previous manual gearshifter was bolted directly to the gearbox, this year's is a remote-linkage setup that puts the stick within easy reach regardless of the driver's height. And lest you worry about the shifter's action feeling disconnected due to the non-direct design, fret not. Compared to the rubbery yet clunky feel of the 2004 car, the '05's shifter is much more precise and simply more satisfying to use whether jockeying in traffic or blasting around a racetrack.

While the handsome style of the '05 Mustang is obviously rooted in the past, behind the galloping horse in the grille is a thoroughly modern source of motivation. In the GT, no less than 300 horses and 315 pound-feet of torque await the driver's command. Compared to the V8 in the '04 GT, these are substantial increases of 40 horsepower and 13 lb-ft, respectively. This 4.6-liter, all-aluminum V8 sports three valves per cylinder which, along with variable valve timing, allows for a deliciously broad spread of power. A nice bonus is that one needn't feed this steed expensive oats; 87 octane fuel is just fine. Even the V6 has more muscle this year; specs for the six-shooter now stand at 200 hp and 235 lb-ft, improvements of 10 horses and 15 lb-ft.

The influence of the first-generation Mustang's dash is obvious, yet it still manages to look contemporary.

Whether you prefer an automatic or a manual gearbox in your new GT, you'll have five gears at your disposal. The do-it-yourself version has the improved shifter mentioned earlier, and the automatic is sourced from the Lincoln LS/Thunderbird. You already know that we like the stick, but the automatic proved to be the big surprise; it didn't let us down once. Under hard acceleration, changes up through the gears were so swift and smooth that there was no letup in the gratifying shove to our backsides. Downshifts were equally eager—no annoying lag, just a quick dip down into the power to get by those semiconscious sorts who tend to dawdle in the passing lane.

The V6 car comes with a choice of a five-speed manual or four-speed automatic. We drove the automatic and found it did a decent job with keeping the V6 responsive, though it wasn't quite as quick-witted as the five-speed in the GT.

At the track we had the chance to sample both the base V6 and GT Mustangs, as well as a couple of 2004 GT models. Starting out with the '04 GT, we were reminded how seriously wrong the seating position is in that car. If a driver isn't completely comfortable behind the wheel (in terms of feeling secure in the seat and having vital controls close at hand), it tends to diminish the experience, especially when trying to concentrate on driving fast. And we were also reminded how that outgoing GT is essentially a straight-line car—cornering was never this Mustang's forte. Granted, Ford did a nice job with the Bullitt and Mach 1 editions in the handling department, but the base GT was hurting in this regard when compared to contemporary sport coupes like the front-wheel-drive Acura RSX or Toyota Celica.

Night and day. That's the difference between the '04 and '05 versions of the Mustang GT when the road throws you a curve. Where the '04 felt like an ornery old pony that was lazy to respond to the reins and not smooth when doing so, the new one handled like a quarter horse, turning crisply into the turns while displaying a flatter and much more composed attitude when charging through them. Many thanks go to the new suspension, which features lighter-weight components (allowing it to react quicker to changes in the road surface), repositioned and lighter coil springs, a stouter rear axle with more effective control arms and bigger brakes. The latter were noticed (and appreciated) as less prone to fading when the going got hot and heavy on the track.

With a hearty output of 300 horsepower, we figure this mill should power the new GT to 60 mph in around 5.5 seconds.

After the adrenaline rush of the track, we just wanted to kick back and be comfy for the long ride back to the hotel. This over-200-mile journey brought to light how easy the '05 Mustang would be to have as a daily driver. Low wind and road noise levels, a supple ride over the bumps and a much more comfortable cabin than before helped us unwind the miles with a minimum of stress.

With the Mustang's competition pretty much nonexistent (those age-old rivals, the Chevy Camaro and Pontiac Firebird were no longer available after 2002), Ford didn't have to make huge changes in the already popular Mustang. But the company did—not only in terms of styling but also in performance, handling and ride dynamics and basic ergonomics.

With pricing slated to be just under $20,000 for the base V6 and around $25,000 for the GT (both nicely equipped, we might add), we expect that once these horses hit the market, the Ford dealers are going to see a stampede of a different kind, that of rabid enthusiasts eager to fill out sales orders.

The GT's 17-inch wheels are shod with 235/55 performance rubber that proved its mettle on the track with a high level of grip and predictability when pushed.

## Featured Vehicle Review
# 2005 Toyota Tacoma

**You couldn't ask for much more in a compact pickup. Always one of the sharpest trucks in the segment, the subtle styling revisions of the 2005 Tacoma make it look better than ever.**

## Compact Crusher

By Ed Hellwig
**Photos courtesy of Toyota Motor Sales U.S.A.**

Toyota engineers claim that they used a "go and see" approach for the design of the latest Tacoma. By this they implied that they went where their customers were and watched them as they used the Tacoma in their daily lives. Whether it was on the job getting beat up by workmen or on the sand serving as a portable beer cooler, they wanted to see firsthand exactly how the Tacoma was used.

After sampling several versions of the 2005 Tacoma, it seems as though Toyota may have left off the latter part of its development mantra, the part that said, "Go and see what your competitors are doing, and then crush them mercilessly with a vastly superior truck that will embarrass lesser pickups into oblivion." It may not have been quite that colorful, but there's no denying the fact that this new Tacoma is far and away one of the best compact trucks ever offered to the American public.

Toyota has had a long history of selling compact trucks in the U.S. and the passion these trucks inspire among their owners is every bit as rabid as that of their domestic competitors. Since becoming the Tacoma in 1995, Toyota's compact pickup has consistently attracted some of the youngest buyers in the category thanks to sharp styling, a bulletproof reliability record and its image as the perfect complement to a pair of dirt bikes or WaveRunners. It wasn't always the biggest or most powerful truck in its class, but when it came to delivering a complete package, the Tacoma rarely let its buyers down.

Giving the Tacoma a full redesign didn't require drastic measures -- just a little more of the stuff it already had, along with a few surprises mixed in, to keep it on top of its game. The all-new Tacoma does just that with a round of across-the-board improvements that boosts its standing among its peers in almost every category. Whether it's engine power, interior room or safety features, the newest Tacoma has more of everything than it had before and even a few things it didn't. After driving several different models in various configurations, it's safe to say that the Tacoma has everything it needs to dominate the category.

Much like their full-size cousins, compact trucks derive much of their practicality from their numerous configurations, and the Tacoma now offers more styles than ever before -- 18 in all. Like most trucks in its class, the new Tacoma comes in regular, extended cab (Toyota calls it an access cab) and crew cab body styles in both two- and four-wheel drive. The Tacoma also continues with the very popular PreRunner models that offer the look and suspension of the four-wheel-drive trucks sans the actual four-wheel-drive running gear. New styles for 2005 include a long-bed version of the crew cab and the high-performance access cab X-Runner street truck.

Regardless of which body style you choose, all Tacomas are larger in most dimensions compared to the previous model. On the outside, the Tacoma is nearly half a foot longer, four inches wider and roughly two inches taller, depending on the model. Most interior dimensions have increased as well, with crew cab models demonstrating the most improvement as their backseats are now comfortable for adult passengers.

In addition to functional improvements like a retuned suspension and a locking rear differential, the optional TRD Off-Road Package adds a set of oversized tires and the obligatory "TRD" decals.

All regular and access cab models are available with either four- or six-cylinder engines, while the crew cab models use the V6 exclusively. On the low end, an all-new 2.7-liter, four-cylinder engine replaces both the 2.4-liter and 2.7-liter engines used previously. Producing 164 horsepower and 183 pound-feet of torque, the new 2.7 offers a significant boost in horsepower and torque while maintaining equivalent fuel efficiency. All V6 models now use a larger 4.0-liter engine in place of the previous 3.4-liter power plant. With 245 hp and 283 lb-ft of torque, the new Tacoma trounces every six-cylinder truck in its class and nearly matches the power of the Dodge Dakota's High-Output 4.7-liter V8. Equipped with the V6 engine, the Tacoma's maximum tow rating is now 6,500 pounds -- up from 5,000 pounds in the previous model.

With 245 horsepower and 283 pound-feet of torque, the Tacoma's V6 is one of the most powerful engines in any compact pickup. Combined with a five-speed automatic transmission, Toyota claims a 0-to-60 time of just 7.5 seconds for a 4x4 crew cab.

All the trucks we drove were equipped with the big V6 engine, and it makes itself known from the first punch of the pedal. With plenty of guts down low and a willingness to spin into the upper rev ranges without getting thrashy, this engine is a terrific all-around performer. It comes mated to either a six-speed manual or a five-speed automatic, giving it all the gears it needs to make the Tacoma move out in a hurry. The base four-cylinder continues with a five-speed manual and a four-speed automatic. Toyota claims that a 4x4 V6 equipped with the automatic transmission can run from zero to 60 mph in just 7.5 seconds, and we don't doubt it after our test-drive. Although the six-speed manual promises even better performance, its action is still typical of a truck -- clunky and awkward through the gears with little incentive to use it more than you need to.

It's too bad that the manual is still so clunky, as the X-Runner sport model is an excellent handler for a truck. All new for 2005, the X-Runner essentially picks up where the old S-Runner left off, offering a sport-tuned pickup for those who want some utility without giving up the fun. It comes as a six-speed V6 access cab only with a lowered suspension and additional structural bracing underneath that gives the truck its name. Retuned Bilstein shocks, firmer springs and thicker sway bars are also included along with a set of 18-inch wheels and tires for added stick.

With its 245-hp V6, lowered suspension, 18-inch wheels and tires and six-speed manual transmission, the X-Runner is a serious sport truck that can really move. An optional Big Brake system is also available that upgrades the stock binders with an oversized track-ready setup for hard-core track junkies.

Apart from the gangly shifter, the X-Runner is an impressive performer. Although we barely probed its limits during our brief test-drive, the feeling behind the wheel is of a truck that feels well planted at every corner, predictable when pushed and surprisingly agile considering its size. The torque of the V6 motor helps give it the punch it needs to back up the handling and a standard limited-slip differential puts the power to the ground in an efficient manner. For those who intend to really push their X-Runner to the limit, Toyota is also offering a Big Brake kit that upgrades the X-Runner with larger 13-inch rotors, four-piston forged calipers, larger brake pads and steel-braided brake lines.

The X-Runner isn't the only model to offer special option packages, however, as Toyota Racing

# 2005 Toyota Tacoma

Adjustable tie-down anchors are a standard feature of the Tacoma's new composite bed along with interior storage compartments and permanent floor anchors.

Crew cabs not only have more rear-seat room than the previous model, they also feature multiple storage compartments located under and behind the flat-folding seat backs.

Looking more like the interior of an upscale SUV than the interior of a compact truck, the Tacoma's cabin sets new class standards for design and materials quality.

A 400W electrical outlet is an optional addition to the bed that makes the Tacoma an ideal companion on the worksite or campsite.

Development (TRD) also put together two additional packages that are available on V6 models only. The TRD Sport Package puts together larger wheels and tires, a retuned suspension, a limited-slip differential and several cosmetic dress-up pieces to give the Tacoma the look of a customized street truck. The TRD Off-Road Package adds retuned springs and shocks, a thicker front sway bar, oversized BF Goodrich tires, foglamps and a locking rear differential. Off-road junkies will also be happy to know that the Tacoma now offers both Hill-start Assist Control (HAC) and Downhill Assist Control (DAC) on all models (X-Runner excepted) equipped with an automatic transmission.

For those with tastes that skew toward a more mainstream truck, Toyota did its part to make the standard models more value-oriented -- never the strongest aspect of the previous model. The least expensive 4x2 regular cab in now outfitted with the kind of standard features you would expect, such as antilock brakes, a CD stereo, multiple power points and a coolant temperature gauge. A revised lineup of option packages makes it easier to upgrade the Tacoma without getting lost in an endless sea of codes and constraints.

Even more impressive than the newly standard features is the overall design and comfort of the interior. With more room in every direction, the Tacoma has lost much of the claustrophobic feeling so typical of most compact trucks. The new truck's spec sheet shows impressive gains in head-, shoulder and hiproom, while its available legroom has tightened up a bit. Getting into access cab models is easier now, thanks to dual rear doors that open wider than before, while crew models are now comfortable for full-size adults in the backseat, thanks to a more relaxed seat back angle and substantial increases in hip- and shoulder room.

The design of the dashboard controls and instrument cluster mimics Toyota's 4Runner SUV, which isn't a bad thing given that it was just redesigned for 2003. There's nothing overly sophisticated about the interior design, but compared to GM's Colorado/Canyon twins the Tacoma looks like it cost $5K more. The quality of the materials sets a new standard for the class, and the seats have the kind of firm, supportive bolstering not typically found on trucks of this type.

Functionality and safety are two more areas where the Tacoma scores big. In addition to the typical stuff like a big center console and plenty of storage bins, the Tacoma also features storage under the seat in extended cab models and built-in cargo compartments behind the seat backs of crew cab models. There's also a new composite cargo bed that comes standard on all models and incorporates built-in storage units, adjustable tie-down anchors and even an optional 400-watt electrical outlet.

On the safety side, the Tacoma comes standard with antilock brakes fortified with Electronic Brakeforce Distribution for smoother stops and BrakeAssist for improved performance during panic situations. While all Tacomas get advanced dual-stage front airbags, crew cab models also offer optional full-length head curtain and front-seat side airbags. The Tacoma is also the first compact truck to add electronic stability control to the options list. An available option on all models, except the X-Runner, Toyota's Vehicle Stability Control (VSC) works in conjunction with an electronic traction control system to provide an added level of vehicle control in panic maneuvers and low traction situations.

If it seems like the Tacoma has a lot of firsts in the category, that's because it does. Toyota seems well apprised of the fact that while the compact truck category has seen little movement in the last five to 10 years, 2005 marks a rekindling of interest in this segment. In addition to GM's new compact trucks that went on sale last fall, both Nissan and Dodge are introducing all-new trucks of their own, and both are promising similar levels of power and features.

# 2005 Toyota Tacoma

While there's no doubt that Dodge and Nissan will have competitive products, they're going to need some pretty special trucks to top the Tacoma this time around, as Toyota's "go and see" approach has yielded a truck with few faults. We'll conduct a proper comparison test to see which compact truck is the real class of the class, but until then, the Tacoma looks like the clear favorite.

# 2005 Acura RL

**MSRP Price Range**

## $48,900

Destination Charge: $570 (all styles)

### Ratings

| Consumer Rating | N/A | |
|---|---|---|
| Editors Rating | 8.5 | |

**What Edmunds.com says:** With tons of standard features, excellent road manners and premium cabin furnishings, the new RL is a worthy competitor to the respected players from Audi, BMW and Lexus.

**Pros:** Quiet cabin, handles well for a large sedan, excellent build and materials quality, unique all-wheel-drive system, innovative navigation system offers real-time traffic information.

**Cons:** Lacks the low-end grunt of a V8, still lacks the prestige of its European competition.

**What's New:** The RL is completely redesigned for 2005, and now sports a 300-horsepower V6 and standard all-wheel drive.

*Crash Test Scores, see pg 530*
*Warranty information, see pg 542*

### Specifications

| Engine/Drivetrain | HP | Torque | EPA Fuel Economy Rating |
|---|---|---|---|
| 6cyl 3.5L A | 300 | 260 | 18 city/26 hwy |

### Body Styles

| Style | MSRP Range |
|---|---|
| Large Sedan | $48,900 |

**Introduction:** Acura had been out of the loop for a while when it came to building a full-size luxury/performance car. In recent years, the company has come up with several vehicles that have been a kind of rebirth for the luxury division of Honda. The TL and TSX are very capable sedans that offer value, performance and luxury all in one package. However, the larger RL has never been a real contender in the luxury sedan world, as competitors have always seemed to offer more luxury, more style and more performance. The one thing the RL has always offered is impressive value, but we're not sure that's the kind of thing that rings true with buyers in this segment who typically have flexible budgets. Acura has shaken things up a bit for 2005 with an all-new and much improved RL. Although the new RL's V6 engine still displaces 3.5 liters, it's not the same old motor. The V6 is now good for 300 horsepower, and it gets that number by using quite a few technological tricks and tweaks. The engine uses variable valve timing technology, as well as a variable flow exhaust system, a new intake system and high compression. Add this to a five-speed shiftable automatic transmission and the car boasts a pretty impressive spec sheet. In the past, the RL was hampered by its front-wheel-drive configuration, but all 2005 models are all-wheel drive. The AWD system (called SH-AWD for Super Handling All-Wheel Drive) typically runs with 70 percent of the power going to the front wheels and the remaining 30 directed to the rear wheels. Under such circumstances as heavy acceleration or hard cornering, more power can be directed to the rear. And like the front wheels, the rear wheels can receive as much as 70 percent of the engine's power. What is unusual is the RL's ability to split the power between the left and right rear wheels. If needed, the AWD system can direct some of the rear wheels' available power (never more than 70-percent total) to just one wheel. Using sensors to determine the position of the car relative to a turn, the car will spin the outside rear wheel faster in order to more accurately point the front of the car in the direction the driver intends. The result is an amazingly capable handler, even when driven aggressively. A North American first is Acura's new satellite-based real-time traffic information system, an innovative feature built into the standard navigation unit. This system provides drivers with up-to-the-minute traffic and road information, which makes navigating large urban areas a breeze. This technology complements a cabin whose premium materials and exacting build quality meet the standards set by Audi, BMW and Lexus. The 2005 RL integrates performance, luxury and technology into a fresh, good-looking package. The fact that you still can't get a V8 in this large sedan may be a turn-off for buyers who crave low-end torque, but for those who appreciate all the other elements that go into a good luxury sedan, the RL is certainly worth consideration.

**Body Styles, Trim Levels and Options:** The RL is a large luxury sedan that seats five. It's available in one fully loaded model that includes leather upholstery, a sunroof, power-adjustable and heated front seats, a memory feature for the driver seat and a 10-speaker Bose surround sound audio system that can play music in both DVD-A and CD formats. The automatic climate control system uses satellite data to help determine time of day and the direction of the sun

# 2005 Acura RL

against the car to appropriately adjust interior comfort levels. Other standard features include 17-inch alloy wheels; adaptive xenon headlights that swivel according to steering input; a voice-activated navigation system with real-time traffic information; a keyless access and startup system; OnStar telematics; and a Bluetooth interface for cell phone users.

**Powertrains and Performance:** The RL comes with only one engine and transmission. Under the hood is a 300-hp, 3.5-liter V6 that uses variable valve timing and a variable flow exhaust system. The transmission is a five-speed automatic with a shift-it-yourself feature. All RLs now have all-wheel drive as standard equipment, and that all-wheel-drive system is truly unique. Not only can the RL split the engine's power from front to rear, but it can split the available power between the left and right wheels for improved handling.

**Safety:** Four-wheel antilock disc brakes, seat-mounted side airbags for front occupants, full-length side curtain airbags and stability control are all standard equipment. OnStar, the in-vehicle communications and emergency assistance service, also comes standard. The RL has not been crash tested.

**Interior Design and Special Features:** The interior of the new RL is befitting of a true luxury car. The high-quality ensemble includes LED gauges and a state-of-the-art navigation system. The center stack is designed for simplicity; one large knob combined with smaller selection buttons makes it very easy to access the RL's impressive computing power. All climate, audio and navigation information is displayed on a large eight-inch screen in the center of the dash that's legible at a glance. An Active Noise Cancellation system uses the Bose audio system to cancel out sound waves from road and exhaust noise.

**Driving Impressions:** The V6 offers plenty of power but lacks the low-end grunt that could be provided by a V8. The engine is nonetheless smooth and very quiet, while the five-speed automatic transmission shifts up and down in an almost invisible fashion. The sophisticated all-wheel-drive system makes the full-size RL a lot of fun to drive hard and virtually insures that the car will go right where the driver intends.

## Competitive Vehicles

Audi A6
$40,900 - $50,500

BMW 5 Series
$41,300 - $55,800

Cadillac STS
$40,300 - $61,815

Mercedes-Benz
E-Class
$48,500 - $60,500

# 2005 Audi A6

**Midsize Sedan**

**MSRP Price Range**

## $40,900 – $50,500
Destination Charge: $720 (all styles)

**#1 Editors' Rating**

### Ratings

| | | |
|---|---|---|
| Consumer Rating | N/A | |
| Editors Rating | 9.1 | |

**What Edmunds.com says:** Solid performance and an elegant cabin design make the A6 a worthy competitor in the luxury sedan class, but BMW's 5 Series is more athletic and Mercedes carries more brand cachet, so it can't be called a class leader just yet.

**Pros:** Heavenly cabin furnishings, crisp handling, all-wheel-drive utility, strong six- and eight-cylinder power plants.

**Cons:** Steering not as sharp as a BMW's, no manual transmission available.

**What's New:** The A6 gets a top-to-bottom redesign for 2005.

**Introduction:** Introduced for the 1998 model year, the A6 is a midsize luxury car designed to go head-to-head with the likes of BMW's 5 Series and the Mercedes E-Class. It's about the size of the Volkswagen Passat, and indeed its exterior body lines are evocative of the general shape of VW's family car. However, the A6 reaches out to a different audience, a wealthier audience, and as such, each one is beautifully furnished with Audi-grade trimmings, including gorgeous wood that's sure to remind you of lush forestland. The A6 has been redesigned for 2005, and the changes stand to make it an even stronger contender in the luxury-car market. The lineup of available engines has been trimmed to two: a 335-horsepower, 4.2-liter V8, and an all-new 3.2-liter, 255-hp V6. Quattro all-wheel drive and a six-speed automanual transmission are now standard. To further enhance the A6's remarkable road feel, the suspension is comprised of an upgraded four-link front suspension and a self-tracking, trapezoidal-link rear setup borrowed from the A8. Audi reports that torsional stiffness is up by more than 34 percent over the previous A6. All of these upgrades were designed to help smooth out unwelcome body roll while turning tight corners and keep the wheels firmly planted on the road. Audi's handsome sedan now boasts a longer wheelbase -- 3.2 inches longer than the previous generation's. This translates into a roomier cabin; head-, shoulder and rear legroom have been bumped up, along with trunk space. The A6 also gets a new single-frame front grille, a tweak that adds a much needed touch of distinctiveness to the car's good looks. A revamped interior -- which, in keeping with Audi tradition, features a wealth of aluminum, leather and wood -- helps make the A6's cabin a heavenly place to be. There's a new multifunction four-spoke steering wheel, and a new Multi Media Interface system that's more user-friendly than either BMW's iDrive and Mercedes-Benz's COMAND systems. A new Advanced Key feature allows drivers to keep the key on their person and simply hit the start button when entering the car, instead of fumbling for the ignition. Other new creature comforts include optional voice control for the Bluetooth hands-free cell phone system; a new audio system with available Bose Surround Sound; and an optional DVD-based navigation system. The 2005 A6 also brings with it an electromechanical parking brake, with a console-mounted button that replaces the previous generation's mechanical arm; a rain sensor; a tire-pressure monitoring system; adaptive bi-xenon headlights; and a function that allows you to customize interior light settings. Like its predecessor, the 2005 A6 has plenty to offer buyers who crave luxury (in fact, no one beats Audi in this area) and like the idea of owning an all-weather vehicle. Serious enthusiasts are still apt to prefer the near telepathic steering of BMW's 5 Series, but the majority of drivers will be quite content with this Audi's combination of sporty handling and comfortable ride quality.

**Body Styles, Trim Levels and Options:** The A6 is sold in two trim levels -- 3.2 and 4.2 -- which correspond to the engine found under the hood. When it comes to dressing up an already nicely standard-equipped A6, four packages are available: The Premium Package includes a power glass sunroof, multifunction steering wheel, bi-xenon headlights, an upgraded Bose stereo system and wood interior trim. The Cold Weather Package provides heated front and

*Crash Test Scores, see pg 530*
*Warranty information, see pg 542*

### Specifications

| Engine/Drivetrain | HP | Torque | EPA Fuel Economy Rating |
|---|---|---|---|
| 8cyl 4.2L A | 335 | 310 | 17 city/23 hwy |
| 6cyl 3.1L A | 255 | 243 | N/A |

### Body Styles

| Style | MSRP Range |
|---|---|
| Midsize Sedan | $40,900–$50,500 |

For the latest full vehicle reports, visit www.edmunds.com/bginfopak

rear seats, a ski sack and headlight washers. The Sports Package will give you a stiffer sport suspension and 18-inch alloy wheels with performance tires. Lastly, the Convenience Package provides auto-dimming/folding exterior mirrors, an auto-dimming interior mirror with compass, memory for the driver seat and mirrors, HomeLink and a trip computer. Separate options include rear parking sensors, rear side airbags, a DVD-based navigation system and voice control for the Bluetooth hands-free cell phone system. Premium leather and sport seats are also available as a la carte extras.

**Powertrains and Performance:** Dropping the twin-turbo 2.7-liter V6 engine option, the new A6 now offers a standard 3.2-liter V6 and an optional 4.2-liter V8. The V6 is rated at 255 horsepower and 243 pound-feet of torque, while the V8 bumps up to 335 hp and a torque rating of 310 lb-ft. Jab the go pedal and both models serve up a competent, quick rush of power with smooth acceleration. The only transmission choice is a six-speed automanual with seven shift stages. While the six-speed works well, true enthusiasts may miss having the option of a true manual transmission. Audi's quattro all-wheel-drive system is standard on all A6s.

**Safety:** The latest generation of ESP (Audi's stability control system, with BrakeAssist and Electronic Brakeforce Distribution) aids drivers in keeping the A6 under control during emergency situations. Front, side and head airbags are also onboard to help keep occupants safe in the event of an unavoidable accident.

**Interior Design and Special Features:** The A6 offers one of the best interiors in its price class. Besides offering standard leather and wood inlays, each cabin is filled with supple, high-quality materials. Aluminum interior trim provides a sporty look, while wood trim is optional in Brown Walnut or Beige Birch. If you bought an A6 for the sake of luxury alone, you wouldn't be disappointed. All models come with the Multi Media Interface (MMI) vehicle management system first seen in the A8. The system's 7.0-inch display is integrated with the standard 10-speaker Bose stereo and the optional navigation system. In practice, it's much easier to use than BMW's iDrive or Mercedes' COMAND.

**Driving Impressions:** While its steering can't match the acuity of BMW's 5 Series, the A6 does provide an excellent ride around town along with tight handling on twistier pavement. Additionally, its quattro system affords it prodigious grip around turns that makes spirited driving that much more fun. Throw in the variable of winter weather, and the A6 will outdo any rear-drive rival.

## Competitive Vehicles

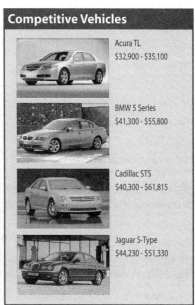

Acura TL
$32,900 - $35,100

BMW 5 Series
$41,300 - $55,800

Cadillac STS
$40,300 - $61,815

Jaguar S-Type
$44,230 - $51,330

# 2005 Buick LaCrosse

**Midsize Sedan**

**MSRP Price Range**

## $22,835 - $28,335
Destination Charge: $660 (all styles)

### Ratings

| Consumer Rating | N/A | |
|---|---|---|
| Editors Rating | 7.5 | |

**What Edmunds.com says:** With more refined power under the hood and a contemporary interior, this replacement for the Regal and Century could go a long way toward reestablishing Buick as a premium brand.

**Pros:** Six-passenger seating availability, supremely quiet ride, powerful and refined engine in CXS model, attractive interior.

**Cons:** Stability control limited to CXS trim, base engine lacks refinement, only comes with a four-speed automatic.

**What's New:** The LaCrosse is an all-new premium sedan replacement for both the Century and Regal sedans.

**Introduction:** Although it has little in common with the concept car by the same name shown at the 2000 North American International Auto Show, the 2005 LaCrosse should do much for Buick's fortunes in the cutthroat midsize sedan segment. It's a direct replacement for the Regal and its budget-oriented Century twin, but a new engine, a higher-quality interior, a longer equipment list and a reworked suspension should allow it to move uptown in image. On the outside, the LaCrosse blends traditional Buick styling cues -- a softly curved hood and a vertical-slat grille -- with modern-day trends. The twin headlamps call to mind the Mercedes-Benz E-Class, while the pull handles on the doors make the LaCrosse look like a contemporary of competing midsize sedans -- always a plus for a Buick. Inside, designers have equipped the new sedan with a clean control layout, interlocking analog gauges and liberal amounts of wood grain trim. The LaCrosse also benefits from the same kind of "QuietTuning" that went into the Rainier, and to that end, it has plenty of sound-deadening material in all the key areas, acoustical laminate on the glass and tightened body panel gap tolerances. As in the Century, buyers will have a choice between front buckets and a bench seat, yielding either five- or six-passenger capacity. The LaCrosse lineup includes an entry-level CX model, a luxury-oriented CXL model and a sporty CXS model. Although Buicks aren't normally known for their inspiring performance, the LaCrosse should rise above its brethren. The 200-horsepower, 3.8-liter (3800) V6 returns as the base engine, but the company says that engineers took extensive measures to ensure smoother, quieter operation. Best of all, it meets the stringent Super Ultra Low Emissions Vehicle (SULEV) standard. Exclusive to the CXS model is a new 3.6-liter DOHC V6. Aided by continuously variable valve timing, it's expected to make about 240 hp and 230 pound-feet of torque. For better or for worse, a four-speed automatic remains the only transmission choice. The LaCrosse rides on the same front strut/rear tri-link suspension as the outgoing Regal and Century, but approximately 80 percent of the components have been retuned to balance the supple ride quality that traditional Buick buyers expect against the controlled handling that mainstream midsize sedan buyers expect. The StabiliTrak stability control system is available on the CXS, and when selected, the LaCrosse scores the second-generation Magnasteer system, which takes steering angle (in addition to vehicle speed) into account when apportioning power assist. In recent years, the Regal and Century have ceased to be major players in the midsize sedan segment -- outside of rental car fleets, anyway. Although the LaCrosse won't be in a position to knock off the Chrysler 300 or Toyota Camry, its attractive styling, modern cabin design, available overhead cam V6 and more composed handling should do their part to increase Buick's presence in this class.

*Crash Test Scores, see pg 530*
*Warranty information, see pg 542*

### Specifications

| Engine/Drivetrain | HP | Torque | EPA Fuel Economy Rating |
|---|---|---|---|
| 6cyl 3.8L A | 200 | 230 | 20 city/29 hwy |
| 6cyl 3.6L A | 240 | 225 | 19 city/28 hwy |

### Body Styles

| Style | MSRP Range |
|---|---|
| Midsize Sedan | $22,835–$28,335 |

**Body Styles, Trim Levels and Options:** The LaCrosse is available in sedan form only in one of three trims -- entry-level CX, luxury-oriented CXL and sporty CXS. The CX includes the basics -- cloth upholstery, a power driver seat, a six-speaker CD stereo and OnStar. The CXL adds leather upholstery, a 60/40-split rear seat back, uplevel exterior trim and alloy wheels. The CXS builds upon the CXL with a more powerful V6, a sport-tuned suspension and larger alloy wheels.

# 2005 Buick LaCrosse

Among the available equipment are a handy remote start feature (as on the Chevrolet Malibu), rear parking assist, an MP3-compatible stereo and satellite radio.

**Powertrains and Performance:** The tried-and-true 200-horsepower, 3.8-liter (3800) V6 powers the CX and CXL models, but Buick says that engineers took extensive measures to ensure smoother, quieter operation. Additionally, adoption of electronic throttle control should make it more responsive underfoot. Exclusive to the CXS model is a new 3.6-liter DOHC V6. Aided by continuously variable valve timing, it's expected to make about 240 hp and 230 pound-feet of torque. A four-speed automatic transmission is standard on all models. Fuel economy estimates for the base engine are 20 mpg city and 29 mpg highway, while the 3.6-liter V6 should return 19 mpg city and 28 mpg highway.

**Safety:** Dual-stage airbags are standard up front, along with OnStar and four-wheel disc brakes. Unfortunately, ABS is standard only on the top-line CXS and must be purchased as an option on other trims. An optional stability control system is available only on the CXS. Other optional safety equipment includes full-length side curtain airbags and a reverse-sensing system.

**Interior Design and Special Features:** The LaCrosse is offered in both five- and six-passenger seating configurations. Extensive high-quality, soft-touch materials adorn the cabin, a welcome change for Buick. Chrome and fake wood accents abound, but their placement is classy and the wood grain is convincing. A tilt steering wheel is standard on all models, and CXL and CXS models include a telescoping function as well. Even though the overall interior feel is certainly on the traditional side, the passenger space is a tremendous improvement over the departed Regal and Century.

**Driving Impressions:** The strengthened structure and retuned suspension do wonders for the ride and handling characteristics of the LaCrosse. CX and CXL models are definitely on the soft end of the handling spectrum, but the sporty CXS strikes a pleasant compromise between day-to-day comfort and agile handling.

## Competitive Vehicles

Chrysler 300
$23,295 - $34,195

Mercury Montego
$24,345 - $28,245

Nissan Altima
$17,250 - $29,200

Pontiac G6
$20,675 - $23,300

# 2005 Buick Terraza

**Midsize Minivan**

**MSRP Price Range**
## $28,110 - $33,855
Destination Charge: $715 (all styles)

### Ratings

| Consumer Rating | N/A | |
|---|---|---|
| Editors Rating | 7.0 | |

**What Edmunds.com says:** Though the Terraza features a slick interior and distinctive styling, it doesn't have the on-road finesse of its minivan competitors.

**Pros:** Smooth ride and handling, lots of nifty interior storage spaces, innovative multimedia storage system, available all-wheel drive.

**Cons:** Engine power and refinement not up to class leaders, no side curtain airbags.

**What's New:** The Terraza is an all-new "crossover sport van." Think of it as a minivan with an SUV-like front end.

*Crash Test Scores, see pg 530*
*Warranty information, see pg 542*

### Specifications

| Engine/Drivetrain | HP | Torque | EPA Fuel Economy Rating |
|---|---|---|---|
| 6cyl 3.5L A | 200 | 220 | N/A |

### Body Styles

| Style | MSRP Range |
|---|---|
| Midsize Minivan | $28,110–$33,855 |

**Introduction:** Just what we've all been waiting for -- a Buick minivan. With Honda and Toyota offering minivans luxurious enough to qualify for Acura and Lexus badges, we suppose it was only a matter of time before Buick made the move into the luxury family van market as well. Banking on the extreme popularity of SUVs, Buick is marketing the new Terraza as a luxury crossover sport van rather than just calling it a minivan. The Terraza takes on a taller stance, and features a longer, more angular nose, in comparison to typical "soccer mom" minivans. Still, a spade is a spade. The Terraza is built off the same platform as GM's other minivans, those being the Chevrolet Uplander, Pontiac Montana SV6 and Saturn Relay, but the addition of Buick's Quiet Tuning measures should provide a more serene cabin environment. Quiet Tuning amounts to extra sound-dampening material applied in various trouble spots and better isolation of engine noise, and Buick hopes discerning clientele will feel right at home in the Terraza. To that end, designers have adorned the Terraza's interior with plenty of leather and wood grain trim. The instrumentation is set against surrounding dark wood grain, and each gauge is trimmed with a thin chrome ring. The double-stitched leather is softer than what you'd find in a Pontiac or Chevrolet, so the line between product offerings is less blurry and more distinct. Inside, there is a useful roof rail system that offers a variety of solutions for storage and entertainment with the pieces being easily moved or added as the owner sees fit. The third-row seats fold down in a 50/50 split and the second-row seats fold forward. Behind the rearmost seats are spacious storage compartments with doors, and second-row occupants have access to storage bins that are built into the rear of the front seats. Increased versatility is found in the collapsible trays between the front seats and second-row captain's chairs -- the trays also house cupholders. In addition to the usual rear DVD entertainment system, the Terraza is available with a PhatNoise mobile digital media system that allows owners to store thousands of MP3s and/or several dozen movies. Another convenient option is a 115-volt AC outlet for all manner of Game Cubes and PlayStations. Seat-mounted side airbags for front occupants are optional, but full-length head curtain airbags are nowhere to be found. An all-wheel-drive version is available, but a 200-hp V6 is the only engine choice. We're not entirely sold on the whole "SUV/van" concept. To our jaded eyes, the Terraza looks more like a minivan with a really big and flat front end. Subjective styling issues aside, the Terraza offers a myriad of interior features and solid overall competence, but still doesn't match the best-in-class offerings in terms of overall refinement, power or safety features.

**Body Styles, Trim Levels and Options:** The Terraza comes in one size and two trim levels, CX and CXL. Standard CX amenities include power windows, air conditioning, an eight-speaker sound system with a CD/MP3 player, a rear-seat DVD entertainment system, the OnStar communications system, cruise control, a power-sliding passenger-side door, keyless entry, a power driver seat, auto-leveling rear suspension, a trip computer, compass, leather seating and sport suspension. The CXL adds rear air conditioning, a power-sliding driver-side door, a 115-volt AC outlet, rear parking assist, dual eight-way power seats with driver's memory, upgraded storage

# 2005 Buick Terraza

and a wood shift knob. An all-wheel-drive system is available. An optional PhatNoise mobile digital media system allows owners to store thousands of MP3s and/or several dozen movies. Other noteworthy options include heated seats, a remote vehicle starting system and XM Satellite Radio.

**Powertrains and Performance:** All Terrazas come equipped with a 3.5-liter V6 that makes 200 horsepower and 220 pound-feet of torque. A four-speed automatic transmission is standard. No other powertrain combinations are available, though buyers in cold climates may want to consider the optional all-wheel-drive system.

**Safety:** All models come standard with four-wheel antilock disc brakes. Side-impact airbags for front occupants and the StabiliTrak stability control system are standard on the CXL, and optional on the CX. Full-length side curtain airbags are not available. The Terraza has not yet been crash tested.

**Interior Design and Special Features:** The Terraza seats seven, and the fold-flat third-row seat offers a 50/50 split. A tasteful color scheme with convincing faux wood accents gives the van a more luxurious ambience than its Chevrolet and Pontiac siblings. The double-stitched leather seats with contrasting piping are particularly elegant. Folding center trays (with cupholders) between the first- and second-row seats offer convenient storage while providing parents with ready access to little ones seated in back. An overhead rail system provides rear-seat access to climate and entertainment functions, and can be outfitted with various storage containers. A rear-seat DVD entertainment system is standard on all Terrazas, and can be upgraded with infrared wireless headphones. A remote vehicle start system, pioneered on the 2004 Chevy Malibu, is optional.

**Driving Impressions:** The V6 power plant is down on power compared to its competitors, but it still manages to provide adequate acceleration. The Terraza's standard sport suspension does a decent job of balancing ride comfort with responsive handling.

## Competitive Vehicles

Chrysler Town and Country
$20,610 - $35,315

Honda Odyssey
$24,490 - $30,490

Nissan Quest
$24,340 - $32,240

Toyota Sienna
$23,225 - $37,495

# 2005 Cadillac STS

**Large Sedan**

**MSRP Price Range**

## $40,300 - $61,815

Destination Charge: $695 (all styles)

### Ratings

| | | |
|---|---|---|
| Consumer Rating | 9.4 | |
| Editors Rating | 8.5 | |

**What Edmunds.com says:** After struggling for years to keep up with the imports, Cadillac has finally hit its stride and the STS proves it. Balanced driving dynamics and edgy-but-attractive styling should make this car a hit with buyers of all ages, especially those looking for a complete package of luxury and performance at a competitive price.

**Pros:** Full-size car at a midsize price, nimble road feel, powerful engine options, available all-wheel drive, optional Bose stereo is one of the best in its class.

**Cons:** Sporty bucket seats might be a bit firm for some, plastic interior panels not quite up to German standards, only one transmission available.

**What's New:** Cadillac's full size sedan is all new for 2005, rounding out the luxury marque's self-proclaimed renaissance with a bevy of performance-oriented credentials, including rear-wheel drive and two powerful engine options. Cutting-edge styling, lavish interior appointments and available all-wheel drive have brought GM's flagship up to par with the best Europe and Japan have to offer.

*Crash Test Scores, see pg 530*
*Warranty information, see pg 542*

### Specifications

| Engine/Drivetrain | HP | Torque | EPA Fuel Economy Rating |
|---|---|---|---|
| 8cyl 4.6L A | 320 | 315 | N/A |
| 6cyl 3.6L A | 260 | 252 | N/A |

### Body Styles

| Style | MSRP Range |
|---|---|
| Large Sedan | $40,300–$61,815 |

**Introduction:** The STS is the 2005 successor to the Seville, which was originally introduced way back in 1956 as a hardtop coupe designed to be the top performance option in the Cadillac lineup. A 305-horsepower V8 engine and exclusive high-end interior trim ensured that the Seville was not only one of the fastest vehicles on the road, but one of the most luxurious as well. Cadillac shook things up several decades later when the all-new Seville was unveiled as a high-performance sport sedan capable of keeping up with the best Europe could offer. Cutting-edge styling, tighter build quality and the addition of a new sport model called the STS made Cadillac the talk of the town. The introduction of the ultrahigh-tech and powerful Northstar V8 a year later further cemented the STS as one of the top performance luxury cars in the world. Another redesign for 1998 saw the Seville pick up a sophisticated array of in-car electronics. By the beginning of the current millennium, though, it had lost some of its appeal, as European and Japanese competitors surpassed it in both luxury and performance. Cadillac has dropped the Seville name for 2005, but the revolutionary new STS definitely shares some DNA with its forebears. This car represents a quantum leap forward in technology, build quality and overall refinement. GM's globally developed Sigma platform cut its teeth as a successful backbone in the CTS, CTS-V and SRX, and was tapped once again to lend some performance cred to the big boy of the Cadillac line. Hard-edged styling introduced a few years ago on the Escalade has been trickling down to the rest of the Cadillac line, and we think it has been applied most successfully here. Clean, elegant lines on the outside work with loads of leather and wood trim in the cabin to form a lasting impression of quality and luxury. Extra attention was given to reducing road noise, and details like a quiet steel dash, triple door seals and even "airfoil" windshield wipers designed in a wind tunnel all contribute to making this the quietest GM vehicle ever built. Engine options include a refined new 255-horse V6 as the standard motor, and the optional 4.6-liter Northstar V8 churning out a smooth 320 ponies for those who expect a little more. A five-speed automatic channels power to the rear wheels and eight-cylinder models are available with all-wheel drive for those who need extra traction come wintertime. Finally, the car is a technophile's dream, thanks to goodies such as a head-up display, active climate control, Bluetooth wireless cell phone connectivity and even an optional 15-speaker Bose 5.1 surround sound audio system. Defining where the STS fits into the luxury sedan marketplace can be a difficult task. Larger than a midsize sedan yet priced low enough to compete with considerably smaller imports, the sporty new Caddy can comfortably compete with the E-Class and 5 Series in virtually every category. For the first time in a generation, GM's premium brand is ready to take on all challengers.

**Body Styles, Trim Levels and Options:** Cadillac gives buyers three STS models to choose from -- V6, V8 and V8 AWD. Every V6 model includes 17-inch wheels, leather seating, aluminum interior trim, eight-way manually adjustable front seats, dual-zone climate control, an eight-speaker Bose sound system and OnStar. The V8 model adds 18-inch wheels, wood interior trim and power-adjustable front seats with multilevel heating and memory. The V8 AWD model

# 2005 Cadillac STS

adds the Magnetic Ride Control system, light-sensitive auto-dimming headlamps, ventilated seats, a DVD-based navigation system, Bluetooth wireless connectivity and a Bose 15-speaker, 5.1 surround sound audio system with an in-dash CD changer -- this stuff is optional on other models.

**Powertrains and Performance:** There are two available engines: a 3.6-liter V6 good for 255 horsepower and 252 pound-feet of torque, and a 4.6-liter Northstar V8 that generates 320 hp and 315 lb-ft of torque. Both engines feature variable valve timing and electronic throttle control. A five-speed automatic with regular and sport shift programs comes standard with either engine. Buyers must decide whether they want rear-wheel drive (to maximize performance and economy) or all-wheel drive for better all-weather traction. One option to consider is Magnetic Ride Control, an adaptive damping system. Thusly equipped, the STS offers decidedly sporty handling characteristics.

**Safety:** Four-wheel antilock disc brakes (with a panic assist feature) and StabiliTrak stability control are standard. Airbags include dual front airbags, seat-mounted side bags for front occupants and head curtain airbags spanning the first and second rows.

**Interior Design and Special Features:** Cadillac has been putting extra effort into interior quality and design as part of its self-proclaimed renaissance, and it shows. Panel fit and finish is top-notch, and premium materials such as eucalyptus wood trim and optional Tuscany leather really make the STS shine. The automatic climate control system monitors interior temperatures in relation to outside conditions, and the driver can stay informed without looking down thanks to a four-color head-up display projected onto the windshield.

**Driving Impressions:** A V8 STS is only about 100 pounds heavier than a comparably equipped 5 Series sedan despite its larger size. It's not exactly sport sedan-quick in its movements, but it can be pushed hard without losing composure. With the rear wheels providing the power, Cadillac's engineers were free to focus on the kind of precise steering feel that's nearly impossible to achieve with front-wheel drive. The result is a delicate feel through the steering wheel without a numb on-center sensation or overly aggressive assistance. The standard V6 is able to get the big sedan up to speed with surprising gusto. Unlike some of its competitors whose six-cylinder offerings provide merely adequate performance, the V6 in the STS rarely feels underpowered. Step up to the V8 and the STS really shows its mettle.

## Competitive Vehicles

Audi A8
$68,500

BMW 5 Series
$39,800 - $58,300

Chrysler 300
$23,295 - $34,195

Lexus GS 300
$38,875

# 2005 Chevrolet Cobalt

**Compact Coupe, Sedan**

**MSRP Price Range**

## $13,625 - $21,430

Destination Charge: $565 (all styles)

### Ratings

| | | |
|---|---|---|
| Consumer Rating | 10.0 | |
| Editors Rating | N/A | |

**What Edmunds.com says:** Positioned several steps upmarket from its Cavalier predecessor, the new Cobalt rides, handles and looks like a more expensive car than it really is.

**Pros:** Smooth ride and sporty handling, torquey four-cylinder engine, premium content for basic-car price.

**Cons:** A few cheap plastic interior parts, odd exterior styling details.

**What's New:** The Cobalt is a replacement for the aged Cavalier and like its predecessor it's available in both coupe and sedan body styles.

Crash Test Scores, see pg 530
Warranty information, see pg 542

### Specifications

| Engine/Drivetrain | HP | Torque | EPA Fuel Economy Rating |
|---|---|---|---|
| 4cyl 2.2L A/M | 145 | 150 | N/A |
| 4cyl 2.0L M | 205 | 200 | N/A |

### Body Styles

| Style | MSRP Range |
|---|---|
| Compact Coupe | $13,625–$21,430 |
| Compact Sedan | $13,625–$18,195 |

**Introduction:** Chevrolet is no stranger to the small-car game. In 1981, the GM division unveiled its answer to the growing number of imports hitting the scene, the Cavalier. The philosophy behind the car was simple: Give customers with limited budgets a well-appointed, reliable car that offers a variety of configurations to suit their needs. Unfortunately, Chevrolet pushed the "if it ain't broke don't fix it" idea a bit too far with the Cavalier. Its first major redesign didn't occur until 1995, a whopping 12 years into its life cycle. By the time the car saw some major revisions, the competition had already outclassed it on nearly every level. The 1995 model, though attractively styled, was still saddled with an ancient platform, and suffered from poor chassis dynamics, crash test scores and an overall lack of refinement. Undaunted, Chevy stuck with the Cavy for another decade. Styling tweaks through the years did little to keep the car fresh, but buyers kept coming back as Chevrolet offered generous rebates and incentives. Recent years have been progressively more difficult for Chevy's small car, as larger and larger rebates have been required to maintain sales volume. Clearly, a major change was needed. The answer was a completely new car -- so new that a name change was in order. Chevy is pinning its hopes on the new Cobalt to win back small-car buyers who demand first-rate accommodations. Rather than stick to one small car to fill a wide array of shoes, Chevy decided to split the market between the Aveo, which serves buyers with a more limited budget, and the new Cobalt, which is positioned as a more upmarket choice. Based on the Delta architecture used for the Saturn Ion, the Cobalt features a conservative and uncluttered appearance inside and out. Though we're still not sold on the coupe's quad round taillamps, the overall look should offend no one. Inside, materials quality, styling and comfort are all light-years ahead of the Cavalier. Reflective of the more upscale positioning, the Cobalt comes loaded with equipment. All but the base models feature keyless entry, antilock brakes and power windows. Coupe and sedan body styles are available, with a sporty SS coupe filling the top spot with a 205-horsepower supercharged engine. Other Cobalts come with a solid-performing 145-hp, 2.2-liter four-cylinder carried over from the Cavalier. The vehicle's stiff structure does wonders for noise and vibration control, and makes for a solid-feeling ride regardless of terrain. Even the doors close with a solid "thunk." Chevy is taking a bit of a risk in aiming the Cobalt at higher-end small cars, but after driving the Cobalt, we think it will succeed. The car is well equipped, competitively priced and, most importantly, very well engineered. Ride and handling is right up there with the class standards, and overall build quality is impressive. The new Cobalt may not have what it takes to overthrow the best-in-class economy sedans and coupes, but it is much closer than any Chevrolet small car has ever been.

**Body Styles, Trim Levels and Options:** The Cobalt is available as a two-door coupe or four-door sedan. Coupes come in base, LS and SS trim, while sedans come in base, LS and LT versions. Base models feature a standard CD player, air conditioning, a driver-seat height adjuster, a split-folding rear seat and 15-inch wheels. The LS adds cruise control; power windows, locks and mirrors; keyless entry; upgraded seats; alloy wheels; upgraded interior lighting; and

antilock brakes. The LT sedan comes loaded with leather seats, a seven-speaker Pioneer sound system, unique interior and exterior chrome trim and 16-inch alloys. The SS coupe features leather seats with color-keyed perforated inserts, unique trim, performance suspension, an A-pillar mounted boost gauge and 18-inch alloy wheels.

**Powertrains and Performance:** A 2.2-liter Ecotec four-cylinder powers all Cobalts, except the SS. With 145 horsepower and 150 pound-feet of torque, the engine compares favorably with most others in the class. It's made entirely of aluminum and boasts dual-overhead camshafts and four valves per cylinder for maximum efficiency and power. The SS coupe features a 2.0-liter supercharged Ecotec that's good for 205 hp and 200 lb-ft of torque. The standard transmission is a five-speed manual with a four-speed automatic available as an option. The automatic is standard on the LT, and not available on the SS.

**Safety:** Antilock brakes are optional on base models, and standard on all other Cobalts. Head-protecting side curtain airbags are optional across the board. Each seating position has a three-point seatbelt standard, and all but base models can be equipped with OnStar telematics. The Cobalt has not yet been crash tested.

**Interior Design and Special Features:** The Cobalt features a modern and stylish interior. Materials quality is competitive with that of other economy cars, and everything is screwed together with care. Chevy's efforts to provide a solid and quiet ride have paid off -- the Cobalt feels more substantial than typical small cars. Though a few plastic bits here and there are of questionable quality, the overall impression is one of a premium compact car.

**Driving Impressions:** The Ecotec four-cylinder is a thoroughly modern and refined engine that provides good power and a smooth delivery. Handling is quite good for a car in this class, with reasonably good manners in corners and a compliant ride around town. In addition to a broad power band, the SS delivers better steering feel and handling response without a noticeable loss of ride quality.

## Competitive Vehicles

Ford Focus
$13,230 - $18,130

Honda Civic
$13,010 - $20,650

Mazda MAZDA3
$13,680 - $17,105

Toyota Corolla
$13,570 - $15,580

# 2005 Chevrolet Corvette

**Compact Convertible, Coupe**

**MSRP Price Range**
## $43,445 - $51,445
Destination Charge: $800 (all styles)

**#1 Editors' Rating**

## Ratings

| | | |
|---|---|---|
| Consumer Rating | 9.7 | |
| Editors Rating | 8.8 | |

**What Edmunds.com says:** The latest Corvette is a world-class performance machine that successfully blends excellent build quality and ergonomics with sexy styling and tremendous value for the dollar.

**Pros:** Performance on par with the world's best sports cars, daily-driver livability, precision build quality, a performance bargain when compared to cars of similar capabilities.

**Cons:** Interior still doesn't look like it belongs in a car of this caliber.

**What's New:** A thoroughly redesigned Corvette debuts this year. Although the basic chassis is based on the previous model, the new Vette shows notable improvement in its performance, features and refinement.

*Crash Test Scores, see pg 530*
*Warranty information, see pg 542*

## Specifications

| Engine/Drivetrain | HP | Torque | EPA Fuel Economy Rating |
|---|---|---|---|
| 8cyl 6.0L M | 400 | 400 | 19 city/23 hwy |

## Body Styles

| Style | MSRP Range |
|---|---|
| Compact Convertible | $51,445 |
| Compact Coupe | $43,445 |

**Introduction:** Debuting in 1953 at the General Motors Motorama in New York City, the Corvette has become one of the longest-running automotive nameplates in history. Although the beautifully styled original '53 was hardly a sports car with its modest six-cylinder engine and two-speed automatic, subsequent models slowly refined the Corvette into America's premier sports car. The 1956 model featured revised bodywork and much improved handling thanks to legendary engineer Zora Arkus-Duntov, but it wasn't until the 1963 "Sting Ray" Corvette that it attained true sports car status. The 1970s weren't particularly kind to the Corvette because of tougher emissions requirements and fuel-economy concerns. Improvement finally arrived in 1984. With its sleek, modern design and a fully removable targa top, the C4 (Corvette fourth generation) was a well-rounded performer, despite some initial problems with its "Cross-Fire" fuel injection system and bone-jarring suspension. A convertible version debuted in '86, while an ultrahigh-performance ZR-1 bowed in 1990. With 375 horsepower, the ZR-1 was one of the fastest cars in the world at the time. In 1997, Chevrolet introduced the fifth-generation Corvette coupe to rave reviews. Stylistically, the C5 wasn't radical, but when it came to performance and refinement, there was no comparison. The standard LS-1 engine in '97 produced 345 hp and 350 pound-feet of torque. A one-piece, hydroformed frame made it stiffer and more capable in the corners than any Corvette before it, and it even had a sizable luggage area beneath the rear hatch. A convertible model debuted a year later, followed by a non-targa roofed hardtop a year after that. Even bigger news came in 2001 when the high-performance Z06 model was reborn (the name originates from an option package on second-generation Corvettes) for enthusiasts willing to sacrifice a little ride quality for all-out performance. The Corvette is once again new for 2005 and is thus designated the C6. Though the basic structure is based on the C5, everything that counts is new. Underhood lies a 400-horsepower LS-2 V8 mated to a standard six-speed manual tranny. The C6 has exposed headlamps -- a design feature not seen on a Vette since 1962. All the suspension bits are new, as is the spacious and well-screwed-together cabin. Three suspension levels are available, including a setup with Magnetic Ride Control and a Z51 package with upgraded brakes, suspension components and transmission gearing. Ride and handling are exceptional, regardless of which suspension package you choose. A convertible model is also available, and can be equipped with a slick power top. The C6 is a thrilling performance machine that offers levels of refinement and value right up there with the very best in its class.

**Body Styles, Trim Levels and Options:** The fiberglass-bodied Corvette comes in two forms: coupe (technically a hatchback) and convertible. The coupe features a removable roof panel for open-air cruising, though true wind-in-the-hair types will want to opt for the soft-top convertible. All Corvettes come well equipped with items such as xenon headlights, leather seating and a removable roof panel. Notable options include the Magnetic Ride Control suspension, a Z51 performance handling package and a DVD-based navigation system. Coupes can be equipped with a transparent roof panel, or both the standard solid panel and

For the latest full vehicle reports, visit www.edmunds.com/bginfopak

the transparent panel. A versatile head-up display is available, along with driver-seat memory, a seven-speaker Bose audio system and automatic climate control.

**Powertrains and Performance:** All coupe and convertible Corvettes come with the 6.0-liter LS-2 V8. Rated at 400 horsepower and 400 pound-feet of torque, this engine unleashes effortless power at any speed. Equipped with the standard six-speed manual transmission, the Corvette will hit 60 mph in a shade over 4 seconds. The car is capable of 186 mph, faster than any production Corvette in history. A four-speed automatic is a no-charge option. To help rein the power in on slippery surfaces, traction and stability control (Active Handling System) are standard equipment.

**Safety:** Antilock disc brakes are standard. Side-impact airbags are optional, but head curtain airbags are not available. The Vette features an Active Handling System (AHS) that can sense a loss of control and apply individual brakes or cut power to help maintain stability. This system has been well programmed to provide non-invasive assistance, and a performance driving mode gives the driver even more control at the track -- while still maintaining a safety net. No crash test data is available.

**Interior Design and Special Features:** Inside, large analog gauges and well-placed radio and climate controls greet passengers. Ergonomics and materials quality are excellent, and seat comfort is top-notch. Luggage space beneath the coupe's rear hatch glass is a healthy 22 cubic feet, more cargo room than most sedans. An innovative keyless access system is standard. Sensors detect the presence of the key fob, and automatically lock or unlock the doors. In fact, there aren't even door handles -- just touch-buttons, inside and out, that unlatch the door. There's no ignition key, either. As long as the keyfob is inside the car, you simply push a dash button to start the engine. Plenty of safeguards are in place to prevent shenanigans caused by a misplaced/lost keyfob, or even a dead battery.

**Driving Impressions:** Endless power from the snarling LS2 combined with a tight suspension results in a sports car that never ceases to put a smile on your face. All three of the suspension packages deliver a compliant ride along with white-knuckled handling abilities. The C6 is a comfortable touring car, as well as a world-class performance machine.

## Competitive Vehicles

BMW M3
$47,100 - $55,600

Chrysler Crossfire SRT-6
$44,820 - $49,120

Dodge Viper
$81,090

Mercedes-Benz CLK55 AMG
$69,900 - $79,950

# 2005 Chevrolet Equinox

Midsize SUV

**MSRP Price Range**

## $21,095 - $24,435

Destination Charge: $565 (all styles)

### Ratings

| | | |
|---|---|---|
| Consumer Rating | 9.2 | |
| Editors Rating | 8.2 | |

**What Edmunds.com says:** A superior successor to the aged Tracker, the Equinox offers flexible interior space, a strong engine and modern styling.

**Pros:** Standard V6 engine, long wheelbase affords plenty of interior room, fore/aft-adjustable rear seats, available side curtain airbags.

**Cons:** Costs as much as the more powerful Saturn Vue, limited drivetrain choices, confusing stereo controls.

**What's New:** The Equinox is an all-new compact SUV from Chevrolet. It shares a platform with the Saturn Vue and offers similar levels of space and versatility for buyers seeking practical suburban transportation.

*Crash Test Scores, see pg 530*
*Warranty information, see pg 542*

### Specifications

| Engine/Drivetrain | HP | Torque | EPA Fuel Economy Rating |
|---|---|---|---|
| 6cyl 3.4L A | 185 | 210 | 19 city/22 hwy |

### Body Styles

| Style | MSRP Range |
|---|---|
| Midsize SUV | $21,095–$24,435 |

**Introduction:** The Equinox is the long-awaited replacement for the Chevy Tracker -- a small, underpowered SUV based on the Suzuki Vitara and Grand Vitara. When the Tracker was last redesigned for 1999, brands like Ford, Jeep, Hyundai, Kia, Mazda and Nissan didn't have small SUV offerings, so the truck-based Tracker was one of a few viable alternatives. Times have changed, though, and all of these manufacturers now have competitive mini-ute offerings. Meanwhile, Honda, Subaru and Toyota have only gotten better at building small SUVs that consumers like. The all-new Equinox will still be built at GM's plant in Ontario (a joint venture with Suzuki), but this time it is not a reworked Suzuki and instead shares most of its architecture with the Saturn Vue. In keeping with traditional Chevy truck thinking, the Equinox will compete against the growing population of mini-SUVs priced under $25,000, but it will be one of the biggest of its kind, thanks to an extra long wheelbase. Inside, it offers innovative storage options and reconfigurable seating that add that extra measure of utility to small SUV ownership. As in the Honda CR-V, the rear seat slides fore and aft (with a nearly 8-inch range of travel) to make way for larger passengers or cargo, and there is an adjustable cargo tray that doubles as a picnic table. Its interior dimensions are comparable to those of competing SUVs, but the Equinox holds slight advantages in rear-seat headroom and legroom categories. Maximum cargo capacity is 69 cubic feet, which puts the Equinox right behind the CR-V. Unlike the Tracker, the Equinox will look every bit like a Chevy truck with a prominent bowtie on the front grille and a bold chrome bar across the front. The overall appearance of the Equinox is rather trucklike. The arched rear pillar combined with the flared rear wheel wells gives the vehicle a much brawnier appearance than soft-looking SUVs like the RAV4, CR-V and Liberty, and more on par with the tougher-looking sheet metal of the Ford Escape and Kia Sorento. Unlike some of the competition, the Equinox does not offer much in the way of powertrain options. A single 3.4-liter V6 engine is standard on all Equinox models, whether front-wheel drive or all-wheel drive. The rest of the equipment list offers more variety, as the Equinox can be equipped with safety items like side curtain airbags and traction control, as well as upscale features like heated leather seats, satellite radio and steering wheel-mounted audio controls. Although several small SUVs can match the Equinox's overall package, it's certainly worth consideration if you're looking for an urban runabout with a flexible cabin design and ample passing power.

**Body Styles, Trim Levels and Options:** Like most Chevrolet trucks, the Equinox is offered in LS and LT trims, both of which are available with either front-wheel drive or all-wheel drive. Standard equipment on the LS includes 16-inch wheels; air conditioning; a height-adjustable driver seat; a six-speaker CD stereo; automatic headlights; power windows, mirrors and locks; an alarm system; and a rear window wiper. The LT adds such features as alloy wheels, ABS, cruise control, foglights and upgraded cloth upholstery. Available options include side curtain airbags, OnStar telematics, satellite radio, an MP3-compatible stereo, leather seating, a power driver seat, heated seats, a trailering package, a sunroof and an auto-dimming rearview mirror.

# 2005 Chevrolet Equinox

**Powertrains and Performance:** All Equinox SUVs come with the same 3.4-liter V6 engine. It's good for 185 horsepower and 210 pound-feet of torque. Towing capacity is rated at 3,500 pounds. The Equinox is available in all-wheel-drive and front-wheel-drive configurations, but only one transmission is offered -- a five speed automatic.

**Safety:** Front disc/rear drum brakes are standard; ABS is optional on LS models and standard on the LT. Traction control is optional on front-drive LS models and standard on LTs. Full-length side curtain airbags are optional on all Equinox models. The Equinox has not been crash tested, yet.

**Interior Design and Special Features:** Inside, Chevrolet designers opted for a simple, industrial look with large, clear gauges and faux aluminum accents. While most of the controls are simple in design, the stereo head unit's collection of small buttons is unnecessarily complicated. Thanks to its long wheelbase, the Equinox offers plenty of room for its occupants, including class-leading rear headroom and legroom. To make way for larger passengers or cargo, the 60/40-split rear seat can slide nearly 8 inches fore and aft. An adjustable rear cargo shelf expands your loading options after a shopping trip and can also function as a picnic table. The Equinox offers 35 cubic feet of luggage space behind its rear seats; fold down the seats and you've got a total of 69 cubic feet.

**Driving Impressions:** The Equinox's 3.4-liter V6 engine has been used in plenty of GM products and has always provided adequate if unrefined power. In the Equinox, you can look forward to spirited acceleration as well as better-than-average fuel economy. The Equinox shares a platform with the Saturn Vue, so expect a comfortable ride and capable, if not altogether nimble, handling characteristics.

## Competitive Vehicles

Ford Escape
$19,265 - $28,005

Honda CR-V
$19,000 - $22,550

Jeep Liberty
$18,380 - $25,875

Kia Sorento
$18,995 - $25,300

# All New for 2005

# 2005 Chevrolet Uplander

**Midsize Minivan**

**MSRP Price Range**

## $23,635 - $31,385

Destination Charge: $715 (all styles)

### Ratings

| Consumer Rating | N/A | |
|---|---|---|
| Editors Rating | 7.0 | |

**What Edmunds.com says:** Although the Uplander features a slick interior and distinctive styling, it doesn't have the on-road finesse of its minivan competitors.

**Pros:** Smooth ride and handling, lots of nifty interior storage spaces, innovative multimedia storage system, available all-wheel-drive.

**Cons:** Engine power and refinement not up to class leaders, no side curtain airbags.

**What's New:** The Uplander is an all-new "crossover sport van" that has roots in the Chevrolet Venture minivan.

*Crash Test Scores, see pg 530*
*Warranty information, see pg 542*

### Specifications

| Engine/Drivetrain | HP | Torque | EPA Fuel Economy Rating |
|---|---|---|---|
| 6cyl 3.5L A | 200 | 220 | N/A |

### Body Styles

| Style | MSRP Range |
|---|---|
| Midsize Minivan | $23,635–$31,385 |

**Introduction:** Chevrolet's Venture minivan has never sold in the numbers General Motors would like -- the offerings from Dodge, Ford and Honda have outsold it for several years running. Part of the problem, according to GM's marketing team, might be due to the "mommy mobile" image minivans confer upon their owners -- some of whom ultimately ditch their vans for SUVs. In response, Chevrolet has introduced the more rugged-sounding Uplander, a "crossover sport van" based on the outgoing Venture's chassis. Compared to the Venture, the Uplander takes on a taller stance and chunkier front fascia more evocative of a truck. The result, Chevy hopes, is a perception that the van is more of a hip and stylish SUV-like van, and not so much a boring soccer mom van. Despite the change in name and outward style, the Uplander does not represent a full redesign of the Venture -- passenger and cargo space are nearly identical. It does, however, incorporate more of the features that today's minivan buyers are looking for, along with a more powerful engine. Additionally, structural upgrades, including a longer, reinforced front end and a stiffer occupant compartment, should improve the van's crashworthiness -- a good thing because the Venture fared poorly in frontal offset crash testing conducted by the IIHS. Seat-mounted side airbags for front occupants are optional, but full-length head curtain airbags are still nowhere to be found. Inside, the Uplander seats seven, and the fold-flat third-row seat offers a 50/50 split, allowing families to carry a mix of passengers and cargo. The Uplander is a more practical place to spend time than the Venture, as Chevrolet has taken Honda's example and installed folding center trays (with cupholders) between the first- and second-row captain's chairs. An overhead rail system provides rear-seat access to climate and entertainment functions, and can be customized to families' liking with various storage containers. In addition to the usual rear DVD entertainment system, the Uplander is available with a PhatNoise mobile digital media system that allows owners to store thousands of MP3s and/or several dozen movies. Another convenient option is a 115-volt AC outlet for plugging in all manner of Game Cubes and Xboxes. For power, the Uplander has a 200-horsepower, 3.5-liter V6 as the one and only engine choice. Although it should be a welcome upgrade from the overworked 3.4-liter motor, don't expect to keep up with Honda Odyssey drivers. A four-speed automatic transmission is standard, and both front-wheel drive and all-wheel drive are available. Seventeen-inch wheels are standard, and the StabiliTrak stability control system is a new option. We're not entirely sold on the whole "SUV/van" concept. To our jaded eyes, the Uplander looks more like a minivan with a really big and flat front end. Subjective styling issues aside, the Uplander offers budding families a myriad of interior features and solid overall competence, but still doesn't match the best-in-class offerings.

**Body Styles, Trim Levels and Options:** The Uplander comes in one size and three different trim levels: base, LS and LT. The base model offers power windows, air conditioning, an eight-speaker sound system with a CD/MP3 player, a rear-seat DVD entertainment system and the OnStar communications system. Upgrades for the LS model include cruise control, keyless entry, rear air conditioning and a built-in child seat. Pop for the LT trim and you'll get a passenger-side power-sliding door, deluxe rear-seat entertainment system with infrared headphones and a 115-volt AC outlet, a power driver seat, steering wheel audio controls, alloy wheels and second-row captain's chairs. The all-wheel-drive system is available on the LT only, and adds automatic load-leveling rear suspension and an inflator kit. The LS and LT can be upgraded with leather seating and heated seats. An optional PhatNoise mobile digital media system allows owners to store thousands of MP3s and/or several dozen movies. Other noteworthy options include dual power-sliding side doors, rear parking assist and a remote vehicle starting system.

**Powertrains and Performance:** All Uplanders come equipped with a 3.5-liter V6 that makes 200 horsepower and 220 pound-feet of torque. A four-speed automatic transmission is standard. No other powertrain combinations are available, but buyers can opt for all-wheel drive.

**Safety:** All models come standard with four-wheel antilock brakes. Side-impact airbags for front occupants are included with the LS and LT, and optional on the base model. Side curtain airbags are not available. The StabiliTrak stability control system is available on the LT when equipped with the optional sport suspension package. The Uplander has not yet been crash tested.

**Interior Design and Special Features:** The Uplander seats seven, and the fold-flat third-row seat offers a 50/50 split. A two-tone color scheme with faux metal accents dramatically brightens the atmosphere of the van. Folding center trays (with cupholders) between the first- and second-row seats are available. An overhead rail system provides rear-seat access to climate and entertainment functions, and can be upgraded with various storage containers. A rear-seat DVD entertainment system is standard on all Uplanders. A remote vehicle start system, pioneered on the Malibu in 2004, is optional.

**Driving Impressions:** The V6 power plant is down on power compared to its competitors, but it still manages to provide adequate acceleration. The Uplander's suspension is on the soft side, though upgrading to the optional sport suspension does provide for a more responsive ride.

## Competitive Vehicles

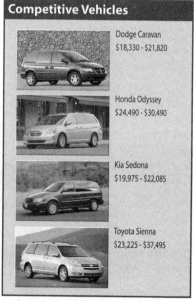

Dodge Caravan
$18,330 - $21,820

Honda Odyssey
$24,490 - $30,490

Kia Sedona
$19,975 - $22,085

Toyota Sienna
$23,225 - $37,495

# 2005 Chrysler 300

**MSRP Price Range**
## $23,295 - $34,195
Destination Charge: $625 (all styles)

## Ratings

| | | |
|---|---|---|
| Consumer Rating | 9.5 | |
| Editors Rating | 8.4 | |

**What Edmunds.com says:** Proving that upscale sedans don't have to be stale-looking and slow, the 300 series offers distinctive styling and V8 power in a practical and affordable package.

**Pros:** Chiseled and masculine good looks, powerful V8 in 300C model, long list of safety features, plenty of luxury and performance for the price paid.

**Cons:** Sluggish acceleration with base V6, limited transmission choices, complex stereo controls.

**What's New:** The 300 is an all-new, rear-wheel-drive flagship sedan for Chrysler; it replaces the Concorde and 300M. In a clear move away from the cab-forward design theme Chrysler championed in the 1990s, the 300 represents the company's bold new direction and makes use of plenty of Mercedes-Benz technology. Available features include Chrysler's Hemi V8, stability control, side curtain airbags and, later in the year, all-wheel drive.

**Introduction:** Continuing Chrysler's proud tradition of letter-series cars, the 300C is a new rear-wheel-drive sedan that reminds us of a time when V8-powered luxury cars ruled the road. Remember when suburban driveways were filled with Chryslers, Buicks and rumbling Mercurys? We do, and apparently Chrysler does as well. This time, though, the company got plenty of engineering help from Mercedes-Benz, so you can expect refined driving dynamics. With its distinct but slightly retro styling, the 300C looks the part of a luxury sedan. The non-letter 300 is essentially the same except it has a V6 under the hood instead of the 300C's muscular V8. Two V6s are available -- a 250-horsepower, 3.5-liter version and a 2.7-liter unit that makes 200 hp. Not only is the 300C powered by a good old-fashioned Hemi, but it adds modern technology to the mix as well. The V8 uses a multidisplacement system, which selectively deactivates four of the engine's cylinders to save fuel in undemanding driving situations. It's all hooked up to a five-speed automatic transmission with AutoStick. But it's not all about power, as the 300 also shoots for excellent ride and handling by utilizing a five-link independent rear suspension and a short-long arm setup in front. Equipment levels vary by style or trim. But the cars do come nicely equipped for the most part, as even the base 300 includes 17-inch wheels, a power driver seat and a telescoping steering wheel. Higher-line models add stability control, leather upholstery and dual-zone automatic climate control. Major options include self-sealing tires, side curtain airbags, adjustable pedals, a navigation system and HID headlights. There's also a six-speaker Boston Acoustics sound system (available with either a 288- or 380-watt amplifier), the first factory-installed system from the venerable stereo maker. And for those who require a fully winterproof sedan, the 300 will also be available with all-wheel drive later in the model year. For the price of a well-equipped Nissan Maxima, Toyota Camry or Volkswagen Passat, Chrysler is offering sedan shoppers a spacious, rear-wheel-drive sedan with a long list of safety features and an undeniable hip factor. For the price of Lexus ES 330 or Acura TL, you can add a 340-hp Hemi V8 to your sedan. Who says your next family sedan has to be boring?

**Body Styles, Trim Levels and Options:** The rear-drive 300 is available only as a four-door sedan, but there are four variations on that theme. The base 300 comes with 17-inch wheels, four-wheel disc brakes, air conditioning, a power driver seat, a CD player, cruise control and a tilt/telescoping steering wheel. The Touring adds a bigger V6, alloy wheels, foglights, ABS, leather upholstery, chrome trim, stability control and BrakeAssist. The plushest of the V6 models, the Limited adds chrome wheels, a power front-passenger seat, heated seats, one-touch up-and-down front windows, dual-zone automatic climate control and an information center. In addition to a V8, the 300C adds dual exhaust tips, 18-inch chrome wheels, larger brakes, tortoise-shell interior accents and a 288-watt Boston Acoustics stereo with an in-dash CD changer. Options on all 300s include adjustable pedals, self-sealing tires and satellite radio. A navigation system is available on Limited and 300C models, and the C is eligible for an even more powerful 380-watt stereo and HID headlights. Snowbelt residents can order all-wheel drive as a midyear option.

*Crash Test Scores, see pg 530*
*Warranty information, see pg 542*

## Specifications

| Engine/Drivetrain | HP | Torque | EPA Fuel Economy Rating |
|---|---|---|---|
| 8cyl 5.7L A | 340 | 390 | 17 city/25 hwy |
| 6cyl 3.5L A | 250 | 250 | 19 city/27 hwy |
| 6cyl 2.7L A | 190 | 190 | 21 city/28 hwy |

## Body Styles

| Style | MSRP Range |
|---|---|
| Large Sedan | $23,295–$34,195 |

For the latest full vehicle reports, visit www.edmunds.com/bginfopak

**Powertrains and Performance:** The base 300 comes with a 200-hp, 2.7-liter V6. Touring and Limited versions upgrade to a 250-hp, 3.5-liter V6. Both V6 engines come with a four-speed automatic transmission, but ordering AWD on models with the 3.5-liter allows you to trade up for a five-speed automatic with automanual functionality. The 300C scores the biggest prize, as Chrysler has stuffed a 340-hp, 5.7-liter Hemi V8 into its engine bay. The five-speed automatic is standard on every 300C.

**Safety:** Active safety features like ABS, traction control and stability control are optional on the base 300, but are standard on the Touring, Limited and C versions. Side curtain airbags, self-sealing tires and adjustable pedals are optional on all models. The 300C also gets rain-sensing wipers as standard fare. Chrysler's new sedan has not yet been crash tested.

**Interior Design and Special Features:** The interior features a simple but elegant layout. The dash area may not be as fancy as some other cars in this segment, but its combination of sporty, semi-retro and luxury motifs is effective. Worth special note are the white-faced gauges and the slick tortoise shell trim in the 300C. Cabin dimensions are generous in all directions, and the 300 offers more rear legroom than any of its competitors. Trunk capacity measures 15.6 cubic feet.

**Driving Impressions:** A rear-wheel-drive V8 family sedan is exactly what American automakers have needed for years to inspire renewed interest in their products. And with plenty of Mercedes-Benz technology in this one, the 300 offers a great deal more refinement than its 1960s ancestors. With their 250-hp V6, the 300 Touring and Limited models are only adequately powered but are still fine choices for those seeking a feature-laden large sedan that handles as well as it rides. Saddled with a small V6, the base model feels sluggish, and we wouldn't recommend it to most buyers.

## Competitive Vehicles

Buick Lacrosse
$22,835 - $28,335

Cadillac CTS
$30,000 - $32,250

Ford Five Hundred
$22,145 - $27,845

Honda Accord
$15,900 - $28,500

# 2005 Chrysler 300C SRT-8

**Large Sedan**

## MSRP Price Range
### *N/A*
Destination Charge: N/A (all styles)

### Ratings

| | | |
|---|---|---|
| Consumer Rating | N/A | |
| Editors Rating | 8.7 | |

**What Edmunds.com says:** Proving that upscale sedans don't have to be stale-looking and slow, the high-performance 300C SRT-8 is a testament to all that Chrysler can do well.

**Pros:** A 425-horsepower Hemi, suspension and braking upgrades that complement the motor, chiseled good looks, plenty of luxury and performance for the price.

**Cons:** No manual transmission available, complex stereo controls.

**What's New:** This high-powered version of the standard 300 is one of the most powerful Chryslers every offered to the public.

**Introduction:** Continuing Chrysler's proud tradition of letter-series cars, the 300C SRT-8 is a performance version of the 300C that reminds us of a time when V8-powered luxury cars ruled the road. Remember when suburban driveways were filled with Chryslers, Buicks and rumbling Mercurys? Then remember how GM, Ford and Chrysler came up with even more powerful versions of those cars. We do, and apparently Chrysler does as well. This time, though, the company got plenty of engineering help from Mercedes-Benz, so you can expect refined driving dynamics. With its distinct but slightly retro styling, the 300C SRT-8 looks the part of a luxury sedan, but with the addition of a tweaked 425-horsepower Hemi, the car takes on a distinctly more intimidating image. The 6.1-liter V8 is the highest specific output engine ever offered by Chrysler. In a fitting nod to the original (and legendary) Hemi of the '60s, the SRT-8 even features an orange-painted cylinder block and black valve covers. Not only is the 300C SRT-8 powered by a good old-fashioned Hemi, but it adds other performance-enhancing features like bigger sway bars, a lowered ride height, more powerful brakes and an improved rear deck spoiler for more downforce. It's all hooked up to a five-speed automatic transmission with AutoStick. But it's not all about power, as the 300 also shoots for excellent ride and handling by utilizing a five-link independent rear suspension and a short-long arm setup in front; the SRT-8 further benefits from stiffer bushings, revised springs and more performance-oriented Electronic Stability Program (ESP). The SRT-8 does come nicely equipped with such features as HID headlights and rear park assist -- many of the features that are optional on other 300s are standard on the 300C SRT-8. There's also a six-speaker Boston Acoustics sound system. The Chrysler 300C SRT-8 is set apart visually with unique styling cues such as body-colored bumpers, door handles and mirrors, as well as special SRT badging. The modified front fascia not only helps to set the look of the SRT-8 apart but helps with brake cooling by directing air over the discs. The regular 300C is certainly no slouch, but with 85 additional horsepower and upgraded chassis components, the SRT-8 is set to rule the roost as the ultimate hot-rod sedan.

**Body Styles, Trim Levels and Options:** The rear-drive 300C SRT-8 is available only as a four-door sedan in one trim level. Standard equipment includes leather upholstery, dual-zone automatic climate control, dual power seats, a trip computer, cruise control and a tilt/telescoping steering wheel. Tunes are supplied by a 380-watt Boston Acoustics stereo with an in-dash CD changer. The SRT-8 rolls on 20-inch forged aluminum wheels shod with high-performance Goodyear F1 tires (all-season tires are an available option) with asymmetrical tread. Tire dimensions are a beefy 245/45R20 in the front and 255/45R20 in the rear. High-intensity discharge headlights are standard, along with rear parking sensors.

**Powertrains and Performance:** The 300C SRT-8 sports a massaged 6.1-liter Hemi V8 that pumps out 425 horsepower and 420 lb-ft of torque. A five-speed automatic with a specially calibrated AutoStick automanual control is standard. The unique Hemi propels the SRT-8 to 60 mph in just a few ticks over 5 seconds.

*Crash Test Scores, see pg 530*
*Warranty information, see pg 542*

### Specifications

| Engine/Drivetrain | HP | Torque | EPA Fuel Economy Rating |
|---|---|---|---|
| 8cyl 6.1L A | 425 | 420 | N/A |

### Body Styles

| Style | MSRP Range |
|---|---|
| Large Sedan | N/A |

For the latest full vehicle reports, visit www.edmunds.com/bginfopak

# 2005 Chrysler 300C SRT-8

**Safety:** The 300C SRT-8 offers standard antilock brakes, stability control (ESP), multistage airbags with an occupant-sensing system and side curtain airbags. While ESP is standard on the 300C, the SRT-8 uses a modified version to give enthusiast drivers more leeway on twisty roads. The 300 sedan has not yet been crash tested.

**Interior Design and Special Features:** The interior features a simple but elegant layout. The dash area may not be as fancy as some other cars in this segment, but its combination of sporty, semi-retro and luxury motifs is effective. Cabin dimensions are generous in all directions, and the 300C SRT-8 offers more rear legroom than any of its competitors. Trunk capacity measures 15.6 cubic feet.

**Driving Impressions:** A rear-wheel-drive V8 family sedan is exactly what American automakers have needed for years to inspire renewed interest in their products. And with plenty of Mercedes-Benz technology in this one, the 300C SRT-8 offers a great deal more refinement than its 1960s ancestors. The 300C is already a blast to drive, and the SRT treatment takes all its visceral aspects to a whole new level. Outstanding power under the hood is matched with powerful Brembo brakes and a tightened suspension system.

## Competitive Vehicles

Cadillac STS
$40,300 - $61,815

Jaguar S-Type R
$58,330

Mercedes-Benz E55 AMG
$79,500

Volvo S60 R
$37,250

# 2005 Dodge Dakota

**Compact Truck**

## MSRP Price Range
## $19,374 - $28,679
Destination Charge: $645 (all styles)

#1 Editors' Rating

## Ratings

| | | |
|---|---|---|
| Consumer Rating | 8.4 | |
| Editors Rating | 8.7 | |

**What Edmunds.com says:** Refinement appears to be the magic word at Dodge these days, and it shows in the all-new Dakota. Excellent powertrain options, nimble suspension and a well thought-out interior score major points, but the aggressive styling isn't for everyone.

**Pros:** Strong engine lineup, choice of part-time or full-time four-wheel drive, comfortable and refined interior, nimble handling.

**Cons:** No long bed or single cab models, club cab's backseat offers barely passable comfort for adults.

**What's New:** The midsize Dakota is all new for 2005. Improvements include a hydroformed boxed steel frame, a coil-over front suspension, three excellent engine options, a five-speed automatic or six-speed manual transmission, revised styling and improved build quality.

*Crash Test Scores, see pg 530*
*Warranty information, see pg 542*

## Specifications

| Engine/Drivetrain | HP | Torque | EPA Fuel Economy Rating |
|---|---|---|---|
| 6cyl 3.7L A/M | 210 | 235 | 17 city/22 hwy |
| 8cyl 4.7L A/M | 230 | 290 | 14 city/19 hwy |
| 8cyl 4.7L A/M | 250 | 300 | N/A |

## Body Styles

| Style | MSRP Range |
|---|---|
| Crew Cab Pickup Truck | $20,774–$28,679 |
| Extended Cab Pickup Truck | $19,374–$27,189 |

**Introduction:** When it comes to searching for the perfect combination of light-duty hauling capability and carlike ride and handling, Dodge has been in a unique position since the company introduced the first midsize Dakota pickup back in 1987. All new and totally redesigned for 2005, the Dakota benefits from three excellent engine options and revised styling that ensure all your neighbors will know you drive a Dodge. A hydroformed fully boxed frame provides eight times more torsional rigidity than the previous design, and an all-new coil-over front suspension and power rack and pinion steering lend the platform a nimble, carlike feel. The tired, old overhead valve six that provided standard power in the Dakota for years is finally gone, replaced by a 3.7-liter single-overhead cam V6 that pumps out a respectable 210 horsepower and 235 lb-ft of torque. The big news in the engine compartment, however, is the availability of not one, but two V8s. The ultrasmooth 4.7-liter, rated for 230 hp and 290 lb-ft of torque, provides more than enough grunt to make the Dakota a spirited performer. However, Dodge has also added an optional high-output version of the 4.7 to the lineup, which utilizes classic hot-rodding tricks to bump output over 250 hp and 300 lb-ft of torque. In order to put all that power to the pavement, buyers can choose from either a five-speed automatic or six-speed manual transmission. Dodge also gives potential buyers two distinctly different four-wheel-drive options, either a traditional part-time 4x4 transfer case with high and low range, or optional first-in-class full-time four-wheel drive that ensures traction in just about any situation. With the decline in popularity of regular cab trucks, Dodge killed that option along with the previously available eight-foot bed. The standard club cab comes equipped with four doors, forward-facing rear seats and a 6-foot-6 bed, while the quad cab model utilizes four full-size doors and a 5-foot-4 bed. Speaking of the Dakota's body, a large crosshair grille is prominently affixed to the front of the truck, followed by the familiar dropped-fender look popularized by the previous-generation Ram and Dakota. The lines of the truck were kept sharp for a more aggressive look, and extensive wind-tunnel development makes this one of the most aerodynamically efficient pickups ever built. A revised A-pillar shape, new sideview mirrors, revised door seals and 20-percent thicker glass were all utilized to help cut wind and road racket. The refinement continues inside, where form is emphasized just as heavily as function. Both cab configurations offer the most interior space in their class, and the rear seats flip up to reveal built-in storage trays for added convenience. The new interior was designed for comfort, and options like plush heated leather seats, steering wheel audio controls and satellite radio make the Dakota more carlike than ever. If you're in the market for a new small pickup this year, the redesigned Dakota should definitely be on your test-drive list.

**Body Styles, Trim Levels and Options:** The Dakota is available in two body styles, both of which have four doors and a backseat. The club cab utilizes rear-opening access doors and has a 6-foot-6 bed, while the more spacious quad cab with four full-size doors has a smaller 5-foot-4 bed. There are three trim levels: ST, SLT and Laramie. The ST comes standard with the 3.7-liter V6 and four-speed automatic transmission, 16-inch steel wheels, air conditioning, a CD player and a cloth interior. The SLT adds alloy wheels, chrome bumpers, a split-fold feature for the rear bench seat and power windows, mirrors and door locks. The high-line Laramie adds a 4.7-liter V8 and five-speed automatic transmission, automatic headlights, leather seating surfaces and remote stereo controls on the steering wheel. Options include a six-speed manual transmission, front bucket seats, heated seats, satellite radio, Bluetooth hands-free cell phone compatibility, full-time four-wheel drive and the high-output 4.7-liter V8.

**Powertrains and Performance:** Three engine options are available, a SOHC 3.7-liter V6 that makes 210 horsepower and 235 pound-feet of torque, a SOHC 4.7-liter V8 that produces 230 hp and 290 lb-ft of torque and a high-output 4.7 cranks out over 250 hp and 300 lb-ft of torque. Five-speed automatic and six-speed manual transmissions are available, and a first-in-class full-time four-wheel-drive system is also being offered for 2005 in addition to the usual 2WD and part-time 4WD configurations. Towing capacity with the V8 engine has been rated at 7,150 pounds.

**Safety:** Rear-wheel ABS is standard on the Dakota; four-wheel ABS is optional. Passive safety features include standard multistage front airbags, optional side curtain airbags and an electronic accident response system. Crash tests have not yet been conducted by the NHTSA.

**Interior Design and Special Features:** Inside, the driving position feels much more carlike than you'd expect. Interior panels are nicely textured two-tone plastic, and the fit and finish is outstanding. Window and door lock switches are comfortably within reach, climate controls are set in a nicely finished bezel and are easy to use and understand, and the shutter-type dash vents are attractive and functional. Cabins are spacious, but adults will still find the rear quarters of the Club Cab cramped.

**Driving Impressions:** On the road, the word refinement springs to mind. The truck is very quiet inside at any speed, with plenty of insulation from wind and road noise. The exhaust emits just a hint of a grumble, which turns into a throaty roar when you stomp on the go-pedal in V8-equipped Dakotas. The chassis feels very stable, and while the ride is a bit taut, it soaks up ruts and bumps with ease. The Dakota is tight and responsive in the corners, which is one of the main reasons for buying a truck in this category over one of the full-size models.

## Competitive Vehicles

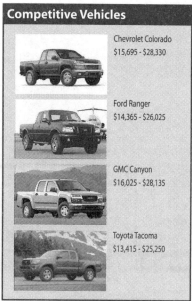

Chevrolet Colorado
$15,695 - $28,330

Ford Ranger
$14,365 - $26,025

GMC Canyon
$16,025 - $28,135

Toyota Tacoma
$13,415 - $25,250

## All New for 2005

# 2005 Dodge Magnum

**Large Wagon**

**MSRP Price Range**
## $21,870 - $31,370
Destination Charge: $625 (all styles)

### Ratings

| | | |
|---|---|---|
| Consumer Rating | 9.2 | |
| Editors Rating | 8.3 | |

**What Edmunds.com says:** Looking for a reason not to buy an SUV? With its available 340-horsepower V8, handsome wagon body and roomy, feature-laden interior, the rear-drive Magnum is one big reason.

**Pros:** Aggressively handsome wagon body style, powerful Hemi V8, quiet ride, roomy interior, lots of safety features, available all-wheel drive.

**Cons:** Sluggish acceleration with base V6, limited transmission choices, complex stereo controls.

**What's New:** The Magnum is an all-new rear-wheel-drive station wagon. Designed to appeal to buyers shopping for a spacious, five-passenger family car, it offers a choice of V6 or V8 power.

*Crash Test Scores, see pg 530*
*Warranty information, see pg 542*

### Specifications

| Engine/Drivetrain | HP | Torque | EPA Fuel Economy Rating |
|---|---|---|---|
| 8cyl 5.7L A | 340 | 390 | 17 city/25 hwy |
| 6cyl 3.5L A | 250 | 250 | 19 city/27 hwy |
| 6cyl 2.7L A | 190 | 190 | 21 city/28 hwy |

### Body Styles

| Style | MSRP Range |
|---|---|
| Large Wagon | $21,870–$31,370 |

**Introduction:** Once stigmatized as stodgy vehicles only your parents would drive, station wagons have waged a comeback in recent years with the help of stylish family vehicles like the Audi A4 Avant, Chrysler PT Cruiser and Subaru Outback. Yet, we suspect that Dodge's new Magnum could be the wagon to shove the revival into the mainstream once and for all, and convince droves of buyers to give up their SUV habit. What's so great about the Magnum? Its long, low stance and flat tail end call to mind the colossal wagons of decades past, but a sharply rising beltline, tapering roof line, short overhangs and prominent wheel arches allow it to pull off a contemporary caricature of its ancestors while giving it an athletic look. Up front, its quad grille strongly resembles that of the Ram and Durango yet manages not to appear too trucklike. Standard 17-inch wheels (or 18s if you go for the V8) complete the Dodge wagon's authoritative stance. The Magnum is about the same size as a Ford Taurus, but a longer wheelbase, rear-wheel-drive configuration and hand-me-down hardware from the Mercedes E-Class put it in a different league where ride and handling characteristics are concerned. The longer wheelbase also translates into extra passenger room, and indeed the Magnum leads its peers when it comes to rear-seat legroom, while offering competitive amounts of head-, hip- and shoulder room. Cargo capacity isn't as impressive, as the Magnum's dropped roof line limits it to 27.8 cubic feet of luggage space behind the rear seats. Power comes from one of three engines -- a 200-horsepower, 2.7-liter V6; a 250-hp, 3.5-liter V6; and, for those who can never get enough, a 340-hp, 5.7-liter V8. Given that a base Magnum weighs in at a hefty 3,800 pounds, the Hemi V8 is certainly the most enticing motor of the three, though the 3.5-liter V6 should be adequate for most buyers. The V8 is also your ticket to a five-speed automatic transmission; the others come with a four-speed auto only. In order to keep its fuel consumption in check, the V8 features Chrysler's Multi Displacement System, which shuts down four of its cylinders during less demanding driving situations. Inside, the Magnum is smartly dressed in a two-tone ensemble accented with faux brushed aluminum. White-faced gauges recessed in separate pods reinforce the wagon's sporty demeanor. Available features include safety items like stability control, side curtain airbags and self-sealing tires, as well as a powerful Boston Acoustics sound system to appeal to your hedonistic side. Buyers living in the Snowbelt can get all-wheel drive starting in the fall of 2004. While sales of seven- and eight-passenger SUVs remain strong, the reality is that most families only need seating for five and a fair amount of luggage space. If you're still waiting for that one perfect wagon that makes both the kids and the adults happy, the Magnum belongs on your test-drive list.

**Body Styles, Trim Levels and Options:** The Magnum is available as a wagon only in one of three trim levels -- SE, SXT and RT. SE models come standard with 17-inch wheels, air conditioning, a CD player, a telescoping steering wheel, cruise control, full power accessories, keyless entry and an outside temperature display. Step up to the SXT and you'll get a bigger V6 engine, along with alloy wheels, antilock brakes, stability control, privacy glass, a power driver seat and a cargo net; most of these items are available on the SE. The high-line RT is your ticket to

For the latest full vehicle reports, visit www.edmunds.com/bginfopak

V8 power, dual exhaust outlets, larger brakes and 18-inch alloy wheels, as well as amenities like leather upholstery and a six-speaker, 288-watt Boston Acoustics sound system. Options include leather upholstery on SE and SXT models; SXT buyers can also get the upgraded stereo. Optional on the RT only are a navigation system and dual-zone automatic climate control. Among the other extras are an MP3-compatible in-dash CD changer, side curtain airbags, adjustable pedals, self-sealing tires, seat heaters, a cargo organizer, a roof rack and a sunroof. Snowbelt residents should also consider all-wheel drive, available as a midyear option.

**Powertrains and Performance:** Engine choices are delineated by trim level. The Magnum SE comes with a 200-hp, 2.7-liter V6. The SXT upgrades to a 3.5-liter V6 good for 250 hp. And for those who can never get enough power, the RT has a 5.7-liter Hemi V8 stuffed under its hood. Output is rated at a prodigious 340 horses and 390 lb-ft of torque. All wagons are rear-wheel drive, unless you specify all-wheel drive as an option. A four-speed automatic transmission comes standard on V6 models; the RT and AWD-equipped SXTs upgrade to a five-speed automatic.

**Safety:** Four-wheel disc brakes are standard across the line. Antilock brakes, traction control and stability control are optional on the base SE model and standard on SXT and RT models. Options on all models include full-length side curtain airbags, self-sealing tires and adjustable pedals. The Magnum has not yet been crash tested.

**Interior Design and Special Features:** Inside, the Magnum's long wheelbase opens up plenty of room for passengers, particularly in the backseat where the Dodge leads its peers in legroom. The Magnum's tapered roof line limits cargo capacity to just 27.8 cubic feet behind the rear seats. Folding those seats opens up 72 cubic feet. Its interior styling isn't revolutionary, but a two-tone color scheme, faux aluminum accents and white-faced gauges give the Magnum a contemporary look.

**Driving Impressions:** With massive amounts of torque flowing to its rear wheels and plenty of Mercedes-derived chassis components, the V8-powered Magnum RT provides serious fun (and serious practicality) for driving enthusiasts-turned-parents. For those who aren't quite ready for the idea of a Hemi-fed wagon, the SXT and its 3.5-liter V6 offer adequate acceleration and an overall pleasant driving experience. The base V6 makes the Magnum SE feel sluggish, do yourself a favor and upgrade to the SXT if at all possible.

## Competitive Vehicles

Infiniti FX35
$34,550 - $36,050

Lexus RX 330
$35,275 - $36,675

Nissan Murano
$28,300 - $30,850

Subaru Outback
$23,470 - $32,620

# 2005 Ford Five Hundred

**Large Sedan**

**MSRP Price Range**
## $22,145 - $27,845
Destination Charge: $650 (all styles)

### Ratings

| | | |
|---|---|---|
| Consumer Rating | 9.7 | |
| Editors Rating | 8.0 | |

**What Edmunds.com says:** Roomy, stylish and practical, the Five Hundred is well suited for family duty, but with its mediocre engine performance and interior materials, it's simply one of many solid choices in the under-$30,000 price bracket.

**Pros:** Spacious cabin, huge trunk, smooth ride quality, available all-wheel drive, plenty of safety features.

**Cons:** Mediocre engine performance, some low-grade interior materials, no stability control.

**What's New:** The Five Hundred is an all-new premium family sedan built on the Volvo S80 platform. Both front- and all-wheel-drive versions are available.

**Introduction:** Although there's still room for basic, economical transportation in the family sedan segment, many consumers now expect their sensible rides to incorporate liberal doses of style, power, convenience items and safety measures. Some buyers even go looking for luxury ambience and sporty handling in a segment once written off for its blandness and lack of originality. Not everyone has been quick to embrace this trend. For the last several years, Ford has been hard-pressed to sell its family cars to anyone besides bargain hunters. Next to the Accord, the Taurus and its Mercury Sable twin suffer for their unrefined drivetrains, subpar braking and handling and low-quality interiors that offer little in the way of style. But help is finally on the way. A larger sedan called the Five Hundred will slide in above the Taurus in a bid for buyers who want a more premium family sedan. While it may not be in a position to pin down the leaders of the family sedan segment, it's a solidly engineered, comfortable and attractive car that will find its place in the mainstream. The Five Hundred is the first Ford product to take advantage of the company's controlling stake in Volvo. It's built on the same platform Volvo uses for its S60 and S80 sedans and makes extensive use of Volvo safety and all-wheel-drive technology. On the outside, the new Ford is about the same size as a Chrysler 300. Their sheet metal is modern but unremarkable in appearance, and for better or worse, heavily derivative of the Volkswagen Passat's. If sitting up high is important to you, then you'll like the view from the driver seat. Ford calls the Five Hundred "a sedan derived from a crossover vehicle," and to that end the seating position is elevated (think Subaru Outback); the car's beltline is relatively low and the side mirrors are large. Front and rear passengers are treated to serious headroom and legroom, and those who buy groceries in bulk will love what they find when they open the trunk -- at 21 cubic feet of capacity, this is the largest cargo hold in the sedan kingdom. The overall interior design is stylish, but materials quality could use improvement. The power source for every Five Hundred is the workhorse 3.0-liter Duratec V6. Output is only 203 horsepower, putting the cars at an immediate disadvantage alongside the powerhouse V6s offered by many competitors. Fortunately, Ford spent money on a couple new transmissions -- a continuously variable transmission (CVT) and a six-speed automatic -- which help the cars get the most out of the available power. Buyers also have a choice of front- or all-wheel drive. Family sedans are supposed to be practical, roomy and loaded with conveniences, and the Five Hundred certainly meets that requirement. But buyers who spend upward of $25,000 will expect to connect to their family sedan on an emotional level, and with its mediocre engine output and interior materials, it remains to be seen how well the Five Hundred will fulfill this part of the deal.

*Crash Test Scores, see pg 530*
*Warranty information, see pg 542*

### Specifications

| Engine/Drivetrain | HP | Torque | EPA Fuel Economy Rating |
|---|---|---|---|
| 6cyl 3.0L A | 203 | 207 | 21 city/29 hwy |

### Body Styles

| Style | MSRP Range |
|---|---|
| Large Sedan | $22,145–$27,845 |

**Body Styles, Trim Levels and Options:** The Five Hundred sedan is available in one of three trims: SE, SEL and Limited. The SE starts you out with 17-inch wheels, a six-way power driver seat, full power accessories, air conditioning, a CD player and cruise control. The SEL adds an eight-way power driver seat, dual-zone automatic climate control, a leather-wrapped steering wheel, wood interior trim, an MP3-compatible in-dash CD changer, a fold-flat front-passenger

For the latest full vehicle reports, visit www.edmunds.com/bginfopak

# 2005 Ford Five Hundred

seat, extra sound insulation and adjustable head restraints and air registers for rear passengers. Step up to the Limited and you'll get 18-inch wheels, leather upholstery, a four-way power passenger seat, seat memory, an upgraded audio system, cream-faced gauges and an analog clock. Options include a moonroof, adjustable pedals and a reverse-sensing system.

**Powertrains and Performance:** Every Five Hundred comes with Ford's 3.0-liter Duratec V6 rated for 203 horsepower and 207 pound-feet of torque. Buyers have two transmission choices. The first of these is a continuously variable transmission (CVT), which has an infinite number of ratios and chooses whichever one best fits a given situation. The other option is a six-speed automatic. Buyers must also decide between front-wheel drive and all-wheel drive. Front-drive SE models and all AWD models come with the CVT. Front-drive SELs and Limiteds get the six-speed automatic.

**Safety:** All Five Hundreds come with a full set of disc brakes, ABS and Electronic Brakeforce Distribution. Optional on all models are side-impact airbags that protect front occupants' torsos and side curtain airbags that protect the heads of front and rear occupants. Traction control is standard, but stability control is not available. This car has not yet been crash tested.

**Interior Design and Special Features:** Scrutinize the cabin and it's apparent that designers put a lot of thought into creating an attractive and functional environment. In lieu of the shapeless dash and seats found in the Taurus, the Five Hundred has the crisp, clean lines popularized by Volkswagen's Passat. The front seats are roomy enough to fit most drivers, yet the cockpit has a snug, almost intimate feel. Rear passengers are treated to equally spacious quarters, making these cars good bets for families with teenagers. The rear seats fold flat in a 60/40-split and this, along with the fold-flat front-passenger seat, allows owners to transport items up to nine feet in length. Trunk capacity leads all sedans on the market at 21 cubic feet.

**Driving Impressions:** The V6 provides enough low-end torque for easy city driving, and the car gets up to speed with minimal fuss. We do expect that eventual owners will wish for a little extra midrange torque for passing at highway speeds and climbing grades. Of the two transmissions, our preference is the CVT, which does a better job of keeping the engine in its power band. Thanks to its Volvo-engineered chassis, the Five Hundred offers a pleasant balance between smooth ride quality and responsive handling. It's not the car to buy if you're looking for entertainment, but if you just want something capable and comfortable, the Five Hundred should satisfy.

## Competitive Vehicles

Chevrolet Malibu
$19,085 - $23,945

Chrysler 300
$23,295 - $34,195

Honda Accord
$15,900 - $28,500

Nissan Altima
$17,250 - $29,200

# 2005 Ford Freestyle

**Midsize Wagon**

**MSRP Price Range**

## $24,945 - $30,245

Destination Charge: $650 (all styles)

### Ratings

| | | |
|---|---|---|
| Consumer Rating | 9.6 | |
| Editors Rating | 8.2 | |

**What Edmunds.com says:** With truly comfortable accommodations for six passengers, plenty of cargo space and refined driving dynamics, the Freestyle has everything going for it except power.

**Pros:** Truly roomy seating for six passengers, plenty of cargo space, balanced ride and handling characteristics, lengthy list of safety features.

**Cons:** So-so acceleration, some low-grade interior materials, no stability control or navigation system.

**What's New:** The Freestyle is an all-new crossover wagon from Ford. Built on a Volvo platform, it incorporates the Swedish brand's safety and all-wheel-drive technology, while offering six- to seven-passenger seating capacity.

**Introduction:** If you had to make a list of the current trends in family transportation, it would surely include wagons and car-based crossover SUVs. Wagons (the stylish ones anyway) are becoming more appealing to sedan buyers who need more cargo room, as well as would-be SUV buyers who realize they don't need all that ground clearance. Car-based SUVs, meanwhile, are a strong draw for would-be SUV buyers who realize they don't need all-terrain capability but don't want to give up the image or convenience of driving one of these vehicles. Ultimately, it's getting harder to draw the line between wagons and SUVs -- features like all-wheel drive, third-row seating and fold-flat seats are available on both sides. Already several manufacturers have attempted to straddle this line, but unlike others before it, Ford's well-packaged Freestyle does so with few if any compromises. Like the new Five Hundred sedan, the Freestyle is built on the same platform as the Volvo S60 and S80 sedans, V70 and XC70 wagons and the XC90 SUV. Chassis tuning is similar to that of the Volvos, and Ford makes no attempt to hide the fact that safety and all-wheel-drive technology is shared between the two brands as well. The Freestyle rides higher than a Taurus but lower than an Explorer, and offers the kind of step-in access you get with a minivan. But Ford's new wagon manages not to look like a minivan -- it has four hinged doors and its squarish front fascia strongly resembles the Explorer's. Inside, the Freestyle offers excellent visibility from the cockpit and "progressive theater seating" for the second and third rows: Each row is two inches higher than the one before it. Depending on whether you select captain's chairs or a 60/40 bench seat in the second row, the wagon can seat six or seven passengers. This kind of seating capacity is nothing remarkable among today's family vehicles, but the Freestyle is one of the few vehicles outside the minivan segment that can honestly seat this many people in comfort. One of our complaints about SUVs like the Explorer and wagons like the Chrysler Pacifica is that when you're carrying a full load of passengers, there's almost no cargo space to speak of. You might be able to fit a few groceries behind the third-row seat, but what if you're shopping for the whole week? The Freestyle provides a satisfying answer to that question, as it has a deep cargo well behind its rearmost seat, allowing owners to fit at least a half-dozen paper grocery bags without dropping the seat. Well-rounded as it is, the Freestyle has a couple of weak spots. With only a 203-horsepower, 3.0-liter V6 providing power to this 4,000-pound vehicle, acceleration is merely adequate. Further, despite the emphasis on style and functionality in the cabin, not all of the materials used are up to import-brand quality standards. If you can get past these drawbacks, though, the safe and roomy Freestyle is definitely worth a look for families of four or more who won't drive a minivan.

**Body Styles, Trim Levels and Options:** The Freestyle comes in three trims -- SE, SEL and Limited. The SE comes 17-inch alloy wheels, privacy glass, seating for six, air conditioning, a CD player, a six-way power driver seat, full power accessories and cruise control. The midgrade SEL adds an MP3-compatible in-dash CD changer, a leather-wrapped steering wheel with auxiliary audio controls, automatic headlights, foglights, heated side mirrors, an auto-dimming rearview

*Crash Test Scores, see pg 530*
*Warranty information, see pg 542*

### Specifications

| Engine/Drivetrain | HP | Torque | EPA Fuel Economy Rating |
|---|---|---|---|
| 6cyl 3.0L A | 203 | 207 | 20 city/27 hwy |

### Body Styles

| Style | MSRP Range |
|---|---|
| Midsize Wagon | $24,945–$30,245 |

mirror, a trip computer, extra sound insulation and body-color door handles and mirrors. If you go for the Limited, you'll get 18-inch wheels, leather upholstery in the first and second rows, wood grain interior trim, dual-zone automatic climate control, an upgraded sound system, power adjustments for both front seats (along with memory for the driver), front seat heaters, 50/50-split capability for the third-row bench and a cargo net. Note that SE and SEL models come with two-tone exterior paint, while the Limited gets a monochromatic paint job. Options include power-adjustable pedals, a three-person bench seat for the second row (provides seven-passenger capacity) and reverse parking sensors.

**Powertrains and Performance:** All Freestyles come with the most updated version of Ford's 3.0-liter Duratec V6, which now includes electronic throttle control. Horsepower comes in at 203, while torque measures 207 pound-feet. A continuously variable transmission (CVT) is standard. Buyers can choose between front-wheel drive and all-wheel drive.

**Safety:** Four-wheel antilock disc brakes with Electronic Brakeforce Distribution are standard, as is traction control. Stability control is not available. On the options list, you'll find both side-impact airbags (for the front) and head curtain airbags (for all three rows). The Freestyle has not yet been crash tested.

**Interior Design and Special Features:** Depending on whether you select captain's chairs or a 60/40 bench seat in the second row, the Freestyle can seat six or seven passengers. The second row offers enough legroom to seat both adults and children comfortably. The captain's chairs can be adjusted fore and aft to provide more room for third-row passengers, but the 60/40 bench seat is nonadjustable. Third-row legroom is adequate when the second-row seats are in the all-the-way-back position and generous when the captain's chairs are scooted up. A deep cargo well provides a good deal of space for groceries, even when all three rows of seating are in use. When you need more room, both the second- and third-row seats fold flat into the floor.

**Driving Impressions:** Acceleration is acceptable for the most part, as the Freestyle has little difficulty getting up to highway speeds. However, we expect that owners will wish for a little more juice for passing maneuvers, especially when the vehicle is loaded up with passengers and gear. Ride dynamics are excellent, as the wagon's fully independent suspension delivers a smooth, refined ride quality and responsive handling in the corners.

## Competitive Vehicles

Honda Pilot
$27,100 - $32,870

Hyundai Santa Fe
$17,999 - $25,499

Subaru Outback
$24,295 - $33,495

Toyota Highlander
$24,080 - $31,380

# 2005 Ford Mustang

**Compact Coupe**

**MSRP Price Range**

## $18,785 - $25,705

Destination Charge: $625 (all styles)

## Ratings

| | | |
|---|---|---|
| Consumer Rating | 9.3 | |
| Editors Rating | 8.2 | |

**What Edmunds.com says:** Not merely a retro reskinning, the newest Mustang improves its performance in all areas and offers V8 enthusiasts a tempting price tag.

**Pros:** Solid V8 power in GT models, about as well mannered as a solid axle suspension can get, slick retro interior, much improved cabin ergonomics.

**Cons:** No side curtain airbags or stability control, seats could use more lateral support.

**What's New:** The Mustang is completely redesigned for 2005.

**Introduction:** The Ford Mustang debuted in April of 1964 and became a national sensation. By the late 1960s, the Mustang competed against the AMC Javelin, Chevrolet Camaro, Dodge Challenger, Plymouth Barracuda and Pontiac Firebird. But, like Elvis Presley, the Mustang had evolved from lightweight and simple into overweight and flashy. By the time the oil crisis of 1973 hit, the Mustang had lost its edge in terms of performance and appeal. Reborn for 1974, the Mustang II rode on a Pinto platform to save development costs and improve fuel economy. Emissions regulations had stifled performance, and the convertible model had disappeared from the lineup. Still, Ford wasn't ready to give up on the Mustang. In 1979, it was completely redesigned. There was even a performance model with a turbocharged 2.3-liter, four-cylinder engine. The new Mustang proved popular, and by 1982, Ford had endowed it with a relatively strong (for the time) V8 engine and the GT designation that continues today. A new car arrived in 1994 wearing retro styling cues such as tribar taillights and a side scoop. Inside, a dual-cowl dashboard provided plenty of pizzazz. A coupe and convertible were available, with either a V6 or V8 engine. Time marched on, however, and the Mustang was in desperate need of a more modern platform by the turn of the century. Enter the 2005 Mustang. The canted nose with its big grille and round headlights recalls the '67 to '69 Mustangs, while the side sculpting, fastback roofline and taillights recall those ponies of the 1965 vintage. Even the triangular side windows are reminiscent of what Carol Shelby did when he made the 1965 Mustang "2 + 2" (a.k.a. the fastback) into his Shelby GT 350. The new Mustang's interior is unique and matches the exterior design theme. Obvious old-school influences are found in the instrument panel -- a dual-hooded dash with aluminum accent panels pays obvious homage to the 1967-'68 Mustang, as do the big speedo and tach, circular air vents and plump, round steering wheel hub. Changeable backlighting illuminates the nostalgic instruments; at the press of a button one can select from white, blue, green and orange hues. For power, the base Mustang uses a 210-horsepower V6, while the GT packs a 300-horse, 4.6-liter V8 with variable valve timing. There's also a new suspension that features lighter weight components, repositioned and lighter coil springs, a stouter rear axle with more effective control arms and bigger brakes. The result is a relatively supple ride and ultracrisp handling. Ford has done a fine job with the new Mustang -- not only in terms of styling, but also in performance, handling, ride dynamics and basic ergonomics.

*Crash Test Scores, see pg 530*
*Warranty information, see pg 542*

## Specifications

| Engine/Drivetrain | HP | Torque | EPA Fuel Economy Rating |
|---|---|---|---|
| 8cyl 4.6L M | 300 | 320 | 17 city/25 hwy |
| 6cyl 4.0L M | 210 | 240 | 19 city/28 hwy |

## Body Styles

| Style | MSRP Range |
|---|---|
| Compact Coupe | $18,785–$25,705 |

**Body Styles, Trim Levels and Options:** Two body styles, coupe and convertible, and four major trim levels are available for the Mustang -- V6 Deluxe, V6 Premium, GT Deluxe and GT Premium. Standard equipment on V6 Deluxe includes keyless entry; 16-inch alloy wheels; air conditioning; power windows, locks and mirrors; cruise control; and a CD player. The V6 Premium adds a 500-watt Shaker 500 premium audio system, upgraded wheels, a power driver seat and, on convertibles, leather seating. The GT Deluxe includes the V6 Deluxe equipment, plus antilock brakes, foglamps, 17-inch alloys, sport seats with driver six-way power adjustment and a leather-wrapped steering wheel. The GT Premium adds the Shaker 500 sound system and leather seats. Interesting options include a Shaker 1000 sound system with nine speakers and 1,000 watts of power, and an interior upgrade package with metallic accents, dark charcoal Aberdeen pattern door panel inserts and instruments with changeable backlighting -- at the press of a button one can select from white, blue, green and orange hues.

**Powertrains and Performance:** Powertrains and Performance: V6 Mustangs include a 4.0-liter V6 with 210 horsepower and 240 lb-ft of torque. Step up to the GT and you'll get a 4.6-liter V8 with 300 hp and 320 lb-ft of torque, three valves per cylinder and variable valve timing. All Mustangs are rear-drive, and can be equipped with either a five-speed manual or a five-speed automatic transmission.

**Safety:** Four-wheel disc brakes are standard on all Mustangs. Antilock brakes and traction control are optional on the V6 models and standard on the GT. A stability control system is not offered. Side-impact airbags for front occupants are optional on all models, but full-length head curtain airbags are not available. The Mustang has not yet been crash tested.

**Interior Design and Special Features:** Interior ergonomics are vastly improved over the previous Mustang. Switches and handles feel substantial, and overall materials quality is top-notch. Retro styling abounds in little touches like the large round speedometer and tach (which feature an appropriate vintage font), dual-hooded dash and a cool steering wheel with a small round airbag hub and metallic spokes. A striking color accent package features red leather seats, red door panel inserts and red floor mats all set against a dark charcoal interior.

**Driving Impressions:** The Mustang turns crisply and eagerly into corners with a flat and composed attitude. The powerful brakes are more fade resistant than before, and control in bumpy corners is improved, despite the continued use of a solid rear axle. The comfortable cabin benefits from low wind and road noise, as well as a surprisingly compliant ride.

## Competitive Vehicles

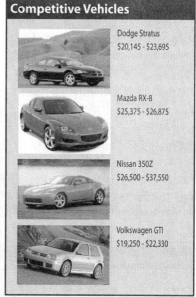

Dodge Stratus
$20,145 - $23,695

Mazda RX-8
$25,375 - $26,875

Nissan 350Z
$26,500 - $37,550

Volkswagen GTI
$19,250 - $22,330

# 2005 Honda Odyssey

**Large Minivan**

**MSRP Price Range**

## $24,995 - $38,295

Destination Charge: $515 (all styles)

 #1 Editors' Rating

## Ratings

| | | |
|---|---|---|
| Consumer Rating | 9.6 | |
| Editors Rating | 8.9 | |

**What Edmunds.com says:** Demonstrating that there's always room for improvement, Honda makes its exceptional Odyssey minivan even better. If you're shopping for a minivan, this is one you won't want to miss.

**Pros:** Agile, carlike handling, a split flat-folding rear bench, optional eight-passenger seating, extensive feature list, smooth and powerful V6, strong reliability record.

**Cons:** High demand forces you to pay sticker price or above.

**What's New:** The top-selling Honda Odyssey minivan is all new for 2005.

Crash Test Scores, see pg 530
Warranty information, see pg 542

## Specifications

| Engine/Drivetrain | HP | Torque | EPA Fuel Economy Rating |
|---|---|---|---|
| 6cyl 3.5L A | 255 | 250 | 20 city/28 hwy |

## Body Styles

| Style | MSRP Range |
|---|---|
| Large Minivan | $24,995–$38,295 |

**Introduction:** There's no disputing the fact that the Honda Odyssey is a great minivan. Having claimed the best-in-class crown from Chrysler shortly after its debut in 1999, the Odyssey reigned supreme for five years thanks to its cavernous interior filled with useful features, pleasant driving characteristics, excellent crash test scores and generally favorable reliability record. And just when you think the best can't get any better, the redesigned Odyssey hits the market offering numerous mechanical improvements as well as increased feature content. The newest Odyssey is quieter, more spacious and offers even more innovative features than before, including increased seating configurations and unique storage solutions. Add the Odyssey's superior handling and Honda's reputation for quality, and you've got a top-rate minivan. Numerous competitors have tried to trump the Odyssey's offerings in recent years, but the Odyssey has not only managed to maintain its great appeal, but build on it as well. But the best part is that all of the new benefits are packed into nearly the same-size overall package. Interior dimensions have expanded, but without a significant increase to the exterior dimensions. The 2005 Odyssey maintains the same exterior length as the previous model, while the exterior width increases by just an inch. Interior length grows by two inches, and interior width gains an additional inch as well. Also new is optional eight-passenger seating with a stowable middle seat in the second row. This optional seat can be converted into a center tray table or removed and stored in the vehicle's new in-floor storage area made even more functional with a rotating "lazy Susan" feature hidden inside. Additionally, the second-row captain's chairs can be pushed together to form a two-passenger bench. In the far back, the third-row seat remains a fold-flat bench, but new for Honda is a one-motion 60/40-split seat instead of the previous one-piece bench. If it sounds like the Odyssey is a great place to spend time in, you're right. With vehicles designed to be everything from no-frills transportation to luxurious, fast sport coupes, the most important thing about minivan design is utility. It's not simply about style or luxury or power. Minivans are about the people inside them -- their comfort, their safety and the way they live. And in the case of the new Odyssey, Honda again approaches the challenge with a special thoughtfulness that has always set it apart from the competition.

**Body Styles, Trim Levels and Options:** The base-level LX model includes 16-inch wheels with wheel covers; power front- and second-row windows; power locks; cruise control; keyless entry; a CD player; a 60/40-split third-row seat; in-floor storage; and a smart maintenance indicator. The EX adds alloy wheels, optional eight-passenger seating, power-sliding doors, an in-dash six-disc CD changer, in-floor storage with a handy "lazy Susan" feature, integrated second-row sunshades, a conversation mirror and a sunglasses holder. Choose the EX with a leather interior and you'll also get a more advanced V6 engine and a power moonroof. Family road-trippers can also add a DVD entertainment system and a navigation system with voice recognition and an integrated rearview camera. The Touring model adds a power liftgate, tri-zone auto climate control, driver-seat memory, a 115-volt AC outlet, a multi-information display, power-adjustable pedals, a leather-wrapped steering wheel, an auto-dimming rearview mirror, foglights,

For the latest full vehicle reports, visit www.edmunds.com/bginfopak

parking sensors, auto headlights, a second-row removable center console (in place of the stowable middle seat), run-flat tires, 17.5-inch wheels and a tire-pressure monitoring system.

**Powertrains and Performance:** The Odyssey offers two V6 engine options. LX and EX models use a 255-horsepower V6 mated to a five-speed automatic transmission. EX models with leather and Touring models use the same engine but are upgraded with Variable Cylinder Management (VCM), which increases fuel efficiency by "shutting off" three of the engine's six cylinders during cruising and deceleration. When more performance is needed, the engine switches back to using all six cylinders. This system can increase fuel economy by as much as 12 percent over the regular V6, according to Honda.

**Safety:** Standard safety features on the Odyssey include stability and traction control (called Vehicle Stability Assist); four-wheel antilock disc brakes with BrakeAssist and Electronic Brakeforce Distribution; side airbags; and three-row side curtain airbags with rollover sensors. Touring models come with run-flat tires and a tire-pressure monitoring system with location and pressure indicators.

**Interior Design and Special Features:** Inside, the Odyssey offers so many unique family-friendly features that driver and passengers alike will be hard-pressed to choose their favorite. From the DVD entertainment system with a whopping nine-inch display screen and wireless headsets with personal surround sound to the optional navigation system with voice recognition (complete with the Zagat survey for restaurants) and an integrated rearview camera, the Honda Odyssey doesn't miss a trick.

**Driving Impressions:** The Odyssey has always been highly regarded for its carlike driving characteristics, and the new minivan is no exception. A high seating position, tight turning radius and nimble suspension make the Odyssey easy to pilot both down the freeway and through the grocery store parking lot.

## Competitive Vehicles

Chevrolet Venture
$23,365 - $30,760

Dodge Grand Caravan
$20,205 - $26,505

Nissan Quest
$23,350 - $32,250

Toyota Sienna
$23,225 - $37,495

# 2005 HUMMER H2 SUT

**Large Truck**

**MSRP Price Range**

**$52,205 - $55,945**
Destination Charge: $850 (all styles)

## Ratings

| | | |
|---|---|---|
| Consumer Rating | 9.0 | |
| Editors Rating | 6.7 | |

**What Edmunds.com says:** The H2 SUV evolves into an even more rugged-looking and versatile vehicle with the new H2 SUT.

**Pros:** Distinctive styling, unmatched off-road capability, stout drivetrain, versatile cargo/passenger space.

**Cons:** Feels massive, some cheap interior materials, dismal fuel economy.

**What's New:** The H2 SUT is a new "sport-utility truck" based upon the H2 SUV.

*Crash Test Scores, see pg 530*
*Warranty information, see pg 542*

## Specifications

| Engine/Drivetrain | HP | Torque | EPA Fuel Economy Rating |
|---|---|---|---|
| 8cyl 6.0L A | 316 | 360 | N/A |

## Body Styles

| Style | MSRP Range |
|---|---|
| Crew Cab Pickup Truck | $52,205–$55,945 |

**Introduction:** The AM General and General Motors partnership has spawned yet another SUV/truck/off-road vehicle, the H2 SUT. For those who aren't familiar with AM General, it's a company that was awarded the original contract to build the Humvee military vehicle. When the Humvee became a household name thanks to its prominent role in Desert Storm, AM General decided to capitalize on its popularity and build a civilian version known as the Hummer (now known as the H1). With a sticker price of well over $100,000, it isn't exactly your average sport-utility, but its unstoppable off-road ability and rugged military styling make it a hit with wannabes and movie stars alike. Unfortunately, the Hummer's transition from all-purpose military vehicle to daily driver wasn't perfect. Despite its imposing size, there is barely enough room for four, and the interior ergonomics are poor. Although the suspension allows it to climb over just about anything, negotiating traffic in the nearly three-ton beast isn't much fun. So how does General Motors figure into the equation? Realizing that AM General had a household name for a product that few could afford, GM stepped in and bought the rights to "Hummer" in 1999. It doesn't own AM General, nor does it build any of the vehicles. What the General did do, however, was design a new SUV called the H2 that uses its extensive inventory of existing truck and SUV parts. Capitalizing on the popularity of the H2 (who can look at an H2 and not know it's a Hummer?), GM designers have crafted a unique pickup truck alternative, a la Chevy Avalanche. The SUT maintains, and perhaps even enhances, the distinctive styling of the original H2 SUV. Basically, the H2's cargo area was opened up to the great outdoors and a removable midgate was added to separate the "pickup bed" from the passenger space. With the midgate closed, the cargo area is a 30-cubic-foot, rubber-lined open bed. Folding the rear seats down and opening the midgate expands the cargo area to 56 cubic feet. Designers also chose to relocate the enormous spare tire to the outside of the tailgate, a huge improvement over the H2 SUV's cargo area-mounted configuration. Almost all of the convenience features found in GM's SUV and truck lineup can be found in the H2 SUT. From dual-zone automatic climate control to a Bose audio system to the OnStar communication system, the SUT is loaded to the hilt with standard features. Of course, its most important feature is still its unmistakable sheet metal, and with colors like Desert Sand and Bright Yellow, those who just want to be seen should have no trouble attracting attention in this creation from Hummer.

**Body Styles, Trim Levels and Options:** The H2 SUT comes in only one body style and one trim level, but two major packages known as the Adventure Series and the Lux Series add numerous features. Niceties like dual-zone automatic climate control, a driver information center and OnStar are standard equipment along with power everything and a keyless entry system. The Adventure Series package adds a self-leveling rear air suspension along with an upgraded audio system, carpeted floor mats, tool and first-aid kits and a front brush guard. The Lux Series package doesn't include the air suspension, but it does add uplevel leather seating, a chrome appearance package, tubular side steps and the Adventure package's audio system

and floor mats. Stand-alone options include heated front and rear seats, an overhead light bar and an integrated DVD-based navigation system.

**Powertrains and Performance:** All H2s are powered by GM's 6.0-liter V8 rated at 316 horsepower and 360 pound-feet of torque. A heavy-duty 4L65-E four-speed automatic transmission handles the shifting chores, while a full-time dual-range transfer case distributes the power to the individual driveshafts. Advanced features include a driver-selectable rear differential locker and a drive-by-wire throttle setup that changes sensitivity when low-range gearing is selected.

**Safety:** The H2 SUT comes standard with ABS and traction control. The advanced traction system allows the SUT to propel itself even if only a single wheel has grip, while driver-selectable settings fine-tune the system to respond better to varying road conditions. The SUT has yet to be crash tested by the IIHS or NHTSA.

**Interior Design and Special Features:** Unlike the awkwardly configured H1, the H2 SUT's interior is arranged like a typical full-size SUV, minus the enclosed cargo area. Power-adjustable captain's chairs reside upfront, while a three-passenger bench seat makes up the second row. The overall design emphasizes the H2's rugged personality, with exposed attachment bolts and an aircraft throttle-style shift lever, but standard equipment like dual-zone climate control and a nine-speaker Bose sound system remind you that the SUT is a thoroughly modern vehicle. A removable midgate separates the passenger area from the open cargo area. At a touch of a button, the driver can lower all four windows and the rear midgate window. A power sunroof is standard on all SUTs. With the midgate closed, the SUT's cargo area consists of a 30-cubic-foot, rubber-lined open bed. Folding the rear seats down and opening the midgate raises capacity to 56 cubic feet.

**Driving Impressions:** Despite being slightly downsized compared to the original H1, the H2 SUT still feels massive on the road. The ride is slightly stiffer than a Suburban's or Avalanche's, but not so much as to be uncomfortable. The SUT's off-road prowess is easily the best in its class, with steep approach and departure angles, plenty of ground clearance and ample wheel travel. Power from the big V8 is watered down by the vehicle's substantial mass.

## Competitive Vehicles

Cadillac Escalade EXT
$52,815

Dodge Ram Pickup 1500
$19,855 - $34,465

Ford F-150
$21,455 - $35,990

Nissan Titan
$22,400 - $34,300

# 2005 Hyundai Tucson

**Compact SUV**

**MSRP Price Range**
## $17,499 - $22,749
Destination Charge: $595 (all styles)

## Ratings

| Consumer Rating | N/A | |
|---|---|---|
| Editors Rating | 7.3 | |

**What Edmunds.com says:** Appealing styling, plenty of standard features and Hyundai's impressive warranty make the Tucson a solid competitor in the compact SUV class.

**Pros:** Generous warranty, standard ABS and stability control, roomy passenger and cargo space, attractive interior, standard side and head curtain airbags.

**Cons:** Low horsepower rating, some cheap interior materials here and there.

**What's New:** The Hyundai Tucson is an all-new compact SUV from Hyundai. It rides on the Elantra platform and is intended for buyers who want a smaller package than the midsize Santa Fe.

Crash Test Scores, see pg 530
Warranty information, see pg 542

## Specifications

| Engine/Drivetrain | HP | Torque | EPA Fuel Economy Rating |
|---|---|---|---|
| 6cyl 2.7L A | 173 | 178 | 20 city/26 hwy |
| 4cyl 2.0L A/M | 140 | 136 | 22 city/27 hwy |

## Body Styles

| Style | MSRP Range |
|---|---|
| Compact SUV | $17,499–$22,749 |

**Introduction:** Hyundai has found surprising success with its Santa Fe, a well-engineered midsize SUV. Early Santa Fes had a few odd quirks, and Hyundai made a point to listen to its customers and upgrade the SUV accordingly. Evidently, Hyundai is still listening to consumers -- this time, it's responding to requests for a smaller vehicle. The answer is the new Tuscon, an all-new compact SUV. Designed to challenge segment stalwarts like Honda's CR-V and Toyota's RAV4, the Tucson offers loads of standard features and a choice of four- or six-cylinder power. The Tucson's styling follows in the tire tracks of the Santa Fe with its sweptback headlights and curving front fenders, although it thankfully doesn't have the "fish mouth" grille of its big brother. For the most part, it's more handsome, if not more conservative, than the Santa Fe. The Tucson boasts a generous standard features list, including full-length side curtain airbags (in addition to seat-mounted side airbags for front occupants). Other notable standard features include four-wheel disc brakes with ABS, traction control, a stability control system, air conditioning and full power equipment. Also standard on all Tucsons is Hyundai's 10-year/100,000-mile warranty. A unique split-folding rear seat is able to fold flat to create a level cargo floor. It does this by lowering the bottom cushion into the footwell, and doesn't even require removal of the head restraints. The all-wheel-drive option uses an Electronic InterActive Torque Management system that routes up to 99 percent of the available power to the front wheels under ideal traction conditions for the sake of fuel economy. As road conditions change, the system automatically diverts up to 50 percent of the power to the rear wheels. A dash-mounted lock button allows the driver to lock the driveline into a set 50/50-split for extra traction when driving in snow. Power is provided by two different engines, a 2.0-liter, inline four-cylinder engine with continuously variable valve timing, which makes 140 horsepower and 136 pound-feet of torque, and an optional 2.7-liter V6 engine that produces 173 hp and 178 lb-ft of torque. The Tucson is joining a crowded class of excellent vehicles. Hyundai hopes its entrant will win the hearts of potential CR-V and RAV4 buyers with its roomy interior, fresh styling and generous helping of standard equipment. With those kinds of credentials, the Tucson may prove just as popular as its big brother, the Santa Fe.

**Body Styles, Trim Levels and Options:** The four-door Tucson compact SUV comes in three trim levels -- entry-level GL, midlevel GLS and top-of-the-line LX. Standard features on the GL include four-wheel disc brakes with ABS, 16-inch alloy wheels, air conditioning, power windows and door locks, keyless entry, cruise control, heated outside mirrors, roof rack side rails, a rear intermittent wiper and a CD stereo system. The GL adds body-side cladding, foglamps, larger tires, a CD/cassette/MP3 stereo, upgraded upholstery and a front wiper de-icer. The LX adds leather seating and an upgraded audio system with an in-dash six-disc CD changer and a subwoofer.

**Powertrains and Performance:** The base GL offers a 2.0-liter, inline four-cylinder engine with continuously variable valve timing. It generates 140 horsepower and 136 pound-feet of torque, and is mated to a five-speed manual transmission or a four-speed automatic with automanual control. The GLS and LX provide a larger, more powerful 2.7-liter V6 engine that produces 173 hp and 178 lb-ft of torque. A four-speed automatic transmission is standard on the GLS and LX. Buyers can get front-wheel drive or all-wheel drive with either engine.

**Safety:** Passengers are well protected as the Tucson comes standard with seat-mounted side-impact airbags for front occupants and side curtain airbags for both front- and rear-seat occupants. Four-wheel antilock disc brakes are also standard on all Tucsons, along with a traction and stability control system. The Tucson has not yet been crash tested.

**Interior Design and Special Features:** The Tucson features a modern interior with high-quality materials and design. Generous passenger space makes for a comfortable ride. Inside, the Tucson offers 22.7 cubic feet of cargo capacity with the rear seat up, and up to 65.5 with the seat folded.

**Driving Impressions:** The Tucson returns a smooth ride and feels more like a sedan than an SUV. The standard four-cylinder is quite weak; we recommend you go with the V6.

## Competitive Vehicles

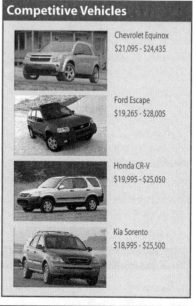

Chevrolet Equinox
$21,095 - $24,435

Ford Escape
$19,265 - $28,005

Honda CR-V
$19,995 - $25,050

Kia Sorento
$18,995 - $25,500

# 2005 Jeep Grand Cherokee

**Midsize SUV**

**MSRP Price Range**

## $26,130 - $34,045

Destination Charge: $645 (all styles)

## Ratings

| | | |
|---|---|---|
| Consumer Rating | 9.8 | |
| Editors Rating | 8.1 | |

**What Edmunds.com says:** The all-new Grand Cherokee manages to retain its classic style and unparalleled off-road ability while delivering a level of luxury never before seen in a Jeep. If you're looking for a true 4x4 that's also refined and comfortable enough to drive in the suburbs, this is a must-see.

**Pros:** Strong engine lineup, unmatched off-road ability, balanced handling, long list of advanced safety equipment, solid warranty.

**Cons:** Hard plastic interior surfaces could use some padding, less cargo capacity than most midsize SUVs.

**What's New:** The Grand Cherokee is all new for 2005. Among the improvements are new four-wheel-drive systems, an independent front suspension, three excellent engine options and better ergonomics and build quality.

Crash Test Scores, see pg 530
Warranty information, see pg 542

## Specifications

| Engine/Drivetrain | HP | Torque | EPA Fuel Economy Rating |
|---|---|---|---|
| 8cyl 5.7L A | 330 | 375 | N/A |
| 8cyl 4.7L A | 230 | 290 | 14 city/20 hwy |
| 6cyl 3.7L A | 210 | 235 | 16 city/21 hwy |

## Body Styles

| Style | MSRP Range |
|---|---|
| Midsize SUV | $26,130–$34,045 |

**Introduction:** Jeep practically invented the sport-utility vehicle way back in the dark days of WWII, when the army needed a tough, maneuverable and lightweight vehicle capable of traversing the nastiest roads and trails on the planet. Sixty years later, the brand is still going strong (thanks to resources from parent company DaimlerChrysler), and while its focus remains on building reliable SUVs with stellar off-road abilities, luxury and refinement have also been incorporated into the mix. The first Grand Cherokee was introduced in 1992 as an answer to the Ford Explorer, and options like leather seats, a powerful V8 engine and an advanced four-wheel-drive system made it an instant hit with daily commuters and desert trekkers alike. Unfortunately, the original Grand Cherokee was a little crude in the fit-and-finish department. Improvements came on the second-generation JGC (1999-2004), but by then, family-oriented buyers had begun to expect carlike handling characteristics and spacious interiors -- attributes that this rugged Jeep simply couldn't deliver as well as a Ford Explorer. Jeep engineers were determined to correct this on the latest version. The third-generation Grand Cherokee offers improved capability and fantastic on-road ride and handling dynamics in a well-appointed package. The all-new exterior design is unmistakably Jeep, thanks to the signature round headlights, seven-slot grille and trapezoidal wheel openings. However, the new body was sculpted with hard edges and prominent lines to convey a more modern and muscular look, and designers spent countless hours in a wind tunnel in an effort to reduce wind and road noise. The nicely finished body panels are mounted on a new platform that incorporates an advanced independent coil-over front suspension, four-wheel antilock disc brakes and standard all-wheel-drive on Laredo and Limited models. The previous generation's tired, old 4.0-liter inline six has been replaced by a more powerful and vastly more refined 3.7-liter V6 borrowed from the Jeep Liberty, and a smooth-shifting five-speed transmission is now standard on all models. For those who desire more power than the V6 can muster, two different V8 engines are available, including a variable-displacement Hemi for the ultimate balance of economy and power. The refinement continues inside, where form is emphasized just as heavily as function. New seats are comfortably padded and available in cloth or two-tone leather, which is complemented by nicely textured two-tone plastic door and trim panels. The chronograph-style four-gauge instrument cluster looks like it belongs in a luxury car, and a gated shifter borrowed from the Mercedes parts bin makes selecting the right gear a breeze. New options for 2005 include auto-dimming headlamps, rear-seat DVD entertainment, satellite navigation and radio, adjustable pedals and dual-zone climate control. Overall, the new Grand Cherokee offers more luxury and comfort than ever before, while maintaining the rugged character that made the Jeep marque what it is today.

**Body Styles, Trim Levels and Options:** The Grand Cherokee is available in two trim levels, Laredo and Limited. Standard Laredo features include power windows and door locks, air conditioning, eight-way power front seats with lumbar support, split-folding rear seat, a reversible cargo floor with water-resistant storage and a CD stereo. The Limited model adds two-tone leather seating, unique 17-inch alloy wheels, an adjustable roof rack, power-adjustable pedals, rain-sensing automatic wipers, a leather-wrapped steering wheel and an in-dash CD changer with MP3 capability. Options include heated front seats, a rear-seat DVD entertainment system, hands-free cell phone compatibility, a DVD-based navigation system, satellite radio, rear park assist and an off-road package with tow hooks and skid plates.

**Powertrains and Performance:** The Laredo comes standard with a 3.7-liter V6 that produces 210 horsepower and 235 pound-feet of torque, while the Limited is equipped with a 4.7-liter V8 capable of pumping out 230 hp and 290 lb-ft of torque. Optional on the Limited is the 5.7-liter Hemi V8, which produces 330 hp and 375 lb-ft of torque. All three engines come standard with a five-speed automatic transmission. Laredo 4x4 models are equipped with the full-time all-wheel-drive, while Limited 4x4s utilize the more advanced Quadra-Trac II that incorporates a two-speed transfer case. Finally, the optional Quadra-Drive II system combines a full-time two-speed transfer case with front/rear/center electronic limited-slip differentials. Towing capacity with the Hemi V8 is rated at 7,200 pounds.

**Safety:** Safety features include four-wheel antilock disc brakes and multistage front airbags (with an occupant weight sensor for the passenger-side front airbag). Side curtain airbags and stability control are optional; buyers can also get an electronic accident response system. Crash tests have not yet been conducted.

**Interior Design and Special Features:** The Grand Cherokee's seats are firm and supportive, and the two-tone perforated leather looks quite contemporary. Wood trim on the center console and door panels is very upscale, and two-tone plastic panels lend a modern touch to the surroundings, even if they are a bit hard. Panel fitment is very good; window and door lock switches are comfortably within reach; climate controls are clearly marked and easy to use; and the chronograph-style gauge cluster adds European flair. This is unquestionably the nicest interior ever put in a Jeep product.

**Driving Impressions:** Smooth is the operative word when describing the new Grand Cherokee. The suspension dampens imperfections in the road well, and the rack and pinion steering provides a solid and responsive road feel. The all-wheel drive grabs pavement with gusto and on tight roads this SUV is very nimble with minimal body roll. Even though the raucous multidisplacement Hemi provides gobs of low-end thrust, the 3.7-liter V6 and 4.7-liter V8 are silky-smooth and provide more than enough power for most applications.

## Competitive Vehicles

Dodge Durango
$26,735 - $35,590

Ford Explorer
$26,770 - $37,530

Nissan Pathfinder
N/A

Toyota 4Runner
$27,495 - $37,495

# 2005 Kia Sportage
Compact SUV

**MSRP Price Range**
## N/A
Destination Charge: N/A (all styles)

### Ratings

| | | |
|---|---|---|
| Consumer Rating | N/A | |
| Editors Rating | N/A | |

**What Edmunds.com says:** Thankfully sharing nothing with its predecessor but its name, the new Sportage offers compact SUV buyers a modern runabout in a stylish and roomy package.

**Pros:** Generous passenger and cargo space, stylish and functional interior, standard side and head curtain airbags, hard-to-beat warranty.

**Cons:** Down on power and cargo capacity versus its competitors.

**What's New:** An all-new Sportage returns after a two-year hiatus. It's now a car-based SUV intended to compete with the Honda CR-V and Toyota RAV4.

*Crash Test Scores, see pg 530*
*Warranty information, see pg 542*

### Specifications

| Engine/Drivetrain | HP | Torque | EPA Fuel Economy Rating |
|---|---|---|---|
| 4cyl 2.0L A/M | 140 | 136 | N/A |
| 6cyl 2.7L A | 173 | 178 | N/A |

### Body Styles

| Style | MSRP Range |
|---|---|
| Compact SUV | N/A |

**Introduction:** The name Sportage doesn't really conjure up warm memories. Many folks remember the Sportage of yesterday, a crude cute-ute that was plagued with quality issues, a weak engine and a cheap interior. Introduced in 1993 (globally), the Sportage was a body-on-frame small SUV. Updates and revisions through the years were made in an effort to keep the truck-based 'ute competitive. The axe fell in 2002 when the aging Sportage disappeared to make way for the new midsize Sorento. Kia realized a gap was left when the Sportage departed, and knew it had to whip up a mini-ute just as modern as the successful Sorento. The all-new Sportage shares nothing with its predecessor. We're not just talkin' basic parts here -- the new SUV even abandons the original's petite dimensions and truck-based body-on-frame structure in favor of a larger design based on a more carlike unibody platform. Kia's goal with the new Sportage is to combine the smooth ride, agile handling and refinement of a passenger car, the style and driving position of an SUV and the interior room of a wagon, all in one versatile package. And it appears the company has succeeded. The Sportage is longer, wider and taller than the average compact SUV. As a result of the generous dimensions, the SUV is able to boast best-in-class second-row headroom, legroom and total interior volume. The stylish interior features quality materials and great ergonomics. A unique split-folding rear seat is able to fold flat to create a level cargo floor. It does this by lowering the bottom cushion into the footwell, and doesn't even require removal of the head restraints. Power is provided by two different engines, a 2.0-liter inline four-cylinder engine with continuously variable valve timing, which makes 140 horsepower and 136 pound-feet of torque, and an optional 2.7-liter V6 engine that produces 173 hp and 178 lb-ft of torque. Front-wheel drive is standard, and a full-time four-wheel-drive system is optional. The all-wheel-drive system senses when one or both front wheels lose grip and automatically diverts up to 50 percent of the engine power to the rear wheels. The system can be manually set to a fixed 50/50-split when extra traction is needed for driving in the snow. The Sportage scores on the safety front by including standard four-wheel disc brakes, seat-mounted side-impact airbags for front occupants and front and rear head-protecting curtain airbags. No longer just a cute little SUV, the Sportage is now a serious competitor in a class of excellent machines. Its combination of carlike ride dynamics, roomy passenger space and all-weather capability make for a compelling package.

**Body Styles, Trim Levels and Options:** The Sportage is a compact four-door SUV offered in both two- and all-wheel-drive configurations. Standard features on the Sportage include four-wheel disc brakes, 16-inch alloy wheels, air conditioning, power windows and locks, tinted glass, a rear wiper and a CD stereo system. Various upgrades include a tire-pressure monitoring system, a premium audio system and leather seating. Automatic climate control is available and includes an air quality management system.

**Powertrains and Performance:** Standard power for the Sportage comes from a 2.0-liter, in-line four-cylinder engine with continuously variable valve timing. It generates 140 horsepower

and 136 pound-feet of torque and is mated to either a five-speed manual transmission or a four-speed automatic with automanual shift capability (2WD only). An optional 2.7-liter V6 produces 173 hp and 178 lb-ft of torque, and is available with the four-speed automatic only. Buyers can get front-wheel drive or all-wheel drive with either engine.

**Safety:** The Sportage boasts six standard airbags -- front and side-impact airbags for both driver and passenger, and side curtain airbags for both front and rear seat occupants. Four-wheel disc brakes are standard, and ABS is optional on all models. A traction and stability control system is also optional. The Sportage has not yet been crash tested.

**Interior Design and Special Features:** Kia designed a functional, roomy and attractive interior for the Sportage. Most of the materials are of good quality and the build quality is solid. A unique rear-seat design allows for a flat load floor by lowering the cushion into the rear footwell; removing the head restraints is not necessary. The Sportage offers 28.4 cubic feet of cargo capacity with the rear seat fold flat. Fold the front passenger seat forward and you'll move up to 39.9 cubic feet of storage space. Although Kia gives you plenty of flexibility for hauling cargo, the Sportage offers less total capacity than its competitors.

**Driving Impressions:** The Sportage provides a carlike ride while returning handling on par with its peers. The four-wheel independent suspension system helps smooth bumps without the jittery feel typical in many SUVs. Power from the standard four-cylinder is adequate at best; we recommend you stick with the larger 2.7-liter V6.

## Competitive Vehicles

Chevrolet Equinox
$21,095 - $24,435

Ford Escape
$19,265 - $28,005

Honda CR-V
$19,995 - $25,050

Toyota RAV4
$18,500 - $21,000

# 2005 Land Rover LR3

**Midsize SUV**

**MSRP Price Range**

**$44,330 - $49,330**
Destination Charge: $665 (all styles)

#**1** Editors' Rating

## Ratings

| Consumer Rating | N/A | |
| --- | --- | --- |
| Editors Rating | 8.6 | |

**What Edmunds.com says:** A powerful V8 engine, cutting-edge suspension technology and interior appointments fit for royalty should land the LR3 in the top tier of luxury SUVs, especially for those who actually plan on traveling off the beaten path.

**Pros:** Highly advanced suspension well suited for on-road cruising and off-road adventures, fold-flat second- and third-row seats, opulent interior, optional 600-watt stereo, powerful V8.

**Cons:** Only one engine available, priced higher than its competitors.

**What's New:** Thanks to a new platform co-designed by Ford, a 300-horse V8 borrowed from Jaguar, sumptuous interior appointments and a wide array of high-tech gadgetry, the all-new midsize LR3 promises to be one of the best Rovers yet.

*Crash Test Scores, see pg 530*
*Warranty information, see pg 542*

## Specifications

| Engine/Drivetrain | HP | Torque | EPA Fuel Economy Rating |
| --- | --- | --- | --- |
| 8cyl 4.4L A | 300 | 315 | 14 city/18 hwy |

## Body Styles

| Style | MSRP Range |
| --- | --- |
| Midsize SUV | $44,330–$49,330 |

**Introduction:** Over the past 50 years, a small British company with a simple green and gold logo has become legendary in the world of off-road exploration. While other marques such as Jeep and Hummer have tried to emulate the mystique and reputation of the venerable Land Rover brand, none have been able to match its reputation for providing luxury and reliability in the most extreme conditions known to man. Once cherished by jungle explorers and Saharan desert-trekkers, Land Rover has undergone a significant makeover in recent years and now represents the creme de la creme of the booming luxury SUV market. This image was helped by a short-lived buyout deal with BMW that lasted just long enough to produce the opulent and exclusive new Range Rover. Unfortunately, the BMW deal came undone before the same magic could be worked on the midsize Discovery, which arrived in the U.S. in 1995 slotted beneath the Range Rover as the more affordable way to obtain a Land Rover. The old Discovery benefited from the same off-road prowess as its big brother, but was otherwise an outdated and overpriced dinosaur in the highly competitive SUV marketplace. Ford came along a few years later and snapped Rover up, hoping to apply the same formula that has proven successful at other legendary British brands recently acquired by the Blue Oval. The all-new LR3 is the first product born out of that relationship, and from what we can tell, it looks more than worthy of carrying the Land Rover badge. When the development began on the LR3, engineers started on the inside and worked their way out. The interior is unmistakably Land Rover, boasting luxurious leather seating and a muted elegance that reflects its British heritage. Three-row seating for seven is available, and a stadium-style layout guarantees every passenger a stellar view of the world passing by. The LR3 can also be ordered with a fixed glass roof that filters out heat and UV rays while letting in the view above, and both the second- and third-row seats can be folded flat for increased cargo capacity. Other interior amenities include a touchscreen navigation system, Bluetooth-enabled communication and an optional 14-speaker, 600-watt Harman Kardon surround sound stereo. All that luxury and technology wouldn't be worth much if it wasn't riding on a proper platform, so the Ford/Rover team designed a new hydroformed backbone that is purportedly one of the strongest in the industry. A V8 borrowed from the Jaguar parts bin channels 300 horsepower through a six-speed automatic transmission, and a cutting-edge four-wheel independent suspension actively dampens each corner of the vehicle separately to accommodate changes in terrain. The LR3 also boasts full-time, dual-range four-wheel drive and ride height control, so it can tackle everything from rain-slick turnpikes to mud-filled bogs with ease. Overall, the new LR3 looks to be a refined and well-engineered addition to the Land Rover lineup, offering a nice balance of luxury and capability with a dash of Ford engineering thrown in for good measure.

**Body Styles, Trim Levels and Options:** The LR3 is offered in two trim levels, SE and HSE. Both come standard with leather upholstery, stadium seating, fold-down rear seats, dual-zone automatic climate control a nine-speaker 300-watt Harman Kardon audio system with a six-disc CD changer and all-wheel drive. HSE models get 19-inch alloy wheels, a 14-speaker 550-watt Logic

For the latest full vehicle reports, visit www.edmunds.com/bginfopak

7 digital surround sound system and rear parking sensors. Optional features include a glass panoramic roof, fold-flat third-row seating and a DVD-based navigation system.

**Powertrains and Performance:** Power for the LR3 comes from an all-aluminum V8 borrowed from the Jaguar parts bin and pumped up to 4.4 liters and 300 horsepower. The six-speed automatic transmission features "intelligent" shift patterns that adapt to changes in road conditions and driving styles, and the sophisticated Terrain Response four-wheel-drive system channels power to the pavement. With a rotary knob controlling five settings (general, snow-grass-gravel, mud and ruts, sand, and rock crawl), the 4WD system optimizes everything from throttle response, traction control, electronic stability control and ABS to the differentials for the conditions. The LR3 also features a fully independent suspension, which utilizes electronically controlled air springs to automatically adapt to virtually any terrain or off-road challenge.

**Safety:** Safety features include adaptive headlights that "look" around corners and adjust up and down to counter the effects of hard braking, four-wheel antilock brakes, traction control, active anti-roll technology, hill-descent control, side-impact and head curtain airbags and even an electronic parking brake. The LR3 has not yet been crash tested.

**Interior Design and Special Features:** The LR3 features a spacious cabin packed with clever storage solutions, as well as either five or seven seats trimmed in English leather. All rear seats fold into the floor when not in use to create a vast, flat-loading space. A commanding driving position and elevated stadium seating give the driver and passengers alike a clear view of their surroundings and an optional glass panoramic roof enhances that view even further. The dash has a simple, geometric look that is very similar to the elegant design employed in the Range Rover. Switches are kept to a minimum, thanks to built-in technology that minimizes the need for driver input, and every tactile surface is thickly padded, as one would expect in a vehicle of this caliber.

**Driving Impressions:** Even with 300 horsepower on tap, the 5,700-pound LR3 is no rocket, but thanks to a stellar four-wheel-drive system and the adaptive six-speed transmission, there is always plenty of power (and traction) available underfoot. The advanced suspension makes for a comfortable ride on the highway and ensures plenty of traction if you ever feel the need to go exploring off-road. Nimble rack and pinion steering lends the Rover a crisp feel behind the wheel. If you're looking for a midsize luxury SUV that can do it all, the LR3 is about as good as it gets.

## Competitive Vehicles

BMW X5
$41,700 - $70,100

Cadillac SRX
$38,340 - $52,035

Mercedes-Benz M-Class
$37,950 - $46,400

Volvo XC90
$34,840 - $41,015

# 2005 Mercedes-Benz C55 AMG

**Compact Sedan**

**MSRP Price Range**
## $53,900
Destination Charge: $720 (all styles)

### Ratings

| | | |
|---|---|---|
| Consumer Rating | 9.2 | |
| Editors Rating | 8.4 | |

**What Edmunds.com says:** Prodigious power, predictable handling and a sharp-looking interior make this one of the most satisfying sport sedans on the market.

**Pros:** Tire-shredding torque available at any speed, crisp and predictable handling, still comfortable despite its sporting intentions.

**Cons:** No manual transmission available, tight backseat, not as involving to drive as Audi's S4.

**What's New:** The new model year brings freshened exterior styling and a new engine that results in a designation change from C32 to C55. A new dash, redesigned seats and tweaked trim pieces help to polish the interior up a bit, as well. A DVD-based navigation system is newly available, and a Harman Kardon sound system replaces last year's Bose unit. The complimentary scheduled maintenance program has been dropped for 2005.

*Crash Test Scores, see pg 530*
*Warranty information, see pg 542*

### Specifications

| Engine/Drivetrain | HP | Torque | EPA Fuel Economy Rating |
|---|---|---|---|
| 8cyl 5.4L A | 362 | 376 | 16 city/22 hwy |

### Body Styles

| Style | MSRP Range |
|---|---|
| Compact Sedan | $53,900 |

**Introduction:** AMG. Those three letters are as revered by auto enthusiasts as ERA or RBI are by baseball fanatics. But what do they stand for and what are they doing affixed to various Mercedes-Benz vehicles? The first two letters stand for the names of the founders: Hans-Werner Aufrecht and Erhard Melcher, and the last letter signifies where the company was born: Grossaspach, Germany, back in 1967. What Mr. A and Mr. M did was modify Mercedes-Benz automobiles for better performance, be it for road use or racing, in which they were heavily involved. As the years went on, AMG became known as a premier tuner of Mercedes-Benz automobiles, and eventually offered interior and exterior modifications, such as custom instruments, steering wheels and seats, as well as ground effects, spoilers and wheels. The company did such a great job that Mercedes-Benz brought it in-house in 1990, and as a result, AMG now has its own high-performance skunk works, similar to rival BMW's "M" division. There is now an AMG version of nearly every Benz model, from the C-Class line's C55 to the CL-Class' CL65, and they all feature powerful engines, agile suspensions and subtle accents inside and out to set them apart from their more common brethren. Transformation of last year's C32 into a C55 begins with the engine. The supercharged V6 of yore has been replaced by a hand-built 5.5-liter V8. A never-ending stream of power is put to the ground via an AMG-fortified five-speed automatic transmission complete with three driver-selectable shift modes: standard, sport or manual. The standard and sport modes provide shifts in traditional fashion with the sport mode serving up a more aggressive shift program. Manual mode allows for driver-controlled shifts through one of two methods: moving the shifter side to side within its gate or actuation of the steering wheel-mounted shift buttons. At around $55,000, the C55 is the least expensive AMG product. Order a couple of options, and the C55 ends up being a mid-to-upper-$60Ks sport sedan. This isn't exactly a bargain four-door, but with a V8 engine and handling that's as sharp as many sports cars, it doesn't seem so steep once you're behind the wheel. Between its stunning performance, sedan practicality and the cachet of its three-pointed-star pedigree, the C55 is more than just your average sport sedan.

**Body Styles, Trim Levels and Options:** The four-door C55 AMG comes in just one well-equipped trim level. Standard features include a sport-tuned suspension, 17-inch wheels and tires, 10-way power sport seats, leather upholstery, a leather-wrapped steering wheel, metallic cabin trim, a revised instrument panel (compared to the regular C-Class), dual-zone automatic climate control, a 10-speaker Harman Kardon stereo with a CD player and a sunroof. Options include a navigation system, satellite radio and an integrated Motorola cell phone.

**Powertrains and Performance:** The C55 AMG packs a hand-built V8 that puts 362 horses and 376 pound-feet of torque at the driver's disposal. An AMG-tweaked five-speed automatic transmission is the sole gearbox choice. Dubbed SpeedShift, this automatic is so quick and smart that most drivers won't miss having a manual tranny, especially in rush-hour traffic. With the 0-to-60-mph dash coming in at around 4.5 seconds and a top speed that's electronically

For the latest full vehicle reports, visit www.edmunds.com/bginfopak

# 2005 Mercedes-Benz C55 AMG

limited to 155 mph, those who need speed should be more than happy with the C55. Braking ability is impressive as well, with stops from 60 mph coming in at less than 120 feet, according to Mercedes.

**Safety:** In addition to expected safety features, such as four-wheel antilock disc brakes and three-point seatbelts with tension limiters for all occupants, the C55 boasts stability control and eight airbags. In government crash tests, the C-Class earned four stars (out of five) for frontal impacts and a full five stars in side impacts. The IIHS gave the C-Class a "Good" rating (the highest possible) and named it a "Best Pick" overall.

**Interior Design and Special Features:** Cabin materials are generally first-rate, with pleasingly textured, soft-touch surfaces all around. A pair of 10-way adjustable sport seats hold the pilot and co-pilot snugly, while a choice of single-tone or two-tone upholstery, metallic accents and unique instrument faces give the C55 its own look inside.

**Driving Impressions:** Simply put, the C55 is a blast to drive. The instantaneous power from the V8 makes for rapid acceleration at nearly any speed, and the tightly wound suspension is well up to the task of getting the power to the ground. As capable as it is in corners, it's not a car that will beat you up on your morning commute. Overall, the C55 is an outstanding combination of dazzling performance and everyday drivability.

## Competitive Vehicles

Audi S4
$45,850 - $55,150

BMW M3
$47,300 - $55,800

Cadillac CTS V-Series
$49,300

Volvo S60 R
$37,250

## All New for 2005

# 2005 Mercedes-Benz CL65 AMG

**Large Coupe**

**MSRP Price Range**

## $177,500

Destination Charge: $720 (all styles)

### Ratings

| | | |
|---|---|---|
| Consumer Rating | 9.6 | |
| Editors Rating | 8.4 | |

**What Edmunds.com says:** One of the finest coupes on the road today, the CL is an artful blend of performance, technology and classic luxury that rarely fails to impress.

**Pros:** Refined beyond belief, dizzying array of high-tech features, classic styling, blinding acceleration, astounding performance that belies its weight.

**Cons:** Big price leap over already fantastic CL55, complex navigation and audio systems.

**What's New:** Yet another version of the CL coupe, the CL65 AMG is a new ultrahigh-performance beast with a 604-horsepower twin-turbo V12. It also boasts a reinforced five-speed automatic tranny, race-derived compound brake rotors with AMG eight-piston calipers, 19-inch wheels and dynamic multicontour seats. The complimentary scheduled maintenance program has been dropped for 2005.

*Crash Test Scores, see pg 530*
*Warranty information, see pg 542*

### Specifications

| Engine/Drivetrain | HP | Torque | EPA Fuel Economy Rating |
|---|---|---|---|
| 12cyl 6.0L A | 604 | 738 | 12 city/19 hwy |

### Body Styles

| Style | MSRP Range |
|---|---|
| Large Coupe | $177,500 |

**Introduction:** AMG. Those three letters are as revered by auto enthusiasts as ERA or RBI are by baseball fanatics. But what do they stand for and what are they doing affixed to various Mercedes-Benz vehicles? The first two letters stand for the names of the founders: Hans-Werner Aufrecht and Erhard Melcher, and the last letter signifies where the company was born: Grossaspach, Germany, back in 1967. What Mr. A and Mr. M did was modify Mercedes-Benz automobiles for better performance, be it for road use or racing, in which they were heavily involved. As the years went on, AMG became known as a premier tuner of Mercedes-Benz automobiles, and eventually offered interior and exterior modifications, such as custom instruments, steering wheels and seats as well as ground effects, spoilers and wheels. The company did such a great job that Mercedes-Benz brought it in-house in 1990 and as a result, AMG now has its own high-performance skunk works, similar to rival BMW's "M" division. There is now an AMG version of nearly every Benz model, from the C-Class' C55 to the CL-Class' CL65, and they all feature powerful engines, agile suspensions and subtle accents inside and out to set them apart from their more common brethren. As indicated by the two numerals (versus the more common three digits) after the model letters, the CL65 is a CL-Class coupe that has been given the AMG treatment. What that means is a horsepower rating of 604 and torque measuring an asphalt-wrinkling 738 pound-feet. Yes, that's seven hundred and thirty-eight. It also boasts a reinforced five-speed automatic tranny, race-derived compound brake rotors with AMG eight-piston calipers, 19-inch wheels and dynamic multicontour seats. Although AMG's engineers are quick to tout the car's overall performance package, there's no getting around the fact that the car's primary source of intrigue lies under its hood. With 6.0 liters of displacement and twin turbochargers, the CL65's V12 engine is the most powerful production engine ever offered by the German automaker. Each engine is hand-built by a single specialist who then signs his name to the carbon-fiber engine cover. The aluminum V12 generates nearly twice the power of a standard Porsche 911 and slots the CL65 in the very exclusive club of 500-plus-hp production cars. An active suspension system, called Active Body Control (ABC), helps this big coupe handle like a much smaller sports car. Via electronic and hydraulic wizardry, the system helps to minimize or eliminate unsettling movements, such as body roll while cornering and squat and dive under acceleration and braking. Another high-tech feature is the Pre-Safe system, which can anticipate an imminent accident and automatically tighten the seatbelts and position the power seats to afford the best protection for the occupants. Beautiful to look at, ride in and drive, the CL65 embodies the spirit of a world-class Grand Touring coupe. Its rivals are few, and after one drive in this coupe, you're not likely to even bother looking much further anyway.

**Body Styles, Trim Levels and Options:** The CL65 is a high-performance version of the standard CL-Class coupe and comes in only one trim level. Of course there are all the luxury amenities you would expect in a flagship coupe, including a DVD-based navigation system, 14-way power-adjustable seats, dual-zone automatic climate control, a Bose sound system

# 2005 Mercedes-Benz CL65 AMG

(with a trunk-mounted CD changer) and generous amounts of leather and wood trim. Sporty accents, such as double-spoke 19-inch alloy wheels and aggressive rocker panel flares, hint at this car's personality. Options include a keyless entry and start system, adaptive cruise control and parking sensors.

**Powertrains and Performance:** The CL65's twin-turbo 6.0-liter V12 puts out astounding levels of power -- 604 horses along with 738 pound-feet of torque. These big numbers mean that this refined yet muscle-bound coupe will hit 60 mph in around 4 seconds, a figure typically associated with exotic sports cars bearing Italian names. The only transmission available is a five-speed automatic, but it does allow for manual shifting if you feel the need to choose gears yourself.

**Safety:** Standard safety equipment includes four-wheel antilock disc brakes; electronic traction and stability control; front, seat-mounted side and side curtain airbags; and emergency braking assist. Seatbelt pre-tensioners and belt-force limiters are used at all four passenger positions. The CL also has the BabySmart feature that deactivates the passenger-side front airbag if a BabySmart-compliant child safety seat is placed on the front-passenger seat. Of course, with the coupe's functional backseat, there's little reason for a small child to be sitting up front in the first place.

**Interior Design and Special Features:** Virtually every luxury and convenience item, including a navigation system and power door-closing assist, is standard on the CL65. Specific wood trim is fitted as well, with dark interiors having burled walnut while lighter cabins are graced with chestnut timber. Most of the switchgear is the same as that of the S-Class, as is the illuminated gauge cluster, shift lever and COMAND control system. However, the quality of materials is even better in the CL, with a leather-trimmed dash, less plastic and even more beautiful wood highlights. Particularly impressive are the CL's unique stainless steel doorsills and outer-edge door trim.

**Driving Impressions:** Step on the throttle and the big Benz gathers itself up on a wave of torque, seemingly accelerating just as fast from 30 to 90 as it does from zero to 60. In spite of a weight of over two tons, the CL65 handles the curves like a much smaller, lighter car, a sensation brought about chiefly by the Active Body Control (ABC) system that quells body roll as well as squat and dive while the car is being driven aggressively. In normal driving, the suspension soaks up the bumps as well as any luxury car, but when it's time to make tracks on a twisty road, the CL tightens up, rising to the challenge.

## Competitive Vehicles

Aston Martin
Vanquish
$234,000 (est.)

Bentley
Continental GT
$150,000 (est.)

Ferrari 575M
$230,000 (est.)

Porsche 911 Turbo
$120,000 (est.)

# 2005 Mercedes-Benz SL65 AMG  Compact Convertible

**MSRP Price Range**

## $179,000
Destination Charge: $720 (all styles)

### Ratings

| Consumer Rating | 8.0 | |
|---|---|---|
| Editors Rating | 8.6 | |

**What Edmunds.com says:** If you're looking for maximum performance and maximum luxury in an open-top vehicle, this is your car.

**Pros:** Blinding acceleration, supercar performance that belies its weight, super-luxury opulence, sultry styling, muscle car-era exhaust note.

**Cons:** Big price leap over already fantastic SL55, complex audio and navigation controls.

**What's New:** As if there weren't enough AMG offerings, Mercedes-Benz adds yet another -- the SL65. With 604 horsepower, however, we won't complain. The SL65 also features a reinforced five-speed automatic tranny, race-bred brakes with AMG eight-piston composite calipers, 19-inch alloys and dynamic multicontour seats. The complimentary scheduled maintenance program has been dropped for 2005.

*Crash Test Scores, see pg 530*
*Warranty information, see pg 542*

### Specifications

| Engine/Drivetrain | HP | Torque | EPA Fuel Economy Rating |
|---|---|---|---|
| 12cyl 6.0L A | 604 | 738 | 12 city/19 hwy |

### Body Styles

| Style | MSRP Range |
|---|---|
| Compact Convertible | $179,000 |

**Introduction:** AMG. Those three letters are as revered by auto enthusiasts as ERA or RBI are by baseball fanatics. But what do they stand for and what are they doing affixed to various Mercedes-Benz vehicles? The first two letters stand for the names of the founders: Hans-Werner Aufrecht and Erhard Melcher, and the last letter signifies where the company was born: Grossaspach, Germany, back in 1967. What Mr. A and Mr. M did was modify Mercedes-Benz automobiles for better performance, be it for road use or racing, in which they were heavily involved. As the years went on, AMG became known as a premier tuner of Mercedes-Benz automobiles, and eventually offered interior and exterior modifications, such as custom instruments, steering wheels and seats as well as ground effects, spoilers and wheels. The company did such a great job that Mercedes-Benz brought it in-house in 1990 and as a result AMG now has its own high-performance skunk works, similar to rival BMW's "M" division. There is now an AMG version of nearly every Benz model, from the C-Class' C55 to the CL-Class' CL65, and they all feature powerful engines, agile suspensions and subtle accents inside and out to set them apart from their more common brethren. With the SL65, Mercedes has taken its legendary roadster and injected it with a major dose of horsepower that elevates it to supercar status. Although AMG's engineers are quick to tout the car's overall performance package, there's no getting around the fact that the car's primary source of intrigue lies under its hood. With 6.0 liters of displacement and twin turbochargers, the SL65's V12 engine is the most powerful production engine ever offered by the German automaker. Each engine is hand-built by a single specialist who then signs his name to the carbon-fiber engine cover. The aluminum V12 generates nearly twice the power of a standard Porsche 911 and slots the SL65 in the very exclusive club of 500-plus-hp production cars. With 604 horsepower and torque measuring an asphalt-wrinkling 738 pound-feet emanating from its twin-turbo V12, this drop top can hang with Ferraris as easily as it will go for a top-down Sunday drive. The SL65 also features a reinforced five-speed automatic tranny, race-bred brakes with AMG eight-piston composite calipers, 19-inch alloys and dynamic multicontour seats. If you're looking for the ultimate combination of open-air fun and unparalleled performance, the SL65 satisfies in ways few other cars can.

**Body Styles, Trim Levels and Options:** The SL65 is a high-performance version of the standard SL luxury roadster. Standard features include 12-way power-adjustable leather sport seats, aluminum trim, dual-zone automatic climate control, xenon headlights, a high-powered Bose stereo with a trunk-mounted CD changer, a navigation system, 19-inch AMG wheels, high-performance tires and lower body sculpting. Options include Distronic, a cruise control system that automatically maintains a set distance between the SL65 and the vehicle in front of it, and Keyless Go, which allows the car to be started without a key.

**Powertrains and Performance:** The SL65's twin-turbo 6.0-liter V12 puts out astounding levels of power -- 604 horses along with 738 pound-feet of torque. These big numbers mean that

# 2005 Mercedes-Benz SL65 AMG

this refined yet muscle-bound roadster will hit 60 mph around 4 seconds, a figure typically associated with exotic sports cars bearing Italian names. The only transmission available is a five-speed automatic, but it does allow for manual shifting if you feel the need to choose gears yourself.

**Safety:** A slew of acronyms that stands for performance- and safety-enhancing technologies are fitted to the SL65, such as ABS (antilock brake system), ASR (traction control), ESP (stability control) and ABC (body roll control). There is also electronic braking, which can react much quicker than a conventional hydraulic system and can even selectively adjust braking force to each wheel when cornering. Should an accident be unavoidable, there's a multitude of airbags to protect the occupants, including side curtain-style bags that cover the head and torso areas and a knee bag for the driver. The SL also has a pop-up roll bar that will deploy if a rollover is imminent.

**Interior Design and Special Features:** AMG sport seats and real metal accents mark the cabin of the SL65. A power-operated, retractable hardtop offers the integrity, insulation and security of a coupe when raised along with the full alfresco experience of a roadster when powered down. The dual-zone climate control is easy to use, but unfortunately the same can't be said for the complex COMAND audio and navigation interface.

**Driving Impressions:** With the SL65, it's not just the acceleration but the effortless acceleration that makes it so impressive. With virtually no drama (provided one is careful with the throttle), the hot-rod Benz can rip from zero to 60 mph in about 4 seconds. When the road gets curvy, the SL65 feels as willing as anything in this price range. Granted, it doesn't offer the same level of feedback as a Porsche or Ferrari in terms of steering feel, and the car's weight (around 4,500 pounds) puts it at a theoretical disadvantage. But the Active Body Control (ABC) technology keeps body movement in check and gives the car a surprisingly nimble demeanor when changing directions quickly.

## Competitive Vehicles

Aston Martin Vanquish
$234,000 (est.)

Ferrari F430
$175,000 (est.)

Ford GT
$139,995

Lamborghini Gallardo
$165,000 (est.)

# 2005 Mercedes-Benz SLK-Class    Compact Convertible

**MSRP Price Range**

## $45,500

Destination Charge: $720 (all styles)

### Ratings

| | | |
|---|---|---|
| Consumer Rating | 9.8 | |
| Editors Rating | 7.8 | |

**What Edmunds.com says:** A fun-to-drive roadster that combines the safety and security of a hardtop, the wind-in-your-hair fun of a convertible and the European-brand cachet of a Mercedes all in one powerful and attractively styled package.

**Pros:** Much improved interior design, sports-carlike handling, strong and sweet-sounding V6, comfort and convenience of retractable hardtop.

**Cons:** Costs more than peers, big blind spots when top is up.

**What's New:** After seven years on the market, Mercedes redesigns the SLK for 2005. Potential buyers should also note that the company's complimentary scheduled maintenance program has been dropped.

**Introduction:** Introduced in 1998 as an answer to the BMW Z3 and Porsche Boxster in the premium small roadster segment, the SLK's most unique feature was its retractable hardtop roof, which offered more security as well as a quieter ride than its competitors' soft tops. In less than 30 seconds, with the touch of a button, one could convert the SLK from a closed coupe to a cool convertible without leaving the driver seat. Improvements over the years kept the car competitive, but after seven years on the market, the SLK was ready for a redesign. With a dramatic new design inspired by Mercedes' Formula One racecars, the second-generation SLK is every bit as eye-catching as the original. It's also slightly larger and more powerful than its predecessor, and still has the fun-to-drive character that made it so likable in the first place. While the previous version had the feel of a leather-lined bobsled, the larger cabin of the '05 version gives you plenty of room to move about. Even more impressive than the added room is the redesigned dashboard with its more cohesive layout, cleaner gauge cluster and higher-quality materials. Overall, the improvements create a more upscale, tasteful-looking cabin that far exceeds the previous model's. An innovative new Airscarf system channels warm air to your neck and shoulders via dedicated registers in the headrests, making the SLK even more comfortable with the top down in chilly weather. Improvements continue under the hood with 268 horsepower on tap, courtesy of an all-new 3.5-liter V6. The SLK can sprint to 60 miles per hour in just 5.6 seconds, according to Mercedes-Benz. Complementing the impressive new power plant is a pair of transmissions that offers excellent flexibility and performance whether you go with the standard six-speed manual or new seven-speed automatic. Other notable improvements under the skin include a new rack and pinion steering system and more powerful brakes. The recirculating-ball steering system used in the previous model was often chastised for its heavy feel and inconsistent feedback, but the new setup is both lighter and more communicative. The SLK now has the power to go head-to-head with a Porsche Boxster and the handling to keep pace with a BMW Z4, and its revamped interior is arguably better than both. Overall, the new SLK offers one of the most compelling combinations of style, performance and comfort available anywhere.

Crash Test Scores, see pg 530
Warranty information, see pg 542

### Specifications

| Engine/Drivetrain | HP | Torque | EPA Fuel Economy Rating |
|---|---|---|---|
| 6cyl 3.5L M | 268 | 258 | 18 city/25 hwy |

### Body Styles

| Style | MSRP Range |
|---|---|
| Compact Convertible | $45,500 |

**Body Styles, Trim Levels and Options:** The SLK comes in one body style: a two-seat roadster with a power-retractable hardtop. Standard equipment includes 17-inch alloy wheels, leather upholstery, automatic climate control, a premium audio system and auto-dimming mirrors. Should this not be enough, there are a number of options to consider, such as bi-xenon headlamps, a navigation system and memory seats. An innovative Airscarf system directs heated air through special vents in the head restraints. The effect is that of an invisible scarf to warm the passenger's neck and shoulders in chilly weather. A 380-watt audio system is available, and includes eleven speakers and surround sound capability.

# 2005 Mercedes-Benz SLK-Class

**Powertrains and Performance:** The SLK offers a 3.5-liter V6 good for 268 hp. The SLK can sprint to 60 miles per hour in just 5.6 seconds, according to Mercedes-Benz. A six-speed manual is standard, and a seven-speed automatic (with automanual shift capability) is optional.

**Safety:** Seat-mounted side airbags are standard equipment, as are four-wheel antilock disc brakes, stability and traction control (called ESP) and the TeleAid system, which alerts emergency personnel if an airbag goes off and can also put you in touch with a live operator to summon medical or police assistance. The SLK also has reinforced A-pillars, integrated roll bars behind each seat and emergency tensioning seatbelt retractors for enhanced rollover protection. BrakeAssist automatically applies full braking force when a panic stop is initiated.

**Interior Design and Special Features:** Good-looking soft-touch material covers the top of the dash, glovebox and doors, while plastics of similar quality fill in the rest. The climate control layout varies depending on whether you add a navigation system (now DVD-based), but both arrangements use easy-to-decipher dials that are usable at a glance. The soft and supportive seats remain comfortable even after several hours of continuous driving. Keep the windows up while the top is down and there's minimal wind buffeting. If that's not enough, consider the new Airscarf system that channels warm air to your neck and shoulders via dedicated registers in the headrests. It actually works quite well, and when combined with traditional seat heaters, the SLK becomes one of the most useful all-weather convertibles on the market.

**Driving Impressions:** The engine's power kicks in early and remains solid throughout thanks to variable camshafts and a two-stage intake manifold. As an added bonus, the stout V6 pours out a satisfying wail that inspires flat-footed runs to redline at every opportunity. The new steering setup is not only lighter to the touch, it returns enough road feel to maintain the car's sporting demeanor during aggressive driving. The revised brakes could still use a better feel through the pedal, but their ability to bring the SLK to a halt in a hurry is never an issue.

## Competitive Vehicles

Audi TT
$33,500 - $43,150

BMW Z4
$33,600 - $40,900

Nissan 350Z
$26,470 - $37,390

Porsche Boxster
$42,600 - $59,900

# 2005 Mercedes-Benz SLK55 AMG Compact Convertible

**MSRP Price Range**
## N/A
Destination Charge: N/A (all styles)

## Ratings

| | | |
|---|---|---|
| Consumer Rating | N/A | |
| Editors Rating | 8.1 | |

**What Edmunds.com says:** A ridiculously fast roadster that blows away the notion that the SLK is just a boulevard cruiser.

**Pros:** Blistering V8 performance, much improved interior design, handles more like a sports car than before, retractable hardtop.

**Cons:** Big blind spots when top is up, no manual gearbox available.

**What's New:** The high-performance SLK55 is an all-new replacement for the SLK32 based on the completely redesigned SLK roadster.

*Crash Test Scores, see pg 530*
*Warranty information, see pg 542*

## Specifications

| Engine/Drivetrain | HP | Torque | EPA Fuel Economy Rating |
|---|---|---|---|
| 8cyl 5.5L A | 360 | 376 | N/A |

## Body Styles

| Style | MSRP Range |
|---|---|
| Compact Convertible | N/A |

**Introduction:** AMG. Those three letters are as revered by auto enthusiasts as ERA or RBI is by baseball fanatics. But what do they stand for and what are they doing affixed to various Mercedes-Benz vehicles? The first two letters stand for the names of the founders: Hans-Werner Aufrecht and Erhard Melcher, and the last letter signifies where the company was born: Grossaspach, Germany, back in 1967. What Mr. A and Mr. M did was modify Mercedes-Benz automobiles for better performance, be it for road use or racing, in which they were heavily involved. As the years went on, AMG became known as a premier tuner of Mercedes-Benz automobiles, and eventually offered interior and exterior modifications, such as custom instruments, steering wheels and seats as well as ground effects, spoilers and wheels. The company did such a great job that Mercedes-Benz brought it in-house in 1990, and as a result AMG now has its own high-performance skunk works, similar to rival BMW's "M" division. There is now an AMG version of nearly every Benz model, from the C-Class' C55 to the CL-Class' CL65, and they all feature powerful engines, agile suspensions and subtle accents inside and out to set them apart from their more common brethren. Perhaps in an effort to quash the SLK's reputation as a "boutique" roadster, Mercedes brought out the muscle-bound, AMG-tuned SLK32 for 2002. The SLK32 AMG brought 349 horsepower to the party by way of a supercharged 3.2-liter V6, its considerable might shipped to the rear tires via a tweaked "SpeedShift" five-speed automatic gearbox. It was also given a massaged suspension, full ground effects and a discreet rear spoiler. With the redesign of the SLK platform for 2005, AMG has turned the fire up a few notches by giving its high-performance version of the new SLK a 360-hp V8 in place of the former supercharged V6. This monster now transmits its might through a seven-speed automatic with Speedshift, a shift program that allows the driver to manually control the tranny. Beyond the newfound power, the SLK55 benefits from the dramatic new styling inspired by Mercedes' Formula One racecars. The new larger cabin of the '05 version gives you plenty of room to stretch out. Even more impressive is the redesigned dashboard with its more cohesive layout, cleaner gauge cluster and higher-quality materials. Overall, the improvements create a more upscale, tasteful-looking cabin that far exceeds the previous model's. The ultrafast SLK55 is certainly enticing, but die-hard enthusiasts may be turned off by its lack of a manual gearbox. Then again, the Speedshift does such a superb job of changing gears that a manual tranny might not be missed at all. The handling is exceptional, allowing you to push the car to its limits, and its straight-line speed is intoxicating. The SLK55 offers a tantalizing combination of speed and style that is simply unmatched by the competition.

**Body Styles, Trim Levels and Options:** The SLK55 comes in one body style: a two-seat roadster with a power-retractable hardtop. Standard equipment includes 18-inch AMG wheels and high-performance tires, napa leather upholstery with Alcantara inserts, power-adjustable sport seats, automatic climate control, a tilt/telescoping steering wheel and a rear spoiler. An innovative Airscarf system directs heated air through special vents in the head restraints -- the

# 2005 Mercedes-Benz SLK55 AMG

effect is that of an invisible scarf to warm the passenger's neck and shoulders in chilly weather. A 380-watt audio system is available, and includes 11 speakers and surround sound capability.

**Powertrains and Performance:** As one would expect, the performance of the SLK55 is thrilling. With its AMG-tuned 5.5-liter V8 making a stupendous 360 horsepower, the AMG-tweaked roadster can leap to 60 mph in just 4.5 ticks of the stopwatch. A seven-speed automatic is standard and includes Speedshift automanual shift capability. Fully equal to the task of keeping all this kinetic energy under control are the massive composite ventilated disc brakes with six-piston calipers up front.

**Safety:** Front and side airbags are standard equipment, as are four-wheel antilock disc brakes, traction and stability control and the TeleAid system (which alerts emergency personnel if an airbag goes off and can put you in touch with a live operator to summon medical or police assistance). The SLK55 also has reinforced A-pillars, integrated roll bars behind each seat and emergency tensioning seatbelt retractors for enhanced rollover protection. BrakeAssist automatically applies full braking force when a panic stop is initiated.

**Interior Design and Special Features:** Attractive soft-touch material covers the top of the dash, glovebox and doors, while plastics of similar quality fill in the rest. The climate control layout varies depending on whether you add a navigation system (now DVD-based), but both arrangements use easy-to-decipher dials that are usable at a glance. The soft and supportive seats remain comfortable even after several hours of continuous driving. Keep the windows up while the top is down and there's minimal wind buffeting. If that's not enough, consider the new Airscarf system that channels warm air to your neck and shoulders via dedicated registers in the headrests. It actually works quite well, and when combined with traditional seat heaters, the SLK becomes one of the most useful all-weather convertibles on the market.

**Driving Impressions:** In spite of the SLK55's ability to surge forward from virtually any speed, the muscle-bound engine is docile around town and will plod through rush-hour traffic without complaint. Additionally, the ride is supple enough so that broken pavement is absorbed without discomfort. The well-sorted suspension never loses its composure on twisty back roads, and the sticky performance tires provide grip to match. The SLK55 is a great combination of near-touring car comfort and sports car performance. Better still, it can serve as either a coupe or convertible without ever forcing the driver to leave his or her seat.

## Competitive Vehicles

Audi S4 Convertible
$55,870 - $56,370

BMW M3 Convertible
$57,495

Chevrolet Corvette Convertible
$52,245

Lotus Elise
$39,985

# 2005 Mercury Mariner
Compact SUV

**MSRP Price Range**
## $21,405 - $26,405
Destination Charge: $590 (all styles)

## Ratings

| | | |
|---|---|---|
| Consumer Rating | 9.5 | |
| Editors Rating | 7.8 | |

**What Edmunds.com says:** Put a Ford Escape in a Mercury outfit and what do you get? An excellent small SUV in pretty dapper digs.

**Pros:** Powerful V6, large cargo capacity, comfortable and stylish interior, carlike handling.

**Cons:** Faux wood trim is unconvincing, fuel-thirsty V6.

**What's New:** The Mariner, based on the successful Ford Escape, is new for 2005.

**Introduction:** Ford introduced the Escape in 2001 to capture buyers in the rapidly growing small SUV segment. It quickly became a best-seller thanks to a desirable combination of size, power and ruggedly handsome styling. Mazda also sells a version of this vehicle, called the Tribute. Feeling a bit left out of the party (and in dire need of an affordable vehicle to get customers into the showroom), Mercury jumps on the bandwagon this year with its own version of the Escape, called the Mariner. The Mariner shares the Escape's basic structure, platform and powertrains. What sets the Mariner apart, though, is style. The handsome front end is decidedly Mercury, and other unique exterior bits like distinctive wheels and sleek rocker moldings move this compact SUV upmarket a few notches. Differences are readily apparent inside, too. Plenty of metallic-look trim adds polish without appearing gaudy. Unfortunately, Mercury stylists couldn't resist the urge to throw some wood grain trim in there, too, and there's just a bit too much of it to seem convincing. Two-tone suede and leather seating steals the show, however, and combined with contrasting stitching, the look is very handsome. One of our main beefs with the Escape has always been its uninspiring style, especially inside. Perhaps unintentionally, Mercury has taken a huge step in the right direction with its upscale treatments. Before you scoff at the idea of a thinly veiled SUV gussy-up job, just think back to 1999 when Cadillac put some jewelry on a Tahoe and called it an Escalade. And we all know how well that idea turned out. Underneath the pretty layers, the Mariner is all-Escape. This is a good thing. The Mariner is intended for those who want the styling and all-wheel-drive capability of a traditional luxury SUV combined with the size, price, practicality and driving characteristics of a midsize car. The Mariner is more suited to on-road driving than off-roading, due to its light-duty 4WD system and unibody construction, and isn't as rugged as some other compact SUVs like the Nissan Xterra and Jeep Liberty. To allay concerns about side-impact safety in small SUVs, full-length side curtain airbags (the Safety Canopy system) are optional. Although long-term reliability is not likely to be as good as that of its Japanese competitors, the well-rounded Mariner is still one of the best compact SUVs available. If you like a bit of class with your compact SUV, the Mariner should fill the bill quite nicely.

*Crash Test Scores, see pg 530*
*Warranty information, see pg 542*

## Specifications

| Engine/Drivetrain | HP | Torque | EPA Fuel Economy Rating |
|---|---|---|---|
| 6cyl 3.0L A | 200 | 193 | 20 city/25 hwy |
| 4cyl 2.3L A | 153 | 152 | 22 city/26 hwy |

## Body Styles

| Style | MSRP Range |
|---|---|
| Compact SUV | $21,405–$26,405 |

**Body Styles, Trim Levels and Options:** Only one four-door body style is available with either front-wheel drive or automatic four-wheel drive. Three trim levels are offered: Convenience, Luxury and Premier. Base Convenience models start you out with a 2.3-liter, four-cylinder engine; 16-inch alloy wheels; a CD player; air conditioning; power accessories keyless entry; and cruise control. The Luxury adds a 3.0-liter V6, a power driver seat, a six-disc CD changer, an alarm system, message center with compass and an auto-dimming rearview mirror. Premier models step up with machined alloy wheels, heated outside mirrors, a MACH premium audio system with subwoofer and heated leather seats with contrasting suedelike inserts. Side curtain airbags and a reverse-sensing system are optional.

For the latest full vehicle reports, visit www.edmunds.com/bginfopak

**Powertrains and Performance:** Standard on the Mariner is a 2.3-liter, inline four-cylinder engine that makes 153 horsepower and 152 pound-feet of torque matched to a four-speed automatic. Standard on Luxury and Premier models is a potent 3.0-liter V6, which makes 200 hp and 193 lb-ft of torque. With this engine, the Mariner can tow up to 3,500 pounds.

**Safety:** ABS is standard on all Mariners, and V6 4WD models have four-wheel disc brakes. A notable safety feature is the optional Safety Canopy system that offers full-length head curtain airbag protection in the event of a side-impact collision or rollover. The mechanically identical Ford Escape has done well in government crash testing, earning a perfect five stars for the driver in frontal impacts and four stars for the front passenger. In side-impact crash tests, it received five stars for both front- and rear-seat occupants. The 2005 Escape earned an "Acceptable" rating (the second-highest) in frontal offset crash tests conducted by the IIHS. In IIHS side-impact tests, this small SUV earned a "Good" rating (the highest) when equipped with side airbags and a "Poor" rating (the worst) without the bags.

**Interior Design and Special Features:** The Mariner boasts a stylish interior with satin aluminum, chrome accents and a two-tone color scheme. The 60/40-split rear seat includes three-point seatbelts and head restraints for all three seating positions. There is 29 cubic feet of cargo space behind the rear seats, and you can fold them down to open up 66 cubic feet of capacity, a good figure for this class.

**Driving Impressions:** Fun to drive, the Mariner offers impressive road manners for a compact SUV. It drives much like a tautly suspended sedan, with little body roll and responsive steering. Mercury provides generous sound insulation, resulting in a surprisingly serene ride out on the open road. The V6 is quite powerful, providing swift acceleration, but fuel economy is mediocre. The standard 2.3-liter four-cylinder delivers adequate acceleration and better mileage than what you'd get with the V6.

## Competitive Vehicles

Honda CR-V
$19,000 - $22,550

Jeep Liberty
$19,265 - $25,110

Nissan Xterra
$18,300 - $28,300

Toyota RAV4
$18,450 - $20,900

# 2005 Mercury Montego

**MSRP Price Range**

## $24,345 - $28,245

Destination Charge: $650 (all styles)

### Ratings

| | | |
|---|---|---|
| Consumer Rating | N/A | |
| Editors Rating | 8.1 | |

**What Edmunds.com says:** Roomy, stylish and practical, the Montego is well suited for family duty, but with its mediocre engine performance and interior materials, it's simply one of many solid choices in the under-$30,000 price bracket.

**Pros:** Spacious cabin, huge trunk, smooth ride quality, available all-wheel drive, plenty of safety features.

**Cons:** Mediocre engine performance, some low-grade interior materials, no stability control.

**What's New:** The Montego is an all-new premium family sedan built on the Volvo S80 platform. Both front- and all-wheel-drive versions are available.

*Crash Test Scores, see pg 530*
*Warranty information, see pg 542*

### Specifications

| Engine/Drivetrain | HP | Torque | EPA Fuel Economy Rating |
|---|---|---|---|
| 6cyl 3.0L A | 203 | 207 | 21 city/29 hwy |

### Body Styles

| Style | MSRP Range |
|---|---|
| Large Sedan | $24,345–$28,245 |

**Introduction:** Although there's still room for basic, economical transportation in the family sedan segment, many consumers now expect their sensible rides to incorporate liberal doses of style, power, convenience items and safety measures. Some buyers even go looking for luxury ambience and sporty handling in a segment once written off for its blandness and lack of originality. Not everyone has been quick to embrace this trend. For the last several years, Mercury has been hard-pressed to sell its family cars to anyone besides bargain hunters. Next to the Accord, the Sable and its Ford Taurus twin suffer for their unrefined drivetrains, subpar braking and handling and low-quality interiors that offer little in the way of style. But help is finally on the way. A larger sedan called the Montego will slide in above the Sable in a bid for buyers who want a more premium family sedan. While it may not be in a position to pin down the leaders of the family sedan segment, both are solidly engineered, comfortable and attractive cars that will find their place in the mainstream. The Montego, and its twin the Ford Five Hundred, are the first Ford products to take advantage of the company's controlling stake in Volvo. They're built on the same platform Volvo uses for its S60 and S80 sedans and make extensive use of Volvo safety and all-wheel-drive technology. On the outside, the new Mercury is about the same size as a Chrysler 300. The sheet metal is modern but unremarkable in appearance and, for better or worse, heavily derivative of the Volkswagen Passat's. If sitting up high is important to you, then you'll like the view from the driver seat. Mercury calls the Montego "a sedan derived from a crossover vehicle," and to that end the seating position is elevated (think Subaru Outback); the car's beltline is relatively low and the side mirrors are large. Front and rear passengers are treated to serious headroom and legroom, and those who buy groceries in bulk will love what they find when they open the trunk -- at 21 cubic feet of capacity, this is the largest cargo hold in the sedan kingdom. The overall interior design is stylish, but materials quality could use improvement. The power source for every Montego is the workhorse 3.0-liter Duratec V6. Output is only 203 horsepower, putting it at an immediate disadvantage alongside the powerhouse V6s offered by many competitors. Fortunately, Ford spent money on a couple of new transmissions -- a continuously variable transmission (CVT) and a six-speed automatic -- which help it get the most out of the available power. Buyers also have a choice of front- or all-wheel drive. Family sedans are supposed to be practical, roomy and loaded with conveniences, and the Montego certainly meets that requirement. But buyers who spend upward of $25,000 will expect to connect to their family sedan on an emotional level, and with its mediocre engine output and interior materials, it remains to be seen how well the Montego will fulfill this part of the deal.

**Body Styles, Trim Levels and Options:** The Montego sedan is available in one of two trims, Luxury and Premier. The Luxury starts you out with 17-inch wheels, a six-way power driver seat, full power accessories, air conditioning, a CD player, cruise control, HID headlamps, dual-zone automatic climate control, wood interior trim and air registers for rear passengers. Step up to the Premier and you'll get 18-inch wheels, leather upholstery, an eight-way driver and four-way

# 2005 Mercury Montego

power passenger seats, seat memory, an upgraded audio system, gray Zapelli wood grain trim and heated seats. Options include a moonroof, adjustable pedals and a reverse-sensing system.

**Powertrains and Performance:** Every Montego comes with Ford's 3.0-liter Duratec V6 rated for 203 horsepower and 207 pound-feet of torque. Buyers have two transmission choices. The first of these is a continuously variable transmission (CVT), which has an infinite number of ratios and chooses whichever one best fits a given situation. The other option is a six-speed automatic. Buyers must also decide between front-wheel drive and all-wheel drive. All front-drive Montegos come with the six-speed automatic, while AWD models get the CVT.

**Safety:** All Montegos come with a full set of disc brakes with ABS and Electronic Brakeforce Distribution. Optional on all models are side-impact airbags that protect front occupants' torsos and side curtain airbags that protect the heads of front and rear occupants. Traction control is standard on all Montegos, but stability control is not available. This car has not yet been crash tested.

**Interior Design and Special Features:** Scrutinize the cabin and it's apparent that designers put a lot of thought into creating an attractive and functional environment. In lieu of the shapeless dash and seats found in the Sable, the Montego has the crisp, clean lines and two-tone interior typical of European sedans. The front seats are roomy enough to fit most drivers, yet the cockpit has a snug, almost intimate feel. Rear passengers are treated to equally spacious quarters, making these cars good bets for families with teenagers. The rear seats fold flat in a 60/40 split and this, along with a fold-flat front-passenger seat, allows owners to carry items up to nine feet in length inside the car. Trunk capacity leads all sedans on the market at 21 cubic feet.

**Driving Impressions:** The V6 provides enough low-end torque for easy city driving, and the car gets up to speed with minimal fuss. We do expect that eventual owners will wish for a little extra midrange torque for passing at highway speeds and climbing grades. Of the two transmissions, our preference is the CVT, which does a better job of keeping the engine in its power band. Thanks to its Volvo-engineered chassis, the Montego offers a pleasant balance between smooth ride quality and responsive handling. It's not the car to buy if you're looking for entertainment, but if you just want something capable and comfortable, the Montego should satisfy.

## Competitive Vehicles

Chrysler 300
$23,295 - $34,195

Honda Accord
$15,900 - $28,800

Nissan Altima
$17,250 - $29,200

Pontiac Bonneville
$27,775 - $35,395

# 2005 MINI Cooper

**Compact Convertible, Coupe**

**MSRP Price Range**

## $16,449 - $24,400

Destination Charge: $550 (all styles)

## Ratings

| Consumer Rating | 9.3 | |
|---|---|---|
| Editors Rating | 7.3 | |

**What Edmunds.com says:** Replete with British charm and German engineering, the born-again Mini Cooper is a stylish, affordable go-kart for adults.

**Pros:** It's a piece of history with modern underpinnings, BMW-engineered suspension and steering, chock-full of comfort and safety features, hatchback utility, free scheduled maintenance for three years/36,000 miles.

**Cons:** Not enough horsepower in base model, questionable seat comfort, not much room for passengers and cargo, some low-grade interior materials.

**What's New:** The big news for 2005 is the arrival of the convertible in both regular and S flavors. Stylish as ever, the drop-top Mini seats four and still has a trunk big enough for a few bags. Other changes include slightly revised front and rear fascias and some reworked option choices. The vanity mirrors are no longer illuminated, a universal remote transmitter is now available and a leather-wrapped steering wheel is now standard. The S version gains 5 horsepower and 7 pound-feet of torque, as well as an external temperature display. Both the five- and six-speed manual transmissions feature shorter gearing this year to improve acceleration. A six-speed automatic transmission will become available on the S versions later in the model year.

*Crash Test Scores, see pg 530*
*Warranty information, see pg 542*

## Specifications

| Engine/Drivetrain | HP | Torque | EPA Fuel Economy Rating |
|---|---|---|---|
| 4cyl 1.6L M | 168 | 162 | N/A |
| 4cyl 1.6L M | 115 | 111 | N/A |

## Body Styles

| Style | MSRP Range |
|---|---|
| Compact Convertible | $20,950–$24,400 |
| Compact Coupe | $16,449–$19,899 |

**Introduction:** In 1959, Alec Issigonis designed a vehicle that combined minimal exterior dimensions with a surprising amount of interior space, thanks to a transverse-mounted engine and a boxy shape. Mini's decades-spanning history may be biblical, but it boils down to a car that was affordable, compact, stylish and fun to drive. Sales in the U.S. were limited to the years between 1960 and 1967, but those who have some connection to Europe always seem to harbor some tender recollection of the British icon. Then, as now, Mini had a wide appeal and reached a diverse audience, its style lending itself to artistic interpretations by pop stars, while its price allowed the middle class to own and enjoy it as well. In 1994, BMW acquired the Rover Group, which included the Land Rover, Rover, MG and Mini brands. BMW wanted entry into the lucrative high-end sport-utility market and sought Land Rover as a foothold, but the acquisition proved to be ill-fated. The company unloaded Land Rover to Ford in 2000, but kept Mini around so it could extend its reach into all segments of the marketplace, including that of the economy hatchback. BMW's goal was to retain the Mini's basic philosophies while raising the engineering bar to Bavarian standards. Enter the latest Mini Cooper. It merges British heritage and facade with German innards (much like the Windsor royals) in the form of technology and construction. Touted as the Next Big Thing, Mini's clever marketing campaign seems to have reached ubiquity. Although the Cooper is no great performance car and has minimal space for passengers and cargo, it has all of the things that made it so popular in the first place: an accessible price, miniature dimensions for urban convenience and fun -- in both its style and its go-kart handling. Mini is making a bold move for 2005 -- chopping the top off the Cooper. A new convertible Cooper is now available, and successfully takes the "cute" factor to yet another level. With a soft canvas top that can be lowered in just 15 seconds, the Mini convertible combines the fun of open-air driving with the one-of-a-kind style that made it famous. The Mini's soft top also not only folds completely away at the flip of a switch, it can also slide back up to 15 inches at the front for those days when you don't want to go completely topless. And even when you do decide to drop the top, there's still over four cubic feet of cargo space in back (six with the top up) -- not bad for a four-seater that's less than 12 feet long. Allow us to suggest that you option your Mini sparingly -- Coopers are eligible for most BMW-grade content, but even with just a few options, you'll end up with one enjoyable hatchback or convertible.

**Body Styles, Trim Levels and Options:** This endearing little bugger is available as either a three-door hatchback or a two-door convertible, and both are available in two versions -- the Cooper and the Cooper S. The base Cooper is outfitted with 15-inch wheels, leatherette upholstery (cloth is a no-cost option), a tilt steering wheel, a centrally mounted speedometer, air conditioning with micron filtration, a six-speaker stereo with CD changer prewiring and power windows, locks and mirrors. The Cooper S adds 16-inch wheels with run-flat performance tires, seat-height adjustment and a leather-wrapped steering wheel; all of these features are available for the base car as well. The extensive options list includes a sport package, leather upholstery and a navigation system. A power-operated top is standard on all convertibles.

# 2005 MINI Cooper

**Powertrains and Performance:** The base car is powered by a 1.6-liter inline four that makes 115 horsepower. This isn't much power by today's standards, but with only 2,300 pounds of car to propel, it's not dreadfully slow. A five-speed manual transmission is standard, and a continuously variable automatic transmission (CVT) with an automanual mode is optional. The sporty Cooper S is aided by a supercharger, allowing it to pump out 168 hp and 162 lb-ft of torque. A six-speed manual gearbox is standard, with a six-speed automatic optional. For those who need more performance, Mini offers the dealer-installed John Cooper Works package, which increases output to 200 hp and 177 lb-ft of torque.

**Safety:** All Minis come with four-wheel antilock disc brakes assisted by Electronic Brakeforce Distribution and Cornering Brake Control. The S model also includes traction control, and should you equip either model with the Sport Package, you'll get Dynamic Stability Control. Other standard safety features include a flat-tire monitor, side airbags for front occupants and head curtain airbags for the front and rear. The convertible version features fixed roll bars perched just behind the rear seat. In government crash tests, the Cooper hatchback earned four stars (out of five) for frontal impacts and four stars for side impacts involving front occupants. In IIHS frontal offset crash testing, the Cooper was named a "Best Pick" among small cars.

**Interior Design and Special Features:** The Cooper's petite cabin looks stylish with its metallic trim, tubular structures and Frisbee-size speedometer in the center of the dash. Although everything looks good, some of the plastics used are low in quality. Passenger and cargo space is predictably tight -- there's just 5.6 cubic feet of cargo capacity with the rear seats in use for the hatchback. Amazingly, the convertible has roughly the same amount of cargo space.

**Driving Impressions:** You can expect lively handling from either Cooper, as the cars borrow suspension bits from the current BMW 3 Series. Additionally, the more performance-oriented Cooper S gets reinforced antiroll bars and firmer springs -- its setup may be too stiff for some, but enthusiasts will love its tight reflexes around corners. Engine power is modest in both Coopers, but they get by just fine in traffic and the Cooper S loves to rev.

## Competitive Vehicles

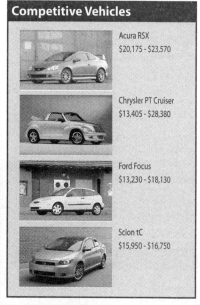

Acura RSX
$20,175 - $23,570

Chrysler PT Cruiser
$13,405 - $28,380

Ford Focus
$13,230 - $18,130

Scion tC
$15,950 - $16,750

# 2005 Nissan Frontier

**MSRP Price Range**

## N/A

Destination Charge: N/A (all styles)

## Ratings

| | | |
|---|---|---|
| Consumer Rating | N/A | |
| Editors Rating | 7.5 | |

**What Edmunds.com says:** Thanks to its Titan under-pinnings and powerful V6, the new Frontier is right up there with the compact pickup class leaders in terms of performance, comfort and utility.

**Pros:** Class-leading V6 engine, larger size for improved passenger and cargo room, innovative bed features, advanced off-road systems.

**Cons:** Fewer model options than competitors, average interior materials.

**What's New:** The Frontier is all new for 2005. Changes include a new and more powerful V6, two new transmissions, advanced off-road systems and a larger size for better passenger comfort.

*Crash Test Scores, see pg 530*
*Warranty information, see pg 542*

## Specifications

| Engine/Drivetrain | HP | Torque | EPA Fuel Economy Rating |
|---|---|---|---|
| 4cyl 2.5L A/M | 154 | 173 | N/A |
| 4cyl 2.5L A/M | N/A | N/A | N/A |
| 6cyl 4.0L A/M | 265 | 284 | N/A |

## Body Styles

| Style | MSRP Range |
|---|---|
| Compact Truck | N/A |

**Introduction:** Nissan has been building trucks for the U.S. market since 1958. Now in its eighth generation of pickup offerings, the company's 2005 Frontier is the first all-new model since the pickup's last major redesign in 1998. Bigger, more powerful and bulging with muscular new lines, the 2005 Frontier now sports the big-truck swagger of the Titan full-size. Its grille is nearly identical to the bigger truck, while its exaggerated fender flares give it even more curves at each corner. The Frontier shares a number of significant features with the Titan, including an innovative spray-in bedliner, Utili-track bed channel tie-down system and fully boxed, all-steel frame. The new Frontier's wheelbase is nearly 10 inches longer than the old Frontier's for improved ride comfort and stability. The 2005 Frontier shares its suspension layout and many component designs with the Titan, including a double-wishbone front suspension and leaf spring rear suspension. The Frontier Crew Cab is identical in length to the extended-cab (King Cab) version, but a larger rear-seating area and forward-hinged rear doors make it a more flexible vehicle for family use -- at the expense of some bed space. The bed measures just under 58.6 inches in length and 61.4 inches in width -- gains of a couple of inches in either direction compared to the standard-bed version of the old crew cab. Interior storage space is also an important consideration when you're buying a pickup, and both the King and Crew Cab feature reconfigurable rear seats. Note that the new Frontier is not available in a regular-cab version. In a sign that Nissan is serious about dominating the compact truck market, the Frontier's top engine is a 4.0-liter V6 with 265 horsepower and 284 pound-feet of torque. With that kind of power onboard, the Frontier boasts a maximum tow rating of over 5,500 pounds, according to Nissan. A 2.5-liter DOHC inline four-cylinder engine is standard on the base Frontier King Cab model. Inside the cabs, ergonomics and materials quality are much improved over the '04 Frontier. Also offered are supplemental front-seat side-impact airbags and available supplemental curtain airbags for side-impact and rollover protection for front and rear outboard passengers. With a tough new look, innovative features and big horsepower under the hood, the new Frontier should provide serious competition for the new trucks from Dodge and Toyota. This is good news for compact pickup buyers, who now have plenty of worthy candidates to test-drive when it comes time to shop.

**Body Styles, Trim Levels and Options:** The Frontier comes in two body styles -- extended cab (known as King Cab) and crew cab. Available trim levels include the base S model and uplevel SE. The base S comes with only basic amenities, along with front bucket seats and folding rear jump seats. The SE adds more features, including air conditioning; a CD stereo; power windows, locks and mirrors; alloy wheels; and cruise control. Leather upholstery and a 300-watt Rockford Fosgate stereo are optional. Compared to the King Cab, the Crew Cab has a larger cabin with expanded rear-seat accommodations as well as a pair of conventional rear doors that offer easier access to those seats.

**Powertrains and Performance:** A 2.5-liter DOHC inline four-cylinder engine is standard on the base Frontier King Cab model. A 4.0-liter V6, which produces a stout 265 hp and 284 lb-ft of torque, is standard in all other models. The V6 design includes Continuous Valve Timing Control (C-VTC) and Nissan variable Induction Control System (NICS). Transmission choices include a standard six-speed manual gearbox and an optional five-speed automatic. Frontier 4x4 models include a shift-on-the-fly four-wheel-drive system with 2Hi/4Hi/4Lo modes operated by an electronically controlled, part-time transfer case.

**Safety:** Four-wheel disc antilock brakes are standard on all Frontiers. Optional are front-seat side-impact airbags and curtain airbags that provide side-impact and rollover protection for front and rear outboard passengers. The Frontier has not yet been crash tested.

**Interior Design and Special Features:** The Frontier's cabin offers straightforward controls, comfortable front seats and an attractive design. The larger overall size results in much improved passenger room, but the overall materials quality is still average. Like the Titan, the Frontier offers a utility bed package that includes a factory-applied spray-in bedliner and the Utili-track tie-down system. The Utili-track system provides cargo hauling flexibility through the use of five special "C" cross-section rails mounted in the bed (two channels in the bed floor, and one each on the bed side rails and the bed header panel). Removable utility cleats slide into the channels, providing a wide range of attachment points for securing cargo. In addition to the tie-down cleats, a full range of accessories are offered for use with the channel system, including bed dividers, sliding cargo trays, modular storage units and bike racks.

**Driving Impressions:** The newfound power of the V6 Frontier is a far cry from the wheezy engines of last year's model. Step on the throttle in this truck and you get instant results, thanks to plenty of low-end torque and well-tuned transmissions. Ride and handling is improved as well; although, it's still a bit bouncy as you might expect from a compact truck. Advanced off-road systems like downhill assist control and hill start assist make off-road models capable performers in the rough stuff.

## Competitive Vehicles

Chevrolet Colorado
$13,625 - $21,430

Dodge Dakota
$19,374 - $28,679

Ford Ranger
$14,365 - $26,025

Toyota Tacoma
$13,415 - $25,250

# 2005 Nissan Pathfinder

Midsize SUV

**MSRP Price Range**

## $24,650 - $34,750

Destination Charge: $560 (all styles)

### Ratings

| | | |
|---|---|---|
| Consumer Rating | N/A | |
| Editors Rating | 7.4 | |

**What Edmunds.com says:** An excellent blend of off-road toughness and everyday comfort, but its concessions toward true backcountry capability might turn off those who want the image more than anything else.

**Pros:** Most powerful V6 in the class, above average off-road ability, well-laid-out interior, flexible seating design, ample storage space throughout.

**Cons:** Tight rear-seat accommodations, on-road handling not as refined as car-based competitors, some odd interior materials.

**What's New:** The Pathfinder has been completely redesigned for 2005 and now includes third-row seating and a larger, more powerful V6.

*Crash Test Scores, see pg 530*
*Warranty information, see pg 542*

### Specifications

| Engine/Drivetrain | HP | Torque | EPA Fuel Economy Rating |
|---|---|---|---|
| 6cyl 4.0L A | 270 | 291 | 16 city/23 hwy |

### Body Styles

| Style | MSRP Range |
|---|---|
| Midsize SUV | $24,650–$34,750 |

**Introduction:** When it was first introduced way back in 1986, the Pathfinder rode on Nissan's small truck chassis giving it the kind of bulletproof hardware and rugged image that consumers craved in an SUV. That configuration, and a distinctive two-door design, made it a hit and put the Pathfinder squarely on the SUV map. But as tastes changed, so did the Pathfinder. Nissan eventually added two more doors and moved to a more paved road-friendly unibody design to help the Pathfinder appeal to a wider range of drivers. Its popularity continued, but for those who liked the original Pathfinder because of its go-anywhere, do-anything capability, the image was somewhat tarnished. For 2005, the redesigned Pathfinder has returned to its roots and once again rides on a body-on-frame truck chassis, a modified version of the Titan's underpinnings. Although it's longer, taller and wider, Nissan's engineers did manage to keep the overall length down compared to its competitors. A third-row seat is now standard equipment, putting the Pathfinder in the same league as most of its peers. The standard V6 was bumped from 3.5 to 4.0 liters, resulting in 270 horsepower and 291 pound-feet of torque. As a result, the Pathfinder now boasts the most powerful V6 in its class. Advanced features like variable valve timing, all-aluminum construction and electronic throttle control assure that it retains a refined feel despite the fact that it's been tuned to provide the kind of low-end torque that an SUV of its size needs. A new four-wheel independent suspension gives the Pathfinder a nice balance between ride comfort and off-road toughness. On pavement, the new model rides just as well as the previous Pathfinder, with only a slightly choppier feel. With a maximum ground clearance of as much as 9.1 inches on 4WD off-road models, steep approach and departure angles and an underbody design that tucks everything underneath up above the frame rails, the Pathfinder is equally capable in the dirt. A new Hill Descent Control (HDC) system maintains a low speed (roughly 3.5 mph) on steep descents, while a Hill Start Assist (HSA) system eliminates the need for fancy footwork on steep climbs by holding the vehicle in place as you go from the brake to the throttle. It also offers four-wheel electronic limited-slip control that moderates the power to all four wheels individually for maximum traction and a low-speed throttle map that offers more precise control while creeping over boulders. Nissan proved with the original Pathfinder that the right image is a strong sales tool that can't be overlooked, and the new version has enough original lines to get it noticed in a sea of like-sized competitors. You might say that the Pathfinder has returned to its roots in more ways than one, but learned enough new tricks along the way to make it a formidable competitor in the cutthroat world of midsize SUVs.

**Body Styles, Trim Levels and Options:** The four-door Pathfinder offers four levels of trim to suit varying desires for simplicity or luxury. The base XE puts together the usual list of expected amenities like 16-inch alloy wheels, power accessories, keyless entry, a CD stereo and cloth seating for seven. The SE adds slightly larger tires, foglights and a power-adjustable driver seat, in addition to a longer options list. A new SE Off-Road trim comes standard with heavy-duty Rancho shocks, underbody skid plates and even larger tires than the standard SE. The top-of-

For the latest full vehicle reports, visit www.edmunds.com/bginfopak

# 2005 Nissan Pathfinder

the-line LE is upgraded with upscale amenities like 17-inch wheels, a sunroof, heated leather seating, a Bose audio system and both side-impact and head curtain airbags. Optional items include a DVD-based navigation system and a rear-seat DVD entertainment system.

**Powertrains and Performance:** The Pathfinder is powered by a 4.0-liter DOHC V6 engine. It makes a stout 270 horsepower and 291 pound-feet of torque. A five-speed automatic is the only transmission and both two- and four-wheel-drive versions are offered. Four-wheel-drive models feature advanced traction systems like Hill Descent Control (HDC), Hill Start Assist (HSA) and electronic limited-slip control that give the Pathfinder excellent off-road ability.

**Safety:** The Pathfinder comes standard with stability control and antilock front disc/rear drum brakes supplemented by Electronic Brakeforce Distribution and BrakeAssist. LE models come standard with side airbags for front occupants and side curtain airbags that protect all three rows. These are optional on all other models. The new Pathfinder has not yet been crash tested.

**Interior Design and Special Features:** The new Pathfinder's larger overall size allows for more passenger room in the first and second rows, while fold-flat seats give it a maximum cargo capacity of 79.2 cubic feet -- slightly more than the 4Runner but a little bit less than the Explorer. There's plenty of space up front for the driver and front passenger, but the second-row seats are snug when it comes to toe and shoulder room. As in most midsize SUVs, the Pathfinder's two-passenger third-row seat isn't adult-friendly. The cargo area features a segment exclusive "easy clean" surface that makes it suitable for wet or muddy items -- it can be hosed out for quick cleaning.

**Driving Impressions:** The V6 provides ample power for just about any type of driving. Body motions are well controlled, the steering is nicely weighted and road irregularities are soaked up with little cabin intrusion. Interior noise levels are low, too, with minimal howl from even the optional off-road tires. The Pathfinder fumbles a bit over bumps and responds to inputs at a slightly slower pace than before, but only those who are intimately familiar with the previous model are apt to notice the difference. Compared to other vehicles in the class, it's a commendable setup that few will find fault with.

## Competitive Vehicles

Chevrolet TrailBlazer
$27,520 - $32,420

Dodge Durango
$26,735 - $35,590

Ford Explorer
$26,770 - $37,530

Toyota 4Runner
$27,495 - $37,495

# 2005 Nissan Xterra

**MSRP Price Range**

## N/A

Destination Charge: N/A (all styles)

## Ratings

| | | |
|---|---|---|
| Consumer Rating | N/A | |
| Editors Rating | 7.5 | |

**What Edmunds.com says:** With newfound power under the hood, a more refined suspension underneath and more passenger space inside, Nissan addresses all the shortcomings of the previous Xterra without taking away any of the appealing attitude that made it a hit in the first place.

**Pros:** One of the most powerful V6s in the class, above average off-road capability, solid passenger room, innovative cargo features.

**Cons:** Still not what we would call refined on the street, a few instances of low-grade interior materials.

**What's New:** The Xterra has been fully redesigned for 2005 with a new platform, a more powerful V6 and a more spacious interior.

**Introduction:** Ever since the mid-'90s, compact SUVs have become a huge market. Most manufacturers offer one, and with so many available, it is often hard to choose the one that is right for you. The majority of compact SUVs for sale lately are so-called "crossover" SUVs, meaning that they are car-based rather than truck-based. The advantages to having a small crossover SUV are that they are comfortable to drive and possess secure handling characteristics, though they tend to lack true off-road ability. Nissan's Xterra, completely redesigned for 2005, is somewhat of a rarity -- it is based on a real truck. It now rides on a modified version of the F-Alpha platform found underneath the full-size Titan truck and Armada SUV. The Xterra features an independent front suspension and leaf-spring and solid axle setup at the rear. Although the overall length is nearly identical to the previous model, the wheelbase is up by two inches for more interior room and a less choppy ride. It's also 2.5 inches wider and nearly two inches taller than its predecessor, making it one of the larger SUVs in the compact class. While the previous model was plagued by a lack of punch, the 2005 Xterra gets a major boost of power in the way of a 4.0-liter V6 that produces 265 horsepower and 284 pound-feet of torque. Two transmissions are offered: a five-speed automatic and a six-speed manual. Four-wheel antilock disc brakes are standard, while an electronic stability control system is offered as an option. Interior space is up thanks to the stretched exterior dimensions. Front seat leg- and headroom are up by nearly an inch, while rear-seat passengers enjoy over 3.5 inches of additional legroom and more than two inches of extra headroom. Interior features include adjustable tie-down hooks in the cargo area, increased storage up front and an optional 300-watt Rockford Fosgate audio system. Safety conscious buyers will be happy to note that in addition to the optional stability control system, the Xterra also offers front-seat side-impact airbags as well as side curtain airbags that protect both rows of seats. The utilitarian interior design leaves out high-end features like onboard navigation and DVD video players, but the Xterra does offer some advanced features under the skin like Hill Descent Control and four-wheel electronic traction control. Compared to other SUVs like the Honda CR-V or Ford Escape, the Xterra's on-pavement performance is not quite as refined, but if serious off-roading is part of your daily routine, the Xterra is one of the better compact SUVs on the market. It also has good build quality and a strong reputation for reliability, giving you peace of mind as you head out on your favorite trail.

Crash Test Scores, see pg 530
Warranty information, see pg 542

**Body Styles, Trim Levels and Options:** The four-door Xterra is available in three trim levels -- S, Off-Road and SE, all of which are offered in both two- and four-wheel drive. The base S comes with basic features like air conditioning, a tilt steering wheel and a CD player. The Off-Road model includes high-performance gas shocks, off-road tires on alloy wheels and special exterior trim. The SE includes power windows, locks and mirrors; cruise control; and upgraded interior trim. A 300-watt Rockford Fosgate audio system with nine speakers, MP3 capability and steering wheel controls is optional.

## Specifications

| Engine/Drivetrain | HP | Torque | EPA Fuel Economy Rating |
|---|---|---|---|
| 6cyl 4.0L A/M | 265 | 284 | N/A |

## Body Styles

| Style | MSRP Range |
|---|---|
| Midsize SUV | N/A |

**Powertrains and Performance:** All Xterra models feature a 4.0-liter V6 that includes electronic throttle control (with secondary mapping in low-range mode on 4WD models), continuous valve timing control (C-VTC) and Nissan's variable Induction Control System (NICS). This engine makes 265 hp and over 284 lb-ft of torque, generous figures for this class. A six-speed manual transmission is standard, with a five-speed automatic optional. Four-wheel-drive versions use a multimode transfer case that offers 2WD and automatic 4WD modes, in addition to low-range gearing, for maximum flexibility in varying conditions.

**Safety:** All Xterras have four-wheel antilock disc brakes fortified with Electronic Brakeforce Distribution and BrakeAssist. Side-impact airbags (for front occupants) and full-length side curtain airbags are optional, as is Vehicle Dynamic Control (VDC), Nissan's stability control system. The Xterra has not yet been crash tested.

**Interior Design and Special Features:** The interior favors function over form, and the ergonomics are solid. The cargo area is highlighted by an easy-to-clean floor and a total of 10 cargo area utility hooks -- six on the floor/sides and four on the ceiling and sides (floor hooks can carry up to 110 pounds). A new adjustable channel system in the cargo floor, similar in design to the Utili-track system offered on the Titan and Frontier pickups, makes it easier to secure bike racks and other accessories or gear. There's also an available built-in first-aid kit and space to securely carry up to one-gallon jugs.

**Driving Impressions:** With more than enough power under the hood, the Xterra is no longer plagued by sluggish performance on the street. Its truck chassis still doesn't deliver the sharp handling that a car chassis would, but it's an acceptable trade-off, given its above-average off-road prowess. If you never plan on leaving the street, there are certainly better compact SUVs on the market, but if weekend adventures call your name often, the Xterra is now a much more capable and willing participant than ever before.

## Competitive Vehicles

Chevrolet Equinox
$21,095 - $24,435

Honda CR-V
$19,995 - $25,050

Jeep Liberty
$19,265 - $25,110

Kia Sorento
$18,995 - $25,500

# 2005 Pontiac G6

**Midsize Sedan**

**MSRP Price Range**

## $20,675 - $23,300

Destination Charge: $625 (all styles)

## Ratings

| | | |
|---|---|---|
| Consumer Rating | 9.6 | |
| Editors Rating | 7.3 | |

**What Edmunds.com says:** With the G6's stylish duds, roomy interior and distinctive features, Pontiac finally has a serious contender in the midsize sedan segment.

**Pros:** Crisp handling, lots of rear-seat room, plenty of standard features, innovative panoramic sunroof.

**Cons:** A few low-buck interior bits, panoramic sunroof takes away rear-seat headroom, down on power compared to class leaders.

**What's New:** The G6 is an all-new midsize sedan replacement for the ancient Grand Am.

**Introduction:** Originally introduced in coupe form in 1973, the Grand Am has carried out Pontiac's midsize sedan duties since the mid-1980s. The most recent Grand Am has roots dating back to 1985, when Pontiac introduced its front-drive "European-inspired" version. Time has not been kind to the Grand Am, as subsequent redesigns in the 1990s did little to bring the car up to class standards. Pontiac knew it needed a competitive replacement, and none too soon. The short answer was to simply make a great Pontiac sedan based on GM's latest-and-greatest midsize platform, the Epsilon architecture. It's taken awhile, but it looks like GM has finally gotten this platform-sharing thing down. We've never been opposed to the idea per se, but in too many instances in the past, cars that shared platforms were just too similar for our tastes. The G6 is the third production car to utilize General Motors' Epsilon platform but it wouldn't be overstating it to say most new car buyers will never see the family resemblance. If it seems like the G6 looks a little bigger than its stablemate, the Chevrolet Malibu, that's because the Pontiac uses the lengthened version of the Epsilon platform like the Malibu Maxx. This long-wheelbase platform provides two main benefits -- more rear-seat room and better handling. The extra length makes for truly big-car backseat space, and passengers will enjoy plenty of legroom. The long wheelbase also helps the G6 deliver a smooth and stable ride. As with most Pontiacs, the G6 is heavy on style -- only this time around the styling is bold without being tacky. The car stands out but does not look garish and, thankfully, the plastic cladding of Pontiacs past has been ditched in favor of clean, simple lines. The G6 offers just enough muscle to back up the sporty looks. The G6 is powered by GM's tried-and-true 3.5-liter V6, good for 200 horsepower. Pontiac is trying to keep (or rebuild) its performance car customer base by offering a shift-it-yourself automatic that will hit redline without upshifting -- in other words, true manual control. A unique option on the G6 is a panoramic sunroof that opens in four sections and remains exposed when it's open. The effect is that it looks like a roof spoiler. Combined with the small antenna that resides at the front edge of the roof, the G6 tends to look a little European. Unfortunately, this sunroof takes up a bit too much rear-seat headroom. Overall, the G6 features a winning combination of bold styling, a cavernous interior and unique features, all at a competitive price.

Crash Test Scores, see pg 530
Warranty information, see pg 542

**Body Styles, Trim Levels and Options:** The four-door G6 comes in two trim levels, base and GT. Generous standard equipment on the base model includes air conditioning; cruise control; power windows, locks and mirrors; keyless entry; a 60/40 split-folding rear seat; a CD player; and a tilt/telescoping steering wheel. The GT adds power-adjustable pedals, an eight-speaker Monsoon sound system, a rear spoiler, alloy wheels and a sport suspension. Notable options include a remote start system, XM Satellite Radio and chrome alloy wheels. Two power sunroof options are available -- a traditional power glass panel, as well as an innovative panoramic roof with four glass panels that fold accordion-style and an electric sunshade.

## Specifications

| Engine/Drivetrain | HP | Torque | EPA Fuel Economy Rating |
|---|---|---|---|
| 6cyl 3.5L A | 200 | 220 | 20 city/25 hwy |

## Body Styles

| Style | MSRP Range |
|---|---|
| Midsize Sedan | $20,675–$23,300 |

For the latest full vehicle reports, visit www.edmunds.com/bginfopak

**Powertrains and Performance:** Standard power comes from a 3.5-liter V6 rated at 200 horse-power and 220 pound-feet of torque. A four-speed automatic transmission is also standard. GT models include a shift-it-yourself feature that offers full manual control of gear changes.

**Safety:** The G6 features standard four-wheel disc brakes. Antilock brakes and traction control are standard on the GT, and optional on the base car. Side curtain airbags are optional across the board, but a stability control system is not available. The G6 has not yet been crash tested.

**Interior Design and Special Features:** The interior of the G6 features stylish seating with generous side bolsters to hold you in place during aggressive cornering. The gauges showcase Pontiac's signature font, and are set in an attractive cluster with chrome rings. Plenty of chrome and metal-look accents brighten up the interior. Overall materials quality is notably good, but a few cheap bits here and there keep the G6 a step below the class standards.

**Driving Impressions:** The 3.5-liter V6 offers plenty of torque down low for easy passing and merging, but can get a bit thrashy at high revs. The suspension returns a surprisingly sporty ride, and the solid structure helps make the interior a serene place to spend time.

## Competitive Vehicles

Honda Accord
$15,900 - $28,500

Mitsubishi Galant
$17,997 - $25,697

Nissan Altima
$17,250 - $29,200

Toyota Camry
$18,045 - $25,405

# 2005 Pontiac Montana SV6 Midsize Minivan

**MSRP Price Range**
## $24,520 - $30,210
Destination Charge: $715 (all styles)

### Ratings

| | | |
|---|---|---|
| Consumer Rating | N/A | |
| Editors Rating | 7.0 | |

**What Edmunds.com says:** Though the Montana SV6 features a slick interior and distinctive styling, it doesn't have the on-road finesse of its minivan competitors.

**Pros:** Smooth ride and handling, lots of nifty interior storage spaces, innovative multimedia storage system, available all-wheel drive.

**Cons:** Engine power and refinement not up to class leaders, no side curtain airbags.

**What's New:** The Montana SV6 is an all-new "crossover sport van" that has roots in the Pontiac Montana minivan.

*Crash Test Scores, see pg 530*
*Warranty information, see pg 542*

### Specifications

| Engine/Drivetrain | HP | Torque | EPA Fuel Economy Rating |
|---|---|---|---|
| 6cyl 3.5L A | 200 | 220 | N/A |

### Body Styles

| Style | MSRP Range |
|---|---|
| Midsize Minivan | $24,520–$30,210 |

**Introduction:** Pontiac's Montana minivan has never sold in the numbers General Motors would like -- the offerings from Dodge, Ford and Honda have outsold it (and its Chevrolet Venture twin) for several years running. Part of the problem, according to GM's marketing team, might be due to the "mommy mobile" image minivans confer upon their owners -- some of whom ultimately ditch their vans for SUVs. In response, Pontiac has introduced the Montana SV6, a "crossover sport van" based on the outgoing Montana's chassis. Compared to the Montana, the SV6 takes on a taller stance, a longer, more angular nose and a more tasteful application of bodyside cladding. The results are not altogether unattractive, and Pontiac will again field the most rugged-looking minivan in the GM lineup. The result, Pontiac hopes, is a perception that the van is more of a hip and stylish SUV-like van, and not so much a boring soccer mom van. Despite the change in name and outward style, the SV6 does not represent a full redesign of the Montana -- passenger and cargo space are nearly identical. It does, however, incorporate more of the features that today's minivan buyers are looking for, along with a more powerful engine. Additionally, structural upgrades, including a longer, reinforced front end and a stiffer occupant compartment, should improve the van's crashworthiness -- a good thing because the Montana fared poorly in frontal offset crash testing conducted by the IIHS. Seat-mounted side airbags for front occupants are optional, but full-length head curtain airbags are still nowhere to be found. Inside, the SV6 seats seven, and the fold-flat third-row seat offers a 50/50 split, allowing families to carry a mix of passengers and cargo. The SV6 is a more practical place to spend time than the old Montana, as Pontiac has taken Honda's example and installed folding center trays (with cupholders) between the first- and second-row captain's chairs. An overhead rail system provides rear-seat access to climate and entertainment functions, and can be customized to families' liking with various storage containers. In addition to the usual rear DVD entertainment system, the SV6 is available with a PhatNoise mobile digital media system that allows owners to store thousands of MP3s and/or several dozen movies. Another convenient option is a 115-volt AC outlet for all manner of Game Cubes and Easy Bake ovens. For power, the SV6 has a 200-horsepower, 3.5-liter V6 as the one and only engine choice. Although it should be a welcome upgrade from the overworked 3.4-liter motor, don't expect to keep up with Honda Odyssey drivers. A four-speed automatic transmission is standard, and both front-wheel drive and all-wheel drive are available. Additionally, 17-inch wheels are standard, and the StabiliTrak stability control system is optional. We're not entirely sold on the whole "SUV/van" concept. To our jaded eyes, the SV6 looks more like a minivan with a really big and flat front end. Subjective styling issues aside, the SV6 offers budding families a myriad of interior features and solid overall competence, but still doesn't match the best-in-class offerings.

**Body Styles, Trim Levels and Options:** The Montana SV6 comes in one size and trim level. Standard equipment includes power windows, air conditioning, an eight-speaker sound system with a CD/MP3 player, a rear-seat DVD entertainment system, the OnStar communications

system, cruise control and keyless entry. An upgrade option package includes a passenger-side power-sliding door, a power driver seat, a sport suspension, rear air conditioning, alloy wheels and additional interior storage. An all-wheel-drive system is available, and includes an automatic load-leveling rear suspension and an inflator kit. An optional PhatNoise mobile digital media system allows owners to store thousands of MP3s and/or several dozen movies. Other noteworthy options include dual power-sliding side doors, leather seating, a 115-volt A/C outlet, trip computer, rear parking assist, heated seats and a remote vehicle starting system.

**Powertrains and Performance:** All Montana SV6s come equipped with a 3.5-liter V6 that makes 200 horsepower and 220 pound-feet of torque. A four-speed automatic transmission is standard. No other powertrain combinations are available, but buyers can opt for all-wheel drive.

**Safety:** All models come standard with four-wheel antilock disc brakes. Side-impact airbags for front occupants are optional. Full-length side curtain airbags are not available. The Stabili-Trak stability control system is available on SV6s equipped with the optional sport suspension. The SV6 has not yet been crash tested.

**Interior Design and Special Features:** The Montana SV6 seats seven, and the fold-flat third-row seat offers a convenient 50/50 split. A pleasing color scheme with faux metal accents dramatically brightens the interior atmosphere of the van. Folding center trays (with cupholders) between the first- and second-row seats are available. An overhead rail system provides rear-seat access to climate and entertainment functions, and can be outfitted with various storage containers. A rear-seat DVD entertainment system is standard on all SV6s, and can be upgraded with infrared wireless headphones. A remote vehicle start system, pioneered on the 2004 Chevy Malibu, is optional.

**Driving Impressions:** The V6 power plant is down on power compared to its competitors, but it still manages to provide adequate acceleration. The SV6's suspension is on the soft side, though upgrading to the optional sport suspension does provide for more responsive handling.

## Competitive Vehicles

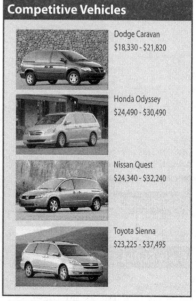

Dodge Caravan
$18,330 - $21,820

Honda Odyssey
$24,490 - $30,490

Nissan Quest
$24,340 - $32,240

Toyota Sienna
$23,225 - $37,495

# 2005 Porsche 911

**Compact Coupe**

**MSRP Price Range**

## $69,300 - $79,100

Destination Charge: N/A (all styles)

## Ratings

| | | |
|---|---|---|
| Consumer Rating | N/A | |
| Editors Rating | 8.6 | |

**What Edmunds.com says:** Still the quintessential sports car after four decades, the 911 has a unique blend of style, performance and sound that's unmatched by anything on the road.

**Pros:** Pinpoint steering, effortless acceleration, awe-inspiring brakes, the rhythmic sound of a powerful flat six, comfortable cockpit.

**Cons:** Relatively small fuel tank, useless rear seats, outlandish option prices.

**What's New:** While the traditional 911 lines have been retained, just about everything else has changed on Porsche's flagship. Notable changes include more powerful engines, a new transmission, variable-ratio rack-and-pinion steering, an adjustable suspension and new seating options in a redesigned passenger compartment.

*Crash Test Scores, see pg 530*
*Warranty information, see pg 542*

## Specifications

| Engine/Drivetrain | HP | Torque | EPA Fuel Economy Rating |
|---|---|---|---|
| 6cyl 3.6L A/M | 325 | 275 | N/A |
| 6cyl 3.8L A/M | 355 | 295 | N/A |

## Body Styles

| Style | MSRP Range |
|---|---|
| Compact Coupe | $69,300–$79,100 |

**Introduction:** A decade after designing the legendary Volkswagen, Dr. Ferdinand Porsche came up with a sports car derivative of his famous "people's car" called the 356. Light and sporty but notoriously underpowered, the 356 developed a loyal following throughout the 1950s and early '60s. Not wanting to offend their die-hard fans, Porsche executives decided a new model needed to be introduced for 1965 that could carry on the rear-engine tradition made famous by the 356. Ferdinand's son Ferry was commissioned with the task of designing the car, and the result was introduced to the world as the all-new 1965 Porsche 911. Forty years later the 911 is celebrated around the world as one of the most legendary sports cars ever built, and the Teutonic road warrior has been completely redesigned to commemorate the occasion. Porsche aficionados and the automotive press alike complained when an all-new 911 debuted in 1999 with slippery new styling and a liquid-cooled engine, claiming the car fell a little too far from the 911 family tree. Porsche has responded by infusing some old-school DNA into the 2005 version that lends the car a much more traditional look. Every body panel except the roof is new, including upright round headlamps that hark back to the much-loved 993, separate turn indicators and foglamps and a sloping front bumper that looks strikingly similar to the aerodynamic front clip on the Carrera GT super car. The rear view features flared wheel wells reminiscent of early turbo cars and wide, brilliantly lit taillamps tucked into either side of the engine cover. The interior has been revised for improved comfort and style, and new high-tech options such as satellite navigation and a Bose surround-sound stereo should make the German sports car a relatively practical choice for commuters with a need for speed. The standard power plant is now a 3.6-liter flat six rated at 325 horsepower and 273 pound-feet of torque while a new Carrera S model receives a 3.8-liter version of the same engine that produces 355 hp and 295 lb-ft of torque. Apart from the larger displacement, the S differs from the standard Carrera by the following standard equipment: an active suspension system, stability control, larger brakes with red calipers, 19-inch wheels instead of the Carrera's 18-inchers, bi-xenon headlamps, a sportier steering wheel, faux aluminum cabin trim and a silver-colored logo mounted on the rear deck lid. While the first of these new-generation 911s will be rear-drive coupes, you'll see the open-roof cabriolet and all-wheel-drive Carrera 4, as well as the race-inspired Turbo, GT2 and GT3 models in coming years. No matter which one you choose, few rivals can match the 911 in terms of performance, luxury and heritage.

**Body Styles, Trim Levels and Options:** The 2005 911 marks the first time since 1977 that Porsche has split the line into two models powered by two distinct engines, a 3.6 flat-six in the standard Carrera and a 3.8-liter version in the high-performance Carrera S. Other features unique to the S include active suspension management technology, larger brakes, 19-inch forged alloy wheels (in place of the standard Carrera's 18s), bi-xenon headlights, a sports steering wheel, aluminum-look interior trim and a silver-colored rear deck logo. To distinguish the two models from behind, the S has twin round tailpipes poking out the rear valance, while the base car sports two oval-shaped units. Other options include ceramic disc brakes borrowed from the GT2 and a Sport Chrono Package that records and displays lap times.

**Powertrains and Performance:** The standard Carrera comes with a 3.6-liter horizontally opposed six that was carried over from 2004, albeit with a revised intake that provides a slim boost in output to 325 horsepower and 275 pound-feet of torque. The next step up the performance ladder is the Carrera S, which has a new 3.8-liter version of the boxer six rated for 355 hp and 295 lb-ft of torque. Both cars come standard with a new six-speed manual transmission; the five-speed Tiptronic automatic offered in past years remains an option. Porsche claims that the Carrera can reach 60 mph in 4.8 seconds, while the S model accomplishes the feat in 4.6.

**Safety:** Six airbags, four-wheel antilock disc brakes and stability control are included on all 911 models. An all-new active suspension management system is optional on the Carrera, and standard on the Carrera S.

**Interior Design and Special Features:** The Cayenne-inspired interior has been completely redesigned with a new steering wheel, single-pod gauge cluster, bucket seats and a hands-free communication system. Both models feature automatic climate control with a pollen filter. Also standard is a new nine-speaker sound system, but a 13-speaker Bose surround-sound system is optional for true audiophiles. A revised driving position, larger foot wells and a new steering column that tilts and telescopes create more head- and legroom than ever before. Optional amenities include heated memory seats with pneumatically adjustable cushions and backrests.

**Driving Impressions:** Driven at normal speeds the 911 delivers a firm but mostly pleasant ride that's suitable for daily commutes, but the growl of the flat six behind the driver is a welcome reminder that this is no vanilla passenger car. Lay into the power, and the 911 comes alive. The variable-rate steering feels slightly numb at certain speeds, but turns in with added precision and is less affected by uneven tarmac. The new brakes are more powerful than ever, and respond promptly thanks to a bigger booster and optional composite rotors. It requires a skilled driver to extract the car's full potential, but thanks to the new Porsche Active Suspension Management system, even those who only scratch the surface will be thrilled with the results.

## Competitive Vehicles

Acura NSX
$89,000

BMW 6 Series
$69,900 - $76,900

Chevrolet Corvette
$43,445 - $51,445

Jaguar XK-Series
$69,830 - $74,830

# 2005 Saab 9-2X

**MSRP Price Range**

## $22,990 - $26,950

Destination Charge: $695 (all styles)

## Ratings

| | | |
|---|---|---|
| Consumer Rating | 8.8 | |
| Editors Rating | 7.8 | |

**What Edmunds.com says:** If you don't mind a strong shot of Subaru with your Saab and are in the market for a sporty wagon, the 9-2X could very well be the ride for you.

**Pros:** Sporty good looks, forgiving ride quality without sacrificing road feel and handling precision, punchy acceleration on turbo models.

**Cons:** Interior more Subaru than Saab, lacks premium features like a navigation system and stability control.

**What's New:** The 9-2X is an all-new sport wagon from Saab. Sporty and versatile, it shares its platform and mechanicals with Subaru's Impreza wagon.

*Crash Test Scores, see pg 530*
*Warranty information, see pg 542*

## Specifications

| Engine/Drivetrain | HP | Torque | EPA Fuel Economy Rating |
|---|---|---|---|
| 4cyl 2.5L M | 165 | 166 | N/A |
| 4cyl 2.0L M | 227 | 217 | N/A |

## Body Styles

| Style | MSRP Range |
|---|---|
| Compact Wagon | $22,990–$26,950 |

**Introduction:** It's no secret that plenty of cars on the road are conceived from another automotive company's parts bin. It seems every company is financially connected to at least one or two others, and with General Motors as its parent company, Saab is no exception. This connection ties Saab to Subaru of America, as GM holds a 20-percent stake in Fuji Heavy Industries, Subaru's parent company. Consequently, when Saab decided to expand its short model lineup, it looked no further than Subaru's successful Impreza sport wagon. Saab's version of the Impreza, the 9-2X sport wagon, is an important addition to the Swedish automaker's two-car portfolio, providing an affordable model geared toward young, active buyers. Simply borrowing the car from Subaru allowed Saab to bring the 9-2X to market that much quicker. Make no mistake, Saab sales haven't been suffering as of late (2003 saw an all-time retail sales record), but as Saab's CEO pointed out, the company also can't allow any more buyers to pass on its limited lineup in favor of a model that it doesn't produce. The new Saab 9-2X has been positioned to seize these new sales opportunities, entering the lineup price-wise below the 9-3 models. The "X" denotes a standard all-wheel-drive system, a main selling point and core Subaru product characteristic. Available only as a wagon, the 9-2X's exterior lines have been smoothed to reduce the Impreza's edgier look. The front and rear treatments are unique to Saab, including the tailgate, spoiler and wraparound lights. Standard 16-inch alloy wheels with 205/55R16 all-season tires were designed exclusively for the 9-2X. In an effort to give the 9-2X upscale dash in place of the Impreza's flash, you won't find any Saabs in Subaru's signature Rally Blue paint; instead look for more refined color options including a dark navy blue. As with the Impreza, two engines are available for the 9-2X: a naturally aspirated, 2.5-liter horizontally opposed four-cylinder rated for 165 horsepower on the base Linear model, and a 227-hp turbocharged 2.0-liter four on the Aero. Discerning buyers will recognize the latter engine as the spunky Impreza WRX power plant. A five-speed manual transmission comes standard on both the Linear and Aero, while both can be optioned out with a four-speed automatic. With a starting price of $22,990 for the 9-2X Linear and $26,950 for the Aero model, some might wonder if Saab has performed enough of an Impreza transformation to encourage buyers to pay the premium. But the company has added a few enticing extras: a four-year/50,000-mile warranty over the three-year/36,000-mile offer from Subaru, plus two years of no-charge scheduled maintenance to sweeten the deal. If you've ever been interested in the Impreza wagon's blend of performance and practicality but wished that it could be delivered in a more refined package, the 9-2X isn't a bad way to go.

**Body Styles, Trim Levels and Options:** The 9-2X is available as a four-door wagon only in two trims, Linear and Aero. Standard items on the Linear include a 16-inch alloy wheels, rear roof spoiler, tinted glass, cloth sport seats, a height-adjustable driver seat, manual air conditioning, full power accessories and a four-speaker, single-CD sound system. Step up to Aero and the goodie bag swells to include metallic-framed gauges; a leather-wrapped steering wheel, shift knob and handbrake; automatic climate control; a cabin air filter; front foglamps; and a six-

For the latest full vehicle reports, visit www.edmunds.com/bginfopak

# 2005 Saab 9-2X

speaker stereo with an in-dash CD changer. Options include 17-inch twin alloy wheels, leather seats, seat heaters, xenon headlights, de-icing wipers and a moonroof.

**Powertrains and Performance:** Two engines are available for the 9-2X: a naturally aspirated, 2.5-liter horizontally opposed four-cylinder rated for 165 horsepower on the base Linear model, and a 227-hp turbocharged 2.0-liter four on the Aero. Subaru fans will recognize the latter engine as the Impreza WRX power plant. A five-speed manual transmission comes standard on both the Linear and Aero, while a four-speed automatic is optional. All-wheel drive is standard across both trims.

**Safety:** Four-wheel antilock disc brakes and side airbags for front occupants are standard on every 9-2X. Also standard are active front head restraints, which help protect against whiplash in the event of a rear-impact collision.

**Interior Design and Special Features:** Inside, the 9-2X boasts design that's sporty and youth-oriented, with bold colors, faux-aluminum trim and a high-contrast palette. The front seats are comfortable and supportive; however, the optional leather upholstery can feel a bit slippery during aggressive cornering. The dashboard is essentially Subaru-issue, but Saab used different plastics for the center stack to give it a slightly different look. A 60/40-split-folding rear seat is at the ready, should you have the need to stow bulky cargo. Maximum cargo capacity is 62 cubic feet -- about the same as an Audi A4 wagon.

**Driving Impressions:** The 9-2X rides much like an Impreza, but the Subaru's extra stiffness has been softened just a bit for the Saab, thanks to retuned springs, shock absorbers and bushings. The gentler ride should be appreciated by most buyers, and the suspension still provides enough road feel and roll control to make the car fun to toss around on back roads. The steering ratio has also been adjusted to provide better control in tighter turns, and the 9-2X proves to be a sharp, precise implement in these situations. Additionally, Saab increased the sound insulation in its sport wagon, which gives the 9-2X a quieter cruising demeanor than the Impreza. The base engine in the Linear provides ample get-up-and-go for everyday driving, but it can feel a bit sluggish during highway passing maneuvers, especially with the automatic transmission. Slight turbo lag results in soft power delivery down low on the Aero model, but once you hit 3,000 rpm, the car jets forth with a fervor unmatched by any other car in the Saab lineup.

## Competitive Vehicles

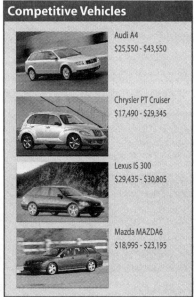

Audi A4
$25,550 - $43,550

Chrysler PT Cruiser
$17,490 - $29,345

Lexus IS 300
$29,435 - $30,805

Mazda MAZDA6
$18,995 - $23,195

# 2005 Saab 9-7X

Midsize SUV

**MSRP Price Range**

## N/A

Destination Charge: N/A (all styles)

| Ratings | | |
|---|---|---|
| Consumer Rating | N/A | |
| Editors Rating | N/A | |

**What Edmunds.com says:** Numerous upgrades give Saab a convincing argument that the 9-7X is more than a rebadged TrailBlazer, but discriminating customers may sniff out this Swedish import's Ohio roots.

**Pros:** Tightly controlled handling, long list of standard luxury features, strong lineup of engines.

**Cons:** Attempts to disguise its domestic origins not altogether successful, hard to justify price premium over Buick and GMC cousins, no stability control.

**What's New:** This all-new SUV from Saab is the Swedish automaker's attempt to tap the distinctly American thirst for large four-wheel-drive family vehicles.

**Introduction:** Conceived to be a key part of Saab's aggressive redevelopment of its product line, the 9-7X aims to attract new customers to its lineup and more importantly keep current Saab owners in the Swedish automaker's family. Saab's market research showed that 39 percent of Saab owners in the U.S. currently have an SUV in their household, while 30 percent of its customers who leave the brand do so to purchase a four-door SUV. In an attempt to keep its claim as the fastest growing European premium car brand in the U.S., Saab desperately needed an SUV to stem the exodus. In the rush to get the 9-7X to market, Saab used the same platform that underpins the Buick Rainier, Chevrolet TrailBlazer and GMC Envoy. The fact that the 9-7X is based on General Motor's midsize SUV platform doesn't make it a completely new vehicle, but extensive modifications to the suspension tuning, exterior styling and interior trim were made to give the 9-7X a look and feel that's uniquely Saab. To achieve this lofty goal, plenty of overtime hours were spent trying to distance the 9-7X's exterior looks from its American cousins. The trademark three-port grille, European-styled headlamps and wraparound rear-quarter windows find their way into the design. Saab stylists also made sure that the profile was clean and uninterrupted, without big bumper offsets or protruding shapes to give the 9-7X a distinctly European flavor. Achieving the road feel of a European sedan using an American truck chassis is no small task, but Saab appears to have made the kind of changes that will yield a responsive SUV. Engineers stiffened the front frame and installed firmer bushings, thicker sway bars and revalved shock absorbers to achieve more stable and responsive handling than the GM-badged versions offer. The 9-7X also uses a quicker 18.5-to-1 steering ratio with street-oriented 18-inch wheels and tires to give it a more sedanlike feel. All-wheel drive and an electronically controlled rear air suspension round out the package. Unfortunately, there are no traditional Saab turbocharged engines available. Instead, the 9-7X comes with either a standard 275-horsepower, 4.2-liter inline six or the optional 300-hp, 5.3-liter V8. Coupled to both of these engines is a four-speed automatic transmission. The Saab 97X comfortably seats five adults. Like most luxury SUVs, the 9-7X comes standard with all the latest amenities including heated leather seats, automatic climate control, a driver information computer, wood accents and the OnStar satellite communications system. It holds up to 41.0 cubic feet of cargo space with the rear seat back up and 80.1 cubic feet with the seat back folded down. A 60/40-split rear bench seat is standard as is a trailer hitch receiver and hitch receiver cover. This faux import comes all the way from the Nordic lands of Moraine, Ohio. While we like what the 9-7X offers in principle, we're not sure that Saab's traditional clientele of highly educated people with discriminating tastes will want to buy a domestically made GM knockoff.

*Crash Test Scores, see pg 530*
*Warranty information, see pg 542*

| Specifications | | | |
|---|---|---|---|
| Engine/Drivetrain | HP | Torque | EPA Fuel Economy Rating |
| 8cyl 5.3L A | 300 | 360 | N/A |
| 6cyl 4.2L A | 275 | 275 | N/A |

| Body Styles | |
|---|---|
| Style | MSRP Range |
| **Midsize SUV** | N/A |

**Body Styles, Trim Levels and Options:** The 9-7X is a midsize four-door SUV that seats five and comes in one trim level. Standard equipment includes 18-inch alloy wheels with Dunlop all-season tires, all-wheel drive, an anti-theft system, leather upholstery, power-adjustable front seats, automatic climate control, an MP3-compatible CD player, front foglights, the

OnStar communications system and no-charge scheduled maintenance for three years or 36,000 miles. Optional equipment includes a rear DVD player with a flip-down screen for rear passengers, a DVD-based navigation system, high-intensity discharge headlights, a sunroof, an in-dash CD changer and satellite radio. Available optional packages include a Convenience Package with adjustable pedals and headlamp washers, as well as a Protection Package with body-side molding and front skid plates.

**Powertrains and Performance:** Being very un-Saab-like, there are no turbocharged power plants available for the 9-7X. Your choice of power comes from either a 275-horsepower, 4.2-liter inline six or a 300-hp, 5.3-liter V8. Coupled to these engines is an electronically controlled four-speed automatic transmission.

**Safety:** Saab packs all the safety features into the 9-7X you'd expect in a Swedish vehicle. Fourwheel ABS, an all-wheel-drive system, dual-stage frontal airbags, a rollover sensing system, daytime running lights and side curtain airbags are standard. The 9-7X has not been crash tested, but the Chevrolet TrailBlazer on which it's based received three stars out of five in NHTSA frontal crash tests for the driver and front passenger and five stars for side-impact protection. The IIHS rated it "Marginal" (second lowest) after conducting its offset frontal impact test.

**Interior Design and Special Features:** Saab drivers will feel right at home in the 9-7X's interior. Traditional brand distinctive design elements such as the instrument panel's cockpit-inspired center stack and driver-oriented controls will be instantly recognizable by aficionados. Wood grain trim on the dash and contrasting seat upholstery and door inserts do their part to give the 9-7X the progressive upscale feel of other Saab models. And, of course, it just wouldn't be a Saab without the center console ignition switch. Those who look closer will see the cabin's GM roots, a resemblance that cheapens the 9-7X next to stylish rivals like the Volkswagen Touareg and Volvo XC90. Cargo capacity measures 41 cubic feet behind the rear seats and 80 cubes when they're folded.

**Driving Impressions:** Achieving the road feel of a European sedan using an American truck chassis is no small task, but Saab has made the kind of changes that will yield a responsive SUV. The 9-7X's stiffened front frame and reworked suspension give it more stable and responsive handling than any of its GM counterparts. Both the standard inline six and optional V8 provide more than ample power, but neither has the refinement of Saab's homegrown turbocharged engines.

## Competitive Vehicles

Buick Rainier
$35,080 - $36,905

Lexus RX330
$35,775 - $37,175

Mercury Mountaineer
$29,685 - $38,530

Volkswagen Touareg
$37,140 - $58,490

# 2005 Saturn Relay

**MSRP Price Range**

## $23,770 - $29,855

Destination Charge: N/A (all styles)

### Ratings

| | | |
|---|---|---|
| Consumer Rating | N/A | |
| Editors Rating | 6.9 | |

**What Edmunds.com says:** Though the Relay features a slick interior and distinctive styling, it doesn't have the on-road finesse of its minivan competitors.

**Pros:** Smooth ride and handling, lots of nifty interior storage spaces, innovative multimedia storage system, available all-wheel drive.

**Cons:** Engine power and refinement not up to class leaders, no side curtain airbags.

**What's New:** The Relay is an all-new "crossover sport van." Think of it as a minivan with an SUV-like front end.

*Crash Test Scores, see pg 530*
*Warranty information, see pg 542*

### Specifications

| Engine/Drivetrain | HP | Torque | EPA Fuel Economy Rating |
|---|---|---|---|
| 6cyl 3.5L A | 200 | 220 | 19 city/27 hwy |

### Body Styles

| Style | MSRP Range |
|---|---|
| Midsize Minivan | $23,770 - $29,855 |

**Introduction:** The Relay is Saturn's first minivan and it marks a kind of departure for the carmaker. Since the brand's introduction, GM has billed Saturn as "a different kind of car company" and for the most part it has stayed true to that formula. With the introduction of the Relay, GM is showing that it is not afraid to bring Saturn a little closer to the fold in order to provide vehicles that family-oriented Saturn customers want. The Relay is Saturn's first all-steel paneled vehicle, and it's not going to be the brand's last. Saturn is calling the Relay a crossover sport van, but really it's a minivan that shares many of its mechanical components with other GM vans like the Chevrolet Uplander, Pontiac Montana SV6 and the more upscale Buick Terraza. Saturn hopes to capture buyers who want the versatility of a minivan but prefer the rugged looks of an SUV. Compared to typical minivans, the Relay takes on a taller stance with a longer, more angular nose. GM hopes the Relay will benefit from Saturn's image as an import fighter, citing the statistic that more than 40 percent of new minivan buyers look to imports for their purchase. The Relay also gives current Saturn owners a way to accommodate growing families without having to change brands -- a key selling point given Saturn's reputation for customer service and the no-haggle shopping experience. With its simple styling, the Relay stays true to the Saturn formula. More upscale-looking than other Saturns, the company's new van offers plenty of luxury along with the expected versatility. Inside, the Relay seats seven, and the fold-flat third-row seat offers a 50/50 split, allowing families to carry a mix of passengers and cargo. The interchangeable overhead console works on a rail system that allows owners to move, rearrange or add storage components as they see fit. In addition to the usual rear DVD entertainment system, the Relay is available with a PhatNoise mobile digital media system that allows owners to store thousands of MP3s and/or several dozen movies. Another convenient option is a 115-volt AC outlet for all manner of Game Cubes and PlayStations. Powered by a 3.5-liter V6, the Relay makes an adequate 200 horsepower. The van is also available with GM's Versatrak all-wheel-drive system as well as the StabiliTrak stability control system. We're not entirely sold on the whole "SUV/van" concept. To our jaded eyes, the Relay looks more like a minivan with a really big and flat front end. Subjective styling issues aside, the Relay offers budding families a myriad of interior features and a solid overall package, but still doesn't match the best-in-class offerings.

**Body Styles, Trim Levels and Options:** The Relay comes in one size and two trim levels, Relay 2 and Relay 3. Standard Relay 2 amenities include power windows, air conditioning, an eight-speaker sound system with a CD/MP3 player, a rear-seat DVD entertainment system, the OnStar communications system, cruise control and keyless entry. The Relay 3 adds rear air conditioning, a power driver seat, alloy wheels and upgraded storage. An all-wheel-drive system is available, and is bundled with a rear load-leveling suspension and front side-impact airbags. An optional PhatNoise mobile digital media system allows owners to store thousands of MP3s and/or several dozen movies on a removable hard drive cartridge. Other noteworthy

options include a remote vehicle startup system, a 115-volt AC outlet, dual power-sliding side doors, rear park assist, XM Satellite Radio, leather seats and a sport suspension.

**Powertrains and Performance:** All Relays come equipped with a 3.5-liter V6 that makes 200 horsepower and 220 pound-feet of torque. A four-speed automatic transmission is standard. No other powertrain combinations are available, though buyers can opt for all-wheel drive.

**Safety:** All models come standard with four-wheel antilock disc brakes. Side-impact airbags for front occupants and the StabiliTrak stability control system are optional. Full-length side curtain airbags are not available. The Relay has not yet been crash tested.

**Interior Design and Special Features:** The Relay seats seven, and the fold-flat third-row seat offers a 50/50 split. A pleasing two-tone color scheme with faux wood accents dramatically brightens the interior atmosphere of the van. Folding center trays (with cupholders) between the first- and second-row seats are available. An overhead rail system provides rear-seat access to climate and entertainment functions, and can be outfitted with various storage containers. A rear-seat DVD entertainment system is standard on all Relays, and can be upgraded with infrared wireless headphones. A remote vehicle start system, pioneered on the 2004 Chevy Malibu, is optional.

**Driving Impressions:** The V6 power plant is down on power compared to its competitors, but it still manages to provide adequate acceleration. The Relay's suspension is on the soft side, though upgrading to the optional sport suspension does provide for more responsive handling.

## Competitive Vehicles

Dodge Grand Caravan
$20,205 - $26,505

Honda Odyssey
$24,995 - $38,295

Nissan Quest
$23,350 - $32,250

Toyota Sienna
$23,225 - $37,495

# 2005 Scion tC

**Compact Coupe**

**MSRP Price Range**

## $15,950 - $16,750
Destination Charge: $515 (all styles)

#1 Editors' Rating

### Ratings

| | | |
|---|---|---|
| Consumer Rating | 9.3 | |
| Editors Rating | 8.4 | |

**What Edmunds.com says:** With a price tag under $17,000, a ton of standard features and a fun-loving personality, we'd bet that the tC is going to be another big hit for the Scion folks.

**Pros:** High quality all around, unexpected safety and luxury features, tight handling, spacious cabin, bargain price.

**Cons:** A couple of odd design elements, drab interior color.

**What's New:** The tC coupe is the latest addition to Toyota's innovative Scion division.

**Introduction:** With the Scion brand, Toyota is making a credible effort to understand the Generation Y market and give it what it wants without pushing it down its throat. Housed within Toyota dealerships, Scion salespeople are instructed to play it straight with consumers -- this means no-haggle pricing similar to Saturn dealers and the ability to get a car the way a customer wants it in about a week. And by offering over three dozen dealer-installed options, Scion hopes to give its buyers unprecedented opportunity to customize their cars on the front end. Unlike the xA and xB, which look like they could've come out of a comic book (and we mean that in a good way -- we like their funky yet practical style), the tC is a more mainstream design. Somehow managing to look a little pudgy yet sleek at the same time, the tC has a generic rectangular grille, headlamps with BMW-like "eyebrows" and a body that boasts crisp, clean lines. Still, there are a few head-turning elements. One is the deeply tinted glass panoramic roof that features a power sunroof above the front seats and a fixed glass portion above the rear compartment. Another is the set of double-spoke, 17-inch alloy wheels that look as good as anything in the aftermarket. Both of these high-end features are standard. Inside the upscale cabin, high-quality materials abound, and features such as metallic accents, damped compartment doors, multiple adjustments for the driver seat and an outside temperature display further this impression. An elegant "waterfall"-style center stack flows into the center console, and both front seats slide forward to allow folks to get into the backseat. On the move, the tC feels eager to run thanks to its standard 2.4-liter inline four-cylinder engine. Borrowed from the Camry, this is a big engine for this class of car, where 1.7 to 2.2 liters is more the norm. With 160 horsepower and 163 pound-feet of torque, the tC's motor handily beats what you'll find in cars like the Civic EX coupe (127 hp and 114 lb-ft), Saturn Ion (140 hp and 145 lb-ft) and VW Golf (115 hp and 122 lb-ft). Out in the real world, the tC's performance makes good on the promise of the spec sheet numbers. A broad power band means that there's strong pull down low and through the midrange, and when coupled to the sweet-shifting five-speed manual gearbox, the tC feels sportier than one might expect. Priced under $17,000, the tC should be yet another hit for Scion. After all, there's the strong Toyota reputation, the spacious and comfortable cabin, fine build quality, entertaining driving dynamics and plenty of standard niceties. Add in the ability to customize with your own personal touch and there's plenty to like about this affordable coupe.

**Body Styles, Trim Levels and Options:** Like the other Scion models, the tC comes in one trim level and is chock-full of unexpected goodies such as one-touch up-and-down power windows, cruise control, air conditioning, keyless entry, mirror-mounted turn signal lights, four-wheel antilock disc brakes and a 160-watt Pioneer sound system with CD player that is (XM) satellite radio-ready. The only factory option is a side airbag package, but there is a multitude of dealer-installed options. This list includes a CD changer, satellite radio, a subwoofer and a lighting kit for the footwell, just to name a few.

*Crash Test Scores, see pg 530*
*Warranty information, see pg 542*

### Specifications

| Engine/Drivetrain | HP | Torque | EPA Fuel Economy Rating |
|---|---|---|---|
| 4cyl 2.4L A/M | 160 | 163 | 23 city/30 hwy |

### Body Styles

| Style | MSRP Range |
|---|---|
| Compact Coupe | $15,950–$16,750 |

**Powertrains and Performance:** Standard power comes from a 2.4-liter inline four-cylinder borrowed from the Camry, with 160 hp and 163 lb-ft of torque. A smooth-shifting five-speed manual gearbox is standard, with a four-speed automatic available as an option. Fuel economy is estimated at 22 mpg city and 29 mpg highway with the manual, and 23 city and 30 highway with the optional automatic.

**Safety:** The tC comes with four-wheel antilock disc brakes (with Electronic Brakeforce Distribution) as standard equipment. Side airbags for front occupants and full-length head curtain airbags are optional. Other standard safety features include a first aid kit, triple side door beams and a driver knee airbag.

**Interior Design and Special Features:** Although the tC is a compact car at just 174 inches long (about the same length as a Honda Civic coupe), a relatively long (106.3-inch) wheelbase provides more than ample legroom, especially for those riding in the back. Rear passengers will also enjoy the split seat backs that can individually recline up to 45 degrees. Although it looks like a coupe, the tC is actually a hatchback, which means flexible cargo capacity. By folding down the rear seats as well as the right front seat, a load floor that stretches 103.6 inches is created, ideal for snowboarders and surfers. Cargo capacity is 12.8 cubic feet with the rear seats in use and a whopping 60 cubic feet when they're folded down.

**Driving Impressions:** The tC features a fully independent suspension (with a double-wishbone setup in the rear that maximizes interior space) and the same tires that are on the Lexus IS 300 -- Z-rated 215/45R17 Bridgestone Potenzas wrapped around those eye-catching 17s. The result is a precise, well-weighted feel and flat, composed cornering. Ride quality is firm, but compliant enough to absorb most bumps and ruts on battered city streets. The 2.4-liter engine's broad power band contributes to the fun with plenty of pull down low and through the midrange.

## Competitive Vehicles

Honda Civic
$13,010 - $20,650

Hyundai Tiburon
$16,999 - $20,497

MINI Cooper
$16,449 - $19,899

Saturn ION Red Line
$20,385

# 2005 Subaru Legacy

**Midsize Sedan, Wagon**

**MSRP Price Range**

## $21,295 - $30,995
Destination Charge: $575 (all styles)

**#1** Editors' Rating

## Ratings

| | | |
|---|---|---|
| Consumer Rating | 9.4 | |
| Editors Rating | 8.7 | |

**What Edmunds.com says:** A tight chassis, a turbocharged engine and a slick cockpit have transformed the all-wheel-drive Legacy into a serious driver's car. Whether you're an enthusiast in need of four doors or a safety-conscious parent in need of some fun, this one is worth a try.

**Pros:** Don't have to pay extra for all-wheel drive, generous standard equipment list, top-notch build and materials quality, excellent power in GT models, great highway ride, sharp handling.

**Cons:** Stability control not available, smaller backseat than most competitors, so-so stereo offerings.

**What's New:** An all-new and vastly improved Legacy is introduced in sedan and wagon body styles. Topping the list of upgrades are a 250-horsepower turbocharged engine, a stylish new interior and a full menu of airbags.

*Crash Test Scores, see pg 530*
*Warranty information, see pg 542*

## Specifications

| Engine/Drivetrain | HP | Torque | EPA Fuel Economy Rating |
|---|---|---|---|
| 4cyl 2.5L A/M | 250 | 250 | N/A |
| 4cyl 2.5L A/M | 168 | 166 | 23 city/30 hwy |

## Body Styles

| Style | MSRP Range |
|---|---|
| Midsize Sedan | $21,295–$29,795 |
| Midsize Wagon | $22,295–$30,995 |

**Introduction:** Known primarily as the wagon that spawned the Outback, the Legacy is the oldest nameplate in the Subaru lineup, dating back to 1990. In recent years, it has been living in the shadow of its armored-wagon offspring. Starved for power and features, the 2000-2004 Legacy wagon was what you bought if you couldn't afford one of Volkswagen's expensive Passat 4Motion wagons, and/or you wouldn't be caught dead in a Taurus. The sedan, meanwhile, offered a winter-friendly alternative to the Accord and Camry, but had little else to distinguish it in the cutthroat family sedan segment. Happily, Subaru has given buyers more reasons to consider its midsize sedan and wagon for 2005: The redesigned Legacy has slimmed down, powered up and slipped into some more stylish threads. Some of the biggest news is under the hood, as GT models feature a modified version of the WRX STi's 2.5-liter turbocharged engine rated for 250 horsepower and 250 lb-ft of torque. Although the continued absence of six-cylinder power in the Legacy might seem like a blow, rest assured that you won't miss it. The turbo four responds with the heart and refinement of a much larger steed. Meanwhile, power delivery rivals V6 engines for smoothness, and the engine is quiet at cruising speeds. For buyers on a tighter budget, Subaru continues to offer a naturally aspirated 2.5-liter four-cylinder. Output has not improved by much; horsepower maxes out at 168 (163 in PZEV-mandated states like California). You can however expect better acceleration this year, as all Legacys lost roughly 100 pounds in the redesign, thanks to the increased use of lighter, stronger materials like aluminum. Additionally, engineers fiddled with the gearing to improve the shift response of the automatic transmission. All-wheel drive remains a staple of the 2005 Legacy lineup, but this is no longer a vehicle that will appeal only to those living in cold climates. Subaru's midsize car has always been known for its fine handling, but this time around the company wanted it behave to like a sporty entry-luxury car. Accordingly, both the sedan and wagon ride beautifully on the highway, while providing a high level of entertainment on twisty back roads. Style and luxury were never within the previous Legacy's grasp, but no apologies need be made for the new cockpits, which are some of the best-looking designs in this price range. They don't break any new ground in styling, but one can't help but like the symmetrical dash design, convincing faux aluminum trim, electroluminescent gauges and three-spoke Momo steering wheel found in GT models. Materials quality is excellent -- you could buy a Legacy and feel like you got a VW. Everything about the way the new Legacy looks, feels and drives is so much more cohesive and satisfying than before. Don't buy a TSX or Mazda 6 without trying this Subaru first.

**Body Styles, Trim Levels and Options:** The Legacy comes in sedan and wagon body styles in either 2.5i or 2.5 GT trim. A Limited Package is available on both trim levels. The 2.5i comes with the base 2.5-liter engine and offers such standard equipment as 16-inch alloy wheels, body-color door handles and moldings, air conditioning, a six-speaker CD stereo, cruise control, a trip computer, tweed upholstery, keyless entry and, on wagons only, roof rails and a cargo cover. Opt for the Limited package and you'll get larger front brakes, a power driver

For the latest full vehicle reports, visit www.edmunds.com/bginfopak

seat, leather upholstery, a leather-wrapped steering wheel, heated seats and mirrors, a wiper de-icer, an in-dash CD changer, dual-zone automatic climate control and dual moonroofs (the sedan gets a single large moonroof). Upgrade to the 2.5 GT and you get a turbocharged engine, along with 17-inch wheels, more powerful brakes, a functional hood scoop, sport seats, a Momo steering wheel and electroluminescent gauges. You'll need to order the Limited Package to get a power driver seat, leather upholstery and a moonroof on the GT.

**Powertrains and Performance:** The 2.5i model is powered by a 2.5-liter horizontally opposed four-cylinder engine that makes 168 horsepower (163 in PZEV-mandated states) and 166 lb-ft of torque. The 2.5 GT uses a 2.5-liter turbocharged engine rated for 250 hp and 250 lb-ft of torque. Either engine can be equipped with a five-speed manual transmission. The 2.5i is eligible for a four-speed automatic while the GT gets a five-speed auto; both come with an automanual mode. All-wheel drive is standard across the board.

**Safety:** All Legacys have four-wheel antilock disc brakes with Electronic Brakeforce Distribution. Stability control is, unfortunately, not available. Front side-impact airbags and full-length side curtain airbags are also standard on all models. The front-seat head restraints feature dynamic whiplash protection.

**Interior Design and Special Features:** Some of the biggest improvements this year are in the cabin. One can't help but like the clean dash design and the convincing faux aluminum trim, not to mention the red-and-white gauges and three-spoke Momo steering wheel in GT models. Build and materials quality is excellent. The front seats offer an optimum blend of cushioning and support. While the backseat is comfortable for two passengers, shoulder room and legroom are still pretty tight for this class. Sedans have an 11.4-cubic-foot trunk with a ski pass-through. The wagon offers 33.5 cubic feet of capacity behind its rear seats and 66 cubes when they're folded.

**Driving Impressions:** The Legacy offers a superb blend of ride comfort and handling acuity. The GT is easily as much fun as an Acura TSX or Mazda 6, and with the confidence of all four wheels putting power to the pavement, this Subaru is a satisfying substitute for the smaller, more expensive Audi A4. The base engine provides adequate acceleration, but serious drivers will want to go for the turbo motor and its vast reserves of lag-free power -- trust us, you won't miss having a V6.

## Competitive Vehicles

Acura TSX
$26,490 - $28,490

Audi A4
$25,550 - $43,550

Chevrolet Malibu Maxx
$21,600 - $24,100

Dodge Magnum
$21,870 - $31,370

# 2005 Subaru Outback
**Midsize Sedan, Wagon**

**MSRP Price Range**
## $24,295 - $33,495
Destination Charge: $575 (all styles)

### Ratings

| | | |
|---|---|---|
| Consumer Rating | 9.4 | |
| Editors Rating | 8.1 | |

**What Edmunds.com says:** Solid all-terrain capability, nimble handling, a varied engine lineup and a luxurious interior make the Outback an excellent all-weather family vehicle. If you're thinking of buying a traditional SUV, you may find this Subaru a better fit.

**Pros:** Standard all-wheel drive, generous standard equipment list, exemplary build and materials quality, strong power from turbo and H6 engines, balanced ride and handling dynamics, capable performance off-road.

**Cons:** Desirable features reserved for top-line models, smaller backseat than most competitors.

**What's New:** An all-new and vastly improved Outback is introduced in sedan and wagon body styles. Highlights include a new turbocharged engine, a stronger H6 motor, a stylish new interior and increased ground clearance for more serious off-highway adventures.

*Crash Test Scores, see pg 530*
*Warranty information, see pg 542*

### Specifications

| Engine/Drivetrain | HP | Torque | EPA Fuel Economy Rating |
|---|---|---|---|
| 6cyl 3.0L A | 250 | 219 | N/A |
| 4cyl 2.5L A/M | 250 | 250 | N/A |
| 4cyl 2.5L A/M | 168 | 166 | N/A |

### Body Styles

| Style | MSRP Range |
|---|---|
| Midsize Sedan | $31,760 |
| Midsize Wagon | $24,295–$33,495 |

**Introduction:** We've been fans of the Outback since its inception. Little did Subaru know that back in 1995, when the Japanese automaker introduced a gussied-up Legacy Wagon called the Outback, that it was about to revolutionize the way Americans thought of sport-utility vehicles. Essentially a trim package that included gray trim, white-lettered tires and a catchy name, the Outback became a phenomenon in 1996 after it was billed "The World's First Sport-Utility Wagon." That's the year Subaru raised the suspension, added large headlight-size foglights and boosted power. Yet one of the earliest and best alternatives to SUV ownership has lost its edge in recent years. Traditional SUVs are more refined and suburb-friendly than they used to be, and by the 2004 model year, the Outback was surrounded by a population of crossover SUVs that could do most of what it did, while offering more room for growing families. For 2005, Subaru will give buyers more reasons to choose its all-terrain wagon and sedan as the redesigned Outback has slimmed down, powered up and slipped into some more stylish digs. Like the Legacy, the Outback takes on a sleeker, more angular look this year, but it has a more aggressive grille, raised hood strakes and, on the wagon, dark tinted rear glass. Additionally, Subaru has decided that buyers are no longer so enthusiastic about the "just in from the woods" aesthetic of the original Outbacks, so all models wear black-letter tires instead of the expected white-letter sidewalls. There's also a longer list of monochromatic paint choices. In spite of its more upscale look, the Outback is actually more rugged than ever before. Ground clearance ranges from 8.4 to 8.7 inches depending on the model you choose -- previously, the tallest Outback stood just 7.9 inches off the ground. Inside, the cockpit has a much more cohesive look along with a classy two-tone ensemble. Meanwhile, there's some big news under the hood. A modified version of the WRX STi's 2.5-liter turbocharged engine with 250 horsepower and 250 lb-ft of torque has joined the lineup. Not only is it a more affordable alternative to the pricey H6, with more torque and an available manual transmission, it's the faster of the two and an obvious choice for weekend enthusiasts. For those who prefer the smoothness of six cylinders, the H6 motor picks up variable valve timing and lift this year so that it, too, is up to 250 hp. For those on a budget, Subaru will continue to offer a naturally aspirated 2.5-liter, four-cylinder engine as well. The 2005 Outback is a wagon with no equal when it comes to off-road capability and, with an upgraded engine lineup and sharpened reflexes, you'll find it fun to drive even when the weather isn't terrible. A small backseat will keep it from competing with larger-capacity SUVs, but for the family of four looking for stylish transportation for all seasons, it could be a perfect fit.

**Body Styles, Trim Levels and Options:** The Outback is available as a wagon or sedan. Wagons come in 2.5i, 2.5 XT, 3.0 R L.L. Bean and 3.0 R VDC Limited. Limited Packages are available on 2.5i and 2.5 XT models. The Outback sedan is available in a single 3.0 R trim. The 2.5i models include 16-inch alloy wheels, air conditioning, a CD player, a power driver seat, cruise control, trip computer and a rear limited-slip differential. Opt for the Limited package and you'll get heated leather seats, a wiper de-icer, a CD changer, dual-zone automatic climate control and

dual moonroofs (the sedan gets a single large moonroof). Upgrade to the 2.5 XT and you get 17-inch wheels, bigger brakes, sport seats, a Momo steering wheel, metallic interior trim and electroluminescent gauges. You'll need to order the Limited Package to get leather upholstery and a moonroof on XT models. The 3.0 models come with a full load of luxury amenities, as well as a tire pressure monitoring system, steering wheel audio controls and mahogany trim; wagons have a fold-down rear armrest. The L.L. Bean model offers perforated leather upholstery, while the VDC wagon is your ticket to stability control and an upgraded stereo.

**Powertrains and Performance:** The 2.5i model is powered by a 2.5-liter horizontally opposed four-cylinder engine that makes 168 horsepower (163 in PZEV states). The 2.5 XT upgrades to a 2.5-liter turbocharged engine with 250 horsepower and 250 lb-ft of torque. The 3.0 models come with a 3.0-liter horizontally opposed six-cylinder (H6); horsepower comes in at 250 while torque maxes out at 219 lb-ft. Either 2.5-liter engine can be equipped with a five-speed manual transmission. A four-speed automatic is available on 2.5i models while 2.5 XT models get a five-speed auto; both come with an automanual mode. The H6 is only available with the five-speed automatic.

**Safety:** All Outbacks have four-wheel antilock disc brakes with Electronic Brakeforce Distribution. Front side-impact airbags and full-length side curtain airbags are also standard. Stability control is reserved only for the top-line 3.0 R VDC Limited wagon. The front head restraints feature dynamic whiplash protection.

**Interior Design and Special Features:** Inside, you can't help but like the clean dash design and the three-spoke Momo steering wheel in XT and 3.0 models. Turbo models have darker interiors with sporty metallic trim, while 3.0 models get matte-finish wood grain trim on the console that matches the real mahogany trim on the steering wheel. The seats are supportive, but the backseat is still a bit tight for adults. Wagons provide 33.5 cubic feet of capacity behind their rear seats; 66 cubes with the seats folded down.

**Driving Impressions:** Out on the road, the '05 Outback rides smoothly and feels even more surefooted in the corners than its agile predecessor. Taken off-road, it can scamper up a rutted hillside with more gusto than just about any crossover SUV on the market. Although the base engine provides only adequate power, acceleration is quick with either the turbo four or the H6.

## Competitive Vehicles

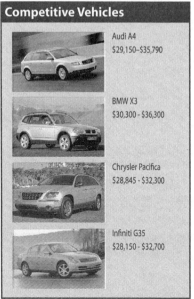

Audi A4
$29,150–$35,790

BMW X3
$30,300 - $36,300

Chrysler Pacifica
$28,845 - $32,300

Infiniti G35
$28,150 - $32,700

# 2005 Suzuki Forenza

**Compact Sedan, Wagon**

**MSRP Price Range**

## $13,449 - $17,949

Destination Charge: $545 (all styles)

### Ratings

| | | |
|---|---|---|
| Consumer Rating | N/A | |
| Editors Rating | 7.5 | |

**What Edmunds.com says:** Comfortable, well equipped and solidly built, the Forenza represents a good value for small car buyers on a budget.

**Pros:** Lots of standard features for the price, comfortable cabin with unexpected conveniences, solid construction, predictable handling.

**Cons:** Subpar fuel economy, similarly priced Aerio makes more power.

**What's New:** A versatile wagon model joins the lineup. Side airbags are now standard on all Forenzas.

**Introduction:** Ever close to General Motors, Suzuki is reaping the benefits of GM's purchase of Daewoo Motor Company. One of two new Suzukis introduced at the 2003 Chicago Auto Show, the Forenza compact sedan is essentially a replacement for the Daewoo Nubira sold in the U.S. from 1999 to 2002 and is built by GM Daewoo Auto & Technology Company in South Korea. Suzuki has long been a back marker in the race to build good, affordable compact cars, but a recent effort that yielded the Aerio sedan and wagon showed that the company is giving it a serious try. In the midst of the highly competitive economy sedan segment, Suzuki's homegrown and distinctive-looking Aerio is a decent car that beckons buyers with a powerful four-cylinder engine, available all-wheel drive and a spacious interior. Knowing this, one can't help but wonder if the segment has room for yet another entry, as solid offerings from Ford, Honda, Hyundai, Mazda, Mitsubishi, Nissan and Toyota make it tough for newcomers to gain a foothold. Suzuki sets the Forenza apart with European-inspired styling penned by Italian designer Pininfarina, a roomy interior and a host of standard features. To our eyes, the Forenza's sheet metal does little to distinguish it from other economy cars, but it's certainly inoffensive. Where features are concerned, the Forenza scores highly, as even the base model comes with body-color bumpers and door handles; four-wheel disc brakes; a height-adjustable driver seat; a padded center armrest; air conditioning; side airbags; an eight-speaker, 140-watt stereo with a CD player and steering-wheel audio controls; and power windows, mirrors and locks. For power, the Forenza offers a 2.0-liter, four-cylinder engine rated for 126 horsepower and 131 pound-feet of torque. Compare that to the Aerio, which starts only slightly higher up the price ladder than the least expensive Forenza and makes 155 hp. Nevertheless, the Forenza gets around as well as any Civic or Corolla and, when equipped with a manual transmission, rarely feels underpowered. Refinement is not a particular strong point of this engine, nor is fuel economy. With a mileage estimate of 22 mpg city/30 mpg highway, the Forenza is one of the thirstiest budget cars on the market. Driving dynamics are better that you might expect, as the Suzuki rides smoothly, handles predictably and stops well. Its reflexes are no match for those of the Ford Focus, Mazda 3 or even the Civic, but much like Hyundai's Elantra, the Forenza is well suited for Point-A-to-B driving. Without question, the Forenza is an important vehicle for Suzuki. And it has all the right features, along with a comfortable, solidly built cabin. The driving experience is fully acceptable as well -- the Forenza offers adequate power and confident handling. Finally, consider the price: The smallest Suzuki puts it all together for a sticker price no other economy car can touch, except perhaps the Hyundai Elantra and Kia Spectra. If value is your biggest priority in shopping for a small sedan or wagon, the Forenza is worth a test-drive.

**Body Styles, Trim Levels and Options:** The Forenza is available as a four-door sedan or a four-door wagon in one of three trim levels -- base S, midlevel LX or high-line EX. Even the S is well equipped, offering such features as body-color bumpers and door handles, four-wheel disc brakes, a height-adjustable driver seat, a padded center armrest, air conditioning, an eight-

*Crash Test Scores, see pg 530*
*Warranty information, see pg 542*

### Specifications

| Engine/Drivetrain | HP | Torque | EPA Fuel Economy Rating |
|---|---|---|---|
| 4cyl 2.0L A/M | 126 | 131 | 22 city/30 hwy |

### Body Styles

| Style | MSRP Range |
|---|---|
| Compact Sedan | $13,449–$17,449 |
| Compact Wagon | $13,949–$17,949 |

For the latest full vehicle reports, visit www.edmunds.com/bginfopak

# 2005 Suzuki Forenza

speaker stereo with a CD player, steering-wheel audio controls and power windows, mirrors and locks. Next up is the LX, which adds alloy wheels, foglights, a leather-wrapped steering wheel and shift knob, a sunroof, cruise control and a remote keyless entry system. The top-level EX adds leather seats and a standard four-speed automatic transmission.

**Powertrains and Performance:** The Forenza comes with only one engine -- a 2.0-liter 16-valve, DOHC, inline four-cylinder making 126 horsepower and 131 pound-feet of torque. A five-speed manual transmission is standard on S and LX models. A four-speed automatic is standard on the top-level EX and optional on the other trim levels.

**Safety:** Side airbags and four-wheel disc brakes are standard, and ABS with Electronic Brakeforce Distribution is optional on all trim levels. Dual-stage airbags and daytime running lights are also standard. In government crash tests, the Forenza earned four stars (out of five) for frontal impact protection. In side-impact tests, it earned three stars for the front and rear, but this year's standard side airbags should increase the protection up front.

**Interior Design and Special Features:** To liven things up a bit, designers used plenty of metallic accents throughout the cabin and an attractive set of gauges. Several features not normally found on a car in this price range include cabin air filtration and an eight-speaker, 140-watt stereo with steering wheel-mounted audio controls. The driver seat is well contoured, and thanks to its two-way seat-bottom tilt, most people will be able to find a comfortable driving position. A padded center armrest provides a comfortable place to rest an elbow on long trips. In the backseat, the accommodations aren't the roomiest of the economy car class, but anyone under 6 feet tall should be OK on short trips. The rear seat offers a 60/40-split-folding arrangement and sedan trunk capacity comes in at 12.4 cubic feet. The wagon offers 24.4 cubic feet.

**Driving Impressions:** Although 126 hp doesn't sound like much these days, the Forenza has no difficulty keeping up in traffic, and if you equip it with the manual gearbox, you'll rarely wish for more power. You may wish for more refinement and better gas mileage, though. Ride quality is smooth over most surfaces, while handling is soft yet predictable in the corners. More expensive economy cars offer more in the way of behind-the-wheel entertainment and overall polish, but the Forenza is well suited for buyers who want a low-priced sedan that can take on the daily commute without fuss.

## Competitive Vehicles

Ford Focus
$13,230 - $18,130

Honda Civic
$13,160 - $20,650

Hyundai Elantra
$13,299 - $15,649

Mazda 3
$13,680 - $17,105

# 2005 Suzuki Reno

**Compact Hatchback/Sedan**

**MSRP Price Range**
## $13,449 - $17,449
Destination Charge: $545 (all styles)

### Ratings

| | | |
|---|---|---|
| Consumer Rating | N/A | |
| Editors Rating | 7.3 | |

**What Edmunds.com says:** Comfortable, well equipped and solidly built, the Reno represents a good value and provides a more youthful alternative to the Forenza wagon.

**Pros:** Lots of standard features for the price, comfortable cabin with unexpected conveniences, solid construction, predictable handling.

**Cons:** Unrefined powertrain, subpar fuel economy, similarly priced Aerio makes more power.

**What's New:** The Reno is an all-new car for 2005. Based on the Forenza, the Reno uses the same engine, transmission and underpinnings but adds a little attitude with a sleeker five-door hatchback body and a flashier interior design.

*Crash Test Scores, see pg 530*
*Warranty information, see pg 542*

### Specifications

| Engine/Drivetrain | HP | Torque | EPA Fuel Economy Rating |
|---|---|---|---|
| 4cyl 2.0L A/M | 126 | 131 | 22 city/30 hwy |

### Body Styles

| Style | MSRP Range |
|---|---|
| Compact Hatchback/Sedan | $13,449–$17,449 |

**Introduction:** The Suzuki Forenza sedan was introduced at the 2003 Chicago Auto Show, and since then it has impressed us with its generous package of amenities, comfortable interior and pleasant driving dynamics. For 2005, a wagon version joins the lineup, along with a sporty five-door hatchback called the Reno. While the Reno doesn't offer much in the way of mechanical or performance upgrades over the Forenza, it does have more of a youthful appearance inside and out. The dash, door panels and color choices are a little more hip than the more traditional Forenza wagon and sedan. Like the Forenza and Verona, the Reno has fresh styling penned by Ital Design. With a base price of around $13,000 the car should be a hit with value-minded shoppers who don't want to give up style and functionality. Still, it won't be easy to gain a foothold in a segment populated by standouts like the Scion xA and xB. Suzuki has attempted to set the Reno apart with a roomy interior and a lengthy list of standard features. Even the base model comes with body-color bumpers and door handles; four-wheel disc brakes; a height-adjustable driver seat; a padded center armrest; air conditioning; side airbags; an eight-speaker, 140-watt stereo with a CD player and steering-wheel audio controls; and power windows, mirrors and locks. For power, the Reno offers a 2.0-liter, four-cylinder engine rated for 126 horsepower and 131 pound-feet of torque. It's no powerhouse but the Reno gets around just fine and, when equipped with a manual transmission, rarely feels underpowered. Unfortunately, fuel economy is not a strong point of this engine, as it turns in lower numbers than most cars in this price range. However, driving dynamics are better that you might expect, as the Reno rides smoothly, handles predictably and stops well. Its reflexes are no match for those of the Ford Focus or Mazda 3, but much like Hyundai's Elantra, the Reno is well suited for Point-A-to-B driving. Finally, consider the price: Suzuki puts it all together for a sticker price no other economy car can touch, except the Hyundai Elantra. If value is your biggest priority in shopping but you still want to drive a car with a little sass, the Reno is worth a test-drive.

**Body Styles, Trim Levels and Options:** The Reno is available only as a five-door hatchback but is offered in three trim levels -- base S, midlevel LX or high-line EX. Even the S is well equipped, offering such features as body-color bumpers and door handles, four-wheel disc brakes, a height-adjustable driver seat, a padded center armrest, air conditioning, cabin air filtration system, an eight-speaker stereo with a CD/MP3 player, steering-wheel audio controls and power windows, mirrors and locks. Next up is the LX, which adds alloy wheels, foglights, a sunroof, cruise control and a remote keyless entry system. An automatic transmission is optional on both the S and LX models. The top-level EX adds leather seats and a standard four-speed automatic transmission. Antilock brakes with Electronic Brakeforce Distribution are optional on all trims.

**Powertrains and Performance:** The Reno comes with only one engine -- a 2.0-liter 16-valve, DOHC, inline four-cylinder making 126 horsepower and 131 pound-feet of torque. A five-speed manual transmission is standard on S and LX models. A four-speed automatic is standard on the top-level EX and optional on the other trim levels. Speed sensitive steering is standard on all Renos.

**Safety:** Side airbags and four-wheel disc brakes are standard, and ABS with Electronic Brakeforce Distribution is optional on all trim levels. Front-seat occupants get seatbelt pre-tensioners and height adjusters, while rear-seat passengers get a full set of head restraints and three-point belts. Dual-stage airbags and daytime running lights are also standard.

**Interior Design and Special Features:** To liven things up a bit, designers used plenty of metallic accents throughout the cabin and an attractive set of gauges. The door panels and dash arrangement are sportier-looking than the Forenza's with more distinctive circular patterns. The Reno has no less than 11 storage compartments and is available with leather seating. Several features not normally found on a car in this price range include foglights and an eight-speaker, 140-watt stereo with steering wheel-mounted audio controls. The driver seat is well contoured, and thanks to its two-way seat-bottom tilt, most people will be able to find a comfortable driving position. A padded center armrest provides a comfortable place to rest an elbow on long trips. In back, passengers are treated to competitive amounts of leg- and shoulder room, along with a fold-down center armrest.

**Driving Impressions:** Although 126 horsepower doesn't sound like much these days, the Reno has no difficulty keeping up in traffic, and if you equip it with the manual gearbox, you'll rarely wish for more power. You may wish for more refinement and better gas mileage, though. Ride quality is smooth over most surfaces, while handling is soft yet predictable in the corners. More expensive economy cars offer more in the way of behind-the-wheel entertainment and overall polish, but the Reno is well suited for buyers who want a low-priced car that can take on the daily commute while offering a little style.

## Competitive Vehicles

Chrysler PT Cruiser
$13,405–$23,455

Ford Focus
$13,230 - $18,130

Mazda MAZDA3
$13,680 - $17,105

Pontiac Vibe
$16,605 - $19,905

# 2005 Toyota Tacoma

**MSRP Price Range**

## $13,415 - $25,250

Destination Charge: $565 (all styles)

### Ratings

| Consumer Rating | N/A | |
| Editors Rating | 7.8 | |

**What Edmunds.com says:** The new Tacoma is far and away one of the best compact trucks ever offered to the American public.

**Pros:** Flexible and refined drivetrains, excellent off-road ability, 18 different body configurations, available stability control, solid build quality and reliability record, well-trimmed interior, unique bed features.

**Cons:** Manual gearbox still vague through the gears, awkward emergency brake.

**What's New:** The Tacoma has been completely redesigned for 2005.

*Crash Test Scores, see pg 530*
*Warranty information, see pg 542*

### Specifications

| Engine/Drivetrain | HP | Torque | EPA Fuel Economy Rating |
| --- | --- | --- | --- |
| 6cyl 4.0L A/M | 245 | 282 | 18 city/22 hwy |
| 4cyl 2.7L A/M | 164 | 183 | 21 city/26 hwy |

### Body Styles

| Style | MSRP Range |
| --- | --- |
| Crew Cab Pickup Truck | $21,675–$25,250 |
| Extended Cab Pickup Truck | $16,855–$23,125 |
| Regular Cab Pickup Truck | $13,415–$17,360 |

**Introduction:** Having made pickups for the U.S. market since 1964 (remember the Stout, anyone?), Toyota introduced its sixth-generation truck, and the Tacoma nameplate, in 1995. An all-new Tacoma debuts this year with across-the-board improvements. Whether it's engine power, interior room or safety features, the newest Tacoma has more of everything than it had before and even a few things it didn't. Like most trucks in its class, the new truck comes in regular, extended cab (Toyota calls it an Access Cab) and crew cab (or Double Cab) body styles in both two- and four-wheel drive. The Tacoma also continues with the popular PreRunner models that offer the look and suspension of the four-wheel-drive trucks sans the actual four-wheel-drive running gear. New styles for 2005 include a long-bed version of the crew cab and the high-performance access cab X-Runner street truck. All regular and access cab models are available with either four- or six-cylinder engines, while the crew cab models use the V6 exclusively. On the low end, an all-new 2.7-liter, four-cylinder engine replaces both the 2.4-liter and 2.7-liter engines used previously. Producing 164 horsepower and 183 pound-feet of torque, the new 2.7 offers a significant boost in horsepower. All V6 models now use a larger 4.0-liter engine in place of the previous 3.4-liter power plant. With 245 hp and 283 lb-ft of torque, the new Tacoma measures up to every six-cylinder truck in its class and nearly matches the power of the Dodge Dakota's High-Output 4.7-liter V8. Off-road junkies will also be happy to know that the Tacoma now offers both Hill-start Assist Control (HAC) and Downhill Assist Control (DAC) on all models (X-Runner excepted) equipped with an automatic transmission. The X-Runner essentially picks up where the old S-Runner left off, offering a sport-tuned pickup for those who want some utility without giving up the fun. It comes as a six-speed V6 access cab only with a lowered suspension and additional structural bracing underneath that gives the truck its name. Toyota also upgraded the base Tacoma to give it a better value proposition -- never the strongest aspect of the previous model. The least expensive 4x2 regular cab in now outfitted with the kind of standard features you would expect, such as antilock brakes, a CD stereo and multiple power points. Even more impressive than the newly standard features is the overall design and comfort of the interior. With more room in every direction, the Tacoma has lost much of the claustrophobic feeling so typical of most compact trucks. There's also a new composite cargo bed that comes standard on all models and incorporates built-in storage units, adjustable tie-down anchors and even an optional 400-watt electrical outlet. Toyota seems well apprised of the fact that while the compact truck category has seen little movement in the last five to 10 years, 2005 marks a rekindling of interest in this segment, with major redesigns for most of the major players. With Toyota's excellent revamp, the Tacoma is now firmly planted in the upper echelon of its class.

**Body Styles, Trim Levels and Options:** The Tacoma comes in three body styles: Regular Cab, Access Cab (extended cab) and Double Cab (crew cab). Each is available with two-wheel or four-wheel drive. Toyota also offers Tacomas with a "PreRunner" designation. PreRunners are 2WD trucks that have the looks and heavy-duty suspension of 4WD models. Toyota also offers

# 2005 Toyota Tacoma

a special 2WD X-Runner access cab sport truck equipped with the V6, a six-speed manual transmission, a sport-tuned suspension and additional structural bracing underneath that gives the truck its name. Standard features on the regular cab include a CD player, a full-size spare tire and a tachometer. Access Cabs add bucket seats, air conditioning and a pair of rear access doors. On top of that, the Double Cab receives keyless entry and power windows, locks and mirrors. An optional SR5 package features color-keyed and chrome trim, intermittent wipers and upgraded interior trim. A JBL audio system with seven speakers is optional on Double Cabs. An available TRD Sport package includes performance suspension and upgraded tires, and a TRD Off-Road package features meaty white-lettered tires and heavy-duty off-road suspension.

**Powertrains and Performance:** All regular and access cab models are available with either four- or six-cylinder engines, while the crew cab models use the V6 exclusively. Standard is a 2.7-liter, four-cylinder engine producing 164 horsepower and 183 pound-feet of torque. The 4.0-liter V6 engine serves up a generous 245 hp and 283 lb-ft of torque. Transmission choices include either a five-speed manual or four-speed automatic for the four-cylinder, while V6 buyers can choose between a six-speed manual and a five-speed automatic. Equipped with the V6 engine, the Tacoma's maximum tow rating is now 6,500 pounds.

**Safety:** Antilock brakes with Electronic Brakeforce Distribution and BrakeAssist are standard on all Tacomas. A stability control system is available on all models, except the X-Runner. Crew cab models also offer optional front-seat side airbags and full-length head curtain airbags. Hill-start Assist Control (HAC) and Downhill Assist Control (DAC) are optional on all models (X-Runner excluded) equipped with an automatic transmission. The Tacoma has not yet been crash tested.

**Interior Design and Special Features:** The design of the dashboard controls and instrument cluster mimics Toyota's 4Runner SUV, which isn't a bad thing. The quality of the materials sets a new standard for the class, and the seats have the kind of firm, supportive bolstering not typically found on trucks of this type. Getting into Access Cabs is easier now, thanks to dual rear doors that open wider than before, while the backseat of the Double Cab is now comfortable for full-size adults.

**Driving Impressions:** While the standard four-cylinder is certainly adequate, the 4.0-liter V6 is a terrific all-around performer, with plenty of guts down low and a willingness to spin into the upper rev ranges without getting thrashy. In terms of handling, the feeling behind the wheel is of a truck that is well planted at every corner, predictable when pushed and surprisingly agile considering its size.

## Competitive Vehicles

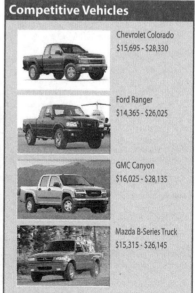

Chevrolet Colorado
$15,695 - $28,330

Ford Ranger
$14,365 - $26,025

GMC Canyon
$16,025 - $28,135

Mazda B-Series Truck
$15,315 - $26,145

# 2005 Volvo S40

**Compact Sedan**

**MSRP Price Range**

**$23,260 - $27,710**

Destination Charge: $685 (all styles)

## Ratings

| | | |
|---|---|---|
| Consumer Rating | 9.1 | |
| Editors Rating | 7.9 | |

**What Edmunds.com says:** Bigger, sportier and more powerful than its predecessor, the new S40 is fun to drive, while adding a much needed dose of style to Volvo's small-car line.

**Pros:** Sharper handling than you would expect from a Volvo, T5 version offers quick acceleration, well-designed interior controls, long list of safety features, available all-wheel drive.

**Cons:** Firm suspension can be choppy on the highway, average performance from the non-turbo engine.

**What's New:** A redesigned S40 was introduced halfway through the 2004 model year as a 2004.5 model. It continues into 2005 unchanged.

**Introduction:** The S40 is Volvo's smallest and most affordable vehicle. It went on sale in Europe in 1996, but wasn't introduced in the U.S. until the 2000 model year. As the years passed, Volvo's small sedan began to show its age. It certainly wasn't a bad car, but it had always suffered for its bland look, lack of powertrain choices and poor packaging. It was too expensive to appeal to Volkswagen Jetta buyers, but not luxurious enough to appeal to the Audi A4 set. Midway through the 2004 model year, though, the prognosis changed: Volvo released a redesigned version of its small sedan. Completely new from the ground up, the new S40 offered improved safety, performance and interior room, as well as slick styling inside and out. Looking more like a sport sedan from Germany than Sweden, the S40 features styling reminiscent of its larger siblings'. Although shorter than its predecessor, the current S40 is wider and has a longer wheelbase, which translates into more interior room. And it's not just space that improved -- just when we thought the typical car dashboard couldn't be improved upon, Volvo came up with the coolest-looking center stack this side of Stockholm. The thin, flowing center piece offers storage space behind it, but it's the wow factor that really gets this interior piece noticed. If you like shopping at IKEA, you'll love the new look. The S40 offers buyers a healthy range of powertrain options. The standard 2.4i model comes with a 2.4-liter, inline five-cylinder engine that is normally aspirated and makes 168 horsepower. A five-speed manual and a five-speed automatic are the available transmissions. An upgraded T5 model offers a turbocharged 2.5-liter inline five that makes 218 hp. Of the two, the T5 is definitely the car serious drivers will prefer. It would be unfair to call the 2.4i underpowered, but once the turbo on the T5 kicks in, the 2.4i is but a distant memory. Available with the same five-speed automatic as the 2.4i, the T5 also offers a six-speed manual gearbox. All-wheel drive is optional on automatic-equipped T5s. Designed specifically with the U.S. market in mind, the S40 shares some of its architecture with the Mazda 3 and the second-generation Ford Focus now on sale in Europe. While engine, drive systems, interior and suspension components are unique to Volvo, the fact remains that Ford, Mazda and Volvo are working more closely with one another. Those skeptical about a Volvo with subtle hints of Ford influence should look to the car's low price for comfort. The S40 looks, acts, feels and performs exactly the way we think an entry-level Volvo should. This small Swede is certainly a worthwhile addition to your shopping list.

**Body Styles, Trim Levels and Options:** The S40 comes in 2.4i and T5 versions. The 2.4i comes with 16-inch alloy wheels, a leather-wrapped steering wheel with telescope adjustment and a CD player. In addition to a more powerful engine, the T5 adds front and rear spoilers, wood grain interior trim, foglights, automatic climate control, a power driver seat and a trip computer -- all of which are optional on the 2.4i. Premium and Sport Packages are available for both trims; they're your ticket to leather upholstery, a moonroof, firmer suspension calibrations and wheel/tire upgrades. Other extras include a 12-speaker Dolby stereo with an in-dash CD changer, a navigation system and bi-xenon headlights.

*Crash Test Scores, see pg 530*
*Warranty information, see pg 542*

## Specifications

| Engine/Drivetrain | HP | Torque | EPA Fuel Economy Rating |
|---|---|---|---|
| 5cyl 2.5L M | 218 | 236 | 22 city/31 hwy |
| 5cyl 2.4L M | 168 | 170 | 22 city/29 hwy |

## Body Styles

| Style | MSRP Range |
|---|---|
| Compact Sedan | $23,260–$27,710 |

For the latest full vehicle reports, visit www.edmunds.com/bginfopak

**Powertrains and Performance:** The 2.4i comes with a naturally aspirated 2.4-liter inline five-cylinder rated for 168 horsepower and 170 pound-feet of torque. Buyers can choose either a five-speed manual or five-speed automatic to go with it. The T5 gets a turbocharged 2.5-liter inline five that makes 218 hp and 236 lb-ft of torque. In addition to the automatic, the T5 is eligible for a six-speed manual gearbox. T5 versions are also available with all-wheel drive, so long as you select the automatic transmission.

**Safety:** Four-wheel antilock disc brakes and traction control are standard on all S40s. Volvo's DTSC stability control system is optional. All models include both side-impact airbags and head curtain airbags, along with whiplash-reducing front seats. Built-in child booster seats are optional. The S40 received a perfect five-star rating in government side-impact crash testing; frontal and offset tests have not yet been performed.

**Interior Design and Special Features:** The S40's interior is unique and styled to appeal to a young audience. The first thing you'll notice is the ultraslim center stack, which has a definite Scandinavian design while also allowing for more storage up front. Interior trim choices include faux metal, faux wood, real aluminum or a transparent material reminiscent of an iMac computer. The ergonomically designed seats are available in different upholstery types, and adults will find adequate legroom in both the front and rear.

**Driving Impressions:** Volvo tuned the S40 to take performance much more seriously than the previous-generation model. Handling is crisp and entertaining, though the standard tires are taxed by more aggressive cornering. The downside to the S40's sharp reflexes is that cruising comfort suffers. The S40 offers adequate power for everyday driving, but weekend enthusiasts should head straight for the spirited T5 model.

## Competitive Vehicles

Acura TSX
$26,490 - $28,490

Audi A4
$25,550 - $43,550

Mazda MAZDA6
$18,995 - $23,195

Mercedes-Benz C-Class
$25,850 - $40,650

# 2005 Volvo V50

**Compact Wagon**

**MSRP Price Range**

## $25,660 - $28,910

Destination Charge: $685 (all styles)

### Ratings

| Consumer Rating | 8.8 | |
| Editors Rating | 8.0 | |

**What Edmunds.com says:** With its winning mix of Volvo safety and Scandinavian style, the V50 deserves to be on your list if you're in the market for a compact family wagon.

**Pros:** Legendary Volvo safety, IKEA-ready interior, crisp handling.

**Cons:** Average performance from the non-turbo engine.

**What's New:** The V50 is an all-new wagon from Volvo. It replaces the previous V40, and shares a platform with the recently redesigned Mazda 3.

**Introduction:** The all-new V50 is a sport wagon that's similar in spirit to Volvo's newly redesigned S40 sport sedan; both stand apart from the rest of Volvo's lineup on the strength of their relatively compact size and affordability. The wagon is Volvo's replacement for its outgoing V40, which was launched in the U.S. in 1999. Beneath the skin, the new Volvo has much in common with the Mazda 3 and the European-market Ford Focus; reflecting Ford's ownership of Volvo and controlling interest in Mazda, the wagon shares a platform with these vehicles. Don't worry about this new blood taking Volvo downmarket, though. From what we've seen thus far, the V50 builds on its borrowed underpinnings to deliver everything we've come to expect from a Volvo and more. Pure Swede to look at, the V50's sheet metal calls to mind the handsome S60 sedan. A sporty exterior and muscular lines speak of Volvo's desire to have the V50 reach the much vaunted youth market. Within its cabin, the wagon offers a simple, stylish layout. Just when you thought the typical car dashboard couldn't be improved upon, Volvo comes up with the coolest-looking center stack this side of Stockholm. The thin, flowing center piece is reminiscent of the latest plasma screen televisions and really sets the interior apart from the competition. If you like shopping at IKEA, you'll appreciate the aesthetic behind this most Scandinavian of interiors. In keeping with its Volvo heritage, the V50 offers a host of safety features. A new front structure boasts four different grades of steel, offering maximum protection for the car's occupants. Side impact and side curtain airbags are standard, as is a whiplash-protection seating system. Two trims are available: the 168-horsepower base 2.4i, and the 218-hp T5 (the T5 may also be had in an all-wheel-drive version). Young couples on a budget will want to check out the V50, which offers style and safety at a reasonable price.

**Body Styles, Trim Levels and Options:** Two trims of the compact V50 wagon are available: the base 2.4i and the sporty T5. Standard items on the 2.4i include tinted windows; power-adjustable heated exterior rearview mirrors; manual climate control; a leather-wrapped steering wheel; and a six-speaker, AM/FM single-CD sound system. Step up to the T5 and you get an eight-way power-adjustable driver seat with lumbar support, automatic climate control, a cargo-area 12-volt power outlet, aluminum trim and steering wheel-mounted audio controls. Options include 17-inch twin alloy wheels, leather upholstery, heated front seats, xenon headlights, windshield and rear-window wiper de-icers and a power moonroof.

**Powertrains and Performance:** Engines are specific to each model. The base 2.4i gets a 168-horsepower, normally aspirated 2.4-liter five-cylinder, while the T5 upgrades to a turbocharged 2.5-liter five-cylinder that generates 218 hp. A five-speed shiftable automatic transmission is standard on the 2.4i. The T5 features a standard six-speed manual tranny as standard, with the five-speed automatic offered as an option. T5 models are also available with all-wheel drive.

**Safety:** In keeping with its Volvo heritage, the V50 comes loaded with safety features. Side airbags for front occupants and side curtain airbags for front and rear occupants are standard. A whiplash protection seating system protects occupants from neck injury in the event of a

*Crash Test Scores, see pg 530*
*Warranty information, see pg 542*

### Specifications

| Engine/Drivetrain | HP | Torque | EPA Fuel Economy Rating |
| --- | --- | --- | --- |
| 5cyl 2.5L M | 218 | 236 | 22 city/31 hwy |
| 5cyl 2.4L A | 168 | 170 | 22 city/30 hwy |

### Body Styles

| Style | MSRP Range |
| --- | --- |
| Compact Wagon | $25,660–$28,910 |

rear-impact collision. Four-wheel antilock disc brakes (with emergency braking assist) and traction control systems are also standard. Stability control is optional on all trims. The V50 has not yet been crash tested.

**Interior Design and Special Features:** Scandinavian to the core, the V50's interior is a study in spartan elegance. A leather-wrapped steering wheel looks both sporty and luxurious, and gauges are pleasantly lit and easy to read. Especially eye-catching is the narrow center stack, which replaces the typical center-piece clutter with spare lines and a "less is more" aesthetic that gives the car a thoroughly modern feel. A 60/40-split-folding rear seat adds versatility, should you need to haul very long items. Overall cargo capacity (62.9 cubic feet) is comparable to what you'd get in an Audi A4 or Volkswagen Passat.

**Driving Impressions:** Handling in the V50 is sporty and tight. Overall, this is a capable wagon that rewards spirited driving with a good deal of fun. In most circumstances, the ride is quiet and comfortable. The 2.4i model offers adequate power for everyday driving, but weekend enthusiasts should head straight for the spirited T5 model. The optional all-wheel-drive system is a good bet for buyers seeking a relatively affordable, premium-brand wagon that can brave the winter snows.

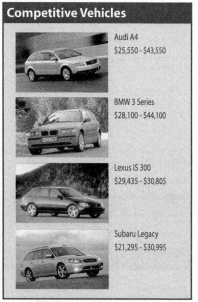

# 2005 Acura MDX

**MSRP Price Range**
## $36,700 - $43,775
Destination Charge: $570 (all styles)

### Ratings

| | | |
|---|---|---|
| Consumer Rating | N/A | |
| Editors Rating | 8.0 | |

**What Edmunds.com says:** A somewhat bland but otherwise utterly capable and perfectly useful crossover SUV.

**Pros:** Room for seven passengers or serious amounts of cargo, gutsy V6 engine, well-balanced suspension, top-rated crash test scores.

**Cons:** Limited off-road capability, below-average tow rating, ho-hum interior design and materials.

**What's New:** This year the MDX receives standard XM Satellite Radio, a Bluetooth hands-free cell phone interface on Touring models, a larger fuel tank and an enhanced stability control system. The optional rear entertainment system now includes an in-dash six-disc CD changer, and the navigation system has an enhanced database. MDXs with navigation also include the OnStar communications system.

**Body Styles, Trim Levels and Options:** The MDX is offered as a four-door only in either base or Touring trim. Base models come well equipped with 17-inch wheels, XM Satellite Radio, heated mirrors, keyless entry, leather seating (heated in front), a power driver seat, front and rear automatic climate control, a CD player and a moonroof. Touring models add a roof rack, a rear wiper, a power front-passenger seat, a driver-seat memory feature, a Bluetooth hands-free cell phone interface and an upgraded audio system with an in-dash six-CD changer. Ordering the Touring model also allows you to specify the optional DVD-based navigation system (with voice recognition and a rearview video camera), the DVD entertainment system for rear passengers, or both.

**Powertrains and Performance:** While most luxury SUVs offer a V8 as the top-line engine, the MDX comes only with a 265-hp, 3.5-liter V6. Though tow capacity suffers (just 3,500 pounds), acceleration is comparable to other SUVs and fuel mileage is superior. A five-speed automatic transmission is standard and it helps the MDX earn an EPA mileage estimate of 17 city/23 highway. Power travels to all four wheels through Acura's Variable Torque Management (VTM) full-time four-wheel-drive system.

**Safety:** The MDX comes standard with four-wheel antilock disc brakes, seat-mounted side airbags for front occupants, head-protecting side-curtain airbags, a tire-pressure monitoring system, stability control and three-point seatbelts in every position. Should an accident prove unavoidable, MDX counters with high crash test scores; it scored five stars (out of five) in the government front- and side-impact tests. The IIHS gave the MDX a "Good" rating (the highest possible) for its performance in the 40-mph frontal offset crash test.

**Interior Design and Special Features:** Perhaps because of its minivan roots, the MDX's interior does little to inspire or awe, but it is quite functional. The second-row rear seats offer ample room, and the third-row seat is fine for children. The spacious cabin also makes the MDX a very practical cargo carrier. The second-row seats are split 60/40, folding nearly flat with one simple latch. The third-row seat is all one unit that folds flat, as well. With both the second- and third-row seats folded down, there's 82 cubic feet of usable space.

**Driving Impressions:** Comfortable on rough city streets, yet firm enough to feel agile in the corners, the MDX offers a pleasing compromise between ride comfort and handling ability. On mild off-road jaunts, the MDX is well up to the task of soaking up big hits as well as smoothing out long, winding stretches of bumpy dirt road. Eight inches of ground clearance allows the MDX to clear small obstacles with ease.

*Crash Test Scores, see pg 530*
*Warranty information, see pg 542*

### Specifications

| Engine/Drivetrain | HP | Torque | EPA Fuel Economy Rating |
|---|---|---|---|
| 6cyl 3.5L A | 265 | 253 | 17 city/23 hwy |

### Body Styles

| Style | MSRP Range |
|---|---|
| Midsize SUV | $36,700–$43,775 |

For the latest full vehicle reports, visit www.edmunds.com/bginfopak

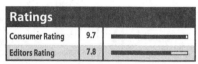

**MSRP Price Range**

## $89,000
Destination Charge: $765 (all styles)

## Ratings

| | | |
|---|---|---|
| Consumer Rating | 9.7 | |
| Editors Rating | 7.8 | |

**What Edmunds.com says:** A 15-year-old exotic that offers competitive performance. Overpriced for what you get, though. Buy a used one and get virtually the same car with less depreciation.

**Pros:** Superb balance and handling, thrilling exhaust note, everyday ergonomics, Honda reliability.

**Cons:** Twitchy at the limit, high cost-to-power ratio, dated interior design.

**What's New:** The NSX continues unchanged for 2005.

**Body Styles, Trim Levels and Options:** The two-door NSX sports car is Acura's most expensive model, but a lack of updates leaves it without the kind of modern amenities you would expect for a car in this price range. Standard features include 17-inch wheels, a removable aluminum roof panel, HID headlights, remote keyless entry, automatic climate control, a 165-watt Bose stereo with a CD changer and leather seating.

**Powertrains and Performance:** The 3.2-liter V6 engine makes 290 horsepower and 224 pound-feet of torque. It's coupled to a close-ratio six-speed manual transmission. A four-speed automatic is also available, but equipping the car as such mandates a smaller 3.0-liter V6 and drops the horsepower rating down to 252. With the six-speed, the NSX can accelerate to 60 mph in about 5 seconds and has a top speed of 175 mph.

**Safety:** The NSX lacks some of the more current safety features, such as side airbags or a stability control system. It does have traction control and antilock brakes. Crash testing has not been performed by the NHTSA or the IIHS.

**Interior Design and Special Features:** The NSX's cabin is comfortable and refined, and one might even call its styling '80s retro, though we don't think that has anything to do with Acura trying to be hip. All controls are logically placed, the seating position is nothing short of perfect, the targa top is easily stored and visibility is certainly acceptable for a midengine sports car. Optional high-impact interior colors like Vivid Blue and Targa Silver are available to capture the flavor of many aftermarket kits.

**Driving Impressions:** Around turns, the NSX still has the goods to hang with just about any other car sold today. Well-balanced, perfectly poised, easy to drive, powerful, graceful—the NSX is a precision instrument that is forgiving enough to make drivers of varying skill feel like pros. The midengine design provides excellent weight distribution, keeping the wheels securely planted around turns. Braking and steering are also NSX strong points. There could definitely be more horsepower, though. Spending nearly $90,000 to get 290 hp doesn't seem quite right.

*Crash Test Scores, see pg 530*
*Warranty information, see pg 542*

## Specifications

| Engine/Drivetrain | HP | Torque | EPA Fuel Economy Rating |
|---|---|---|---|
| 6cyl 3.2L M | 290 | 224 | 17 city/24 hwy |
| 6cyl 3.0L A | 252 | 210 | 17 city/24 hwy |

## Body Styles

| Style | MSRP Range |
|---|---|
| Compact Coupe | $89,000 |

# 2005 Acura RL

**MSRP Price Range**

## $48,900

Destination Charge: $570 (all styles)

## Ratings

| | | |
|---|---|---|
| Consumer Rating | N/A | |
| Editors Rating | 8.5 | |

**What Edmunds.com says:** With tons of standard features, excellent road manners and premium cabin furnishings, the new RL is a worthy competitor to the respected players from Audi, BMW and Lexus.

**Pros:** Quiet cabin, handles well for a large sedan, excellent build and materials quality, unique all-wheel-drive system, innovative navigation system offers real-time traffic information.

**Cons:** Lacks the low-end grunt of a V8, still lacks the prestige of its European competition.

**What's New:** The RL is completely redesigned for 2005, and now sports a 300-horsepower V6 and standard all-wheel drive.

**Body Styles, Trim Levels and Options:** The RL is a large luxury sedan that seats five. It's available in one fully loaded model that includes leather upholstery, a sunroof, power-adjustable and heated front seats, a memory feature for the driver seat and a 10-speaker Bose surround sound audio system that can play music in both DVD-A and CD formats. The automatic climate control system uses satellite data to help determine time of day and the direction of the sun against the car to appropriately adjust interior comfort levels. Other standard features include 17-inch alloy wheels; adaptive xenon headlights that swivel according to steering input; a voice-activated navigation system with real-time traffic information; a keyless access and startup system; OnStar telematics; and a Bluetooth interface for cell phone users.

**Powertrains and Performance:** The RL comes with only one engine and transmission. Under the hood is a 300-hp, 3.5-liter V6 that uses variable valve timing and a variable flow exhaust system. The transmission is a five-speed automatic with a shift-it-yourself feature. All RLs now have all-wheel drive as standard equipment, and that all-wheel-drive system is truly unique. Not only can the RL split the engine's power from front to rear, but it can split the available power between the left and right wheels for improved handling.

**Safety:** Four-wheel antilock disc brakes, seat-mounted side airbags for front occupants, full-length side curtain airbags and stability control are all standard equipment. OnStar, the in-vehicle communications and emergency assistance service, also comes standard. The RL has not been crash tested.

**Interior Design and Special Features:** The interior of the new RL is befitting of a true luxury car. The high-quality ensemble includes LED gauges and a state-of-the-art navigation system. The center stack is designed for simplicity; one large knob combined with smaller selection buttons makes it very easy to access the RL's impressive computing power. All climate, audio and navigation information is displayed on a large eight-inch screen in the center of the dash that's legible at a glance. An Active Noise Cancellation system uses the Bose audio system to cancel out sound waves from road and exhaust noise.

*Crash Test Scores, see pg 530*
*Warranty information, see pg 542*

**Driving Impressions:** The V6 offers plenty of power but lacks the low-end grunt that could be provided by a V8. The engine is nonetheless smooth and very quiet, while the five-speed automatic transmission shifts up and down in an almost invisible fashion. The sophisticated all-wheel-drive system makes the full-size RL a lot of fun to drive hard and virtually insures that the car will go right where the driver intends.

## Specifications

| Engine/Drivetrain | HP | Torque | EPA Fuel Economy Rating |
|---|---|---|---|
| 6cyl 3.5L A | 300 | 260 | 18 city/26 hwy |

## Body Styles

| Style | MSRP Range |
|---|---|
| Large Sedan | $48,900 |

**MSRP Price Range**

## $20,175 - $23,570
Destination Charge: $570 (all styles)

### Ratings

| | | |
|---|---|---|
| Consumer Rating | 9.7 | ▮▮▮▮▮▮▮▮▮▮ |
| Editors Rating | 8.0 | ▮▮▮▮▮▮▮▮▯ |

**What Edmunds.com says:** With an overall feeling of refinement, and exemplary steering, Acura's RSX is a car you can drive to work everyday and still cut loose in it over the weekend.

**Pros:** High-revving Type-S engine, nimble handling, sharp steering, clean interior design, plenty of standard equipment.

**Cons:** Modest torque output, tight rear-seat headroom, forgettable exterior design.

**What's New:** For 2005, the RSX receives a number of changes. Horsepower for the Type-S is bumped up to 210, thanks to new high-performance camshafts, a larger intake duct, large diameter exhaust pipe and a high-flow catalytic converter. The six-speed transmission on the Type-S gets a lower final drive ratio and carbon synchronizers (instead of brass) on fifth and sixth gears for a smoother shift feel. Suspension upgrades on all models include a 7mm lower ride height, revised stabilizer bars and inversely wound springs. The steering and braking systems have been refined for better feel and response, and the Type-S gets a larger diameter front strut tower brace and 17-inch wheels. Front and rear fascias have also been redesigned, along with the side sills, grille, headlamps and taillamps. The Type-S gets a rear spoiler, as well. Inside, you'll find new deeply bolstered seats with thicker cushioning and new trim accents. Overall body rigidity has increased by 15 percent in front and 21 percent in the rear.

**Body Styles, Trim Levels and Options:** The RSX two-door sport hatchback comes in two trim levels: base and Type-S. Both are well equipped. With the base RSX, you get standard features such as 16-inch alloy wheels; automatic climate control; power windows, locks and mirrors; cruise control; a power moonroof; a leather-wrapped steering wheel; and a CD player. These items, plus 17-inch wheels, stronger brakes, firmer suspension tuning, a rear spoiler and an in-dash six-disc CD changer come on the Type-S. Leather seats are standard on the Type-S, though you can upgrade the base car's cloth with leather if you so desire.

**Powertrains and Performance:** Both the RSX and RSX Type-S feature 2.0-liter, four-cylinder engines. Like most Honda and Acura engines, they are smooth and high-revving. The base RSX puts out 160 horsepower at 6,500 rpm and 141 pound-feet of torque at 4,000 rpm. For the Type-S, Acura tunes the engine to bring horsepower up to 210 (at 7,800 rpm) and 143 lb-ft of torque. V6-equipped sport coupes like the Hyundai Tiburon GT and Mitsubishi Eclipse GT produce significantly more torque and, as such, are a bit more tractable for city driving than the RSX, but both will have you paying more at the fuel pump. The base RSX comes equipped with either a five-speed manual or an optional five-speed automatic transmission. The automatic features Acura's Sequential SportShift, a special mode that allows the driver to select individual gears quickly by moving the transmission lever into a special gate. The Type-S has an exclusive six-speed manual.

**Safety:** The RSX comes with standard antilock brakes and side airbags, in addition to the federally mandated safety features. In government crash tests, the RSX received five out of five stars for driver and front-passenger protection in a frontal impact. In side-impact tests, it received four stars for front-occupant protection.

**Interior Design and Special Features:** Drivers wanting to relax after strafing twisty roads should enjoy the RSX's driver-oriented cockpit, contemporary materials, easy-to-use automatic climate controls and large metallic-faced gauges. Front-seat occupants will be comfortable, but adults sitting in back will find headroom is lacking. The RSX has 17.8 cubic feet of luggage space, about a cube more than an Eclipse or Celica.

**Driving Impressions:** Neither engine offers an abundance of torque, and the Type-S motor, in particular, needs to be revved quite high in order to achieve maximum acceleration. The six-speed shifter, however, is quite exemplary in its feel and quickness. On curvy roads, the Type-S feels secure and buttoned down, though the base car is still pretty sporty. The Acura's ride quality is a little on the stiff side compared to a coupe like the Eclipse, but those looking to add a dose of sport to their daily commute will not be disappointed.

*Crash Test Scores, see pg 530*
*Warranty information, see pg 542*

### Specifications

| Engine/Drivetrain | HP | Torque | EPA Fuel Economy Rating |
|---|---|---|---|
| 4cyl 2.0L M | 210 | 143 | 23 city/31 hwy |
| 4cyl 2.0L A/M | 160 | 141 | 25 city/34 hwy |

### Body Styles

| Style | MSRP Range |
|---|---|
| Compact Coupe | $20,175–$23,570 |

# Acura

# 2005 Acura TL

**Midsize Sedan**

**MSRP Price Range**
## $32,900 - $35,100
Destination Charge: $570 (all styles)

**#1 Editors' Rating**

## Ratings

| | | |
|---|---|---|
| Consumer Rating | 9.8 | |
| Editors Rating | 8.9 | |

**What Edmunds.com says:** Luxurious, extremely well equipped and enjoyable to drive, the stylish TL should be on your test-drive list if you're shopping for a sedan under $40K.

**Pros:** Luxurious interior, long list of standard equipment, powerful V6 engine, slick-shifting six-speed manual, pleasant blend of ride comfort and fun, superb sound system.

**Cons:** Can't match the athleticism of some German rivals, V6 could use more low-end torque.

**What's New:** The front seatbelt buckles are now mounted to the seat frame, and sensors in the front-passenger seat alert the driver when an occupant is out of a safe position for the side airbag.

**Body Styles, Trim Levels and Options:** Standard equipment includes 17-inch wheels and all-season tires, high-intensity discharge headlights, leather upholstery, aluminum trim, a 10-way power driver seat, a four-way power front-passenger seat, heated seats and a telescoping steering wheel. A 225-watt 5.1 surround-sound audio system that can play both CDs and DVD-Audio discs is also included, along with satellite radio, Bluetooth hands-free phone compatibility, steering-wheel audio controls and a power sunroof. In addition, manual-shift TLs have front Brembo brakes and larger stabilizer bars. Among the few options are high-performance tires on manual-shift TLs and a DVD-based navigation system with an 8-inch touchscreen, voice recognition technology and solar-sensing technology that enhances the performance of the climate control system. Also worth consideration is the A-SPEC kit, which adds performance springs and shocks that lower the car about an inch, 18-inch wheels, an aero body kit, a rear spoiler, a sport steering wheel and special exterior badging. Automatic-equipped TLs also pick up the Brembo brakes when equipped with this package.

**Powertrains and Performance:** All TLs come with a 3.2-liter V6 engine with VTEC (variable valve timing and lift). Horsepower measures 270, while torque comes in at 238 lb-ft. Transmission choices include a six-speed manual and a five-speed automatic.

**Safety:** Standard safety features include four-wheel antilock disc brakes with Electronic Brakeforce Distribution and BrakeAssist, as well as stability control, seat-mounted side airbags for front occupants and side curtain airbags for front and rear occupants. In front offset crash tests conducted by the IIHS, the TL earned a top rating of "Good" and a "Best Pick" designation. In government crash tests, the TL received a perfect five stars for everything but front-seat side impacts, where it earned a four-star rating.

**Interior Design and Special Features:** Inside, the TL feels as luxurious as an Audi or Lexus. The cockpit has a stylish two-tone color scheme, aluminum inlays and an attractive set of bright blue electroluminescent gauges. Materials quality is excellent; most surfaces are soft-touch, and the standard leather upholstery is quite supple. The sophisticated Panasonic audio system plays music through six channels when you load up DVD-Audio discs.

**Driving Impressions:** All TLs are entertaining to drive, thanks to their prodigious horsepower, but cars equipped with the slick-shifting six-speed manual are the most rewarding on back roads. In city driving situations, however, the TL would benefit from a tad more low-end torque. The suspension manages to deliver both a comfortable ride and tight handling around corners. Enthusiasts will prefer the sharper reflexes and rear-drive layout of cars like the BMW 3 Series, but in stock form Acura's driving dynamics are well balanced.

*Crash Test Scores, see pg 530*
*Warranty information, see pg 542*

## Specifications

| Engine/Drivetrain | HP | Torque | EPA Fuel Economy Rating |
|---|---|---|---|
| 6cyl 3.2L A/M | 270 | 238 | 20 city/29 hwy |

## Body Styles

| Style | MSRP Range |
|---|---|
| Midsize Sedan | $32,900–$35,100 |

For the latest full vehicle reports, visit www.edmunds.com/bginfopak

**MSRP Price Range**

## N/A

Destination Charge: N/A (all styles)

### Ratings

| | | |
|---|---|---|
| Consumer Rating | N/A | |
| Editors Rating | 8.2 | |

**What Edmunds.com says:** Between its long list of high-end features, well-trimmed interior, agile handling and willing engine, the TSX is one of the best values on the market when it comes to affordable sport sedans.

**Pros:** An engine that loves to rev and sounds good doing it, sharp handling, slick six-speed manual transmission, upscale interior look and feel, long list of standard equipment, top-of-the-line navigation system for those who want it.

**Cons:** Forgettable styling, not much power until the engine gets revved up.

**What's New:** Acura adds XM Satellite Radio, heated door mirrors and a four-way power passenger seat to the standard features list. The steering wheel-mounted audio and cruise controls are now illuminated.

**Body Styles, Trim Levels and Options:** The TSX is available in only one trim but with its extensive list of standard features you're not likely to want anything more. Included on every model are items like 17-inch alloy wheels; xenon headlights; heated, power-adjustable driver and passenger seats; leather upholstery; an eight-speaker, 360-watt audio system with XM Satellite Radio and an in-dash CD changer; dual-zone automatic climate control; and a sunroof. A DVD-based navigation system with voice-activated software is the only option.

**Powertrains and Performance:** All TSXs come with a 2.4-liter, DOHC four-cylinder making 200 horsepower and 166 pound-feet of torque. While this engine is strong at high rpm, there is considerably less power down low. Keep it above 3,000 rpm, however, and it rewards you with solid thrust that extends right up to its lofty 7,110-rpm redline and smooth power delivery. Transmission choices include a six-speed manual or a five-speed automatic with Sportshift feature.

**Safety:** Four wheel antilock disc brakes, traction control and a stability control system are all standard. Side-impact airbags for front passengers and side curtain airbags for both front and rear occupants are also standard. In crash tests conducted by the IIHS, the TSX received a rating of "Good," the highest possible, and a "Best Pick" designation. In government tests, the TSX earned a perfect five-star rating on all counts, except rear side impacts, where it received a four-star rating.

**Interior Design and Special Features:** Inside, the TSX offers a well-trimmed interior that looks and feels more upscale than you would expect in a car that costs less than $30,000. The driver-oriented cockpit has large, easy-to-read gauges and controls and performance-engineered front bucket seats that feel great. An Acura premium sound system is also standard that includes a 360-watt amplifier, in-dash six-disc CD changer, XM Satellite Radio and illuminated steering wheel-mounted controls.

**Driving Impressions:** The TSX's 2.4-liter four delivers all the sophistication you'd expect from an Acura. While a four-cylinder is usually not ideal in a luxury car, this one is so refined that some owners may give up on V6s altogether. The smooth six-speed manual transmission is well suited to the 200-hp four and shifts are precise and the gates easy to find. Handling is equally impressive, if not more so. The TSX rides benefits from a double-wishbone suspension up front with a multilink setup in back. Equipped with 17-inch wheels and tires and standard stability control, the car slices through turns with barely a hint of body roll and the VSA does its work without being intrusive. The steering provides quick, precise action and torque steer in this front-wheel-drive sport sedan is almost nonexistent. During more subdued driving, the TSX never forgets its luxury branding and delivers a solid, compliant ride that always feels just right.

*Crash Test Scores, see pg 530*
*Warranty information, see pg 542*

### Specifications

| Engine/Drivetrain | HP | Torque | EPA Fuel Economy Rating |
|---|---|---|---|
| 4cyl 2.4L A/M | 200 | 166 | 22 city/31 hwy |

### Body Styles

| Style | MSRP Range |
|---|---|
| Midsize Sedan | N/A |

## Audi

# 2005 Audi A4

### Compact Convertible, Sedan, Wagon

**MSRP Price Range**

## $25,800 - $44,250

Destination Charge: $720 (all styles)

### Ratings

| | | |
|---|---|---|
| Consumer Rating | 8.6 | |
| Editors Rating | 8.2 | |

**What Edmunds.com says:** The A4 is luxurious, sporty, winterproof and a few grand cheaper than BMW's 3 Series. As such, it's one of our favorite entry-luxury cars.

**Pros:** Classy, well-constructed interiors, sharp handling, precise steering, available all-wheel drive, generous maintenance program.

**Cons:** Engines short on low-end torque, sport package makes for a choppy ride.

**What's New:** A4 sedans and Avants get new bi-xenon headlamps along with a new satellite/navigation/AM and FM radio antenna. Satellite radio (XM or Sirius) is now optional on the A4 Cabriolet. OnStar is no longer an available option.

*Crash Test Scores, see pg 530*
*Warranty information, see pg 542*

### Specifications

| Engine/Drivetrain | HP | Torque | EPA Fuel Economy Rating |
|---|---|---|---|
| 6cyl 3.0L A/M | 220 | 221 | 20 city/28 hwy |
| 4cyl 1.8L A/M | 170 | 166 | 23 city/30 hwy |

### Body Styles

| Style | MSRP Range |
|---|---|
| Compact Convertible | $35,750–$44,250 |
| Compact Sedan | $25,800–$34,790 |
| Compact Wagon | $29,150–$35,790 |

**Body Styles, Trim Levels and Options:** A4s are sold in two trim levels—1.8T and 3.0—which correspond to the engine under the hood. The sedan and cabriolet models are available in front-wheel-drive or quattro all-wheel-drive configuration, while all wagons are AWD. Standard equipment on 1.8Ts includes dual-zone automatic climate control, an in-dash six-CD changer, one-touch windows, 16-inch wheels and, for convertibles, an automatic top. Step up to the 3.0 and you'll get leather seating with 12-way power adjustments and real wood interior trim. The 1.8Ts can be upgraded with the Premium Package that adds the amenities of the 3.0 along with a sunroof and an auto-dimming mirror. The Sport Package adds a firmer suspension and 17-inch wheels and tires, while the Cold Weather Package throws in seat heaters and a ski sack. Other options include a Bose sound system, HID headlights and a CD-based navigation system.

**Powertrains and Performance:** Engine choices correspond to model names—hence, you can choose either the 1.8T, a 170-horsepower turbocharged inline four, or the 3.0, a 220-horsepower V6. All-wheel-drive 1.8T and 3.0 models can be equipped with either a six-speed manual or a five-speed automatic transmission. Front-wheel-drive V6s are equipped with a continuously variable transmission only, while the 1.8T comes standard with a five-speed manual and offers the CVT as an option. Compared with competitors like the BMW 330i and Infiniti G35, A4s feels sluggish off the line, especially the portly Cabriolet.

**Safety:** Safety features include a superb set of four-wheel antilock disc brakes, Electronic Brakeforce Distribution, BrakeAssist and stability control. Additionally, the A4 is equipped with side airbags for the driver and front passenger. Sedans and wagons also come with side curtain airbags for the front and rear (seat-mounted rear side airbags are optional), while convertibles get a rollover protection system. In government crash testing, the A4 sedan received five stars for front-seat occupants in the side-impact category and four stars for the rear. In IIHS frontal offset crash testing, the A4 was named a "Best Pick" in its class.

**Interior Design and Special Features:** Audi interiors are some of the finest in the luxury car kingdom and the A4 is no exception. High-quality materials, solid construction and a sleek, modern design make this a car you'll love every time you get in. The seats can be on the firm side and a few of the controls take some time to get used to, but the overall design is one of the best in the segment. Wagons offer 27.8 cubic feet of luggage capacity with the rear seats up and 60.6 when they're folded.

**Driving Impressions:** The A4 is one of the most balanced cars in the entry-luxury segment in terms of ride and handling. It's comfortable in day-to-day driving as the suspension soaks up most bumps and potholes. On winding back roads, top-notch underpinnings result in excellent handling. While the A4 isn't as razor-sharp as some peers, the extra grip afforded by quattro could justify the trade-off for many drivers, particularly those who live in harsh climates.

**MSRP Price Range**
## $40,900 - $50,500
Destination Charge: $720 (all styles)

### Ratings

| | | |
|---|---|---|
| Consumer Rating | N/A | |
| Editors Rating | 9.1 | |

**What Edmunds.com says:** Solid performance and an elegant cabin design make the A6 a worthy competitor in the luxury sedan class, but BMW's 5 Series is more athletic and Mercedes carries more brand cachet, so it can't be called a class leader just yet.

**Pros:** Heavenly cabin furnishings, crisp handling, all-wheel-drive utility, strong six- and eight-cylinder power plants.

**Cons:** Steering not as sharp as a BMW's, no manual transmission available.

**What's New:** The A6 gets a top-to-bottom redesign for 2005.

**Body Styles, Trim Levels and Options:** The A6 is sold in two trim levels—3.2 and 4.2—which correspond to the engine found under the hood. When it comes to dressing up an already nicely standard-equipped A6, four packages are available: The Premium Package includes a power glass sunroof, multifunction steering wheel, bi-xenon headlights, an upgraded Bose stereo system and wood interior trim. The Cold Weather Package provides heated front and rear seats, a ski sack and headlight washers. The Sports Package will give you a stiffer sport suspension and 18-inch alloy wheels with performance tires. Lastly, the Convenience Package provides auto-dimming/folding exterior mirrors, an auto-dimming interior mirror with compass, memory for the driver seat and mirrors, HomeLink and a trip computer. Separate options include rear parking sensors, rear side airbags, a DVD-based navigation system and voice control for the Bluetooth hands-free cell phone system. Premium leather and sport seats are also available as a la carte extras.

**Powertrains and Performance:** Dropping the twin-turbo 2.7-liter V6 engine option, the new A6 now offers a standard 3.2-liter V6 and an optional 4.2-liter V8. The V6 is rated at 255 horsepower and 243 pound-feet of torque, while the V8 bumps up to 335 hp and a torque rating of 310 lb-ft. Jab the go pedal and both models serve up a competent, quick rush of power with smooth acceleration. The only transmission choice is a six-speed automanual with seven shift stages. While the six-speed works well, true enthusiasts may miss having the option of a true manual transmission. Audi's quattro all-wheel-drive system is standard on all A6s.

**Safety:** The latest generation of ESP (Audi's stability control system, with BrakeAssist and Electronic Brakeforce Distribution) aids drivers in keeping the A6 under control during emergency situations. Front, side and head airbags are also onboard to help keep occupants safe in the event of an unavoidable accident.

**Interior Design and Special Features:** The A6 offers one of the best interiors in its price class. Besides offering standard leather and wood inlays, each cabin is filled with supple, high-quality materials. Aluminum interior trim provides a sporty look, while wood trim is optional in Brown Walnut or Beige Birch. If you bought an A6 for the sake of luxury alone, you wouldn't be disappointed. All models come with the Multi Media Interface (MMI) vehicle management system first seen in the A8. The system's 7.0-inch display is integrated with the standard 10-speaker Bose stereo and the optional navigation system. In practice, it's much easier to use than BMW's iDrive or Mercedes' COMAND.

**Driving Impressions:** While its steering can't match the acuity of BMW's 5 Series, the A6 does provide an excellent ride around town along with tight handling on twistier pavement. Additionally, its quattro system affords it prodigious grip around turns that makes spirited driving that much more fun. Throw in the variable of winter weather, and the A6 will outdo any rear-drive rival.

*Crash Test Scores, see pg 530*
*Warranty information, see pg 542*

### Specifications

| Engine/Drivetrain | HP | Torque | EPA Fuel Economy Rating |
|---|---|---|---|
| 8cyl 4.2L A | 335 | 310 | 17 city/23 hwy |
| 6cyl 3.1L A | 255 | 243 | N/A |

### Body Styles

| Style | MSRP Range |
|---|---|
| Midsize Sedan | $40,900–$50,500 |

# 2005 Audi A8

**MSRP Price Range**
## $66,590 - $69,900
Destination Charge: $720 (all styles)

## Ratings

| | | |
|---|---|---|
| Consumer Rating | 9.3 | ████████████ |
| Editors Rating | 9.0 | ████████████ |

**What Edmunds.com says:** It may not have the name recognition of its German peers, but the A8 matches or beats them in just about every meaningful category.

**Pros:** Superb driving dynamics, plenty of passenger space, exquisite interior, standard all-wheel drive.

**Cons:** Inconvenient glovebox location for the CD changer.

**What's New:** A standard wheelbase version of the A8 is introduced this year for those who don't need all the size of the A8 L, along with a tire-pressure monitor, rain-sensing wipers and LED lighting for the door handles and mirror controls. New optional equipment includes a keyless entry and start system, a wood steering wheel and shift knob, satellite radio and power door closers for the front and rear side doors. Horsepower has been bumped up to 335 (from 330).

**Body Styles, Trim Levels and Options:** Two versions of the A8 are offered, a standard-wheelbase sedan and the long-wheelbase L sedan for those who need maximum rear legroom. The question with this car isn't what's standard, it's what isn't. Most anyone with a big thirst for luxury and convenience features should be well sated by the A8. A DVD-based navigation system and bi-xenon headlights are on the long standard features roster, as is a 12-speaker Bose audio system with CD changer (located in the glovebox) that was designed exclusively for the A8. Other coddling features include a pair of vanity mirrors for the rear-seat passengers, heated seats (front and rear) and steering wheel, power lumbar support for all four outboard seats and window shades for the rear side and back windows. Options for what is already an opulent interior include wood steering wheel trim, a keyless ignition and power door closers.

**Powertrains and Performance:** The A8's 4.2-liter, 40-valve V8 generates 335 horsepower and 317 pound-feet of torque. The V8 is matched to a six-speed Tiptronic automatic transmission and drives all four wheels through Audi's quattro system. Audi claims that the A8 L will sprint to 60 mph in just 6.3 seconds and run down the quarter-mile in 14.2 ticks, putting it about equal in acceleration to its executive express rivals, Mercedes-Benz's S500 and BMW's 745Li.

**Safety:** Peace-of-mind features include stability control, 10 airbags (including four side, front knee and full-length head curtain) and a first aid kit in the rear center armrest. The A8 hasn't been crash tested.

**Interior Design and Special Features:** Whether you sit in the pilot's seat or stretch out (and with 42 inches of rear legroom in the L, we mean stretch out) in the back, everything you see and touch in the A8 bespeaks the highest quality. Generous fillets of dark or light wood, suede trim and aluminum accents are arranged attractively. With 16-way power adjustment (including upper seat back angle for the shoulders) and a power tilt/telescoping steering wheel, finding a comfortable driving position is easy for short and tall folk alike.

**Driving Impressions:** Throttle response is gratifying, to say the least. Whether taking off from a stoplight or jetting up to cruising speed on the freeway, a solid rush of power is always on tap. And the six-shooter gearbox might as well be a CVT, so seamless are its gear changes. True to its autobahn-bred heritage, the A8 is utterly relaxed at felonious velocities, so a watchful eye on the speedo is well advised. Powerfully reassuring brakes that are easily modulated have no problem reining in the A8. The air suspension is well sorted; left in automatic, the system works just fine providing a soft but not mushy ride and solid composure through the twisty bits. And when used in the dynamic setting, body lean is kept to an absolute minimum, making the A8 feel more like Audi's sporty TT coupe than the company's flagship sedan.

*Crash Test Scores, see pg 530*
*Warranty information, see pg 542*

## Specifications

| Engine/Drivetrain | HP | Torque | EPA Fuel Economy Rating |
|---|---|---|---|
| 8cyl 4.2L A | 335 | 317 | 18 city/24 hwy |

## Body Styles

| Style | MSRP Range |
|---|---|
| Large Sedan | $66,590–$69,900 |

**MSRP Price Range**

## $45,850 - $55,150

Destination Charge: $720 (all styles)

### Ratings

| | | |
|---|---|---|
| Consumer Rating | 9.3 | ████████████ |
| Editors Rating | 8.4 | ███████████ |

**What Edmunds.com says:** Though not quite as enthralling as BMW's frenetic M3, the S4 still offers entertaining performance along with a more livable personality.

**Pros:** Broad power band, confident handling, high-quality materials and attractive cabin design, available as a sedan, wagon or convertible.

**Cons:** Not the tire smoker you would expect, small backseat, priced close to more established rivals.

**What's New:** For 2005, the S4 gets a new satellite/navigation/AM/FM antenna.

**Body Styles, Trim Levels and Options:** The S4 is available as a sedan, wagon or convertible in one well-equipped trim level. Standard features include 18-inch wheels and tires, xenon headlights, 12-way power-adjustable Recaro seats, Silk Nappa leather upholstery, dual-zone automatic climate control, heated mirrors and a 10-speaker audio system with an in-dash CD changer. Convertibles are equipped with more conventional leather-upholstered sport seats in place of the Recaros, along with a power-operated soft top. Among the available options are an upgraded 215-watt Bose stereo, a navigation system and OnStar telematics.

**Powertrains and Performance:** All S4s are fitted with a 4.2-liter, 340-horsepower V8 that channels the power to Audi's quattro all-wheel-drive system through either a six-speed manual gearbox or a six-speed Tiptronic automatic. The latter transmission allows manual-style shifting via steering wheel-mounted paddles. Audi claims that an S4 sedan equipped with the manual tranny can sprint from zero to 60 mph in 5.3 seconds.

**Safety:** Safety features include a superb set of four-wheel antilock disc brakes, Electronic Brakeforce Distribution, BrakeAssist and stability control. Additionally, the S4 is equipped with side airbags for the driver and front passenger. There are also side curtain airbags for the front and rear; seat-mounted side airbags for the rear are optional. In government crash testing, the A4 sedan on which the S4 is based received five stars (the highest rating) for front-seat occupants in the side-impact category and four stars for the rear. And in frontal offset crash testing, the Audi earned the highest rating of "Good" and was named a "Best Pick."

**Interior Design and Special Features:** Audi interiors are some of the finest in the luxury car arena; one look at the S4's cabin and the high quality of materials used is quickly apparent. Tasteful accents abound, such as gray birch wood trim and gray instrument facings. The S4's serious performance intentions are reinforced by standard Recaro front seats in the sedan and wagon, which feature aggressive bolstering to hold one in place during spirited runs through the twisties. Although the rear seat is fine for small children, adults seated back there will likely complain about a shortage of legroom. The Avant wagon provides up to 61 cubic feet of cargo space with the rear seats folded.

**Driving Impressions:** As one would expect, with a 340-horse V8, performance is thrilling, and on winding back roads, the S4's top-notch underpinnings result in excellent handling while still providing a supple ride. While the Audi isn't quite as razor-sharp as BMW's M3, the extra grip afforded by its all-wheel drive could justify the trade-off for many enthusiasts, particularly those who live in parts of the country where rain- or snow-slicked roads are a part of life.

*Crash Test Scores, see pg 530*
*Warranty information, see pg 542*

### Specifications

| Engine/Drivetrain | HP | Torque | EPA Fuel Economy Rating |
|---|---|---|---|
| 8cyl 4.2L A/M | 340 | 302 | 18 city/24 hwy |

### Body Styles

| Style | MSRP Range |
|---|---|
| Compact Convertible | $53,950–$55,150 |
| Compact Sedan | $45,850–$47,050 |
| Compact Wagon | $46,850–$48,050 |

# Audi

# 2005 Audi TT

**MSRP Price Range**

## $33,500 - $43,150

Destination Charge: $720 (all styles)

### Ratings

| | | |
|---|---|---|
| Consumer Rating | 9.6 | |
| Editors Rating | 7.3 | |

**What Edmunds.com says:** For buyers seeking the ultimate performance sport coupe or roadster, the TT may disappoint, but if you're willing to give up a little performance in the name of style, the TT is a real head-turner.

**Pros:** One-of-a-kind styling, cutting-edge interiors, sophisticated DSG transmission, strong V6 engine, available all-wheel drive.

**Cons:** Confusing interior controls, roadster's hefty curb weight limits handling, useless backseat in coupe.

**What's New:** Satellite radio is now available on both TT coupes and roadsters.

*Crash Test Scores, see pg 530*
*Warranty information, see pg 542*

### Specifications

| Engine/Drivetrain | HP | Torque | EPA Fuel Economy Rating |
|---|---|---|---|
| 6cyl 3.2L A | 250 | 236 | 22 city/27 hwy |
| 4cyl 1.8L M | 225 | 207 | 20 city/29 hwy |
| 4cyl 1.8L A | 180 | 173 | 21 city/29 hwy |

### Body Styles

| Style | MSRP Range |
|---|---|
| Compact Convertible | $35,500–$43,150 |
| Compact Coupe | $33,500–$40,150 |

**Body Styles, Trim Levels and Options:** Coupe and roadster body styles are offered in three levels of trim based on engine output. Base 180-horsepower models come standard with a long list of features that includes automatic climate control, leather seats, a CD player, 16-inch wheels, xenon headlights and a manual top on roadster versions. Midgrade 225-hp models add 17-inch wheels and a power-operated top on roadsters. Top-of-the-line 250-hp versions add a firmer suspension, minor exterior enhancements, a modified exhaust system and an aluminum shifter cover. Options include a Bose sound system, heated seats, a navigation system and 18-inch wheels and tires.

**Powertrains and Performance:** Three engines are available on the TT. Front-wheel-drive coupes and roadsters get a 1.8-liter turbocharged inline four that generates 180 hp and 173 pound-feet of torque. A six-speed automatic is standard; a six-speed manual is optional. Quattro all-wheel-drive models come with one of two engines. The first is a 225-hp version of the 1.8-liter four; it comes with a standard six-speed manual but a six-speed automatic is optional. The other choice is a 3.2-liter V6 that delivers 250 hp and 236 lb-ft of torque; it's coupled to Audi's six-speed Direct Shift Gearbox (DSG). This electronically controlled manual transmission provides the smoothness and convenience of an automatic along with the ability to perform quick manual shifts via steering wheel-mounted paddles.

**Safety:** All TTs come with four-wheel antilock disc brakes and electronic stability control. Side and head airbags are standard, and Audi contends that the protection level of the roadster in a rollover is equal to that of the coupe. In government side-impact crash testing, the TT received a perfect five stars for protection of front occupants.

**Interior Design and Special Features:** Aluminum and leather dominate a decidedly industrial theme that blends retro and modern design elements into one enticing package. A standard power glass windblocker ensures that chilly nights along the beach are pleasant for roadster owners. Trunk capacity ranges from 6.4 cubic feet in quattro roadsters to 13.8 cubes in front-drive coupes.

**Driving Impressions:** Driven back-to-back with its competitors, the TT's hefty curb weight and soft suspension are immediately evident, though the added horsepower and advanced transmission of the 250-hp, 3.2-liter model help the TT keep up with peers like the Infiniti G35 and BMW Z4 when it comes to straight-line acceleration. The compliant suspension yields a blissfully secure ride, but pick up the pace and the TT tends to wallow through dips and turns. Overall, Audi has engineered an excellent compromise between comfort and performance, but for the most part, this is a cruiser not a bruiser.

# 2005 Audi allroad quattro

**MSRP Price Range**
## $40,250 - $47,250
Destination Charge: $720 (all styles)

### Ratings

| | | |
|---|---|---|
| Consumer Rating | N/A | |
| Editors Rating | 7.9 | |

**What Edmunds.com says:** For luxury car buyers who seek extra utility without the added bulk of a full-blown SUV, Audi's allroad delivers excellent all-weather capability in an elegant package. However, many car-based SUVs now offer more comfort and flexibility than the allroad and many of them do it for less money.

**Pros:** Elegant interior, powerful engines, flexibility of adjustable-height suspension, competent off-road performance.

**Cons:** High base price, turbo lag in V6 version, suspension can be harsh over bumps, lousy fuel economy in city driving.

**What's New:** Black fender panels and the optional OnStar system are no longer available.

**Body Styles, Trim Levels and Options:** The allroad is sold in two trim levels powered by either a twin-turbo V6 or a V8. Standard equipment for both includes dual-zone automatic climate control, a full set of one-touch windows, 12-way power front seats (with memory for the driver), an in-dash six-CD changer, a split-folding rear seat, genuine wood interior trim and 17-inch wheels. The options list includes a couple of premium packages that bundle popular features like leather upholstery, a sunroof, xenon headlights and auto-dimming mirrors. The V8 version also comes with 18-inch wheels and higher-grade leather seating. A 200-watt Bose sound system, a navigation system, satellite radio (XM or Sirius), a parking assist system and hands-free phone compatibility are among the a la carte extras.

**Powertrains and Performance:** The 250-horsepower, 2.7-liter twin-turbo V6 generates 258 pound-feet of torque over a broad rpm band. Turbo lag is evident when scooting away from stoplights, but thereafter, forward thrust is prodigious. The engine can be paired with a six-speed manual transmission or a five-speed Tiptronic automanual. The 4.2-liter V8 sports 300 horsepower and 280 lb-ft of torque and is paired with a five-speed Tiptronic automatic. As expected, the V8 furnishes more off-the-line grunt and cruises effortlessly at high speeds. The standard quattro all-wheel-drive system distributes the power to all four wheels and automatically adjusts power distribution for surefooted handling in low-traction environments. The height-adjustable pneumatic suspension offers four settings, ranging from 5.6 inches of ground clearance for efficient high-speed travel and easy entry and exit to a maximum of 8.2 inches for low-speed travel on rugged terrain.

**Safety:** Active safety features include four-wheel antilock disc brakes, Electronic Brakeforce Distribution and stability control (ESP). Additionally, side airbags (for front occupants) and a side curtain protection system (for the front and rear) are standard. Rear-seat-mounted side airbags are optional.

**Interior Design and Special Features:** Top-quality materials cover every inch of the cabin and the overall layout is simple yet elegant. The many stereo and climate controls aren't immediately intuitive, but once learned, they pose little annoyance. Cargo capacity is 36.4 cubic feet with the second-row seats in use, and 73.2 cubes when they're folded.

**Driving Impressions:** Like it or not, the allroad makes for an interesting drive. The same twin-turbo engine that leaves you waiting in city traffic allows you to blast down empty highways. The V8 is more muscular, delivering immediate thrust off the line but fuel economy dips even lower. Although the allroad is generally smooth-riding, the suspension can feel overly harsh over bumps and ruts and overly soft when rounding corners. The quattro all-wheel-drive system and adjustable suspension allow the wagon to get through snow and light-duty off-road trails with little difficulty.

Crash Test Scores, see pg 530
Warranty information, see pg 542

### Specifications

| Engine/Drivetrain | HP | Torque | EPA Fuel Economy Rating |
|---|---|---|---|
| 8cyl 4.2L A | 300 | 280 | N/A |
| 6cyl 2.7L A/M | 250 | 258 | N/A |

### Body Styles

| Style | MSRP Range |
|---|---|
| Midsize Wagon | $40,250–$47,250 |

# 2005 BMW 3 Series
### Compact Convertible, Coupe, Sedan, Wagon

**MSRP Price Range**
## $29,300 – $44,600
Destination Charge: $695 (all styles)

#1 Editors' Rating

## Ratings

| | | |
|---|---|---|
| Consumer Rating | 9.4 | |
| Editors Rating | 8.3 | |

**What Edmunds.com says:** If you've got the bucks to spend, this is unequivocally the best car in the entry-luxury category.

**Pros:** Still the standard when it comes to perfectly sorted vehicle dynamics, high-quality interior materials exude luxury, wide range of configurations to suit any style, available all-wheel drive for sedan and wagon.

**Cons:** Still costs more than most of its competitors, limited rear-seat space and cargo capacity, confusing array of options and packages.

**What's New:** A power moonroof and Myrtle wood trim are now standard on all models. Brushed aluminum column trim is available as a no-cost option. Front lumbar support has been added to the Premium Package for all 325 models; a power top is now standard on the 325Ci convertible; and new star-spoke wheels are standard on the 325Ci coupe and convertible. The 330Ci convertible gets an auto-dimming rearview mirror, lumbar support and a universal garage door opener as standard. This year, the sequential manual gearbox (SMG) is available only on 3.0-liter models, and only in combination with the Sport Package. Buyers can now order both the Performance and Premium Packages together. Lastly, a flat tire warning and white indicator lights are now standard on all models.

*Crash Test Scores, see pg 530*
*Warranty information, see pg 542*

## Specifications

| Engine/Drivetrain | HP | Torque | EPA Fuel Economy Rating |
|---|---|---|---|
| 6cyl 3.0L M | 225 | 214 | 21 city/30 hwy |
| 6cyl 2.5L M | 184 | 175 | 20 city/29 hwy |

## Body Styles

| Style | MSRP Range |
|---|---|
| Compact Convertible | $39,000–$44,600 |
| Compact Coupe | $31,700–$37,300 |
| Compact Sedan | $29,300–$37,450 |
| Compact Wagon | $31,200–$32,950 |

**Body Styles, Trim Levels and Options:** The lineup includes the 325i sedan and wagon, 330i sedan, 325xi all-wheel-drive sedan and wagon, 330xi all-wheel-drive sedan, 325Ci coupe and convertible and 330Ci coupe and convertible. Standard features on 325 models include 16-inch wheels, automatic climate control, leatherette (vinyl, that is) upholstery, one-touch power windows, a power moonroof, automatic headlights, heated mirrors, a CD player and keyless entry. Additionally, coupes have a sport-tuned suspension, and coupes and wagons have a split-folding rear seat (optional on sedans). The 330 models add 17-inch wheels, a sport suspension (optional on the 330Ci convertible and not available on the 330xi), and a Harman Kardon sound system. The 330Ci convertible also gets power leather seats. You can get any of these features in one form or another on other models; a DVD-based navigation system, bi-xenon headlights and parking sensors are stand-alone extras for the entire lineup. There are also several wheel and tire upgrade packages. The 330i sedan is eligible for the Performance Package, which incorporates a few drivetrain modifications, even tighter suspension tuning, 18-inch wheels and suede upholstery.

**Powertrains and Performance:** All 325 models are powered by a 2.5-liter inline six that makes 184 horsepower and 175 pound-feet of torque. All 330s use a 3.0-liter engine that generates 225 hp and 214 lb-ft of torque. On 330i sedans with the Performance Package, output goes up to 235 hp and 222 lb-ft. Transmission choices include either a five-speed or six-speed manual, depending on the model, and a five-speed automatic. BMW's Sequential Manual Gearbox (SMG) is also available on 3.0-liter rear-drive models equipped with the Sport Package. Either engine is more than ample for everyday travel, though the 3.0-liter is by far our favorite as it's able to propel a manual-shift 330i to 60 mph in just 6.3 seconds.

**Safety:** Included on every model are four-wheel antilock disc brakes, stability control, dynamic brake control, front side-impact airbags and head curtain airbags (convertibles get rollover protection) for the front and rear; rear side-impact bags are optional. The 3 Series earned a "Good" rating (the highest) in IIHS frontal offset crash testing, as well as four stars for the driver and five stars for the front passenger in government frontal impact testing.

**Interior Design and Special Features:** The 3 Series' interiors provide a restrained show of luxury, wherein the emphasis is on driver comfort and involvement (hence the supportive seats and clean analog gauges). Materials are high in quality and build quality is exceptional; indeed, even the standard vinyl upholstery looks and feels better than you would expect.

**Driving Impressions:** The 3 Series never fails to impress us. Its world-class suspension, steering and brakes provide hours of entertainment on twisty two-lane highways—beyond simply feeling rock-solid when hustled around turns, this car communicates with the driver in a manner that inspires confidence no matter what kind of driving you're doing. And you don't have to give up a comfortable ride to get this kind of athleticism.

# 2005 BMW 5 Series

## Ratings

| | | |
|---|---|---|
| Consumer Rating | N/A | |
| Editors Rating | 8.4 | |

**What Edmunds.com says:** Controversial styling and BMW's continued use of the confounding iDrive system are the only blemishes on this otherwise outstanding luxury sport sedan.

**Pros:** One of the most satisfying midsize sport sedans you can buy, ultrarefined engines, multiple transmissions, tastefully appointed cabin, exceptional build quality, strong resale value.

**Cons:** Styling may not appeal to 5 Series loyalists, iDrive system still more hassle than it's worth, costs more than most competitors.

**What's New:** For 2005, the interior of all models receives more extensive wood trim on the center console, and adjustable front lumbar support is now standard on the 530i and 545i. Poplar wood trim is now included on the 525i and 530i. Anthracite Maple wood trim is a no-cost option. The 525i receives 17-inch Star Spoke cast-alloy wheels, and park distance control is now standard on the 545i. Active Steering is now offered as a stand-alone option on all models. The 545i now comes standard with the six-speed manual transmission, with the six-speed steptronic automatic available as a no-cost option. BMW's innovative SMG sequential manual gearbox is available on the 530i and 545i.

**Body Styles, Trim Levels and Options:** The 5 Series sedan comes in three models: 525i, 530i and 545i. Standard equipment includes automatic climate control, a CD player, a full set of one-touch power windows, rain-sensing windshield wipers and heated power mirrors. Ten-way power front seats are standard, with 12-way power front sport seats and four-way power lumbar support, and 20-way power multifunction comfort front seats with memory as options. The iDrive vehicle management system is integrated into all 5 Series models, while a DVD-based navigation system with voice command and adaptive cruise control are optional. On the audio side, buyers will be able to get a glovebox-mounted CD/DVD changer, as well as a premium-grade Harman Kardon Logic 7 sound system. Other options to consider include adaptive bi-xenon headlights, and a sport package with various wheel/run-flat tire upgrades (up to 18 inches in diameter), firmer suspension tuning and Active Front Steering (AFS).

**Powertrains and Performance:** BMW's 2.5-liter six-cylinder generates 184 horsepower, while the 3.0-liter is rated at 225 hp. The top-of-the-line 545i features the same 4.4-liter V8 found in the flagship 7 Series rated at 325 hp. All models get a six-speed manual standard with a six-speed Steptronic automatic an available option. The 530i and 545i can also be had with BMW's sequential manual gearbox (SMG), a sophisticated transmission that combines the control of a manual gearbox with the ease of an automatic. Performance from the base 2.5-liter is refined, if not exhilarating. The 3.0-liter engine provides the best compromise between speed and efficiency, while the V8 delivers outstanding performance at just about any speed.

**Safety:** Standard safety equipment includes a head protection system and side-impact airbags for both the front and rear seats. Dynamic Stability Control (DSC), electronic brake proportioning, cornering and braking stability enhancements and four-wheel antilock disc brakes are standard across the model line. Active front head restraints and Advanced Safety Electronics (ASE) that govern the deployment of safety systems are optional. The 5 Series was named a "Best Pick" in IIHS frontal offset crash testing.

**Interior Design and Special Features:** The driver-oriented 5 Series cockpit greets passengers with a dignified show of luxury. As in the 7 Series, the multifunction iDrive interface integrates the audio, climate and navigation systems, but basic functions can be accomplished without going through iDrive. Build and materials quality is outstanding. Supportive seating is provided in both the front and rear, and even adults won't mind sitting in the backseat.

**Driving Impressions:** The 5 Series is an extremely balanced machine that can handle aggressive driving maneuvers as well as it does dilapidated highways. The active steering system hasn't dulled BMW's trademark steering feel, and even vehicles equipped with the optional run-flat tires maintain a livable ride quality. Equipped with the V8, this is a true enthusiast's sedan that will outpace many sports cars.

*Crash Test Scores, see pg 530*
*Warranty information, see pg 542*

## Specifications

| Engine/Drivetrain | HP | Torque | EPA Fuel Economy Rating |
|---|---|---|---|
| 8cyl 4.4L M | 325 | 330 | 17 city/25 hwy |
| 6cyl 3.0L M | 225 | 214 | 20 city/30 hwy |
| 6cyl 2.5L M | 184 | 175 | 19 city/28 hwy |

## Body Styles

| Style | MSRP Range |
|---|---|
| Midsize Sedan | $41,300–$55,800 |

# 2005 BMW 6 Series

**MSRP Price Range**

## $69,900 - $76,900

Destination Charge: $695 (all styles)

### Ratings

| | | |
|---|---|---|
| Consumer Rating | N/A | |
| Editors Rating | 8.1 | |

**What Edmunds.com says:** The 6 Series may not have the sleek, sexy sheet metal of its Mercedes-Benz rivals, but its satisfying combination of performance, luxury and technology will put you on top of the world.

**Pros:** Nimble handling for a big coupe, smooth and quiet ride, endless power from ultrasmooth V8, elegant interior design, supportive seats, large trunk in coupe.

**Cons:** iDrive controller is improved but still a nuisance, small backseat, only one engine option.

**What's New:** Park distance control is now standard on both the coupe and convertible, and active cruise control is a new option. Active steering is now a stand-alone option on all models. Shadowline high-gloss exterior trim is now included in the Sport package on the 645Ci convertible.

*Crash Test Scores, see pg 530*
*Warranty information, see pg 542*

### Specifications

| Engine/Drivetrain | HP | Torque | EPA Fuel Economy Rating |
|---|---|---|---|
| 8cyl 4.4L M | 325 | 330 | 17 city/25 hwy |

### Body Styles

| Style | MSRP Range |
|---|---|
| Midsize Convertible | $76,900 |
| Midsize Coupe | $69,900 |

**Body Styles, Trim Levels and Options:** Available in coupe and convertible body styles, the 6 Series comes in just one well-equipped level of trim. Standard equipment includes automatic climate control, a CD player with MP3 compatibility, a full set of one-touch power windows, rain-sensing windshield wipers and heated power mirrors. The seats feature multiple power adjustments and electric heaters for a perfect fit and a warm backside. The iDrive vehicle management system is integrated into the console, while a DVD-based navigation system with voice command and park distance control also comes standard. Active cruise control is optional. On the audio side, buyers can opt for a glovebox-mounted CD changer, as well as a premium-grade Harman Kardon Logic 7 sound system. An optional sport package adds BMW's unique Active Front Steering system along with bolstered sport seats and larger wheel and tires.

**Powertrains and Performance:** There is only one engine offered this year: a 4.4-liter V8 rated to produce 325 horsepower and 330 pound-feet of torque. Shared with the 7 Series sedan, the eight-cylinder uses the latest in advanced engine technology to produce a broad band of power while remaining remarkably smooth and silent. Three different transmissions allow you to choose varying levels of performance and driving effort. There's a six-speed manual for do-it-yourself enthusiasts, a six-speed automatic for those who don't really care how the shifts get done and a six-speed paddle-shifted Sequential Manual Gearbox (SMG) that offers a combination of both. Regardless of which transmission you choose, the 645i delivers outstanding performance with a 0-to-60 time of 5.6 seconds in the coupe.

**Safety:** Four-wheel antilock disc brakes fortified with Electronic Brakeforce Distribution are standard along with stability and traction control (BMW's DSC). Run-flat tires are optional along with adaptive headlights for better visibility. Other safety features include front side-impact in both cars, full-length side curtain airbags (coupe only) and a rollover protection system (convertible only).

**Interior Design and Special Features:** Utilization of BMW's iDrive control system reduces button clutter to a minimum, making for a clean dash design but confusing operation of some controls. BMW's trademark analog gauges stare out from behind the steering wheel, while an optional head-up display offers to project pertinent vehicle info onto the windshield for less distraction. Thanks to its generous dimensions and standard panorama roof (coupes only) the 6 Series is spacious for two, but four adults make for a tight fit.

**Driving Impressions:** Although it's not quite as nimble as BMW's smaller 3 Series coupe, the 645i is a very capable performer when driven hard. Its combination of modest weight and ample power make for quick acceleration from any speed. The Active Roll Stabilization system keeps the big coupe flat around corners, and the lightweight suspension does its part to maintain traction and soak up the bumps. The wide range of transmissions allows you to outfit the 6 Series in a way that best suits your particular driving style, so consider the options carefully.

# 2005 BMW 7 Series

**MSRP Price Range**
## $69,900 - $117,300
Destination Charge: $695 (all styles)

### Ratings

| | | |
|---|---|---|
| Consumer Rating | 8.2 | |
| Editors Rating | 7.9 | |

**What Edmunds.com says:** A brilliant luxury sedan scarred by senselessly complicated interior controls and awkward exterior styling.

**Pros:** Superb driving dynamics, world-class drivetrain, highly advanced safety systems, dizzying array of features, sumptuous furnishings.

**Cons:** Toys can be distracting from the task at hand, confusing secondary controls, odd styling details.

**What's New:** Park distance control and adaptive headlights are now standard on all models. Comfort Access is a new option, and allows the driver to lock and unlock the doors without pressing any remote buttons. Also new this year is a Rear Entertainment package that includes a rear-seat iDrive controller and screen, as well as a trunk-mounted six-disc DVD changer.

**Body Styles, Trim Levels and Options:** Four versions of the 7 Series sedan are offered: the standard-wheelbase 745i and 760i, and the long-wheelbase 745Li and 760Li. Standard fare on the 745i includes 18-inch wheels, bi-HID headlights, park distance control, adaptive headlights, leather upholstery, matte-finish cherry wood interior trim, a 14-way power driver seat and 12-way front-passenger seat, a navigation system, a 10-speaker sound system with a CD player, dual-zone climate control, one-touch windows and a moonroof. The 745Li adds 20-way adjustable front seats and dynamic front headrests (both optional on the 745i). Both cars are eligible for a long list of options—the only difference is that the 745Li can be had with power rear seats to complement the extra legroom in the back. Otherwise, options include 19-inch wheels, Active Cruise Control, an adaptive ride package with a self-leveling rear suspension and Electronic Damping Control, "soft-close" doors and trunk lid, heating and cooling for the front seats and a premium sound system with an in-dash CD changer. Almost all of the above items come standard on the 760i and 760Li. A Rear Entertainment package is also available, and features a rear-seat iDrive controller and screen, along with a trunk-mounted six-disc DVD changer.

**Powertrains and Performance:** The 745i and 745Li are powered by a 4.4-liter V8 with 325 horsepower and 330 pound-feet of torque, along with impressive EPA mileage ratings of 18 city/26 highway. The 760i and 760Li offer a 6.0-liter V12 with direct-injection technology—the first V12 production engine to do so. Mileage numbers are lower than the 745i at 15 city/22 highway, but power is impressive at 438 hp and 444 lb-ft of torque.

**Safety:** Included on every model are four-wheel antilock disc brakes, an electronic stability control system, front side-impact airbags, head protection airbags for front and rear occupants and active knee protection.

**Interior Design and Special Features:** Inside, the cabin has a clean appearance, thanks to the minimal center stack controls, though not all interior materials are as upscale as they should be. The iDrive system was designed to consolidate the vehicle's control systems into one easy-to-use interface, but its confusing operation makes it more trouble than it's worth. Backseat passengers will be just as comfortable as those in front, as the rear seat back contours perfectly support your lower back and shoulders, while headroom and legroom are abundant. Go for the 745Li or 760Li and you'll get 5.6 inches of increased wheelbase, most of it going into rear-seat legroom.

**Driving Impressions:** Even at high speeds, the 7 Series cabin is devoid of engine and wind noise. Steering feel is typical BMW with relatively high weighting and excellent feedback. Body roll is held in check during cornering via the standard Active Roll Stabilization system. While it may be a stretch to call the 7 nimble, words like "confident" and "dynamic" are perfectly suited to this sedan.

*Crash Test Scores, see pg 530*
*Warranty information, see pg 542*

### Specifications

| Engine/Drivetrain | HP | Torque | EPA Fuel Economy Rating |
|---|---|---|---|
| 8cyl 4.4L A | 325 | 330 | 18 city/26 hwy |
| 12cyl 6.0L A | 438 | 444 | 18 city/26 hwy |

### Body Styles

| Style | MSRP Range |
|---|---|
| Large Sedan | $69,900–$117,300 |

# 2005 BMW M3

**MSRP Price Range**
## $47,300 - $55,800
Destination Charge: $695 (all styles)

## Ratings

| | | |
|---|---|---|
| Consumer Rating | N/A | |
| Editors Rating | 8.4 | |

**What Edmunds.com says:** Phenomenal BMW handling combined with an equally awe-inspiring engine make this high-performance Motorsport creation one of our all-time favorites.

**Pros:** Remarkable engine, racecarlike handling, sumptuous interior, available Sequential Manual Gearbox.

**Cons:** Uninspired exhaust whine, having to pay extra for basics like power seats and an alarm system.

**What's New:** Aluminum trim is now standard on all models, with Titan Shadow trim available at no extra charge.

**Body Styles, Trim Levels and Options:** The M3 in offered in both coupe and convertible form. Standard features on the coupe include 18-inch wheels with Z-rated rubber, automatic climate control, 10-way adjustable sport seats, leather and cloth upholstery, one-touch power windows, heated power mirrors, a CD player, an auto-dimming rearview mirror, automatic headlights, rain-sensing wipers and keyless entry. The convertible adds power seat adjustments and full leather upholstery; these items are optional on the coupe. Additionally, the drop top comes with a fully automatic soft top (with heated rear glass); a removable hardtop is available. Among the other options are seat heaters, bi-xenon headlights, a navigation system, a premium sound system, parking sensors, BMW Assist and an alarm system.

**Powertrains and Performance:** The M3 is propelled by a magnificent 3.2-liter, six-cylinder engine rated to produce 333 horsepower and 262 pound-feet of torque. A six-speed manual transmission is standard, while a six-speed sequential manual gearbox (SMG) is offered as an option. The SMG offers both manual and automatic driving modes, and although it is by definition a manual transmission (no torque converter), its clutch is electronically controlled, such that there's no clutch pedal. Drivers can use either steering column-mounted paddles or the shift lever to change gears in manual mode. Unlike other systems, SMG allows you to alter the quickness of the shifts, and in its most aggressive shift program, it's said to be faster than Ferrari's Formula One setup.

**Safety:** Safety features include four-wheel antilock disc brakes, stability control, front side-impact airbags, head curtain airbags for the front (coupe only) and a rollover protection system (convertible only); rear side-impact bags are optional. The 3 Series earned a "Good" rating from the IIHS in 40-mph frontal offset crash testing.

**Interior Design and Special Features:** Aggressive driving is aided by heavily bolstered front bucket seats, a thick M Sport steering wheel with attractive blue and red stitching and distinctive red-needled M instrumentation. The rest of the interior is pretty much standard-issue 3 Series, and that means high-quality materials and tight construction.

**Driving Impressions:** We've always loved the near telepathic feel of the 3 Series' suspension, and the M3 is all that and more. The near insurmountable grip and predictable motions inspire cornering speeds that will leave even the most experienced drivers second-guessing themselves. Keep the throttle set in "sport" mode and the M3 will tackle your favorite set of switchbacks as fast as any production car on the road.

*Crash Test Scores, see pg 530*
*Warranty information, see pg 542*

## Specifications

| Engine/Drivetrain | HP | Torque | EPA Fuel Economy Rating |
|---|---|---|---|
| 6cyl 3.2L M | 333 | 262 | 16 city/24 hwy |

## Body Styles

| Style | MSRP Range |
|---|---|
| Compact Convertible | $55,800 |
| Compact Coupe | $47,300 |

# 2005 BMW X3

**MSRP Price Range**

## $30,300 - $36,300

Destination Charge: N/A (all styles)

### Ratings

| | | |
|---|---|---|
| Consumer Rating | N/A | |
| Editors Rating | 8.1 | |

**What Edmunds.com says:** Looking for a small SUV that performs like a sport sedan? The X3 shouldn't disappoint, so long as you don't mind its big price tag and so-so cabin ambience.

**Pros:** World-class engines, nimble handling, precise steering, comfortable cabin, solid build quality.

**Cons:** Expensive for a compact sport-ute, limited cargo space, some economy-grade interior materials, overly stiff ride with Sport Package.

**What's New:** No significant changes for 2005.

**Body Styles, Trim Levels and Options:** The X3 is a compact four-door SUV that comes in two trim levels that correspond to their respective engines—either 2.5i or 3.0i. The base 2.5i comes with all the features like automatic climate control, leatherette (vinyl, that is) upholstery, one-touch power windows, automatic headlights, heated mirrors, a CD player and keyless entry. The 3.0i models add larger wheels and tires and an upgraded audio system. Options on both models include full leather upholstery, a DVD-based navigation system, bi-xenon headlights and rear parking sensors. Order the Sport Package on either model and you'll get a firmer suspension and a more aggressive wheel/tire set.

**Powertrains and Performance:** The 2.5i is powered by a 2.5-liter inline six that makes 184 horsepower and 175 pound-feet of torque. The 3.0i uses a 3.0-liter engine that generates 225 hp and 214 lb-ft of torque. Both models come standard with a six-speed manual transmission; a five-speed Steptronic automatic is optional. Also standard on all models is an all-wheel-drive system dubbed xDrive that automatically distributes power to the wheels with the most traction for optimum performance in all conditions.

**Safety:** Both X3 models feature standard four-wheel antilock disc brakes, Dynamic Stability Control (DSC), Hill Descent Control (HDC) and a full complement of front, side and side curtain airbags. The X3 has not yet been crash tested.

**Interior Design and Special Features:** An updated version of the 3 Series cabin, the X3's interior is still instantly recognizable as a BMW. Large analog gauges greet the driver, and the supportive seats provide a commanding view of the road. The climate controls are still more complex than we would like, but the overall look is very clean and uncluttered. Unfortunately, not all of the materials are up to the premium standards set by the 3 Series, giving the X3 a more economy-grade feel than its price tag would indicate. Passenger space is about average for the category, with a smaller cargo hold than most compact SUVS.

**Driving Impressions:** It may be an SUV but it sure doesn't drive like one. Much like its bigger brother, the X5, the X3 feels more like a sporty sedan behind the wheel than a lumbering off-road machine. Typically precise steering combined with a tightly controlled suspension and perfect traction results in a sport-ute that gives up little in the way of driving dynamics. The downside to this is that the ride quality can be overly stiff on vehicles equipped with the Sport Package. However, if you're looking for the closest thing to a sports car with a high seating position, this is your vehicle.

Crash Test Scores, see pg 530
Warranty information, see pg 542

### Specifications

| Engine/Drivetrain | HP | Torque | EPA Fuel Economy Rating |
|---|---|---|---|
| 6cyl 2.5L A/M | 184 | 175 | N/A |
| 6cyl 3.0L A/M | 225 | 214 | N/A |

### Body Styles

| Style | MSRP Range |
|---|---|
| Midsize SUV | $30,300 - $36,300 |

# 2005 BMW X5

**MSRP Price Range**

## $41,700 – $70,100

Destination Charge: $695 (all styles)

### Ratings

| | | |
|---|---|---|
| Consumer Rating | 8.8 | |
| Editors Rating | 8.0 | |

**What Edmunds.com says:** If you want a vehicle that looks utilitarian but doesn't drive that way, you can't do much better than the X5—just don't expect much in the way of practicality.

**Pros:** Rides and drives like a BMW sedan, multiple drivetrain choices, top safety scores, high-end cabin furnishings.

**Cons:** Not much cargo space, lousy fuel economy for a car-based SUV, expensive option packages.

**What's New:** Front lumbar supports and automatic climate control are now standard on all models, while the 4.4i gets standard park distance control. The optional auto-dimming rearview mirror now includes a digital compass. High-gloss dark wood trim is standard on the 3.0i and replaces high-gloss light wood trim as standard on the 4.4i. Anthracite wood trim and high-gloss light wood trim are available at no extra charge.

*Crash Test Scores, see pg 530*
*Warranty information, see pg 542*

### Specifications

| Engine/Drivetrain | HP | Torque | EPA Fuel Economy Rating |
|---|---|---|---|
| 8cyl 4.8L A | 355 | 360 | N/A |
| 8cyl 4.4L A | 315 | 324 | 16 city/22 hwy |
| 6cyl 3.0L M | 225 | 214 | 15 city/21 hwy |

### Body Styles

| Style | MSRP Range |
|---|---|
| Midsize SUV | $41,700–$70,100 |

**Body Styles, Trim Levels and Options:** The X5 is offered as a four-door sport-utility in three trim levels—the 3.0i, the 4.4i and the 4.8is. Standard features on the 3.0i include 17-inch wheels, a power driver seat, wood trim, a tilt/telescoping steering wheel, power-folding and reclining rear seats, one-touch windows, automatic climate control, a CD player and a full-size spare tire. The 4.4i adds 18-inch wheels (losing the full-size spare), leather upholstery, park distance control and a power front-passenger seat—all this stuff is optional for the 3.0i. The 4.8is adds 20-inch wheels, front and rear heated seats and a panoramic moonroof. Additional options for 3.0i and 4.4i models include larger wheels, a sport suspension, automatic xenon headlights, an Alcantara/napa leather combo or full napa, heated power front sport seats, heated rear seats, rain-sensing wipers, auto-dimming mirrors, a moonroof, a premium sound system and a cartridge-style CD changer. Other notable options include a DVD-based navigation system and an adjustable ride height suspension that better enables the X5 to handle light off-roading.

**Powertrains and Performance:** The 3.0i is powered by a 225-horsepower, 3.0-liter inline six that comes standard with a six-speed manual transmission; a five-speed automatic is optional. Although its numbers don't indicate it, this engine has surprising vigor, given its broad, smooth power band. Power fiends can go with either the 4.4i and its 315-hp 4.4-liter V8, or the 4.8is and its 355-hp 4.8-liter V8. These engines only come with a six-speed automatic. Fuel economy is nothing to brag about—the 3.0i is rated at 15 mpg city/21 highway; the 4.4i's efficient V8 allows it to post a slightly better 16/22 rating. Towing capacity is 5,953 pounds for both models. All-wheel drive is standard on all X5s.

**Safety:** Every X5 has stability control, dynamic brake control, Hill Descent Control, front side-impact airbags, head protection airbags for front and rear occupants and an extra set of brakelights that activates during panic stops. In government crash testing, the BMW earned a perfect five stars for driver and front-passenger protection in frontal impacts. In side-impact testing, it earned four stars for front-occupant protection and five stars for the rear. The X5 earned a "Good" rating (the highest possible) in IIHS frontal offset crash testing.

**Interior Design and Special Features:** When it's time to haul the family, the X5 isn't much better than a typical luxury sedan. Rear-seat accommodations are average at best, with the Acura MDX, Infiniti FX, Lexus RX 330 and Volvo XC90 offering more space and comfort. With the second-row seats folded, the X5's maximum cargo capacity peaks at a very disappointing 54.4 cubic feet.

**Driving Impressions:** Ground clearance is limited and there is no low-range transfer case—so the X5 is definitely an all-weather vehicle rather than an all-terrain vehicle. Accept it as a fast, agile, stylish vehicle for spirited runs through the suburbs, and you won't be disappointed.

For the latest full vehicle reports, visit www.edmunds.com/bginfopak

**MSRP Price Range**
## $34,300 - $41,300
Destination Charge: $695 (all styles)

## Ratings

| | | |
|---|---|---|
| Consumer Rating | N/A | |
| Editors Rating | 7.8 | |

**What Edmunds.com says:** The Z4's body lines may not be as sexy as those of the Mercedes SLK, but for the money, you'd be hard-pressed to find a more entertaining luxury roadster.

**Pros:** Exhilarating driving dynamics, long list of standard safety features, refined drivetrains, excellent build quality.

**Cons:** Options are expensive, odd styling, firm ride, notable wind and road noise.

**What's New:** Light Poplar Grain wood trim is available as a no-charge option on all Z4s. White indicator lights are standard across the board, and foglights and cruise control are now standard on the 2.5i. The 3.0i includes automatic climate control as standard equipment this year. Leather seating is no longer part of the 2.5i's Premium Package and is a stand-alone option, while all models receive additional black accents for the interior. The Sequential Manual Gearbox (SMG) is only available on the 3.0i, and requires the Sport Package. Last year's Convenience Package is history, though its contents are now either standard or part of the Premium Package.

**Body Styles, Trim Levels and Options:** BMW offers the Z4 roadster in two trim levels—2.5i and 3.0i. The 2.5i includes 16-inch wheels with run-flat tires, a manually operated soft top (with rear glass), height-adjustable sport seats with leatherette upholstery (or rather, vinyl), cruise control, rain-sensing windshield wipers, a tilt-telescoping steering wheel, a CD player and power windows, mirrors and locks. The 3.0i adds 17-inch wheels, leather upholstery, a center armrest, aluminum interior trim, a premium audio system, automatic climate control and heated mirrors. Any of these features can be added to a 2.5i. Note that wheel-tire upgrades are part of the Sport Package, which also includes a lowered sport suspension, Dynamic Drive Control (a feature that quickens throttle and steering response), and on the 3.0i, 18-inch wheels. Other options include a power-operated top, bi-HID headlights, seat heaters, power seats, a DVD-based navigation system and wood interior trim. Dealer-installed items include a hardtop, a wind deflector, a CD changer, satellite radio and an alarm system.

**Powertrains and Performance:** The 2.5i model is powered by a 2.5-liter, inline six-cylinder engine that makes 184 hp and 175 lb-ft of torque, while the 3.0i uses a 3.0-liter straight six that generates 225 hp and 214 lb-ft of torque. BMW gets a lot out of its engines, and most drivers will be satisfied with the 2.5, which starts to feel winded only at very high speeds. Enthusiasts, of course, will want to go with the 3.0 and its smooth, continuous power supply. A five-speed manual transmission is standard on 2.5s, while 3.0s get a six-speed. If you don't want to deal with a clutch, you can opt for a five-speed automatic (with a Steptronic automanual gate) or, on the 3.0 only, a Sequential Manual Gearbox (SMG).

**Safety:** Every model comes with four-wheel antilock disc brakes, run-flat tires and a sophisticated stability control system. Passive safety features include rollover protection, side airbags, active knee protection and child-seat anchor points for the passenger seat.

**Interior Design and Special Features:** The Z4's simple cockpit features a sweeping dash with a clean set of analog gauges, bolstered sport seats and little else to distract you from the road. Plenty of metallic trim comes standard, but wood trim is available for those who want to dress up their roadster a bit. Both the manual and power-operated convertible tops are easy to use, and the trunk has a generous 9-cubic-foot capacity (made possible by the elimination of the spare tire in favor of run-flat tires).

**Driving Impressions:** With its stiff chassis, large brakes and multiple transmission options, the Z4 provides great driving pleasure—easily managed when driven near the limit on twisty roads. Ride quality is smooth, but commuters may find Sport Package-equipped Z4s too firm for comfort. Wind and road noise can also be bothersome at highway speeds, but once you turn off onto your favorite back road, it becomes a distant memory.

*Crash Test Scores, see pg 530*
*Warranty information, see pg 542*

## Specifications

| Engine/Drivetrain | HP | Torque | EPA Fuel Economy Rating |
|---|---|---|---|
| 6cyl 3.0L M | 225 | 214 | 21 city/29 hwy |
| 6cyl 2.5L M | 184 | 175 | 20 city/28 hwy |

## Body Styles

| Style | MSRP Range |
|---|---|
| Compact Convertible | $34,300–$41,300 |

# 2005 Buick Century

**MSRP Price Range**

## $22,040 - $26,030

Destination Charge: $660 (all styles)

### Ratings

| | | |
|---|---|---|
| Consumer Rating | 7.6 | |
| Editors Rating | 7.2 | |

**What Edmunds.com says:** Although roomy and comfortable, the aging Century can't match the competition when it comes to refinement, features and resale value.

**Pros:** Roomy interior, easy to decipher controls, low base price.

**Cons:** Mushy seats, engine lacks power and refinement, lacks the features of its more modern competitors.

**What's New:** Changes for the Century's final production year are minimal; Glacier Blue Metallic replaces Graphite Metallic and a Special Edition option package has been added.

**Body Styles, Trim Levels and Options:** The Century is offered in several trim levels. Standard equipment includes remote keyless entry, manual dual-zone air conditioning with air filtration, programmable power door locks, power windows, automatic on/off headlamps with daytime running lamps, a tilt steering wheel and a theft-deterrent system. The Custom package adds a power driver seat, cruise control, rear-seat assist handles and floor mats. The Limited package builds on the Custom features with leather seating, steering wheel-mounted audio controls and chrome wheel covers. The new Special Edition is the top-line Century this year, and boasts dual-zone automatic climate control, 16-inch touring tires mounted on chrome alloys, ABS, traction control and a tire inflation monitor. Additional options include the OnStar communications system and an upgraded CD/cassette stereo.

**Powertrains and Performance:** The Century is powered by a 3.1-liter V6 that makes 175 horsepower. With V6 family sedans like the Honda Accord and Nissan Altima now making at least 240 hp (and their four-cylinder versions making at least 160), this Buick is certainly on the short end of the power spectrum. Fuel economy, however, is good for a V6 with a rating of 20 city/29 highway. A smooth-shifting four-speed automatic transmission puts the power to the pavement through the front wheels, and traction control is included with the optional ABS.

**Safety:** All Centurys come with four-wheel disc brakes; ABS and a side-impact airbag (for the driver only) are optional. The National Highway Traffic Safety Administration gave the Century four stars (out of a possible five) for driver-side front-impact protection and three stars for front-passenger protection. Side-impact tests resulted in a three-star rating for both front and rear passengers. The Insurance Institute for Highway Safety gave the Century an "Acceptable" rating for in frontal offset crash testing.

**Interior Design and Special Features:** Inside, occupants will find easy-to-use controls, inoffensive styling and plenty of room up front. The seats are more like couch cushions than car seats, so don't expect much in the way of firm support. The quality of the cabin materials could be better, but overall build quality tends to be better than average. Trunk space is quite generous for a midsize sedan with a maximum capacity of 16.7 cubic feet.

*Crash Test Scores, see pg 530*
*Warranty information, see pg 542*

**Driving Impressions:** The Century offers a pleasant ride over most surfaces, but road feel is minimal and large potholes tend to upset the soft suspension. The standard V6 provides adequate acceleration from a standstill, but freeway passing maneuvers tax its ability to move the sizable sedan. The Buick's forgiving ride and efficient engine make it a solid highway cruiser, but more demanding situations reveal the car's aging design.

### Specifications

| Engine/Drivetrain | HP | Torque | EPA Fuel Economy Rating |
|---|---|---|---|
| 6cyl 3.1L A | 175 | 195 | 20 city/30 hwy |

### Body Styles

| Style | MSRP Range |
|---|---|
| Midsize Sedan | $22,040–$26,030 |

For the latest full vehicle reports, visit www.edmunds.com/bginfopak

# 2005 Buick LaCrosse

**MSRP Price Range**
**$22,835 - $28,335**
Destination Charge: $660 (all styles)

## Ratings

| Consumer Rating | N/A | |
|---|---|---|
| Editors Rating | 7.5 | |

**What Edmunds.com says:** With more refined power under the hood and a contemporary interior, this replacement for the Regal and Century could go a long way toward reestablishing Buick as a premium brand.

**Pros:** Six-passenger seating availability, supremely quiet ride, powerful and refined engine in CXS model, attractive interior.

**Cons:** Stability control limited to CXS trim, base engine lacks refinement, only comes with a four-speed automatic.

**What's New:** The LaCrosse is an all-new premium sedan replacement for both the Century and Regal sedans.

**Body Styles, Trim Levels and Options:** The LaCrosse is available in sedan form only in one of three trims—entry-level CX, luxury-oriented CXL and sporty CXS. The CX includes the basics—cloth upholstery, a power driver seat, a six-speaker CD stereo and OnStar. The CXL adds leather upholstery, a 60/40-split rear seat back, uplevel exterior trim and alloy wheels. The CXS builds upon the CXL with a more powerful V6, a sport-tuned suspension and larger alloy wheels. Among the available equipment are a handy remote start feature (as on the Chevrolet Malibu), rear parking assist, an MP3-compatible stereo and satellite radio.

**Powertrains and Performance:** The tried-and-true 200-horsepower, 3.8-liter (3800) V6 powers the CX and CXL models, but Buick says that engineers took extensive measures to ensure smoother, quieter operation. Additionally, adoption of electronic throttle control should make it more responsive underfoot. Exclusive to the CXS model is a new 3.6-liter DOHC V6. Aided by continuously variable valve timing, it's expected to make about 240 hp and 230 pound-feet of torque. A four-speed automatic transmission is standard on all models. Fuel economy estimates for the base engine are 20 mpg city and 29 mpg highway, while the 3.6-liter V6 should return 19 mpg city and 28 mpg highway.

**Safety:** Dual-stage airbags are standard up front, along with OnStar and four-wheel disc brakes. Unfortunately, ABS is standard only on the top-line CXS and must be purchased as an option on other trims. An optional stability control system is available only on the CXS. Other optional safety equipment includes full-length side curtain airbags and a reverse-sensing system.

**Interior Design and Special Features:** The LaCrosse is offered in both five- and six-passenger seating configurations. Extensive high-quality, soft-touch materials adorn the cabin, a welcome change for Buick. Chrome and fake wood accents abound, but their placement is classy and the wood grain is convincing. A tilt steering wheel is standard on all models, and CXL and CXS models include a telescoping function as well. Even though the overall interior feel is certainly on the traditional side, the passenger space is a tremendous improvement over the departed Regal and Century.

**Driving Impressions:** The strengthened structure and retuned suspension do wonders for the ride and handling characteristics of the LaCrosse. CX and CXL models are definitely on the soft end of the handling spectrum, but the sporty CXS strikes a pleasant compromise between day-to-day comfort and agile handling.

*Crash Test Scores, see pg 530*
*Warranty information, see pg 542*

## Specifications

| Engine/Drivetrain | HP | Torque | EPA Fuel Economy Rating |
|---|---|---|---|
| 6cyl 3.8L A | 200 | 230 | 20 city/29 hwy |
| 6cyl 3.6L A | 240 | 225 | 19 city/28 hwy |

## Body Styles

| Style | MSRP Range |
|---|---|
| Midsize Sedan | $22,835–$28,335 |

# 2005 Buick LeSabre

Large Sedan

**MSRP Price Range**
## $26,545 - $32,205
Destination Charge: $725 (all styles)

### Ratings

| | | |
|---|---|---|
| Consumer Rating | 8.4 | |
| Editors Rating | 7.8 | |

**What Edmunds.com says:** A crowd-pleasing large sedan that offers space, safety and surprisingly good mileage in a high-value and economical package.

**Pros:** Room for six, excellent mileage from V6, smooth ride, huge trunk, solid crash test scores.

**Cons:** Dated interior styling, can be slow when fully loaded, no split-folding rear seat.

**What's New:** The 2005 model year brings no major changes for the LeSabre.

**Body Styles, Trim Levels and Options:** The 2005 LeSabre is comprised of two models—Custom and Limited. Custom includes the usual round of sedan basics, such as power windows, locks and mirrors; air conditioning; remote keyless entry; cruise control; tilt steering; a power driver seat; and an AM/FM stereo with CD player. The Limited adds side airbags, traction control, 16-inch aluminum wheels, rain-sensing wipers, the OnStar communication system, dual-zone automatic climate control and heated seats. Four-wheel-disc brakes with ABS are standard on both trim levels.

**Powertrains and Performance:** The only available powertrain in the LeSabre is the trusty 3.8-liter V6, which is mated to a smooth-shifting four-speed automatic transmission. The engine makes a respectable 205 horsepower and manages to earn an EPA mileage rating of 20 city/29 highway. Acceleration is brisk for the most part, but a full load of passengers and luggage slows the sedan down considerably.

**Safety:** Safety has also been an enduring LeSabre trait, and the 2005 LeSabre doesn't disappoint. The model received high marks in crashworthiness from the Insurance Institute of Highway Safety (IIHS), and was one of the IIHS's "Best Picks" in the large family car class. The National Highway Transportation Safety Administration (NHTSA) gave the LeSabre a perfect five stars for frontal impacts and four stars for side impacts, respectively. The LeSabre continues to offer OnStar, the 24-hour on-demand navigation and assistance service as standard equipment on all models, along with the options of the StabiliTrak stability control system and side airbags.

**Interior Design and Special Features:** Typical Buick buyers place a priority on comfort, and the LeSabre delivers. The front seats are wide, soft and flat, accommodating a large range of body types. Six-passenger seating is standard, while front buckets are available. As this is a full-size car, rear-seat occupants are equally taken care of. And even though legroom back there isn't best in class, it is still comfortable for three adults. The trunk has a commendable 18-cubic-foot capacity.

**Driving Impressions:** The LeSabre's 3.8-liter V6 delivers smooth power and plenty of low-end torque for passing. The steering is well weighted and responsive, but doesn't offer much feedback to the driver. The LeSabre handles the road well for a large sedan, but don't expect anything more than a pleasant cruise behind the wheel.

*Crash Test Scores, see pg 530*
*Warranty information, see pg 542*

### Specifications

| Engine/Drivetrain | HP | Torque | EPA Fuel Economy Rating |
|---|---|---|---|
| 6cyl 3.8L A | 205 | 230 | N/A |

### Body Styles

| Style | MSRP Range |
|---|---|
| Large Sedan | $26,545–$32,205 |

For the latest full vehicle reports, visit www.edmunds.com/bginfopak

# Large Sedan

# 2005 Buick Park Avenue

**MSRP Price Range**

## $35,555 – $40,730

Destination Charge: $795 (all styles)

| Ratings | | |
|---|---|---|
| Consumer Rating | 9.2 | |
| Editors Rating | 7.9 | |

**What Edmunds.com says:** When shopping for an extra-large, luxury-laden sedan of domestic heritage, it's hard to go wrong with the shapely Park Avenue.

**Pros:** Spacious and comfortable interior, strong V6 engine, solid safety scores, good value.

**Cons:** Floaty ride without Gran Touring package, dated interior design.

**What's New:** A special-edition appearance package and optional 17-inch chrome wheels are the only notable changes for the Park Avenue.

**Body Styles, Trim Levels and Options:** There are two trim levels: the well-equipped base Park Avenue and the upscale Ultra model. A variety of luxury sedan features are standard on both models, such as dual-zone automatic climate control, keyless entry, cruise control and 10-way power seats for both driver and passenger. The base model comes with an AM/FM stereo with cassette, with the option of adding a CD player, while the Ultra gets the cassette and CD standard. Optional equipment on base models includes a memory package, rain-sensing windshield wipers, traction control, stability control and OnStar. Ultra models include all these features as standard equipment. Additional features optional on both models include a head-up display, rear parking assist and a power sunroof. One particular option that we feel base owners should strongly consider, and Ultra owners will receive as standard, is the Gran Touring package, which adds programmable-effort power steering, a beefier suspension, larger brake rotors and either 16-inch or 17-inch alloy wheels with touring tires.

**Powertrains and Performance:** The base model comes with a 3.8-liter V6 that puts out 205 horsepower. A supercharged version of the same engine is standard in the Ultra that offers 240 hp and considerably more torque for quick takeoff. Both engines are connected to a standard four-speed automatic transmission. Standard models are adequately powered for leisurely driving, while the Ultra delivers surprisingly quick acceleration for its size.

**Safety:** The Park Avenue has been awarded high marks in the Insurance Institute for Highway Safety's (IIHS) frontal offset crash tests, and four stars across the board in the National Highway Transportation Safety Association's (NHTSA) frontal and side-impact crash tests. The Park Avenue's safety factor is further enhanced with standard seat-mounted side airbags for the driver and front passenger. As on most premium GM models, the OnStar mobile communications system is offered, as is the StabiliTrak stability control system for added safety in adverse driving situations.

**Interior Design and Special Features:** Although it has been updated over the years, the Park Avenue's interior sticks with traditional design cues like a broad, flat dashboard and plain analog gauges. The radio features large numbers and dials for easy tuning, but the climate control system can be a bit cumbersome with its numerous push-buttons. Roomy seating areas make the Park Avenue comfortable for adults, while the spacious trunk makes loading luggage a snap.

**Driving Impressions:** This sedan might look sleek, but it's soft and pudgy underneath. Still, the powerful supercharged V6 moves the Park Avenue Ultra to speed with verve. The speed-sensitive steering provides surprisingly good levels of feedback and heft, and the brake pedal offers the proper amount of feel and resistance. When this Buick is equipped with the Gran Touring package, you can expect a firmer ride and better body control.

*Crash Test Scores, see pg 530*
*Warranty information, see pg 542*

## Specifications

| Engine/Drivetrain | HP | Torque | EPA Fuel Economy Rating |
|---|---|---|---|
| 6cyl 3.8L A | 240 | 280 | 18 city/28 hwy |
| 6cyl 3.8L A | 205 | 230 | 20 city/29 hwy |

## Body Styles

| Style | MSRP Range |
|---|---|
| Large Sedan | $35,555–$40,730 |

# 2005 Buick Rainier

**MSRP Price Range**

## $35,080 - $36,905

Destination Charge: $685 (all styles)

### Ratings

| | | |
|---|---|---|
| Consumer Rating | 9.2 | |
| Editors Rating | 6.6 | |

**What Edmunds.com says:** Quiet and powerful, especially in V8 form, the Rainier fails to look and act the part of a luxury SUV in most other respects.

**Pros:** Exceptionally quiet ride, strong optional V8, easy to get in and out, decent off-road ability.

**Cons:** Subpar build and materials quality, sloppy handling, lacks key safety features, not enough storage space.

**What's New:** The CXL Plus trim level is dropped in favor of a single CXL model; a CD/MP3 player stereo is newly optional; real wood replaces the fake stuff for the steering wheel and shift knob; and various upgrades help spruce things up inside. Full-length head curtain airbags make their way to the options list, though Buick has dropped last year's seat-mounted side airbags (which provided torso protection for front occupants).

**Body Styles, Trim Levels and Options:** The five-passenger Rainier comes well equipped in one trim, CXL. Standard equipment includes 17-inch alloy wheels, four-wheel ventilated disc brakes with ABS, leather upholstery, wood accents in the cabin, power seats, memory for the seats and mirrors, dual-zone automatic climate control, a CD player and OnStar telematics. Various options include a Bose sound system, adjustable pedals, seat heaters, a DVD-based navigation system, a rear DVD entertainment system and a sunroof.

**Powertrains and Performance:** Two engines are available in the Rainier. The standard power plant is GM's 4.2-liter inline six that makes 275 hp and 275 lb-ft of torque. For added towing power, an optional 5.3-liter V8 offers 290 hp and 325 lb-ft of torque. Two-wheel-drive models equipped with the 5.3-liter V8 can tow up to 6,700 pounds. Both engines use the same transmission—a four-speed electronically controlled automatic that delivers seamless, well-timed shifts in almost all situations.

**Safety:** Four-wheel antilock disc brakes are standard. Full-length head curtain airbags are optional, but seat-mounted side airbags (for front occupants) are not available. The Rainier earned five stars for both front and rear passenger side-impact protection when equipped with side airbags. Frontal impacts resulted in a three-star rating for the driver and front passenger. The IIHS rated the Rainier's mechanical twin, the Chevy TrailBlazer, as "Marginal" (the second lowest score on a four-point scale) after conducting its frontal offset crash test.

**Interior Design and Special Features:** Inside, the Rainier looks similar to its GM cousins but offers sporty gauges similar to those found in the Rendezvous, along with real wood trim. There's adequate room for five passengers, but you're out of luck if you need a third-row seat. Seat comfort is average front and rear. But the Buick's cabin is certainly quiet compared to a TrailBlazer, Envoy or any other SUV for that matter, as it includes extra sound-deadening material and laminated glass. With the rear seat folded down, there's 80 cubic feet of cargo space.

*Crash Test Scores, see pg 530*
*Warranty information, see pg 542*

**Driving Impressions:** The Rainier's standard inline six is smooth and powerful, and should be more than adequate for most shoppers. Those who wish for a little more grunt will be pleased with the Rainier's optional V8. With 290 hp available across a wide-rpm range, you'll rarely find yourself wishing for more. With its tough truck-based underpinnings, the Rainier has a fair amount of real off-road capability. For the majority of buyers who won't be off-roading in their Buick, it offers a smooth, comfortable ride. Handling is not what it should be in a premium SUV, however, as the Rainier's poorly tuned rear suspension gives it a skittish feel when taking turns at higher speeds. Placed in similar situations, competitors like the Mercury Mountaineer and Toyota 4Runner feel much more confident.

### Specifications

| Engine/Drivetrain | HP | Torque | EPA Fuel Economy Rating |
|---|---|---|---|
| 6cyl 4.2L A | 275 | 275 | N/A |

### Body Styles

| Style | MSRP Range |
|---|---|
| Midsize SUV | $35,080–$36,905 |

**MSRP Price Range**

## $26,585 - $39,220
Destination Charge: $685 (all styles)

### Ratings

| | | |
|---|---|---|
| Consumer Rating | 8.3 | |
| Editors Rating | 6.8 | |

**What Edmunds.com says:** The Rendezvous is a well-rounded family vehicle with plenty of space for passengers and cargo. However, with no genuine off-road ability and less convenience than a minivan, it doesn't quite live up to its billing as the ultimate crossover vehicle.

**Pros:** Usable third-row seats that fold flat, comfortable ride, plenty of interior storage, refined 3.6-liter engine, good fuel economy.

**Cons:** Weak standard V6 engine, good-looking but cheap-feeling interior materials, limited off-road ability compared to SUVs.

**What's New:** The larger 3.6-liter V6 is now available on the front-wheel-drive CXL model, while the top-of-the-line Ultra is now offered in both front- and all-wheel-drive versions. New tire and wheel combinations round out the changes for 2005.

**Body Styles, Trim Levels and Options:** The Rendezvous comes in three trim levels: base CX, midlevel CXL and top-of-the-line Ultra. Each can be had in either front- or all-wheel drive. All Rendezvous models include the basics and then some, such as power windows, mirrors and locks; air conditioning; automatic headlights; a CD player; lumbar support for the driver and front passenger; and a split-folding bench seat in the second row. The CXL adds leather upholstery, power seats and dual-zone climate control. The Ultra further ups the content level with standard second-row captain's chairs, a third-row seat, XM Satellite Radio and a head-up display. Lower level trims can add the Ultra's captain's chairs, third-row seat and satellite radio as options, while all models can be upgraded with DVD-based entertainment and touchscreen navigation systems.

**Powertrains and Performance:** The base engine in the CX and CXL is GM's workhorse 3.4-liter V6. Output figures of 185 horsepower and 210 pound-feet of torque are respectable, but considerably less than what rivals offer. An upgraded 3.6-liter V6 comes standard on the Ultra and is optional on front-wheel-drive CXLs. It boasts an advanced overhead cam design that allows it to produce a more competitive 245 hp. A four-speed automatic is the only transmission available. Fuel mileage is above average, as front-drive models get a 19 city/26 highway rating with the base engine and an 18/25 rating with the 3.6-liter. All-wheel-drive models come in at 18/24 with either engine.

**Safety:** Antilock brakes, traction control and side airbags for front occupants are optional on the CX 2WD and standard on the CX AWD, CXL and Ultra. The Rendezvous received an "Acceptable" rating (second highest) in 40-mph frontal offset crash testing conducted by the IIHS, and a perfect five-star rating in side-impact crash tests conducted by the NHTSA.

**Interior Design and Special Features:** The Rendezvous offers an expansive cabin and serious cargo capacity. The interior design aims for an elegant, upscale look, and, to a certain degree, it succeeds. Materials quality is better than in most GM products, with the Ultra model exhibiting the most extensive amount of chrome, wood and leather trim. Storage space up front is best in class. When it's time to work, Rendezvous is ready with up to 109 cubic feet of cargo volume and a 3,500-pound maximum towing capacity.

**Driving Impressions:** Although the Rendezvous' standard V6 engine manages to move the sport-ute with ease around town, acceleration at higher speeds could best be described as leisurely. The more powerful 3.6-liter V6 provides the kind of power you would expect from a vehicle in this category, as it's able to pass effortlessly at any speed. Highway cruising yields a comfortable ride quality without the typical "float" associated with some Buick sedans. Push the Rendezvous a little bit harder, however, and the physics of its tall, narrow body take over, resulting in considerably more body roll in corners. The Versatrak all-wheel-drive system works well in winter weather.

*Crash Test Scores, see pg 530*
*Warranty information, see pg 542*

### Specifications

| Engine/Drivetrain | HP | Torque | EPA Fuel Economy Rating |
|---|---|---|---|
| 6cyl 3.6L A | 245 | 235 | N/A |
| 6cyl 3.4L A | 185 | 210 | N/A |

### Body Styles

| Style | MSRP Range |
|---|---|
| Midsize SUV | $26,585–$39,220 |

# 2005 Buick Terraza

Midsize Minivan

**MSRP Price Range**
## $28,110 - $33,855
Destination Charge: $715 (all styles)

### Ratings

| Consumer Rating | N/A | |
|---|---|---|
| Editors Rating | 7.0 | |

**What Edmunds.com says:** Though the Terraza features a slick interior and distinctive styling, it doesn't have the on-road finesse of its minivan competitors.

**Pros:** Smooth ride and handling, lots of nifty interior storage spaces, innovative multimedia storage system, available all-wheel drive.

**Cons:** Engine power and refinement not up to class leaders, no side curtain airbags.

**What's New:** The Terraza is an all-new "crossover sport van." Think of it as a minivan with an SUV-like front end.

**Body Styles, Trim Levels and Options:** The Terraza comes in one size and two trim levels, CX and CXL. Standard CX amenities include power windows, air conditioning, an eight-speaker sound system with a CD/MP3 player, a rear-seat DVD entertainment system, the OnStar communications system, cruise control, a power-sliding passenger-side door, keyless entry, a power driver seat, auto-leveling rear suspension, a trip computer, compass, leather seating and sport suspension. The CXL adds rear air conditioning, a power-sliding driver-side door, a 115-volt AC outlet, rear parking assist, dual eight-way power seats with driver's memory, upgraded storage and a wood shift knob. An all-wheel-drive system is available. An optional PhatNoise mobile digital media system allows owners to store thousands of MP3s and/or several dozen movies. Other noteworthy options include heated seats, a remote vehicle starting system and XM Satellite Radio.

**Powertrains and Performance:** All Terrazas come equipped with a 3.5-liter V6 that makes 200 horsepower and 220 pound-feet of torque. A four-speed automatic transmission is standard. No other powertrain combinations are available, though buyers in cold climates may want to consider the optional all-wheel-drive system.

**Safety:** All models come standard with four-wheel antilock disc brakes. Side-impact airbags for front occupants and the StabiliTrak stability control system are standard on the CXL, and optional on the CX. Full-length side curtain airbags are not available. The Terraza has not yet been crash tested.

**Interior Design and Special Features:** The Terraza seats seven, and the fold-flat third-row seat offers a 50/50 split. A tasteful color scheme with convincing faux wood accents gives the van a more luxurious ambience than its Chevrolet and Pontiac siblings. The double-stitched leather seats with contrasting piping are particularly elegant. Folding center trays (with cupholders) between the first- and second-row seats offer convenient storage while providing parents with ready access to little ones seated in back. An overhead rail system provides rear-seat access to climate and entertainment functions, and can be outfitted with various storage containers. A rear-seat DVD entertainment system is standard on all Terrazas, and can be upgraded with infrared wireless headphones. A remote vehicle start system, pioneered on the 2004 Chevy Malibu, is optional.

**Driving Impressions:** The V6 power plant is down on power compared to its competitors, but it still manages to provide adequate acceleration. The Terraza's standard sport suspension does a decent job of balancing ride comfort with responsive handling.

*Crash Test Scores, see pg 530*
*Warranty information, see pg 542*

### Specifications

| Engine/Drivetrain | HP | Torque | EPA Fuel Economy Rating |
|---|---|---|---|
| 6cyl 3.5L A | 200 | 220 | N/A |

### Body Styles

| Style | MSRP Range |
|---|---|
| Midsize Minivan | $28,110–$33,855 |

For the latest full vehicle reports, visit www.edmunds.com/bginfopak

# 2005 Cadillac CTS

**MSRP Price Range**

## $30,000 - $32,250
Destination Charge: $695 (all styles)

### Ratings

| | | |
|---|---|---|
| Consumer Rating | 9.0 | 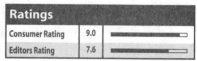 |
| Editors Rating | 7.6 | |

**What Edmunds.com says:** Sharp reflexes and a powerful V6 make the CTS a viable choice among entry-level luxury sport sedans, but it still can't match the class leaders when it comes to overall execution and fun behind the wheel.

**Pros:** Excellent handling, spacious cabin, wide array of available features, alternative look.

**Cons:** Interior still can't match the class leaders, larger size keeps it from providing nimble feel of its competitors.

**What's New:** The base 3.2-liter V6 engine has been dropped; a 2.8-liter V6 will become the base engine later in the model year. A six-speed manual transmission is now standard regardless of engine choice. Package contents have been shuffled, and "synthetic leather" will be added to the options list later this year.

**Body Styles, Trim Levels and Options:** The CTS comes equipped one way, but two option packages are offered to add varying levels of luxury and sport. Standard equipment includes leather seating, side and head curtain airbags, an eight-way power-adjustable driver seat, dual-zone climate control, an AM/FM cassette stereo with a CD player, the OnStar communications system, ABS and traction control. Upgrades include a power passenger seat, an audible theft-deterrent system, two-driver memory package, HomeLink and wood trim on the steering wheel and shift lever. Additional options include an upgraded Bose audio package with a DVD-based navigation system, heated front seats, HID headlamps, a power sunroof and machine-finished aluminum wheels. A stand-alone sport package is available that includes a sport-tuned suspension, restyled 17-inch wheels and tires, speed-sensitive power steering, high-performance brake linings and the StabiliTrak stability control system.

**Powertrains and Performance:** A 3.6-liter V6 rated at 255 hp and 252 lb-ft of torque is standard on the CTS. An entry-level 2.8-liter V6 (210 hp and 195 lb-ft of torque) will become available later in the model year. Power is directed to the rear wheels through either a six-speed manual or five-speed automatic transmission.

**Safety:** The CTS offers standard four-wheel antilock disc brakes, traction control, seat-mounted side airbags for front occupants and side curtain airbags that protect both front and rear passengers; stability control is optional. In tests conducted by the National Highway Traffic Safety Administration, the CTS earned four out of five stars for driver and front-passenger protection in frontal impacts. Side-impact tests resulted in a four-star rating for front passengers and a five-star rating for rear passengers. The IIHS named the CTS a "Best Pick" after conducting its 40-mph frontal offset crash test.

**Interior Design and Special Features:** Although the CTS competes in the entry-level luxury sport sedan category, its physical dimensions more closely resemble that of larger midsize luxury sedans like BMW's 5 Series and Audi's A6. The result is a spacious cabin that easily swallows five adults. The bucket seats in front are supremely comfortable, offering a wide range of movement, supportive side bolsters and a power lumbar adjustment. Still, the CTS can't match its European competitors for overall design elegance.

**Driving Impressions:** Anyone expecting a soft, cushy ride from this Cadillac is going to be surprised. The CTS is a true sport sedan, with a tightly controlled ride and sharp steering. The six-speed manual's shifter has a solid feel to it, and the 3.6-liter V6 gives the CTS some serious punch. Ride quality isn't quite as refined as that of some competitors, but even so, the CTS makes for a swift and entertaining conveyance that should appeal to entry-luxury buyers looking for something a little different. If you want hard-core performance, however, you'll want to check out the high-powered CTS-V model.

*Crash Test Scores, see pg 530*
*Warranty information, see pg 542*

### Specifications

| Engine/Drivetrain | HP | Torque | EPA Fuel Economy Rating |
|---|---|---|---|
| 6cyl 3.6L M | 255 | 252 | 17 city/27 hwy |
| 6cyl 2.8L M | 210 | 194 | 17 city/27 hwy |

### Body Styles

| Style | MSRP Range |
|---|---|
| Midsize Sedan | $30,000–$32,250 |

# 2005 Cadillac CTS-V

**Midsize Sedan**

**MSRP Price Range**
## $49,300
Destination Charge: $695 (all styles)

### Ratings

| | | |
|---|---|---|
| Consumer Rating | 9.4 | |
| Editors Rating | 8.0 | |

**What Edmunds.com says:** It may be a little rough around the edges, but the fast and nimble CTS-V is one of the most promising signs yet that Cadillac is ready to take on the world.

**Pros:** V8 muscle, do-it-yourself gearbox, composed chassis, inexpensive compared to its peers, spacious cabin for day-to-day livability.

**Cons:** Can't keep its feet planted during hard launches, awkward interior design, average interior materials.

**What's New:** No significant changes for the CTS-V this year.

**Body Styles, Trim Levels and Options:** The high-performance, four-door CTS-V is available in one well-equipped model. Standard features include 18-inch wheels and 245/45WR18 Goodyear tires, ventilated Brembo brakes, a driver-adjustable stability control system, high-intensity discharge headlamps, leather upholstery, aluminum and chrome-finish trim, laterally bolstered sport seats, a 160-mph speedometer, dual-zone automatic climate control and a CD player. A DVD-based navigation system is also standard. A sunroof is among the scant list of options.

**Powertrains and Performance:** Engineers from GM's performance division took the liberty of installing a 5.7-liter LS-6 V8 and a six-speed manual transmission. Output is rated at 400 horsepower at 6,000 rpm and 395 pound-feet of torque at 4,800 rpm. The CTS-V needs just 5.1 seconds to reach 60 mph, and an enlarged dual-exhaust system ensures that both the driver and surrounding motorists will experience the full brunt of the V8's deep rumble.

**Safety:** Four-wheel ventilated discs with four-piston calipers and ABS are standard, as is a stability control system with driver-selectable levels of intervention. Also included are seat-mounted side-impact airbags for front occupants and side curtain airbags that protect front and rear occupants. In government crash tests, the CTS earned four out of five stars for driver and front-passenger protection in frontal impacts. Side-impact tests resulted in a four-star rating for front passengers and a five-star rating for rear passengers. In frontal offset crash testing conducted by the IIHS, the Cadillac earned a "Good" rating (the best possible) and was named a "Best Pick."

**Interior Design and Special Features:** Inside the cockpit, the standard CTS instrumentation has been swapped out for a chrome-ringed set with a 180-mph speedometer. The three-spoke steering wheel has aluminum trim, while the door handles and shift knob get a satin chrome finish—these are nice touches, but as in the regular CTS, the overall design is awkward and materials quality is mediocre for this class. In service of the more aggressive driving a CTS V-Series owner will likely be doing, the seats offer extra lateral bolstering, and the center console armrest has been lowered for better access to the shifter. A spacious backseat allows this performance sedan to pull double duty as a family car when needed.

*Crash Test Scores, see pg 530*
*Warranty information, see pg 542*

### Specifications

| Engine/Drivetrain | HP | Torque | EPA Fuel Economy Rating |
|---|---|---|---|
| 8cyl 5.7L M | 400 | 395 | 16 city/25 hwy |

### Body Styles

| Style | MSRP Range |
|---|---|
| Midsize Sedan | $49,300 |

**Driving Impressions:** The CTS-V delivers blistering acceleration at any speed, and the standard manual gearbox provides the perfect means of enjoying it. Fast as it is, though, the sedan is subject to unnerving wheel hop during hard launches, making it seem unrefined alongside European rivals. Fortunately, the suspension displays no such flaws when it comes to keeping the car well planted on the street, where the CTS-V is every bit as entertaining as an M5. The brakes are quite strong, but inconsistent pedal feel can make them tricky to modulate. While unable to deliver performance with the cold precision of its German peers, the CTS-V still represents one of the best blends of fun and affordability in its class.

# 2005 Cadillac DeVille

**MSRP Price Range**
## $45,695 - $51,250
Destination Charge: $795 (all styles)

### Ratings

| Ratings | | |
|---|---|---|
| Consumer Rating | 9.3 | |
| Editors Rating | 7.4 | |

**What Edmunds.com says:** A traditional Cadillac for the traditional Cadillac buyer, the Deville offers a plush ride, plenty of room and surprisingly adept road manners, not to mention all the latest high-tech features.

**Pros:** Smooth and strong power from Northstar V8, spacious and comfortable cabin, admirable handling for a sedan of its size, easy-to-use DVD navigation system.

**Cons:** Lacks the upscale image of its competition, interior materials should be better for the price.

**What's New:** The DeVille receives no major changes for 2005.

**Body Styles, Trim Levels and Options:** The DeVille is available in three models: the base DeVille, a ritzy DeVille High Luxury Sedan (DHS) and a sporty five-passenger DeVille Touring Sedan (DTS). Designed to provide an affordable entry point to DeVille ownership, the base model offers tri-zone automatic climate control, leather upholstery, power front seats and one-touch windows. In terms of luxury features, the DHS is the one to get, as it nets you heated and cooled front seats, seat memory for the driver, a heated rear bench, lumbar adjustment for outboard rear passengers, a power rear sunshade, rain-sensing wipers, a Bose sound system and audio controls mounted on a wood-trimmed steering wheel. The performance-oriented DTS features a continuously variable road-sensing suspension (CVRSS) that monitors and adjusts individual shock damping according to road surface changes for maximum comfort and performance. Popular stand-alone options on the DeVille include a DVD-based navigation system and six-disc CD changer. XM Satellite Radio is also available.

**Powertrains and Performance:** Even with its relatively slim and trim shape, the DeVille is still a sizable sedan, so the 4.6-liter Northstar V8 engine is a welcome sight under the hood. Standard DeVilles and the DHS get a 275-horsepower version, while the sportier DTS gets upgraded to 290 hp. A four-speed automatic transmission is standard on all models.

**Safety:** On hand to maintain optimum vehicle control on the DTS (optional on the DeVille and DHS) is StabiliTrak 2.0, GM's advanced stability and traction control system. A vast array of onboard sensors can detect if the vehicle is deviating from the driver's intended path and selectively apply individual brakes to restore control. All DeVilles also include standard front side-impact airbags. Side airbags for rear passengers are optional. Should you need assistance in an emergency (or just need tickets to the basketball game), GM's OnStar communications system comes standard. If you frequently drive on dark roads, you may want to consider the optional Night Vision head-up display, which uses infrared imaging to help drivers see beyond the normal range of the headlights. Rear parking sensors are also available.

**Interior Design and Special Features:** Interior room is outstanding, with both five- and six-passenger models available. Front-seat passengers are coddled in sumptuous leather seats. Rear passengers are given just as much legroom as front passengers, and the trunk can hold several suitcases without a problem. The overall interior design isn't up to the standards of the DeVille's European or Japanese competition, but the majority of the controls are easy to decipher, and build quality is generally good, if not exceptional.

**Driving Impressions:** Despite its considerable size and softly tuned suspension, the DeVille carries itself well. There's plenty of power on hand for quick passes, while the suspension manages to offer a compliant ride and solid handling. Road and wind noise is barely noticeable and the sheer volume of room in the cabin makes it a terrific highway cruiser.

*Crash Test Scores, see pg 530*
*Warranty information, see pg 542*

### Specifications

| Engine/Drivetrain | HP | Torque | EPA Fuel Economy Rating |
|---|---|---|---|
| 8cyl 4.6L A | 290 | 295 | 18 city/22 hwy |
| 8cyl 4.6L A | 275 | 300 | 18 city/22 hwy |

### Body Styles

| Style | MSRP Range |
|---|---|
| Large Sedan | $45,695–$51,250 |

# 2005 Cadillac Escalade

**MSRP Price Range**
## $52,865 - $55,765
Destination Charge: $850 (all styles)

## Ratings

| | | |
|---|---|---|
| Consumer Rating | 9.3 | |
| Editors Rating | 7.9 | |

**What Edmunds.com says:** With its brash styling, class-leading V8 power, well-sorted vehicle dynamics and plush interior, the Escalade is an SUV worthy of the Cadillac name.

**Pros:** Endless V8 power, plush ride quality, more nimble than you might think, comfortable seats, plenty of cargo capacity, all the latest technological gadgets, best-in-class towing capacity.

**Cons:** Poor mileage, a few noticeable instances of cost cutting, must pay a premium to get the big engine.

**What's New:** Changes this year include a redesigned gauge cluster and door panels, touchscreen capability with the optional navigation system and a more user-friendly driver information system. Additionally, burled walnut trim replaces last year's Zebrano wood.

**Body Styles, Trim Levels and Options:** In keeping with its premium image, the seven-passenger Escalade comes in one trim level only. The standard features list is extensive, including everything from electronic stability control to a Bose audio system and satellite radio. Options include a DVD entertainment system, a DVD-based navigation system, chrome wheels and a second-row bench seat (instead of the standard twin buckets) to increase passenger capacity to eight.

**Powertrains and Performance:** Escalade buyers can choose between an all-wheel-drive model and a less expensive two-wheel-drive model. The 2WD version comes standard with a 5.3-liter V8 rated at 295 horsepower and 330 pound-feet of torque. Stepping up to the AWD version lands you a high-output 6.0-liter V8 with 345 horsepower and 380 lb-ft of torque, making it one of the most powerful SUV engines on the market. Both engines use a four-speed automatic transmission. The maximum tow rating for AWD models is 8,100 pounds, while 2WD versions can lug up to 7,400 pounds. Acceleration with either engine is surprisingly brisk for such a large vehicle, but buyers who tow heavy trailers on a regular basis will want the added muscle of the 6.0-liter V8. On the flip side, those who don't need the extra oomph will find the smaller V8 perfectly adequate and more fuel-efficient.

**Safety:** All Escalades come standard with the StabiliTrak stability control system as well as four-wheel antilock disc brakes, side airbags for the driver and front passenger and OnStar telematics. Other safety features include high-intensity discharge (HID) headlamps, a tire-pressure monitoring system and rear parking sensors. In tests conducted by the National Highway Traffic Safety Administration, the Escalade earned four out of five stars for driver and front-passenger protection in frontal impacts.

**Interior Design and Special Features:** As you would expect in a luxury SUV, the Escalade's interior features plenty of soft leather and shiny wood accents. Some of the cabin's design cues and materials are too derivative of a Chevy Tahoe, but the Cadillac still pulls off the role of a luxury vehicle. The front bucket seats feel like big lounge chairs, and well-cushioned second-row buckets are standard fare—a bench seat for the second row is a no-cost option. There's plenty of room for four or five adults to stretch out and even the optional third-row seats are comfortable enough for shorter trips.

*Crash Test Scores, see pg 530*
*Warranty information, see pg 542*

## Specifications

| Engine/Drivetrain | HP | Torque | EPA Fuel Economy Rating |
|---|---|---|---|
| 8cyl 6.0L A | 345 | 380 | 13 city/15 hwy |
| 8cyl 5.3L A | 295 | 330 | 14 city/16 hwy |

## Body Styles

| Style | MSRP Range |
|---|---|
| Large SUV | $52,865–$55,765 |

**Driving Impressions:** Despite its imposing size, the Escalade handles itself admirably. Body roll is kept well under control and the continuous adjustments made by the standard Road Sensing Suspension (RSS) maintain an excellent balance between ride quality and road feel. The steering can feel a bit numb on the highway, but it lightens up nicely during low-speed maneuvers. Both engines provide ample passing power and the four-speed automatic transmission does an excellent job of choosing the right gears.

For the latest full vehicle reports, visit www.edmunds.com/bginfopak

**MSRP Price Range**

## $58,165 - $69,535
Destination Charge: $850 (all styles)

### Ratings

| | | |
|---|---|---|
| Consumer Rating | 9.6 | ▬▬▬▬▬▬▬▬▫ |
| Editors Rating | 7.9 | ▬▬▬▬▬▬▭ |

**What Edmunds.com says:** With its brash styling, class-leading V8 power, well-sorted vehicle dynamics and cavernous interior, the ESV is the Escalade of choice for those who want maximum utility and luxury.

**Pros:** Endless V8 power, plush ride quality, feels relatively nimble around turns, comfortable seats, plenty of cargo capacity, all the latest technological gadgets, best-in-class towing capacity.

**Cons:** Poor mileage, huge size makes it cumbersome in tight spots, a few noticeable instances of cost cutting.

**What's New:** Changes this year include a redesigned gauge cluster, touchscreen capability with the optional navigation system, a more user-friendly driver information system and a refreshed door panel appearance. Additionally, walnut burled wood trim replaces last year's Zebrano wood.

**Body Styles, Trim Levels and Options:** The seven-passenger Escalade ESV comes in one trim level only, but a limited-production Platinum edition offers several additional features for those looking for something more distinctive. The standard features list includes everything you would expect in a luxury sport-utility. There's leather upholstery, tri-zone automatic climate control, a multifunction driver information center, second-row captain's chairs, the OnStar communications system, satellite radio, power-adjustable pedals, a thundering Bose audio system and the StabiliTrak electronic stability and traction control system just to name a few. The short options list consists of a rear DVD video entertainment system, a second-row bench seat that increases passenger capacity to eight, a sunroof and chromed aluminum wheels. The Platinum edition adds more wood and chrome trim to the interior, a dual-screen DVD system, navigation system, a chrome grille and a lowered suspension finished off with 20-inch chrome wheels.

**Powertrains and Performance:** The ESV comes in all-wheel-drive only, and its sole power plant is a high-output 6.0-liter V8 engine. With 345 horsepower and 380 pound-feet of torque, the only other SUVs that can match it also wear Cadillac emblems. The maximum tow rating is 7,800 pounds. Acceleration is surprisingly brisk for such a large vehicle, but you pay for it with low fuel mileage, which is estimated at 12 city/16 highway.

**Safety:** All Escalades come standard with the StabiliTrak stability control system as well as four-wheel antilock disc brakes, side airbags for the driver and front passenger and the OnStar communications system. Additional safety enhancements include high-intensity Discharge (HID) headlamps, a tire-pressure monitoring system, rear parking sensors and a front-passenger sensor that can detect the presence of a child and depower the airbag accordingly. In tests conducted by the National Highway Traffic Safety Administration, the standard Escalade earned four out of five stars for driver and front-passenger protection in frontal impacts.

**Interior Design and Special Features:** As you would expect in a luxury SUV, the ESV's interior features plenty of soft leather and shiny wood accents. There's plenty of room for five adults to stretch out and even those banished to the third-row seats will find enough room to rest in comfort. The limited-production Platinum edition adds unique leather, wood and chrome accents along with a premium headliner and a dual-screen DVD entertainment system.

**Driving Impressions:** Despite its imposing size, the Escalade ESV handles itself admirably. Body roll is kept well under control and the continuous adjustments made by the standard Road Sensing Suspension (RSS) maintain an excellent balance between ride quality and road feel. The steering can feel a bit numb on the highway, but it lightens up nicely during low-speed maneuvers. The enormous 6.0-liter V8 provides ample passing power, while the four-speed automatic transmission does an excellent job of choosing the right gears. Overall, a very comfortable and competent cruiser that rarely gets out of sorts no matter what you throw at it.

*Crash Test Scores, see pg 530*
*Warranty information, see pg 542*

### Specifications

| Engine/Drivetrain | HP | Torque | EPA Fuel Economy Rating |
|---|---|---|---|
| 8cyl 6.0L A | 345 | 380 | 13 city/15 hwy |

### Body Styles

| Style | MSRP Range |
|---|---|
| Large SUV | $58,165–$69,535 |

# 2005 Cadillac Escalade EXT

**MSRP Price Range**

## $53,045

Destination Charge: $850 (all styles)

### Ratings

| | | |
|---|---|---|
| Consumer Rating | 8.0 | |
| Editors Rating | 7.8 | |

**What Edmunds.com says:** It's gaudy, expensive and sucks gas like a '70s Eldorado. Still, well-sorted vehicle dynamics and a plush interior make the Escalade EXT an SUV worthy of the Cadillac name.

**Pros:** Huge power from its big V8, solid handling for its size, innovative packaging offers excellent utility, features galore.

**Cons:** Poor fuel mileage, a few noticeable instances of cost cutting, steep price tag.

**What's New:** Changes this year include a redesigned gauge cluster, touch-screen capability with the optional navigation system, a more user-friendly driver information system and a refreshed door panel appearance. Walnut burled wood trim replaces last year's Zebrano wood. A sliding load floor for the cargo bed is also new for 2005.

**Body Styles, Trim Levels and Options:** In keeping with its premium image, the Escalade EXT comes in only one trim level. The standard feature list is extensive, including everything from electronic stability control to a thundering Bose audio system. Both leather-upholstered front seats are heated and offer 10-way power adjustment. Additional standard equipment includes XM Satellite Radio, a towing package and a tire-pressure monitoring system. A rear-seat DVD entertainment system, a touchscreen DVD-based navigation system and chrome wheels are available options.

**Powertrains and Performance:** Unlike the standard Escalade that offers a choice of two- or all-wheel drive, the EXT comes in AWD only. The only available engine is the high-output 6.0-liter V8 that boasts 345 horsepower and 380 pound-feet of torque. A heavy-duty four-speed automatic transmission takes care of the shifting. As you might expect, the powerful V8 moves the big sport-ute with little hesitation, but those looking for a quiet, refined power plant might find it a little raucous at higher rpm. The transmission downshifts quickly and rarely fails to provide crisp, clean upshifts under acceleration. The EXT's maximum towing capacity is 7,300 pounds.

**Safety:** All EXTs come standard with the StabiliTrak stability control system as well as four-wheel antilock disc brakes, side airbags for the driver and front passenger and the OnStar communications system. A standard tire-pressure monitoring system alerts drivers of abnormally low pressures that could result in a blowout. Other key safety items include high-intensity discharge (HID) headlights and rear parking sensors. In frontal impact tests conducted by the National Highway Traffic Safety Administration, the Escalade EXT earned three out of five stars for driver protection and four stars for front-passenger protection.

**Interior Design and Special Features:** Like the standard Escalade, the EXT features an extensive array of luxury amenities. Soft leather covers nearly every inch of the cabin, while wood accents grace the steering wheel, dashboard and door panels. Of course, the EXT's most unique feature is the convertible Midgate, a removable partition between the rear seats and the utility bed that allows you to extend the bed from a bit over 5 feet to a full 8 feet with just a few latches. It's a snap to use, and it gives the EXT a level of utility that no other luxury sport-ute can match. When you're not using the extra bed length, this Cadillac can seat four or five passengers in comfort.

*Crash Test Scores, see pg 530*
*Warranty information, see pg 542*

### Specifications

| Engine/Drivetrain | HP | Torque | EPA Fuel Economy Rating |
|---|---|---|---|
| 8cyl 6.0L A | 345 | 380 | 13 city/15 hwy |

### Body Styles

| Style | MSRP Range |
|---|---|
| Crew Cab Pickup Truck | $53,045 |

**Driving Impressions:** Despite its bulky size, the EXT is a competent handler. Body roll is kept well under control, and the continuous adjustments made by the standard Road Sensing Suspension maintain an excellent balance between ride quality and road feel. The steering can feel a bit detached on the highway, but it lightens up nicely during low-speed maneuvers. The massive Vortec V8 provides ample passing power while the four-speed automatic transmission does an excellent job of choosing the right gears.

**MSRP Price Range**

## $38,340 - $52,035

Destination Charge: $695 (all styles)

### Ratings

| | | |
|---|---|---|
| Consumer Rating | 9.1 | |
| Editors Rating | 8.1 | |

**What Edmunds.com says:** Roomy on the inside and a superb handler on the street, the SRX is a desirable alternative to the premium import crossover SUVs.

**Pros:** Potent engine lineup, roomy and comfortable interior, optional third-row seat, excellent ride and handling dynamics.

**Cons:** Questionable interior design and materials, missing key convenience features, mediocre fuel mileage with V8.

**What's New:** No major changes for the SRX this year.

**Body Styles, Trim Levels and Options:** Cadillac gives buyers two SRX models to choose from—V6 and V8. Every V6 model includes leather seating, StabiliTrak stability control, side airbags for front occupants, head curtain airbags for the first two rows and OnStar telematics. The V8 models add such features as wood trim pieces, seat heaters, power-adjustable pedals, a power front-passenger seat and a six-disc CD changer; this stuff is optional on the V6. Options for both models include all-wheel drive, Magnetic Ride Control, a third-row seat, the extra-large UltraView sunroof, a DVD rear entertainment system (with the screen mounted on the center console), a DVD-based navigation system and XM Satellite Radio.

**Powertrains and Performance:** There are two available engines: a 3.6-liter V6 good for 260 horsepower and 252 pound-feet of torque, and a 4.6-liter Northstar V8 that generates 320 hp and 315 lb-ft of torque. Both engines feature variable valve timing and electronic throttle control. A five-speed automatic with regular and sport shift programs, as well as a separate automanual gate, comes standard with either engine. Buyers must decide whether they want rear-wheel drive (to maximize performance and economy) or all-wheel drive (for driving in the snow). One option to consider is Magnetic Ride Control, an adaptive damping system also available on the XLR and Corvette. Thusly equipped, the SRX offers decidedly sporty handling characteristics.

**Safety:** Four-wheel antilock disc brakes (with a panic assist feature) and stability control are standard. Airbags include seat-mounted side bags for front occupants and head curtain airbags spanning the first and second rows. In tests conducted by the National Highway Traffic Safety Administration, the SRX earned four out of five stars for driver and front-passenger protection in frontal impacts. Side-impact tests resulted in a perfect five-star rating for front and rear passengers.

**Interior Design and Special Features:** Inside, the SRX provides comfortable accommodations for its passengers, but both the design and the materials leave something to be desired; the available wood trim helps create a more luxurious ambience. There is plenty of room to go around in the second row, though occupants of the third-row seat may feel more cramped than in some competitors. The optional UltraView sunroof allows both front and rear passengers to experience open-air driving. The rearmost bench folds flat into the floor, yielding 32.4 cubic feet of capacity behind the second-row seats. Fold the second-row seats and you've got 70 cubes.

**Driving Impressions:** Handling is nothing short of exceptional, as the body feels tight and responsive, giving the 4,400-pound vehicle a tossable feel on par with only the X5 and FX35/45. We have also been impressed by the well-weighted steering and progressive brakes. Fortunately, this doesn't come at the expense of ride quality, which is smooth and comfortable. If you love to drive but need more space than either the BMW X5 or Infiniti FX35/45 can provide, this is probably the best alternative.

*Crash Test Scores, see pg 530*
*Warranty information, see pg 542*

### Specifications

| Engine/Drivetrain | HP | Torque | EPA Fuel Economy Rating |
|---|---|---|---|
| 8cyl 4.6L A | 320 | 315 | 15 city/20 hwy |
| 6cyl 3.6L A | 255 | 254 | 16 city/21 hwy |

### Body Styles

| Style | MSRP Range |
|---|---|
| Large SUV | $38,340–$52,035 |

# Cadillac

# 2005 Cadillac STS

**MSRP Price Range**

## $40,300 - $61,815

Destination Charge: $695 (all styles)

### Ratings

| | | |
|---|---|---|
| Consumer Rating | 9.4 | |
| Editors Rating | 8.5 | |

**What Edmunds.com says:** After struggling for years to keep up with the imports, Cadillac has finally hit its stride and the STS proves it. Balanced driving dynamics and edgy-but-attractive styling should make this car a hit with buyers of all ages, especially those looking for a complete package of luxury and performance at a competitive price.

**Pros:** Full-size car at a midsize price, nimble road feel, powerful engine options, available all-wheel drive, optional Bose stereo is one of the best in its class.

**Cons:** Sporty bucket seats might be a bit firm for some, plastic interior panels not quite up to German standards, only one transmission available.

**What's New:** Cadillac's full size sedan is all new for 2005, rounding out the luxury marque's self-proclaimed renaissance with a bevy of performance-oriented credentials, including rear-wheel drive and two powerful engine options. Cutting-edge styling, lavish interior appointments and available all-wheel drive have brought GM's flagship up to par with the best Europe and Japan have to offer.

**Body Styles, Trim Levels and Options:** Cadillac gives buyers three STS models to choose from—V6, V8 and V8 AWD. Every V6 model includes 17-inch wheels, leather seating, aluminum interior trim, eight-way manually adjustable front seats, dual-zone climate control, an eight-speaker Bose sound system and OnStar. The V8 model adds 18-inch wheels, wood interior trim and power-adjustable front seats with multilevel heating and memory. The V8 AWD model adds the Magnetic Ride Control system, light-sensitive auto-dimming headlamps, ventilated seats, a DVD-based navigation system, Bluetooth wireless connectivity and a Bose 15-speaker, 5.1 surround sound audio system with an in-dash CD changer—this stuff is optional on other models.

**Powertrains and Performance:** There are two available engines: a 3.6-liter V6 good for 255 horsepower and 252 pound-feet of torque, and a 4.6-liter Northstar V8 that generates 320 hp and 315 lb-ft of torque. Both engines feature variable valve timing and electronic throttle control. A five-speed automatic with regular and sport shift programs comes standard with either engine. Buyers must decide whether they want rear-wheel drive (to maximize performance and economy) or all-wheel drive for better all-weather traction. One option to consider is Magnetic Ride Control, an adaptive damping system. Thusly equipped, the STS offers decidedly sporty handling characteristics.

**Safety:** Four-wheel antilock disc brakes (with a panic assist feature) and StabiliTrak stability control are standard. Airbags include dual front airbags, seat-mounted side bags for front occupants and head curtain airbags spanning the first and second rows.

**Interior Design and Special Features:** Cadillac has been putting extra effort into interior quality and design as part of its self-proclaimed renaissance, and it shows. Panel fit and finish is top-notch, and premium materials such as eucalyptus wood trim and optional Tuscany leather really make the STS shine. The automatic climate control system monitors interior temperatures in relation to outside conditions, and the driver can stay informed without looking down thanks to a four-color head-up display projected onto the windshield.

Crash Test Scores, see pg 530
Warranty information, see pg 542

### Specifications

| Engine/Drivetrain | HP | Torque | EPA Fuel Economy Rating |
|---|---|---|---|
| 8cyl 4.6L A | 320 | 315 | N/A |
| 6cyl 3.6L A | 260 | 252 | N/A |

### Body Styles

| Style | MSRP Range |
|---|---|
| Large Sedan | $40,300–$61,815 |

**Driving Impressions:** A V8 STS is only about 100 pounds heavier than a comparably equipped 5 Series sedan despite its larger size. It's not exactly sport sedan-quick in its movements, but it can be pushed hard without losing composure. With the rear wheels providing the power, Cadillac's engineers were free to focus on the kind of precise steering feel that's nearly impossible to achieve with front-wheel drive. The result is a delicate feel through the steering wheel without a numb on-center sensation or overly aggressive assistance. The standard V6 is able to get the big sedan up to speed with surprising gusto. Unlike some of its competitors whose six-cylinder offerings provide merely adequate performance, the V6 in the STS rarely feels underpowered. Step up to the V8 and the STS really shows its mettle.

For the latest full vehicle reports, visit www.edmunds.com/bginfopak

**MSRP Price Range**

**$75,835**

Destination Charge: $815 (all styles)

## Ratings

| | | |
|---|---|---|
| Consumer Rating | 9.5 | ████████████ |
| Editors Rating | 8.0 | ██████████░ |

**What Edmunds.com says:** Its design makes it stand out from the crowd, but its performance and craftsmanship aren't quite as extraordinary.

**Pros:** Eye-catching design, forgiving ride quality, hardtop convenience, nearly every feature is standard.

**Cons:** Interior doesn't always reflect the price, not as sporty as its Corvette underpinnings might suggest, minimal cargo space, can be cramped for taller drivers.

**What's New:** Buyers now have the choice of two interior wood trim finishes: Dark Eucalyptus, along with last year's Light Eucalyptus.

**Body Styles, Trim Levels and Options:** The XLR is available as a two-door roadster only. Virtually every luxury feature comes standard, including navigation system, traction control, stability control, high-intensity discharge headlights, rear parking sensors, headlamp washers, dual-zone climate control, a 250-watt sound system with an in-dash CD changer and a seven-inch color touchscreen for driver information, entertainment and navigation system control. The XLR boasts a posh cabin complete with Eucalyptus wood trim and aluminum accents in addition to leather seating. XM Satellite Radio is the lone option.

**Powertrains and Performance:** The XLR comes with an advanced 4.6-liter Northstar V8 that uses variable valve timing and a low restriction intake to generate 320 horsepower and 310 pound-feet of torque. To insure the noise from all that power stays under the hood, Cadillac developed a new acoustic engine cover that also gives the engine bay a perfectly finished look. Using a modified version of the five-speed automatic transmission found in the CTS sedan, the XLR offers both a shift-it-yourself feature and a fully automatic mode. The transmission is mounted in the rear to help achieve proper weight distribution.

**Safety:** The XLR comes with a host of safety features, most designed to keep the car from getting into an accident in the first place. Four-wheel ABS is standard, as are stability control and side airbags. Because the XLR is a two-seater, the passenger-side front airbag can be switched off to accommodate children in safety seats.

**Interior Design and Special Features:** Inside, the XLR uses a rather simple design approach. Clean-looking but certainly not bland, the XLR's interior is modern and warm. Standard features include such gee-whiz technology as a head-up display, adaptive cruise control, a voice-activated DVD navigation system, heated and cooled seats plus optional XM radio and a Bose audio system. The color touchscreen is mounted high in the center stack and helps to keep the dash uncluttered by eliminating the need for numerous single-use buttons.

**Driving Impressions:** As fast as the XLR is when pushed, those expecting a Corvette in Cadillac's clothing will be disappointed. Not only does the XLR return less enthusiastic responses to the throttle than its corporate cousin, its soft suspension tuning results in considerable body roll during hard cornering and plenty of nose dive under heavy braking. Magnetic Ride control (MR) shocks are standard equipment, but even with their split-second adjustability, the XLR still feels less willing to tackle the turns than an SL. An overly large steering wheel makes it feel all the more ponderous, but at least the level of steering assist isn't overly aggressive. Acceleration is excellent and the sound of the Northstar V8 at full throttle is as good or better than anything in its class. At highway speeds wind buffeting is intrusive with the top down, but not so much that it deters from the XLR's otherwise exemplary all-around performance.

*Crash Test Scores, see pg 530*
*Warranty information, see pg 542*

## Specifications

| Engine/Drivetrain | HP | Torque | EPA Fuel Economy Rating |
|---|---|---|---|
| 8cyl 4.6L A | 320 | 310 | 17 city/21 hwy |

## Body Styles

| Style | MSRP Range |
|---|---|
| Compact Convertible | $75,835 |

# 2005 Chevrolet Astro

**MSRP Price Range**

## $24,300 - $31,445

Destination Charge: $740 (all styles)

## Ratings

| | | |
|---|---|---|
| Consumer Rating | 8.8 | |
| Editors Rating | 6.6 | |

**What Edmunds.com says:** Other than its ability to mimic an SUV in terms of towing ability and cargo space, there's not much about the Astro van that makes it a viable choice over its numerous competitors.

**Pros:** Big-van capacity in a small-van package, available all-wheel drive, high-towing ability.

**Cons:** Engineered in the early '80s, iffy crash test scores, cramped front footwells.

**What's New:** No significant changes for the Astro this year.

**Body Styles, Trim Levels and Options:** Astro passenger vans come in three levels of trim: base, LS and LT. Base models come standard with air conditioning, power window and door locks, a tilt steering wheel, cruise control and cloth upholstery. LS models add keyless entry and an upgraded audio system with a CD player. Step up to the LT and you get a better cloth interior, rear air conditioning, an overhead console with map lights and an outside temperature gauge, a power-adjustable driver seat, a leather-wrapped steering wheel and a Homelink programmable garage door transmitter. LT vans also offer the option of seven-passenger seating with captain's chairs in the second row, as well as leather upholstery.

**Powertrains and Performance:** A 190-horsepower, 4.3-liter V6 is the only engine available, sending power through a smooth-shifting four-speed automatic transmission. Standard rear-wheel drive allows the Astro to boast a maximum towing capacity of 5,400 pounds. A full-time all-wheel-drive system is optional. This system transfers power to the front wheels when it detects rear-wheel slippage for maximum traction in adverse weather situations.

**Safety:** All Astro vans come standard with four-wheel antilock disc brakes. The National Highway Traffic Safety Administration gave the Astro three out of five stars for protection of the driver in a frontal crash and four stars for the front passenger. The Insurance Institute for Highway Safety rated the Astro "Poor," the lowest of four rankings, after administering its frontal offset crash test.

**Interior Design and Special Features:** With only minor changes since its debut 20 years ago, the Astro's interior is dated to say the least. Overall interior room is generous, with 170 cubic feet of total cargo space, but small front footwells make the driver and front passenger feel more cramped than in most minivans. The standard seating arrangement holds eight passengers, but optional captain's chairs reduce capacity to seven.

**Driving Impressions:** Taller than many of its rivals, the Astro van is admittedly more trucklike in temperament, but delivers a pleasant highway ride with competent handling. The 4.3-liter V6 engine provides plenty of thrust down low, but it runs out of breath quickly.

*Crash Test Scores, see pg 530*
*Warranty information, see pg 542*

## Specifications

| Engine/Drivetrain | HP | Torque | EPA Fuel Economy Rating |
|---|---|---|---|
| 6cyl 4.3L A | 190 | 250 | 16 city/18 hwy |

## Body Styles

| Style | MSRP Range |
|---|---|
| Large Minivan | $24,300–$31,445 |

For the latest full vehicle reports, visit www.edmunds.com/bginfopak

## MSRP Price Range
### $33,320 - $42,195
Destination Charge: $850 (all styles)

### Ratings

| | | |
|---|---|---|
| Consumer Rating | 9.8 | |
| Editors Rating | 7.4 | |

**What Edmunds.com says:** Combining the comforts of a Suburban with the practicality of a Silverado, the Avalanche is a crossover vehicle that creatively provides the best of both worlds.

**Pros:** Versatile and innovative cab configuration, strong V8 engines, substantial towing ability, comfortable daily driver.

**Cons:** Some cheap interior pieces, lifeless steering, fewer drivetrain choices than comparable trucks.

**What's New:** Changes for 2005 include a new optional touchscreen navigation system and a chrome exterior accent package. Interior trim has been split up into LS and LT levels. Steering wheel radio controls and OnStar are now standard on all models.

**Body Styles, Trim Levels and Options:** The Avalanche comes in both half-ton and three-quarter-ton configurations with either two- or four-wheel drive, and a choice of two trim levels—LS and LT. Standard LS equipment includes dual-zone manual air conditioning and a 40/20/40-split bench front seat. LT upgrades include a Bose sound system, power-adjustable pedals, automatic climate control and leather seating. Notable options include a sunroof, XM Satellite Radio and a rear-seat DVD video system. Hard-core off-road enthusiasts can upgrade the Avalanche with the Z71 package that adds retuned springs and shocks, underbody skid plates, heavy-duty shocks, a rear locking differential and larger wheels and tires. Those who never plan to venture off-road can order the half-ton version with the Z66 sport suspension package that adds specially tuned springs and shocks, traction control, a rear locking differential and 17-inch wheels and tires.

**Powertrains and Performance:** All half-ton models feature a 5.3-liter Vortec V8 rated at 295 horsepower and 330 pound-feet of torque hooked to a four-speed automatic transmission. Three-quarter-ton versions get a heavy-duty four-speed automatic and an 8.1-liter V8 that cranks out 320 hp and 440 lb-ft of torque. The maximum trailer weight rating for the three-quarter-ton model is 12,000 pounds, while the half-ton can pull up to 8,200 pounds.

**Safety:** All models come standard with four-wheel antilock disc brakes. Side airbags and electronic stability control are available as options. In government crash tests, the Avalanche earned three stars (out of five) for driver protection in a frontal impact and four stars for front-passenger protection.

**Interior Design and Special Features:** Built on the same chassis as the Suburban, the Avalanche features a similar interior design. The gauges are simple, easy-to-read analog dials, while the climate and stereo controls are both placed high in the dash for easy adjustment. Switching the Avalanche from five- or six-passenger SUV to a two- or three-passenger pickup is a simple operation that can be performed in just a few minutes without hand tools. The rear cargo area has drainage holes so it can be hosed out, and there are two auxiliary storage compartments in the sides of the bed.

**Driving Impressions:** As rough and tough as the Avalanche looks on the outside, the driving experience is as pleasant as any SUV's. Half-ton models have a soft, forgiving ride quality and quiet cabins that make them comfortable as daily drivers. Three-quarter-ton models are a bit stiffer, as you would expect, but not so much as to make them uncomfortable around town. The Avalanche suffers from the same numb steering exhibited by most GM trucks, but its light weighting does make for easy maneuvering in tight spots.

*Crash Test Scores, see pg 530*
*Warranty information, see pg 542*

### Specifications

| Engine/Drivetrain | HP | Torque | EPA Fuel Economy Rating |
|---|---|---|---|
| 8cyl 8.1L A | 320 | 440 | N/A |
| 8cyl 5.3L A | 295 | 330 | 14 city/18 hwy |

### Body Styles

| Style | MSRP Range |
|---|---|
| Crew Cab Pickup Truck | $33,320–$42,195 |

# 2005 Chevrolet Aveo

**Compact Coupe, Sedan**

**MSRP Price Range**

## $9,455 - $12,795

Destination Charge: $540 (all styles)

### Ratings

| | | |
|---|---|---|
| Consumer Rating | 9.3 | |
| Editors Rating | 6.1 | |

**What Edmunds.com says:** Refined road manners and a spacious interior make this one of the better subcompacts on the market.

**Pros:** Low price, nimble handling, ample headroom, logical control layout, available MP3 player, loads of cargo room in hatchback models.

**Cons:** Not much power, imprecise manual shifter, side airbags not available.

**What's New:** Chevrolet fiddles with the trim levels—last year's base model is now the LS, while last year's LS model is now the LT.

**Body Styles, Trim Levels and Options:** The Aveo comes in four-door sedan and five-door hatchback configurations, and both are available in one of three trim levels—Special Value, LS and LT. Special Value models come in at around $10,000 and offer basics like power steering, an AM/FM stereo, tilt steering wheel, split-folding rear seat, 14-inch steel wheels, tinted glass, body-color mirrors and door handles and, on hatchbacks, a rear wiper. LS models add air conditioning and carpeted floor mats, as well as the availability of major options such as ABS, CD/MP3 player, alloy wheels and an automatic transmission. The LT adds power windows and locks, a CD/MP3 player, remote keyless entry, heated outside mirrors, alloy wheels and upgraded seat fabric.

**Powertrains and Performance:** Aveo features a 1.6-liter dual-overhead cam, 16-valve, inline four-cylinder that delivers 103 hp and 107 lb-ft of torque. A large intake resonator, dual-muffler exhaust system and other sound-damping technologies help reduce engine noise. A five-speed manual transmission is standard, and there's also an optional four-speed automatic with an electronic "hold" feature for second-gear starts when driving on slippery surfaces. Fuel mileage estimates are 28 mpg in the city and 34 on the highway with the manual gearbox and 26/35 with the automatic—comparable to the Hyundai Accent but less efficient than the Toyota Echo and Scion xA.

**Safety:** The Aveo comes with three-point seatbelts for all five passengers with pre-tensioners in the front. ABS is optional on LS and LT models, and it includes Electronic Brakeforce Distribution for shorter stopping distances. Side airbags are not available. Government crash tests produced an excellent five-star rating for driver and front-passenger protection in frontal impacts. In side-impact tests, the Aveo earned a middling three out of five stars for both the front and rear.

**Interior Design and Special Features:** Though bare-bones in appearance and feel, the interior has a user-friendly control layout and a few thoughtful features for a car in this price range. The back of each front headrest has a hook for holding a shopping bag, and the five-door hatch has a flip-forward rear seat that allows for a maximum cargo capacity of 42 cubic feet. Even the sedan comes with a 60/40-split-folding rear seat and offers a decent 11.7-cubic-foot trunk capacity.

*Crash Test Scores, see pg 530*
*Warranty information, see pg 542*

### Specifications

| Engine/Drivetrain | HP | Torque | EPA Fuel Economy Rating |
|---|---|---|---|
| 4cyl 1.6L M | 103 | 107 | 27 city/35 hwy |

### Body Styles

| Style | MSRP Range |
|---|---|
| Compact Coupe | $9,455–$12,795 |
| Compact Sedan | $9,455–$12,570 |

**Driving Impressions:** Subcompacts have a well-deserved reputation for poor handling and wobbly rides. While the Aveo is certainly no thrill ride, it provides better overall vehicle dynamics than most of its competitors. The steering is direct, the suspension well tuned and the standard engine—while loud and buzzy—is adequate for day-to-day commuting. We normally recommend that buyers in this class opt for a manual transmission, but in the Aveo's case, the automatic is the better bet: The manual tranny's gear ratios are too wide, leaving the car underpowered on highway grades and ultimately compromising fuel economy.

**MSRP Price Range**

## $21,165 - $26,435

Destination Charge: $685 (all styles)

| Ratings | | |
|---|---|---|
| Consumer Rating | 5.4 | |
| Editors Rating | 5.4 | |

**What Edmunds.com says:** Although it does offer a strong running V6, the Blazer is otherwise outclassed by nearly every other sport-ute on the market. An option only if the low price is too hard for you to overlook.

**Pros:** Unique Xtreme and ZR2 suspension packages, competent drivetrain, cheap price.

**Cons:** Aged platform, spotty build quality, low-grade interior parts, uncomfortable rear seats, poor resale value.

**What's New:** The Blazer is available exclusively as a two-door this year, as four-doors are now sold as fleet vehicles only.

**Body Styles, Trim Levels and Options:** The Blazer is offered in base, Xtreme or ZR2 trim with two doors only. Base models offer either two- or four-wheel drive and come standard with air conditioning and an AM/FM CD stereo. The Xtreme trim comes in two-wheel drive only and adds an exterior appearance package, unique wheels and upgraded sport suspension. The ZR2 off-road package adds a wide stance frame, stronger gears and axles, heavy-duty shocks and springs, skid plates and a brush guard. Various options include a power driver seat, upgraded tires and a power sunroof.

**Powertrains and Performance:** All Blazers come standard with a 4.3-liter V6 engine rated at 190 horsepower and 250 pound-feet of torque. A five-speed manual transmission is standard, with a four-speed automatic as an available option. The Blazer is rated to tow up to a maximum of 5,500 pounds. All 4x4 models can be equipped with the AutoTrac push-button electronic transfer case.

**Safety:** All Blazers feature four-wheel antilock disc brakes as standard equipment. In government crash tests, the sport-ute earned three stars (out of five) for the driver and four for the front passenger in frontal impacts and a perfect five stars in side impacts. In 40-mph frontal offset crash testing conducted by the IIHS, the Blazer earned a "Poor" rating (the lowest), as the passenger compartment wasn't well maintained during the impact.

**Interior Design and Special Features:** There's lots of cargo space inside the Blazer, with the spare tire mounted outside the tailgate. Sadly, the Blazer's interior is marred by chintzy plastic and precious little footroom in front of a rather low and mushy seat. Adult passengers won't find the rear accommodations much better.

**Driving Impressions:** Considering its aged design, the Blazer offers a reasonably controlled ride on the pavement, although there's noticeable body roll when cornering. The transmission shifts smoothly and the engine is strong off the line, but it runs out of breath in the higher-rpm ranges. The sport-tuned Xtreme model tightens up the handling, but the long-throw shifter and numb steering keep it from being anything special.

*Crash Test Scores, see pg 530*
*Warranty information, see pg 542*

## Specifications

| Engine/Drivetrain | HP | Torque | EPA Fuel Economy Rating |
|---|---|---|---|
| 6cyl 4.3L M | 190 | 250 | 15 city/21 hwy |

## Body Styles

| Style | MSRP Range |
|---|---|
| Compact SUV | $21,165–$26,435 |

# Chevrolet
# 2005 Chevrolet Cavalier
### Compact Coupe, Sedan

**MSRP Price Range**
## $10,325 - $17,710
Destination Charge: $565 (all styles)

## Ratings

| | | |
|---|---|---|
| Consumer Rating | 9.5 | |
| Editors Rating | 5.0 | |

**What Edmunds.com says:** Despite various revisions, there's no hiding the fact that this car was engineered more than a decade ago, leaving it hopelessly outclassed by nearly every other car on the market.

**Pros:** Low price, torquey four-cylinder engine, optional satellite radio and OnStar.

**Cons:** Ancient design inside and out, cheap interior materials, poor build quality, low resale value, poor side-impact and front-offset crash test results, ABS no longer standard.

**What's New:** No major changes as the Cavalier gallops into the automotive sunset.

**Body Styles, Trim Levels and Options:** The Cavalier is available as a two-door coupe or four-door sedan in three different trim levels: base, LS and LS Sport. Additionally, the coupe is available in a Special Value trim. Base models feature a standard AM/FM stereo and air conditioning. The Special Value model includes a CD player, but has the restriction of no other available options. The LS and LS Sport models add a tilt steering wheel, power windows, keyless entry, cruise control and floor mats. Other options include antilock brakes, cruise control, OnStar, XM Satellite Radio, side airbags and a sunroof on coupe models.

**Powertrains and Performance:** Unlike years past, there is only one engine available for 2005. The 2.2-liter Ecotec four-cylinder powers all Cavaliers. With 140 horsepower and 150 pound-feet of torque, the engine compares favorably with most others in the class. It's made entirely of aluminum and boasts dual-overhead camshafts and four valves per cylinder for maximum efficiency and power. The standard transmission is a five-speed manual with a four-speed automatic available as an option on all but the Special Value model. EPA mileage estimates are 24 city/32 highway for the automatic and 25 city/33 highway for the manual.

**Safety:** Antilock brakes are optional on all models, except the Special Value coupe. Side airbags for front occupants are available on LS and LS Sport models as an option. Each seating position has a three-point seatbelt standard, and LS and LS Sport Cavaliers can be equipped with OnStar telematics. Crash tests conducted by the National Highway Traffic Safety Administration (NHTSA) produced middling results. The Cavalier earned four out of five stars for the driver and front passenger in the frontal impact crash test but only one star for the driver in the side-impact test (a Cavalier equipped with side airbags has yet to be tested). The Insurance Institute for Highway Safety (IIHS) gave the Cavalier a rating of "Poor," its lowest, after conducting its 40-mph frontal offset crash test.

**Interior Design and Special Features:** The Cavalier's interior has never been one of its strong points. The seats aren't very comfortable and the build quality leaves a lot to be desired. The fact that both OnStar and XM Satellite Radio are available gives the Cavalier a slight technological edge over its competitors, but it doesn't make up for the dated appearance of everything else.

*Crash Test Scores, see pg 530*
*Warranty information, see pg 542*

**Driving Impressions:** The Ecotec four-cylinder is a thoroughly modern engine that provides good power and a smooth delivery. It may not have quite the same kick as the old 2.4-liter, but it's significantly more refined and gets much better mileage. The handling is acceptable for a car in this class, with reasonably good manners in corners and a compliant ride around town, but expect a harsher ride over bumps and ruts than you would in newer competitors.

## Specifications

| Engine/Drivetrain | HP | Torque | EPA Fuel Economy Rating |
|---|---|---|---|
| 4cyl 2.2L M | 140 | 150 | 25 city/33 hwy |

## Body Styles

| Style | MSRP Range |
|---|---|
| Compact Coupe | $10,325–$17,510 |
| Compact Sedan | $14,610–$17,710 |

**MSRP Price Range**
## $13,625 - $21,430
Destination Charge: $565 (all styles)

### Ratings

| | | |
|---|---|---|
| Consumer Rating | 10.0 | ████████ |
| Editors Rating | N/A | ▭▭▭▭▭▭▭ |

**What Edmunds.com says:** Positioned several steps upmarket from its Cavalier predecessor, the new Cobalt rides, handles and looks like a more expensive car than it really is.

**Pros:** Smooth ride and sporty handling, torquey four-cylinder engine, premium content for basic-car price.

**Cons:** A few cheap plastic interior parts, odd exterior styling details.

**What's New:** The Cobalt is a replacement for the aged Cavalier and like its predecessor it's available in both coupe and sedan body styles.

**Body Styles, Trim Levels and Options:** The Cobalt is available as a two-door coupe or four-door sedan. Coupes come in base, LS and SS trim, while sedans come in base, LS and LT versions. Base models feature a standard CD player, air conditioning, a driver-seat height adjuster, a split-folding rear seat and 15-inch wheels. The LS adds cruise control; power windows, locks and mirrors; keyless entry; upgraded seats; alloy wheels; upgraded interior lighting; and antilock brakes. The LT sedan comes loaded with leather seats, a seven-speaker Pioneer sound system, unique interior and exterior chrome trim and 16-inch alloys. The SS coupe features leather seats with color-keyed perforated inserts, unique trim, performance suspension, an A-pillar mounted boost gauge and 18-inch alloy wheels.

**Powertrains and Performance:** A 2.2-liter Ecotec four-cylinder powers all Cobalts, except the SS. With 145 horsepower and 150 pound-feet of torque, the engine compares favorably with most others in the class. It's made entirely of aluminum and boasts dual-overhead camshafts and four valves per cylinder for maximum efficiency and power. The SS coupe features a 2.0-liter supercharged Ecotec that's good for 205 hp and 200 lb-ft of torque. The standard transmission is a five-speed manual with a four-speed automatic available as an option. The automatic is standard on the LT, and not available on the SS.

**Safety:** Antilock brakes are optional on base models, and standard on all other Cobalts. Head-protecting side curtain airbags are optional across the board. Each seating position has a three-point seatbelt standard, and all but base models can be equipped with OnStar telematics. The Cobalt has not yet been crash tested.

**Interior Design and Special Features:** The Cobalt features a modern and stylish interior. Materials quality is competitive with that of other economy cars, and everything is screwed together with care. Chevy's efforts to provide a solid and quiet ride have paid off—the Cobalt feels more substantial than typical small cars. Though a few plastic bits here and there are of questionable quality, the overall impression is one of a premium compact car.

**Driving Impressions:** The Ecotec four-cylinder is a thoroughly modern and refined engine that provides good power and a smooth delivery. Handling is quite good for a car in this class, with reasonably good manners in corners and a compliant ride around town. In addition to a broad power band, the SS delivers better steering feel and handling response without a noticeable loss of ride quality.

Crash Test Scores, see pg 530
Warranty information, see pg 542

### Specifications

| Engine/Drivetrain | HP | Torque | EPA Fuel Economy Rating |
|---|---|---|---|
| 4cyl 2.2L A/M | 145 | 150 | N/A |
| 4cyl 2.0L M | 205 | 200 | N/A |

### Body Styles

| Style | MSRP Range |
|---|---|
| Compact Coupe | $13,625–$21,430 |
| Compact Sedan | $13,625–$18,195 |

# 2005 Chevrolet Colorado

**MSRP Price Range**

## $15,695 - $28,330

Destination Charge: $635 (all styles)

### Ratings

| | | |
|---|---|---|
| Consumer Rating | 8.2 | ▬▬▬▬▬ |
| Editors Rating | 6.9 | ▬▬▬▬ |

**What Edmunds.com says:** It has the features and the looks necessary to become the dominant truck in the compact class, but next to the all-new pickups from Dodge, Nissan and Toyota, the Colorado comes up short in power, interior room and overall fit and finish.

**Pros:** Versatile size, fuel-efficient engine lineup, available side curtain airbags and locking differential, standard ABS.

**Cons:** Not much low-end torque, no six- or eight-cylinder engine option, low tow ratings, subpar build and materials quality.

**What's New:** No major changes this year.

**Body Styles, Trim Levels and Options:** The Colorado comes in regular, extended and crew cab body styles, and all are offered in both two- and four-wheel drive. Regular and extended cab models have a six-foot bed, while the crew cab gets a five-foot bed. There are two basic trim levels: base and LS. Base models come with air conditioning, a 60/40-split cloth bench seat and an AM/FM stereo. Upgraded LS models add titanium-colored trim, tilt steering, cruise control and a CD stereo. Both the Z85 heavy-duty and Z71 off-road packages add a torsion bar front suspension with heavier-duty shocks. Of these two packages, the Z71 offers the tallest ride height, along with a locking rear differential, oversize tires and skid plates on 4WD models. There's also a ZQ8 sport package that features a lowered suspension, quicker-ratio steering, 17-inch alloy wheels wearing 235/50 performance tires and color-keyed wheel flares, grille and bumpers. Other notable options include OnStar, XM Satellite Radio and a six-disc CD changer.

**Powertrains and Performance:** Two engines are available: a 2.8-liter inline four-cylinder and a 3.5-liter inline five-cylinder. Both are built out of lightweight aluminum and both feature dual-overhead cams, four valves per cylinder and electronic throttle control. The 2.8-liter engine is standard on all models and is rated at 175 horsepower and 220 lb-ft of torque. The optional 3.5-liter engine offers 220 hp and 225 lb-ft of torque. A five-speed manual transmission is standard, but a four-speed automatic is also available on all models. Four-wheel-drive models feature a dual-range transfer case with push-button controls.

**Safety:** The Colorado is the first compact truck to offer roof-mounted side curtain airbags. Dual-stage driver and front-passenger airbags are standard along with four-wheel antilock brakes. Traction control is optional on 2WD trucks. In government crash tests, the Colorado earned four stars (out of five) for both the driver and front passenger in frontal impact testing, and four out of five stars in side-impact testing for front passengers, and five stars for rear passengers.

*Crash Test Scores, see pg 530*
*Warranty information, see pg 542*

**Interior Design and Special Features:** It may be a fresh design, but it's still a compact pickup so don't expect anything fancy in the Colorado's cabin. Simple rotary climate controls and a large stereo faceplate make the interior seem instantly familiar as soon as you get in. The gauges are similarly basic, but functional in their design.

### Specifications

| Engine/Drivetrain | HP | Torque | EPA Fuel Economy Rating |
|---|---|---|---|
| 5cyl 3.5L A | 220 | 225 | N/A |
| 4cyl 2.8L M | 175 | 185 | N/A |

### Body Styles

| Style | MSRP Range |
|---|---|
| Crew Cab Pickup Truck | $21,185–$28,330 |
| Extended Cab Pickup Truck | $18,040–$23,905 |
| Regular Cab Pickup Truck | $15,695–$21,255 |

**Driving Impressions:** The inline engines deliver smooth, refined power, but their off-the-line punch and odd exhaust note are a little disappointing. Still, either engine provides the kind of midrange torque and higher-rpm horsepower necessary for most day-to-day driving. Shifts from the four-speed automatic are firm and well timed, and although it's still fairly vague through the gears, the new five-speed manual gearbox is about as good as you're going to find in a compact truck. The stock suspension tuning is on the soft side, but if you're intent on going fast or bashing boulders, the sport and off-road packages provide suitable performance.

# 2005 Chevrolet Corvette

**MSRP Price Range**
## $43,445 - $51,445
Destination Charge: $800 (all styles)

**#1 Editors' Rating**

## Ratings

| | | |
|---|---|---|
| Consumer Rating | 9.7 | ■■■■■■■■■ |
| Editors Rating | 8.8 | ■■■■■■■■ |

**What Edmunds.com says:** The latest Corvette is a world-class performance machine that successfully blends excellent build quality and ergonomics with sexy styling and tremendous value for the dollar.

**Pros:** Performance on par with the world's best sports cars, daily-driver livability, precision build quality, a performance bargain when compared to cars of similar capabilities.

**Cons:** Interior still doesn't look like it belongs in a car of this caliber.

**What's New:** A thoroughly redesigned Corvette debuts this year. Although the basic chassis is based on the previous model, the new Vette shows notable improvement in its performance, features and refinement.

**Body Styles, Trim Levels and Options:** The fiberglass-bodied Corvette comes in two forms: coupe (technically a hatchback) and convertible. The coupe features a removable roof panel for open-air cruising, though true wind-in-the-hair types will want to opt for the soft-top convertible. All Corvettes come well equipped with items such as xenon headlamps, leather seating and a removable roof panel. Notable options include the Magnetic Ride Control suspension, a Z06 performance handling package and a DVD-based navigation system. Coupes can be equipped with a transparent roof panel, or both the standard solid panel and the transparent panel. A versatile head-up display is available, along with driver-seat memory, a seven-speaker Bose audio system and automatic climate control.

**Powertrains and Performance:** All coupe and convertible Corvettes come with the 6.0-liter LS-2 V8. Rated at 400 horsepower and 400 pound-feet of torque, this engine unleashes effortless power at any speed. Equipped with the standard six-speed manual transmission, the Corvette will hit 60 mph in a shade over 4 seconds. The car is capable of 186 mph, faster than any production Corvette in history. A four-speed automatic is a no-charge option. To help rein the power in on slippery surfaces, traction and stability control (Active Handling System) are standard equipment.

**Safety:** Antilock disc brakes are standard. Side-impact airbags are optional, but head curtain airbags are not available. The Vette features an Active Handling System (AHS) that can sense a loss of control and apply individual brakes or cut power to help maintain stability. This system has been well programmed to provide non-invasive assistance, and a performance driving mode gives the driver even more control at the track—while still maintaining a safety net. No crash test data is available.

**Interior Design and Special Features:** Inside, large analog gauges and well-placed radio and climate controls greet passengers. Ergonomics and materials quality are excellent, and seat comfort is top-notch. Luggage space beneath the coupe's rear hatch glass is a healthy 22 cubic feet, more cargo room than most sedans. An innovative keyless access system is standard. Sensors detect the presence of the key fob, and automatically lock or unlock the doors. In fact, there aren't even door handles—just touch-buttons, inside and out, that unlatch the door. There's no ignition key, either. As long as the keyfob is inside the car, you simply push a dash button to start the engine. Plenty of safeguards are in place to prevent shenanigans caused by a misplaced/lost keyfob, or even a dead battery.

**Driving Impressions:** Endless power from the snarling LS2 combined with a tight suspension results in a sports car that never ceases to put a smile on your face. All three of the suspension packages deliver a compliant ride along with white-knuckled handling abilities. The C6 is a comfortable touring car, as well as a world-class performance machine.

*Crash Test Scores, see pg 530*
*Warranty information, see pg 542*

## Specifications

| Engine/Drivetrain | HP | Torque | EPA Fuel Economy Rating |
|---|---|---|---|
| 8cyl 6.0L M | 400 | 400 | 19 city/28 hwy |

## Body Styles

| Style | MSRP Range |
|---|---|
| Compact Convertible | $51,445 |
| Compact Coupe | $43,445 |

# 2005 Chevrolet Equinox

Midsize SUV

**MSRP Price Range**

## $21,095 - $24,435

Destination Charge: $565 (all styles)

### Ratings

| | | |
|---|---|---|
| Consumer Rating | 9.2 | |
| Editors Rating | 8.2 | |

**What Edmunds.com says:** A superior successor to the aged Tracker, the Equinox offers flexible interior space, a strong engine and modern styling.

**Pros:** Standard V6 engine, long wheelbase affords plenty of interior room, fore/aft-adjustable rear seats, available side curtain airbags.

**Cons:** Costs as much as the more powerful Saturn Vue, limited drivetrain choices, confusing stereo controls.

**What's New:** The Equinox is an all-new compact SUV from Chevrolet. It shares a platform with the Saturn Vue and offers similar levels of space and versatility for buyers seeking practical suburban transportation.

**Body Styles, Trim Levels and Options:** Like most Chevrolet trucks, the Equinox is offered in LS and LT trims, both of which are available with either front-wheel drive or all-wheel drive. Standard equipment on the LS includes 16-inch wheels; air conditioning; a height-adjustable driver seat; a six-speaker CD stereo; automatic headlights; power windows, mirrors and locks; an alarm system; and a rear window wiper. The LT adds such features as alloy wheels, ABS, cruise control, foglights and upgraded cloth upholstery. Available options include side curtain airbags, OnStar telematics, satellite radio, an MP3-compatible stereo, leather seating, a power driver seat, heated seats, a trailering package, a sunroof and an auto-dimming rearview mirror.

**Powertrains and Performance:** All Equinox SUVs come with the same 3.4-liter V6 engine. It's good for 185 horsepower and 210 pound-feet of torque. Towing capacity is rated at 3,500 pounds. The Equinox is available in all-wheel-drive and front-wheel-drive configurations, but only one transmission is offered—a five speed automatic.

**Safety:** Front disc/rear drum brakes are standard; ABS is optional on LS models and standard on the LT. Traction control is optional on front-drive LS models and standard on LTs. Full-length side curtain airbags are optional on all Equinox models. The Equinox has not been crash tested, yet.

**Interior Design and Special Features:** Inside, Chevrolet designers opted for a simple, industrial look with large, clear gauges and faux aluminum accents. While most of the controls are simple in design, the stereo head unit's collection of small buttons is unnecessarily complicated. Thanks to its long wheelbase, the Equinox offers plenty of room for its occupants, including class-leading rear headroom and legroom. To make way for larger passengers or cargo, the 60/40-split rear seat can slide nearly 8 inches fore and aft. An adjustable rear cargo shelf expands your loading options after a shopping trip and can also function as a picnic table. The Equinox offers 35 cubic feet of luggage space behind its rear seats; fold down the seats and you've got a total of 69 cubic feet.

**Driving Impressions:** The Equinox's 3.4-liter V6 engine has been used in plenty of GM products and has always provided adequate if unrefined power. In the Equinox, you can look forward to spirited acceleration as well as better-than-average fuel economy. The Equinox shares a platform with the Saturn Vue, so expect a comfortable ride and capable, if not altogether nimble, handling characteristics.

*Crash Test Scores, see pg 530*
*Warranty information, see pg 542*

### Specifications

| Engine/Drivetrain | HP | Torque | EPA Fuel Economy Rating |
|---|---|---|---|
| 6cyl 3.4L A | 185 | 210 | 19 city/25 hwy |

### Body Styles

| Style | MSRP Range |
|---|---|
| Midsize SUV | $21,095–$24,435 |

**MSRP Price Range**
## $25,400 - $32,410
Destination Charge: $775 (all styles)

### Ratings

| | | |
|---|---|---|
| Consumer Rating | N/A | |
| Editors Rating | 6.7 | |

**What Edmunds.com says:** The Express (and its twin, the GMC Savanna) is pretty much the only game in town if you're looking for a full-size van that doesn't look and drive like it was designed two decades ago.

**Pros:** Strong powertrains, dual-passenger access doors, multiple wheelbase and passenger configurations, optional all-wheel drive.

**Cons:** Plasticky interior, awkward handling.

**What's New:** The StabiliTrak stability control system will become standard later in the model year, but only on one-ton regular-wheelbase vans.

**Body Styles, Trim Levels and Options:** The standard-wheelbase (135-inch) Express comes in half-ton, three-quarter-ton and one-ton configurations, while the extended-wheelbase version (155-inch) requires either three-quarter-ton or one-ton running gear. There are two trim levels: base and LS. Base models are geared toward fleet service so standard equipment is limited to air conditioning, an AM/FM stereo and a theft-deterrent system. The more livable LS models include rear-seat climate controls, power windows and door locks, cloth upholstery, cruise control, a tilt steering wheel and keyless entry. Optional equipment includes power driver and front passenger seats, the OnStar communications system and an upgraded audio system with an in-dash six-disc CD changer.

**Powertrains and Performance:** Express vans offer a choice of three power plants and either rear- or all-wheel drive. The standard engine on two-wheel-drive half-ton models is a 4.3-liter V6 rated at 195 horsepower and 260 pound-feet of torque. A 5.3-liter V8 with 295 hp and 325 lb-ft of torque is standard on all-wheel-drive half-tons and optional on rear-drive versions. Three-quarter- and one-ton models come standard with a 6.0-liter V8 rated at 300 hp and 360 lb-ft of torque. All half-ton models use a four-speed automatic transmission, while three-quarter-ton and one-ton models get a heavy-duty version. The maximum trailer towing capacity on half-ton models is 6,300 pounds. Standard-wheelbase three-quarter-ton models can tow up to 9,800 pounds while extended-wheelbase versions are limited to 7,400 pounds. Standard-wheelbase one-ton vans can tow up to 9,800 pounds, and extended-wheelbase one-ton vans max out at 9,400 pounds.

**Safety:** All Express vans have four-wheel antilock disc brakes standard. Light-duty models (GVWR less than 8,600 pounds) feature a front-passenger sensing system that will deactivate the front airbag if it senses a small adult or child sitting up front. Heavy-duty models use a manual airbag deactivation switch for the front passenger. StabiliTrak stability control is standard, from mid-2005 on, on one-ton regular-wheelbase vans only.

**Interior Design and Special Features:** The interior is built for pure functionality, and while it may not be pretty, it sure gets the job done. All controls are simple to use and well within reach of the driver, but the footwells remain as cramped as ever. Buyers can opt for 60/40-split driver-side doors for easier passenger access to the rear seats. The standard configuration seats 12, with 8- or 15-passenger arrangements also available, depending on which model you choose.

**Driving Impressions:** A reinforced frame, larger sway bars, rack and pinion steering (half-ton models only) and standard four-wheel antilock disc brakes give the Express a leg up on the competition when it comes to ride and handling. Although Chevy's van is still far from nimble, it's a better choice for day-to-day driving than Ford's aged Econoline. And with three strong V8 engines to choose from, merging and passing maneuvers come easily, even when you're hauling a heavy load.

*Crash Test Scores, see pg 530*
*Warranty information, see pg 542*

### Specifications

| Engine/Drivetrain | HP | Torque | EPA Fuel Economy Rating |
|---|---|---|---|
| 8cyl 6.0L A | 300 | 360 | N/A |
| 8cyl 5.3L A | 295 | 325 | 13 city/17 hwy |
| 6cyl 4.3L A | 195 | 260 | 14 city/18 hwy |

### Body Styles

| Style | MSRP Range |
|---|---|
| Large Van | $30,304–$31,644 |
| Midsize Van | $25,400–$32,410 |

# 2005 Chevrolet Impala

**MSRP Price Range**

## $22,220 - $28,425

Destination Charge: $660 (all styles)

## Ratings

| | | |
|---|---|---|
| Consumer Rating | 9.7 | |
| Editors Rating | 7.2 | |

**What Edmunds.com says:** Although suitably quick in 240-horse SS form, Chevrolet's full-size sedan still lags behind the competition when it comes to driving dynamics and overall refinement.

**Pros:** Six-passenger seating availability, good crash test scores, torquey and efficient V6 engines.

**Cons:** Vague steering, soggy suspension on base and LS models, low-buck interior.

**What's New:** OnStar is now standard on all models, and a new Sport Appearance Package is optional on the base Impala. Other than that, changes are limited to minor trim updates.

**Body Styles, Trim Levels and Options:** Available as a sedan only, the Impala comes in three trim levels—base, LS and SS. Base models include 16-inch wheels; a front bench seat; dual-zone air conditioning; power locks, mirrors and windows; a tilt steering wheel and keyless entry. Moving up to the LS model adds ABS, alloy wheels, a floor console, cloth bucket seats with six-way power adjustment for the driver, a leather-wrapped steering wheel and a tire inflation monitor. The SS comes with monochromatic exterior paint and adds a lowered suspension, 17-inch wheels and leather upholstery. Optional equipment includes leather seating for the LS, a trip computer, an upgraded audio system with a CD player, satellite radio and a sunroof.

**Powertrains and Performance:** Base-model Impalas are powered by a 3.4-liter V6 engine that produces 180 horsepower and 205 pound-feet of torque. Stepping up to LS trim gets you a 3.8-liter V6 that makes 200 hp and 225 lb-ft of torque. Both models employ a responsive four-speed automatic transmission that sends the power through the front wheels. The SS has a supercharged version of the 3.8-liter V6 making an impressive 240 hp and 280 lb-ft of torque. To handle the extra power, the SS uses a heavy-duty version of GM's four-speed automatic.

**Safety:** Occupant safety is a big selling point for the Impala. In crash tests conducted by the National Highway Traffic Safety Administration (NHTSA), the Impala earned five stars (out of five) for both the driver and front passenger in frontal impact testing, and four out of five stars in side-impact testing. In frontal offset crash testing, the Impala earned a "Good" rating, the highest possible. Antilock brakes and traction control are standard on the LS and SS, and optional on the base model. A side airbag for the driver only is optional on all Impalas.

**Interior Design and Special Features:** As one of the few six-passenger sedans on the market, the Impala does have an edge on the competition when it comes to interior space. That's about the only edge, however, as the rest of the interior is a mix of cheap plastics and bland design that pales in comparison to the more modern offerings from Toyota and Chrysler. Even the sporty SS provides no real styling upgrades, except for a new set of gauges and a few "SS" logos.

**Driving Impressions:** Despite its modest weight, the Impala still suffers in the handling department, at least in base and LS form. The way it floats and wallows through turns, you'd think you were in one of the enormous land yachts of the '60s. Vague steering and flat seats certainly don't add much to the driving experience. The V6 engines get it going at a reasonable rate, but refinement is not a strong point. The SS is the best choice for those who like to drive, as its supercharged engine offers brisk acceleration, while a reworked suspension and 17-inch wheels improve handling.

Crash Test Scores, see pg 530
Warranty information, see pg 542

## Specifications

| Engine/Drivetrain | HP | Torque | EPA Fuel Economy Rating |
|---|---|---|---|
| 6cyl 3.8L A | 240 | 280 | 18 city/28 hwy |
| 6cyl 3.8L A | 200 | 225 | 20 city/30 hwy |
| 6cyl 3.4L A | 180 | 205 | 21 city/32 hwy |

## Body Styles

| Style | MSRP Range |
|---|---|
| Large Sedan | $22,220–$28,425 |

For the latest full vehicle reports, visit www.edmunds.com/bginfopak

# Midsize Sedan

# 2005 Chevrolet Malibu

**MSRP Price Range**
## $19,085 - $23,945
Destination Charge: $625 (all styles)

### Ratings

| | | |
|---|---|---|
| Consumer Rating | 8.6 | |
| Editors Rating | 7.0 | |

**What Edmunds.com says:** Roomy, affordable and well equipped, the Malibu delivers excellent value but lacks some of the performance and refinement of the class leaders.

**Pros:** Pros: Smooth ride quality, above-average fuel economy with V6, plenty of passenger and cargo space, ample safety and convenience features, innovative remote start feature.

**Cons:** Lackluster interior, subpar brakes and steering, down on power compared to competitors, no manual transmission available.

**What's New:** The side curtain airbag option now includes front-seat side-impact airbags.

**Body Styles, Trim Levels and Options:** The four-door Malibu is available in three different trim levels—base, LS and LT. The base model comes well equipped with air conditioning; a CD player; a height-adjustable driver seat; a tilt-and-telescoping steering wheel; power windows, mirrors and door locks; and a 60/40-split folding rear seat. The midlevel LS adds features like alloy wheels, power-adjustable pedals, cruise control, keyless entry, premium cloth seats, front map lights, a cargo net in the trunk, lumbar support for the driver and an upgraded stereo with a driver information center. The LT is the top-of-the-line Malibu, and it adds even more luxury features like a remote vehicle starter, heated leather seats, automatic climate control, 16-inch wheels, foglights and front and rear reading lights. Options include an in-dash CD changer, satellite radio, a sunroof and OnStar. A remote vehicle starter is optional on base and LS models.

**Powertrains and Performance:** The base Malibu comes with GM's 2.2-liter Ecotec engine rated at 145 horsepower. LS and LT models get a 200-hp, 3.5-liter V6. Both engines are mated to a four-speed automatic transmission. LS and LT Malibu come with traction control; it's optional on base models. Fuel economy estimates are 23 mpg city/33 mpg highway with the base four and 22/30 with the V6.

**Safety:** Base Malibu come with front disc/rear drum brakes, while LS and LT models feature four-wheel discs; ABS and traction control are optional on the base model and standard on the LS and LT. Front-seat side-impact airbags and full-length head-protecting side curtain airbags are optional on base and LS models and standard on the LT. In government crash testing, this family sedan earned four out of five stars for frontal impact protection. In IIHS testing, the Malibu earned the top score of "Good" for frontal offset crashes and an "Acceptable" rating (second highest) for side impacts when equipped with side airbags (without the bags, it rated "Poor").

**Interior Design and Special Features:** Inside, the Malibu offers broad, flat seats with plenty of head-, shoulder and legroom in both the front and back. Both adjustable pedals and a tilt-and-telescoping steering wheel are included in most Malibus, allowing drivers of all sizes to get comfortable behind the wheel. The cabin design is functional but bland with a straightforward control layout. Trunk space is generous at 15.4 cubic feet, and a 60/40-split rear seat and fold-flat front-passenger seat make it easy to expand cargo space when needed.

**Driving Impressions:** Power is adequate with the base four-cylinder, but most buyers will want to step up to the V6, which offers plenty of torque for merging and passing despite its modest ratings. A softly tuned but composed suspension gives the Malibu a smooth ride and predictable handling in the corners. Unfortunately, the car's electric steering ruins the fun by providing too much power assist much of the time. The brakes perform adequately in traffic, but stopping distances are a bit long.

*Crash Test Scores, see pg 530*
*Warranty information, see pg 542*

### Specifications

| Engine/Drivetrain | HP | Torque | EPA Fuel Economy Rating |
|---|---|---|---|
| 6cyl 3.5L A | 200 | 220 | 23 city/32 hwy |
| 4cyl 2.2L A | 145 | 155 | 24 city/34 hwy |

### Body Styles

| Style | MSRP Range |
|---|---|
| Midsize Sedan | $19,085–$23,945 |

# 2005 Chevrolet Malibu Maxx

**MSRP Price Range**
## $21,350 - $24,495
Destination Charge: $625 (all styles)

## Ratings

| | | |
|---|---|---|
| Consumer Rating | 9.4 | ████████████████ |
| Editors Rating | 7.0 | ███████████ |

**What Edmunds.com says:** Spacious and well equipped, the Malibu Maxx is a well-executed design that adds the functionality of a wagon without giving up sedan drivability.

**Pros:** Hatchback configuration makes for easy loading, spacious interior with adjustable rear seats, plenty of safety and convenience features, innovative remote start feature, standard V6.

**Cons:** Lackluster interior, subpar braking and steering, less cargo space than true wagons or SUVs.

**What's New:** The side curtain airbag option now includes front-seat side-impact airbags.

**Body Styles, Trim Levels and Options:** The Malibu Maxx comes only as a four-door wagon and is available in two different trim levels—LS and LT. The LS is well equipped and offers features like 16-inch alloy wheels; air conditioning; a six-speaker stereo with a CD player and driver information center; a tilt-and-telescoping steering wheel; power-adjustable pedals; premium cloth seats with height and lumbar adjustment for the driver; power windows, mirrors and door locks; keyless entry; a multiadjustable 60/40-split folding rear seat; a fixed rear skylight with retractable shade; and a rear cargo shelf. The LT adds luxury features like a remote vehicle starter, front heated leather seats, automatic climate control, foglights and heated outside mirrors. Options include an in-dash CD changer, satellite radio, separate rear audio controls, a rear-seat DVD player and OnStar telematics.

**Powertrains and Performance:** Standard on every Malibu Maxx is a 3.5-liter V6 that makes 200 horsepower and 220 pound-feet of torque. A four-speed automatic is the only transmission available. Fuel economy estimates are 21 mpg for city driving and 29 mpg on the highway.

**Safety:** Safety is a strong point for the Malibu Maxx. Four-wheel antilock disc brakes and traction control are standard. Front side-impact airbags and full-length side head curtain airbags are optional on the LS and standard on the LT. Other key standard items include a tilt-and-telescoping steering wheel and adjustable pedals.

**Interior Design and Special Features:** Inside, the Malibu Maxx offers plenty of passenger space; the head-, shoulder and legroom in the front and rear seats are competitive with what the roomiest midsize sedans offer. The Maxx is six inches longer than the Malibu sedan, and the 60/40-split rear seat reclines and offers seven inches of fore/aft travel. A standard fixed sunroof over the rear seats contributes to the cabin's open feel. Cargo capacity behind the rear seats measures 22.8 cubic feet, and a parcel shelf allows for two-tier loading. Though not particularly upscale or stylish in feel, the cabin is at least functional with a straightforward control layout.

*Crash Test Scores, see pg 530*
*Warranty information, see pg 542*

## Specifications

| Engine/Drivetrain | HP | Torque | EPA Fuel Economy Rating |
|---|---|---|---|
| 6cyl 3.5L A | 200 | 220 | 22 city/30 hwy |

## Body Styles

| Style | MSRP Range |
|---|---|
| Midsize Coupe | $21,350–$24,495 |

**Driving Impressions:** The Malibu Maxx shares underpinnings with the agile Saab 9-3, but it's not exactly what we would call sporty. The steering feel is on the wobbly side, but in most driving conditions the Malibu is a competent and comfortable performer. Although its V6 might seem down on power compared to the competition its generous low-end torque and quick-shifting transmission do a good job of making it feel more powerful than its numbers suggest. Braking performance is adequate in everyday traffic, but the Maxx's stopping distances are longer than they should be for a car in this class.

For the latest full vehicle reports, visit www.edmunds.com/bginfopak

**MSRP Price Range**
## $22,150 - $28,225
Destination Charge: $660 (all styles)

### Ratings

| | | |
|---|---|---|
| Consumer Rating | 9.1 | ▆▆▆▆▆▆▆▆▭ |
| Editors Rating | 7.2 | ▆▆▆▆▆▆▭ |

**What Edmunds.com says:** Generally a lackluster coupe in terms of styling and handling, but the supercharged SS version restores some of the excitement to this once-famous nameplate.

**Pros:** Spacious interior, low sticker price, strong acceleration with supercharged V6.

**Cons:** Mediocre performance on non-supercharged models, bland interior with cheap materials, no passenger side-impact airbag, ABS not standard.

**What's New:** This year the SS badge is reserved for the supercharged Monte Carlo; last year's non-supercharged SS is now the LT. The Competition Yellow Sport Appearance, Dale Earnhardt "Intimidator" Special Edition and Dale Earnhardt Jr. packages are no longer available, nor are body side moldings and the deck lid lock cylinder. OnStar is now standard equipment on all models.

**Body Styles, Trim Levels and Options:** The Monte Carlo is a two-door coupe that comes in three trim levels: LS, LT and SS. The base LS model comes with 16-inch wheels, dual-zone manual air conditioning, power door locks and windows, a tilt steering wheel and remote keyless entry. Stepping up to the LT model gets you foglights, rocker-panel moldings, alloy wheels, ABS, traction control, a tire-pressure monitor and dual exhaust outlets. Inside, LT models add cruise control, a leather-wrapped steering wheel with audio controls and upgraded cloth seats. On top of those items, the SS offers 17-inch wheels, a lowered suspension and full-perimeter ground effects. Options include leather seats, an upgraded audio system with a CD player, satellite radio, power front seats, heated exterior mirrors and a power sunroof.

**Powertrains and Performance:** The base engine in LS coupe is a 3.4-liter V6 rated at 180 horsepower. The midlevel LT has a 3.8-liter V6 good for 200 hp. The top-dog SS benefits from a supercharged version of the 3.8-liter that pumps out 240 horses and 280 pound-feet of torque. A four-speed automatic transmission is standard regardless of which model you choose, but the SS gets a heavy-duty version to manage the extra power. Expect fuel economy around 20 mpg in the city and close to 30 mpg on the highway with any of the engines.

**Safety:** Antilock brakes and traction control are standard on LT and SS models, and optional on the LS. A side airbag for the driver is optional on all Monte Carlos. In government crash tests, the Monte Carlo received five stars (out of five) for protection of the driver and front passenger in a frontal collision. Side-impact crash tests resulted in a three-star rating for front-passenger protection and four stars for rear-occupant protection.

**Interior Design and Special Features:** As far as coupes go, the Monte Carlo is spacious and comfortable. The seats are wide and can accommodate a variety of drivers, and even the rear seats are usable. There's not a hint of elegant design to be found anywhere, but for those who value function over form, the Monte's ergonomics won't disappoint. The SS benefits from a sportier six-gauge instrument panel, as well as special badging throughout the cabin.

**Driving Impressions:** The Monte Carlo handles well enough to suit its intended buyer. Large four-wheel antilock disc brakes and meaty performance tires give it respectable stopping power and grip, but the lifeless steering doesn't communicate enough road feel to make this big coupe feel sporty. The fact that it only comes with an automatic transmission doesn't help either, but at least the V6s are torquey off the line. If you like to drive, the SS is your best bet, as its boosted V6 delivers brisk acceleration at just about any speed, while a reworked suspension and 17-inch wheels and tires provide improved handling.

*Crash Test Scores, see pg 530*
*Warranty information, see pg 542*

### Specifications

| Engine/Drivetrain | HP | Torque | EPA Fuel Economy Rating |
|---|---|---|---|
| 6cyl 3.8L A | 240 | 280 | 18 city/28 hwy |
| 6cyl 3.8L A | 200 | 225 | 20 city/30 hwy |
| 6cyl 3.4L A | 180 | 205 | 21 city/32 hwy |

### Body Styles

| Style | MSRP Range |
|---|---|
| Large Coupe | $22,150–$28,225 |

# 2005 Chevrolet SSR

**MSRP Price Range**

## $42,430

Destination Charge: $625 (all styles)

### Ratings

| | | |
|---|---|---|
| Consumer Rating | 7.9 | |
| Editors Rating | 7.7 | |

**What Edmunds.com says:** Combining the styling elements of a late-'40s Chevy pickup, the attitude of a muscle car and the fun of a roadster, the SSR is an entertaining answer to a question nobody asked.

**Pros:** Quick folding convertible hardtop, street rod style, aggressive exhaust note, comfortable seats.

**Cons:** Seats only two and yet weighs nearly 5,000 pounds, costs almost as much as a Corvette.

**What's New:** Big news for the SSR—more power for 2005. Last year's 5.3-liter V8 is ditched in favor of a 6.0-liter aluminum engine with 390 hp. Newly optional this year is a six-speed manual Tremec transmission with an Eaton limited-slip differential. Other changes include a new CD/MP3 stereo and gas struts for the hood.

**Body Styles, Trim Levels and Options:** All SSRs come as retractable-hardtop roadsters, offering the security and comfort of a coupe when the roof is raised along with the al fresco experience of a convertible when the top is dropped. There is just a single well-equipped version of the SSR, though an LS Preferred Equipment option package is available for those who desire heated seats, upgraded Bose sound (including an in-dash CD changer) and auto-dimming mirrors. Also available is wood trim for the cargo bed, another tip of the hat to the pickups of the late 1940s.

**Powertrains and Performance:** The sole powertrain for the SSR is a 6.0-liter aluminum V8 rated at 390 horsepower and 405 pound-feet of torque. The big V8 sends the power to the rear wheels via either a heavy-duty four-speed automatic gearbox, or a six-speed manual Tremec transmission. A limited-slip differential is standard, but differs depending upon which transmission you choose—an 8.6-inch Zexel-torsen unit with the automatic, and a 9.5-inch Eaton unit with the manual. Towing capacity is rated at a relatively meager 2,500 pounds, so it can't pull much more than a Wave Runner.

**Safety:** Side airbags, antilock brakes and traction control highlight the safety features list, but stability control is not available. The SSR hasn't been crash tested.

**Interior Design and Special Features:** Leather seating and tasteful aluminum-look trim offer modern-day comfort and visual appeal, as does the four-spoke steering wheel that features controls for the trip computer and audio system functions. Touches of nostalgia abound; the automatic's gear selector looks like it could have come from a 1968 Corvette, while an optional row of small gauges mounted down on the console remind one of a Camaro of similar vintage. Passenger space is a bit snug, however; the power seat controls are so close to the door that only child-size hands can operate them without opening the door first.

**Driving Impressions:** Accompanied by an exhaust note that would do an old Chevelle SS proud, the SSR's brawny V8 does an admirable job of motivating a vehicle that weighs 700 pounds more than a Caddy DeVille. When hustled along curvy roads, the SSR holds its own, feeling composed if not exactly agile. With an agreeable combination of handling, ride and performance, the SSR should satisfy anyone looking for a comfortable and stylish cruiser.

*Crash Test Scores, see pg 530*
*Warranty information, see pg 542*

### Specifications

| Engine/Drivetrain | HP | Torque | EPA Fuel Economy Rating |
|---|---|---|---|
| 8cyl 6.0L A | 390 | 405 | N/A |

### Body Styles

| Style | MSRP Range |
|---|---|
| Regular Cab Pickup Truck | $42,430 |

For the latest full vehicle reports, visit www.edmunds.com/bginfopak

**MSRP Price Range**

## $18,635 - $37,920
Destination Charge: $850 (all styles)

### Ratings

| | | |
|---|---|---|
| Consumer Rating | 8.8 | |
| Editors Rating | 7.9 | |

**What Edmunds.com says:** Powerful drivetrains, stout underpinnings and unique options make the Silverado a pickup worth considering, but the Dodge Ram, Ford F-150 and Nissan Titan have it beat when it comes to interior design and overall refinement.

**Pros:** Roomy extended and crew cab models, strong V8 engines, innovative features, slick hybrid electric option.

**Cons:** Cheap interior materials, questionable build quality.

**What's New:** Quadrasteer is no longer available on 2WD models, standard wheel sizes have been bumped up to 17 inches, and on extended and crew cab models; a power sunroof that includes HomeLink and a deluxe overhead console are new options. Chevy takes a step backward this year with the return of rear drum brakes, as opposed to last year's four-wheel disc setup. A gasoline/electric hybrid model is also introduced in limited quantities this year. Basically a "mild" hybrid, the system provides no power boost, but does allow for automatic engine startup and shutdown at stops. This truck also comes with four 120-volt AC power outlets and is the only Silverado with rear disc brakes this year. The hybrid truck is only available in Western states and Florida.

**Body Styles, Trim Levels and Options:** Three cab styles—regular, extended and crew cab—are available in five levels of trim: Work Truck, Base, LS, LT and Z71. Designed to be affordable on-the-job companions, Work Trucks offer few amenities, but you do get dual-zone manual air conditioning and an AM/FM radio. Base models offer a few more features like cruise control and a CD player. The midgrade LS trim includes upgrades like deluxe cloth upholstery, power windows and locks and remote keyless entry. LT trucks add aluminum wheels, leather upholstery, automatic climate control and Bose audio. The Z71 version is intended for off-roaders and builds upon the LS with heavier-duty suspension components, skid plates and all-terrain tires. Available on 4WD models is the Quadrasteer four-wheel steering system, which gives the Silverado unmatched stability while towing, as well as a significantly reduced turning circle.

**Powertrains and Performance:** Four engine choices are available for the half-ton Silverado—a 195-horsepower, 4.3-liter V6; a 285-hp, 4.8-liter V8; a 295-hp, 5.3-liter V8; and a 310-hp, 5.3-liter V8 on 4WD extended cab models only. A five-speed manual transmission is standard on regular cabs with the V6 engine. Optional on that model and standard on all other Silverados is a four-speed automatic. The maximum towing capacity with the 5.3-liter V8 is 9,000 pounds (8,300 pounds on Quadrasteer-equipped models). Four-wheel drive is available on all models; although, only LS and LT trim levels can be ordered with the optional Autotrac automatic 4WD system. A hybrid powertrain option is available on LS extended cabs with the 5.3-liter, but the system does not provide any power boost. Its main function is to conserve fuel via automatic engine shutdown and startup at stops, as well as provide on-the-job power through four 120-volt AC outlets.

**Safety:** All Silverados include four-wheel antilock brakes as standard equipment. The Silverado received a rating of "Marginal" (third lowest out of four possible rankings) in the Insurance Institute for Highway Safety's offset crash test. In government crash tests, the Silverado received four stars (out of five) for driver protection in frontal impacts and three stars for the front passenger.

**Interior Design and Special Features:** Inside, Silverado buyers will find a logically laid-out interior, with clear, uncluttered gauges. Materials quality is unimpressive, and build quality, though improved over the last few years, is still below that of the competition. The cabin is roomy, particularly on crew cab models.

**Driving Impressions:** The Silverado is comfortable enough to be a daily driver, yet it's still powerful enough to use as a dedicated work truck. Acceleration is adequate, especially with either of the Vortec V8s, and the automatic transmission shifts with authority. The steering feels vague on center, but it's light and precise enough for easy maneuvering. The automatic engine shutdown and startup feature works seamlessly in the hybrid truck. Additionally, the hybrid's electric power steering feels at least as good as the traditional setup.

*Crash Test Scores, see pg 530*
*Warranty information, see pg 542*

### Specifications

| Engine/Drivetrain | HP | Torque | EPA Fuel Economy Rating |
|---|---|---|---|
| 8cyl 5.3L A | 310 | 335 | 16 city/21 hwy |
| 8cyl 5.3L A | 295 | 335 | 16 city/21 hwy |
| 8cyl 5.3L A | 295 | 330 | 16 city/21 hwy |
| 8cyl 4.8L A | 285 | 295 | 16 city/21 hwy |
| 6cyl 4.3L A/M | 195 | 260 | 16 city/20 hwy |

### Body Styles

| Style | MSRP Range |
|---|---|
| Crew Cab Pickup Truck | $30,090–$37,920 |
| Extended Cab Pickup Truck | $23,690–$36,470 |
| Regular Cab Pickup Truck | $18,635–$29,715 |

# 2005 Chevrolet Silverado 1500HD Large Truck

**MSRP Price Range**
## $31,495 - $39,185
Destination Charge: $850 (all styles)

### Ratings

| Consumer Rating | N/A | |
|---|---|---|
| Editors Rating | 7.8 | |

**What Edmunds.com says:** A powerful drivetrain and stout underpinnings make the Silverado 1500HD crew cab a good option for buyers who like the size of a half-ton pickup but require extra towing capacity. If you don't plan to tow, the Nissan Titan and Dodge Ram are better overall trucks.

**Pros:** Roomy crew cab can carry six passengers, strong 6.0-liter V8 engine, highest tow rating of any half-ton pickup, innovative features.

**Cons:** Dated interior with low-grade materials, questionable build quality.

**What's New:** The heavy-duty 1500HD crew cab is back once again this year for buyers who like the size of the light-duty 1500 crew cab, but need more power and towing capacity. As on other half-ton Silverados, a power sunroof is a new option, and includes a HomeLink universal transmitter and deluxe overhead console.

**Body Styles, Trim Levels and Options:** The Silverado 1500HD comes in the crew cab body style only, and is available in two levels of trim: LS and LT. Intended as a truck for recreational use rather than hard-core work duty, the crew cab configuration provides a spacious passenger cabin without the harsh ride typical of most workhorse crew cabs. Well-equipped LS models include cruise control, keyless entry, an AM/FM/CD stereo, dual-zone manual air conditioning and a driver message center that monitors multiple vehicle systems. LT models add power-adjustable driver and passenger seats (with driver memory), automatic climate control, a Bose sound system with rear audio controls and the OnStar communications system. The optional Quadrasteer four-wheel steering system dramatically improves the truck's turning radius and provides additional stability when towing heavy loads at highway speeds.

**Powertrains and Performance:** Under the hood rests a 6.0-liter V8 rated at 300 horsepower and 360 pound-feet of torque. While these used to be impressive numbers, Dodge, Ford and Nissan all offer V8s with as much or more power. Handling the shifting needs of the 6.0-liter V8 is a heavy-duty four-speed automatic transmission. With overdrive and a tow/haul mode that adjusts shift points for better performance under load, this transmission-engine combo allows the 1500HD to tow up to 10,200 pounds. Larger four-wheel disc brakes borrowed from the three-quarter-ton lineup assure that you'll be able to haul the load down to speed as quickly as the burly V8 engine gets it going.

**Safety:** Chevy's dual-stage airbags deploy with varying levels of force depending on the crash severity, while the passenger sensor will deactivate the passenger-side airbag if it detects the presence of a child. All Silverados include four-wheel antilock brakes as standard equipment. In IIHS frontal offset crash testing, the Silverado earned a "Marginal" rating (the second-lowest on a scale of four).

**Interior Design and Special Features:** Inside, Silverado buyers will find a logically laid-out interior, with an easy-to-use dual-zone climate control system and clear, uncluttered gauges. Materials quality is unimpressive, and build quality, though improved over the last few years, is still behind the competition. The large cabin offers room for six passengers, and the four-door configuration makes getting in and out much easier than most extended cab trucks. The Silverado also offers an optional Bose audio system and XM Satellite Radio, as well as a rear-seat DVD entertainment system.

*Crash Test Scores, see pg 530*
*Warranty information, see pg 542*

### Specifications

| Engine/Drivetrain | HP | Torque | EPA Fuel Economy Rating |
|---|---|---|---|
| 8cyl 6.0L A | 300 | 360 | N/A |

### Body Styles

| Style | MSRP Range |
|---|---|
| Crew Cab Pickup Truck | $31,495–$39,185 |

**Driving Impressions:** Despite its hefty tow rating, the 1500HD is still comfortable enough to be a daily driver. The big V8 provides swift acceleration and the heavy-duty automatic transmission shifts with authority. The steering feels vague on center, but the new Quadrasteer system is amazing in its ability to make this big truck feel small. A combination of torsion bars up front and leaf springs in the rear give the Silverado a comfortable, if not refined, ride in most situations.

**MSRP Price Range**

**$38,570**

Destination Charge: $850 (all styles)

| Ratings | | |
|---|---|---|
| Consumer Rating | 4.3 | |
| Editors Rating | 7.3 | |

**What Edmunds.com says:** With the retirement of Ford's F-150 Lightning, the SS is now the second-fastest domestic sport truck. But second place doesn't mean much when the 500-hp SRT-10 Ram is first.

**Pros:** Sport truck performance coupled to extended-cab utility, more than adequate towing ability.

**Cons:** Down on power and performance compared to Ram SRT-10, all-wheel drive adds weight, interior lacks a distinctive design.

**What's New:** The only notable change for 2005 is an optional power sunroof with a HomeLink universal transmitter and overhead console.

**Body Styles, Trim Levels and Options:** The SS is offered in just one style; extended cab pickup. All SS Silverados come fully loaded with all-wheel drive, a stiffer suspension (compared to other Silverados), 20-inch aluminum wheels, leather upholstery, heated power seats, air conditioning and a seven-speaker sound system with a CD player and Bose speakers. The front fascia is more aggressive-looking than a typical Silverado, as it incorporates a wide center air-scoop and two rectangular side scoops. Front and rear bumpers as well as side moldings are body-color to give the truck a monochromatic appearance. Options include an in-dash CD changer, automatic climate control, OnStar, XM Satellite Radio and a power sunroof.

**Powertrains and Performance:** The SS is offered with just one engine, a 6.0-liter Vortec V8 making 345 horsepower and 380 pound-feet of torque. Off-the-line performance is enhanced by a 3.06 first gear ratio in the standard four-speed automatic transmission. All-wheel drive makes hard starts a no-brainer, as the truck merely hooks up and moves out the second you mash the pedal. Shifts from the automatic are firm and acceleration is swift—just steer clear of any SRT-10-badged pickups. Towing capacity is 7,500 pounds.

**Safety:** The SS offers ABS as standard equipment, as well as dual-stage front airbags. The full-time all-wheel-drive system does its work without driver input and offers a locking rear differential. Government crash testing resulted in a three-star rating (out of five) for the driver in frontal impacts and four stars for the passenger. In 40-mph frontal offset crash testing, Chevy's full-size pickup garnered a "Marginal" rating (the second lowest of four).

**Interior Design and Special Features:** Inside, the SS is essentially an LT Silverado with a few additional "SS" styling cues. We weren't expecting any styling revelations in a pickup, but two-tone upholstery and/or some faux metal trim on the dash and doors would have gone a long way toward giving the cab a more distinctive SS identity. As it is, the interior is offered only in a Dark Charcoal color scheme. The standard leather seats have an "SS" emblem embroidered into the headrest. Instruments are white-faced with orange needles. While not exactly a success in terms of styling, the SS cabin will please those with families, as the roomy extended-cab configuration can easily accommodate a couple of kids in the backseat.

**Driving Impressions:** The SS gets around corners easily enough for a pickup, but not in a manner that will encourage you to seek out twisty roads—the body doesn't settle easily and the 20-inch tires do little to reduce body roll. Straight-line acceleration is much more impressive (that is, when the Ram SRT-10 is out of the discussion), and the 6.0-liter Vortec motor pulls smoothly and effortlessly whenever pressed.

*Crash Test Scores, see pg 530*
*Warranty information, see pg 542*

| Specifications | | | |
|---|---|---|---|
| Engine/Drivetrain | HP | Torque | EPA Fuel Economy Rating |
| 8cyl 6.0L A | 345 | 380 | 12 city/16 hwy |

| Body Styles | |
|---|---|
| Style | MSRP Range |
| Extended Cab Pickup Truck | $38,570 |

# 2005 Chevrolet Silverado 2500HD Large Truck

**MSRP Price Range**

## $24,245 - $40,425

Destination Charge: $850 (all styles)

### Ratings

| | | |
|---|---|---|
| Consumer Rating | 9.1 | |
| Editors Rating | 7.8 | |

**What Edmunds.com says:** With its numerous powertrain and cab configurations, and stout towing and hauling capacities, the Silverado HD is a hard truck to beat for those who need maximum functionality and capability.

**Pros:** Powerful engine lineup, multiple drivetrain configurations, substantial towing and hauling capacities.

**Cons:** Spotty build quality, mediocre interior design and materials.

**What's New:** This year all heavy-duty Silverados receive a redesigned hood and grille. On extended and crew cab models, a power sunroof is a new option, and it includes a HomeLink universal transmitter and deluxe overhead console.

**Body Styles, Trim Levels and Options:** The 2500HD is available in regular, extended and crew cab body styles. From there, you can pick two- or four-wheel drive and a short or long box (except for regular cabs, which are long boxes only). There are four trim levels: Work Truck, base, LS and LT. Work Trucks offer manual dual-zone air conditioning, a 40/20/40-split bench seat and ABS. Base models come with a tilt steering wheel, cruise control, an AM/FM/CD stereo, an upgraded driver message center and tinted glass. Midgrade LS models add power windows and door locks, remote keyless entry and a leather-wrapped steering wheel. Top-of-the-line LTs come with power heated leather seats, OnStar, satellite steering wheel controls, a Bose audio system, a self-dimming rearview mirror with a built-in compass and power heated exterior mirrors.

**Powertrains and Performance:** The HD's base engine is a 6.0-liter V8 rated at 300 horsepower and 360 pound-feet of torque. Chevrolet offers two even more powerful options: an 8.1-liter V8 and the 6.6-liter Duramax turbodiesel. The 8.1-liter engine boasts an impressive 330 hp and 450 lb-ft of torque, while the Duramax diesel makes as much as 310 hp and 605 lb-ft of torque when equipped with an automatic transmission. The standard transmission for the 6.0-liter V8 is a five-speed manual with a heavy-duty four-speed automatic optional. The 8.1-liter V8 and Duramax diesel can be hooked up to either a six-speed manual or a heavy-duty five-speed automatic. Being heavy-duty trucks, these brutes can certainly pull—the maximum towing capacity of the 2500HD with the 6.0-liter engine is 10,600 pounds, while the 8.1-liter V8 and Duramax diesel can tow up to 12,000 pounds.

**Safety:** All heavy-duty Silverados include four-wheel antilock disc brakes as standard equipment. In frontal crash tests conducted by the National Highway Traffic Safety Administration, the Silverado earned a three-star rating (out of five) for driver protection and four stars for the front passenger. In the Insurance Institute for Highway Safety's frontal offset crash test, the Silverado was given an overall rating of "Marginal," the second lowest score.

*Crash Test Scores, see pg 530*
*Warranty information, see pg 542*

### Specifications

| Engine/Drivetrain | HP | Torque | EPA Fuel Economy Rating |
|---|---|---|---|
| 8cyl 6.0L A/M | 300 | 360 | N/A |

### Body Styles

| Style | MSRP Range |
|---|---|
| Crew Cab Pickup Truck | $29,045–$40,425 |
| Extended Cab Pickup Truck | $26,945–$38,035 |
| Regular Cab Pickup Truck | $24,245–$29,920 |

**Interior Design and Special Features:** Inside, Silverado buyers will find a logically laid-out interior, with an easy-to-use climate control system and clear, uncluttered gauges. Materials quality is unimpressive, and build quality, though improved over the last few years, is still behind the competition. The large cabin offers plenty of room, comfortable bucket seats and a four-door configuration on extended cab models that makes getting in and out of the backseat much easier.

**Driving Impressions:** The 2500HD is a reasonably comfortable truck for everyday use, but don't expect the plush ride of its light-duty siblings. Any of the three available engines provides swift acceleration and ample towing power, but the Duramax diesel is probably the best choice for those who tow heavy loads.

# 2005 Chevrolet Silverado 3500

**MSRP Price Range**
## $28,505 - $41,040
Destination Charge: $850 (all styles)

| Ratings | | |
|---|---|---|
| Consumer Rating | N/A | |
| Editors Rating | 7.8 | |

**What Edmunds.com says:** Although the Silverado still has the capacity to tackle just about any job, its newer competition manages a slight edge when it comes to refinement and maximum towing power.

**Pros:** Multiple drivetrain configurations, substantial towing and hauling capacities, compliant ride quality.

**Cons:** Interior design is showing its age, low-quality interior materials, below-average build quality.

**What's New:** This year all heavy-duty Silverados receive a redesigned hood and grille. On extended and crew cab models, a power sunroof is a new option, and includes a HomeLink universal transmitter and deluxe overhead console.

**Body Styles, Trim Levels and Options:** The 3500 is available in regular, extended and crew cab body styles with 8-foot boxes and either single or dual rear-wheel configurations. Single rear-wheel models come in 4WD only, while dual rear-wheel versions offer two-wheel drive on extended and crew cab models. There are four trim levels: Work Truck, base, LS and LT. Work Trucks offer basics like 16-inch steel wheels, a vinyl 40/20/40 bench seat, dual-zone manual air conditioning and an AM/FM radio. Base models add chrome-finish wheels, grille and bumpers, cloth upholstery, cruise control and a CD player. Midgrade LS models add power windows and door locks, keyless entry and a leather-wrapped steering wheel. Top-of-the-line LTs come with power-heated leather seats, OnStar, satellite steering wheel controls, a Bose audio system, a self-dimming rearview mirror with a built-in compass and power-heated exterior mirrors.

**Powertrains and Performance:** The 3500's base engine is a 6.0-liter V8 rated at 300 horsepower and 360 pound-feet of torque. If that's not enough grunt under the hood for you, Chevrolet offers two more powerful options: an 8.1-liter V8 and a 6.6-liter Duramax turbodiesel V8. The 8.l-liter engine boasts an impressive 330 hp and 450 lb-ft of torque, while the Duramax diesel makes 300 hp and 520 lb-ft of torque. The standard transmission for the 6.0-liter V8 is a five-speed manual with a heavy-duty four-speed automatic optional. The 8.1-liter V8 and Duramax diesel can be hooked up to either a six-speed manual or a heavy-duty five-speed automatic. Maximum towing capacity is 12,000 pounds with either the 8.1 or Duramax (15,500 pounds for fifth-wheel trailers).

**Safety:** All Silverados feature standard four-wheel antilock disc brakes. In government crash tests, the Silverado earned a three-star rating (out of five) for driver protection and four stars for the front passenger. In frontal offset crash testing, the Silverado was given an overall rating of "Marginal" (second lowest).

**Interior Design and Special Features:** Silverado buyers will find a logically laid-out interior, with an easy-to-use dual-zone climate control system and clear, uncluttered gauges. Materials quality is unimpressive, but build quality, though improved over the last few years, is still below the competition. However, the cabin is roomy, particularly on extended cab models and the recently redesigned front seats are comfortable on long trips. Standard rear doors on the extended cab make entry and exit to the rear bench seat easy.

**Driving Impressions:** The 3500HD is a dedicated work truck, so don't expect the plush ride of its lighter-duty siblings. Any of the three available engines provide swift acceleration and ample towing power, but the Duramax diesel is probably the best choice for those who tow heavy loads.

*Crash Test Scores, see pg 530*
*Warranty information, see pg 542*

| Specifications | | | |
|---|---|---|---|
| Engine/Drivetrain | HP | Torque | EPA Fuel Economy Rating |
| 8cyl 6.0L A/M | 300 | 360 | N/A |

| Body Styles | |
|---|---|
| Style | MSRP Range |
| Crew Cab Pickup Truck | $30,605–$41,040 |
| Extended Cab Pickup Truck | $28,505–$38,875 |
| Regular Cab Pickup Truck | $28,995–$31,355 |

# 2005 Chevrolet Suburban

**MSRP Price Range**

## $37,850 - $47,550

Destination Charge: $850 (all styles)

### Ratings

| | | |
|---|---|---|
| Consumer Rating | 8.9 | ███████████████░ |
| Editors Rating | 7.4 | ████████████░░░░ |

**What Edmunds.com says:** With its capable suspension, excellent powertrain and standard room for nine, the Suburban remains one of the best family-haulers available anywhere. Add Quadrasteer and it becomes an excellent tow vehicle as well.

**Pros:** Choice of powerful V8 engines, available Quadrasteer four-wheel steering system, cavernous cargo space, room for nine.

**Cons:** Massive size can be tough in tight confines, vague steering feel, cheap interior plastics.

**What's New:** Revisions for 2005 include a new optional touchscreen navigation system. Rear barn doors are no longer available, as all models now come standard with an overhead rear liftgate (with separate liftglass). The Z71 off-road package is now available on two-wheel-drive models.

**Body Styles, Trim Levels and Options:** The Suburban is offered in half-ton (1500) and three-quarter-ton (2500) configurations with either two- or four-wheel drive. Two trim levels are available: LS and LT. Standard equipment for LS models includes tri-zone manual air conditioning, cruise control, a driver message center, keyless entry, a leather-wrapped tilt steering wheel and an AM/FM/CD stereo. LT models add automatic climate control, leather seating with 10-way power adjustments for the driver and front passenger and an upgraded audio system with an in-dash CD changer. Options like a Bose audio system, XM Satellite Radio, navigation system and a rear-seat DVD video system make the Suburban a family-friendly vehicle.

**Powertrains and Performance:** All half-ton models feature a 5.3-liter Vortec V8 rated at 295 horsepower and 330 pound-feet of torque mated to a four-speed automatic transmission. Three-quarter-ton versions can be equipped with either a 6.0-liter V8 rated at 300 hp and 360 lb-ft of torque or an 8.1-liter V8 that cranks out 320 hp and 445 lb-ft of torque. Both engines get heavy-duty versions of the standard four-speed automatic. Equipped with the 6.0-liter engine, the Suburban can tow up to 9,900 pounds, while the 8.1-liter engine can pull up to 12,000 pounds when properly equipped. The maximum tow rating on half-ton models is 8,400 pounds. If you order the optional Quadrasteer four-wheel steering system, the Suburban will enjoy improved stability while towing, as well as a dramatically reduced turning radius.

**Safety:** The standard dual-stage airbags deploy based on crash severity and a passenger seat safety system can sense the presence of a child riding up front and disable the airbag to prevent injury. Also available is the StabiliTrak stability control system on all half-ton models. Side airbags and the OnStar communications system are optional. In crash tests conducted by the National Highway Traffic Safety Administration (NHTSA), the Suburban received four stars (out of five) for protection of the driver and front passenger in front-impact crashes.

**Interior Design and Special Features:** All Suburban interiors are spacious with solid ergonomics and plenty of creature comforts. There's room for nine if you stick with bench seats; ordering the optional captain's chairs drops capacity to seven passengers. There's a little more plastic than we would like in the cabin, and build quality could be better, but overall it's still a pleasant environment for a family vehicle.

**Driving Impressions:** We've been impressed with the current-generation Suburban's smooth, comfortable ride quality and easy-to-drive nature. Thanks to a stiff frame and a well-insulated cabin, Chevrolet's big SUV is generally quiet and rattle-free, making it a great long-distance cruiser. The ride of the heavy-duty 2500 models is a little less forgiving for rear-seat passengers, but they're still comfortable enough to be daily drivers.

*Crash Test Scores, see pg 530*
*Warranty information, see pg 542*

### Specifications

| Engine/Drivetrain | HP | Torque | EPA Fuel Economy Rating |
|---|---|---|---|
| 8cyl 6.0L A | 325 | 365 | N/A |
| 8cyl 5.3L A | 295 | 335 | 14 city/18 hwy |

### Body Styles

| Style | MSRP Range |
|---|---|
| Large SUV | $37,850–$47,550 |

# 2005 Chevrolet Tahoe

**MSRP Price Range**
## $35,000 - $44,570
Destination Charge: $850 (all styles)

### Ratings

| | | |
|---|---|---|
| Consumer Rating | 9.3 | ▬▬▬▬▬▬▬▬▬□ |
| Editors Rating | 7.3 | ▬▬▬▬▬▬▬▭▭ |

**What Edmunds.com says:** With room for up to nine passengers, gutsy V8 engines and a long list of available options, it's no wonder the Tahoe is the best-selling full-size sport-ute on the market.

**Pros:** Strong engines, roomy and versatile interior, numerous available amenities.

**Cons:** Spotty build quality, interior materials could use improvement.

**What's New:** A touchscreen navigation system is optional on Tahoe this year, and all models now come standard with the overhead rear liftgate (with separate rear lift-glass). The Z71 off-road package can now be had with two-wheel drive.

**Body Styles, Trim Levels and Options:** The Tahoe is available in a four-door body style and comes in three trim levels. The base LS boasts standard features like tri-zone manual climate control, a CD player, keyless entry, a driver information center, heated outside mirrors, side-mounted assist steps and Homelink. The LS comes with two rows of seating and can accommodate up to six thanks to a front bench seat; an optional third-row bench brings capacity to nine. Uplevel LT models get the third-row seat standard, while adding automatic climate control; front captain's chairs with heaters and 10-way power adjustment; leather upholstery; a six-CD changer and Bose speakers; power-heated side mirrors with turn signal indicators and puddle lamps; and adjustable pedals. The off-road-oriented Z71 model offers a specially tuned suspension and most of the LT's equipment. Available options include a towing package, second-row bucket seats, a DVD-based entertainment system, a sunroof, satellite radio and OnStar telematics.

**Powertrains and Performance:** A 4.8-liter V8 is standard on the LS, and it offers 285 horsepower and 295 pound-feet of torque. Optional on the LS and standard on the LT and Z71 is the 5.3-liter V8 that ups the ante with 295 hp and 330 lb-ft of torque. The standard transmission is a four-speed automatic with a tow/haul mode for improved performance under heavy loads. Four-wheel-drive models feature the push-button Autotrac transfer case, which provides both 2WD and automatic 4WD modes for driving on the street. The Tahoe can tow up to 7,800 pounds when properly equipped.

**Safety:** Four-wheel antilock disc brakes are standard, and the StabiliTrak stability control system is optional on models equipped with the 5.3-liter engine. Front-seat side-impact airbags are optional on all Tahoes. In government frontal impact crash testing, the Tahoe scored three out of a possible five stars on the driver side and four out of five on the passenger side.

**Interior Design and Special Features:** Inside, the Tahoe provides a simple layout with easy-to-read analog instrumentation, user-friendly controls and well-cushioned seats. The quality of the materials, however, could stand improvement, as many of the plastics look and feel cheap. Second-row bucket seats are available when you order leather upholstery, as is a DVD-based entertainment system. An available 50/50-split third-row seat allows the Tahoe to seat anywhere from seven to nine people. With no third row and the second-row seats folded, the Tahoe offers 104 cubic feet of cargo volume.

**Driving Impressions:** Either of the Tahoe's Vortec V8 engines delivers ample power in most situations. Those who pull a trailer often would be wise to opt for the 5.3-liter engine, as it provides a substantial bump in torque despite only 10 additional horsepower compared to the 4.8-liter V8. The suspension delivers a stable, smooth ride, regardless of whether the Tahoe travels on or off pavement, while the steering is light enough to maneuver the big sport-ute easily in tight situations.

*Crash Test Scores, see pg 530*
*Warranty information, see pg 542*

### Specifications

| Engine/Drivetrain | HP | Torque | EPA Fuel Economy Rating |
|---|---|---|---|
| 8cyl 5.3L A | 295 | 335 | 14 city/18 hwy |
| 8cyl 4.8L A | 285 | 295 | 14 city/18 hwy |

### Body Styles

| Style | MSRP Range |
|---|---|
| Large SUV | $35,000–$44,570 |

# 2005 Chevrolet TrailBlazer

**Midsize SUV**

**MSRP Price Range**
## $27,520 - $32,420
Destination Charge: $685 (all styles)

### Ratings

| | | |
|---|---|---|
| Consumer Rating | 9.3 | |
| Editors Rating | 6.4 | |

**What Edmunds.com says:** A strong drivetrain, plenty of room inside and a long features list make this an attractive family vehicle, but some cheap interior materials and iffy handling keep it from gaining our full recommendation.

**Pros:** Strong engine performance, comfortable highway ride, extensive features list, user-friendly controls.

**Cons:** Skittish handling around corners, numb steering, generic interior design with mediocre materials.

**What's New:** The TrailBlazer gets a host of minor interior improvements this year. Seating has been restyled and boasts comfort and quality improvements. Detail changes include revised chrome accents, trim enhancements and a new instrument panel appearance. Among the new options are an audio system with CD/MP3 compatibility and full-length side curtain airbags (which replace last year's front-seat side airbags).

**Body Styles, Trim Levels and Options:** The TrailBlazer offers two trim levels—LS and LT. Base LS models come decently equipped, offering such features as 16-inch wheels, dual-zone manual air conditioning, a CD player, automatic headlights and power windows and locks. Items like cruise control, keyless entry and a roof rack are optional. LT models have all of the above, plus a power driver seat, premium cloth upholstery, foglamps, power side mirrors and an auto-dimming rearview mirror with compass. Major options include leather upholstery, a sunroof, a rear-seat DVD entertainment system, a DVD-based navigation system, a Bose sound system, an in-dash CD changer, satellite radio and OnStar telematics.

**Powertrains and Performance:** The TrailBlazer's standard 4.2-liter inline six puts out 275 horsepower and 275 lb-ft of torque. That's more power than most of its competitors' V8s and allows the TrailBlazer to tow 6,300 pounds on properly equipped two-wheel-drive models or 6,100 pounds in four-wheel-drive configuration. The 4WD models get the Autotrac system, which can be set to engage four-wheel drive automatically when slippage is detected at the rear wheels. A rear locking differential is optional on all TrailBlazers.

**Safety:** Four-wheel antilock disc brakes are standard, and there are three-point seatbelts in all seating positions. Full-length side curtain airbags are optional. If equipped with the optional airbags, the TrailBlazer rates a perfect five stars for side impacts involving the front occupants. Rear side-impact safety is also excellent, with a score of five stars. Frontal impact testing resulted in three-star ratings for both driver and front-passenger protection. The IIHS rated the TrailBlazer "Marginal" (the second-lowest ranking on a four-point scale) in 40-mph frontal offset crash testing. Power-adjustable pedals are optional on the LT.

**Interior Design and Special Features:** The TrailBlazer offers ample interior room, with five adults able to fit comfortably. If you need seven-passenger capacity, you'll want to look at the longer-wheelbase TrailBlazer EXT. Although most of the controls are easy to use, the overall interior design is drab compared to the cabins of competitors like the Ford Explorer and Toyota 4Runner, and some of the TrailBlazer's interior materials look and feel cheap. The cargo bay holds 41 cubic feet, and if you fold down the 60/40-split rear seat, you've got 80 cubes at your disposal.

**Driving Impressions:** The TrailBlazer is great for freeway on-ramps and highway passing, but stop-and-go driving reveals a lack of low-end grunt from the standard inline six that keeps it from earning unanimous praise. The sport-ute's suspension is another mixed bag. Its soft tuning results in an extremely comfortable ride around town and on the highway. But push it hard into a corner, or take a bump too fast in the dirt, and the TrailBlazer's soft setup gets out of sorts quickly. Additionally, the steering offers little in the way of road feel.

*Crash Test Scores, see pg 530*
*Warranty information, see pg 542*

### Specifications

| Engine/Drivetrain | HP | Torque | EPA Fuel Economy Rating |
|---|---|---|---|
| 6cyl 4.2L A | 275 | 275 | 16 city/21 hwy |

### Body Styles

| Style | MSRP Range |
|---|---|
| Midsize SUV | $27,520–$32,420 |

For the latest full vehicle reports, visit www.edmunds.com/bginfopak

# 2005 Chevrolet TrailBlazer EXT

**MSRP Price Range**

## $29,790 - $34,220
Destination Charge: $685 (all styles)

### Ratings

| | | |
|---|---|---|
| Consumer Rating | 9.5 | |
| Editors Rating | 6.5 | |

**What Edmunds.com says:** Strong drivetrains, loads of room inside and a long features list make this an attractive family vehicle, but some cheap interior materials and iffy handling keep it from gaining our full recommendation.

**Pros:** Class-leading engine power, soft highway ride, room for seven, extensive features list, simple controls.

**Cons:** Skittish handling around corners, numb steering, generic interior design with mediocre materials.

**What's New:** The TrailBlazer EXT gets minor interior revisions this year. Seating has been restyled and boasts comfort and quality improvements. Detail changes include revised chrome accents, trim enhancements and a new instrument panel appearance. A stereo system with CD/MP3 compatibility and full-length side curtain airbags (replacing last year's front-seat side airbags) are new options this year. Power rear-quarter windows are also new for 2005.

**Body Styles, Trim Levels and Options:** The four-door TrailBlazer EXT seats seven and comes in two trim levels—LS and LT. Base LS models come with 17-inch wheels, dual-zone manual air conditioning, a CD player and power windows and locks. Items like cruise control, keyless entry and a roof rack are optional. LT models have all of the above, along with a power driver seat, premium cloth upholstery, foglamps, power side mirrors and an auto-dimming rearview mirror with compass. Major options include leather upholstery, a sunroof, a rear-seat DVD entertainment system, a DVD-based navigation system, a Bose sound system, an in-dash CD changer, satellite radio and OnStar telematics.

**Powertrains and Performance:** The TrailBlazer EXT's standard 4.2-liter inline six puts out 275 horsepower and 275 lb-ft of torque. That's more power than most of its competitors'V8s, but those who tow a trailer will appreciate the added low-end grunt of the optional Vortec 5.3-liter V8, which kicks out 290 hp and 326 lb-ft or torque. Properly equipped, V8-powered EXTs can tow up to 7,100 pounds; six-cylinder versions max out at 6,000 pounds. Buyers have a choice between two- and four-wheel drive; 4WD models get the Autotrac system, which can be set to engage all four wheels automatically when slippage is detected at the rear wheels. A rear locking differential is optional on all models.

**Safety:** Four-wheel antilock disc brakes are standard, and there are three-point seatbelts in all seating positions. Side curtain airbags that protect front and rear occupants are optional. The regular-wheelbase TrailBlazer rated a perfect five stars for side impacts involving the front occupants. Rear side-impact safety is also excellent, with a score of five stars. Frontal impact testing resulted in three-star ratings for both driver and front-passenger protection. The IIHS rated the TrailBlazer "Marginal" (the second-lowest ranking on a four-point scale) in 40-mph frontal offset crash testing. Power-adjustable pedals are optional on the LT.

**Interior Design and Special Features:** The TrailBlazer EXT has a longer wheelbase than the regular TrailBlazer, and this allows it to accommodate a third-row seat, bringing passenger capacity to seven. Fold down both rows of seats in a TrailBlazer EXT and you'll have 107 cubic feet of cargo space—the most in the midsize SUV segment. Most controls are simple to use, but a drab design and some low-grade materials leave the Chevy's cabin several steps behind the competition.

**Driving Impressions:** While the inline six provides adequate power for most driving, the V8 is our choice, as it provides loads of torque for easy passing and merging and extra stamina when hauling heavy loads. Soft suspension tuning gives the TrailBlazer EXT an extremely comfortable ride around town and on the highway. But push it hard into a corner, or take a bump too fast in the dirt, and the sport-ute's soft setup gets out of sorts quickly.

*Crash Test Scores, see pg 530*
*Warranty information, see pg 542*

### Specifications

| Engine/Drivetrain | HP | Torque | EPA Fuel Economy Rating |
|---|---|---|---|
| 8cyl 5.5L A | 300 | 330 | 16 city/19 hwy |
| 6cyl 4.2L A | 275 | 275 | 15 city/19 hwy |

### Body Styles

| Style | MSRP Range |
|---|---|
| Large SUV | $29,790–$34,220 |

# 2005 Chevrolet Uplander

**Midsize Minivan**

**MSRP Price Range**
## $23,635 - $31,385
Destination Charge: $715 (all styles)

## Ratings

| | | |
|---|---|---|
| Consumer Rating | N/A | |
| Editors Rating | 7.0 | |

**What Edmunds.com says:** Although the Uplander features a slick interior and distinctive styling, it doesn't have the on-road finesse of its minivan competitors.

**Pros:** Smooth ride and handling, lots of nifty interior storage spaces, innovative multimedia storage system, available all-wheel-drive.

**Cons:** Engine power and refinement not up to class leaders, no side curtain airbags.

**What's New:** The Uplander is an all-new "crossover sport van" that has roots in the Chevrolet Venture minivan.

**Body Styles, Trim Levels and Options:** The Uplander comes in one size and three different trim levels: base, LS and LT. The base model offers power windows, air conditioning, an eight-speaker sound system with a CD/MP3 player, a rear-seat DVD entertainment system and the OnStar communications system. Upgrades for the LS model include cruise control, keyless entry, rear air conditioning and a built-in child seat. Pop for the LT trim and you'll get a passenger-side power-sliding door, deluxe rear-seat entertainment system with infrared headphones and a 115-volt AC outlet, a power driver seat, steering wheel audio controls, alloy wheels and second-row captain's chairs. The all-wheel-drive system is available on the LT only, and adds automatic load-leveling rear suspension and an inflator kit. The LS and LT can be upgraded with leather seating and heated seats. An optional PhatNoise mobile digital media system allows owners to store thousands of MP3s and/or several dozen movies. Other noteworthy options include dual power-sliding side doors, rear parking assist and a remote vehicle starting system.

**Powertrains and Performance:** All Uplanders come equipped with a 3.5-liter V6 that makes 200 horsepower and 220 pound-feet of torque. A four-speed automatic transmission is standard. No other powertrain combinations are available, but buyers can opt for all-wheel drive.

**Safety:** All models come standard with four-wheel antilock brakes. Side-impact airbags for front occupants are included with the LS and LT, and optional on the base model. Side curtain airbags are not available. The StabiliTrak stability control system is available on the LT when equipped with the optional sport suspension package. The Uplander has not yet been crash tested.

**Interior Design and Special Features:** The Uplander seats seven, and the fold-flat third-row seat offers a 50/50 split. A two-tone color scheme with faux metal accents dramatically brightens the atmosphere of the van. Folding center trays (with cupholders) between the first- and second-row seats are available. An overhead rail system provides rear-seat access to climate and entertainment functions, and can be upgraded with various storage containers. A rear-seat DVD entertainment system is standard on all Uplanders. A remote vehicle start system, pioneered on the Malibu in 2004, is optional.

**Driving Impressions:** The V6 power plant is down on power compared to its competitors, but it still manages to provide adequate acceleration. The Uplander's suspension is on the soft side, though upgrading to the optional sport suspension does provide for a more responsive ride.

*Crash Test Scores, see pg 530*
*Warranty information, see pg 542*

## Specifications

| Engine/Drivetrain | HP | Torque | EPA Fuel Economy Rating |
|---|---|---|---|
| 6cyl 3.5L A | 200 | 220 | N/A |

## Body Styles

| Style | MSRP Range |
|---|---|
| Midsize Minivan | $23,635–$31,385 |

For the latest full vehicle reports, visit www.edmunds.com/bginfopak

**Midsize Minivan**

# 2005 Chevrolet Venture

**MSRP Price Range**

## $23,365 - $30,760

Destination Charge: $715 (all styles)

### Ratings

| | | |
|---|---|---|
| Consumer Rating | 8.8 | |
| Editors Rating | 6.6 | |

**What Edmunds.com says:** Not terribly refined, but loaded with value, the Chevy Venture is a solid minivan if you don't need all the latest features and gadgets.

**Pros:** Carlike ride and handling, power-sliding doors, eight-passenger seating option, available DVD entertainment system.

**Cons:** Flimsy modular seats, poor interior fit and finish, ABS not standard, coarse engine character, mixed crash test results.

**What's New:** The regular wheelbase and all-wheel-drive Ventures are history, leaving the extended-length front-wheel-drive model as the sole option.

**Body Styles, Trim Levels and Options:** The Venture comes in one size and three different trim levels: Plus, LS and LT. The Plus model offers power windows, an overhead console, cruise control and a chrome grille. Upgrades for the LS model include side-impact airbags for front occupants, antilock brakes, remote keyless entry, a 60/40-split bench seat for the second row, a 50/50-split bench in the third row, a CD player, a rear-window defogger, floor mats, power rear-quarter windows and a longer list of available options. Pop for LT trim and you'll get a power driver seat, a power passenger-side door, second-row captain's chairs, rear audio and climate controls, a rear-seat DVD entertainment system, satellite steering wheel controls and traction control. A sport appearance package is available with select colors and adds a rear spoiler, body-color side moldings, 16-inch aluminum wheels and an upgraded suspension.

**Powertrains and Performance:** All Ventures come equipped with a 3.4-liter V6 that makes 185 horsepower and 210 pound-feet of torque. A four-speed automatic transmission is standard. Mileage is above average with EPA mileage ratings of 19 city/26 highway.

**Safety:** LS and LT models come standard with four-wheel antilock brakes and side-impact airbags for front occupants; both items are optional on the Plus. Side curtain airbags and stability control are not available. The Venture has received mixed crash test results. In government crash tests, the van received four out of five stars for driver and front-passenger protection in frontal impacts. Side-impact tests resulted in a five-star rating for front occupants and a four-star rating for rear occupants. In frontal offset crash testing conducted by the IIHS, the Venture received an overall rating of "Poor," the lowest possible.

**Interior Design and Special Features:** Like most minivans, the Venture's interior is geared toward simplicity and ease of use. The climate controls are a simple three-dial design, and the gauges are clear analog dials, but much of the switchgear is made of a cheap plastic that doesn't look or feel particularly sturdy. An optional DVD entertainment system will keep the kids entertained for hours. It's also worth mentioning that all Ventures can be equipped with a disappearing third-row seat that makes loading bulky items onto the cargo area's flat floor a snap.

**Driving Impressions:** The standard V6 power plant is down on power compared to its competitors, but it still manages to provide adequate acceleration. The transmission shifts quickly with little prodding, but the engine note does get a little harsh at higher rpm. The Venture handles well for a minivan, especially with the optional sport suspension. Larger bumps and road obstacles tend to upset the ride quality more so than in most other minivans, but overall the Venture exhibits likable driving dynamics.

*Crash Test Scores, see pg 530*
*Warranty information, see pg 542*

### Specifications

| Engine/Drivetrain | HP | Torque | EPA Fuel Economy Rating |
|---|---|---|---|
| 6cyl 3.4L A | 185 | 210 | 19 city/26 hwy |

### Body Styles

| Style | MSRP Range |
|---|---|
| Midsize Minivan | $23,365–$30,760 |

# 2005 Chrysler 300

**Large Sedan**

**MSRP Price Range**
## $23,295 - $34,195
Destination Charge: $625 (all styles)

### Ratings

| | | |
|---|---|---|
| Consumer Rating | 9.5 | |
| Editors Rating | 8.4 | |

**What Edmunds.com says:** Proving that upscale sedans don't have to be stale-looking and slow, the 300 series offers distinctive styling and V8 power in a practical and affordable package.

**Pros:** Chiseled and masculine good looks, powerful V8 in 300C model, long list of safety features, plenty of luxury and performance for the price paid.

**Cons:** Sluggish acceleration with base V6, limited transmission choices, complex stereo controls.

**What's New:** The 300 is an all-new, rear-wheel-drive flagship sedan for Chrysler; it replaces the Concorde and 300M. In a clear move away from the cab-forward design theme Chrysler championed in the 1990s, the 300 represents the company's bold new direction and makes use of plenty of Mercedes-Benz technology. Available features include Chrysler's Hemi V8, stability control, side curtain airbags and, later in the year, all-wheel drive.

*Crash Test Scores, see pg 530*
*Warranty information, see pg 542*

### Specifications

| Engine/Drivetrain | HP | Torque | EPA Fuel Economy Rating |
|---|---|---|---|
| 8cyl 5.7L A | 340 | 390 | 17 city/25 hwy |
| 6cyl 3.5L A | 250 | 250 | 19 city/27 hwy |
| 6cyl 2.7L A | 190 | 190 | 21 city/28 hwy |

### Body Styles

| Style | MSRP Range |
|---|---|
| Large Sedan | $23,295–$34,195 |

**Body Styles, Trim Levels and Options:** The rear-drive 300 is available only as a four-door sedan, but there are four variations on that theme. The base 300 comes with 17-inch wheels, four-wheel disc brakes, air conditioning, a power driver seat, a CD player, cruise control and a tilt/telescoping steering wheel. The Touring adds a bigger V6, alloy wheels, foglights, ABS, leather upholstery, chrome trim, stability control and BrakeAssist. The plushest of the V6 models, the Limited adds chrome wheels, a power front-passenger seat, heated seats, one-touch up-and-down front windows, dual-zone automatic climate control and an information center. In addition to a V8, the 300C adds dual exhaust tips, 18-inch chrome wheels, larger brakes, tortoise-shell interior accents and a 288-watt Boston Acoustics stereo with an in-dash CD changer. Options on all 300s include adjustable pedals, self-sealing tires and satellite radio. A navigation system is available on Limited and 300C models, and the C is eligible for an even more powerful 380-watt stereo and HID headlights. Snowbelt residents can order all-wheel drive as a midyear option.

**Powertrains and Performance:** The base 300 comes with a 200-hp, 2.7-liter V6. Touring and Limited versions upgrade to a 250-hp, 3.5-liter V6. Both V6 engines come with a four-speed automatic transmission, but ordering AWD on models with the 3.5-liter allows you to trade up for a five-speed automatic with automanual functionality. The 300C scores the biggest prize, as Chrysler has stuffed a 340-hp, 5.7-liter Hemi V8 into its engine bay. The five-speed automatic is standard on every 300C.

**Safety:** Active safety features like ABS, traction control and stability control are optional on the base 300, but are standard on the Touring, Limited and C versions. Side curtain airbags, self-sealing tires and adjustable pedals are optional on all models. The 300C also gets rain-sensing wipers as standard fare. Chrysler's new sedan has not yet been crash tested.

**Interior Design and Special Features:** The interior features a simple but elegant layout. The dash area may not be as fancy as some other cars in this segment, but its combination of sporty, semi-retro and luxury motifs is effective. Worth special note are the white-faced gauges and the slick tortoise shell trim in the 300C. Cabin dimensions are generous in all directions, and the 300 offers more rear legroom than any of its competitors. Trunk capacity measures 15.6 cubic feet.

**Driving Impressions:** A rear-wheel-drive V8 family sedan is exactly what American automakers have needed for years to inspire renewed interest in their products. And with plenty of Mercedes-Benz technology in this one, the 300 offers a great deal more refinement than its 1960s ancestors. With their 250-hp V6, the 300 Touring and Limited models are only adequately powered but are still fine choices for those seeking a feature-laden large sedan that handles as well as it rides. Saddled with a small V6, the base model feels sluggish, and we wouldn't recommend it to most buyers.

# 2005 Chrysler 300C SRT-8

## Ratings

| | | |
|---|---|---|
| Consumer Rating | N/A | |
| Editors Rating | 8.7 | |

**What Edmunds.com says:** Proving that upscale sedans don't have to be stale-looking and slow, the high-performance 300C SRT-8 is a testament to all that Chrysler can do well.

**Pros:** A 425-horsepower Hemi, suspension and braking upgrades that complement the motor, chiseled good looks, plenty of luxury and performance for the price.

**Cons:** No manual transmission available, complex stereo controls.

**What's New:** This high-powered version of the standard 300 is one of the most powerful Chryslers every offered to the public.

**Body Styles, Trim Levels and Options:** The rear-drive 300C SRT-8 is available only as a four-door sedan in one trim level. Standard equipment includes leather upholstery, dual-zone automatic climate control, dual power seats, a trip computer, cruise control and a tilt/telescoping steering wheel. Tunes are supplied by a 380-watt Boston Acoustics stereo with an in-dash CD changer. The SRT-8 rolls on 20-inch forged aluminum wheels shod with high-performance Goodyear F1 tires (all-season tires are an available option) with asymmetrical tread. Tire dimensions are a beefy 245/45R20 in the front and 255/45R20 in the rear. High-intensity discharge headlights are standard, along with rear parking sensors.

**Powertrains and Performance:** The 300C SRT-8 sports a massaged 6.1-liter Hemi V8 that pumps out 425 horsepower and 420 lb-ft of torque. A five-speed automatic with a specially calibrated AutoStick automanual control is standard. The unique Hemi propels the SRT-8 to 60 mph in just a few ticks over 5 seconds.

**Safety:** The 300C SRT-8 offers standard antilock brakes, stability control (ESP), multistage airbags with an occupant-sensing system and side curtain airbags. While ESP is standard on the 300C, the SRT-8 uses a modified version to give enthusiast drivers more leeway on twisty roads. The 300 sedan has not yet been crash tested.

**Interior Design and Special Features:** The interior features a simple but elegant layout. The dash area may not be as fancy as some other cars in this segment, but its combination of sporty, semi-retro and luxury motifs is effective. Cabin dimensions are generous in all directions, and the 300C SRT-8 offers more rear legroom than any of its competitors. Trunk capacity measures 15.6 cubic feet.

**Driving Impressions:** A rear-wheel-drive V8 family sedan is exactly what American automakers have needed for years to inspire renewed interest in their products. And with plenty of Mercedes-Benz technology in this one, the 300C SRT-8 offers a great deal more refinement than its 1960s ancestors. The 300C is already a blast to drive, and the SRT treatment takes all its visceral aspects to a whole new level. Outstanding power under the hood is matched with powerful Brembo brakes and a tightened suspension system.

*Crash Test Scores, see pg 530*
*Warranty information, see pg 542*

## Specifications

| Engine/Drivetrain | HP | Torque | EPA Fuel Economy Rating |
|---|---|---|---|
| 8cyl 6.1L A | 425 | 420 | N/A |

## Body Styles

| Style | MSRP Range |
|---|---|
| Large Sedan | N/A |

# 2005 Chrysler Crossfire

**Compact Convertible, Coupe**

**MSRP Price Range**

## $29,045 - $39,120

Destination Charge: $875 (all styles)

### Ratings

| | | |
|---|---|---|
| Consumer Rating | 9.4 | |
| Editors Rating | 7.8 | |

**What Edmunds.com says:** DaimlerChrysler's first attempt at infusing Chrysler products with Mercedes underpinnings and heritage results in a fun-to-drive coupe and roadster.

**Pros:** Sleek and sexy styling, exceptional handling dynamics, quiet interior.

**Cons:** Needs more low-end torque, steering not as precise as its competitors, interior surfaces feel cheap, some confusing controls.

**What's New:** A hot roadster and a lower-priced base model join the Crossfire lineup.

**Body Styles, Trim Levels and Options:** The Crossfire is available in coupe and convertible body styles, both of which come in either base or Limited trim. Base models are available only with a manual transmission, and come with such features as stability control; dual-zone air conditioning; a four-speaker CD stereo; cloth upholstery; a height-adjustable driver seat; a leather-wrapped steering wheel; power windows, mirrors and locks; and on convertibles, a power top with defrostable rear glass. Limited models add an eight-speaker, 240-watt Infinity stereo system, power-adjustable leather seats with heaters, more sound insulation, a tire-pressure display and various upgraded trim pieces. The standard wheel/tire arrangement calls for 18s in front (225/40ZR Michelin Pilots) and 19s in back (sized 255/35); buyers can get all-season tires as a low-cost option. Also optional is a DVD-based navigation system on Limited models.

**Powertrains and Performance:** All models are powered by a Mercedes-engineered 3.2-liter V6 that produces 215 horsepower and 229 pound-feet of torque. Base models are available only with a six-speed manual transmission. Limited buyers have their choice of the slick six-speed manual or a five-speed automatic.

**Safety:** Standard safety equipment includes four-wheel antilock disc brakes with BrakeAssist, traction and stability control and side airbags that protect passengers' heads and torsos. No official crash test data is available.

**Interior Design and Special Features:** If you're considering a Crossfire for reasons beyond pure performance, you'll be pleasantly surprised by its comfortable and quiet cabin. Entry and exit take some getting used to because of the low roof that curves down to meet the side windows, but once inside, headroom is plentiful due to the car's domed shape. Because of the car's swooping shape, rearward visibility is seriously limited, especially in the coupe. The handsome two-tone cockpit is accented with metallic trim and certainly calls to mind its Mercedes-Benz heritage. Peer closer, however, and you'll see that most of the trim is merely silver plastic; the brushed metal shift knob for the six-speed is a notable exception. Moreover, some of the controls such as the radio's numerous unlabeled buttons are difficult to use. The coupe's rear hatch won't hold more than a couple of suitcases, but then, such is the reality when choosing to drive a sporty two-seater.

*Crash Test Scores, see pg 530*
*Warranty information, see pg 542*

### Specifications

| Engine/Drivetrain | HP | Torque | EPA Fuel Economy Rating |
|---|---|---|---|
| 6cyl 3.2L A/M | 215 | 229 | 21 city/28 hwy |

### Body Styles

| Style | MSRP Range |
|---|---|
| Compact Convertible | $34,085–$39,120 |
| Compact Coupe | $29,045–$34,820 |

**Driving Impressions:** The Crossfire coupe and convertible are both quick but certainly not fast. Low-end torque is somewhat lacking, with most of the usable power available between 3,000 and 5,000 rpm. The delivery is smooth throughout, however, and the slick-shifting six-speed makes it fun to mix up the gears in order to keep the engine on the boil. The Crossfire's stiff body structure and oversized tires give it crisp handling characteristics when exercised on back roads. We'd like a little more communication from the steering, but as it is, the Crossfire is a delight to drive. And on those occasions when you merely want to cruise down the highway, the Crossfire obliges with a smooth and quiet ride.

**Compact Convertible, Coupe** | **2005 Chrysler Crossfire SRT-6**

**MSRP Price Range**

## $44,820 - $49,120

Destination Charge: $875 (all styles)

### Ratings

| Ratings | | |
|---|---|---|
| Consumer Rating | 8.7 | |
| Editors Rating | 7.8 | |

**What Edmunds.com says:** The most expensive Chrysler product offered to date, the fast and nimble Crossfire SRT-6 is a bargain if you ever wanted a Mercedes SLK32 but shied away from its mid-$50K price tag.

**Pros:** Sleek and sexy styling, exceptional handling dynamics, prodigious power.

**Cons:** Interior surfaces feel cheap, several confusing controls, no manual transmission offered.

**What's New:** The first Chrysler to wear the SRT badge, the new Crossfire SRT-6 boasts a 330-horsepower supercharged V6 engine and a reworked suspension. Both coupe and convertible body styles are available.

**Body Styles, Trim Levels and Options:** The Crossfire SRT-6 is available in two flavors: convertible and coupe. Notable standard features include Nappa Pearl leather seats with Alcantara suede inserts and bolsters, dual power seats and an Infinity Modulus audio system based on Infinity's Modulus home theater surround sound system. Other standard items include a power fabric top with a power hard tonneau cover for the SRT-6 convertible, manual dual-zone climate control, heated seats and a universal garage door opener. The standard wheel/tire arrangement calls for 18-inch wheels in front (with Z-rated 225/40R18 Michelin Pilot Sports) and 19s in back (with 255/35 rubber). All-season tires are optional.

**Powertrains and Performance:** SRT-6 performance comes courtesy a hand-built 3.2-liter supercharged V6 with 330 horsepower and 310 lb-ft of torque. The only transmission choice is a sport-oriented five-speed automatic with manual-shift capability. Save for a few calibration changes, this is the same drivetrain used in the 2004 Mercedes-Benz SLK32 AMG, and just as in the Benz, acceleration is very quick: The coupe can hit 60 mph in about five seconds.

**Safety:** Standard safety equipment includes four-wheel antilock disc brakes with BrakeAssist, side airbags, traction control and a performance-tuned stability control system. A tire-pressure monitor is also standard.

**Interior Design and Special Features:** If you're considering a Crossfire for reasons beyond pure performance, you'll be pleasantly surprised by its comfortable cabin. Sadly, a fair amount of tire noise tends to spoil freeway cruising. Entry and exit take some getting used to because of the low roof that curves down to meet the side windows, but once inside, headroom is plentiful due to the car's domed shape. Because of the car's swooping shape, rearward visibility is seriously limited, especially in the coupe. The handsome two-tone cockpit is accented with metallic trim and certainly calls to mind its Mercedes-Benz heritage. Peer closer, however, and you'll see that most of the trim is merely silver plastic. Moreover, some of the controls such as the radio's numerous unlabeled buttons are difficult to use. The trunk won't hold more than a couple of suitcases, but then, such is the reality when choosing to drive a sporty two-seater.

**Driving Impressions:** The standard Crossfire is already a competent handler, but the SRT-6 goodies manage to bump the thrill meter up several notches, albeit at the cost of ride quality. The SRT-6 has, without a doubt, one of the stiffest rides we've experienced. Power is plentiful at all speeds, with 90 percent of peak torque available from 2,300 to 6,200 rpm. The engine provides a delightful soundtrack under full throttle yet will cruise down the highway in relative silence. Skimming off speed is no problem, as larger brakes provide excellent pedal and short stopping distances. The real fun begins when the road turns twisty, where the SRT-6 exhibits a flat attitude through the corners while its massive tires provide immense grip. Although still not as communicative as that of some peers, the steering offers considerably more road feel and precision than the standard Crossfire's, and contributes to an overall enjoyable package.

*Crash Test Scores, see pg 530*
*Warranty information, see pg 542*

### Specifications

| Engine/Drivetrain | HP | Torque | EPA Fuel Economy Rating |
|---|---|---|---|
| 6cyl 3.2L A | 330 | 310 | 17 city/22 hwy |

### Body Styles

| Style | MSRP Range |
|---|---|
| Compact Convertible | $49,120 |
| Compact Coupe | $44,820 |

# 2005 Chrysler PT Cruiser

**Compact Convertible, Wagon**

**MSRP Price Range**

## $13,405 - $28,380

Destination Charge: $590 (all styles)

### Ratings

| | | |
|---|---|---|
| Consumer Rating | 9.1 | |
| Editors Rating | 7.2 | |

**What Edmunds.com says:** A practical wagon with some Hollywood style, the PT Cruiser can also be fun to drive, especially in turbo form.

**Pros:** Distinctive styling inside and out, spacious cabin with multiconfigurable rear seats, smooth ride, spirited acceleration on turbo models, reasonable pricing.

**Cons:** Acceleration can be sluggish with base engine, awkward seating position for shorter drivers, unimpressive fuel economy.

**What's New:** A convertible joins the PT Cruiser lineup for 2005.

**Body Styles, Trim Levels and Options:** The PT Cruiser comes in four-door wagon and two-door convertible body styles. Wagons come in base, Touring, Limited and GT trim levels. The convertible is offered in base, Touring and GT trim. The base PT wagon comes well equipped with a cassette stereo and power windows. The base convertible picks up a bit more equipment, including full power accessories, a CD player and a power top. Touring models add rear headrests, a thermometer and compass, foglights, deep-tint glass, keyless entry, power locks and mirrors, 16-inch alloy wheels and a touring suspension. The Limited ups the ante with leather-suede seats (with power height adjustment for the driver), side airbags, a moonroof, cruise control and chrome wheels. The sporty GT comes standard with sport-tuned suspension, 17-inch wheels, tuned exhaust and leather seats.

**Powertrains and Performance:** The base engine is a 2.4-liter inline four that makes 150 horsepower and 162 pound-feet of torque. It's available with either a five-speed manual or four-speed automatic transmission on wagons, and a manual gearbox only on the heavier convertible. Optional on Touring and Limited models is a turbocharged version of that engine, which puts out 180 hp. If that's not enough, the performance-oriented GT offers a higher-boost version good for 220 ponies. Turbo-equipped Touring and Limited Cruisers come standard with the four-speed automatic, while the GT can take either a manual or automatic.

**Safety:** Side airbags for front occupants, antilock brakes and traction control are available on all PT Cruisers. You can get four-wheel disc brakes on all Cruisers, except the base model. NHTSA crash test scores for a PT Cruiser with side airbags come in at four stars (out of a possible five) for frontal and side impacts.

**Interior Design and Special Features:** Inside you'll find a spacious and versatile cabin with a retro-themed and symmetrical dash. Taller drivers will find plenty of room to get comfortable in the cockpit, but shorter drivers may not care for the somewhat flat seat design and elevated driving position. The rear seats in both variants are slightly elevated to provide a nice view, and adults will find plenty of head- and legroom. An adjustable rear parcel shelf makes it easy to secure items behind the rear seat in the PT wagon. Remove the rear seats and the PT wagon boasts an impressive 64.2 cubic feet of cargo capacity, about as much as a compact SUV.

**Driving Impressions:** Equipped with either turbocharged engine, the PT Cruiser doesn't feel like a sports car, but it does accelerate smartly once the turbo is spooled up. All PTs are easy to steer (though you'll notice the car's wide turning radius in parking lots), and the suspension consistently soaks up road irregularities, yielding a smooth, composed ride. Body roll is evident during cornering, but the PT can still hustle through the curves at a rapid clip, particularly the GT, which has firmer suspension tuning and stickier tires. Strong and reassuring brakes round out the PT's compliant road manners.

Crash Test Scores, see pg 530
Warranty information, see pg 542

### Specifications

| Engine/Drivetrain | HP | Torque | EPA Fuel Economy Rating |
|---|---|---|---|
| 4cyl 2.4L A/M | 220 | 245 | 19 city/25 hwy |
| 4cyl 2.4L A | 180 | 210 | 19 city/25 hwy |
| 4cyl 2.4L A/M | 150 | 165 | 20 city/25 hwy |

### Body Styles

| Style | MSRP Range |
|---|---|
| Compact Convertible | $19,405–$28,380 |
| Compact Wagon | $13,405–$23,455 |

**MSRP Price Range**

## $24,315 - $36,315

Destination Charge: $680 (all styles)

### Ratings

| | | |
|---|---|---|
| Consumer Rating | 8.6 | |
| Editors Rating | 7.3 | |

**What Edmunds.com says:** The Pacifica offers an enticing blend of performance, style and comfort that any midsize family is sure to find appealing but a rash of repair issues on early models prevents it from getting our full recommendation.

**Pros:** Exceptional comfort for four, drives more like a sedan than a minivan, top-notch safety scores, upscale interior design.

**Cons:** Average room for six, not as family-friendly as most minivans, spotty reliability on early models.

**What's New:** A midlevel Touring model is added to the Pacifica lineup, and the base model loses some of its standard equipment to accommodate a new lower price. Rear parking assist is now optional.

**Body Styles, Trim Levels and Options:** The Pacifica is available in three models—base, Touring and Limited. The base model comes with a 3.8-liter V6 engine; two-row, five-passenger seating; cloth upholstery; a CD player; full power accessories and keyless entry. The Touring adds a 3.5-liter single-overhead cam V6 engine; 17-inch alloy wheels; three-row six-passenger seating (with second-row captain's chairs); and a 10-way power driver seat. Limited models build upon the Touring with standard all-wheel drive, a monochromatic exterior, 19-inch wheels, heated leather seats, a power moonroof and a power liftgate. Entertainment options include an upgraded 385-watt Infinity audio system, Sirius Satellite Radio and a rear-seat DVD entertainment system. An innovative DVD-based navigation system is offered with the screen mounted in the instrument cluster for easy viewing by the driver.

**Powertrains and Performance:** The base front-wheel-drive Pacifica is powered by a 3.8-liter V6 with 210 horsepower and 240 lb-ft of torque. All-wheel-drive base and all Touring and Limited versions come with Chrysler's 3.5-liter V6, which makes 250 horsepower and 250 pound-feet of torque. AWD models use a viscous coupling center differential, and the system has the ability to send up to 90 percent of the power to the front or rear wheels if the conditions warrant. All Pacificas come with a four-speed automatic transmission.

**Safety:** Safety features include optional side curtain airbags for all three rows, ABS, a knee airbag for the driver and an optional tire-pressure monitoring system. The Pacifica has earned a perfect five-star sweep in front- and side-impact crash tests conducted by the NHTSA (when equipped with side curtain airbags). In addition, the Pacifica achieved a "Best Pick" rating from the Insurance Institute for Highway Safety (IIHS) in its frontal offset crash test.

**Interior Design and Special Features:** Touring and Limited Pacificas can seat up to six people, but the seats are arranged in three rows of two. Base models include a three-passenger rear bench seat and no third-row seat. The second- and third-row chairs can be tumbled easily to fold flat into the floor, maximizing level loading space with an extra storage bin under the cargo area. Lack of legroom in the third row limits it to occasional use only.

**Driving Impressions:** The Pacifica delivers a confident over-the-road feel that most minivans, and SUVs for that matter, would find hard to match. The steering provides solid feedback, and the suspension imparts a sense of surefooted control that borders on fun. We're not going to go too far out on a limb and call it "sporty," but for a vehicle that's specifically designed for family duty, it's surprisingly entertaining. While power from either V6 is adequate, the Pacifica can feel sluggish at times due to its hefty curb weight.

*Crash Test Scores, see pg 530*
*Warranty information, see pg 542*

### Specifications

| Engine/Drivetrain | HP | Torque | EPA Fuel Economy Rating |
|---|---|---|---|
| 6cyl 3.8L A | 210 | 240 | 18 city/25 hwy |
| 6cyl 3.5L A | 250 | 250 | 17 city/23 hwy |

### Body Styles

| Style | MSRP Range |
|---|---|
| Large Wagon | $24,315–$36,315 |

# 2005 Chrysler Sebring

**MSRP Price Range**

## $19,350 - $31,020

Destination Charge: $625 (all styles)

### Ratings

| | | |
|---|---|---|
| Consumer Rating | N/A | |
| Editors Rating | 7.0 | |

**What Edmunds.com says:** An average-performing sedan, coupe and convertible lost in a sea of higher-caliber vehicles. Low prices make the Sebring family attractive, but most shoppers should consider other options before signing on the bottom line.

**Pros:** Solid ride and handling characteristics in sedan and coupe, large trunk, low pricing.

**Cons:** Unrefined drivetrains, sloppy handling in convertible, uncomfortable backseats in sedan and coupe, subpar build and materials quality.

**What's New:** The Limited sedan receives automatic climate control and automatic headlamps. A CD audio unit with navigation system is optional.

*Crash Test Scores, see pg 530*
*Warranty information, see pg 542*

### Specifications

| Engine/Drivetrain | HP | Torque | EPA Fuel Economy Rating |
|---|---|---|---|
| 6cyl 3.0L A | 198 | 205 | 20 city/28 hwy |
| 6cyl 2.7L A | 200 | 190 | 21 city/28 hwy |
| 4cyl 2.4L A | 150 | 160 | 22 city/30 hwy |
| 4cyl 2.4L A | 142 | 155 | 21 city/28 hwy |

### Body Styles

| Style | MSRP Range |
|---|---|
| Midsize Convertible | $25,410–$31,020 |
| Midsize Coupe | $22,145–$24,520 |
| Midsize Sedan | $19,350–$22,360 |

**Body Styles, Trim Levels and Options:** The Sebring comes in sedan, coupe and convertible body styles. Sedans come in Base, Touring and Limited trim. Base and Touring models have air conditioning, a CD stereo, cruise control and power windows, locks and mirrors. Top-of-the-line Limited trim adds foglights, electroluminescent gauges, a leather-wrapped steering wheel and shift knob, an eight-way power driver seat and trip computer. The coupe offers two trim levels—Base and Limited. Base coupes come with air conditioning, power windows, a four-disc CD changer, cruise control, a tilt steering wheel and 16-inch wheels. Limited trim adds an Infinity audio system, a leather-wrapped shift knob and steering wheel and four-wheel disc brakes. The convertible has four trims from which to choose: base, GTC, Touring and Limited. Standard on the base is air conditioning and a six-speaker stereo. The GTC trim offers a CD player and cruise control. The Touring has a leather-wrapped shift knob, faux wood accents and leather seats. The Limited adds an upgraded Infinity audio system and auto-dimming mirrors.

**Powertrains and Performance:** Both the Sebring sedan and convertible offer two engines: a 2.4-liter inline four-cylinder rated at 150 horsepower and 167 pound-feet of torque, and a 2.7-liter V6 with 200 hp and 190 lb-ft of torque. For the sedan, both engines are available only with a four-speed automatic transmission; the convertible offers a five-speed manual option with the V6 engine in GTC trim. The coupe offers both transmissions, and a standard 2.4-liter inline four that provides 147 horses and 158 lb-ft of torque. Optional is a 3.0-liter V6 that generates 200 hp and 205 lb-ft of torque.

**Safety:** Antilock brakes and traction control are standard on the Limited convertible and optional on all other Sebrings. Side curtain airbags are optional on the coupe and sedan. In NHTSA frontal impact crash testing, the Sebring sedan netted an impressive five out of five stars for both the driver and front passenger. In side-impact testing, the sedan earned three stars for the front and rear. The Sebring convertible rated three stars for the driver and front passenger in NHTSA frontal impact tests; in side-impact testing, it scored three stars in front and four in the rear. In testing by the IIHS, the sedan picked up an "Acceptable" rating (the second highest of four). Finally, the Sebring coupe earns four stars from the NHTSA regarding both driver and passenger-side frontal impact testing; in side-impact testing, it scores three stars in front and five stars in rear.

**Interior Design and Special Features:** In spite of their crisp body lines, the Sebring offers little in the way of interior style. Materials quality is also lacking. The convertible is one of the few drop tops on the market than can seat four comfortably.

**Driving Impressions:** The Sebrings don't stand out in their segments in terms of outright performance, but they do provide a relaxed, moderately entertaining drive (when configured with V6 power). The coupe rides smoothly on the highway, but the sedan and convertible are not as composed.

# 2005 Chrysler Town and Country

**MSRP Price Range**
## $20,610 - $35,315
Destination Charge: $665 (all styles)

## Ratings

| | | |
|---|---|---|
| Consumer Rating | 9.1 | |
| Editors Rating | 8.5 | |

**What Edmunds.com says:** Pleasing to drive and ride in, the T&C has finally come to the table with the all-important fold-flat third seat, allowing families to get the most out of its expansive interior. While it still can't match the rock-solid reliability of import rivals, this otherwise well-qualified van is worth consideration.

**Pros:** Excellent ride and handling, good low-end pull from 3.8-liter V6, roomy and luxurious interior, innovative fold-flat second- and third-row seats.

**Cons:** Unimpressive reliability history, major safety features remain optional on lower-level models, no stability control.

**What's New:** The Town & Country gets revised styling, a handful of new features, a much lower base price and—oh yeah, the Stow 'n Go fold-flat second- and third-row seating system.

**Body Styles, Trim Levels and Options:** The Town & Country offers four trim levels—base, LX, Touring and Limited. The base model is the only standard-wheelbase T&C; the other three are extended-wheelbase. Base models are equipped with basic amenities like cruise control, tilt steering, air conditioning, power windows and locks, an AM/FM/CD stereo and a 3.3-liter V6 engine. Moving up to the LX model adds Stow 'n Go fold-flat seating in the second and third rows. The Touring adds dual power-sliding doors, power liftgate, power driver seat, ABS and a 3.8-liter V6 engine. The top-of-the-line Limited model is further upgraded with three-zone automatic climate control, leather seats with ultrasuede accents, a DVD-based navigation system, rear park assist, three-row side curtain airbags and an Infinity audio system. A rear DVD entertainment system is optional on Touring and Limited models.

**Powertrains and Performance:** A 3.3-liter, 180-horsepower V6 comes standard on base and LX models. Standard on Touring and Limited models is a 215-hp, 3.8-liter V6. A four-speed automatic is the sole transmission. A T&C with the 3.8-liter V6 is a sprightly performer, with crisp response down low and through the midrange. Towing capacity maxes out at 3,800 pounds with the optional towing package.

**Safety:** ABS with traction control is optional on the base and LX, and standard on Touring and Limited models. Full-length side curtain airbags are optional on base, LX and Touring models, and standard on the Limited. All T&Cs include a new driver's knee airbag. The structurally identical Grand Caravan has posted four (out of five) stars in frontal impact testing and five stars for side impacts. Offset crash testing produced an overall "Acceptable" rating (the second highest on a scale of four).

**Interior Design and Special Features:** The star of the show is definitely the Stow 'n Go fold-flat seating and storage system, but the cabin also sports a number of other neat optional features, such as a movable center console equipped with power points and a power rear liftgate. The seats are generally comfortable, and drivers will find most controls within easy reach. Extended versions have 26 cubic feet of cargo capacity behind the 60/40-split third-row seats, and a maximum of 168 cubes with all second- and third-row seats folded into the floor.

**Driving Impressions:** The Town & Country's most endearing qualities continue to be its agile handling and supple ride characteristics. We suspect that this van will surprise and win over a lot of folks who expect the minivan driving experience to be an exercise in lethargic vehicle dynamics. The 3.3-liter V6 engine provides adequate acceleration, but larger families and those who tow a trailer will prefer the added power of the 3.8-liter V6.

*Crash Test Scores, see pg 530*
*Warranty information, see pg 542*

## Specifications

| Engine/Drivetrain | HP | Torque | EPA Fuel Economy Rating |
|---|---|---|---|
| 6cyl 3.8L A | 215 | 245 | 18 city/25 hwy |
| 6cyl 3.3L A | 180 | 210 | 19 city/26 hwy |

## Body Styles

| Style | MSRP Range |
|---|---|
| Large Minivan | $24,960–$35,315 |
| Midsize Minivan | $20,610–$23,420 |

# 2005 Dodge Caravan

**Midsize Minivan**

**MSRP Price Range**
## $18,330 - $21,820
Destination Charge: $665 (all styles)

### Ratings

| | | |
|---|---|---|
| Consumer Rating | 8.3 | |
| Editors Rating | 8.3 | |

**What Edmunds.com says:** Enjoyable to drive and ride in, the Caravan offers no-frills minivan transportation for the family on a tight budget.

**Pros:** Surprisingly agile handling, quiet ride in V6 models, low price.

**Cons:** Some cheap interior bits, reliability record not as strong as some competitors', limited availability of major safety features.

**What's New:** The Caravan gets a styling refresh and a hefty base price reduction.

**Body Styles, Trim Levels and Options:** With only two trim levels to choose from, picking out a Caravan is relatively easy (there's also a cargo van version, the CV, that offers options for configuring a Caravan as a work-oriented vehicle). Pricing starts at around $19,000, which nets a base SE equipped with a four-cylinder engine, 15-inch steel wheels, sliding door alert system and an AM/FM stereo with CD player. Stepping up to the SXT model adds 16-inch alloy wheels, dual-zone manual air conditioning (with separate controls for the rear), power door locks with keyless entry, second-row bucket seats and a tilt steering wheel. Many of the features fitted to the SXT can be had as options on the SE, including power windows, locks and mirrors.

**Powertrains and Performance:** The Caravan SE is motivated by a 2.4-liter inline four, rated at 150 hp. This engine may be adequate for a small passenger car, but it is definitely lacking as a power source for a minivan. The SXT's 3.3-liter, 180-horse V6 is strongly recommended. In addition to more muscle, another benefit of the V6 is its quiet performance in contrast to the four which gets buzzy when pushed. The V6 is standard on SXT and CV models. A four-speed automatic transmission is the sole gearbox. In terms of fuel economy, you can expect 21 mpg in the city and 27 mpg on the highway with the four-cylinder, and 19 mpg city, 26 highway with the V6.

**Safety:** Antilock brakes are optional on the SXT only. All Caravans include a new driver knee airbag. Side curtain airbags and adjustable pedals are optional on both the SE and SXT. The Caravan has posted good crash test scores in government crash testing, netting four out of five stars for driver and front-passenger protection in frontal impacts. In side impacts, it earned four stars for front-occupant protection and a perfect five stars for rear-occupant protection. Although the Caravan's passive (surviving an accident) safety is commendable, it lags behind some competitors in active (avoiding an accident) safety—no traction or stability control system is available, and ABS is still an extra cost option.

*Crash Test Scores, see pg 530*
*Warranty information, see pg 542*

**Interior Design and Special Features:** Optional on the Caravan are power-adjustable pedals, a feature that allows shorter folks to get comfortable in the driver seat without having the airbag-equipped steering wheel too close to their bodies. When in family-shuttle mode, 15.3 cubic feet of luggage space is found behind the third-row seat. When it's time to make a trip to the home improvement superstore, removing the second- and third-row seats (which are by no means light) will open up 147 cubes of available cargo space.

### Specifications

| Engine/Drivetrain | HP | Torque | EPA Fuel Economy Rating |
|---|---|---|---|
| 6cyl 3.3L A | 180 | 210 | 19 city/26 hwy |
| 4cyl 2.4L A | 150 | 167 | 21 city/27 hwy |

### Body Styles

| Style | MSRP Range |
|---|---|
| Midsize Minivan | $18,330–$21,820 |

**Driving Impressions:** The Caravan's most endearing qualities continue to be its agile handling and supple ride characteristics. We suspect that these vans will surprise and win over a lot of folks who expect the minivan driving experience to be an exercise in lethargic vehicle dynamics.

**MSRP Price Range**
## $19,374 - $28,679
Destination Charge: $645 (all styles)

**#1 Editors' Rating**

| Ratings | | |
|---|---|---|
| Consumer Rating | 8.4 | |
| Editors Rating | 8.7 | |

**What Edmunds.com says:** Refinement appears to be the magic word at Dodge these days, and it shows in the all-new Dakota. Excellent powertrain options, nimble suspension and a well thought-out interior score major points, but the aggressive styling isn't for everyone.

**Pros:** Strong engine lineup, choice of part-time or full-time four-wheel drive, comfortable and refined interior, nimble handling.

**Cons:** No long bed or single cab models, club cab's backseat offers barely passable comfort for adults.

**What's New:** The midsize Dakota is all new for 2005. Improvements include a hydroformed boxed steel frame, a coil-over front suspension, three excellent engine options, a five-speed automatic or six-speed manual transmission, revised styling and improved build quality.

**Body Styles, Trim Levels and Options:** The Dakota is available in two body styles, both of which have four doors and a backseat. The club cab utilizes rear-opening access doors and has a 6-foot-6 bed, while the more spacious quad cab with four full-size doors has a smaller 5-foot-4 bed. There are three trim levels: ST, SLT and Laramie. The ST comes standard with the 3.7-liter V6 and four-speed automatic transmission, 16-inch steel wheels, air conditioning, a CD player and a cloth interior. The SLT adds alloy wheels, chrome bumpers, a split-fold feature for the rear bench seat and power windows, mirrors and door locks. The high-line Laramie adds a 4.7-liter V8 and five-speed automatic transmission, automatic headlights, leather seating surfaces and remote stereo controls on the steering wheel. Options include a six-speed manual transmission, front bucket seats, heated seats, satellite radio, Bluetooth hands-free cell phone compatibility, full-time four-wheel drive and the high-output 4.7-liter V8.

**Powertrains and Performance:** Three engine options are available, a SOHC 3.7-liter V6 that makes 210 horsepower and 235 pound-feet of torque, a SOHC 4.7-liter V8 that produces 230 hp and 290 lb-ft of torque and a high-output 4.7 cranks out over 250 hp and 300 lb-ft of torque. Five-speed automatic and six-speed manual transmissions are available, and a first-in-class full-time four-wheel-drive system is also being offered for 2005 in addition to the usual 2WD and part-time 4WD configurations. Towing capacity with the V8 engine has been rated at 7,150 pounds.

**Safety:** Rear-wheel ABS is standard on the Dakota; four-wheel ABS is optional. Passive safety features include standard multistage front airbags, optional side curtain airbags and an electronic accident response system. Crash tests have not yet been conducted by the NHTSA.

**Interior Design and Special Features:** Inside, the driving position feels much more carlike than you'd expect. Interior panels are nicely textured two-tone plastic, and the fit and finish is outstanding. Window and door lock switches are comfortably within reach, climate controls are set in a nicely finished bezel and are easy to use and understand, and the shutter-type dash vents are attractive and functional. Cabins are spacious, but adults will still find the rear quarters of the Club Cab cramped.

**Driving Impressions:** On the road, the word refinement springs to mind. The truck is very quiet inside at any speed, with plenty of insulation from wind and road noise. The exhaust emits just a hint of a grumble, which turns into a throaty roar when you stomp on the go-pedal in V8-equipped Dakotas. The chassis feels very stable, and while the ride is a bit taut, it soaks up ruts and bumps with ease. The Dakota is tight and responsive in the corners, which is one of the main reasons for buying a truck in this category over one of the full-size models.

*Crash Test Scores, see pg 530*
*Warranty information, see pg 542*

## Specifications

| Engine/Drivetrain | HP | Torque | EPA Fuel Economy Rating |
|---|---|---|---|
| 8cyl 4.7L A/M | 240 | 290 | 14 city/19 hwy |
| 8cyl 4.7L A/M | 250 | 300 | N/A |
| 6cyl 3.7L A/M | 210 | 235 | 17 city/22 hwy |

## Body Styles

| Style | MSRP Range |
|---|---|
| Crew Cab Pickup Truck | $20,774–$28,679 |
| Extended Cab Pickup Truck | $19,374–$27,189 |

# 2005 Dodge Durango

**MSRP Price Range**

## $26,735 - $35,590

Destination Charge: $645 (all styles)

### Ratings

| | | |
|---|---|---|
| Consumer Rating | 9.0 | |
| Editors Rating | 8.1 | |

**What Edmunds.com says:** With its tough-truck styling, available Hemi V8 and roomy interior, the Durango offers an appealing combination of power, comfort and utility. If you don't mind its big thirst at the pump, it's a great value.

**Pros:** Strong V8 engines, agile handling, excellent ride quality, capable off-road, lots of cargo capacity, simple controls.

**Cons:** Lousy mileage, sloppy fit and finish, needs more second-row legroom and storage, no stability control or parking sensors.

**What's New:** Two trim levels have been added—SXT and SLT Adventurer. The SXT features roof rails, running boards and side moldings. The Adventurer includes a Thule roof rack, side steps, slush mats, cargo liner and organizer and unique wheels. Cloth heated seats are standard on all models this year (except the Limited, which sticks with leather heated seats). A full-screen navigation system is newly available.

*Crash Test Scores, see pg 530*
*Warranty information, see pg 542*

### Specifications

| Engine/Drivetrain | HP | Torque | EPA Fuel Economy Rating |
|---|---|---|---|
| 8cyl 4.7L A | 235 | 295 | 15 city/21 hwy |
| 6cyl 3.7L A | 215 | 235 | 15 city/21 hwy |

### Body Styles

| Style | MSRP Range |
|---|---|
| Large SUV | $26,735–$35,590 |

**Body Styles, Trim Levels and Options:** The four-door Durango is offered in five trim levels—ST, SXT, SLT, SLT Adventurer and top-of-the-line Limited—with either two- or four-wheel drive. The base ST comes standard with power windows, locks and mirrors; air conditioning; heated seats; an AM/FM/CD stereo; and speed control. The SXT builds upon the ST with roof side rails, gray body side moldings, running boards and a CD changer. The SLT adds a power driver seat, rear air conditioning, wood grain cabin accents, body-color front and rear fascias, foglamps and a third-row seat. The SLT Adventurer includes a Thule roof rack with a choice of six rack systems, tubular side steps, slush mats, a cargo liner and organizer, and unique alloy wheels. Spring for the Limited and leather seating, automatic climate control, high-output audio system with steering wheel-mounted controls, auto-dimming mirrors, universal garage opener, a memory system (for the driver seat, mirror, stereo and climate settings), power-adjustable pedals and a security system are all standard.

**Powertrains and Performance:** The standard power plant for two-wheel-drive Durangos is a 3.7-liter V6 that supplies 215 horsepower and 235 pound-feet of torque. Standard on four-wheel-drive models is a 4.7-liter V8 with 235 horses and 295 lb-ft. For maximum towing and hauling power, an optional 5.7-liter Hemi V8 is available that generates 335 hp and 370 lb-ft of torque. All three engines use automatic transmissions; the V6 runs through a four-speed gearbox, while the V8s have five-speed units that feature a tow/haul mode that reduces gear hunting. When equipped with the Hemi V8, the Durango has an 8,950-pound tow rating.

**Safety:** Four-wheel antilock disc brakes are standard. Side curtain airbags (which protect the head and upper torso in side-impact collisions) that cover all three rows are optional, as are power-adjustable pedals. In government crash testing, the Durango earned a perfect five-star rating for frontal impacts.

**Interior Design and Special Features:** Modern in design and functional throughout, the seven-passenger Durango was designed with family usage in mind, as there are numerous cupholders throughout the cabin. The front seats are roomy and comfortable, but adults will find legroom and storage areas in short supply in the second row. Meanwhile, the third-row seat is suited for kids only. Cargo capacity should be more than ample for most buyers; there's 68.4 cubic feet when the third seat is folded into the floor. The standard single-piece third-row bench is hard to fold, but a 50/50-split design is a low-cost option. Other family-friendly extras include a DVD entertainment system, a 384-watt Infinity sound system and satellite radio.

**Driving Impressions:** In spite of its generous proportions, the Durango manages to deliver both a smooth, composed ride and nimble handling around corners. Dodge's SUV is similarly adept in off-road situations, offering plenty of wheel travel and a playful demeanor. The base V6 provides barely adequate power, so if you want quick acceleration opt for the 4.7-liter V8. Equipped with the top-of-the-line Hemi V8, the Durango is one of the quickest SUVs in its price range.

# 2005 Dodge Grand Caravan

**MSRP Price Range**
## $20,205 - $30,175
Destination Charge: $680 (all styles)

## Ratings

| | | |
|---|---|---|
| Consumer Rating | 8.6 | |
| Editors Rating | 8.5 | |

**What Edmunds.com says:** Pleasant to drive and ride in, the Grand Caravan finally steps up to the plate with fold-flat rear seating, allowing families to get the most out of its expansive interior. Reliability and resale value are still in question, but this Dodge is worth a test-drive if you're shopping for a minivan.

**Pros:** Excellent ride and handling characteristics, good low-end pull from 3.8-liter V6, roomy cabin, nifty fold-flat second- and third-row seats.

**Cons:** Unimpressive reliability history, low resale value, can't get stability control.

**What's New:** This year the Grand Caravan receives a styling refresh and a new Stow 'n Go seating and storage system with fold-flat second- and third-row seats, as well as a hefty base price reduction.

**Body Styles, Trim Levels and Options:** The Grand Caravan is available in three main trim levels—SE, SE Plus and high-line SXT (there's also a cargo van version, the CV, which offers several options for configuring a Grand Caravan as a work vehicle). The SE comes with 15-inch steel wheels, antilock brakes, a second-row bench seat (for two passengers), a single-piece third-row bench, dual manual-sliding doors, cruise control and a tilt steering wheel. The SE Plus adds the Stow 'n Go fold-flat seating feature, keyless entry, and power windows, mirrors and locks. The top-level SXT features dual power-sliding doors, traction control, a rear heating and air conditioning system, power driver seat, 16-inch alloy wheels and a 3.8-liter V6 engine. A variety of options are available on all Grand Caravans, including automatic climate control, leather upholstery, an Infinity sound system and a rear DVD entertainment system.

**Powertrains and Performance:** A 180-horsepower, 3.3-liter V6 powers SE and SE Plus models. The SXT includes the more powerful 215-hp, 3.8-liter V6. A four-speed automatic transmission is standard on all models. A Grand Caravan with the 3.8-liter V6 is a sprightly performer, with crisp response down low and through the midrange. Towing capacity maxes out at 3,800 pounds with the optional towing package.

**Safety:** Antilock brakes are standard across the line, and the SXT includes traction control. Stability control is not available. Side curtain airbags (with coverage for all three rows) are optional across the line. All Grand Caravans include a new driver's knee airbag. In government crash testing, the Grand Caravan posted four (out of five) stars for frontal impact protection and a perfect five stars for side-impact protection. Frontal offset crash testing produced an overall "Acceptable" rating (the second highest on a scale of four).

**Interior Design and Special Features:** The star of the show is definitely the Stow 'n Go fold-flat seating and storage system, but the cabin also sports a number of other neat optional features, such as a movable center console equipped with power points and a power rear lift-gate. The seats are generally comfortable, and drivers will find most controls within easy reach. Grand Caravans have 26 cubic feet of cargo capacity behind the 60/40-split third-row seat, and a maximum of 168 cubes with all second- and third-row seats folded into the floor.

**Driving Impressions:** The Grand Caravan's most endearing qualities continue to be its agile handling and supple ride characteristics. We suspect that these vans will surprise and win over a lot of folks who expect the minivan driving experience to be an exercise in lethargic vehicle dynamics. The 3.3-liter V6 engine provides adequate acceleration, but larger families and those who tow a trailer will prefer the added power of the 3.8-liter V6.

*Crash Test Scores, see pg 530*
*Warranty information, see pg 542*

## Specifications

| Engine/Drivetrain | HP | Torque | EPA Fuel Economy Rating |
|---|---|---|---|
| 6cyl 3.8L A | 215 | 245 | 18 city/25 hwy |
| 6cyl 3.3L A | 180 | 210 | 19 city/26 hwy |

## Body Styles

| Style | MSRP Range |
|---|---|
| Large Minivan | $20,205–$30,175 |

# 2005 Dodge Magnum

**Large Wagon**

**MSRP Price Range**

## $21,870 - $31,370
Destination Charge: $625 (all styles)

### Ratings

| | | |
|---|---|---|
| Consumer Rating | 9.2 | |
| Editors Rating | 8.3 | |

**What Edmunds.com says:** Looking for a reason not to buy an SUV? With its available 340-horsepower V8, handsome wagon body and roomy, feature-laden interior, the rear-drive Magnum is one big reason.

**Pros:** Aggressively handsome wagon body style, powerful Hemi V8, quiet ride, roomy interior, lots of safety features, available all-wheel drive.

**Cons:** Sluggish acceleration with base V6, limited transmission choices, complex stereo controls.

**What's New:** The Magnum is an all-new rear-wheel-drive station wagon. Designed to appeal to buyers shopping for a spacious, five-passenger family car, it offers a choice of V6 or V8 power.

**Body Styles, Trim Levels and Options:** The Magnum is available as a wagon only in one of three trim levels—SE, SXT and RT. SE models come standard with 17-inch wheels, air conditioning, a CD player, a telescoping steering wheel, cruise control, full power accessories, keyless entry and an outside temperature display. Step up to the SXT and you'll get a bigger V6 engine, along with alloy wheels, antilock brakes, stability control, privacy glass, a power driver seat and a cargo net; most of these items are available on the SE. The high-line RT is your ticket to V8 power, dual exhaust outlets, larger brakes and 18-inch alloy wheels, as well as amenities like leather upholstery and a six-speaker, 288-watt Boston Acoustics sound system. Options include leather upholstery on SE and SXT models; SXT buyers can also get the upgraded stereo. Optional on the RT only are a navigation system and dual-zone automatic climate control. Among the other extras are an MP3-compatible in-dash CD changer, side curtain airbags, adjustable pedals, self-sealing tires, seat heaters, a cargo organizer, a roof rack and a sunroof. Snowbelt residents should also consider all-wheel drive, available as a midyear option.

**Powertrains and Performance:** Engine choices are delineated by trim level. The Magnum SE comes with a 200-hp, 2.7-liter V6. The SXT upgrades to a 3.5-liter V6 good for 250 hp. And for those who can never get enough power, the RT has a 5.7-liter Hemi V8 stuffed under its hood. Output is rated at a prodigious 340 horses and 390 lb-ft of torque. All wagons are rear-wheel drive, unless you specify all-wheel drive as an option. A four-speed automatic transmission comes standard on V6 models; the RT and AWD-equipped SXTs upgrade to a five-speed automatic.

**Safety:** Four-wheel disc brakes are standard across the line. Antilock brakes, traction control and stability control are optional on the base SE model and standard on SXT and RT models. Options on all models include full-length side curtain airbags, self-sealing tires and adjustable pedals. The Magnum has not yet been crash tested.

**Interior Design and Special Features:** Inside, the Magnum's long wheelbase opens up plenty of room for passengers, particularly in the backseat where the Dodge leads its peers in legroom. The Magnum's tapered roof line limits cargo capacity to just 27.8 cubic feet behind the rear seats. Folding those seats opens up 72 cubic feet. Its interior styling isn't revolutionary, but a two-tone color scheme, faux aluminum accents and white-faced gauges give the Magnum a contemporary look.

**Driving Impressions:** With massive amounts of torque flowing to its rear wheels and plenty of Mercedes-derived chassis components, the V8-powered Magnum RT provides serious fun (and serious practicality) for driving enthusiasts-turned-parents. For those who aren't quite ready for the idea of a Hemi-fed wagon, the SXT and its 3.5-liter V6 offer adequate acceleration and an overall pleasant driving experience. The base V6 makes the Magnum SE feel sluggish, do yourself a favor and upgrade to the SXT if at all possible.

Crash Test Scores, see pg 530
Warranty information, see pg 542

### Specifications

| Engine/Drivetrain | HP | Torque | EPA Fuel Economy Rating |
|---|---|---|---|
| 8cyl 5.7L A | 340 | 390 | 17 city/25 hwy |
| 6cyl 3.5L A | 250 | 250 | 19 city/27 hwy |
| 6cyl 2.7L A | 190 | 190 | 21 city/28 hwy |

### Body Styles

| Style | MSRP Range |
|---|---|
| Large Wagon | $21,870–$31,370 |

For the latest full vehicle reports, visit www.edmunds.com/bginfopak

**MSRP Price Range**
## $13,615 - $16,750
Destination Charge: $545 (all styles)

### Ratings

| | | |
|---|---|---|
| Consumer Rating | 8.9 | |
| Editors Rating | 5.8 | |

**What Edmunds.com says:** Those looking for a polished economy car would be better served elsewhere, but the Neon does have some likable traits, namely capable handling, a powerful audio system and a reasonable price.

**Pros:** More fun in the curves than you might expect, strong brakes, good ride quality, rockin' sound system.

**Cons:** Lacks refinement levels of competitors, numerous low-grade interior components, can't get power rear windows.

**What's New:** Trim levels are reduced to SE and SXT; the R/T is dropped in favor of an SRT appearance package. SXT models feature a new Kicker audio system.

**Body Styles, Trim Levels and Options:** The four-door Neon sedan is available in two trim levels, SE and SXT. Base SE models come with a cassette player, a split-folding rear seat and a tilt steering wheel. Air conditioning and a CD player are optional. Moving up to the SXT adds an air conditioner; power front windows, mirrors and locks; CD player instead of the cassette player; and 15-inch alloy wheels. A Kicker audio system with eight speakers, a CD changer, cruise control and ABS are optional. The SXT trim qualifies for the SRT Design appearance package. The package includes new foglights, dual exhaust and a rear spoiler. There's also a Mopar ground effects kit available.

**Powertrains and Performance:** A 2.0-liter, 132-horsepower inline four powers all Neons. Transmission choices include a four-speed automatic or a five-speed manual. Fuel economy is good for this class, as manual-shift Neons are rated to get 29 mpg in the city and 36 on the highway. Getting the automatic lowers mileage considerably—25 mpg city and 32 highway.

**Safety:** Front disc/rear drum brakes are standard, and ABS is optional on both the SE and SXT. Side airbags for front occupants are also optional. In frontal impact crash testing, the Neon scored four out of five stars; in side-impact tests, it got three stars for front and rear passenger protection. In frontal offset crash testing, the Neon earned only a "Marginal" rating, the second lowest possible.

**Interior Design and Special Features:** The cabin has a mix of soft-touch and cheap plastic surfaces. If one chooses the option of power windows, they still are only for the benefit of front passengers—rear windows are still moved up and down by a good old-fashioned crank. An in-dash six-disc CD changer is optional on the SXT. Audiophiles will be pleased to know that the Kicker audio system packs 208 watts and has eight speakers with a separate amp.

**Driving Impressions:** In general, the Neon is not as quiet as other economy sedans, exhibiting plenty of wind, road and engine noise. It still lags behind most rivals in refinement, especially the Honda Civic, Mazda 3 and Toyota Corolla, and acceleration is nothing to get excited about, either. Handling is solid for a small front-driver, with the Neon demonstrating an eagerness for the twisties through its well-weighted steering. The car provides both a comfortable ride for commuting and a fair amount of agility around corners all for a very reasonable price.

*Crash Test Scores, see pg 530*
*Warranty information, see pg 542*

### Specifications

| Engine/Drivetrain | HP | Torque | EPA Fuel Economy Rating |
|---|---|---|---|
| 4cyl 2.0L A/M | 132 | 130 | 25 city/32 hwy |

### Body Styles

| Style | MSRP Range |
|---|---|
| Compact Sedan | $13,615–$16,750 |

# Dodge

# 2005 Dodge Neon SRT-4 Compact Sedan

**MSRP Price Range**

## $20,650

Destination Charge: $545 (all styles)

## Ratings

| | | |
|---|---|---|
| Consumer Rating | 8.9 | |
| Editors Rating | 7.5 | |

**What Edmunds.com says:** A ridiculously fast econobox with the suspension to back it up, the SRT-4 is undeniably the most performance you can buy for $20K.

**Pros:** More power than a $20K car has any business having, near perfect suspension tuning, throaty exhaust snarl, serious seat bolstering.

**Cons:** Lacks refinement, some low-grade interior components.

**What's New:** A new option this year is the Kicker/SRT Livin' Loud audio system that included a six-disc CD changer, two one-inch Neodymium tweeters, two 75-watt 5.5-inch full-range speakers, two 90-watt 6x9 coaxials and a 10-inch 100-watt SVC amplified subwoofer.

**Body Styles, Trim Levels and Options:** The SRT-4 comes only in a four-door sedan body style. Standard features include air conditioning, a CD stereo, power windows (front only), power mirrors, 17-inch alloy wheels shod with 17-inch performance tires, an auxiliary boost gauge, metallic interior accents, foglights and sport seats. Key options include a power sunroof, a premium Kicker/SRT Livin' Loud audio system and side airbags.

**Powertrains and Performance:** The SRT-4 is fitted with a turbocharged, 2.4-liter inline four that boasts ratings of 230 horsepower and 250 pound-feet of torque. The sole transmission is a five-speed manual, and a limited-slip differential is standard. With this type of power in a small car, acceleration is almost scary; according to Dodge, the SRT-4 will blast from zero to 60 mph in under 6 seconds. Top speed is north of 140 mph.

**Safety:** Four-wheel antilock disc brakes are standard and side airbags are optional. In frontal impact testing, the Neon scored four out of five stars; in side-impact tests, it got three stars. In frontal offset crash testing, the Neon earned only a "Marginal" rating, the second lowest on a scale of four.

**Interior Design and Special Features:** The most notable interior feature is the pair of Viper-inspired sport seats with side bolsters so prominent you practically have to crawl around them just to get in. A few other upgrades such as a boost gauge and satin silver metallic accents separate the SRT-4 from plebian Neons. The rear seats are relatively tight for adults, so don't expect to shove too many friends back there. All interior controls are simple to use, but materials quality is iffy and build quality generally isn't much better.

**Driving Impressions:** The SRT-4 is the most fun you can have behind the wheel for $20,000. Under full boost, first gear disappears in a torrent of tire smoke, but the big 17-inch tires dig in for second and never let up from there on out. The car pulls strongly through 6,000 rpm with only a minimal drop-off in power as it approaches its 6,240-rpm redline. The only notable weak spot is the shifter, as it takes its time getting into gear, allowing the turbo to lag behind on every shift. The antilock disc brakes are fully up to the task of keeping the easily gotten velocity in check; we recorded a stellar 116-foot stopping distance from 60 mph. The car's speed is undeniable, but there's more to the SRT-4 than just horsepower. A full complement of thick sway bars and retuned springs provide flat cornering and crisp transitions. Ride quality has been compromised, but not by much, as it remains compliant enough for everyday driving—just don't expect to sip your morning coffee without a few tongue scaldings.

*Crash Test Scores, see pg 530*
*Warranty information, see pg 542*

## Specifications

| Engine/Drivetrain | HP | Torque | EPA Fuel Economy Rating |
|---|---|---|---|
| 4cyl 2.4L M | 220 | 245 | 22 city/30 hwy |

## Body Styles

| Style | MSRP Range |
|---|---|
| Compact Sedan | $20,650 |

# 2005 Dodge Ram Pickup 1500

**MSRP Price Range**
## $20,180 - $34,140
Destination Charge: $850 (all styles)

### Ratings

| | | |
|---|---|---|
| Consumer Rating | 7.8 | |
| Editors Rating | 8.1 | |

**What Edmunds.com says:** Still the king of big-truck attitude, the Ram 1500 can handle the diverse duties of comfortable daily driver and capable workhorse with equal ease.

**Pros:** Optional "Hemi" V8, sharp steering, compliant ride, spacious interior, available side curtain airbags.

**Cons:** Poor fuel mileage, cramped rear seat, fewer body configurations than its competition, ABS not standard.

**What's New:** The 3.7-liter V6 and 4.7-liter V8 receive a standard six-speed manual transmission. Crew cab models can be equipped with a power sunroof and Sirius Satellite Radio this year.

**Body Styles, Trim Levels and Options:** Ram 1500s are available in two cab styles (regular and Quad), two bed lengths (6 feet 3 inches and 8 feet even) and three trim levels (base ST, midlevel SLT, luxury Laramie). Additionally, a Sport package is optional on the SLT and Laramie. The Ram ST comes with air conditioning, AM/FM/cassette stereo, antilock rear brakes and a 40/20/40-split front seat. Stepping up to the SLT adds cruise control, larger (265/70R17) tires, chrome wheels, trip computer and power windows, locks and mirrors. The luxurious Laramie adds the following: leather seating, power driver (and passenger on Quad Cab) seat, Homelink transmitter system, a 240-watt 11-speaker sound system (with a CD changer and steering wheel-mounted controls), keyless entry/anti-theft system, four-wheel antilock brakes and alloy wheels. Sport models feature a monochromatic paint scheme along with a unique grille and 20-inch wheels with 275/55R20 rubber. The Off-Road package adds skid plates, anti-spin rear differential, heavy-duty cooling and all-terrain tires, while the Work Special group replaces the standard exterior chrome trim with painted components.

**Powertrains and Performance:** Three engines see duty in the Ram 1500: a 3.7-liter V6 (215 horsepower and 235 pound-feet of torque), a 4.7-liter V8 (235 horses and 295 lb-ft) and a 5.7-liter Hemi V8 (345 ponies and 375 lb-ft of torque). Two-wheel-drive regular-cab Rams come standard with the V6, all others get the 4.7-liter V8. A six-speed manual is standard on the two smaller engines; a five-speed automatic is optional on the V6 and 4.7 V8 and is the sole gearbox for the 5.7 V8. Properly equipped, a Ram Quad Cab can tow up to 9,300 pounds and haul a payload of 2,090 pounds.

**Safety:** Side curtain airbags are optional on all Rams and all center seats have three-point seatbelts. Four-wheel antilock brakes are optional. Crash test scores are impressive, with the Ram garnering a "Good" rating (the highest possible) in frontal offset crash testing conducted by the IIHS, and five stars from the government for driver and front-passenger protection in frontal impacts.

**Interior Design and Special Features:** The Ram's cabin features white-faced gauges, simple twist-knob climate controls and a huge center armrest/bin. In Quad Cab models, the rear seats fold up to reveal a flat load floor for carrying large items inside. The Ram also boasts impressive overall build and materials quality that approaches the class-leading Toyota Tundra in many respects.

**Driving Impressions:** For such a big vehicle, the Ram is nimble and easy to drive. The suspension can still be a bit bouncy at times, but when loaded up with passengers and cargo, the Ram's ride quality is downright comfortable. The 5.7-liter Hemi is a big improvement over the old, lethargic yet thirsty 5.9-liter V8. With the Hemi, there's plenty of power for hills and hauling, but as expected, fuel mileage still isn't great—typically around 12 mpg. Unless you plan on heavy towing, the more efficient 4.7-liter V8 would probably serve your needs just fine.

*Crash Test Scores, see pg 530*
*Warranty information, see pg 542*

### Specifications

| Engine/Drivetrain | HP | Torque | EPA Fuel Economy Rating |
|---|---|---|---|
| 8cyl 4.7L A/M | 240 | 300 | 14 city/19 hwy |
| 6cyl 3.7L M | 215 | 235 | 16 city/21 hwy |

### Body Styles

| Style | MSRP Range |
|---|---|
| Crew Cab Pickup Truck | $24,190–$34,140 |
| Regular Cab Pickup Truck | $20,180–$31,245 |

# 2005 Dodge Ram Pickup 1500 SRT-10

**Large Truck**

## MSRP Price Range

### $45,000 - $50,000
Destination Charge: $850 (all styles)

### Ratings

| | | |
|---|---|---|
| Consumer Rating | N/A | |
| Editors Rating | 8.5 | |

**What Edmunds.com says:** If you loved the muscle cars of the 1960s but were too young or too poor to get in on the high-test fun, the SRT-10 offers a second chance at piloting a truly brawny Dodge.

**Pros:** Ridiculous V10 power, sharp handling for a truck, cool Hurst shifter on regular cab model, macho good looks, roomy interiors.

**Cons:** Lousy fuel economy.

**What's New:** A Quad Cab (crew cab) model joins the regular cab SRT-10 this year. The Quad includes a super-duty four-speed automatic transmission, auxiliary transmission oil cooler, heavy-duty torque converter, and special front and rear strut and spring assemblies. A special braking system incorporates heavy-duty Ram components and unique four-piston calipers. The regular cab SRT-10 gets a new 4.56 axle ratio for improved launch feel and low-end acceleration. Also new this year is an aluminum body-color tonneau cover, with spoiler, over the pickup bed. The cover is optional on the regular cab, and standard on the Quad.

**Body Styles, Trim Levels and Options:** Dodge's powerful sport truck is available as a two-wheel-drive regular cab or crew cab in just one trim level. The SRT-10 Ram comes loaded with such features as 22-inch alloy wheels wrapped in massive 305/40YR22 Pirelli tires, leather/suede-upholstered sport seats, a 12-speaker 500-watt audio system, air conditioning and full power accessories, so options are few. Exterior paint choices are limited to red, black and silver.

**Powertrains and Performance:** The Ram SRT-10 comes with the Viper's 8.3-liter V10 under the hood—an engine that's good for 500 horsepower. It also delivers 525 lb-ft of torque and propels the regular cab from a standstill to 60 mph in 5.4 seconds. Power flows to the rear wheels via a modified version of the Viper's T56 six-speed manual transmission with a Hurst shifter on top in the regular cab, and a heavy-duty four-speed automatic in the crew cab. The SRT-10 is also lowered one inch in the front and over two inches in the rear compared to a standard Ram pickup. The revised suspension incorporates Bilstein shocks, performance springs and a rear sway bar in anticipation of increased cornering loads.

**Safety:** Four-wheel ABS is standard, and the truck's massive disc brakes utilize 15-inch rotors in front and 14-inch rotors in the rear. Dual-stage airbags are also standard, and side curtain airbags are available as well. In government crash tests, the standard Ram earned four out of five stars for driver protection in a frontal collision and five out of five stars for protection of the front passenger. Offset frontal crash tests conducted by the IIHS resulted in a "Good" rating, the highest possible.

**Interior Design and Special Features:** Inside, the Ram SRT-10 is fairly straightforward—there's only so much you can do with a pickup cab. However, Dodge has installed white-faced gauges, drilled metallic pedals, a Hurst shifter (in the regular cab) and leather/suede sport seats to distinguish its performance truck from other Rams. Otherwise, it's the familiar Ram design, and that means easy-to-use controls and better-than-average build and materials quality.

Crash Test Scores, see pg 530
Warranty information, see pg 542

### Specifications

| Engine/Drivetrain | HP | Torque | EPA Fuel Economy Rating |
|---|---|---|---|
| 10cyl 8.3L A/M | 500 | 525 | N/A |

### Body Styles

| Style | MSRP Range |
|---|---|
| Crew Cab Pickup Truck | $50,000 |
| Regular Cab Pickup Truck | $45,000 |

**Driving Impressions:** When piloting the SRT-10, it is readily apparent that you're behind the wheel of a really serious machine. The regular cab's clutch is heavy, similar to that of an old muscle car, and the 505-cubic-inch engine rumbles and shakes the cab with as much mechanical noise as there is exhaust burble. As much brawn as there is under the hood, it's surprising how little exhaust noise there is at idle and low rpm. However, find an open stretch of road, drop the Hurst shifter from fourth to third, nail the gas pedal and suddenly it sounds like the truck is tearing a hole in the sky. With nothing less than purebred racecar urgency, the Ram jets forward like it's being shot out of a catapult, pinning the driver to the seat. Handling is tighter than you'd ever expect in a truck, and the brakes are fully capable of reining in the SRT-10's prodigious power.

# 2005 Dodge Ram Pickup 2500

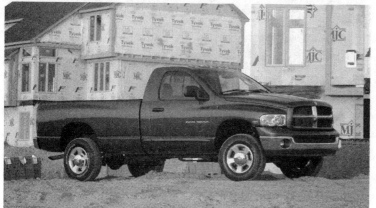

**MSRP Price Range**
## $24,565 - $34,775
Destination Charge: $850 (all styles)

## Ratings

| | | |
|---|---|---|
| Consumer Rating | 9.8 | |
| Editors Rating | 8.0 | |

**What Edmunds.com says:** The heavy-duty Ram offers serious diesel power, stout suspensions and a well-built, functional interior—all of which make it an impressive package for hard-core truck users.

**Pros:** Powerful engine lineup, huge payload and towing capacities, comfortable interior, compliant ride, available side curtain airbags.

**Cons:** Stunted standard bed, cramped rear seat, fewer body configurations that the competition.

**What's New:** The big news (literally) for 2005 is the new Power Wagon, which features class-exclusive electric locking front and rear differentials, and an electronic disconnecting front sway bar. Other Power Wagon extras include 33-inch BF Goodrich off-road tires, a 12,000-pound winch, a two-inch taller stance and a unique suspension. Other changes for the Ram 2500 this year include an even more powerful version of the Cummins turbodiesel engine, now rated at a whopping 600 lb-ft of torque, and the availability of a power sunroof and Sirius Satellite Radio on Quad Cabs.

**Body Styles, Trim Levels and Options:** Heavy-duty Rams are available in two cab styles (regular and Quad), two bed lengths (a standard 6-foot, 3-inch bed or an 8-foot-long bed) and four trim levels (base ST, midlevel SLT, leather-clad Laramie, and off road-ready Power Wagon). The regular cab comes only with the long bed, while the Quad Cab can be had with either the standard or long bed. The Ram ST comes with air conditioning, AM/FM/cassette stereo and a 40/20/40-split front seat. Stepping up to the SLT adds an overhead console, a CD player, carpeted floor mats, cloth upholstery, cruise control, chrome wheels and keyless entry. The luxurious Laramie is further upgraded with power-adjustable pedals, a HomeLink transmitter system, a 240-watt 11-speaker sound system (with a CD changer and steering wheel-mounted controls), leather seating with six-way power driver and front passenger adjustments and cast aluminum wheels. The Power Wagon includes electric locking front and rear differentials, an electronic disconnecting front sway bar, a 12,000-pound winch, 33-inch tires on unique alloys, matte finish wheel flares and a two-inch taller stance.

**Powertrains and Performance:** Dodge's 5.7-liter Hemi V8 is the standard engine for the 2500. Rated at 345 horsepower and 375 pound-feet of torque, it outmuscles both of GM's and Ford's standard offerings. Two Cummins diesel engines are also offered: a standard 5.9-liter inline six with 250 hp and 460 lb-ft of torque and a high-output version of the same engine rated at 325 hp and a towering 600 lb-ft of torque. The Hemi V8 and standard 5.9-liter diesel come with a five-speed manual, while the high-output diesel gets a six-speed manual standard. A five-speed automatic is optional for the V8, while either of the diesels can be equipped with a four-speed overdrive automatic. A Ram 2500 regular cab with the high-output Cummins has a 2,770-pound payload rating and a 13,600-pound tow rating.

**Safety:** Side curtain airbags are optional on all Rams. All center seats have three-point seatbelts. Optional on the SLT and standard on the Laramie are power-adjustable pedals, which allow shorter folk to find a comfortable driving position without having to sit too close to the steering wheel. The trucks also feature standard antilock disc brakes. Although heavy-duty versions of the Ram have not been crash tested, the Ram 1500 received a "Good" rating (the highest possible) from the IIHS.

**Interior Design and Special Features:** Interior room is generous, and the overall design is very functional with comfortable seats and simple controls. If you've got more cargo than passengers, you can fold up the rear seats and take advantage of the Ram's flat load floor.

**Driving Impressions:** Although it's built to take on the most demanding tasks, the Ram 2500 is still a surprisingly comfortable truck for daily use. Between its quick steering and supple ride, it's nearly as comfortable as most half-tons. The Hemi engine is a competent all-around engine, but for serious towing and hauling, one of the Cummins diesels is essential.

*Crash Test Scores, see pg 530*
*Warranty information, see pg 542*

## Specifications

| Engine/Drivetrain | HP | Torque | EPA Fuel Economy Rating |
|---|---|---|---|
| 8cyl 5.7L M | 330 | 375 | N/A |

## Body Styles

| Style | MSRP Range |
|---|---|
| Crew Cab Pickup Truck | $26,945–$34,775 |
| Regular Cab Pickup Truck | $24,565–$32,020 |

# 2005 Dodge Ram Pickup 3500

**MSRP Price Range**

## $26,450 - $40,920

Destination Charge: $850 (all styles)

#1 Editors' Rating

### Ratings

| | | |
|---|---|---|
| Consumer Rating | 9.4 | |
| Editors Rating | 8.4 | |

**What Edmunds.com says:** The heavy-duty Ram offers serious diesel power, stout suspensions and a well-built, functional interior—all of which make it an impressive package for hard-core truck users.

**Pros:** Powerful engine lineup, huge payload and towing capacities, comfortable interior, compliant ride, available side-curtain airbags.

**Cons:** Stunted standard bed, fewer body configurations than the competition.

**What's New:** Changes for the Ram 3500 include an even more powerful version of the Cummins turbodiesel engine, now rated at a whopping 600 lb-ft of torque, and the availability of a power sunroof and Sirius Satellite Radio on Quad Cabs.

**Body Styles, Trim Levels and Options:** Heavy-duty Rams are available in two cab styles (regular and Quad), two bed lengths (a standard 6-foot-3-inch bed or an 8-foot-long bed) and three trim levels (base ST, midlevel SLT and leather-clad Laramie). The regular cab comes only with the long bed, while the Quad Cab can be had with either the standard or long bed. The Ram ST comes with air conditioning, AM/FM/cassette stereo and a 40/20/40-split front seat. Stepping up to the SLT adds an overhead console, a CD player, carpeted floor mats, cloth upholstery, cruise control, chrome wheels and keyless entry. The luxurious Laramie is further upgraded with power-adjustable pedals, a HomeLink transmitter system, a 240-watt 11-speaker sound system (with a CD changer and steering wheel-mounted controls), leather seating with six-way power driver and front-passenger adjustments and cast aluminum wheels. Notable options include a DVD-based navigation system and Bluetooth hands-free cell phone capability.

**Powertrains and Performance:** Dodge's 5.7-liter Hemi V8 is the standard engine for the 3500. Rated at 345 horsepower and 375 pound-feet of torque, it out-muscles both of GM's and Ford's standard offerings. Two Cummins diesels engines are also offered: a standard 5.9-liter inline six with 250 hp and 460 lb-ft of torque, and a high-output version of the same engine rated at 325 hp and a towering 600 lb-ft of torque. The Hemi V8 and standard Cummins diesel come with a five-speed manual, while the high-output diesel gets a six-speed manual standard. A five-speed automatic is optional for the V8, and either of the diesels can be equipped with a four-speed overdrive automatic. A Ram 3500 regular cab with dual rear wheels and the high-output Cummins has a 5,020-pound payload rating and a 16,400-pound tow rating.

**Safety:** Side curtain airbags are optional on all Rams. All center seats have three-point seatbelts. Optional on the SLT and standard on the Laramie are power-adjustable pedals, which allow shorter folk to find a comfortable driving position without having to sit too close to the steering wheel. The trucks also feature ABS and four-wheel disc brakes. Although heavy-duty versions of the Ram have not been crash tested, the Ram 1500 received a "Good" rating (the highest possible) from the IIHS.

*Crash Test Scores, see pg 530*
*Warranty information, see pg 542*

### Specifications

| Engine/Drivetrain | HP | Torque | EPA Fuel Economy Rating |
|---|---|---|---|
| 8cyl 5.7L M | 330 | 375 | N/A |
| 6cyl 5.9L M | 325 | 600 | N/A |

### Body Styles

| Style | MSRP Range |
|---|---|
| Crew Cab Pickup Truck | $29,660–$40,920 |
| Regular Cab Pickup Truck | $26,450–$33,150 |

**Interior Design and Special Features:** Interior room is generous, and the overall design is very functional with comfortable seats and simple controls. If you've got more cargo than passengers, you can fold up the rear seats and take advantage of the Ram's flat load floor.

**Driving Impressions:** Although it's built to take on the most demanding tasks, the Ram 3500 is still a surprisingly comfortable truck for daily use. Between its quick steering and supple ride, it's nearly as comfortable as most half-tons. The Hemi engine is a competent all-around engine, but for serious towing and hauling, one of the Cummins diesels is essential.

# 2005 Dodge Stratus

**Body Styles, Trim Levels and Options:** Coupes and sedans are available in base SXT and sporty R/T versions. The SXT comes with air conditioning, power windows and locks, cruise control, a four-disc CD changer, keyless entry and 16-inch alloy wheels. Stepping up to the R/T brings a V6, a firmer suspension and 17-inch alloys wrapped with performance tires (optional on the coupe). A sunroof is optional on the R/T as is an eight-way adjustable driver seat (six-way on the coupe) and leather seating. The R/T coupe has an upgraded audio system with seven Infinity speakers, steering wheel-mounted audio controls and foglights.

**Powertrains and Performance:** Stratus coupes share an engine with the Mitsubishi Eclipse; the SXT uses a 2.4-liter inline four producing 147 horsepower and the R/T sports a 3.0-liter V6 rated at 200 ponies. Both engines can be had with either a five-speed manual or four-speed automatic transmission. The sedans have Chrysler engines. The SXT has a 2.4-liter inline four good for 150 hp, while the R/T version receives a 200-hp 2.7-liter V6. All sedans come with a four-speed automatic transmission. Expect adequate, albeit noisy, acceleration with either four-cylinder engine. We recommend going with the V6 in both the coupe and sedan, as both engines get the Stratus up to speed quite nicely in most situations, though not with the refinement of most imports.

**Safety:** Side curtain airbags are optional on all Stratus models. Antilock brakes with traction control are standard on the R/T sedan and optional on other models. Crash test scores for the Stratus sedan are excellent; it garnered a "Good" (the highest possible) rating in frontal offset testing as well as five stars (out of five) ratings in front crash tests. Side impacts were rated at just three out of five stars, but this was without the optional airbags. The coupe didn't fare quite as well. It scored four stars in frontal impacts and, for side impacts, three stars for front passengers and five stars for rear-seat passengers.

**Interior Design and Special Features:** In spite of their crisp body lines, neither the coupe nor the sedan has much in the way of style in the cockpit. Materials quality is also lacking. The sedan, at least, has white-faced gauges that give it a somewhat sporty feel. Although most drivers will find adequate room up front, the rear-seat accommodations leave plenty to be desired with minimal room to spread out and mediocre cushioning. Both the coupe and sedan boast 16 cubic feet of trunk space.

**Driving Impressions:** Neither the sedan nor the coupe stands out in its segment in terms of outright performance, but the Stratus does provide a relaxed, moderately entertaining drive (when configured with V6 power) along with a low out-the-door price. The R/T sedan handles well in the corners with minimal body roll, and the coupe, while softer, is also a steady companion when the road turns curvy. The coupe rides smoothly on the highway, but the sedan is not as composed, often transferring harshness directly to the occupant compartment.

**MSRP Price Range**
## $20,145 - $23,695
Destination Charge: $625 (all styles)

### Ratings

| | | |
|---|---|---|
| Consumer Rating | 9.1 | |
| Editors Rating | 6.1 | |

**What Edmunds.com says:** A mediocre midsize sedan and coupe lost in a crowd of better-qualified vehicles. Still fair game for bargain hunters, but most shoppers should look elsewhere.

**Pros:** Low pricing, solid ride and handling characteristics, large trunk.

**Cons:** Unrefined drivetrains, uncomfortable backseats, subpar build and materials quality, looks positively dull next to the Magnum.

**What's New:** The Stratus sedan now offers a Sport Appearance Package on the SXT that mimics the look of the R/T by offering sport instruments, chrome wheels and a spoiler.

*Crash Test Scores, see pg 530*
*Warranty information, see pg 542*

### Specifications

| Engine/Drivetrain | HP | Torque | EPA Fuel Economy Rating |
|---|---|---|---|
| 6cyl 3.0L A/M | 200 | 205 | 20 city/28 hwy |
| 6cyl 2.7L A | 200 | 190 | 21 city/28 hwy |
| 4cyl 2.4L A | 150 | 167 | 22 city/30 hwy |
| 4cyl 2.4L M | 147 | 158 | 24 city/32 hwy |
| 4cyl 2.4L A | 142 | 155 | 21 city/28 hwy |

### Body Styles

| Style | MSRP Range |
|---|---|
| Midsize Coupe | $20,905–$23,695 |
| Midsize Sedan | $20,145–$21,625 |

# 2005 Dodge Viper

**Compact Convertible**

**MSRP Price Range**

## $81,495

Destination Charge: $800 (all styles)

### Ratings

| | | |
|---|---|---|
| Consumer Rating | 9.3 | |
| Editors Rating | 7.5 | |

**What Edmunds.com says:** Still the king of speed, the Viper has softened some of its rough edges without losing its unique character in the process.

**Pros:** Neck-straining acceleration, race-car-caliber brakes, track-ready suspension, decent ergonomics for a supercar, exclusivity of limited production.

**Cons:** No traction control or side airbags, too extreme for a daily driver, awkward shifter, exploiting its capabilities requires elevated driver skills.

**What's New:** No major changes for 2005.

**Body Styles, Trim Levels and Options:** The Viper comes only as a two-seat roadster. Standard equipment includes racing-style seats; power-adjustable pedals; full instrumentation; power windows, locks and mirrors; tilt steering; keyless entry; and a seven-speaker, 300-watt audio system with an in-dash six-disc changer. There are no options; the only choice a customer need make is color.

**Powertrains and Performance:** An 8.3-liter (505-cubic-inch) V10 engine sports heroic output numbers: 500 horsepower and 525 pound-feet of torque. The power is transferred to the fat rear tires via a Tremec six-speed manual transmission and a standard limited-slip differential. Its performance numbers are equally impressive, as the Viper is able to reach 60 mph in just 4.0 seconds and run the quarter-mile is 12.0 seconds flat.

**Safety:** In spite of the recent redesign, there are no side airbags, nor is there traction or stability control. Massive four-wheel antilock disc brakes assure rapid stops and a passenger-side airbag cutoff switch makes it feasible for small children to ride along in a pinch.

**Interior Design and Special Features:** Although the cockpit was improved with 2003's revamping, it still feels like a Viper inside, except with build and materials quality more befitting an $80,000 car. A large center-mounted tachometer sits next to a 220-mph speedometer. Additional gauges reside between the speedometer and center console, angled toward the driver. Pedals, which are power-adjustable, are placed directly in front of the driver, and there's also a dead pedal. Seat comfort is surprisingly good and the controls are user-friendly; there's even a real center console storage compartment (but no cupholders—as specifically requested by Viper owners). The audio system has a fully integrated head unit, complete with an in-dash six-disc CD changer. Adding a race-car feel is a red starter button that's used to fire the beast's V10 engine to life.

**Driving Impressions:** The Viper is one of the fastest production cars in the world. Its 500-horsepower V10 pushes it to triple-digit speeds in the blink of an eye and it doesn't stop there. Massive rear tires make fast starts easier than you might think, although the shifter is a bit awkward so concentration is required to hit the gates just right. Pushing the Viper to the limit still requires the skill of a seasoned driver, but even rookie pilots will admire the car's unbelievable abilities. Ultraquick steering, racing-style seats and powerful Brembo brakes add to the race-carlike feel. It's not comfortable enough to be used as an everyday driver, but for those who can afford to have it on the side, the Viper is a supercar that answers to nothing.

*Crash Test Scores, see pg 530*
*Warranty information, see pg 542*

### Specifications

| Engine/Drivetrain | HP | Torque | EPA Fuel Economy Rating |
|---|---|---|---|
| 10cyl 8.3L M | 500 | 525 | 12 city/20 hwy |

### Body Styles

| Style | MSRP Range |
|---|---|
| Compact Convertible | $81,495 |

For the latest full vehicle reports, visit www.edmunds.com/bginfopak

# 2005 Ford Crown Victoria

**MSRP Price Range**
## $24,190 - $30,275
Destination Charge: $725 (all styles)

### Ratings

| | | |
|---|---|---|
| Consumer Rating | 9.0 | ▭ |
| Editors Rating | 8.0 | ▭ |

**What Edmunds.com says:** One of the last traditional rear-drive, body-on-frame full-size sedans, the Crown Vic is a favorite of taxi cab drivers, police departments and those looking for a lot of room at a reasonable price. However, those with more money to spend on a V8 sedan will prefer the modern, stylish Chrysler 300C.

**Pros:** Low price, rear-wheel-drive performance, standard ABS, room for six, comfortable ride, excellent crash test results.

**Cons:** Large size makes it difficult to park and maneuver, dated interior styling.

**What's New:** No major changes for the Crown Victoria this year.

**Body Styles, Trim Levels and Options:** Ford's full-size Crown Victoria comes in three trim levels—base, LX and LX Sport. The base model comes equipped with basics like air conditioning, a power driver seat and a cassette stereo. Upgrades like remote keyless entry and a CD player are available as options. Step up to the LX to get them standard, as well as an overhead console with compass and alloy wheels. Select the Premier group to add such equipment as a power passenger seat, automatic climate control, a leather-wrapped steering wheel and an auto-dimming rearview mirror to the LX. The LX Sport comes with a handling and performance package that includes performance tires, revised suspension components, a 3.27 axle ratio (compared to the standard 2.73 gears), dual exhaust, leather trim for the seats and a floor-mounted shift level with console. Traction control is available on all trim levels.

**Powertrains and Performance:** Despite its size, the two-ton Crown Victoria is no slouch in terms of acceleration thanks to its 4.6-liter V8 engine that pumps out 224 horsepower and 265 pound-feet of thrust. This engine makes 239 hp and 276 lb-ft of torque in the LX Sport. The only transmission offered is a four-speed automatic. Fuel economy is acceptable for a large V8 sedan, as the Crown Vic rates 18 mpg for city driving and 25 mpg on the highway.

**Safety:** All Crown Vics come with four-wheel antilock disc brakes and Electronic Brakeforce Distribution (EBD). Side airbags are available but only on the LX and LX Sport trim levels. The Crown Victoria has done well in National Highway Traffic Safety Administration crash tests; it earned five stars for driver and front passenger protection and four stars in side-impact testing. The big sedan also earned the top rating of "Good" in frontal offset crash testing conducted by the IIHS. With a crash-severity sensor, safety belt pre-tensioners, dual-stage airbags and seat-position sensors, the Crown Vic offers most of the latest safety innovations despite its older design.

**Interior Design and Special Features:** If you've ridden in a taxi cab recently, you know that the Crown Victoria's strength is not innovative interior design. For better or for worse, it's basic, roomy and comfortable. A cavernous trunk of 20.6 cubic feet will swallow any luggage you might have. The Crown Vic can seat six passengers thanks to a column-mounted shifter and standard front bench seat.

**Driving Impressions:** As you might expect, responsive handling is not the Crown Victoria's forte. Various improvements over the years provide a comfortable ride, but there's no getting around the vehicle's substantial weight and dimensions, nor its old-tech underpinnings. If you're looking for nothing more than a family cruiser, the Vic will suffice, but if a car with a somewhat involving driving experience is your desire, look elsewhere.

*Crash Test Scores, see pg 530*
*Warranty information, see pg 542*

### Specifications

| Engine/Drivetrain | HP | Torque | EPA Fuel Economy Rating |
|---|---|---|---|
| 8cyl 4.6L A | 239 | 276 | 18 city/25 hwy |
| 8cyl 4.6L A | 224 | 265 | 18 city/25 hwy |

### Body Styles

| Style | MSRP Range |
|---|---|
| Large Sedan | $24,190–$30,275 |

# 2005 Ford Econoline Wagon

**Large/Midsize Van**

**MSRP Price Range**

## $24,790 - $32,140

Destination Charge: $735 (all styles)

## Ratings

| | | |
|---|---|---|
| Consumer Rating | 10.0 | |
| Editors Rating | 5.0 | |

**What Edmunds.com says:** Although the Econoline still provides one of the most spacious interiors on the market for big families, its lack of significant upgrades leaves it a step behind GM's more modern full-size vans.

**Pros:** Massive people-hauling and cargo-toting ability, powerful engines, wide range of configurations, comfortable seats.

**Cons:** Trucklike fuel economy, unwieldy size, limited second-row legroom, lots of wind noise.

**What's New:** Changes this year are limited to minor transmission and interior trim revisions. All engines now feature electronic throttle control.

**Body Styles, Trim Levels and Options:** There are three models to choose from: the base-model E-150, the tougher E-350 Super Duty and the E-350 Super Duty Extended. Each of these vehicles is offered in either XL or XLT trim; E-150s and standard-length E-350s are also available in high-line Chateau trim. Both XL and XLT come standard with items like tilt steering, air conditioning and a Class One trailer-towing package. Chateau models come with second-row captain's chairs, a CD player, keyless entry and running boards. Available options include an upgraded tow package, leather upholstery and an in-dash six-CD changer.

**Powertrains and Performance:** Four different engines are available depending on which model you choose. The E-150 offers a choice of either a 4.6-liter V8 or a 5.4-liter V8. The 4.6-liter produces 225 horsepower and 286 pound-feet of torque, while the 5.4-liter makes 255 hp and 350 lb-ft of torque. E-350 Super Duty and Super Duty Extended models have the 5.4-liter V8 as standard. To upgrade, you can go with the 6.8-liter, 305-hp V10 or the new 6.0-liter, 235-hp Power Stroke turbodiesel V8. Trailer ratings range from 6,600 pounds for an E-150 to 10,000 pounds for an E-350 Super Duty. A four-speed automatic handles the shifting duties, except on vans with the turbodiesel, which get a five-speed auto.

**Safety:** All Econolines come standard with four-wheel ABS, but that's about it when it comes to high-tech safety features. It earned four out of five stars for both the driver and passenger in NHTSA's frontal crash test.

**Interior Design and Special Features:** Inside, the Econoline offers comfortable seating (particularly if your van has the optional captain's chairs), though legroom is a bit tight for those sitting in the second row. Depending on which model you choose, the Econoline can seat seven, eight, 12 (E-350) or 15 passengers (E-350 Extended). Cargo space is prodigious, with anywhere from 257 to 309 cubic feet at your disposal.

**Driving Impressions:** Driving an Econoline, despite its passenger seating, differs little from piloting a delivery vehicle, so it's not a logical choice for everyday motoring—though quite a few families happily employ their vans exactly that way. The virtues of sitting tall with a panoramic view of the road ahead can outweigh many a minor inconvenience. And despite their old-fashioned suspension designs, Econolines feel relatively stable and confident on the highway. Excessive wind noise tends to drown out conversation in the cabin, however.

*Crash Test Scores, see pg 530*
*Warranty information, see pg 542*

## Specifications

| Engine/Drivetrain | HP | Torque | EPA Fuel Economy Rating |
|---|---|---|---|
| 8cyl 5.4L A | 255 | 350 | 14 city/17 hwy |
| 8cyl 4.6L A | 225 | 286 | 15 city/19 hwy |

## Body Styles

| Style | MSRP Range |
|---|---|
| Large Van | $29,330–$31,185 |
| Midsize Van | $24,790–$32,140 |

# 2005 Ford Escape

**MSRP Price Range**

## $19,265 - $28,005
Destination Charge: $590 (all styles)

### Ratings

| | | |
|---|---|---|
| Consumer Rating | 9.0 | ████████████░ |
| Editors Rating | 7.8 | ██████████░░░ |

**What Edmunds.com says:** Still one of our favorites in the category, the Escape is a very capable small SUV thanks to its powerful V6 and hybrid electric engines, spacious cabin and carlike handling.

**Pros:** Powerful V6, quick and efficient hybrid model, large cargo capacity, comfortable interior, carlike handling, optional side curtain airbags.

**Cons:** Small gas tank size limits cruising range, so-so interior materials quality.

**What's New:** For 2005, the Escape gets a freshened look and some new mechanicals. Last year's base 2.0-liter engine is replaced by a new 153-horsepower, 2.3-liter, four-cylinder engine that's available with either a four-speed automatic or five-speed manual transmission. This new engine is a more viable choice for budget-conscious buyers, and like the V6, it can be matched with a new electronically controlled all-wheel-drive system. Meanwhile, the V6 engine has been tweaked to provide improved throttle response. Antilock brakes are now standard across the line. Interior updates include a floor-mounted shifter, new gauges, upgraded seats and additional storage. The most significant improvement inside is the addition of the optional Safety Canopy rollover protection system. Further, the vehicle's structure has been modified to better absorb offset frontal impacts, and the backseat gets a full set of three-point belts. On the outside, all Escapes have reworked front and rear fascias with a new grille design and headlights. Finally, an XLT Sport model joins the lineup.

**Body Styles, Trim Levels and Options:** Only one four-door body style is available with either front-wheel drive or all-wheel drive. Five trim levels are offered: XLS, XLT, XLT Sport, Hybrid and Limited. XLS versions start you out with basic amenities like air conditioning, a CD player and power windows, mirrors and locks. XLT and Hybrid models add 16-inch alloy wheels, a power driver seat, upgraded cloth upholstery, cruise control and an in-dash CD changer. The new XLT Sport versions have two-tone exterior paint, black step bars and machined aluminum wheels. The high-line Limited comes with body-color exterior trim, heated front seats and sideview mirrors, leather upholstery and an auto-dimming rearview mirror.

**Powertrains and Performance:** Standard on the Escape XLS is a 2.3-liter inline four-cylinder engine that makes 153 horsepower and 152 pound-feet of torque. It is matched to either a five-speed manual transmission or a four-speed automatic. There's also the more potent 3.0-liter V6, which makes 200 hp and 193 lb-ft of torque. It is standard on XLT, XLT Sport and Limited models and comes with an automatic transmission only. With this setup, the Escape can tow up to 3,500 pounds. The Escape Hybrid power plant consists of a 2.3-liter gasoline engine and two electric drive motor/generators. The hybrid features an elegantly simple continuously variable "transmission" of sorts, called a power split device. There are no gears to shift, drive belts, torque converter or clutch. The motors work in concert with the gas engine, through a planetary gearset, to provide seamless power and maximum efficiency. Hybrid fuel mileage is rated at 36 city and 31 highway for 2WD, and 33/29 for the 4WD.

**Safety:** ABS is standard on all Escapes, and V6 models have four-wheel disc brakes. A new safety feature is the optional Safety Canopy system that offers full-length head curtain airbag protection in the event of a side-impact collision or rollover. A reverse-sensing system is optional on the Limited. The Escape has done well in government crash testing, earning a perfect five stars for the driver in frontal impacts and four stars for the front passenger. In side-impact crash tests, it received five stars for both front- and rear-seat occupants. Less impressive is the Escape's "Acceptable" rating (the second-highest) in the frontal offset crash test.

**Interior Design and Special Features:** The Escape has never been known for its exciting interior, but for 2005, the cabin gets a few enhancements, including a floor-mounted shifter, new gauges, revised seat cushions and additional storage areas. There is 33 cubic feet of cargo space behind the rear seats, and you can fold them down to open up 65 cubic feet of capacity, a good figure for this class.

**Driving Impressions:** Fun to drive, the Ford Escape offers impressive road manners for a compact SUV. It drives much like a tautly suspended sedan, with little body roll and responsive steering. The V6 is quite powerful, providing swift acceleration, but fuel economy is mediocre. The Hybrid model is just as quick, and returns outstanding fuel mileage.

*Crash Test Scores, see pg 530*
*Warranty information, see pg 542*

### Specifications

| Engine/Drivetrain | HP | Torque | EPA Fuel Economy Rating |
|---|---|---|---|
| 6cyl 3.0L A | 200 | 193 | 20 city/25 hwy |
| 4cyl 2.3L A/M | 153 | 152 | 22 city/25 hwy |
| 4cyl 2.3L A | 133 | 129 | 33 city/29 hwy |

### Body Styles

| Style | MSRP Range |
|---|---|
| Compact SUV | $19,265–$28,005 |

# Ford
# 2005 Ford Excursion
**Large SUV**

**MSRP Price Range**
## $37,165 - $50,420
Destination Charge: $795 (all styles)

## Ratings

| | | |
|---|---|---|
| Consumer Rating | 8.7 | |
| Editors Rating | 6.4 | |

**What Edmunds.com says:** Unless you really need the Excursion's towing ability and huge interior, you're better off with the smaller Expedition or GM's Suburban/Yukon XL twins.

**Pros:** Substantial passenger and cargo capacity, impressive towing ability, diesel engine option.

**Cons:** Unwieldy size, trucklike driving characteristics, poor fuel economy, high sticker price.

**What's New:** Alloy wheels replace chrome steel wheels on XLS models, and the front fascia appearance has been slightly revised.

**Body Styles, Trim Levels and Options:** The four-door Excursion offers eight- or nine-passenger seating with either two- or four-wheel drive. XLS, XLT, Eddie Bauer and Limited trims are available. XLS models come well equipped with a rear air conditioner, cruise, ABS and a front bench seat that gives your rig nine-person seating capacity. XLT versions add power rear-quarter windows, rear audio controls, automatic headlights, a trip computer and front captain's chairs. Eddie Bauer models include special trim, foglights, turn signal sideview mirrors, automatic climate control and power-adjustable pedals. Limited models up the ante with body-color trim, a premium audio system, a reversible cargo mat and heated front seats. A notable option for the XLT, Eddie Bauer and Limited is a DVD-based rear-seat entertainment system. Other options include an in-dash six-disc CD changer for all trim levels except for Limited trim and second-row captain's chairs (available on Eddie Bauer and Limited). We'd recommend that you opt for the reverse-sensing system to help maneuver this behemoth.

**Powertrains and Performance:** Three engines are available on two-wheel-drive and four-wheel-drive Excursions. Standard on all models is a 5.4-liter V8 that makes 255 horsepower at 4,500 rpm and 350 pound-feet of torque at 2,500 rpm. Optional engines include a 6.8-liter V10 or a 6.0-liter turbodiesel V8. The V10 produces 310 hp and 425 lb-ft of torque. The Power Stroke turbodiesel generates 325 hp and 560 lb-ft of torque. All are matched to a four-speed automatic transmission, except the turbodiesel which gets a five-speed automatic. When properly equipped, the Excursion can tow up to 11,000 pounds.

**Safety:** The Excursion comes standard with four-wheel antilock disc brakes. Optional equipment includes power-adjustable foot pedals and a reverse-sensing system. Designed to be as crash-compatible with regular passenger cars as possible, the Excursion includes a Blockbeam at the front of the frame to help dissipate crash energy during a collision with a smaller vehicle. The Excursion hasn't been crash tested by the NHTSA or IIHS.

*Crash Test Scores, see pg 530*
*Warranty information, see pg 542*

**Interior Design and Special Features:** Donated by the Super Duty pickup truck, the rather industrial dashboard of the Excursion prioritizes function over form. Eddie Bauer models dress things up a bit with a two-tone color scheme, while Limiteds get cherrywood trim to jazz up the interior. The Excursion can carry nine passengers in XLS or XLT trim, but all other models are restricted to eight because of the front captain's chairs. Maximum cargo space is 146.4 cubic feet.

**Driving Impressions:** The Excursion is one of the largest vehicles on the road, and as you'd expect, it doesn't take kindly to life in urban areas. Ride quality isn't bad, but GM's full-size SUVs seem downright plush in comparison. Steering feel is vague, so be prepared to make continual corrections to keep the Excursion from drifting into other lanes on the highway. If you can give up the size, the Expedition is a far better daily driver in every respect.

## Specifications

| Engine/Drivetrain | HP | Torque | EPA Fuel Economy Rating |
|---|---|---|---|
| 8cyl 6.0L A | 325 | 560 | N/A |
| 8cyl 5.4L A | 255 | 350 | N/A |
| 10cyl 6.8L A | 310 | 425 | N/A |

## Body Styles

| Style | MSRP Range |
|---|---|
| Large SUV | $37,165–$50,420 |

**MSRP Price Range**

## $31,395 - $43,860

Destination Charge: $795 (all styles)

### Ratings

| | | |
|---|---|---|
| Consumer Rating | 7.0 | |
| Editors Rating | 7.8 | |

**What Edmunds.com says:** Roomy on the inside and agile out on the road, the Expedition is a solid choice among full-size SUVs.

**Pros:** Well-thought-out interior with plenty of room for passengers and their belongings, handy fold-flat third-row seat, impressive handling for its size, great crash test scores.

**Cons:** Poor fuel economy, ride quality suffers on rough roads, some low-grade interior materials.

**What's New:** Various changes for 2005 include revised option packages and trim equipment, a redesigned instrument panel cluster display and a more powerful 5.4L V8. A Limited trim level debuts this year, and includes unique body-color exterior trim, special interior trim and power-adjustable leather seats.

**Body Styles, Trim Levels and Options:** Six trim levels are available: XLS, XLT, XLT Sport, NBX, Eddie Bauer and Limited. The base XLS model is a no-frills workhorse that comes with a front bench seat, CD player, air conditioning, a third-row seat and power-adjustable pedals. The XLT offers most features buyers are looking for including power accessories, a rear air conditioner and other comfort features while the Sport version adds tubular step bars, Shadow Gray exterior trim and a revised grille. The NBX model includes skid plates, off-road shocks, tubular step bars and power-adjustable front captain's chairs. To add even more features, choose the Eddie Bauer model with leather upholstery (optional on XLT models), automatic climate control, a reverse-sensing system and an in-dash six-disc CD changer. The Limited adds unique wheels and exterior trim, eight-way power heated and cooled front seats and copious wood trim. Optional goodies include a load-leveling air suspension, second-row captain's chairs, a CD-based navigation system, a rear DVD entertainment system, a power-folding third-row seat, heated and cooled front seats and tire-pressure monitors.

**Powertrains and Performance:** All Expeditions come standard with a 5.4-liter V8 that makes 301 horsepower and 365 pound-feet of torque. First introduced in the 2004 F-150, this new version of last year's engine is extremely smooth, quiet and rich in midrange torque. A four-speed automatic transmission is standard across the line; all trims are available with either two- or four-wheel drive. A heavy-duty rear differential gives the Expedition a maximum tow rating of 8,900 pounds.

**Safety:** The Expedition received double five-star ratings in front crash tests performed by the NHTSA. All Expeditions come standard with four-wheel antilock disc brakes enhanced with Electronic BrakeAssist and Brakeforce Distribution. Optional safety systems include a tire-pressure monitor system, side- and head-impact protection for first- and second-row passengers and the AdvanceTrac stability control system that was upgraded this year with class-exclusive Roll Stability Control for added protection against rollover accidents.

**Interior Design and Special Features:** Expeditions seat anywhere from seven to nine passengers, depending on whether you go with captain's chairs or bench seats. Sticking with the 40/20/40 second-row bench seat will allow you to scoot the middle section forward for easier access to a little one. The Expedition's 60/40 third-row seat is one of the more comfortable in the full-size SUV class and it folds flat with a quick and easy release handle.

**Driving Impressions:** The Expedition's fully independent suspension and rack and pinion steering system provide solid handling for a vehicle of its size. It still feels like a big SUV, but the excessive body roll and numb steering of previous models are now gone, and overall, it's a comfortable cruiser. The new 5.4-liter engine brings much needed punch that brings it closer in line with its competitors.

*Crash Test Scores, see pg 530*
*Warranty information, see pg 542*

### Specifications

| Engine/Drivetrain | HP | Torque | EPA Fuel Economy Rating |
|---|---|---|---|
| 8cyl 5.4L A | 301 | 365 | 14 city/19 hwy |

### Body Styles

| Style | MSRP Range |
|---|---|
| Large SUV | $31,395–$43,860 |

# 2005 Ford Explorer

**MSRP Price Range**

## $26,770 - $37,530

Destination Charge: $645 (all styles)

## Ratings

| | | |
|---|---|---|
| Consumer Rating | 8.6 | |
| Editors Rating | 7.8 | |

**What Edmunds.com says:** A functional interior, ample passenger space, strong powertrains and a well-controlled ride all contribute to the Explorer's well-deserved reputation as a practical midsize SUV with few faults.

**Pros:** Excellent ride and handling characteristics for a truck-based SUV, strong optional V8, comfortable cabin with user-friendly layout and seating for up to seven, good crash test scores.

**Cons:** Dull cabin design with some low-grade materials, low resale value, confusing controls on high-line models, lousy fuel economy.

**What's New:** For 2005, the Explorer receives minor interior and exterior trim changes, and the AdvanceTrac stability control system is upgraded with roll stability control for better protection against rollover accidents.

Crash Test Scores, see pg 530
Warranty information, see pg 542

## Specifications

| Engine/Drivetrain | HP | Torque | EPA Fuel Economy Rating |
|---|---|---|---|
| 8cyl 4.6L A | 239 | 282 | 15 city/20 hwy |
| 6cyl 4.0L A | 210 | 254 | 15 city/20 hwy |

## Body Styles

| Style | MSRP Range |
|---|---|
| Midsize SUV | $26,770–$37,530 |

**Body Styles, Trim Levels and Options:** The four-door Explorer is available in XLS, XLS Sport, XLT, XLT Sport, NBX, Eddie Bauer and Limited trims. The XLS comes with front bucket seats, air conditioning, cruise control, a CD player, keyless entry and power windows and mirrors. The XLS Sport includes alloy wheels, running boards, wheel lip moldings and an upgraded center console. XLT models get a power driver seat, auto-dimming mirror and automatic headlights, while the XLT Sport adds special platinum gloss exterior trim and 17-inch machine-finished wheels with all-terrain tires. NBX trim includes an off-road package with skid plates and heavier-duty shocks, special exterior badging, unique 17-inch wheels, a Yakima roof rack, rubber floor mats and upgraded cloth upholstery. Eddie Bauer and Limited models come with leather upholstery, seat heaters, a power front-passenger seat, power-adjustable pedals, automatic climate control and an upgraded sound system with an in-dash CD changer. Major options on the Explorer include a third-row seat, rear air conditioner and a rear DVD entertainment system.

**Powertrains and Performance:** The base engine is a 4.0-liter V6 good for 210 horsepower. Optional on all models, except the XLS and XLS Sport, is a 4.6-liter V8 engine good for 239 hp and 282 lb-ft of torque. A five-speed automatic transmission and two-, four- or all-wheel drive are available with either engine. Towing capacity tops out at 7,140 pounds. Fuel economy estimates are 14 to 15 mpg in the city and 19 to 21 mpg on the highway.

**Safety:** Four-wheel antilock disc brakes are standard; the AdvanceTrac stability control system now offers additional rollover protection and is optional on all trims, except XLS and XLS Sport. Any Explorer can be outfitted with the Safety Canopy system that includes front and rear side curtain airbags and a rollover sensor. Power-adjustable pedals are optional on XLT models and standard on the Eddie Bauer and Limited, while a reverse-sensing system can be added to all but the XLS models. In government crash testing, the Explorer received four stars for frontal impacts involving the driver and a perfect five stars for the front passenger. The Ford picked up a "Good" rating (the best possible) in frontal offset testing.

**Interior Design and Special Features:** Depending on the model you choose, the interior trim of the Explorer can range from bland to plush. All the controls are neatly arranged, and the gauges are legible, but it's function over form. It's feasible to carry two adults in the third-row seats, but choosing the third-row option also reduces available cargo space. Seven-passenger Explorers max out at 81.3 cubic feet of cargo space, while five-passenger versions offer a more competitive 88 cubic feet.

**Driving Impressions:** Any Explorer is a joy to drive, as SUVs go. Taking much of the credit for this praise is the rear independent suspension, which provides a smooth ride and keeps the wheels planted on rough pavement. Power from either the V6 or V8 engine is acceptable, though we prefer the added refinement of the V8.

For the latest full vehicle reports, visit www.edmunds.com/bginfopak

# 2005 Ford Explorer Sport Trac

**MSRP Price Range**

## $23,820 - $31,090

Destination Charge: $645 (all styles)

## Ratings

| | | |
|---|---|---|
| Consumer Rating | 9.1 | |
| Editors Rating | 7.1 | |

**What Edmunds.com says:** Part SUV, part truck, the Sport Trac is much better at the former than it is at the latter.

**Pros:** SUV comfort and pickup truck bed convenience, workhorse V6, features galore, available side curtain airbags.

**Cons:** Ancient underpinnings deliver sloppy ride and handling, can't carry as much as a real pickup, subpar off-road ability.

**What's New:** The new model year brings few changes for the Sport Trac. All audio systems now feature MP3 and satellite radio compatibility.

**Body Styles, Trim Levels and Options:** Available with two- or four-wheel drive, the four-door Sport Trac is offered in XLS, XLT, XLT Premium and Adrenalin trim. Base XLS models are well equipped with dark tinted rear glass, roof rails, skid plates (4WD only), air conditioning, power locks and windows and a CD stereo. The XLT adds power side mirrors, remote keyless entry, a leather-wrapped tilt steering wheel, cruise control and carpeted floor mats. The top-line XLT Premium includes monochromatic exterior trim, a six-way power driver seat, power lumbar support for the driver and front passenger, unique alloy wheels and a special center console that features rear audio and climate controls. The Adrenalin version features a 510-watt stereo system, step bars and upgraded wheels, monochromatic paint and unique "Adrenalin" badges. Other available options offered on the Sport Trac include an in-dash six-disc CD changer, a cargo cage/bed extender and a moonroof.

**Powertrains and Performance:** The only engine available in the Explorer Sport Trac is a 4.0-liter single-overhead cam V6 making 210 horsepower at 5,250 rpm and 240 pound-feet of torque at 3,000 rpm. A five-speed automatic transmission is standard on all models. Shift-on-the-fly four-wheel drive is optional. Towing capacity is 5,300 pounds.

**Safety:** Four-wheel antilock disc brakes are standard on all Sport Tracs. An optional Safety Canopy system provides head curtain airbag protection for the both front and rear passengers in a rollover accident, as well as certain side-impact collisions. Child safety-seat anchors are provided for the rear seats along with safety locks for the rear doors.

**Interior Design and Special Features:** Based on the previous-generation Explorer's dash design, and sharing many interior features with the Ranger pickup, the Sport Trac received minor interior upgrades for 2004 including a revised gauge cluster. The interior is similar in size to the newest compact crew cab pickups, allowing the Sport Trac to accommodate four adults in relative comfort. Audiophiles will want to check out the Adrenalin model that features a 510-watt, nine-speaker audio system.

**Driving Impressions:** Athletic the Sport Trac is not. Its ride quality is decent, but otherwise the soft suspension makes the truck feel floaty when driving around corners. Unlike the current-generation Explorer, the Sport Trac is stuck with a low-tech rear suspension that leads to a jarring ride when driving over bumps. Off pavement, the Sport Trac is a poor performer thanks to low-hanging components that frequently scrape over rocky terrain. Although it won't win any awards for refinement, the stout V6 delivers strong low and midrange power.

*Crash Test Scores, see pg 530*
*Warranty information, see pg 542*

## Specifications

| Engine/Drivetrain | HP | Torque | EPA Fuel Economy Rating |
|---|---|---|---|
| 6cyl 4.0L A | 210 | 242 | 16 city/21 hwy |

## Body Styles

| Style | MSRP Range |
|---|---|
| Crew Cab Pickup Truck | $23,820–$31,090 |

# 2005 Ford F-150

**MSRP Price Range**

## $19,800 - $36,065

Destination Charge: $795 (all styles)

### Ratings

| | | |
|---|---|---|
| Consumer Rating | 9.3 | |
| Editors Rating | 8.0 | |

**What Edmunds.com says:** A class leader when it comes to ride and handling, the F-150 is dragged down by its excessive weight and lack of key safety features.

**Pros:** Exceptional ride and handling characteristics, attractive and functional interior designs, multiple cab and bed configurations, the most payload and towing capacity in the half-ton class.

**Cons:** Feels sluggish even with larger V8, no available side airbags, not much interior storage space.

**What's New:** New packages this year include a Work Truck Group with argent bumpers and a vinyl bench seat, and a King Ranch Group with exclusive interior and exterior trim. A 4.2-liter V6 has been added as the base engine, along with a five-speed manual transmission.

*Crash Test Scores, see pg 530*
*Warranty information, see pg 542*

### Specifications

| Engine/Drivetrain | HP | Torque | EPA Fuel Economy Rating |
|---|---|---|---|
| 8cyl 5.4L A | 300 | 365 | 15 city/19 hwy |
| 8cyl 4.6L A | 231 | 293 | 15 city/19 hwy |
| 6cyl 4.2L M | 202 | 260 | 15 city/20 hwy |

### Body Styles

| Style | MSRP Range |
|---|---|
| Crew Cab Pickup Truck | $29,580–$36,065 |
| Extended Cab Pickup Truck | $24,475–$33,640 |
| Regular Cab Pickup Truck | $19,800–$31,145 |

**Body Styles, Trim Levels and Options:** The F-150 is available in three body styles (regular cab, extended cab and crew cab), three bed lengths (five-and-a-half-foot, six-and-a-half-foot and eight-foot) and five different trim levels (XL, STX, XLT, FX4 and Lariat). Both regular and extended cab trucks come standard with reverse-opening rear doors for easier cab access, while the crew cab features forward-hinged full-size doors. The base XL is your standard work truck with a vinyl or cloth interior and minimal amenities. The STX is similarly equipped but adds body-colored bumpers, sportier wheels and a few additional features, such as a stepside bed and an upgraded sound system. The volume leader in the lineup is the midgrade XLT, as it offers the widest array of available options, as well as an upgraded interior. The FX4 is geared toward off-road enthusiasts as it includes underbody skid plates, retuned springs and heavy-duty shocks, as well as 18-inch wheels and an upgraded interior. Top-of-the-line Lariat models cater to buyers looking for an upscale look and feel with interior features like brushed aluminum and wood highlights, optional leather heated seats, satellite steering wheel controls, white-faced gauges and automatic climate control. Exterior details include two-tone paint, chrome bumpers and 18-inch aluminum wheels.

**Powertrains and Performance:** There are three engine choices: the standard 4.2-liter V6, a 4.6-liter V8 and an optional 5.4-liter V8. The 4.2-liter V6 makes 202 horsepower and 260 pound-feet of torque. The 4.6-liter engine provides 231 hp and 293 lb-ft of torque, while the 5.4-liter V8 produces 300 hp and 365 lb-ft of torque. Both V8 engines are matched to four-speed automatic transmissions, with the 5.4-liter engine getting a heavy-duty version to handle its increased power output. The V6 gets a standard five-speed manual. Maximum towing capacity is 9,900 pounds.

**Safety:** All F-150s include Ford's personal safety system that combines multistage airbags, seatbelt pre-tensioners and seat position sensors to achieve the best possible protection based on crash severity. Antilock brakes are also standard across the board, and adjustable pedals are available as an option. Unlike some of its competitors, the F-150 does not offer side airbags or electronic stability control. Frontal impact testing by the NHTSA resulted in a perfect five-star rating. In offset-frontal crash testing conducted by the IIHS, the F-150 earned a rating of "Good," the highest available, and a "Best Pick" designation.

**Interior Design and Special Features:** FX4 and Lariat models with bucket seats use a floor-mounted shifter while all other configurations have a standard column shifter. An optional overhead console uses interchangeable modules so owners can add whatever features they find most useful. Regular cab models have handy reverse-opening access doors for getting to the storage area behind the seat.

**Driving Impressions:** Thanks to a stiff frame and rack and pinion steering, the F-150 delivers impressive ride and handling for a truck. Excessive weight bogs down the 4.2-liter V6 and 4.6-liter V8 engines, so upgrading to the 5.4-liter V8 is a must.

# 2005 Ford F-250 Super Duty

**MSRP Price Range**

## $22,570 - $36,780
Destination Charge: $795 (all styles)

### Ratings

| | | |
|---|---|---|
| Consumer Rating | 8.8 | |
| Editors Rating | 7.8 | |

**What Edmunds.com says:** Class-leading payload and towing capacity and a wide variety of configurations and special-edition models help make the aging Super Duty a viable option for those who need a hard-core pickup civilized enough for everyday use.

**Pros:** Rugged construction, multiple configurations, competent off-road capabilities, high towing and payload capacities, diesel leads the class in power and fuel economy.

**Cons:** Noisy drivetrains, gas engines' poor mileage, vague steering, spotty build quality.

**What's New:** Among the changes for 2005 are a new front suspension for improved handling, a standard TorqueShift five-speed automatic transmission on all models and increased towing and hauling capacities across the board. The Harley-Davidson edition package sees minor cosmetic upgrades.

**Body Styles, Trim Levels and Options:** The Super Duty comes in Regular Cab, SuperCab and Crew Cab body styles. SuperCab models have small rear-opening doors, while the Crew Cab has four full-size swing-out doors. A plethora of optional equipment is available, including electronic shift-on-the-fly four-wheel drive, a heavy-duty suspension package and telescoping trailer-towing mirrors. To match your desired level of opulence, there are three trim levels available: XL, XLT and Lariat. XL models are work trucks, and as such come with a vinyl bench seat in front, manual windows, mirrors and locks, a basic AM/FM radio and no air conditioner. The XLT adds cloth upholstery, a 40/20/40 front bench, air conditioning, a CD player and a full set of power controls. High-line Lariats come with leather upholstery, a power driver seat and keyless entry.

**Powertrains and Performance:** The F-250 offers three different engines. The base engine is a 5.4-liter V8 that generates 300 horsepower and 365 pound-feet of torque. An optional 6.8-liter V10 generates 355 hp and 455 lb-ft of torque. A six-speed manual is standard with these engines, but a five-speed automatic is also available. The best choice for those who do serious towing and hauling, though, is the 6.0-liter Power Stroke diesel V8 rated at 325 hp and 570 lb-ft. The diesel is mated to a five-speed automatic with a specially tuned tow-haul mode and newly revised programming. Properly equipped, an F-250 can tow up to 15,000 pounds.

**Safety:** Four-wheel disc brakes with ABS are standard. The Super Duty also offers power-adjustable pedals. As of yet, there is no NHTSA or IIHS crash test data on the Super Duties.

**Interior Design and Special Features:** On the inside, the Super Duty trucks look much like their half-ton counterparts. The seats are comfortable and supportive, but the base grade upholstery feels a little downmarket. Everything else is covered in hard gray plastic, and while the fit of the panels is mediocre, it will probably hold up pretty well under extreme working conditions. Five or six adults can ride inside with little problem as long as you choose the SuperCab or Crew Cab body. In addition, there are many interior convenience features designed for today's business owners. For example, a fold-down armrest and utility bin are designed to house a portable fax machine or laptop computer.

**Driving Impressions:** The F-250 is actually quite civil on the highway, as it soaks up heavy ruts and bumps with ease while providing a quiet ride. The new coil spring suspension and large-diameter wheels have reinvigorated the platform, as handling is now crisp and precise on the open road or on tighter city streets. The steering can still feel a little vague, though, so some extra attention is required to keep the big truck headed in the right direction. The Power Stroke diesel provides incredible power, and even with a 15,000-pound trailer hitched to the back, acceleration is smooth and linear thanks to its broad power curve.

*Crash Test Scores, see pg 530*
*Warranty information, see pg 542*

### Specifications

| Engine/Drivetrain | HP | Torque | EPA Fuel Economy Rating |
|---|---|---|---|
| 8cyl 5.4L M | 300 | 365 | N/A |

### Body Styles

| Style | MSRP Range |
|---|---|
| Crew Cab Pickup Truck | $26,165–$36,780 |
| Extended Cab Pickup Truck | $24,755–$34,135 |
| Regular Cab Pickup Truck | $22,570–$28,915 |

# 2005 Ford F-350 Super Duty

**MSRP Price Range**

## $23,315 - $38,645

Destination Charge: $795 (all styles)

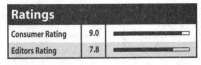

## Ratings

| | | |
|---|---|---|
| Consumer Rating | 9.0 | |
| Editors Rating | 7.8 | |

**What Edmunds.com says:** Class-leading payload and towing capacity along with a wide variety of configurations and special-edition models make the aging Super Duty a viable option for those who need a hard-core pickup civilized enough for everyday use.

**Pros:** Rugged construction, multiple configurations, competent off-road capabilities, high towing and payload capacities, diesel leads the class in power and fuel economy.

**Cons:** Noisy drivetrains, gas engines' poor mileage, vague steering, spotty build quality.

**What's New:** The F-350 benefits from a new front suspension for improved handling, a standard TorqShift five-speed automatic on all trims, and increased towing and hauling capacities increased across the board. The Harley-Davidson edition package sports cosmetic revisions this year.

**Body Styles, Trim Levels and Options:** The Super Duty comes in Regular Cab, SuperCab and Crew Cab body styles. SuperCab models have small rear-opening doors, while the Crew Cab has four full-size swing-out doors. A plethora of optional equipment is available, including electronic shift-on-the-fly four-wheel drive, a heavy-duty suspension package and telescoping trailer-towing mirrors. To match your desired level of opulence, there are three trim levels available: XL, XLT and Lariat. XL models are work trucks, and as such come with a vinyl bench seat in front; manual windows, mirrors and locks; a basic AM/FM radio; and no air conditioner. The XLT adds cloth upholstery, a 40/20/40 front bench, air conditioning, a CD player and a full set of power controls. High-line Lariats come with leather upholstery, a power driver seat and keyless entry.

**Powertrains and Performance:** The F-350 offers three different engines. The base engine is a 5.4-liter V8 that generates 300 horsepower and 365 pound-feet of torque. An optional 6.8-liter V10 generates 355 hp and 455 lb-ft of torque. A six-speed manual is standard with these engines, but a five-speed automatic with a tow-haul mode is also available. The best choice for those who do serious towing and hauling, though, is the 6.0-liter Power Stroke diesel rated at 325 hp and 570 lb-ft. The diesel is mated to the five-speed automatic only. Properly equipped, an F-250 can tow up to 15,000 pounds.

**Safety:** Four-wheel disc brakes with ABS are standard. The Super Duty also offers power-adjustable pedals. As of yet, there is no NHTSA or IIHS crash test data on the Super Duties.

**Interior Design and Special Features:** Inside, the roomy cabs have large, comfortable seats and generous seat-track travel. Five or six adults can ride inside with little problem as long as you choose the SuperCab or Crew Cab body. In addition, there are many interior convenience features designed for today's business owners. For example, a fold-down armrest and utility bin are designed to house a portable fax machine or laptop computer. Materials quality is nothing special, as the base grade upholstery feels a little downmarket while the dash and door panels are covered in hard gray plastic. The leather upholstery in the Lariat is nice enough, but the Harley Davidson and King Ranch packages provide even richer hides.

Crash Test Scores, see pg 530
Warranty information, see pg 542

## Specifications

| Engine/Drivetrain | HP | Torque | EPA Fuel Economy Rating |
|---|---|---|---|
| 8cyl 5.4L M | 300 | 365 | N/A |
| 10cyl 6.8L M | 362 | 457 | N/A |

## Body Styles

| Style | MSRP Range |
|---|---|
| Crew Cab Pickup Truck | $27,115–$38,645 |
| Extended Cab Pickup Truck | $25,835–$36,125 |
| Regular Cab Pickup Truck | $23,315–$30,840 |

**Driving Impressions:** The F-350 is actually quite civil on the highway, as it soaks up heavy ruts and bumps with ease. The new coil spring front suspension and large-diameter wheels have reinvigorated the platform, as handling is now crisp and precise on the open road or on tighter city streets. The steering is still pretty vague, however, so extra attention is required to keep the truck centered at highway speeds. The PowerStroke provides incredible power, and even with a 15,000-pound trailer hitched to the back, acceleration is smooth and linear thanks to the diesel's broad power curve. On the inside, the Super Duty trucks look much like their half-ton counterparts. Out on the road, the cabin is quiet and rattle-free.

For the latest full vehicle reports, visit www.edmunds.com/bginfopak

**Large Sedan**

# 2005 Ford Five Hundred

**MSRP Price Range**
## $22,145 - $27,845
Destination Charge: $650 (all styles)

### Ratings

| | | |
|---|---|---|
| Consumer Rating | 9.7 | |
| Editors Rating | 8.0 | |

**What Edmunds.com says:** Roomy, stylish and practical, the Five Hundred is well suited for family duty, but with its mediocre engine performance and interior materials, it's simply one of many solid choices in the under-$30,000 price bracket.

**Pros:** Spacious cabin, huge trunk, smooth ride quality, available all-wheel drive, plenty of safety features.

**Cons:** Mediocre engine performance, some low-grade interior materials, no stability control.

**What's New:** The Five Hundred is an all-new premium family sedan built on the Volvo S80 platform. Both front- and all-wheel-drive versions are available.

**Body Styles, Trim Levels and Options:** The Five Hundred sedan is available in one of three trims: SE, SEL and Limited. The SE starts you out with 17-inch wheels, a six-way power driver seat, full power accessories, air conditioning, a CD player and cruise control. The SEL adds an eight-way power driver seat, dual-zone automatic climate control, a leather-wrapped steering wheel, wood interior trim, an MP3-compatible in-dash CD changer, a fold-flat front-passenger seat, extra sound insulation and adjustable head restraints and air registers for rear passengers. Step up to the Limited and you'll get 18-inch wheels, leather upholstery, a four-way power passenger seat, seat memory, an upgraded audio system, cream-faced gauges and an analog clock. Options include a moonroof, adjustable pedals and a reverse-sensing system.

**Powertrains and Performance:** Every Five Hundred comes with Ford's 3.0-liter Duratec V6 rated for 203 horsepower and 207 pound-feet of torque. Buyers have two transmission choices. The first of these is a continuously variable transmission (CVT), which has an infinite number of ratios and chooses whichever one best fits a given situation. The other option is a six-speed automatic. Buyers must also decide between front-wheel drive and all-wheel drive. Front-drive SE models and all AWD models come with the CVT. Front-drive SELs and Limiteds get the six-speed automatic.

**Safety:** All Five Hundreds come with a full set of disc brakes, ABS and Electronic Brakeforce Distribution. Optional on all models are side-impact airbags that protect front occupants' torsos and side curtain airbags that protect the heads of front and rear occupants. Traction control is standard, but stability control is not available. This car has not yet been crash tested.

**Interior Design and Special Features:** Scrutinize the cabin and it's apparent that designers put a lot of thought into creating an attractive and functional environment. In lieu of the shapeless dash and seats found in the Taurus, the Five Hundred has the crisp, clean lines popularized by Volkswagen's Passat. The front seats are roomy enough to fit most drivers, yet the cockpit has a snug, almost intimate feel. Rear passengers are treated to equally spacious quarters, making these cars good bets for families with teenagers. The rear seats fold flat in a 60/40-split and this, along with the fold-flat front-passenger seat, allows owners to transport items up to nine feet in length. Trunk capacity leads all sedans on the market at 21 cubic feet.

**Driving Impressions:** The V6 provides enough low-end torque for easy city driving, and the car gets up to speed with minimal fuss. We do expect that eventual owners will wish for a little extra midrange torque for passing at highway speeds and climbing grades. Of the two transmissions, our preference is the CVT, which does a better job of keeping the engine in its power band. Thanks to its Volvo-engineered chassis, the Five Hundred offers a pleasant balance between smooth ride quality and responsive handling. It's not the car to buy if you're looking for entertainment, but if you just want something capable and comfortable, the Five Hundred should satisfy.

*Crash Test Scores, see pg 530*
*Warranty information, see pg 542*

### Specifications

| Engine/Drivetrain | HP | Torque | EPA Fuel Economy Rating |
|---|---|---|---|
| 6cyl 3.0L A | 203 | 207 | 21 city/29 hwy |

### Body Styles

| Style | MSRP Range |
|---|---|
| Large Sedan | $22,145–$27,845 |

# Ford

# 2005 Ford Focus

### Compact Coupe, Sedan, Wagon

**MSRP Price Range**

## $13,230 - $18,130

Destination Charge: $545 (all styles)

## Ratings

| | | |
|---|---|---|
| Consumer Rating | 9.2 | |
| Editors Rating | 7.7 | |

**What Edmunds.com says:** The Focus is a wonderful small car that's fun to drive, frugal with fuel and offered in such a wide variety of configurations it would be hard not to find one that suits your needs.

**Pros:** Spacious and comfortable interior, fun-to-drive character, sharp steering, smooth ride, impressive selection of body configurations and features.

**Cons:** Generic interior styling, performance-bargain 2.3-liter engine now limited to ST sedan, can't match competitors' records for quality and reliability.

**What's New:** The new model year ushers in some significant changes for the Focus. Exteriors have been updated with revised fascias and trim, and the car's oddball interior design has been replaced by more sedate and sophisticated furnishings. Last year's diverse engine lineup has been scrapped in favor of an all-new PZEV-rated 2.0-liter power plant good for 136 horsepower. A performance-oriented ST sedan has been added to take the place of the discontinued SVT Focus hatchbacks; it features a 151-hp incarnation of last year's excellent 2.3-liter PZEV engine. The 2.3-liter loses its squeaky-clean PZEV rating, however. In other news, the typically confusing array of trim levels and packages has been organized into logical and consistent trim lines, standardized across all body styles. New audio systems, increased interior storage and tweaked suspension tuning round out this year's midcycle makeover.

*Crash Test Scores, see pg 530*
*Warranty information, see pg 542*

## Specifications

| Engine/Drivetrain | HP | Torque | EPA Fuel Economy Rating |
|---|---|---|---|
| 4cyl 2.3L M | 151 | 154 | 22 city/31 hwy |
| 4cyl 2.0L M | 136 | 133 | 26 city/35 hwy |

## Body Styles

| Style | MSRP Range |
|---|---|
| Compact Coupe | $13,230–$17,130 |
| Compact Sedan | $13,830–$17,930 |
| Compact Wagon | $17,030–$18,130 |

**Body Styles, Trim Levels and Options:** Ford offers the Focus in four body styles: a three-door ZX3 hatchback, a five-door ZX5 hatchback, a ZX4 sedan and a ZXW wagon. The hatchbacks and sedan come in three basic trim levels—S, SE and SES—while the wagon is available in SE and SES trims only. Additionally, an ST sedan is available for buyers seeking a sportier Focus. The S includes basics like a CD player, 15-inch steel wheels and black exterior trim. The SE adds upgraded suspension tuning; power windows, locks and mirrors; keyless entry; air conditioning; a CD/MP3 player; and an overhead console. The uplevel SES includes 16-inch alloy wheels, foglamps, body-color exterior trim, a CD/MP3 changer, cruise control, tachometer and a tilt/telescoping steering wheel. The top-line ST sedan adds four-wheel disc brakes with ABS and traction control, a performance-tuned suspension, sport seats and distinctive trim inside and out.

**Powertrains and Performance:** The standard drivetrain in hatchbacks, wagons and all sedans except the ST is a refined 2.0-liter four-cylinder rated for 136 hp (130 in California emissions states). The ST sedan features a 2.3-liter four good for 151 hp. A five-speed manual transmission is standard across the line, and a four-speed automatic is optional on all but the base S ZX3 hatchback and the ST sedan. Fuel economy is average for this class, as both engines have EPA mileage ratings in the mid-to-upper 20s for city driving and mid-30s for highway travel.

**Safety:** All models come with advanced dual-stage front airbags, seatbelt pre-tensioners for front occupants and three-point belts in all five seating positions. Optional safety equipment includes side airbags, antilock brakes and traction control (standard on the ST). In NHTSA crash testing, both the hatchback and sedan did well in all tests with the exception of rear side impacts where the ZX3 received only one star. In frontal offset testing (conducted by the IIHS), the Focus earned a "Good" score, the highest possible.

**Interior Design and Special Features:** he Focus is roomy for its class, offering generous accommodations for its front and rear passengers, even in three-door ZX3 models. Though ergonomically sound, the interior design in the 2005 version lacks the panache of previous Focus models. Buyers seeking a more sedate cabin environment may find it to their liking, however. Sound quality from the stock audio systems is surprisingly good, and downright exceptional with the optional Audiophile system. The ST's sport seats are quite comfy, and the unique interior trim is certainly eye-catching.

**Driving Impressions:** Regardless of trim, the Focus offers a smooth ride and above-average handling. Although the four-wheel fully independent suspension allows for noticeable body roll while cornering, the Focus stays planted and inspires confidence. The steering system is surprisingly quick, fluid and responsive, always providing plenty of feedback from the road surface. If you're looking for a comfortable economy car that still knows how to have a good time, you might be surprised by how well the Focus satisfies your needs.

# 2005 Ford Freestar

**MSRP Price Range**

## $21,610 - $32,710
Destination Charge: $685 (all styles)

### Ratings

| | | |
|---|---|---|
| Consumer Rating | 9.1 | |
| Editors Rating | 6.5 | |

**What Edmunds.com says:** The Freestar has all the right safety features, but with better appointed, more refined minivans available from Chrysler, Honda, Nissan, Toyota and even Kia, it ultimately doesn't measure up.

**Pros:** Plenty of safety features, upscale looks inside and out, roomy interior, dealers' willingness to discount.

**Cons:** Unrefined powertrains with less horsepower and worse fuel mileage than most competitors, low-grade interior materials, hard-to-remove second-row seats, can't get a navigation system.

**What's New:** For 2005 trim levels have been renamed and package content has been slightly refined. A lift-gate spoiler is available on the SES, and Class I and Class II towing packages are available on all models.

**Body Styles, Trim Levels and Options:** The Freestar is available in five trim levels—S, SE, SES, SEL and Limited. S models start you out with ABS, a second-row bench seat, a fold-flat third-row seat, air conditioning, keyless entry and power windows and locks. The SE adds a CD player, cruise control and privacy glass. Step up to the SES and you get a rear air conditioner, a power driver seat, foglamps and a unique exterior appearance package. The SEL provides second-row captain's chairs, rear-seat audio controls, audio controls on the steering wheel and luxury-oriented chrome exterior trim. Finally, the top-line Limited offers upgraded interior trim with leather upholstery, automatic climate control and two-tone paint.

**Powertrains and Performance:** Two engines are available. The base 3.9-liter V6 produces an adequate 193 horsepower, while offering a healthy 240 pound-feet of torque. An available large-displacement 4.2-liter V6 makes just 202 hp, but offers 263 lb-ft of torque. Both engines are torque-rich and deliver adequate power for most situations, but they tend to run out of breath at higher speeds. A four-speed automatic is standard on all models. Either V6 can get 23 mpg during highway travel, but city mileage is unimpressive, rating just 17 mpg with the 3.9-liter and 16 mpg with the 4.2-liter.

**Safety:** Four-wheel antilock disc brakes with Electronic Brakeforce Distribution are standard on all Freestars. Available safety features include side curtain airbags that span all three rows of seating, and the AdvanceTrac stability and traction control system, which now incorporates a panic brake assist feature. The Windstar earned five stars across the board in government crash tests, and picked up a "Good" rating (the highest), as well as a "Best Pick" designation, in 40-mph frontal offset crash testing by the IIHS.

**Interior Design and Special Features:** Ford designers have equipped the Freestar with a shapely dash and steering wheel, and attractive materials—the result is a much more refined, classier-looking minivan. Unfortunately, materials quality is still below average in this segment. While the cabin dimensions are basically the same as those of the Windstar, the addition of a fold-flat third-row seat allows for more flexible use of the available space (although the seat folds only as a single piece, rather than allowing a 60/40-split). Legroom in the second row can be tight for adults and children alike, and the seats themselves are hard to remove when you need to make way for cargo.

**Driving Impressions:** The Freestar meets the minimum requirements of most minivan buyers: It provides adequate power and a comfortable ride. It's heavier than most minivans and therefore isn't as adept when negotiating corners and freeway entrance ramps. Either engine offers enough power for easy around-town travel, but their vigor diminishes during highway passing maneuvers. Neither one scores well in the refinement department, as they're noisier than most other six-cylinder motors in this segment.

*Crash Test Scores, see pg 530*
*Warranty information, see pg 542*

### Specifications

| Engine/Drivetrain | HP | Torque | EPA Fuel Economy Rating |
|---|---|---|---|
| 6cyl 4.2L A | 202 | 263 | 18 city/23 hwy |
| 6cyl 3.9L A | 193 | 240 | 18 city/23 hwy |

### Body Styles

| Style | MSRP Range |
|---|---|
| Midsize Minivan | $21,610–$32,710 |

**Ford**

# 2005 Ford Freestyle

**Midsize Wagon**

**MSRP Price Range**

## $24,945 - $30,245

Destination Charge: $650 (all styles)

## Ratings

| | | |
|---|---|---|
| Consumer Rating | 9.6 | |
| Editors Rating | 8.2 | |

**What Edmunds.com says:** With truly comfortable accommodations for six passengers, plenty of cargo space and refined driving dynamics, the Freestyle has everything going for it except power.

**Pros:** Truly roomy seating for six passengers, plenty of cargo space, balanced ride and handling characteristics, lengthy list of safety features.

**Cons:** So-so acceleration, some low-grade interior materials, no stability control or navigation system.

**What's New:** The Freestyle is an all-new crossover wagon from Ford. Built on a Volvo platform, it incorporates the Swedish brand's safety and all-wheel-drive technology, while offering six- to seven-passenger seating capacity.

*Crash Test Scores, see pg 530*
*Warranty information, see pg 542*

## Specifications

| Engine/Drivetrain | HP | Torque | EPA Fuel Economy Rating |
|---|---|---|---|
| 6cyl 3.0L A | 203 | 207 | 20 city/27 hwy |

## Body Styles

| Style | MSRP Range |
|---|---|
| Midsize Wagon | $24,945–$30,245 |

**Body Styles, Trim Levels and Options:** The Freestyle comes in three trims—SE, SEL and Limited. The SE comes 17-inch alloy wheels, privacy glass, seating for six, air conditioning, a CD player, a six-way power driver seat, full power accessories and cruise control. The midgrade SEL adds an MP3-compatible in-dash CD changer, a leather-wrapped steering wheel with auxiliary audio controls, automatic headlights, foglights, heated side mirrors, an auto-dimming rearview mirror, a trip computer, extra sound insulation and body-color door handles and mirrors. If you go for the Limited, you'll get 18-inch wheels, leather upholstery in the first and second rows, wood grain interior trim, dual-zone automatic climate control, an upgraded sound system, power adjustments for both front seats (along with memory for the driver), front seat heaters, 50/50-split capability for the third-row bench and a cargo net. Note that SE and SEL models come with two-tone exterior paint, while the Limited gets a monochromatic paint job. Options include power-adjustable pedals, a three-person bench seat for the second row (provides seven-passenger capacity) and reverse parking sensors.

**Powertrains and Performance:** All Freestyles come with the most updated version of Ford's 3.0-liter Duratec V6, which now includes electronic throttle control. Horsepower comes in at 203, while torque measures 207 pound-feet. A continuously variable transmission (CVT) is standard. Buyers can choose between front-wheel drive and all-wheel drive.

**Safety:** Four-wheel antilock disc brakes with Electronic Brakeforce Distribution are standard, as is traction control. Stability control is not available. On the options list, you'll find both side-impact airbags (for the front) and head curtain airbags (for all three rows). The Freestyle has not yet been crash tested.

**Interior Design and Special Features:** Depending on whether you select captain's chairs or a 60/40 bench seat in the second row, the Freestyle can seat six or seven passengers. The second row offers enough legroom to seat both adults and children comfortably. The captain's chairs can be adjusted fore and aft to provide more room for third-row passengers, but the 60/40 bench seat is nonadjustable. Third-row legroom is adequate when the second-row seats are in the all-the-way-back position and generous when the captain's chairs are scooted up. A deep cargo well provides a good deal of space for groceries, even when all three rows of seating are in use. When you need more room, both the second- and third-row seats fold flat into the floor.

**Driving Impressions:** Acceleration is acceptable for the most part, as the Freestyle has little difficulty getting up to highway speeds. However, we expect that owners will wish for a little more juice for passing maneuvers, especially when the vehicle is loaded up with passengers and gear. Ride dynamics are excellent, as the wagon's fully independent suspension delivers a smooth, refined ride quality and responsive handling in the corners.

**MSRP Price Range**
## $139,995
Destination Charge: $1250 (all styles)

### Ratings

| | | |
|---|---|---|
| Consumer Rating | 9.1 | ████████████ |
| Editors Rating | 7.1 | ████████ |

**What Edmunds.com says:** As a 21st-century update to an American racing legend, the GT succeeds because of its timeless design, world-class performance and relatively low price.

**Pros:** World-class performance, striking looks, easy-going nature, a theoretical bargain (if you can get one at MSRP).

**Cons:** Awkward entry/exit procedure, some interior materials don't live up to MSRP, seats could provide more lateral support.

**What's New:** The Ford GT is an all-new supercar that pays homage to the original GT40 that dominated international sports car racing in the mid- to late-1960s. It will be produced in limited numbers (approximately 3,500 units over a two-year production run) and offer performance on par with the world's most exclusive—and expensive—supercars.

**Body Styles, Trim Levels and Options:** The Ford GT is a midengine, two-seat sports car available in a single trim. The chassis is constructed of aluminum and rides on a double wishbone suspension, front and rear. The exterior body panels are constructed of super-plastic-formed aluminum, and the vehicle rolls on 18-inch front, 19-inch rear wheels. Standard equipment includes air conditioning, power windows, antilock brakes and an AM/FM/CD audio system. Options are limited, but include an upgraded McIntosh audio system with a four-channel amplifier and single-slot CD player. Other options, such as BBS forged aluminum wheels, red or gray painted brake calipers and a full-length racing stripe (or side stripe delete option) allow buyers a bit of personalization when ordering their GT.

**Powertrains and Performance:** A hand-built, all-aluminum 5.4-liter V8 powers the GT. It makes a total of 550 hp at 6,500 rpm with the help of a Lysholm supercharger and intercooler. Peak torque is 500 pound-feet at 3,750 rpm. The engine is hooked to a six-speed Ricardo manual transmission, no automatic or sequential manual transmission is offered. The GT's combination of horsepower, torque and 315/40 series rear tires allows the car to slingshot to 60 mph in around 3.5 seconds and shred the quarter-mile in well under 12 seconds.

**Safety:** Antilock brakes are standard, but stability control and traction control are unavailable on the Ford GT. The passenger seat includes both a child seat tether and ISOFIX mounting hardware. High-intensity discharge headlights are standard.

**Interior Design and Special Features:** The interior is a combination of retro design and advanced materials. The wide gauge cluster, metal shift knob and large toggle switches pay homage to the car's 40-year history, but the magnesium center console with illuminated climate controls offers a futuristic twist. The carbon-fiber seats, center-mounted tachometer and supercharged engine, as seen through the cabin's rear glass, are clear indicators of the Ford GT's primary purpose. A large, red button is used to fire the 550-hp V8.

**Driving Impressions:** While rear visibility and the entry/exit process are typical of an exotic car, the GT's on-road behavior is closer to a Corvette in terms of drivability and ease of use. The clutch pedal and shifter operates smoothly, the steering provides excellent feedback without unnecessary heaviness, and the engine remains docile when idling through slow-moving traffic. Conversely, when driven like a racecar, either at a track or on open roads, the Ford GT provides the kind of stability and confidence that makes other exotics feel nervous and unsure. Everything happens in a smooth, progressive manner, giving the GT an advantage over its direct competitors and making it competitive with cars costing three-to-four times as much.

*Crash Test Scores, see pg 530*
*Warranty information, see pg 542*

### Specifications

| Engine/Drivetrain | HP | Torque | EPA Fuel Economy Rating |
|---|---|---|---|
| 8cyl 5.4L M | 550 | 500 | 13 city/21 hwy |

### Body Styles

| Style | MSRP Range |
|---|---|
| Compact Coupe | $139,995 |

# 2005 Ford Mustang

**MSRP Price Range**

## $18,785 - $25,705

Destination Charge: $625 (all styles)

### Ratings

| | | |
|---|---|---|
| Consumer Rating | 9.3 | |
| Editors Rating | 8.2 | |

**What Edmunds.com says:** Not merely a retro reskinning, the newest Mustang improves its performance in all areas and offers V8 enthusiasts a tempting price tag.

**Pros:** Solid V8 power in GT models, about as well mannered as a solid axle suspension can get, slick retro interior, much improved cabin ergonomics.

**Cons:** No side curtain airbags or stability control, seats could use more lateral support.

**What's New:** The Mustang is completely redesigned for 2005.

**Body Styles, Trim Levels and Options:** Two body styles, coupe and convertible, and four major trim levels are available for the Mustang—V6 Deluxe, V6 Premium, GT Deluxe and GT Premium. Standard equipment on V6 Deluxe includes keyless entry; 16-inch alloy wheels; air conditioning; power windows, locks and mirrors; cruise control; and a CD player. The V6 Premium adds a 500-watt Shaker 500 premium audio system, upgraded wheels, a power driver seat and, on convertibles, leather seating. The GT Deluxe includes the V6 Deluxe equipment, plus antilock brakes, foglamps, 17-inch alloys, sport seats with driver six-way power adjustment and a leather-wrapped steering wheel. The GT Premium adds the Shaker 500 sound system and leather seats. Interesting options include a Shaker 1000 sound system with nine speakers and 1,000 watts of power, and an interior upgrade package with metallic accents, dark charcoal Aberdeen pattern door panel inserts and instruments with changeable backlighting—at the press of a button one can select from white, blue, green and orange hues.

**Powertrains and Performance:** Powertrains and Performance: V6 Mustangs include a 4.0-liter V6 with 210 horsepower and 240 lb-ft of torque. Step up to the GT and you'll get a 4.6-liter V8 with 300 hp and 320 lb-ft of torque, three valves per cylinder and variable valve timing. All Mustangs are rear-drive, and can be equipped with either a five-speed manual or a five-speed automatic transmission.

**Safety:** Four-wheel disc brakes are standard on all Mustangs. Antilock brakes and traction control are optional on the V6 models and standard on the GT. A stability control system is not offered. Side-impact airbags for front occupants are optional on all models, but full-length head curtain airbags are not available. The Mustang has not yet been crash tested.

**Interior Design and Special Features:** Interior ergonomics are vastly improved over the previous Mustang. Switches and handles feel substantial, and overall materials quality is top-notch. Retro styling abounds in little touches like the large round speedometer and tach (which feature an appropriate vintage font), dual-hooded dash and a cool steering wheel with a small round airbag hub and metallic spokes. A striking color accent package features red leather seats, red door panel inserts and red floor mats all set against a dark charcoal interior.

**Driving Impressions:** The Mustang turns crisply and eagerly into corners with a flat and composed attitude. The powerful brakes are more fade resistant than before, and control in bumpy corners is improved, despite the continued use of a solid rear axle. The comfortable cabin benefits from low wind and road noise, as well as a surprisingly compliant ride.

*Crash Test Scores, see pg 530*
*Warranty information, see pg 542*

### Specifications

| Engine/Drivetrain | HP | Torque | EPA Fuel Economy Rating |
|---|---|---|---|
| 8cyl 4.6L M | 300 | 320 | 17 city/25 hwy |
| 6cyl 4.0L M | 210 | 240 | 19 city/28 hwy |

### Body Styles

| Style | MSRP Range |
|---|---|
| Compact Coupe | $18,785–$25,705 |

# 2005 Ford Ranger

**MSRP Price Range**

## $14,365 - $26,025
Destination Charge: $620 (all styles)

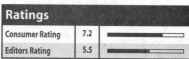

### Ratings

| | | |
|---|---|---|
| Consumer Rating | 7.2 | |
| Editors Rating | 5.5 | |

**What Edmunds.com says:** Old, tired and completely outclassed by its competition, the Ranger only deserves a look if you're content with a cheap price and passable performance.

**Pros:** Multiple trim levels and options, functional interior, cheap price.

**Cons:** Dated platform, weak engines, choppy ride, lack of modern features and amenities, no crew cab body style.

**What's New:** The flareside pickup bed option is no longer available. Package updates and revised wheel and tire options round out the changes this year.

**Body Styles, Trim Levels and Options:** The Ranger is available in regular or extended cab (called SuperCab) body styles. Regular cabs can be ordered with either a 6- or a 7-foot bed. SuperCabs come only with a 6-footer and can be equipped with reverse-opening rear access doors. Trim levels include XL, youth-oriented Edge and Tremor and XLT, which is available with several packages, including FX4. The XL is basic—cloth upholstery and an AM/FM radio are among the few amenities. The Edge and XLT are the next step up, and they're your ticket to the Power Equipment Group, which offers keyless entry and power windows, locks and mirrors. The Edge has body-colored bumpers, while the XLT gets a more traditional chrome finish. Both have a CD player, but the Edge version is MP3-compatible. A Deluxe package for the Edge sets you up with full power accessories, a CD changer and a 290-watt stereo. The Tremor package gets its name from its 510-watt Pioneer stereo system. Two versions of the XLT FX4 are available: Off Road and Level II. The Off Road package includes heavy-duty shocks, skid plates, tow hooks, 16-inch all-terrain tires and a limited-slip rear axle. The Level II gets a Torsen limited-slip differential, Bilstein shocks, BF Goodrich all-terrain tires and Alcoa wheels.

**Powertrains and Performance:** Three engine choices are available. The base engine is a 143-horsepower, 2.3-liter inline four. Next up is a 3.0-liter V6 rated for 148 hp and 180 lb-ft of torque. At the top of the engine chart is a 4.0-liter overhead cam V6 rated for 207 hp and 238 lb-ft of torque. Properly equipped, a 4.0-liter Ranger can tow up to 5,740 pounds. Transmission choices include a five-speed manual or a five-speed automatic, and most models offer a choice of two- or four-wheel drive.

**Safety:** The Ranger comes standard with four-wheel antilock brakes and a passenger airbag cutoff switch. Two-wheel-drive SuperCabs received four stars (out of five) in NHTSA frontal and side-impact crash tests. Regular cab models earned a five-star side-impact rating.

**Interior Design and Special Features:** Controls are easy to spot, understand and use, and the available white-faced gauges adds a little extra style. Although we've found the Ranger's front seats uncomfortable in the past, Ford made improvements for the 2004 model year. SuperCabs can be equipped with small jump seats in the rear, suitable only for children or small adults.

**Driving Impressions:** The Ranger is a decent performer when equipped with the 4.0-liter V6, but it tends to feel underpowered with the 3.0-liter V6 or the base four-cylinder, especially if you get the automatic transmission. Rangers are quite capable off-road, especially when equipped with one of the FX4 packages. Ride and handling characteristics on pavement are tolerable, but when driven back-to-back with newer offerings from GM, Dodge, Nissan and Toyota, the Ranger's age shows.

*Crash Test Scores, see pg 530*
*Warranty information, see pg 542*

### Specifications

| Engine/Drivetrain | HP | Torque | EPA Fuel Economy Rating |
|---|---|---|---|
| 6cyl 4.0L M | 207 | 238 | 15 city/19 hwy |
| 6cyl 3.0L M | 148 | 185 | 18 city/23 hwy |
| 6cyl 3.0L M | 148 | 180 | 18 city/23 hwy |
| 4cyl 2.3L M | 143 | 154 | 24 city/29 hwy |

### Body Styles

| Style | MSRP Range |
|---|---|
| Extended Cab Pickup Truck | $17,065–$26,025 |
| Regular Cab Pickup Truck | $14,365–$20,675 |

# 2005 Ford Taurus

**Midsize Sedan, Wagon**

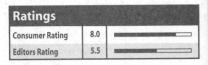

**MSRP Price Range**

## $20,685 - $23,545

Destination Charge: $660 (all styles)

## Ratings

| | | |
|---|---|---|
| Consumer Rating | 8.0 | |
| Editors Rating | 5.5 | |

**What Edmunds.com says:** No longer a top contender in the midsize car segment, the Taurus is still a decent buy if a low initial price is more important to you than overall refinement and resale value.

**Pros:** Low price, roomy interior, good crash test scores, available as a sedan or a wagon.

**Cons:** Low-grade interior materials, poor expected resale value, doesn't ride, handle or stop as well as top competitors.

**What's New:** The Taurus receives a few changes this year, most in the name of simplification. Trim levels have been pared down to just SE and SEL, last year's huge array of packages has been consolidated and a comprehensive wood trim package is now standard on the SEL. Later in the model year, a tire-pressure monitor system will become standard on all models with alloy wheels.

*Crash Test Scores, see pg 530*
*Warranty information, see pg 542*

## Specifications

| Engine/Drivetrain | HP | Torque | EPA Fuel Economy Rating |
|---|---|---|---|
| 6cyl 3.0L A | 200 | 207 | N/A |
| 6cyl 3.0L A | 153 | 185 | N/A |

## Body Styles

| Style | MSRP Range |
|---|---|
| Midsize Sedan | $20,685–$22,595 |
| Midsize Wagon | $22,555–$23,545 |

**Body Styles, Trim Levels and Options:** The Taurus comes in two trim levels, SE and SEL, and two body styles, sedan and wagon. Standard items on the SE include remote keyless entry; air conditioning; cassette stereo; power locks, windows, and mirrors; cruise control; a trip computer; and a front bench seat (allowing the car to seat up to six). Move up to SEL trim and you get all of these items standard, along with a keyless entry keypad on the driver-side door, body-color rearview mirrors with approach lamps, alloy wheels, perimeter alarm system and a stereo with CD player. Additional SEL features include a power driver seat, wood trim accents and front bucket seats with a center console and floor shifter. SE models can be upgraded with a Preferred Equipment package that includes alloy wheels, rear spoiler and power driver seat. The SEL offers an available Premium package with a six-disc CD changer, automatic climate control, leather seating, rear spoiler, power passenger seat and auto headlamps.

**Powertrains and Performance:** There are two V6 engines offered: the 3.0-liter "Vulcan" and the 3.0-liter "Duratec." The main difference between the two is the cylinder head design; the base Vulcan has two valves per cylinder, while the Duratec has four. The latter is rated at 200 horsepower and 207 pound-feet of torque, while the Vulcan makes just 153 hp and 185 lb-ft of torque. Both engines are mated to a four-speed automatic transmission. Expect to average 20 mpg in the city and 27 mpg on the highway with either engine.

**Safety:** A new optional Safety/Security package bundles side airbags, antilock brakes and traction control into one group. Notably, only wagons are equipped with four-wheel disc brakes; all sedans have rear drums. The Taurus earned a perfect five-star rating in NHTSA frontal crash testing and three stars in side-impact tests. In 40-mph frontal offset testing conducted by the IIHS, the Taurus has earned a "Good" rating and was named a "Best Pick" among family cars.

**Interior Design and Special Features:** Taurus cabins have a dated look and feel, but most controls are easy to find and use. The broad, flat seats aren't especially supportive but can accommodate occupants of all sizes. Carrying six passengers is a legitimate prospect if your Taurus has the front bench seat. The front bench seat also includes a flip/fold center compartment with cupholders and storage cubbies. The sedan has a spacious 17-cubic-foot trunk. The wagon's optional rear-facing third-row seat can be used to carry two additional children. When it's not in use, you'll have 38.8 cubic feet of luggage space.

**Driving Impressions:** Both engines are noisier than most competing V6s, but the Duratec at least offers strong acceleration. The automatic transmission gets the job done but is slow to downshift. Ride quality is generally comfortable, but can be harsh over more severe bumps and ruts. Braking distances are longer than those of most peers, and neither the suspension nor the steering is suited for brisk driving around corners.

# 2005 Ford Thunderbird

**MSRP Price Range**

## $37,460 - $38,505
Destination Charge: $605 (all styles)

### Ratings

| | | |
|---|---|---|
| Consumer Rating | 8.8 | |
| Editors Rating | 6.9 | |

**What Edmunds.com says:** Fun to drive and fun to be seen driving, the Thunderbird successfully straddles a fine line between luxury and performance.

**Pros:** Silky-smooth V8, cool retro styling, relaxed yet capable handling, available hardtop.

**Cons:** Minimal trunk space, lackluster interior design, no manual transmission offered.

**What's New:** New this year are 50th anniversary exterior badges, newly styled aluminum applique trim on the doors and center stack, new map pockets on the seat backs and a handful of color changes.

**Body Styles, Trim Levels and Options:** The Thunderbird is sold exclusively as a two-seat roadster in Deluxe and Premium trim. Deluxe models include most of the features buyers will need, such as 17-inch wheels, leather upholstery, power seats, dual-zone climate control and an eight-speaker sound system with an in-dash CD changer. Step up to a Premium Thunderbird and you'll get heated seats, chrome wheels and the option to get a color accent package for the interior.

**Powertrains and Performance:** A 3.9-liter V8 powers the Thunderbird's rear wheels through a five-speed automatic transmission. With the help of variable cam timing, the V8 produces 280 horsepower and 286 pound-feet of torque. Buyers who like to choose their own gears can get a SelectShift automanual feature as an option. Fuel economy estimates are 18 mpg in the city and 24 mpg on the highway. While not fast like a sports car, the Thunderbird's V8 power and well-sorted suspension give it surprisingly nimble handling when the road turns curvy.

**Safety:** The Thunderbird comes equipped with standard side airbags that protect the head and chest. And when you want to include small children in the fun, there's a deactivation switch for the passenger-side front and side airbags, along with child-seat anchors. All T-Birds come with four-wheel antilock disc brakes and traction control. In government crash tests, the Thunderbird earned four stars for the driver and a perfect five stars for the front passenger in the frontal impact category, and five stars in the side-impact category.

**Interior Design and Special Features:** Inside, you'll find that many of the buttons and switches, as well as the instrument cluster, are lifted directly from Lincoln's LS luxury sedan, but attractive white-faced gauges and aluminum accents somewhat offset the lack of imaginative design in the cockpit. The leather seat trim has what Ford calls a "Thunderbird tuck and roll," and the driver seat has six-way power adjustment and adjustable lumbar support. While the standard interior color is black, there's an available option package in which the seats, lower instrument panel, steering-wheel top and shift knob match or contrast the exterior color.

**Driving Impressions:** Most critics call the Thunderbird a boulevard cruiser, and while it's no sports car, it will handle a twisty road with more capability than most owners will require. The V8 provides plenty of smooth, quiet power for navigating the urban jungle, and the steering offers surprising levels of road feel and response. Even the somewhat soft suspension, which is tuned to provide a comfortable ride, maintains its composure well when pushed, quelling body roll, dive and squat. Watch out, though, for excessive cabin buffeting with the top down at freeway speeds. When it's time to put the soft top up, you'll find the cabin surprisingly quiet for a convertible.

*Crash Test Scores, see pg 530*
*Warranty information, see pg 542*

### Specifications

| Engine/Drivetrain | HP | Torque | EPA Fuel Economy Rating |
|---|---|---|---|
| 8cyl 3.9L A | 280 | 286 | 17 city/23 hwy |

### Body Styles

| Style | MSRP Range |
|---|---|
| Midsize Convertible | $37,460–$38,505 |

# 2005 GMC Canyon

Compact Truck

**MSRP Price Range**

## $16,025 - $28,135
Destination Charge: $635 (all styles)

### Ratings

| | | |
|---|---|---|
| Consumer Rating | 8.5 | |
| Editors Rating | 6.9 | |

**What Edmunds.com says:** It has the features and the looks necessary to get the attention of compact pickup buyers, but next to the all-new pickups from Dodge, Nissan and Toyota, the Colorado comes up short in power, interior room and overall fit and finish.

**Pros:** Versatile size, fuel-efficient engine lineup, simple controls, available side curtain airbags and locking differential, standard ABS.

**Cons:** Not much low-end torque, no six- or eight-cylinder engine option, low tow ratings, subpar build and materials quality, generic interior design.

**What's New:** No major changes this year.

Crash Test Scores, see pg 530
Warranty information, see pg 542

### Specifications

| Engine/Drivetrain | HP | Torque | EPA Fuel Economy Rating |
|---|---|---|---|
| 5cyl 3.5L A | 220 | 225 | 18 city/23 hwy |
| 4cyl 2.8L M | 175 | 185 | 18 city/25 hwy |

### Body Styles

| Style | MSRP Range |
|---|---|
| Crew Cab Pickup Truck | $21,290–$28,135 |
| Extended Cab Pickup Truck | $18,370–$24,795 |
| Regular Cab Pickup Truck | $16,025–$22,120 |

**Body Styles, Trim Levels and Options:** The Canyon comes in regular, extended and crew cab body styles, and all are offered in both two- and four-wheel drive. Regular and extended cab models have a six-foot bed while the crew cab gets a five-foot bed only. There are two basic trim levels: SL and SLE. SL models come standard with air conditioning, a 60/40 cloth bench seat and an AM/FM stereo. Upgraded SLE models add titanium-colored trim, tilt steering, cruise control, full carpeting and a CD stereo. Both the Z85 heavy-duty and Z71 off-road packages add a torsion bar front suspension with heavier-duty shocks. Of these two packages, the Z71 offers the tallest ride height, along with a locking rear differential, oversize tires and skid plates on 4WD models. Other notable options include the OnStar communications system; a power convenience package that includes power windows, locks and mirrors, along with keyless entry, XM Satellite Radio and a six-disc CD changer.

**Powertrains and Performance:** Two engines are available: a 2.8-liter inline four-cylinder and a 3.5-liter inline five-cylinder. Both are built out of lightweight aluminum and both feature dual-overhead cams, four valves per cylinder and electronic throttle control. The 2.8-liter engine is standard on all models and is rated at 175 horsepower and 220 pound-feet of torque. The optional 3.5-liter engine offers 220 hp and 225 lb-ft of torque. A five-speed manual transmission is standard, but a four-speed automatic is also available on all models. Four-wheel-drive models feature a dual-range transfer case with push-button controls.

**Safety:** The Canyon was the first compact truck to offer roof-mounted side curtain airbags. Dual-stage driver and front passenger airbags are standard along with four-wheel antilock brakes. Traction control is optional on 2WD trucks. In government crash tests, the Canyon earned four stars (out of five) for driver and front-passenger protection in frontal impacts. In side-impact testing, it received four stars for front-occupant protection in side impacts, and five stars for rear passengers.

**Interior Design and Special Features:** Trucks may have gotten more hospitable in recent years, but don't expect anything fancy in the Canyon's cabin. Simple rotary climate controls and a large stereo faceplate make the interior seem instantly familiar as soon as you get in. The gauges are similarly basic, but functional in their design. Materials range from average to substandard in quality, and build quality can be inconsistent.

**Driving Impressions:** The new inline engines deliver smooth, refined power, but their off-the-line punch and odd exhaust note is a little disappointing. Either engine provides the kind of midrange torque and higher-rpm horsepower necessary for most day-to-day driving. Shifts from the four-speed automatic are firm and well timed, and although it's still fairly vague through the gears, the new five-speed manual gearbox is about as good as you're going to find in a compact truck. The stock suspension tuning is on the soft side, but if you're really intent on bashing boulders, the off-road package provides suitable performance.

# 2005 GMC Envoy

**MSRP Price Range**
## $29,750 - $36,135
Destination Charge: $685 (all styles)

### Ratings

| | | |
|---|---|---|
| Consumer Rating | 9.4 | |
| Editors Rating | 6.4 | |

**What Edmunds.com says:** A solid effort from GMC, but it still falls short of more well-rounded midsize SUVs like the Ford Explorer and Toyota 4Runner.

**Pros:** Extensive list of available options, strong six-cylinder engine, user-friendly interior design.

**Cons:** Numb steering, some low-grade interior pieces, sloppy handling around corners.

**What's New:** For 2005, seating has been restyled and boasts comfort and quality improvements. A touch-screen DVD-based navigation system is now available. Among the new options are an audio system with CD/MP3 compatibility and full-length side curtain airbags (which replace last year's front-seat side airbags).

**Body Styles, Trim Levels and Options:** The four-door Envoy seats five and comes in two trim levels: SLE and SLT. Base SLE versions come with a cloth interior; dual-zone manual air conditioning; a CD player; power windows, mirrors and locks; keyless entry; and 17-inch wheels. SLT models are loaded with just about every feature available including a driver information center, automatic climate control, leather seating and a leather-wrapped steering wheel with radio and climate controls, just to name a few. The Envoy also offers a rear-seat DVD entertainment system, a DVD-based navigation system, air suspension, upgraded audio systems, XM Satellite Radio and heated front seats as options.

**Powertrains and Performance:** All Envoys are powered by a 4.2-liter dual-overhead-cam inline six-cylinder engine. Rated at 275 horsepower and 275 pound-feet of torque, this engine outpowers most of its competitors' V8s, let alone their V6 offerings. It's connected to a well-designed four-speed automatic transmission that delivers firm, precise shifts. Both two-wheel-drive and four-wheel-drive models are available. Properly equipped, the Envoy can tow 6,300 pounds. Fuel economy is better than average for a truck-based utility vehicle; 4WD models rate 15 mpg city/21 mpg highway, while 2WD models have a 16/22 EPA estimate.

**Safety:** Four-wheel antilock disc brakes are standard on all Envoys, while full-length head curtain airbags are optional. There are three-point seatbelts at all five seating locations. The Envoy has fared well in the NHTSA side-impact crash tests, scoring five stars (the best possible) for both front and rear passengers. Frontal impact tests resulted in a three-star rating for driver and front-passenger protection. The IIHS rated the vehicle "Marginal" (second lowest) after conducting its frontal offset crash test.

**Interior Design and Special Features:** Inside, the Envoy's cabin offers plenty of room for five adult passengers. Brushed nickel accents grace the console and instrument panel, and wood accents add a touch of class to the uplevel SLT trim. Materials quality has been improved, but unfortunately, cheap plastic still dominates the dashboard and door panels. The 60/40-split rear seats fold for cargo-loading flexibility; with the seats folded, the Envoy has a maximum cargo-carrying capacity of 80 cubic feet.

**Driving Impressions:** Out on the road, the Envoy delivers a well-cushioned ride that most shoppers will like. Unfortunately, the steering offers little in the way of road feel, and handling is sloppy around corners. An electronically controlled rear air suspension is available as an option to help maintain a level stance when hauling heavy loads. Off-road, the Envoy is capable of tackling the typical obstacles one encounters while trying to access trailheads and campsites. Ultimately, the most enjoyable aspect of this utility vehicle is its brawny inline six. With a generous 275 horsepower and 275 pound-feet of torque, it makes for easy passing and acceleration.

*Crash Test Scores, see pg 530*
*Warranty information, see pg 542*

### Specifications

| Engine/Drivetrain | HP | Torque | EPA Fuel Economy Rating |
|---|---|---|---|
| 6cyl 4.2L A | 275 | 275 | 16 city/21 hwy |

### Body Styles

| Style | MSRP Range |
|---|---|
| Midsize SUV | $29,750–$36,135 |

# 2005 GMC Envoy XL

**MSRP Price Range**

## $31,420 - $37,785

Destination Charge: $685 (all styles)

## Ratings

| | | |
|---|---|---|
| Consumer Rating | 8.5 | |
| Editors Rating | 6.2 | |

**What Edmunds.com says:** If true seven-passenger capacity and serious cargo space are your top priorities in shopping for a midsize SUV, the Envoy XL has the competition beat. Just make sure you test-drive the well-rounded Ford Explorer and Dodge Durango before making a decision.

**Pros:** Strong six- or eight-cylinder power, clean interior design, plenty of passenger and cargo room.

**Cons:** Sloppy handling around corners, numb steering, some cheap interior materials.

**What's New:** For 2005, seating has been restyled and boasts comfort and quality improvements. A touchscreen DVD-based navigation system is now available. A stereo system with CD/MP3 compatibility and full-length side curtain airbags (replacing last year's front-seat side airbags) are new options this year.

*Crash Test Scores, see pg 530*
*Warranty information, see pg 542*

## Specifications

| Engine/Drivetrain | HP | Torque | EPA Fuel Economy Rating |
|---|---|---|---|
| 8cyl 5.3L A | 300 | 330 | 15 city/19 hwy |
| 6cyl 4.2L A | 275 | 275 | 16 city/19 hwy |

## Body Styles

| Style | MSRP Range |
|---|---|
| Large SUV | $31,420–$37,785 |

**Body Styles, Trim Levels and Options:** The four-door, seven-passenger Envoy XL comes in two well-appointed trim levels: SLE and SLT. Base SLE versions come with a deluxe cloth interior, dual-zone manual climate control and a six-speaker AM/FM stereo with CD player. SLT models are loaded with just about every feature available including a driver information center, automatic climate control, leather seating and a leather-wrapped steering wheel with auxiliary radio and climate controls, just to name a few. Optional items include a DVD-navigation system, XM Satellite Radio and power-adjustable pedals.

**Powertrains and Performance:** Bracing horsepower comes via the sport-ute's standard Vortec 4.2-liter dual-overhead-cam inline six. Rated at 275 horsepower and 275 pound-feet of torque, this engine outmuscles most of its competitors' V8s, let alone their V6 offerings. Envoy XL buyers also get the option of a brawny V8, in the form of a Vortec 5.3-liter that generates 290 hp and 326 lb-ft of torque. With this optional V8, the XL is able to provide trailering capacities of 7,000 pounds for two-wheel-drive models and 6,700 pounds for four-wheel-drive models, while standard models are rated to tow 6,000 pounds in 2WD form and 5,800 pounds when equipped with 4WD. EPA fuel economy ratings are 15 mpg city/20 mpg highway for six-cylinder models and 14 city/19 highway for V8-equipped versions.

**Safety:** The Envoy XL comes standard with four-wheel antilock disc brakes and three-point seatbelts for all seating positions. Head curtain airbags are optional on all models. In government frontal impact testing, the standard-length Envoy received three stars out of five for driver and front-passenger protection, and five stars for front and rear side-impact protection. The IIHS rated the standard-length Envoy "Marginal" (the second lowest) after conducting its frontal offset crash test.

**Interior Design and Special Features:** Inside, the Envoy XL's spacious cabin offers room for seven passengers. Brushed nickel accents grace the console and instrument panel, and wood accents add a touch of class to the uplevel SLT trim, but the low-grade plastics used on the dash and door panels are still noticeable. Cargo capacity is tops among midsize SUVs—there is 23.4 cubic feet of space behind the third-row seats, and with both the second- and third-row seats folded, there is a maximum of 107 cubic feet.

**Driving Impressions:** The standard 4.2-liter six is impressive enough on its own, so there's no going wrong with either of the XL's engine options. Unfortunately, the suspension isn't quite so competent, as it tends to feel overly soft when cornering and rough in off-road situations. Less enthusiastic driving generates a smooth, comfortable ride, so it's not all bad, but overall, we consider the Ford Explorer's driving dynamics superior in most respects.

# 2005 GMC Envoy XUV

**MSRP Price Range**

## $31,505 - $37,840

Destination Charge: $685 (all styles)

## Ratings

| | | |
|---|---|---|
| Consumer Rating | 9.1 | ▬▬▬▬▬▬▬ |
| Editors Rating | 6.5 | ▬▬▬▬▬▬ |

**What Edmunds.com says:** If you're looking to haul five people and the occasional eight-foot dresser in a mid-size SUV, the Envoy XUV has the competition beat—in fact, there really is no competition.

**Pros:** Strong six- or eight-cylinder power, clean interior design, reconfigurable cargo area.

**Cons:** Spongy suspension, numb steering, some low-grade interior materials, odd exterior proportions.

**What's New:** Seating has been restyled and boasts comfort and quality improvements this year. A touch-screen DVD-based navigation system is now available, and the SLT trim includes burled wood accents inside. A stereo system with CD/MP3 compatibility and full-length side curtain airbags (replacing last year's front-seat side airbags) are also new this year.

**Body Styles, Trim Levels and Options:** The Envoy XUV comes in two well-appointed trim levels: SLE and SLT. Base SLE versions come with 17-inch alloy wheels, a cloth interior, dual-zone manual climate controls and a six-speaker AM/FM stereo with a CD player. SLT models are loaded with just about every feature available, including a driver information center, automatic climate control, power front seats (with memory for the driver), leather upholstery and a leather-wrapped steering wheel with auxiliary radio and climate controls, just to name a few. Options include a DVD-based navigation system, an in-dash CD changer, power-adjustable pedals and a load-leveling rear suspension.

**Powertrains and Performance:** As with the other Envoy models, the XUV can be had in either two- or four-wheel drive, and with either six- or eight-cylinder power. The standard Vortec 4200 (4.2-liter) inline six provides 275 horsepower and 275 pound-feet of torque—sufficient to tow up to 5,800 pounds. With 290 horses and 326 lb-ft, the optional 5.3-liter V8 can pull up to 5,900 pounds. Both engines use a quick-shifting four-speed automatic transmission. The base engine is rated by the EPA at 15 city/20 highway for 2WD (15/19 4WD) while the V8 is rated at 15 city/19 highway (14/18 4WD).

**Safety:** The Envoy XUV comes standard with four-wheel antilock disc brakes and three-point seatbelts at all seating positions. Head curtain airbags for front and rear occupants are optional on all models. In government crash tests, the standard Envoy earned three stars out of five for protection of the driver and front passenger in frontal collisions. In side-impact tests, it earned a perfect five stars for protection for both front and rear passenger protection. The IIHS gave the standard Envoy a rating of "Marginal" (second lowest out of four) after conducting its 40-mph frontal offset crash test.

**Interior Design and Special Features:** The Envoy XUV's spacious cabin offers room for five passengers. Brushed nickel accents grace the console and instrument panel, and wood accents add a touch of class to the uplevel SLT trim. Like other Envoys, though, the XUV has some low-grade plastics that aren't befitting a mid-$30Ks price tag. When it comes to hauling cargo, a flip of a switch opens the XUV's sizable rear roof hatch, creating an open bed for hauling bulky objects. When maximum cargo capacity is required, owners can lower the partition window (between the cargo bay and passenger compartment), fold down the Midgate and drop the rear seats.

**Driving Impressions:** The standard 4.2-liter six provides enough power for most day-to-day driving, but if you're planning to do any towing or heavy hauling on a regular basis, the V8 is the way to go. Both are matched to a well-tuned automatic transmission that provides excellent performance in all situations. Unfortunately, the suspension isn't quite so competent, as it tends to feel overly soft when cornering, and rough in off-road situations. Less enthusiastic driving generates a smooth, comfortable ride, so it's not all bad, but overall, we consider the Ford Explorer's and Dodge Durango's driving dynamics superior in most respects.

*Crash Test Scores, see pg 530*
*Warranty information, see pg 542*

## Specifications

| Engine/Drivetrain | HP | Torque | EPA Fuel Economy Rating |
|---|---|---|---|
| 8cyl 5.3L A | 300 | 330 | 15 city/19 hwy |
| 6cyl 4.2L A | 275 | 275 | 16 city/19 hwy |

## Body Styles

| Style | MSRP Range |
|---|---|
| Large SUV | $31,505–$37,840 |

# 2005 GMC Safari

**MSRP Price Range**

## $24,195 - $31,340
Destination Charge: $740 (all styles)

### Ratings

| | | |
|---|---|---|
| Consumer Rating | 6.1 | |
| Editors Rating | 6.6 | |

**What Edmunds.com says:** Other than its ability to mimic an SUV in terms of towing ability and cargo space, there's not much about the Safari van that makes it a viable choice over its numerous competitors.

**Pros:** Standard eight-passenger seating, 5,400-pound trailer rating, torquey V6.

**Cons:** Poor fuel economy, intrusive engine cover makes for small footwells, overall lack of refinement.

**What's New:** No significant changes for the Safari this year.

**Body Styles, Trim Levels and Options:** Safari passenger vans come in three levels of trim: base, SLE and SLT. Base models come standard with air conditioning, power window and door locks, a tilt steering wheel, cruise control, cloth upholstery and an AM/FM stereo. SLE models add keyless entry and an upgraded audio system with a CD player. Step up to the SLT and you get an upgraded cloth interior, rear air conditioning, an overhead console with map lights and an outside temperature gauge, a power-adjustable driver seat, a leather-wrapped steering wheel and a Homelink programmable garage door transmitter. SLT vans also offer the option of seven-passenger seating with captain's chairs in the second row, as well as leather upholstery.

**Powertrains and Performance:** A 190-horsepower, 4.3-liter V6 is the only engine available, sending power through a smooth-shifting four-speed automatic transmission. Standard rear-wheel drive allows the Safari to boast a maximum towing capacity of 5,400 pounds. A full-time all-wheel-drive system is optional. This system transfers power to the front wheels when it detects rear-wheel slippage for maximum traction in adverse weather situations.

**Safety:** All Safari vans come standard with four-wheel antilock disc brakes. The National Highway Traffic Safety Administration gave the Safari three out of five stars for protection of the driver in a frontal crash and four stars for the front passenger. The Insurance Institute for Highway Safety rated the Safari "Poor," its lowest ranking, after administering its frontal offset crash test.

**Interior Design and Special Features:** With only minor changes since its debut in 1985, the Safari interior is dated-looking to say the least. Overall interior room is generous, with 170 cubic feet of total cargo space, but small front footwells make the driver and front passenger feel more cramped than in most minivans. The standard seating arrangement holds eight passengers, but optional captain's chairs reduce capacity to seven.

**Driving Impressions:** Taller than many of their rivals, Safaris are admittedly more trucklike in temperament, but deliver a pleasant highway ride with competent handling. The 4.3-liter V6 engine provides plenty of thrust down low, but it runs out of breath quickly.

*Crash Test Scores, see pg 530*
*Warranty information, see pg 542*

### Specifications

| Engine/Drivetrain | HP | Torque | EPA Fuel Economy Rating |
|---|---|---|---|
| 6cyl 4.3L A | 190 | 250 | 16 city/20 hwy |

### Body Styles

| Style | MSRP Range |
|---|---|
| Large Van | $24,195–$31,340 |

For the latest full vehicle reports, visit www.edmunds.com/bginfopak

**MSRP Price Range**

## $25,530 - $32,540
Destination Charge: $775 (all styles)

### Ratings

| | | |
|---|---|---|
| Consumer Rating | N/A | |
| Editors Rating | 6.7 | |

**What Edmunds.com says:** Powerful Vortec engines and some unique features make the Savana (and its twin, the Chevrolet Express) pretty much the only game in town if you're looking for a full-size van that doesn't look and drive like it was designed two decades ago.

**Pros:** Strong powertrains, dual-passenger access doors, multiple wheelbase and passenger configurations, optional all-wheel drive.

**Cons:** Plasticky interior, handling still awkward despite improvements.

**What's New:** The StabiliTrak stability control system becomes standard later in the model year, but only on one-ton regular wheelbase vans.

**Body Styles, Trim Levels and Options:** The standard wheelbase (135-inch) Savana comes in half-ton, three-quarter-ton and one-ton configurations, while the extended wheelbase version (155-inch) requires either three-quarter-ton or one-ton running gear. There are two trim levels: base and SLE. Base models feature air conditioning, an AM/FM stereo and a theft-deterrent system. The more livable SLE models include rear-seat climate controls, power windows and door locks, cloth upholstery, cruise control, a tilt steering wheel and keyless entry. Optional equipment includes power driver and front-passenger seats, the OnStar communications system and an upgraded audio system with an in-dash six-disc CD changer.

**Powertrains and Performance:** Savana vans offer a choice of three power plants and all-wheel drive. The standard engine on two-wheel-drive half-ton models is a 4.3-liter V6 rated at 195 horsepower and 260 pound-feet of torque. A 5.3-liter V8 with 295 hp and 325 lb-ft of torque is standard on all-wheel-drive half-tons and optional on two-wheel-drive versions. Three-quarter- and one-ton models come standard with a 6.0-liter V8 rated at 300 hp and 360 lb-ft of torque. All half-ton models use a four-speed automatic transmission, while three-quarter-ton and one-ton models get a heavy-duty version. The maximum trailer towing capacity on half-ton models is 6,300 pounds. Standard wheelbase three-quarter-ton models can tow up to 9,800 pounds while extended wheelbase versions are limited to 7,400 pounds. Standard wheelbase one-ton vans can tow up to 9,800 pounds, and extended wheelbase one-ton vans max out at 9,400 pounds.

**Safety:** All Savana vans have four-wheel antilock disc brakes standard. Light-duty models (GVW less than 8,600 pounds) feature a front-passenger sensing system that will deactivate the front airbag if it senses a small child sitting up front. Heavy-duty models use a manual airbag deactivation switch for the front passenger. StabiliTrak stability control is standard, from mid-2005 on, on one-ton regular wheelbase vans. Oddly, this system is not available on any other Savana.

**Interior Design and Special Features:** The interior is built for pure functionality, and while it may not be pretty, it sure gets the job done. All controls are simple to use and well within reach of the driver, but the footwells remain as cramped as ever. The standard configuration seats 12, with 8- or 15-passenger arrangements also available, depending on which model you choose.

**Driving Impressions:** A reinforced frame, larger stabilizer bars, rack-and-pinion steering (half-ton models only) and a recently upgraded brake system give the Savana a leg up on Ford's Econoline when it comes to ride and handling. Although the Savana is still far from nimble, the numerous improvements made last year make day-to-day driving a much more enjoyable experience. The powerful brakes require less effort than most full-size vans and the power of its available V8 engines really make a difference when it comes to merging and passing.

*Crash Test Scores, see pg 530*
*Warranty information, see pg 542*

### Specifications

| Engine/Drivetrain | HP | Torque | EPA Fuel Economy Rating |
|---|---|---|---|
| 8cyl 6.0L A | 300 | 360 | N/A |
| 8cyl 5.3L A | 295 | 325 | 13 city/17 hwy |
| 6cyl 4.3L A | 195 | 260 | 14 city/18 hwy |

### Body Styles

| Style | MSRP Range |
|---|---|
| Large Van | $30,434–$31,774 |
| Midsize Van | $25,530–$32,540 |

# 2005 GMC Sierra 1500

**Large Truck**

**MSRP Price Range**
## $18,635 - $41,735
Destination Charge: $850 (all styles)

### Ratings

| | | |
|---|---|---|
| Consumer Rating | N/A | |
| Editors Rating | 7.8 | |

**What Edmunds.com says:** Like its Silverado cousin, the Sierra is a solid truck in terms of its drivetrain, roomy interior and unique features, but the Dodge Ram, Ford F-150 and Nissan Titan have it beat when it comes to interior design and overall refinement.

**Pros:** Roomy extended and crew cab models, strong V8 engines, innovative features, slick hybrid electric option.

**Cons:** Lags the competition in terms or refinement and power, spotty fit and finish, low-grade interior materials.

**What's New:** Quadrasteer is no longer available on 2WD models, standard wheel sizes have been bumped up to 17 inches and, on extended and crew cab models, a power sunroof that includes HomeLink and a deluxe overhead console in now optional. GMC takes a step backward this year with the return of rear drum brakes, as opposed to last year's four-wheel disc setup. Big changes for the Denali this year—Quadrasteer is no longer available, and the Denali is now a crew cab model only. A gasoline/electric hybrid model is also introduced this year. Basically a "mild" hybrid, the system provides no power boost, but does allow for automatic engine startup and shutdown at stops. This truck also comes with four 120-volt AC power outlets and is the only Silverado with rear disc brakes this year. The hybrid truck is only available in Western states and Florida.

*Crash Test Scores, see pg 530*
*Warranty information, see pg 542*

### Specifications

| Engine/Drivetrain | HP | Torque | EPA Fuel Economy Rating |
|---|---|---|---|
| 8cyl 6.0L A | 345 | 380 | 15 city/18 hwy |
| 8cyl 5.3L A | 310 | 335 | 15 city/18 hwy |
| 8cyl 5.3L A | 295 | 335 | 17 city/20 hwy |
| 8cyl 4.8L A | 285 | 295 | 17 city/20 hwy |
| 6cyl 4.3L A/M | 195 | 260 | 16 city/20 hwy |

### Body Styles

| Style | MSRP Range |
|---|---|
| Crew Cab Pickup Truck | $30,655–$41,735 |
| Extended Cab Pickup Truck | $24,635–$36,795 |
| Regular Cab Pickup Truck | $18,635–$29,435 |

**Body Styles, Trim Levels and Options:** Three cab styles are available in four different trim levels and two bed lengths. Regular cabs can be outfitted with Work Truck, Base or SLE trim, while extended cabs come in Work Truck, Base, SLE or SLT trim. The light-duty crew cab models are available in either SLE, SLT or Denali trim. True to their name, Work Trucks offer only the basics, but you still get manual dual-zone air conditioning and ABS. Base Sierras include a few more amenities like cruise control and a CD player. The SLE trim adds upgrades like power windows and locks, remote keyless entry and foglamps. SLT trucks add aluminum wheels, leather upholstery, automatic climate control and Bose audio. Top-level Denali models include nearly every available option as standard, as well as unique trim and a 345-hp V8 engine.

**Powertrains and Performance:** Several engine choices are available for the Sierra, ranging from a 195-horsepower, 4.3-liter V6 to a 345-hp, 6.0-liter V8 in the Denali. In between, you'll find a 285-hp, 4.8-liter V8 and a 295-hp, 5.3-liter V8. All Sierras come standard with a four-speed automatic, except V6-equipped regular cabs, which come with a five-speed manual. The maximum towing capacity with the 5.3-liter is 9,000 pounds (8,300 pounds on Quadrasteer-equipped models), while the Denali is rated at 8,100 pounds. Either two- or four-wheel drive is available on all models; the Denali comes with full-time all-wheel drive. A hybrid powertrain option is available on SLE extended cabs with the 5.3-liter, but the system does not provide any power boost. Its main function is to conserve fuel via automatic engine shutdown and startup at stops, as well as provide on-the-job power through four 120-volt AC outlets.

**Safety:** Four-wheel antilock brakes are standard. In government crash tests, the Sierra earned four stars (out of five) for driver protection in frontal impacts and three stars for the front passenger. In IIHS frontal offset crash testing, the Sierra was given an overall rating of "Marginal"—the second lowest of four.

**Interior Design and Special Features:** Inside, Sierra buyers will find a logically laid-out interior, with clear, uncluttered gauges. Materials quality is unimpressive, and build quality, though improved over the last few years, is still below that of the competition. The cabin is roomy, particularly on crew cab models.

**Driving Impressions:** The Sierra is comfortable enough to be a daily driver, yet it's still powerful enough to use as a dedicated work truck. Acceleration is adequate, especially with either of the Vortec V8s, and the automatic transmission shifts with authority. The steering feels vague on center, but it's light and precise enough for easy maneuvering. The automatic engine shutdown and startup feature works seamlessly in the hybrid truck. Additionally, the hybrid's electric power steering feels at least as good as the traditional setup.

# 2005 GMC Sierra 1500HD

**MSRP Price Range**
## $32,130 - $39,645
Destination Charge: $850 (all styles)

## Ratings

| | | |
|---|---|---|
| Consumer Rating | N/A | |
| Editors Rating | 7.8 | |

**What Edmunds.com says:** A powerful drivetrain and stout underpinnings make the Sierra 1500HD (and its Silverado twin) a good option for buyers who like the size of a half-ton pickup but require extra towing capacity. If you don't plan to tow, the Nissan Titan and Dodge Ram are better overall trucks.

**Pros:** Roomy crew cab can carry six passengers, strong 6.0-liter V8 engine, has the highest tow rating of any half-ton pickup, innovative features.

**Cons:** Spotty fit and finish, dated interior with low-grade materials.

**What's New:** The heavy-duty 1500HD crew cab is back once again this year for buyers who like the size of the light-duty 1500 crew cab, but need more power and towing capacity. As on other half-ton Sierras, a power sunroof is a new option, and it includes a HomeLink universal transmitter and deluxe overhead console.

**Body Styles, Trim Levels and Options:** The Sierra 1500HD comes in the crew cab body style only, and is available in two levels of trim: SLE and SLT. Intended as a truck for recreational use rather than hard-core work duty, the crew cab configuration provides a spacious passenger cabin without the harsh ride typical of most workhorse crew cabs. Well-equipped SLE models include cruise control, keyless entry, an AM/FM/CD stereo, dual-zone manual air conditioning and a driver message center that monitors multiple vehicle systems. SLT models add power-adjustable driver and passenger seats (with driver memory), automatic climate control, a Bose sound system with rear audio controls and the OnStar communications system. The optional Quadrasteer four-wheel steering system dramatically improves the truck's turning radius and provides additional stability when towing heavy loads at highway speeds.

**Powertrains and Performance:** Under the hood rests a 6.0-liter V8 rated at 300 horsepower and 360 pound-feet of torque. While these used to be impressive numbers, Dodge, Ford and Nissan all offer V8s with as much or more power. Handling the shifting needs of the 6.0-liter V8 is a heavy-duty four-speed automatic transmission. With overdrive and a tow/haul mode that adjusts shift points for better performance under load, this transmission-engine combo allows the 1500HD to tow up to 10,200 pounds. Larger four-wheel disc brakes borrowed from the three-quarter-ton lineup assure that you'll be able to haul the load down to speed as quickly as the burly V8 engine gets it going.

**Safety:** GMC's dual-stage airbags deploy with varying levels of force depending on the crash severity, while the passenger sensor will deactivate the passenger-side airbag if it detects the presence of a child. All Sierras include four-wheel antilock brakes as standard equipment. In IIHS frontal offset crash testing, the Sierra earned a "Marginal" rating (the second-lowest on a scale of four).

**Interior Design and Special Features:** Inside, Sierra buyers will find a logically laid-out interior, with easy-to-use dual-zone climate controls and clear, uncluttered gauges. Materials quality is unimpressive, and build quality, though improved over the last few years, is still behind the competition. The large cabin offers room for six passengers and the four-door configuration makes getting in and out much easier than most extended cab trucks. The Sierra also offers an optional Bose audio system and XM Satellite Radio, as well as a rear-seat DVD entertainment system.

**Driving Impressions:** Despite its hefty tow rating, the 1500HD is still comfortable enough to be a daily driver. The big V8 provides swift acceleration and the heavy-duty automatic transmission shifts with authority. The steering feels vague on center, but the new Quadrasteer system is amazing in its ability to make this big truck feel small. A combination of torsion bars up front and leaf springs in the rear give the Silverado a comfortable, if not refined, ride in most situations.

*Crash Test Scores, see pg 530*
*Warranty information, see pg 542*

## Specifications

| Engine/Drivetrain | HP | Torque | EPA Fuel Economy Rating |
|---|---|---|---|
| 8cyl 6.0L A | 300 | 360 | N/A |

## Body Styles

| Style | MSRP Range |
|---|---|
| Crew Cab Pickup Truck | $32,130–$39,645 |

# 2005 GMC Sierra 2500HD

**MSRP Price Range**

## $24,235 - $40,885

Destination Charge: $850 (all styles)

### Ratings

| | | |
|---|---|---|
| Consumer Rating | 9.1 | |
| Editors Rating | 7.9 | |

**What Edmunds.com says:** With its numerous powertrain and cab configurations, and stout towing and hauling capacities, the Sierra HD is a hard truck to beat for those who need maximum functionality and capability.

**Pros:** Powerful engine lineup, multiple drivetrain configurations, substantial towing and hauling capacities.

**Cons:** Spotty build quality, mediocre design and interior materials.

**What's New:** On extended and crew cab models, a power sunroof is a new option, and it includes a HomeLink universal transmitter and deluxe overhead console.

**Body Styles, Trim Levels and Options:** The 2500HD is available in regular, extended and crew cab body styles in both two- and four-wheel drive. Short or long boxes are available except on regular cabs, which are long boxes only. There are four trim levels: Work Truck, base, SLE and SLT. True to their name, Work Trucks offer only the basics, but you still get manual dual-zone air conditioning, a 40/20/40-split bench seat and ABS. Base models come standard with a tilt steering wheel, cruise control, an AM/FM/CD stereo, driver message center and tinted glass. Midgrade SLE models add power windows and door locks, remote keyless entry, power-heated exterior mirrors, foglamps and a leather-wrapped steering wheel. Top-of-the-line SLTs add automatic climate control, a six-way power-adjustable driver seat, satellite steering wheel controls and OnStar.

**Powertrains and Performance:** The HD's base engine is a 6.0-liter V8 rated at 300 horsepower and 360 pound-feet of torque. If that's not enough grunt under the hood, GMC offers two even more powerful options: an 8.1-liter V8 and the 6.6-liter Duramax turbodiesel V8. The 8.1-liter V8 boasts an impressive 330 hp and 450 lb-ft of torque, while the Duramax diesel makes up to 310 hp and 605 lb-ft of torque when equipped with the automatic transmission. The standard transmission for the 6.0-liter V8 is a five-speed manual with a heavy-duty four-speed automatic being optional. The 8.1-liter V8 and Duramax diesel can be hooked up to either a six-speed manual or a heavy-duty five-speed automatic. Being heavy-duty trucks, these brutes can certainly pull—the maximum towing capacity of the 2500HD with the 6.0-liter engine is 10,600 pounds, while the 8.1-liter V8 and Duramax diesel can tow up to 12,000 pounds.

**Safety:** Four-wheel antilock disc brakes are standard. In frontal crash tests conducted by the National Highway Traffic Safety Administration, a Sierra earned a three-star rating (out of five) for driver protection and four stars for the front passenger. In the Insurance Institute for Highway Safety's frontal offset crash test, the Sierra was given an overall rating of "Marginal," the second lowest.

*Crash Test Scores, see pg 530*
*Warranty information, see pg 542*

### Specifications

| Engine/Drivetrain | HP | Torque | EPA Fuel Economy Rating |
|---|---|---|---|
| 8cyl 6.0L A/M | 300 | 360 | N/A |

### Body Styles

| Style | MSRP Range |
|---|---|
| Crew Cab Pickup Truck | $30,130–$40,885 |
| Extended Cab Pickup Truck | $28,030–$38,300 |
| Regular Cab Pickup Truck | $24,235–$30,475 |

**Interior Design and Special Features:** Inside, Sierra buyers will find a logically laid-out interior with an easy-to-use dual-zone climate control system and clear, uncluttered gauges. Materials quality is unimpressive, and build quality, though improved over the last few years, is still behind the competition. The large cabin offers plenty of room, comfortable bucket seats and a four-door configuration on extended cab models that makes getting in and out of the backseat much easier.

**Driving Impressions:** The 2500HD is a reasonably comfortable truck for everyday use, but don't expect the plush ride of its light-duty siblings. Any of the three available engines provide swift acceleration and ample towing power, but the Duramax diesel is probably the best choice for those who tow heavy loads. The manual transmissions are about what you would expect in a big truck, but the automatics shift smoothly and crisply no matter how heavy the load.

# GMC
# 2005 GMC Sierra 3500

**MSRP Price Range**
## $28,985 - $41,500
Destination Charge: $850 (all styles)

### Ratings

| | | |
|---|---|---|
| Consumer Rating | 9.5 | ████████████ |
| Editors Rating | 7.9 | █████████▒ |

**What Edmunds.com says:** Although the Sierra still has the capacity to tackle just about any job, its newer competition manages a slight edge when it comes to refinement and maximum towing power.

**Pros:** Multiple drivetrain configurations, substantial towing and hauling capacities, compliant ride quality.

**Cons:** Interior design is showing its age, spotty build quality, cheap interior materials.

**What's New:** On extended and crew cab models, a power sunroof is a new option, and includes a HomeLink universal transmitter and deluxe overhead console.

**Body Styles, Trim Levels and Options:** The 3500 is only available as a long box, but buyers can still choose between regular, extended and crew cab body styles and either two- or four-wheel drive (regular cabs are 4WD only). There are four trim levels: Work Truck, Base, SLE and SLT. Work Trucks are intended for jobsite use and offer basics like 16-inch steel wheels, a vinyl 40/20/40-split bench seat, dual-zone manual air conditioning and an AM/FM radio. Base models add chrome-finish wheels, grille and bumpers, cloth upholstery, cruise control and a CD player. Midgrade SLE models add foglights, privacy glass, power windows and door locks, a self-dimming rearview mirror with a built-in compass, keyless entry, an upgraded six-speaker stereo, power-heated exterior mirrors and a leather-wrapped steering wheel. Top-of-the-line SLTs add automatic climate control, a six-way power-adjustable bucket seats, leather uphol-stery, seat heaters, a Bose sound system with an in-dash CD changer, steering wheel audio controls, a trip computer and OnStar telematics.

**Powertrains and Performance:** The 3500's base engine is a 6.0-liter V8 rated at 300 horse-power and 360 pound-feet of torque. GMC offers two even more powerful options: an 8.1-liter V8 and the 6.6-liter Duramax turbodiesel V8. The 8.1-liter engine boasts an impressive 330 hp and 450 lb-ft of torque, while the Duramax diesel also generates up to 310 hp and 605 lb-ft of torque when equipped with an automatic transmission. The standard transmission for the 6.0-liter V8 is a five-speed manual; a heavy-duty four-speed automatic is optional. The 8.1-liter V8 and Duramax diesel can be hooked up to either a six-speed manual or a heavy-duty five-speed automatic. Maximum towing capacity is 12,000 pounds with either the 8.1 or Duramax (15,500 pounds for fifth-wheel trailers).

**Safety:** Four-wheel antilock disc brakes are standard. In government crash tests, the Sierra earned a four-star rating (out of five) for driver protection in frontal impacts and three stars for the front passenger. In frontal offset crash testing, the Sierra was given an overall rating of "Marginal," the second lowest on a scale of four.

**Interior Design and Special Features:** Inside, Sierra buyers will find a logically laid-out interior with an easy-to-use dual-zone climate control system and clear, uncluttered gauges. Materials quality is unimpressive, and build quality, though improved over the last few years, is still below the competition. The large cabin offers plenty of room, comfortable bucket seats and a four-door configuration on extended cab models that makes getting in and out of the backseat much easier.

**Driving Impressions:** The 3500 is a dedicated work truck, so don't expect the plush ride of its light-duty siblings. Any of the three available engines provide swift acceleration and ample towing power, but the Duramax diesel is the best choice for those who tow heavy loads. The manual transmissions are about what you would expect in a big truck, but the automatics shift smoothly and crisply no matter how heavy the load.

*Crash Test Scores, see pg 530*
*Warranty information, see pg 542*

### Specifications

| Engine/Drivetrain | HP | Torque | EPA Fuel Economy Rating |
|---|---|---|---|
| 8cyl 6.0L A/M | 300 | 360 | N/A |

### Body Styles

| Style | MSRP Range |
|---|---|
| Crew Cab Pickup Truck | $31,730–$41,500 |
| Extended Cab Pickup Truck | $29,630–$39,335 |
| Regular Cab Pickup Truck | $28,985–$31,910 |

# 2005 GMC Yukon

**Large SUV**

**MSRP Price Range**

## $35,460 - $49,860

Destination Charge: $850 (all styles)

### Ratings

| | | |
|---|---|---|
| Consumer Rating | N/A | |
| Editors Rating | 7.3 | |

**What Edmunds.com says:** With room for up to nine passengers, gutsy V8 engines and numerous passenger amenities, the Yukon is a full-featured family sport-ute that's tough to beat.

**Pros:** Strong engines, roomy and versatile interior, rugged chassis, numerous available amenities.

**Cons:** Spotty build quality, interior materials could be better.

**What's New:** A touchscreen navigation system is a new option this year, while all models now come standard with an overhead rear liftgate (with separate liftglass).

**Body Styles, Trim Levels and Options:** The Yukon comes in three trim levels—SLE, SLT and Denali. The base SLE boasts standard features like tri-zone manual climate control, keyless entry, cruise control and a CD player. Uplevel SLT models add leather seats front and rear, rear audio controls, adjustable pedals and heated side mirrors with turn signal indicators and puddle lamps. Top-of-the-line Denali models come standard with just about every feature available, although items like a DVD-based entertainment system, second-row captain's chairs and a sunroof are still optional.

**Powertrains and Performance:** There are three available engines. The 4.8-liter V8, offering 285 horsepower and 295 pound-feet of torque, is standard on the SLE. Optional on the SLE and standard on the SLT is the 5.3-liter V8 that ups the ante with 295 hp and 330 lb-ft of torque. The Denali comes standard with a 6.0-liter V8 rated at 320 hp and 365 lb-ft of torque. The standard transmission is a four-speed automatic with a tow/haul mode for improved performance under heavy loads. SLE and SLT buyers have the choice of two- or four-wheel drive, while Denali models get a heavy-duty gearbox and permanent all-wheel drive. The standard Yukon can tow up to 7,800 pounds while the Denali can handle up to 8,200 pounds.

**Safety:** The Yukon has a tire-pressure monitoring system, dual-stage front airbags (with a passenger sensing system) and four-wheel antilock disc brakes. Side airbags and the StabiliTrak stability control system are standard on the Denali and optional on other trims. In government crash testing, the Yukon rated three out of a possible five stars for driver protection in frontal impacts and four out of five for the passenger.

**Interior Design and Special Features:** Inside, the Yukon offers comfortable seating and simple controls, but the quality of interior materials could stand improvement. Second-row bucket seats are available when you order leather upholstery, as is a DVD-based entertainment system. An optional 50/50-split third-row seat gives the Tahoe nine-passenger seating capacity. With no third row and the second-row seats folded forward, the Tahoe offers 104 cubic feet of cargo volume.

*Crash Test Scores, see pg 530*
*Warranty information, see pg 542*

**Driving Impressions:** Any one of the Yukon's V8 engines delivers ample power in most situations. Those who pull a trailer often would be wise to opt for the 5.3-liter engine, as it provides a substantial bump in torque despite only 10 additional horsepower compared to the 4.8-liter V8. For the ultimate in luxury and towing power, the Denali is the best of this bunch, though Ford's Expedition and Nissan's Armada boast higher maximum tow ratings. The suspension delivers a stable, smooth ride, regardless of whether it travels on or off pavement, while the steering is light enough to maneuver the big sport-ute easily in tight situations.

### Specifications

| Engine/Drivetrain | HP | Torque | EPA Fuel Economy Rating |
|---|---|---|---|
| 8cyl 6.0L A | 335 | 375 | N/A |
| 8cyl 5.3L A | 295 | 330 | 15 city/19 hwy |
| 8cyl 4.8L A | 285 | 295 | 16 city/20 hwy |

### Body Styles

| Style | MSRP Range |
|---|---|
| Large SUV | $35,460–$49,860 |

# 2005 GMC Yukon XL

**MSRP Price Range**
## $38,510 - $51,510
Destination Charge: $850 (all styles)

### Ratings

| | | |
|---|---|---|
| Consumer Rating | 9.1 | |
| Editors Rating | 7.3 | |

**What Edmunds.com says:** One of our favorite big SUVs, thanks to strong engines, a smooth ride and excellent functionality and feature content.

**Pros:** Huge interior, strong lineup of V8 engines, available Quadrasteer four-wheel steering system, extensive list of optional features.

**Cons:** Some cheap interior materials considering the price, bulky size makes it unwieldy for daily use.

**What's New:** Revisions for 2005 include a new optional touchscreen navigation system. Rear barn doors are no longer available, as all models now come with an overhead rear liftgate (with separate liftglass).

**Body Styles, Trim Levels and Options:** The standard Yukon XL is offered in half-ton (1500) and three-quarter-ton (2500) configurations with either two- or four-wheel drive, while the upscale Denali XL is offered as a half-ton, all-wheel-drive model only. There are two trim levels for the standard model: SLE and SLT. Standard equipment for SLE models includes tri-zone manual air conditioning, cruise control, a driver message center, keyless entry, a leather-wrapped tilt steering wheel and a CD player. SLT models add automatic climate control, leather seating, a redesigned floor console with integrated rear passenger stereo and climate controls and an upgraded audio system. Top-of-the-line Denali models come standard with just about every feature available, although items like a DVD-based entertainment system and a sunroof are still optional.

**Powertrains and Performance:** All half-ton models feature a 5.3-liter V8 rated at 295 horsepower and 330 pound-feet of torque mated to a four-speed automatic transmission. Three-quarter-ton versions can be equipped with either a 6.0-liter V8 rated at 300 hp and 360 lb-ft of torque or an 8.1-liter V8 that cranks out 320 hp and 445 lb-ft of torque. The XL Denali features an upgraded version of the 6.0-liter V8 rated at 320 hp and 365 lb-ft of torque. Both 6.0-liter V8s and the 8.1-liter V8 get a heavy-duty version of the standard four-speed automatic. The half-ton Yukon XL can tow up to 8,400 pounds (8,000 is the limit on the Denali). Three-quarter-ton models equipped with the 6.0-liter engine can tow up to 9,900 pounds. Vehicles with the 8.1-liter engine can pull up to 12,000 pounds. The Quadrasteer four-wheel steering system is optional on three-quarter-ton models for improved stability and a decreased turning radius.

**Safety:** The Yukon XL offers airbags that deploy based on crash severity, a tire-pressure monitoring system (half-tons only) and a passenger-seat safety system that can sense the presence of a child riding up front and disable the airbag to prevent injury. Also available is the StabiliTrak stability control system on half-ton models (standard on Denali). In crash tests conducted by the NHTSA, the Yukon XL received four stars (out of five) for protection of the driver and front passenger in front-impact crashes.

**Interior Design and Special Features:** The interior of the Yukon XL is spacious with solid ergonomics and plenty of creature comforts. There's room for nine if you stick with bench seats, but ordering the optional captain's chairs drops capacity to seven passengers. Like many GMC trucks there's a little more plastic than we would like and the build quality could be better, but overall it's still a pleasant environment for a family vehicle.

**Driving Impressions:** We're impressed with the Yukon XL's smooth, comfortable ride quality and easy-to-drive nature. Thanks to a stiff frame and a well-insulated cabin, this big SUV is generally quiet and rattle-free, making it a great long-distance cruiser. The ride of the heavy-duty three-quarter-ton models is a little less forgiving for rear-seat passengers, but they're still comfortable enough to be daily drivers.

*Crash Test Scores, see pg 530*
*Warranty information, see pg 542*

### Specifications

| Engine/Drivetrain | HP | Torque | EPA Fuel Economy Rating |
|---|---|---|---|
| 8cyl 6.0L A | 335 | 375 | 13 city/17 hwy |
| 8cyl 5.3L A | 295 | 335 | 15 city/20 hwy |

### Body Styles

| Style | MSRP Range |
|---|---|
| Large SUV | $38,510–$51,510 |

# Honda
# 2005 Honda Accord
### Midsize Coupe, Sedan

**MSRP Price Range**
## $16,195 - $28,800
Destination Charge: $515 (all styles)

## Ratings

| | | |
|---|---|---|
| Consumer Rating | 8.7 | ▮▮▮▮▮▮▮▮▯ |
| Editors Rating | 8.1 | ▮▮▮▮▮▮▮▮▯ |

**What Edmunds.com says:** No other sedan puts together all the elements of a family car as well as the Accord.

**Pros:** Roomy and stylish interior, tight build quality, smooth ride, powerful and efficient hybrid model, good crash test scores.

**Cons:** Tepid handling, brakes should be more powerful.

**What's New:** Honda takes a bold leap for 2005 with the introduction of the Hybrid Accord. Rather than add a hybrid motor to its four-cylinder, Honda bolts its third-generation IMA system to the Accord's already-potent V6. In one fell swoop the Accord hybrid has become the class leader in fuel economy (30 city, 38 highway) and power (255 horsepower). Other changes for the Accord this year include new wheel cover designs for the LX and EX trims, a new coin pocket design, illuminated steering wheel controls and improved rear styling in sedans with redesigned taillamps. In addition, front-seat side airbags and full-length head curtain airbags are now available on all trim levels all the way down to the base DX model.

*Crash Test Scores, see pg 530*
*Warranty information, see pg 542*

## Specifications

| Engine/Drivetrain | HP | Torque | EPA Fuel Economy Rating |
|---|---|---|---|
| 6cyl 3.0L A/M | 240 | 212 | 21 city/30 hwy |
| 4cyl 2.4L A/M | 160 | 161 | 24 city/34 hwy |

## Body Styles

| Style | MSRP Range |
|---|---|
| Midsize Coupe | $19,775–$28,800 |
| Midsize Sedan | $16,195–$28,700 |

**Body Styles, Trim Levels and Options:** The Accord comes as a two-door coupe or a four-door sedan. Trim levels include DX (sedan only), LX, Hybrid and EX. The DX includes power windows and a CD stereo with two speakers. The LX adds air conditioning, cruise control, power locks and mirrors, keyless entry and six speakers. V6-equipped LX models include a few extra goodies, like 16-inch wheels, an in-dash CD changer and a power driver seat. The Hybrid is similar to the LX V6 in features, and adds unique instrumentation and dual-zone automatic climate control. Top-line EX models get a power sunroof, alloy wheels, unique interior trim and steering wheel-mounted audio controls. Get the EX V6 sedan, and you're living large with heated leather seats, a power passenger seat, satellite radio and dual-zone climate control. The EX V6 coupe with the six-speed manual transmission includes 17-inch alloy wheels and a premium sound system.

**Powertrains and Performance:** Most Accords come with either a 160-horsepower, 2.4-liter inline four or a 240-hp, 3.0-liter V6. Select the Hybrid sedan, which pairs an electric motor with the standard V6, and you'll get a combined 255 hp and 232 lb-ft of torque. Four-cylinder engines can be had with either a five-speed manual or five-speed automatic transmission; V6 and Hybrid models come only with the automatic. A short-throw six-speed manual is available on the V6-powered EX coupe.

**Safety:** Antilock brakes are standard on all Accords, and side and head curtain airbags are either standard or optional on every model. In government crash testing, the Accord received a perfect five stars for protection against frontal impacts. The Accord coupe earned a full five stars for side-impact crash protection for both front and rear occupants; the sedan received four stars for side impacts involving front occupants. In IIHS testing, the Accord earned a "Good" rating (the best possible) for its performance in the 40-mph frontal offset crash test; in side-impact tests, it received a "Good" rating when equipped with side airbags and a "Poor" rating (the lowest) without them.

**Interior Design and Special Features:** Honda has done a nice job of tailoring the interior to meet the needs of the American family. The seating arrangements are top-notch, and the interior design and materials quality continues the high-caliber standards established by previous-generation Accords. The backseat is among the roomiest in the segment, and our only complaint is that the trunk is a bit smaller than that of some peers.

**Driving Impressions:** With 255 hp available, the Accord Hybrid can beat just about any other family car in terms of acceleration; however, most buyers will be perfectly content with the power and refinement of the four-cylinder engine. The suspension provides a comfortable ride as well as decent levels of road grip while cornering, though cars like the Nissan Altima or Mazda 6 beat out the Accord in terms of handling sharpness and driving enjoyment.

**MSRP Price Range**
## $19,995 - $25,050
Destination Charge: $515 (all styles)

### Ratings

| | | |
|---|---|---|
| Consumer Rating | 8.9 | |
| Editors Rating | 8.3 | |

**What Edmunds.com says:** With ample power, room and refinement, the CR-V has almost all you need in a mini sport-utility, as long as you keep on the beaten path.

**Pros:** Highly versatile and roomy interior, stable handling, comfortable ride, good crash test scores standard airbags and stability control.

**Cons:** Limited off-road ability, not as big inside as some of its competitors, no V6 option.

**What's New:** All models get redesigned headlamps and front fascias along with antilock brakes, stability control, side airbags and minor interior styling refinements. A five-speed automatic transmission replaces last year's four-speed unit. The EX receives new alloy wheels, and all models now wear 16-inch wheels. A Special Edition trim debuts that includes heated leather seats, heated mirrors, a leather-wrapped steering wheel and shift knob, as well as body-color bumpers, side molding, door handles and hard spare tire cover.

**Body Styles, Trim Levels and Options:** The CR-V is offered as a four-door compact SUV that seats up to five. There are three trim levels: LX, EX and SE (Special Edition). As with most Honda products, the LX trim should be fine for most consumers, while the more posh EX and SE are there for those who prefer all the extras. On the LX, you'll find power windows and locks, cruise control, air conditioning, a CD player, rear heater ducts and a cargo area-mounted 12-volt accessory outlet. EX models add keyless entry, alloy wheels, a moonroof, steering wheel audio controls, an outside temperature gauge and privacy glass. The SE includes heated leather seats and mirrors, a leather-wrapped steering wheel and shift knob and, on the outside, body-colored bumpers, side moldings, door handles and hard spare tire cover.

**Powertrains and Performance:** Under the hood you'll find a 2.4-liter inline four with Honda's latest i-VTEC architecture. While its power output—160 horsepower and 162 pound-feet of torque—can't equal the grunt of some V6s found in other competitors, we've found that the CR-V has more than adequate acceleration for almost all situations. Two transmissions are available: a five-speed manual or a five-speed automatic. LX models come in either front-wheel drive or all-wheel drive. EX and SE models are all-wheel-drive only. Honda calls its all-wheel-drive system Real Time 4WD, but lacking a dual-range transfer case, it's AWD by definition. The system powers the front wheels only under normal conditions. If the front wheels begin to slip, power is immediately transferred to the rear wheels until traction is regained.

**Safety:** All CR-Vs include antilock brakes, stability control and side airbags as standard equipment. The CR-V earned five stars from the NHTSA for front and side impacts, the highest rating possible. In addition, the IIHS awarded a "Good" rating, also the highest possible, for the CR-V's performance in the 40-mph frontal offset crash test.

**Interior Design and Special Features:** Besides having a multitude of storage areas and cubbies, the CR-V is quite generous in its allotment of interior room for passengers and cargo. The rear quarters are surprisingly comfy considering the vehicle's overall size. Each side of the 60/40-split bench seat can be moved forward or back 6.7 inches, and the seat backs can be reclined up to 45 degrees. For maximum cargo room, both rear seats can be tumbled forward to clear up to 72 cubic feet of space.

**Driving Impressions:** Around-town driving reveals a softly tuned setup that favors comfort over performance. The CR-V is more of a confident cruiser, able to take just about anything the road can dish out, but never enticing you to push it harder. Four-wheel-drive CR-Vs are perfect for negotiating wet or snowy road conditions. However, when taken on terrain more rugged than a gravel road, the CR-V quickly gets wobbly in the knees. Though it has more ground clearance than the Honda Element, this isn't the mini SUV to get if you regularly venture into the wilderness.

*Crash Test Scores, see pg 530*
*Warranty information, see pg 542*

### Specifications

| Engine/Drivetrain | HP | Torque | EPA Fuel Economy Rating |
|---|---|---|---|
| 4cyl 2.4L A/M | 160 | 162 | 23 city/29 hwy |

### Body Styles

| Style | MSRP Range |
|---|---|
| Midsize SUV | $19,995–$25,050 |

Honda

# 2005 Honda Civic

**Compact Coupe, Sedan**

**MSRP Price Range**

## $13,160 - $20,650

Destination Charge: $515 (all styles)

 #1 Editors' Rating

## Ratings

| | | |
|---|---|---|
| Consumer Rating | 9.8 | |
| Editors Rating | 8.0 | |

**What Edmunds.com says:** Still the class of its class, the Civic is the most refined, solidly built economy car on the market.

**Pros:** Fuel-efficient and environmentally friendly engines, roomy interior, reputation for durability and quality, impressive crash test scores.

**Cons:** Top-of-the-line models are pricey, antilock brakes not available on DX or LX.

**What's New:** A Special Edition package is introduced for both the sedan and coupe; it features an upgraded audio system with MP3 capability, six-disc CD changer and an auxiliary jack for portable music devices. SE models also include a leather-wrapped steering wheel, a wing spoiler and alloy wheels.

**Body Styles, Trim Levels and Options:** The Civic comes as a coupe, sedan or hatchback. For the coupe and sedan, there are four main trim levels: the base DX (sedan only), base Value Package (coupe), LX and EX. The basic DX offers little more than an AM/FM radio. The VP adds air conditioning and a CD player. If you can swing it, the LX is the better choice, and you'll get most of the features you need, including cruise control; keyless entry; power windows, locks and mirrors; and a tachometer. Going with the EX nets you a moonroof, antilock brakes, variable wipers, a driver seat-height adjuster and alloy wheels. There are also four specialty models: the HX coupe, SE coupe and sedan, Si hatchback and Hybrid sedan. The frugal HX coupe is equipped similarly to the DX coupe, while the SE matches closely to the LX sedan, with the addition of a premium audio system and cosmetic enhancements. The Si hatchback boasts standard rear disc brakes, a sport-tuned suspension, sport seats and special gauges. The Hybrid, in addition to its special powertrain, is most similar to the EX, less the moonroof.

**Powertrains and Performance:** DX, VP and LX models are powered by a 115-horsepower, 1.7-liter four-cylinder engine. The EX powers up to 127 hp, while the lean-burn 117-hp HX boasts more miserly fuel economy. The HX and Hybrid can be equipped with a continuously variable transmission. The 1.3-liter gasoline-electric powertrain found in the Civic Hybrid makes 93 hp and boasts the best fuel economy figures of the Civic range—45 city and 51 highway for manual transmission-equipped cars. The 160-hp Si is the most powerful Civic and comes matched to a close-ratio five-speed manual transmission.

**Safety:** The Civic has a perfect five-star rating for frontal impacts. When equipped with side airbags, the coupe earns a full five stars for side impacts, while the sedan gets four stars with or without the bags. The IIHS gave the Civic a "Good" rating (its best) for frontal offset crash results. Dual front seatbelt pre-tensioners, three-point seatbelts for all five occupants and optional side airbags with a cutoff system that can detect a child or occupant out of position are all offered. ABS isn't offered on DX, VP, HX or LX trims.

**Interior Design and Special Features:** The Civic's interior is one of the best found in the economy class. It's roomy for the driver and passengers, and possesses a straightforward design and high-quality materials. If you plan on frequently moving bulky items, the Si hatchback, with its 35.7-cubic-foot cargo hold, is the logical choice.

**Driving Impressions:** With the sedan and coupes, the driving experience isn't the most exciting to be found in this class. The suspension is tuned for a refined and comfortable ride, not necessarily performance. The interior is roomy and quiet, however, and this allows the Civic to be an excellent car for both commuting and long-distance trips. The Si hatchback is more fun, though not as much as other sporty coupes.

*Crash Test Scores, see pg 530*
*Warranty information, see pg 542*

## Specifications

| Engine/Drivetrain | HP | Torque | EPA Fuel Economy Rating |
|---|---|---|---|
| 4cyl 2.0L M | 160 | 132 | 26 city/30 hwy |
| 4cyl 1.7L A/M | 127 | 114 | 31 city/38 hwy |
| 4cyl 1.7L A/M | 117 | 111 | 35 city/40 hwy |
| 4cyl 1.7L A/M | 115 | 110 | 29 city/38 hwy |
| 4cyl 1.3L M | 93 | 116 | 46 city/51 hwy |
| 4cyl 1.3L A | 93 | 105 | 48 city/47 hwy |

## Body Styles

| Style | MSRP Range |
|---|---|
| Compact Coupe | $13,560–$19,470 |
| Compact Sedan | $13,160–$20,650 |

**MSRP Price Range**

## N/A

Destination Charge: N/A (all styles)

## Ratings

| | | |
|---|---|---|
| Consumer Rating | N/A | |
| Editors Rating | 8.1 | |

**What Edmunds.com says:** Intended to accommodate the lifestyles of the young and active, the Element is a spunky small SUV with a thoughtfully designed interior wrapped up in a unique shell.

**Pros:** Spacious, waterproof interior, optional all-wheel drive, smooth four-cylinder engine, balanced handling.

**Cons:** Only seats four, clamshell doors hinder entry/exit for rear-seat passengers, ABS restricted to high-line EX.

**What's New:** Side airbags are now standard on the EX, and all audio systems are equipped with MP3 and WMA playback capability. XM Satellite Radio is newly available. Power mirrors, cruise control and new wheel covers have been added to the LX. New features for the EX include a tailpipe finisher, black and blue plastic panels and a new side sill treatment for reduced chipping.

**Body Styles, Trim Levels and Options:** The four-door Element comes in three trim levels—DX, LX and EX. With the DX, you'll get power windows and locks, an easy-to-clean urethane utility floor, removable and folding rear seats, waterproof front seats and a driver-seat height adjuster. The LX adds power mirrors, cruise control, wheel covers, air conditioning and a CD player. The EX has all of these features plus alloy wheels, an additional cargo area-mounted power point, remote keyless entry, waterproof rear seats, front armrests and a 270-watt audio system. Vehicles with all-wheel drive come with a removable rear sunroof.

**Powertrains and Performance:** Behind the Element's bulldoglike snout is the same 2.4-liter inline four found in the CR-V. Boasting Honda's latest i-VTEC variable valve timing and lift technology, output is rated at 160 horsepower and 161 pound-feet of torque. The Element is available in both front-wheel-drive and all-wheel-drive configurations, and can be equipped with either a four-speed automatic or five-speed manual transmission.

**Safety:** Four-wheel disc brakes are standard. EX versions get antilock brakes and front side-impact airbags as standard. In government crash tests, the Element earned a perfect five stars for frontal impact protection. In side-impact tests, it earned five stars for front occupants and four stars for the rear (but with a higher than normal likelihood of head injury). In frontal offset crash testing conducted by the IIHS, the Element earned the top rating of "Good." In IIHS side-impact tests of small SUVs, it earned a "Poor" rating (the lowest), though the vehicle tested did not have the optional side airbags.

**Interior Design and Special Features:** Although the Element, at 71.5 inches, is some 3 inches wider than a CR-V, it is configured to seat four, not five. With stadium-style seating for the rear passengers, those riding in back will enjoy plenty of room and high visibility. With the rear seats removed, cargo capacity is a quite impressive 75 cubic feet. Though the wide opening provided by the clamshell doors is useful, using the rear doors is not as convenient as one might think. To open them, the front doors must be opened first, leading to some annoyance for the front passengers as they always have to open their doors in order to allow people in or out of the rear-seating area.

**Driving Impressions:** The Element is no speed demon, but it does offer peppy performance with enough smoothness to make everyday commuting a pleasant experience. From behind the wheel, the Element feels as tall and boxy as it is. The steering offers positive feedback and the wide track keeps the Element stable in evasive maneuvers. The only thing that could detract from the fun on the open road is the boxy, high roof that is prone to wind noise.

*Crash Test Scores, see pg 530*
*Warranty information, see pg 542*

## Specifications

| Engine/Drivetrain | HP | Torque | EPA Fuel Economy Rating |
|---|---|---|---|
| 4cyl 2.4L A/M | 160 | 161 | 22 city/26 hwy |

## Body Styles

| Style | MSRP Range |
|---|---|
| Compact SUV | N/A |

# Honda
# 2005 Honda Insight

**MSRP Price Range**
*N/A*
Destination Charge: N/A (all styles)

## Ratings

| | | |
|---|---|---|
| Consumer Rating | N/A | |
| Editors Rating | N/A | |

**What Edmunds.com says:** Newer hybrid competitors may have eclipsed the Insight in terms of technology and power, but the Insight is still the class leader when it comes to fuel economy and high-tech construction.

**Pros:** Amazing fuel economy, quick steering, lots of standard equipment, exotic aluminum construction, low production numbers make for exclusivity.

**Cons:** Batteries drain fast under continual electric motor assist, highly susceptible to strong crosswinds, small payload capacity.

**What's New:** The Insight continues into 2005 with no changes.

**Body Styles, Trim Levels and Options:** The two-door, two-passenger Insight comes fully equipped with power windows, mirrors and locks, keyless entry; a CD player; and a rear window defroster and wiper. Automatic climate control air conditioning is optional (a manual heater-only system is standard). Cruise control, unfortunately, is not offered.

**Powertrains and Performance:** The most revolutionary thing about the Insight is its gasoline-electric hybrid powertrain or, in Honda's terms, the Integrated Motor Assist (IMA) system. IMA combines the efforts of a 1.0-liter, 12-valve, inline three-cylinder VTEC-E gasoline engine and a lightweight permanent-magnet electric motor capable of recharging its own power supply—a bank of 120 D-size nickel-metal hydride batteries (with a total output of 144 volts) housed under the cargo floor. The gas engine does the bulk of the work, supplying 67 horsepower at 5,700 rpm and 66 pound-feet of torque at 4,800 rpm. Mounted between the gas engine and the transmission, the electric motor provides only supplemental power. Yet, the motor's contributions at low rpm are what make the Insight feel livable, as it improves the total torque output to 91 lb-ft at 2,000 rpm, while adding 6 extra horsepower. There are two transmissions available: a five-speed manual or a continuously variable automatic transmission (CVT). With the five-speed, the Insight is rated at 60 mpg in the city and 66 on the highway and is ULEV-certified. The CVT offers 57 city/56 highway, and has the even more squeaky clean SULEV rating.

**Safety:** In government crash testing, the Insight earned four stars (out of a possible five) for frontal and side-impact safety. Antilock brakes are standard, but side airbags are not available.

**Interior Design and Special Features:** The Insight's cabin combines quasi-futuristic aesthetics with forthright functionality. The digital instrument cluster includes a meter to show you when the electric motor is assisting and when it's charging the battery pack, a meter to show instantaneous fuel economy, and another display to show you the average mpg. If you're the driver of said car, you can't keep your eyes off this stuff. Whether you feel excited by the challenge or merely guilty, you're motivated to improve the numbers before you. This challenge makes driving the Insight like piloting a high-tech video game.

**Driving Impressions:** The Insight's power is adequate for most driving. However, the battery charge will drain quickly if you hold a high gear too long under heavy IMA assist. IMA assist and regenerative braking work much better with the CVT. The Insight is highly susceptible to crosswinds, and the narrow tires easily track any groove in the pavement. On the plus side, the car's small dimensions and light, accurate steering make it a breeze to maneuver in crowded areas.

*Crash Test Scores, see pg 530*
*Warranty information, see pg 542*

## Specifications

| Engine/Drivetrain | HP | Torque | EPA Fuel Economy Rating |
|---|---|---|---|
| 4cyl 1.0L A/M | 73 | 91 | 57 city/56 hwy |

## Body Styles

| Style | MSRP Range |
|---|---|
| Compact Coupe | N/A |

# 2005 Honda Odyssey

**MSRP Price Range**
## $24,995 - $38,295
Destination Charge: $515 (all styles)

#1 Editors' Rating

## Ratings

| | | |
|---|---|---|
| Consumer Rating | 9.6 | ▭ |
| Editors Rating | 8.9 | ▭ |

**What Edmunds.com says:** Demonstrating that there's always room for improvement, Honda makes its exceptional Odyssey minivan even better. If you're shopping for a minivan, this is one you won't want to miss.

**Pros:** Agile, carlike handling, a split flat-folding rear bench, optional eight-passenger seating, extensive feature list, smooth and powerful V6, strong reliability record.

**Cons:** High demand forces you to pay sticker price or above.

**What's New:** The top-selling Honda Odyssey minivan is all new for 2005.

**Body Styles, Trim Levels and Options:** The base-level LX model includes 16-inch wheels with wheel covers; power front- and second-row windows; power locks; cruise control; keyless entry; a CD player; a 60/40-split third-row seat; in-floor storage; and a smart maintenance indicator. The EX adds alloy wheels, optional eight-passenger seating, power-sliding doors, an in-dash six-disc CD changer, in-floor storage with a handy "lazy Susan" feature, integrated second-row sunshades, a conversation mirror and a sunglasses holder. Choose the EX with a leather interior and you'll also get a more advanced V6 engine and a power moonroof. Family road-trippers can also add a DVD entertainment system and a navigation system with voice recognition and an integrated rearview camera. The Touring model adds a power liftgate, tri-zone auto climate control, driver-seat memory, a 115-volt AC outlet, a multi-information display, power-adjustable pedals, a leather-wrapped steering wheel, an auto-dimming rearview mirror, foglights, parking sensors, auto headlights, a second-row removable center console (in place of the stowable middle seat), run-flat tires, 17.5-inch wheels and a tire-pressure monitoring system.

**Powertrains and Performance:** The Odyssey offers two V6 engine options. LX and EX models use a 255-horsepower V6 mated to a five-speed automatic transmission. EX models with leather and Touring models use the same engine but are upgraded with Variable Cylinder Management (VCM), which increases fuel efficiency by "shutting off" three of the engine's six cylinders during cruising and deceleration. When more performance is needed, the engine switches back to using all six cylinders. This system can increase fuel economy by as much as 12 percent over the regular V6, according to Honda.

**Safety:** Standard safety features on the Odyssey include stability and traction control (called Vehicle Stability Assist); four-wheel antilock disc brakes with BrakeAssist and Electronic Brakeforce Distribution; side airbags; and three-row side curtain airbags with rollover sensors. Touring models come with run-flat tires and a tire-pressure monitoring system with location and pressure indicators.

**Interior Design and Special Features:** Inside, the Odyssey offers so many unique family-friendly features that driver and passengers alike will be hard-pressed to choose their favorite. From the DVD entertainment system with a whopping nine-inch display screen and wireless headsets with personal surround sound to the optional navigation system with voice recognition (complete with the Zagat survey for restaurants) and an integrated rearview camera, the Honda Odyssey doesn't miss a trick.

**Driving Impressions:** The Odyssey has always been highly regarded for its carlike driving characteristics, and the new minivan is no exception. A high seating position, tight turning radius and nimble suspension make the Odyssey easy to pilot both down the freeway and through the grocery store parking lot.

*Crash Test Scores, see pg 530*
*Warranty information, see pg 542*

## Specifications

| Engine/Drivetrain | HP | Torque | EPA Fuel Economy Rating |
|---|---|---|---|
| 6cyl 3.5L A | 255 | 250 | 20 city/28 hwy |

## Body Styles

| Style | MSRP Range |
|---|---|
| Large Minivan | $24,995–$38,295 |

# 2005 Honda Pilot

**MSRP Price Range**
## $27,350 - $34,120
Destination Charge: $515 (all styles)

## Ratings

| | | |
|---|---|---|
| Consumer Rating | 9.7 | |
| Editors Rating | 8.3 | |

**What Edmunds.com says:** One of the best crossover SUVs available, the Pilot is an excellent choice for large, active families in need of versatility.

**Pros:** Roomy interior with eight-passenger seating, versatile storage and cargo-hauling abilities, many standard features, comfortable ride, smooth power delivery.

**Cons:** Mediocre towing capacity, side curtain airbags not available, feels big behind the wheel.

**What's New:** The Pilot receives a new 250-hp engine for 2005, along with numerous functional changes. A tire-pressure monitoring system has been added, and EX models with leather get vehicle stability control. Slightly increased fuel capacity helps extend driving range, and a revised power steering pump provides improved on-center steering feel. Inside the cabin, the instrument panel has been tweaked with ambient lighting and a six-disc CD changer for all EX trims. A driver footrest has been added, and leather-upholstered EX models can now be had with a sunroof. The LX now has standard keyless entry, and all models get an integrated remote key and fob. Honda has made slight frame changes this year that resulted in improved IIHS crash test ratings.

**Body Styles, Trim Levels and Options:** The four-door, eight-passenger Pilot comes in two trim levels: LX and EX. As is typical of Honda offerings, nearly everything comes standard. This includes air conditioning; cruise control; power windows, mirrors and locks; keyless entry; a rear window defroster; and a CD player. Going with the EX adds alloy wheels, auto-off headlamps, an eight-way power driver seat with lumbar, extra interior storage, automatic climate control, Homelink and steering wheel-mounted audio controls. On EX models with leather (EX-L), a sunroof and heated seats and side mirrors come standard, with either a DVD-based navigation system or a DVD entertainment system available as options. If the nav system is ordered, the Pilot comes with a center stack-mounted 6-inch LCD display screen. The entertainment system includes a 7-inch flip-down LCD screen for second- and third-row occupants. Unfortunately, the nav and entertainment systems cannot be ordered together.

**Powertrains and Performance:** The Pilot comes equipped with a 3.5-liter V6 that makes 250 horsepower. More power can be found in some domestic SUV offerings, but all are thirstier at the gas pump. Expect a 0-to-60 mph time of about 8 seconds. The engine's power is routed through a five-speed automatic transmission. Equipped with the optional dealer-installed tow package, the Pilot's trailer towing rating is 3,500 pounds.

**Safety:** Antilock brakes with Electronic Brakeforce Distribution (EBD) come standard, along with side airbags for front occupants. Head-protecting side curtain airbags are not available. Honda considers stability control a luxury item and restricts it to the top-rung EX-L. In government crash tests, the Pilot earned a perfect five-star rating across the board. In frontal offset crash testing conducted by the IIHS, the Pilot received the highest rating of "Good."

**Interior Design and Special Features:** The Pilot seats eight passengers. The second- and third-row seats are positioned theater-style, meaning that they are elevated to give occupants a better outside view. Legroom for second-row passengers is quite good, but the tight third row is best suited for children. Both the second and third rows are split 60/40 and can be folded flat to expand the Pilot's cargo capacity. Maximum cargo capacity is 90 cubic feet.

*Crash Test Scores, see pg 530*
*Warranty information, see pg 542*

**Driving Impressions:** As the Pilot features a stiff unibody structure and a fully independent suspension, it is quite smooth and comfortable on normal roads. However, with a curb weight of more than two tons, there is no denying the Pilot's bulk, and some drivers might find it a bit clumsy to drive. In terms of off-road ability, the Pilot can take on common hazards such as boat ramps, washed-out gullies and rough roads, but not much more.

## Specifications

| Engine/Drivetrain | HP | Torque | EPA Fuel Economy Rating |
|---|---|---|---|
| 6cyl 3.5L A | 255 | 250 | 17 city/22 hwy |

## Body Styles

| Style | MSRP Range |
|---|---|
| Midsize SUV | $27,350–$34,120 |

**MSRP Price Range**

## $32,950

Destination Charge: $515 (all styles)

**#1 Editors' Rating**

### Ratings

| | | |
|---|---|---|
| Consumer Rating | 9.5 | |
| Editors Rating | 8.2 | |

**What Edmunds.com says:** A sports car that makes few compromises, the S2000 is one of the more visceral cars sold in America. And yes, that's a good thing.

**Pros:** Agile chassis, rev-happy engine, minimalist design, optional hardtop, high level of performance for the price.

**Cons:** Could still use some additional low-end torque, shrill engine note at high rpm.

**What's New:** The S2000 returns for 2005 unchanged.

**Body Styles, Trim Levels and Options:** There is only one version of Honda's roadster. All cars have a power-operated top with a defrostable glass rear window, lightweight 17-inch wheels, leather seats, keyless entry, air conditioning, a digital instrument panel, a CD audio system and HID headlights. An optional aluminum hardtop—it weighs just 44 pounds—is also available.

**Powertrains and Performance:** In response to criticism that the S2000 lacks off-the-line grunt, Honda bumped the engine displacement from 2.0 to 2.2 liters last year. This change gave the car more accessible torque—163 lb-ft at 6,500 rpm compared to the previous 153 lb-ft at 7,500 rpm. Horsepower held steady at 240, but it peaks at 7,700 rpm, 600 rpm fewer than the 2.0-liter engine. Power is routed to the rear wheels though a six-speed close-ratio transmission.

**Safety:** Fitting its minimalist theme, the S2000 lacks some of the latest safety features, such as stability control, traction control and side airbags. Four-wheel antilock disc brakes are standard, though. The S2000 scored well in government crash tests, earning four stars (out of a best score of five) for protection against frontal impacts and five stars for side impacts.

**Interior Design and Special Features:** The interior is pure business—there is no silly fake wood or fancy navigation system to detract from the driver's full enjoyment of the car's abilities. Spend any significant time behind the wheel of this driver's car, and you'll wonder why so many other roadsters and sports cars don't cater to the pilot with such one-dimensional purpose. Nearly all the controls you'll ever need are mounted within a finger extension of the steering wheel. Honda slightly enlarged the cockpit last year, though it still retains a snug fit better suited for hard runs on back roads than daily commuting. The laterally bolstered seats hold the driver and passenger in tightly during aggressive cornering.

**Driving Impressions:** There's virtually no perceptible flex despite the S2000's roofless architecture, and body roll is kept to an absolute minimum by the sophisticated double-wishbone suspension front and rear. A fifty-fifty front-to-rear weight distribution gives the car exceptional balance and predictable manners in the corners. In fact, the car is so well mannered, it's almost scary. You find yourself diving into turns faster than you ever thought possible. There is a slight hint of twitchiness at the limit, but with such a short wheelbase, you can't expect it to be completely drama-free.

*Crash Test Scores, see pg 530*
*Warranty information, see pg 542*

### Specifications

| Engine/Drivetrain | HP | Torque | EPA Fuel Economy Rating |
|---|---|---|---|
| 4cyl 2.2L M | 240 | 162 | 20 city/25 hwy |

### Body Styles

| Style | MSRP Range |
|---|---|
| Compact Convertible | $32,950 |

# 2005 HUMMER H2

**Large SUV**

**MSRP Price Range**

## $51,150 - $55,390

Destination Charge: $850 (all styles)

### Ratings

| | | |
|---|---|---|
| Consumer Rating | 9.1 | |
| Editors Rating | 6.6 | |

**What Edmunds.com says:** Despite its more civilized design, this Hummer still maintains the head-turning looks and unstoppable off-road prowess that made the original famous.

**Pros:** Distinctive styling, unmatched off-road capability, stout drivetrain.

**Cons:** Feels massive, poor visibility, some cheap interior materials, limited cargo room, horrible fuel economy.

**What's New:** A new stereo system with an integrated DVD-based navigation system is optional, as is XM Satellite Radio.

**Body Styles, Trim Levels and Options:** The H2 comes in only one body style and one trim level, but two major packages known as the Adventure Series and the Lux Series add numerous options. Features like dual-zone automatic climate control, a driver information center and OnStar are standard equipment, along with power everything and a keyless entry system. The Adventure Series package adds a self-leveling rear air suspension along with an upgraded audio system, carpeted floor mats, tool and first aid kits and a front brush guard. The Lux Series package doesn't include the air suspension, but it does add uplevel leather seating, a chrome appearance package, a brushed-aluminum roof rack, tubular side steps and the Adventure package's audio system and floor mats. Other stand-alone options include heated front and rear seats, a power sunroof, an overhead light bar and a DVD-based navigation system.

**Powertrains and Performance:** All H2s are powered by GM's 6.0-liter V8 rated at 316 horsepower and 360 lb-ft of torque. A heavy-duty 4L65-E four-speed automatic transmission handles the shifting chores, while a full-time dual-range transfer case distributes the power to the individual driveshafts. Advanced features include a driver-selectable rear differential locker and a drive-by-wire throttle setup that changes sensitivity when low-range gearing is selected.

**Safety:** The H2 comes standard with an ABS/traction control system. The advanced traction system allows the H2 to propel itself even if only a single wheel has grip, while driver-selectable settings fine-tune the system to respond better to varying road conditions. The H2 has yet to be tested by the IIHS or NHTSA.

**Interior Design and Special Features:** Unlike the awkwardly configured H1, the H2's interior is arranged like a typical full-size SUV. Power-adjustable captain's chairs reside upfront, while a three-passenger bench seat makes up the second row. A bulky full-size spare cuts the third row down to just one solitary jump seat, but it can be removed to make way for extra cargo. The overall design emphasizes the H2's rugged personality, with exposed attachment bolts and an aircraft-style shift lever, but standard equipment like dual-zone climate control and a nine-speaker Bose sound system remind you that the H2 is a thoroughly modern vehicle.

Crash Test Scores, see pg 530
Warranty information, see pg 542

### Specifications

| Engine/Drivetrain | HP | Torque | EPA Fuel Economy Rating |
|---|---|---|---|
| 8cyl 6.0L A | 316 | 360 | 13 city/13 hwy |

### Body Styles

| Style | MSRP Range |
|---|---|
| Large SUV | $51,150–$55,390 |

**Driving Impressions:** Despite being slightly downsized compared to the original, the H2 still feels massive on the road. The ride is slightly stiffer than that of a Suburban or Tahoe, but not so much as to be uncomfortable. The H2's off-road prowess is easily the best in its class, with steep approach and departure angles, plenty of ground clearance and ample wheel travel. Power from the big V8 is watered down by the vehicle's substantial mass, and fuel mileage often drops to the single digits during stop-and-go driving.

For the latest full vehicle reports, visit www.edmunds.com/bginfopak

**Large Truck**

**MSRP Price Range**
### $52,205 - $55,945
Destination Charge: $850 (all styles)

### Ratings

| | | |
|---|---|---|
| Consumer Rating | 9.0 | |
| Editors Rating | 6.7 | |

**What Edmunds.com says:** The H2 SUV evolves into an even more rugged-looking and versatile vehicle with the new H2 SUT.

**Pros:** Distinctive styling, unmatched off-road capability, stout drivetrain, versatile cargo/passenger space.

**Cons:** Feels massive, some cheap interior materials, dismal fuel economy.

**What's New:** The H2 SUT is a new "sport-utility truck" based upon the H2 SUV.

**Body Styles, Trim Levels and Options:** The H2 SUT comes in only one body style and one trim level, but two major packages known as the Adventure Series and the Lux Series add numerous features. Niceties like dual-zone automatic climate control, a driver information center and OnStar are standard equipment along with power everything and a keyless entry system. The Adventure Series package adds a self-leveling rear air suspension along with an upgraded audio system, carpeted floor mats, tool and first-aid kits and a front brush guard. The Lux Series package doesn't include the air suspension, but it does add uplevel leather seating, a chrome appearance package, tubular side steps and the Adventure package's audio system and floor mats. Stand-alone options include heated front and rear seats, an overhead light bar and an integrated DVD-based navigation system.

**Powertrains and Performance:** All H2s are powered by GM's 6.0-liter V8 rated at 316 horse-power and 360 pound-feet of torque. A heavy-duty 4L65-E four-speed automatic transmission handles the shifting chores, while a full-time dual-range transfer case distributes the power to the individual driveshafts. Advanced features include a driver-selectable rear differential locker and a drive-by-wire throttle setup that changes sensitivity when low-range gearing is selected.

**Safety:** The H2 SUT comes standard with ABS and traction control. The advanced traction system allows the SUT to propel itself even if only a single wheel has grip, while driver-selectable settings fine-tune the system to respond better to varying road conditions. The SUT has yet to be crash tested by the IIHS or NHTSA.

**Interior Design and Special Features:** Unlike the awkwardly configured H1, the H2 SUT's interior is arranged like a typical full-size SUV, minus the enclosed cargo area. Power-adjustable captain's chairs reside upfront, while a three-passenger bench seat makes up the second row. The overall design emphasizes the H2's rugged personality, with exposed attachment bolts and an aircraft throttle-style shift lever, but standard equipment like dual-zone climate control and a nine-speaker Bose sound system remind you that the SUT is a thoroughly modern vehicle. A removable midgate separates the passenger area from the open cargo area. At a touch of a button, the driver can lower all four windows and the rear midgate window. A power sunroof is standard on all SUTs. With the midgate closed, the SUT's cargo area consists of a 30-cubic-foot, rubber-lined open bed. Folding the rear seats down and opening the midgate raises capacity to 56 cubic feet.

**Driving Impressions:** Despite being slightly downsized compared to the original H1, the H2 SUT still feels massive on the road. The ride is slightly stiffer than a Suburban's or Avalanche's, but not so much as to be uncomfortable. The SUT's off-road prowess is easily the best in its class, with steep approach and departure angles, plenty of ground clearance and ample wheel travel. Power from the big V8 is watered down by the vehicle's substantial mass.

*Crash Test Scores, see pg 530*
*Warranty information, see pg 542*

### Specifications

| Engine/Drivetrain | HP | Torque | EPA Fuel Economy Rating |
|---|---|---|---|
| 8cyl 6.0L A | 316 | 360 | 13 city/13 hwy |

### Body Styles

| Style | MSRP Range |
|---|---|
| Crew Cab Pickup Truck | $52,205–$55,945 |

# Hyundai

# 2005 Hyundai Accent

**Compact Coupe, Sedan**

**MSRP Price Range**

## $9,999 - $11,399

Destination Charge: $545 (all styles)

| Ratings | | |
|---|---|---|
| Consumer Rating | N/A | |
| Editors Rating | 7.1 | |

**What Edmunds.com says:** A decent buy for those determined to own a brand-new car with full-warranty coverage, though we'd encourage prospective owners to shop the used car market before closing the deal.

**Pros:** Excellent warranty, low price, nicely appointed interior, standard side airbags, solid build quality, smooth ride.

**Cons:** Weak tires, low handling limits, buzzy engine.

**What's New:** Trim levels are revised and ABS is finally available.

**Body Styles, Trim Levels and Options:** The Accent is available either as a two-door hatchback or four-door sedan. The hatchback is offered in two levels of trim—GLS and GT—while the sedan comes in GLS trim only. The GLS hatchback and sedan come with 13-inch steel wheels, body-side moldings, tinted glass, a tachometer, a cassette player, a rear defroster, power steering, variable intermittent wipers and a folding rear seat. The GT hatchback offers 14-inch alloy wheels, a sport suspension, cloth sport seats, body-color rocker moldings, white-faced gauges, front foglamps, a rear spoiler and a leather-wrapped steering wheel and shift knob. All Accents can be equipped with air conditioning, floor mats, a rear spoiler, mudguards or a cargo net for the trunk.

**Powertrains and Performance:** Hyundai offers one engine for the Accent—a 1.6-liter inline four-cylinder that makes 104 horsepower and 106 pound-feet of torque. A five-speed manual transmission is standard, and a four-speed automatic is optional. We've tried both transmissions and have found them equally acceptable in their operation—if you drive in an area with heavy traffic, we'd recommend the automatic. Mileage is rated at 29 city/33 highway with a manual and 26/35 with an automatic.

**Safety:** The Accent offers standard side airbags and front seatbelt pre-tensioners. Antilock brakes are optional on all models. In government crash testing, the sedan earned four out of five stars for driver and front-passenger protection in frontal impacts. Side-impact tests resulted in five stars for front and four stars for rear-passenger protection. The hatchback earned five stars for the driver, and four stars in all other tests.

**Interior Design and Special Features:** Interiors feature an easy-to-read instrument panel and a center stack with straightforward climate and radio controls. The GT features white-faced gauges and more upscale sport seats. The hatchbacks offer 16.9 cubic feet of luggage capacity with the backseat in use.

*Crash Test Scores, see pg 530*
*Warranty information, see pg 542*

**Driving Impressions:** Along with passable acceleration, the Accent provides a fine ride, and its small size makes it easy to maneuver in crowded urban areas. But don't go looking for revelations in handling when the road turns twisty. The Accent's base tires are small, and neither they nor the suspension deal well with quick transitions—resulting in limited grip and considerable body roll.

## Specifications

| Engine/Drivetrain | HP | Torque | EPA Fuel Economy Rating |
|---|---|---|---|
| 4cyl 1.6L A/M | 103 | 106 | 26 city/35 hwy |

## Body Styles

| Style | MSRP Range |
|---|---|
| Compact Coupe | $9,999–$11,399 |
| Compact Sedan | $10,499–$11,299 |

For the latest full vehicle reports, visit www.edmunds.com/bginfopak

**MSRP Price Range**
## $13,299 - $15,649
Destination Charge: $545 (all styles)

### Ratings

| | | |
|---|---|---|
| Consumer Rating | N/A | |
| Editors Rating | 7.7 | |

**What Edmunds.com says:** Between its low cost, solid performance, numerous features and long warranty, the Elantra presents one of the best values on the market in the economy class.

**Pros:** Solidly built, powerful engine for its class, long list of standard features, comfortable interior, ultralow price tag, generous warranty.

**Cons:** Floaty ride on the freeway with base suspension, hard to find equipped with ABS, poor offset crash test score.

**What's New:** This year Hyundai adds a GLS version of the five-door hatchback to the Elantra line.

**Body Styles, Trim Levels and Options:** The Elantra sedan and five-door hatchback are available in GLS or GT trim. Standard equipment on the GLS is generous by economy car standards and includes side airbags; air conditioning; power windows, mirrors and locks; remote keyless entry; a center armrest with storage; and a 60/40-split-folding rear seat. The GLS hatchback also includes a sport suspension and four-wheel disc brakes. In addition to the above items, GT models provide four-wheel disc brakes, alloy wheels, leather seats, cruise control, foglights, an instrument panel with unique illumination and trip computer, a European front grille, a six-speaker CD audio system and a rear spoiler (different designs for the sedan and hatchback). Among the factory options are cruise control and a CD player on GLS models, and antilock brakes and a sunroof on all trims.

**Powertrains and Performance:** The Elantra is one of the more powerful economy cars on the market. Its 2.0-liter DOHC inline four-cylinder engine is fitted with continuously variable valve timing and is available in ULEV and SULEV versions to meet varying emission standards. ULEV Elantras are rated at 138 horsepower; for SULEV versions, the rating drops slightly, to 132. Regardless of which version you end up with, this Hyundai has ample zip for its price tag with good power off the line and reasonable passing power. Drivers have their choice of either a five-speed manual or a four-speed automatic.

**Safety:** Side airbags (for front occupants) are standard on all Elantras, and antilock brakes are optional. In government crash testing, the Elantra earned five stars out of five for protection of the driver and four stars for the front passenger in the frontal impact category. In side-impact tests, the Elantra received five stars for protection of the front occupants and four stars for rear-occupant protection. In 40-mph frontal offset crash testing by the IIHS, it earned a "Poor" rating (the lowest possible).

**Interior Design and Special Features:** Inside, every Elantra has a simple layout—though not exciting, the switchgear is high in quality and all of the controls are right where you expect them to be. GT models have a more upscale flavor with leather wrappings on the seats, steering wheel and shift knob, as well as purple nighttime illumination for the gauges. Hatchbacks offer 28 cubic feet of cargo capacity with the rear seats in use and 37 cubes when they're folded.

**Driving Impressions:** The Elantra excels at Point-A-to-B driving where a comfortable ride and light, easy handling are assets. In GT form, the suspension has slightly thicker front and rear stabilizer bars and firmer shocks and springs, giving the Elantra a somewhat tauter feel on curvy roads; the trade-off is that a bit more harshness invades the cabin when the car hits a bump.

*Crash Test Scores, see pg 530*
*Warranty information, see pg 542*

### Specifications

| Engine/Drivetrain | HP | Torque | EPA Fuel Economy Rating |
|---|---|---|---|
| 4cyl 2.0L A/M | 138 | 136 | 24 city/32 hwy |

### Body Styles

| Style | MSRP Range |
|---|---|
| Compact Coupe | $13,599–$15,649 |
| Compact Sedan | $13,299–$15,649 |

# 2005 Hyundai Santa Fe

**MSRP Price Range**

## $21,499 - $25,999

Destination Charge: N/A (all styles)

### Ratings

| | | |
|---|---|---|
| Consumer Rating | N/A | |
| Editors Rating | 7.3 | |

**What Edmunds.com says:** The Santa Fe offers a consumer-friendly blend of space, comfort, features, performance and value that make it a compact SUV worth considering.

**Pros:** Reasonable price, strong warranty, roomy interior, long list of standard features, solid construction, good crash test scores.

**Cons:** Thirsty at the pump for a small car-based SUV, soft suspension limits handling ability.

**What's New:** The base trim level has been dropped. The 2.7-liter V6 is now standard (the LX still gets the 3.5-liter V6), as is an automatic transmission. Also newly standard this year are four-wheel antilock brakes and traction control. Exterior changes include a new grille surround, side cladding, taillamps, tailgate handle, rear bumper design and alloy wheels. Inside, there is new seat fabric, an upgraded two-tone color scheme and a revised instrument cluster. A power driver seat is now standard on the LX, and a compass is included with the optional sunroof.

**Body Styles, Trim Levels and Options:** The four-door Santa Fe is sold in GLS and LX trims. Standard equipment on the GLS includes side airbags; air conditioning; power windows, mirrors and locks; a CD player; 16-inch alloy wheels; a full-size spare tire; foglights; and a CD-cassette combo. Options on the GLS include a power sunroof and a Monsoon sound system with an in-dash CD changer. The Monsoon stereo comes standard on the high-line LX, along with automatic climate control, a power driver seat, leather upholstery, heated seats and an auto-dimming mirror with a HomeLink remote transmitter; a sunroof remains optional.

**Powertrains and Performance:** The standard power plant is a 2.7-liter V6 rated at 170 horsepower and 181 lb-ft of torque; it's paired with a four-speed automatic transmission. Standard on the LX is a 3.5-liter V6 good for 200 hp and 219 lb-ft of torque. This engine comes with a five-speed automatic. Buyers can choose between front-wheel drive (2WD) and all-wheel drive. Although the smaller V6 is rated for up to 26 mpg on the highway, the 3.5-liter turns in dismal fuel numbers for a small SUV application—just 16-17 mpg in the city and 21-22 on the highway.

**Safety:** Four-wheel antilock disc brakes, traction control and side airbags (for front occupants) are standard on all models. Outboard occupants get headrests and three-point seatbelts, but the rear center position has only a lap belt. In government crash tests, the Santa Fe earned a perfect five stars for driver protection in frontal impacts and four stars for the front passenger. Side-impact testing resulted in a five-star rating for front passenger protection. In frontal offset crash testing conducted by the IIHS, the Santa Fe received a "Good" rating (the highest possible); in IIHS side-impact testing, it earned an "Acceptable" rating (the second highest).

**Interior Design and Special Features:** Inside, the Santa Fe has spacious accommodations for five and a 29.4-cubic-foot cargo bay; fold down the 60/40-split rear seats, and you get a generous 78 cubes. The cabin boasts a sharp two-tone color scheme and feels high in quality, as Hyundai has fitted it with low-gloss plastics and solid switchgear.

**Driving Impressions:** The Santa Fe has just what most family-oriented buyers want: adequate power and a smooth, quiet ride. Handling is on the bland side—with noticeable body roll around corners and numb steering—but unless you're a driving enthusiast, you won't care. If you opt for AWD, you'll have a bargain-priced, all-weather family vehicle.

*Crash Test Scores, see pg 530*
*Warranty information, see pg 542*

### Specifications

| Engine/Drivetrain | HP | Torque | EPA Fuel Economy Rating |
|---|---|---|---|
| 6cyl 2.7L A | 170 | 181 | 20 city/26 hwy |
| 6cyl 3.5L A | 200 | 219 | 17 city/22 hwy |

### Body Styles

| Style | MSRP Range |
|---|---|
| Midsize SUV | $21,499 - $25,999 |

# 2005 Hyundai Sonata

**MSRP Price Range**

## $15,999 - $19,799
Destination Charge: $595 (all styles)

### Ratings

| | | |
|---|---|---|
| Consumer Rating | N/A | |
| Editors Rating | 6.6 | |

**What Edmunds.com says:** A decent buy if you can't spend over $20,000 on a midsize sedan, but the Sonata offers no revelations in performance or interior accommodations.

**Pros:** Excellent warranty, pleasant highway ride, refined V6 engine, lots of storage space.

**Cons:** Noisy four-cylinder engine, bland interior design and materials, tight rear-seat legroom, tepid handling.

**What's New:** For 2005, trim levels have been slightly revised, and an auto-dimming rearview mirror with a HomeLink remote transmitter has been added to the LX.

**Body Styles, Trim Levels and Options:** The midsize Sonata sedan is sold in three trim levels—GL, GLS and LX. The GL offers 15-inch wheels; foglights; side airbags; a CD player; air conditioning; power windows, locks and mirrors; a 60/40-split-folding rear seat; keyless entry; and cruise control. The GLS adds 16-inch alloy wheels, rear disc brakes, a power antenna, upgraded cloth upholstery, a leather-wrapped steering wheel and shift knob, wood grain trim, heated mirrors and a cassette player along with the CD player. The high-line LX tacks on leather upholstery, an auto-dimming rearview mirror with a HomeLink remote transmitter, a power driver seat and automatic climate control. Antilock brakes are optional on all trim levels; traction control is coupled with ABS on the GLS and LX. A moonroof is a stand-alone extra.

**Powertrains and Performance:** Sonata buyers have two engine choices: A 138-horsepower, 2.4-liter inline four is standard on the base GL. As it comes up short in power and refinement, we feel that most buyers will be happier with the 170-hp, 2.7-liter V6—it's standard on the GLS and LX. Although the V6 is weaker than most six-cylinders currently offered in the family sedan segment, it's smooth and quiet, and offers decent acceleration and enough thrust for confident merging on the highway. The four-cylinder engine can be mated to a five-speed manual transmission or a four-speed automatic with a manual-shift mode, while the V6 comes only with the automatic. Mileage ratings are 22 mpg city/30 mpg highway with the four-cylinder and 19/27 with the V6.

**Safety:** Antilock brakes are optional across the line, and V6-equipped vehicles get rear disc brakes. Side airbags for front occupants and three-point seatbelts for all five seating positions are standard in every Sonata. In government crash testing, the Sonata earned four out of five stars across the board. In frontal offset crash testing conducted by the IIHS, the Sonata received an "Acceptable" rating (the second highest possible). In IIHS side-impact tests, the Sonata returned a rating of "Poor," the lowest, even with its standard side airbags.

**Interior Design and Special Features:** Inside the monochromatic cabin are plush seats that provide a comfortable driving position. Interior materials are on the economy side, but they're acceptable in a car that costs less than $20,000. Drivers will find logically arranged radio and climate controls, plenty of storage nooks and, in GLS and LX models, warm faux-wood accents and a leather-wrapped steering wheel and shift knob. The spacious 14-cubic-foot trunk offers an extremely low lift-over height and closes with struts rather than parcel-crushing hinges.

**Driving Impressions:** Although not as refined as an Accord or Camry, the value-priced Sonata targets the same sort of buyer—commuters and families who want comfortable transportation for the day-to-day grind. The ride is stable and smooth, though bumps and ruts are transmitted to the cabin more harshly than they should be. Around-town maneuvers are accomplished with ease, and a tight 34.4-foot turning radius makes the Sonata an affable companion in parking lots.

*Crash Test Scores, see pg 530*
*Warranty information, see pg 542*

### Specifications

| Engine/Drivetrain | HP | Torque | EPA Fuel Economy Rating |
|---|---|---|---|
| 6cyl 2.7L A | 170 | 181 | 19 city/23 hwy |
| 4cyl 2.4L A/M | 138 | 147 | 22 city/30 hwy |

### Body Styles

| Style | MSRP Range |
|---|---|
| Midsize Sedan | $15,999–$19,799 |

# 2005 Hyundai Tiburon
**Compact Coupe**

**MSRP Price Range**

*N/A*

Destination Charge: N/A (all styles)

## Ratings

| | | |
|---|---|---|
| Consumer Rating | N/A | |
| Editors Rating | 7.8 | |

**What Edmunds.com says:** With clean styling, optional V6 power and a generous warranty, the Tiburon would seem to have no faults, but a few too many pounds and a less-than-athletic suspension keep it from attaining class-leading sport coupe status.

**Pros:** Solid V6 power, predictable driving dynamics, clean interior styling, generous standard equipment list, reasonable price, great warranty.

**Cons:** Considerable weight takes its toll on performance, thirsty at the pumps in V6 form.

**What's New:** For 2005, Hyundai shuffles the Tiburon's trim levels and revises the interior and exterior styling. Outside, the Tiburon receives a new grille and lower fascia, new headlamps and foglamps, redesigned side mirrors, a revised side garnish, new taillamps and new badging. Interior updates include new seat cloth, floor mats, overhead console and center air vent controls. Cars with the six-speed manual transmission get a new shift knob as well.

**Body Styles, Trim Levels and Options:** The Tiburon coupe is available in GS, GT and SE trims. Standard equipment for the GS includes air conditioning, six-speaker stereo with CD player, side airbags, cruise control, sport seats, power windows and locks, keyless entry, four-wheel disc brakes, 16-inch alloy wheels and a rear spoiler. The GT adds leather, automatic climate control, a seven-speaker Infinity sound system, sport suspension, 17-inch wheels and a more dramatic rear spoiler. The sporty SE includes red front brake calipers, ABS, foglamps, high rear spoiler, aluminum pedals, manual-control air conditioning, metal grain interior trim, a Kenwood CD/MP3 audio system, cruise control, and a leather-wrapped steering wheel and shift knob. The SE also features auxiliary torque, voltmeter and vacuum gauges.

**Powertrains and Performance:** The base engine is a 2.0-liter DOHC inline four with continuously variable valve timing. This engine makes 138 hp and 136 lb-ft of torque. While this engine isn't the pinnacle of refinement, it feels surprisingly energetic when revved. For optimal performance, you'll want to get the five-speed manual rather than the four-speed automatic. Step up to the GT or SE, and you're rewarded with a 2.7-liter DOHC V6 rated at 172 hp and 181 lb-ft of torque. The GT is available with a five-speed manual or a four-speed automatic, while the SE can be had with either a six-speed manual or the automatic. All Tiburons feature a fully independent suspension with MacPherson struts in the front and a multilink rear. The GT and SE feature a tauter ride, thanks to higher spring rates, stiffer shock absorbers and larger front and rear antiroll bars.

**Safety:** All Tiburons come standard with seat-mounted side airbags for front occupants. Four-wheel disc brakes are standard; antilock brakes are standard on the SE and optional on all other models.

**Interior Design and Special Features:** The Tiburon has a simple but handsome cockpit. At first glance, it's evident that the interior designers wanted to impart a high-quality look and feel to the cabin. Everything is laid out in a straightforward fashion free of gimmickry. Fiddle with the climate control knobs, and the silky fluidity with which they move would do a Honda proud. Bolstered sport seats help keep occupants in place during enthusiastic cornering, and the large speedometer and tachometer are easy to read at a glance

**Driving Impressions:** When the Tiburon is driven hard, it lacks the athleticism of an Acura RSX or Mini Cooper S—its V6 is confident but not eager; its steering is a bit slow and numb, and with a curb weight of about 3,000 pounds in GT and SE form, it's heavy for a sport coupe. However, when driven in a relaxed manner, this Hyundai performs capably and delivers a smooth ride. Factor in a generous standard features list, competitive pricing and elegant styling, and the Tiburon is definitely worth a test-drive.

*Crash Test Scores, see pg 530*
*Warranty information, see pg 542*

## Specifications

| Engine/Drivetrain | HP | Torque | EPA Fuel Economy Rating |
|---|---|---|---|
| 4cyl 2.0L A/M | 138 | 136 | 24 city/30 hwy |
| 6cyl 2.7L A/M | 172 | 181 | 19 city/26 hwy |

## Body Styles

| Style | MSRP Range |
|---|---|
| Compact Coupe | N/A |

For the latest full vehicle reports, visit www.edmunds.com/bginfopak

**Compact SUV**

# 2005 Hyundai Tucson

**MSRP Price Range**
## $17,499 - $22,749
Destination Charge: $595 (all styles)

## Ratings

| Ratings | | |
|---|---|---|
| Consumer Rating | N/A | |
| Editors Rating | 7.3 | |

**What Edmunds.com says:** Appealing styling, plenty of standard features and Hyundai's impressive warranty make the Tucson a solid competitor in the compact SUV class.

**Pros:** Generous warranty, standard ABS and stability control, roomy passenger and cargo space, attractive interior, standard side and head curtain airbags.

**Cons:** Low horsepower rating, some cheap interior materials here and there.

**What's New:** The Hyundai Tucson is an all-new compact SUV from Hyundai. It rides on the Elantra platform and is intended for buyers who want a smaller package than the midsize Santa Fe.

**Body Styles, Trim Levels and Options:** The four-door Tucson compact SUV comes in three trim levels—entry-level GL, midlevel GLS and top-of-the-line LX. Standard features on the GL include four-wheel disc brakes with ABS, 16-inch alloy wheels, air conditioning, power windows and door locks, keyless entry, cruise control, heated outside mirrors, roof rack side rails, a rear intermittent wiper and a CD stereo system. The GL adds body-side cladding, foglamps, larger tires, a CD/cassette/MP3 stereo, upgraded upholstery and a front wiper de-icer. The LX adds leather seating and an upgraded audio system with an in-dash six-disc CD changer and a subwoofer.

**Powertrains and Performance:** The base GL offers a 2.0-liter, inline four-cylinder engine with continuously variable valve timing. It generates 140 horsepower and 136 pound-feet of torque, and is mated to a five-speed manual transmission or a four-speed automatic with automanual control. The GLS and LX provide a larger, more powerful 2.7-liter V6 engine that produces 173 hp and 178 lb-ft of torque. A four-speed automatic transmission is standard on the GLS and LX. Buyers can get front-wheel drive or all-wheel drive with either engine.

**Safety:** Passengers are well protected as the Tucson comes standard with seat-mounted side-impact airbags for front occupants and side curtain airbags for both front- and rear-seat occupants. Four-wheel antilock disc brakes are also standard on all Tucsons, along with a traction and stability control system. The Tucson has not yet been crash tested.

**Interior Design and Special Features:** The Tucson features a modern interior with high-quality materials and design. Generous passenger space makes for a comfortable ride. Inside, the Tucson offers 22.7 cubic feet of cargo capacity with the rear seat up, and up to 65.5 with the seat folded.

**Driving Impressions:** The Tucson returns a smooth ride and feels more like a sedan than an SUV. The standard four-cylinder is quite weak; we recommend you go with the V6.

*Crash Test Scores, see pg 530*
*Warranty information, see pg 542*

## Specifications

| Engine/Drivetrain | HP | Torque | EPA Fuel Economy Rating |
|---|---|---|---|
| 6cyl 2.7L A | 173 | 178 | 20 city/26 hwy |
| 4cyl 2.0L A/M | 140 | 136 | 22 city/27 hwy |

## Body Styles

| Style | MSRP Range |
|---|---|
| Compact SUV | $17,499–$22,749 |

# 2005 Hyundai XG350

**Midsize Sedan**

## MSRP Price Range
### $24,399 - $25,999
Destination Charge: N/A (all styles)

## Ratings

| | | |
|---|---|---|
| Consumer Rating | N/A | |
| Editors Rating | N/A | |

**What Edmunds.com says:** If upscale features are more important to you than tight handling and a mainstream name, the XG350 is worth a look. However, most buyers would be better served by a well-optioned Accord or Camry.

**Pros:** Classy interior materials, long list of standard features, low price, excellent warranty.

**Cons:** Flaccid handling, easily confused automatic transmission, conservative styling, no side curtain airbags.

**What's New:** The XG350L receives a standard eight-disc CD changer.

**Body Styles, Trim Levels and Options:** Hyundai's XG350 flagship sedan is available in two trim levels—base and L. The base car comes with 16-inch alloy wheels, four-wheel antilock disc brakes, traction control, side airbags, leather upholstery, dual power seats, automatic climate control, a CD player, a leather-wrapped steering wheel, a 60/40-split-folding rear seat, a full-size spare tire with matching alloy wheel and power windows, locks and mirrors. The L adds a sunroof, an eight-disc CD changer, seat heaters, an auto-dimming rearview mirror, memory for the driver seat and mirror settings and a faux wood- and leather-wrapped steering wheel. The L version also gets unique 12-spoke alloy wheels

**Powertrains and Performance:** Every XG350 is powered by a 3.5-liter V6 that generates 194 horsepower and 216 pound-feet of torque. This engine is smooth, quiet and reasonably powerful compared with the other offerings in the family sedan segment, though touchy throttle response mars the driving experience somewhat. A five-speed automatic with a sequential-shift manual mode is standard. Despite the XG's non-sporting personality, the manual mode actually works quite well. Fuel economy is rated at 18 mpg in the city and 26 on the highway.

**Safety:** Four-wheel antilock disc brakes, traction control and side airbags for front occupants are standard. Full-length head curtain airbags are not available. The XG earned a "Good" rating (the highest possible) in IIHS' 40-mph offset crash testing. In government crash tests the XG earned a perfect five stars for frontal impacts, and four for side impacts.

**Interior Design and Special Features:** Overall, the cabin imparts a sense of traditional luxury. Materials quality is high, especially considering the price, and storage space is generous. Although roomy, the rear seats are contoured more for two passengers than three and toe room is tight. Still, backseat riders will appreciate the rear vents and 12-volt power point. The trunk offers decent capacity at 14.5 cubic feet and even has non-luggage-crushing external strut hinges.

**Driving Impressions:** The XG350 is suitable for the average driver who prefers comfort over performance as it provides a smooth ride over almost any surface. If you push it harder, however, its non-athletic personality is immediately evident, as its suspension wallows over bumps and ruts and allows plenty of body roll when cornering, and its steering maintains a limp, uncommunicative feel. While we think the XG is worth your consideration if a dressed-up cabin and a lengthy standard features list are your top priorities, we'll readily acknowledge that it's unlikely to please those looking for a fun-to-drive midsize sedan.

*Crash Test Scores, see pg 530*
*Warranty information, see pg 542*

## Specifications

| Engine/Drivetrain | HP | Torque | EPA Fuel Economy Rating |
|---|---|---|---|
| 6cyl 3.5L A | 194 | 216 | 18 city/26 hwy |

## Body Styles

| Style | MSRP Range |
|---|---|
| Midsize Sedan | $24,399 - $25,999 |

# 2005 Infiniti FX35

**MSRP Price Range**

## $34,750 - $36,250
Destination Charge: $590 (all styles)

### Ratings

| | | |
|---|---|---|
| Consumer Rating | N/A | |
| Editors Rating | N/A | |

**What Edmunds.com says:** A stylish melding of form and function, the FX35 offers carlike handling and all-weather capability in a package that will never be mistaken for your average Explorer.

**Pros:** Standout styling, handles like a sport sedan, roomy interior for four, long list of standard features, strong V6.

**Cons:** Minimal cargo room, large blind spots, tricky at-the-limit handling, doesn't feel as upscale as some peers, no third-row seat available.

**What's New:** New options for 2005 include a lane departure warning system, Intelligent Cruise Control and a new Intelligent Key. Roof-mounted side-curtain airbags with rollover protection are now standard.

**Body Styles, Trim Levels and Options:** The FX35 is a four-door midsize SUV offered in one trim level. Standard equipment includes eight-way power driver and front-passenger seats, a leather-wrapped steering wheel and shift knob, dual-zone automatic climate control, keyless entry, HID headlights, an in-dash six-disc CD changer and 18-inch aluminum wheels. There are three significant option packages for adding additional equipment. The Premium Package adds items like leather seating, a power tilt and telescoping steering wheel, heated seats and mirrors, a sunroof, a 300-watt Bose audio system, steering wheel audio controls, auto headlights and a programmable Homelink remote transmitter. The Sport Package is identical to the Premium Package, except for the addition of 20-inch aluminum wheels. For more gadgets, the Technology Package augments the equipment in the Sport Package with a DVD navigation system, intelligent keyless entry (that uses electronic signals in place of a conventional keyless remote), a DVD entertainment system, radar-based adaptive cruise control, a rearview backup camera and a tire-pressure monitoring system. An available Lane Departure Warning System (LDW) works to alert the driver to any unintended movement of the vehicle out of a designated traffic lane.

**Powertrains and Performance:** The FX35 is available with either rear- or all-wheel drive. Both models use a 280-hp, 3.5-liter V6 engine and a five-speed automatic transmission with a manual-shift mode. All-wheel-drive models use an electronically controlled system that automatically directs power to the wheels with the most traction.

**Safety:** Safety highlights include four-wheel vented disc brakes with ABS, BrakeAssist and Electronic Brakeforce Distribution. Front-seat side-impact airbags are standard, along with front and rear head-curtain airbags. Electronic traction and stability control systems also come standard. All-wheel-drive versions feature a snow mode for smoother take-offs on slippery roads.

**Interior Design and Special Features:** With plenty of passenger room and a clean design, the FX35's interior is comfortable and easy to get used to. Although leather upholstery is available, the interior has more of a sporty flavor than a luxurious one, as aluminum trim takes the place of wood accents. The center console features a few too many buttons of similar shape and size. The sloping roofline makes for tight headroom in back, but the seat backs recline for added space when needed. Cargo room is tight as there's just 65 cubic feet of room compared to 80 cubic feet or more in most midsize SUVs.

**Driving Impressions:** Built specifically to excel on the pavement where most owners will use it most, the FX handles more like a sedan than an SUV. Minimal body roll, quick steering and the powerful V6 engine all combine to provide a driving experience that few other sport-utes can match. When driven at the upper end of its performance limits, the FX isn't as easy to control as a BMW X5, but the vast majority of drivers will find its road manners exceptional. If you like driving but need the utility of an SUV, the FX is one of the most enjoyable compromises available.

*Crash Test Scores, see pg 530*
*Warranty information, see pg 542*

### Specifications

| Engine/Drivetrain | HP | Torque | EPA Fuel Economy Rating |
|---|---|---|---|
| 6cyl 3.5L A | 280 | 270 | 17 city/23 hwy |

### Body Styles

| Style | MSRP Range |
|---|---|
| Midsize SUV | $34,750–$36,250 |

# 2005 Infiniti FX45

**MSRP Price Range**

### $45,250

Destination Charge: $590 (all styles)

## Ratings

| | | |
|---|---|---|
| Consumer Rating | N/A | |
| Editors Rating | 7.4 | |

**What Edmunds.com says:** If you like the styling, the rest of the vehicle isn't likely to let you down, as the FX45 delivers surprisingly adept handling and spirited performance for an SUV.

**Pros:** Standout styling, handles like a sport sedan, potent V8 engine, roomy interior for four, long list of standard features.

**Cons:** Cabin lacks the upscale feel of the competition, minimal cargo room, large blind spots, tricky at-the-limit handling, no third-row seating available.

**What's New:** New options for 2005 include a lane departure warning system, Intelligent Cruise Control and a new Intelligent Key. Roof-mounted side curtain airbags with rollover protection are now standard.

**Body Styles, Trim Levels and Options:** The FX45 is a midsize SUV offered in one trim level. The long standard features list is highlighted by full leather seating and trim, power eight-way driver and front-passenger seats, dual-zone automatic climate control, heated front seats, HID headlights, 20-inch aluminum wheels and an in-dash six-disc CD changer. For additional features, there are two significant options packages. The Premium Package adds a sunroof, a Bose 300-watt audio system, steering wheel audio controls, auto headlights and a programmable Homelink remote transmitter. The Technology Package augments the equipment in the Premium Package with a DVD navigation system, intelligent keyless entry that uses electronic signals instead of a conventional keyless remote, a DVD entertainment system, radar cruise control, a rearview backup camera and a tire-pressure monitoring system. An available Lane Departure Warning System (LDW) works to alert the driver to any unintended movement of the vehicle out of a designated traffic lane.

**Powertrains and Performance:** All FX45s feature a 4.5-liter V8 engine that produces 315 hp and 329 lb-ft of torque. A five-speed automatic transmission with manual-shift capability sends the power to the ground via an electronically controlled all-wheel-drive system. Performance is impressive for an SUV, as the FX can accelerate to 60 mph in just 6.5 seconds. Not surprisingly, fuel mileage is considerably less impressive with EPA ratings of 15 mpg city and 19 mpg on the highway.

**Safety:** Safety highlights include four-wheel vented disc brakes with ABS, BrakeAssist and Electronic Brakeforce Distribution. Front-seat side-impact airbags are standard, along with front and rear head curtain airbags. Electronic traction and stability control systems also come standard. A snow mode for the all-wheel-drive system delivers smoother take-offs on slippery roads.

*Crash Test Scores, see pg 530*
*Warranty information, see pg 542*

**Interior Design and Special Features:** With plenty of passenger room and a clean design, the FX's interior is comfortable and easy to get used to. The accommodations are as luxurious as those of some peers, though, as aluminum trim replaces the usual wood inlays. The center console features a few too many buttons for our tastes, but once you're accustomed to their placement, the layout proves functional. The sloping roofline makes for tight headroom in back, but the seat backs recline for added space when needed. Cargo room is tight, as there's just 65 cubic feet of capacity compared to 80 cubic feet or more in most midsize SUVs. The optional 11-speaker Bose stereo sounds incredible, as it envelops the driver and front passenger in a rich soundstage.

## Specifications

| Engine/Drivetrain | HP | Torque | EPA Fuel Economy Rating |
|---|---|---|---|
| 8cyl 4.5L A | 315 | 329 | 15 city/19 hwy |

## Body Styles

| Style | MSRP Range |
|---|---|
| Midsize SUV | $45,250 |

**Driving Impressions:** The 4.5-liter motor delivers effortless acceleration and a thrilling exhaust note that's unexpected in an SUV. The FX also handles surprisingly well for its size, but the trade-off is a stiff suspension that can be uncomfortable on rough streets. Further, when driven at the upper end of its performance limits, the FX isn't as easy to control as a BMW X5, though the vast majority of drivers will find its handling characteristics exceptional. For a softer ride, consider the FX35 with its smaller wheels and more forgiving setup.

## Midsize Coupe, Sedan

# 2005 Infiniti G35

**MSRP Price Range**
### $30,700 - $32,500
Destination Charge: $590 (all styles)

## Ratings

| | | |
|---|---|---|
| Consumer Rating | N/A | |
| Editors Rating | 8.0 | |

**What Edmunds.com says:** Fast, stylish and relatively affordable, the rear-drive G35 sedan and the coupe offer high levels of performance and luxury.

**Pros:** Powerful V6, balanced and capable handling, roomy cabin, reasonable price.

**Cons:** Average interior materials quality, touchy brakes.

**What's New:** The sedan receives exterior styling revisions with a new hood, grille, bumpers, side sills, taillights and wheels. Coupes and sedans with an automatic transmission also get more power—280 hp (up from 260) and 270 lb-ft of torque (also up from 260)—and the sport suspension package now includes 18-inch alloy wheels and drilled aluminum pedals. G35s equipped with a manual transmission get even more power, for a total of 298 horsepower. All G35s get a redesigned instrument panel and console area with aluminum or wood trim, and the manual transmission has been improved to provide a lower shifting effort. A Sport Coupe model debuts this year and includes a new sport-tuned suspension, viscous limited-slip differential, 19-inch forged alloy wheels and drilled aluminum pedals.

**Body Styles, Trim Levels and Options:** The G35 is available in coupe or sedan form. The sedan is available in rear-wheel- or all-wheel drive. There are no trim levels to choose between in the sedan, but coupes are available in base or Sport trim. All sedans come with 17-inch wheels, automatic climate control, one-touch auto up-down front windows, an in-dash six-disc CD changer, keyless entry and a rear-seat trunk pass-through. In addition to that, base coupes get high-intensity discharge headlamps and heated, power-adjustable seats. Additionally, sedans equipped with a manual gearbox and all coupes get a sport-tuned suspension, 18-inch wheels and drilled aluminum pedals; manual-shift coupes also pick up Brembo brakes. The Sport Coupe model adds an even firmer performance-tuned suspension, a viscous limited-slip differential and 19-inch alloys. All leather-upholstered G35s are eligible for a premium package that includes dual-zone climate control with rear vents, an upgraded 225-watt Bose sound system, a sunroof, automatic headlights and an auto-dimming rearview mirror. Among the other options are a DVD-based navigation system and either Sirius or XM Satellite Radio.

**Powertrains and Performance:** Though the G35 comes with just one engine, it should satisfy all but the most power-hungry drivers. This smooth-revving 3.5-liter V6 makes 280 horsepower and 270 pound-feet of torque in both the coupe and sedan when hitched to the five-speed automatic transmission. Models equipped with the six-speed manual transmission get a 298-hp version of this engine. Automatic-equipped G35 sedans are eligible for an electronically controlled all-wheel-drive system that includes a "snow mode," which evenly splits the power 50/50 to the front and rear wheels.

**Safety:** All G35s come standard with four-wheel antilock disc brakes with brakeforce distribution and BrakeAssist, torso-protecting side airbags, head-protecting side curtain airbags and front seatbelts with pre-tensioners and load limiters. Vehicle Dynamic Control (VDC), a stability control system, is also standard. In frontal offset crash testing conducted by the IIHS, the G35 earned the top score of "Good."

**Interior Design and Special Features:** Thanks to a long wheelbase, the G35 offers a spacious cabin. The sedan's passenger compartment measures 101.4 cubic feet, with ample amounts of front and rear headroom, legroom and shoulder room. The coupe is also roomy in front; those seated in back will find adequate legroom, but the sloping rear glass limits the available headroom for adults. The sedan offers 14.5 cubic feet of trunk capacity, while the coupe's hatchback holds just 7.8 cubes.

**Driving Impressions:** As expected, the G35 offers a very entertaining ride. Acceleration is strong, and the prodigious midrange torque is something not often found in this class of car. Handling, too, is on par with the best and you'll likely find yourself leaving the windows down just to hear the exhaust note of the coupe. We highly recommend taking a look at the G35 if you're shopping for an entry-level luxury sport sedan or coupe.

*Crash Test Scores, see pg 530*
*Warranty information, see pg 542*

## Specifications

| Engine/Drivetrain | HP | Torque | EPA Fuel Economy Rating |
|---|---|---|---|
| 6cyl 3.5L A/M | 280 | 270 | 19 city/26 hwy |
| 6cyl 3.5L A/M | 298 | 260 | N/A |

## Body Styles

| Style | MSRP Range |
|---|---|
| Midsize Coupe | $32,400–$33,000 |
| Midsize Sedan | $30,700–$32,500 |

# 2005 Infiniti Q45

Large Sedan

**MSRP Price Range**

## $55,900

Destination Charge: $590 (all styles)

## Ratings

| | | |
|---|---|---|
| Consumer Rating | 9.5 | |
| Editors Rating | 8.2 | |

**What Edmunds.com says:** Fast, luxurious and priced thousands of dollars less than most peers, the Q is a solid buy for comfort seekers on a budget. But if owning the best is what matters to you, drive the competition first.

**Pros:** Elegant and spacious interior, long list of standard luxury features, strong V8, excellent value.

**Cons:** Unnecessarily complex interior controls, small trunk capacity, not as athletic as some competitors.

**What's New:** For 2005, Infiniti's flagship sedan receives updated exterior styling with new front and rear fascias, a new hood, headlights with integrated foglamps, a new trunk deck lid, LED taillights and fine-line chrome trim. Instead of offering Luxury and Premium models this year, Infiniti will sell a base Q45 (with all the Luxury equipment) with an optional Premium Package. Inside, the Q45 features new "sport contour," double-stitched seats and a new instrument cluster, along with a metal-trimmed shifter bezel, metal knobs and dark maple wood and chrome accents. The transmission has been recalibrated for better response, and the performance-tuned active dampening suspension, previously available only at the Premium level, is now standard on all models. Base models get a new 17-inch alloy wheel design this year. Other enhancements include standard rain- and speed-sensing wipers, a revised DVD-based navigation system (also standard), and new brake-operated "pre-crash" front seatbelts, which tighten under emergency braking.

*Crash Test Scores, see pg 530*
*Warranty information, see pg 542*

## Specifications

| Engine/Drivetrain | HP | Torque | EPA Fuel Economy Rating |
|---|---|---|---|
| 8cyl 4.5L A | 340 | 333 | 17 city/25 hwy |

## Body Styles

| Style | MSRP Range |
|---|---|
| Large Sedan | $55,900 |

**Body Styles, Trim Levels and Options:** This year Infiniti is offering the Q45 sedan in a single trim. The base Q comes with 17-inch alloy wheels, an adaptive suspension with driver-selectable settings, a powerful set of high-intensity discharge headlights, a DVD-based navigation system, a 10-way power driver seat and eight-way power front-passenger seat, front seat heaters, leather upholstery, genuine wood trim, a sunroof, a voice recognition system for various controls, rain-sensing wipers, a rearview backup camera, a 300-watt Bose stereo with eight speakers, an in-dash CD changer and satellite radio (either XM or Sirius). Opt for the Premium Package and you'll get 18-inch wheels, adaptive cruise control (called Intelligent Cruise Control), heated and cooled front seats, power-adjustable and heated rear seats, rear air conditioning controls and a power-operated rear-window shade along with manual shades for the side windows.

**Powertrains and Performance:** The rear-drive Q45 is powered by a muscular 4.5-liter V8 that produces 340 hp and 333 lb-ft of torque. This power is routed through a five-speed automatic transmission with a manual-shift mode. The Q45 can go from zero to 60 mph in 6.7 seconds, about average for the segment.

**Safety:** The Q45 features a myriad of standard safety features, including dual-stage front airbags with seatbelt sensors that help tailor deployment to collision severity. Front-seat occupants get front-seat active head restraints, while the seats themselves are equipped with supplemental side-impact airbags. Side curtain airbags protect front and rear outboard occupants. Other features include four-wheel antilock disc brakes with BrakeAssist and Electronic Brakeforce Distribution (EBD). Stability and traction control are also standard. Every Q45 comes with Infiniti's RearView Monitor, which helps avert parking lot mishaps by projecting the images from a rear-mounted camera to the car's center display screen whenever the transmission is in reverse.

**Interior Design and Special Features:** Step inside, and you're greeted with an exquisite cabin draped in soft leather and dark maple wood trim. The electroluminescent gauges are both beautiful to look at and easy to read. Passenger room is ample throughout, and the spectacular Bose stereo fills the cabin with near perfect sound reproduction. Although visually appealing and technologically innovative, the Q's climate and radio controls are needlessly complicated, routed as they are through a joystick-controlled LCD—good thing voice command comes standard. Trunk capacity (13.7 cubic feet) is a bit meager compared to the competition.

**Driving Impressions:** The Q's V8 engine feels strong once it revs up a bit, though it doesn't feel as quick off the line as competitors' V8s. As you'd expect of a large luxury sedan, the ride is delightfully quiet and comfortable on the highway. The active dampening suspension system provides a nice balance between ride comfort and handling ability, but don't expect the sharp reflexes of an Audi A8 or BMW 7 Series.

# Large SUV

**MSRP Price Range**
## $47,750 - $50,750
Destination Charge: N/A (all styles)

### Ratings

| | | |
|---|---|---|
| Consumer Rating | N/A | |
| Editors Rating | 8.4 | |

**What Edmunds.com says:** If the styling suits you, the rest of this import luxury liner should, too, as the QX56 more than measures up to its domestic competitors.

**Pros:** Powerful and refined V8 power, good balance of ride and handling, class-leading towing capacity, roomy second-row seats, handy video parking monitor.

**Cons:** Some low-grade cabin trim, typical big SUV thirst.

**What's New:** No significant changes this year for the QX56.

**Body Styles, Trim Levels and Options:** The QX56 is a full-size four-door luxury SUV with one trim level and either two- or four-wheel drive. As expected, standard features are plentiful, including 18-inch chrome wheels, xenon headlights, leather seating for seven, real wood trim, a DVD-based navigation system, a 10-speaker Bose audio system, dual-zone automatic climate control, a separate rear air conditioner, one-touch power windows and a power rear liftgate. The short list of options includes a bench seat for the second row (increasing capacity to eight), satellite radio (XM or Sirius), a power sunroof and a very handy rear backup camera system packaged with adaptive cruse control. A DVD entertainment system is also available to entertain backseat passengers.

**Powertrains and Performance:** Power comes by way of a 5.6-liter DOHC V8 with 315 hp and 390 lb-ft of torque. A five-speed automatic handles shifting duties, sending the power to either the rear wheels or all four wheels via Infiniti's All-Mode all-wheel-drive system. Maximum towing capacity is 8,900 pounds. As expected, fuel economy is not very good with EPA ratings of 13 mpg city and 18-19 mpg highway.

**Safety:** Side curtain airbags offer protection to all three rows of passengers, and seat-mounted side-impact airbags protect front-seat passengers. A reverse-sensing system is standard, and a useful rear video camera is optional. All QX56s include ABS, traction and stability control and a tire-pressure monitor. Power-adjustable pedals help owners find an ideal driving position and are linked to the standard memory system.

**Interior Design and Special Features:** The QX56 interior is swathed in leather and thick carpeting. The steering wheel is trimmed in wood and aluminum, and the console features a generous plank of either dark Macore or blonde Apaya wood trim. Unfortunately, hard plastics on the dash and doors somewhat detract from the upscale ambience. Second-row captain's chairs are standard, along with a removable center console and third-row fold-flat bench seat. A fold-flat second-row bench seat is optional. Big as it feels on the inside, the QX56 has less maximum cargo capacity than an Escalade or Navigator, with just over 97 cubic feet of space. But if you're planning to seat passengers in all three rows, the Infiniti has the advantage, with a generous 20 cubic feet behind the third row.

**Driving Impressions:** Around town, the QX56 moves out briskly and effortlessly storms up freeway on-ramps to blend into fast-moving traffic. The five-speed automatic provides seamless gear changes and steps down promptly when a burst of power is needed for quick passing. Far from being a one-trick pony, the QX56 has a chassis to match its potent power plant. An independent suspension all around provides the well-damped ride quality that luxury buyers would expect along with surprisingly nimble handling for a vehicle of its size. Body lean is noticeable when cornering, but it's nothing excessive—just a reminder to the driver that in spite of the QX56's sure handling, there is still a lot of sheet metal getting tossed around.

*Crash Test Scores, see pg 530*
*Warranty information, see pg 542*

### Specifications

| Engine/Drivetrain | HP | Torque | EPA Fuel Economy Rating |
|---|---|---|---|
| 8cyl 5.6L A | 315 | 390 | 13 city/19 hwy |

### Body Styles

| Style | MSRP Range |
|---|---|
| Large SUV | $47,450 - $50,750 |

# 2005 Isuzu Ascender

**Large SUV**

**MSRP Price Range**
## $25,959 - $38,914
Destination Charge: N/A (all styles)

## Ratings

| | | |
|---|---|---|
| Consumer Rating | N/A | |
| Editors Rating | 6.6 | |

**What Edmunds.com says:** Capable, roomy and packing optional V8 power, the Ascender's longer warranty makes it worth considering over its nearly identical Chevrolet and GMC cousins.

**Pros:** Strong six- and eight-cylinder engines, simple interior design, plenty of passenger and cargo room, long warranty.

**Cons:** Spongy suspension, numb steering, low-grade interior materials, odd exterior proportions, poor expected resale value.

**What's New:** New options include XM Satellite Radio and a side curtain airbag system (available midyear). The 5.3-liter V8 now includes Displacement-on-Demand technology to improve fuel economy and is rated for five more horsepower this year for a total of 300.

**Body Styles, Trim Levels and Options:** The Ascender SUV comes in five-passenger and seven-passenger versions, each of which is available in three trim levels: base S, midlevel LS and high-line Limited. Two-wheel-drive S models include standard features such as power windows and locks, and dual-zone climate control with rear-seat climate controls. Select the Preferred Equipment Package to pick up power-heated mirrors, a power driver seat, keyless entry and side airbags, or order a four-wheel-drive S model to get them standard. Midgrade LS models get all of the above, plus 17-inch wheels, a moonroof, automatic climate control, steering wheel-mounted audio controls, an in-dash CD changer, a power front-passenger seat, OnStar and rear-seat audio controls. The Limited includes upgraded exterior mirrors, running boards, automatic wipers, leather seating, heated front seats, driver-adjustable pedals (in the seven-passenger version) and a premium Bose audio system.

**Powertrains and Performance:** Bracing horsepower comes via the sport-ute's standard 4.2-liter inline six. Rated at 275 horsepower and 275 pound-feet of torque, this engine outmuscles many of its competitors' V8s, let alone their V6 offerings. On LS and Limited versions of the seven-passenger Ascender, a 5.3-liter V8 is also available. It generates 300 hp and 330 lb-ft of torque and includes Displacement-on-Demand technology (DoD), which saves fuel by using only half of the engine's cylinders while cruising. Both engines come with a four-speed automatic transmission, and both two- and four-wheel-drive configurations are available. With the V8, the Ascender can tow up to 7,100 pounds.

**Safety:** Side airbags for front passengers are standard on LS and Limited models and optional on the S. Side curtain airbags are available as a midyear option. All Ascenders come with four-wheel antilock disc brakes, and 2WD LS and Limited models get traction control. Government crash tests of the Ascender's five-passenger Envoy twin yielded three out of five stars for frontal impact protection and a perfect five stars for side impacts (when equipped with side airbags). The IIHS rated the SUV "Marginal" (the second lowest of four) in frontal offset crash testing.

*Crash Test Scores, see pg 530*
*Warranty information, see pg 542*

## Specifications

| Engine/Drivetrain | HP | Torque | EPA Fuel Economy Rating |
|---|---|---|---|
| 6cyl 4.2L A | 275 | 275 | 16 city/21 hwy |
| 8cyl 5.3L A | 300 | 330 | 15 city/20 hwy |

## Body Styles

| Style | MSRP Range |
|---|---|
| Large SUV | $25,959 - $38,914 |

**Interior Design and Special Features:** The "smaller" Ascender should appeal to those people not needing a full three rows of seating. Interior materials and detailing are similar to those of the Envoy, which is to say below average, though the Limited trim adds leather and wood trim. Should you need to haul stuff, the big Ascender has 22.3 cubic feet of cargo room behind the third-row seat. With the second- and third-row seats lowered, it has 100 cubic feet of capacity, considerably more than most midsize SUVs.

**Driving Impressions:** The standard 4.2-liter is impressive enough on its own, so there's no going wrong with either of the Isuzu's engine options. Unfortunately, the suspension isn't quite so competent, as it tends to feel overly soft when cornering and rough in off-road situations. Less enthusiastic driving generates a smooth, comfortable ride.

For the latest full vehicle reports, visit www.edmunds.com/bginfopak

# 2005 Jaguar S-Type

**MSRP Price Range**

## $44,230 - $51,330

Destination Charge: $665 (all styles)

### Ratings

| | |
|---|---|
| Consumer Rating | 9.7 |
| Editors Rating | 7.4 |

**What Edmunds.com says:** A solid all-around luxury sedan, the S-Type is exactly what you would expect from Jaguar in terms of style, form and function.

**Pros:** Elegantly appointed interiors, solid all-around performance, classic British styling, full load of standard safety equipment.

**Cons:** A few cheap interior bits, high price, fussy J-gate shifter.

**What's New:** The S-Type gets minor styling revisions in the form of smaller taillights, a tighter-looking deck lid and a restyled front fascia. New exterior panels have tighter fits, while the hood is now made of aluminum. Interior upgrades include new Bronze Madrona trim, a revised instrument panel and an optional aluminum trim package. Eight-cylinder models get a new VDP package that adds premium heated leather seats, burled walnut trim and unique 17-inch alloy wheels.

**Body Styles, Trim Levels and Options:** Jaguar's S-Type sedan is available in two trims: 3.0 V6 and 4.2 V8 (a high-performance R version is also available). Standard equipment includes leather seats, bird's eye maple trim, dual-zone automatic climate control, a 140-watt sound system with a CD player, heated exterior mirrors and alloy wheels. Stepping up to the 4.2 V8 model adds more power adjustments for the front seats; 17-inch wheels; a power moonroof; a memory function for the seats, mirrors, pedals and steering column; a programmable garage door opener; and auto-dimming mirrors. The V8 sedan can also be had with a new VDP Edition package, which offers premium leather upholstery with contrasting piping on the seats, deep-pile carpeted floor mats, heated seats, burled walnut trim and an electric rear sunshade. On the outside, the VDP Edition adds chrome mirrors, xenon headlights and unique alloy wheels. Both models are eligible for a sport package that adds sport seats, unique wood trim, a sport steering wheel, special alloy wheels, body-color exterior trim, larger brakes and Jaguar's Computer Active Technology Suspension (CATS) system. Additional options include a DVD-based navigation system and adaptive cruise control.

**Powertrains and Performance:** The S-Type's standard 3.0-liter V6 makes 235 horsepower and is mated to a six-speed automatic transmission that drives the rear wheels. Models equipped with the 4.2-liter V8 boast 293 hp and come standard with the same six-speed automatic.

**Safety:** Standard equipment includes seat-mounted side-impact airbags for front occupants and full-length side curtain airbags, the former of the dual-stage variety and all connected to an advanced adaptive restraint technology system. Four-wheel antilock disc brakes with panic assist are standard, along with stability control, traction control and power-adjustable pedals. Rear parking sensors and rain-sensitive wipers are included on all S-Types.

**Interior Design and Special Features:** With a cabin slathered in real wood and sumptuous leather, the S-Type has few competitors that are as opulently trimmed. Some of the switchgear and controls are hard to use, however, and seem more suited for a Ford than a Jaguar. S-Types equipped with the navigation system have a touchscreen that controls most stereo, climate, DVD navigation and telephone features, requiring drivers to cycle through tedious menus. Jaguar has done away with a traditional handbrake, replacing it with an electronic parking brake operated using a switch on the console. For the first time ever on a Jaguar sedan, there's a high-tech aluminum fascia option, in place of traditional wood.

**Driving Impressions:** Both S-Types display surprisingly nimble driving dynamics along with a comfortable ride quality and smooth power delivery. The V8 is the way to go if you like to go everywhere fast, but most people will find the performance of the V6 perfectly acceptable. The six-speed automatic not only delivers smooth shifts, it gives the S-Type respectable fuel mileage as well.

*Crash Test Scores, see pg 530*
*Warranty information, see pg 542*

### Specifications

| Engine/Drivetrain | HP | Torque | EPA Fuel Economy Rating |
|---|---|---|---|
| 8cyl 4.2L A | 294 | 303 | 18 city/26 hwy |
| 6cyl 3.0L A | 235 | 216 | 18 city/ 26 hwy |

### Body Styles

| Style | MSRP Range |
|---|---|
| Midsize Sedan | $44,230–$51,330 |

# Jaguar

# 2005 Jaguar S-Type R

**Midsize Sedan**

**MSRP Price Range**

## $58,330

Destination Charge: $665 (all styles)

## Ratings

| | | |
|---|---|---|
| Consumer Rating | 9.6 | ████████████ |
| Editors Rating | 7.8 | ████████ |

**What Edmunds.com says:** Traditional English styling, combined with performance typically reserved for its German rivals, gives the S-Type R unique appeal in a segment full of worthy competitors.

**Pros:** Endless torque from supercharged V8, sure-footed handling, understated styling enhancements over the regular S-Type, luxurious interior, competitive price.

**Cons:** A few cheap interior bits, smallish rear seat, no manual transmission available.

**What's New:** S-Type R gets minor styling revisions in the form of smaller taillights, a tighter-looking deck lid and a restyled front fascia. New exterior panels have tighter fits, while the hood is now made of aluminum. Interior upgrades include a new instrument panel with clearer displays and optional aluminum trim.

**Body Styles, Trim Levels and Options:** The S-Type R is available only as a four-door sedan in one trim level. Owing to its luxury roots, nearly every type of comfort and convenience feature comes standard including 16-way power-adjustable sport seats, 18-inch alloy wheels, an active suspension, power-adjustable pedals, a leather-wrapped performance steering wheel, a rear parking sensor, bird's eye maple wood trim, automatic dual-zone climate control, xenon head-lights and a 10-speaker Alpine audio system. A DVD-based navigation system and adaptive cruise control are the only options.

**Powertrains and Performance:** The standard engine is a supercharged 4.2-liter V8 rated at 390 horsepower and 399 lb-ft of torque. A six-speed automatic transmission sends the power to the rear wheels. Performance is exemplary, with a 0-to-60 time of just 5.3 seconds, according to Jaguar, and an electronically limited top speed of 155 mph. Mileage is about average for the category, with an EPA rating of 16 mpg city/23 mpg highway.

**Safety:** Standard safety equipment on the S-Type R includes seat-mounted side airbags for front occupants, side curtain airbags for the front and rear, anti-whiplash seats, electronic stability and traction control and high-performance Brembo brakes with emergency braking assist.

**Interior Design and Special Features:** Slathered in real bird's eye maple wood trim and sumptuous leather, the S-Type R's interior has few competitors when it comes to outright opulence. The sporty gray wood trim gives the car a less traditional look in tune with its hot-rod image. For the first time ever on a Jaguar sedan, there's a high-tech aluminum trim option this year, in place of traditional wood. The cabin features an optional touchscreen telematics system that controls the stereo, climate, optional DVD navigation and telephone features, requiring the driver to cycle through tedious menus. Jaguar has done away with a traditional handbrake, replacing it with an electronic parking brake operated using a switch on the console.

**Driving Impressions:** The S-Type R is a real thrill ride. Between its explosive V8, taut handling, hefty steering and powerful brakes, the S Type R is the kind of sedan that makes you seek out every twist and turn. As adept as it is in the turns, however, it doesn't punish you during more sedate driving, as its suspension offers an acceptable compromise between hard-edged performance and everyday comfort. Sure, a manual transmission would give an added measure of sport sedan feel, but as it is, you're not apt to miss it much.

*Crash Test Scores, see pg 530*
*Warranty information, see pg 542*

## Specifications

| Engine/Drivetrain | HP | Torque | EPA Fuel Economy Rating |
|---|---|---|---|
| 8cyl 4.2L A | 390 | 399 | 17 city/24 hwy |

## Body Styles

| Style | MSRP Range |
|---|---|
| Midsize Sedan | $58,330 |

For the latest full vehicle reports, visit www.edmunds.com/bginfopak

**MSRP Price Range**
## $30,330 - $36,330
Destination Charge: $665 (all styles)

## Ratings

| | | |
|---|---|---|
| Consumer Rating | N/A | |
| Editors Rating | 6.4 | |

**What Edmunds.com says:** Priced to compete with the entry-luxury offerings from Audi, BMW and Mercedes, the all-wheel-drive X-Type falls short in most areas, from driving dynamics to cabin furnishings. Only worth considering if you've got to have the style of a Jaguar.

**Pros:** Comfortable highway ride, attractive styling inside and out, standard all-wheel drive, large trunk.

**Cons:** Doesn't handle as well as competitors, engines short on torque, low-grade interior materials, some hard-to-use controls, tight entry to rear seat.

**What's New:** Jaguar expands the X-Type lineup for 2005 with a new station wagon body style and two packages, the Sport and the VDP Edition. The wagon is dubbed the Sportwagon, and features a standard 3.0-liter V6. The new Sport package includes aggressive body styling, 18-inch wheels, sport suspension, sport seats and dynamic stability control. Carbon-fiber interior trim can be added in place of the standard wood, along with sport seats trimmed in half black leather, half in Alcantara. The VDP Edition includes a memory system for the driver seat and mirrors, rain-sensing wipers, a premium audio system, heated seats, unique trim and a trip computer.

**Body Styles, Trim Levels and Options:** The four-door X-Type sedan is available in two models, 2.5 and 3.0, while the wagon is available only as a 3.0. Standard equipment on the 2.5 includes 16-inch alloy wheels, leather upholstery, a power driver seat, real wood trim, automatic climate control, a six-speaker CD stereo and one-touch power windows. The 3.0 model adds 17-inch wheels a power moonroof, split-folding rear seat, auto headlamps and a wood and leather steering wheel. On the options list, you'll find the Sport Package, which offers stability control, revised suspension settings, bigger wheels and tires and more aggressive exterior styling. The VDP Edition includes special wheels, chrome mirror caps, a seat and mirror memory system, an Alpine audio system with a trunk-mounted CD changer, walnut trim and heated, 10-way power seats with color-contrast piping. Among the stand-alone options are rear parking sensors and a DVD-based navigation system.

**Powertrains and Performance:** X-Type buyers get a choice of two engines. The 2.5 model has a 2.5-liter V6, which generates 194 horsepower and 180 pound-feet of torque. The 3.0 model upgrades to a 3.0-liter V6, which kicks out 231 hp and 209 lb-ft of torque. The X-Type is also the only Jaguar currently available with a manual transmission; it's standard on the 2.5-liter model and available as a no-cost option in the 3.0-liter model. The other transmission choice is a five-speed automatic. All-wheel drive is standard on all X-Types.

**Safety:** A full complement of safety features is provided on the X-Type, including seat-mounted side airbags for front occupants, side curtain airbags for front and rear passengers and four-wheel antilock disc brakes with Electronic Brakeforce Distribution. Stability control is optional. In government crash testing, the X-Type earned four out of five stars in all frontal and side-impact categories. In frontal offset crash testing, it received a "Good" rating (the best possible).

**Interior Design and Special Features:** Inside, the X-Type comes with an ample array of luxury features—leather upholstery, real wood trim, automatic climate control and one-touch windows are part of the basic package. Unfortunately, many of the interior materials are low in quality compared to other entry-level luxury sedans. Although a sloping roof line cuts down on headroom, the X-Type can accommodate four adults, provided they can negotiate the tight rear door openings. The sedan's capacity is generous at 16 cubic feet, while the wagon offers up to 50 cubic feet with the rear seats folded.

**Driving Impressions:** Compared to most other entry-level luxury sedans and wagons, the X-Type comes up short. Neither V6 engine feels particularly powerful, nor is the five-speed automatic especially quick on the draw. Those seeking maximum performance should go with the available manual gearbox. The Jaguar's ride quality is smooth and comfortable on the highway, but it can be harsh over bumps and ruts. Opting for the Sport Package gives the X-Type a fair amount of agility in the turns.

*Crash Test Scores, see pg 530*
*Warranty information, see pg 542*

## Specifications

| Engine/Drivetrain | HP | Torque | EPA Fuel Economy Rating |
|---|---|---|---|
| 6cyl 3.0L A | 227 | 206 | 18 city/25 hwy |
| 6cyl 2.5L M | 192 | 178 | 19 city/28 hwy |

## Body Styles

| Style | MSRP Range |
|---|---|
| Midsize Sedan | $30,330–$34,330 |
| Midsize Wagon | $36,330 |

# 2005 Jaguar XJ-Series

**MSRP Price Range**

## $60,830 - $89,330

Destination Charge: $665 (all styles)

### Ratings

| | | |
|---|---|---|
| Consumer Rating | 9.1 | |
| Editors Rating | 8.0 | |

**What Edmunds.com says:** An all-aluminum body and high-tech air suspension combined with classic Jaguar styling give the XJ a fighting chance against its German rivals.

**Pros:** Supple ride quality, powerful V8 engines, roomy interior, more athletic than you might think.

**Cons:** Fussy interior controls, clumsy transmission shifter, CD changer is still in the trunk.

**What's New:** Long-wheelbase models are added to the lineup in standard, Vanden Plas and Super V8 trim.

**Body Styles, Trim Levels and Options:** All Jaguar XJs are four-door sedans, but four distinct styles are available. The standard XJ8 model, offered in both short- and long-wheelbase (XJ8 L) derivatives, offers a long list of amenities that includes traction control, four-zone climate control, adjustable pedals, walnut-trimmed interior and a self-leveling suspension all for a starting price just under $62,000. The long-wheelbase Vanden Plas ups the plush factor with 16-way power seats, unique 18-inch wheels, an upgraded audio system, richer wood trim, thicker carpeting, heated seats, xenon headlights and a power rear sunshade. For driving enthusiasts, the Super V8 model offers all the luxury and room of the Vanden Plas, along with a supercharged V8 engine, more powerful brakes, a rear DVD entertainment system, DVD navigation, adaptive cruise control and unique 19-inch wheels.

**Powertrains and Performance:** Both the XJ8 and Vanden Plas come with Jaguar's 4.2-liter V8 engine which is good for 294 horsepower and 303 pound-feet of torque. The Super V8 has a supercharged V8 which puts out nearly 100 more hp—an impressive rating of 390 hp. Both engines use a six-speed automatic transmission and a Jaguar traditional "J" gateshifter.

**Safety:** All XJs come standard with such safety features as antilock brakes, BrakeAssist, front and rear seatbelt pre-tensioners and front, side and head curtain airbags. Sensors monitor the front occupants' weight and position to the point that the airbags will deploy at a lesser rate or not at all if it is deemed unsafe for the occupant. The XJ-Series sedans have not been crash tested.

**Interior Design and Special Features:** Although loaded up with modern technology, the XJ still offers a rich and warm interior befitting a proper British luxury sedan. Vanden Plas models offer 16-way power seats versus the standard 12-way seats that come standard in the XJ8. A DVD-based navigation system is optional on all models, though only the top-line Vanden Plas and Super V8 offer rear-seat DVD video screens. An electronic parking brake that automatically sets and releases itself as the shift lever is moved into and out of park is standard in all XJs.

*Crash Test Scores, see pg 530*
*Warranty information, see pg 542*

### Specifications

| Engine/Drivetrain | HP | Torque | EPA Fuel Economy Rating |
|---|---|---|---|
| 8cyl 4.2L A | 390 | 399 | 17 city/24 hwy |
| 8cyl 4.2L A | 294 | 303 | 18 city/28 hwy |

### Body Styles

| Style | MSRP Range |
|---|---|
| Large Sedan | $60,830–$89,330 |

**Driving Impressions:** The XJ's significant technological features are immediately noticeable when it comes to the vehicle's ride and handling. Wind noise is virtually nonexistent, and the XJ's interior is extremely quiet, especially at highway speeds. The combination of a powerful V8 and the weight savings from the XJ's aluminum construction yield a lively, fun-to-drive car, especially in Super V8 form. Thankfully, comfort is a top priority as well; all XJ variants offer a tight, smooth and refined driving experience.

**Compact Convertible, Coupe**

# 2005 Jaguar XK-Series

**MSRP Price Range**
## $69,830 - $74,830
Destination Charge: $665 (all styles)

### Ratings

| Ratings | | |
|---|---|---|
| Consumer Rating | 9.0 | ▉▉▉▉▉▉▉▉▉░ |
| Editors Rating | 7.4 | ▉▉▉▉▉▉▉▉░░ |

**What Edmunds.com says:** Smooth, sleek and sexy, the XK maintains considerable appeal despite its advanced age.

**Pros:** Divine exterior shape, smooth V8 engine, good balance between luxury and performance.

**Cons:** Some low-grade interior materials, cowl shake in the convertible, useless rear seats.

**What's New:** Subtle refinements for the XK-Series this year include freshened exterior styling elements, new wheel designs and a standard driver-controlled automatic speed limiter.

**Body Styles, Trim Levels and Options:** Available as a coupe or a convertible, the XK offers a lengthy list of standard equipment. Among the highlights are 18-inch wheels, leather upholstery, 12-way power-heated seats with memory for the driver, automatic climate control, reverse-parking sensors, one-touch power windows and a 320-watt Alpine stereo with a six-disc CD changer in the trunk. The convertible has a power-operated top. Options include xenon headlamps, adaptive cruise control and a DVD-based navigation system.

**Powertrains and Performance:** All XKs get a smooth 4.2-liter V8 engine rated for 294 horsepower and 303 pound-feet of torque. A standard six-speed automatic transmission routes power to the rear wheels. Fuel economy is good for a V8-powered car—expect about 18 mpg in the city and up to 26 mpg on the highway.

**Safety:** Reining in the horses are four-wheel ventilated disc brakes at all four corners, supplemented by ABS and BrakeAssist. Stability and traction control are standard, as are seat-mounted side airbags for front occupants. Missing from the equipment list of this $70,000 vehicle are side curtain airbags and a rollover protection system for the convertible. The XK has not been crash tested.

**Interior Design and Special Features:**

**Driving Impressions:** The 4.2-liter V8 offers plenty of acceleration in just about any situation, and the six-speed automatic delivers smooth shifts without fail. The double-wishbone suspension provides a luxurious, well-controlled ride that is perfect for highway cruising. Want to take a quick drive up the coast or into the mountains with that special someone? We can think of few cars more romantic than an XK8. At the same time, those who want a sporting driving experience should look elsewhere at cars like the Mercedes SL500, Cadillac XLR or even Jaguar's own performance-tuned XKR.

*Crash Test Scores, see pg 530*
*Warranty information, see pg 542*

### Specifications

| Engine/Drivetrain | HP | Torque | EPA Fuel Economy Rating |
|---|---|---|---|
| 8cyl 4.2L A | 294 | 303 | 18 city/26 hwy |

### Body Styles

| Style | MSRP Range |
|---|---|
| Compact Convertible | $74,830 |
| Compact Coupe | $69,830 |

# 2005 Jaguar XKR

**MSRP Price Range**
## $81,330 - $86,330
Destination Charge: $665 (all styles)

## Ratings

| | | |
|---|---|---|
| Consumer Rating | 9.7 | |
| Editors Rating | 7.5 | |

**What Edmunds.com says:** Still more a grand tourer than a sports car, the supercharged XKR is nonetheless smooth, sleek and sexy.

**Pros:** Divine exterior shape, supercharged V8 power, comfortable seats, opulent interior.

**Cons:** Cramped interior space, some low-grade interior materials.

**What's New:** Subtle refinements for the XK-Series this year include freshened exterior styling elements, new wheel designs and a standard driver-controlled automatic speed limiter.

**Body Styles, Trim Levels and Options:** Available as a coupe or convertible, the XKR comes fully loaded. Standard equipment includes 18-inch wheels, a computer-controlled active suspension, high-intensity discharge headlamps, leather upholstery, wood and aluminum trim, 12-way power sport seats with heaters and memory for the driver, automatic climate control, a 320-watt Alpine stereo with a six-disc CD changer mounted in the trunk and a DVD-based navigation system. A power-operated top is standard on the convertible. On the options list, you'll find an assortment of pricey 20-inch wheels, Recaro seats, adaptive cruise control, a Momo steering wheel and shift knob, drilled aluminum pedals and a handling package that sets you up with Brembo brakes (with visible red calipers) and firmer suspension settings.

**Powertrains and Performance:** The XKR's 4.2-liter V8 is energized by an Eaton supercharger, twin air-to-liquid intercoolers and minor structural changes over the normally aspirated version in the XK8. Output is rated at a prodigious 390 horsepower and 399 pound-feet of torque. A standard six-speed automatic transmission routes power to the rear wheels. EPA ratings are 16 mpg in the city and 23 mpg on the highway.

**Safety:** Four-wheel ventilated disc brakes supplemented by ABS and BrakeAssist are standard; a higher-performance Brembo set is optional. Other standard safety features include stability and traction control and seat-mounted side airbags for front occupants. Missing from the equipment list of this $80,000 vehicle is a rollover protection system in the convertible.

**Interior Design and Special Features:** The XKR's cockpit is an attractive blend of luxury and sport, with supple leather used on the seats, center console, door panels and steering wheel. The leather is matched up with extensive use of burl walnut wood. You can opt for Recaro sport seats, drilled aluminum pedals and a Momo steering wheel and gearshift knob. Amongst all the rich surfaces, you'll find some low-grade plastics that seem more appropriate for a Ford than a Jaguar. Front occupants will find ample room to stretch out, but the small rear seats are best left to shopping bags.

*Crash Test Scores, see pg 530*
*Warranty information, see pg 542*

## Specifications

| Engine/Drivetrain | HP | Torque | EPA Fuel Economy Rating |
|---|---|---|---|
| 8cyl 4.2L A | 390 | 399 | 16 city/23 hwy |

## Body Styles

| Style | MSRP Range |
|---|---|
| Compact Convertible | $86,330 |
| Compact Coupe | $81,330 |

**Driving Impressions:** Given the XKR's ability to sprint to 60 mph in under 5.5 seconds and flash through the quarter-mile in under 14 ticks, this cat should be quick enough for anyone short of an Air Force test pilot. The six-speed automatic is quick on the draw, though the traditional J-gate shifter is not well suited for manual shifting. Although the XKR has serious wheels and tires, it's still not a full-on sports car. The steering is light, precise and quick, and the XKR handles curves with ease, with the active suspension keeping body roll to a minimum. Still, it doesn't urge you on like a true sports car would. Fine for most people, but enthusiasts will prefer the 911 or even an SL500 roadster.

**MSRP Price Range**
**$26,130 - $34,045**
Destination Charge: $645 (all styles)

## Ratings

| | | |
|---|---|---|
| Consumer Rating | 9.8 | |
| Editors Rating | 8.1 | |

**What Edmunds.com says:** The all-new Grand Cherokee manages to retain its classic style and unparalleled off-road ability while delivering a level of luxury never before seen in a Jeep. If you're looking for a true 4x4 that's also refined and comfortable enough to drive in the suburbs, this is a must-see.

**Pros:** Strong engine lineup, unmatched off-road ability, balanced handling, long list of advanced safety equipment, solid warranty.

**Cons:** Hard plastic interior surfaces could use some padding, less cargo capacity than most midsize SUVs.

**What's New:** The Grand Cherokee is all new for 2005. Among the improvements are new four-wheel-drive systems, an independent front suspension, three excellent engine options and better ergonomics and build quality.

**Body Styles, Trim Levels and Options:** The Grand Cherokee is available in two trim levels, Laredo and Limited. Standard Laredo features include power windows and door locks, air conditioning, eight-way power front seats with lumbar support, split-folding rear seat, a reversible cargo floor with water-resistant storage and a CD stereo. The Limited model adds two-tone leather seating, unique 17-inch alloy wheels, an adjustable roof rack, power-adjustable pedals, rain-sensing automatic wipers, a leather-wrapped steering wheel and an in-dash CD changer with MP3 capability. Options include heated front seats, a rear-seat DVD entertainment system, hands-free cell phone compatibility, a DVD-based navigation system, satellite radio, rear park assist and an off-road package with tow hooks and skid plates.

**Powertrains and Performance:** The Laredo comes standard with a 3.7-liter V6 that produces 210 horsepower and 235 pound-feet of torque, while the Limited is equipped with a 4.7-liter V8 capable of pumping out 230 hp and 290 lb-ft of torque. Optional on the Limited is the 5.7-liter Hemi V8, which produces 330 hp and 375 lb-ft of torque. All three engines come standard with a five-speed automatic transmission. Laredo 4x4 models are equipped with the full-time all-wheel-drive, while Limited 4x4s utilize the more advanced Quadra-Trac II that incorporates a two-speed transfer case. Finally, the optional Quadra-Drive II system combines a full-time two-speed transfer case with front/rear/center electronic limited-slip differentials. Towing capacity with the Hemi V8 is rated at 7,200 pounds.

**Safety:** Safety features include four-wheel antilock disc brakes and multistage front airbags (with an occupant weight sensor for the passenger-side front airbag). Side curtain airbags and stability control are optional; buyers can also get an electronic accident response system. Crash tests have not yet been conducted.

**Interior Design and Special Features:** The Grand Cherokee's seats are firm and supportive, and the two-tone perforated leather looks quite contemporary. Wood trim on the center console and door panels is very upscale, and two-tone plastic panels lend a modern touch to the surroundings, even if they are a bit hard. Panel fitment is very good; window and door lock switches are comfortably within reach; climate controls are clearly marked and easy to use; and the chronograph-style gauge cluster adds European flair. This is unquestionably the nicest interior ever put in a Jeep product.

**Driving Impressions:** Smooth is the operative word when describing the new Grand Cherokee. The suspension dampens imperfections in the road well, and the rack and pinion steering provides a solid and responsive road feel. The all-wheel drive grabs pavement with gusto and on tight roads this SUV is very nimble with minimal body roll. Even though the raucous multidisplacement Hemi provides gobs of low-end thrust, the 3.7-liter V6 and 4.7-liter V8 are silky-smooth and provide more than enough power for most applications.

*Crash Test Scores, see pg 530*
*Warranty information, see pg 542*

## Specifications

| Engine/Drivetrain | HP | Torque | EPA Fuel Economy Rating |
|---|---|---|---|
| 8cyl 5.7L A | 330 | 375 | 14 city/21 hwy |
| 8cyl 4.7L A | 230 | 290 | 14 city/20 hwy |
| 6cyl 3.7L A | 210 | 235 | 16 city/21 hwy |

## Body Styles

| Style | MSRP Range |
|---|---|
| Midsize SUV | $26,130–$34,045 |

# 2005 Jeep Liberty

**Compact SUV**

**MSRP Price Range**

## $19,265 - $25,110

Destination Charge: $610 (all styles)

### Ratings

| | | |
|---|---|---|
| Consumer Rating | 9.2 | |
| Editors Rating | 7.7 | |

**What Edmunds.com says:** A thoroughly capable and comfortable compact SUV if you like to bash boulders, but if you're like most people and spend 99 percent of your time on the pavement, the Liberty lags behind its more carlike competitors.

**Pros:** Extremely capable off-road, creative interior design, economical diesel engine option, still a Jeep at heart.

**Cons:** Gas engines are rather thirsty at the pump, not as "carlike" on the street as most of its competitors, less cargo space than some of its competitors.

**What's New:** An all-new diesel engine option makes its debut for 2005. Exterior appearance changes this year include a new front fascia, grille, foglamps, fender flares and body side moldings. Interior upgrades include relocated power window switches, new instrument panel cluster graphics and trim bezels and improved seat comfort. The Renegade model gets a flatter hood, taller grille, off-road foglamps and taillamp guards, as well as functional rock rails and four skid plates. A new six-speed manual transmission replaces last year's five-speed unit.

*Crash Test Scores, see pg 530*
*Warranty information, see pg 542*

### Specifications

| Engine/Drivetrain | HP | Torque | EPA Fuel Economy Rating |
|---|---|---|---|
| 6cyl 3.7L A/M | 210 | 235 | 17 city/22 hwy |
| 4cyl 2.8L M | 160 | 295 | 22 city/27 hwy |
| 4cyl 2.4L M | 150 | 165 | 20 city/24 hwy |

### Body Styles

| Style | MSRP Range |
|---|---|
| Compact SUV | $19,265–$25,110 |

**Body Styles, Trim Levels and Options:** The four-door Liberty is offered in three trim levels: Sport, Limited and Renegade. The Sport is bare-bones; standard features include 16-inch wheels, a 12-volt power outlet and an AM/FM/CD stereo. The Renegade offers additional goodies such as air conditioning, higher-grade upholstery, a leather-wrapped steering wheel, power windows and cruise control. Renegade-only features include unique exterior styling, functional rock rails and a full set of skid plates. The more exclusive Limited trim gets you amenities such as 17-inch chrome wheels and a power driver seat. Available options include a power sunroof, leather upholstery, heated seats, an in-dash six-disc CD player with Infinity speakers, a DVD-based navigation system and UConnect, Chrysler's hands-free in-vehicle communication system.

**Powertrains and Performance:** The Liberty offers three engines: a 2.4-liter inline four-cylinder that generates 150 horses and 165 pound-feet of torque, a 3.7-liter V6 rated at 210 hp and 235 lb-ft of torque and a 2.8-liter diesel four-cylinder that produces 160 hp and a eye-opening 295 lb-ft of torque. The diesel improves the Liberty's fuel economy by about 25 percent, while also reducing CO2 emissions by 20 percent. The base four-cylinder comes with a six-speed manual transmission only, while the upgraded V6 and diesel offer both a manual and a four-speed automatic. Each engine is available in two- and four-wheel-drive configurations.

**Safety:** Four-wheel antilock disc brakes come standard on the Liberty, while side curtain airbags are available as an option on all models. In government crash tests, the Liberty earned a perfect five stars for driver protection in a frontal impact, and four stars for front-passenger protection. Side-impact testing resulted in a five-star rating for both front and rear passengers. In frontal offset crash testing by the IIHS, the Liberty was given a "Marginal" rating, the second lowest of four.

**Interior Design and Special Features:** The Liberty provides ample room for four adults inside (five in a pinch), with satin aluminum accents and chrome-ringed, black-on-white gauges. A full-size spare is hung on the nifty rear cargo door, which features a single-action swing-gate/flipper-glass system. There's a total of 29 cubic feet of cargo space available behind the Liberty's 35/65-split-folding rear seat and 69 cubic feet when that seat is folded down.

**Driving Impressions:** As the base four-cylinder really isn't enough to propel this pudgy SUV, most buyers should stick with either the V6 or the diesel. The V6 provides good acceleration but drinks plenty at the gas pump. The diesel is equally speedy, and its excellent fuel economy makes for fewer fill-ups. Like other Jeeps, the Liberty is a sensational off-roader. However, the heft required to make it a surefooted billy goat in the rough hobbles it somewhat on the highway and in the city. Its performance on pavement is tolerable enough, but the steering is heavy and numb, and the Liberty exhibits considerable body roll around corners. On the plus side, its long suspension travel does a good job of smoothing out bumps and potholes.

# 2005 Jeep Wrangler

**MSRP Price Range**

## $17,900 - $29,040

Destination Charge: $610 (all styles)

### Ratings

| | | |
|---|---|---|
| Consumer Rating | 9.2 | |
| Editors Rating | 6.9 | |

**What Edmunds.com says:** It has a stiff ride, offers about the same noise isolation as a motorcycle and has a soft top that's a nail-buster to operate, but if you're dying for a cheap convertible or an off-roader that can go just about anywhere, it's hard to beat the Wrangler.

**Pros:** Cheap, fun to drive, classic styling, go-anywhere capability.

**Cons:** Soft top a handful to manipulate, poor ergonomics, difficult ingress-egress, slow steering, bouncy suspension on the street, can't get ABS on the Unlimited.

**What's New:** A Rubicon version of the Unlimited joins the lineup. All Wranglers get a new six-speed manual transmission to replace the old five-speed unit. The Sahara version of the Wrangler is dropped for 2005.

**Body Styles, Trim Levels and Options:** The regular-length Wrangler comes as a two-door sport-ute in four trims: SE, X, Sport and Rubicon. An extended-wheelbase Unlimited also has two doors and comes in standard and Rubicon trims. The SE is a real stripper with carpeting and high-back vinyl bucket seats as its most notable standard features. The X trim adds a four-speaker AM/FM/CD stereo, cloth upholstery and fold-and-tumble bench seating in back. The Sport trim's features list includes a full-length center console, foglamps and full doors with roll-up windows. The Wrangler Unlimited features unique cloth seats, a painted center stack, a bright grille and body-color fenders. Rubicon models forgo some of the nicer amenities in favor of hard-core off-road features like black fender flares, diamond-plate side sills, heavy-duty axles, front and rear differential lockers and 16-inch cast-aluminum wheels. Options available across the line are a hardtop (included are full doors with roll-up windows and a rear-window wiper and defroster) and a lockable rear storage box.

**Powertrains and Performance:** SE models are powered by a 2.4-liter inline four-cylinder mated to a six-speed manual transmission. This engine kicks out 147 horsepower and 165 pound-feet of torque, and is also available with a four-speed automatic transmission. All other trim levels are powered by a more vigorous 4.0-liter inline six-cylinder that cranks out 190 horses and 235 lb-ft of torque. The new six-speed manual transmission is standard with this engine, but a four-speed automatic transmission is optional. Maximum towing capacity is 2,000 pounds on regular-size Wranglers and 3,500 on the Unlimited.

**Safety:** Four-wheel disc brakes are standard on Rubicon models, optional for all others. ABS is optional on X and Sport (but not the Unlimited). In government frontal impact crash tests, the Wrangler earned four stars for both driver and front-passenger protection. In frontal offset frontal impact testing, the Wrangler received an "Acceptable" rating, the second highest of four.

**Interior Design and Special Features:** The interior blends nicely with its exterior in terms of functionality and ruggedness; you're not going to find any soft-touch plastic or supple leather. Maximum cargo capacity with the rear seats folded is 46 cubic feet for the hardtop, 47.2 for soft-top models. The Unlimited is 15 inches longer than the standard-issue Wrangler, and the result is additional passenger and cargo space out back.

**Driving Impressions:** Nobody will mistake the Wrangler for a smooth-running family sedan; it's very much a truck, thanks to its high step-in height, slow steering ratio and abundant wind and road noise. On the street, its small size and tight turning radius make it fun to maneuver, but it can get a little scary at freeway speeds in high crosswinds. However, there's no denying its performance off-road. The suspension allows for an incredible amount of wheel articulation that's further aided by steep approach and departure angles. The added hardware on the Rubicon model makes it one of the most capable off-road vehicles you can buy.

*Crash Test Scores, see pg 530*
*Warranty information, see pg 542*

### Specifications

| Engine/Drivetrain | HP | Torque | EPA Fuel Economy Rating |
|---|---|---|---|
| 6cyl 4.0L A/M | 190 | 235 | 16 city/20 hwy |
| 4cyl 2.4L M | 147 | 165 | 18 city/20 hwy |

### Body Styles

| Style | MSRP Range |
|---|---|
| Compact SUV | $17,900–$29,040 |

# 2005 Kia Amanti

**MSRP Price Range**

## $25,200

Destination Charge: N/A (all styles)

### Ratings

| | | |
|---|---|---|
| Consumer Rating | N/A | |
| Editors Rating | 7.8 | |

**What Edmunds.com says:** It's not the fastest or the most stylish car on the block, but Kia's Amanti is a solid alternative for shoppers who want a large sedan that's safe, well equipped and reasonably priced.

**Pros:** Class-leading amenities, spacious interior, long warranty, good value for the money.

**Cons:** Weak V6 considering its size, doesn't register very high on the prestige meter.

**What's New:** Heated seats have been added to the optional Leather package, and a tire-pressure monitor has been added to the optional Convenience package. The Amanti now includes an analog clock on the instrument panel.

**Body Styles, Trim Levels and Options:** The Amanti is a large four-door sedan available in a single trim level. The standard equipment list includes 16-inch alloy wheels, a full-size spare tire, dual-zone automatic climate control, a CD player, cloth-upholstered seats with eight-way power adjustment and memory for the driver (four-way power for the passenger), wood grain trim, steering wheel-mounted audio and cruise controls and a full set of one-touch up-down windows. Opt for the Leather package and you'll get leather upholstery, heated seats, a 270-watt Infinity sound system with an in-dash CD changer, a trip computer with a 4-inch LCD screen, and memory settings for the mirrors. Additional features are available in the Convenience package, which offers a sunroof, an auto-dimming rearview mirror with a HomeLink remote transmitter and a tire-pressure monitor.

**Powertrains and Performance:** The Amanti is powered by a 3.5-liter V6 rated at 195 horsepower and 217 pound-feet of torque. A five-speed automatic gives the Amanti solid performance despite its modest horsepower. The transmission includes a manual-shift mode with an LED indicator in the instrument panel.

**Safety:** Four-wheel antilock disc brakes are standard, and stability and traction control (Electronic Stability Program), Electronic Brakeforce Distribution and BrakeAssist are optional. Seat-mounted side airbags protect front occupants, while full-length side curtain airbags protect all outboard occupants. The Amanti also has active front headrests that move up and forward in the event of a rear-end collision, and an anti-lockout system that keeps the doors from being locked while the key is still in the ignition. A tire-pressure monitoring system is included in the optional convenience package.

**Interior Design and Special Features:** The interior offers the highest level of amenities ever offered in a Kia such as dual-zone automatic climate control, an eight-way power-adjustable driver seat and a 270-watt audio system. The front seats offer more head- and legroom than any other full-size sedan. In back, occupants will find plenty of headroom as well, but slightly less shoulder and legroom than the Crown Victoria and LeSabre. The Amanti comes standard with a ski pass-through and trunk lid that utilizes concealed hinges with gas struts to keep from damaging cargo.

*Crash Test Scores, see pg 530*
*Warranty information, see pg 542*

### Specifications

| Engine/Drivetrain | HP | Torque | EPA Fuel Economy Rating |
|---|---|---|---|
| 6cyl 3.5L A | 195 | 217 | 17 city/25 hwy |

### Body Styles

| Style | MSRP Range |
|---|---|
| Midsize Sedan | $25,200 |

**Driving Impressions:** Like most vehicles in its class, the Amanti is tuned to provide a smooth, quiet ride with maximum isolation from the road. With only 195 horsepower, it lags behind some of its more powerful competitors, but there's enough power on tap for most driving situations. Its overall refinement level doesn't quite match the class-leading Toyota Avalon, but for those looking for an excellent value in this segment, the Amanti is a compelling choice.

# Midsize Sedan

# 2005 Kia Optima

**MSRP Price Range**
## $15,900 - $19,895
Destination Charge: $560 (all styles)

### Ratings

| | | |
|---|---|---|
| Consumer Rating | N/A | |
| Editors Rating | 8.0 | |

**What Edmunds.com says:** The Optima trails its Japanese competitors when it comes to performance and interior accommodations, but remains a decent buy for those seeking a stylish, well-equipped family sedan for less than $20,000.

**Pros:** Low price, pleasant highway ride, refined V6, lots of storage space, excellent warranty.

**Cons:** Noisy four-cylinder engine, tepid handling, some cheap interior bits, tight rear legroom, ABS isn't available on four-cylinder models.

**What's New:** For 2005, the Optima wears clear turn signal lenses up front, the sunroof on the EX gains a one-touch opening feature and the optional leather seats get new stitching.

**Body Styles, Trim Levels and Options:** The midsize Optima sedan is sold in two trim levels—LX and EX. The LX comes with 15-inch wheels (16s on V6 models); side airbags; a CD player; air conditioning; power windows, locks and mirrors; a 60/40-split-folding rear seat; and cruise control. The EX comes with quite a bit more. On the outside, there are alloy wheels, foglights, heated side mirrors, keyless entry and a power sunroof. Inside, you'll find upgraded cloth upholstery, a power driver seat, wood grain trim, automatic climate control, an auto-dimming rearview mirror and a 120-watt sound system with a CD and cassette player. Options include a sound system upgrade for LX models, a leather upholstery package (with a power front-passenger seat) for EX models and antilock brakes for vehicles equipped with the V6 engine (available on both trims).

**Powertrains and Performance:** Optima buyers have two engine choices—a base 138-horsepower, 2.4-liter inline four-cylinder or a 170-hp, 2.7-liter V6. In our experience, the four-cylinder comes up short in power and refinement. While the V6 won't inspire thrills, it's smooth and quiet, and offers decent acceleration with enough thrust for confident merging on the highway. The four-cylinder can be mated to a five-speed manual transmission or a four-speed automatic with a manual-shift mode; the V6 comes with the automatic only. Mileage ratings are 22 mpg city/30 highway with the four-cylinder and 20/27 with the V6.

**Safety:** Vehicles equipped with the V6 get four-wheel disc brakes with ABS as an option. Side airbags for front occupants and three-point seatbelts for all five seating positions are standard in every Optima. In government crash tests, the Optima earned four stars for driver and front-passenger protection in a frontal impact. The IIHS gave the Optima a rating of "Acceptable" (the second highest of four) after conducting its frontal offset crash test.

**Interior Design and Special Features:** Inside, the Optima offers attractive if not upscale accommodations—the seats are plush and most drivers will be able to find a comfortable driving position. Interior materials are on the economy side, but they're acceptable in a car that costs less than $20,000. Drivers will find logically arranged radio and climate controls, along with plenty of storage areas for cell phones and spare change. The 14-cubic-foot trunk offers a low lift-over height and closes with struts and hidden hinges to avoid crushing cargo.

**Driving Impressions:** The Optima will appeal to commuters who want comfortable transportation for the day-to-day grind. The ride is stable and smooth, though bumps and ruts are transmitted to the cabin a little more harshly than they should be. The steering, while light and somewhat flighty on the highway, is nonetheless linear and direct, and around-town maneuvers are accomplished with ease.

*Crash Test Scores, see pg 530*
*Warranty information, see pg 542*

### Specifications

| Engine/Drivetrain | HP | Torque | EPA Fuel Economy Rating |
|---|---|---|---|
| 6cyl 2.7L A | 170 | 181 | 20 city/27 hwy |
| 4cyl 2.4L A/M | 138 | 147 | 22 city/30 hwy |

### Body Styles

| Style | MSRP Range |
|---|---|
| Midsize Sedan | $15,900–$19,895 |

## Kia
# 2005 Kia Rio

**Compact Sedan, Wagon**

**MSRP Price Range**
## $9,740 - $12,390
Destination Charge: $540 (all styles)

### Ratings

| | | |
|---|---|---|
| Consumer Rating | N/A | |
| Editors Rating | 6.7 | |

**What Edmunds.com says:** The Rio and Rio Cinco are the lowest-priced sedan and wagon on the market, and they feel that way. Buy one only if you must have a new-car warranty; otherwise, spend your money on a nice used car.

**Pros:** Small price, big warranty, peppy engine.

**Cons:** Unrefined handling, five-speed manual's rubbery shift action, mediocre fuel economy.

**What's New:** No major changes for the Rio this year.

**Body Styles, Trim Levels and Options:** The Rio is offered in two models—a sedan and a wagon called the Rio Cinco, which is basically a five-door hatchback. Standard equipment on the sedan includes 14-inch wheels with plastic wheel covers, a driver-seat height adjuster, a fold-down driver armrest, variable intermittent wipers and rear defrost. The wagon is a bit better equipped, as it also comes with alloy wheels, a CD player, power steering, a tachometer, steering wheel tilt adjustment, vanity mirrors, map lights, a sunglass holder and body-side moldings; the alloy wheels and CD player are available as stand-alone extras on the sedan, and everything else is part of the Upgrade Package. Other options you may want to consider for both models include air conditioning, ABS, and power windows and locks.

**Powertrains and Performance:** Every Rio is powered by a 1.6-liter, inline four-cylinder engine that generates 104 horsepower and 104 pound-feet of torque, and buyers have their choice of a five-speed manual or four-speed automatic transmission. Either way, you won't have a lot of power to work with off the line, but let the engine rev up and you'll have ample pep for everyday driving. Fuel economy isn't very good for a subcompact—the Rio is rated for 26 mpg city/33 highway with a manual gearbox and 25/32 with an automatic. The Scion xA, Toyota Echo and Hyundai Accent are superior in this regard.

**Safety:** As you would expect, safety features are minimal; antilock brakes at least are optional. All Rios have height-adjustable seatbelts in front and child-seat anchors in the back. Should you decide to put three people in the backseat, the center passenger will make do with a lap belt. The Rio's crash test scores were decent, as the car earned four out of five stars for driver and front-passenger protection in frontal impacts and three stars for front- and rear-occupant protection in side impacts.

**Interior Design and Special Features:** On the inside, the Rio feels bare, but you can take comfort in its simple layout and thoughtful features (the driver-seat height adjuster, for example). Controls are generally large and easy to find, and the seats are relatively comfortable. The rear seat feels like a park bench but offers more hip- and shoulder room than other subcompacts' backseats. The Rio Cinco earns its keep by offering 24.8 cubic feet of luggage space (compared to the sedan's 9.2-cubic-foot trunk); fold down the 60/40-split rear seat and you'll have 44.3 cubes.

*Crash Test Scores, see pg 530*
*Warranty information, see pg 542*

**Driving Impressions:** The Rio offers basic transportation and little more—pretty much what you'd expect from one of the cheapest cars on the market. Provided you keep engine rpm up, everyday driving maneuvers can be accomplished with relative ease, and the Rio can stay with the flow of traffic on the highway.

### Specifications

| Engine/Drivetrain | HP | Torque | EPA Fuel Economy Rating |
|---|---|---|---|
| 4cyl 1.6L A/M | 104 | 104 | 25 city/32 hwy |

### Body Styles

| Style | MSRP Range |
|---|---|
| Compact Sedan | $9,740–$10,615 |
| Compact Wagon | $11,365–$12,390 |

For the latest full vehicle reports, visit www.edmunds.com/bginfopak

**Midsize Minivan**

**MSRP Price Range**
## $20,200 - $22,600
Destination Charge: $640 (all styles)

### Ratings

| | | |
|---|---|---|
| Consumer Rating | N/A | |
| Editors Rating | 8.0 | |

**What Edmunds.com says:** While mainstream minivans may offer all the latest gadgets, Kia's Sedona continues to stuff all essential ingredients of a family vehicle into a value-priced package.

**Pros:** Excellent value, roomy interior with lots of cupholders and storage bins, solid build quality, lengthy warranty coverage.

**Cons:** Handling and steering response could be better, missing a few key minivan features, ABS not standard, below-average fuel mileage.

**What's New:** Second-row captain's chairs are now available on the LX, while all models get larger rear drum brakes.

**Body Styles, Trim Levels and Options:** The Sedona is offered in two well-equipped trim levels, LX and EX. The LX comes with 15-inch wheels, body-color bumpers, door handles and side molding, seven-passenger seating (with a second-row bench seat), adjustable seat height and lumbar for the driver, one-touch power front windows, power door locks and mirrors, front and rear air conditioning, cruise control, a CD player, a folding/expanding center tray (between the front seats), 10 cupholders and three power points. A roof rack and second-row captain's chairs are optional. The EX adds keyless entry, second-row captain's chairs, an eight-way power driver seat, four-way power passenger seat, power rear-quarter windows, a CD/cassette player combo, foglights, automatic headlights, alloy wheels, a roof rack and various leather and wood trim throughout the interior. Options include leather upholstery and a sunroof. Both models are eligible for optional ABS and a rear spoiler.

**Powertrains and Performance:** Powering all Sedonas is a 3.5-liter V6 that generates 195 horsepower. This might not sound like enough power to hang with the many 200-plus-hp vans out there. However, thanks to a five-speed automatic, the Kia makes the most of its 195 horses and never feels slow; off-the-line power is excellent. Fuel economy, on the other hand, is not good, rating just 15 mpg in the city and 20 on the highway—the culprit here is the Sedona's hefty 4,700-pound curb weight.

**Safety:** Front disc/rear drum brakes are standard, but ABS costs extra. We highly recommend spending the money on this worthwhile safety item. Side airbags are not available, but the Sedona swept up during government crash testing, earning five-star ratings in all categories. IIHS testing wasn't as encouraging, though, as the van was rated "Acceptable" in the 40-mph offset crash test (the second highest out of four) and received a "Poor" rating for bumper strength. The latter score isn't a major safety concern but does suggest that repair costs would be high in minor front- or rear-end collisions.

**Interior Design and Special Features:** In addition to abundant storage and cupholders, the Sedona offers comfortable, flexible seating. Both front seats, for instance, offer ratcheting armrests. The second- and third-row seats can slide fore and aft by several inches, allowing owners to position the seats to accommodate longer legs or extra cargo. Unfortunately, the third-row bench does not fold flat into the floor, and the seats are more difficult to remove than most. Cargo capacity is 21.8 cubic feet with all seats in use, 70.6 cubes with the third-row bench removed and 127.5 with all rear seats removed.

**Driving Impressions:** Despite its hefty curb weight, the Sedona feels comfortable and stable in everyday driving situations. However, steering response is a little weak, and there's a bit too much body roll when driving around twists and turns.

*Crash Test Scores, see pg 530*
*Warranty information, see pg 542*

### Specifications

| Engine/Drivetrain | HP | Torque | EPA Fuel Economy Rating |
|---|---|---|---|
| 6cyl 3.5L A | 195 | 218 | 16 city/22 hwy |

### Body Styles

| Style | MSRP Range |
|---|---|
| Midsize Minivan | $20,200–$22,600 |

# Kia

# 2005 Kia Sorento
Midsize SUV

**MSRP Price Range**
## $18,995 - $25,500
Destination Charge: $640 (all styles)

**#1** Editors' Rating

## Ratings

| | | |
|---|---|---|
| Consumer Rating | N/A | |
| Editors Rating | 8.6 | |

**What Edmunds.com says:** Good-looking, comfortable, rugged and well equipped, the Sorento is one of the best buys among small and midsize SUVs.

**Pros:** Great value, long list of standard features, high-quality interior materials, solid construction, true off-road capability, lengthy warranty coverage.

**Cons:** Mediocre fuel economy, harsh ride over sharp bumps.

**What's New:** The optional sport package now includes blacked-out headlamps and, on LX models, a premium audio system. A five-speed automatic transmission replaces last year's four-speed unit.

**Body Styles, Trim Levels and Options:** The four-door Sorento is offered in two trim levels, LX and EX. Standard equipment on the LX includes 16-inch wheels (with a full-size spare tire); skid plates; air conditioning; power windows, mirrors and locks; cruise control; a 60/40-split rear seat; a CD player; and an overhead console with four 12-volt outlets. The EX adds alloy wheels, two-tone cladding, body-color exterior trim, foglights, keyless entry, a power sunroof, a power driver seat, an auto-dimming rearview mirror, an upgraded sound system, brushed metal and chrome interior trim and a cargo net. The EX is available with a luxury package that adds an in-dash CD changer, automatic climate control, automatic headlights, leather seats (heated in front), a leather-wrapped steering wheel and an automatic 4WD system. A sport package includes a five-speed manual transmission, side step bars, alloy wheels, blacked-out headlamps, a roof rack, leather-wrapped steering wheel, keyless entry and, on the LX, the upgraded sound system.

**Powertrains and Performance:** Powering all Sorentos is a 3.5-liter V6 that cranks out 192 horsepower. A five-speed automatic routes power to the rear or all four wheels, depending on whether you choose 2WD or 4WD. A five-speed manual transmission is included with the optional sport package. Towing capacity (just 3,500 pounds) is unimpressive given the Sorento's body-on-frame construction.

**Safety:** Four-wheel disc brakes are standard, an antilock system is optional. Also included are front and rear side curtain airbags, and three-point belts and headrests in all seating positions. In government crash tests, the Sorento earned four stars out of five for driver and front-passenger protection in frontal impacts. The sport-ute earned a perfect five stars for front- and rear-occupant protection in side impacts. In offset crash testing by the IIHS, the Sorento earned a rating of "Acceptable," the second-highest.

**Interior Design and Special Features:** Inside the cabin, soft-touch surfaces abound on the dash and door panels, and the front-passenger airbag is seamlessly integrated into the dash, giving the cabin an upscale feel. The rear seat is wide enough for three adults in a pinch, though knee and toe room are tight. Cargo space is on par with other midsize SUVs with the rear seat up (31.4 cubic feet), but when it's folded, the resulting space measures only 66.4 cubes.

*Crash Test Scores, see pg 530*
*Warranty information, see pg 542*

**Driving Impressions:** Though acceleration at freeway speeds tapers off to just adequate, the Kia will cruise happily at 75 mph all day long. Driven on pavement, the Sorento's independent front and solid axle rear suspension design provide a firm, mostly agreeable ride, though sharp impacts can intrude into the cabin. Accurate, well-weighted steering and a minimum of body roll keep the Kia well planted around corners. With body-on-frame architecture, a low-range transfer case on 4WD models and meaty 16-inch tires, the Sorento can easily take on off-road trails of moderate difficulty.

## Specifications

| Engine/Drivetrain | HP | Torque | EPA Fuel Economy Rating |
|---|---|---|---|
| 6cyl 3.5L A/M | 192 | 217 | 16 city/19 hwy |

## Body Styles

| Style | MSRP Range |
|---|---|
| Midsize SUV | $18,995–$25,500 |

For the latest full vehicle reports, visit www.edmunds.com/bginfopak

**MSRP Price Range**

## $12,620 - $15,970
Destination Charge: $540 (all styles)

### Ratings

| | | |
|---|---|---|
| Consumer Rating | N/A | |
| Editors Rating | 7.5 | |

**What Edmunds.com says:** With its lengthy equipment list, high-quality interior and better-than-average performance, the Spectra sedan and hatchback are an excellent low-cost alternative to a Honda Civic or Toyota Matrix.

**Pros:** Low price, spunky engine, well-finished interior, standard side-curtain airbags, excellent warranty.

**Cons:** Obtrusive engine noise at high speeds, ABS not available on LX model.

**What's New:** A five-door hatchback model dubbed the Spectra5 joins the lineup, along with a sporty SX sedan. Both models come with a front spoiler, black mesh grille, black headlight bezels, upgraded tires, 16-inch alloys, side sills, rear valance panel and rear spoiler. Inside, there is leather wrapping for the steering wheel and shift knob, gray sport cloth upholstery, metallic trim pieces and metal pedals. A sport-tuned suspension is also included, and models with a manual transmission get a front strut tower bar as well.

**Body Styles, Trim Levels and Options:** The Spectra sedan is available in LX, EX and SX trims, while the five-door Spectra5 hatchback is available in one trim only. The LX features a standard six-speaker CD stereo, height-adjustable driver seat, tilt steering wheel and 60/40 rear seat. Additional amenities on the EX version include air conditioning, power windows and locks, heated power mirrors and keyless entry. The EX is also your ticket to options like antilock brakes, cruise control and alloy wheels. The SX sedan and Spectra5 hatchback add front and rear spoilers, side sills, rear valance, black grille, black headlight bezels, upgraded tires and 16-inch alloys and a sport-tuned suspension (on manual transmission models, a front strut tower bar is also included). Inside, leather trim on the steering wheel and shift knob add a sporty touch, as do sport cloth seats, metal-look trim, and metal pedals.

**Powertrains and Performance:** The Spectra features a 2.0-liter DOHC engine with 138 hp and 135 lb-ft of torque. Buyers can choose a five-speed manual or four-speed automatic transmission. Fuel economy is a respectable 25 mpg city/34 mpg highway.

**Safety:** Only EX, SX and Spectra5 models are eligible for antilock brakes. Four-wheel disc brakes are standard on all models. All Spectras feature standard front-seat-mounted side airbags and full-length side-curtain airbags. In government crash tests, the Spectra earned a rating of four stars (out of five) for front impacts, as well as front-seat side impacts. The rear-seat side-impact rating is three stars.

**Interior Design and Special Features:** The Spectra offers a simple cabin layout with logically arranged controls and top-notch build and materials quality. The front seats are downright comfortable with enough shoulder, hip- and legroom to accommodate large adults. The Spectra5 boasts an accommodating station wagonlike cargo area.

**Driving Impressions:** The 2.0-liter inline four provides more than enough muscle for the small sedan and hatchback, making lane changes and passing on the freeway a breeze. The downside is that engine noise can be obtrusive at speeds of 70 mph and above. The LX and EX Spectras offer a smooth ride, effective brakes and competent if not exactly sporty handling. The Spectra5 and SX sedan kick it up a notch with tighter handling while also retaining the supple ride quality of the less sporting sedans.

*Crash Test Scores, see pg 530*
*Warranty information, see pg 542*

### Specifications

| Engine/Drivetrain | HP | Torque | EPA Fuel Economy Rating |
|---|---|---|---|
| 4cyl 2.0L A/M | 138 | 136 | 25 city/34 hwy |

### Body Styles

| Style | MSRP Range |
|---|---|
| Compact Coupe | $14,995–$15,970 |
| Compact Sedan | $12,620–$15,970 |

# 2005 Kia Sportage

**Compact SUV**

**MSRP Price Range**
## N/A
Destination Charge: N/A (all styles)

### Ratings

| | | |
|---|---|---|
| Consumer Rating | N/A | |
| Editors Rating | N/A | |

**What Edmunds.com says:** Thankfully sharing nothing with its predecessor but its name, the new Sportage offers compact SUV buyers a modern runabout in a stylish and roomy package.

**Pros:** Generous passenger and cargo space, stylish and functional interior, standard side and head curtain airbags, hard-to-beat warranty.

**Cons:** Down on power and cargo capacity versus its competitors.

**What's New:** An all-new Sportage returns after a two-year hiatus. It's now a car-based SUV intended to compete with the Honda CR-V and Toyota RAV4.

**Body Styles, Trim Levels and Options:** The Sportage is a compact four-door SUV offered in both two- and all-wheel-drive configurations. Standard features on the Sportage include four-wheel disc brakes, 16-inch alloy wheels, air conditioning, power windows and locks, tinted glass, a rear wiper and a CD stereo system. Various upgrades include a tire-pressure monitoring system, a premium audio system and leather seating. Automatic climate control is available and includes an air quality management system.

**Powertrains and Performance:** Standard power for the Sportage comes from a 2.0-liter, in-line four-cylinder engine with continuously variable valve timing. It generates 140 horsepower and 136 pound-feet of torque and is mated to either a five-speed manual transmission or a four-speed automatic with automanual shift capability (2WD only). An optional 2.7-liter V6 produces 173 hp and 178 lb-ft of torque, and is available with the four-speed automatic only. Buyers can get front-wheel drive or all-wheel drive with either engine.

**Safety:** The Sportage boasts six standard airbags—front and side-impact airbags for both driver and passenger, and side curtain airbags for both front and rear seat occupants. Four-wheel disc brakes are standard, and ABS is optional on all models. A traction and stability control system is also optional. The Sportage has not yet been crash tested.

**Interior Design and Special Features:** Kia designed a functional, roomy and attractive interior for the Sportage. Most of the materials are of good quality and the build quality is solid. A unique rear-seat design allows for a flat load floor by lowering the cushion into the rear footwell; removing the head restraints is not necessary. The Sportage offers 28.4 cubic feet of cargo capacity with the rear seat fold flat. Fold the front passenger seat forward and you'll move up to 39.9 cubic feet of storage space. Although Kia gives you plenty of flexibility for hauling cargo, the Sportage offers less total capacity than its competitors.

**Driving Impressions:** The Sportage provides a carlike ride while returning handling on par with its peers. The four-wheel independent suspension system helps smooth bumps without the jittery feel typical in many SUVs. Power from the standard four-cylinder is adequate at best; we recommend you stick with the larger 2.7-liter V6.

*Crash Test Scores, see pg 530*
*Warranty information, see pg 542*

### Specifications

| Engine/Drivetrain | HP | Torque | EPA Fuel Economy Rating |
|---|---|---|---|
| 4cyl 2.0L A/M | 140 | 136 | N/A |
| 6cyl 2.4L A/M | 173 | 178 | N/A |

### Body Styles

| Style | MSRP Range |
|---|---|
| Compact SUV | N/A |

# 2005 Land Rover Freelander

## MSRP Price Range
### $26,830
Destination Charge: $665 (all styles)

### Ratings

| | | |
|---|---|---|
| Consumer Rating | N/A | |
| Editors Rating | 7.2 | |

**What Edmunds.com says:** With less capability than true dirt runners and less of a prestige factor than BMW's X3, it's hard to make much of a case for the Freelander.

**Pros:** Excellent on-road handling for an SUV, permanent all-wheel drive, still capable off-road.

**Cons:** Expensive for a compact SUV, tight on cargo space, V6 engine on the weak side, no side airbags, SE3's hard top is hard to install.

**What's New:** The HSE trim level is history, leaving only the SE four-door, and the SE3 two-door. A new premium package includes last year's HSE content at an overall lower price. The SE receives a power sunroof, foglights and a full-size spare tire as standard equipment.

**Body Styles, Trim Levels and Options:** The Freelander comes in two body styles: a two-door version with a detachable roof called the SE3, and a four-door version available in SE trim. Major standard equipment on the SE and SE3 models includes 17-inch alloy wheels; a roof rack; air conditioning; steering wheel-mounted stereo controls; cruise control; power windows, mirrors and locks; and keyless entry. Additionally, the SE comes with leather upholstery, while the youth-oriented SE3 gets a durable vinyl upholstery (leather is optional), a power sunroof and foglamps. A premium package includes perforated leather seating, a Harman Kardon sound system, in-dash six-disc CD changer, 18-inch alloys and side rubstrips.

**Powertrains and Performance:** A dual-overhead cam all-aluminum 2.5-liter V6 engine is the only power plant available. It makes 174 horsepower and 177 pound-feet of torque, and is connected to a five-speed automatic transmission with sport and automanual shift modes. Maximum tow rating is 2,500 pounds, a bit low for this class of vehicle. Fuel economy is not very good for a small SUV, as Freelanders get just 17 mpg in city driving and 21 mpg on the highway.

**Safety:** Safety is addressed by four-wheel antilock brakes with Electronic Brakeforce Distribution and standard all-wheel drive. Hill Descent Control helps prevent uncontrolled slides on off-road trails. Unlike other vehicles in the price point, the Land Rover lacks stability control, or side or head-curtain airbags. The Freelander earned an "Acceptable" rating (the second highest on a scale of four) from the IIHS in the 40-mph frontal offset crash test. In side-impact testing of small SUVs also conducted by the IIHS, the Freelander received a "Poor" rating (the lowest).

**Interior Design and Special Features:** The Freelander's historically drab, downmarket interior got a much needed upgrade last year; the dash, instruments, switchgear and door trim panels were all revised, and new front seats offered more comfort and support. The Freelander has 19.3 cubic feet of cargo capacity with the rear seat in use and a meager 46.6 cubes with it folded. That's substantially less than most players in this market, so if you regularly carry even a few large items,(or several smaller ones), be sure to look at the competition. In the SE3 models, the roof section over the rear seats can be removed to create a partial top-down driving experience. Unfortunately, reinstalling the top can be a pain, as the process requires tools and plenty of patience.

**Driving Impressions:** The stout suspension that does so well in the rough stuff also manages to provide a tightly controlled ride on the street. There's more body roll in corners than we would like, but the Freelander remains stable and controllable. The steering provides more feedback than most competitors' setups, as well, although some might find the weighting a bit too heavy for day-to-day driving. With limited ground clearance and no low-range gearing, the Freelander isn't as capable off-road as other Land Rovers, or the Liberty or Xterra, but it can handle moderate trails with little difficulty.

Crash Test Scores, see pg 530
Warranty information, see pg 542

### Specifications

| Engine/Drivetrain | HP | Torque | EPA Fuel Economy Rating |
|---|---|---|---|
| 6cyl 2.5L A | 174 | 177 | 18 city/21 hwy |

### Body Styles

| Style | MSRP Range |
|---|---|
| Compact SUV | $26,830 |

# 2005 Land Rover LR3

**Midsize SUV**

**MSRP Price Range**
## $44,330 - $49,330
Destination Charge: $665 (all styles)

**#1 Editors' Rating**

### Ratings

| | | |
|---|---|---|
| Consumer Rating | N/A | |
| Editors Rating | 8.6 | |

**What Edmunds.com says:** A powerful V8 engine, cutting-edge suspension technology and interior appointments fit for royalty should land the LR3 in the top tier of luxury SUVs, especially for those who actually plan on traveling off the beaten path.

**Pros:** Highly advanced suspension well suited for on-road cruising and off-road adventures, fold-flat second- and third-row seats, opulent interior, optional 600-watt stereo, powerful V8.

**Cons:** Only one engine available, priced higher than its competitors.

**What's New:** Thanks to a new platform co-designed by Ford, a 300-horse V8 borrowed from Jaguar, sumptuous interior appointments and a wide array of high-tech gadgetry, the all-new midsize LR3 promises to be one of the best Rovers yet.

**Body Styles, Trim Levels and Options:** The LR3 is offered in two trim levels, SE and HSE. Both come standard with leather upholstery, stadium seating, fold-down rear seats, dual-zone automatic climate control a nine-speaker 300-watt Harman Kardon audio system with a six-disc CD changer and all-wheel drive. HSE models get 19-inch alloy wheels, a 14-speaker 550-watt Logic 7 digital surround sound system and rear parking sensors. Optional features include a glass panoramic roof, fold-flat third-row seating and a DVD-based navigation system.

**Powertrains and Performance:** Power for the LR3 comes from an all-aluminum V8 borrowed from the Jaguar parts bin and pumped up to 4.4 liters and 300 horsepower. The six-speed automatic transmission features "intelligent" shift patterns that adapt to changes in road conditions and driving styles, and the sophisticated Terrain Response four-wheel-drive system channels power to the pavement. With a rotary knob controlling five settings (general, snow-grass-gravel, mud and ruts, sand, and rock crawl), the 4WD system optimizes everything from throttle response, traction control, electronic stability control and ABS to the differentials for the conditions. The LR3 also features a fully independent suspension, which utilizes electronically controlled air springs to automatically adapt to virtually any terrain or off-road challenge.

**Safety:** Safety features include adaptive headlights that "look" around corners and adjust up and down to counter the effects of hard braking, four-wheel antilock brakes, traction control, active anti-roll technology, hill-descent control, side-impact and head curtain airbags and even an electronic parking brake. The LR3 has not yet been crash tested.

**Interior Design and Special Features:** The LR3 features a spacious cabin packed with clever storage solutions, as well as either five or seven seats trimmed in English leather. All rear seats fold into the floor when not in use to create a vast, flat-loading space. A commanding driving position and elevated stadium seating give the driver and passengers alike a clear view of their surroundings and an optional glass panoramic roof enhances that view even further. The dash has a simple, geometric look that is very similar to the elegant design employed in the Range Rover. Switches are kept to a minimum, thanks to built-in technology that minimizes the need for driver input, and every tactile surface is thickly padded, as one would expect in a vehicle of this caliber.

*Crash Test Scores, see pg 530*
*Warranty information, see pg 542*

**Driving Impressions:** Even with 300 horsepower on tap, the 5,700-pound LR3 is no rocket, but thanks to a stellar four-wheel-drive system and the adaptive six-speed transmission, there is always plenty of power (and traction) available underfoot. The advanced suspension makes for a comfortable ride on the highway and ensures plenty of traction if you ever feel the need to go exploring off-road. Nimble rack and pinion steering lends the Rover a crisp feel behind the wheel. If you're looking for a midsize luxury SUV that can do it all, the LR3 is about as good as it gets.

### Specifications

| Engine/Drivetrain | HP | Torque | EPA Fuel Economy Rating |
|---|---|---|---|
| 8cyl 4.4L A | 300 | 315 | 14 city/18 hwy |

### Body Styles

| Style | MSRP Range |
|---|---|
| Midsize SUV | $44,330–$49,330 |

# 2005 Land Rover Range Rover

**MSRP Price Range**
**$73,085**
Destination Charge: $665 (all styles)

## Ratings

| | | |
|---|---|---|
| Consumer Rating | N/A | |
| Editors Rating | 8.0 | |

**What Edmunds.com says:** Designed and engineered by BMW, the Range Rover offers a satisfying blend of on-road comfort and off-road capability in a stylish and well-trimmed package. If you can afford the price of admission, this is one luxury SUV that won't disappoint.

**Pros:** Comfortable ride and handling on and off the pavement, classy yet rugged interior, spacious backseat, high level of off-road capability.

**Cons:** High price, cabin ergonomics still aren't the best, engine could use more low-end torque, a few low-grade interior materials.

**What's New:** The Range Rover's electronic systems—navigation, audio and telecommunications—are all new and completely integrated using fiber optics. The new DVD-based navigation system uses a VGA display, which is brighter and has better resolution than last year's LCD unit. A 4x4 driver interface graphically displays vehicle settings and positions, such as the angle of the front wheels, the suspension setting and the direction of travel. The Harman Kardon Logic 7 audio system has been boosted to 710 watts playing through 14 speakers. A Bluetooth wireless cell phone interface has also been added.

**Body Styles, Trim Levels and Options:** The four-door Range Rover comes in two trims: the HSE and the limited-edition Westminster Edition. The HSE is decked with a deep list of standard features that includes 19-inch wheels, high-intensity discharge headlights, three-zone automatic climate control, leather upholstery, wood trim, a leather-wrapped steering wheel, a 12-way power-adjustable driver seat, a 10-way power front-passenger seat, a Bluetooth wireless interface and park distance control. The standard DVD-based navigation system uses a VGA display with touchscreen capability. Entertainment is provided by a 14-speaker, 710-watt Harman Kardon sound system. Step up to the Westminster Edition, and you're rewarded with goodies such as pearlescent paint, 20-inch wheels, rain-sensing windshield wipers and leather Contour seats. Two optional packages are available. The Luxury Interior Package offers amenities such as 16-way power contour seats with upgraded leather and heated front and rear seats. The Heated Accessories Package offers multilevel heated front and rear seats, a ski bag and a heated steering wheel.

**Powertrains and Performance:** A BMW-engineered 4.4-liter V8 motivates the Range Rover; it makes 282 horsepower and 324 pound-feet of torque. Power delivery is smooth, but the engine has less low-end torque than the larger V8s offered in the Range Rover's competitors. The only transmission choice is a five-speed automatic, featuring a sequential-shift manual mode. Maximum towing capacity is set at 7,000 pounds. A permanent four-wheel-drive system and a height-adjustable suspension are standard features, along with low-range gearing and a maximum of 11.1 inches of ground clearance for serious off-roading.

**Safety:** Standard safety items include four-wheel antilock brakes, stability control, BrakeAssist, Electronic Brakeforce Distribution, seat-mounted side airbags for front occupants, full-length side curtain airbags and front and rear and parking sensors.

**Interior Design and Special Features:** Inside, the Range Rover's unique personality comes through, as it has the upscale ambience of a luxury SUV and the rugged feel of a serious off-road vehicle. Most materials are premium-grade, but there are a few instances of cost-cutting. The seating position is notably upright, but both front and rear passengers will find the accommodations supportive and roomy. Rear-seaters get their own climate controls and power-adjustable headrests. Don't expect too much by way of cargo space, though. The Range Rover falls short of its competitors in this area, offering a mere 63 cubic feet of capacity.

**Driving Impressions:** Built for the bush but bought for bragging rights, Range Rovers are more likely to be found in Beverly Hills than Botswana. Acknowledging that reality, the current Range Rover employs a unibody design and has a self-adjusting air suspension that monitors vehicle loads and road conditions. When driven on pavement, the Range Rover feels stable and comfortable. In terms of boulder-bashing, it still has few equals, thanks to its generous ground clearance and wheel travel.

*Crash Test Scores, see pg 530*
*Warranty information, see pg 542*

## Specifications

| Engine/Drivetrain | HP | Torque | EPA Fuel Economy Rating |
|---|---|---|---|
| 8cyl 4.4L A | 282 | 325 | 12 city/16 hwy |

## Body Styles

| Style | MSRP Range |
|---|---|
| Midsize SUV | $73,085 |

# 2005 Lexus ES 330

**Midsize Sedan**

**MSRP Price Range**
## $31,975
Destination Charge: $650 (all styles)

| Ratings | | |
|---|---|---|
| Consumer Rating | 9.3 | |
| Editors Rating | 8.0 | |

**What Edmunds.com says:** A supple ride and a gorgeous interior make this one entry-level luxury sedan that you'll never want to upgrade from.

**Pros:** Comprehensive array of luxury and convenience features, superb ride quality, silent cabin, advanced safety technology, excellent reputation for reliability.

**Cons:** Bland driving characteristics, many of the most desirable options are expensive, no split-folding rear seat.

**What's New:** Lexus polished up some of the details on the ES 330 for 2005. Revised exterior styling includes a new front and rear appearance with updated lighting and trim. Inside, color revisions and new wood availability keep things fresh. New 17-inch wheels are available in either chrome or alloy finish. A memory function now applies to both the driver and front-passenger seats, and heated and ventilated front seats are a new option. A revised steering wheel with auxiliary audio controls debuts, as does voice activation technology for the optional navigation system.

*Crash Test Scores, see pg 530*
*Warranty information, see pg 542*

| Specifications | | | |
|---|---|---|---|
| Engine/Drivetrain | HP | Torque | EPA Fuel Economy Rating |
| 6cyl 3.3L A | 225 | 240 | 21 city/29 hwy |

| Body Styles | |
|---|---|
| Style | MSRP Range |
| Midsize Sedan | $31,975 |

**Body Styles, Trim Levels and Options:** The five-passenger, four-door ES 330 is sold in just one trim level. Many luxury features are standard, including power front seats with memory, automatic dual-zone climate control, a power moonroof, Homelink, a full set of auto-dimming mirrors, one-touch up-and-down windows on all doors, leather seating and burled walnut or golden bird's eye maple wood trim. Other optional items include a DVD-based navigation system with voice activation, a premium Mark Levinson audio system, a powered rear sunshade, heated and ventilated seats, high-intensity discharge headlights and an in-dash six-disc CD changer. Power-adjustable pedals with a memory function are also available. A new 17-inch wheel and performance tire option dresses up the exterior appearance, while also providing a bit of an improvement in the handling department.

**Powertrains and Performance:** The ES 330's 3.3-liter V6 engine is rated at 225 horsepower and 240 pound-feet of torque and is matched to a five-speed automatic transmission. An adaptive variable suspension system is optional, and helps the ES balance a silky-smooth ride with respectable cornering ability.

**Safety:** The ES 330 has solid NHTSA crash test scores, earning five stars (the best possible) in every category except for rear-side impacts, which warranted four stars. It has also earned a "Good" rating from the IIHS for front-offset impact safety, its highest rating. The ES 330 comes with a full complement of airbags, including seat-mounted side airbags for front passengers and side-curtain airbags for all outboard passengers. The front seatbelts have pre-tensioners and load limiters. Lexus offers standard four-wheel antilock disc brakes with Electronic Brakeforce Distribution (EBD). Vehicle Skid Control (VSC), which helps prevent dangerous spins and skids, is optional, and includes traction control and BrakeAssist.

**Interior Design and Special Features:** The ES 330's cabin is quite warm and inviting. In terms of the overall design and the materials used, you're not likely to find anything better in this class—the leather is soft, the wood trim is rich and every surface the driver is likely to touch returns an impression of quality. Besides that, the backseat is roomy, the trunk is large and there should be enough luxury features to keep you and your occupants content.

**Driving Impressions:** Around town, the ES 330 floats plenty and absorbs road anomalies, providing a cushion-soft ride. When pushed harder, it offers little to get excited about—the handling limits are quite modest, though we expect most owners won't be too concerned with that particular aspect. Although cars like the Acura TL, Chrysler 300, Nissan Maxima and Volkswagen Passat W8 offer faster engines, the ES 330 should prove sufficiently quick for buyers who are more interested in tranquility than maximum performance.

**MSRP Price Range**

**$38,875**
Destination Charge: $650 (all styles)

## Ratings

| | | |
|---|---|---|
| Consumer Rating | 6.9 | |
| Editors Rating | 7.5 | |

**What Edmunds.com says:** A capable and comfortable car, but considering that the IS 300 is sportier and the ES 330 nearly as luxurious for less, the GS 300 doesn't make much sense.

**Pros:** Silky engine, available Mark Levinson audio system, commendable blend of luxury and handling.

**Cons:** Average acceleration, doesn't communicate with the driver enough given the sporting mission of the car.

**What's New:** The GS 300 continues into 2005 with no changes.

**Body Styles, Trim Levels and Options:** This midsize four-door luxury sedan comes in just one trim level. Luxury touches include standard dual-zone automatic climate control, a power tilting and telescoping steering wheel, 10-way power front seats, an auto-dimming rearview mirror, a moonroof and an in-dash CD changer. Cloth seating is standard, however, so you'll have to pay extra for leather. It's available as a stand-alone option, but quite likely you'll find it packaged into cars with the optional navigation and Mark Levinson premium sound systems. This impressive-sounding ML system includes 10 speakers and an in-dash six-disc CD changer.

**Powertrains and Performance:** The GS 300 uses a 3.0-liter inline six that develops 220 horsepower and 220 pound-feet of torque. A five-speed automatic is the only transmission available. To take advantage of the transmission's five forward gears, the GS 300 features manual-style upshift and downshift buttons on the steering wheel spokes, controlled by the thumb and forefinger of either hand. The EPA rates the GS 300 with fuel mileage estimates of 18 city/25 highway.

**Safety:** Safety equipment includes seat-mounted side and head curtain airbags (for front occupants only), four-wheel antilock disc brakes with BrakeAssist, traction control and stability control. The NHTSA has not tested the GS, though the IIHS has given the car a "Good" rating (the best possible) for its performance in the frontal offset crash test.

**Interior Design and Special Features:** A roomy cabin provides the driver and front passenger with space to stretch out. Impressive amounts of leg- and shoulder room accommodate the long-limbed and broad-shouldered in the front seats. Rear-seat passengers don't fare as well, however, and get less room than what is offered in the ES 330. The cabin is outfitted with rich wood trim and handsome light-sensitive gauges housed in chrome-ringed pods. Materials quality is excellent, and everything is assembled with precision.

**Driving Impressions:** The GS 300 sparkles on the open road. Its silent cabin, devoid of any noise, harshness or vibration, is a portrait of tranquility. During modest cornering, the chassis is solid and the multilink suspension keeps the tires pressed tight to the ground at all times. A noticeable amount of body roll limits high-speed antics. The 3.0-liter, inline six-cylinder engine is smooth, but with a curb weight of more than 3,600 pounds, the GS 300 offers only mediocre acceleration. If you're looking for speed, the GS 430 would be a better choice.

*Crash Test Scores, see pg 530*
*Warranty information, see pg 542*

## Specifications

| Engine/Drivetrain | HP | Torque | EPA Fuel Economy Rating |
|---|---|---|---|
| 6cyl 3.0L A | 220 | 220 | 18 city/25 hwy |

## Body Styles

| Style | MSRP Range |
|---|---|
| Midsize Sedan | $38,875 |

# 2005 Lexus GS 430

**Midsize Sedan**

**MSRP Price Range**

## $47,975

Destination Charge: $650 (all styles)

### Ratings

| | | |
|---|---|---|
| Consumer Rating | N/A | |
| Editors Rating | 7.8 | |

**What Edmunds.com says:** A premium sedan to consider if you can't decide which you like more, luxury or sport.

**Pros:** Powerful engine, extensive list of safety features onboard, available Mark Levinson audio system, Lexus quality and refinement.

**Cons:** Navigation system makes for clumsy control of the audio and climate control system, doesn't communicate with the driver enough given the sporting mission of the car.

**What's New:** The GS 430 continues into 2005 with no changes.

**Body Styles, Trim Levels and Options:** The five-passenger GS 430 luxury sedan comes with a high level of standard features. Highlights include 10-way power and heated front seats, auto-dimming mirrors, dual-zone automatic climate control, leather upholstery, satellite audio controls for the six-CD changer audio system, a memory system for the driver seat, HID headlights and a moonroof. Popular options include chrome 16- or 17-inch wheels, a wood-trimmed steering wheel, a DVD-based navigation system and an impressive-sounding 10-speaker Mark Levinson premium audio system.

**Powertrains and Performance:** The GS 430 packs Lexus' 4.3-liter V8, the same one used in the LS 430. With 300 horsepower and 325 pound-feet of torque on tap, the car can accelerate from zero to 60 mph in about 6.0 seconds, a solid effort for this class of car. Variable Valve Timing with intelligence (VVT-i) is used to provide optimal fuel efficiency and allows the GS 430 to earn Ultra Low Emission Vehicle (ULEV) certification. A five-speed automatic is the only transmission available. Fuel mileage estimates are 18 mpg in the city and 23 on the highway.

**Safety:** Standard equipment includes stability control, traction control and four-wheel anti-lock disc brakes with BrakeAssist. Should these items be unable to prevent an accident, the GS comes with a full brace of airbags. The NHTSA has not tested the GS, though the IIHS has given the car a "Good" rating (the highest possible) for its performance in the frontal offset crash test.

**Interior Design and Special Features:** As you might expect from a luxury sedan in this price range, the interior is replete with a virtual laundry list of luxury features. The roomy cabin is outfitted with gleaming California walnut wood trim and handsome light-sensitive gauges housed in chrome-ringed pods. Materials quality is excellent, and everything is assembled with precision. Impressive amounts of leg- and shoulder room accommodate the long-limbed and broad-shouldered in the front seats. Rear-seat passengers don't fare as well, however, as there is considerably less legroom.

**Driving Impressions:** With plenty of horsepower and torque on tap, the GS 430 accelerates briskly and it makes quick work of highway passing. The car is happiest on the open road, where its silent cabin—devoid of any noise, harshness or vibration—is a portrait of tranquility. The four-wheel independent double-wishbone suspension is configured to favor a supple, smooth ride over a taut, sporty one, which is great for the passengers, but a tad stultifying for the driver.

*Crash Test Scores, see pg 530*
*Warranty information, see pg 542*

### Specifications

| Engine/Drivetrain | HP | Torque | EPA Fuel Economy Rating |
|---|---|---|---|
| 8cyl 4.3L A | 300 | 325 | 18 city/23 hwy |

### Body Styles

| Style | MSRP Range |
|---|---|
| Midsize Sedan | $47,975 |

For the latest full vehicle reports, visit www.edmunds.com/bginfopak

# Midsize SUV

# 2005 Lexus GX 470

**MSRP Price Range**

*N/A*

Destination Charge: N/A (all styles)

## Ratings

| | | |
|---|---|---|
| Consumer Rating | N/A | |
| Editors Rating | 8.0 | |

**What Edmunds.com says:** A luxurious sport-ute that offers a near perfect blend of on- and off-road capability. You won't miss the LX 470.

**Pros:** Luxurious cabin furnishings, plush ride quality, fine road manners, smooth drivetrain, exceptional off-road ability should you need it, costs less than highly regarded European competitors.

**Cons:** Very tight quarters in optional third-row seat, side-hinged cargo door impedes curbside loading.

**What's New:** A Sport model joins the lineup that includes the Kinetic Dynamic Suspension System, smoked bezel headlamps, foglamp trim, black pearl emblems, a chrome license plate garnish and exhaust tip and alloy wheels with a dark graphite finish. Inside, the Sport features black bird's eye maple wood and graphite metallic trim. Other GX option changes this year include an upgraded navigation system with better graphics and additional functions, Bluetooth compatibility and voice commands for the climate control, audio and navigation systems. All models also receive a more powerful V8 engine good for 270 horsepower (up from 235).

**Body Styles, Trim Levels and Options:** The Lexus GX 470 is a midsize, four-door luxury SUV available in base and Sport trims. With the optional third-row seat, it can accommodate up to eight passengers. Standard features on the base model include 17-inch wheels, heated outside mirrors, illuminated running boards, leather seating, bird's eye maple wood trim, heated and power-adjustable front seats, dual-zone automatic climate control, a moonroof, one-touch up-and-down side windows and a power tilt-and-telescoping steering wheel. The standard audio system has an in-dash six-disc CD changer; you can also upgrade to the 240-watt Mark Levinson premium audio system. The Sport includes unique exterior trim and wheels, as well as the Kinetic Dynamic Suspension System, a computer-controlled suspension system designed to provide a smooth ride and excellent handling. Inside, the Sport features black bird's eye maple wood and graphite metallic trim. Another noteworthy optional item includes a DVD-based navigation system with a rear backup camera and voice recognition technology.

**Powertrains and Performance:** The only available engine is a 4.7-liter V8 that makes 270 horsepower and 330 pound-feet of torque. It's connected to a five-speed automatic that applies continuous power to all four wheels. Should a tire start to slip, the GX automatically redirects torque to the wheels with the most grip. A number of features, such as a two-speed transfer case and a hill descent feature, ensure that the GX can take on off-road trails without much difficulty. Properly equipped, the GX can tow up to 6,500 pounds.

**Safety:** The GX 470 comes standard with four-wheel antilock disc brakes with BrakeAssist and Electronic Brakeforce Distribution (EBD). It also has traction control, a stability control system and a tire-pressure monitoring system. Front side-impact and front and rear head curtain airbags are standard. In IIHS frontal offset crash testing, the GX 470 earned a rating of "Good," the highest.

**Interior Design and Special Features:** As with most other Lexus products, the interior design is warm and luxurious with rich bird's eye maple inlays and soft leather upholstery. While seat comfort is good for first- and second-row passengers, the optional third-row seat is for children only. Unlike in some other SUVs, the third-row seat does not fold into the floor but its 50/50 halves can be folded and secured upright on either side of the cargo bay. Or, you can remove them entirely. Cargo capacity measures 49.7 cubic feet behind the second row. The GX 470's high stance detracts from rearward visibility, but the optional rear backup camera solves that problem.

**Driving Impressions:** Thanks to a rear air suspension and an Adaptive Variable Suspension (AVS), the standard GX 470 delivers a luxurious ride and stable handling both on- and off-road. Even when the AVS is set in "sport" mode, though, the standard GX doesn't feel particularly sporting, so the Sport model is worth considering if sharp handling on pavement is your main priority.

*Crash Test Scores, see pg 530*
*Warranty information, see pg 542*

## Specifications

| Engine/Drivetrain | HP | Torque | EPA Fuel Economy Rating |
|---|---|---|---|
| 8cyl 4.7L A | 270 | 330 | N/A |

## Body Styles

| Style | MSRP Range |
|---|---|
| Midsize SUV | N/A |

**MSRP Price Range**

*$29,435 - $30,805*

Destination Charge: $545 (all styles)

## Ratings

| | | |
|---|---|---|
| Consumer Rating | 10.0 | |
| Editors Rating | 7,4 | |

**What Edmunds.com says:** Can't match the BMW 3 Series, but its combination of price, performance and premium features make the IS 300 a very intriguing sport sedan or wagon.

**Pros:** Outstanding driving dynamics, slick interior decor, competitive pricing.

**Cons:** Small rear seat and trunk, not much storage space, aging design struggles to keep up with its more modern competition.

**What's New:** The IS 300 continues into 2005 largely unchanged. A limited-slip differential is no longer available with the manual transmission.

*Crash Test Scores, see pg 530*
*Warranty information, see pg 542*

## Specifications

| Engine/Drivetrain | HP | Torque | EPA Fuel Economy Rating |
|---|---|---|---|
| 6cyl 3.0L A/M | 215 | 218 | 18 city/24 hwy |

## Body Styles

| Style | MSRP Range |
|---|---|
| Compact Sedan | $29,435–$30,805 |
| Compact Wagon | $30,805 |

**Body Styles, Trim Levels and Options:** The IS 300 is available as a sedan or a wagon dubbed the SportCross. Each version comes standard with 17-inch wheels, auto-dimming mirrors, automatic climate control, HID headlights and an in-dash six-disc CD changer. Available options include leather seating (or a leather and fake-suede combo) with power front seats, a navigation system, heated front seats, a moonroof and a variety of tire-and-wheel packages.

**Powertrains and Performance:** Power comes from a DOHC 3.0-liter inline six-cylinder engine. Equipped with variable valve timing, the engine spins out 215 horsepower and 218 pound-feet of torque. When the IS debuted, buyers could have any transmission they wanted as long as it was the five-speed automatic. Much of the motoring press complained, so Lexus began offering a five-speed-manual sedan in 2002. Subsequent consumer interest in the five-speed has been minimal, however, and you might have a hard time finding them on dealer lots.

**Safety:** Seat-mounted side airbags for front occupants and full-length side curtain airbags are standard equipment. So are traction control and four-wheel antilock disc brakes with EBD and BrakeAssist. Vehicle Skid Control (VSC), a stability control system that can help reduce dangerous spins and skids, is an option on automatic-equipped cars. As for crash tests, the NHTSA has given four stars (out of a possible five) for driver and front-passenger safety in frontal impacts, and five stars each for side impacts to the front and rear. The IIHS gave the car a "Good" rating (its highest) in its frontal offset crash test, and named the IS 300 a "Best Pick" overall.

**Interior Design and Special Features:** The IS 300's cabin wears distinctive features like a chrome-plated shift knob, chronograph-inspired gauge cluster and race-carlike drilled aluminum pedals. The gauge cluster features the speedometer as the main dial with three smaller gauges inside it. The smaller ones (real-time fuel mileage, battery volts and coolant temperature) look cool but are hard to read due to their size. Additionally, some of the interior plastics seem low-grade given the class of car. People who frequently use their sedans to ferry multiple adults might find that this Lexus' backseat is not particularly well suited to the task as it has considerably less rear legroom than the ES 330. The trunk (10.1 cubic feet) is also a size smaller than what is typically offered. The SportCross wagon offers 21.8 cubic feet of cargo room for those who need the extra space.

**Driving Impressions:** We consider the IS 300 to be an excellent vehicle when it comes to driver enjoyment. The car's behavior is unlike anything else Lexus sells. The body structure is extremely stiff, and the suspension has been tuned to provide sticky handling without overly degrading ride quality on the street. The IS 300 is an easy car to pilot aggressively, thanks to its responsive steering, strong brakes, nimble size and excellent driving position.

# Large Sedan

# 2005 Lexus LS 430

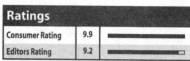

**MSRP Price Range**

## $55,675

Destination Charge: $650 (all styles)

#1 Editors' Rating

### Ratings

| | | |
|---|---|---|
| Consumer Rating | 9.9 | |
| Editors Rating | 9.2 | |

**What Edmunds.com says:** With refinement and comfort levels equal to or better than the German uber-sedans, the LS provides an exceptional luxury sedan experience without the holier-than-thou attitude.

**Pros:** Superb ride quality, impressive array of standard and optional luxury features, premium interior materials, Lexus reliability, top-notch dealer service.

**Cons:** Not as athletic as some competitors, adding options raises the price to unLexus-like levels.

**What's New:** After last year's major refresh, Lexus chose to keep changes simple this year. The lone change is to the optional 18-inch alloy wheels, which are now available as a stand-alone extra.

**Body Styles, Trim Levels and Options:** As the Lexus flagship, the LS 430 offers plenty of standard and optional features. All cars come with 17-inch wheels, adaptive headlights that swivel during cornering, dual-zone climate control (with oscillating air registers), a 14-way power driver seat with memory and 10-way power for the front passenger, auto-dimming mirrors, an in-dash CD changer, a moonroof, a rear sunshade and a power trunk closer. On the options list, you'll find two upgraded leather upholstery trims, heated and cooled front seats, a voice-activated navigation system with rear backup camera and a 240-watt Mark Levinson premium audio system. The Custom Luxury package includes these items and tacks on rear-seat heaters and power door closers. Buyers have their choice of laser-based adaptive cruise control, or a radar-based system that includes the Pre-Collision system, which detects and prepares for unavoidable impacts. Still not enough? The aptly named Ultra Luxury package gives you all of that plus SmartAccess, which allows you to start the car without a key, Lexus Link telematics, a smoother-riding air suspension, upgraded power-adjustable, heated/cooled rear seats and a separate rear climate control system.

**Powertrains and Performance:** A 4.3-liter V8 engine powers the LS 430, offering 290 horse-power and 320 pound-feet of torque. Variable Valve Timing with intelligence (VVT-i) eliminates the compromise between high-rpm horsepower and low-end torque while allowing the car to be ULEV-certified. The engine is matched to a six-speed automatic transmission (with an automanual gate) driving the rear wheels, and thanks to very slippery aerodynamics, the LS has an 18/25 mpg EPA fuel mileage rating.

**Safety:** A full complement of airbags (side, head curtain and knee), four-wheel antilock brakes with BrakeAssist, traction control, the VSC stability control system and a tire-pressure monitor are all in place to ensure maximum safety. There's also Pre-Collision, which uses radar to detect unavoidable collisions and then prepares for impact by tightening the seatbelts, applying maximum braking force and activating sport mode on air suspension-equipped LS 430s.

**Interior Design and Special Features:** The LS 430's cabin is warm and luxurious given its high-quality leather, abundance of rich walnut or maple trim, sharp electroluminescent gauges and wonderfully comfortable seats. There is plenty of headroom and legroom for both front and rear passengers, and the large trunk holds 20.2 cubic feet of luggage.

**Driving Impressions:** A serene car in nearly all situations, the LS 430 is great for urban commuting and long-distance drives. The suspension neatly soaks up road irregularities, especially when equipped with the air suspension setup found in the Ultra Luxury package. Previous LS 400s weren't known for inspired driving dynamics, and while capable when the road turns twisty, the 430 does little to engage its driver on an emotional level. If you want passion from your super-luxury sedan, an Audi A8 or a BMW 7 Series will suit you better.

*Crash Test Scores, see pg 530*
*Warranty information, see pg 542*

### Specifications

| Engine/Drivetrain | HP | Torque | EPA Fuel Economy Rating |
|---|---|---|---|
| 8cyl 4.3L A | 290 | 320 | 18 city/25 hwy |

### Body Styles

| Style | MSRP Range |
|---|---|
| Large Sedan | $55,675 |

# 2005 Lexus LX 470

Midsize SUV

**MSRP Price Range**

**$64,775**

Destination Charge: $650 (all styles)

#1 Editors' Rating

## Ratings

| | | |
|---|---|---|
| Consumer Rating | 9.2 | |
| Editors Rating | 8.8 | |

**What Edmunds.com says:** Yes, it costs well over $60,000. But for the money, you'd be hard-pressed to find a more versatile, luxurious and capable vehicle.

**Pros:** Quiet and refined demeanor, capable backwoods performer, slick adjustable suspension, splendid interior materials, Lexus build quality.

**Cons:** High price, lack of horsepower.

**What's New:** Satellite radio is now an available option

**Body Styles, Trim Levels and Options:** The LX 470 is a full-size four-door SUV based on the Toyota Land Cruiser. Standard equipment includes power-adjustable and heated front seats, illuminated running boards, automatic climate control, a DVD-based navigation system, auto-dimming mirrors, a moonroof and a rear backup camera system. The base audio system has a dash-mounted six-CD changer; an optional Mark Levinson audio system exists for those who need the utmost in audio quality. Other options include the Night View enhanced nighttime vision system, the Lexus Link emergency communications service, a roof rack, satellite radio and a dealer-installed DVD entertainment system for rear-seat passengers.

**Powertrains and Performance:** Every LX 470 is four-wheel drive and uses a 4.7-liter V8 that produces 235 horsepower and 320 pound-feet of torque. Matched to a standard five-speed automatic transmission, this V8 is smooth but taxed by the vehicle's substantial 5,600-pound curb weight, especially with a full load of passengers. Nevertheless, most buyers will find it perfectly adequate for day-to-day driving. Fuel mileage is rated at 13 city/17 highway and, properly equipped, the LX 470 can tow a load up to 5,000 pounds.

**Safety:** Standard equipment includes four-wheel antilock disc brakes, front seat-mounted side airbags and side curtain airbags for front- and second-row occupants. To help avoid an accident, Lexus has fortified the brakes with Electronic Brakeforce Distribution (EBD) and BrakeAssist. There is also VDC, Lexus' stability control system. The LX has not been crash tested by the NHTSA nor the IIHS.

**Interior Design and Special Features:** You get a sense that no expense was spared in creating its luxurious cabin. Indeed, the LX 470's walnut wood trim is radiant in its luster and the perforated leather sumptuous in its suppleness. Materials used in the construction of the interior are generally of the highest quality. Three rows of seating come standard. The 60/40-split second row can be folded forward, and the 50/50-split rear bench can be removed entirely. So done, there is 90.4 cubic feet of cargo room available.

**Driving Impressions:** Ride and handling characteristics are as close to perfect as any large SUV has ever come. On the street, the ride is as smooth and buttery as you like, depending on which of the four modes you choose for the Adaptive Variable Suspension (AVS), which automatically adjusts shock absorber firmness according to driving style, road conditions and vehicle load. Even on challenging off-road trails composed of severe bumps and ruts, the LX 470 retains its compliant, forgiving ride quality.

*Crash Test Scores, see pg 530*
*Warranty information, see pg 542*

## Specifications

| Engine/Drivetrain | HP | Torque | EPA Fuel Economy Rating |
|---|---|---|---|
| 8cyl 4.7L A | 235 | 320 | 13 city/17 hwy |

## Body Styles

| Style | MSRP Range |
|---|---|
| Midsize SUV | $64,775 |

For the latest full vehicle reports, visit www.edmunds.com/bginfopak

# Midsize SUV

# 2005 Lexus RX 330

**MSRP Price Range**

## $35,775 - $37,175
Destination Charge: $650 (all styles)

### Ratings

| Consumer Rating | 9.7 | |
|---|---|---|
| Editors Rating | 8.3 | |

**What Edmunds.com says:** A luxurious SUV that effectively combines sport, utility, comfort and technology in a stylish package with a strong reputation for reliability.

**Pros:** Well-appointed interior, rides more like a sedan than an SUV, loaded with high-tech features, solid reputation for reliability, excellent dealer service.

**Cons:** Less powerful than some of its competitors, soft ride makes for merely adequate handling in corners, no third-row seat option.

**What's New:** The power rear hatch is now standard on all models, as is wood and leather trim for the shift knob and steering wheel. The power passenger seat is upgraded from four-way to eight-way while the optional navigation system gets Bluetooth capability and voice actuated control. Last year's standard six-disc CD changer moves to the options list, making way for a standard single-CD setup.

**Body Styles, Trim Levels and Options:** The RX 330 is available in a single trim with either front-wheel drive or all-wheel drive. The standard equipment list includes items such as power-adjustable front seats, stability and traction control, second-row seats that slide and recline, dual-zone automatic climate control and a power rear hatch. The options list is extensive, with most major components bundled together into packages. One package adds a navigation system along with a Mark Levinson audio system, while another adds 18-inch wheels and tires, air suspension and leather upholstery among other things. Notable options include xenon headlights that swivel when you turn, a rear-mounted camera for seeing what's behind you while backing up, and a rear-seat DVD entertainment system with wireless headphones.

**Powertrains and Performance:** The RX 330 is powered by a 3.3-liter V6 rated at 230 horsepower and 242 pound-feet of torque. Equipped with the available Performance Package, and its automanual shifter, Lexus claims the RX 330 is the fastest crossover SUV on the market with a 0-to-60-mph time of 7.7 seconds for the front-wheel-drive version. Like its predecessor, the RX 330 offers a full-time all-wheel-drive system that automatically adjusts the division of power between the front and rear wheels based on available traction.

**Safety:** The RX 330 features standard front, side, head and even driver knee airbags. Standard stability and traction control systems also lend an added measure of active safety to the RX's considerable repertoire of safety devices. Crash testing conducted by the NHTSA resulted in a five-star rating (out of five) for all but the front passenger, which received a four-star rating. Testing by the IIHS turned in a rating of "Good," the highest available, and "Best Pick" status for its class.

**Interior Design and Special Features:** Inside the RX 330, three round, chrome-rimmed gauges house the vital information, while an angular center pod tapering into an attractive center console houses the audio/nav system and climate control functions. Metallic-looking surfaces combined with rich wood really drive the RX's luxury theme home. Along with its sleek exterior, the RX 330's cabin presents a sporty, youthful look. There's also a 40/20/40-split rear seat that slides and reclines for maximum passenger comfort. In back, the RX offers 84.7 cubic feet of cargo space as well as a standard power-operated liftgate.

**Driving Impressions:** As expected, the RX 330 delivers all the smoothness and sophistication one would expect from Lexus. The V6 offers plenty of power and refinement, and the five-speed transmission handles it well. Occasionally, the five-speed seems to get confused, but its overall performance is solid. Due to the luxurious intent of the RX 330, handling is a little on the soft side with plenty of body lean when cornering; although, the vehicle never feels floaty or uncontrollable. Handling is improved significantly with the Performance Package and its air suspension upgrade. With that option, cornering is nearly flat, but ride quality is not compromised—it still feels like a Lexus.

*Crash Test Scores, see pg 530*
*Warranty information, see pg 542*

### Specifications

| Engine/Drivetrain | HP | Torque | EPA Fuel Economy Rating |
|---|---|---|---|
| 6cyl 3.3L A | 230 | 242 | 20 city/26 hwy |

### Body Styles

| Style | MSRP Range |
|---|---|
| Midsize SUV | $35,775–$37,175 |

# 2005 Lexus SC 430

**MSRP Price Range**

## $63,175

Destination Charge: $650 (all styles)

### Ratings

| | | |
|---|---|---|
| Consumer Rating | 9.7 | |
| Editors Rating | 8.0 | |

**What Edmunds.com says:** Though not particularly invigorating to drive, the Lexus SC 430 counters with a serene top-down experience for a price considerably less than the competition.

**Pros:** Long list of comfort and convenience features, beautifully finished interior, silky V8 engine, retractable hardtop, Lexus quality.

**Cons:** Sparse cargo space, cramped (and nearly useless) rear seats, doesn't inspire anything more than leisurely cruising.

**What's New:** The 2005 SC 430 receives new shock absorbers for improved ride comfort and driving performance. All-season run-flat tires are now an available option in addition to the summer-use run-flats offered previously.

**Body Styles, Trim Levels and Options:** Though available in just one body style and trim level, the SC 430 comes packed with luxurious amenities. Standard features include 18-inch wheels, a navigation system, supple leather seats with driver and passenger memory functions, an astounding 240-watt nine-speaker premium audio system, a sophisticated climate control system and either bird's eye maple or walnut trim. With a press of a button, the aluminum-alloy roof rises to provide shelter from the vagaries of the environment. Once closed, the top seals tight to transform the SC 430 into a hardtop coupe possessing superior structural rigidity and little wind noise while cruising down the freeway. Options on the SC 430 include run-flat tires and a rear spoiler.

**Powertrains and Performance:** The SC 430 is powered by the same 4.3-liter V8 engine that Lexus uses in the LS and GS sedans. It produces 300 horsepower and 325 pound-feet of torque. It's connected to a five-speed automatic transmission that drives the rear wheels. Zero-to-60 mph acceleration comes in at around 6.5 seconds.

**Safety:** Four-wheel antilock disc brakes with a panic-assist feature and Electronic Brakeforce Distribution (EBD) are standard, as are seatbelt pre-tensioners and front- and side-impact airbags. The SC 430 also comes with traction control and stability control. The optional run-flat tires allow the car to be driven up to 100 miles at 55 mph without air pressure. Neither the NHTSA nor the IIHS has crash tested the SC 430.

**Interior Design and Special Features:** The interior is the highlight of the car. Beautiful to look at, the cockpit is filled with real wood and leather, and spring-loaded wooden covers can hide much of the center stack. From a more practical standpoint, however, the SC falls a little short. Owners will find that the trunk doesn't offer much room, as it holds just 8.8 cubic feet of cargo. Ordering the optional run-flat tires and ditching the spare bumps the trunk size up to 9.4 cubic feet. Keep in mind that these numbers are with the top up; with the top retracted, luggage space is very scarce. Additionally, the SC's undersized rear seats are basically just for show rather than actual use.

*Crash Test Scores, see pg 530*
*Warranty information, see pg 542*

### Specifications

| Engine/Drivetrain | HP | Torque | EPA Fuel Economy Rating |
|---|---|---|---|
| 8cyl 4.3L A | 300 | 325 | 18 city/23 hwy |

### Body Styles

| Style | MSRP Range |
|---|---|
| Compact Convertible | $63,175 |

**Driving Impressions:** The 4.3-liter V8 allows the SC to leap from nearly any speed. It climbs to redline with no discernable strain. The exhaust note is nearly imperceptible, a trait that's either pleasing or disappointing depending on your point of view. Shifts from the five-speed automatic are always crisp, but with no manual-shift mode, spirited driving takes more attention than it should. The suspension setup echoes the traits of the drivetrain, filtering out every bump and ripple in the road in an attempt to maintain civility at all times. This, in turn, results in less road feel and reduced driver confidence when pushing the SC 430 hard into the corners.

# 2005 Lincoln Aviator

**MSRP Price Range**
## $40,615 - $43,565
Destination Charge: $740 (all styles)

## Ratings

| | | |
|---|---|---|
| Consumer Rating | N/A | |
| Editors Rating | 7.4 | |

**What Edmunds.com says:** A surprisingly enjoyable luxury sport-ute that takes all that's right about the Navigator and applies it to a smaller, more manageable package.

**Pros:** Excellent performance from the standard V8, sharp handling dynamics for an SUV, stylish and feature-laden interior that's doesn't sacrifice utility.

**Cons:** Interior lacks the rock solid build quality of equivalently priced luxury SUVs, engine noise intrusive at high rpm.

**What's New:** The AdvanceTrac stability control system is now standard and includes a new Roll Stability Control feature. The model lineup has been pared down to one well-equipped trim with separate option packages for those who want additional luxury features. Seventeen-inch alloy wheels are now standard, and there is a new chrome grille surround and slots.

**Body Styles, Trim Levels and Options:** The Aviator comes in one well-equipped model. Standard features include dual-zone climate control, a CD player, leather upholstery, power-adjustable pedals and rear park assist. Available upgrades include HID headlamps, heated and cooled seats, an in-dash CD changer and 17-inch chrome wheels. Other popular options include a moonroof, DVD entertainment system, DVD-based navigation system with THX-Certified audio and a class III trailer hitch. The Aviator comes with three rows of seating with your choice of bench or bucket seats in the second row.

**Powertrains and Performance:** Powering the Aviator is a 32-valve, 4.6-liter V8 that cranks out 302 horsepower and 300 pound-feet of torque. A five-speed automatic sends this considerable thrust to either the rear wheels on two-wheel-drive versions, or all four in the case of the all-wheel-drive Aviator. The muscle-bound V8, along with the Aviator's stout body-on-frame design, gives the Lincoln a serious towing advantage over its less rugged competition with a maximum capacity of 7,300 pounds (7,100 pounds for AWD models).

**Safety:** Hefty antilock disc brakes, a tire-pressure monitoring system and side curtain airbags that cover the first and second rows are standard. The standard AdvanceTrac stability control system features Roll Stability Control for additional protection against rollover accidents. Like its Explorer platform mate, the Aviator has been named a "Best Pick" by the IIHS for frontal offset crash protection. The NHTSA has not tested an Aviator, but the Explorer's scores—a perfect five stars for side impacts, four stars for frontal impacts involving the driver and five stars for frontal impacts involving the passenger—are indicative of the Lincoln's crashworthiness.

**Interior Design and Special Features:** The cabin is all Lincoln and features a symmetrical dash, plenty of real wood trim, power-adjustable pedals and leather seating. In addition to providing a choice of buckets or a bench for the second row, the Aviator also boasts more third-seat legroom than the full-size Cadillac Escalade. Controls are illuminated at night by white LEDs (that vary in intensity according to ambient light), and the steering wheel has controls for the audio and climate control systems. The Aviator can carry 77 cubic feet of cargo, a figure equal to the Lexus GX 470's capacity.

**Driving Impressions:** Around town, the powerful V8 moves the Aviator with authority. Any anxiety about passing or merging is quickly forgotten in this vehicle, as it builds speed quickly and smoothly. As impressive as the engine is, what really gives the Aviator an upscale feel is its combination of a precisely tuned suspension, stiff chassis and smooth steering. The result is a vehicle that soaks up even the biggest road hazards with minimal intrusion into the cabin and a suspension that tracks well over just about any surface.

*Crash Test Scores, see pg 530*
*Warranty information, see pg 542*

## Specifications

| Engine/Drivetrain | HP | Torque | EPA Fuel Economy Rating |
|---|---|---|---|
| 8cyl 4.6L A | 302 | 300 | 13 city/19 hwy |

## Body Styles

| Style | MSRP Range |
|---|---|
| Midsize SUV | $40,615–$43,565 |

# 2005 Lincoln LS

**Midsize Sedan**

**MSRP Price Range**

## $32,475 - $43,425

Destination Charge: $635 (all styles)

### Ratings

| | | |
|---|---|---|
| Consumer Rating | N/A | |
| Editors Rating | 7.7 | |

**What Edmunds.com says:** A smooth, comfortable American sedan with a good heart, but it lacks the refinement and athleticism of its competition.

**Pros:** Confident steering and handling, optional V8 delivers plenty of smooth and quiet power, comfortable and roomy interior, optional THX-certified sound system.

**Cons:** Lack of a manual transmission keeps it from true sport sedan status, build quality lags behind German and Japanese competitors, not as nimble as other sport sedans in its class.

**What's New:** The LS features a new front fascia for 2005, and the automatic transmission has been tweaked yet again for improved shift feel and quality.

**Body Styles, Trim Levels and Options:** Available trim levels range from basic V6 to loaded V8. You can choose the base version, the V6 Luxury, with a host of standard features like dual-zone climate control, leather upholstery and power seats. The V6 Premium package gets you American burl walnut interior trim, memory seats, power-folding mirrors and an in-dash six-disc CD changer. Step up to the V8 Sport and you'll get most of the features of the V6 Premium, along with 17-inch wheels, the automanual transmission and aluminum interior trim. Go the whole hog with the V8 Ultimate and receive a power moonroof, AdvanceTrac stability control and heated and cooled front seats. Other options include a DVD-based navigation system and a THX-certified audio system.

**Powertrains and Performance:** Buyers can choose from two power plants. The first is a 3.0-liter V6 that produces 232 horsepower and 220 pound-feet of torque. Next up is a 3.9-liter V8 that boasts 280 hp at 6,000 rpm and 250 lb-ft of torque at 2,000 rpm. Both are mated to a five-speed automatic transmission; V8 models come with an automanual gate for drivers who want to do their own shifting.

**Safety:** Traction control is standard across the line, while the AdvanceTrac stability control system is standard on the V8 Ultimate, but optional on all other trims. The four-wheel antilock disc brakes are equipped with Electronic Brakeforce Distribution (EBD) and BrakeAssist. Side airbags for front passengers are standard on all models; full-length head curtain airbags and rear parking sensors are optional. In NHTSA crash testing, the LS scored a perfect five stars for driver and front passenger protection. Side-impact tests resulted in a four-star score for front-seat occupants and five stars for rear-seat passengers. In 40-mph frontal offset crash testing by the IIHS, the LS received a "Good" rating (the best possible).

**Interior Design and Special Features:** Materials quality is not up to the level of import competitors, but real wood, faux titanium and chrome accents add some visual interest to the LS cockpit. The leather upholstery is soft to the touch, and although the well-cushioned chairs provide excellent comfort during highway cruising, their lack of lateral support makes them unsuitable for more spirited driving. The backseat offers more room than most entry-level luxury sedans, as even six-footers will find ample head-, leg- and foot room.

*Crash Test Scores, see pg 530*
*Warranty information, see pg 542*

### Specifications

| Engine/Drivetrain | HP | Torque | EPA Fuel Economy Rating |
|---|---|---|---|
| 8cyl 3.9L A | 280 | 286 | 18 city/25 hwy |
| 6cyl 3.0L A | 232 | 220 | 20 city/26 hwy |

### Body Styles

| Style | MSRP Range |
|---|---|
| Midsize Sedan | $32,475–$43,425 |

**Driving Impressions:** The V6 has ample power to get the LS up to speed amidst everyday traffic and is a solid choice for those on a budget, but the V8 is where the fun lies. Smooth and gutsy off the line, it remains quiet while providing strong acceleration from almost any speed. The Lincoln's handling is commendable considering its size, but as the turns get smaller the LS begins to feel bigger. Excellent highway manners make it a terrific car for eating up long stretches of pavement, but as a sport sedan it's average at best.

For the latest full vehicle reports, visit www.edmunds.com/bginfopak

# 2005 Lincoln Navigator

**MSRP Price Range**

## $49,790 - $56,440

Destination Charge: $795 (all styles)

### Ratings

| | | |
|---|---|---|
| Consumer Rating | 9.4 | ▬▬▬▬▬▬▬▬ |
| Editors Rating | 7.9 | ▬▬▬▬▬▬ |

**What Edmunds.com says:** A spacious and stylish full-size luxury SUV, but the Escalade is more powerful and the Lexus LX 470 more refined.

**Pros:** Lots of room for passengers and cargo, handles well for its size, stylish interior, smooth drivetrain, extensive list of luxury features.

**Cons:** A few low-grade interior materials, still can't match the Escalade's power, some confusing controls.

**What's New:** A revised version of last year's 5.4-liter V8 engine mated to an all-new six-speed automatic transmission gives the Navigator a boost in performance and refinement. The AdvanceTrac stability control system now features Roll Stability Control and is standard on all Navigators. Design changes include a new front fascia, revised side cladding and running boards. A new 18-inch chrome wheel design is also available.

**Body Styles, Trim Levels and Options:** Two trim levels are available: Luxury and Ultimate. Luxury models come with leather upholstery, automatic dual-zone climate control, an in-dash six-disc changer, roof rack and power-folding side mirrors. Still not satisfied? Opting for the Ultimate sets you up with heated and cooled front seats, a power liftgate, power-folding third-row seats and a power moonroof. Options for both models include a 40/20/40 second-row bench seat (in lieu of the standard captain's chairs), a DVD-based navigation system, a THX-certified audio system, a rear-seat DVD entertainment system and a Class III/IV tow hitch. Power-deploying running boards, a signature Navigator feature, are also available.

**Powertrains and Performance:** The Navigator is powered by a 5.4-liter V8 engine rated for 300 horsepower. A six-speed automatic transmission is standard. As the Navigator weighs almost 5,800 pounds, acceleration is adequate but certainly not brisk, and fuel mileage leaves something to be desired. As with other truck-based SUVs, buyers have a choice between two-wheel drive (rear-drive) and four-wheel drive. Properly equipped, the Navigator can tow up to 8,600 pounds.

**Safety:** The Navigator comes standard with side curtain airbags and four-wheel disc brakes with ABS, Electronic Brakeforce Distribution and BrakeAssist. The AdvanceTrac stability control system, which features Roll Stability Control to help reduce the chance of a rollover accident, is standard on all models. The Lincoln earned a perfect five stars in frontal crash testing conducted by the NHTSA.

**Interior Design and Special Features:** The shapely dash has a dual-cowl dash design evocative of a 1961 Lincoln Continental and a pleasing blend of warm and cool tones. The sparingly applied walnut trim is convincing, and the leather seat upholstery looks and feels good. Unfortunately, closer inspection reveals a number of cheap plastics, and some of the controls are hard to use. The Navigator makes no such compromises when it comes to hauling passengers, though, as its third-row seat offers class-leading legroom—giving it a usable capacity of seven or eight people. Cargo capacity ranges from 17.9 cubic feet with all the seats in use to 104.7 cubic feet with all rear seats folded down.

**Driving Impressions:** Acceleration is adequate in most situations, but when pushed on the highway, the Lincoln's V8 runs out of breath more quickly than its Cadillac rival. Although not as plush-riding as the Cadillac or the Lexus LX 470, the Navigator has a composed, confident feel on the road, and body lean is well controlled around corners.

*Crash Test Scores, see pg 530*
*Warranty information, see pg 542*

### Specifications

| Engine/Drivetrain | HP | Torque | EPA Fuel Economy Rating |
|---|---|---|---|
| 8cyl 5.4L A | 300 | 365 | 13 city/18 hwy |

### Body Styles

| Style | MSRP Range |
|---|---|
| Large SUV | $49,790–$56,440 |

# Lincoln

# 2005 Lincoln Town Car
Large Sedan

**MSRP Price Range**
## $41,875 - $50,245
Destination Charge: $795 (all styles)

## Ratings

| | | |
|---|---|---|
| Consumer Rating | 8.8 | |
| Editors Rating | 8.3 | |

**What Edmunds.com says:** If you want a big American luxury car for a reasonable price, the Town Car is the only game in town, but equivalently priced European and Japanese luxury sedans are better in almost every respect.

**Pros:** Roomy interior, quiet cabin, throaty V8 engine, huge trunk, availability of a long-wheelbase model.

**Cons:** Interior looks ancient compared to equivalently priced European and Japanese luxury sedans, poor resale value.

**What's New:** Lincoln juggles the Town Car's trim levels again this year; the base car is now the Signature, and the Signature Limited represents the loaded version. A Signature L fills the long-wheelbase slot for 2005. (Another long-wheelbase Town Car, the Executive L, is available but it is restricted to commercial fleet sales only.) The navigation radio option now includes a THX-certified audio system and satellite radio compatibility. Additionally, a new two-spoke steering wheel debuts this year.

*Crash Test Scores, see pg 530*
*Warranty information, see pg 542*

## Specifications

| Engine/Drivetrain | HP | Torque | EPA Fuel Economy Rating |
|---|---|---|---|
| 8cyl 4.6L A | 239 | 287 | 18 city/25 hwy |

## Body Styles

| Style | MSRP Range |
|---|---|
| Large Sedan | $41,875–$50,245 |

**Body Styles, Trim Levels and Options:** The Lincoln Town Car is offered in Signature and Signature Limited trim. The Signature is available in regular- or long-wheelbase (called the L) form, while the Signature Limited comes with the regular wheelbase only. Standard equipment includes 17-inch alloy wheels, dual-zone climate control with heat and air conditioning vents for rear passengers, leather upholstery, eight-way power front seats, power-adjustable pedals, a CD player, an analog clock for the dashboard, automatic headlamps and rear parking sensors. The Signature Limited adds heated front seats, driver seat memory, a wood-and-leather steering wheel, an upgraded audio system and a full power open/close trunk. The Signature L adds a six-inch wheelbase extension for increased rear-seat room and builds upon the standard Signature model's equipment list with dual rear-seat power points, four-way rear head restraints, heated rear seats and remote controls for audio, climate and the front-passenger seat. Various options include HID headlights, chrome wheels, a trunk-mounted CD changer and a navigation system paired with a TXH-certified audio system; dealers can install a Sirius Satellite Radio receiver.

**Powertrains and Performance:** All Town Cars are powered by a 4.6-liter V8 rated at 239 horsepower and 287 pound-feet of torque. A standard four-speed automatic transmission sends the power to the rear wheels. Fuel economy is rated at 17 mpg in the city and 25 mpg on the highway.

**Safety:** Heading up the list of Town Car safety features is the Personal Safety System, which is comprised of dual-stage front airbags, seat-mounted side airbags and three-point seatbelts for all outboard seating positions. All-speed traction control is standard, as is four-wheel ABS with Electronic Brakeforce Distribution and BrakeAssist technology, which applies full braking power in a panic stop. Also on the list of standard items are traction control and power-adjustable pedals.

**Interior Design and Special Features:** Boasting large interior dimensions and a massive trunk (20.6 cubic feet), the Town Car's primary mission is to transport multiple passengers to their destination silently and comfortably. Buyers can also select the L version, which offers a whopping 47 inches of rear legroom thanks to its 6-inch-longer wheelbase.

**Driving Impressions:** Thrust from the Town Car's V8 should be fully adequate for most buyers. Passing maneuvers are accomplished with ease, and freeway cruising at 80 mph is hushed. The Town Car has no peer when it comes to transporting large (or large numbers of) people. Besides offering a comfortable ride, this Lincoln is a decent handler—the steering has some feel to it, and the body doesn't roll too much around corners. Compared to premium luxury flagships like the BMW 7 Series, Infiniti Q45, Lexus LS 430 and Mercedes S-Class, the Town Car's mediocre levels of refinement quickly stand out, but none of those cars can match the Lincoln's under-$50,000 price tag.

# 2005 Mazda MAZDA3

**MSRP Price Range**
**$13,680 - $17,105**
Destination Charge: $545 (all styles)

#1 Editors' Rating

## Ratings

| | | |
|---|---|---|
| Consumer Rating | 9.3 | |
| Editors Rating | 8.4 | |

**What Edmunds.com says:** Good looks, strong engines and sharp handling add up to an economy car that feels anything but cheap.

**Pros:** Fun-to-drive character, stylish interior design, strong engines, hatchback utility.

**Cons:** Ride might be too stiff for some, a few ergonomic quirks, tight rear legroom.

**What's New:** All new for 2004, the Mazda 3 receives only minor changes for 2005. The four-door "i" model gets a new 15-inch wheel cover design, and Sirius Satellite Radio is now available on all models.

**Body Styles, Trim Levels and Options:** The 3 is available as a sedan in base "i" or upgraded "s" trim, while the four-door hatchback model comes in "s" trim only. Base sedans have basic features like a tilt-and-telescoping steering wheel, full carpeting, a 60/40-split-folding rear seat and an AM/FM CD stereo. Options include air conditioning, 16-inch alloy wheels, a sunroof and a six-disc CD changer. Upgraded "s" models come standard with power windows, locks and mirrors; 16-inch alloys; cruise control; keyless entry; a leather-wrapped steering wheel with satellite audio and cruise controls; and higher-grade cloth upholstery. Hatchbacks come standard with the Sport Appearance package that adds 17-inch wheels and additional bodywork; it's optional on the sedan. Full leather seating is also an option, along with a DVD navigation system and xenon headlights.

**Powertrains and Performance:** Base sedans use a 2.0-liter, four-cylinder engine rated to produce 148 horsepower (144 in Calif.), while the upgraded "s" models use a 2.3-liter four-cylinder that bumps the horsepower number to 160. Both engines can be equipped with either a five-speed manual or a four-speed automatic transmission with manual-shift capability.

**Safety:** All models feature four-wheel disc brakes and seatbelt pre-tensioners for the front seats. Antilock brakes with Electronic Brakeforce Distribution (EBD) are optional on all models as are front side-impact airbags and full-length side curtain airbags. The NHTSA gave the 3 a four-star rating (out of a possible five) for frontal impact protection and a three-star rating for side impacts.

**Interior Design and Special Features:** Unlike most economy cars, the 3 offers a distinctive interior design that is both comfortable and functional. The sharp-looking gauges are housed in their own individual binnacles, while the center stack augments the typical three-dial design with a sleek radio treatment that gives the car a more upscale appearance than most cars in its class. There's enough room for taller drivers to get comfortable up front, and the rear seats are acceptably spacious for a car in this class. Trunk space is up on sedan models, but the hatchback is still short on cargo space until you fold the rear seats.

**Driving Impressions:** Liquid-filled suspension bushings, an electrohydraulic steering system and a multilink rear suspension design are just a few of the 3's upgrades that deliver refined road manners that will surprise those expecting the typically flabby ride and handling of most economy cars. Tightly controlled in turns and solid at speed, the suspension leans toward the sporty end of the spectrum. On par with the Honda Civic in overall driving dynamics, the Mazda 3 is a top choice if you're looking for a compact car that's entertaining behind the wheel.

Crash Test Scores, see pg 530
Warranty information, see pg 542

## Specifications

| Engine/Drivetrain | HP | Torque | EPA Fuel Economy Rating |
|---|---|---|---|
| 4cyl 2.3L M | 160 | 150 | 25 city/32 hwy |
| 4cyl 2.0L M | 148 | 135 | 28 city/35 hwy |

## Body Styles

| Style | MSRP Range |
|---|---|
| Compact Sedan/Hatchback | $13,680–$17,105 |

# Mazda

# 2005 Mazda MAZDA6
### Midsize Sedan, Wagon

**MSRP Price Range**
## $18,995 - $26,795
Destination Charge: $545 (all styles)

## Ratings

| | | |
|---|---|---|
| Consumer Rating | 9.2 | |
| Editors Rating | 8.1 | |

**What Edmunds.com says:** Tired of the dull, sensible, vanilla-flavored family car? If you're willing to give up some passenger room, the Mazda 6 promises to add a dash of zing to your daily commute whether you're looking for a sedan, hatchback or wagon.

**Pros:** More fun to drive than most family cars, slick-shifting manual transmission, smooth power delivery, nicely appointed interior, multiple body styles.

**Cons:** Tight rear-seat accommodations, engines lack the vigor of competitors, interior materials aren't always top quality.

**What's New:** New hatchback and wagon body styles were added to the lineup at the end of 2004 and carry over unchanged for 2005. The optional automatic transmission on all V6 models has been upgraded from a five-speed to a six-speed unit.

Crash Test Scores, see pg 530
Warranty information, see pg 542

## Specifications

| Engine/Drivetrain | HP | Torque | EPA Fuel Economy Rating |
|---|---|---|---|
| 6cyl 3.0L A/M | 220 | 192 | 20 city/27 hwy |
| 4cyl 2.3L A/M | 160 | 155 | 23 city/28 hwy |

## Body Styles

| Style | MSRP Range |
|---|---|
| Midsize Sedan | $18,995–$26,125 |
| Midsize Wagon | $22,895–$26,795 |

**Body Styles, Trim Levels and Options:** The 6 is available as a sedan, wagon or four-door hatchback. Sedans and hatchbacks come in either base "i" and high-line "s" trim; the wagon comes in s trim only. Standard equipment on the i includes a tilt/telescoping steering wheel, air conditioning, a CD stereo, steering wheel-mounted audio controls, cruise control and power windows, mirrors and locks. The s model adds a V6 engine, 17-inch alloy wheels, lumbar adjustment for the driver and automatic climate control. Both models are eligible for the Luxury Package, which adds leather upholstery, a power driver seat, red electroluminescent gauges and heated seats and mirrors; and the Sport Package, which provides foglights, an underbody kit, faux titanium interior trim and a rear spoiler. Separate options include a moonroof and a Bose stereo with an in-dash CD changer.

**Powertrains and Performance:** Standard on the base model is a 2.3-liter, four-cylinder engine that makes 160 horsepower. A five-speed manual transmission is also standard and a four-speed automatic is optional. The s model upgrades to a 220-hp, 3.0-liter V6. Unlike most V6-powered midsize sedans, this one can be equipped with a five-speed manual, or you can go for the optional six-speed automatic.

**Safety:** All models come with four-wheel disc brakes and whiplash-reducing front seats. ABS with Electronic Brakeforce Distribution and traction control are standard on the s model and optional on the i. Optional on both models are side airbags for front occupants and full-length side curtain airbags. In government crash tests, the 6 received a perfect five stars for frontal impact protection. In side-impact tests, the 6 earned just three stars for front-occupant protection and four stars for rear passengers, but the vehicle tested did not have side airbags. In IIHS frontal offset crash testing, the Mazda earned the top rating of "Good." In IIHS side-impact testing, it rated "Poor," but again the vehicle tested did not have side airbags.

**Interior Design and Special Features:** Inside, the 6 has a clean and contemporary design with solid build quality and easy-to-operate controls. Most materials are attractive, but they're a step or two below the premium-quality stuff in the Accord and Passat. Rear-seat occupants benefit from a center armrest, but shoulder room is a bit tight for this class. A 60/40-split rear seat folds to expand the sedan's 17.6-cubic-foot trunk capacity, while the hatchback boasts a 22-cubic-foot cargo hold that expands to 59 cubes. Roomiest of all is the wagon, which offers 33.7 cubic feet behind the rear seat and 61 with the seat folded.

**Driving Impressions:** Like most other Mazdas, the 6 is a thrill behind the wheel. Neither engine is as powerful as competing motors, but their smooth, quiet power delivery offsets this, particularly on V6 models. A communicative steering rack goes a long way toward making the 6 fun to drive on the highway or from corner to corner on back roads. The suspension achieves a superb balance between ride quality and handling, and as a result, the 6 is comfortable enough for weekday commutes and highly entertaining on weekend road trips.

For the latest full vehicle reports, visit www.edmunds.com/bginfopak

**MSRP Price Range**

## $15,315 - $26,145
Destination Charge: $620 (all styles)

### Ratings

| | | |
|---|---|---|
| Consumer Rating | N/A | |
| Editors Rating | 5.8 | |

**What Edmunds.com says:** Unless the Mazda name holds a special place in your heart, there's no reason to consider this ancient compact pickup when there are several equally capable and infinitely more modern competitors available for the same price.

**Pros:** Torquey 4.0-liter V6 engine, versatile size, tough underpinnings.

**Cons:** Dated platform, no crew cab model, limited lineup doesn't match many consumers' needs, uncomfortable seats.

**What's New:** Dual Sport and SE models now come standard with conveniences like cruise control, a leather-wrapped tilt steering wheel, a bed liner and power mirrors.

**Body Styles, Trim Levels and Options:** Available as either a regular cab or an extended cab with four doors, the Mazda Truck is further broken down into base, SE and Dual Sport trim levels. Base models are available as either a 2WD regular cab or a 4WD two-door extended cab and come standard with a tachometer, sliding rear window, AM/FM stereo and 15-inch steel wheels (16-inch on 4WD models). The SE trim level is offered on extended cab models only in both two- and four-wheel-drive configurations and features alloy wheels, air conditioning and a CD player. Dual Sport models offer all three body styles but are 2WD only. A standard raised suspension gives all Dual Sport models the look of a 4WD without the added expense. Various options packages are also available like the Power Package that bundles together keyless entry and power windows, locks and mirrors, and the Convenience Package with tilt steering, cruise control and a bed liner.

**Powertrains and Performance:** Three engines are available. The B2300 is powered by a 2.3-liter, four-cylinder engine that develops 143 horsepower and 154 pound-feet of torque. The B3000 has a 3.0-liter V6 that makes 150 hp and 180 lb-ft of torque. The top-level B4000 features a 4.0-liter SOHC V6 with 207 hp and 238 lb-ft of torque. A five-speed manual is standard, while a five-speed automatic is optional on all trim levels, except for the B2300 extended cab. Four-cylinder models are fine for cargo-hauling or light towing duties with a tow rating of 2,240 pounds, but with its maximum rating of 5,900 pounds, the 4.0-liter V6 is the engine you want for heavy-duty chores.

**Safety:** Antilock brakes are standard on all models. In government crash tests, the Mazda Truck earned four stars out of five for driver and front-passenger protection in frontal and side-impact crashes. The IIHS gave this compact pickup a rating of "Acceptable" (the second highest of four) after conducting its frontal offset impact tests.

**Interior Design and Special Features:** Even after a freshening last year, the interior is still not up to class standards. The seats are still low, flat and unsupportive, so don't expect long-range comfort. Extended cab models have twin jump seats in the rear; the side-facing rear seats on this model are by no means comfortable for adults, but they can be used by extra passengers in a pinch. Four-door extended cab versions make access to the rear passenger area considerably easier.

**Driving Impressions:** Budget buyers will prefer the B2300 for fuel economy and low purchase cost, and the B3000 represents a sensible blend of power and efficiency. The stout B4000 V6 offers the most power and torque for off-roading and towing. All models are easy to drive, but the basic platform and underpinnings are outdated, resulting in a rough, harsh ride.

*Crash Test Scores, see pg 530*
*Warranty information, see pg 542*

### Specifications

| Engine/Drivetrain | HP | Torque | EPA Fuel Economy Rating |
|---|---|---|---|
| 6cyl 4.0L A/M | 207 | 238 | 15 city/19 hwy |
| 6cyl 3.0L M | 154 | 180 | 18 city/23 hwy |
| 4cyl 2.3L M | 143 | 154 | 24 city/29 hwy |

### Body Styles

| Style | MSRP Range |
|---|---|
| Extended Cab Pickup Truck | $18,860–$26,145 |
| Regular Cab Pickup Truck | $15,315–$19,500 |

# Mazda
# 2005 Mazda MPV
### Compact Minivan

**MSRP Price Range**
## $22,940 - $28,505
Destination Charge: $545 (all styles)

## Ratings

| | | |
|---|---|---|
| Consumer Rating | 9.1 | |
| Editors Rating | 7.6 | |

**What Edmunds.com says:** A stylish and capable van if that's all you need, but compared to newer class leaders, the MPV lacks the size, features and refinement to compete for the top spot.

**Pros:** Manageable size, lots of interior storage, decidedly unminivan looks, roll-down windows in the sliding doors.

**Cons:** Lacks the features, passenger/cargo space and power found in its competitors, noisy engine, clunky transmission.

**What's New:** The MPV received a handful of changes for 2004 and moves into 2005 with only a few option package alterations.

**Body Styles, Trim Levels and Options:** The MPV is a four-door, seven-passenger minivan with two available trims. The base LX includes 16-inch alloy wheels, dual manual-sliding doors with roll-down windows, steering wheel-mounted stereo controls, a CD player and front and rear air conditioning. A power driver seat, side airbags for front occupants and traction control are options. Step up to the ES and get all of the above standard, along with 17-inch wheels and leather upholstery. Options on both models include power-sliding doors, an in-dash CD changer, a DVD-based rear entertainment system and a sunroof.

**Powertrains and Performance:** The standard drivetrain is a 200-horsepower, 3.0-liter V6 paired with a five-speed automatic transmission. Towing capacity is 2,000 pounds, or 3,000 pounds with the optional four-seasons driving package. EPA estimates are 18 mpg city and 24 mpg on the highway.

**Safety:** Four-wheel antilock disc brakes are standard on all models, while traction control and side airbags are standard on the ES and optional on the LX. In government crash tests, the MPV earned a perfect five-star rating in all front- and side-impact categories. In frontal offset crash testing conducted by the IIHS, the MPV received an "Acceptable" rating (the second highest out of four).

**Interior Design and Special Features:** The interior is equipped with three rows of seating for seven passengers. The second and third rows can be reconfigured for multiple seating arrangements. The second row features two comfortable captain's chairs that have their own flip-up armrests. As in the Honda Odyssey, the right-side second-row captain's chair can be released by a handle, allowing it to slide along tracks to meet up flush with the other seat, creating a bench. Both second-row seats are removable. For maximum convenience, the third-row seat easily folds flat into the floor, creating a spacious cargo hold without requiring owners to remove the seats entirely.

*Crash Test Scores, see pg 530*
*Warranty information, see pg 542*

**Driving Impressions:** The MPV's handling is almost carlike, thanks to its nicely weighted steering and smooth ride. Although the Mazda's relatively compact size makes it more maneuverable on tight city streets, vans like the Honda Odyssey and Dodge Grand Caravan ultimately offer sportier handling. The 3.0-liter V6 provides adequate acceleration in most situations but is quite noisy under heavy acceleration. Those who plan to carry heavy passenger loads or tow a trailer should consider competing vans, all of which can be had with larger engines. The MPV's five-speed automatic transmission is often indecisive, hampering acceleration efforts with early upshifts and late downshifts.

## Specifications

| Engine/Drivetrain | HP | Torque | EPA Fuel Economy Rating |
|---|---|---|---|
| 6cyl 3.0L A | 200 | 200 | 18 city/25 hwy |

## Body Styles

| Style | MSRP Range |
|---|---|
| Compact Minivan | $22,940–$28,505 |

For the latest full vehicle reports, visit www.edmunds.com/bginfopak

## Ratings

| | | |
|---|---|---|
| Consumer Rating | 9.5 | ▬▬▬▬▬▬▬ |
| Editors Rating | 7.8 | ▬▬▬▬▬ |

**What Edmunds.com says:** Still the standard when it comes to delivering top-down thrills without breaking the bank.

**Pros:** Huge fun factor, precise steering and handling, low base price, economical to operate.

**Cons:** Small trunk, drones on the freeway, tight cabin.

**What's New:** New exterior colors—Nordic Green and Razor Blue—are the only changes on the Miata for 2005.

**Body Styles, Trim Levels and Options:** The Miata comes one way: two doors, two seats, convertible top. Base and LS models are available. Standard equipment includes 16-inch alloy wheels, four-wheel disc brakes, air conditioning, a CD player and power windows and mirrors. The LS adds a limited-slip differential, leather upholstery, cruise control, power locks, keyless entry and an upgraded stereo with Bose speakers. Note that the base model is eligible for a convenience package that provides power door locks, cruise, keyless entry and tweeter speakers. A suspension package for both models includes Bilstein shocks and firmer suspension settings; the base model also picks up the limited-slip differential. Two Appearance Packages are offered, but we don't think either one really adds to the appeal of the car. Finally, for those who live in harsh climates, Mazda offers a detachable hardtop.

**Powertrains and Performance:** The Miata's 1.8-liter, four-cylinder engine makes 142 horsepower at 7,000 rpm and 125 pound-feet of torque at 5,000 rpm. A five-speed manual transmission drives the rear wheels, but a six-speed is available on the LS. In our experience, the six-speed adds little to the driving experience; we're happy with the five-speed, though you can't get the suspension package with it. Should you really dislike shifting the car yourself, any Miata can be equipped with a four-speed automatic transmission.

**Safety:** Antilock brakes aren't available on base models, but can be ordered as an option on the LS model—it's required when the automatic transmission is ordered. Unlike most premium German roadsters, the Miata is not available with side airbags, head airbags or stability control. In government frontal impact crash tests, the Miata earned four stars out of five for driver protection and a perfect five stars for protection of the front passenger. Side-impact tests resulted in a three-star rating.

**Interior Design and Special Features:** The Miata's cockpit is snug, seemingly more so when the top is raised. Still, it is comfortable enough for two to take day trips or go on a weekend getaway. If you pack sparingly, the tight trunk has enough room for your belongings. The Miata is basic inside, but conveniences such as cruise control, an in-dash CD changer and leather upholstery are available. The top can be raised or lowered from the driver seat in a matter of seconds, making the Miata an ideal companion for spontaneous adventures.

**Driving Impressions:** Cross-country trips on American interstates are not the Miata's forte, as the engine tends to drone at highway cruising speeds. However, with a lowered top and an open road, the Miata has few equals. The engine is perfectly matched to the suspension and steering, making the car a joy to pilot on curvy two-lane roads. When equipped with the Suspension Package, the Miata's performance envelope is even more impressive.

*Crash Test Scores, see pg 530*
*Warranty information, see pg 542*

## Specifications

| Engine/Drivetrain | HP | Torque | EPA Fuel Economy Rating |
|---|---|---|---|
| 4cyl 1.8L M | 142 | 125 | 23 city/29 hwy |

## Body Styles

| Style | MSRP Range |
|---|---|
| Compact Convertible | $22,098–$24,903 |

# 2005 Mazda MAZDASPEED MX-5 Miata  Compact Convertible

**MSRP Price Range**
## $25,780 - $26,580
Destination Charge: $545 (all styles)

## Ratings

| | | |
|---|---|---|
| Consumer Rating | N/A | |
| Editors Rating | 8.0 | |

**What Edmunds.com says:** The standard Miata is a sporty yet affordable roadster. Aided by a turbocharger and an array of chassis upgrades, the Mazdaspeed version is a full-blown sports car that still fits the budget of an enthusiast with a day job.

**Pros:** Fun-to-drive character, excellent steering response and handling, thrilling acceleration, excellent build and materials quality.

**Cons:** Tight cockpit is a squeeze for taller drivers, small trunk, engine drones on the highway.

**What's New:** The Mazdaspeed Miata's formula remains the same for 2005, with the exception of a new wheel design and two new color options.

**Body Styles, Trim Levels and Options:** The Mazdaspeed Miata comes one way: two doors, two seats, convertible top. Standard equipment includes unique 17-inch Racing Hart alloy wheels, air conditioning, a Bose stereo with CD player, unique black and red upholstery, cruise control, full power accessories and keyless entry. The only major option is leather seating. Special styling and trim enhancements abound, most of which serve as a reminder you're in a Mazdaspeed Miata—that is, assuming the surge of turbocharged power goes unnoticed.

**Powertrains and Performance:** The Mazdaspeed Miata's 1.8-liter, turbocharged and intercooled four-cylinder engine makes 178 horsepower and 166 pound-feet of torque. A beefed-up six-speed manual transmission drives the rear wheels through a Bosch torque-sensing limited-slip differential. Naturally, an automatic transmission is not available.

**Safety:** Unlike most premium German roadsters, the Mazdaspeed Miata is not available with side airbags or stability control. Four-wheel antilock disc brakes are standard, though. In government frontal impact crash tests, the Miata earned four stars out of five for driver protection and a perfect five stars for protection of the front passenger. Side-impact tests resulted in a three-star rating.

**Interior Design and Special Features:** The Miata's cockpit is snug with the top down and borders on cramped when the top is raised. Still, it is comfortable enough for two moderately sized adults to take day trips or go on weekend getaways. If you pack sparingly, the small trunk will have enough room for your belongings. The simple silver-faced gauges and round vents give the interior a slight retro appeal. Plenty of silver-finish trim pieces and red accents give the Mazdaspeed Miata interior a customized appearance. Materials quality is excellent and quality construction is evident throughout the cockpit. The climate and audio controls are straightforward in their layout, but some of the small buttons can be tricky to adjust while driving. The manual top can be raised or lowered from the driver seat in a matter of seconds, making the Miata an ideal companion for spontaneous adventures.

*Crash Test Scores, see pg 530*
*Warranty information, see pg 542*

## Specifications

| Engine/Drivetrain | HP | Torque | EPA Fuel Economy Rating |
|---|---|---|---|
| 4cyl 1.8L M | 178 | 166 | 20 city/26 hwy |

## Body Styles

| Style | MSRP Range |
|---|---|
| Compact Convertible | $25,780–$26,580 |

**Driving Impressions:** Cross-country trips on American interstates are not the Miata's forte, as the engine tends to drone at highway cruising speeds. However, with a lowered top and an open road, the Miata has few equals. The engine is perfectly matched to the suspension and steering, making the car a joy to pilot on curvy two-lane roads. Thanks to the Mazdaspeed treatment under the hood, this Miata is equally thrilling when the road becomes straight as well. The three-spoke steering wheel feels great in your hands as does the short-throw shifter of the six-speed manual transmission. Amidst the super-sensitive road feel and quick gear changes that come with driving this car, you rapidly get accustomed to that wonderful glued-to-the-road feeling that defines the Miata. Weekday commuters should note that the Mazdaspeed version's stiffer suspension makes for a harsher ride over bumps and ruts, however.

# 2005 Mazda RX-8

**MSRP Price Range**

## $25,375 - $26,875

Destination Charge: $545 (all styles)

| Ratings | | |
|---|---|---|
| Consumer Rating | 9.3 | |
| Editors Rating | 8.2 | |

**What Edmunds.com says:** Regardless of how many doors the RX-8 has, it is ultimately a sport coupe that offers sensational handling without the stiffness typically associated with cars of this type.

**Pros:** Low base price, agile handling yet still comfortable enough for daily use, smooth rotary engine fun to wind out on the open road, room for four in a pinch.

**Cons:** Option packages add considerable expense, iffy interior ergonomics, poor gas mileage.

**What's New:** Mazda's four-door sports car was all new in 2004, and is back for 2005 with no changes except for the addition of a satellite radio-compatible head unit.

**Body Styles, Trim Levels and Options:** The RX-8 is available in two variants—a 197-horsepower base model with an automatic and a 238-hp performance model with a six-speed manual. The automatic version comes standard with basic amenities like air conditioning, 16-inch wheels and power windows, locks and mirrors. The six-speed manual model adds a limited-slip differential, a sport-tuned suspension and 18-inch wheels and tires. There are three available option packages for buyers looking to upgrade their RX-8. On six-speed models, the Sport package adds xenon headlights, stability and traction control and foglights, while automatic-equipped versions also get a limited-slip differential, larger brakes, a retuned suspension and 18-inch wheels and tires as part of the deal. The Touring package builds on the Sport package by adding a sunroof, Bose audio, Homelink and auto-dimming mirrors. The top-of-the-line Grand Touring package adds all of the above equipment along with a six-way power-adjustable and heated driver seat, leather upholstery and heated side mirrors. Additional available options include a navigation system and an in-dash six-disc CD changer.

**Powertrains and Performance:** Both versions of the RX-8 are motivated by a 1.3-liter rotary engine that sends power to the rear wheels. When connected to the four-speed automatic transmission, the engine is tuned to produce 197 hp, while manual transmission versions get a 238-hp version of this power plant. Coupled with the vehicle's light weight, the RX-8 delivers exhilarating performance along with ultrasmooth power delivery.

**Safety:** All RX-8s come with standard front and side airbags for the driver and front passenger, as well as side curtain airbags. Four-wheel antilock disc brakes are also standard, while stability control is optional. The NHTSA gave the RX-8 a four-star rating (out of a possible five) for driver protection in frontal impacts and five stars for the front passenger. The Mazda received four stars across the board for side-impact protection.

**Interior Design and Special Features:** Although it looks like a coupe, the RX-8 actually has four doors. The rear openings are hinged at the back and there is no center pillar between the two sets of doors. The wide opening that results makes for easy access to the rear seats that are surprisingly roomy considering the overall size of the car. The interior carries a circular design theme with three round gauges. A circular central dash pod houses the stereo, and three round knobs work the climate control functions.

**Driving Impressions:** Although the RX-8 has the look of a race-tuned sports car, its demeanor on the road is considerably more docile. There's plenty of grip in the corners and solid feedback through the steering wheel, but it won't beat you up on daily commutes. The rotary engine requires high engine speeds to make its peak power, but the delivery is ultrasmooth and noise levels are kept well in check. Overall, the RX-8 is one of the best examples of a car that's fun to drive while still remaining livable on a day-to-day basis.

*Crash Test Scores, see pg 530*
*Warranty information, see pg 542*

## Specifications

| Engine/Drivetrain | HP | Torque | EPA Fuel Economy Rating |
|---|---|---|---|
| cyl 1.3L M | 238 | 159 | 18 city/24 hwy |
| cyl 1.3L A | 197 | 164 | 18 city/24 hwy |

## Body Styles

| Style | MSRP Range |
|---|---|
| Compact Coupe | $25,375–$26,875 |

# 2005 Mazda Tribute
**Compact SUV**

**MSRP Price Range**
## $19,630 - $24,390
Destination Charge: $590 (all styles)

### Ratings

| | | |
|---|---|---|
| Consumer Rating | 9.0 | |
| Editors Rating | 7.8 | |

**What Edmunds.com says:** Roomy on the inside, stylish on the outside and fun to drive wherever it goes, the Tribute is one of our favorite small SUVs.

**Pros:** Roomy and comfortable interior, peppy V6 engine, drives more like a car than a truck, long list of standard features.

**Cons:** Mediocre fuel economy and driving range on V6 models.

**What's New:** Extensive changes for the Tribute this year include a new base engine, restyled exterior and a new electronic four-wheel-drive system. A floor-mounted shifter replaces the awkward column shifter, and ABS is now standard on all models.

**Body Styles, Trim Levels and Options:** The four-door Tribute is available in two trim levels—base i and high-line s. The i comes with the new 2.3-liter, four-cylinder engine and a decent amount of standard equipment, including 16-inch alloy wheels, a roof rack, air conditioning, a CD player and power windows, mirrors and locks. Besides a V6 engine, the s adds privacy glass, a height-adjustable driver seat and cruise control. Key options include leather upholstery, a power driver seat, a power moonroof and a class II towing package with 3,500-pound capacity. A rear-seat DVD entertainment system can be ordered on any Tribute as long as a sunroof isn't involved.

**Powertrains and Performance:** Two engines are available in the Tribute. The i comes equipped with a 153-hp, 2.3-liter, inline four-cylinder engine matched to a five-speed manual or four-speed automatic transmission. The s gets a 200-hp, 3.0-liter V6 engine. A four-speed automatic is standard with the V6. All models are available with either front-wheel drive (2WD) or an electronic four-wheel-drive system (4WD). Note that 4WD models require an automatic tranny, even with the base four-cylinder engine.

**Safety:** Four-wheel antilock brakes with Electronic Brakeforce Distribution and BrakeAssist are standard on all models. Side-curtain airbags are optional on the s. The Tribute scored very well in governmental crash testing, earning a perfect five stars for the driver and four stars for the front passenger in the frontal impact category, and five stars across the board for side impacts. Frontal offset crash testing conducted by the IIHS told a different story, however, as the Tribute earned a "Marginal" rating (the second lowest of four). The Tribute did earn a "Good" in IIHS side-impact testing when equipped with side airbags.

**Interior Design and Special Features:** Tribute cabins are roomy and functional with plenty of room for four passengers and a simple control layout. All radios come standard with Sirius Satellite Radio capability this year. In general, materials quality is not as impressive as that of other Mazdas, but considering the economical nature of this small SUV, most buyers won't find it lacking. Cargo capacity is generous for a small SUV with 30 cubic feet behind the rear seats and a total of 66 cubic feet when the seats are folded.

*Crash Test Scores, see pg 530*
*Warranty information, see pg 542*

### Specifications

| Engine/Drivetrain | HP | Torque | EPA Fuel Economy Rating |
|---|---|---|---|
| 6cyl 3.0L A | 200 | 193 | 20 city/25 hwy |
| 4cyl 2.3L A/M | 153 | 152 | 22 city/25 hwy |

### Body Styles

| Style | MSRP Range |
|---|---|
| Compact SUV | $19,630–$24,390 |

**Driving Impressions:** Mazda markets the Tribute as the Miata of SUVs, and the claim isn't far off the mark. With a wide track and powerful V6, the Tribute handles better than most SUVs on the road, driving more like a sporty car than a truck. Ride quality is smooth, making this SUV a suitable choice for commuting or hauling around the family. Equipped with 4WD, the Tribute can easily take on snow and ice during the winter. One of the few drawbacks to this Mazda is the V6 engine's mediocre gas mileage. This year's new 153-hp four-cylinder is a good option for buyers on tighter budgets—expect adequate acceleration and better mileage than what you'd get with the V6.

**MSRP Price Range**
## $25,850 - $39,150
Destination Charge: $720 (all styles)

### Ratings

| | | |
|---|---|---|
| Consumer Rating | 9.4 | |
| Editors Rating | 7.0 | |

**What Edmunds.com says:** A variety of body styles and trim levels assure that you're bound to find something to your liking, but none can match the Audi A4 for interior style or the BMW 3 Series for athleticism.

**Pros:** State-of-the-art safety and luxury features, three body styles to choose from, pleasing power from top V6 engine.

**Cons:** More expensive than competitors, ordinary cabin furnishings, small backseat.

**What's New:** The new model year brings freshened exterior styling to the C-Class. A new dash, redesigned seats and tweaked trim pieces help to polish the interior up a bit, as well. A new audio system with six speakers and a CD player is standard across the board. Further updates include an improved short-throw six-speed manual transmission and revised suspension tuning. A DVD-based navigation system is newly available, while the C320 wagon has been discontinued. The complimentary scheduled maintenance program has been dropped for 2005.

**Body Styles, Trim Levels and Options:** A hatchback duo (the C230 and C320 Sport Coupes), a handful of sedans (C230 and C320 Sport Sedans, and the C240 and C320 Luxury Sedans) and a single wagon (the C240 Luxury Wagon) make up the C-Class. Sporty and affordable, the coupes and the C230 Sport Sedan come with 17-inch wheels, a sport-tuned suspension, cloth sport seats, dual-zone climate control and a CD stereo. C240 versions are more mild-mannered, offering 16-inch wheels, softer suspension tuning, leather/cloth seating and genuine wood trim, along with V6 power. Step up to the C320 to enjoy a 10-speaker Bose stereo and 10-way power seats with memory. To this, the C320 Sport Sedan adds 17-inch wheels, a firmer suspension and sport seats. The options lists are extensive, allowing buyers to add full leather upholstery, bi-xenon headlights, a DVD-based navigation system and, on coupes only, a panoramic sunroof.

**Powertrains and Performance:** Three engines see duty in the C-Class lineup. The C230 has a 189-horsepower, 1.8-liter supercharged inline four. The C240 has not a 2.4, but a 2.6-liter V6 with 168 hp. And the C320 employs a 3.2-liter V6 good for 215 hp. Two transmission choices—a six-speed manual or five-speed automatic—are available on all Sport models; Luxury models come with the automatic only. All coupes are rear-wheel drive, but sedans and wagons offer a choice between rear-drive and 4Matic all-wheel drive.

**Safety:** In addition to expected safety features, such as four-wheel antilock disc brakes and three-point seatbelts with tension limiters for all occupants, every C-Class boasts stability control and eight airbags that include head-protecting side curtain airbags. In government crash tests, the C-Class scored four out of five stars for driver and front-passenger protection in frontal impacts and five stars (for the front and rear) for side impacts. The IIHS gave the C-Class a "Good" rating (its highest) for its performance in the 40-mph frontal offset crash test, and named it a "Best Pick" overall.

**Interior Design and Special Features:** In the past, C-Class interiors were nothing special, but this year's upgrades include new gauges, controls and seats—finally giving the entry-level Benz the slick look it should have always had. As the cars are compact in size, there isn't a lot of legroom in the backseat, and adult occupants are apt to complain. With a generous maximum cargo capacity of 63.6 cubic feet, the wagons provide utility in a smart-looking package. And if you flip down the seats in the sport coupes, the hatchback will swallow 38.1 cubes worth of luggage.

**Driving Impressions:** As you would expect, the C-Class is a comfortable car that excels at pampering its occupants. It's also more sporting than previous small Benzes, and the sport sedans and sport coupes, in particular, are fun to drive, though don't expect the razor-sharp manners of a BMW 3 Series. Both the 1.8-liter supercharged four-cylinder and the 3.2-liter V6 deliver solid, refined performance, but the midgrade 2.6-liter V6 is a bit lethargic.

*Crash Test Scores, see pg 530*
*Warranty information, see pg 542*

### Specifications

| Engine/Drivetrain | HP | Torque | EPA Fuel Economy Rating |
|---|---|---|---|
| 6cyl 3.2L A/M | 215 | 221 | 19 city/26 hwy |
| 6cyl 2.6L A | 168 | 177 | 19 city/25 hwy |
| 4cyl 1.8L M | 189 | 192 | 24 city/32 hwy |

### Body Styles

| Style | MSRP Range |
|---|---|
| Compact Coupe | $25,850–$28,250 |
| Compact Sedan | $29,250–$39,150 |
| Compact Wagon | $34,150–$35,350 |

## Mercedes-Benz

# 2005 Mercedes-Benz C55 AMG Compact Sedan

**MSRP Price Range**
## $53,900
Destination Charge: $720 (all styles)

### Ratings

| | | |
|---|---|---|
| Consumer Rating | 9.2 | |
| Editors Rating | 8.4 | |

**What Edmunds.com says:** Prodigious power, predictable handling and a sharp-looking interior make this one of the most satisfying sport sedans on the market.

**Pros:** Tire-shredding torque available at any speed, crisp and predictable handling, still comfortable despite its sporting intentions.

**Cons:** No manual transmission available, tight backseat, not as involving to drive as Audi's S4.

**What's New:** The new model year brings freshened exterior styling and a new engine that results in a designation change from C32 to C55. A new dash, redesigned seats and tweaked trim pieces help to polish the interior up a bit, as well. A DVD-based navigation system is newly available, and a Harman Kardon sound system replaces last year's Bose unit. The complimentary scheduled maintenance program has been dropped for 2005.

*Crash Test Scores, see pg 530*
*Warranty information, see pg 542*

**Body Styles, Trim Levels and Options:** The four-door C55 AMG comes in just one well-equipped trim level. Standard features include a sport-tuned suspension, 17-inch wheels and tires, 10-way power sport seats, leather upholstery, a leather-wrapped steering wheel, metallic cabin trim, a revised instrument panel (compared to the regular C-Class), dual-zone automatic climate control, a 10-speaker Harman Kardon stereo with a CD player and a sunroof. Options include a navigation system, satellite radio and an integrated Motorola cell phone.

**Powertrains and Performance:** The C55 AMG packs a hand-built V8 that puts 362 horses and 376 pound-feet of torque at the driver's disposal. An AMG-tweaked five-speed automatic transmission is the sole gearbox choice. Dubbed SpeedShift, this automatic is so quick and smart that most drivers won't miss having a manual tranny, especially in rush-hour traffic. With the 0-to-60-mph dash coming in at around 4.5 seconds and a top speed that's electronically limited to 155 mph, those who need speed should be more than happy with the C55. Braking ability is impressive as well, with stops from 60 mph coming in at less than 120 feet, according to Mercedes.

**Safety:** In addition to expected safety features, such as four-wheel antilock disc brakes and three-point seatbelts with tension limiters for all occupants, the C55 boasts stability control and eight airbags. In government crash tests, the C-Class earned four stars (out of five) for frontal impacts and a full five stars in side impacts. The IIHS gave the C-Class a "Good" rating (the highest possible) and named it a "Best Pick" overall.

**Interior Design and Special Features:** Cabin materials are generally first-rate, with pleasingly textured, soft-touch surfaces all around. A pair of 10-way adjustable sport seats hold the pilot and co-pilot snugly, while a choice of single-tone or two-tone upholstery, metallic accents and unique instrument faces give the C55 its own look inside.

**Driving Impressions:** Simply put, the C55 is a blast to drive. The instantaneous power from the V8 makes for rapid acceleration at nearly any speed, and the tightly wound suspension is well up to the task of getting the power to the ground. As capable as it is in corners, it's not a car that will beat you up on your morning commute. Overall, the C55 is an outstanding combination of dazzling performance and everyday drivability.

### Specifications

| Engine/Drivetrain | HP | Torque | EPA Fuel Economy Rating |
|---|---|---|---|
| 8cyl 5.4L A | 362 | 376 | 16 city/22 hwy |

### Body Styles

| Style | MSRP Range |
|---|---|
| Compact Sedan | $53,900 |

For the latest full vehicle reports, visit www.edmunds.com/bginfopak

# 2005 Mercedes-Benz CL-Class

**MSRP Price Range**
## $93,900 - $127,900
Destination Charge: $720 (all styles)

#1 Editors' Rating

### Ratings

| | | |
|---|---|---|
| Consumer Rating | 8.9 | |
| Editors Rating | 8.2 | |

**What Edmunds.com says:** One of the finest coupes on the road today, the CL is an artful blend of performance, technology and classic luxury that rarely fails to impress.

**Pros:** Ultrarefined in every respect, dizzying array of high-tech features, classic styling, impressive performance.

**Cons:** Complex navigation and audio systems, cramped rear seat.

**What's New:** The complimentary scheduled maintenance program has been dropped for 2005.

**Body Styles, Trim Levels and Options:** The CL is a two-door coupe available in two trim levels: CL500 and CL600. Both feature nearly all the luxury amenities you would expect in a flagship coupe including high-intensity discharge headlamps, a DVD-based navigation system, dual-zone automatic climate control, an eight-speaker Bose sound system, 14-way power-adjustable seats and generous amounts of leather and wood trim. Options include ventilated seats that feature built-in fans to keep one's backside cool on sultry days and a power lumbar support that also inflates and deflates twice a minute, providing a slow massage to keep fatigue at bay on a long trip. Also available is a keyless entry and start system (called Keyless Go), adaptive cruise control, parking sensors and special designo packages for a more customized interior look.

**Powertrains and Performance:** The CL500 is powered by a 5.0-liter, 302-horsepower (and 339 pound-feet of torque) V8 that delivers power through an all-new seven-speed automatic transmission—an industry first. Not to be outdone, the CL600 has a 5.5-liter V12 fed by twin turbochargers that produces an astounding 493 hp and 590 lb-ft or torque. Mercedes claims that these staggering numbers allow the CL600 to accelerate to 60 mph in just 4.5 seconds.

**Safety:** Standard safety equipment includes four-wheel antilock disc brakes; electronic traction and stability control; front, side and side curtain airbags; and emergency braking assist. Seatbelt pre-tensioners and belt-force limiters are used at all four passenger positions.

**Interior Design and Special Features:** Virtually every luxury and convenience item, including a navigation system and power door-closing assist, is standard on every CL. Specific wood trim is fitted as well, with dark interiors having burled walnut, while lighter cabins are graced with chestnut timber. Most of the switchgear is the same as that in the S-Class, as is the illuminated gauge cluster, shift lever and COMAND control system. However, the quality of materials is even better in the CL, with a leather-trimmed dash, less plastic and even more beautiful wood highlights. Particularly impressive are the CL's unique stainless steel doorsills and outer-edge door trim.

**Driving Impressions:** Step on the throttle, and the Mercedes gathers itself up on a wave of torque, seemingly accelerating just as fast from 30 to 90 as it does from zero to 60. No matter which model you drive, the power delivery is the same, seamless and unflustered, the only variable being the rapidity of acceleration. In spite of a weight of over two tons, the CL handles the curves like a much smaller, lighter car, a sensation brought about chiefly by the Active Body Control (ABC) system that quells body roll as well as squat and dive while the car is being driven aggressively. In normal driving, the suspension soaks up the bumps as well as any luxury car, but when you're ready to make time on a twisty road, the CL tightens up, rising to the challenge.

*Crash Test Scores, see pg 530*
*Warranty information, see pg 542*

### Specifications

| Engine/Drivetrain | HP | Torque | EPA Fuel Economy Rating |
|---|---|---|---|
| 8cyl 5.0L A | 302 | 339 | 16 city/24 hwy |
| 12cyl 5.5L A | 493 | 590 | 13 city/19 hwy |

### Body Styles

| Style | MSRP Range |
|---|---|
| Large Coupe | $93,900–$127,900 |

# 2005 Mercedes-Benz CL55 AMG

**Large Coupe**

**MSRP Price Range**

## $118,900

Destination Charge: $720 (all styles)

### Ratings

| | | |
|---|---|---|
| Consumer Rating | N/A | |
| Editors Rating | 8.3 | |

**What Edmunds.com says:** One of the finest coupes on the road today, the CL55 is an artful blend of performance, technology and classic luxury that will embarrass many sports cars.

**Pros:** As refined a coupe as you're ever going to find, exotic car performance, dizzying array of high-tech features, comfortable enough to drive everyday.

**Cons:** Complex navigation and audio systems, cramped rear seat.

**What's New:** The complimentary scheduled maintenance program has been dropped for 2005.

**Body Styles, Trim Levels and Options:** The CL55 is a high-performance version of the standard CL and comes in only one trim level. Of course there are all the luxury amenities you would expect in a flagship coupe, including a DVD-based navigation system, 14-way power-adjustable seats, dual-zone automatic climate control, a Bose sound system (with a trunk-mounted CD changer) and generous amounts of leather and wood trim. Sporty accents, such as double-spoke 18-inch alloy wheels and aggressive rocker panel flares, hint at this car's personality. Options include active, ventilated seats that feature built-in fans to keep one's backside cool on sultry days and lateral bolsters that move to hold you in during spirited driving. Also available is a keyless start system, adaptive cruise control, parking sensors and special designo packages for a more customized interior look.

**Powertrains and Performance:** The CL55's supercharged 5.5-liter V8 puts out astounding levels of power—493 horses along with 516 pound-feet of torque. These big numbers mean that this refined yet muscle-bound coupe will hit 60 mph in just 4.5 seconds, a figure typically associated with exotic sports cars bearing Italian names. The only transmission available is a five-speed automatic, but it does allow for manual shifting if you ever feel the need to choose gears yourself.

**Safety:** Standard safety equipment includes four-wheel antilock disc brakes; electronic traction and stability control; front, seat-mounted side and side curtain airbags; and emergency braking assist. Seatbelt pre-tensioners and belt-force limiters are used at all four passenger positions.

**Interior Design and Special Features:** Virtually every luxury and convenience item, including a navigation system and power door-closing assist, is standard on the CL55. Specific wood trim is fitted as well, with dark interiors having burled walnut while lighter cabins are graced with chestnut timber. Most of the switchgear is the same as that in the S-Class, as is the illuminated gauge cluster, shift lever and COMAND control system. However, the quality of materials is even better in the CL, with a leather-trimmed dash, less plastic and even more beautiful wood highlights. Particularly impressive are the CL's unique stainless steel doorsills and outer-edge door trim.

*Crash Test Scores, see pg 530*
*Warranty information, see pg 542*

### Specifications

| Engine/Drivetrain | HP | Torque | EPA Fuel Economy Rating |
|---|---|---|---|
| 8cyl 5.4L A | 493 | 516 | 14 city/22 hwy |

### Body Styles

| Style | MSRP Range |
|---|---|
| Large Coupe | $118,900 |

**Driving Impressions:** Step on the throttle and the big Benz gathers itself up on a wave of torque, seemingly accelerating just as fast from 30 to 90 as it does from zero to 60. In spite of a weight of over two tons, the CL55 handles the curves like a much smaller, lighter car, a sensation brought about chiefly by the Active Body Control (ABC) system that quells body roll as well as squat and dive while the car is being driven aggressively. In normal driving, the suspension soaks up the bumps as well as any luxury car, but when it's time to make tracks on a twisty road, the CL tightens up, rising to the challenge.

**Large Coupe**

# 2005 Mercedes-Benz CL65 AMG

**MSRP Price Range**

## $177,500

Destination Charge: $720 (all styles)

### Ratings

| | | |
|---|---|---|
| Consumer Rating | 9.6 | ■■■■■■■■■ |
| Editors Rating | 8.4 | ■■■■■■■ |

**What Edmunds.com says:** One of the finest coupes on the road today, the CL is an artful blend of performance, technology and classic luxury that rarely fails to impress.

**Pros:** Refined beyond belief, dizzying array of high-tech features, classic styling, blinding acceleration, astounding performance that belies its weight.

**Cons:** Big price leap over already fantastic CL55, complex navigation and audio systems.

**What's New:** Yet another version of the CL coupe, the CL65 AMG is a new ultrahigh-performance beast with a 604-horsepower twin-turbo V12. It also boasts a reinforced five-speed automatic tranny, race-derived compound brake rotors with AMG eight-piston calipers, 19-inch wheels and dynamic multicontour seats. The complimentary scheduled maintenance program has been dropped for 2005.

**Body Styles, Trim Levels and Options:** The CL65 is a high-performance version of the standard CL-Class coupe and comes in only one trim level. Of course there are all the luxury amenities you would expect in a flagship coupe, including a DVD-based navigation system, 14-way power-adjustable seats, dual-zone automatic climate control, a Bose sound system (with a trunk-mounted CD changer) and generous amounts of leather and wood trim. Sporty accents, such as double-spoke 19-inch alloy wheels and aggressive rocker panel flares, hint at this car's personality. Options include a keyless entry and start system, adaptive cruise control and parking sensors.

**Powertrains and Performance:** The CL65's twin-turbo 6.0-liter V12 puts out astounding levels of power—604 horses along with 738 pound-feet of torque. These big numbers mean that this refined yet muscle-bound coupe will hit 60 mph in around 4 seconds, a figure typically associated with exotic sports cars bearing Italian names. The only transmission available is a five-speed automatic, but it does allow for manual shifting if you feel the need to choose gears yourself.

**Safety:** Standard safety equipment includes four-wheel antilock disc brakes; electronic traction and stability control; front, seat-mounted side and side curtain airbags; and emergency braking assist. Seatbelt pre-tensioners and belt-force limiters are used at all four passenger positions. The CL also has the BabySmart feature that deactivates the passenger-side front airbag if a BabySmart-compliant child safety seat is placed on the front-passenger seat. Of course, with the coupe's functional backseat, there's little reason for a small child to be sitting up front in the first place.

**Interior Design and Special Features:** Virtually every luxury and convenience item, including a navigation system and power door-closing assist, is standard on the CL65. Specific wood trim is fitted as well, with dark interiors having burled walnut while lighter cabins are graced with chestnut timber. Most of the switchgear is the same as that of the S-Class, as is the illuminated gauge cluster, shift lever and COMAND control system. However, the quality of materials is even better in the CL, with a leather-trimmed dash, less plastic and even more beautiful wood highlights. Particularly impressive are the CL's unique stainless steel doorsills and outer-edge door trim.

**Driving Impressions:** Step on the throttle and the big Benz gathers itself up on a wave of torque, seemingly accelerating just as fast from 30 to 90 as it does from zero to 60. In spite of a weight of over two tons, the CL65 handles the curves like a much smaller, lighter car, a sensation brought about chiefly by the Active Body Control (ABC) system that quells body roll as well as squat and dive while the car is being driven aggressively. In normal driving, the suspension soaks up the bumps as well as any luxury car, but when it's time to make tracks on a twisty road, the CL tightens up, rising to the challenge.

*Crash Test Scores, see pg 530*
*Warranty information, see pg 542*

### Specifications

| Engine/Drivetrain | HP | Torque | EPA Fuel Economy Rating |
|---|---|---|---|
| 12cyl 6.0L A | 604 | 738 | 12 city/19 hwy |

### Body Styles

| Style | MSRP Range |
|---|---|
| Large Coupe | $177,500 |

---

Mercedes-Benz

# 2005 Mercedes-Benz CLK-Class Compact Convertible, Coupe

**MSRP Price Range**
## $45,250 - $61,200
Destination Charge: $720 (all styles)

### Ratings

| | | |
|---|---|---|
| Consumer Rating | 8.9 | |
| Editors Rating | 7.8 | |

**What Edmunds.com says:** A stylish, if expensive, melding of comfort and performance suitable for all but the most serious driving enthusiasts.

**Pros:** Solid chassis, composed ride, comfortable front seats, fast power top operation in Cabriolet.

**Cons:** High price, some subpar plastic trim, a few hard-to-use controls.

**What's New:** This year the CLK's standard eight-speaker Bose audio system is scrapped in favor of a 10-speaker Harman Kardon unit, while the navigation system is now DVD-based. The 320 model gets upgraded standard wheels, and offers a lighting package with foglights that illuminate with the turn signals, or when the steering wheel is turned. The 500's five-speed automatic is replaced with a new seven-speed unit with steering wheel shift controls. Also, ventilated front seats are now optional. The complimentary scheduled maintenance program has been dropped for 2005.

*Crash Test Scores, see pg 530*
*Warranty information, see pg 542*

### Specifications

| Engine/Drivetrain | HP | Torque | EPA Fuel Economy Rating |
|---|---|---|---|
| 8cyl 5.0L A | 302 | 339 | 17 city/22 hwy |
| 6cyl 3.2L A | 215 | 229 | 20 city/26 hwy |

### Body Styles

| Style | MSRP Range |
|---|---|
| Compact Convertible | $52,700–$61,200 |
| Compact Coupe | $45,250–$53,750 |

**Body Styles, Trim Levels and Options:** The two-door CLK is available in two models—CLK320 and CLK500—both of which come in coupe and convertible body styles. The 320 has a 3.2-liter V6 underhood, while the 500 uses the 5.0-liter V8 from the senior Benzes. Highlights of the standard features list include 10-way power front seats, leather upholstery, dual-zone climate control, a 10-speaker Harman Kardon sound system and a power-adjustable tilt/telescoping steering wheel. Options include Distronic, an adaptive cruise control system that automatically maintains a set distance between the CLK and the vehicle in front of it; Keyless Go, which allows the car to be started without a key; a glovebox-mounted CD changer; and rear parking sensors.

**Powertrains and Performance:** A choice of V6 (3.2 liters, 215 horsepower) or V8 power (5.0 liters, 302 hp) is offered. According to Mercedes, the CLK500 will rocket to 60 mph in just 5.7 seconds, and the CLK320 will hit that same velocity in 7.4 seconds. A five-speed automatic gearbox with TouchShift automanual control is fitted to the CLK320, while a seven-speed unit, with steering wheel shift controls, is found in the CLK500.

**Safety:** To help drivers avoid an accident, Mercedes' stability control system, dubbed "ESP," is standard, as are four-wheel antilock disc brakes with BrakeAssist technology. Should a collision occur, no less than eight airbags are at the ready, including the side curtain variety that helps protect the heads of both front and rear occupants.

**Interior Design and Special Features:** Sometimes, grabbing the seatbelts in a two-door car is a bit of a reach for those in front. This problem is alleviated in the CLK, as automatic seatbelt "presenters" offer the belts after the door(s) is shut. Other conveniences include an Easy Entry system that powers the front seats forward and up, making it easier to get in back. Also, in the coupe, the rear seats now fold down completely providing a flat load floor that allows long items to be carried inside the car. The convertible features large side windows and a slim roof design for good top-up visibility, and the top can be quickly lowered or raised simply by pressing a button on the key fob.

**Driving Impressions:** While not as athletic as the two-seat SLK, the CLK feels more nimble than the larger CL-Class, which benefits from active suspension technology. Though the CLK320 offers more than adequate performance, driving enthusiasts are apt to prefer the cheaper BMW 3 Series coupe, which offers more power and sharper handling. The V8-powered CLK500 provides the better combination of performance and sophistication for the dollar, rewarding the buyer with vigorous acceleration and composed road manners. In terms of striking a balance between sporting performance and practicality, the CLK500 is likely Mercedes' best overall two-door package—top up or down.

# 2005 Mercedes-Benz CLK55 AMG
### Compact Convertible, Coupe

**MSRP Price Range**
## $69,900 - $80,850
Destination Charge: $720 (all styles)

## Ratings

| | | |
|---|---|---|
| Consumer Rating | 6.4 | |
| Editors Rating | 8.1 | |

**What Edmunds.com says:** As close as it gets to a four-seat SL55, the high-performance CLK55 offers a desirable blend of performance and comfort for the well-to-do enthusiast with a day job and a family.

**Pros:** Thrilling performance, rock-solid chassis, compliant ride, comfortable front seats, fast power-top operation in Cabriolet form.:

**Cons:** High price, some subpar plastic trim, a few hard-to-use controls.

**What's New:** The complimentary scheduled maintenance program has been dropped for 2005.

**Body Styles, Trim Levels and Options:** Available in coupe and convertible form, the CLK55 comes loaded with standard features such as leather upholstery, aluminum trim, 10-way power front seats, seat heaters, dual-zone automatic climate control, a premium stereo and a power-adjustable tilt/telescoping steering wheel. Exclusive double-spoke 17-inch wheels along with black mesh inserts in the front fascia and aggressive side sill sculpting give the CLK55 the proper AMG attitude. Options include rear parking sensors; Distronic, an adaptive cruise control system that automatically maintains a set distance between the CLK and the vehicle in front of it; and Keyless Go, which allows the car to be started without a key.

**Powertrains and Performance:** An AMG-tweaked 5.4-liter V8 sends 362 horsepower and 376 pound-feet of torque to the rear wheels. According to Mercedes, all this power sends the CLK55 to 60 mph from standstill in just 5.0 seconds. A SpeedShift five-speed automatic gearbox offers manual-style gear changes via buttons on the back of the steering wheel spokes. No manual gearbox is available on the CLK55.

**Safety:** To help drivers avoid an accident, Mercedes' stability control system (called ESP) is standard as are four-wheel antilock brakes with BrakeAssist technology. Should a collision occur, no less than eight airbags are at the ready, including the side curtain variety that helps protect the heads of the outboard occupants in a side-impact collision.

**Interior Design and Special Features:** The CLK55 cockpit is distinguished by AMG sport seats and steering wheel, two-tone upholstery and aluminum accents. To make fastening seatbelts easier, automatic seatbelt "presenters" offer the belts after the door(s) is shut. Other conveniences include an Easy Entry system that powers the front seats forward and up, making it easier to get in back. In the coupe, the rear seats fold down completely (like a wagon's) providing a lower, flatter load floor that allows long items to be carried inside the car. The convertible features larger side windows and a slimmer roof design for increased top-up visibility, and that top can be quickly lowered or raised simply by pressing a button on the key fob.

**Driving Impressions:** With scalding acceleration, composed handling and a firm but comfortable ride, the CLK55 offers virtually supercar performance, along with seating for four and daily-driver usability. It's too big for serious corner carving but, when it comes to swallowing huge chunks of highway, few coupes do it as effortlessly as this AMG-tuned coupe and cabriolet.

*Crash Test Scores, see pg 530*
*Warranty information, see pg 542*

## Specifications

| Engine/Drivetrain | HP | Torque | EPA Fuel Economy Rating |
|---|---|---|---|
| 8cyl 5.4L A | 362 | 376 | 15 city/22 hwy |

## Body Styles

| Style | MSRP Range |
|---|---|
| Compact Convertible | $80,850 |
| Compact Coupe | $69,900 |

# Mercedes-Benz

# 2005 Mercedes-Benz E-Class — Midsize Sedan, Wagon

**MSRP Price Range**
**$48,500 - $60,500**
Destination Charge: $720 (all styles)

#1 Editors' Rating

## Ratings

| | | |
|---|---|---|
| Consumer Rating | 8.6 | |
| Editors Rating | 8.4 | |

**What Edmunds.com says:** Although it costs more than its peers, a combination of excellent driving dynamics, numerous safety and luxury features and high style make the E-Class one of our favorites.

**Pros:** Sleek and dignified design inside and out, pleasing blend of ride and handling, sophisticated safety features, all-wheel drive available on both sedans and wagons.

**Cons:** More expensive than competitors, confusing control layout, electronically controlled brakes lack progressive feel.

**What's New:** Diesel Mercedes fans, rejoice! After years of waiting, a Mercedes-Benz diesel is once again available in the States, as the E320 CDI joins the lineup. For now, this model is only 45-state certified, meaning that you won't be able to buy it in California, Maine, Massachusetts, New York or Vermont. The complimentary scheduled maintenance program has been dropped for 2005.

*Crash Test Scores, see pg 530*
*Warranty information, see pg 542*

## Specifications

| Engine/Drivetrain | HP | Torque | EPA Fuel Economy Rating |
|---|---|---|---|
| 8cyl 5.0L A | 302 | 339 | 17 city/25 hwy |
| 6cyl 3.2L A | 221 | 232 | 20 city/28 hwy |
| 6cyl 3.2L A | 201 | 369 | 27 city/37 hwy |

## Body Styles

| Style | MSRP Range |
|---|---|
| Midsize Sedan | $48,500–$59,400 |
| Midsize Wagon | $50,750–$60,500 |

**Body Styles, Trim Levels and Options:** The E-Class is available in both sedan and wagon form in one of three trim levels—E320, E320 CDI and E500. The E320 and E500 can be had in either body style; the E320 CDI is a sedan only. Standard features on the E320 and E320 CDI include 16-inch wheels, leather upholstery, wood interior trim, 10-way power seats, dual-zone automatic climate control, a 10-speaker CD stereo and a full set of one-touch windows. E500 models add 17-inch wheels, an adaptive suspension, four-zone climate control and an upgraded Bose sound system—most of this is optional on the E320 models. A number of high-tech options are available, including the Keyless Go entry and startup system, self-adjusting Drive Dynamic seats, adaptive cruise control and a DVD-based navigation system.

**Powertrains and Performance:** E-Class buyers have three engine choices. The E320 comes with a 3.2-liter V6 rated at 221 horsepower and 232 pound-feet of torque. The diesel engine in the E320 CDI is a 3.2-liter with 201 hp and an impressive 369 lb-ft of torque. If that's not enough, you can step up to the E500 and its 5.0-liter V8, which pumps out 302 hp and 339 lb-ft of torque. A five-speed automanual transmission is fitted to each engine. Power flows to the rear wheels on standard models; if you opt for the 4Matic all-wheel-drive version, power is sent to all four wheels.

**Safety:** In addition to expected premium features like stability control and head- and torso-protecting side airbags, the E-Class boasts electronic braking. This system provides a more precise interface between the brakes and other active safety systems. Stopping distances are convincingly short, but the brakes can't match the progressive feel of conventional setups. Should an accident occur, crash sensors help determine the type and severity of an accident and deploy airbags and seatbelt tensioners accordingly. In government crash tests, the E-Class earned four stars (out of five) for frontal impacts and a perfect five stars for side impacts. In IIHS frontal offset crash testing, the midsize Benz was named a "Best Pick" in its class.

**Interior Design and Special Features:** The well-appointed cabin features a two-tone dash with wood accents, top-grade materials and nicely dampened controls. One of the most extravagant options is the Drive Dynamic front seats, which not only adapt for comfort but automatically provide additional lateral support during cornering. Two adults can easily fit in the backseat, but larger occupants may find thigh support and foot room in short supply.

**Driving Impressions:** The V6 is a confident, refined unit with ample power for most any situation. Money no object, the smooth and silent 5.0-liter V8 is also a great choice. The CDI is the best of both worlds—efficient at the pump and plenty powerful. All E-Class cars demonstrate exemplary road manners with a comfortable, controlled ride. Although this Benz doesn't have quite the athletic feel of BMW's 5 Series, those who like to take the back roads will not be disappointed by the car's grip and response around turns.

# 2005 Mercedes-Benz E55 AMG

**Body Styles, Trim Levels and Options:** The E55 comes only as a four-door sedan sold in a single trim level. Subtle enhancements set the E55 apart from its other E-Class stablemates, such as more aggressive front and rear fascias, flared rocker panels and gorgeous dual-spoke 18-inch wheels. Interior upgrades include dark bird's eye maple trim, premium-grade leather upholstery and an Alcantara suede headliner and pillar trim. Other amenities include 10-way power-adjustable front sport seats with memory and heating, four-zone climate control and a 10-speaker sound system with a CD player. A number of high-tech options are offered, such as Keyless Go and a Distronic adaptive cruise control system that automatically maintains a preset distance between the Benz and the car in front of it.

**Powertrains and Performance:** Rated at 469 horsepower and 516 pound-feet of torque, the E55's supercharged 5.5-liter V8 is one of the most powerful production engines ever offered in the U.S. Mercedes claims a 0-to-60-mph time of just 4.5 seconds—we're talking Ferrari territory here. The never-ending stream of power is put to the ground via an AMG-fortified five-speed automatic transmission complete with three driver-selectable shift modes: standard, sport or manual.

**Safety:** In addition to expected premium features such as stability control and side curtain airbags, the E55 boasts electronic braking (first seen in the 2003 SL500). This system provides a more precise interface between the brakes and the antilock and stability control hardware, enabling more effective individual wheel braking. In government crash tests, the E-Class received four stars (out of five) for driver and front-passenger protection in frontal impacts and five stars for side impacts.

**Interior Design and Special Features:** Already well laid out in standard E-Class guise, the E55 adds dark wood trim, higher-quality leather and 10-way power-adjustable sport seats to the mix. Four inflatable air bladders offer infinitely adjustable thigh and lateral support. Combined with the three-stage seat heaters and optional ventilation, these seats can't be beat. The rest of the interior is standard E-Class, which means plenty of high-quality materials and an elegant if not completely intuitive control setup.

**Driving Impressions:** This is a car that blurs the lines between luxury sedan and sports car like few other four-doors on the road. Its ability to effortlessly summon triple-digit speeds while retaining all the poise you would expect of a Mercedes is nothing short of phenomenal, and the fact that it remains equally as amicable around town makes it all the more impressive. We have a few minor quibbles—the steering is a bit overboosted, with a jiggly on-center feel that never seems quite right. And the electronically controlled brakes could be a bit smoother in their actuation. Hard-core enthusiasts might consider the E55's lack of a manual transmission a roadblock to super sedan supremacy, but then again, 469 horsepower does have a way of changing your mind in a hurry.

**MSRP Price Range**
**$79,500**
Destination Charge: $720 (all styles)

## Ratings

| | | |
|---|---|---|
| Consumer Rating | N/A | |
| Editors Rating | 8.6 | |

**What Edmunds.com says:** The speed of an exotic and the practicality of a four-door make this AMG creation one of the most enticing Mercedes yet.

**Pros:** Endless tire-smoking power from supercharged V8, composed handling at any speed, luxurious interior, state-of-the-art safety features, everyday drivability.

**Cons:** Firm ride for a luxury sedan, touchy brakes, some confusing controls.

**What's New:** The complimentary scheduled maintenance program has been dropped for 2005.

*Crash Test Scores, see pg 530*
*Warranty information, see pg 542*

## Specifications

| Engine/Drivetrain | HP | Torque | EPA Fuel Economy Rating |
|---|---|---|---|
| 8cyl 5.4L A | 469 | 516 | 14 city/21 hwy |

## Body Styles

| Style | MSRP Range |
|---|---|
| Midsize Sedan | $79,500 |

Mercedes-Benz
# 2005 Mercedes-Benz G-Class Midsize SUV

**MSRP Price Range**
## $77,700
Destination Charge: $720 (all styles)

### Ratings

| | | |
|---|---|---|
| Consumer Rating | N/A | |
| Editors Rating | 6.2 | |

**What Edmunds.com says:** Although extremely capable in the wild, its primitive nature on the street makes it more of a high-priced novelty than a true luxury SUV.

**Pros:** Go-anywhere capability, powerful V8 engine, surprisingly quiet on the highway.

**Cons:** Heavy steering and accelerator pedal efforts, no side airbags, poor ergonomics, uncomfortable rear seat, not much cargo room.

**What's New:** The complimentary scheduled maintenance program has been dropped for 2005.

**Body Styles, Trim Levels and Options:** The G500 is available as a four-door sport-utility only. Just about every luxury feature comes standard, including 18-inch wheels, dual-zone automatic climate control, a premium nine-speaker sound system (with a CD changer mounted in the cargo bay), a navigation system, rear parking assist, heated front and rear seats and full leather upholstery and wood trim.

**Powertrains and Performance:** The G500 employs a 5.0-liter gasoline V8 engine that pumps out 292 horsepower and 336 pound-feet of torque. Peak torque arrives before 3,000 rpm, promising brisk acceleration and stout off-road grunt. The five-speed automatic transmission delivers firm shifts and offers manual gear selection. A permanent four-wheel-drive system with low-range gearing sends power to all four wheels via fully lockable front, center and rear differentials. Should you want to tow, this SUV can lug up to 7,000 pounds.

**Safety:** Standard safety equipment includes four-wheel antilock disc brakes, electronic traction and stability control, seatbelt pre-tensioners, a front-passenger detection system and emergency brake assist. Side airbags are not available, and the rear center seating position has only a lap belt.

**Interior Design and Special Features:** A navigation system, front and rear heated seats, a Harman Kardon audio system with a six-disc CD changer, power everything, rear park assist and sunroof all come standard, along with enough leather and wood to make the driver think he's sitting in an S-Class sedan. Unfortunately, the stereo and navigation systems are operated via Mercedes' confusing all-in-one COMAND interface. What's more, owners must adapt to a rigidly upright seating position more suited to a Jeep Wrangler than a luxury vehicle. Rear cargo space maxes out at 80 cubic feet, slightly less than most midsize SUVs.

**Driving Impressions:** With the V8 working in tandem with the smooth and alert automatic gearbox, brisk acceleration is available whether from a standstill or on the highway when swift passing response is needed. But due to a stiff gas pedal, it takes a serious lead foot just to maintain speed in the G—good thing cruise control is standard. The heavy steering likewise requires some muscle. A few modern-day tweaks have made the live-axle setup bearable around town, but it's not enough to mask the low-tech design. The tall, upright body still exhibits significant body roll, and road hazards come booming through the cabin with annoying frequency.

*Crash Test Scores, see pg 530*
*Warranty information, see pg 542*

### Specifications

| Engine/Drivetrain | HP | Torque | EPA Fuel Economy Rating |
|---|---|---|---|
| 8cyl 5.0L A | 292 | 336 | 13 city/14 hwy |

### Body Styles

| Style | MSRP Range |
|---|---|
| Midsize SUV | $77,700 |

For the latest full vehicle reports, visit www.edmunds.com/bginfopak

**Midsize SUV**

# 2005 Mercedes-Benz G55 AMG

**MSRP Price Range**

**$99,900**

Destination Charge: $720 (all styles)

## Ratings

| | | |
|---|---|---|
| Consumer Rating | N/A | |
| Editors Rating | 6.3 | |

**What Edmunds.com says:** Just when we thought the G-Class couldn't get any more ridiculous, along comes the AMG-tuned version.

**Pros:** Go-anywhere capability, powerful V8 engine, surprisingly quiet ride on the highway.

**Cons:** Heavy steering and accelerator pedal efforts, no side airbags, fussy navigation system, minimal cargo capacity.

**What's New:** The G55 gets a supercharged 5.5-liter V8 with 469 horsepower this year. The complimentary scheduled maintenance program has been dropped for 2005.

**Body Styles, Trim Levels and Options:** The high-performance G55 is available as a four-door sport-utility only. Just about every luxury feature comes standard, including 18-inch wheels and performance tires, an aluminum brush guard, a premium Harman Kardon sound system with a CD changer mounted in the cargo bay, a navigation system, rear parking sensors, 10-way power-adjustable seats with heaters and full leather upholstery and wood trim.

**Powertrains and Performance:** The G55's AMG-tweaked 5.5-liter, supercharged V8 sends 469 horsepower and 516 pound-feet of torque to the wheels. The five-speed automatic transmission delivers firm shifts and offers manual gear selection. A permanent four-wheel-drive system with low-range gearing sends power to all four wheels via fully lockable front, center and rear differentials. Should you want to tow, this SUV can lug up to 7,000 pounds.

**Safety:** Standard safety equipment includes four-wheel antilock disc brakes, emergency brake assist, electronic traction and stability control and a front-passenger detection system. Side airbags are not available, and the rear center passenger makes do with a lap belt.

**Interior Design and Special Features:** Rugged origins notwithstanding, the G55 comes standard with a navigation system, heated seats front and rear, a Harman Kardon audio system with a six-disc CD changer, power everything, rear park assist, a sunroof and enough leather and wood to make one think that he's sitting in an S-Class sedan. Unfortunately, the stereo and navigation systems are operated via Mercedes' confusing all-in-one "COMAND" interface. The seats offer passable comfort, but occupants must conform to a rigidly upright seating position more suited to a Jeep than a high-dollar luxury vehicle. Rear cargo space maxes out at 80 cubic feet, slightly less than that of most midsize SUVs.

**Driving Impressions:** With a muscular V8 working in tandem with the smooth and alert automatic gearbox, thrilling acceleration is available whenever you want it, be it from a stop or when executing passing maneuvers. But due to a stiff gas pedal, it takes a serious lead foot just to maintain speed in the G—good thing cruise control is standard. The heavy steering likewise requires some muscle. Modern-day tweaks and AMG modifications have made the live-axle setup bearable around town, but it's not enough to mask the low-tech design. The tall, upright body still exhibits significant body roll, and road hazards come booming through the cabin with annoying frequency.

*Crash Test Scores, see pg 530*
*Warranty information, see pg 542*

## Specifications

| Engine/Drivetrain | HP | Torque | EPA Fuel Economy Rating |
|---|---|---|---|
| 8cyl 5.4L A | 469 | 516 | 12 city/14 hwy |

## Body Styles

| Style | MSRP Range |
|---|---|
| Midsize SUV | $99,900 |

# 2005 Mercedes-Benz M-Class

Midsize SUV

**MSRP Price Range**
## $37,950 - $46,400
Destination Charge: $720 (all styles)

### Ratings

| | | |
|---|---|---|
| Consumer Rating | 7.9 | |
| Editors Rating | 7.0 | |

**What Edmunds.com says:** Now in its eighth year, the M-Class provides solid on-road performance along with excellent all-weather capability and a safe, feature-laden cabin. Drive it back to back with newer car-based competitors, though, and it's obvious that its road manners no longer set the standard among luxury SUVs.

**Pros:** Strong range of engines, extensive array of safety features, comfortable for five, surefooted in bad weather.

**Cons:** On-road handling surpassed by newer crossover SUVs, expensive for what you get.

**What's New:** Besides the addition of a Special Edition package that bundles together desirable features, the M-Class is unchanged. The complimentary scheduled maintenance program has been dropped for 2005.

**Body Styles, Trim Levels and Options:** The M-Class is available as a four-door SUV in two levels of trim. The standard ML350 features 17-inch alloy wheels, automatic climate control, a six-way manually adjustable driver seat and burled walnut interior trim. The ML500 gets standard leather seating, eight-way power-adjustable and heated front seats and a standard DVD-based navigation system. Although the M-Class offers plenty of standard luxury and style, there are numerous options available, including a power glass sunroof, rain-sensing windshield wipers and a sport appearance package. Other options include a third-row seat, high-intensity discharge headlamps and an upgraded Bose sound system with a cargo bay-mounted CD changer. For those interested in a full measure of features, a new Special Edition package bundles together desirable options while adding sporty elements like a "power dome" hood and thickly bolstered seats.

**Powertrains and Performance:** The ML350 is powered by a 232-hp, 3.5-liter V6, while the ML500 comes standard with a 288-hp, 5.0-liter V8. Both engines are mated to a driver-adaptive five-speed automatic transmission with a manual-shift gate. The ML350 will accelerate to 60 mph in under nine seconds, while the ML500 can accomplish the same feat in just over 7 seconds. Both models are rated to tow a maximum of 5,000 pounds. A dual-range four-wheel-drive system is standard.

**Safety:** Standard safety features include the TeleAid communications system, traction and stability control, four-wheel antilock disc brakes and eight airbags (including four side-impact bags for torso protection and two full-length head curtains). In frontal offset impact crash testing conducted by the IIHS, the ML received a "Good" rating (the highest possible) and was named a "Best Pick" among midsize SUVs.

**Interior Design and Special Features:** The M-Class has a tasteful, modern look that doesn't sacrifice functionality. Although there are lapses here and there, materials quality is generally good, and the overall layout is easy to get comfortable with. A DVD-based navigation system is available, but don't go looking for an in-dash CD changer—it's back in the cargo bay. Second-row passenger space is about average for the class, while the optional third-row seat is for children only. Cargo capacity stands at 34.7 cubic feet with the second seat up and 81.2 cubic feet with it flipped down.

*Crash Test Scores, see pg 530*
*Warranty information, see pg 542*

### Specifications

| Engine/Drivetrain | HP | Torque | EPA Fuel Economy Rating |
|---|---|---|---|
| 8cyl 5.0L A | 288 | 325 | 14 city/17 hwy |
| 6cyl 3.7L A | 232 | 254 | 15 city/18 hwy |

### Body Styles

| Style | MSRP Range |
|---|---|
| Midsize SUV | $37,950–$46,400 |

**Driving Impressions:** Body-on-frame construction gives the M-Class a choppier ride and slower reflexes compared with the newer, car-based SUVs it competes with, but for the most part the Benz delivers stable and predictable on-road handling. Minimal ground clearance precludes it from any serious off-road adventures, but as an all-weather vehicle it excels.

**MSRP Price Range**
## $75,300 - $124,750
Destination Charge: N/A (all styles)

### Ratings

| | | |
|---|---|---|
| Consumer Rating | N/A | |
| Editors Rating | 8.3 | |

**What Edmunds.com says:** After a minor refresh last year, the S-Class is once again a top choice when it comes to a no-compromise luxury sedan.

**Pros:** Elegantly appointed and spacious cabin, feels nimble for its size, state-of-the-art safety features, strong resale value.

**Cons:** Complicated COMAND system, not as athletic as some of its competitors, a few low-grade interior materials.

**What's New:** Mercedes 4Matic all-wheel-drive system is now a no-cost option on the S430 and S500 models. The complimentary scheduled maintenance program has been dropped for 2005.

**Body Styles, Trim Levels and Options:** The four-door S-Class includes three models: the S430, S500 and S600. All models come with most of the luxury features you would expect in a sedan of this caliber including 14-way power-adjustable front seats, a DVD navigation system, Bose premium audio system and rich leather and wood trim. Notable options include ventilated front seats with a massage feature, a keyless entry and start system (called Keyless Go), adaptive cruise control and a Sport package that includes larger wheels and tires, resculpted bumpers and side skirts.

**Powertrains and Performance:** The S430 is powered by a 4.3-liter, 275-horsepower V8, while the S500 offers more power courtesy of its 5.0-liter V8 that's rated at 302 hp. Both engines use a new seven-speed automatic transmission—an industry first. The top-of-the-line S600 uses a twin-turbocharged 5.5-liter V12 rated to produce 493 hp and 590 lb-ft of torque; it's paired with a five-speed automatic. Mercedes claims that the S600 can hit 60 mph in about 4.5 seconds, placing it in a league usually occupied by exotic sports cars. The S430 and S500 are available with either the standard rear-drive setup or the fully automatic 4Matic all-wheel-drive system as a no-cost option. Note that 4Matic-equipped cars use a five-speed automatic instead of the seven-speed.

**Safety:** The 2003 model year brought "Pre-Safe," which determines accident probability by using sensors in the stability control system and the BrakeAssist feature. Should an accident seem unavoidable, the system applies split-second tensioning of the seatbelts, moves the front passenger seat and power-adjustable individual rear seats to the most favorable positions and closes the sunroof (if the vehicle is skidding). If the accident is averted at the last moment, the seatbelt tensioning is cancelled and the seats are reset to their original positions. Of course, Pre-Safe joins a list of already impressive safety features that includes four-wheel antilock disc brakes, electronic traction and stability control, seat-mounted side-impact airbags for front occupants and side curtain airbags that protect both front and rear passengers.

**Interior Design and Special Features:** Virtually every luxury and convenience item to be found in an automobile, including a DVD-based navigation system and power door-closing assist, is standard on each S-Class sedan. Still, there are optional designo interior trim packages which include more dramatic leather and wood combinations, as well as dynamic multicontour front seats, four-zone climate control and power-adjustable rear seats.

**Driving Impressions:** The S-Class has that enviable quality of feeling smaller and more nimble than its substantial size suggests. Strong acceleration, precise handling and a relaxing ride remain strong virtues of Mercedes' senior sedan. The S600 provides truly exceptional performance in a straight line, but BMW's 760Li is still a more involving driving experience. Buyers needing all-weather capability can opt for the 4Matic all-wheel-drive system at no cost on the S430 and S500.

*Crash Test Scores, see pg 530*
*Warranty information, see pg 542*

### Specifications

| Engine/Drivetrain | HP | Torque | EPA Fuel Economy Rating |
|---|---|---|---|
| 8cyl 4.3L A | 275 | 295 | 17 city/24 hwy |
| 8cyl 5.0L A | 302 | 339 | 16 city/22 hwy |
| 12cyl 5.5L A | 493 | 590 | 13 city/19 hwy |

### Body Styles

| Style | MSRP Range |
|---|---|
| Large Sedan | $75,300 - $124,750 |

# 2005 Mercedes-Benz S55 AMG

**Large Sedan**

**MSRP Price Range**

## $111,900

Destination Charge: $720 (all styles)

### Ratings

| | | |
|---|---|---|
| Consumer Rating | N/A | |
| Editors Rating | N/A | |

**What Edmunds.com says:** Combining performance more akin to that of an Italian sports car along with S-Class luxury and room, the S55 has few rivals in the ultraperformance luxury sedan arena.

**Pros:** -class performance, state-of-the-art safety features, spacious and comfortable cabin.

**Cons:** Complicated COMAND system, six-figure price tag.

**What's New:** The complimentary scheduled maintenance program has been dropped for 2005.

**Body Styles, Trim Levels and Options:** The four-door S55 comes in one well-appointed trim level. The long list of standard features includes a DVD-based navigation system, 14-way power front seats, dual-zone automatic climate control, extensive leather and wood interior trim, a high-powered CD audio system and even illuminated vanity mirrors for all four seating positions. Among the options are "active, ventilated" seats that feature built-in fans to keep one's backside cool on sultry days, Distronic cruise control that automatically maintains a preset distance from the car in front of it and Parktronic that lets you know when you're approaching a potentially damaging object in a parking lot.

**Powertrains and Performance:** The S55's supercharged 5.5-liter V8 produces a stunning 493 hp and 505 lb-ft of torque. The power is managed by an AMG-tweaked five-speed automatic that furnishes 35-percent quicker gear changes and a "Speedshift" feature that allows manual-shift capability without having to take your hands off the wheel. Mercedes claims that this high-performance super-luxury sedan will hit 60 mph in about 4.5 seconds, a figure typically associated with exotic sports cars bearing Italian names.

**Safety:** Mercedes'"Pre-Safe" system is standard. It determines accident probability by using sensors belonging to the stability control system and the BrakeAssist feature. Should an accident appear unavoidable, the system applies split-second tensioning of the seatbelts, moves the front passenger seat and power-adjustable individual rear seats to the most favorable positions and closes the sunroof (if the vehicle is skidding). If the accident is averted at the last moment, the seatbelt tensioning is cancelled and the seats reset to their original positions. Of course, Pre-Safe joins a list of already impressive safety features that includes four-wheel antilock disc brakes, electronic traction and stability control and seat-mounted side and side curtain airbags that protect the heads and torsos of both front and rear passengers.

**Interior Design and Special Features:** Virtually every luxury and convenience item to be found in an automobile, including a DVD-based navigation system and power door-closing assist, is standard on the S55. Still, there are optional designo interior trim packages which provide more dramatic leather and wood combinations, as well as dynamic multicontour front seats, four-zone climate control and power-adjustable rear seats.

*Crash Test Scores, see pg 530*
*Warranty information, see pg 542*

**Driving Impressions:** The S55 has that enviable quality of feeling smaller and more nimble than its substantial size suggests. Acceleration rivals that of many exotic sports cars and even its handling could be described as nimble. Although it's still not the kind of car you buy for the sole purpose of weekend jaunts through the hills, it will make the occasional detour home from the office a most pleasurable trip indeed.

### Specifications

| Engine/Drivetrain | HP | Torque | EPA Fuel Economy Rating |
|---|---|---|---|
| 8cyl 5.5L A | 493 | 505 | 14 city/22 hwy |

### Body Styles

| Style | MSRP Range |
|---|---|
| Large Sedan | $111,900 |

# 2005 Mercedes-Benz SL-Class

**MSRP Price Range**

## $89,900 - $127,500

Destination Charge: $720 (all styles)

## Ratings

| | | |
|---|---|---|
| Consumer Rating | 9.3 | ▭ |
| Editors Rating | 8.5 | ▭ |

**What Edmunds.com says:** Between its elegant styling, impressive performance and cutting-edge technology, the SL roadster still reigns as the quintessential luxury drop top.

**Pros:** Seductive style, quick-folding retractable hardtop, commendable performance, ride and handling.

**Cons:** Heavy for a "sports car," limited cargo capacity.

**What's New:** The complimentary scheduled maintenance program has been dropped for 2005.

**Body Styles, Trim Levels and Options:** The standard SL-Class roadster line consists of the V8-powered SL500 and the V12-powered SL600. Standard equipment on both models includes multiadjustable leather seats, automatic dual-zone climate control, bi-xenon headlights, a power-retractable hardtop and a high-powered CD stereo system. Options include a Sport package for the SL500 that adds 18-inch AMG wheels, high-performance tires and lower body sculpting, Parktronic electronic parking assist, "Distronic" cruise control (which automatically keeps the Benz a fixed distance from the car ahead of it on the freeway) and "Keyless Go," a device that lets you access and run the car without a conventional key. The SL600 ups the ante with exclusive wheels and interior trim, along with a few additional standard features.

**Powertrains and Performance:** The SL500 sports a 5.0-liter V8 that pumps out 302 horsepower and 339 pound-feet of torque. No manual gearbox is available, but the standard seven-speed automatic allows manual-style gear changes. The SL500 can sprint from zero to 60 mph in around 6 seconds and hit a (electronically limited) top speed of 155 mph. The 493 horses and 590 lb-ft of torque produced by the SL600's twin-turbocharged 5.5-liter V12 will slingshot that Benz to 60 mph in just 4.5 seconds, though its (electronically limited) top speed is the same.

**Safety:** A slew of acronyms that stand for performance- and safety-enhancing technologies are fitted to every SL, such as ABS (antilock brake system), ASR (traction control), ESP (stability control) and ABC (body roll control). And the SL is the first car to have electronic braking, which can react much quicker than a conventional hydraulic system and can even selectively adjust braking force to each wheel when cornering. Should an accident be unavoidable, there's a multitude of airbags to protect the occupants, including side curtain-style bags that cover the head and torso areas and a knee bag for the driver. The SL also has a pop-up roll bar that will deploy if a rollover is imminent.

**Interior Design and Special Features:** A power-operated, retractable hardtop is standard and offers the integrity, insulation and security of a coupe when raised along with the full al fresco experience of a roadster when powered down. The dual-zone climate control is easy to use, but unfortunately the same can't be said for the complex COMAND audio and navigation interface.

**Driving Impressions:** Apart from the electronically controlled brakes that feel a bit touchy at first, the current SL offers the driver a rewarding experience behind the wheel that rarely grows tiring. Handling is exceptional with almost no body roll and excellent grip. Although the standard SL500 provides brisk acceleration, those looking for the ultimate in top-down performance may want to consider the world-beating performance of the SL600's V12.

*Crash Test Scores, see pg 530*
*Warranty information, see pg 542*

## Specifications

| Engine/Drivetrain | HP | Torque | EPA Fuel Economy Rating |
|---|---|---|---|
| 8cyl 5.0L A | 302 | 339 | 16 city/23 hwy |
| 12cyl 5.5L A | 493 | 590 | 13 city/19 hwy |

## Body Styles

| Style | MSRP Range |
|---|---|
| Compact Convertible | $89,900–$127,500 |

# 2005 Mercedes-Benz SL55 AMG

**Compact Convertible**

**MSRP Price Range**

## $121,500

Destination Charge: $720 (all styles)

### Ratings

| | | |
|---|---|---|
| Consumer Rating | 9.3 | |
| Editors Rating | 8.6 | |

**What Edmunds.com says:** If you're looking for maximum performance and maximum luxury in an open-top vehicle, this is your car.

**Pros:** Supercar performance, super-luxury opulence, sultry styling, muscle car-era exhaust note.

**Cons:** Complex audio and navigation controls, cramped rear seat.

**What's New:** The complimentary scheduled maintenance program has been dropped for 2005.

**Body Styles, Trim Levels and Options:** The SL55 is a high-performance version of the standard SL luxury roadster. Standard features include 12-way power-adjustable leather sport seats, aluminum trim, dual-zone automatic climate control, xenon headlights, a high-powered Bose stereo with a trunk-mounted CD changer, a navigation system, 18-inch AMG wheels, high-performance tires and lower body sculpting. Options include Distronic, a cruise control system that automatically maintains a set distance between the SL55 and the vehicle in front of it, and Keyless Go, which allows the car to be started without a key.

**Powertrains and Performance:** A supercharged 5.5-liter V8 sends 493 horsepower and 516 pound-feet of torque to the rear wheels. All this power sends the SL55 to 60 mph from standstill in just 4.7 seconds. A SpeedShift five-speed automatic gearbox offers manual-style gear changes via buttons on the back of the steering wheel spokes.

**Safety:** A slew of acronyms that stand for performance- and safety-enhancing technologies are fitted to the SL55, such as ABS (antilock brake system), ASR (traction control), ESP (stability control) and ABC (body roll control). There is also electronic braking, which can react much quicker than a conventional hydraulic system and can even selectively adjust braking force to each wheel when cornering. Should an accident be unavoidable, there's a multitude of airbags to protect the occupants, including side curtain-style bags that cover the head and torso areas and a knee bag for the driver. The SL also has a pop-up roll bar that will deploy if a rollover is imminent.

**Interior Design and Special Features:** AMG sport seats and real metal accents mark the cabin of the SL55. A power-operated, retractable hardtop offers the integrity, insulation and security of a coupe when raised along with the full alfresco experience of a roadster when powered down. The dual-zone climate control is easy to use, but unfortunately the same can't be said for the complex COMAND audio and navigation interface.

**Driving Impressions:** With the SL55, it's not just the acceleration but the effortless acceleration that makes it so impressive. With virtually no drama (provided one is careful with the throttle), the hot-rod Benz can rip from zero to 60 mph in only 4.7 seconds. When the road gets curvy, the SL55 feels as willing as anything in this price range (Porsche 911 Turbo, BMW Z8, Maserati Spyder). Granted, it doesn't offer the same level of feedback as the Porsche or Maserati in terms of steering feel, and the car's weight (around 4,200 pounds) puts it at a theoretical disadvantage. But the Active Body Control (ABC) technology keeps body movement in check and gives the car a surprisingly nimble demeanor when changing directions quickly.

*Crash Test Scores, see pg 530*
*Warranty information, see pg 542*

### Specifications

| Engine/Drivetrain | HP | Torque | EPA Fuel Economy Rating |
|---|---|---|---|
| 8cyl 5.4L A | 493 | 516 | 14 city/20 hwy |

### Body Styles

| Style | MSRP Range |
|---|---|
| Compact Convertible | $121,500 |

**Compact Convertible**

# 2005 Mercedes-Benz SL65 AMG

**MSRP Price Range**

## $179,000
Destination Charge: $720 (all styles)

### Ratings

| | | |
|---|---|---|
| Consumer Rating | 8.0 | |
| Editors Rating | 8.6 | |

**What Edmunds.com says:** If you're looking for maximum performance and maximum luxury in an open-top vehicle, this is your car.

**Pros:** Blinding acceleration, supercar performance that belies its weight, super-luxury opulence, sultry styling, muscle car-era exhaust note.

**Cons:** Big price leap over already fantastic SL55, complex audio and navigation controls.

**What's New:** As if there weren't enough AMG offerings, Mercedes-Benz adds yet another—the SL65. With 604 horsepower, however, we won't complain. The SL65 also features a reinforced five-speed automatic tranny, race-bred brakes with AMG eight-piston composite calipers, 19-inch alloys and dynamic multicontour seats. The complimentary scheduled maintenance program has been dropped for 2005.

**Body Styles, Trim Levels and Options:** The SL65 is a high-performance version of the standard SL luxury roadster. Standard features include 12-way power-adjustable leather sport seats, aluminum trim, dual-zone automatic climate control, xenon headlights, a high-powered Bose stereo with a trunk-mounted CD changer, a navigation system, 19-inch AMG wheels, high-performance tires and lower body sculpting. Options include Distronic, a cruise control system that automatically maintains a set distance between the SL65 and the vehicle in front of it, and Keyless Go, which allows the car to be started without a key.

**Powertrains and Performance:** The SL65's twin-turbo 6.0-liter V12 puts out astounding levels of power—604 horses along with 738 pound-feet of torque. These big numbers mean that this refined yet muscle-bound roadster will hit 60 mph around 4 seconds, a figure typically associated with exotic sports cars bearing Italian names. The only transmission available is a five-speed automatic, but it does allow for manual shifting if you feel the need to choose gears yourself.

**Safety:** A slew of acronyms that stands for performance- and safety-enhancing technologies are fitted to the SL65, such as ABS (antilock brake system), ASR (traction control), ESP (stability control) and ABC (body roll control). There is also electronic braking, which can react much quicker than a conventional hydraulic system and can even selectively adjust braking force to each wheel when cornering. Should an accident be unavoidable, there's a multitude of airbags to protect the occupants, including side curtain-style bags that cover the head and torso areas and a knee bag for the driver. The SL also has a pop-up roll bar that will deploy if a rollover is imminent.

**Interior Design and Special Features:** AMG sport seats and real metal accents mark the cabin of the SL65. A power-operated, retractable hardtop offers the integrity, insulation and security of a coupe when raised along with the full alfresco experience of a roadster when powered down. The dual-zone climate control is easy to use, but unfortunately the same can't be said for the complex COMAND audio and navigation interface.

**Driving Impressions:** With the SL65, it's not just the acceleration but the effortless acceleration that makes it so impressive. With virtually no drama (provided one is careful with the throttle), the hot-rod Benz can rip from zero to 60 mph in about 4 seconds. When the road gets curvy, the SL65 feels as willing as anything in this price range. Granted, it doesn't offer the same level of feedback as a Porsche or Ferrari in terms of steering feel, and the car's weight (around 4,500 pounds) puts it at a theoretical disadvantage. But the Active Body Control (ABC) technology keeps body movement in check and gives the car a surprisingly nimble demeanor when changing directions quickly.

*Crash Test Scores, see pg 530*
*Warranty information, see pg 542*

### Specifications

| Engine/Drivetrain | HP | Torque | EPA Fuel Economy Rating |
|---|---|---|---|
| 12cyl 6.0L A | 604 | 738 | 12 city/19 hwy |

### Body Styles

| Style | MSRP Range |
|---|---|
| Compact Convertible | $179,000 |

Mercedes-Benz

# 2005 Mercedes-Benz SLK-Class
### Compact Convertible

**MSRP Price Range**
## $45,500
Destination Charge: $720 (all styles)

## Ratings

| | | |
|---|---|---|
| Consumer Rating | 9.8 | |
| Editors Rating | 7.8 | |

**What Edmunds.com says:** A fun-to-drive roadster that combines the safety and security of a hardtop, the wind-in-your-hair fun of a convertible and the European-brand cachet of a Mercedes all in one powerful and attractively styled package.

**Pros:** Much improved interior design, sports-carlike handling, strong and sweet-sounding V6, comfort and convenience of retractable hardtop.

**Cons:** Costs more than peers, big blind spots when top is up.

**What's New:** After seven years on the market, Mercedes redesigns the SLK for 2005. Potential buyers should also note that the company's complimentary scheduled maintenance program has been dropped.

**Body Styles, Trim Levels and Options:** The SLK comes in one body style: a two-seat roadster with a power-retractable hardtop. Standard equipment includes 17-inch alloy wheels, leather upholstery, automatic climate control, a premium audio system and auto-dimming mirrors. Should this not be enough, there are a number of options to consider, such as bi-xenon headlamps, a navigation system and memory seats. An innovative Airscarf system directs heated air through special vents in the head restraints. The effect is that of an invisible scarf to warm the passenger's neck and shoulders in chilly weather. A 380-watt audio system is available, and includes eleven speakers and surround sound capability.

**Powertrains and Performance:** The SLK offers a 3.5-liter V6 good for 268 hp. The SLK can sprint to 60 miles per hour in just 5.6 seconds, according to Mercedes-Benz. A six-speed manual is standard, and a seven-speed automatic (with automanual shift capability) is optional.

**Safety:** Seat-mounted side airbags are standard equipment, as are four-wheel antilock disc brakes, stability and traction control (called ESP) and the TeleAid system, which alerts emergency personnel if an airbag goes off and can also put you in touch with a live operator to summon medical or police assistance. The SLK also has reinforced A-pillars, integrated roll bars behind each seat and emergency tensioning seatbelt retractors for enhanced rollover protection. BrakeAssist automatically applies full braking force when a panic stop is initiated.

**Interior Design and Special Features:** Good-looking soft-touch material covers the top of the dash, glovebox and doors, while plastics of similar quality fill in the rest. The climate control layout varies depending on whether you add a navigation system (now DVD-based), but both arrangements use easy-to-decipher dials that are usable at a glance. The soft and supportive seats remain comfortable even after several hours of continuous driving. Keep the windows up while the top is down and there's minimal wind buffeting. If that's not enough, consider the new Airscarf system that channels warm air to your neck and shoulders via dedicated registers in the headrests. It actually works quite well, and when combined with traditional seat heaters, the SLK becomes one of the most useful all-weather convertibles on the market.

*Crash Test Scores, see pg 530*
*Warranty information, see pg 542*

**Driving Impressions:** The engine's power kicks in early and remains solid throughout thanks to variable camshafts and a two-stage intake manifold. As an added bonus, the stout V6 pours out a satisfying wail that inspires flat-footed runs to redline at every opportunity. The new steering setup is not only lighter to the touch, it returns enough road feel to maintain the car's sporting demeanor during aggressive driving. The revised brakes could still use a better feel through the pedal, but their ability to bring the SLK to a halt in a hurry is never an issue.

## Specifications

| Engine/Drivetrain | HP | Torque | EPA Fuel Economy Rating |
|---|---|---|---|
| 6cyl 3.5L M | 268 | 258 | 18 city/25 hwy |

## Body Styles

| Style | MSRP Range |
|---|---|
| Compact Convertible | $45,500 |

For the latest full vehicle reports, visit www.edmunds.com/bginfopak

## Compact Convertible

# 2005 Mercedes-Benz SLK55 AMG

**MSRP Price Range**

**N/A**

Destination Charge: $720 (all styles)

### Ratings

| Ratings | | |
|---|---|---|
| Consumer Rating | N/A | |
| Editors Rating | 8.1 | |

**What Edmunds.com says:** A ridiculously fast roadster that blows away the notion that the SLK is just a boulevard cruiser.

**Pros:** Blistering V8 performance, much-improved interior design, handles more like a sports car than before, retractable hardtop.

**Cons:** Big blind spots when top is up, no manual gearbox available.

**What's New:** The high-performance SLK55 is an all-new replacement for the SLK32 based on the completely redesigned SLK roadster.

**Body Styles, Trim Levels and Options:** The SLK55 comes in one body style: a two-seat roadster with a power-retractable hardtop. Standard equipment includes 18-inch AMG wheels and high-performance tires, napa leather upholstery with Alcantara inserts, power-adjustable sport seats, automatic climate control, a tilt/telescoping steering wheel and a rear spoiler. An innovative Airscarf system directs heated air through special vents in the head restraints—the effect is that of an invisible scarf to warm the passenger's neck and shoulders in chilly weather. A 380-watt audio system is available, and includes 11 speakers and surround sound capability.

**Powertrains and Performance:** As one would expect, the performance of the SLK55 is thrilling. With its AMG-tuned 5.5-liter V8 making a stupendous 360 horsepower, the AMG-tweaked roadster can leap to 60 mph in just 4.5 ticks of the stopwatch. A seven-speed automatic is standard and includes Speedshift automanual shift capability. Fully equal to the task of keeping all this kinetic energy under control are the massive composite ventilated disc brakes with six-piston calipers up front.

**Safety:** Front and side airbags are standard equipment, as are four-wheel antilock disc brakes, traction and stability control and the TeleAid system (which alerts emergency personnel if an airbag goes off and can put you in touch with a live operator to summon medical or police assistance). The SLK55 also has reinforced A-pillars, integrated roll bars behind each seat and emergency tensioning seatbelt retractors for enhanced rollover protection. BrakeAssist automatically applies full braking force when a panic stop is initiated.

**Interior Design and Special Features:** Attractive soft-touch material covers the top of the dash, glovebox and doors, while plastics of similar quality fill in the rest. The climate control layout varies depending on whether you add a navigation system (now DVD-based), but both arrangements use easy-to-decipher dials that are usable at a glance. The soft and supportive seats remain comfortable even after several hours of continuous driving. Keep the windows up while the top is down and there's minimal wind buffeting. If that's not enough, consider the new Airscarf system that channels warm air to your neck and shoulders via dedicated registers in the headrests. It actually works quite well, and when combined with traditional seat heaters, the SLK becomes one of the most useful all-weather convertibles on the market.

**Driving Impressions:** In spite of the SLK55's ability to surge forward from virtually any speed, the muscle-bound engine is docile around town and will plod through rush-hour traffic without complaint. Additionally, the ride is supple enough so that broken pavement is absorbed without discomfort. The well-sorted suspension never loses its composure on twisty back roads, and the sticky performance tires provide grip to match. The SLK55 is a great combination of near-touring car comfort and sports car performance. Better still, it can serve as either a coupe or convertible without ever forcing the driver to leave his or her seat.

*Crash Test Scores, see pg 530*
*Warranty information, see pg 542*

### Specifications

| Engine/Drivetrain | HP | Torque | EPA Fuel Economy Rating |
|---|---|---|---|
| 8cyl 5.5L A | 360 | 376 | N/A |

### Body Styles

| Style | MSRP Range |
|---|---|
| Compact Convertible | N/A |

# 2005 Mercury Grand Marquis

**Large Sedan**

**MSRP Price Range**
## $24,425 - $30,780
Destination Charge: $725 (all styles)

## Ratings

| | | |
|---|---|---|
| Consumer Rating | N/A | |
| Editors Rating | 8.0 | |

**What Edmunds.com says:** A perennial best-seller among older folks who appreciate its large size and reasonable price, the Grand Marquis offers a Lincoln Town Car experience for under $30,000.

**Pros:** Spacious interior, comfortable ride, good crash test scores.

**Cons:** Large size makes it difficult to park and maneuver, some low-grade interior materials.

**What's New:** Minor changes this year include a new instrument panel applique, a revised steering wheel design and new wheel choices.

**Body Styles, Trim Levels and Options:** The Grand Marquis comes as a four-door sedan only in two levels of trim—GS and LS. Each trim is further broken down into base and Convenience lines for the GS, and Premium and Ultimate for the LS. Base GS models include all the family-sedan basics, like air conditioning; a CD player; a power driver seat; keyless entry; power windows, mirrors and locks; cruise control; a tilt steering wheel; and 16-inch wheels. The GS Convenience adds traction control and power-adjustable pedals. The LS Premium adds alloy wheels, a power front-passenger seat, automatic climate control and an auto-dimming rearview mirror. The LS Ultimate includes a wood and leather steering wheel and rear air suspension. Options on both LS models include leather, seat heaters, laminated side glass, a CD changer and a handling package, which offers a bump in power as well as firmer suspension tuning for better handling.

**Powertrains and Performance:** Only one engine and transmission are offered. Standard models use a 224-horsepower, 4.6-liter V8 and a four-speed automatic. Opt for the handling package on either LS model, and the same engine is upgraded to produce 239 hp, along with a boost in torque. Fuel economy is good for a large V8-powered sedan—expect about 17 mpg in the city and up to 25 mpg on the highway.

**Safety:** You can sleep better at night knowing that the Grand Marquis scores well in National Highway Traffic Safety Administration crash tests; it earned a perfect five stars in frontal impact testing and four stars in side-impact testing. With a crash-severity sensor, safety belt pretensioners, dual-stage airbags and seat-position sensors, the Grand Mark protects occupants like few smaller cars can. Four-wheel antilock disc brakes are standard on every Grand Marquis, and traction control is standard on all cars except the base GS. Side airbags for front occupants are optional.

**Interior Design and Special Features:** A roomy cabin is one of the biggest selling points for the Grand Marquis, and adults will find plentiful head-, shoulder, hip- and legroom. Bench seating allows this big sedan to accommodate up to six people. A cavernous trunk of 20.6 cubic feet will swallow any luggage they might have with them. Controls and instrumentation are simple in design, though not particularly stylish, and some of the materials are low in quality.

**Driving Impressions:** Want a chrome-encrusted, rear-drive V8-powered American sedan without the premium charged for a Lincoln or the trendy Chrysler 300C? The Grand Marquis fits the bill perfectly. The standard V8 provides plenty of acceleration in just about any situation, and the car's smooth, forgiving ride spares occupants from harsh impacts over bumps. The large size of this Mercury can make it unwieldy in tight spots, but the car's relatively responsive steering helps drivers keep it on track.

Crash Test Scores, see pg 530
Warranty information, see pg 542

## Specifications

| Engine/Drivetrain | HP | Torque | EPA Fuel Economy Rating |
|---|---|---|---|
| 8cyl 4.6L A | 224 | 275 | 18 city/25 hwy |

## Body Styles

| Style | MSRP Range |
|---|---|
| Large Sedan | $24,425–$30,780 |

For the latest full vehicle reports, visit www.edmunds.com/bginfopak

**MSRP Price Range**
## $21,405 - $26,405
Destination Charge: $590 (all styles)

### Ratings

| | | |
|---|---|---|
| Consumer Rating | 9.5 | |
| Editors Rating | 7.8 | |

**What Edmunds.com says:** Put a Ford Escape in a Mercury outfit and what do you get? An excellent small SUV in pretty dapper digs.

**Pros:** Powerful V6, large cargo capacity, comfortable and stylish interior, carlike handling.

**Cons:** Faux wood trim is unconvincing, fuel-thirsty V6.

**What's New:** The Mariner, based on the successful Ford Escape, is new for 2005.

**Body Styles, Trim Levels and Options:** Only one four-door body style is available with either front-wheel drive or automatic four-wheel drive. Three trim levels are offered: Convenience, Luxury and Premier. Base Convenience models start you out with a 2.3-liter, four-cylinder engine; 16-inch alloy wheels; a CD player; air conditioning; power accessories keyless entry; and cruise control. The Luxury adds a 3.0-liter V6, a power driver seat, a six-disc CD changer, an alarm system, message center with compass and an auto-dimming rearview mirror. Premier models step up with machined alloy wheels, heated outside mirrors, a MACH premium audio system with subwoofer and heated leather seats with contrasting suedelike inserts. Side curtain airbags and a reverse-sensing system are optional.

**Powertrains and Performance:** Standard on the Mariner is a 2.3-liter, inline four-cylinder engine that makes 153 horsepower and 152 pound-feet of torque matched to a four-speed automatic. Standard on Luxury and Premier models is a potent 3.0-liter V6, which makes 200 hp and 193 lb-ft of torque. With this engine, the Mariner can tow up to 3,500 pounds.

**Safety:** ABS is standard on all Mariners, and V6 4WD models have four-wheel disc brakes. A notable safety feature is the optional Safety Canopy system that offers full-length head curtain airbag protection in the event of a side-impact collision or rollover. The mechanically identical Ford Escape has done well in government crash testing, earning a perfect five stars for the driver in frontal impacts and four stars for the front passenger. In side-impact crash tests, it received five stars for both front- and rear-seat occupants. The 2005 Escape earned an "Acceptable" rating (the second-highest) in frontal offset crash tests conducted by the IIHS. In IIHS side-impact tests, this small SUV earned a "Good" rating (the highest) when equipped with side airbags and a "Poor" rating (the worst) without the bags.

**Interior Design and Special Features:** The Mariner boasts a stylish interior with satin aluminum, chrome accents and a two-tone color scheme. The 60/40-split rear seat includes three-point seatbelts and head restraints for all three seating positions. There is 29 cubic feet of cargo space behind the rear seats, and you can fold them down to open up 66 cubic feet of capacity, a good figure for this class.

**Driving Impressions:** Fun to drive, the Mariner offers impressive road manners for a compact SUV. It drives much like a tautly suspended sedan, with little body roll and responsive steering. Mercury provides generous sound insulation, resulting in a surprisingly serene ride out on the open road. The V6 is quite powerful, providing swift acceleration, but fuel economy is mediocre. The standard 2.3-liter four-cylinder delivers adequate acceleration and better mileage than what you'd get with the V6.

*Crash Test Scores, see pg 530*
*Warranty information, see pg 542*

### Specifications

| Engine/Drivetrain | HP | Torque | EPA Fuel Economy Rating |
|---|---|---|---|
| 6cyl 3.0L A | 200 | 193 | 20 city/25 hwy |
| 4cyl 2.3L A | 153 | 152 | 22 city/26 hwy |

### Body Styles

| Style | MSRP Range |
|---|---|
| Compact SUV | $21,405–$26,405 |

# 2005 Mercury Montego

**Large Sedan**

**MSRP Price Range**

## $24,345 - $28,245

Destination Charge: $650 (all styles)

### Ratings

| | | |
|---|---|---|
| Consumer Rating | N/A | |
| Editors Rating | 8.1 | |

**What Edmunds.com says:** Roomy, stylish and practical, the Montego is well suited for family duty, but with its mediocre engine performance and interior materials, it's simply one of many solid choices in the under-$30,000 price bracket.

**Pros:** Spacious cabin, huge trunk, smooth ride quality, available all-wheel drive, plenty of safety features.

**Cons:** Mediocre engine performance, some low-grade interior materials, no stability control.

**What's New:** The Montego is an all-new premium family sedan built on the Volvo S80 platform. Both front- and all-wheel-drive versions are available.

**Body Styles, Trim Levels and Options:** The Montego sedan is available in one of two trims, Luxury and Premier. The Luxury starts you out with 17-inch wheels, a six-way power driver seat, full power accessories, air conditioning, a CD player, cruise control, HID headlamps, dual-zone automatic climate control, wood interior trim and air registers for rear passengers. Step up to the Premier and you'll get 18-inch wheels, leather upholstery, an eight-way driver and four-way power passenger seats, seat memory, an upgraded audio system, gray Zapelli wood grain trim and heated seats. Options include a moonroof, adjustable pedals and a reverse-sensing system.

**Powertrains and Performance:** Every Montego comes with Ford's 3.0-liter Duratec V6 rated for 203 horsepower and 207 pound-feet of torque. Buyers have two transmission choices. The first of these is a continuously variable transmission (CVT), which has an infinite number of ratios and chooses whichever one best fits a given situation. The other option is a six-speed automatic. Buyers must also decide between front-wheel drive and all-wheel drive. All front-drive Montegos come with the six-speed automatic, while AWD models get the CVT.

**Safety:** All Montegos come with a full set of disc brakes with ABS and Electronic Brakeforce Distribution. Optional on all models are side-impact airbags that protect front occupants' torsos and side curtain airbags that protect the heads of front and rear occupants. Traction control is standard on all Montegos, but stability control is not available. This car has not yet been crash tested.

**Interior Design and Special Features:** Scrutinize the cabin and it's apparent that designers put a lot of thought into creating an attractive and functional environment. In lieu of the shapeless dash and seats found in the Sable, the Montego has the crisp, clean lines and two-tone interior typical of European sedans. The front seats are roomy enough to fit most drivers, yet the cockpit has a snug, almost intimate feel. Rear passengers are treated to equally spacious quarters, making these cars good bets for families with teenagers. The rear seats fold flat in a 60/40 split and this, along with a fold-flat front-passenger seat, allows owners to carry items up to nine feet in length inside the car. Trunk capacity leads all sedans on the market at 21 cubic feet.

*Crash Test Scores, see pg 530*
*Warranty information, see pg 542*

### Specifications

| Engine/Drivetrain | HP | Torque | EPA Fuel Economy Rating |
|---|---|---|---|
| 6cyl 3.0L A | 203 | 207 | 21 city/29 hwy |

### Body Styles

| Style | MSRP Range |
|---|---|
| Large Sedan | $24,345–$28,245 |

**Driving Impressions:** The V6 provides enough low-end torque for easy city driving, and the car gets up to speed with minimal fuss. We do expect that eventual owners will wish for a little extra midrange torque for passing at highway speeds and climbing grades. Of the two transmissions, our preference is the CVT, which does a better job of keeping the engine in its power band. Thanks to its Volvo-engineered chassis, the Montego offers a pleasant balance between smooth ride quality and responsive handling. It's not the car to buy if you're looking for entertainment, but if you just want something capable and comfortable, the Montego should satisfy.

# 2005 Mercury Monterey

**MSRP Price Range**

## $29,010 - $34,910
Destination Charge: $685 (all styles)

### Ratings

| | | |
|---|---|---|
| Consumer Rating | N/A | |
| Editors Rating | 6.5 | |

**What Edmunds.com says:** Intended to provide a luxury minivan experience, the Monterey is both safe and stylish, but key omissions on the features list, an underachieving V6 and a general lack of refinement, make it less appealing than upscale vans from Chrysler, Honda and Toyota.

**Pros:** Extensive list of safety and convenience features, sharp interior design, torquey V6 engine.

**Cons:** Unimpressive fuel economy numbers, less horse-power than top competitors despite larger engine, lacks overall refinement and a few key features, expensive compared to similarly equipped peers.

**What's New:** Heated and cooled leather seats with perforated suede inserts are now standard on the Premier, while the AdvanceTrac stability control system and a liftgate spoiler are optional on both Luxury and Premier models. A power liftgate has been added to the options list of the Luxury, while all models can be equipped with Class I and Class II towing packages.

**Body Styles, Trim Levels and Options:** The Monterey comes in one size and three trim levels: Convenience, Luxury and top-of-the-line Premier. Standard equipment on the base-level Convenience version includes a tilt steering wheel, cruise control, dual-zone climate control, front console cupholders and storage, a fold-flat third-row bench and front and rear parking assist. All of the above comes standard on the Luxury model, along with first- and second-row leather trim; a leather-wrapped steering wheel with audio controls; power-adjustable pedals; memory for the driver seat, pedals and mirrors; an anti-theft system; side-impact and head curtain airbags; first-row floor console storage; third-row reading lamps; black roof rails; and dual power-sliding doors. On top of all of this, the Premier adds driver and passenger heated and cooled seats, front-passenger lumbar adjustment, first- and second-row leather seats with perforated suede inserts, automatic climate control, power liftgate and unique split-spoke design aluminum roof rails. Optional on both the Luxury and Premier are a rear DVD entertainment system and self-sealing tires.

**Powertrains and Performance:** The Monterey has just one available engine: a 4.2-liter V6 engine that delivers 201 horsepower and a generous 263 pound-feet of torque. The Monterey comes standard with a four-speed automatic transmission, and is capable of towing up to 3,500 pounds when properly equipped. EPA fuel estimates are 16 mpg city and 22 mpg highway, which is below average in the minivan segment.

**Safety:** Four-wheel antilock disc brakes with Electronic Brakeforce Distribution are standard on all Montereys. Available safety features include side curtain airbags that span all three rows of seating and the AdvanceTrac stability and traction control system, which also incorporates a panic brake assist feature. The Monterey earned five stars across the board in government crash tests, and picked up a "Good" rating (the highest), as well as a "Best Pick" designation, in 40-mph frontal offset crash testing by the IIHS.

**Interior Design and Special Features:** Mercury designers equipped the Monterey with a shapely dash and steering wheel, and the plastics are higher in quality than what was used in its predecessor—the result is a much more refined, classier-looking minivan. Still, if you look closely, some of the materials are still subpar for this segment. The fold-flat third-row seat allows for more flexible use of the interior space, but unfortunately, the seat folds only as a single piece, rather than allowing a 60/40-split.

**Driving Impressions:** With driving characteristics nearly identical to those of the Ford Free-star, the Monterey offers adequate power and a comfortable ride. Independent MacPherson struts up front and a semi-independent rear suspension provide satisfactory handling, but ride quality is not quite as composed as that of minivans with four-wheel independent suspensions. The torque-rich engine provides plenty of initial grunt, but runs out of breath at higher engine speeds and turns in disappointing fuel mileage.

*Crash Test Scores, see pg 530*
*Warranty information, see pg 542*

### Specifications

| Engine/Drivetrain | HP | Torque | EPA Fuel Economy Rating |
|---|---|---|---|
| 6cyl 4.2L A | 201 | 263 | 16 city/22 hwy |

### Body Styles

| Style | MSRP Range |
|---|---|
| **Midsize Minivan** | $29,010–$34,910 |

# 2005 Mercury Mountaineer

Midsize SUV

**MSRP Price Range**

## $29,685 - $38,530

Destination Charge: $645 (all styles)

## Ratings

| | | |
|---|---|---|
| Consumer Rating | N/A | |
| Editors Rating | 7.9 | |

**What Edmunds.com says:** Stylish and safe with seating for seven, the Mercury Mountaineer is a good bet for family shoppers who want a little bit of everything in their SUV.

**Pros:** Excellent ride and handling characteristics for a truck-based SUV, strong optional V8, comfortable cabin with user-friendly layout, good crash test scores.

**Cons:** Some low-grade materials, low resale value, confusing controls on high-line models, lousy fuel economy.

**What's New:** The AdvanceTrac stability control system has been improved with a new Roll Stability Control system and is now standard on all Mountaineers. A newly available Designer Series package includes suede interior trim, scuff plates and 17-inch chrome wheels. The roof rack has been redesigned, and now includes raised side rails. The 40/20/40-split second-row seat now has reclining outboard seats, and an eight-way power driver seat is available.

**Body Styles, Trim Levels and Options:** The Mountaineer is offered as a four-door SUV with three trim levels: Convenience, Luxury and Premier. Convenience is well equipped with such features as 16-inch alloy wheels, roof rails, a third-row seat, air conditioning, a CD player, cruise control and power windows, mirrors and locks. Leather upholstery and a rear air conditioner are optional on the base model. Luxury models receive 17-inch alloys, dual-zone automatic climate control, heated leather seats, an auto-dimming rearview mirror, power-adjustable pedals and power seating with driver-side memory. The top-of-the-line Premier adds a power sunroof, reverse-sensing system, side curtain airbags, unique exterior trim and an upgraded stereo with an in-dash CD changer. Notable options on the Luxury and Premier include a DVD entertainment system for rear-seat passengers and a quad seating option that sets you up with second-row captain's chairs.

**Powertrains and Performance:** As on the Explorer, the standard engine is a 4.0-liter single-overhead cam V6 good for 210 horsepower and 254 pound-feet of torque. An optional 4.6-liter V8 is rated for 239 hp and 282 lb-ft of torque. All-wheel drive is available with either engine. Properly equipped, a Mountaineer can tow up to 6,980 pounds.

**Safety:** Four-wheel antilock disc brakes and a tire-pressure monitor are standard on all models, along with the AdvanceTrac stability control system that now includes a Roll Stability Control feature to help lessen the chances of a rollover accident. Luxury and Premier models come with power-adjustable pedals, which are optional on Convenience models. Standard on the Premier and optional on other Mountaineers is a security group with a reverse-sensing system and a Safety Canopy System that adds side curtain airbags. In government crash tests, the Mountaineer received a four-star rating for the driver and a perfect five-star rating for the front passenger. In IIHS frontal offset crash testing, the Mountaineer earned a "Good" rating (the highest possible) and was named a "Best Pick."

**Interior Design and Special Features:** The interior is simple and straightforward in design, with room for seven adults and comfortable seats that offer a commanding view outward. Some controls are placed in odd locations and are difficult to use, and not all of the materials used in the cabin impart a sense of quality. With the third-row seat folded, the Mountaineer offers 44.5 cubic feet of cargo capacity; drop the second-row seats as well, and you've got 81.7 cubes at your disposal.

*Crash Test Scores, see pg 530*
*Warranty information, see pg 542*

## Specifications

| Engine/Drivetrain | HP | Torque | EPA Fuel Economy Rating |
|---|---|---|---|
| 8cyl 4.6L A | 239 | 282 | 15 city/20 hwy |
| 6cyl 4.0L A | 210 | 254 | 16 city/21 hwy |

## Body Styles

| Style | MSRP Range |
|---|---|
| Midsize SUV | $29,685–$38,530 |

**Driving Impressions:** More softly tuned than the Explorer, the Mountaineer is designed to spend far more of its time on the pavement than on the dirt. A four-wheel independent suspension gives the Mountaineer a firmly buttoned-down ride and keeps the tires in contact with the road surface even over rough bumps. Either engine is powerful enough to keep up with traffic, but the V8 is more refined and offers more grunt off the line. Handling is excellent, as the Mercury feels predictable and stable in corners and higher-speed turns.

**MSRP Price Range**

## $21,055 - $25,130
Destination Charge: $670 (all styles)

### Ratings

| | | |
|---|---|---|
| Consumer Rating | 9.0 | ████████████░ |
| Editors Rating | 5.5 | ███████░░░░░ |

**What Edmunds.com says:** No longer a top contender in the midsize car segment, the Sable is still a decent buy if a low initial price is more important to you than overall refinement and resale value.

**Pros:** Low price, above-average levels of safety and cabin space, available as a sedan or a wagon.

**Cons:** Low-grade interior materials; poor resale value; doesn't ride, handle or stop as well as other cars in its class.

**What's New:** The new model year brings few changes for the Sable. The model lineup has been simplified to GS and LS trims for sedans, and LS trim for the wagon. A CD player is now standard on the LS, along with wood trim and ABS. Oddly, power-adjustable pedals have been dropped altogether. Sable wagon production ends midyear, so if you can't find one at the Mercury dealership, consider buying its twin, the Ford Taurus wagon.

**Body Styles, Trim Levels and Options:** The Sable is available as a sedan or station wagon. Sedans can be ordered in GS or LS trim levels; the wagon is only available as an LS. The GS comes with remote keyless entry; air conditioning; cassette stereo; power windows, mirrors and locks; cruise control; a trip computer; and a front bench seat (allowing the car to seat six). The LS adds a keyless entry keypad on the driver door, body-color rearview mirrors with approach lamps, alloy wheels, perimeter alarm system and a stereo with a CD player. Additional LS features include a power driver seat, wood trim accents and front bucket seats with a center console and floor shifter. An available LS Premium package includes a cassette deck in place of the standard CD player, automatic climate control, leather seating and automatic headlamps. A Platinum Edition Feature Vehicle package is also available, and includes unique alloy wheels, satin aluminum finish interior trim, two-tone leather seating and monochromatic exterior trim. A CD changer is optional.

**Powertrains and Performance:** Engine choices include a 3.0-liter Vulcan V6 and a 3.0-liter Duratec V6. The main difference between the two is the cylinder head design; the base Vulcan has two valves per cylinder, while the Duratec has four. This greatly affects output and performance, as the base engine manages just 153 horsepower, while the heartier Duratec puts out 200 hp. Regardless of engine choice, the Sable comes standard with a four-speed automatic transmission. Fuel economy estimates for both engines are 20 mpg city and 27 mpg highway.

**Safety:** The Sable has earned a good reputation for safety, thanks to its solid performances in crash testing. Both the sedan and wagon earned a five-star rating for frontal crash testing and three stars for side impacts. The IIHS named the Sable a "Best Pick" after conducting its 40-mph frontal offset crash test. Side airbags for front occupants are optional on all models. ABS and traction control is standard on LS models, and optional on the GS. You can only get four-wheel disc brakes on wagons; sedans have rear drum brakes.

**Interior Design and Special Features:** Sable cabins have a dated look, but most controls are easy to find and use. The broad, flat seats aren't especially supportive but can accommodate occupants of all sizes. Carrying six passengers is a legitimate prospect if your Sable has the front bench seat. The front bench seat also includes a flip/fold center compartment with cupholders and storage cubbies. The sedan has a spacious 17-cubic-foot trunk. The wagon's rear-facing third-row seat can be used to carry two additional children. When it's not in use, you'll have 38.8 cubic feet of luggage space.

**Driving Impressions:** Both engines are noisier than most competing V6s, but the Duratec at least offers strong acceleration. Ride quality is generally comfortable, but can be harsh over more severe bumps and ruts. Braking distances are longer than those of most peers, and neither the suspension nor the steering is suited for brisk driving around corners.

*Crash Test Scores, see pg 530*
*Warranty information, see pg 542*

### Specifications

| Engine/Drivetrain | HP | Torque | EPA Fuel Economy Rating |
|---|---|---|---|
| 6cyl 3.0L A | 200 | 200 | 20 city/27 hwy |
| 6cyl 3.0L A | 155 | 185 | 20 city/28 hwy |

### Body Styles

| Style | MSRP Range |
|---|---|
| Midsize Sedan | $21,055–$24,020 |
| Midsize Wagon | $25,130 |

# 2005 MINI Cooper

**Compact Convertible, Coupe**

**MSRP Price Range**

## $16,449 - $24,400

Destination Charge: $550 (all styles)

### Ratings

| | | |
|---|---|---|
| Consumer Rating | 9.3 | |
| Editors Rating | 7.8 | |

**What Edmunds.com says:** Replete with British charm and German engineering, the born-again Mini Cooper is a stylish, affordable go-kart for adults.

**Pros:** It's a piece of history with modern underpinnings, BMW-engineered suspension and steering, chock-full of comfort and safety features, hatchback utility, free scheduled maintenance for three years/36,000 miles.

**Cons:** Not enough horsepower in base model, questionable seat comfort, not much room for passengers and cargo, some low-grade interior materials.

**What's New:** The big news for 2005 is the arrival of the convertible in both regular and S flavors. Stylish as ever, the drop-top Mini seats four and still has a trunk big enough for a few bags. Other changes include slightly revised front and rear fascias and some reworked option choices. The vanity mirrors are no longer illuminated, a universal remote transmitter is now available and a leather-wrapped steering wheel is now standard. The S version gains 5 horsepower and 7 pound-feet of torque, as well as an external temperature display. Both the five- and six-speed manual transmissions feature shorter gearing this year to improve acceleration. A six-speed automatic transmission will become available on the S versions later in the model year.

**Body Styles, Trim Levels and Options:** This endearing little bugger is available as either a three-door hatchback or a two-door convertible, and both are available in two versions—the Cooper and the Cooper S. The base Cooper is outfitted with 15-inch wheels, leatherette upholstery (cloth is a no-cost option), a tilt steering wheel, a centrally mounted speedometer, air conditioning with micron filtration, a six-speaker stereo with CD changer prewiring and power windows, locks and mirrors. The Cooper S adds 16-inch wheels with run-flat performance tires, seat-height adjustment and a leather-wrapped steering wheel; all of these features are available for the base car as well. The extensive options list includes a sport package, leather upholstery and a navigation system. A power-operated top is standard on all convertibles.

**Powertrains and Performance:** The base car is powered by a 1.6-liter inline four that makes 115 horsepower. This isn't much power by today's standards, but with only 2,300 pounds of car to propel, it's not dreadfully slow. A five-speed manual transmission is standard, and a continuously variable automatic transmission (CVT) with an automanual mode is optional. The sporty Cooper S is aided by a supercharger, allowing it to pump out 168 hp and 162 lb-ft of torque. A six-speed manual gearbox is standard, with a six-speed automatic optional. For those who need more performance, Mini offers the dealer-installed John Cooper Works package, which increases output to 200 hp and 177 lb-ft of torque.

**Safety:** All Minis come with four-wheel antilock disc brakes assisted by Electronic Brakeforce Distribution and Cornering Brake Control. The S model also includes traction control, and should you equip either model with the Sport Package, you'll get Dynamic Stability Control. Other standard safety features include a flat-tire monitor, side airbags for front occupants and head curtain airbags for the front and rear. The convertible version features fixed roll bars perched just behind the rear seat. In government crash tests, the Cooper hatchback earned four stars (out of five) for frontal impacts and four stars for side impacts involving front occupants. In IIHS frontal offset crash testing, the Cooper was named a "Best Pick" among small cars.

*Crash Test Scores, see pg 530*
*Warranty information, see pg 542*

**Interior Design and Special Features:** The Cooper's petite cabin looks stylish with its metallic trim, tubular structures and Frisbee-size speedometer in the center of the dash. Although everything looks good, some of the plastics used are low in quality. Passenger and cargo space is predictably tight—there's just 5.6 cubic feet of cargo capacity with the rear seats in use for the hatchback. Amazingly, the convertible has roughly the same amount of cargo space.

### Specifications

| Engine/Drivetrain | HP | Torque | EPA Fuel Economy Rating |
|---|---|---|---|
| 4cyl 1.6L M | 168 | 162 | 27 city/35 hwy |
| 4cyl 1.6L M | 115 | 111 | 28 city/36 hwy |

### Body Styles

| Style | MSRP Range |
|---|---|
| Compact Convertible | $20,950–$24,400 |
| Compact Coupe | $16,449–$19,899 |

**Driving Impressions:** You can expect lively handling from either Cooper, as the cars borrow suspension bits from the current BMW 3 Series. Additionally, the more performance-oriented Cooper S gets reinforced antiroll bars and firmer springs—its setup may be too stiff for some, but enthusiasts will love its tight reflexes around corners. Engine power is modest in both Coopers, but they get by just fine in traffic and the Cooper S loves to rev.

# 2005 Mitsubishi Eclipse

**MSRP Price Range**

## $19,449 - $25,849

Destination Charge: $595 (all styles)

## Ratings

| | | |
|---|---|---|
| Consumer Rating | N/A | |
| Editors Rating | 6.5 | |

**What Edmunds.com says:** More of a comfortable cruiser than a high-winding, apex-strafing sport coupe.

**Pros:** Comfortable ride quality, plenty of standard equipment, smooth V6 power in GT and GTS trim.

**Cons:** Sloppy handling compared to its competitors, uninspired interior design, side airbags and antilock brakes are available only on the GTS model.

**What's New:** New for 2005 is the REMIX Edition that features a unique shift knob and steering wheel, leather front seating surfaces, a 210-watt Infinity stereo with six-disc CD changer, 16-inch alloy wheels, chrome exhaust tip, color-keyed door mirrors and REMIX Edition badges. The base RS model has been dropped for 2005.

**Body Styles, Trim Levels and Options:** The Eclipse is offered in three trim levels: GS, GT and GTS. Standard equipment on every model includes power windows, mirrors and door locks; an anti-theft system; air conditioning; a height-adjustable driver seat; a CD player; auto-off headlights; and alloy wheels. Additional standard features include 16-inch wheels, a rear spoiler, cruise control, remote keyless entry and a split-folding rear seat. Next up is the GT, which adds 17-inch wheels, four-wheel disc brakes, ground effects, a chrome exhaust tip and foglights. The top-dog GTS packs a sunroof, leather seating surfaces, a power driver seat, rear window wiper and washer and a 210-watt, seven-speaker Infinity audio system with an in-dash CD changer. GS buyers can get many of these features by ordering the REMIX package, which adds a unique shift knob and steering wheel, leather, the aforementioned Infinity sound system (with CD changer), a chrome exhaust tip, color-keyed mirrors and REMIX Edition badges.

**Powertrains and Performance:** The GS model comes with a four-cylinder engine that displaces 2.4 liters and produces 147 horsepower (142 hp with the automatic). The GT model is equipped with a 3.0-liter V6 engine making 200 horsepower. The GTS is slightly more muscular than the GT, as it sports 210 horses. All models can be equipped with either a five-speed manual or four-speed automatic transmission with a sequential-shift Sportronic mode. The V6 delivers its power in a smooth manner that's great for cruising but a little lackluster when it comes to more spirited driving.

**Safety:** Three major safety features—antilock brakes, side airbags and traction control—are only available on the top trim level, the GTS. In the government crash tests, the Eclipse scored four (out of five) stars for driver and front-passenger protection in frontal impacts and five stars for side-impact protection.

**Interior Design and Special Features:** Featuring a symmetrical cockpit, the Eclipse's interior is dull in appearance and heavy on low-grade interior materials. There is a unique top-mounted display for the audio system, but you still have to look down to fiddle with the buttons on the stereo, so it doesn't help much. The front seats are softly padded, which is beneficial for long commutes, but more aggressive drivers will be begging for additional side support. Rear passengers will want more of just about everything, including headroom, legroom and thigh support.

**Driving Impressions:** Eclipses, particularly with the V6 engine, are pleasant to drive, thanks to a smooth power delivery and a compliant suspension. Power from the four-cylinder is certainly adequate, and the V6's torque curve makes it an easy car to drive around town and on the highway. In terms of handling, the car is better suited for cruising rather than hard driving. The suspension is softly tuned, and driver involvement is minimal.

*Crash Test Scores, see pg 530*
*Warranty information, see pg 542*

## Specifications

| Engine/Drivetrain | HP | Torque | EPA Fuel Economy Rating |
|---|---|---|---|
| 6cyl 3.0L A/M | 210 | 205 | 20 city/27 hwy |
| 6cyl 3.0L A/M | 200 | 205 | 20 city/27 hwy |
| 4cyl 2.4L M | 147 | 158 | 23 city/31 hwy |
| 4cyl 2.4L A | 142 | 155 | 21 city/28 hwy |

## Body Styles

| Style | MSRP Range |
|---|---|
| Compact Coupe | $19,449–$25,849 |

# Mitsubishi

# 2005 Mitsubishi Eclipse Spyder
### Compact Convertible

**MSRP Price Range**
## $24,899 - $30,699
Destination Charge: $595 (all styles)

## Ratings

| | | |
|---|---|---|
| Consumer Rating | 5.6 | |
| Editors Rating | 6.6 | |

**What Edmunds.com says:** A comfortable and affordable drop top, but those seeking real performance should look elsewhere.

**Pros:** Comfortable ride quality, smooth V6 power in GT trim, easy-to-use convertible top, minimal wind buffeting with the top down.

**Cons:** Sloppy handling compared to its competitors, uninspired interior design, intolerable rear seats, side airbags and antilock brakes are available only on GTS model.

**What's New:** New for 2005 is the REMIX Edition that features a unique shift knob and steering wheel, leather front seating surfaces, a six-disc CD changer, 16-inch alloy wheels, chrome exhaust tip, color-keyed door mirrors, alloy fuel door and REMIX Edition badge.

*Crash Test Scores, see pg 530*
*Warranty information, see pg 542*

## Specifications

| Engine/Drivetrain | HP | Torque | EPA Fuel Economy Rating |
|---|---|---|---|
| 6cyl 3.0L A/M | 210 | 205 | 20 city/28 hwy |
| 4cyl 2.4L M | 147 | 158 | 23 city/31 hwy |
| 4cyl 2.4L A | 142 | 155 | 21 city/28 hwy |

## Body Styles

| Style | MSRP Range |
|---|---|
| Compact Convertible | $24,899–$30,699 |

**Body Styles, Trim Levels and Options:** The Eclipse Spyder is offered in three trim levels: GS, GT and GTS. Standard equipment on the base GS includes a power-operated convertible top, 16-inch alloy wheels, air conditioning, a height-adjustable driver seat, adjustable lumbar support, a 210-watt Infinity stereo with a CD player, auto-off headlights, a rear spoiler, cruise control, keyless entry, an anti-theft system and power windows, mirrors and door locks. Next up is the GT, which adds a V6 engine, 17-inch wheels, four-wheel disc brakes, ground effects, a chrome exhaust tip and foglights. In addition to more power, the top dog GTS also packs leather seating surfaces, a power driver seat, an in-dash CD changer, ABS and side airbags. Leather upholstery is optional on the GS and GT. Also available on the GS model only is a special REMIX version that adds a unique shift knob and steering wheel, leather, the CD changer, 16-inch SXC alloy wheels, a chrome exhaust tip, color-keyed mirrors and REMIX Edition badges.

**Powertrains and Performance:** The GS model comes with a four-cylinder engine that displaces 2.4 liters and produces 147 horsepower (142 hp with the automatic). The GT model comes equipped with a 3.0-liter V6 engine making 200 hp. The GTS is slightly more muscular than the GT, as it sports 210 horses. All models can be equipped with either a five-speed manual or a four-speed automatic transmission (with a sequential-shift Sportronic mode). Equipped with either transmission, the V6 delivers its power in a smooth manner that's great for cruising but a little lackluster when it comes to more spirited driving.

**Safety:** Three major safety features, antilock brakes, side airbags and traction control are only available on the top trim level, the GTS. No crash test data is currently available for the Eclipse Spyder. However, in government crash testing, the coupe version of the Eclipse scored four (out of five) stars for driver and front-passenger protection in frontal impacts.

**Interior Design and Special Features:** Featuring a symmetrical cockpit design, the interior is dull in appearance and heavy on low-grade interior materials. At least the convertible top is simple to use; push the buttons in the two latches to release it, and then let the automatic mechanism take over. Once the top is in its well, you'll need to take some time to attach the soft tonneau cover for a finished look. The top includes a glass rear window with a defroster. The two-passenger backseat makes it possible to take the kids along for the ride, but families are apt to find the quarters cramped—convertible versions of the Chrysler PT Cruiser and Toyota Solara offer more room.

**Driving Impressions:** The Eclipse Spyder is generally pleasant to drive, thanks to a smooth power delivery and a compliant suspension. It may have a sporty image, but the Eclipse is better off cruising the highway than it is tearing up a twisty canyon road. Wind buffeting with the top down is kept well in check, so that long, open-air drives aren't a problem.

**MSRP Price Range**

## $25,399 - $33,199
Destination Charge: $595 (all styles)

### Ratings

| | | |
|---|---|---|
| Consumer Rating | N/A | |
| Editors Rating | 8.0 | |

**What Edmunds.com says:** A solid all-around package for those who crave non-traditional styling more than ultimate cargo- or people-toting capacity.

**Pros:** Rides like a car, roomy seating, torquey V6 power plant, solid build and materials quality, good crash test scores.

**Cons:** Less cargo capacity than the class leaders, polarizing interior design, no third-row seat available.

**What's New:** Following on the heels of a significant midyear refresh for 2004, there are few new features for this year. Side airbags are now standard on all models, and an anti-theft system is included on the XLS.

**Body Styles, Trim Levels and Options:** There are three trim levels: base LS, midlevel XLS and top-of-the-line Limited. The LS offers your typical standard features like power windows, locks and mirrors along with remote keyless entry, air conditioning and a 140-watt CD stereo; all-wheel-drive versions also get a full-size spare tire and towing preparation (both items are optional on 2WD models). The XLS adds a power driver seat, upgraded cloth upholstery and a 315-watt stereo with an in-dash six-disc CD changer. The Limited upgrades to leather upholstery and an automatic climate control system with separate rear controls. All trim levels offer an available towing package, while the XLS and Limited models offer additional options like a rear DVD entertainment system, a sunroof and heated seats and mirrors.

**Powertrains and Performance:** All Endeavors come with a 3.8-liter V6 coupled to a four-speed automatic transmission. Output is rated at 225 horsepower and a substantial 250 lb-ft of torque. Although many vehicles in this class offer substantially more horsepower, the Endeavor's ample torque gives it an equally powerful feel. Two-wheel-drive models are front-wheel drive, and all-wheel-drive models utilize a full-time system with a viscous center differential.

**Safety:** Antilock brakes are standard on all except the LS 2WD, on which they're optional. Side airbags for front occupants and a tire-pressure monitoring system are standard on all models. The Endeavor scored well in IIHS frontal offset crash testing, earning the top mark of "Good." In government crash tests, it earned a perfect five stars for driver protection in frontal impacts and four stars for the front passenger. The Mitsu scored five stars across the board for side-impact protection.

**Interior Design and Special Features:** A large center console dominates the interior, giving the Endeavor a slightly different look than most other sport-utes. In keeping with the exterior's bold and unique design, sporty faux metallic trim is used throughout the cabin. A small screen placed atop the dash provides vital radio, compass and climate information, but it doesn't support an optional navigation system. Like most other sport-utes in its class, the Endeavor uses a flip-up rear hatch along with a separate lift-glass for added convenience. Cargo capacity maxes out at 75 cubic feet, less than either the Honda Pilot's or Ford Explorer's.

**Driving Impressions:** Due to the Endeavor's impressive 250 lb-ft of torque, the 3.8-liter engine feels responsive off the line and into the midrange. The transmission can be a little slow to downshift on highway grades, but overall the Endeavor performs as well as most other vehicles in the class. Its car-based chassis provides a comfortable ride on the street and reasonably adept handling on mildly rutted dirt roads. The steering is a little slower to react than we'd like, but the weighting seems perfectly balanced for everyday errand running or commuting.

*Crash Test Scores, see pg 530*
*Warranty information, see pg 542*

### Specifications

| Engine/Drivetrain | HP | Torque | EPA Fuel Economy Rating |
|---|---|---|---|
| 6cyl 3.8L A | 225 | 250 | 17 city/23 hwy |

### Body Styles

| Style | MSRP Range |
|---|---|
| Midsize SUV | $25,399–$33,199 |

# 2005 Mitsubishi Galant

**Midsize Sedan**

**MSRP Price Range**
## $18,699 - $26,299
Destination Charge: $595 (all styles)

### Ratings

| | | |
|---|---|---|
| Consumer Rating | 6.0 | |
| Editors Rating | 7.7 | |

**What Edmunds.com says:** Roomy for four and enjoyable to drive, the Galant does without a few key features while sacrificing some practicality and refinement for the sake of style. Though unlikely to unseat any of the class leaders, it's still worth a look if you're not one to follow the crowd.

**Pros:** Excellent balance between ride quality and handling, strong V6, stylish and comfortable cockpit, roomy backseat, superb Infinity sound system.

**Cons:** No manual transmission or full side curtain airbags, some interior materials feel cheap, not enough storage areas, no folding rear seat.

**What's New:** The Galant receives seat-mounted side airbags with head protection as standard equipment on all models. A power driver seat with lumbar adjustment is now standard equipment on the LS. Rear floor heater ducts have been added, and Blackwood trim replaces Metal Mesh and Birdseye wood on the GTS.

**Body Styles, Trim Levels and Options:** The Galant is offered in four trim levels—DE, ES, LS and GTS. The DE comes with air conditioning; power windows, mirrors and locks; keyless entry; a 140-watt CD stereo; and a height-adjustable driver seat. The ES adds body-color exterior trim, cruise control, faux titanium trim and a couple extra speakers (for a total of six). The ES is eligible for the Diamond Package, which provides alloy wheels, a 270-watt Infinity stereo, an in-dash CD changer and faux titanium center stack controls with blue backlighting; and the Leather Package, which adds leather upholstery and a power driver seat. Next up the line is the LS; it offers much the same equipment and options as the ES, along with a V6 engine and a power driver seat. Spring for the loaded GTS and all of the above items are included, along with 17-inch wheels, projector-beam headlights, clear-lens taillights, a rear spoiler, a sunroof, white-faced gauges and Blackwood interior trim.

**Powertrains and Performance:** The DE and ES trims come with a 2.4-liter, four-cylinder engine good for 160 horsepower (155 hp in California). LS and GTS models come with a 3.8-liter V6 rated at 230 hp and 250 pound-feet of torque. A four-speed automatic transmission is standard on all Galants; V6 models get a manual-shift mode.

**Safety:** All models come with four-wheel disc brakes and side airbags with head protection (for front occupants). ABS with Electronic Brakeforce Distribution is standard on the LS and GTS and optional on the ES. Traction control is standard on the LS and GTS. In government crash tests, the Galant earned a perfect five stars across the board, except in the rear side-impact test in which it earned four stars. Frontal offset crash testing conducted by the IIHS resulted in an overall rating of "Good," the highest. IIHS side-impact testing resulted in a "Poor" rating (the lowest); however, the Galant tested did not have this year's side airbags.

**Interior Design and Special Features:** The interior is clean and contemporary, and bright blue backlighting gives it a distinctive look at night. Controls are easy to find and reach. The seats are softly cushioned and roomy, but some people may wish for firmer support. Trunk capacity is just 13.3 cubic feet, but the opening is wide. Although there is a ski pass-through, the rear seats do not fold.

**Driving Impressions:** The V6 comes through with plenty of torque, making it easy to execute passing maneuvers on the highway. Heavier than its competitors, though, the Galant doesn't feel quite as fast as the V6 Altima, nor is the power delivery as refined as that of the Accord or Camry. If you decide to go with the four-cylinder engine, you can expect adequate acceleration, but again, less refinement than you'd get in other import sedans. The Galant's ride and handling characteristics should please consumers looking for the best of both worlds—a quiet, comfortable ride on the highway, and agile handling around twists and turns.

*Crash Test Scores, see pg 530*
*Warranty information, see pg 542*

### Specifications

| Engine/Drivetrain | HP | Torque | EPA Fuel Economy Rating |
|---|---|---|---|
| 6cyl 3.8L A | 230 | 250 | 19 city/27 hwy |
| 4cyl 2.4L A | 160 | 157 | 23 city/30 hwy |

### Body Styles

| Style | MSRP Range |
|---|---|
| Midsize Sedan | $18,699–$26,299 |

For the latest full vehicle reports, visit www.edmunds.com/bginfopak

**MSRP Price Range**
## $13,999 - $19,099
Destination Charge: $575 (all styles)

### Ratings

| | | |
|---|---|---|
| Consumer Rating | N/A | |
| Editors Rating | 7.3 | |

**What Edmunds.com says:** A midpack player in base and O-Z Rally trim, the more powerful and fun-to-drive Ralliart model gives the Lancer the boost it needs to compete with the class leaders.

**Pros:** Spacious and nicely appointed interior, smooth power delivery, comfortable ride, spirited acceleration in Ralliart model.

**Cons:** Base engine lacks punch, ABS and side airbags not available on all models, small trunk.

**What's New:** The Sportback wagon, introduced just last year, has been discontinued for 2005. The LS sedan is also gone. The O-Z Rally receives newly designed O-Z racing wheels, and the ES Convenience package is upgraded with color-keyed mirrors, cruise control and intermittent wipers. The Sun & Sound package is now available on the O-Z Rally.

**Body Styles, Trim Levels and Options:** The Lancer is available in sedan form only. Trim levels include base ES, faux-sport O-Z Rally and true-sport Ralliart trim. ES sedans come with air conditioning; power windows, locks, and mirrors; a tilt steering wheel; simulated wood grain trim; a height-adjustable driver seat; and a 140-watt stereo with a CD player. The O-Z Rally sedan adds O-Z racing alloy wheels, ground effects, white-faced gauges, simulated carbon-fiber trim and embroidered floor mats. Top-of-the-line Ralliart models add fog lamps, lower body kit moldings, a sport grille, 16-inch alloy wheels, a tuned exhaust system, a sport suspension and sport seats. The ES can be equipped with a convenience package with keyless entry, a 60/40-split-folding rear seat, color-keyed exterior trim pieces and cruise control. O-Z Rally and Ralliart buyers can further upgrade with the Sun and Sound package, which provides a power sunroof, side airbags and a 315-watt Infinity stereo.

**Powertrains and Performance:** The ES and O-Z Rally sedans are powered by a 120-horse-power, 2.0-liter inline four-cylinder. The Ralliart sedan upgrades to a 2.4-liter engine tuned to produce 162 hp and 162 pound-feet of. A five-speed manual transmission is standard on all models, with a four-speed automatic available as an option.

**Safety:** Antilock brakes are standard on the Ralliart models, and not available on the ES or O-Z Rally. Side airbags are optional on the O-Z Rally and Ralliart sedans. In government crash testing, the Lancer scored four (out of five) stars for driver and front passenger protection in frontal impacts. In side-impact tests, the Lancer received two stars for front-occupant protection (without side airbags) and four stars for rear-occupant protection. In frontal offset crash testing conducted by the IIHS, the Lancer received a "Good" rating (the highest possible).

**Interior Design and Special Features:** The Lancer's interior is surprisingly stylish and constructed with quality materials. This car also has one of the roomiest cabins in its class. Rear-seat legroom, at 36.6 inches, is virtually equal to many larger midsize sedans. Ralliart models provide an all-black interior with carbonlike accents and sport bucket front seats.

**Driving Impressions:** Like its Galant sibling, the smooth-riding Lancer does a fine job of isolating passengers from nasty jolts on the roadway. Base models provide adequate power around town, but highway travel will make you wish you had more than 120 hp. With 162 horses to go around, the Ralliart model is much more enjoyable, especially when equipped with the slick-shifting five-speed manual. Although standard Lancers offer modest handling capability, the sport-tuned Ralliart model has sharper reflexes and is fun to drive.

*Crash Test Scores, see pg 530*
*Warranty information, see pg 542*

### Specifications

| Engine/Drivetrain | HP | Torque | EPA Fuel Economy Rating |
|---|---|---|---|
| 4cyl 2.4L A/M | 162 | 162 | 22 city/28 hwy |
| 4cyl 2.0L A/M | 120 | 130 | 25 city/31 hwy |

### Body Styles

| Style | MSRP Range |
|---|---|
| Compact Sedan | $13,999–$19,099 |

# 2005 Mitsubishi Lancer Evolution
### Compact Sedan

**MSRP Price Range**

## $27,629 - $34,199

Destination Charge: $575 (all styles)

### Ratings

| | | |
|---|---|---|
| Consumer Rating | N/A | |
| Editors Rating | 8.2 | |

**What Edmunds.com says:** The Evo has established itself as one of the most thrilling sedans on the market this side of an M5. If you're willing to sacrifice a little ride quality and interior ambience for all-out performance, the Evo is hard to beat.

**Pros:** One of the best-handling sedans available at any price, razor-sharp steering, ample turbocharged power, sophisticated all-wheel-drive system, stripped-down RS model offers serious bang for the buck.

**Cons:** Spartan interior, unforgiving highway ride, not much in the way of upscale amenities, no side airbags.

**What's New:** A new MR edition debuts that features a six-speed manual transmission, BBS one-piece forged alloy wheels, Bilstein shocks and an aluminum roof for a lower center of gravity. The all-wheel-drive system for all Evos now includes a front helical limited-slip differential and electronic active center differential (ACD). All models get a power boost of 5 horsepower and 13 pound-feet of torque. A larger cupholder is new this year, and all models get aluminum side-impact bars (to save weight). The standard Evo loses its HID headlamps (now optional), and all Evos lose the intercooler water spray feature (due to packaging for the ACD). The MR and RS get an aluminum roof panel, and the RS also gets thinner sheet metal in the deck lid (again, to save weight). Inside, all models get a revised meter cluster to include the ACD display.

*Crash Test Scores, see pg 530*
*Warranty information, see pg 542*

### Specifications

| Engine/Drivetrain | HP | Torque | EPA Fuel Economy Rating |
|---|---|---|---|
| 4cyl 2.0L M | 276 | 286 | 19 city/26 hwy |

### Body Styles

| Style | MSRP Range |
|---|---|
| Compact Sedan | $27,629–$34,199 |

**Body Styles, Trim Levels and Options:** The Lancer Evolution is available in three trims: RS, standard and MR Edition. The standard Evo offers features such as 17-inch wheels; air conditioning; power windows, mirrors and locks; a CD player; and a tilt steering wheel. The RS edition is essentially a stripped-down iteration of the standard car, and deletes ABS and power windows and locks, but adds HID headlights, additional gauges and unique trim, along with thinner sheet metal and aluminum panels to save weight. The MR includes Bilstein shocks, BBS wheels, exclusive trim pieces and unique badging. Options include leather seating, a 315-watt Infinity sound system, a power sunroof and a carbon-fiber rear spoiler.

**Powertrains and Performance:** All Evos come with a turbocharged and intercooled DOHC 2.0-liter inline four conservatively rated at an impressive 276 horsepower and 286 pound-feet of torque. Power is delivered via a five-speed manual transmission on base and RS models, and a six-speed unit in the MR. An automatic transmission is not available. Standard on every Evo is a full-time all-wheel-drive system with an adjustable active center differential and limited-slip front and rear differentials. Expect 0-to-60 times of around 5.7 seconds. Braking is achieved through a Brembo system that uses 12.6-inch ventilated front discs with four-piston calipers and 11.8-inch ventilated discs and two-piston calipers out back. There is also a Sports ABS system that works in combination with Electronic Brakeforce Distribution to provide stopping power on par with the world's best sports cars.

**Safety:** The standard version of the Evo includes ABS; however, this feature is deleted on the RS and MR. Side airbags are not available. In NHTSA frontal crash tests, the standard Lancer received four out of five stars for protection of the driver and front passenger. Side-impact tests resulted in a subpar two-star rating for front passenger protection and four stars for rear passengers. In IIHS frontal offset crash testing, the Lancer earned the top rating of "Good" and was named a "Best Pick."

**Interior Design and Special Features:** Inside, the Evolution lives up to its race-winning image with well-bolstered Recaro seats. A thick-rimmed, leather-covered, Momo steering wheel and large, easy-to-read gauges help keep the driver focused on the task at hand. Gauges glow red and are illuminated at all times to insure they remain legible day or night. The shifter is covered with leather and offers a short throw to accommodate the free-revving engine.

**Driving Impressions:** With its ultraquick steering and race-tuned suspension, few cars can match the Lancer Evolution's bang for the buck. The learning curve is as short as they come given that the car reacts with quick, predictable movements at every turn. Of course, at day's end the firm suspension can take its toll on your backside. This, along with the lack of cruise control, makes the Evo less than ideal for road trips, but its all-out performance nature will surely attract enthusiasts with a need for speed. The engine suffers almost no turbo lag and pulls hard from almost any rpm.

**MSRP Price Range**

## $35,799

Destination Charge: N/A (all styles)

### Ratings

| | | |
|---|---|---|
| Consumer Rating | N/A | |
| Editors Rating | 6.3 | |

**What Edmunds.com says:** An old-school sport-ute that excels off-road, but when it comes to overall performance and passenger-carrying ability, it can't match its more modern rivals.

**Pros:** High-quality interior materials, sharp cabin design, large cargo capacity, excellent off-road capability.

**Cons:** Serious lack of power compared to rivals, mediocre on-road handling, cramped third-row seat, no side curtain airbags.

**What's New:** The Montero receives new 17-inch painted alloy wheels this year.

**Body Styles, Trim Levels and Options:** The four-door Montero comes in Limited trim only. Standard equipment includes leather upholstery, a 315-watt Infinity audio system with a CD changer, 17-inch alloy wheels, power-adjustable front seats, a sunroof, a trip computer, automatic climate control and a leather-and-wood steering wheel. A DVD entertainment system is optional, which deletes the standard six-disc CD changer and sunroof.

**Powertrains and Performance:** The only engine available on the Montero is a 3.8-liter V6 that generates 215 hp and 248 lb-ft of torque. It's matched to a five-speed automatic transmission with "Sportronic" shifting that allows manual gear selection. Mitsubishi's "ActiveTrac" four-wheel-drive system comes standard and offers both full- or part-time operation. The Montero's 5,000-pound towing capacity is modest compared to V8-powered midsizers like the Dodge Durango and Ford Explorer.

**Safety:** Antilock brakes with Electronic Brakeforce Distribution (EBD) and a stability control system are standard. Side airbags for front occupants are also included, but full-length side curtain airbags are not available. Frontal crash testing conducted by the NHTSA returned a four-star (out of five) rating for the driver, and three stars for the passenger. Side-impact testing resulted in a perfect five-star rating, front and rear. In frontal offset crash testing, the Montero earned an "Acceptable" rating (second highest) from the Insurance Institute for Highway Safety.

**Interior Design and Special Features:** Although the overall design is a bit dated, quality materials give the Montero's cabin a rugged, upscale feel. Maximum cargo capacity is a solid 91.7 cubic feet. A third-row seat is standard, though its flat cushioning and shortage of legroom limit its use to carrying small children. An optional entertainment system is available for rear passengers' amusement.

**Driving Impressions:** On the road, the Montero's suspension is firm enough to keep it under control during evasive maneuvers, but don't expect carlike handling. The dual-wishbone front and multilink rear suspension results in an overall feel that is soft and forgiving, but minor road irregularities can transmit a surprising amount of harshness throughout the otherwise isolated cabin. The Montero's off-road prowess is exceptional. Whether it's rugged washboard pathways, fast fire roads or technical rock-strewn riverbeds, this truck never flinches as it stays the course.

*Crash Test Scores, see pg 530*
*Warranty information, see pg 542*

### Specifications

| Engine/Drivetrain | HP | Torque | EPA Fuel Economy Rating |
|---|---|---|---|
| 6cyl 3.8L A | 215 | 248 | 15 city/19 hwy |

### Body Styles

| Style | MSRP Range |
|---|---|
| Large SUV | $35,799 |

# 2005 Mitsubishi Outlander

**MSRP Price Range**

## $17,799 - $25,179

Destination Charge: $720 (all styles)

### Ratings

| | | |
|---|---|---|
| Consumer Rating | N/A | |
| Editors Rating | 7.6 | |

**What Edmunds.com says:** With its unique looks, pleasant handling characteristics and roomy, user-friendly interior, Mitsubishi's compact SUV has no trouble winning over its share of fans.

**Pros:** Roomy and functional interior, comfortable ride, peppy around town, solid handling.

**Cons:** Could use some more power, less cargo capacity than competitors, ABS limited to the most expensive models.

**What's New:** The Outlander now offers a manual transmission on the base LS model. A new Limited trim line debuts, and all models feature slightly revised rear styling. Standard equipment enhancements on all Outlanders include advanced airbags and four-wheel disc brakes. Leather-trimmed seats are standard on the Limited, and both the XLS and Limited ride on 17-inch alloy wheels.

*Crash Test Scores, see pg 530*
*Warranty information, see pg 542*

### Specifications

| Engine/Drivetrain | HP | Torque | EPA Fuel Economy Rating |
|---|---|---|---|
| 4cyl 2.4L A/M | 160 | 162 | 21 city/27 hwy |

### Body Styles

| Style | MSRP Range |
|---|---|
| Midsize SUV | $17,799–$25,179 |

**Body Styles, Trim Levels and Options:** The Outlander is a compact four-door SUV offered in three trims. The base LS is well equipped with the usual array of power windows, locks and mirrors; AM/FM/CD stereo; air conditioning; a tilt steering wheel; cruise control; and 16-inch wheels. Stepping up to the XLS trim level adds a two-tone color scheme, white-faced gauges, an auto-dimming rearview mirror and upgraded cloth upholstery. The Limited adds unique interior and exterior trim enhancements, as well as leather seating.

**Powertrains and Performance:** Every Outlander comes with a 2.4-liter, four-cylinder engine rated at 160 horsepower and 162 pound-feet of torque. A five-speed manual transmission is standard on the LS. Optional on the LS and standard on all other models is a four-speed automatic with Sportronic that allows manual gear changes by moving the shift lever into a separate gate. Outlanders can be had with either front-wheel drive or all-wheel drive.

**Safety:** Antilock brakes are optional only on the XLS AWD, and standard on the Limited AWD. Daytime running lights are standard on all models. In government crash tests, the Outlander received four out of five stars for driver and front passenger protection in a frontal collision. Side-impact tests resulted in a five-star rating for front passenger protection and a four-star rating for rear passengers. In frontal offset tests conducted by the IIHS, the Outlander received an overall rating of "Good" (its highest). It received a "Poor" rating (the lowest) from the IIHS for side-impact protection on models without side airbags.

**Interior Design and Special Features:** The cabin's overall look is clean and functional, with deeply recessed gauges and easy-to-reach three-dial climate controls. Extensive use of soft-touch materials adds an upscale, comfortable feel, while numerous storage bins and map pockets keep it practical. The two-tone color scheme and faux metal accents look great, but the optional leather upholstery isn't quite as impressive. Maximum cargo capacity is 60 cubic feet.

**Driving Impressions:** The 2.4-liter engine has enough power to give the small sport-ute a quick start in traffic and keep it humming along on the highway. The engine is sufficiently refined and high-rpm passing maneuvers, though not especially quick, don't elicit much racket from under the hood. The automatic transmission's shift points are perfectly acceptable in the normal drive mode, but for those who like to have a little bit more control, the automanual mode works well. If you want total control, get an LS model with the manual gearbox. Driven on tight winding roads and wide-open highways, the Outlander proves to be a very competent and comfortable handler. It drives more like a car than an SUV, with only moderate body roll and a solid feel for the road.

For the latest full vehicle reports, visit www.edmunds.com/bginfopak

**MSRP Price Range**
## $26,500 - $37,550
Destination Charge: $560 (all styles)

### Ratings

| | | |
|---|---|---|
| Consumer Rating | 8.7 | |
| Editors Rating | 7.8 | |

**What Edmunds.com says:** Nissan's crown jewel. For the money, this is one of the best performance buys on the market.

**Pros:** Smooth and powerful V6 engine, excellent handling, available drop-top version, a bargain compared to anything that can run with it.

**Cons:** Rough ride on Track model, some low-grade interior materials, lack of luggage space, poor rearward visibility.

**What's New:** Enhancements for 2005 include a standard tire-pressure monitor, heated outside mirrors and a driver-seat height adjuster for both front and rear portions of the bottom cushion. Clutch pedal effort has been reduced this year, and the five-speed automatic transmission now features downshift rev matching. The navigation system has a faster processor for improved route calculation times. A special 35th Anniversary edition includes 18-inch alloy wheels, Brembo brakes, front chin spoiler, rear spoiler, available two-tone leather seats and a choice of three exterior colors, including a new Ultra Yellow. A slight bump in horsepower is also part of the package.

**Body Styles, Trim Levels and Options:** The 350Z is available as both a two-seat coupe and a roadster. The coupe comes in base, Enthusiast, Performance, Touring and Track versions, while the roadster is limited to Enthusiast and Touring trim levels. Base models come with items like an automatic climate control system with air conditioning; 17-inch alloys; power windows, locks and mirrors; a tire-pressure monitor; a CD player; and remote keyless entry. Going with an Enthusiast model sets you up with high-intensity discharge headlights, cruise control, traction control, an auto-dimming rearview mirror, a limited-slip rear differential and, on the roadster, a power-operated soft top and wind deflector. Performance models add Vehicle Dynamic Control (VDC) and 18-inch wheels. For even more performance, the Track model has front and rear spoilers, 18-inch lightweight wheels and upgraded brakes. The Touring model offers an upgraded audio system, power and heated seats, leather upholstery and, on the roadster only, side airbags. A special 35th Anniversary edition includes 18-inch alloys, Brembo brakes, available two-tone leather and a slight bump in horsepower. The Touring version of the roadster is eligible for unique Burnt Orange leather seats with net inserts that allow the driver to literally feel the breeze on his back.

**Powertrains and Performance:** The front-engine, rear-drive 350Z features a strong and flexible 3.5-liter V6. Similar to the engines found in the Nissan Maxima and Altima 3.5 SE, the Z's engine has variable valve timing and an electronically controlled throttle. It makes 287 horsepower and 274 pound-feet of torque, enough to propel the Z to 60 miles per hour in just 5.6 seconds. A six-speed close-ratio manual transmission is standard, and a five-speed automatic with downshift rev matching is available.

**Safety:** Four-wheel ventilated disc brakes with ABS are standard on all models; the Track model gets an upgraded set of four-piston Brembo calipers and larger rotors. Side and head-protecting side curtain airbags are optional on all coupes. Regular side airbags are standard on Touring roadsters and optional on Enthusiast versions.

**Interior Design and Special Features:** Inside, the contemporarily styled body is a driver-oriented cabin that combines both classic and cutting-edge designs. The instrument panel features three gauge pods similar to the original 240Z, while a rear suspension brace resides prominently in the cargo area. While this brace certainly improves body rigidity, it also compromises valuable luggage space. All of the controls a driver might need are close at hand, but some of the materials used in the cockpit seem low-grade for this price range.

**Driving Impressions:** There's nothing special or gimmicky about getting started—just turn the key, buckle your seatbelt and go. Around town, the V6 is quite docile, and the clutch isn't overly stiff. Open it up a bit, and the dual-exhaust pipes produce an enjoyable and throaty V6 growl. Power delivery is linear and athletic, with the most fun coming on around 4,000 rpm. During cornering, outright grip is high, and the car feels well balanced. Overall, the car offers handling equal to some of the best sports cars available.

*Crash Test Scores, see pg 530*
*Warranty information, see pg 542*

### Specifications

| Engine/Drivetrain | HP | Torque | EPA Fuel Economy Rating |
|---|---|---|---|
| 6cyl 3.5L A/M | 287 | 274 | 19 city/26 hwy |

### Body Styles

| Style | MSRP Range |
|---|---|
| **Compact Convertible** | $34,150–$37,550 |
| **Compact Coupe** | $26,500–$34,300 |

# 2005 Nissan Altima

Midsize Sedan

**MSRP Price Range**

***$17,250 - $29,200***

Destination Charge: $560 (all styles)

## Ratings

| | | |
|---|---|---|
| Consumer Rating | 9.1 | |
| Editors Rating | 7.7 | |

**What Edmunds.com says:** Once a frumpy wallflower, the Altima is now a midsize sedan to be desired, especially when equipped with the 250-horsepower V6.

**Pros:** Sports car power in a midsize sedan body, excellent handling, roomy and comfortable interior, high level of features, distinctive styling.

**Cons:** Considerable road noise, overboosted steering, no stability control, ABS still an extra-cost option.

**What's New:** All Altimas receives exterior styling enhancements, including new smoked headlamps and taillights, new wheel designs and a restyled front fascia and grille, along with a much needed interior redesign. The 3.5-liter V6 gets five more horsepower and three more lb-ft of torque, for a total of 250 and 249, respectively, and is now available with a five-speed automatic transmission. A new performance-oriented SE-R model joins the lineup along with a leather-lined 3.5 SL model. A newly optional DVD-based navigation system and two new exterior colors round out the changes.

**Body Styles, Trim Levels and Options:** Six models are offered: the base 2.5, 2.5 S, 2.5 S with SL Package, 3.5 SE, 3.5 SL and SE-R. The 2.5 is a bare-bones model with few features. The S adds air conditioning; cruise control; a stereo with a CD player; power windows, locks and mirrors; and keyless entry. SL upgrades include leather seating, trip computer, power driver seat, security system and a Bose audio system with an in-dash six-disc CD changer and steering wheel controls. The 3.5 SE isn't as loaded as the SL trims, but has a few more features than the S, such as a trip computer and V6 engine. The sporty SE-R gets new gauges, dark chrome trim, leather-trimmed sport seats and xenon headlights. Options include a leather seating, a Bose audio system, high-intensity discharge (HID) headlights, a power sunroof and a DVD-based navigation system—most are bundled together in pricey packages.

**Powertrains and Performance:** The 2.5 models are powered by a 2.5-liter inline four-cylinder engine, while the 3.5 SE, 3.5 SL and SE-R have a 3.5-liter V6. The four-cylinder engine puts out 175 horsepower and 180 pound-feet of torque, while the V6 cranks out 250 horses and 249 lb-ft of twist. The SE-R model uses minor engine enhancements that push horsepower and torque to 260 and 251, respectively. The 2.5 models qualify as Partial-credit Zero Emissions Vehicle (PZEV) in California emissions states, but said designation reduces horsepower to 170 and torque to 175 lb-ft. Transmission choices include a five-speed manual (six-speed on SE-R only), and either a four or five-speed automatic, depending on model.

**Safety:** The Altima offers optional side-impact airbags and head-protecting side curtain airbags. Other features include standard four-wheel disc brakes and optional antilock brakes (standard on V6 automatic models). Traction control is optional on V6 automatic models only. In government crash tests, the Altima received four stars (out of five) for driver and front-passenger protection in frontal impacts. Side-impact scores (on cars without side airbags) are three stars for front-seat occupants and four stars for rear-seat riders. In frontal offset crash testing conducted by the IIHS, the Altima received an overall rating of "Good," the best ranking possible.

**Interior Design and Special Features:** The dashboard features a sporty three-pod instrument layout and an uncluttered center stack. Thoughtful features include a tilt-and-telescoping steering wheel and, on higher-end models, a trip computer and steering wheel-mounted audio controls. Last year's sea-of-plastic interior has been finessed with a new instrument panel, three-spoke steering wheel, center console, trim finishes, seat upholstery and headliner. Both the front and rear seats are comfortable and roomy, and the trunk has a generous 15.6-cubic-foot capacity.

**Driving Impressions:** Both engines render the Altima fun to drive, and its capable suspension gives the Nissan a more sporting character than most family sedans. True enthusiasts will want to check out the SE-R performance model as it offers the most aggressively tuned suspension and additional power.

***Crash Test Scores, see pg 530***
***Warranty information, see pg 542***

## Specifications

| Engine/Drivetrain | HP | Torque | EPA Fuel Economy Rating |
|---|---|---|---|
| 6cyl 3.5L A/M | 260 | 251 | 20 city/30 hwy |
| 6cyl 3.5L A/M | 250 | 249 | 20 city/30 hwy |
| 4cyl 2.5L A/M | 175 | 180 | 23 city/29 hwy |

## Body Styles

| Style | MSRP Range |
|---|---|
| Midsize Sedan | $17,250-$29,200 |

# 2005 Nissan Armada

**MSRP Price Range**

## $33,600 - $41,500
Destination Charge: $650 (all styles)

### Ratings

| | | |
|---|---|---|
| Consumer Rating | N/A | |
| Editors Rating | 7.9 | |

**What Edmunds.com says:** Other than its odd proportions, the Armada sizes up favorably with its domestic competition on nearly every front.

**Pros:** Spacious interior, monster motor, lots of storage areas up front, fold-flat third-row seat, comfortable ride quality around town, solid tow rating.

**Cons:** Leather seats not as comfortable as their cloth counterparts, dismal fuel mileage, cumbersome to park.

**What's New:** For 2005, the Armada receives active head restraints and seatbelt pre-tensioners for the first row, a unique wheel finish for SE models and metallic interior accent trim for all models. A power liftgate has been added to the SE Sunroof Package while a new RearView Monitor is now included in the Technology Package.

**Body Styles, Trim Levels and Options:** The Armada is available only as a four-door SUV. There are two trim levels: SE and LE, both of which are available with either two- or four-wheel drive. Base SEs come standard with 18-inch alloy wheels, a body-color grille, cloth seating, second- and third-row seat bench seats, full-length side curtain airbags, a tire-pressure monitoring system, power-adjustable pedals, rear parking sensors, an eight-speaker stereo with an in-dash CD changer and an auto-dimming rearview mirror. The SE can be equipped with the Off-Road Package, which adds Rancho shocks, a lower final drive ratio, 17-inch wheels and all-terrain tires, foglights and skid plates; or the Tow Package, which in addition to trailering preparation, provides a self-leveling rear suspension. The high-line LE model offers a chrome grille, heated leather seats, a power driver seat with memory, second-row bucket seats, seat-mounted side airbags for front occupants and an upgraded 10-speaker Bose audio system. The leather upholstery, side airbags and Bose stereo can all be added to the SE, while a sunroof and a rear DVD entertainment system are optional on both models. Options exclusive to the LE include a power rear liftgate, a DVD-based navigation system and dual-zone automatic climate control.

**Powertrains and Performance:** All Armadas come with a 5.6-liter V8 paired with a five-speed automatic transmission. Rated at 305 horsepower and 385 pound-feet of torque, the Endurance V8 uses dual-overhead cams and a variable intake manifold to produce a broad band of power and an impressive 9,100-pound maximum tow rating. Four-wheel-drive models use a push-button transfer case with dual-range gears.

**Safety:** The Armada comes standard with four-wheel antilock disc brakes, electronic stability control, rear parking sensors and side curtain airbags that protect all three rows of passengers. A vehicle rollover sensor will deploy the side curtain airbags when it senses an imminent rollover accident. Seat-mounted side airbags for front occupants are optional on the SE and standard on the LE. The Armada has not been crash tested.

**Interior Design and Special Features:** The Armada offers seating for up to eight passengers and easy-to-use, fold-flat second and third-row seats. There's plenty of storage space up front and an unprecedented number of overhead storage bins. A DVD-based navigation system is optional, as is a rear-seat DVD entertainment system and a rear power liftgate. With both the second- and third-row seats folded flat, there's 97.1 cubic feet of cargo space.

**Driving Impressions:** While the powerful V8 does give the Armada a "light on its feet" feel when accelerating, the massive girth of this truck is obvious when cornering or coming to an abrupt stop. Still, ride quality is smooth and comfortable on the highway, and the well-weighted steering makes the Armada easy enough to maneuver in everyday driving situations. The big V8 has a nice throaty rumble when pressed and at the same time delivers smooth power on par with Toyota's iForce V8.

*Crash Test Scores, see pg 530*
*Warranty information, see pg 542*

### Specifications

| Engine/Drivetrain | HP | Torque | EPA Fuel Economy Rating |
|---|---|---|---|
| 8cyl 5.6L A | 305 | 385 | 13 city/19 hwy |

### Body Styles

| Style | MSRP Range |
|---|---|
| Large SUV | $33,600–$41,500 |

# 2005 Nissan Frontier

**MSRP Price Range**

*N/A*

Destination Charge: N/A (all styles)

## Ratings

| | | |
|---|---|---|
| Consumer Rating | N/A | |
| Editors Rating | 7.5 | |

**What Edmunds.com says:** Thanks to its Titan under-pinnings and powerful V6, the new Frontier is right up there with the compact pickup class leaders in terms of performance, comfort and utility.

**Pros:** Class-leading V6 engine, larger size for improved passenger and cargo room, innovative bed features, advanced off-road systems.

**Cons:** Fewer model options than competitors, average interior materials.

**What's New:** The Frontier is all new for 2005. Changes include a new and more powerful V6, two new trans-missions, advanced off-road systems and a larger size for better passenger comfort.

**Body Styles, Trim Levels and Options:** The Frontier comes in two body styles—extended cab (known as King Cab) and crew cab. Available trim levels include the base S model and uplevel SE. The base S comes with only basic amenities, along with front bucket seats and fold-ing rear jump seats. The SE adds more features, including air conditioning; a CD stereo; power windows, locks and mirrors; alloy wheels; and cruise control. Leather upholstery and a 300-watt Rockford Fosgate stereo are optional. Compared to the King Cab, the Crew Cab has a larger cabin with expanded rear-seat accommodations as well as a pair of conventional rear doors that offer easier access to those seats.

**Powertrains and Performance:** A 2.5-liter DOHC inline four-cylinder engine is standard on the base Frontier King Cab model. A 4.0-liter V6, which produces a stout 265 hp and 284 lb-ft of torque, is standard in all other models. The V6 design includes Continuous Valve Timing Control (C-VTC) and Nissan variable Induction Control System (NICS). Transmission choices include a standard six-speed manual gearbox and an optional five-speed automatic. Frontier 4x4 models include a shift-on-the-fly four-wheel-drive system with 2Hi/4Hi/4Lo modes oper-ated by an electronically controlled, part-time transfer case.

**Safety:** Four-wheel disc antilock brakes are standard on all Frontiers. Optional are front-seat side-impact airbags and curtain airbags that provide side-impact and rollover protection for front and rear outboard passengers. The Frontier has not yet been crash tested.

**Interior Design and Special Features:** The Frontier's cabin offers straightforward controls, comfortable front seats and an attractive design. The larger overall size results in much improved passenger room, but the overall materials quality is still average. Like the Titan, the Frontier offers a utility bed package that includes a factory-applied spray-in bedliner and the Utili-track tie-down system. The Utili-track system provides cargo hauling flexibility through the use of five special "C" cross-section rails mounted in the bed (two channels in the bed floor, and one each on the bed side rails and the bed header panel). Removable utility cleats slide into the channels, providing a wide range of attachment points for securing cargo. In addition to the tie-down cleats, a full range of accessories are offered for use with the channel system, including bed dividers, sliding cargo trays, modular storage units and bike racks.

**Driving Impressions:** The newfound power of the V6 Frontier is a far cry from the wheezy en-gines of last year's model. Step on the throttle in this truck and you get instant results, thanks to plenty of low-end torque and well-tuned transmissions. Ride and handling is improved as well; although, it's still a bit bouncy as you might expect from a compact truck. Advanced off-road systems like downhill assist control and hill start assist make off-road models capable performers in the rough stuff.

*Crash Test Scores, see pg 530*
*Warranty information, see pg 542*

## Specifications

| Engine/Drivetrain | HP | Torque | EPA Fuel Economy Rating |
|---|---|---|---|
| 4cyl 2.5L A/M | 154 | 173 | N/A |
| 6cyl 4.0L A/M | 265 | 284 | N/A |

## Body Styles

| Style | MSRP Range |
|---|---|
| Compact Truck | N/A |

**MSRP Price Range**
## $27,100 - $29,350
Destination Charge: $560 (all styles)

### Ratings

| | | |
|---|---|---|
| Consumer Rating | 9.5 | |
| Editors Rating | 8.0 | |

**What Edmunds.com says:** Although it's more upscale than before, the Maxima remains one of the best combinations of performance, luxury and value in the midsize sedan segment.

**Pros:** Roomy interior, lots of upscale options, sweet V6, available with a manual transmission.

**Cons:** So-so center stack ergonomics, premium price without the premium nameplate.

**What's New:** Improved manual transmission shift feel (thanks to a shorter shift stroke), black-tone brake calipers, additional chrome accents inside and new softer leather upholstery. Auto-dimming outside mirrors are now available, and a new 12-volt power point resides at the base of the center stack.

**Body Styles, Trim Levels and Options:** The Maxima is offered in 3.5 SL or 3.5 SE trim. The SE is a sportier version with slightly stiffer suspension and 18-inch wheels on the outside and a metallic-trimmed interior on the inside. It's loaded with standard features that include an eight-speaker CD stereo, side impact airbags, one-touch up/down front windows and keyless entry. The more luxurious SL sports wood trim, heated leather seats, a 320-watt Bose audio system and xenon headlights, just to name a few. The optional Elite Package affixes even more luxury to the Maxima by changing the rear-seating area into a more comfortable two-passenger setup. This package adds a rear center console that features controls for the seat heaters as well as a switch to operate the power rear sunshade. Additional options on both models include a DVD-based navigation system and XM or Sirius Satellite Radio.

**Powertrains and Performance:** The Maxima still sports the same award-winning, 24-valve, 3.5-liter V6 engine as in previous editions, but now that engine is good for 265 horsepower. More importantly, the Maxima offers 15 horsepower more than the V6 Altima. The 3.5 SE is available with a six-speed manual transmission or a five-speed automatic; the SL comes only with the automatic.

**Safety:** The Maxima offers four-wheel disc brakes with ABS, BrakeAssist and Electronic Brakeforce Distribution. All Maximas with an automatic transmission have the option of adding an electronic stability and traction control system. A torque-sensitive limited-slip differential is optional when you select the six-speed manual in order to provide additional traction during cornering maneuvers or slippery conditions. Side airbags and head curtain airbags (front and rear) are standard as are foglights and cornering lights.

**Interior Design and Special Features:** Inside, the Maxima's vast interior seems downright cavernous. The five-passenger version provides wide and supportive front seats, but finding an optimal driving position can be difficult even with the eight-way power-adjustable seat. While the dashboard features a sleek, modern design, its functionality is spotty as most of the buttons are the same size, shape and color, making it hard to figure out how to operate certain features without consulting the manual and/or taking your eyes off the road.

**Driving Impressions:** Although the suspension provides a comfortable ride, it lacks a true performance feel that you might expect from this self-proclaimed sport sedan. Ride quality, at least, is smooth and comfortable. The steering is communicative and well weighted, but there are other midsize sedans that provide a better feel for the road. The brakes are strong and easy to modulate. Acceleration is strong at any speed, regardless of which transmission you choose.

*Crash Test Scores, see pg 530*
*Warranty information, see pg 542*

### Specifications

| Engine/Drivetrain | HP | Torque | EPA Fuel Economy Rating |
|---|---|---|---|
| 6cyl 3.5L A/M | 265 | 255 | 20 city/28 hwy |

### Body Styles

| Style | MSRP Range |
|---|---|
| Midsize Sedan | $27,100–$29,350 |

# 2005 Nissan Murano

**MSRP Price Range**

## $26,850 - $30,900

Destination Charge: N/A (all styles)

### Ratings

| | | |
|---|---|---|
| Consumer Rating | N/A | |
| Editors Rating | 8.1 | |

**What Edmunds.com says:** The Murano is a likable crossover SUV that blends unique styling with a spacious, comfortable interior and a fun-to-drive character. If it wasn't for the power-sapping CVT transmission, it would get our top recommendation.

**Pros:** Sharp handling, strong standard engine, comfortable and practical interior.

**Cons:** Continuously variable transmission detracts from performance, SE model rides harshly, no third-row seat.

**What's New:** For 2005, the Murano receives a rollover sensor for the side curtain airbags, and a new S model with fewer features and a lower price. New options packages and an Intelligent Key entry and ignition system are newly available.

*Crash Test Scores, see pg 530*
*Warranty information, see pg 542*

### Specifications

| Engine/Drivetrain | HP | Torque | EPA Fuel Economy Rating |
|---|---|---|---|
| 6cyl 3.5L A | 245 | 246 | 20 city/24 hwy |

### Body Styles

| Style | MSRP Range |
|---|---|
| Midsize SUV | $26,850 - $30,900 |

**Body Styles, Trim Levels and Options:** The five-passenger Murano comes in three trim levels: base S, luxury-oriented SL and sporty SE. The S trim includes 18-inch wheels, cloth seating, dual-zone climate control, a CD player and steering wheel-mounted audio controls. The SL adds a cargo cover and net, and a 10-way power driver seat with power lumbar. The SE adds a sport-tuned suspension and HID headlamps. The optional Premium Package includes a roof rack, adjustable pedals, a Bose stereo system with a six-disc CD changer, while the Dynamic Control Package adds a tire-pressure monitoring system and stability control. Other stand-alone options include a sunroof and a DVD-based navigation system.

**Powertrains and Performance:** Available with front- or all-wheel drive, the Murano is powered by a 3.5-liter DOHC V6 similar to the one found in the Altima and Maxima. It makes 245 horsepower and 246 pound-feet of torque. The sole transmission choice is a continuously variable transmission (CVT). Benefits of the CVT include smoother operation and greater fuel efficiency than a traditional automatic.

**Safety:** The Murano comes with a comprehensive list of standard safety features, including front seat-mounted side airbags, head-protecting side curtain airbags for all outboard occupants and active head restraints. Additional safety features include an optional stability control system (dubbed Vehicle Dynamic Control), a traction control system and four-wheel antilock disc brakes supplemented by BrakeAssist and Electronic Brakeforce Distribution. In government crash tests, the Murano earned four stars (out of five) for driver and front-passenger protection in frontal impacts. In side-impact testing, it earned five stars for front-occupant protection and four stars for the rear. Testing conducted by the IIHS returned a top-rating of "Good" for offset frontal impacts

**Interior Design and Special Features:** Immediately noticeable when you climb aboard is the distinctive "floating dash" design, which is complemented by the real aluminum trim liberally sprinkled around the cabin. The gauges glow orange and are clearly marked. Split-folding rear seats are pretty standard these days, but in the Murano, they have a reclining feature and a remote flip-down function, allowing the seats to be easily released from the rear cargo area. For storage, there's a two-tiered lockable center console box roomy enough to hold a laptop computer, door pockets with a flip-out function, as well as assorted nooks and crannies for items such as cell phones, sunglasses and coins. With the rear seats down, the cargo bay offers a healthy 81.6 cubic feet of space.

**Driving Impressions:** Acceleration is lively for the most part, though the CVT can make for sluggish starts in traffic. Handling is sharp, even compared to other car-based crossover SUVS. Buyers can choose between the sport-tuned SE model or the more softly calibrated SL form. Unless you're really into driving your SUV fast on a curvy road, we'd suggest the SL for day-to-day comfort.

# 2005 Nissan Pathfinder

**MSRP Price Range**
## $24,650 - $34,750
Destination Charge: $560 (all styles)

### Ratings

| | | |
|---|---|---|
| Consumer Rating | N/A | |
| Editors Rating | 7.4 | |

**What Edmunds.com says:** An excellent blend of off-road toughness and everyday comfort, but its concessions toward true backcountry capability might turn off those who want the image more than anything else.

**Pros:** Most powerful V6 in the class, above average off-road ability, well-laid-out interior, flexible seating design, ample storage space throughout.

**Cons:** Tight rear-seat accommodations, on-road handling not as refined as car-based competitors, some odd interior materials.

**What's New:** The Pathfinder has been completely redesigned for 2005 and now includes third-row seating and a larger, more powerful V6.

**Body Styles, Trim Levels and Options:** The four-door Pathfinder offers four levels of trim to suit varying desires for simplicity or luxury. The base XE puts together the usual list of expected amenities like 16-inch alloy wheels power accessories, keyless entry, a CD stereo and cloth seating for seven. The SE adds slightly larger tires, foglights and a power-adjustable driver seat, in addition to a longer options list. A new SE Off-Road trim comes standard with heavy-duty Rancho shocks, underbody skid plates and even larger tires than the standard SE. The top-of-the-line LE is upgraded with upscale amenities like 17-inch wheels, a sunroof, heated leather seating, a Bose audio system and both side-impact and head curtain airbags. Optional items include a DVD-based navigation system and a rear-seat DVD entertainment system.

**Powertrains and Performance:** The Pathfinder is powered by a 4.0-liter DOHC V6 engine. It makes a stout 270 horsepower and 291 pound-feet of torque. A five-speed automatic is the only transmission and both two- and four-wheel-drive versions are offered. Four-wheel-drive models feature advanced traction systems like Hill Descent Control (HDC), Hill Start Assist (HSA) and electronic limited-slip control that give the Pathfinder excellent off-road ability.

**Safety:** The Pathfinder comes standard with stability control and antilock front disc/rear drum brakes supplemented by Electronic Brakeforce Distribution and BrakeAssist. LE models come standard with side airbags for front occupants and side curtain airbags that protect all three rows. These are optional on all other models. The new Pathfinder has not yet been crash tested.

**Interior Design and Special Features:** The new Pathfinder's larger overall size allows for more passenger room in the first and second rows, while fold-flat seats give it a maximum cargo capacity of 79.2 cubic feet—slightly more than the 4Runner but a little bit less than the Explorer. There's plenty of space up front for the driver and front passenger, but the second-row seats are snug when it comes to toe and shoulder room. As in most midsize SUVs, the Pathfinder's two-passenger third-row seat isn't adult-friendly. The cargo area features a segment exclusive "easy clean" surface that makes it suitable for wet or muddy items—it can be hosed out for quick cleaning.

**Driving Impressions:** The V6 provides ample power for just about any type of driving. Body motions are well controlled, the steering is nicely weighted and road irregularities are soaked up with little cabin intrusion. Interior noise levels are low, too, with minimal howl from even the optional off-road tires. The Pathfinder fumbles a bit over bumps and responds to inputs at a slightly slower pace than before, but only those who are intimately familiar with the previous model are apt to notice the difference. Compared to other vehicles in the class, it's a commendable setup that few will find fault with.

*Crash Test Scores, see pg 530*
*Warranty information, see pg 542*

### Specifications

| Engine/Drivetrain | HP | Torque | EPA Fuel Economy Rating |
|---|---|---|---|
| 6cyl 4.0L A | 270 | 291 | 16 city/23 hwy |

### Body Styles

| Style | MSRP Range |
|---|---|
| Midsize SUV | $24,650–$34,750 |

# 2005 Nissan Quest

**Large Minivan**

**MSRP Price Range**
## $23,350 - $32,250
Destination Charge: $560 (all styles)

### Ratings

| | | |
|---|---|---|
| Consumer Rating | N/A | |
| Editors Rating | 8.0 | |

**What Edmunds.com says:** With its non-traditional sheet metal, innovative features and strong V6 engine, the Quest provides a stylish alternative to the class-leading Honda Odyssey and Toyota Sienna, but can't match their level of refinement or user-friendly nature.

**Pros:** Flat-folding rear seats, head airbag protection for all occupants, smooth 240-horse V6, innovative roof system.

**Cons:** Inconvenient control layout, some low-grade plastics, third-row seat isn't split-folding, can't get a second-row bench seat.

**What's New:** Revisions to the Quest for 2005 include adjustable armrests for the leather-appointed front seats, a standard roof rack on the 3.5 S and new active front head restraints on all trims. Satellite radio is now available, and the theft-deterrent system is now standard on all models. The S also receives a power-sliding passenger-side door, power liftgate, power rear-quarter windows and a reverse-sensing system. Bose audio has been added to the Leather package on the 3.5 SL. The SL also receives the five-speed automatic transmission as standard equipment. A new low-priced base model debuts this year, slotted just below the S.

**Body Styles, Trim Levels and Options:** The Quest comes in four trim levels—3.5 base, 3.5 S, 3.5 SL and 3.5 SE. The base model comes standard with 16-inch wheels, cloth upholstery, auto up/down front windows, cruise control, remote keyless entry, front and side curtain airbags, a tire-pressure monitoring system and an eight-speaker AM/FM/CD stereo. The S adds a power-sliding passenger-side door, power liftgate, power rear quarter windows and a reverse-sensing system. The midlevel SL adds alloy wheels, an eight-way power driver seat, steering wheel and rear-seat audio controls, an auto-dimming rearview mirror and power-adjustable pedals. Top-of-the-line SEs are further upgraded with 17-inch wheels, leather seating, dual power-sliding doors, automatic headlights, a power front passenger seat, a 10-speaker Bose audio system with an in-dash CD changer and fixed skylights over the rear-seating area. Available options include a rear DVD entertainment system (dual screen on the SE) and a DVD-based navigation system.

**Powertrains and Performance:** Power is provided by a 3.5-liter V6 engine rated for 240 horsepower. Two transmissions are available—a four-speed automatic on the base and S, and a five-speed automatic on the SL and SE models. Although the five-speed tranny provides better acceleration, the four-speed's lower gearing allows it to achieve slightly better fuel economy: EPA estimates are 19 mpg city/26 mpg highway with the four-speed and 18 city/25 highway with the five-speed.

**Safety:** Four-wheel antilock brakes, full-length side curtain airbags, BrakeAssist, Electronic Brakeforce Distribution and traction control come standard on all Quests. An electronic stability control system comes standard on SE models along with side-impact airbags for front occupants; the airbags are optional on the midlevel SL. In government crash testing, the Quest earned a perfect five stars across the board. In frontal offset crash testing conducted by the IIHS, the Quest received a rating of "Good" (the highest).

**Interior Design and Special Features:** Inside, the Quest provides seating for seven passengers. Nissan's minivan offers flat-folding seats for both the second and third rows—a segment "must-have" these days. Maximum cargo capacity measures 149 cubic feet on base, S and SL models (144 on the SE). Interesting features include a center-mounted instrument cluster built below a 6.3-inch information display screen designed to provide stereo and climate controls right at your fingertips. Unfortunately, the myriad of buttons look too similar and can be difficult to use while driving. The SE model comes with Skyview windows—five fixed rectangular openings cut into the Quest's roof to give the rear-seating area an open feel.

**Driving Impressions:** While the V6 engine feels powerful around town and on the highway, the five-speed automatic makes a noticeable difference in how that power is delivered and is a worthwhile upgrade. The Quest is a willing player in the corners, but overall ride and handling are a few steps behind the class-leading Odyssey.

*Crash Test Scores, see pg 530*
*Warranty information, see pg 542*

### Specifications

| Engine/Drivetrain | HP | Torque | EPA Fuel Economy Rating |
|---|---|---|---|
| 6cyl 3.5L A | 240 | 242 | 19 city/26 hwy |

### Body Styles

| Style | MSRP Range |
|---|---|
| Large Minivan | $23,350–$32,250 |

For the latest full vehicle reports, visit www.edmunds.com/bginfopak

# 2005 Nissan Sentra

## Ratings

| | | |
|---|---|---|
| Consumer Rating | 8.9 | ▭ |
| Editors Rating | 6.9 | ▭ |

**What Edmunds.com says:** Packed with features, the Sentra offers a lot for the money, but a cramped rear seat and an aging interior design leave it a step behind the competition.

**Pros:** Functional cabin design, powerful 2.5-liter engine, nimble handling, lots of standard features.

**Cons:** Generic styling, small backseat, SE-R Spec V model commands premium price.

**What's New:** The base 1.8 model receives the body-colored door handles and upper instrument panel storage bin from the upper-level models. A trip computer and cruise control are now included on the 1.8 S, and all models receive new seat fabrics. There's also a new color for the gauge cluster housing on the SE-R, and a new shift knob for the SE-R Spec V.

**Body Styles, Trim Levels and Options:** There are five Sentra models available—1.8, 1.8 S, 2.5 S, SE-R and SE-R Spec V. The 1.8 is truly an economy car as it offers only the most basic features. Moving up to the 1.8 S scores you power windows, locks and mirrors; remote keyless entry; a split-folding rear seat; cruise control; a trip computer; air conditioning; an eight-way adjustable driver seat; and a CD stereo. Along with a larger engine, the 2.5 S adds an upgraded stereo, a vehicle security system and side airbags. The base SE-R performance model features larger 16-inch wheels, foglights and a rear spoiler, while the top-line SE-R Spec V gets even larger 17-inch wheels, sport seats and optional Brembo brakes.

**Powertrains and Performance:** The base 1.8 and 1.8 S both use a 126-horsepower, 1.8-liter, four-cylinder engine. The 1.8-liter makes most of its torque at low engine speeds, resulting in spirited in-town response. All 1.8 and 1.8 S models sold in California emissions states earn squeaky-clean SULEV status. The 2.5 S and SE-R models use a larger 2.5-liter engine that makes 165 hp and 170 lb-ft of torque. The Spec V bumps those figures to 175 and 180, respectively. The 1.8 and 1.8 S come standard with a five-speed manual transmission. A four-speed automatic is standard on the 2.5 S and SE-R and optional on the 1.8 and 1.8 S. The high-strung SE-R Spec V packs an exclusive six-speed manual only.

**Safety:** The 1.8 and 1.8 S have front disc/rear drum brakes, while the remaining trim levels have discs all around. ABS and front seat-mounted side airbags are standard on the 2.5 S; they're optional on everything else, except the 1.8. In NHTSA testing, the Sentra earned four stars (out of a possible five) for driver and front-passenger protection in frontal impacts. The IIHS gave the car an "Acceptable" (second highest) score for its performance in the 40-mph frontal offset crash test.

**Interior Design and Special Features:** The front seats are comfortable for most drivers, and the dash is laid out in a clean fashion, making it easy to find and use the controls. The cabin imparts a comfortable if not upscale feel, but the cramped rear seats put the squeeze on even average-size passengers. Trunk space is listed at 11.6 cubic feet, placing it near the bottom of the compact sedan segment.

**Driving Impressions:** In 1.8 and 1.8 S trim, there is little to get excited about in terms of the driving experience, but there's enough power for daily commutes and errands. The 2.5 S and SE-R models add serious power that makes the Sentra one of the fastest cars in its class. The upgraded suspension on the SE-R and Spec V makes for a bumpier ride on the highway, but enthusiast drivers will appreciate the improved cornering ability. In general, the Sentra is more fun to drive than most economy cars, but you have to step up to at least the 2.5 S model to get the full effect.

*Crash Test Scores, see pg 530*
*Warranty information, see pg 542*

## Specifications

| Engine/Drivetrain | HP | Torque | EPA Fuel Economy Rating |
|---|---|---|---|
| 4cyl 2.5L M | 175 | 180 | 23 city/29 hwy |
| 4cyl 2.5L A | 165 | 175 | 23 city/28 hwy |
| 4cyl 1.8L A/M | 126 | 129 | 28 city/35 hwy |

## Body Styles

| Style | MSRP Range |
|---|---|
| Compact Sedan | $12,600–$17,700 |

# Nissan
# 2005 Nissan Titan

**MSRP Price Range**
## $22,650 - $35,100
Destination Charge: $650 (all styles)

## Ratings

| | | |
|---|---|---|
| Consumer Rating | N/A | ▬▬▬▬▬▬▬▬ |
| Editors Rating | 8.3 | ▬▬▬▬▬▬▬ |

**What Edmunds.com says:** With a stout V8, roomy interior and loads of innovative and useful features, the Titan is an impressive full-size that every truck buyer should consider.

**Pros:** One of the best drivetrains in its class, smooth-riding suspension, spacious and functional cabin, innovative design features, available stability control and side airbags.

**Cons:** Limited drivetrain and body style choices, no heavy-duty models, burly exhaust note can get annoying on long drives.

**What's New:** Crew cab models receive a standard power up/down rear window with defroster, while all models get a tailgate with dampended assist. Other changes include new active head restraints for the driver and front passenger, new badging on the front doors and a unique wheel finish for SE models. The LE receives brushed aluminum interior trim accents and a leather-appointed bench seat is available in place of the buckets. The popular spray-in bedliner is now available as a stand-alone option on the XE.

*Crash Test Scores, see pg 530*
*Warranty information, see pg 542*

## Specifications

| Engine/Drivetrain | HP | Torque | EPA Fuel Economy Rating |
|---|---|---|---|
| 8cyl 5.6L A | 305 | 379 | 14 city/19 hwy |

## Body Styles

| Style | MSRP Range |
|---|---|
| Crew Cab Pickup Truck | $25,500–$35,100 |
| Extended Cab Pickup Truck | $22,650–$32,300 |

**Body Styles, Trim Levels and Options:** There are just two body styles: an extended cab (King Cab) with a 6-foot-5-inch bed and a crew cab with a 5-foot-5 bed. Both are available in two- or four-wheel-drive configurations and three trim levels: XE, SE and LE. Base XE models come well equipped with air conditioning, cruise control, a 40/20/40-split bench seat and a CD stereo. The midgrade SE adds captain's chairs and a flow-through center console, along with power windows, locks and mirrors; keyless entry; an overhead console; and chrome trim for the exterior. Top-of-the-line LE models add power-adjustable leather seats, a Rockford Fosgate audio system, power-adjustable pedals, an auto-dimming rearview mirror with integrated compass and garage door opener, tubular side steps and a utility package for the bed. Notable options include a DVD-based navigation system, a DVD rear entertainment system, a sunroof and the first ever factory-applied spray-in bedliner. There's also an off-road package that includes Rancho shocks, heavy-duty skid plates, lower differential gears, BFGoodrich all-terrain tires and a push-button rear locking differential. A tow package adds a heavy-duty radiator, upgraded springs, extending tow mirrors and an electronic stability/traction control system.

**Powertrains and Performance:** The Titan offers only one drivetrain combination: an all-aluminum 5.6-liter V8 hooked to a five-speed automatic transmission. The V8 is rated at 305 hp and 379 lb-ft of torque thanks to advanced features like dual-overhead cams and a variable intake system that provides 90 percent of its available torque at 2,500 rpm. With the optional tow package, the Titan is rated to pull up to 9,500 pounds. The standard five-speed automatic transmission features a tow/haul mode for handling heavy loads. Four-wheel-drive models get a part-time transfer case with ultralow gearing.

**Safety:** Standard safety features include a tire-pressure monitoring system and four-wheel antilock disc brakes with Electronic Brakeforce Distribution and BrakeAssist. Seat-mounted side-impact airbags and roof-mounted side curtain airbags are also available on all models while electronic stability control can be added to SE and LE trim levels.

**Interior Design and Special Features:** The Titan features a spacious and functional interior design with easy-to-use controls and numerous storage bins. SE and LE trim levels offer captain's chairs with a floor-mounted transmission shifter and a flow-through center console (a bench seat with a column shifter is standard on base models and optional on the SE). The rear load floor is flat for hauling large items inside the cab, and the rear doors on extended cab models open 180 degrees for easier access. Crew cab models feature a standard power up/down rear window with defroster.

**Driving Impressions:** A tightly controlled ride and a gutsy engine make the Titan feel smaller than you might think. The five-speed transmission keeps the engine in the heart of its power band for strong acceleration that rivals any of its competitors. Strong brakes and solid road feel further contribute to the Titan's ability to handle everything from heavy loads to daily errand-running.

# 2005 Nissan Xterra

**Body Styles, Trim Levels and Options:** The four-door Xterra is available in three trim levels—S, Off-Road and SE, all of which are offered in both two- and four-wheel drive. The base S comes with basic features like air conditioning, a tilt steering wheel and a CD player. The Off-Road model includes high-performance gas shocks, off-road tires on alloy wheels and special exterior trim. The SE includes power windows, locks and mirrors; cruise control; and upgraded interior trim. A 300-watt Rockford Fosgate audio system with nine speakers, MP3 capability and steering wheel controls is optional.

**Powertrains and Performance:** All Xterra models feature a 4.0-liter V6 that includes electronic throttle control (with secondary mapping in low-range mode on 4WD models), continuous valve timing control (C-VTC) and Nissan's variable Induction Control System (NICS). This engine makes 265 hp and over 284 lb-ft of torque, generous figures for this class. A six-speed manual transmission is standard, with a five-speed automatic optional. Four-wheel-drive versions use a multimode transfer case that offers 2WD and automatic 4WD modes, in addition to low-range gearing, for maximum flexibility in varying conditions.

**Safety:** All Xterras have four-wheel antilock disc brakes fortified with Electronic Brakeforce Distribution and BrakeAssist. Side-impact airbags (for front occupants) and full-length side curtain airbags are optional, as is Vehicle Dynamic Control (VDC), Nissan's stability control system. The Xterra has not yet been crash tested.

**Interior Design and Special Features:** The interior favors function over form, and the ergonomics are solid. The cargo area is highlighted by an easy-to-clean floor and a total of 10 cargo area utility hooks—six on the floor/sides and four on the ceiling and sides (floor hooks can carry up to 110 pounds). A new adjustable channel system in the cargo floor, similar in design to the Utili-track system offered on the Titan and Frontier pickups, makes it easier to secure bike racks and other accessories or gear. There's also an available built-in first-aid kit and space to securely carry up to one-gallon jugs.

**Driving Impressions:** With more than enough power under the hood, the Xterra is no longer plagued by sluggish performance on the street. Its truck chassis still doesn't deliver the sharp handling that a car chassis would, but it's an acceptable trade-off, given its above-average off-road prowess. If you never plan on leaving the street, there are certainly better compact SUVs on the market, but if weekend adventures call your name often, the Xterra is now a much more capable and willing participant than ever before.

## MSRP Price Range
### N/A
Destination Charge: N/A (all styles)

### Ratings

| | | |
|---|---|---|
| Consumer Rating | N/A | |
| Editors Rating | 7.5 | |

**What Edmunds.com says:** With newfound power under the hood, a more refined suspension underneath and more passenger space inside, Nissan addresses all the shortcomings of the previous Xterra without taking away any of the appealing attitude that made it a hit in the first place.

**Pros:** One of the most powerful V6s in the class, above average off-road capability, solid passenger room, innovative cargo features.

**Cons:** Still not what we would call refined on the street, a few instances of low-grade interior materials.

**What's New:** The Xterra has been fully redesigned for 2005 with a new platform, a more powerful V6 and a more spacious interior.

*Crash Test Scores, see pg 530*
*Warranty information, see pg 542*

### Specifications

| Engine/Drivetrain | HP | Torque | EPA Fuel Economy Rating |
|---|---|---|---|
| 6cyl 4.0L A/M | 265 | 284 | N/A |

### Body Styles

| Style | MSRP Range |
|---|---|
| Midsize SUV | N/A |

# 2005 Pontiac Aztek

**Midsize SUV**

**MSRP Price Range**

## $21,375 - $24,290

Destination Charge: $685 (all styles)

### Ratings

| | | |
|---|---|---|
| Consumer Rating | 8.5 | |
| Editors Rating | 6.8 | |

**What Edmunds.com says:** Although functional as a minivan/sport-utility crossover, the Aztek's ungainly handling and weak engine make it hard to recommend over more refined wagons and sport-utes.

**Pros:** Versatile interior, available all-wheel drive.

**Cons:** Some cheap interior materials, poor visibility, awkward styling.

**What's New:** No major changes for the Aztek.

**Body Styles, Trim Levels and Options:** The Aztek offers just one body style and two basic configurations—front-wheel drive or all-wheel drive. From there, three major options packages can be specified for varying degrees of features. The base package offers air conditioning, power windows and door locks and a CD player. Choose another package to add cruise control, carpeted floor mats, multiple cargo tie-downs and storage nets and a removable console cooler. The top-level package decks out the Aztek with a premium cloth interior, a trip computer, an overhead console, a tire inflation monitoring system, the OnStar communications system, a six-way power driver seat, steering wheel audio controls, a slide-out rear cargo tray and a theft deterrent system. Notable options include a DVD entertainment system, heated front seats, leather upholstery, XM Satellite Radio, a six-disc CD changer and a sunroof.

**Powertrains and Performance:** The Aztek gives you a choice of either the standard front-wheel-drive model or an upgraded all-wheel-drive version. Both are powered by GM's tried-and-true 3.4-liter V6 that produces 185 horsepower and is backed by a four-speed automatic transmission. The Aztek is rated to pull 3,500 pounds with the optional trailer-towing option that includes heavy-duty engine cooling, a high-output alternator and an auto-leveling rear suspension.

**Safety:** ABS is optional on front-wheel-drive Azteks, and standard on all-wheel-drive models. The National Highway Traffic Safety Administration gave the Aztek three stars for driver protection and four stars for front-passenger protection in its frontal impact crash test. The Insurance Institute for Highway Safety gave the Aztek a rating of "Marginal," the second lowest out of four, after conducting its offset frontal impact test.

**Interior Design and Special Features:** Two seating configurations are offered—front bucket seats with a choice of a three-passenger 50/50-split bench seat or dual captain's chairs in the second row. The rear 50/50-split bench is of a lightweight modular design that can be folded, flipped forward or removed to create extra room. The Aztek has a wide, low and flat cargo floor with 93.5 cubic feet of storage when the rear seats are removed. Drop the tailgate and the Aztek can accommodate four full sheets of 3/4-inch plywood. A dozen cargo anchors, a rear convenience net and storage areas built into the side trim and tailgate help keep track of loose ends.

*Crash Test Scores, see pg 530*
*Warranty information, see pg 542*

**Driving Impressions:** While its sporty exterior conveys a sense of performance, the Aztek's minivan-derived hardware underneath doesn't back it up. The suspension delivers a soft, forgiving ride over harsh surfaces, but on smoother pavement it feels floaty. Body roll is excessive in turns and the steering provides little feedback. The V6 engine has solid off-the-line power, but it drops off quickly thereafter.

### Specifications

| Engine/Drivetrain | HP | Torque | EPA Fuel Economy Rating |
|---|---|---|---|
| 6cyl 3.4L A | 185 | 210 | 19 city/26 hwy |

### Body Styles

| Style | MSRP Range |
|---|---|
| Midsize SUV | $21,375–$24,290 |

For the latest full vehicle reports, visit www.edmunds.com/bginfopak

# 2005 Pontiac Bonneville

**MSRP Price Range**

## *$27,775 - $35,395*

Destination Charge: $725 (all styles)

## Ratings

| | | |
|---|---|---|
| Consumer Rating | 8.7 | |
| Editors Rating | 7.5 | |

**What Edmunds.com says:** If traditional Pontiac styling twists your crank, and you want a large sedan packed with performance and features, the Bonneville is your kind of ride. However, the rear-drive Chrysler 300 offers a better package overall.

**Pros:** Loads of gee-whiz features, solid handling, powerful V8 in GXP, excellent crash test scores, large trunk.

**Cons:** Average interior materials, overly complicated controls, poor resale value.

**What's New:** The OnStar communications system is now standard on all Bonnevilles.

**Body Styles, Trim Levels and Options:** Three models are available: SE, SLE and GXP The base SE comes nicely equipped with 16-inch wheels and tires; four-wheel disc brakes with ABS; keyless entry; a six-way power-adjustable driver seat; power windows, mirrors and door locks; a six-speaker AM/FM/CD stereo; and a tire-pressure monitor. The midlevel SLE adds a programmable driver information center, a leather-wrapped steering wheel with satellite stereo controls, traction control and 17-inch aluminum wheels. The top-level GXP loads up the standard equipment list with 18-inch wheels, a sport-tuned suspension, dual-zone climate control, leather/suede upholstery, carbon-fiber trim, a power front-passenger seat and a high-powered Monsoon audio system. Satellite radio is optional on all models.

**Powertrains and Performance:** Standard on the SE and SLE is GM's 3800 Series II V6 that not only pumps out 205 horsepower through a four-speed automatic transmission, but also can get an impressive 29 miles per gallon on the highway. Move to the GXP and you get a vigorous 275 hp and 300 pound-feet of torque from a 4.46-liter Northstar V8. An automatic transmission is also standard on the GXP, but it has a more aggressive 3.71 final drive ratio for quicker starts.

**Safety:** All Bonnevilles offer standard four-wheel antilock disc brakes and optional side airbags (standard on the GXP). Traction control is standard on all but the base SE model, and the GXP gets the StabiliTrak stability control system. In government crash testing, the Bonneville received four out of five stars for driver protection in a frontal impact and a perfect five stars for front-passenger protection. Side-impact tests returned a five-star rating for both front and rear passengers. The IIHS gave the Bonneville a "Good" rating (its best) and named it a "Best Pick" in its category.

**Interior Design and Special Features:** All controls are canted toward the driver in true Pontiac tradition, with full instrumentation backlit in the brand-signature red lighting. It's easy to see at night, but the endless array of buttons and knobs can be a little overwhelming at times. If your needs call for six-passenger capability, a 55/45-split bench seat with center storage armrest is available on the SE (in cloth only). Rear-seat room is excellent with good support and a useful fold-down armrest that includes two cupholders.

**Driving Impressions:** The Bonneville's standard V6 is plenty adequate for confident merging and passing, but those who want serious power will definitely want to upgrade to the GXP and its potent Northstar V8. Despite its large size, the Bonneville is a competent handler. Push an SE or SLE model hard and it will get out of sorts easily, but less aggressive drivers will find either one comfortable and competent for everyday driving chores. The steering leans toward the lighter side to the detriment of road feel, but the brakes have a good solid feel. Without question, enthusiasts will prefer the dynamics of the GXP, as its sport suspension and 18-inch wheels give it better control and response in the turns.

*Crash Test Scores, see pg 530*
*Warranty information, see pg 542*

## Specifications

| Engine/Drivetrain | HP | Torque | EPA Fuel Economy Rating |
|---|---|---|---|
| 8cyl 4.6L A | 275 | 300 | 17 city/24 hwy |
| 6cyl 3.8L A | 205 | 230 | 20 city/29 hwy |

## Body Styles

| Style | MSRP Range |
|---|---|
| Large Sedan | $27,775–$35,395 |

# 2005 Pontiac G6

**Midsize Sedan**

**MSRP Price Range**

## $20,675 - $23,300

Destination Charge: $625 (all styles)

### Ratings

| | | |
|---|---|---|
| Consumer Rating | 9.6 | |
| Editors Rating | 7.3 | |

**What Edmunds.com says:** With the G6's stylish duds, roomy interior and distinctive features, Pontiac finally has a serious contender in the midsize sedan segment.

**Pros:** Crisp handling, lots of rear-seat room, plenty of standard features, innovative panoramic sunroof.

**Cons:** A few low-buck interior bits, panoramic sunroof takes away rear-seat headroom, down on power compared to class leaders.

**What's New:** The G6 is an all-new midsize sedan replacement for the ancient Grand Am.

**Body Styles, Trim Levels and Options:** The four-door G6 comes in two trim levels, base and GT. Generous standard equipment on the base model includes air conditioning; cruise control; power windows, locks and mirrors; keyless entry; a 60/40 split-folding rear seat; a CD player; and a tilt/telescoping steering wheel. The GT adds power-adjustable pedals, an eight-speaker Monsoon sound system, a rear spoiler, alloy wheels and a sport suspension. Notable options include a remote start system, XM Satellite Radio and chrome alloy wheels. Two power sunroof options are available—a traditional power glass panel, as well as an innovative panoramic roof with four glass panels that fold accordion-style and an electric sunshade.

**Powertrains and Performance:** Standard power comes from a 3.5-liter V6 rated at 200 horsepower and 220 pound-feet of torque. A four-speed automatic transmission is also standard. GT models include a shift-it-yourself feature that offers full manual control of gear changes.

**Safety:** The G6 features standard four-wheel disc brakes. Antilock brakes and traction control are standard on the GT, and optional on the base car. Side curtain airbags are optional across the board, but a stability control system is not available. The G6 has not yet been crash tested.

**Interior Design and Special Features:** The interior of the G6 features stylish seating with generous side bolsters to hold you in place during aggressive cornering. The gauges showcase Pontiac's signature font, and are set in an attractive cluster with chrome rings. Plenty of chrome and metal-look accents brighten up the interior. Overall materials quality is notably good, but a few cheap bits here and there keep the G6 a step below the class standards.

**Driving Impressions:** The 3.5-liter V6 offers plenty of torque down low for easy passing and merging, but can get a bit thrashy at high revs. The suspension returns a surprisingly sporty ride, and the solid structure helps make the interior a serene place to spend time.

*Crash Test Scores, see pg 530*
*Warranty information, see pg 542*

### Specifications

| Engine/Drivetrain | HP | Torque | EPA Fuel Economy Rating |
|---|---|---|---|
| 6cyl 3.5L A | 200 | 220 | 20 city/30 hwy |

### Body Styles

| Style | MSRP Range |
|---|---|
| Midsize Sedan | $20,675–$23,300 |

For the latest full vehicle reports, visit www.edmunds.com/bginfopak

**MSRP Price Range**

## N/A

Destination Charge: N/A (all styles)

### Ratings

| | | |
|---|---|---|
| Consumer Rating | N/A | ▭ |
| Editors Rating | 7.8 | ▬▬▬ |

**What Edmunds.com says:** Old-school GTO fans may not like the Euro-style looks of the modern-day incarnation, but there's no denying that under its skin beats the heart of a true muscle car.

**Pros:** Powerful V8, rear-wheel drive, tight build quality, loaded with standard features.

**Cons:** Forgettable styling, handling should be a bit sharper, no sunroof or navigation system available.

**What's New:** For 2005, the GTO receives a new engine—the 6.0-liter LS2 V8. The new V8 produces 400 horsepower, up from 350, and 395 lb-ft of torque, up from 365. More rumble comes from a new split dual-exhaust system, and new exterior options include two new colors and an available hood scoop.

**Body Styles, Trim Levels and Options:** The Pontiac GTO is offered as a 2+2 sport coupe in one generously appointed trim level. The standard features list includes full leather trim (seats, steering wheel, shift handle); a premium Blaupunkt audio system with an in-dash six-disc CD changer; keyless entry; eight-way power-adjustable front seats; a trip computer; power windows, locks and mirrors; air conditioning; cruise control; and 17-inch aluminum wheels. Aside from choosing a transmission, there are no additional options.

**Powertrains and Performance:** There is only one engine available on the GTO—a 6.0-liter V8 rated at 400 horsepower and 395 pound-feet of torque. The standard transmission is a four-speed overdrive automatic, but a six-speed, close-ratio manual transmission is available as an option. Regardless of which transmission is selected, all GTOs come with a limited-slip differential and electronic traction control.

**Safety:** All GTOs come standard with four-wheel antilock disc brakes, electronic traction control, multistage front airbags and an emergency mode that shuts down the vehicle's systems and unlocks the doors in the event of an airbag deployment. Side airbags are not available, nor is stability control. The GTO has not been crash tested.

**Interior Design and Special Features:** Unlike the original GTO, this modern-day version is no stripper. Comfortable leather-trimmed seats; a 200-watt, 10-speaker sound system; and a comprehensive trip computer all come standard. The overall design is straightforward with large analog gauges and an easy-to-use climate control system. Access to the rear seats is tight as you might expect, but they are quite comfy once you're seated.

**Driving Impressions:** On the street, the GTO has a luxury carlike ride quality, and when pushed a bit, it seems to handle predictably and respectably, despite a fair amount of body roll. But when driven more aggressively, the car feels heavy and the steering a little slow and numb. Blazing engine performance and powerful brakes, however, showcase true muscle car roots.

*Crash Test Scores, see pg 530*
*Warranty information, see pg 542*

### Specifications

| Engine/Drivetrain | HP | Torque | EPA Fuel Economy Rating |
|---|---|---|---|
| 6cyl 6.0L A/M | 400 | 395 | N/A |

### Body Styles

| Style | MSRP Range |
|---|---|
| Midsize Coupe | N/A |

# 2005 Pontiac Grand Am

Midsize Coupe

**MSRP Price Range**
## $22,365 - $23,615
Destination Charge: $625 (all styles)

### Ratings

| | | |
|---|---|---|
| Consumer Rating | 9.3 | |
| Editors Rating | 7.2 | |

**What Edmunds.com says:** A viable import alternative, but don't expect Camry- or Accord-like resale values or build quality.

**Pros:** Lots of standard features, roomy interior, crisp handling.

**Cons:** Five-speed manual no longer available, cheap interior pieces, iffy crash test scores.

**What's New:** The sedan has been dropped from the lineup along with the base four-cylinder engine and the manual transmission.

**Body Styles, Trim Levels and Options:** The Grand Am is available in GT coupe form exclusively (an SE sedan is available to fleet customers only). Generous standard equipment includes cruise control; power windows, locks and mirrors; keyless entry; air conditioning; and a Monsoon premium sound system. Various upgrades are available, including XM Satellite Radio, a power sunroof and chrome alloy wheels. A unique appearance package is also on the options sheet that features a special composite performance hood and an aggressive rear spoiler.

**Powertrains and Performance:** Standard power comes from a Ram Air 3.4-liter V6 rated at 175 horsepower and 205 lb-ft of torque. A four-speed automatic transmission is also standard; no manual transmission is offered.

**Safety:** The Grand Am GT features standard four-wheel antilock disc brakes and traction control. In government frontal impact crash testing, the Grand Am received four out of five stars for driver and front-passenger protection. Side-impact tests resulted in a rating of three out of five stars for front- and rear-passenger protection. In offset frontal impact crash testing performed by the IIHS, the Grand Am received a "Poor" rating (the lowest possible).

**Interior Design and Special Features:** On the inside, Grand Ams feature traditional Pontiac design cues. Although it is intended to mimic a jet fighter cockpit, we don't recall F-16s having so much cheap plastic. Interior room is comparable to your average sporty coupe, with nicely bolstered seats that offer solid support for spirited driving. A split-folding rear seat is standard.

**Driving Impressions:** The 3.4-liter V6 is an old GM standby with plenty of torque down low for easy passing and merging. The suspension is stiffer than that of most import coupes, returning a surprisingly sporty ride that's only occasionally harsh.

*Crash Test Scores, see pg 530*
*Warranty information, see pg 542*

### Specifications

| Engine/Drivetrain | HP | Torque | EPA Fuel Economy Rating |
|---|---|---|---|
| 6cyl 3.4L A | 175 | 205 | 20 city/29 hwy |

### Body Styles

| Style | MSRP Range |
|---|---|
| Midsize Coupe | $22,365–$23,615 |

# 2005 Pontiac Grand Prix

**MSRP Price Range**

## $22,900 - $26,560
Destination Charge: $660 (all styles)

### Ratings

| | | |
|---|---|---|
| Consumer Rating | 8.3 | |
| Editors Rating | 6.9 | |

**What Edmunds.com says:** Fast and fun to drive, the Grand Prix is still too rough around the edges to steal the hearts of import buyers.

**Pros:** Strong supercharged V6, nimble handling, attractive gauges, easy-to-use controls, big trunk, fold-flat front-passenger seat.

**Cons:** Build and materials quality still needs some work, tight backseat, noisy engine.

**What's New:** The changes are all in the details for 2005. Option packages have been shuffled a bit, as have the wheel choices. New radio units include a CD/MP3 player and a DVD-based navigation system with six-disc CD changer. Remote vehicle start is now available in all models.

**Body Styles, Trim Levels and Options:** The Grand Prix is available as a four-door sedan in one of three trim levels—Base, GT and GTP. The base model comes with 16-inch wheels, foglights, a CD player, cruise control and power windows, mirrors and locks. The GT adds ABS, alloy wheels and a power driver seat, while opening up options like leather upholstery, a sunroof and a head-up display. Along with a supercharged engine, the GTP gets 17-inch alloy wheels and On-Star telematics. The GTP is eligible for the enthusiast-oriented Competition Group. The Comp G package retrofits the GTP with a more aggressive 3.29-to-1 final drive ratio, an automanual transmission mode, firmer suspension tuning, performance tires, an enthusiast-oriented stability control system (StabiliTrak Sport), upgraded steering that varies effort levels in response to cornering forces, red brake calipers and, inside the cockpit, a head-up display. Other options include dual-zone automatic climate control, a nine-speaker Monsoon stereo, an in-dash CD changer, a navigation system and satellite radio.

**Powertrains and Performance:** A pair of 3.8-liter V6s serves duty in the Grand Prix. In the base and GT models, the standard V6 makes 200 horsepower and 225 pound-feet of torque. The GTP has a supercharged version rated for 260 ponies and 280 lb-ft of torque. Both engines come with a four-speed automatic gearbox. GTPs equipped the Competition Group have a manual-shift mode as well. Mileage ratings are 18-20 in the city and 28-30 on the highway.

**Safety:** Antilock brakes and traction control are optional on the base model and standard on the GT and the GTP. Stability control is available as part of the Competition Group package for the GTP. Front and rear side curtain airbags are optional on the GT and GTP. In government crash tests, the Grand Prix earned three out of five stars for side impacts (front and rear), but the car tested did not have the side curtain airbags. Frontal crash tests resulted in a three out of five stars rating for the driver, and four stars for the passenger.

**Interior Design and Special Features:** Inside, there's a definite cockpit theme, as the center stack curves to meet the driver and the gauges and displays are all in red. Control layouts are simple and intuitive, even the trip computer. The front seats are broad and comfortable, though taller adults may find headroom limited. The backseat is cramped, with a low bench and tight foot room making it a last resort for adults. At least there's plenty of cargo space, thanks to a 16-cubic-foot trunk, a 60/40-split rear seat and a fold-flat front-passenger seat.

**Driving Impressions:** Even the base engine furnishes brisk response at low- and midrange speeds, but we certainly enjoy the rush of the supercharged V6. The four-speed automatic shifts smartly on its own, and we like that the automanual mode in the GTP Comp G allows full manual operation. Ride quality is comfortable enough for weekday commutes. Although all Grand Prixs are excellent handlers, the responsive GTP Comp G is definitely the car for the enthusiast.

*Crash Test Scores, see pg 530*
*Warranty information, see pg 542*

### Specifications

| Engine/Drivetrain | HP | Torque | EPA Fuel Economy Rating |
|---|---|---|---|
| 6cyl 3.8L A | 260 | 280 | 18 city/28 hwy |
| 6cyl 3.8L A | 200 | 230 | 20 city/30 hwy |

### Body Styles

| Style | MSRP Range |
|---|---|
| Midsize Sedan | $22,900–$26,560 |

# 2005 Pontiac Montana
**Midsize Minivan**

**MSRP Price Range**
## $26,040 - $30,420
Destination Charge: $715 (all styles)

## Ratings

| | | |
|---|---|---|
| Consumer Rating | 8.5 | |
| Editors Rating | 6.6 | |

**What Edmunds.com says:** If you can stomach the heavy doses of plastic trim both inside and out, the Montana offers peppy performance and comfortable passenger accommodations in a feature-laden package.

**Pros:** Available eight-passenger seating, optional rear parking assist, sporty handling, numerous optional entertainment features (MP3, DVD, XM Satellite Radio).

**Cons:** Weak offset crash test scores, ABS not standard, can't get side curtain airbags, cheap interior materials, unrefined powertrain character.

**What's New:** The Montana's model lineup goes under the knife this year—trimmed away are the regular-wheelbase and all-wheel-drive models.

**Body Styles, Trim Levels and Options:** The Montana comes in two basic trim levels: Base and MontanaVision. The base van is well equipped with features like air conditioning, cruise control, power windows and door locks, a tilt steering wheel, keyless entry and an AM/FM/CD stereo. The high-line MontanaVision model is upgraded with ABS, side airbags, a power-adjustable driver seat, rear air conditioning and audio controls, a driver information center, a leather-wrapped steering wheel with satellite audio controls and, of course, the MontanaVision rear DVD entertainment system. Notable options include a leather seat package, power-sliding rear doors and a parking distance monitor that lets you know how close you are to objects behind the vehicle—a real help in tight parking lots.

**Powertrains and Performance:** All Montanas come equipped with a 3.4-liter V6 that makes 185 horsepower and 210 pound-feet of torque. A four-speed automatic transmission is standard. An optional towing package, which provides towing capacity up to 3,500 pounds, includes heavy-duty cooling, a firmer suspension with rear level control and a heavy-duty alternator.

**Safety:** The Montana has received mixed crash test results. In tests conducted by the National Highway Transportation Safety Administration (NHTSA), a 2002 model Montana received four out of five stars for protection of the driver and front passenger in a frontal impact crash. Side-impact tests resulted in a five-star rating for front passengers and a four-star rating for rear passengers. But after undergoing the Insurance Institute for Highway Safety's (IIHS) frontal offset crash test, the Montana received an overall rating of "Poor," the lowest possible. Side airbags and ABS are optional on the base model, and standard on the MontanaVision. Side curtain airbags are not available.

**Interior Design and Special Features:** Like most minivans, the Montana's interior is geared toward simplicity and ease of use. The climate controls are a simple three-dial design and the gauges are clear analog dials, but much of the switchgear is a cheap gray plastic that doesn't look or feel particularly sturdy. Multiple seating configurations allow seven- or eight-passenger capacity, and the optional MontanaVision DVD entertainment system will keep the kids entertained for hours. It's also worth mentioning that all Montanas can be equipped with a disappearing third-row seat that makes loading bulky items onto the cargo area's flat floor a snap.

*Crash Test Scores, see pg 530*
*Warranty information, see pg 542*

## Specifications

| Engine/Drivetrain | HP | Torque | EPA Fuel Economy Rating |
|---|---|---|---|
| 6cyl 3.4L A | 185 | 210 | 19 city/26 hwy |

## Body Styles

| Style | MSRP Range |
|---|---|
| Midsize Minivan | $26,040–$30,420 |

**Driving Impressions:** The standard V6 engine is down on power compared to its competitors, but it still manages to provide adequate acceleration. The transmission shifts quickly with little prodding, but the engine note does get a bit harsh at higher rpm. The Montana handles well for a minivan, especially with the optional sport suspension. Larger bumps and ruts tend to upset the Montana more than most other minivans, but overall it's fun to drive—as minivans go.

For the latest full vehicle reports, visit www.edmunds.com/bginfopak

**MSRP Price Range**
## $24,520 - $30,210
Destination Charge: $715 (all styles)

### Ratings

| | | |
|---|---|---|
| Consumer Rating | N/A | |
| Editors Rating | 7.0 | |

**What Edmunds.com says:** Though the Montana SV6 features a slick interior and distinctive styling, it doesn't have the on-road finesse of its minivan competitors.

**Pros:** Smooth ride and handling, lots of nifty interior storage spaces, innovative multimedia storage system, available all-wheel drive.

**Cons:** Engine power and refinement not up to class leaders, no side curtain airbags.

**What's New:** The Montana SV6 is an all-new "crossover sport van" that has roots in the Pontiac Montana minivan.

**Body Styles, Trim Levels and Options:** The Montana SV6 comes in one size and trim level. Standard equipment includes power windows, air conditioning, an eight-speaker sound system with a CD/MP3 player, a rear-seat DVD entertainment system, the OnStar communications system, cruise control and keyless entry. An upgrade option package includes a passenger-side power-sliding door, a power driver seat, a sport suspension, rear air conditioning, alloy wheels and additional interior storage. An all-wheel-drive system is available, and includes an automatic load-leveling rear suspension and an inflator kit. An optional PhatNoise mobile digital media system allows owners to store thousands of MP3s and/or several dozen movies. Other noteworthy options include dual power-sliding side doors, leather seating, a 115-volt A/C outlet, trip computer, rear parking assist, heated seats and a remote vehicle starting system.

**Powertrains and Performance:** All Montana SV6s come equipped with a 3.5-liter V6 that makes 200 horsepower and 220 pound-feet of torque. A four-speed automatic transmission is standard. No other powertrain combinations are available, but buyers can opt for all-wheel drive.

**Safety:** All models come standard with four-wheel antilock disc brakes. Side-impact airbags for front occupants are optional. Full-length side curtain airbags are not available. The Stabili-Trak stability control system is available on SV6s equipped with the optional sport suspension. The SV6 has not yet been crash tested.

**Interior Design and Special Features:** The Montana SV6 seats seven, and the fold-flat third-row seat offers a convenient 50/50 split. A pleasing color scheme with faux metal accents dramatically brightens the interior atmosphere of the van. Folding center trays (with cupholders) between the first- and second-row seats are available. An overhead rail system provides rear-seat access to climate and entertainment functions, and can be outfitted with various storage containers. A rear-seat DVD entertainment system is standard on all SV6s, and can be upgraded with infrared wireless headphones. A remote vehicle start system, pioneered on the 2004 Chevy Malibu, is optional.

**Driving Impressions:** The V6 power plant is down on power compared to its competitors, but it still manages to provide adequate acceleration. The SV6's suspension is on the soft side, though upgrading to the optional sport suspension does provide for more responsive handling.

*Crash Test Scores, see pg 530*
*Warranty information, see pg 542*

### Specifications

| Engine/Drivetrain | HP | Torque | EPA Fuel Economy Rating |
|---|---|---|---|
| 6cyl 3.5L A | 200 | 220 | N/A |

### Body Styles

| Style | MSRP Range |
|---|---|
| Midsize Minivan | $24,520–$30,210 |

# 2005 Pontiac Sunfire

**Compact Coupe**

**MSRP Price Range**

## $10,895 - $15,085

Destination Charge: $565 (all styles)

### Ratings

| | | |
|---|---|---|
| Consumer Rating | 8.6 | |
| Editors Rating | 4.9 | |

**What Edmunds.com says:** Despite a peppy engine and a few neat options, this decade-old economy coupe is outclassed by newer competitors.

**Pros:** Low price, torquey four-cylinder engine, optional satellite radio and OnStar.

**Cons:** Overall design showing its age, low resale value, poor side-impact and front-offset crash test results.

**What's New:** Other than revised package content, the Sunfire continues unchanged.

**Body Styles, Trim Levels and Options:** The Sunfire is available as a two-door coupe only, but three different options packages allow varying levels of feature content. The base package includes a standard AM/FM stereo, rear spoiler and air conditioning, while the midlevel 1SB package adds a tilt steering wheel, carpeted floor mats, an easy-entry front-passenger seat and a CD player to the standard equipment list. The top-level 1SC package decks the Sunfire out with an overhead console, a leather-wrapped steering wheel, cruise control, keyless entry, alloy wheels, ABS and upgraded cloth bucket seats with adjustable lumbar support for the driver. Available options include power windows, side-impact airbags, the OnStar communications system, a sunroof and a Monsoon premium stereo.

**Powertrains and Performance:** Unlike years past, there is only one engine available for 2005—the 2.2-liter Ecotec four-cylinder. With 140 horsepower and 150 pound-feet of torque, it compares favorably with most other vehicles in its class. It's made entirely of aluminum and boasts dual-overhead camshafts and four valves per cylinder for maximum efficiency and power. The standard transmission is a five-speed manual with a four-speed automatic available as part of an option package. EPA mileage estimates are 24 city/32 highway for the four-speed automatic and 25 city/33 highway for cars equipped with the five-speed manual.

**Safety:** Side-impact airbags and ABS are available on models equipped with certain option packages. Crash tests conducted by the National Highway Traffic Safety Administration (NHTSA) produced middling results. The Sunfire earned four out of five stars for the driver and front passenger in frontal crash tests, but only one star for the driver in the side-impact test (a Sunfire equipped with side airbags has yet to be tested). The Insurance Institute for Highway Safety (IIHS) gave the Sunfire a rating of "Poor," its lowest, after conducting its frontal offset crash test.

**Interior Design and Special Features:** The Sunfire's interior has never been one of its strong points. The seats aren't very comfortable, and the build and materials quality leaves a lot to be desired. Although most cars in this class lack much design flair, the Sunfire still manages to pale in comparison. The fact that both OnStar and XM Satellite Radio are available gives the Sunfire a slight technological edge over its competitors, but it doesn't make up for the dated appearance of everything inside and out.

*Crash Test Scores, see pg 530*
*Warranty information, see pg 542*

### Specifications

| Engine/Drivetrain | HP | Torque | EPA Fuel Economy Rating |
|---|---|---|---|
| 4cyl 2.2L M | 140 | 150 | 26 city/37 hwy |

### Body Styles

| Style | MSRP Range |
|---|---|
| Compact Coupe | $10,895–$15,085 |

**Driving Impressions:** Unlike its less technologically advanced predecessors, the Ecotec four-cylinder is a thoroughly modern engine that provides good power and a smooth delivery. The five-speed shifter isn't the most precise unit we've tested, so if you can afford it, go with the smooth-shifting four-speed automatic instead. The handling is acceptable for a car in this class, with reasonably good manners in corners and a compliant suspension that delivers a decent highway ride. But expect a harsher ride over bumps and ruts than you would in newer competitors.

**MSRP Price Range**

## $17,000 - $20,325
Destination Charge: $560 (all styles)

### Ratings

| | | |
|---|---|---|
| Consumer Rating | 9.5 | |
| Editors Rating | 7.6 | |

**What Edmunds.com says:** Here's one Pontiac that hits its mark. The Vibe blends performance, practicality and affordability into a tastefully styled, but still fun sport wagon package.

**Pros:** Comfortable ride, unique features, roomy backseat, versatile cargo area, good gas mileage, available stability control.

**Cons:** All-wheel-drive version is sluggish, Toyota's version likely to have better resale value.

**What's New:** New options this year include programmable power locks, OnStar, a tire-pressure monitor, leather seating, stability control and side curtain airbags. The Moon and Tunes Value package now includes an integrated subwoofer.

**Body Styles, Trim Levels and Options:** The Vibe comes as a four-door wagon in three levels of trim: base, AWD and GT. Base and AWD models come standard with air conditioning, dual front airbags, AM/FM/CD stereo, tilt steering and tinted windows. AWD models add standard ABS and a four-speed automatic transmission. GT versions get standard 16-inch wheels and four-wheel disc brakes with ABS. A Moon and Tunes package adds a power sunroof and an upgraded audio system with an integrated subwoofer, while a Power Group Value package adds power windows and door locks, cruise control and keyless entry. Leather seating, OnStar and XM Satellite Radio are also available.

**Powertrains and Performance:** The Vibe offers two different engines and three transmissions. Base models come with a 1.8-liter, 130-horsepower four-cylinder mated to either the standard five-speed manual or an optional four-speed automatic. All-wheel-drive versions come with the automatic only, and due to different exhaust routing, make just 123 hp. Top-of-the-line GT models get a 180-horsepower version of the same 1.8-liter four-cylinder and a standard six-speed manual transmission.

**Safety:** All Vibes come with dual-stage front airbags for the driver and front passenger. Seat-mounted side airbags for front occupants and full-length side curtain airbags are optional across the line. ABS brakes are standard on AWD and GT models, and optional on the base model. Stability control is optional on all front-wheel-drive models. The Vibe earned a perfect five stars in the NHTSA's frontal impact testing, five stars for side impacts involving front occupants and four stars for side impacts involving rear occupants.

**Interior Design and Special Features:** All Vibe models feature interiors that are both stylish and functional. Chrome-ringed gauges and metallic dash trim spice things up in front, while in back, the 60/40-split bench seat provides roomy accommodations for adult passengers and folds completely flat to create 54.1 cubic feet of usable cargo space. Other useful features include a front-passenger seat that folds flat for carrying extra-long items, a 115-volt AC power outlet for plugging in household devices and adjustable tie-down anchors in the cargo area. A DVD-based navigation system with a remotely mounted six-disc CD changer is available as a stand-alone option.

**Driving Impressions:** The Vibe offers an elevated driving position that affords a great view of the road, but the ergonomics can be a bit awkward for some. The handling isn't particularly sporty but it is responsive, while the ride quality is smooth and comfortable on a day-to-day basis. Acceleration from the base motor is a bit sluggish, especially with the added weight of the all-wheel-drive system, but the GT is fast for a compact wagon, provided you let its higher-strung engine rev a bit.

*Crash Test Scores, see pg 530*
*Warranty information, see pg 542*

### Specifications

| Engine/Drivetrain | HP | Torque | EPA Fuel Economy Rating |
|---|---|---|---|
| 4cyl 1.8L M | 173 | 127 | 25 city/32 hwy |
| 4cyl 1.8L M | 130 | 125 | 29 city/36 hwy |
| 4cyl 1.8L A | 123 | 118 | 26 city/31 hwy |

### Body Styles

| Style | MSRP Range |
|---|---|
| Compact Wagon | $17,000–$20,325 |

# 2005 Porsche 911 Compact Coupe

**MSRP Price Range**

## $69,300 - 79,100

Destination Charge: N/A (all styles)

### Ratings

| | | |
|---|---|---|
| Consumer Rating | N/A | |
| Editors Rating | 8.6 | |

**What Edmunds.com says:** Still the quintessential sports car after four decades, the 911 has a unique blend of style, performance and sound that's unmatched by anything on the road.

**Pros:** Pinpoint steering, effortless acceleration, awe-inspiring brakes, the rhythmic sound of a powerful flat six, comfortable cockpit.

**Cons:** Relatively small fuel tank, useless rear seats, outlandish option prices.

**What's New:** While the traditional 911 lines have been retained, just about everything else has changed on Porsche's flagship. Notable changes include more powerful engines, a new transmission, variable-ratio rack-and-pinion steering, an adjustable suspension and new seating options in a redesigned passenger compartment.

**Body Styles, Trim Levels and Options:** The 2005 911 marks the first time since 1977 that Porsche has split the line into two models powered by two distinct engines, a 3.6 flat-six in the standard Carrera and a 3.8-liter version in the high-performance Carrera S. Other features unique to the S include active suspension management technology, larger brakes, 19-inch forged alloy wheels (in place of the standard Carrera's 18s), bi-xenon headlights, a sports steering wheel, aluminum-look interior trim and a silver-colored rear deck logo. To distinguish the two models from behind, the S has twin round tailpipes poking out the rear valance, while the base car sports two oval-shaped units. Other options include ceramic disc brakes borrowed from the GT2 and a Sport Chrono Package that records and displays lap times.

**Powertrains and Performance:** The standard Carrera comes with a 3.6-liter horizontally opposed six that was carried over from 2004, albeit with a revised intake that provides a slim boost in output to 325 horsepower and 275 pound-feet of torque. The next step up the performance ladder is the Carrera S, which has a new 3.8-liter version of the boxer six rated for 355 hp and 295 lb-ft of torque. Both cars come standard with a new six-speed manual transmission; the five-speed Tiptronic automatic offered in past years remains an option. Porsche claims that the Carrera can reach 60 mph in 4.8 seconds, while the S model accomplishes the feat in 4.6.

**Safety:** Six airbags, four-wheel antilock disc brakes and stability control are included on all 911 models. An all-new active suspension management system is optional on the Carrera, and standard on the Carrera S.

**Interior Design and Special Features:** The Cayenne-inspired interior has been completely redesigned with a new steering wheel, single-pod gauge cluster, bucket seats and a hands-free communication system. Both models feature automatic climate control with a pollen filter. Also standard is a new nine-speaker sound system, but a 13-speaker Bose surround-sound system is optional for true audiophiles. A revised driving position, larger foot wells and a new steering column that tilts and telescopes create more head- and legroom than ever before. Optional amenities include heated memory seats with pneumatically adjustable cushions and backrests.

*Crash Test Scores, see pg 530*
*Warranty information, see pg 542*

### Specifications

| Engine/Drivetrain | HP | Torque | EPA Fuel Economy Rating |
|---|---|---|---|
| 6cyl 3.6L A/M | 325 | 275 | N/A |
| 6cyl 3.8L A/M | 355 | 295 | N/A |

### Body Styles

| Style | MSRP Range |
|---|---|
| Compact Coupe | $69,300–$79,100 |

**Driving Impressions:** Driven at normal speeds the 911 delivers a firm but mostly pleasant ride that's suitable for daily commutes, but the growl of the flat six behind the driver is a welcome reminder that this is no vanilla passenger car. Lay into the power, and the 911 comes alive. The variable-rate steering feels slightly numb at certain speeds, but turns in with added precision and is less affected by uneven tarmac. The new brakes are more powerful than ever, and respond promptly thanks to a bigger booster and optional composite rotors. It requires a skilled driver to extract the car's full potential, but thanks to the new Porsche Active Suspension Management system, even those who only scratch the surface will be thrilled with the results.

# 2005 Porsche Boxster

**MSRP Price Range**
## $43,800 - $53,100
Destination Charge: N/A (all styles)

### Ratings

| | | |
|---|---|---|
| Consumer Rating | N/A | [_____] |
| Editors Rating | 8.0 | [▬▬▬▬▬▬▬▬▬___] |

**What Edmunds.com says:** A midengine design and classic Porsche styling, not to mention sublime steering and brakes, give the Boxster appeal that's hard to ignore.

**Pros:** Supreme handling characteristics, pinpoint steering, plenty of usable power especially in "S" model, usable cargo compartment, fast power top operation.

**Cons:** Options are costly, doesn't look much different than the old model, interior controls still a little busy.

**What's New:** The Boxster is significantly updated for 2005. Notable changes include more power for both models, new manual transmissions and a restyled exterior with larger front and side air intakes, a new headlamp treatment, revised door sills and larger side windows. The brakes have been upgraded, stability control is now standard across the board and head-protecting side airbags have been added.

**Body Styles, Trim Levels and Options:** This two-seat roadster comes as either the Boxster or the Boxster S. The standard equipment list on both models includes such features as leather-trimmed seats with power recline; automatic climate control; leather-covered steering wheel, gearshift knob, armrests and handbrake handle; an in-dash CD player; and a power top. Optional equipment includes full leather seating, a Bose digital sound system, bi-xenon headlights, rear parking assist, a three-piece wind deflector, heated seats, a navigation system and a removable aluminum hardtop. Standard Boxsters also offer an optional sport suspension, while both models offer optional 18-inch wheels.

**Powertrains and Performance:** Both models use a horizontally opposed six-cylinder engine. In the standard Boxster, it displaces 2.7 liters and produces 240 horsepower. The Boxster S uses a 3.2-liter version of the same engine with 280 hp. A five-speed manual transmission is fitted to the Boxster, while the Boxster S gets a six-speed unit. An automatic, Porsche's five-speed Tiptronic S automanual, is also available for either car. Other Boxster S upgrades include higher-rate springs and shocks, longer control arms and standard lightweight 17-inch wheels. Porsche claims that the standard Boxster will sprint to 60 mph in 5.9 seconds, while the S accomplishes the same feat in just 5.2 ticks of the watch.

**Safety:** Side airbags and four-wheel antilock disc brakes are standard on both Boxsters. Electronic stability control, dubbed PSM, is also standard. The side airbag system includes a head-protecting airbags that deploy from the door window sills. To date, no crash tests of the Boxster have been conducted.

**Interior Design and Special Features:** The Boxster's seats are firm and supportive, and substantial bolstering holds occupants in place on tight turns. Like the 911, the Boxster's cabin is good-looking but a little confusing at first glance. The new gauge cluster is well laid out, but the climate and radio controls are still a little hard to decipher. Materials quality has been improved, however, so at least now you feel like in you're in a high-dollar sports car. With two cargo areas (one up front and one in back), there is an ample cargo space available.

**Driving Impressions:** As a commuter vehicle, the Boxster's tight steering, brakes and clutch can make it a chore around town. Buy a BMW Z4 or Mercedes SLK if your primary driving environment resembles the mega-mall parking lot. Rather, the Porsche Boxster shines as a weekend-getaway vehicle, providing comfort and space for two adults and their luggage with driving characteristics that are thoroughly enjoyable at speed.

*Crash Test Scores, see pg 530*
*Warranty information, see pg 542*

### Specifications

| Engine/Drivetrain | HP | Torque | EPA Fuel Economy Rating |
|---|---|---|---|
| 6cyl 2.7L A/M | 240 | 199 | N/A |
| 6cyl 3.2L A/M | 280 | 236 | N/A |

### Body Styles

| Style | MSRP Range |
|---|---|
| **Compact Convertible** | $43,800–$53,100 |

# 2005 Porsche Cayenne

Midsize SUV

**MSRP Price Range**
## $41,100 - $89,300
Destination Charge: N/A (all styles)

### Ratings

| | | |
|---|---|---|
| Consumer Rating | N/A | |
| Editors Rating | 7.8 | |

**What Edmunds.com says:** Awkward-looking but thrilling behind the wheel, the Cayenne is a thoroughly capable vehicle that makes good on its Porsche nameplate.

**Pros:** Sports car performance, available adjustable ride height and suspension damping control, solid off-road capability and towing capacity, slightly more cargo room than a Range Rover.

**Cons:** Can't match the Rover in the dirt, annoying turbo lag on top end model, you have to pay a little extra for the name.

**What's New:** The base Cayenne receives a six-speed manual transmission and Porsche's Drive-Off Assistant System, otherwise known as a "hill-holder" clutch. All Cayenne models now feature a power rear tailgate and body-colored side sills and fascias. An optional panoramic power sunroof debuts this year, along with an available rearview camera system. A comprehensive performance upgrade package is available on the Turbo model through Porsche's Tequipment program. Highlights include a horsepower increase to 500 and upgraded brakes.

**Body Styles, Trim Levels and Options:** Three versions of the four-door Cayenne are offered: base, S and Turbo. Base and S models come with features such as 18-inch alloy wheels, leather seating, power seats, dual-zone automatic climate control and a 350-watt, 15-speaker Bose audio system. The Turbo adds adaptive suspension with automatic ride height and damping adjustment (Porsche Active Suspension Management), bi-HID headlights, a CD-based navigation system, heated seats front and rear, seat memory, sonar front/rear parking assist and power adjustment for the steering wheel. In keeping with Porsche tradition, there are a number of options available to increase functionality and personality, including four-zone climate control, bolstered sport seats, various wheel/tire upgrades and trailering preparation.

**Powertrains and Performance:** The base Cayenne uses a 3.2-liter V6 rated to produce 250 horsepower and 228 pound-feet of torque. The midgrade Cayenne S is upgraded with a 4.5-liter V8 rated at 340 hp and 310 lb-ft of torque. Top-of-the-line Turbos boast 450 hp and 460 lb-ft of torque from a twin-turbocharged version of the S model's V8. The Tequipment upgrade boosts horsepower to 500 on the Turbo. Power is sent to all four wheels via a permanent four-wheel-drive system that's fully integrated with the stability control system. Acceleration is, fittingly, sports-carlike; the S does zero to 60 mph in 7.2 seconds while the Turbo dispatches that sprint in just 5.6 seconds. Maximum towing capacity for all three models is a substantial 7,700 pounds. The base Cayenne is available with a six-speed manual transmission. You can also get a six-speed automatic on the base model; the automatic is standard on S and Turbo models.

**Safety:** Standard safety features on all models include seat-mounted side airbags in the front, full-length side curtain airbags, four-wheel antilock disc brakes and stability control. The Cayenne has not been crash tested.

**Interior Design and Special Features:** In a nod to its Porsche heritage, the Cayenne's ignition switch is on the dash's left side, and the instrument cluster would look equally at home in a 911. For those unfamiliar with the legendary sports car, this means that the gauge cluster is nearly perfect, but the climate and radio controls are an indecipherable cluster of buttons and knobs. With a maximum cargo capacity of 63 cubic feet, the Cayenne has slightly more capacity than the Range Rover but slightly less than the Infiniti FX45.

**Driving Impressions:** Strange as it seems, the Cayenne does live up to the Porsche name in terms of acceleration and handling. The transmission shifts with precision and the engine growls reassuringly under full throttle. Turbo lag is annoying on the top-line model, but otherwise the drivetrain offers little to complain about. It may sound like a cliche, but out on the road the Cayenne is truly the Porsche of SUVs, exhibiting tight body control in the corners. The Cayenne is also a capable SUV when it comes to off-highway work as long as you specify the optional off-road package.

*Crash Test Scores, see pg 530*
*Warranty information, see pg 542*

### Specifications

| Engine/Drivetrain | HP | Torque | EPA Fuel Economy Rating |
|---|---|---|---|
| 6cyl 3.2L A/M | 250 | 228 | N/A |
| 8cyl 4.5L A/M | 340 | 310 | N/A |
| 8cyl 4.5L A/M | 450 | 460 | N/A |

### Body Styles

| Style | MSRP Range |
|---|---|
| Midsize SUV | $41,100 - $89,300 |

For the latest full vehicle reports, visit www.edmunds.com/bginfopak

**MSRP Price Range**
## $22,990 - $26,950
Destination Charge: $695 (all styles)

### Ratings

| | | |
|---|---|---|
| Consumer Rating | 8.8 | ▬▬▬▬▬▬▬▬▬▬▬▭ |
| Editors Rating | 7.8 | ▬▬▬▬▬▬▬▬▬▭▭ |

**What Edmunds.com says:** If you don't mind a strong shot of Subaru with your Saab and are in the market for a sporty wagon, the 9-2X could very well be the ride for you.

**Pros:** Sporty good looks, forgiving ride quality without sacrificing road feel and handling precision, punchy acceleration on turbo models.

**Cons:** Interior more Subaru than Saab, lacks premium features like a navigation system and stability control.

**What's New:** The 9-2X is an all-new sport wagon from Saab. Sporty and versatile, it shares its platform and mechanicals with Subaru's Impreza wagon.

**Body Styles, Trim Levels and Options:** The 9-2X is available as a four-door wagon only in two trims, Linear and Aero. Standard items on the Linear include a 16-inch alloy wheels, rear roof spoiler, tinted glass, cloth sport seats, a height-adjustable driver seat, manual air conditioning, full power accessories and a four-speaker, single-CD sound system. Step up to Aero and the goodie bag swells to include metallic-framed gauges; a leather-wrapped steering wheel, shift knob and handbrake; automatic climate control; a cabin air filter; front foglamps; and a six-speaker stereo with an in-dash CD changer. Options include 17-inch twin alloy wheels, leather seats, seat heaters, xenon headlights, de-icing wipers and a moonroof.

**Powertrains and Performance:** Two engines are available for the 9-2X: a naturally aspirated, 2.5-liter horizontally opposed four-cylinder rated for 165 horsepower on the base Linear model, and a 227-hp turbocharged 2.0-liter four on the Aero. Subaru fans will recognize the latter engine as the Impreza WRX power plant. A five-speed manual transmission comes standard on both the Linear and Aero, while a four-speed automatic is optional. All-wheel drive is standard across both trims.

**Safety:** Four-wheel antilock disc brakes and side airbags for front occupants are standard on every 9-2X. Also standard are active front head restraints, which help protect against whiplash in the event of a rear-impact collision.

**Interior Design and Special Features:** Inside, the 9-2X boasts design that's sporty and youth-oriented, with bold colors, faux-aluminum trim and a high-contrast palette. The front seats are comfortable and supportive; however, the optional leather upholstery can feel a bit slippery during aggressive cornering. The dashboard is essentially Subaru-issue, but Saab used different plastics for the center stack to give it a slightly different look. A 60/40-split-folding rear seat is at the ready, should you have the need to stow bulky cargo. Maximum cargo capacity is 62 cubic feet—about the same as an Audi A4 wagon.

**Driving Impressions:** The 9-2X rides much like an Impreza, but the Subaru's extra stiffness has been softened just a bit for the Saab, thanks to retuned springs, shock absorbers and bushings. The gentler ride should be appreciated by most buyers, and the suspension still provides enough road feel and roll control to make the car fun to toss around on back roads. The steering ratio has also been adjusted to provide better control in tighter turns, and the 9-2X proves to be a sharp, precise implement in these situations. Additionally, Saab increased the sound insulation in its sport wagon, which gives the 9-2X a quieter cruising demeanor than the Impreza. The base engine in the Linear provides ample get-up-and-go for everyday driving, but it can feel a bit sluggish during highway passing maneuvers, especially with the automatic transmission. Slight turbo lag results in soft power delivery down low on the Aero model, but once you hit 3,000 rpm, the car jets forth with a fervor unmatched by any other car in the Saab lineup.

*Crash Test Scores, see pg 530*
*Warranty information, see pg 542*

### Specifications

| Engine/Drivetrain | HP | Torque | EPA Fuel Economy Rating |
|---|---|---|---|
| 4cyl 2.5L M | 165 | 166 | N/A |
| 4cyl 2.0L M | 227 | 217 | N/A |

### Body Styles

| Style | MSRP Range |
|---|---|
| Compact Wagon | $22,990–$26,950 |

# Saab

# 2005 Saab 9-3

**MSRP Price Range**

## $26,850 - $42,600

Destination Charge: $720 (all styles)

## Ratings

| | | |
|---|---|---|
| Consumer Rating | 8.3 | |
| Editors Rating | 7.5 | |

**What Edmunds.com says:** Roomy and fun to drive, the 9-3 is a solid buy among entry-level luxury cars. Just don't expect the razor-sharp reflexes and highly refined interiors of its German and Japanese competitors.

**Pros:** Handles well for a front-drive car, frugal yet powerful engines, generous passenger room, class-leading trunk space.

**Cons:** Suspension should be stiffer on Aero models, ride can be harsh over bumps, interiors lack upscale look and feel, weak stereos.

**What's New:** A new in-dash DVD-based navigation system is added to the options list. The 9-3 convertible is now available in entry-level Linear trim.

Crash Test Scores, see pg 530
Warranty information, see pg 542

## Specifications

| Engine/Drivetrain | HP | Torque | EPA Fuel Economy Rating |
|---|---|---|---|
| 4cyl 2.0L M | 210 | 221 | 22 city/30 hwy |
| 4cyl 2.0L M | 175 | 195 | 23 city/34 hwy |

## Body Styles

| Style | MSRP Range |
|---|---|
| Compact Convertible | $37,100–$42,600 |
| Compact Sedan | $26,850–$32,850 |

**Body Styles, Trim Levels and Options:** The 9-3 is available as a four-door sedan or a two-door convertible. Sedans and convertibles come in Linear, Arc and Aero trim. The base Linear offers full leather seating, a 150-watt stereo, keyless entry, the OnStar system, stability control and 15-inch alloy wheels. Midlevel Arc models feature a mix of real walnut trim and leather, while adding power front seats, automatic climate control, an upgraded 300-watt audio system and 16-inch alloy wheels. The sporty Aero model adds bolstered sport seats, chrome instrument surrounds and interior trim, a lower body kit, a lowered sport suspension and 17-inch twin-spoke alloy wheels. Convertibles come with a fully automatic power top. Options include seat heaters and bi-xenon headlights on all 9-3s, a new in-dash DVD-based navigation system on all Arc and Aero models and, on the sedan only, a sunroof and rear parking sensors.

**Powertrains and Performance:** Two different versions of the 9-3's turbocharged 2.0-liter in-line four-cylinder engine are available. Standard on Linear models is a low-pressure turbo with an output of 175 horsepower and 195 pound-feet of torque. Standard on Arc and Aero models is an upgraded engine with a high-pressure turbo that raises output to 210 hp and 221 lb-ft of torque. Linear and Arc models get a standard five-speed manual gearbox, while Aeros get a six-speed manual. A five-speed automatic with manual-shift capability is optional on all 9-3s.

**Safety:** The 9-3 features adaptive-force front airbags, active head restraints and seat-mounted side torso airbags. Side curtain airbags in the sedan protect passengers in both the front and rear seats in side-impact collisions. Convertibles get the DynaCage rollover protection system that integrates pop-up roll bars, reinforced A-pillars and the front seatbelt pre-tensioners. Four-wheel antilock disc brakes, Electronic Brakeforce Distribution and traction and stability control are standard on all models. The 9-3 was named a "Best Pick" in IIHS frontal offset crash testing.

**Interior Design and Special Features:** Some climate and stereo controls can be difficult to operate, but a standard "profiler" system allows drivers to program a host of individual settings that can be recalled at the press of a button. There's plenty of room for four to sit comfortably in the sedan, but legroom can be tight for adults seated in the back of the convertible. With 14.8 cubic feet of trunk space in the sedan and 12.4 cubes in the convertible, the 9-3 can carry more than most other cars in its class.

**Driving Impressions:** The 9-3 is one of the better-handling front-drive cars on the road. A stiff chassis translates into a car that's easy to place in the corners and satisfyingly precise on the highway. Still, we wish the sporty Aero model felt a little sharper when driven aggressively on twisty roads. The low-pressure turbo provides adequate acceleration for most driving situations, while the high-pressure 2.0-liter delivers a strong pull throughout its power band. The automatic downshifts quickly but can be slow on upshifts, while the manual transmissions shift just fine but tend to feel rubbery through the gates.

**Midsize Sedan, Wagon**

**MSRP Price Range**
## $32,550 - $40,750
Destination Charge: $720 (all styles)

### Ratings

| | | |
|---|---|---|
| Consumer Rating | 8.1 | |
| Editors Rating | 6.7 | |

**What Edmunds.com says:** A likable sedan in numerous ways, but it lags behind the competition when it comes to providing class-leading luxury or performance. In wagon form, however, its seductive style and superior functionality make it a more attractive proposition.

**Pros:** Best-in-class crash scores, long list of standard features, plush highway ride, supportive seats, large trunk.

**Cons:** Turbo lag at low speeds, suspension too soft for aggressive driving, interior materials could use improvement.

**What's New:** An in-dash DVD-based navigation system is added to the options list. Arc models receive a new 16-inch wheel design.

**Body Styles, Trim Levels and Options:** The 9-5 offers two body styles—sedan and wagon—and three trim levels—Linear, Arc and Aero. Base Linear trim is offered only on the wagon; standard equipment includes 16-inch wheels, leather upholstery, walnut trim, heated power-adjustable seats, dual-zone automatic climate control, a CD player, a sunroof, a 60/40-split folding rear seat and OnStar telematics. The Arc adds three-position driver-seat memory, an auto-dimming rearview mirror and a 240-watt Harman Kardon audio system. Top-of-the-line Aero models are further upgraded with 17-inch wheels, a sport-tuned suspension, bolstered sport seats, metallic dash trim and a sport steering wheel. An optional Touring package is available that includes bi-xenon headlights, rear parking assist, auto-dimming exterior mirrors and rain-sensing wipers. Ventilated front seats are optional on Arc and Aero models, as is a new in-dash DVD-based navigation system.

**Powertrains and Performance:** Each trim level of the 9-5 gets its own unique engine. The Linear is powered by a 185-horsepower, turbocharged 2.3-liter inline four-cylinder, while the Arc uses a higher-boost version of the same engine that produces 220 hp. The performance-oriented Aero gets an even higher-output version with a rating of 250 hp. All 9-5s come standard with a five-speed manual transmission, while a five-speed automatic is optional.

**Safety:** All 9-5s feature adaptive-force front airbags, active head restraints and seat-mounted side airbags that protect the heads and torsos of front occupants. Four-wheel antilock disc brakes, Electronic Brakeforce Distribution and stability and traction control are standard on all models. In government crash testing, the 9-5 earned a perfect five stars for driver and front-passenger protection in frontal impacts. In side-impact tests, the Saab received five stars for front-occupant protection and four stars for the rear. The IIHS gave the 9-5 a "Good" rating (the best possible) in frontal offset crash testing and named it a "Best Pick."

**Interior Design and Special Features:** Most drivers will find the 9-5's seats exceptionally comfortable, especially those equipped with the optional heating and ventilation feature. Materials quality could use improvement in some spots, but passenger room is excellent all around. A split-folding rear seat and nearly 16 cubic feet of trunk space give the 9-5 an added level of versatility. The wagon supplies 37 cubes of luggage capacity with the rear seats in use and 73 cubes when they're folded.

**Driving Impressions:** Although its turbo power plant and sporty looks might suggest otherwise, the 9-5 feels more at home on the highway than it does ripping through a twisty canyon. Aero models can hold their own once you get used to the front-wheel-drive power, but an intrusive stability control system and excessive body roll discourage aggressive driving. Unlike most sport sedans and wagons, the 9-5 is preferable with the automatic transmission, as it makes better use of the turbo engine's unusual power band.

*Crash Test Scores, see pg 530*
*Warranty information, see pg 542*

### Specifications

| Engine/Drivetrain | HP | Torque | EPA Fuel Economy Rating |
|---|---|---|---|
| 4cyl 2.3L M | 250 | 258 | 21 city/29 hwy |
| 4cyl 2.3L A | 220 | 228 | 19 city/28 hwy |
| 4cyl 2.3L M | 185 | 207 | 21 city/29 hwy |

### Body Styles

| Style | MSRP Range |
|---|---|
| Midsize Sedan | $36,250–$39,950 |
| Midsize Wagon | $32,550–$40,750 |

# 2005 Saab 9-7X

**MSRP Price Range**

## N/A

Destination Charge: N/A (all styles)

### Ratings

| | | |
|---|---|---|
| Consumer Rating | N/A | |
| Editors Rating | N/A | |

**What Edmunds.com says:** Numerous upgrades give Saab a convincing argument that the 9-7X is more than a rebadged TrailBlazer, but discriminating customers may sniff out this Swedish import's Ohio roots.

**Pros:** Tightly controlled handling, long list of standard luxury features, strong lineup of engines.

**Cons:** Attempts to disguise its domestic origins not altogether successful, hard to justify price premium over Buick and GMC cousins, no stability control.

**What's New:** This all-new SUV from Saab is the Swedish automaker's attempt to tap the distinctly American thirst for large four-wheel-drive family vehicles.

**Body Styles, Trim Levels and Options:** The 9-7X is a midsize four-door SUV that seats five and comes in one trim level. Standard equipment includes 18-inch alloy wheels with Dunlop all-season tires, all-wheel drive, an anti-theft system, leather upholstery, power-adjustable front seats, automatic climate control, an MP3-compatible CD player, front foglights, the OnStar communications system and no-charge scheduled maintenance for three years or 36,000 miles. Optional equipment includes a rear DVD player with a flip-down screen for rear passengers, a DVD-based navigation system, high-intensity discharge headlights, a sunroof, an in-dash CD changer and satellite radio. Available optional packages include a Convenience Package with adjustable pedals and headlamp washers, as well as a Protection Package with body-side molding and front skid plates.

**Powertrains and Performance:** Being very un-Saab-like, there are no turbocharged power plants available for the 9-7X. Your choice of power comes from either a 275-horsepower, 4.2-liter inline six or a 300-hp, 5.3-liter V8. Coupled to these engines is an electronically controlled four-speed automatic transmission.

**Safety:** Saab packs all the safety features into the 9-7X you'd expect in a Swedish vehicle. Fourwheel ABS, an all-wheel-drive system, dual-stage frontal airbags, a rollover sensing system, daytime running lights and side curtain airbags are standard. The 9-7X has not been crash tested, but the Chevrolet TrailBlazer on which it's based received three stars out of five in NHTSA frontal crash tests for the driver and front passenger and five stars for side-impact protection. The IIHS rated it "Marginal" (second lowest) after conducting its offset frontal impact test.

**Interior Design and Special Features:** Saab drivers will feel right at home in the 9-7X's interior. Traditional brand distinctive design elements such as the instrument panel's cockpit-inspired center stack and driver-oriented controls will be instantly recognizable by aficionados. Wood grain trim on the dash and contrasting seat upholstery and door inserts do their part to give the 9-7X the progressive upscale feel of other Saab models. And, of course, it just wouldn't be a Saab without the center console ignition switch. Those who look closer will see the cabin's GM roots, a resemblance that cheapens the 9-7X next to stylish rivals like the Volkswagen Touareg and Volvo XC90. Cargo capacity measures 41 cubic feet behind the rear seats and 80 cubes when they're folded.

*Crash Test Scores, see pg 530*
*Warranty information, see pg 542*

### Specifications

| Engine/Drivetrain | HP | Torque | EPA Fuel Economy Rating |
|---|---|---|---|
| 6cyl 4.2L A | 275 | 275 | N/A |
| 8cyl 5.3L A | 300 | 360 | N/A |

### Body Styles

| Style | MSRP Range |
|---|---|
| Midsize SUV | N/A |

**Driving Impressions:** Achieving the road feel of a European sedan using an American truck chassis is no small task, but Saab has made the kind of changes that will yield a responsive SUV. The 9-7X's stiffened front frame and reworked suspension give it more stable and responsive handling than any of its GM counterparts. Both the standard inline six and optional V8 provide more than ample power, but neither has the refinement of Saab's homegrown turbocharged engines.

**Compact Coupe, Sedan**

# 2005 Saturn ION

**MSRP Price Range**
## $11,995 - $18,145
Destination Charge: $565 (all styles)

| Ratings | | |
|---|---|---|
| Consumer Rating | N/A | |
| Editors Rating | 5.5 | |

**What Edmunds.com says:** Saturn has taken negative feedback to heart and made significant enhancements to the Ion. The result is a more polished machine that is much more competitive with its peers.

**Pros:** Low price, customer-focused dealers, large trunk capacity, coupe's innovative rear access doors, solid ride and handling dynamics.

**Cons:** Limited rear legroom, dash layout takes some getting used to, interior materials still aren't class-leading.

**Body Styles, Trim Levels and Options:** The Ion is available in two body styles: sedan and quad coupe. The sedan is available in three numerical trim levels—1, 2 and 3—while the quad coupe comes only in two levels of trim—2 or 3. The Ion 1 is your average econobox with 14-inch steel wheels, manual windows and locks and an AM/FM radio. The Ion 2 adds basic comfort options including air conditioning, power locks, a height-adjustable driver seat and a CD player, along with 15-inch wheels. Add the Convenience Package to get power windows and mirrors, cruise control and keyless entry. The Ion 3 takes a sportier step forward adding 16-inch alloy wheels, full power accessories and an anti-theft system. Leather upholstery is optional on the Ion 3, and both 2 and 3 models can get a sunroof and an in-dash CD changer.

**Powertrains and Performance:** Both the sedan and coupe feature a 2.2-liter, four-cylinder engine rated for 140 horsepower and 145 pound-feet of torque. Both models come standard with a five-speed manual transmission, with a four-speed automatic available as an option. Fuel economy estimates for manual-shift Ions are 26 mpg city and 35 mpg highway; automatic-equipped models are rated 24 city/32 highway.

**Safety:** Antilock brakes with traction control are optional, as is a head curtain side airbag system that unfolds from the roof rail to provide coverage for both front and rear outboard occupants. Also available is GM's OnStar communication system, which can summon aid automatically if the airbags deploy. In government crash testing, the Ion earned a perfect five stars for driver and front-passenger protection in frontal impacts. In side-impact testing, an Ion sedan without head curtain airbags earned three stars for the protection of rear occupants (front-occupant protection wasn't tested). The coupe earned a four-star rating front and rear.

**Interior Design and Special Features:** The speedometer and other related instruments are housed in a center-mounted pod, freeing up space in front of the driver for better sight lines and more steering-wheel adjustability. Nevertheless, this unusual layout takes some getting used to. The Ion coupe has two additional dual rear-access doors (RADs), hence the name "quad coupe," that makes it easier for rear passengers to get in and out. Material and trim enhancements for 2005, as well as new seats for level 2 and 3 models, make the Ion interior a comfortable place to spend time.

**Driving Impressions:** The engine provides adequate, if not entirely refined, power throughout the rev range. The four-speed automatic transmission is responsive, but the manual box is still a little rough through the gates. Built on a completely different platform than its S-Series predecessor, the Ion displays commendable ride and handling characteristics. It's soft enough to soak up rough roads, yet it still handles itself well in tight turns and freeway off-ramps. We've previously criticized the Ion's steering, which never seemed to provide the right amount of power assist, but revisions for 2005 have yielded much improved road feel.

**What's New:** Significant changes accompany the Ion into 2005. A revised front fascia on sedans, as well as various other exterior trim and wheel upgrades, spruce up the Ion's outward appearance. Inside, new front and rear seats (on level 2 and 3 models) provide substantial comfort improvements, and a new steering wheel replaces last year's go-kartlike unit. Interior trim and materials have also been refined. Substantial improvements to noise, vibration and harshness (NVH) have been made possible through the use of Quiet Steel for the plenum and dash, an acoustic engine cover, and other powertrain and insulation enhancements. The electric power steering has been recalibrated, and various suspension revisions improve ride and handling. A four-speed automatic transmission replaces last year's five-speed unit and the coupe's CVT unit.

*Crash Test Scores, see pg 530*
*Warranty information, see pg 542*

## Specifications

| Engine/Drivetrain | HP | Torque | EPA Fuel Economy Rating |
|---|---|---|---|
| 4cyl 2.2L A/M | 140 | 145 | 25 city/32 hwy |

## Body Styles

| Style | MSRP Range |
|---|---|
| Compact Coupe | $15,495–$18,145 |
| Compact Sedan | $11,995–$17,370 |

# 2005 Saturn ION Red Line

**Compact Coupe**

**MSRP Price Range**

## $20,885

Destination Charge: N/A (all styles)

## Ratings

| | | |
|---|---|---|
| Consumer Rating | N/A | |
| Editors Rating | 6.7 | |

**What Edmunds.com says:** With over 200 horsepower, upgraded running gear and a price under $20,000, the Ion Red Line has all the right credentials to compete in the rapidly growing sport-compact class.

**Pros:** Smooth supercharged engine, lots of performance for the price, easily accessible rear seat, customer-focused dealers.

**Cons:** Limited rear legroom, dash layout takes some getting used to, interior materials still need improvement.

**What's New:** Significant changes accompany the Ion Red Line into 2005. Inside, interior trim and materials have been refined. Substantial improvements to noise, vibration and harshness (NVH) have been made possible through the use of Quiet Steel for the plenum and dash, and various powertrain and insulation enhancements.

**Body Styles, Trim Levels and Options:** A performance version of the Ion, the Red Line is offered in quad coupe form in a single trim level. Standard features include 17-inch forged alloy wheels with 45-series performance tires, a lowered track-tuned suspension, four-wheel anti-lock disc brakes, air conditioning, leather and cloth sport seats, an MP3-compatible CD player and power door locks and windows. All Red Lines have black interiors. Buyers can choose from a variety of rear spoiler options.

**Powertrains and Performance:** Under the hood is a supercharged and intercooled 2.0-liter version of GM's Ecotec inline four-cylinder engine. Output is rated at 205 horsepower and 200 pound-feet of torque. A heavy-duty Getrag five-speed manual transmission with a short-throw shifter is standard; an automatic is not available. The suspension, which is 10mm lower than the setup on the standard Ion, incorporates firmer spring and bushing rates, and larger stabilizer bars and rear shocks. The Ion Red Line's electric power steering features different programming to provide increased driver feedback and better feel.

**Safety:** Four-wheel antilock disc brakes are standard on the Ion Red Line. On the options list, you'll find a head curtain side airbag system that protects both front and rear outboard occupants, and the OnStar communications system. In government crash testing, the Ion earned a perfect five stars for driver and front-passenger protection in frontal impacts. In side-impact testing, an Ion coupe without head curtain airbags earned four stars front and rear.

**Interior Design and Special Features:** The Red Line retains the standard Ion's center-mounted instrument pod but gains a sportier cockpit ensemble with a black color scheme, a unique shift knob and bolstered sport seats to better keep occupants in place during hard cornering. Like other Ion coupes, it has two additional rear-access doors (RADs), hence the name "quad coupe." These extra doors make it easier to get people and cargo in and out of the backseat. Material and trim enhancements for 2005 make the Ion Red Line interior a more comfortable place to spend time.

**Driving Impressions:** While the standard Ion offers little to get excited about, the Red Line presents a high level of performance for the price. With 205 horsepower and a low 2,930-pound curb weight, this coupe is able to run with just about anything in its price range. Saturn promises 0-60 times of about 6.3 seconds, with a quarter-mile of 14.8 seconds. Braking is also strong at 119 feet from 60 to zero. The performance-tuned suspension still delivers a comfortable ride, while also providing excellent dynamic ability at the track. The steering, in particular, is impressive in its just-right firmness and solid feel at speed.

*Crash Test Scores, see pg 530*
*Warranty information, see pg 542*

## Specifications

| Engine/Drivetrain | HP | Torque | EPA Fuel Economy Rating |
|---|---|---|---|
| 4cyl 2.0L A | 205 | 200 | 23 city/29 hwy |

## Body Styles

| Style | MSRP Range |
|---|---|
| Compact Coupe | $20,885 |

For the latest full vehicle reports, visit www.edmunds.com/bginfopak

**MSRP Price Range**
## $23,770 - $29,855
Destination Charge: N/A (all styles)

## Ratings

| | | |
|---|---|---|
| Consumer Rating | N/A | |
| Editors Rating | 6.9 | |

**What Edmunds.com says:** Though the Relay features a slick interior and distinctive styling, it doesn't have the on-road finesse of its minivan competitors.

**Pros:** Smooth ride and handling, lots of nifty interior storage spaces, innovative multimedia storage system, available all-wheel drive.

**Cons:** Engine power and refinement not up to class leaders, no side curtain airbags.

**What's New:** The Relay is an all-new "crossover sport van." Think of it as a minivan with an SUV-like front end.

**Body Styles, Trim Levels and Options:** The Relay comes in one size and two trim levels, Relay 2 and Relay 3. Standard Relay 2 amenities include power windows, air conditioning, an eight-speaker sound system with a CD/MP3 player, a rear-seat DVD entertainment system, the OnStar communications system, cruise control and keyless entry. The Relay 3 adds rear air conditioning, a power driver seat, alloy wheels and upgraded storage. An all-wheel-drive system is available, and is bundled with a rear load-leveling suspension and front side-impact airbags. An optional PhatNoise mobile digital media system allows owners to store thousands of MP3s and/or several dozen movies on a removable hard drive cartridge. Other noteworthy options include a remote vehicle startup system, a 115-volt AC outlet, dual power-sliding side doors, rear park assist, XM Satellite Radio, leather seats and a sport suspension.

**Powertrains and Performance:** All Relays come equipped with a 3.5-liter V6 that makes 200 horsepower and 220 pound-feet of torque. A four-speed automatic transmission is standard. No other powertrain combinations are available, though buyers can opt for all-wheel drive.

**Safety:** All models come standard with four-wheel antilock disc brakes. Side-impact airbags for front occupants and the StabiliTrak stability control system are optional. Full-length side curtain airbags are not available. The Relay has not yet been crash tested.

**Interior Design and Special Features:** The Relay seats seven, and the fold-flat third-row seat offers a 50/50 split. A pleasing two-tone color scheme with faux wood accents dramatically brightens the interior atmosphere of the van. Folding center trays (with cupholders) between the first- and second-row seats are available. An overhead rail system provides rear-seat access to climate and entertainment functions, and can be outfitted with various storage containers. A rear-seat DVD entertainment system is standard on all Relays, and can be upgraded with infrared wireless headphones. A remote vehicle start system, pioneered on the 2004 Chevy Malibu, is optional.

**Driving Impressions:** The V6 power plant is down on power compared to its competitors, but it still manages to provide adequate acceleration. The Relay's suspension is on the soft side, though upgrading to the optional sport suspension does provide for more responsive handling.

*Crash Test Scores, see pg 530*
*Warranty information, see pg 542*

## Specifications

| Engine/Drivetrain | HP | Torque | EPA Fuel Economy Rating |
|---|---|---|---|
| 6cyl 3.5L A | 200 | 220 | N/A |

## Body Styles

| Style | MSRP Range |
|---|---|
| Midsize Minivan | $23,770 - $29,855 |

# 2005 Saturn VUE

**MSRP Price Range**

## $17,630 – $24,890

Destination Charge: $575 (all styles)

### Ratings

| | | |
|---|---|---|
| Consumer Rating | N/A | ▭▭▭▭▭ |
| Editors Rating | 6.6 | ▰▰▰▰▱ |

**What Edmunds.com says:** A well-thought-out and capable mini sport-ute, the Vue's unimpressive interior and sloppy steering keep it from challenging the class leaders in this segment.

**Pros:** Strong V6, spacious cabin, comfortable ride, excellent crash test scores, good fuel economy.

**Cons:** Too many low-grade and ill-fitting interior materials, undersized front seats, vague steering.

**What's New:** Revised interior and exterior trim details freshen up the interior of Saturn's SUV. Four-cylinder models get new machined alloy wheels in place of last year's painted alloys, along with new seat fabric, and a four-speed automatic transmission in place of the former CVT unit. All-wheel drive is no longer available on four-cylinder Vues.

*Crash Test Scores, see pg 530*
*Warranty information, see pg 542*

### Specifications

| Engine/Drivetrain | HP | Torque | EPA Fuel Economy Rating |
|---|---|---|---|
| 6cyl 3.5L A | 250 | 242 | 20 city/28 hwy |
| 4cyl 2.2L A/M | 143 | 152 | 22 city/28 hwy |

### Body Styles

| Style | MSRP Range |
|---|---|
| Midsize SUV | $17,630–$24,890 |

**Body Styles, Trim Levels and Options:** The Vue is available in four-cylinder and V6 models with either front- or all-wheel drive; interior trim is largely dictated by the engine. Base four-cylinder models come with 16-inch wheels, air conditioning, a tilt steering wheel, a height-adjustable driver seat, cloth interior and a four-speaker AM/FM stereo. Moving up to the six-cylinder models adds features like alloy wheels (16-inch on front-drive models, 17-inch on AWD models); power windows, locks and mirrors; cruise control; keyless entry; and an upgraded six-speaker, MP3-compatible CD stereo. Optional equipment on all models includes an in-dash six-disc CD changer, satellite radio, a DVD entertainment system, leather upholstery, a sunroof and the OnStar communications system. Order the Seat Comfort Package to pick up a power driver seat, heated front seats and adjustable lumbar support.

**Powertrains and Performance:** The base model Vue is powered by a 2.2-liter four-cylinder rated at 143 horsepower. Transmission choices include a five-speed manual or a four-speed automatic. Note that the four-cylinder Vue is front-wheel-drive only. For additional power and capability, there's a 3.5-liter V6 rated for 250 hp and 242 pound-feet of torque. Available in front-drive and AWD configurations, the V6 Vue is the most powerful SUV in its class. A five-speed automatic transmission is standard with the V6. Fuel mileage is above average—you can expect 19-24 mpg in the city and 25-29 mpg on the highway.

**Safety:** Head curtain airbags that protect both front and rear passengers are optional on all Vues. ABS is standard on V6 models and optional on four-cylinder models. In government testing, the Vue earned a perfect five stars for driver protection in frontal impacts and four stars for front-passenger protection. Side-impact tests resulted in a five-star rating for front and rear passengers. The IIHS gave the Vue a rating of "Good" (its best) in frontal offset crash testing. In IIHS side-impact tests of small SUVs, the Vue earned a "Poor" rating (the lowest), but the vehicle tested did not have head curtain airbags.

**Interior Design and Special Features:** Continual improvements to the interior help inch the Vue up toward having an attractive cabin, but in general, materials quality is still below that of most competitors. However, passenger room is excellent, and a low step-in height makes getting in and out easy. A foldable front-passenger seat allows the transport of extra-long cargo, while folding down the rear seats provides 63.5 cubic feet of cargo space.

**Driving Impressions:** Knowing full well that the Vue would remain almost exclusively on the pavement, Saturn engineers gave the Vue a fully independent suspension that delivers a comfortable, forgiving ride. The wide stance keeps body roll down, but the electric power steering system doesn't deliver much road feel. The four-cylinder engine is sufficiently powerful, while the V6 offers a substantial power boost that makes the Vue extremely quick on its feet for a small SUV.

## Compact Coupe

# 2005 Scion tC

**MSRP Price Range**
## $15,950 - $16,750
Destination Charge: $515 (all styles)

#1
Editors'
Rating

### Ratings

| | | |
|---|---|---|
| Consumer Rating | 9.3 | ▭ |
| Editors Rating | 8.4 | ▭ |

**What Edmunds.com says:** With a price tag under $17,000, a ton of standard features and a fun-loving personality, we'd bet that the tC is going to be another big hit for the Scion folks.

**Pros:** High quality all around, unexpected safety and luxury features, tight handling, spacious cabin, bargain price.

**Cons:** A couple of odd design elements, drab interior color.

**What's New:** The tC coupe is the latest addition to Toyota's innovative Scion division.

**Body Styles, Trim Levels and Options:** Like the other Scion models, the tC comes in one trim level and is chock-full of unexpected goodies such as one-touch up-and-down power windows, cruise control, air conditioning, keyless entry, mirror-mounted turn signal lights, four-wheel antilock disc brakes and a 160-watt Pioneer sound system with CD player that is (XM) satellite radio-ready. The only factory option is a side airbag package, but there is a multitude of dealer-installed options. This list includes a CD changer, satellite radio, a subwoofer and a lighting kit for the footwell, just to name a few.

**Powertrains and Performance:** Standard power comes from a 2.4-liter inline four-cylinder borrowed from the Camry, with 160 hp and 163 lb-ft of torque. A smooth-shifting five-speed manual gearbox is standard, with a four-speed automatic available as an option. Fuel economy is estimated at 22 mpg city and 29 mpg highway with the manual, and 23 city and 30 highway with the optional automatic.

**Safety:** The tC comes with four-wheel antilock disc brakes (with Electronic Brakeforce Distribution) as standard equipment. Side airbags for front occupants and full-length head curtain airbags are optional. Other standard safety features include a first aid kit, triple side door beams and a driver knee airbag.

**Interior Design and Special Features:** Although the tC is a compact car at just 174 inches long (about the same length as a Honda Civic coupe), a relatively long (106.3-inch) wheelbase provides more than ample legroom, especially for those riding in the back. Rear passengers will also enjoy the split seat backs that can individually recline up to 45 degrees. Although it looks like a coupe, the tC is actually a hatchback, which means flexible cargo capacity. By folding down the rear seats as well as the right front seat, a load floor that stretches 103.6 inches is created, ideal for snowboarders and surfers. Cargo capacity is 12.8 cubic feet with the rear seats in use and a whopping 60 cubic feet when they're folded down.

**Driving Impressions:** The tC features a fully independent suspension (with a double-wishbone setup in the rear that maximizes interior space) and the same tires that are on the Lexus IS 300—Z-rated 215/45R17 Bridgestone Potenzas wrapped around those eye-catching 17s. The result is a precise, well-weighted feel and flat, composed cornering. Ride quality is firm, but compliant enough to absorb most bumps and ruts on battered city streets. The 2.4-liter engine's broad power band contributes to the fun with plenty of pull down low and through the midrange.

*Crash Test Scores, see pg 530*
*Warranty information, see pg 542*

### Specifications

| Engine/Drivetrain | HP | Torque | EPA Fuel Economy Rating |
|---|---|---|---|
| 4cyl 2.4L A/M | 160 | 163 | 23 city/30 hwy |

### Body Styles

| Style | MSRP Range |
|---|---|
| Compact Coupe | $15,950–$16,750 |

# Scion

# 2005 Scion xA

**MSRP Price Range**

## $12,480 - $13,280

Destination Charge: $515 (all styles)

### Ratings

| | | |
|---|---|---|
| Consumer Rating | 9.0 | |
| Editors Rating | 7.8 | |

**What Edmunds.com says:** Roomy and well equipped, the spunky Scion xA is one of the best buys for 2005 in the economy car segment.

**Pros:** Handles well for an economy car, lengthy standard equipment list, comfortable seats, easy to load cargo, better deal than Toyota's Echo.

**Cons:** The cool stuff costs extra, modest passing power with automatic transmission.

**What's New:** The Scion xA carries over unchanged for 2005. Sales are now nationwide.

*Crash Test Scores, see pg 530*
*Warranty information, see pg 542*

### Specifications

| Engine/Drivetrain | HP | Torque | EPA Fuel Economy Rating |
|---|---|---|---|
| 4cyl 1.5L A/M | 108 | 105 | 31 city/37 hwy |

### Body Styles

| Style | MSRP Range |
|---|---|
| Compact Coupe | $12,480–$13,280 |

**Body Styles, Trim Levels and Options:** The xA is sold as a single trim level. Each one comes with ABS; air conditioning; power windows, locks, mirrors and steering; a six-speaker Pioneer stereo with a CD player; a rear wiper; rear defroster; a tachometer; and a 60/40-split-folding rear seat. The only factory option is a side airbag package, but there are about 40 dealer-installed options. This list includes a CD changer with multicolor head unit illumination, satellite radio, a subwoofer, alloy wheels, a roof rack, keyless entry and a lighting kit for the footwell, just to name a few. Those seeking to eke out a bit more performance can opt for a strut tower brace and/or a cold air intake.

**Powertrains and Performance:** Under the hood is a 1.5-liter inline four-cylinder with variable valve timing. It's the same engine used in the Echo and xB, and it makes 108 horsepower. This isn't a lot by modern-day standards, and as the xA weighs almost 300 pounds more than the Echo, acceleration isn't as spirited. Still, the xA has enough get-up-and-go for city driving, and it cruises along nicely on the highway. Passing maneuvers require a little more effort, particularly on cars with the four-speed automatic. A five-speed manual is the other transmission choice. Gas mileage is rated at 31 city/37 highway with the automatic and 32/38 with the manual.

**Safety:** The xA comes with antilock brakes (with Electronic Brakeforce Distribution), three-point belts in all five seating positions and a first aid kit. Side airbags for front occupants and full-length head curtain airbags are optional. An xA without side airbags earned four out of five stars in all government front- and side-impact crash tests.

**Interior Design and Special Features:** Inside, the xA is perfectly agreeable for an economy car. Various surfaces have been trimmed in faux aluminum that's more attractive than the stuff you'll find in some Toyotas. Lots of hard plastic is inevitable at this price, but most of it is low in gloss. The gauge cluster is mounted in the center of the dash and takes some getting used to. As in the xB and Echo, a tall cabin design yields a spacious feel and allows occupants to sit tall. Although the xA's backseat isn't as roomy as the xB's, its accommodations are certainly on par with those of the Matrix and Honda Civic. With the rear seats in use, there isn't much cargo space—fold the seats and you'll have 32.8 cubic feet.

**Driving Impressions:** Although the xA is built on the same platform as the Echo (a car we've never considered a good handler), it's amazing what a set of 15-inch wheels and tires and a rear stabilizer bar can do. On the highway, the xA feels nicely connected to the road. Driven enthusiastically around a few twists and turns, the xA is more entertaining than its economy origins would suggest. While enthusiasts would be better served by a Focus or Civic, most drivers will be satisfied with the Scion's ride and handling.

For the latest full vehicle reports, visit www.edmunds.com/bginfopak

# 2005 Scion xB

## Ratings

| | | |
|---|---|---|
| Consumer Rating | 9.4 | |
| Editors Rating | 8.2 | |

**What Edmunds.com says:** It looks like nothing else on the market and it can haul serious amounts of people and cargo. A must-drive if you're light on cash but don't travel light.

**Pros:** Massive interior for its size, unusual mini-truck styling, long list of standard equipment, comes with standard stability control, handles well for a budget-priced vehicle.

**Cons:** The cool stuff costs extra, modest passing power with automatic transmission, can't get xA's side airbags.

**What's New:** No changes for the ultrahip xB, other than nationwide availability.

**Body Styles, Trim Levels and Options:** The xB is sold as a single trim level. Each one comes with ABS; air conditioning; power windows, locks, mirrors and steering; a six-speaker Pioneer stereo with a CD player; a 60/40-split folding and removable rear seat; keyless entry; a rear wiper; rear defroster; a tachometer; and a ground effects kit. There are about 40 dealer-installed options. This list includes a CD changer with multicolor head unit illumination, satellite radio, a subwoofer, alloy wheels, a roof rack and a lighting kit for the foot wells, just to name a few. Those seeking to eke out a bit more performance can opt for a strut tower brace and/or a cold air intake.

**Powertrains and Performance:** Power comes from a 1.5-liter inline four-cylinder with variable valve timing. It's the same engine used in the Echo and xA, and it makes 108 horsepower. This isn't a lot, and as the xB weighs almost 400 pounds more than the Echo, acceleration isn't as spirited. Still, it has enough get-up-and-go for city driving, and it cruises along nicely on the highway. Merging and passing maneuvers require a little more effort, particularly on cars with the four-speed automatic. A five-speed manual is the other transmission choice. Fuel economy is in the 30-mpg range.

**Safety:** The xB comes with stability and traction control, antilock brakes with Electronic Brakeforce Distribution, three-point belts in all five seating positions and a first aid kit. It has not yet been crash tested.

**Interior Design and Special Features:** Being tall (64.6 inches) and boxy has its advantages, and the xB treats its passengers to incredible amounts of head- and legroom. Even when the front chairs are adjusted for a normal-size driver and passenger, those seated in the rear (there's room for three) are still able to stretch out their legs. And stylish as the xB is, these attributes make it a great vehicle for anyone with a baby on board. With the rear seats in use, the xB can hold 21 cubic feet of cargo; fold or remove these seats and the number goes up to 43. Apart from being spacious, the cabin is agreeable in appearance. Lots of hard plastic is inevitable in this price range, but most of it is low in gloss. The center-mounted gauge pod takes some getting used to, but is otherwise unobtrusive.

**Driving Impressions:** Although the xB is built on the same platform as the Echo (a car we've never considered a good handler), it's amazing what a set of 15-inch wheels and tires and a rear stabilizer bar can do. On the highway, the xB feels nicely connected to the road and offers a reasonably smooth ride. Some wind buffeting is inevitable with its anti-aerodynamic design, but not enough to make it feel unsafe. Driven enthusiastically around twists and turns, the xB is more entertaining than its dimensions and price would suggest.

*Crash Test Scores, see pg 530*
*Warranty information, see pg 542*

## Specifications

| Engine/Drivetrain | HP | Torque | EPA Fuel Economy Rating |
|---|---|---|---|
| 4cyl 1.5L A/M | 108 | 105 | 30 city/34 hwy |

## Body Styles

| Style | MSRP Range |
|---|---|
| Compact Wagon | $13,680–$14,480 |

# 2005 Subaru Baja

**MSRP Price Range**
## $22,195 - $27,095
Destination Charge: $575 (all styles)

### Ratings

| | | |
|---|---|---|
| Consumer Rating | 9.1 | |
| Editors Rating | 7.6 | |

**What Edmunds.com says:** An interesting car-and-pickup blend that comes up a bit short in outright functionality.

**Pros:** Comfortable ride, stable handling, turbo model's peppy performance, convenience of an open bed, unlikely to be lost in a parking lot.

**Cons:** Midgate's glass isn't removable, limited towing and hauling capability.

**What's New:** New features this year include a 12-volt power outlet in the console, a net pocket on the rear seat back and pre-wiring for roof-mounted rally lights. The leather package now includes a hard bed cover.

**Body Styles, Trim Levels and Options:** The Baja is a four-door utility vehicle available in two trims—Baja Sport and Baja Turbo. The Baja Sport is the most affordably priced, and it offers 16-inch alloy wheels; foglights; air conditioning; a CD player; cruise control; a moonroof; power windows, locks and mirrors; and keyless entry. Step up to the Baja Turbo and you get a more powerful turbocharged engine along with an upgraded six-speaker audio system with an in-dash CD changer. Among the available options are a tubular bed extender, a bed-mounted bike rack, roof-mounted rally lights and a sunroof. Turbo models are eligible for a Leather Package that provides leather upholstery, heated front seats and a hard bed cover.

**Powertrains and Performance:** The Baja Sport is equipped with a 2.5-liter, four-cylinder engine that delivers 165 horsepower and 166 pound-feet of torque. The Baja Turbo boasts a turbocharged version that produces 210 hp and 235 lb-ft of twist. A five-speed manual transmission is standard; a four-speed automatic is optional. Automatic-equipped Baja Turbos also get an automanual gate that allows for manual shifting when the driver desires. All Subaru vehicles sold in the United States come with standard all-wheel drive, and the Baja is no exception. This Subaru can carry a maximum payload of 1,050 pounds, and has a 2,400-pound towing capacity. This is about half of what a typical compact pickup can pull, but it's enough to easily accommodate a personal watercraft or a couple of motorcycles.

**Safety:** The Baja comes standard with four-wheel antilock disc brakes and pre-tensioners and load limiters for the front seatbelts. Side airbags are not available. No crash test data is available for the Baja.

**Interior Design and Special Features:** The Baja's cargo box is smaller than the beds of traditional compact pickups, but this car-based pickup does offer a handsome interior that scores high marks for style, comfort and ergonomics. Utility is maximized via the Switchback feature; to use, flip up the bottom cushion of the rear seat, fold the rear seat back forward and fold the trapdoor flat into the rear seat. The rear window is fixed, however, and that puts limits on the shape and height of items that can fit. An optional tailgate extender is available that increases cargo bed length to 75 inches.

Crash Test Scores, see pg 530
Warranty information, see pg 542

### Specifications

| Engine/Drivetrain | HP | Torque | EPA Fuel Economy Rating |
|---|---|---|---|
| 4cyl 2.5L A/M | 210 | 235 | 18 city/23 hwy |
| 4cyl 2.5L A/M | 165 | 166 | 21 city/28 hwy |

### Body Styles

| Style | MSRP Range |
|---|---|
| Crew Cab Pickup Truck | $22,195–$27,095 |

**Driving Impressions:** Acceleration can be a bit sluggish in Bajas with the base engine, so those looking for a little excitement would be advised to check out the Turbo model, which has ample power for just about any situation. Based on the previous-generation Outback, the Baja has a fully independent suspension and rides much more like a car than a truck. It has a comfortable ride around town and never feels unstable when going around corners. Heavy-duty suspension components and 8.2 inches of ground clearance allow it to tackle rutted dirt roads and sandy washes without a problem, but don't expect to do any serious boulder bashing.

**MSRP Price Range**
## $21,295 - $28,195
Destination Charge: $575 (all styles)

| Ratings | | |
|---|---|---|
| Consumer Rating | 8.9 | |
| Editors Rating | 8.0 | |

**What Edmunds.com says:** Practical, well built and enjoyable to drive, the Forester offers an excellent balance of upscale features and all-weather drivability.

**Pros:** Standard all-wheel drive, two engine choices, availability of upscale features, class-leading crash test scores.

**Cons:** Price can be higher than some of the competition, tight on legroom in the backseat.

**What's New:** The base engine is enhanced this year with electronic throttle control, and a new four-speed automatic transmission is available. An air filtration system is now standard on all Foresters. Also new this year is the 2.5 XS L.L. Bean Edition, which includes a myriad of interior and exterior trim enhancements, rugged cargo area trim and a self-leveling rear suspension.

**Body Styles, Trim Levels and Options:** The Forester is available in four trim levels: 2.5 X, 2.5 XS, 2.5 XS L.L. Bean Edition and 2.5 XT. The X comes with power windows, locks and mirrors; air conditioning with air filtration; cruise control; tilt steering; 16-inch wheels and tires; 100-watt AM/FM/weather band CD audio; and remote keyless entry. XS models have automatic climate control, alloy wheels, an eight-way power driver seat, an in-dash six-disc CD changer, a leather-wrapped steering wheel and shifter and upgraded interior upholstery and carpet. The XS L.L. Bean Edition is your ticket to leather upholstery, as well as unique wheels and exterior trim and a self-leveling rear suspension; an automatic transmission is standard on this model. The XT offers all the regular XS equipment along with a 210-hp turbocharged engine, functional hood scoop and body-color side cladding. An optional premium package adds leather upholstery and a moonroof to the XT.

**Powertrains and Performance:** Standard on X and XS models is a 2.5-liter horizontally opposed four-cylinder engine that makes 165 horsepower and 166 pound-feet of torque. If you need extra power, opt for the XT model, which has a turbocharged version of the 2.5-liter engine good for 210 hp and 235 lb-ft of torque. Both engines give you the choice of a five-speed manual or four-speed automatic transmission. Like all Subarus, the Forester comes standard with full-time all-wheel drive. Manual transmission-equipped vehicles have a Hill Holder clutch feature that keeps the vehicle from rolling back on steep inclines.

**Safety:** ABS is standard on all Foresters; additionally, all models except the base X have four-wheel disc brakes. Active head restraints and side-impact airbags round out the Forester's safety features. The IIHS gave the Forester a "Good" rating (its best) for frontal offset and side-impact crashes, and named it a "Best Pick" in the compact SUV class. The Subaru also earned a perfect five stars in all front- and side-impact testing conducted by the NHTSA. If safety is of utmost importance in your selection of a small SUV, this is the one to get.

**Interior Design and Special Features:** The Forester earns praise for the high-quality look and feel of its interior. Even the base X model is well equipped and user-friendly, and leather-equipped models feel downright luxurious. The front seats are supportive with adequate room for most adults, but the rear quarters are a little tight for adults, and kids riding in bulky safety seats. Rear cargo room with the seats folded measures 64.1 cubic feet, a bit shy of the major players in this class.

**Driving Impressions:** The base 2.5-liter engine provides adequate performance, but for those seeking maximum acceleration, we recommend the thrilling turbocharged XT paired with the standard five-speed manual transmission. In terms of handling, the Forester is stable and predictable even when pushed to its limits. The steering is a bit vague at speed, and the soft suspension tuning results in some body roll, but for day-to-day driving, the Forester is comfortable and controllable enough to suit most drivers.

*Crash Test Scores, see pg 530*
*Warranty information, see pg 542*

| Specifications | | | |
|---|---|---|---|
| Engine/Drivetrain | HP | Torque | EPA Fuel Economy Rating |
| 4cyl 2.5L A/M | 210 | 235 | 19 city/23 hwy |
| 4cyl 2.5L A/M | 165 | 166 | 21 city/26 hwy |

| Body Styles | |
|---|---|
| Style | MSRP Range |
| Compact Wagon | $21,295–$28,195 |

# 2005 Subaru Impreza

**Compact Sedan, Wagon**

**MSRP Price Range**
## $18,095 - $27,395
Destination Charge: $575 (all styles)

### Ratings

| | | |
|---|---|---|
| Consumer Rating | 9.0 | |
| Editors Rating | 7.0 | |

**What Edmunds.com says:** From the RS wagon to the WRX, the all-wheel-drive Impreza is a practical, fun-to-drive alternative to the typically dull cars that populate its segment of the market.

**Pros:** A stout 227 horsepower in the WRX, all-wheel-drive grip, a variety of sedans and wagons to choose from, fun to drive.

**Cons:** Tight rear quarters, limited availability of side airbags.

**What's New:** The 2.5 RS now has drive-by-wire electronic throttle control and a new four-speed automatic transmission. The dashboard center stack/console has been redesigned with improved cupholders and fancier metallic trim. The 2.5 RS wagon, which boasts the RS sedan's upgraded suspension tuning, alloy wheels and sport seats, has replaced last year's 2.5 TS wagon. The WRX picks up automatic climate control, redesigned alloy wheels and body-color ground effects. Smoke-tinted headlight lenses and revised exterior colors round out the changes.

**Body Styles, Trim Levels and Options:** The Impreza is available in sedan and wagon body styles and three basic trim levels: the 2.5 RS sedan and wagon, the Outback Sport wagon and the WRX sedan and wagon. Standard equipment levels are above average. The 2.5 RS sedan and wagon have 16-inch alloy wheels, a sport-tuned suspension, air conditioning, sport seats with height adjustment for the driver, a CD player, a leather-wrapped steering wheel, and power windows, locks and mirrors. The Outback Sport adds a two-tone paint scheme, softer suspension tuning and a bit more ground clearance, massive foglights and a power point and tie-downs in the cargo bay. The high-performance WRX adds a functional hood scoop, limited-slip rear differential, an even stiffer suspension, bigger brakes and unique wheels. Inside the cockpit are alloy pedals, a six-disc CD changer, automatic climate control and a Momo leather-wrapped steering wheel.

**Powertrains and Performance:** Powering the 2.5 RS sedan and wagon, as well as the Outback Sport, is a 2.5-liter, 165-horsepower horizontally opposed four-cylinder engine. A smaller, though more powerful, engine can be found in the WRX sedan and wagon. This turbocharged 2.0-liter mill (also a flat four) kicks out an impressive 227 horsepower—enough to push the WRX sedan to 60 mph in just over 6 seconds. For all models, transmission choices are a five-speed manual or a four-speed automatic. All-wheel drive is standard on all Imprezas, but three different systems are used depending on the model and the transmission choice.

**Safety:** All Imprezas have standard four-wheel antilock disc brakes, three-point seatbelts for rear passengers and pre-tensioners and force limiters for the front seatbelts. Side airbags are standard on the WRX but aren't available on other trims. In government crash testing, the Impreza earned four stars (out of a possible five) for driver safety in frontal impacts and five stars for front-passenger safety. Five stars were awarded for front-seat side-impact safety. The IIHS gave the car a "Good" rating (its best) for front offset crash protection and named it a "Best Pick."

*Crash Test Scores, see pg 530*
*Warranty information, see pg 542*

### Specifications

| Engine/Drivetrain | HP | Torque | EPA Fuel Economy Rating |
|---|---|---|---|
| 4cyl 2.5L A/M | 165 | 166 | 23 city/30 hwy |
| 4cyl 2.0L A/M | 227 | 217 | 20 city/27 hwy |

### Body Styles

| Style | MSRP Range |
|---|---|
| Compact Sedan | $18,095–$27,395 |
| Compact Wagon | $18,095–$25,395 |

**Interior Design and Special Features:** Though by no means a match for the cockpit of a Volkswagen Jetta, the Impreza's dash is modern enough in appearance, and the materials used are of good quality. For cargo, the wagons can hold 27.9 cubic feet of stuff, or 61.6 cubic feet with the rear seats folded flat.

**Driving Impressions:** There's no question that the WRX sedan and wagon are an absolute blast to drive. Slight turbo lag results in soft power delivery at low rpm, but once past 3,000 rpm, the WRX blasts off. Handling is superb thanks to a well-tuned suspension, grippy tires and the standard all-wheel drive. Although not nearly as fast, the 2.5 RS sedan and wagon are equally enjoyable to toss around on a twisty road. The Outback Sport may have a sportier look, but the less expensive RS wagon is the better handler.

**MSRP Price Range**

## $32,295

Destination Charge: $575 (all styles)

### Ratings

| | | |
|---|---|---|
| Consumer Rating | 9.2 | |
| Editors Rating | 8.0 | |

**What Edmunds.com says:** With its powerful engine, driver-controlled all-wheel-drive system and track-ready suspension, the WRX STi represents the ultimate in affordable all-wheel-drive performance.

**Pros:** Stunning acceleration, slightly more forgiving ride than that of Mitsubishi Evolution, high-quality cabin trim.

**Cons:** Handling not quite as sharp as Evolution's, vague gearshifter.

**What's New:** The WRX STi receives a host of detail changes, including a new helical limited-slip front differential, power steering oil cooler and revised alloy wheels. Interior improvements include a redesigned center stack/console layout, full-auto climate control and revised front seats. Last, but not least, an audio system with six premium speakers and a six-disc CD changer is now standard.

**Body Styles, Trim Levels and Options:** The Impreza WRX STi comes only as a sedan. Standard equipment includes Brembo brakes, xenon headlights, 17-inch wheels with 225/45 performance tires, an aluminum hood with functional hood scoop, a large rear wing and ground effects. Inside the cockpit are alloy pedals; automatic climate control; a six-speaker stereo with an in-dash CD changer; keyless entry; sport seats; power windows, locks and mirrors; cruise control; and a Momo leather-wrapped steering wheel. The short options list includes an auto-dimming rearview mirror, carbon-fiber cockpit accents and a turbo boost gauge.

**Powertrains and Performance:** The STi uses a larger 2.5-liter version of the standard WRX's turbocharged flat-four. With this layout comes a unique, muscular growl that announces serious output to the tune of 300 hp and a stout 300 lb-ft of torque. Sending the power to all four wheels is a six-speed manual gearbox, the only transmission available on the STi. Subaru's World Rally Championship racing technology trickles down to the street, as the STi has a driver-controlled center differential (DCCD). Worked by a thumbwheel on the center console, the DCCD allows the pilot to control the power split between the front and rear axles, for optimum traction in varied conditions.

**Safety:** The WRX STi features four-wheel antilock disc brakes, Electronic Brakeforce Distribution (EBD), side airbags for front occupants and pre-tensioners and force limiters for the front seatbelts. In government crash tests, the Impreza earned four stars (out of a possible five) for driver protection in frontal impacts and five stars for front-passenger safety. The Subaru also earned four stars for front-occupant protection in side impacts. The Insurance Institute for Highway Safety gave the car a "Good" rating (the highest) for front offset crash protection and named it a "Best Pick" overall.

**Interior Design and Special Features:** With heavily bolstered two-tone seats and a fat three-spoke steering wheel, the STi's cockpit won't be mistaken for a standard WRX's. Aluminum pedals and controls for the intercooler sprayer and center differential further hint at the serious performance nature of the STi. Creature comforts have been kept to a minimum, but this year's models do get standard automatic climate control and a premium audio system complete with a six-disc CD changer.

**Driving Impressions:** With so much usable power, the STi is scary quick. Zero to 60 mph takes less than 5.0 seconds and the quarter-mile is eaten up in under 14 seconds. Equally impressive is the Subie's braking ability. Stopping from 60 mph takes only 110 feet of asphalt—a world-class effort. In addition to its fat power band and strong brakes, the STi offers excellent steering feedback, commendable handling and a forgiving nature. The gearshift's action could be more precise and the STi's suspension tuning isn't perfect, but these are minor drawbacks given the STi's overall performance capabilities.

*Crash Test Scores, see pg 530*
*Warranty information, see pg 542*

### Specifications

| Engine/Drivetrain | HP | Torque | EPA Fuel Economy Rating |
|---|---|---|---|
| 4cyl 2.5L M | 300 | 300 | 18 city/24 hwy |

### Body Styles

| Style | MSRP Range |
|---|---|
| Compact Sedan | $32,295 |

# 2005 Subaru Legacy

**Midsize Sedan, Wagon**

**MSRP Price Range**

**$21,295 - $30,995**

Destination Charge: $575 (all styles)

#1 Editors' Rating

### Ratings

| | | |
|---|---|---|
| Consumer Rating | 9.4 | |
| Editors Rating | 8.7 | |

**What Edmunds.com says:** A tight chassis, a turbo-charged engine and a slick cockpit have transformed the all-wheel-drive Legacy into a serious driver's car. Whether you're an enthusiast in need of four doors or a safety-conscious parent in need of some fun, this one is worth a try.

**Pros:** Don't have to pay extra for all-wheel drive, generous standard equipment list, top-notch build and materials quality, excellent power in GT models, great highway ride, sharp handling.

**Cons:** Stability control not available, smaller backseat than most competitors, so-so stereo offerings.

**What's New:** An all-new and vastly improved Legacy is introduced in sedan and wagon body styles. Topping the list of upgrades are a 250-horsepower turbo-charged engine, a stylish new interior and a full menu of airbags.

*Crash Test Scores, see pg 530*
*Warranty information, see pg 542*

### Specifications

| Engine/Drivetrain | HP | Torque | EPA Fuel Economy Rating |
|---|---|---|---|
| 4cyl 2.5L A/M | 250 | 250 | 19 city/25 hwy |
| 4cyl 2.5L A/M | 168 | 166 | 23 city/30 hwy |

### Body Styles

| Style | MSRP Range |
|---|---|
| Midsize Sedan | $21,295–$29,795 |
| Midsize Wagon | $22,295–$30,995 |

**Body Styles, Trim Levels and Options:** The Legacy comes in sedan and wagon body styles in either 2.5i or 2.5 GT trim. A Limited Package is available on both trim levels. The 2.5i comes with the base 2.5-liter engine and offers such standard equipment as 16-inch alloy wheels, body-color door handles and moldings, air conditioning, a six-speaker CD stereo, cruise control, a trip computer, tweed upholstery, keyless entry and, on wagons only, roof rails and a cargo cover. Opt for the Limited package and you'll get larger front brakes, a power driver seat, leather upholstery, a leather-wrapped steering wheel, heated seats and mirrors, a wiper de-icer, an in-dash CD changer, dual-zone automatic climate control and dual moonroofs (the sedan gets a single large moonroof). Upgrade to the 2.5 GT and you get a turbocharged engine, along with 17-inch wheels, more powerful brakes, a functional hood scoop, sport seats, a Momo steering wheel and electroluminescent gauges. You'll need to order the Limited Package to get a power driver seat, leather upholstery and a moonroof on the GT.

**Powertrains and Performance:** The 2.5i model is powered by a 2.5-liter horizontally opposed four-cylinder engine that makes 168 horsepower (163 in PZEV-mandated states) and 166 lb-ft of torque. The 2.5 GT uses a 2.5-liter turbocharged engine rated for 250 hp and 250 lb-ft of torque. Either engine can be equipped with a five-speed manual transmission. The 2.5i is eligible for a four-speed automatic while the GT gets a five-speed auto; both come with an automanual mode. All-wheel drive is standard across the board.

**Safety:** All Legacys have four-wheel antilock disc brakes with Electronic Brakeforce Distribution. Stability control is, unfortunately, not available. Front side-impact airbags and full-length side curtain airbags are also standard on all models. The front-seat head restraints feature dynamic whiplash protection.

**Interior Design and Special Features:** Some of the biggest improvements this year are in the cabin. One can't help but like the clean dash design and the convincing faux aluminum trim, not to mention the red-and-white gauges and three-spoke Momo steering wheel in GT models. Build and materials quality is excellent. The front seats offer an optimum blend of cushioning and support. While the backseat is comfortable for two passengers, shoulder room and legroom are still pretty tight for this class. Sedans have an 11.4-cubic-foot trunk with a ski pass-through. The wagon offers 33.5 cubic feet of capacity behind its rear seats and 66 cubes when they're folded.

**Driving Impressions:** The Legacy offers a superb blend of ride comfort and handling acuity. The GT is easily as much fun as an Acura TSX or Mazda 6, and with the confidence of all four wheels putting power to the pavement, this Subaru is a satisfying substitute for the smaller, more expensive Audi A4. The base engine provides adequate acceleration, but serious drivers will want to go for the turbo motor and its vast reserves of lag-free power—trust us, you won't miss having a V6.

**Midsize Wagon**

**MSRP Price Range**
## $24,295 - $33,495
Destination Charge: $575 (all styles)

### Ratings

| | | |
|---|---|---|
| Consumer Rating | 9.4 | |
| Editors Rating | 8.1 | |

**What Edmunds.com says:** Solid all-terrain capability, nimble handling, a varied engine lineup and a luxurious interior make the Outback an excellent all-weather family vehicle. If you're thinking of buying a traditional SUV, you may find this Subaru a better fit.

**Pros:** Standard all-wheel drive, generous standard equipment list, exemplary build and materials quality, strong power from turbo and H6 engines, balanced ride and handling dynamics, capable performance off-road.

**Cons:** Desirable features reserved for top-line models, smaller backseat than most competitors.

**What's New:** An all-new and vastly improved Outback is introduced in sedan and wagon body styles. Highlights include a new turbocharged engine, a stronger H6 motor, a stylish new interior and increased ground clearance for more serious off-highway adventures.

**Body Styles, Trim Levels and Options:** The Outback is available as a wagon or sedan. Wagons come in 2.5i, 2.5 XT, 3.0 R L.L. Bean and 3.0 R VDC Limited. Limited Packages are available on 2.5i and 2.5 XT models. The Outback sedan is available in a single 3.0 R trim. The 2.5i models include 16-inch alloy wheels, air conditioning, a CD player, a power driver seat, cruise control, trip computer and a rear limited-slip differential. Opt for the Limited package and you'll get heated leather seats, a wiper de-icer, a CD changer, dual-zone automatic climate control and dual moonroofs (the sedan gets a single large moonroof). Upgrade to the 2.5 XT and you get 17-inch wheels, bigger brakes, sport seats, a Momo steering wheel, metallic interior trim and electroluminescent gauges. You'll need to order the Limited Package to get leather upholstery and a moonroof on XT models. The 3.0 models come with a full load of luxury amenities, as well as a tire pressure monitoring system, steering wheel audio controls and mahogany trim; wagons have a fold-down rear armrest. The L.L. Bean model offers perforated leather upholstery, while the VDC wagon is your ticket to stability control and an upgraded stereo.

**Powertrains and Performance:** The 2.5i model is powered by a 2.5-liter horizontally opposed four-cylinder engine that makes 168 horsepower (163 in PZEV states). The 2.5 XT upgrades to a 2.5-liter turbocharged engine with 250 horsepower and 250 lb-ft of torque. The 3.0 models come with a 3.0-liter horizontally opposed six-cylinder (H6); horsepower comes in at 250 while torque maxes out at 219 lb-ft. Either 2.5-liter engine can be equipped with a five-speed manual transmission. A four-speed automatic is available on 2.5i models while 2.5 XT models get a five-speed auto; both come with an automanual mode. The H6 is only available with the five-speed automatic.

**Safety:** All Outbacks have four-wheel antilock disc brakes with Electronic Brakeforce Distribution. Front side-impact airbags and full-length side curtain airbags are also standard. Stability control is reserved only for the top-line 3.0 R VDC Limited wagon. The front head restraints feature dynamic whiplash protection.

**Interior Design and Special Features:** Inside, you can't help but like the clean dash design and the three-spoke Momo steering wheel in XT and 3.0 models. Turbo models have darker interiors with sporty metallic trim, while 3.0 models get matte-finish wood grain trim on the console that matches the real mahogany trim on the steering wheel. The seats are supportive, but the backseat is still a bit tight for adults. Wagons provide 33.5 cubic feet of capacity behind their rear seats; 66 cubes with the seats folded down.

**Driving Impressions:** Out on the road, the '05 Outback rides smoothly and feels even more surefooted in the corners than its agile predecessor. Taken off-road, it can scamper up a rutted hillside with more gusto than just about any crossover SUV on the market. Although the base engine provides only adequate power, acceleration is quick with either the turbo four or the H6.

*Crash Test Scores, see pg 530*
*Warranty information, see pg 542*

### Specifications

| Engine/Drivetrain | HP | Torque | EPA Fuel Economy Rating |
|---|---|---|---|
| 6cyl 3.0L A | 250 | 219 | 19 city/25 hwy |
| 4cyl 2.5L A/M | 250 | 250 | 19 city/24 hwy |
| 4cyl 2.5L A/M | 168 | 166 | 22 city/28 hwy |

### Body Styles

| Style | MSRP Range |
|---|---|
| Midsize Wagon | $24,295–$33,495 |

# 2005 Suzuki Aerio

Compact Sedan, Wagon

**MSRP Price Range**
## $13,449 - $17,749
Destination Charge: $545 (all styles)

### Ratings

| | | |
|---|---|---|
| Consumer Rating | N/A | |
| Editors Rating | 6.8 | |

**What Edmunds.com says:** As the most affordable all-wheel-drive car on the market, the Aerio may suit buyers in harsh climates, but in most other respects it lags behind its more refined competition.

**Pros:** Available as a sedan or wagon, optional all-wheel drive, roomy interior, powerful standard engine, long list of standard features, solid crash test scores.

**Cons:** Some low-grade interior plastics, sloppy handling.

**What's New:** The Aerio receives a new front bumper, grille and foglamp design, as well as a new rear spoiler on sedans, new clear-lens taillights on the SX and new alloy wheels. Inside, all models get standard automatic climate control, a new instrument panel with analog gauges in place of the former digital setup, new steering wheel with audio controls, redesigned console, upgraded seat fabric and a sunglasses holder. Also, side airbags are now standard on all Aerios. The base S model gains power door locks, keyless entry, a rear spoiler and additional interior trim accents.

*Crash Test Scores, see pg 530*
*Warranty information, see pg 542*

### Specifications

| Engine/Drivetrain | HP | Torque | EPA Fuel Economy Rating |
|---|---|---|---|
| 4cyl 2.3L A/M | 155 | 152 | 25 city/31 hwy |

### Body Styles

| Style | MSRP Range |
|---|---|
| Compact Sedan | $13,449–$17,449 |
| Compact Wagon | $15,449–$17,749 |

**Body Styles, Trim Levels and Options:** The Aerio is offered as a sedan in S and LX trim, and a wagon version in SX trim. With the S, you get 14-inch steel wheels with covers; color-keyed front and rear bumpers; daytime running lights; automatic climate control; a seven-speaker stereo with a CD player and steering wheel controls; power windows, locks and mirrors; keyless entry; tilt steering wheel; rear spoiler; and split-folding rear seats. With the LX and SX, you get all of the above, plus 15-inch alloy wheels, foglamps, color-keyed door handles and mirrors, chrome exhaust tips, an in-dash six-disc CD changer with seven speakers, cruise control, reading lamps, an underseat storage bin and front-seat back pockets. Optional equipment for all models includes floor mats and four-wheel ABS; the LX and SX have the additional option of AWD.

**Powertrains and Performance:** All Aerios come with a 2.3-liter inline four engine that produces 155 horsepower and 152 pound-feet of torque. A five-speed manual transmission is standard on front-wheel-drive Aerios, and a four-speed automatic is optional. If you opt for the all-wheel-drive system, the automatic comes standard.

**Safety:** Side airbags are standard on all Aerios, and antilock brakes are optional. In crash tests conducted by the NHTSA, the Aerio earned four stars (out of five) for the driver, and three stars for the front passenger. Side-impact testing (without side airbags) returned a perfect five-star rating for the front seat, and four stars for the back. In frontal offset crash testing conducted by the IIHS, the Aerio earned a "Good" rating, the highest possible.

**Interior Design and Special Features:** With an overall height three to four inches greater than other vehicles in its class, the Aerio boasts a surprising amount of passenger and cargo room, and passengers will find it easy to get in and out. Sedans offer a generous 14.6 cubic feet of trunk space; wagons provide 21 cubic feet with the rear seats in use and 64 cubic feet when they're folded. Interior plastics are low in quality compared to the class leaders in the economy car segment. In the past, all Aerios had a hard-to-read digital instrument panel, but Suzuki has replaced it with an analog gauge pack this year, while adding a couple of sorely needed storage areas.

**Driving Impressions:** Solid power from the standard four-cylinder engine makes the Aerio impressively peppy for daily commutes; match it with either the automatic or the manual, and you can't lose. The Aerio provides a smooth ride on the highway, but the cost is excessive body roll around corners that is accentuated by the car's tall stance. Opting for the all-wheel-drive system on LX and SX models gives the Aerio true all-weather capability.

# Compact Sedan, Wagon
# 2005 Suzuki Forenza

**MSRP Price Range**
## $13,449 - $17,949
Destination Charge: $545 (all styles)

### Ratings

| | | |
|---|---|---|
| Consumer Rating | N/A | |
| Editors Rating | 7.5 | |

**What Edmunds.com says:** Comfortable, well equipped and solidly built, the Forenza represents a good value for small car buyers on a budget.

**Pros:** Lots of standard features for the price, comfortable cabin with unexpected conveniences, solid construction, predictable handling.

**Cons:** Subpar fuel economy, similarly priced Aerio makes more power.

**What's New:** A versatile wagon model joins the lineup. Side airbags are now standard on all Forenzas.

**Body Styles, Trim Levels and Options:** The Forenza is available as a four-door sedan or a four-door wagon in one of three trim levels—base S, midlevel LX or high-line EX. Even the S is well equipped, offering such features as body-color bumpers and door handles, four-wheel disc brakes, a height-adjustable driver seat, a padded center armrest, air conditioning, an eight-speaker stereo with a CD player, steering-wheel audio controls and power windows, mirrors and locks. Next up is the LX, which adds alloy wheels, foglights, a leather-wrapped steering wheel and shift knob, a sunroof, cruise control and a remote keyless entry system. The top-level EX adds leather seats and a standard four-speed automatic transmission.

**Powertrains and Performance:** The Forenza comes with only one engine—a 2.0-liter 16-valve, DOHC, inline four-cylinder making 126 horsepower and 131 pound-feet of torque. A five-speed manual transmission is standard on S and LX models. A four-speed automatic is standard on the top-level EX and optional on the other trim levels.

**Safety:** Side airbags and four-wheel disc brakes are standard, and ABS with Electronic Brakeforce Distribution is optional on all trim levels. Dual-stage airbags and daytime running lights are also standard. In government crash tests, the Forenza earned four stars (out of five) for frontal impact protection. In side-impact tests, it earned three stars for the front and rear, but this year's standard side airbags should increase the protection up front.

**Interior Design and Special Features:** To liven things up a bit, designers used plenty of metallic accents throughout the cabin and an attractive set of gauges. Several features not normally found on a car in this price range include cabin air filtration and an eight-speaker, 140-watt stereo with steering wheel-mounted audio controls. The driver seat is well contoured, and thanks to its two-way seat-bottom tilt, most people will be able to find a comfortable driving position. A padded center armrest provides a comfortable place to rest an elbow on long trips. In the backseat, the accommodations aren't the roomiest of the economy car class, but anyone under 6 feet tall should be OK on short trips. The rear seat offers a 60/40-split-folding arrangement and sedan trunk capacity comes in at 12.4 cubic feet. The wagon offers 24.4 cubic feet.

**Driving Impressions:** Although 126 hp doesn't sound like much these days, the Forenza has no difficulty keeping up in traffic, and if you equip it with the manual gearbox, you'll rarely wish for more power. You may wish for more refinement and better gas mileage, though. Ride quality is smooth over most surfaces, while handling is soft yet predictable in the corners. More expensive economy cars offer more in the way of behind-the-wheel entertainment and overall polish, but the Forenza is well suited for buyers who want a low-priced sedan that can take on the daily commute without fuss.

*Crash Test Scores, see pg 530*
*Warranty information, see pg 542*

### Specifications

| Engine/Drivetrain | HP | Torque | EPA Fuel Economy Rating |
|---|---|---|---|
| 4cyl 2.0L A/M | 126 | 131 | 22 city/30 hwy |

### Body Styles

| Style | MSRP Range |
|---|---|
| Compact Sedan | $13,449–$17,449 |
| Compact Wagon | $13,949–$17,949 |

# 2005 Suzuki Grand Vitara

**MSRP Price Range**
## $18,399 - $22,599
Destination Charge: $595 (all styles)

### Ratings

| | | |
|---|---|---|
| Consumer Rating | N/A | |
| Editors Rating | 7.0 | |

**What Edmunds.com says:** An aging compact SUV increasingly outdistanced by the competition.

**Pros:** Standard V6, impressive list of features, low-range transfer case with the 4WD option.

**Cons:** Harsh suspension, unimpressive brakes, cramped rear seats, lack of cargo space.

**What's New:** This year the Grand Vitara receives a three-point seatbelt for the rear center seat.

**Body Styles, Trim Levels and Options:** The four-door Grand Vitara comes in two trim levels—LX and EX—with your choice of either two- or four-wheel drive. Both come with plenty of standard equipment, including keyless remote entry; privacy glass; air conditioning with automatic climate control; a seven-speaker audio system with CD player; an adjustable center armrest with storage; steering wheel-mounted audio controls; a tilt steering wheel; a cargo cover; split-folding rear seats; cruise control; power windows, mirrors and locks; and heated mirrors. The EX adds 16-inch alloy wheels, a sunroof, foglights and a rear spoiler.

**Powertrains and Performance:** The Grand Vitara features a 2.5-liter, 24-valve V6 engine producing 165 horsepower and 162 pound-feet of torque. Transmission choices consist of a five-speed manual or four-speed automatic. Towing capacity is a meager 1,500 pounds. EPA fuel mileage estimates are 19 mpg for city driving and 21-22 on the highway.

**Safety:** The Grand Vitara offers four-wheel ABS as an option. Side airbags are not available. In crash tests conducted by the IIHS, the Grand Vitara received an overall "Acceptable" rating (the second highest possible). Government crash testing resulted in four out of five stars for driver and front-passenger protection in frontal impact, and five stars for front- and rear-occupant protection in side impacts.

**Interior Design and Special Features:** The Grand Vitara doesn't live up to its grand title when it comes to cargo space. The Suzuki's maximum cargo space of 50.2 cubic feet pales in comparison to the Toyota RAV4 and its 68 cubic feet of cargo space—the vehicles are virtually the same size on the outside. Passenger space is similarly cramped, and even shorter adults are apt to complain if asked to sit in the backseat. The rest of the cabin design is practical if not attractive, and the materials are of merely average quality.

**Driving Impressions:** With an available low-range transfer case, the Grand Vitara has a hill climbing and descending capability not usually found with other compact SUVs. But its low-tech suspension (a five-link rear suspension with a solid axle) degrades ride quality for normal driving conditions. Whether you're seeking an on- or off-road capable compact SUV, there are superior choices to consider.

*Crash Test Scores, see pg 530*
*Warranty information, see pg 542*

### Specifications

| Engine/Drivetrain | HP | Torque | EPA Fuel Economy Rating |
|---|---|---|---|
| 6cyl 2.5L A/M | 165 | 162 | 19 city/22 hwy |

### Body Styles

| Style | MSRP Range |
|---|---|
| Compact SUV | $18,399–$22,599 |

For the latest full vehicle reports, visit www.edmunds.com/bginfopak

**MSRP Price Range**
## $13,449 - $17,449
Destination Charge: $545 (all styles)

### Ratings

| | | |
|---|---|---|
| Consumer Rating | N/A | ▭ |
| Editors Rating | 7.3 | ▬ |

**What Edmunds.com says:** Comfortable, well equipped and solidly built, the Reno represents a good value and provides a more youthful alternative to the Forenza wagon.

**Pros:** Lots of standard features for the price, comfortable cabin with unexpected conveniences, solid construction, predictable handling.

**Cons:** Unrefined powertrain, subpar fuel economy, similarly priced Aerio makes more power.

**What's New:** The Reno is an all-new car for 2005. Based on the Forenza, the Reno uses the same engine, transmission and underpinnings but adds a little attitude with a sleeker five-door hatchback body and a flashier interior design.

**Body Styles, Trim Levels and Options:** The Reno is available only as a five-door hatchback but is offered in three trim levels—base S, midlevel LX or high-line EX. Even the S is well equipped, offering such features as body-color bumpers and door handles, four-wheel disc brakes, a height-adjustable driver seat, a padded center armrest, air conditioning, cabin air filtration system, an eight-speaker stereo with a CD/MP3 player, steering-wheel audio controls and power windows, mirrors and locks. Next up is the LX, which adds alloy wheels, foglights, a sunroof, cruise control and a remote keyless entry system. An automatic transmission is optional on both the S and LX models. The top-level EX adds leather seats and a standard four-speed automatic transmission. Antilock brakes with Electronic Brakeforce Distribution are optional on all trims.

**Powertrains and Performance:** The Reno comes with only one engine—a 2.0-liter 16-valve, DOHC, inline four-cylinder making 126 horsepower and 131 pound-feet of torque. A five-speed manual transmission is standard on S and LX models. A four-speed automatic is standard on the top-level EX and optional on the other trim levels. Speed sensitive steering is standard on all Renos.

**Safety:** Side airbags and four-wheel disc brakes are standard, and ABS with Electronic Brakeforce Distribution is optional on all trim levels. Front-seat occupants get seatbelt pretensioners and height adjusters, while rear-seat passengers get a full set of head restraints and three-point belts. Dual-stage airbags and daytime running lights are also standard.

**Interior Design and Special Features:** To liven things up a bit, designers used plenty of metallic accents throughout the cabin and an attractive set of gauges. The door panels and dash arrangement are sportier-looking than the Forenza's with more distinctive circular patterns. The Reno has no less than 11 storage compartments and is available with leather seating. Several features not normally found on a car in this price range include foglights and an eight-speaker, 140-watt stereo with steering wheel-mounted audio controls. The driver seat is well contoured, and thanks to its two-way seat-bottom tilt, most people will be able to find a comfortable driving position. A padded center armrest provides a comfortable place to rest an elbow on long trips. In back, passengers are treated to competitive amounts of leg- and shoulder room, along with a fold-down center armrest.

**Driving Impressions:** Although 126 horsepower doesn't sound like much these days, the Reno has no difficulty keeping up in traffic, and if you equip it with the manual gearbox, you'll rarely wish for more power. You may wish for more refinement and better gas mileage, though. Ride quality is smooth over most surfaces, while handling is soft yet predictable in the corners. More expensive economy cars offer more in the way of behind-the-wheel entertainment and overall polish, but the Reno is well suited for buyers who want a low-priced car that can take on the daily commute while offering a little style.

*Crash Test Scores, see pg 530*
*Warranty information, see pg 542*

### Specifications

| Engine/Drivetrain | HP | Torque | EPA Fuel Economy Rating |
|---|---|---|---|
| 4cyl 2.0L A/M | 126 | 131 | 22 city/30 hwy |

### Body Styles

| Style | MSRP Range |
|---|---|
| Compact Sedan/Hatchback | $13,449–$17,449 |

# 2005 Suzuki Verona

**Midsize Sedan**

**MSRP Price Range**

## $17,449 - $20,949

Destination Charge: $545 (all styles)

### Ratings

| | | |
|---|---|---|
| Consumer Rating | N/A | |
| Editors Rating | 6.2 | |

**What Edmunds.com says:** A low price and a standard six-cylinder engine may make the Verona appealing to bargain hunters, but most shoppers will be happier with a better-performing four-cylinder Accord or Camry.

**Pros:** Low price, smooth power delivery, comfortable ride quality, strong brakes, attractive interior design, simple controls.

**Cons:** Weak acceleration, sloppy handling in the corners, lots of wind noise, some low-grade interior materials, no side curtain airbags.

**What's New:** New standard features for 2005 include a tire-pressure monitoring system, side-impact airbags, a trunk-mounted tool case and iridium spark plugs. A power sunroof is now standard on the LX model.

**Body Styles, Trim Levels and Options:** The four-door Verona is offered in three trim levels: the base S model, the midlevel LX and the top-of-the-line EX. The S comes standard with power windows and door locks, heated power mirrors, cruise control, a leather-wrapped steering wheel and shifter, keyless entry, a tilt steering wheel, a six-way adjustable driver seat, air conditioning, an in-dash CD/cassette player and floor mats. Step up to the LX and you get automatic climate control, a power sunroof, 16-inch alloy wheels and antilock brakes. The top-of-the-line Verona EX features heated leather seats, faux wood accents, an auto-dimming rearview mirror and an eight-way adjustable power driver seat. Options include antilock brakes for S models and an electronic traction control system on the EX.

**Powertrains and Performance:** All trim levels come with a 155-horsepower inline six-cylinder engine. The all-aluminum, dual-overhead cam 24-valve power plant also generates 177 pound-feet of torque at 4,000 rpm. The front-wheel-drive Verona uses a four-speed automatic transmission that adapts to suit the driver's particular driving style. EPA mileage estimates 20 mpg in the city and 28 mpg on the highway. A manual transmission is not available.

**Safety:** All models come with four-wheel disc brakes. LX and EX models get standard antilock brakes (optional on the S), while traction control is an option on the EX only. Side airbags for front occupants are standard across the board. Crash tests by the IIHS returned a rating of "Acceptable," the second highest, for offset frontal impacts. Side-impact tests, however, resulted in a rating of "Poor," the lowest. It is important to note, however, that this test was conducted on a 2004 Verona without side airbags, which are now standard.

**Interior Design and Special Features:** Inside, the Verona offers a pleasing two-tone ensemble not unlike that of the Honda Accord. The material used on the dash and door tops has an upscale grain pattern and is soft to the touch. White-faced gauges light up in a soothing lime-green color that matches the readouts for the automatic climate control and stereo head unit. Unfortunately, not all of the materials return an impression of quality, as various plastics feel glossy and cheap. Both the front and rear seats provide passable comfort for adults, though taller passengers may find the legroom a bit tight in the back.

*Crash Test Scores, see pg 530*

*Warranty information, see pg 542*

### Specifications

| Engine/Drivetrain | HP | Torque | EPA Fuel Economy Rating |
|---|---|---|---|
| 6cyl 2.5L A | 155 | 177 | 20 city/28 hwy |

### Body Styles

| Style | MSRP Range |
|---|---|
| Midsize Sedan | $17,449–$20,949 |

**Driving Impressions:** The driving experience is the least enjoyable aspect of the Verona. The trouble begins under the hood, as the car's 2.5-liter inline six feels slow in most driving situations, particularly those that call for a quick burst of acceleration. Power delivery, at least, is smooth, and the four-speed automatic does a commendable job with gear selection. Overly soft suspension tuning yields a cushy highway ride that any grizzled commuter will appreciate, but the trade-off is a sedan that feels weak-kneed around twists and turns. The brake pedal is also on the soft side, but stopping distances are short.

For the latest full vehicle reports, visit www.edmunds.com/bginfopak

**MSRP Price Range**
## $20,399 - $27,799
Destination Charge: $595 (all styles)

## Ratings

| | | |
|---|---|---|
| Consumer Rating | N/A | |
| Editors Rating | 7.3 | |

**What Edmunds.com says:** By offering a third-row seat in a compact SUV, Suzuki answers a question not many people are asking.

**Pros:** Affordable base price, competent on- and off-road handling, available seven-passenger seating.

**Cons:** Cramped second- and third-row seating, dated design, low-grade interior plastics, side airbags not available.

**What's New:** The XL-7 gets a tire-pressure monitoring system and a chrome "S" badge on the spare tire cover.

**Body Styles, Trim Levels and Options:** The four-door XL-7 is available in four trim levels: LX, LX III, EX and EX III. The LX is the five-passenger base model and is well equipped with power door locks, mirrors and windows; remote keyless entry; cruise control; automatic climate control; daytime running lights; an adjustable center armrest; a seven-speaker stereo system with an in-dash CD player and steering wheel-mounted stereo controls; and tinted privacy glass. The LX III adds a two-person third-row seat plus rear air conditioning. The EX is a loaded five-passenger version that gets all the LX equipment along with 16-inch alloy wheels, running boards, four-wheel ABS, leather seating, heated mirrors, a power sunroof and an in-dash six-CD changer. The EX III gives you all this, plus third-row accommodations and rear air conditioning. Heated seats are optional on EX and EX III models equipped with four-wheel drive.

**Powertrains and Performance:** All XL-7 models are equipped with a 2.7-liter V6 engine that produces 185 horsepower and 180 pound-feet of torque. LX models are available with a five-speed manual or a five-speed automatic transmission, while EX models are available only with the automatic. Fuel economy ratings are 17-18 mpg for city driving and 20 mpg on the highway—about average for a truck-based compact SUV. Towing capacity is a respectable 3,000 pounds. Buyers have a choice between two-wheel drive and a part-time four-wheel-drive system with a dual-range transfer case.

**Safety:** The XL-7 comes standard with antilock brakes, but side airbags aren't available. In 40-mph frontal offset crash testing conducted by the IIHS, the XL-7 earned a "Good" score (the highest possible). The NHTSA hasn't crash tested the XL-7.

**Interior Design and Special Features:** Equipped with the optional third-row seating, the XL-7 can pack in seven passengers. It's not until you start shopping larger SUVs (with their larger price tags) that you'll find this feature. However, due to the Suzuki's smaller dimensions, legroom is very tight in both the second and third rows and there's little room for cargo with all the rear seats in use. With the third-row bench out of the way, you'll have up to 40 cubic feet of cargo capacity behind the second-row seats, while folding these seats opens up 75 cubic feet of space.

**Driving Impressions:** The XL-7 handles competently on- and off-road. Ride quality is decent for a truck-based SUV, but car-based SUVs like the Ford Escape and Honda CR-V have more refined road manners. The 185-horsepower V6 provides some initial off-the-line grunt, but it gets wheezy at higher engine speeds, particularly when climbing highway grades

*Crash Test Scores, see pg 530*
*Warranty information, see pg 542*

## Specifications

| Engine/Drivetrain | HP | Torque | EPA Fuel Economy Rating |
|---|---|---|---|
| 6cyl 2.7L A/M | 185 | 184 | 18 city/22 hwy |

## Body Styles

| Style | MSRP Range |
|---|---|
| Midsize SUV | $20,399–$27,799 |

# 2005 Toyota 4Runner

**Midsize SUV**

**MSRP Price Range**
**$27,495 - $37,495**
Destination Charge: $565 (all styles)

#1 Editors' Rating

## Ratings

| | | |
|---|---|---|
| Consumer Rating | 9.3 | |
| Editors Rating | 8.5 | |

**What Edmunds.com says:** Highly capable whether on the pavement or in the dirt, the 4Runner is a well-rounded midsize SUV, and one of our favorites, particularly with the third-row seat option.

**Pros:** Powerful engine lineup, well mannered on pavement, above average off-road capability, comfortable, well-trimmed cabin, long list of standard equipment.

**Cons:** Cargo capacity isn't much more than what many compact SUVs offer, cramped third-row seat.

**What's New:** The base V6 now comes with a five-speed automatic, while the optional V8 has been upgraded to deliver 270-hp and 330 pound-feet of torque. A rollover sensor now comes with the optional head curtain airbag system. A limited-slip differential has been added to the stability control system. SR5 models now feature a chrome grille, color-keyed bumpers and black running boards, while the Sport model get a color-keyed grille. All Limiteds receive color-keyed bumpers, illuminated black running boards and a black roof rack.

*Crash Test Scores, see pg 530*
*Warranty information, see pg 542*

## Specifications

| Engine/Drivetrain | HP | Torque | EPA Fuel Economy Rating |
|---|---|---|---|
| 8cyl 4.7L A | 270 | 320 | 18 city/21 hwy |
| 6cyl 4.0L A | 245 | 282 | 18 city/21 hwy |

## Body Styles

| Style | MSRP Range |
|---|---|
| Midsize SUV | $27,495–$37,495 |

**Body Styles, Trim Levels and Options:** The four-door 4Runner comes in three distinct trim levels—SR5, Sport and Limited. Standard features on the base SR5 include 16-inch wheels, fender flares and body cladding, automatic climate control with rear vents, a CD player, remote keyless entry, a telescoping steering wheel, cruise control, a trip computer, running boards and full skid plate protection. Stepping up to the Sport Edition adds larger 17-inch wheels, X-REAS shocks (used to help quell body roll in turns), a hood scoop, a leather-wrapped steering wheel with stereo and cruise controls, high-contrast seat fabrics and color-keyed exterior mirrors. High-dollar Limited models pick up illuminated running boards, dual-zone automatic climate control, leather upholstery, rear-seat audio controls and an auto-dimming rearview mirror with compass. Options include a DVD-based navigation system and a third-row seat. The X-REAS shocks are optional for the Limited and come with a height-adjustable rear air suspension.

**Powertrains and Performance:** All 4Runners are available with either two- or four-wheel drive and one of two engines. The standard 4.0-liter V6 makes 245 horsepower and 283 pound-feet of torque. The optional 4.7-liter V8 generates 270 hp and 330 lb-ft of torque. All 4Runners get a five-speed automatic transmission. Towing capacity is 7,300 pounds on V8 models, while V6 models top out at 5,000 pounds. Fuel mileage on V6 models is 17-18 mpg in the city and 21 on the highway. V8 versions rate 15-16 mpg in the city and 19-20 on the highway.

**Safety:** All 4Runners comes with standard four-wheel antilock disc brakes with BrakeAssist (BA) and Electronic Brakeforce Distribution (EBD). Stability control (called VSC) is also standard—a rarity in this class. Front seat-mounted side airbags and overhead side curtain airbags for front and rear passengers are optional on all models. In government crash testing, the 4Runner earned four out of five stars in the frontal impact category and a perfect five stars for side impacts. In IIHS offset frontal testing, the 4Runner received a rating of "Good," the highest.

**Interior Design and Special Features:** The 4Runner offers roomy quarters for four to five passengers, plus a couple extra kids if you opt for the third-row seat. The overall design of the interior is both aesthetically pleasing and seriously functional with most controls easy to find and use. Our only major ergonomic complaint concerns the climate controls, which look like intuitive dials but work more like joysticks. Maximum cargo capacity is 75 cubic feet, which trails behind most of the 4Runner's midsize competitors.

**Driving Impressions:** Both engines move the 4Runner out quickly; although the V8 is a must if you plan on doing any serious towing, most buyers will be happy with the less expensive and more fuel-efficient V6. When driven on pavement, the 4Runner delivers a smooth, controlled ride, and handling around turns is surprisingly tight and responsive for a traditional body-on-frame SUV. Taken off-road, this Toyota is right at home, tackling steep passes with little drama.

Midsize Sedan

# 2005 Toyota Camry

**MSRP Price Range**

***$18,045 - $25,405***

Destination Charge: $540 (all styles)

## Ratings

| | | |
|---|---|---|
| Consumer Rating | 9.1 | |
| Editors Rating | 7.7 | |

**What Edmunds.com says:** It won't win any design awards or run circles around its competitors, but when it comes to practicality, value and refinement, few midsize sedans can top the Camry.

**Pros:** Roomy, comfortable, quiet, plenty of safety and luxury features, high resale value, strong reputation for reliability.

**Cons:** Costs more than most competitors, base V6 isn't as powerful as others in the class.

**What's New:** In an effort to make Camry ownership more affordable, Toyota adds an entry-level Standard model to the lineup this year. All models receive freshened exterior styling with a new grille, headlamps, taillamps and wheel designs. All Camrys now have antilock brakes as standard equipment, and the optional automatic transmission for all models is now a five-speed unit. Inside, all Camrys feature Optitron gauges, steering wheel audio controls, a rear center headrest and upgraded seat fabrics. The XLE V6 now includes standard leather seating.

**Body Styles, Trim Levels and Options:** Available trims include Standard, LE, SE and XLE. The entry-level Standard offers basics such as power locks and windows, cruise control and a CD player, but has limited option availability. The LE adds upgrades like keyless entry, a power driver seat and color-keyed exterior mirrors. The sporty SE is similarly equipped, but features different interior trim and upholstery, a sport-tuned suspension, 17-inch alloy wheels, a rear spoiler, foglamps and a unique grille. Step up to the XLE, and you get automatic climate control, an auto-dimming rearview mirror, upgraded audio system and, on the XLE V6, leather seating. Various options include a sunroof, leather seating, heated front seats, a DVD-based navigation system and an in-dash six-disc CD changer.

**Powertrains and Performance:** Three engines are available. The first is a 2.4-liter four-cylinder that makes 157 horsepower. It's mated to either a five-speed manual or five-speed automatic transmission, and should be powerful enough for the majority of buyers. A 3.0-liter V6 that generates 210 hp is also available on the LE and XLE, while a 225-hp, 3.3-liter V6 is available on SE model only. Six-cylinder Camrys come with the automatic only.

**Safety:** Antilock brakes are standard on all Camrys. Optional on all models are side airbags for front passengers and head-protecting side curtain airbags for all outboard passengers. Stability control is available on V6 models. In government frontal impact crash tests, the Camry earned a perfect five stars for driver protection and four stars for front-passenger protection. Side-impact testing resulted in a three-star rating for front-occupant protection (without side airbags) and a five-star rating for the rear. In IIHS offset frontal impact testing, the Camry earned a "Good" rating (the highest possible) and was named a "Best Pick." In IIHS side-impact tests, the Camry received a "Good" rating (the highest) when equipped with side airbags (without the bags, it rated "Poor").

**Interior Design and Special Features:** The Camry's interior offers excellent build quality, high-quality materials and a straightforward design that won't leave you thumbing through the owner's manual to figure out where everything is located. Additionally, the Camry boasts competitive amounts of head-, leg- and shoulder room, including the roomiest backseat of any midsize family sedan. The optional navigation system is one of the best around with simple controls and a large, easy-to-read screen.

**Driving Impressions:** Never one to impress with its power or handling, the Camry instead stakes its reputation on delivering a smooth, quiet ride quality that makes it feel more expensive than it is. Power from the four-cylinder engine is average compared to the Accord and Altima, but it's delivered in such a refined fashion that only those who demand above-average acceleration are likely to complain. Same goes for the V6 engines, though the more powerful SE V6 has no trouble hanging with the competition. The SE model does provide a slightly more athletic feel, but those looking for a true sport sedan should try a Mazda 6 or Nissan Altima.

*Crash Test Scores, see pg 530*
*Warranty information, see pg 542*

## Specifications

| Engine/Drivetrain | HP | Torque | EPA Fuel Economy Rating |
|---|---|---|---|
| 6cyl 3.3L A | 225 | 240 | 20 city/29 hwy |
| 6cyl 3.0L A | 210 | 220 | 21 city/29 hwy |
| 4cyl 2.4L A/M | 160 | 163 | 24 city/34 hwy |

## Body Styles

| Style | MSRP Range |
|---|---|
| Midsize Sedan | $18,045-$25,405 |

# 2005 Toyota Camry Solara
### Midsize Convertible, Coupe

**MSRP Price Range**
## $19,220 - $29,650
Destination Charge: $540 (all styles)

### Ratings

| | | |
|---|---|---|
| Consumer Rating | 9.2 | |
| Editors Rating | 8.0 | |

**What Edmunds.com says:** The new standard for elegance, refinement and value in the midsize coupe and convertible segment, but it's better enjoyed from the inside.

**Pros:** Unsurpassed build quality, smooth and efficient drivetrains, stylish interiors, high-quality materials throughout, extensive safety features.

**Cons:** Average performance credentials, middle-of-the-road styling, can't get the V6 with a manual transmission.

**What's New:** A leather-wrapped steering wheel, shift knob and parking brake handle are now standard on the SE convertible.

**Body Styles, Trim Levels and Options:** The Camry Solara is available as a coupe or convertible. The coupe is offered in three trim levels—SE, SE Sport and SLE—while the convertible comes in SE and SLE versions only. The base SE coupe is well equipped with power windows, locks and mirrors; keyless entry; cruise control; satellite steering wheel audio controls; a six-speaker CD stereo; 16-inch wheels and tires; and a multifunction trip computer. The SE Sport adds a performance-oriented suspension, 17-inch wheel and tires, an exterior body kit, graphite-style interior trim, a unique gauge cluster and a leather-wrapped steering wheel and shift knob; most of this equipment is also included on the SE convertible along with a power cloth top. Top-of-the-line SLE coupes and convertibles add automatic climate control, wood-style trim, a power-adjustable driver seat, a moonroof, a JBL premium audio system with a six-disc CD changer and, on V6 models, leather seating.

**Powertrains and Performance:** The standard coupe engine is a 2.4-liter four-cylinder rated at 157 horsepower and 162 pound-feet of torque. It's mated to either a five-speed manual or a four-speed automatic, and is EPA-rated at 23 city/33 highway for the manual and 23 city/32 highway with the automatic. Optional on coupes and standard on convertibles is a 3.3-liter V6 rated for 225 hp and 240 lb-ft of torque. No manual is available with this engine, but the automatic is a five-speed unit with a manual-shift gate for those who like to pick their own gears. The EPA mileage estimate for all V6 models is 20 city/28 highway.

**Safety:** All Solaras come standard with front and side-impact airbags and four-wheel antilock disc brakes. Side curtain airbags that protect both front and rear passengers are available on coupes as well. A combined electronic stability and traction control system is optional on SLE models with the V6 engine. Government crash testing of the coupe returned a perfect five-star rating across the board.

Crash Test Scores, see pg 530
Warranty information, see pg 542

### Specifications

| Engine/Drivetrain | HP | Torque | EPA Fuel Economy Rating |
|---|---|---|---|
| 6cyl 3.3L A | 225 | 240 | 20 city/32 hwy |
| 4cyl 2.4L A/M | 157 | 162 | 23 city/32 hwy |

### Body Styles

| Style | MSRP Range |
|---|---|
| Midsize Convertible | $26,380–$29,650 |
| Midsize Coupe | $19,220–$26,095 |

**Interior Design and Special Features:** All trim levels feature an upscale interior design with bright metallic accents and exceptional build quality. Sport models get sharp-looking graphite accents, while top-line SLE versions add premium wood trim. The front seats offer plenty of room for even the tallest drivers, but the rear seats are still better left for short trips. Buyers should note that coupes can seat three passengers in back, while the convertible can accommodate just two. When you're ready for an open-air ride, the convertible's power top automatically stows beneath its own tonneau cover. Overall, these are some of the nicest interiors you'll find in this price range by far.

**Driving Impressions:** The Solara's suspension tuning delivers a well-controlled ride that's still quite comfortable. The added stiffness of the SE Sport model gives it enough capability in the turns to have some fun while still maintaining the civilized ride quality of the other models. Power from the V6 is smoother than ever, but enthusiast drivers will be left wishing for a manual gearbox.

**MSRP Price Range**

### $17,670 - $23,035
Destination Charge: $540 (all styles)

## Ratings

| | | |
|---|---|---|
| Consumer Rating | 9.1 | |
| Editors Rating | 7.4 | |

**What Edmunds.com says:** A distinctive and entertaining sport coupe, but you better be small and easily impressed as the cabin is tight and the features list short.

**Pros:** Rev-happy engine in the GT-S, ultraprecise steering, razor-sharp handling and strong brakes make for a thrill ride in the canyons.

**Cons:** Mediocre interior materials, difficult-to-master GT-S six-speed shifter, short features list, poor rearward visibility.

**What's New:** This is the Celica's final year of production. For 2005, the cassette player is no longer standard, though it is still available as an option with the JBL premium audio system on the GT-S.

**Body Styles, Trim Levels and Options:** The front-drive Celica is a two-door hatchback with two available trim levels: GT and GT-S. Though the GT has an attractive price, its feature list is rather scant. You'll get the basics like air conditioning and a CD player, but power windows and locks, cruise control and a rear wiper are all optional. These features are standard on the GT-S, along with its higher-horsepower engine. The GT-S also has bigger brakes, alloy wheels, foglamps, a JBL sound system, a leather-wrapped steering wheel and sport pedals. On either car, you can order upgraded 16-inch alloy wheels, high-intensity discharge headlamps, a sunroof, a rear wing, keyless entry and leather seats (GT-S only). An "Action Package" is also available on both models, and it adds numerous exterior body enhancements.

**Powertrains and Performance:** The base GT is equipped with a 1.8-liter, four-cylinder dual-overhead camshaft engine rated at 140 horsepower and 125 pound-feet of torque. The GT-S gets a more powerful 1.8-liter four-cylinder that produces 180 hp and 122 lb-ft of torque. The GT comes standard with a five-speed manual gearbox, while the GT-S features a six-speed manual. Optional on both trims is a four-speed automatic transmission. The GT-S' version has E-shift steering wheel-mounted buttons which allows for "manual" shifting.

**Safety:** GT models come with front disc/rear drum brakes, while GT-S models wear a full set of discs. Both Celicas offer antilock brakes and side-impact airbags as optional equipment. In government crash tests, the Celica earned four out of five stars for protection of the driver and front passenger in frontal impacts and three stars for side impacts.

**Interior Design and Special Features:** The Celica's interior is stylish, functional and comfortable for two adults and a healthy amount of their gear. A simple, down-swept dash layout, big analog gauges, sporty bucket seats, faux-drilled metal pedals and fashionable metallic silver accents add to Celica's cockpit ambience, but materials quality is less than impressive. Both the GT and GT-S offer a center console big enough to hold eight CD cases, as well as two oversize cups. The rear seats are small and barely offer enough room to squeeze in extra passengers, but folded down, they allow a considerable amount of cargo space.

**Driving Impressions:** The Celica's suspension, steering and braking systems provide outstanding handling and performance. There's little body roll, excellent road feel and few surprises when it's pushed hard. The GT-S leans heavily in favor of performance over comfort, so be prepared to make the trade-off if you want the extra performance. The standard GT is still an entertaining drive despite its more forgiving setup.

*Crash Test Scores, see pg 530*
*Warranty information, see pg 542*

## Specifications

| Engine/Drivetrain | HP | Torque | EPA Fuel Economy Rating |
|---|---|---|---|
| 4cyl 1.8L A/M | 180 | 130 | 23 city/30 hwy |
| 4cyl 1.8L A/M | 140 | 125 | 29 city/36 hwy |

## Body Styles

| Style | MSRP Range |
|---|---|
| Compact Coupe | $17,670–$23,035 |

# 2005 Toyota Corolla

**MSRP Price Range**

### $13,680 - $17,455
Destination Charge: $540 (all styles)

## Ratings

| | | |
|---|---|---|
| Consumer Rating | 9.3 | |
| Editors Rating | 8.0 | |

**What Edmunds.com says:** A solid economy sedan that many will purchase on the basis of name alone. Next to its peers, though, the Corolla costs too much and lacks personality.

**Pros:** Refined and roomy interior, excellent gas mileage and crash test scores, long list of safety features, spunky XRS model, illustrious reliability record.

**Cons:** Awkward driver-seat position, bland personality, gets pricey when even basic features are desired, sedan body style only.

**What's New:** A sporty new XRS model debuts boasting a 170-horsepower engine and a sport-tuned suspension. Additionally, all Corollas receive a restyled front fascia and rear taillights. The LE model now has Lexus-like Optitron instrumentation, along with a cloth-trimmed center console and sun visors. Side curtain airbags, stability control and a JBL audio system are all new options.

*Crash Test Scores, see pg 530*
*Warranty information, see pg 542*

## Specifications

| Engine/Drivetrain | HP | Torque | EPA Fuel Economy Rating |
|---|---|---|---|
| 4cyl 1.8L M | 170 | 127 | 25 city/32 hwy |
| 4cyl 1.8L A/M | 130 | 125 | 29 city/38 hwy |

## Body Styles

| Style | MSRP Range |
|---|---|
| Compact Sedan | $13,680–$17,455 |

**Body Styles, Trim Levels and Options:** The five-passenger Corolla comes as a sedan only. Trim levels include the base CE, the better-equipped LE, the somewhat sporty S and the truly sporty XRS. Standard features in the CE include air conditioning, a CD player, power mirrors, an outside temperature gauge, 60/40-split-folding rear seats and 15-inch wheels. Go with the LE to gain fake-wood trim, Optitron gauges, a driver-seat height adjuster and remote keyless entry. The S model includes "sporty" trim such as body-color rocker panels and door handles, smoked headlights, foglights, special gauges and a leather-wrapped steering wheel. The XRS adds a 170-horsepower engine, sport seats, four-wheel disc brakes, tire pressure monitors and cruise control.

**Powertrains and Performance:** Power for CE, LE and S models comes in the form of a 130-horsepower, 1.8-liter four-cylinder engine. Thanks to a variable valve timing system (Toyota's VVT-i), this engine provides decent acceleration. Transmission choices are either a five-speed manual or a four-speed automatic. The XRS features a 170-horsepower 1.8-liter with variable valve timing and lift (VVTL-i) mated to a six-speed manual transmission; an automatic is not available on this model.

**Safety:** The Corolla comes with multistage front airbags that deploy at various levels, depending on impact. Full-length side curtain airbags and front side-impact airbags are optional, as are antilock brakes with Electronic Brakeforce Distribution (standard on the XRS). Stability control is optional on models equipped with an automatic transmission and ABS. In the NHTSA's crash tests, the Corolla earned five stars (the best score possible) for frontal impact protection and four stars for side-impact protection. In 40-mph frontal offset crash testing by the IIHS, it received a "Good" rating (the highest possible) and was named a "Best Pick" among small cars.

**Interior Design and Special Features:** Every Corolla's interior is furnished with high-quality materials and user-friendly controls that wouldn't seem out of place in a more expensive car. Even with the car's tall cabin design, room in the front seats is only average with a somewhat awkward seating position for the driver. Meanwhile, two adults can sit comfortably in the backseat without ducked heads or pulled-up legs. Trunk capacity measures a generous 13.6 cubic feet.

**Driving Impressions:** We've found the Corolla's performance acceptable, with a good off-the-line punch and decent passing power at speed. During highway driving, the Corolla is a quiet cruiser, with very little ambient engine noise and even less wind noise. Though not as sporty as some competitors, this Toyota offers an appealing compromise between handling and comfort. It rides smoothly enough to be used as a commuter car, while maintaining its composure when occasionally pushed around the corners. For those seeking a little extra entertainment without giving up Corolla reliability, the 170-horse XRS model is a good bet.

# Compact Coupe, Sedan

# 2005 Toyota ECHO

**MSRP Price Range**

## $10,355 - $11,685

Destination Charge: $540 (all styles)

### Ratings

| | | |
|---|---|---|
| Consumer Rating | 9.5 | |
| Editors Rating | 7.0 | |

**What Edmunds.com says:** With its cheap interior and wobbly handling, the Echo doesn't seem like much of a bargain, especially when you consider the more capable, better-packaged offerings from Hyundai and Toyota's own Scion division.

**Pros:** Good gas mileage, speedy acceleration, roomy and functional interior, Toyota reliability.

**Cons:** Cartoonish styling, annoying gauge placement, shaky handling, deceptively low base pricing.

**What's New:** There are no changes for the Echo this year.

**Body Styles, Trim Levels and Options:** The Echo is available as a two-door coupe or a four-door sedan. Standard equipment is basic, including an AM/FM radio, a tilt steering wheel, dual manual outside mirrors and 14-inch steel wheels. For many of the features people take for granted these days, you'll have to go to the options list. Here, you'll find an all-weather package (including a heavy-duty battery and rear window defogger), antilock brakes, air conditioning, side airbags, a CD player and keyless entry. Power steering is an option, as are power windows, power mirrors, a tachometer and a split-folding rear seat. Even the clock is optional. If you're hoping to enhance the looks of the Echo, there are upgrade packages available that include sport body cladding; 15-inch wheels are a stand-alone option.

**Powertrains and Performance:** The Echo comes with a 1.5-liter, four-cylinder engine. Thanks to dual-overhead cams and a variable valve timing system, it makes 108 horsepower and 105 pound-feet of torque. Though these aren't big numbers, the Echo weighs only about 2,000 pounds. Consequently, acceleration is spirited. Fuel mileage is impressive, too; expect to get about 40 mpg on the highway. You can equip the Echo with an optional four-speed automatic transmission, or you can stand pat with the standard five-speed manual.

**Safety:** Antilock brakes and side airbags are optional on the Echo. In government crash testing, the Echo earned four out of five stars for driver and front-passenger protection in frontal impacts. In side-impact testing, the car received three stars for front-occupant protection and four stars for the rear.

**Interior Design and Special Features:** Without question, the Echo's most impressive attribute is the amount of room afforded by its cabin and trunk. The tall greenhouse and narrow roof pillars offer unobstructed visibility and acres of headroom. Front seating is comfortable as long as the "propped up" feel doesn't bother you, and there is plenty of storage available. Meanwhile, the Echo can easily accommodate a pair of adults in the rear seat, though parents may find it difficult to install bulky child safety seats.

**Driving Impressions:** Because of its standard 14-inch tires, tall stance and high center of gravity, handling is not the Echo's forte. Even moderate crosswinds severely hamper the car's ability to stay in its own lane. We'd definitely recommend going with the optional 15-inch wheels and tires if your budget allows. The Echo does have a couple of advantages in cramped urban settings, as its small size makes it easy to park in tight spaces, while its soft suspension does a fair job of filtering out bumps and ruts.

*Crash Test Scores, see pg 530*
*Warranty information, see pg 542*

### Specifications

| Engine/Drivetrain | HP | Torque | EPA Fuel Economy Rating |
|---|---|---|---|
| 4cyl 1.5L A/M | 108 | 105 | 33 city/39 hwy |

### Body Styles

| Style | MSRP Range |
|---|---|
| Compact Coupe | $10,355–$11,155 |
| Compact Sedan | $10,885–$11,685 |

# 2005 Toyota Highlander

**MSRP Price Range**

## $24,080 - $31,380

Destination Charge: $565 (all styles)

### Ratings

| | | |
|---|---|---|
| Consumer Rating | 7.8 | |
| Editors Rating | 7.6 | |

**What Edmunds.com says:** With its fuel-efficient engine lineup, full complement of safety features and available third-row seat, the Highlander is one of our top recommendations to those who need SUV utility but don't want any unnecessary bulk or fuel bills.

**Pros:** Seats up to seven, carlike ride and handling, smooth and powerful V6 engine, fuel-efficient four-cylinder engine, lots of safety features.

**Cons:** Limited towing and off-road ability, bland personality.

**What's New:** New standard features this year include a roof rack with cross bars, remote keyless entry and a cargo cover. Standard on the Limited and optional on the base is a new windshield wiper de-icer grid.

**Body Styles, Trim Levels and Options:** The four-door Highlander comes in two trims: base and Limited. The base models are decently equipped with items like 16-inch wheels; stability control; power windows, locks and mirrors; cruise control; air conditioning; keyless entry; and a CD player. Step up to the Limited and you'll gain automatic headlights, 17-inch alloy wheels, heated outside mirrors, a windshield wiper de-icer, a power-adjustable driver seat, a fold-flat third-row seat, a premium sound system and HomeLink. On the Limited, you can also order leather seating, an in-dash CD changer, a rear DVD entertainment system and heated front seats.

**Powertrains and Performance:** There are two engine choices: a standard 2.4-liter four-cylinder or a 3.3-liter V6. The four-cylinder makes 160 horsepower and 165 pound-feet of torque, while the smooth V6 puts out 230 ponies and 242 lb-ft of torque. A four-speed automatic transmission is standard on four-cylinder models, while V6 Highlanders upgrade to a five-speed unit. Tow ratings are on the light side, the maximum being 3,500 pounds on a properly equipped V6 model. The Highlander comes in both front-wheel-drive (2WD) and all-wheel-drive configurations. Fuel mileage is above average for a midsize utility vehicle; a 2WD four-cylinder Highlander rates 22 mpg city/27 mpg highway, while an all-wheel-drive V6 model rates 18/24.

**Safety:** All Highlanders come with four-wheel antilock disc brakes equipped with Electronic Brakeforce Distribution (EBD) and BrakeAssist, Toyota's VSC stability control system, a tire-pressure warning system and whiplash-reducing front seats. Optional on all models are seat-mounted side airbags for front occupants and side curtain airbags for the first and second rows. In government crash testing, the Highlander scored four stars (out of a possible five) for frontal impact protection. In side-impact tests, it received four stars for front occupants and five stars for rear-seat riders. In frontal offset crash testing administered by the IIHS, the Toyota earned a "Good" rating (the best possible).

Crash Test Scores, see pg 530
Warranty information, see pg 542

### Specifications

| Engine/Drivetrain | HP | Torque | EPA Fuel Economy Rating |
|---|---|---|---|
| 6cyl 3.3L A | 230 | 242 | 19 city/25 hwy |
| 4cyl 2.4L A | 160 | 165 | 22 city/27 hwy |

### Body Styles

| Style | MSRP Range |
|---|---|
| Midsize SUV | $24,080–$31,380 |

**Interior Design and Special Features:** The Highlander's passenger accommodations are reasonably spacious, but newer competitors offer more room in the second row. Ordering the third-row seat allows the Toyota to seat two additional passengers, preferably small ones, for a total capacity of seven. When it's time to haul groceries, the third-row seat folds flat into the floor (without requiring removal of the headrests), opening up 38.5 cubic feet of cargo space. Drop the 60/40-split second-row seats, and there are 81.4 cubes to go around.

**Driving Impressions:** A fully independent suspension delivers an excellent combination of comfort and control; although, like the Camry, the Highlander favors ride quality over handling. Even so, it weighs less than other crossover SUVs, giving a nimble feel alongside its peers. The base four-cylinder engine provides adequate power for those who travel light, but most buyers will prefer the V6, which provides smooth, strong acceleration in all situations.

# 2005 Toyota Land Cruiser

**MSRP Price Range**

## $55,025

Destination Charge: $565 (all styles)

### Ratings

| | | |
|---|---|---|
| Consumer Rating | 8.4 | |
| Editors Rating | 8.7 | |

**What Edmunds.com says:** An SUV that does everything well. But before you buy, make sure you have a need for all of the Land Cruiser's abilities.

**Pros:** Go-anywhere capability, smooth ride quality, strong and smooth V8, versatile interior with luxurious appointments.

**Cons:** Quality and capability don't come cheap; Toyota's Sequoia is bigger yet less expensive.

**What's New:** All Land Cruisers now ride on a set of 18-inch aluminum wheels.

**Body Styles, Trim Levels and Options:** The full-size, eight-passenger Land Cruiser comes only one way—loaded up. The highlights include four-wheel drive, leather seating, power-adjustable and heated front seats, a JBL audio system with an in-dash CD changer, a moonroof and separate automatic climate control systems for front and rear passengers. On the short factory options list, you'll find a roof rack and running board package, a DVD-based navigation system with rearview backup camera and a side and head curtain airbag package. A rear-seat DVD entertainment system is available from the dealer.

**Powertrains and Performance:** Power comes from a 4.7-liter V8 that generates 235 horsepower and 320 pound-feet of torque. While certainly not the most powerful engine in this class, the Land Cruiser's smooth acceleration satisfies, and passing maneuvers are rarely a problem. A five-speed automatic transmission is standard, as is four-wheel drive with low-range gearing for off-roading. Should you want to tow, the Land Cruiser can lug 6,500 pounds. EPA fuel economy ratings are 13 mpg in the city and 17 on the highway.

**Safety:** The Land Cruiser comes standard with Toyota's Star Safety System, which includes Vehicle Stability Control (VSC) and traction control (TRAC), an anti-lock brake system (ABS) with Electronic Brakeforce Distribution (EBD) and BrakeAssist. On the options list, you'll find an airbag package with regular side airbags for front occupants, along with side curtain airbags and a rollover sensor that offer chest and head protection for first- and second-row outboard passengers.

**Interior Design and Special Features:** Thanks to the multitude of features and comfortable seating in the first and second rows, this is a very enjoyable SUV to spend time in. Total passenger capacity is eight. When not in use, the third row can be split in half, folded to either side of the cargo bay and stored in an upright position; when it's removed entirely, the Toyota sports a maximum cargo capacity of 97.5 cubic feet. If the Land Cruiser isn't luxurious enough for you, consider its cousin, the Lexus LX 470.

**Driving Impressions:** Unlike many luxury SUVs, this one comes with a locking center differential and a button on the dash that lowers the antenna to clear low-hanging branches. First and foremost, the Land Cruiser is designed to be driven off-road. The magic is in how composed it behaves on pavement, where most buyers travel. While not best in the class in terms of urban driving dynamics, it certainly beats most truck-based competitors when it comes time to run to the grocery store.

*Crash Test Scores, see pg 530*
*Warranty information, see pg 542*

### Specifications

| Engine/Drivetrain | HP | Torque | EPA Fuel Economy Rating |
|---|---|---|---|
| 8cyl 4.7L A | 235 | 320 | 13 city/17 hwy |

### Body Styles

| Style | MSRP Range |
|---|---|
| Midsize SUV | $55,025 |

# 2005 Toyota MR2 Spyder

**Compact Convertible**

**MSRP Price Range**

## $25,145 - $26,145
Destination Charge: $540 (all styles)

### Ratings

| | | |
|---|---|---|
| Consumer Rating | 7.9 | |
| Editors Rating | 6.0 | |

**What Edmunds.com says:** Though better suited as a weekend car than a daily driver, the MR2 Spyder is the perfect alternative for those suffering from Mazda Miata burnout.

**Pros:** Lively and precise handling dynamics, scores high on the fun scale, available SMT transmission, affordable compared to other European-brand roadsters.

**Cons:** Severe lack of storage space, bland interior design, not many safety features available.

**What's New:** Say good-bye to the MR2 (again). This is the final year of production for the fun, little convertible. The only changes this year are to the audio system, which now has an amber-colored display screen and a standard six-disc CD changer in place of the cassette player.

**Body Styles, Trim Levels and Options:** The MR2 Spyder comes in just one trim level that includes most of the features you're likely to want. Air conditioning, antilock brakes, power windows and door locks, a six-disc CD changer and a tilt steering wheel are all standard. An optional limited-slip differential makes this mighty mite all the more fun to fling through corners. Like most other convertibles, the MR2 has a glass rear window with a defroster. However, the rag top is a bit more cumbersome than those on the Honda S2000 or Mazda Miata, as it is necessary to get out of the car before putting it up or down.

**Powertrains and Performance:** The Spyder's midship-mounted 1.8-liter, twin-cam, 16-valve, four-cylinder engine produces 138 horses at 6,400 rpm and 125 pound-feet of torque at 4,400 rpm, thanks in part to variable valve timing. Expect 0-to-60-mph times in the 7- to 8-second range. There are two transmissions available that apply power to the rear wheels. The first is a standard five-speed manual transmission. The second is a sequential-shift six-speed manual transmission (SMT). A rare feature in this price range, the SMT combines the convenience of an automatic transmission with the interaction and efficiency of a manual.

**Safety:** Four-wheel antilock disc brakes are standard. Premium features such as stability control, traction control or side airbags are not available. There is no crash test data available from either the NHTSA or the IIHS for the MR2 Spyder.

**Interior Design and Special Features:** The interior of the MR2 is one of its few weak points. The look is bland, and the materials used aren't very plush. The car's more pressing problem, however, is its dearth of storage and luggage space. The hard-to-access bin behind the seats holds just 1.5 cubic feet of cargo, and the "trunk" is nearly useless unless the spare tire is removed.

**Driving Impressions:** Being a diminutive midengined roadster, the MR2 Spyder possesses excellent handling and quick responses. It is quite nimble and a joy to drive on twisting canyon roads. But because of its small cockpit and minimal storage space, this car works best as a weekend getaway car rather than a daily commuter. If you do expect frequent drives in heavy traffic, you might want to consider the SMT.

*Crash Test Scores, see pg 530*
*Warranty information, see pg 542*

### Specifications

| Engine/Drivetrain | HP | Torque | EPA Fuel Economy Rating |
|---|---|---|---|
| 4cyl 1.8L M | 138 | 125 | 25 city/33 hwy |

### Body Styles

| Style | MSRP Range |
|---|---|
| Compact Convertible | $25,145–$26,145 |

For the latest full vehicle reports, visit www.edmunds.com/bginfopak

## Ratings

| | | |
|---|---|---|
| Consumer Rating | 9.3 | |
| Editors Rating | 7.5 | |

**What Edmunds.com says:** Versatile and affordable, the Matrix is the best compact wagon for hauling people and cargo in its price class.

**Pros:** Versatile cargo area, roomy rear seats, good gas mileage, generous standard equipment list, availability of all-wheel drive and stability control.

**Cons:** Modest torque output, less fun to drive than its styling suggests.

**What's New:** The Matrix receives a revised front bumper, taillights and grille to freshen up the exterior, along with a new audio head unit design, optional side curtain airbags and other minor interior changes. Stability control is also newly optional.

**Body Styles, Trim Levels and Options:** Three trim levels are available: base, XR and XRS. Base-level cars have the necessities such as air conditioning and a CD player, but most of the worthwhile features are optional. Go with the XR or XRS to get standard power locks and windows, keyless entry and a rear wiper. Other options include 16- or 17-inch aluminum alloy wheels, an all-weather package, a DVD-based navigation system, a power moonroof and two different premium sound systems.

**Powertrains and Performance:** The Matrix comes with a 1.8-liter, four-cylinder engine. Buyers of the base and XR are offered a choice of either front-wheel drive or full-time all-wheel drive. With front-wheel drive, the engine makes 130 horsepower and 125 lb-ft of torque and earns ultralow emission vehicle (ULEV) certification. All-wheel-drive models get a less impressive LEV rating and make slightly less power (123 hp). A four-speed automatic is the only transmission available with AWD, while front-drive cars can also be ordered with a five-speed manual. The front-drive XRS is the sportiest trim. It comes standard with a 180-hp version of the 1.8-liter engine, four-wheel disc brakes and a six-speed manual transmission; no automatic is available. Fuel economy is excellent, as even AWD models can get 30 mpg on the highway.

**Safety:** Antilock brakes are standard on the Matrix XRS and all-wheel-drive models, and optional on front-drive base and XR models. Seat-mounted side airbags for front occupants and full-length side curtain airbags are optional across the line. Stability control is another worthwhile option. In NHTSA crash testing, the Matrix earned five stars (the best score possible) for driver and front-passenger protection in frontal impacts. For side impacts, it received five stars for front-passenger protection and four stars for rear-passenger protection.

**Interior Design and Special Features:** For cargo, the Matrix is very similar to a compact SUV. The tailgate opens upward, and the rear glass can be raised independently. The main cargo area and rear seat backs are unapologetically coated in hard plastic, the idea being that it's a lot easier to clean dirt and mud off one long expanse of plastic than out of matted carpet. A special cargo-floor track features eight adjustable tie-down hooks. Underneath the floor is a hidden storage compartment. The 60/40-split rear seats can be folded flat, thereby expanding cargo room to 53.2 cubic feet. The front-passenger seat also folds forward, allowing items more than 8 feet long to be carried with the tailgate closed.

**Driving Impressions:** Despite Toyota's claims, the Matrix isn't particularly sporty. With the base and XR cars, acceleration is only average. AWD-equipped cars come off as particularly taxed because of their extra weight and obligatory automatic transmissions. Even the XRS with its 180-hp engine isn't particularly rewarding as most of its power is made in the high reaches of the rev range. Handling, too, is modest. The Matrix's ride quality, however, is smooth and comfortable.

*Crash Test Scores, see pg 530*
*Warranty information, see pg 542*

## Specifications

| Engine/Drivetrain | HP | Torque | EPA Fuel Economy Rating |
|---|---|---|---|
| 4cyl 1.8L M | 170 | 127 | 25 city/32 hwy |
| 4cyl 1.8L A/M | 130 | 125 | 28 city/33 hwy |
| 4cyl 1.8L A | 123 | 118 | 26 city/31 hwy |

## Body Styles

| Style | MSRP Range |
|---|---|
| Compact Wagon | $14,760–$18,750 |

# 2005 Toyota Prius

**MSRP Price Range**

## $20,875

Destination Charge: $540 (all styles)

### Ratings

| | | |
|---|---|---|
| Consumer Rating | 9.1 | |
| Editors Rating | 8.3 | |

**What Edmunds.com says:** A full-featured midsize family sedan that just so happens to be the most fuel-efficient and earth-friendly sedan on the market as well. The fact that it starts at just $20K makes it all the more attractive.

**Pros:** Outstanding mileage, ultralow emissions, generous amount of interior room, hatchback utility, reasonable price, excellent build quality.

**Cons:** Less power than other midsize sedans, some confusing controls, real-world driving results in lower mileage than the window sticker suggests.

**What's New:** A rear wiper is now standard, the sun visor material has been changed from vinyl to fabric, and the Smart Entry and Start system has been renamed the Smart Key System.

**Body Styles, Trim Levels and Options:** The Prius is available as a four-door hatchback only. There is only one well-appointed trim level. The standard features list includes power windows, locks and mirrors; automatic climate control; a tilt steering wheel with satellite audio and climate controls; a six-speaker CD stereo; cruise control; trip computer; and 15-inch aluminum wheels. Options like a DVD-based navigation system, Bluetooth hands-free phone technology and a nine-speaker JBL premium audio system with a six-disc CD changer are also available, along with an auto-dimming mirror and xenon headlights. The available Smart Key system allows you to lock/unlock the doors and start the car—all with the key safely in your pocket or purse. The optional voice command system permits voice control of features ranging from temperature adjustment to Bluetooth cell phone dialing.

**Powertrains and Performance:** There is only one engine and transmission combination available. The Hybrid Synergy Drive power plant consists of a 1.5-liter gasoline engine and two electric drive motor/generators. The gas engine produces 76 horsepower and 82 pound-feet of torque, while the electric motors generate the equivalent of 67 hp and 295 lb-ft of torque. Net horsepower is 110, mainly because the two power sources hit their peak at different times. Regardless, power delivery is smooth and consistent from rest all the way to top speed. The Prius features an elegantly simple continuously variable "transmission" of sorts, called a power split device. It provides the ease of a conventional automatic transmission, but there are no gears to shift, drive belts, torque converter or clutch. The motors work in concert with the gas engine, through a planetary gearset, to provide seamless power and maximum efficiency at all times. Fuel mileage is rated at 60 city and 51 highway, though real-world mileage is typically in the mid 40s.

**Safety:** All models come standard with four-wheel antilock brakes with BrakeAssist and traction control. Electronic stability control and side-impact/side curtain airbags are optional. Government crash tests resulted in a four-star (out of five) rating for everything but the driver in the frontal test, which earned five stars.

*Crash Test Scores, see pg 530*
*Warranty information, see pg 542*

**Interior Design and Special Features:** Materials quality is impressive, and the overall look is upscale. The gauge cluster is positioned toward the center of the dashboard, but the display is clear and easy to see. The optional touchscreen DVD-based navigation system is not only Toyota's most comprehensive system ever, it can be voice-operated as well.

**Driving Impressions:** As you might expect, the Prius is no speed demon, but when it comes to the kind of daily driving that most drivers encounter, there's more than enough power to get around. The continuously variable transmission (CVT) takes some getting used to since it doesn't shift gears, but it does make the best use of the hybrid drivetrain's power. Cabin noise is minimal, and the suspension is comfortably soft without feeling too floaty.

### Specifications

| Engine/Drivetrain | HP | Torque | EPA Fuel Economy Rating |
|---|---|---|---|
| 4cyl 1.5L A | 110 | 82 | 60 city/51 hwy |

### Body Styles

| Style | MSRP Range |
|---|---|
| Compact Coupe | $20,875 |

Compact SUV

# 2005 Toyota RAV4

**MSRP Price Range**

***$18,550 - $21,000***

Destination Charge: $565 (all styles)

## Ratings

| | | |
|---|---|---|
| Consumer Rating | 9.5 | |
| Editors Rating | 7.4 | |

**What Edmunds.com says:** With ample power under the hood, nimble handling on the street and a generous standard features list, the RAV4 is a worthy adversary for mini-utes like the Honda CR-V and Ford Escape.

**Pros:** Steers and handles like a car, thoughtful cabin design, exemplary build and materials quality, ABS and stability control standard, refined and fuel-efficient engine.

**Cons:** Somewhat cramped interior, high repair costs in low-speed rear collisions, not much off-road ability.

**What's New:** The JBL 3-in-1 audio system has been discontinued, and the sport package receives a unique metal mesh grille and silver sport pedals.

**Body Styles, Trim Levels and Options:** The four-door RAV4 is offered in a single trim level and comes with front-wheel drive (2WD) or all-wheel drive (AWD). All RAV4s come with 16-inch wheels, ABS, stability control, air conditioning, a height-adjustable driver seat, cruise control, a six-speaker CD stereo and power windows, mirrors and locks. Upgrade to the "L" package and you'll also get heated mirrors, a leather-wrapped steering wheel, dark tinted glass, foglights and body-color bumpers and door handles. The "L" package is also your ticket to leather upholstery and heated seats if you want them. A sport package adds a mesh grille, a hood scoop, color-keyed door handles, a roof rack, silver sport pedals, heated mirrors, gray-painted bumpers and overfenders and sport fabric seats. Other options include alloy wheels, a sunroof and keyless entry. Larger tires are also available on AWD models.

**Powertrains and Performance:** Both 2WD and AWD versions of the RAV4 are powered by a 2.4-liter, four-cylinder engine that delivers 161 horsepower and 165 pound-feet of torque. Buyers can choose either a five-speed manual transmission or a four-speed automatic. Fuel economy is excellent, and buyers can expect to get 22 to 25 mpg in the city and 27 to 31 mpg on the highway.

**Safety:** Four-wheel antilock disc brakes are standard, as is Toyota's VSC stability control system. Side airbags for front occupants and full-length side curtain airbags are optional. The RAV4 fared well in government crash tests, earning four out of five stars for frontal impact protection and a perfect five stars for side impacts. It also earned a "Good" rating (the highest) in frontal offset and side-impact crash testing by the IIHS (the RAV4 is the first vehicle to earn a "Best Pick" designation for both frontal and side-impact tests). One other item of note is the RAV4's lack of a rear bumper. Low-speed crashes that damage the rear of the vehicle can lead to high repair costs.

**Interior Design and Special Features:** Inside, buyers will find a set of stylish white-faced gauges. As usual, all controls are simple and straightforward to use. Thoughtful design elements include adjustable cupholders and well-placed storage bins. There's plenty of room for four passengers, but throw in a fifth and things get a little tight. Behind the rear seat, the RAV4 can hold 29.2 cubic feet of cargo. Remove the 50/50-split bench seat, which also slides, tumbles, folds and reclines, and the vehicle can hold an impressive 68.3 cubic feet.

**Driving Impressions:** Intended for a life on pavement, the RAV4 really shines in this environment, where its taut suspension, quick steering and tight turning radius come together to produce one of the best-handling SUVs we've ever driven. Minimal body lean and sticky street tires combined with the traction of all-wheel drive provide reassuring handling in almost all situations. With a capable and refined 2.4-liter engine installed under the hood, the RAV4 has the power to complement its sharp reflexes.

***Crash Test Scores, see pg 530***
***Warranty information, see pg 542***

## Specifications

| Engine/Drivetrain | HP | Torque | EPA Fuel Economy Rating |
|---|---|---|---|
| **4cyl 2.4L A/M** | **161** | **165** | **24 city/29 hwy** |

## Body Styles

| Style | MSRP Range |
|---|---|
| **Compact SUV** | **$18,550–$21,000** |

Toyota

# 2005 Toyota Sequoia

**Large SUV**

**MSRP Price Range**
## $32,470 - $44,960
Destination Charge: $565 (all styles)

### Ratings

| | | |
|---|---|---|
| Consumer Rating | 9.5 | |
| Editors Rating | 8.3 | |

**What Edmunds.com says:** A thoroughly capable and comfortable full-size SUV, but if you need to tow a heavy load the competition does it better.

**Pros:** Refined drivetrain, surprisingly agile handling, versatile and comfortable interior, Toyota reputation for reliability.

**Cons:** Nondescript styling, low towing capacity for a full-size SUV.

**What's New:** The standard 4.7-liter V8 now delivers 282 horsepower and 325 pound-feet of torque and is hooked to a five-speed automatic transmission. The Sequoia also gets a new front fascia and grille, redesigned taillamps, an in-glass antenna and color-keyed fender flares. A new sport package for the SR5 includes foglamps, tubular running boards, a height-adjustable rear suspension, a front skid plate, the JBL premium sound system and 16-inch alloy wheels. A new Limited Luxury package includes second-row leather bucket seats, a removable center console, unique wood trim, electroluminescent gauges, the height-adjustable rear suspension and memory for the driver seat and outside mirrors. Other additions include available push-button engagement for the 4WD system and an optional navigation system. There's also a new rollover sensor that triggers the side and head curtain airbags in the event of a rollover accident. A third-row center headrest has been added to all Sequoias.

*Crash Test Scores, see pg 530*
*Warranty information, see pg 542*

### Specifications

| Engine/Drivetrain | HP | Torque | EPA Fuel Economy Rating |
|---|---|---|---|
| 8cyl 4.7L A | 282 | 325 | 14 city/17 hwy |
| 8cyl 4.7L A | 240 | 315 | 14 city/18 hwy |

### Body Styles

| Style | MSRP Range |
|---|---|
| Large SUV | $32,470–$44,960 |

**Body Styles, Trim Levels and Options:** There are only two trim levels, base SR5 and Limited. The SR5 is well equipped with features like power windows, seats, mirrors and locks; a CD and cassette audio system; cruise control; 16-inch wheels and automatic climate control. Limited models come fully equipped with leather seating, a premium JBL audio system, power sunroof, a multifunction display, an auto-dimming rearview mirror, heated front seats, 17-inch alloy wheels and keyless entry. On both trucks, you can also get an in-dash six-disc CD changer, a rear-seat DVD-based entertainment system and an available rear load-leveling suspension. A sport package with tubular running boards, a skid plate, the load-leveling suspension and various other extras is available on the SR5, while Limited buyers can get a luxury package with second-row bucket seats, electroluminescent gauges, upgraded wood trim and seat memory.

**Powertrains and Performance:** Under the hood rests a slightly modified version of the V8 from the Tundra pickup. Displacing 4.7 liters and rated at 282 horsepower and 325 pound-feet of torque, this engine lives up to Toyota's tradition of smooth powertrains that deliver seamless power with minimal apparent effort. Despite the available torque, the Sequoia's maximum towing capacity tops out at 6,500 pounds (6,200 on four-wheel-drive models)—less than most of its heavier-duty competition.

**Safety:** The Sequoia comes standard with stability and traction control, as well as four-wheel antilock disc brakes with EBD and panic assist. Optional are seat-mounted side airbags for front occupants and side curtain airbags for first- and second-row occupants. Besides providing added protection in side impacts, these airbags will also deploy in the event of a rollover. The Sequoia received five out of five stars for driver and front-passenger protection in government frontal impact testing.

**Interior Design and Special Features:** Most Sequoias seat eight, though opting for the Limited model's luxury package drops capacity to seven. Second-row passengers are given plenty of room, and the 60/40-split bench seat can be reclined, folded or tumbled completely forward. Although there's significantly more third-row legroom than in the Tahoe, the Toyota's narrower body makes three across too close for comfort. Toyota lists maximum cargo capacity at 128.1 cubic feet, but that's with the second-row seats unbolted from the floor. With the second-row seats in use, capacity measures 73.6 cubes.

**Driving Impressions:** Whether on city streets or dirt trails, the Sequoia handles well for a full-size SUV, providing both a smooth ride and easy maneuverability around turns. Engaging the four-wheel-drive system requires nothing more than pushing the big oval button on the dash marked "4WD." Some Sequoias still use a floor-mounted lever for engaging the locking center differential and low-range gears in the transfer case, but for the majority of drivers, that big button on the dash is all you'll ever need.

For the latest full vehicle reports, visit www.edmunds.com/bginfopak

# 2005 Toyota Sienna

**MSRP Price Range**
## $23,225 - $37,495
Destination Charge: $565 (all styles)

### Ratings

| | | |
|---|---|---|
| Consumer Rating | 9.6 | |
| Editors Rating | 8.8 | |

**What Edmunds.com says:** If you want Lexus-like luxury in your family hauler, the Sienna has your number. With tons of innovative features and even more available options, this Toyota is one of our top recommendations to buyers shopping in the minivan segment.

**Pros:** Smooth ride, refined V6, fold-flat 60/40 third-row seat, seven- and eight-passenger seating configurations, great fuel economy, available all-wheel drive.

**Cons:** A bit too much lean in the corners, seat comfort and noise isolation could be better, expensive option packages.

**What's New:** XLE and XLE Limited models now offer a power-adjustable passenger seat.

**Body Styles, Trim Levels and Options:** The Sienna comes in four trim levels—CE, LE, XLE and top-of-the-line XLE Limited; CE and LE seat seven or eight. LE, XLE and XLE Limited are eligible for all-wheel drive. The CE includes ABS, a rear air conditioner, CD player, telescoping steering wheel, dual-sliding doors with power windows and keyless entry. The LE adds driver lumbar, cruise control, heated power mirrors, privacy glass, a roof rack and a fold-flat front-passenger seat—most of this is optional on the CE. The XLE includes alloy wheels, power-sliding doors, a power liftgate, auto headlamps, three-zone automatic climate control, power-adjustable front seats, rear audio controls and a removable center console. The XLE Limited trim level gets larger 17-inch wheels, rear disc brakes, stability control, adaptive cruise control, a moonroof, leather upholstery, heated front seats, a CD changer, a park-assist system and rear window shades. All-wheel-drive models automatically receive 17-inch wheels, run-flat tires, stability control and upgraded brakes. An entertainment system is available to LE, XLE and XLE Limited buyers, and you can get a navigation system for the XLE and XLE Limited.

**Powertrains and Performance:** The Sienna benefits from a smooth 3.3-liter V6 engine with 230 horsepower coupled to a five-speed automatic transmission. This refined combination results in good fuel mileage with EPA figures of 19 mpg in the city and 27 on the highway for front-drive models and 18/24 for all-wheel-drive vans. The AWD system requires no driver intervention—if a wheel begins to slip, power is automatically transferred to the wheels with more grip.

**Safety:** Antilock brakes are standard across the line. Stability and traction control are included on XLE Limited and AWD models, and optional on all other Siennas. Airbag protection includes seat-mounted side airbags for front occupants and side curtain airbags that cover all three rows—standard on XLE Limited and optional on other trims. In government crash testing, the Sienna earned perfect five-star ratings across the board. Frontal offset testing by the IIHS returned a rating of "Good," the highest.

**Interior Design and Special Features:** The Sienna's interior is swathed in high-quality fabric on lower trim levels and leather and faux wood on high-end models. Most controls are simple to use, and storage space is abundant. Seven-passenger vans allow owners to push the second-row captain's chairs together to create a bench seat, though the setup isn't as user-friendly as the Odyssey's or MPV's. The eight-passenger version uses a 40/20/40-split bench in the second row, enabling you to pull the middle seat 13 inches closer to the front seats for easier access to a baby. The Sienna provides 149 cubic feet of cargo capacity—second only to the Chrysler minivans.

**Driving Impressions:** The V6 is quite powerful when cruising around the suburbs, and especially when merging onto the freeway. Though the ride is supremely plush, overall handling isn't quite up to the sporty level of the Honda Odyssey.

*Crash Test Scores, see pg 530*
*Warranty information, see pg 542*

### Specifications

| Engine/Drivetrain | HP | Torque | EPA Fuel Economy Rating |
|---|---|---|---|
| 6cyl 3.3L A | 230 | 242 | 19 city/26 hwy |

### Body Styles

| Style | MSRP Range |
|---|---|
| Large Minivan | $23,225–$37,495 |

# 2005 Toyota Tacoma

**MSRP Price Range**

## $13,415 - $25,250

Destination Charge: $565 (all styles)

### Ratings

| | | |
|---|---|---|
| Consumer Rating | N/A | |
| Editors Rating | 7.8 | |

**What Edmunds.com says:** The new Tacoma is far and away one of the best compact trucks ever offered to the American public.

**Pros:** Flexible and refined drivetrains, excellent off-road ability, 18 different body configurations, available stability control, solid build quality and reliability record, well-trimmed interior, unique bed features.

**Cons:** Manual gearbox still vague through the gears, awkward emergency brake.

**What's New:** The Tacoma has been completely redesigned for 2005.

**Body Styles, Trim Levels and Options:** The Tacoma comes in three body styles: Regular Cab, Access Cab (extended cab) and Double Cab (crew cab). Each is available with two-wheel or four-wheel drive. Toyota also offers Tacomas with a "PreRunner" designation. PreRunners are 2WD trucks that have the looks and heavy-duty suspension of 4WD models. Toyota also offers a special 2WD X-Runner access cab sport truck equipped with the V6, a six-speed manual transmission, a sport-tuned suspension and additional structural bracing underneath that gives the truck its name. Standard features on the regular cab include a CD player, a full-size spare tire and a tachometer. Access Cabs add bucket seats, air conditioning and a pair of rear access doors. On top of that, the Double Cab receives keyless entry and power windows, locks and mirrors. An optional SR5 package features color-keyed and chrome trim, intermittent wipers and upgraded interior trim. A JBL audio system with seven speakers is optional on Double Cabs. An available TRD Sport package includes performance suspension and upgraded tires, and a TRD Off-Road package features meaty white-lettered tires and heavy-duty off-road suspension.

**Powertrains and Performance:** All regular and access cab models are available with either four- or six-cylinder engines, while the crew cab models use the V6 exclusively. Standard is a 2.7-liter, four-cylinder engine producing 164 horsepower and 183 pound-feet of torque. The 4.0-liter V6 engine serves up a generous 245 hp and 283 lb-ft of torque. Transmission choices include either a five-speed manual or four-speed automatic for the four-cylinder, while V6 buyers can choose between a six-speed manual and a five-speed automatic. Equipped with the V6 engine, the Tacoma's maximum tow rating is now 6,500 pounds.

**Safety:** Antilock brakes with Electronic Brakeforce Distribution and BrakeAssist are standard on all Tacomas. A stability control system is available on all models, except the X-Runner. Crew cab models also offer optional front-seat side airbags and full-length head curtain airbags. Hill-start Assist Control (HAC) and Downhill Assist Control (DAC) are optional on all models (X-Runner excluded) equipped with an automatic transmission. The Tacoma has not yet been crash tested.

*Crash Test Scores, see pg 530*
*Warranty information, see pg 542*

### Specifications

| Engine/Drivetrain | HP | Torque | EPA Fuel Economy Rating |
|---|---|---|---|
| 6cyl 4.0L A/M | 245 | 282 | 18 city/22 hwy |
| 4cyl 2.7L A/M | 164 | 183 | 21 city/26 hwy |

### Body Styles

| Style | MSRP Range |
|---|---|
| Crew Cab Pickup Truck | $21,675–$25,250 |
| Extended Cab Pickup Truck | $16,855–$23,125 |
| Regular Cab Pickup Truck | $13,415–$17,360 |

**Interior Design and Special Features:** The design of the dashboard controls and instrument cluster mimics Toyota's 4Runner SUV, which isn't a bad thing. The quality of the materials sets a new standard for the class, and the seats have the kind of firm, supportive bolstering not typically found on trucks of this type. Getting into Access Cabs is easier now, thanks to dual rear doors that open wider than before, while the backseat of the Double Cab is now comfortable for full-size adults.

**Driving Impressions:** While the standard four-cylinder is certainly adequate, the 4.0-liter V6 is a terrific all-around performer, with plenty of guts down low and a willingness to spin into the upper rev ranges without getting thrashy. In terms of handling, the feeling behind the wheel is of a truck that is well planted at every corner, predictable when pushed and surprisingly agile considering its size.

**MSRP Price Range**
## $15,955 - $33,075
Destination Charge: $565 (all styles)

### Ratings

| | | |
|---|---|---|
| Consumer Rating | 8.6 | |
| Editors Rating | 7.3 | |

**What Edmunds.com says:** If you have to drive a truck everyday and heavy-duty towing isn't a concern, a Tundra should be in your driveway.

**Pros:** Smooth and refined V8, Toyota build quality and reliability, nimble off-road, most carlike of the full-size trucks.

**Cons:** Lacks serious brawn for towing and hauling, narrow cabin, chintzy interior materials.

**What's New:** The base engine is now a 245-hp, 4.0-liter V6 that uses either a six-speed manual or optional five-speed automatic. The optional 4.7-liter V8 now makes 282 hp and is coupled with a standard five-speed automatic transmission. Two-wheel-drive regular cabs are now available with a V8 engine, while four-wheel-drive Access Cabs can no longer be equipped with a V6. Regular cabs equipped with the V8 get a color-keyed grille and chrome front bumper, as well as vinyl flooring and a cloth bench seat. Two new alloy wheel designs are available on Access Cab and Double Cab models, and all Tundras get new headlamps and rear combination lamps. Inside, new gauges and an available navigation system with JBL audio spruce things up a bit. In addition, Double Cabs can now get a 60/40-split bench front seat for true six-passenger seating. Front side-impact airbags and full-length head curtain airbags are now available on Double Cabs.

**Body Styles, Trim Levels and Options:** The Toyota Tundra is available in regular, extended (Access Cab) and crew cab (Double Cab) versions. Regular cabs come only in long bed form, while Access and Double Cabs come only as short beds. Access Cabs have two "suicide" rear doors for easier rear-seat access, while Double Cabs feature four full-size doors and, thanks to their longer wheelbase, equal bed length. There are also three trim levels: base, SR5 and Limited. Available only on regular cabs, the base trim's amenities are limited to antilock brakes, 16-inch steel wheels, a cloth bench seat and a CD player. The SR5 adds body-color bumpers, a chrome grille and air conditioning; V8-equipped models also get cruise control. Available with a V8 only, the Limited offers alloy wheels, an in-dash CD changer and power windows, mirrors and locks. Compared to domestic full-size trucks, the Tundra's options list is short. The convenience package for SR5 models includes full power accessories, cruise, a sliding rear window and keyless entry. You can also get a towing package, a cold-weather package, an off-road package and a sport suspension package. On Limited trucks, there are optional leather-upholstered captain's chairs with a power driver seat. A DVD entertainment system is available for Double Cab models. For added style, Toyota also offers a stepside bed on V8-powered Access Cabs.

**Powertrains and Performance:** Two dual-overhead-cam engines are available: a 4.0-liter V6 and a 4.7-liter V8. The V6 makes 245 horsepower and 282 pound-feet of torque, while the V8 musters 282 hp and 325 lb-ft of torque. The V6 comes with either a six-speed manual or an optional five-speed automatic. The V8 is offered with the five-speed automatic only. Either engine can be had with four-wheel drive. Maximum towing capacity is 7,100 pounds.

**Safety:** The brakes—discs up front and drums in the rear—are equipped with standard ABS. Side-impact airbags for front occupants and full-length side curtain airbags with a rollover sensor are optional on Double Cabs. In government crash tests, the Tundra received a four-star rating (out of five) for driver and front-passenger protection in frontal impacts. The Toyota earned a perfect five stars for front-occupant protection in side impacts. The IIHS gave the truck a "Good" rating (its best) for frontal offset crashes.

**Interior Design and Special Features:** The Access Cab's rear-seat area is useful, but it's smaller than the quarters in other full-size extended cabs. The Double Cab's 60/40-split rear seat boasts legroom on par with its domestic competitors and a reclined seat back for better comfort. Up front, the Tundra offers a typical blend of solid-feeling switchgear, though the materials used are often of mediocre quality, and overall style is bland.

**Driving Impressions:** The V6 is powerful enough for light-duty use, and the V8 certainly has enough oats for everyday driving and typical towing and hauling. Slightly smaller than other full-size trucks, the Tundra is more maneuverable in crowded areas. The standard suspension is softly tuned—it's comfortable for commuting, but less suitable for hauling heavy loads.

*Crash Test Scores, see pg 530*
*Warranty information, see pg 542*

### Specifications

| Engine/Drivetrain | HP | Torque | EPA Fuel Economy Rating |
|---|---|---|---|
| 8cyl 4.7L A | 282 | 325 | 15 city/19 hwy |
| 6cyl 4.0L A/M | 245 | 282 | 16 city/20 hwy |

### Body Styles

| Style | MSRP Range |
|---|---|
| Crew Cab Pickup Truck | $26,120–$33,075 |
| Extended Cab Pickup Truck | $22,410–$31,165 |
| Regular Cab Pickup Truck | $15,955–$21,760 |

# 2005 Volkswagen GTI

Compact Coupe

**MSRP Price Range**

## $19,510 - $22,330

Destination Charge: $575 (all styles)

### Ratings

| | | |
|---|---|---|
| Consumer Rating | N/A | |
| Editors Rating | 7.9 | |

**What Edmunds.com says:** The GTI may have introduced the idea of budget performance, but its aging design has been surpassed by a number of cheaper and faster competitors.

**Pros:** Fun to drive, reasonably priced, lots of standard equipment, premium cabin materials, utility of hatchback design, available six-speed manual.

**Cons:** More expensive and slower than many of its peers.

**What's New:** With an all-new GTI on the way next year, there are no changes to the current platform for 2005.

**Body Styles, Trim Levels and Options:** VW offers two GTI models—1.8T and VR6. The 1.8T comes with 16-inch alloy wheels, a full-size spare, height-adjustable sport seats, an eight-speaker CD stereo, a tilt and telescoping steering wheel, keyless entry with alarm, cruise control and power windows, locks and mirrors. The VR6 adds a bigger engine, 17-inch wheels (optional for the 1.8T) and a trip computer. Options for both models include leather upholstery, a sunroof, seat heaters and the Monsoon sound system. Luxury items like automatic climate control, rain-sensing wipers and a self-dimming rearview mirror are available only on the VR6.

**Powertrains and Performance:** Engine choices are specific to each trim level. Our favorite is the 180-horsepower, turbocharged 1.8-liter inline four in the GTI 1.8T. Besides providing a broad torque band (174 pound-feet from 1,950 to 5,000 rpm), the 1.8T is lighter than the VR6 engine and better suited to the GTI's chassis. It's available with a five-speed manual or five-speed automatic. But if you've got to have the most power, the 24-valve 2.8-liter VR6—and its 200 hp and 195 lb-ft of torque—is unlikely to disappoint. This model targets enthusiast-type drivers and only comes with a six-speed manual transmission.

**Safety:** Four-wheel antilock disc brakes, traction control, and side and head curtain airbags are standard on all GTIs. Stability control is optional on the 1.8T and standard on the VR6. As the GTI is a performance version of the Golf hatchback, the latter's crash test scores apply here: the NHTSA gave the Golf a perfect five stars for driver and front-passenger protection in frontal impact crash tests. The IIHS gave the Golf an "Acceptable" rating (the second highest of four) in frontal offset crash testing.

**Interior Design and Special Features:** The GTI's cabin has a premium feel that you won't find in comparably priced sport coupes and hatchbacks. Interior materials are high in quality, and everything is assembled with care. The height-adjustable front seats are roomy with plenty of bolstering to keep you in place on spirited drives. The rear seat is definitely tight for three people, but the nicely contoured bench can certainly accommodate two, and legroom is surprisingly adequate for a compact. Getting in back is easy, thanks to a front passenger seat that flips forward. With the 60/40-split rear seat in use, the hatch provides 18 cubic feet of capacity; with the seat folded, there are 41.8 cubes.

*Crash Test Scores, see pg 530*
*Warranty information, see pg 542*

### Specifications

| Engine/Drivetrain | HP | Torque | EPA Fuel Economy Rating |
|---|---|---|---|
| 6cyl 2.8L M | 200 | 195 | 21 city/30 hwy |
| 4cyl 1.8L A/M | 180 | 173 | 22 city/29 hwy |

### Body Styles

| Style | MSRP Range |
|---|---|
| Compact Coupe | $19,510–$22,330 |

**Driving Impressions:** The GTI rides on a sport-tuned version of the Golf's independent front strut/rear torsion beam suspension. The VR6 model also has front and rear stabilizer bars to help it manage the extra weight. In practice, both cars strike a pleasant balance between everyday ride comfort and agile, responsive handling on curvy roads. However, the GTI has softer suspension tuning and weighs more than other sport coupes, and as a result, its overall performance suffers.

**MSRP Price Range**

## $15,830 - $20,655

Destination Charge: $575 (all styles)

### Ratings

| | | |
|---|---|---|
| Consumer Rating | N/A | |
| Editors Rating | 7.0 | |

**What Edmunds.com says:** Though pricier than the average economy car, the Golf offers far more amenities, refined driving dynamics and a very fuel-efficient diesel option, all of which make it an attractive hatchback.

**Pros:** Long list of standard features, high-quality cabin materials, utility of hatchback design, fuel-efficient diesel engine, fun to drive.

**Cons:** More expensive than its peers, mediocre performance of base four-cylinder, some controls difficult to use.

**What's New:** With an all-new Golf on the way next year, there are no major changes for the current model.

**Body Styles, Trim Levels and Options:** Volkswagen offers the Golf two-door in GL trim, while the four-door hatchback is available in GL and GLS trim. Standard GL features include air conditioning, four-wheel antilock disc brakes, side airbags, head curtain airbags, headrests in all five seating positions, a tilt and telescoping steering wheel, driver-seat height adjustment, a CD player, cruise control, keyless entry with alarm system and power windows, locks and mirrors. GLS trim adds a sunroof, alloy wheels, upgraded upholstery, a premium Monsoon sound system and a front center armrest with storage. Options include stability control (ESP) with BrakeAssist, and heated seats and windshield washer jets.

**Powertrains and Performance:** All Golf buyers have two engine choices—either a 2.0-liter inline four-cylinder that makes 115 horsepower, or a 1.9-liter diesel four-cylinder (TDI) that's rated for 100 hp and an impressive 177 pound-feet of torque. Both engines provide adequate power for easy around-town acceleration and are available with a five-speed manual or four-speed automatic. Golfs equipped with the 2.0-liter four can feel sluggish at highway speeds, and fuel economy is below that of Civics and Corollas (23 mpg city/29 highway with the automatic, 24/31 with the manual). In contrast, the TDI is a serious fuel miser (34/45 auto, 42/49 manual) and has plenty of torque for passing and merging—it's ideal for commuters.

**Safety:** Four-wheel antilock disc brakes, side airbags (for front occupants) and head curtain airbags (front and rear) are standard on all Golfs. Stability control is optional. VW's hatchback earned a perfect five stars for driver and front-passenger protection in the NHTSA's frontal impact crash tests. It wasn't tested for side impacts, though given its full complement of airbags and its Jetta platform mate's four-star ratings, it probably would have done well. The IIHS gave it an "Acceptable" rating (the second highest of four) in frontal offset crash testing.

**Interior Design and Special Features:** Every Golf's interior is filled with high-quality materials and assembled with care; at night, you'll get to enjoy VW's signature blue-red cabin illumination. The front seats are roomy, and both are height-adjustable. The rear seat is definitely tight for three people, but the nicely contoured bench can certainly accommodate two adults; and compared to the Jetta, legroom is surprisingly adequate. Getting in back is easy in two-door models, thanks to a front passenger seat that flips forward. With the 60/40-split rear seat in use, the hatch provides 18 cubic feet of capacity; fold the seat and you'll have 41.8 cubes at your disposal.

**Driving Impressions:** For the most part, the Golf provides a pleasant balance between highway comfort and responsive handling. More demanding drivers may find the ride a bit floaty with much body roll when cornering—if that's you, take a spin in the GTI, the performance version of the Golf.

*Crash Test Scores, see pg 530*
*Warranty information, see pg 542*

### Specifications

| Engine/Drivetrain | HP | Torque | EPA Fuel Economy Rating |
|---|---|---|---|
| 4cyl 2.0L A/M | 115 | 122 | 24 city/30 hwy |
| 4cyl 1.9L A/M | 100 | 177 | 32 city/43 hwy |

### Body Styles

| Style | MSRP Range |
|---|---|
| Compact Coupe | $15,830–$20,655 |

# 2005 Volkswagen Jetta

**Compact Sedan, Wagon**

**MSRP Price Range**
## $17,680 - $25,045
Destination Charge: $575 (all styles)

## Ratings

| | | |
|---|---|---|
| Consumer Rating | N/A | |
| Editors Rating | 6.9 | |

**What Edmunds.com says:** The Jetta is no longer priced like an economy car; yet its powerful engine lineup, near ideal balance between ride and handling and premium cabin materials make it one of our top recommendations to small car buyers.

**Pros:** Powerful 1.8T engine, fuel-efficient TDI power plant, fun to drive, comfortable ride, rich interior materials, loads of standard safety features, solid build quality.

**Cons:** More expensive than most small sedans and wagons, tight rear-seat legroom, weak base four-cylinder, spotty reliability.

**What's New:** The GLI VR6 model is no longer available, but the GLI 1.8T can now be had with an automatic transmission.

*Crash Test Scores, see pg 530*
*Warranty information, see pg 542*

## Specifications

| Engine/Drivetrain | HP | Torque | EPA Fuel Economy Rating |
|---|---|---|---|
| 4cyl 2.0L A/M | 115 | 122 | 24 city/30 hwy |
| 4cyl 1.9L A/M | 100 | 177 | 33 city/44 hwy |
| 4cyl 1.8L A/M | 180 | 173 | 22 city/29 hwy |

## Body Styles

| Style | MSRP Range |
|---|---|
| Compact Sedan | $17,680–$25,045 |
| Compact Wagon | $18,680–$23,275 |

**Body Styles, Trim Levels and Options:** The Jetta sedan is offered in GL, GLS and GLI versions, while the wagon comes only in GL and GLS trims. Standard features on GL models include a height-adjustable driver seat; tilt and telescoping steering wheel; power windows, mirrors and locks; cruise control; a CD player; a full-size spare tire; and, for 1.8T-equipped cars, traction control. Options include stability control (ESP), heated seats and a Monsoon sound system. The next step up is the GLS, which adds a center armrest, Monsoon sound system as standard, a sunroof and alloy wheels. All GL options are available on the GLS, along with a leather interior. GLS 1.8T models can be fitted with a sport package (firmer suspension, 17-inch wheels), and GLS 1.8T wagons are eligible for a premium package with power seats, automatic climate control, an auto-dimming rearview mirror and rain-sensing wipers. Finally, the sporty GLI sedan has all the GLS content, except the sunroof (optional), and adds unique trim, 17-inch wheels, a sport suspension, ESP and heated sport seats.

**Powertrains and Performance:** GL and GLS buyers have their choice of three engines: a 115-horsepower, 2.0-liter, four-cylinder engine; a 1.9-liter diesel four (called TDI for turbo direct injection) that makes 100 hp and 177 pound-feet of torque (not available in California emissions states); or a delightful 180-hp, turbocharged, 1.8-liter four-cylinder (called 1.8T). Meanwhile, the performance-oriented GLI sedan comes only with the 1.8T. GL and GLS models are available with a five-speed manual, or one of two automatic transmissions—the base four and TDI get a four-speed auto, while the 1.8T has a five-speed unit. The sporty GLI has a standard six-speed manual but can also be equipped with the five-speed automatic this year. Acceleration with the base 2.0-liter is sluggish and gas mileage is only average, but the torquey TDI is a serious fuel miser (up to 46 mpg) and ideal for commuters. The 1.8T makes any Jetta a rousing good time, while delivering mileage about equal to the 2.0-liter.

**Safety:** Four-wheel antilock disc brakes, side airbags for front occupants and full-length head curtain airbags are standard across the line; stability control is either standard or optional, depending on the model. The Jetta earned five stars in government frontal impact crash tests and four stars in side-impact testing. The IIHS rated the car "Acceptable" (second highest) after conducting its offset frontal impact crash test.

**Interior Design and Special Features:** Each Jetta's cabin is filled with high-quality materials and assembled with care. The front seats are roomy, but the rear bench, though nicely contoured, is tight on legroom. The wagon has 34 cubic feet of capacity with the rear seats up and 51.9 cubes when they're folded.

**Driving Impressions:** Out on the road, the Jetta manages to provide both comfortable ride quality and agile handling. If the regular suspension is too soft for your taste, try the optional sport suspension or the enthusiast-oriented GLI model.

For the latest full vehicle reports, visit www.edmunds.com/bginfopak

**Compact Coupe, Convertible**  # 2005 Volkswagen New Beetle

**MSRP Price Range**
## $16,570 - $26,525
Destination Charge: N/A (all styles)

### Ratings

| | | |
|---|---|---|
| Consumer Rating | N/A | |
| Editors Rating | 7.0 | |

**What Edmunds.com says:** The image car in VW's lineup (and the original retro-mobile), the New Beetle offers a unique combination of safety, fun and upscale features for its price range.

**Pros:** Cute yet classic styling, range of engine choices, long list of standard features, excellent crash test scores.

**Cons:** Tight rear-seat accommodations, limited cargo room, Turbo S model priced much higher than comparable performance coupes.

**What's New:** Changes for 2005 include a new optional six-speed automatic transmission with the 2.0 and 1.8T engines, a standard MP3 connector for the radio and a satellite radio (either XM or Sirius) option. The 1.8T engine gets squeaky-clean with a ULEV emissions rating. Color changes (always an important factor in any New Beetle purchase) are as follows: Shadow Blue replaces Galactic Blue, Tornado Red replaces Uni Red, and Blue Lagoon is no longer available.

**Body Styles, Trim Levels and Options:** The two-door New Beetle is available in two-door hatchback and convertible body styles. Hatchbacks come in GL, GLS and Turbo S trim; convertibles are either GL or GLS. GL models come with 16-inch wheels; air conditioning; power windows, locks and mirrors; cruise control; seat-height adjusters; a tilt and telescoping steering wheel; and a manually folding top on convertibles. The GLS adds a sunroof, a center armrest with storage, alloy wheels, foglights and a power-operated top on the convertible. The Turbo S has all of the above items, plus unique 17-inch wheels, leather seating, a sport-tuned suspension, distinctive body add-ons and a unique interior.

**Powertrains and Performance:** GL and GLS buyers can choose one of three engines. First up is a 115-horsepower, 2.0-liter inline four-cylinder. More interesting is the 100-hp, 1.9-liter diesel four (called TDI) that gets close to 50 mpg on the highway and makes an impressive 177 lb-ft of torque (not available in California emissions states), or the 150-hp, 1.8-liter turbocharged four (called the 1.8T). All of these engines have adequate power for easy city driving, though the 1.8T is the most fun, and it provides fuel economy on par with the base 2.0-liter. The performance-oriented Turbo S gets a 180-hp version of the 1.8T. A five-speed manual transmission is standard on all trims, except the Turbo S, which gets a six-speed gearbox only. A six-speed automatic with Tiptronic automanual shifting ability is optional on 2.0 and 1.8T engines. A Direct Shift Gearbox (DSG) is available on the TDI, essentially a six-speed manual tranny with an electronically controlled clutch. It can be operated in a full auto mode like a traditional automatic or manually shifted.

**Safety:** Standard on all New Beetles are four-wheel antilock disc brakes, side airbags for front occupants, head curtain airbags and active front head restraints. Convertibles have a rollover protection system. Stability control is optional on GL and GLS models and standard on the Turbo S. In government crash testing, the Beetle earned five stars in both frontal impact categories. It received a "Good" rating (and "Best Pick" status) from the IIHS in frontal offset crash testing.

**Interior Design and Special Features:** Though smaller inside than the Golf, the Beetle (seats four, 12 cubic feet of hatch space) compensates with style: its tablelike dashboard, huge circular speedometer and round vents distinguish it from everything else on the road. The convertible's top is easy to fold and well insulated from wind and road noise. With its top down, the bug has a classic but polished appearance, thanks to the handsome aluminum trim along the beltline.

**Driving Impressions:** Like other VWs, the Beetle is both fun to drive and comfortable for long trips. The Turbo S has a slightly stiffer suspension—it's still too soft for performance freaks, but just about right for most drivers who want a little more sport from their Bug.

*Crash Test Scores, see pg 530*
*Warranty information, see pg 542*

### Specifications

| Engine/Drivetrain | HP | Torque | EPA Fuel Economy Rating |
|---|---|---|---|
| 4cyl 2.0L A/M | 115 | 125 | N/A |
| 4cyl 1.9L A/M | 100 | 177 | N/A |
| 4cyl 1.8L A/M | 150 | 162 | N/A |
| 4cyl 1.8L A/M | 180 | 173 | N/A |

### Body Styles

| Style | MSRP Range |
|---|---|
| Compact Coupe, Convertible | $16,570–$26,525 |

# 2005 Volkswagen Passat

**Midsize Sedan, Wagon**

**MSRP Price Range**
## $22,070 - $33,615
Destination Charge: $575 (all styles)

### Ratings

| | | |
|---|---|---|
| Consumer Rating | 9.0 | |
| Editors Rating | 8.1 | |

**What Edmunds.com says:** With its fun-to-drive character, upscale interior and wide range of features, the Passat is one of our favorite midsize sedans and wagons. Don't buy your next family car without driving one of these first.

**Pros:** Better handling dynamics than most sedans in its class, excellent value in GL or GLS trim, roomy interior with upscale feel, outstanding build and materials quality, available all-wheel drive, unique diesel engine option.

**Cons:** Upper-level models are expensive compared to Japanese rivals, less rear-seat room and storage than competitors, V6 is down on power.

**What's New:** The top-of-the-line W8 model has been discontinued. The GLX loses its standard telematics system. New 16-inch "Rockstar" alloy wheels are standard on the GLS (in place of the former 15s), and new 17-inch "Bistar" alloys are optional on the GLS and GLX.

*Crash Test Scores, see pg 530*
*Warranty information, see pg 542*

### Specifications

| Engine/Drivetrain | HP | Torque | EPA Fuel Economy Rating |
|---|---|---|---|
| 6cyl 2.8L A/M | 190 | 206 | 19 city/27 hwy |
| 4cyl 2.0L A | 134 | 247 | 27 city/38 hwy |
| 4cyl 1.8L A/M | 170 | 166 | 21 city/30 hwy |

### Body Styles

| Style | MSRP Range |
|---|---|
| Midsize Sedan | $22,070–$32,615 |
| Midsize Wagon | $23,070–$33,615 |

**Body Styles, Trim Levels and Options:** VW offers the Passat sedan and wagon in three trim levels—GL, GLS and GLX. The GL comes with 15-inch wheels, a driver-seat height adjuster, air conditioning, a CD player, cruise control, power windows and locks, keyless entry, power-heated mirrors and a full-size spare. Options include a premium sound system and a dealer-installed CD changer. The GLS adds a sunroof, 16-inch alloy wheels and an upgraded Monsoon stereo; options include seat heaters, leather upholstery and a CD changer. All of the above are standard on the GLX, except the CD changer, which remains optional. Additionally, GLX models come with power seats, automatic climate control and an auto-dimming rearview mirror.

**Powertrains and Performance:** Of the three engine choices, our favorite is the 1.8-liter turbocharged inline four (called 1.8T) that delivers 170 horsepower. It's standard on the GL and GLS. The other choice on GL and GLS models is a 134-hp, 2.0-liter turbocharged direct injection (TDI) diesel four-cylinder, which is unfortunately not yet available in California, New York, Vermont, Maine or Massachusetts. Though low on horsepower, the diesel offers an impressive 247 pound-feet of torque while delivering fuel mileage in the high 30s. Standard on the GLX is a 190-hp 2.8-liter V6. The V6 is smooth, but it's down on horsepower compared to other six-cylinders in this class. All of the above engines come with either a five-speed manual or a five-speed automatic, except the TDI, which comes with the automatic only. Optional on select GLX and GLS models is the 4Motion all-wheel-drive system.

**Safety:** All models come with four-wheel antilock disc brakes, traction control, side airbags for front occupants and full-length head curtain airbags. Stability control is standard on the GLX and optional on other models. In government crash testing, the Passat earned a perfect five stars for driver and front-passenger protection in frontal impacts and four stars in the side-impact categories. The IIHS gave it a "Good" rating for the frontal offset crash test and named it a "Best Pick" among midsize cars.

**Interior Design and Special Features:** Even at the GL trim level, the Passat's cabin is comfortable and upscale in feel. The rear seat is a little tight compared to the competition, but it's perfectly adequate for two adults. Wagons provide 39 cubic feet of luggage space; fold down the 60/40-split rear seat and you'll have 56.5 cubic feet (54.6 for 4Motion models).

**Driving Impressions:** With a well-balanced suspension and perfectly weighted steering, the Passat is one of the most entertaining midsize cars around. Some drivers might find body roll a bit excessive around turns, but the trade-off for excellent ride quality is worthwhile.

**Large Sedan**

# 2005 Volkswagen Phaeton

**MSRP Price Range**

## $66,950 - $96,100

Destination Charge: $615 (all styles)

### Ratings

| | | |
|---|---|---|
| Consumer Rating | 9.1 | |
| Editors Rating | 8.8 | |

**What Edmunds.com says:** It competes favorably with Germany's finest on nearly every level, but without the prestigious brand name, it's hard to swallow the price.

**Pros:** Powerful engine lineup, rock-solid build quality, exquisitely trimmed interior, standard all-wheel drive, a features list any Mercedes would be proud to call its own.

**Cons:** Excessive weight impedes handling, poor fuel economy, premium price for a non-premium brand.

**What's New:** Changes to VW's flagship sedan include a new style front grille, new soft-close doors, active cruise control and standard cell phone preparation for the W12 model (optional on V8). The V8 model also receives revised 18-inch alloy wheels and wood upgrades (Myrtle and Walnut).

**Body Styles, Trim Levels and Options:** The four-door Phaeton is offered in one long-wheelbase body style only. Equipment levels vary depending on which engine is chosen, but all Phaetons come standard with a four-zone automatic climate control system, high-intensity discharge headlamps, heated windshield washer nozzles, entry-exit lights at all doors, an oversize sunroof and a 10-speaker premium sound system with a glovebox-mounted six-CD changer. Choose the V8 Phaeton and 17-inch alloy wheels will adorn the exterior, while interior features include 12-way power memory heated front seats with four-way power-adjustable lumbar support; ambient lighting; eucalyptus wood trim; a leather-wrapped, hand-stitched steering wheel with multifunction controls; a full set of self-dimming mirrors with memory; stainless steel pedals; power rear-window sunshades and side manual sunshades; and a trunk pass-through with ski bag. The 12-cylinder Phaeton adds 18-inch alloy wheels with all-season tires, quad exhaust pipes (versus dual pipes on the V8), an upgraded 12-speaker sound system with digital sound processing and additional window tinting. The W12 also benefits from 18-way power-adjustable front seats that are heated and ventilated and have a 10-minute massage function. The rear seats are heated, too.

**Powertrains and Performance:** The Phaeton is available with two engine options: a 4.2-liter V8 which delivers 335 horsepower, or a 6.0-liter W12 which makes an impressive 420 hp. The V8 engine comes mated to a six-speed automatic transmission with manual-shift capability, while the W12 receives a five-speed automatic that also offers manual shifting. Both cars are limited to a top speed of 135 mph. All-wheel drive is standard on all Phaetons.

**Safety:** The Phaeton has a total of eight airbags, including full-length side curtain airbags. Also standard are four-wheel antilock disc brakes with emergency brake assist, electronic park assist, VW's ESP stability control and a tire-pressure monitoring system. OnStar, an in-vehicle communication service, is also included.

**Interior Design and Special Features:** Inside, the Phaeton's luxurious cabin is trimmed in wood ranging from walnut to eucalyptus, Italian leather and chrome and brushed metal. Buyers can choose between a four-seat or five-seat configuration, with a wood-trimmed console resting between the rear seats on the four-passenger setup. An integrated vehicle management system uses a 7-inch color screen that incorporates the navigation system, onboard trip computer, stereo system and climate control system.

**Driving Impressions:** Fine-tuning the ride for the Phaeton is an air suspension that includes continuous damping control, which allows the vehicle to automatically adapt to the road surfaces and driving conditions without the driver's input. The competent suspension, along with the standard all-wheel-drive system and eager engine, makes for an entertaining ride, but the car's excessive weight keeps it from delivering the athletic feel of its competitors.

*Crash Test Scores, see pg 530*
*Warranty information, see pg 542*

### Specifications

| Engine/Drivetrain | HP | Torque | EPA Fuel Economy Rating |
|---|---|---|---|
| 8cyl 4.2L A | 335 | 317 | 16 city/22 hwy |
| 12cyl 6.0L A | 420 | 406 | 12 city/19 hwy |

### Body Styles

| Style | MSRP Range |
|---|---|
| Large Sedan | $66,950–$96,100 |

# 2005 Volkswagen Touareg Midsize SUV

**MSRP Price Range**
## $37,140 - $58,490
Destination Charge: $615 (all styles)

## Ratings

| Ratings | | |
|---|---|---|
| Consumer Rating | 8.7 | |
| Editors Rating | 7.6 | |

**What Edmunds.com says:** An enticing blend of the pavement-dwelling crossover and the rugged off-roader swathed in Volkswagen style.

**Pros:** Upscale interior, polished road manners, true off-road capability, solid construction, lengthy standard equipment list, available V10 diesel.

**Cons:** Lousy fuel economy with gas engines, not a lot of room in the backseat, no in-dash CD changer.

**What's New:** The Touareg's standard V6 engine goes from 220 hp to 240 hp. The optional navigation system will change from CD-based to DVD-based later in the model year. The formerly standard tire-pressure monitoring system is now optional, and satellite radio is available across the board. A self-dimming rearview mirror debuts this year, along with a full-size rear-mounted spare tire and new style 18-inch alloy wheels.

**Body Styles, Trim Levels and Options:** The Touareg comes in three trim levels—V6, V8 and V10 TDI. The V6 comes with 17-inch alloy wheels, dual-zone automatic climate control, heated leatherette seats, telescoping steering wheel, genuine wood and aluminum accents, a 10-speaker sound system with CD player, one-touch front windows and an auto-dimming rearview mirror. The V8 adds 18-inch wheels and power leather seats (optional on the V6), while opening up options like 19-inch wheels, four-zone climate control, heated rear seats and premium napa leather. Options on all Touaregs include bi-xenon headlights, parking sensors and a navigation system.

**Powertrains and Performance:** Three engines are available. The base motor is a 240-horse-power, 3.2-liter V6. Next up is a 310-hp, 4.2-liter V8, the same one used in the Audi A6 and A8. The top-dog engine choice is the V10 TDI turbodiesel, which boasts 310 hp and 553 lb-ft of torque. Note that the TDI is not yet available in California emissions states. All engines are paired with a six-speed automatic transmission with sport and automanual modes. Towing capacity is 7,716 pounds for all Touaregs. The 4XMotion four-wheel-drive system is standard, and it includes low-range gearing for serious off-roading. Another option to consider is the air suspension, which increases the Touareg's standard 8.3 inches of ground clearance to a maximum of 11.8, while offering a variety of lower height settings for less intense terrain, along with continuous damping control to flatten the SUV's cornering attitude.

**Safety:** Every model comes with four-wheel antilock disc brakes with BrakeAssist and Electronic Brakeforce Distribution, stability control, hill descent and incline rollback control. Passive safety features include side airbags for front occupants, full-length head curtain airbags and seatbelt pre-tensioners in all outboard positions. Crash testing by the NHTSA returned a four-star rating (out of five) for frontal impacts (both driver and passenger) and five-stars for side impacts (front and rear).

*Crash Test Scores, see pg 530*
*Warranty information, see pg 542*

## Specifications

| Engine/Drivetrain | HP | Torque | EPA Fuel Economy Rating |
|---|---|---|---|
| 8cyl 4.2L A | 310 | 302 | 14 city/18 hwy |
| 6cyl 3.2L A | 240 | 229 | 15 city/20 hwy |
| 10cyl 4.9L A | 310 | 553 | 17 city/23 hwy |

## Body Styles

| Style | MSRP Range |
|---|---|
| Midsize SUV | $37,140–$58,490 |

**Interior Design and Special Features:** Inside, the Touareg builds upon the styling cues established in the Passat. Each one has an upscale two-tone ensemble accented by real wood and aluminum. Most surfaces are soft-touch, and what hard surfaces there are (lower dash, console and doors) feel smooth and substantial to the touch. The backseat isn't overly roomy, and we encourage families to try before they buy. Cargo capacity is average—31 cubic feet with the rear seats up and 71 cubes when they're folded.

**Driving Impressions:** Even if you never leave the pavement, the Touareg should satisfy. Acceleration ranges from adequate in the base V6 model, to ample in the V8, to explosive in the V10 TDI. Ride quality is smooth and stable, and although heavy, the VW feels agile around corners, particularly when equipped with the air suspension. Taken off-road, the Touareg amazes, as it tackles steep passes and deep ruts normally reserved for rough-and-tumble Jeeps.

**Compact Sedan**

**MSRP Price Range**
## $23,260 - $27,710
Destination Charge: $685 (all styles)

### Ratings

| | | |
|---|---|---|
| Consumer Rating | 9.1 | |
| Editors Rating | 7.9 | |

**What Edmunds.com says:** Bigger, sportier and more powerful than its predecessor, the new S40 is fun to drive, while adding a much needed dose of style to Volvo's small-car line.

**Pros:** Sharper handling than you would expect from a Volvo, T5 version offers quick acceleration, well-designed interior controls, long list of safety features, available all-wheel drive.

**Cons:** Firm suspension can be choppy on the highway, average performance from the non-turbo engine.

**What's New:** A redesigned S40 was introduced halfway through the 2004 model year as a 2004.5 model. It continues into 2005 unchanged.

**Body Styles, Trim Levels and Options:** The S40 comes in 2.4i and T5 versions. The 2.4i comes with 16-inch alloy wheels, a leather-wrapped steering wheel with telescope adjustment and a CD player. In addition to a more powerful engine, the T5 adds front and rear spoilers, wood grain interior trim, foglights, automatic climate control, a power driver seat and a trip computer—all of which are optional on the 2.4i. Premium and Sport Packages are available for both trims; they're your ticket to leather upholstery, a moonroof, firmer suspension calibrations and wheel/tire upgrades. Other extras include a 12-speaker Dolby stereo with an in-dash CD changer, a navigation system and bi-xenon headlights.

**Powertrains and Performance:** The 2.4i comes with a naturally aspirated 2.4-liter inline five-cylinder rated for 168 horsepower and 170 pound-feet of torque. Buyers can choose either a five-speed manual or five-speed automatic to go with it. The T5 gets a turbocharged 2.5-liter inline five that makes 218 hp and 236 lb-ft of torque. In addition to the automatic, the T5 is eligible for a six-speed manual gearbox. T5 versions are also available with all-wheel drive, so long as you select the automatic transmission.

**Safety:** Four-wheel antilock disc brakes and traction control are standard on all S40s. Volvo's DTSC stability control system is optional. All models include both side-impact airbags and head curtain airbags, along with whiplash-reducing front seats. Built-in child booster seats are optional. The S40 received a perfect five-star rating in government side-impact crash testing; frontal and offset tests have not yet been performed.

**Interior Design and Special Features:** The S40's interior is unique and styled to appeal to a young audience. The first thing you'll notice is the ultraslim center stack, which has a definite Scandinavian design while also allowing for more storage up front. Interior trim choices include faux metal, faux wood, real aluminum or a transparent material reminiscent of an iMac computer. The ergonomically designed seats are available in different upholstery types, and adults will find adequate legroom in both the front and rear.

**Driving Impressions:** Volvo tuned the S40 to take performance much more seriously than the previous-generation model. Handling is crisp and entertaining, though the standard tires are taxed by more aggressive cornering. The downside to the S40's sharp reflexes is that cruising comfort suffers. The S40 offers adequate power for everyday driving, but weekend enthusiasts should head straight for the spirited T5 model.

*Crash Test Scores, see pg 530*
*Warranty information, see pg 542*

### Specifications

| Engine/Drivetrain | HP | Torque | EPA Fuel Economy Rating |
|---|---|---|---|
| 5cyl 2.5L M | 218 | 236 | 22 city/31 hwy |
| 5cyl 2.4L M | 168 | 170 | 22 city/29 hwy |

### Body Styles

| Style | MSRP Range |
|---|---|
| Compact Sedan | $23,260–$27,710 |

**MSRP Price Range**
## $27,235 - $33,285
Destination Charge: $685 (all styles)

### Ratings

| | | |
|---|---|---|
| Consumer Rating | N/A | |
| Editors Rating | 7.9 | |

**What Edmunds.com says:** An elegant luxury sedan or a sleek sport sedan? The S60 can fill both of these roles, though not with the grace of some German rivals.

**Pros:** Superb front-seat comfort, wide variety of safety and luxury features, balanced ride and handling characteristics, available all-wheel drive.

**Cons:** Doesn't handle with true sport sedan precision, expensive optional equipment, turbo lag and torque steer in the T5 model, tight rear legroom.

**What's New:** The S60 gets a revised front fascia this year with new headlamps, grille and bumper. Color-keyed side moldings, lower rocker sills and bumpers are also new, along with LED taillamps. Other changes include new flat-blade windshield wipers, revised front seats, a new center console and an improved audio system. A trip computer is newly standard, and real wood replaces the fake stuff in the Premium Package. The Sport Package gets a new wheel design, and run-flat tires are a new option. The headlamp washers have been redesigned, and the interior air quality sensor is now a stand-alone option. The 2.5T gets new wheels and available rear park assist. A wood steering wheel is also available. The Four-C chassis from the S60R is now optional on all S60s. The T5 gets a bump in horsepower, up to 257, as well as larger disc brakes and new seat fabric. The T5 also receives speed-sensitive steering and a sport suspension as standard. Black mesh inlays replace the aluminum pieces in the Premium Package, except with the graphite interior color.

*Crash Test Scores, see pg 530*
*Warranty information, see pg 542*

### Specifications

| Engine/Drivetrain | HP | Torque | EPA Fuel Economy Rating |
|---|---|---|---|
| 5cyl 2.5L A | 208 | 236 | N/A |
| 5cyl 2.4L M | 257 | 258 | N/A |
| 5cyl 2.4L M | 168 | 166 | N/A |

### Body Styles

| Style | MSRP Range |
|---|---|
| Compact Sedan | $27,235–$33,285 |

**Body Styles, Trim Levels and Options:** Four trim levels are available—base 2.4, midlevel 2.5T, winter-friendly 2.5T AWD and upscale T5. The four vary on the basis of standard equipment and engine type. The 2.4 is equipped with 15-inch alloy wheels, a trip computer, dual-zone climate control, a CD player, power-fold rear headrests, one-touch front windows and a tilt/telescoping, leather-wrapped steering wheel. The 2.5T and 2.5T AWD get 16-inch wheels, a power driver seat with memory, automatic climate control and faux wood interior accents. The T5 comes with upgraded trim and a power passenger seat. Options include an excellent 13-speaker Dolby sound system with a four-disc CD changer, a DVD-based navigation system, an adaptive suspension, 17-inch wheels, leather upholstery, heated seats and a sunroof.

**Powertrains and Performance:** The S60 2.4 comes with a 2.4-liter five-cylinder engine that produces 168 horsepower (165 in California where it's SULEV-certified). The 2.5T, as you might guess, is turbocharged, and it makes a healthy 208 hp. The 2.5T AWD has the same engine, but power is routed through an electronically controlled all-wheel-drive system. The T5 is the most powerful S60 with its 257-hp, 2.3-liter turbocharged engine. Both the 2.4 and T5 can be equipped with either a five-speed manual or a five-speed automatic transmission, while the 2.5T and 2.5T AWD are available only with the automatic. Automanual functionality is available on all models except the 2.4.

**Safety:** Safety features include side airbags for front occupants, side curtain airbags for front and rear passengers, anti-submarine seats and whiplash-reducing head restraints. Stability control is standard on the T5 and optional for all other models. In government crash testing, the S60 scored four out of five stars for the driver and front passenger in the frontal impact category. Side-impact scores were five stars for both front- and rear-seat occupants. In frontal offset crash testing, the S60 received a "Good" rating overall (the best possible).

**Interior Design and Special Features:** The S60's interior is functional but doesn't feel upscale unless you add options like leather upholstery. The controls are nicely weighted; although, the pictograms depicting the various functions can be difficult to understand. There is seating for five, but rear passengers may find legroom tight. The front seats always receive the highest accolades, with a blend of cushioning and support and a myriad of controls that allow variously sized bodies to fit comfortably.

**Driving Impressions:** The base S60 2.4 offers adequate power, though most people are apt to prefer the more powerful 2.5T models. The T5 should be your choice if you like to do things quickly but don't mind some turbo lag. All S60s provide a smooth, serene ride that veers more toward comfort than sport. The Volvo holds the road well when driven around twists and turns, but when pushed hard, it can't maintain the composure of sportier rivals. What's more, bumps and ruts tend to upset the chassis more so than in other entry-luxury sedans. The steering is relatively quick but lacks road feel, while the brakes provide strong stopping power.

# Compact Sedan

# 2005 Volvo S60 R

**MSRP Price Range**
**$37,250**
Destination Charge: $685 (all styles)

## Ratings

| | | |
|---|---|---|
| Consumer Rating | 9.5 | |
| Editors Rating | 8.2 | |

**What Edmunds.com says:** Need a handsome family vehicle that's fast enough to surprise unsuspecting BMW drivers? The S60 R fulfills both roles.

**Pros:** Impressive 300-horsepower turbo engine, excellent balance and grip when driven briskly, luxurious interior with lots of safety features, reasonable price, stealth appeal.

**Cons:** Not as razor-sharp as high-performance German offerings, tight rear legroom.

**What's New:** Changes for this year include restyled front and rear clips and new headlamps. Color-keyed side moldings and lower sills are now standard, while the interior air quality sensor is now a stand-alone option.

**Body Styles, Trim Levels and Options:** Most desirable features come standard on the S60 R. The equipment list includes bi-xenon headlights, 17-inch wheels with 235/45ZR17 tires, leather upholstery, bolstered sport seats, a three-spoke steering wheel with tilt/telescope adjustment, aluminum inlays, dual-zone automatic climate control, a CD player, a trip computer and a split-folding rear seat. On the options list, you'll find 18-inch wheels with 235/40 rubber, premium leather, a sunroof, a four-disc CD changer, a DVD-based navigation system, Volvo's On Call telematics and an integrated child booster seat.

**Powertrains and Performance:** Every S60 R is powered by a turbocharged 2.5-liter inline five-cylinder that pumps out 300 horsepower and 295 pound-feet of torque when paired with the standard close-ratio six-speed manual transmission. A five-speed automatic (with automanual functionality) is optional—buyers should take note that peak torque drops to 258 lb-ft when the automatic is selected. Acceleration is quite brisk in the S60 R, with ample juice to pick off the occasional unsuspecting BMW driver. Volvo claims a 0-to-60-mph time of 5.4 seconds with the manual gearbox. Volvo's Four-C (Continuously Controlled Chassis Concept) system comes standard; it includes an electronically controlled all-wheel-drive system, as well as an adaptive suspension that Volvo says can adjust the shock valving up to 500 times per second for improved grip, reduced body roll and better overall balance.

**Safety:** As the S60 R is intended to pull double duty for driving enthusiasts who are also parents, all the usual Volvo safety features are included—stability control, side-impact airbags for front occupants, full-length head curtain airbags and whiplash-reducing seats. The S60 R is based on the regular S60, which earned four out of five stars in the NHTSA's frontal impact crash tests, a perfect five stars for side impacts and a "Good" rating in IIHS frontal offset crash testing.

**Interior Design and Special Features:** Inside, the S60 R offers more upscale furnishings than regular S60s, namely more heavily bolstered leather sport seats, stylish silver and blue gauges and real aluminum trim. Comfort is exceptional in front, but rear passengers may find legroom a bit tight. The control layout is more complex than in other cars, and new owners may need to sit down with the owner's manual in order to master everything. Trunk capacity is 13.9 cubic feet.

**Driving Impressions:** Considerably faster than other Volvos, the S60 R is also a much better handler. Taken out on your favorite back roads, the R is ready to play—its high level of balance and grip instills confidence in the driver. While still unable to communicate with its pilot in the indelible manner of a BMW, the S60 R is sized right (four doors) to make it a good choice for enthusiasts with families. And it rides comfortably enough to be used as an everyday commuter car.

*Crash Test Scores, see pg 530*
*Warranty information, see pg 542*

## Specifications

| Engine/Drivetrain | HP | Torque | EPA Fuel Economy Rating |
|---|---|---|---|
| 5cyl 2.5L M | 300 | 295 | N/A |

## Body Styles

| Style | MSRP Range |
|---|---|
| Compact Sedan | $37,250 |

# 2005 Volvo S80

**MSRP Price Range**

## $35,900 - $48,515

Destination Charge: $685 (all styles)

### Ratings

| | | |
|---|---|---|
| Consumer Rating | N/A | |
| Editors Rating | 8.2 | |

**What Edmunds.com says:** When it comes to ride comfort, feature content and uncompromised safety, the S80 excels, but for those who prefer a little sport in their sedans, the S80 will leave you wishing for more.

**Pros:** Loaded with outstanding safety innovations and features, quick on its feet in T6 trim, spacious backseat, soothing ride.

**Cons:** Suspension still doesn't feel athletic even with Four-C system, turbo lag can be annoying around town, gets pricey with options.

**What's New:** The base 2.9 model has been dropped in favor of the 2.5T model introduced late in the 2004 model year. Inside, real walnut trim replaces the faux trim used in last year's models, and you can now load six discs at a time into the in-dash CD changer. Satellite radio and run-flat tires are new options on all S80s, while 2.5T buyers can now get sport seats. A new safety feature called the Blind Spot Information System (BLIS) is offered later in the model year.

**Body Styles, Trim Levels and Options:** The four-door S80 is available in four trim levels—2.5T, 2.5T AWD, T6 and T6 Premier. The 2.5T and 2.5T AWD come with 16-inch alloy wheels, traction control, dual-zone climate control, a power-adjustable driver seat with memory, a tilt/telescoping steering wheel with satellite cruise and audio controls and an eight-speaker CD stereo. Moving up to the T6 adds 17-inch wheels, leather upholstery, burled walnut trim, a power passenger seat, a sunroof, stability control and Volvo's On Call telematics system. The top-of-the-line T6 Premier is further upgraded with rain-sensing windshield wipers and a dual-screen rear-seat DVD entertainment system. Available options on all models include a DVD navigation system, the Four-C adjustable suspension, run-flat tires, high-intensity discharge (HID) headlights, a premium 10-speaker Dolby audio system and heated front and rear seats. A rear-seat refrigerator is optional on the T6 Premier.

**Powertrains and Performance:** The base 2.5T models are powered by a 2.5-liter turbocharged five-cylinder with 208 hp and 236 lb-ft of torque. The T6 and T6 Premier models use a twin turbocharged version of the same engine that generates 268 horsepower and 280 lb-ft of torque. All S80s are front-wheel drive, except for the 2.5T AWD, which has an electronically controlled all-wheel-drive system. A five-speed automatic transmission is standard on the 2.5T models, while all T6 models get a four-speed unit.

**Safety:** Four-wheel antilock brakes with Electronic Brakeforce Distribution and emergency braking assist are standard. Stability control is standard on both T6 models and optional on the 2.5T models. Every S80 comes with side airbags for front passengers, head curtain airbags for front and rear passengers and whiplash-reducing headrests. Additionally, the T6 models are equipped with shatter-resistant laminated side window glass. The S80 received perfect marks in all government crash tests, as well as a "Good" score, the highest possible, in IIHS frontal offset tests.

**Interior Design and Special Features:** Comfort is a Volvo hallmark, and the S80 boasts soft, supportive seats and plenty of room to stretch out. The rear seat is exceptionally roomy, and there are heating and air conditioning vents in the B-pillars to keep the rear passengers at the perfect temperature. The control layout in the S80 could be better, but once you learn where everything is it works well. The dual-screen DVD system in the T6 Premier makes long drives with the kids a no-hassle affair, but even if you're just heading across town, the S80 will deliver you there in perfect comfort.

**Driving Impressions:** Overall, the S80 handles adequately for a large front-wheel-drive car; the all-wheel-drive model is a good option for those living in harsh climates. The optional Four-C adjustable suspension tightens up things a bit on twisty roads, but it's still not a true sport sedan.

*Crash Test Scores, see pg 530*
*Warranty information, see pg 542*

### Specifications

| Engine/Drivetrain | HP | Torque | EPA Fuel Economy Rating |
|---|---|---|---|
| 6cyl 2.9L A | 268 | 280 | 19 city/26 hwy |
| 5cyl 2.5L A | 208 | 236 | 20 city/28 hwy |

### Body Styles

| Style | MSRP Range |
|---|---|
| Midsize Sedan | $35,900–$48,515 |

**Compact Wagon**

# 2005 Volvo V50

**MSRP Price Range**
## $25,660 - $28,910
Destination Charge: $685 (all styles)

### Ratings

| | | |
|---|---|---|
| Consumer Rating | 8.8 | ███████████▒ |
| Editors Rating | 8.0 | ██████████▒▒ |

**What Edmunds.com says:** With its winning mix of Volvo safety and Scandinavian style, the V50 deserves to be on your list if you're in the market for a compact family wagon.

**Pros:** Legendary Volvo safety, IKEA-ready interior, crisp handling.

**Cons:** Average performance from the non-turbo engine.

**What's New:** The V50 is an all-new wagon from Volvo. It replaces the previous V40, and shares a platform with the recently redesigned Mazda 3.

**Body Styles, Trim Levels and Options:** Two trims of the compact V50 wagon are available: the base 2.4i and the sporty T5. Standard items on the 2.4i include tinted windows; power-adjustable heated exterior rearview mirrors; manual climate control; a leather-wrapped steering wheel; and a six-speaker, AM/FM single-CD sound system. Step up to the T5 and you get an eight-way power-adjustable driver seat with lumbar support, automatic climate control, a cargo-area 12-volt power outlet, aluminum trim and steering wheel-mounted audio controls. Options include 17-inch twin alloy wheels, leather upholstery, heated front seats, xenon headlights, windshield and rear-window wiper de-icers and a power moonroof.

**Powertrains and Performance:** Engines are specific to each model. The base 2.4i gets a 168-horsepower, normally aspirated 2.4-liter five-cylinder, while the T5 upgrades to a turbocharged 2.5-liter five-cylinder that generates 218 hp. A five-speed shiftable automatic transmission is standard on the 2.4i. The T5 features a standard six-speed manual tranny as standard, with the five-speed automatic offered as an option. T5 models are also available with all-wheel drive.

**Safety:** In keeping with its Volvo heritage, the V50 comes loaded with safety features. Side airbags for front occupants and side curtain airbags for front and rear occupants are standard. A whiplash protection seating system protects occupants from neck injury in the event of a rear-impact collision. Four-wheel antilock disc brakes (with emergency braking assist) and traction control systems are also standard. Stability control is optional on all trims. The V50 has not yet been crash tested.

**Interior Design and Special Features:** Scandinavian to the core, the V50's interior is a study in spartan elegance. A leather-wrapped steering wheel looks both sporty and luxurious, and gauges are pleasantly lit and easy to read. Especially eye-catching is the narrow center stack, which replaces the typical center-piece clutter with spare lines and a "less is more" aesthetic that gives the car a thoroughly modern feel. A 60/40-split-folding rear seat adds versatility, should you need to haul very long items. Overall cargo capacity (62.9 cubic feet) is comparable to what you'd get in an Audi A4 or Volkswagen Passat.

**Driving Impressions:** Handling in the V50 is sporty and tight. Overall, this is a capable wagon that rewards spirited driving with a good deal of fun. In most circumstances, the ride is quiet and comfortable. The 2.4i model offers adequate power for everyday driving, but weekend enthusiasts should head straight for the spirited T5 model. The optional all-wheel-drive system is a good bet for buyers seeking a relatively affordable, premium-brand wagon that can brave the winter snows.

*Crash Test Scores, see pg 530*
*Warranty information, see pg 542*

### Specifications

| Engine/Drivetrain | HP | Torque | EPA Fuel Economy Rating |
|---|---|---|---|
| 5cyl 2.5L M | 218 | 236 | 22 city/31 hwy |
| 5cyl 2.4L A | 168 | 170 | 22 city/30 hwy |

### Body Styles

| Style | MSRP Range |
|---|---|
| Compact Wagon | $25,660–$28,910 |

# 2005 Volvo V70

**MSRP Price Range**
## $28,760 - $36,010
Destination Charge: $685 (all styles)

### Ratings

| | | |
|---|---|---|
| Consumer Rating | N/A | |
| Editors Rating | 7.2 | |

**What Edmunds.com says:** Comfortable, safe and roomier than most other luxury-brand wagons in its price range, the V70 is a smart choice in family transportation.

**Pros:** Superb front-seat comfort, wide variety of safety and luxury features, balanced ride and handling characteristics, lots of cargo space.

**Cons:** Tight rear legroom, turbo lag and torque steer in T5 model, pricey optional equipment.

**What's New:** The 2.5T AWD model has been discontinued. New this year are revised headlamps and taillamps, color-keyed side moldings and lower sills, front grille and flat blade windshield wipers. The audio systems and front seats have been revised. The center console is new, and real wood replaces the fake stuff in the Premium Package. Run-flat tires are newly available, and a trip computer is now standard. The headlamp washers have been redesigned, rear park assist is newly optional and satellite radio preparation is available as a stand-alone option. The 2.5T gets color-keyed bumpers with chrome inserts, the geartronic transmission and foglamps as standard equipment. A wood steering wheel is newly optional. The T-5 gets more power this year, up to 257 horsepower. Speed-sensitive steering is standard, and black mesh inlays replace the aluminum pieces in the Premium Package.

Crash Test Scores, see pg 530
Warranty information, see pg 542

### Specifications

| Engine/Drivetrain | HP | Torque | EPA Fuel Economy Rating |
|---|---|---|---|
| 5cyl 2.5L A | 208 | 236 | 20 city/28 hwy |
| 5cyl 2.4L A | 257 | 258 | 18 city/25 hwy |
| 5cyl 2.4L M | 168 | 170 | 22 city/30 hwy |

### Body Styles

| Style | MSRP Range |
|---|---|
| Midsize Wagon | $28,760–$36,010 |

**Body Styles, Trim Levels and Options:** The V70 wagon comes in three trim levels—base 2.4, midlevel 2.5T, winter-friendly 2.5T AWD and upscale T5. The 2.4 comes with 15-inch alloy wheels, dual-zone climate control, a trip computer, a CD player, power-fold rear headrests, one-touch front windows and a tilt/telescoping leather-wrapped steering wheel. In addition, the 2.5T gets 16-inch wheels, a power driver seat with memory, automatic climate control and faux wood interior accents. The T5 is trimmed with black mesh inlays and gets a power passenger seat and an auto-dimming rearview mirror. Options include an excellent 13-speaker Dolby Pro Logic sound system with a four-disc CD changer, a DVD-based navigation system, 17-inch wheels, leather upholstery, heated seats, Volvo's On Call telematics, a sunroof and bi-xenon headlights. A versatility package adds a third-row seat, bumping maximum passenger capacity from five to seven.

**Powertrains and Performance:** The V70 2.4 comes with a 2.4-liter, five-cylinder engine that produces 168 horsepower (165 in California where it's SULEV-certified). The 2.5T, as you might guess, is turbocharged, and it makes a healthy 208 hp. The T5 is the most powerful V70 with its 257-hp, 2.3-liter turbocharged engine. Both the 2.4 and T5 can be equipped with either a five-speed manual or a five-speed automatic transmission, while the 2.5T is available only with the automatic. Automanual functionality is included on 2.5T and automatic-equipped T5 models.

**Safety:** The V70 boasts a long list of safety features, among these side airbags for front occupants, head curtain airbags for front and rear passengers, anti-submarine seats and whiplash-reducing front headrests. Stability control is standard on the T5 and optional on all other V70s. The V70 has not been crash tested.

**Interior Design and Special Features:** The V70's interior is similar in design to that of the S60 sedan. The controls are nicely weighted, although the pictograms depicting the various functions can be difficult to understand. The V70 offers wonderfully comfortable accommodations for front passengers, though legroom is a bit tight for rear passengers. Fold the rear seats down, and there are 71.4 cubic feet of cargo space at your disposal. As an added bonus, the Volvo's front-passenger seat folds flat, as well. If you have more bodies than cargo, you can purchase the optional rear-facing third-row bench, which seats two children.

**Driving Impressions:** All V70s offer a level of performance and confidence not associated with the wagons of yesteryear. The base 2.4 offers adequate power for everyday driving, though most people are apt to prefer the more powerful 2.5T model. The T5 should be your choice if you like to do things quickly but don't mind some turbo lag. On twisty roads, the V70 feels planted and predictable, though if you're looking for true performance, the fast and nimble V70 R is a better bet. Ride quality is smooth on all but the harshest pavement. The steering isn't overly communicative, but its quick ratio makes this wagon easy to maneuver.

# Midsize Wagon

# 2005 Volvo V70 R

**MSRP Price Range**

***$38,750***

Destination Charge: $685 (all styles)

## Ratings

| | | |
|---|---|---|
| Consumer Rating | N/A | |
| Editors Rating | 8.2 | |

**What Edmunds.com says:** Need a handsome family wagon that's fast enough to surprise unsuspecting BMW drivers? The V70 R fulfills both roles.

**Pros:** Impressive 300-horsepower turbo engine, excellent balance and grip when driven briskly, luxurious interior with lots of safety features, reasonable price, stealth appeal.

**Cons:** Tight rear legroom.

**What's New:** New this year are color-keyed front, side and rear moldings. The audio systems have been revised, rear park assist is newly optional and the interior air quality sensor is a stand-alone option. The V70 R can now be equipped with a subwoofer or a rear-facing third-row seat in the cargo area.

**Body Styles, Trim Levels and Options:** Most desirable features come standard on the V70 R. The equipment list includes bi-xenon headlights, 17-inch wheels with 235/45ZR17 tires, leather upholstery, bolstered sport seats, a three-spoke steering wheel with tilt/telescope adjustment, aluminum inlays, dual-zone automatic climate control, a CD player, a trip computer and a split-folding rear seat. On the options list, you'll find higher-grade leather upholstery, a sunroof, a four-disc CD changer, a DVD-based navigation system, Volvo's On Call telematics and an integrated child booster seat.

**Powertrains and Performance:** Every V70 R is powered by a turbocharged 2.5-liter inline five-cylinder that pumps out 300 horsepower and 295 pound-feet of torque when paired with the standard close-ratio six-speed manual transmission. A five-speed automatic (with automanual functionality) is optional—buyers should take note that peak torque drops to 258 lb-ft when the automatic is selected. In any case, acceleration is quite brisk in the V70, with ample juice to pick off the occasional unsuspecting BMW driver. Volvo claims a 0-to-60-mph time of 5.4 seconds with the manual gearbox. Volvo's Four-C (Continuously Controlled Chassis Concept) system comes standard; it includes an electronically controlled all-wheel-drive system, as well as an adaptive suspension that Volvo says can adjust the shock valving up to 500 times per second for improved grip, reduced body roll and better overall balance.

**Safety:** As the V70 R is intended to pull double duty for driving enthusiasts who are also parents, all the usual Volvo safety features are included—stability control, side-impact airbags for front occupants, full-length head curtain airbags and whiplash-reducing seats. The V70 R is based on the standard V70, which has not been crash tested.

**Interior Design and Special Features:** Inside, the V70 R offers more upscale furnishings than regular V70s, namely laterally bolstered leather sport seats, stylish silver and blue gauges and real aluminum trim. Comfort is exceptional in front, but rear passengers may find legroom a bit tight. An optional rear-facing third-row bench can seat two additional children on carpool days. The control layout is more complex than in other cars, and new owners may need to sit down with the owner's manual in order to master everything. Cargo capacity is 37.5 cubic feet; fold down the rear seats and you've got 71.5 cubic feet.

**Driving Impressions:** Considerably faster than other Volvos, the V70 R is also a much better handler. Taken out on your favorite back roads, the R is ready to play—its high level of balance and grip instills confidence in the driver. And it still rides comfortably enough to be used as an everyday commuter vehicle. Better yet, the midsize V70 R is priced (under $40,000) and sized right to make it a good value for enthusiasts with families.

***Crash Test Scores, see pg 530***
***Warranty information, see pg 542***

## Specifications

| Engine/Drivetrain | HP | Torque | EPA Fuel Economy Rating |
|---|---|---|---|
| 5cyl 2.5L M | 300 | 295 | 18 city/25 hwy |

## Body Styles

| Style | MSRP Range |
|---|---|
| Midsize Wagon | $38,750 |

# 2005 Volvo XC70

**MSRP Price Range**

## $34,810

Destination Charge: $685 (all styles)

### Ratings

| | | |
|---|---|---|
| Consumer Rating | 9.5 | |
| Editors Rating | 7.3 | |

**What Edmunds.com says:** A viable alternative for those who need an all-weather wagon but don't want the bulk and poor handling of most SUVs.

**Pros:** Superb seat comfort, extensive array of safety equipment, solid construction, strong brakes, excellent snow vehicle.

**Cons:** High price, lacks the true off-road capability of an SUV, tight legroom in backseat.

**What's New:** Stone Gray bumpers and lower side trim replace last year's Slate Blue bumpers and trim. The grille has been redesigned, along with new headlamps (with new washers) and taillamps. Also new this year are brushed aluminum roof rails, flat-blade windshield wipers and aluminum skid plates. The front seats have been redesigned, along with the cruise control interface, center console and audio systems. A trip computer is now standard, and rear park assist, satellite radio preparation, a wood steering wheel, integrated booster seats, a rear-facing third-row seat, and a 40/20/40 rear seat are all stand-alone options. Real wood inlays replace last year's fake pieces in the Premium Package. A blind spot information system is added to the options list later in the model year.

**Body Styles, Trim Levels and Options:** The XC70 comes as a four-door wagon in one trim level. Standard equipment includes cloth seats, a trip computer, dual-zone climate control, a leather-wrapped tilt-telescoping steering wheel with cruise and audio controls, a CD stereo, heated front seats and simulated wood trim. Notable options include a DVD-based navigation system, a premium audio system, leather seating, bi-xenon headlights and a sunroof. You can also get a rear-facing third-row seat large enough for two children.

**Powertrains and Performance:** Only one engine is offered, a 2.5-liter turbocharged five-cylinder. It's rated at 208 horsepower and 236 lb-ft of torque and sends power to all four wheels in varying degrees depending on available traction. Under normal conditions, 95 percent of the engine's power is routed to the front wheels for the sake of fuel efficiency. A five-speed automatic with Geartronic manual selection and a winter mode is the only transmission choice. EPA mileage ratings are 18 mpg in the city and 25 mpg on the highway.

**Safety:** Like all Volvos, the XC70 comes standard with numerous safety features that include side-impact airbags for front occupants, side curtain airbags for front and rear passengers, pre-tensioning seatbelts in all five seating positions, a whiplash protection system and four-wheel antilock disc brakes. A traction and stability control system is also an option, along with integrated child booster seats.

**Interior Design and Special Features:** In standard trim, the XC70 doesn't look or feel particularly luxurious, but leather upholstery is available for those who want a more upscale cabin. The front seats provide excellent comfort, but legroom in the second row is tight. Interior ergonomics are generally good, although a few oddly placed controls take some getting used to. With the rear seats folded down, the XC70 has 71.5 cubic feet of cargo room—slightly less than the capacity of most midsize SUVs but considerably more than most other wagons offer.

**Driving Impressions:** With its soft, forgiving suspension, the XC70 provides a smooth, isolated ride on all surfaces. Sharp handling isn't in the XC's repertoire, but light steering and a relatively small size make for easy maneuvering. The turbocharged engine is economical and smooth with adequate power for most situations, but the automatic transmission is sometimes slow on the draw. The fully automatic all-wheel-drive system assures surefootedness in inclement weather along with the economy of front-drive operation while on dry pavement.

*Crash Test Scores, see pg 530*
*Warranty information, see pg 542*

### Specifications

| Engine/Drivetrain | HP | Torque | EPA Fuel Economy Rating |
|---|---|---|---|
| 5cyl 2.5L A | 208 | 236 | 19 city/24 hwy |

### Body Styles

| Style | MSRP Range |
|---|---|
| Midsize Wagon | $34,810 |

# 2005 Volvo XC90

**MSRP Price Range**

## $34,840 - $41,015
Destination Charge: $685 (all styles)

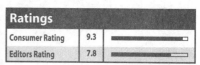

### Ratings

| | | |
|---|---|---|
| Consumer Rating | 9.3 | |
| Editors Rating | 7.8 | |

**What Edmunds.com says:** Easy to drive and easy on the eyes, Volvo's first foray into the SUV arena has everything it needs to compete in this highly competitive category.

**Pros:** Safe as a bank vault, plush ride, solid performance from V8 model, feels smaller than it is, high-quality interior materials, ample cargo room.

**Cons:** Turbocharged T6 engine not well suited to SUV duty, third-row seating takes up too much second-row space.

**What's New:** A V8-powered model joins the lineup this year featuring a new six-speed automatic transmission. Improved rain-sensing, flat-blade windshield wipers are standard, as is a HomeLink remote transmitter. The front seats have been redesigned, and a tire-pressure warning system will become standard later in the model year.

**Body Styles, Trim Levels and Options:** The XC90 comes in three models—2.5T, T6 and V8. The 2.5T comes with a power driver seat with memory, cloth upholstery, dual-zone climate control and a CD player. A premium package adds leather upholstery, a moonroof, a power passenger seat, an in-dash CD changer and an auto-dimming mirror. If you opt for the T6 trim, all of the above are included, but its premium package will also get you a Dolby Pro Logic II Surround system with 12 speakers, 18-inch wheels, a wood steering wheel and power-retractable side mirrors. The V8 model gets unique 18-inch wheels, body-colored door handles, twin exhaust pipes and most of the T6's optional equipment as standard. Individual options include a DVD-based navigation system, bi-HID headlamps, parking sensors and a DVD entertainment system.

**Powertrains and Performance:** Buyers get to choose between three engines. The 2.5T models come with a turbocharged 208-horsepower, 2.5-liter inline five-cylinder mated to a five-speed automanual transmission. This engine serves the XC90 fine around town, but once on the highway, you may wish for more power. T6 models get a twin-turbo 2.9-liter inline six that makes 268 horsepower and is paired with a four-speed automanual. The top-of-the-line model gets a 4.4-liter V8 with 315 hp and a standard six-speed automatic for optimum performance. You can choose either front- (2WD) or all-wheel drive on 2.5Ts, while T6s and V8s come standard with AWD.

**Safety:** The XC90's Roll Stability Control system uses a gyro-sensor to calculate the SUV's roll speed and angle; if it's determined that a rollover is imminent, the stability control system is activated. In the event the vehicle does roll over, an inflatable curtain covers all three rows. The XC90 is equipped with a crossmember that's lower than that found on most SUVs—it sits at the height of the beam in a car. In the event of a collision, this crossmember strikes the oncoming car's protective structure, activating its crumple zone to give the cars' occupants maximum protection. The Volvo earned a "Good" rating (the highest) and "Best Pick" status in IIHS frontal offset crash testing.

**Interior Design and Special Features:** The XC90's interior places its emphasis on versatility. You can order it as a five- or seven-seater; in both variations the second row (and third row if equipped) folds down to create a flat floor. The middle seat in the second row can be equipped with an integrated child booster cushion; in seven-seaters, the child seat slides forward, allowing for contact between parents and tykes. Cargo capacity tops out at 92 cubic feet.

**Driving Impressions:** The XC90 rides on the same underpinnings as most of Volvo's sedans. Appropriately, ride quality is soft and comfortable. It lacks the silky, fluid quality of the Lexus RX 330 and the quasi-sport sedan demeanor of a BMW X5, but like the Acura MDX, it offers an appealing compromise of comfort and handling that will satisfy most drivers.

*Crash Test Scores, see pg 530*
*Warranty information, see pg 542*

### Specifications

| Engine/Drivetrain | HP | Torque | EPA Fuel Economy Rating |
|---|---|---|---|
| 8cyl 4.4L M | 315 | 325 | N/A |
| 6cyl 2.9L A | 268 | 280 | 15 city/20 hwy |
| 5cyl 2.5L A | 208 | 236 | 18 city/24 hwy |

### Body Styles

| Style | MSRP Range |
|---|---|
| Midsize SUV | $34,840–$41,015 |

# Segment Analysis & Comparison Charts

## Figuring out which car or truck is right for you can be a daunting task.

You may be focused solely on price, or you may be considering everything from cargo capacity to fuel mileage to ride quality. Regardless of which factors you feel are crucial in your purchase decision, the most efficient method for narrowing your choices is to compare the various cars in a given segment.

To aid you in finding the right car, and to ensure you don't pass over a vehicle that might be perfect for you, we've compiled the following comparison charts that cover every major vehicle segment. Included in these charts is basic horsepower, pricing and fuel mileage information. We've also included passenger and cargo capacities, as well as the editor ratings for each vehicle.

Finally, we've identified the Most Wanted winners and Top Rated vehicles for each category. The Most Wanted winners are the vehicles we feel best represent the segment, and are the cars we would pick if it were our money on the line. The Top Rated vehicles are those that score the highest when systematically evaluated and rated by our team of road test editors. Oftentimes, the Most Wanted winner and Top Rated vehicle are the same in a given category, but because Most Wanted is a more emotionally based decision, while Top Rated is based on logic and critical analysis, they can differ. Obviously, we can't guarantee you'll feel the same as we do when it comes to a segment's "best" vehicle, but we would suggest you at least consider these Most Wanted picks if you haven't already.

If you're in the early phases of your next vehicle purchase use these charts get a feel for what models deserve a closer look. Once you've narrowed your list down to a few primary candidates, use the specific vehicle pages to learn more about what car or truck is right for you. You can also reference these charts at any point in the research process just to confirm how a specific model stacks up against its primary competitors in terms of pricing, fuel mileage, horsepower or editor ratings.

Good luck and happy shopping!

## Top 10 Things to Consider Before Buying

**Size/Market Segment:** Sedans come in three basic sizes -- compact, midsize and large (or full-size). Market segments include economy, family, entry-level luxury, luxury and sport. Some models don't fit neatly into any one group.

**Price:** Compact economy sedans cost $10,000 to $20,000. Midsize family sedans start under $20,000 and top off in the low-$30Ks. Large non-luxury sedans run from the mid-$20Ks to the mid-$30Ks. Entry-level luxury sedans run from $25,000 to $40,000. Anything above that is considered luxury. Sport sedans are spread across all price brackets.

**Engines/Fuel Economy:** You'll see four-, five-, six-, eight- and even 12-cylinder engines in this group; turbos are common. Compacts are the best bets for gas mileage, especially the gas-electric hybrids and diesels.

**Safety:** Family shoppers should look at crash test scores and check the availability of features like ABS, side airbags and stability control. Most luxury sedans will have you covered in these areas.

**Luxury and Convenience Features:** Luxuries like auto climate control, heated seats, in-dash CD changers, navigation systems and one-touch windows can often be found in *non*-luxury sedans. Look for them as you shop.

**Passenger Capacity/Interior Space:** Most compact and midsize sedans can transport four adults in reasonable comfort. Taller families and those with five to carry should consider a large sedan.

**Luggage Capacity:** Compacts offer 12-13 cubic feet of trunk space, midsize sedans offer 14-16 and large sedans offer 17-21. If you'll be hauling anything bulky, get a sedan with folding seats or a ski pass-through.

**Do You Need All-Wheel Drive?** Some sport sedans come with all-wheel drive for the sake of stability during high-speed maneuvers. General consumers should only pay extra for AWD if they regularly drive in snow.

**Manual vs. Automatic Transmission:** Most drivers prefer the ease of an automatic, but a manual gearbox usually offers increased performance. Some automatics offer an automanual mode, which simulates manual shifting.

**Operating Costs:** Sedans are the standard by which all other vehicles are judged; although their price and size vary widely, those looking for low-cost transportation will inevitably end up with four doors and a trunk. Low-priced compact and midsize sedans are the cheapest to own; they don't use much gas, they don't cost a lot to insure, and their lack of complexity keeps repair bills down. Luxury sedans may come with a free maintenance plan but expect higher costs as they age. Sport sedans may cost more to insure and maintain.

## Sedans Under $15,000

**Market Leaders:** Although the economy sedan segment houses some of the least expensive cars on the market, competition has grown heated in recent years, resulting in cars that are downright enjoyable to own and drive. The top players are the Ford Focus, Honda Civic, Hyundai Elantra, Mazda 3, Nissan Sentra and Toyota Corolla. The leader of this group is the Civic, which offers a range of fuel-efficient engine choices (including a gas-electric hybrid), polished road manners, a roomy cabin with excellent ergonomics and high-grade materials, excellent crashworthiness and a longstanding reputation for quality. Close behind the Civic you'll find the Elantra, a true value leader that offers many of the Civic's attributes at a lower price, and the Mazda 3, a replacement for the Protegé that builds upon its predecessor's standing as the sportiest of family sedans. A powerful engine lineup and sharp styling inside and out should assure the 3's status as the choice of budget-conscious driving enthusiasts. The Sentra offers the most powerful engine in this group (165 horsepower), responsive handling and a logical interior layout, while cramped seating and a somewhat jarring ride are its main shortcomings. The Corolla is a fully competent but unexceptional economy sedan; performance and seat comfort are nothing to write home about, yet the car's upscale interior and legendary reliability history make it a smart choice nonetheless. Although early models were plagued by recalls and repair issues, the Focus remains a favorite of ours due to its fun-to-drive nature and spacious cabin with user-friendly controls and well-cushioned seats. Just don't expect build quality on par with the top imports. Kia's Spectra has never been especially well regarded in the economy sedan segment, but a redesign last year has given the small Korean sedan a whole new lease on life. The new Spectra offers an all-new engine, a comfortable and nicely finished interior, class-leading standard safety features and crisp new styling, making it a top choice for value-conscious consumers. Chevrolet has finally killed off its aged Cavalier and replaced it with the new Cobalt, which is based on the same architecture as the Saturn Ion. Standard power comes from a 145-hp, 2.2-liter four that was carried over from the Cavalier, although a stout 205-hp, supercharged 2.0-liter four comes standard in the high-performance SS model. Available as a coupe or sedan in several trim levels, the Cobalt looks, rides and handles like a more expensive car than it really is, but whether it can compete with more established nameplates like the Civic and Corolla remains to be seen.

If you're looking for more cargo room than a traditional sedan can provide, a four-door hatchback may be a better fit for you. The Mazda 3, Focus ZX5, Elantra and Scion xA are all good bets in this category. The Mazda 3, Focus ZX5 and Elantra hatchbacks offer all the attributes of their sedan counterparts, along with 17 to 19 cubic feet of cargo space behind the rear seats. A newcomer to the segment, the smaller Scion xA was initially sold only in California, but as it makes its way to the rest of the country, we expect it to be a car people talk about. It's about a half-size smaller than the others on the outside, but it doesn't feel that way on the inside, where a tall cabin design allows both front and rear occupants to get comfortable. Down on power, the xA is small on price, while offering a lengthy standard equipment list, a long list of affordable options, a solidly constructed cabin and adroit handling for a car with modest running gear.

Several manufacturers offer performance versions of their small sedans aimed at enthusiasts who can spend a little more. With a high-boost turbo four-cylinder conservatively rated at 276 hp, a standard all-wheel-drive system and a track-ready suspension, Mitsubishi's Lancer Evolution is the undisputed leader of this niche. Although the Evo's stiff ride and lack of cruise control make it ill-suited for road trips, serious drivers will love the way it behaves when the pavement turns twisty. For those on a budget, Dodge's 230-hp Neon SRT-4 should more than satisfy. It might not have AWD, but its broad power band, tight suspension and powerful brakes should be a perfect match for weekend racers. Less experienced drivers should consider alternatives like the Sentra SE-R Spec V (175 hp), Focus ST sedan (151 hp), Lancer Ralliart (162 hp) and the stock Mazda 3 (160 hp)—all of which can still show you a good time.

**Others to Consider:** If you decide to pick from the rest, the standard Mitsubishi Lancer is one of the better choices; a roomy and refined car, its main drawback is a lack of power on non-Ralliart versions (just 120 hp). The Suzuki Aerio's interior materials and driving dynamics need improvement, but the car's 155-hp engine and optional all-wheel drive are definite advantages. Dodge's standard Neon is sorely lacking in refinement, but its surprisingly good handling may appeal to some buyers. Another Suzuki, the Forenza, offers a long list of standard equipment and a classy interior, but it's down on power and costs almost as much as the Aerio. Saturn's Ion sedan offers a decent equipment list and a comfortable ride, but substandard build and materials quality make it hard for us to recommend it.

Step down a half-size and you'll find entry-level offerings like the Chevrolet Aveo, Hyundai Accent, Kia Rio and Toyota Echo. Backed by a long warranty, the well-rounded Accent is the pick of the litter, while the Aveo offers the best driving dynamics but makes do with average warranty coverage. Still, it does come in a four-door hatchback body style, giving it a measure of utility over the others. The Rio also has a long warranty but is ill-mannered out on the road. The Echo is as reliable and well built as any other Toyota, but poor packaging forces buyers to spend too much on options just to get the basics.

## Sedans Under $25,000

**Market Leaders:** For the buyer looking to get the best value in a family sedan, the major players in this category continue to be the Honda Accord, Mazda 6, Nissan Altima, Toyota Camry and Volkswagen Passat. However, there are two new strong candidates from Chrysler and Ford. Chrysler's 300 sedan offers a pair of V6 engine options, as well as a 5.7-liter Hemi V8 for serious power fiends with more flexible budgets. Dramatic styling, rear-wheel drive and a huge interior further distance this American sedan from its foreign competition. The Ford Five Hundred is another new domestic sedan, but in contrast to the 300 Ford's new four-door is more traditionally styled and comes with a 200-horsepower V6 only. Smart interior packaging makes it very space-efficient inside and optional all-wheel drive keeps it all-weather-friendly. A more upscale version is available in the form of the Mercury Montego. For sheer driving pleasure, check out Mazda's nimble and confident 6. This car feels like a European sport sedan thanks to its communicative steering, responsive handling and willing drivetrain. At 220 hp for the optional V6 model, it's down on horsepower compared to the Altima and Accord, but the 6 never feels slow. Other performance players include Nissan's Altima and the redesigned Subaru Legacy. The Altima's optional V6 offers 245 hp and even the standard four-cylinder engine manages an impressive 180 horses while a new interior for 2005 improves one of its few faults. The Legacy features a standard 165-hp four-cylinder or an optional 250-hp turbocharged power plant. Standard all-wheel drive, an upscale exterior design and good-looking interior materials make the new Legacy worth a look. For a near luxury appearance, the Passat offers plush cloth or optional leather and most interior surfaces have a soft-touch feel that belie the car's low-$20,000 price range. The Passat also offers a sporty ride due to its communicative steering, and horsepower from the base turbocharged four-cylinder engine is more than adequate, thus negating the need to spring for the more expensive V6. Volvo's new S40 also impresses when it comes to top-quality interior materials. Add to that a simple but elegant design, a legendary safety record and optional all-wheel drive and this is yet another sedan to consider. Last, but certainly not least (in terms of total sales) are the Honda Accord and Toyota Camry. Think of these two as fraternal twins separated at birth. They don't look alike, but when judged with an eye for engineering, reliability and overall value, they are hard to distinguish. The Accord gets the nod in terms of driving dynamics and user-friendly controls while the Camry has a slight advantage in the areas of refinement and reliability, but the distances separating even these characteristics are hardly worth mentioning.

Those driven by an environmental conscience or simply a desire for a practical midsize car should seriously consider the redesigned Toyota Prius. Now a midsize four-door hatchback, the Prius is almost as big inside as a Camry while offering passable power for all manner of driving, even greater fuel-efficiency (a combined EPA rating of 55 mpg), and easy access to cargo. It's also worth noting that the Accord is available as a hybrid for the first time this year, utilizing a V6 gasoline engine equipped with variable displacement technology along with an electric motor to boost overall horsepower over the standard V6 model while simultaneously increasing fuel economy into the mid-30s. While the Prius is perfect for techies or consumers looking to obtain the best fuel mileage possible, the Accord Hybrid is geared toward performance enthusiasts also looking to save a little money at the pump. It will be priced about $4,000 higher than a nicely equipped V6 EX model, but will come loaded with every option available except a sunroof.

Finally, if performance is foremost on your mind, you'd be remiss if you didn't consider Subaru's Impreza WRX. A 227-hp turbocharged version of the standard Impreza sedan, the all-wheel-drive WRX is a joy to drive hard on back roads. It also comes in right around $25,000, making it one of the best performance buys on the market. For those seeking a higher level of performance, Subaru offers the WRX STi, which picks up a larger 300-hp engine and an even stiffer suspension. Its handling isn't quite as sharp as that of its chief competitor, Mitsubishi's Lancer Evolution, but it's easier to live with day to day than the hard-nosed Evo. As both the regular WRX and the STi are compact in size, neither is an ideal choice for family duty. But if you're a parent who loves to drive, rest assured that the backseat can accommodate a pair of child safety seats.

**Others to Consider:**Even beyond the models mentioned above, the midsize family sedan category is loaded with worthy competitors. Chevrolet's Malibu is inexpensive, packed with features and plenty powerful thanks to a strong optional V6. For a little more fun behind the wheel, check out Pontiac's new G6. It starts below $24K even in GT trim and features a sleek look and performance-oriented ride and handling. The new Buick LaCrosse offers a more luxurious experience for about the same price as the G6. A long features list and a sharp-looking interior make it worth checking out. Chevrolet Impala, Ford Crown Victoria and Mercury Grand Marquis are all large sedans that offer plenty of room for five adults, but in terms of refinement and reliability none can match the Japanese competition. Kia's new Amanti is an excellent alternative to the domestics if you're shopping for a large car. It's just as spacious on the inside and comes loaded with safety features, including stability control and side curtain airbags.

Other American offerings like the Chrysler Sebring/Dodge Stratus are closely aligned with the Accord/Camry sedans in terms of size, but they still don't measure up when refinement, reliability and value are taken into account. If you're looking for one-of-a-kind style, Mitsubishi's Galant may do the trick. Much like the Altima, it combines big V6 power and sporty handling with a big cabin, but its mediocre materials quality and polarizing interior design relegate it to alternative status. Pontiac's Grand Prix is similar in personality. Although its interior design and ergonomics put it several steps above most domestic sedans in this price range, it's let down by a cramped backseat and iffy materials quality. A pair of platform-sharing Koreans, the Hyundai Sonata and the Kia Optima, provides plenty of interior space and features, along with more value and quality than you might think—don't overlook them if price is a primary concern. Hyundai's XG350 is geared toward bargain hunters seeking more interior room and a higher level of luxury. Suzuki's Verona offers pleasant cabin accommodations and a convincingly low price, but a weak engine and a lack of safety features make it hard for us to recommend.

Those looking for a smaller sedan in this segment might consider the non-turbo Subaru Impreza (with standard all-wheel drive), the four-door Volkswagen Golf (hatchback) or Jetta (sedan). The Golf and Jetta are pricey for this segment, but like their older brother, the Passat, they have a high-quality interior that might justify the cost for some buyers.

## Sedans Under $35,000

**Market Leaders:** There are, in essence, three subcategories of sedans in this segment: small luxury/sport sedans, midsize luxury/sport sedans and full-size luxury/sport sedans. And there are still a few that escape these classifications, such as the Buick LeSabre (full-size family car) and Subaru Outback (midsize all-wheel-drive family car).

For those looking for an enjoyable smaller sedan, there is the ever popular BMW 3 Series. There are three chief reasons why this car remains a favorite among Edmunds staffers and other driving enthusiasts—dynamite performance, timeless design and fine build quality. But there are a number of other sprightly choices as well. Acura's bargain-priced yet eminently entertaining TSX is right there with the BMW in terms of the fun factor. Saab's recently revamped 9-3 offers a broad spread of turbocharged power along with comfy seats and roomy accommodations. Always a strong contender, Audi's A4 offers one of the nicest cabins this side of $50,000 and the availability of its quattro all-wheel drive.

The midsize cars offer perhaps the best combination of practicality and sporty driving dynamics, and there are plenty of worthy candidates. The Acura TL has a more athletic personality while still providing room and comfort for all within. In a similar vein are the Nissan Maxima and its upscale cousin, Infiniti's I35, which both couple powerful performance with spacious cabins. Emphasizing sharp handling over a plush ride is the Infiniti G35 that offers purists a rarity in this class—the sporty dynamics of a rear-wheel-drive chassis.

Leaning more heavily toward luxury is the Lexus ES 300, whose plush ride and classy cabin might be mistaken for that of its much costlier brethren, the LS 430. A little left of center with its inline five-cylinder engine is Volvo's swoopy S60, known for immensely comfortable seating and a long-standing reputation for top-notch safety. Cadillac's sporty CTS sedan is available with a variety of engines, including a 220-horsepower V6, 255-hp V6 and even a variant of the fire-breathing 400-horsepower LS6 V8.

**Others to Consider:** Although Jaguar's diminutive X-Type falls short of the leaders in terms of driving dynamics, passenger space and cabin refinement, it offers standard all-wheel drive and Jaguar's seductive styling. Mercedes-Benz's C-Class is a solid pick with safety and luxury features galore, but go easy on the options as this small, entry-level luxury sedan's sticker can rapidly approach $40K. If you can live with its tight backseat and somewhat austere cabin, the 215-horsepower, rear-drive Lexus IS 300 should prove to be a reliable and most entertaining ride.

Midsize mixed-bag offerings abound. Lincoln's LS offers a roomy cabin and strong performance, although it lags behind the leaders in terms of overall polish and outright agility. Saab's

9-5 has the traditional Swedish virtues of supportive seats and excellent crash protection, but has soft handling and some low-grade interior trim that prevent A-list status. A pair of General Motors full-size sedans are worthy of consideration; Pontiac's extroverted Bonneville which (in GXP form) can be had with Cadillac's stellar Northstar V8, and Buick's LeSabre, a traditional American family car (read: six-passenger capacity with pillow-soft seats and suspension). Toyota's Avalon is an Americanized Toyota, meaning it has a large cabin with soft seats and a quiet, but isolated driving experience.

## Sedans Under $45,000

**Market Leaders:** If you're looking for a midsize luxury sedan, there are several models that offer strong performance, ample passenger room and all the latest features. At the top of the list rest an American upstart and a German standby. The all-new Cadillac STS replaces the Seville in GM's premium car lineup, and is based on the same nimble rear-wheel-drive platform as the successful CTS and SRX. This is perhaps the best rendition of Caddy's aggressive new styling yet, and an opulent leather- and wood-laden interior coupled with features like the stellar Northstar V8 and optional all-wheel drive make the STS a true standout among its peers. Also new for 2005 is the Audi A6, which features unique front-end styling and a choice of V6 and V8 power plants that drive all four wheels. A six-speed automanual transmission is now standard, and the interior offers typical Audi fit and finish. Burled walnut trim accents the leather seating surfaces nicely, but new aluminum interior accents are now available for those who appreciate a more modern look. No matter which you choose, the new A6 promises to be nimble, luxurious and more powerful than ever before. Its chief German rival, the BMW 5 Series, continues its reign as the top-selling sport sedan in the category. It features flawless handling, a smooth six-cylinder engine (a powerful 4.4-liter V8 is optional) and a choice of either a manual or automatic transmission. In addition to its distinctive new sheet metal there's also a revised version of the iDrive vehicle interface that debuted on the flagship 7 Series. It's still not the most intuitive means of tuning the stereo or adjusting the fan, but once you're on the road all the electronic gadgetry will be the last thing on your mind. On a slightly different note, Jaguar's S-Type sedan has more traditional style and comfort than electronic wizardry. With its distinctive shape and lavish interior, it offers all the luxury of its German counterparts along with a uniquely British style. The S-Type is also offered in high-performance "R" trim that adds a nearly 400-horsepower V8 and a sport-tuned suspension for those who desire serious speed and style. The S-Type may not enjoy the long-standing reputations of its BMW and Audi competitors, but strong performance and ample luxury more than make up for its lack of pedigree.

**Other to consider:** If none of the top choices seem appealing, there are several other cars in the category that warrant some attention. Acura has finally redesigned its flagship RL and, unlike its lackluster predecessor, the new version is a sedan worth considering. With a 300-hp V6, standard all-wheel drive and a much improved interior, the RL offers the kind of performance and features you would expect in a sedan of its caliber. Volvo's S80 has plenty of kick as well as a compliant ride, comfortable interior and plenty of high-end features. And as you might expect, it's also one of the safest sedans available at any price. The Lincoln Town Car soldiers on as one of the last remaining large luxury cars on the market. It lacks the refinement and technology found in many of the cars in this category, but if you want maximum space above all else the Town Car is your ride.

## Sedans Over $45,000

**Market Leaders:** This class includes the flagship sedans from the world's top luxury carmakers. Nearly all of them come standard with V8 engines, automatic transmissions and more features than you'll ever need. As fiercely contested as this segment is, there are a few models that stand out as the clear front-runners, namely the Audi A8L, Lexus LS 430, Mercedes-Benz E- and S-Classes and BMW's 7 Series. The Audi A8L was totally redesigned last year and blends elegant styling, strong performance and a beautifully crafted interior into one cohesive package that leaves little to be desired. There's ample passenger room both front and rear, a relatively easy-to-use onboard computer interface and standard all-wheel drive. While previous versions of the A8 were overlooked due to their small cabins and uninspired design, the latest version has more than enough style, space and performance to satisfy even the most finicky luxury sedan buyer. Mercedes' E- and S-Class sedans both feature powerful engines, sharp handling and the latest technological enhancements. The midsize E-Class, whether in base E320, midlevel E500 or performance-tuned E55 form, delivers exacting performance, uncompromised safety and plenty of creature comforts. The flagship S-Class isn't quite as nimble, but with all the amenities and a larger cabin, the S-Class is the quintessential Mercedes sedan. While not as adventurous in the styling department, Lexus continues to refine its flagship LS 430 over the years with smoother engines and better transmissions than ever before. Never a performance icon, the LS 430 focuses on providing a serene driving environment that coddles passengers in soft leather seats and near total silence. Factor in world-class build quality and top-rated dealer service and it's easy to see why the LS 430 remains a perennial class-leader. BMW's full-size 7 Series may wear a controversial look, but underneath the skin it's all BMW. From the smooth and powerful V8 to the surprisingly athletic handling, the 7 Series is the most sporting of all the big luxury sedans. Whether you choose the standard 745i, stretched 745Li or V12-powered 760Li, rest assured that all provide a satisfying feel from the driver seat and plenty of comfort for those just going along for the ride.

**Others to consider:** Volkswagen, once known for building budget-oriented basic transportation, has jumped onto the luxury bandwagon in a big way with its Phaeton sedan. Based on the same successful platform as the Audi A8, the Phaeton offers a more sedate look on the outside while providing an incredibly plush wood and leather-lined interior fit for royalty. Power comes from either a 335-hp V8 or 420-hp W12, and all-wheel drive is standard. The only drawbacks of this big cruiser are the Passat-styling and VW badge in the grille, both of which make it look like a lesser vehicle than its mechanical glories deserve.

Thanks to a full redesign for 2004, Jaguar's flagship XJ sedan is now a worthy competitor to the dominant Germans. Its all-aluminum body sits atop a sophisticated air suspension that delivers a compliant ride and admirable handling. Increased dimensions in every direction give this previously cramped sedan ample passenger room while the distinctively British style of the previous model remains. For the utmost in passenger space, Cadillac's DeVille offers a more traditional luxury sedan experience that foregoes sport sedan handling in favor of maximum comfort. There's almost as much space in back as there is in the front and its computer-controlled suspension assures a smooth ride no matter how rough the road. The remaining players in this segment are two cars that suffer from identity crisis—the Infiniti Q45 and Lexus GS 430. The Q45 is not quite as big as the top players, yet it still doesn't manage to offer up a more nimble feel or swifter acceleration in exchange. The GS 430 from Lexus is getting a full redesign for 2006 so unless you're looking for a good deal it's best to stay away from this one for now.

# Sedan Under $15,000

| Vehicle | Price Range | Base Drivetrain | EPA Fuel Rating (mpg) | Cargo/ Trunk Capacity | The Drive | The Ride | Design | Cargo/ Passenger Space | Overall Rating |
|---------|-------------|-----------------|-----------------------|-----------------------|-----------|----------|--------|------------------------|----------------|
| **Mazda MAZDA3** | $13,680-$16,615 | 2.0L 4cyl 5M Inline 4 FWD | 28 city 35 hwy | 11 cu. ft. | 8.6 | 8.8 | 8.3 | 7.5 | **8.4** |
| **Honda Civic** | $13,160-$20,650 | 1.7L 4cyl 5M Inline 4 FWD | 32 city 38 hwy | 13 cu. ft. | 7.9 | 9.3 | 7.9 | 7.5 | **8.0** |
| **Toyota Corolla** | $13,680-$17,455 | 1.8L 4cyl 5M Inline 4 FWD | 32 city 40 hwy | 14 cu. ft. | 7.6 | 8.5 | 8.3 | 8.0 | **8.0** |
| **Ford Focus** | $13,830-$17,930 | 2.0L 4cyl 5M Inline 4 FWD | N/A | 15 cu. ft. | 7.6 | 7.5 | 7.6 | 8.0 | **7.7** |
| **Hyundai Elantra** | $13,299-$15,649 | 2.0L 4cyl 5M Inline 4 FWD | 26 city 34 hwy | 13 cu. ft. | 7.4 | 8.3 | 7.4 | 8.0 | **7.7** |
| **Kia Spectra** | $12,620-$15,970 | 2.0L 4cyl 5M Inline 4 FWD | 25 city 32 hwy | 12 cu. ft. | 7.1 | 7.8 | 7.6 | 8.0 | **7.5** |
| **Suzuki Forenza** | $13,449-$17,449 | 2.0L 4cyl 5M Inline 4 FWD | 22 city 30 hwy | 12 cu. ft. | 6.6 | 7.3 | 7.8 | 8.8 | **7.5** |
| **Mitsubishi Lancer** | $13,999-$19,099 | 2.0L 4cyl 5M Inline 4 FWD | N/A | 11 cu. ft. | 7.0 | 7.8 | 7.4 | 7.5 | **7.3** |
| **Suzuki Reno** | $13,449-$17,449 | 2.0L 4cyl 5M Inline 4 FWD | 22 city 30 hwy | 9 cu. ft. | 6.6 | 7.3 | 7.5 | 8.3 | **7.3** |

| Vehicle | Price Range | Base Drivetrain | EPA Fuel Rating (mpg) | Cargo/ Trunk Capacity | The Drive | The Ride | Design | Cargo/ Passenger Space | Overall Rating |
|---|---|---|---|---|---|---|---|---|---|
| Hyundai Accent | $10,499-$11,299 | 1.6L 4cyl 5M Inline 4 FWD | 29 city 33 hwy | 12 cu. ft. | 5.8 | 7.8 | 8.4 | 7.0 | 7.1 |
| Toyota ECHO | $10,885-$11,685 | 1.5L 4cyl 5M Inline 4 FWD | 35 city 43 hwy | 14 cu. ft. | 6.8 | 7.8 | 6.9 | 6.8 | 7.0 |
| Nissan Sentra | $12,600-$17,700 | 1.8L 4cyl 5M Inline 4 FWD | 28 city 36 hwy | 12 cu. ft. | 7.3 | 5.8 | 7.1 | 6.8 | 6.9 |
| Suzuki Aerio | $13,449-$17,449 | 2.3L 4cyl 5M Inline 4 FWD | 25 city 31 hwy | 15 cu. ft. | 6.6 | 8.0 | 6.4 | 6.8 | 6.8 |
| Kia Rio | $9,740-$10,615 | 1.6L 4cyl 5M Inline 4 FWD | 26 city 33 hwy | 9 cu. ft. | 5.6 | 7.3 | 7.4 | 7.0 | 6.7 |
| Chevrolet Aveo | $9,455-$12,570 | 1.6L 4cyl 5M Inline 4 FWD | N/A | 7 cu. ft. | 5.9 | 5.3 | 6.1 | 7.3 | 6.1 |
| Dodge Neon | $13,615-$16,750 | 2.0L 4cyl 5M Inline 4 FWD | 29 city 36 hwy | 13 cu. ft. | 6.4 | 5.8 | 5.3 | 6.5 | 5.8 |
| Saturn ION | $11,995-$17,370 | 2.2L 4cyl 5M Inline 4 FWD | 26 city 33 hwy | 15 cu. ft. | 6.0 | 4.8 | 5.1 | 6.3 | 5.5 |
| Chevrolet Cobalt | $13,625-$18,195 | 2.2L 4cyl 5M Inline 4 FWD | N/A | 14 cu. ft. | N/A | N/A | N/A | N/A | N/A |

# Sedan Under $25,000

| Vehicle | Price Range | Base Drivetrain | EPA Fuel Rating (mpg) | Cargo/ Trunk Capacity | The Drive | The Ride | Design | Cargo/ Passenger Space | Overall Rating |
|---|---|---|---|---|---|---|---|---|---|
| Subaru Legacy | $21,295-$29,795 '1 Editors' Rating | 2.5L 4cyl 5M Horizontally Opposed AWD | 23 city 30 hwy | 11 cu.ft. | 8.5 | 8.8 | 8.9 | 8.5 | 8.7 |
| Chrysler 300 | $23,295-$34,195 | 2.7L 6cyl 4A V6 RWD | 21 city 28 hwy | 16 cu.ft. | 8.4 | 9.0 | 8.5 | 7.8 | 8.4 |
| Toyota Prius | $20,295-20,875 | 1.5L 4cyl CVT | 60 city 51 hwy | 16 cu.ft. | 7.8 | 8.3 | 8.1 | 9.5 | 8.3 |
| Honda Accord | $16,195-$28,700 | 2.4L 4cyl 5M Inline 4 FWD | N/A | 14 cu.ft. | 7.8 | 8.8 | 7.9 | 8.5 | 8.1 |
| Mazda MAZDA6 | $18,995-$26,125 | 2.3L 4cyl 5M Inline 4 FWD | 23 city 31 hwy | 15 cu.ft. | 8.5 | 8.5 | 8.0 | 7.0 | 8.1 |
| Mercury Montego | $24,345-$28,245 | 3L 6cyl 6A V6 FWD | 21 city 29 hwy | 21 cu.ft. | 7.4 | 8.3 | 7.9 | 9.8 | 8.1 |
| Volkswagen Passat | $22,070-$32,615 | 1.8L 4cyl 5M Inline 4 FWD | 22 city 31 hwy | 15 cu.ft. | 7.8 | 9.0 | 8.5 | 7.5 | 8.1 |
| Ford Crown Victoria | $24,190-$30,275 | 4.6L 8cyl 4A V8 RWD | 18 city 25 hwy | 21 cu.ft. | 7.5 | 9.3 | 7.8 | 7.8 | 8.0 |
| Ford Five Hundred | $22,145-$27,845 | 3L 6cyl 6A V6 FWD | N/A | 21 cu.ft. | 7.4 | 8.0 | 7.6 | 9.8 | 8.0 |

| Vehicle | Price Range | Base Drivetrain | EPA Fuel Rating (mpg) | Cargo/ Trunk Capacity | The Drive | The Ride | Design | Cargo/ Passenger Space | Overall Rating |
|---|---|---|---|---|---|---|---|---|---|
| Kia Optima | $15,900-$19,895 | 2.4L 4cyl 5M Inline 4 FWD | 23 city 30 hwy | 14 cu.ft. | 7.5 | 8.3 | 8.4 | 7.8 | 8.0 |
| Mercury Grand Marquis | $24,425-$30,780 | 4.6L 8cyl 4A V8 RWD | 18 city 25 hwy | 21 cu.ft. | 7.4 | 9.3 | 7.9 | 7.8 | 8.0 |
| Volvo S40 | $23,260-$27,710 | 2.4L 5cyl 5M Inline 5 FWD | 22 city 29 hwy | 14 cu.ft. | 7.6 | 8.3 | 8.6 | 6.8 | 7.9 |
| Kia Amanti | $25,200 | 3.5L 6cyl 5A FWD | 17 city 25 hwy | 16 cu.ft. | 7.3 | 8.3 | 8.1 | 8.0 | 7.8 |
| Mitsubishi Galant | $18,699-$26,299 | 2.4L 4cyl 4A Inline 4 FWD | 23 city 30 hwy | 13 cu.ft. | 8.3 | 8.3 | 7.4 | 7.3 | 7.7 |
| Nissan Altima | $17,250-$29,200 | 2.5L 4cyl 5M Inline 4 FWD | 24 city 31 hwy | 16 cu.ft. | 8.1 | 7.8 | 7.4 | 7.5 | 7.7 |
| Toyota Camry | $18,045-$25,405 | 2.4L 4cyl 5M Inline 4 FWD | 24 city 33 hwy | 17 cu.ft. | 7.6 | 7.5 | 7.6 | 8.3 | 7.7 |
| Buick LaCrosse | $22,835-$28,335 | 3.8L 6cyl 4A V6 FWD | 20 city 29 hwy | 16 cu.ft. | 7.1 | 8.0 | 7.3 | 8.3 | 7.5 |
| Pontiac G6 | $20,675-$23,300 | 3.5L 6cyl 4A V6 FWD | N/A | 14 cu.ft. | 7.0 | 8.3 | 7.3 | 7.3 | 7.3 |

# Sedan Under $25,000

| Vehicle | Price Range | Base Drivetrain | EPA Fuel Rating (mpg) | Cargo/ Trunk Capacity | The Drive | The Ride | Design | Cargo/ Passenger Space | Overall Rating |
|---------|-------------|-----------------|------------------------|------------------------|-----------|----------|--------|-------------------------|----------------|
| Buick Century | $22,040-$26,030 | 3.1L 6cyl 4A V6 FWD | 20 city 30 hwy | 17 cu.ft. | 7.0 | 8.0 | 7.0 | 7.5 | 7.2 |
| Chevrolet Impala | $22,220-$28,425 | 3.4L 6cyl 4A V6 FWD | N/A | 19 cu.ft. | 7.8 | 7.0 | 6.6 | 7.5 | 7.2 |
| Chevrolet Malibu | $19,085-$23,945 | 2.2L 4cyl 4A Inline 4 FWD | N/A | 15 cu.ft. | 7.1 | 7.5 | 6.5 | 7.0 | 7.0 |
| Chrysler Sebring | $19,350-$22,360 | 2.4L 4cyl 4A Inline 4 FWD | 22 city 30 hwy | 16 cu.ft. | 6.9 | 7.8 | 6.6 | 7.0 | 7.0 |
| Subaru Impreza | $18,095-$27,395 | 2.5L 4cyl 5M Horizontally Opposed AWD | N/A | 11 cu.ft. | 8.4 | 7.8 | 6.3 | 5.8 | 7.0 |
| Pontiac Grand Prix | $22,900-$26,560 | 3.8L 6cyl 4A V6 FWD | N/A | 16 cu.ft. | 7.6 | 6.3 | 7.1 | 5.8 | 6.9 |
| Volkswagen Jetta | $17,680-$25,045 | 2.0L 4cyl 5M Inline 4 FWD | 24 city 31 hwy | 13 cu.ft. | 7.4 | 7.0 | 8.0 | 4.5 | 6.9 |
| Hyundai Sonata | $15,999-$19,799 | 2.4L 4cyl 5M Inline 4 FWD | N/A | 14 cu.ft. | 6.5 | 7.0 | 6.5 | 7.3 | 6.6 |
| Suzuki Verona | $17,449-$20,949 | 2.5L 6cyl 4A Inline 6 FWD | 20 city 28 hwy | 13 cu.ft. | 5.5 | 6.5 | 6.9 | 6.3 | 6.2 |

| Vehicle | Price Range | Base Drivetrain | EPA Fuel Rating (mpg) | Cargo/ Trunk Capacity | The Drive | The Ride | Design | Cargo/ Passenger Space | Overall Rating |
|---|---|---|---|---|---|---|---|---|---|
| **Dodge Stratus** | $20,145-$21,625 | 2.4L 4cyl 4A Inline 4 FWD | 22 city 30 hwy | 16 cu. ft. | 5.5 | 7.3 | 5.9 | 7.0 | **6.1** |
| **Hyundai XG350** | $24,399-$25,999 | 3.5L 6cyl 5A V6 FWD | 17 city 26 hwy | 15 cu. ft. | 4.8 | 6.8 | 6.8 | 6.5 | **6.0** |
| **Ford Taurus** | $20,685-$22,595 | 3.0L 6cyl 4A V6 FWD | N/A | 17 cu. ft. | 4.4 | 5.8 | 5.3 | 7.5 | **5.5** |
| **Mercury Sable** | $21,055-$24,020 | 3.0L 6cyl 4A V6 FWD | 20 city 28 hwy | 16 cu. ft. | 4.4 | 5.8 | 5.3 | 7.5 | **5.5** |

# Sedan Under $35,000

| Vehicle | Price Range | Base Drivetrain | EPA Fuel Rating (mpg) | Cargo/ Trunk Capacity | The Drive | The Ride | Design | Cargo/ Passenger Space | Overall Rating |
|---|---|---|---|---|---|---|---|---|---|
| Acura TL | $32,900–$35,100 | 3.2L 6cyl 5A V6 FWD | 20 city 29 hwy | 13 cu.ft. | 9.0 | 9.3 | 8.9 | 8.5 | 8.9 |
| BMW 3 Series | $29,300–$37,450 | 2.5L 6cyl 5M Inline 6 RWD | 20 city 29 hwy | 11 cu.ft. | 9.3 | 7.8 | 8.6 | 6.3 | 8.3 |
| Acura TSX | N/A | 2.4L 4 cyl 5A FWD | 22 city 31 hwy | 13 cu.ft. | 8.3 | 8.5 | 8.3 | 7.5 | 8.2 |
| Audi A4 | $25,800–$47,050 | 1.8L 4cyl 5M Inline 4 FWD | 22 city 31 hwy | 13 cu.ft. | 8.1 | 8.5 | 8.8 | 7.3 | 8.2 |
| Subaru Outback | $31,670 | 3.0L 6cyl 5A Horizontally Opposed AWD | N/A | 11.4 cu.ft. | 8.0 | 8.3 | 8.3 | 7.8 | 8.1 |
| Infiniti G35 | $30,700–$32,500 | 3.5L 6cyl 5A RWD | 18 city 26 hwy | 14.8 cu.ft. | 8.6 | 8.0 | 7.4 | 8.0 | 8.0 |
| Lexus ES 330 | $31,975 | 3.3L 6cyl 5A V6 FWD | 21 city 29 hwy | 15 cu.ft. | 7.5 | 8.3 | 8.6 | 7.5 | 8.0 |
| Nissan Maxima | $27,100–$29,350 | 3.5L 6cyl 5A V6 FWD | 20 city 28 hwy | 16 cu.ft. | 8.4 | 8.3 | 7.6 | 7.5 | 8.0 |
| Volvo S60 | $27,235–$33,285 | 2.4L 5cyl 5M Inline 5 FWD | N/A | 14 cu.ft. | 7.3 | 8.5 | 8.3 | 8.3 | 7.9 |

For the latest full vehicle reports, visit www.edmunds.com/bginfopak

| Vehicle | Price Range | Base Drivetrain | EPA Fuel Rating (mpg) | Cargo/ Trunk Capacity | The Drive | The Ride | Design | Cargo/ Passenger Space | Overall Rating |
|---------|-------------|-----------------|------------------------|------------------------|-----------|----------|--------|-------------------------|----------------|
| Buick LeSabre | $26,545-$32,205 | 3.8L 6cyl 4A V6 FWD | N/A | 18 cu.ft. | 7.8 | 8.8 | 7.5 | 7.8 | 7.8 |
| Lincoln LS | $32,475-$43,425 | 3L 6cyl 5A V6 RWD | 20 city 26 hwy | 14 cu.ft. | 8.0 | 7.8 | 7.6 | 7.3 | 7.7 |
| Cadillac CTS | $30,000-$32,250 | 2.8L 6cyl 6M V6 RWD | 17 city 27 hwy | 13 cu.ft. | 7.9 | 7.8 | 7.0 | 8.0 | 7.6 |
| Pontiac Bonneville | $27,775-$35,395 | 3.8L 6cyl 4A V6 FWD | N/A | 18 cu.ft. | 7.4 | 8.3 | 7.1 | 8.0 | 7.5 |
| Saab 9-3 | $26,850-$32,850 | 2.0L 4cyl 5M Inline 4 FWD | 23 city 34 hwy | 15 cu.ft. | 7.3 | 8.3 | 7.5 | 7.8 | 7.5 |
| Lexus IS 300 | $29,435-$30,805 | 3.0L 6cyl 5M Inline 6 RWD | 18 city 25 hwy | 10 cu.ft. | 8.6 | 7.0 | 8.0 | 4.3 | 7.4 |
| Mercedes-Benz C-Class | $29,250-$39,150 | 1.8L 4cyl 6M Inline 4 RWD | N/A | 12 cu.ft. | 7.5 | 7.3 | 6.5 | 6.8 | 7.0 |
| Jaguar X-Type | $30,330-$34,330 | 2.5L 6cyl 5M V6 AWD | N/A | 16 cu.ft. | 6.6 | 6.8 | 7.0 | 4.8 | 6.4 |

# Sedan Under $45,000

| Vehicle | Price Range | Base Drivetrain | EPA Fuel Rating (mpg) | Cargo/ Trunk Capacity | The Drive | The Ride | Design | Cargo/ Passenger Space | Overall Rating |
|---------|-------------|-----------------|----------------------|----------------------|-----------|----------|--------|------------------------|----------------|
| **Audi A6** | $40,900-$50,500 | 3.1L 6cyl 6A V6 AWD | N/A | 16 cu. ft. | 8.9 | 9.3 | 9.3 | 9.0 | **9.1** |
| **Cadillac STS** | $40,300-$61,815 | 3.6L 6cyl 5A V6 RWD | N/A | 14 cu. ft. | 8.9 | 8.8 | 8.5 | 7.8 | **8.5** |
| **BMW 5 Series** | $41,300-$55,800 | 2.5L 6cyl 6M Inline 6 RWD | 19 city 28 hwy | 14 cu. ft. | 8.9 | 8.5 | 8.3 | 7.8 | **8.4** |
| **Lincoln Town Car** | $41,875-$50,245 | 4.6L 8cyl 4A V8 RWD | 18 city 25 hwy | 21 cu. ft. | 7.6 | 9.3 | 8.4 | 8.8 | **8.3** |
| **Volvo S80** | $35,900-$48,515 | 2.5L 5cyl 5A Inline 5 FWD | N/A | 14 cu. ft. | 8.0 | 8.8 | 8.5 | 7.5 | **8.2** |
| **Buick Park Avenue** | $35,555-$40,730 | 3.8L 6cyl 4A V6 FWD | 20 city 29 hwy | 19 cu. ft. | 7.8 | 8.8 | 7.6 | 7.8 | **7.9** |
| **Lexus GS 300** | $38,875 | 3.0L 6cyl 5A Inline 6 RWD | 18 city 25 hwy | 15 cu. ft. | 7.3 | 8.3 | 7.5 | 7.5 | **7.5** |
| **Jaguar S-Type** | $44,230-$51,330 | 3.0L 6cyl 6A V6 RWD | N/A | 14 cu. ft. | 8.0 | 8.3 | 7.1 | 6.3 | **7.4** |
| **Saab 9-5** | $36,250-$39,950 | 2.3L 4cyl 5A Inline 4 FWD | 19 city 28 hwy | 16 cu. ft. | 6.3 | 7.5 | 7.0 | 6.8 | **6.7** |

| Vehicle | Price Range | Base Drivetrain | EPA Fuel Rating (mpg) | Cargo/ Trunk Capacity | The Drive | The Ride | Design | Cargo/ Passenger Space | Overall Rating |
|---|---|---|---|---|---|---|---|---|---|
| **Lexus LS 430** #1 Editors' Rating | $55,675 | 4.3L 8cyl 6A V8 RWD | 18 city 25 hwy | 20 cu. ft. | 8.9 | 9.5 | 9.5 | 8.8 | **9.2** |
| **Audi A8** | $66,590–$69,900 | 4.2L 8cyl 6A V8 AWD | 18 city 24 hwy | 15 cu. ft. | 8.5 | 9.8 | 9.4 | 8.3 | **9.0** |
| **Volkswagen Phaeton** | $66,950–$96,100 | 4.2L 8cyl 6A V8 AWD | 16 city 22 hwy | 13 cu. ft. | 8.4 | 9.8 | 9.1 | 8.0 | **8.8** |
| **Acura RL** | $48,900 | 3.5L 6cyl 5A V6 AWD | 18 city 26 hwy | 13 cu. ft. | 8.9 | 9.5 | 8.3 | 7.5 | **8.5** |
| **Mercedes-Benz E-Class** | $48,500–$59,400 | 3.2L 6cyl 5A V6 RWD | 20 city 28 hwy | 16 cu. ft. | 8.6 | 9.5 | 8.8 | 6.8 | **8.4** |
| **Mercedes-Benz S-Class** | $75,300–$124,750 | 4.3L 8cyl 7A RWD | 13-17 city 19-24 hwy | 15 cu. ft. | 8.4 | 9.3 | 8.1 | 7.3 | **8.3** |
| **Infiniti Q45** | $55,900 | 4.5L 8cyl 5A V8 RWD | 17 city 25 hwy | 14 cu. ft. | 7.6 | 9.8 | 8.3 | 8.3 | **8.2** |
| **Jaguar XJ-Series** | $60,830–$89,330 | 4.2L 8cyl 6A V8 RWD | 18 city 28 hwy | 16 cu. ft. | 8.3 | 8.8 | 8.0 | 7.0 | **8.0** |
| **BMW 7 Series** | $69,900–$117,300 | 4.4L 8cyl 6A V8 RWD | 18 city 26 hwy | 18 cu. ft. | 8.9 | 9.0 * | 6.6 | 8.0 | **7.9** |

# Sedan Over $45,000

| Vehicle | Price Range | Base Drivetrain | EPA Fuel Rating (mpg) | Cargo/ Trunk Capacity | The Drive | The Ride | Design | Cargo/ Passenger Space | Overall Rating |
|---------|-------------|-----------------|----------------------|----------------------|-----------|----------|--------|-----------------------|----------------|
| **Lexus GS 430** | $47,975 | 4.3L 8cyl 5A V8 RWD | 18 city 23 hwy | 15 cu. ft. | 7.9 | 8.5 | 7.6 | 7.5 | **7.8** |
| **Cadillac DeVille** | $45,695-$51,250 | 4.6L 8cyl 4A V8 FWD | N/A | 19 cu. ft. | 7.0 | 8.5 | 6.9 | 8.0 | **7.4** |

## Top 10 Things to Consider Before Buying

**Size/Segment:** Wagons come in three sizes -- compact, midsize and, occasionally, large. Market segments include economy, crossover, luxury and sport. Some models don't fit neatly into any one group.

**Price:** Compacts range from economy models that start in the low teens and top off in the low $20Ks, to luxury models that run from the mid-$20Ks to around $40,000. Midsize wagons start in the low-$20Ks and can reach the $60,000 vicinity. There are only a few large wagons, and you can expect to pay anywhere between $25,000 and $35,000, depending on how you equip them.

**Engines/Fuel Economy:** This group includes four-, five-, six- and eight-cylinder engines, and turbo versions are common. Gas mileage is in the 20s for most wagons, but V8 wagons often dip below that.

**Safety:** Family shoppers should look at crash test scores and check the availability of features like ABS, side airbags and stability control. Most luxury wagons will have you covered in these areas.

**Luxury and Convenience Features:** Luxuries like auto climate control, heated seats, in-dash CD changers, leather upholstery and one-touch windows can often be found in non-luxury wagons. Look for them as you shop.

**Passenger Capacity/Interior Space:** Most wagons can seat four adults in comfort; five are possible if children are involved. A few models offer a two-person third-row seat, but most are suitable for children only. A few large wagons offer flexible seating options, including a choice of a bench seat or buckets in the second row and split-folding third-row seats.

**Do You Need All-Wheel Drive?** General consumers should only pay extra for all-wheel drive if they regularly drive in snow. AWD may provide handling benefits in sport wagons, but it lowers fuel economy.

**Cargo Capacity:** Most wagons have almost as much cargo space as comparable SUVs (sometimes more). Shoppers should look for adjustable roof racks, flip-up rear glass, grocery hooks and nets and cargo tie-downs.

**Wagon vs. SUV:** Wagons are typically cheaper to own and easier to drive than SUVs. Unless you need to go off-road, tow a trailer or seat more than five people, go with a wagon.

**Operating Costs:** Wagons under $30,000 are a good bet for budget-minded consumers; they typically cost less to buy than SUVs (and some minivans), while offering comparable cargo space for a family of four or five and much better gas mileage. Maintenance and insurance costs are generally modest for non-luxury nameplates. Luxury and sport wagons may cost a bit more to maintain and insure.

## Wagons Under $15,000

**Segment Leaders:** There aren't many true wagons to choose from in this price range, and buyers would be wise to look at similarly priced four-door hatchbacks as well as compact wagons priced between $15,000 and $20,000. Of the wagons that come in well under $15,000, the Scion xB and Suzuki Forenza are our favorites. Built on the Toyota Echo platform, the xB is styled to look like a miniature truck, at once distinguishing it from any other economy car on the market. The vehicle's tall, boxy profile pays off big inside the cabin where occupants are treated to enormous amounts of headroom and legroom. With the front chairs adjusted for an average-size driver and front passenger, those seated in the rear (there's room for three) still have plenty of room to stretch out their legs. Behind the rear seats, there's 22 cubic feet of cargo capacity to stow camping gear, groceries or a stroller. Owners can fold or remove the rear seats to open a maximum capacity of 43 cubic feet. As far as the driving experience goes, the xB proves to be more enjoyable than most cars in this price range. And reliable Toyota genes mean that the xB will continue going strong long after the styling ceases to be cutting-edge. Topping it all off is a generous list of standard features that includes ABS, Electronic Brakeforce Distribution, stability and traction control, air conditioning, a six-speaker Pioneer stereo with a CD player and full power accessories. Without question, the xB is one of the best buys for 2005 regardless of price range or market segment. Of course, if you can afford to spend a little more, you might prefer the larger, more powerful Suzuki Forenza or Toyota Matrix. Both offer additional cargo capacity compared to the xB, as well as the option of all-wheel drive. The Suzuki offers an interesting array of standard features including an eight-speaker stereo with CD, four-wheel disc brakes and options such as leather seating surfaces and Electronic Brakeforce Distribution. While the Forenza is apt to be the more affordable of the two, the Matrix (and its more expensive twin, the Pontiac Vibe) would likely be more satisfying to own, thanks to its greater refinement under the hood and in the cabin, superior cockpit ergonomics and durable plastic load floor with embedded cargo tracks.

**Others to Consider:** The other choice among small, inexpensive wagons is the Kia Rio Cinco. Unlike the xB, the Rio Cinco is a traditional economy wagon in terms of its styling, interior layout and short standard features list. On the plus side, it costs considerably less money than the xB and compensates for Kia's less-than-spectacular quality record with five-year/60,000-mile basic warranty coverage and 10-year/100,000-mile drivetrain coverage. Seat yourself in a Rio, and it definitely feels like a budget-priced car, but the front seats offer passable comfort and most controls are easy to use. Out on the road, the wagon offers little more than basic transportation, and we encourage prospective buyers to investigate the used car market before settling on this Kia.

## Wagons Under $25,000

**Market Leaders:** Buyers shopping for a wagon in this price range will find that sizes range from compact all the way up to full-size. While wagons may have been viewed as stodgy and archaic a few short years ago, new entries in the field have reinvigorated the segment and high-performance haulers are becoming more common. On the top of the performance wagon list is the all-new Dodge Magnum, which has the tendency to draw crowds with its uniquely aggressive front-end styling and low-slung roofline. The rear-wheel-drive five-passenger family car boasts a nimble road feel, a highly adaptable storage area and optional all-wheel drive for snowbound drivers. The SE and SXT models come standard with V6 power and

17-inch alloy wheels, while the high-performance RT model includes unique 18-inch wheels, leather interior trim and, of course, the venerable 340-horsepower Hemi V8 engine. Another sporty wagon that attains similar goals in a totally different way is the Subaru Legacy and its more rugged stablemate, the Outback, both of which are all new and vastly improved for 2005. An extremely tight and nimble chassis, standard all-wheel drive, improved fit and finish and a powerful 250-hp turbocharged engine have turned the Legacy and Outback wagons into fast, nimble wagons that are fun to drive. Other improvements include a highly refined and futuristic cockpit that looks German in origin and a GT package on the Legacy that includes a functional hood scoop and Momo steering wheel, among other high-performance goodies. If you desire a truly nimble sport sedan but are forced to deal with the realities of a station wagon, either of these vehicles would be an excellent choice.

Compact wagons are also enjoying unprecedented popularity in the U.S right now, and as a result, general consumers have plenty to choose from in this segment. For those seeking the best overall package of space, practicality and quality, you really can't go wrong with the Pontiac Vibe/Toyota Matrix twins. Designed and engineered by Toyota, the Vibe and Matrix offer roomy accommodations for four to five people and a durable cargo floor (with numerous adjustable tie-down points). The driving experience is nothing special, but an available 180-hp engine and optional all-wheel drive give these wagons wide-ranging appeal.

Without question, Volkswagen's Passat dominates the midsize group. Cabins are roomy, upscale in feel and constructed of the highest-quality materials. Engine choices include a frugal diesel four, a spirited turbocharged four and a smooth V6. Out on the road, the Passat is exceptionally well balanced, offering both a smooth ride and agility in the corners, and the rear hatch opens up to reveal a cavernous cargo area big enough to swallow golf bags and suitcases with equal aplomb.

A relatively new entry in this market segment is the crossover, which combines the space and go-anywhere attitude of an SUV with the stable, low-slung handling of a wagon. One of the newest and most refined takes on this theme is the all-new Ford Freestyle, which rides on Volvo-engineered underpinnings while offering a comfortable and spacious interior and available all-wheel drive. The car's looks blur the line between station wagon and SUV perfectly, and options such as rear air conditioning and a rear-seat entertainment center make this crossover a solid choice for families.

**Others to Consider:** For economy-minded buyers seeking a sportier driving experience, the Ford Focus is a great choice. Reliability was hit or miss on early Focus models, so if this is of utmost importance to you stick with the imports, but otherwise Ford's sporty world car offers a pleasurable driving experience and powerful engine for a bargain price. Those who can spend a bit more should look at the Chrysler PT Cruiser, Volkswagen Jetta, Saab 9-2x and its cousin, the Subaru Impreza. Although most people think of retro styling when they think of the PT Cruiser, this wagon is a practical family vehicle in its own right. A tall cabin design provides roomy seating more befitting of a midsize car, and when hauling needs dictate, the rear seats can be flipped, folded or removed entirely. There is a range of engine choices, including a base 150-hp four-cylinder, a 180-hp turbo and, on a special performance-oriented GT model, a 215-hp turbo. The Impreza family makes an interesting case for itself among compact wagons. The entry-level TS model tends to be more expensive than its peers, but standard all-wheel drive and a reputation for quality and durability make them excellent choices for cold climates. Meanwhile, the 227-hp Impreza WRX wagon is a legitimate sports car designated for driving enthusiasts who need a fair amount of cargo space. If you like the speed and stability of the Subaru platform but desire a little more luxury and style, the new Saab 9-2x should fit the bill perfectly. Riding on the same nimble platform as the WRX, but with Saab exterior styling and several different trim and comfort levels available in the cabin, the affordable 9-2x is a strong contender in the sport wagon category. Chevrolet's Malibu Maxx also warrants consideration. Nimble handling and low pricing are its main advantages, but it also offers unusual conveniences like a fore/aft-adjustable rear seat and a remote-start feature. Finally, for those who want a small wagon that's entertaining to drive and upscale on the inside, there's the Jetta. It costs more than other small wagons and has developed a reputation for spotty reliability, but its overall level of refinement is unmatched by its peers.

## Wagons Under $35,000

**Market Leaders:** With the continuing popularity of sport-utility vehicles, the number of upper-tier wagons remains small, but those that remain offer attractive blends of utility, performance and safety. For those who need a little extra cargo room but don't want to give up the fun-to-drive nature of a sport sedan you can't go wrong with the Audi A4 Avant. With standard all-wheel drive, the choice of a turbocharged four-cylinder or V6 engine and sharp handling, the A4 gives up little to its sedan counterpart when it comes to performance. Add in Audi's high-quality cabins and a stylish exterior and it's easy to see why this is one wagon that won't leave you dreaming about your younger days. For a more traditional wagon, look no further than the midsize entries from Volvo and Saab. The Volvo V70 couples the company's legendary safety record with a comfortable cabin, plenty of cargo space and a sleek look. A range of efficient five-cylinder engines is offered along with either front- or all-wheel drive, and a high-performance V70 R is available that offers surprising power and handling for a wagon. If you want a Volvo but don't need the space of the V70, there's also the smaller and newly redesigned V50. The V50 wagon features nimble suspension and a 168-horse engine backed by a five-speed automatic in standard trim, and a more powerful turbocharged engine and six-speed manual trans in the high-performance T-5 package. Either way you get great style, safety and performance at a reasonable price. BMW's 3 Series wagon offers a similar blend of performance and practicality. Only one engine is offered but it can be coupled with all-wheel drive if you need the all-weather capabilities. Its cargo area doesn't swallow much, but if you desire performance above all else the 3 Series is a solid performer. Much the same can be said about Saab's 9-5 wagon as it, too, offers agile handling, a wide range of engines, excellent safety features and a spacious cabin that can accommodate up to five passengers and considerable cargo.

If you're up for an altogether different wagon experience, Chrysler's Pacifica may be worth a look. This large wagon seats up to six passengers, but is most comfortable for four, thanks to a bucket seat configuration in both the first and second rows. Interior space is comparable to that of a minivan, and with fold-flat third-row seats and an optional rear DVD entertainment system, the Pacifica is almost as practical. All-wheel drive is also available. Downsides include high pricing by Chrysler standards, cramped third-row seats and a hefty curb weight that saps engine performance and detracts from fuel economy.

**Other to consider:** If you can deal with its high asking price, Mercedes' C-Class wagon is a fine choice for those seeking an upscale yet versatile family vehicle. The compact Benz wagon offers a refined driving experience, a comfortable interior, a long list of safety features and an impressive amount of cargo capacity for its size. Other than price, disadvantages include interior materials that don't feel as luxurious as they should and less-than-ideal ergonomics. Rounding out the segment is the Lexus IS 300 Sportcross, which is much like the Audi and

BMW in size and purpose. If you only need a little extra room and desire maximum performance, the Sportcross delivers on both counts.

# Wagon Over $35,000

**Market Leaders:** Mercedes has this segment nearly all to itself as its German rivals have largely taken the year off when it comes to midsize wagons. Regardless of the state of its competition, the E-Class wagon is well prepared to take on all contenders. Available in both six-cylinder E320 trim and eight-cylinder E500 spec, the E-Class wagon sports a sleek shape, top-notch interior and serene driving dynamics. In addition, the E-Class wagon boasts a number of state-of-the-art components, such as Keyless Go, Distronic adaptive cruise control and a DVD-based navigation system. Two powertrain configurations are available, the 320 with its 221-horsepower V6 in either rear- or all-wheel drive ("4Matic") and the 500 which sports a 302-horse V8 coupled to the 4Matic system.

Yes, these wagons don't come cheap, ranging from around $51,000 to $62,000, but almost every luxury and safety feature you might desire is standard. With seven-passenger capacity and performance that essentially mirrors that of the superb E-Class sedan, we doubt if anyone considering one of these wagons will second-guess their decision over an SUV.

Another wagon worth considering in this price range is Audi's allroad. Based on the previous-generation A6 sedan, the allroad is a more rugged version of your typical luxury wagon. It features an adjustable air suspension that allows multiple ride heights for adventures on and off the beaten path. It offers a choice of either the standard 2.7-liter, twin-turbo V6 or a 4.2-liter V8. With 250 hp the V6 is hardly underpowered, but the additional low-end power of the larger 300-hp V8 gives it the feel of a true luxury wagon. Of course, Audi's reputation for exquisite interior design doesn't hurt either. With nearly every surface covered in top-quality materials, the allroad has an interior befitting a wagon in this price range. If you're looking for something a little less traditional, the allroad is worth looking into.

**Others to Consider:** Volvo's XC70 is the only other wagon in this category. Like the allroad, the XC70 is a more rugged version of Volvo's standard V70 wagon. The XC70 boasts increased ride height, additional body cladding and standard all-wheel drive. A 2.5-liter turbocharged five-cylinder engine is the only available power plant. With only 208 hp it's down on power compared to the Mercedes and the Audi, but during normal driving the XC moves out with little trouble. Its cabin is trimmed in high-quality materials and there are standard side torso and side curtain airbags for safety. With the introduction of the Volvo's XC90 SUV, there's a little less room in the lineup for a rugged wagon, but for those who would rather stay a little closer to the ground the XC70 is worth considering.

# Wagon Under $15,000

| Vehicle | Price Range | Base Drivetrain | EPA Fuel Rating (mpg) | Cargo Capacity | The Drive | The Ride | Design | Cargo/ Passenger Space | Overall Rating |
|---------|-------------|-----------------|----------------------|----------------|-----------|----------|--------|------------------------|----------------|
| **Scion xB** | $13,680-$14,480 | 1.5L 4cyl 5M Inline 4 FWD | N/A | 21.2 cu.ft. | 8.4 | 9.0 | 8.5 | 6.3 | **8.2** |
| **Scion xA** | $12,480-$13,280 | 1.5L 4cyl 5M Inline 4 FWD | 31 city 37 hwy | 11.9 cu.ft. | 7.6 | 8.8 | 8.0 | 7.0 | **7.8** |
| **Suzuki Forenza** | $13,949-$17,949 | 2.0L 4cyl 5M Inline 4 FWD | 21 city 28 hwy | 24.4 cu.ft. | 6.6 | 7.3 | 7.8 | 8.8 | **7.5** |
| **Toyota Matrix** | $14,760-$18,750 | 1.8L 4cyl 5M Inline 4 FWD | 29 city 36 hwy | 21.8 cu.ft. | 6.8 | 7.8 | 7.4 | 8.8 | **7.5** |
| **Chrysler PT Cruiser** | $13,405-$23,455 | 2.4L 4cyl 5M Inline 4 FWD | 21 city 29 hwy | 21.9 cu.ft. | 6.6 | 6.0 | 7.8 | 8.3 | **7.2** |
| **Kia Rio** | $11,365-$12,390 | 1.6L 4cyl 5M Inline 4 FWD | 26 city 33 hwy | 24.8 cu.ft. | 5.6 | 7.3 | 7.4 | 7.0 | **6.7** |

| Vehicle | Price Range | Base Drivetrain | EPA Fuel Rating (mpg) | Cargo Capacity | The Drive | The Ride | Design | Cargo/ Passenger Space | Overall Rating |
|---|---|---|---|---|---|---|---|---|---|
| Subaru Legacy | $22,295-$30,995 | 2.5L 4cyl 4A Horizontally Opposed AWD | 22 city 30 hwy | 33.5 cu.ft. | 8.5 | 8.8 | 8.9 | 8.5 | 8.7 |
| Subaru Outback | $24,295-$33,495 | 2.5L 4cyl 5M Horizontally Opposed AWD | N/A | 33.5 cu.ft. | 8.4 | 8.5 | 8.5 | 8.5 | 8.4 |
| Dodge Magnum | $21,870-$31,370 | 2.7L 6cyl 4A V6 RWD | 21 city 28 hwy | 27.2 cu.ft. | 8.0 | 8.8 | 8.3 | 8.3 | 8.3 |
| Ford Freestyle | $24,945-$30,245 | 3L 6cyl CVT V6 FWD | N/A | 17.6 cu.ft. | 8.0 | 8.8 | 7.6 | 9.5 | 8.2 |
| Mazda MAZDA6 | $22,895-$26,795 | 3L 6cyl 5M V6 FWD | 19 city 26 hwy | 33.7 cu.ft. | 8.5 | 8.5 | 8.0 | 7.0 | 8.1 |
| Volkswagen Passat | $23,070-$33,615 | 1.8L 4cyl 5M Inline 4 FWD | 22 city 31 hwy | 39 cu.ft. | 7.8 | 9.0 | 8.5 | 7.5 | 8.1 |
| Subaru Forester | $21,295-$28,195 | 2.5L 4cyl 5M Horizontally Opposed AWD | 21 city 27 hwy | 32 cu.ft. | 8.1 | 7.8 | 8.3 | 7.5 | 8.0 |
| Saab 9-2X | $22,990-$26,950 | 2.5L 4cyl 5M Horizontally Opposed AWD | N/A | 27.9 cu.ft. | 8.6 | 8.5 | 7.4 | 6.8 | 7.8 |
| Ford Focus | $17,030-$18,130 | 2.0L 4cyl 5M Inline 4 FWD | N/A | 35.6 cu.ft. | 7.6 | 7.5 | 7.6 | 8.0 | 7.7 |

# Wagon Under $25,000

| Vehicle | Price Range | Base Drivetrain | EPA Fuel Rating (mpg) | Cargo Capacity | The Drive | The Ride | Design | Cargo/ Passenger Space | Overall Rating |
|---|---|---|---|---|---|---|---|---|---|
| Pontiac Vibe | $17,000-$20,325 | 1.8L 4cyl 5M Inline 4 FWD | 29 city 36 hwy | 19.3 cu.ft. | 6.8 | 7.8 | 7.8 | 8.8 | 7.6 |
| Chrysler Pacifica | $24,315-$36,315 | 3.8L 6cyl 4A V6 FWD | 18 city 25 hwy | 13 cu.ft. | 7.1 | 8.3 | 7.4 | 7.3 | 7.3 |
| Chevrolet Malibu Maxx | $21,350-$24,495 | 3.5L 6cyl 4A V6 FWD | N/A | 22.8 cu.ft. | 7.1 | 7.5 | 6.5 | 7.5 | 7.0 |
| Subaru Impreza | $18,095-$25,395 | 2.5L 4cyl 5M Horizontally Opposed AWD | N/A | 11 cu.ft. | 8.4 | 7.8 | 6.3 | 5.8 | 7.0 |
| Volkswagen Jetta | $18,680-$23,275 | 2.0L 4cyl 5M Inline 4 FWD | 24 city 30 hwy | 34 cu.ft. | 7.4 | 7.0 | 8.0 | 4.5 | 6.9 |
| Suzuki Aerio | $15,449-$17,749 | 2.3L 4cyl 5M Inline 4 FWD | 25 city 31 hwy | 14.6 cu.ft. | 6.6 | 8.0 | 6.4 | 6.8 | 6.8 |
| Ford Taurus | $22,555-$23,545 | 3.0L 6cyl 4A V6 FWD | N/A | 38.8 cu.ft. | 4.4 | 5.8 | 5.3 | 7.5 | 5.5 |

# Wagon Under $35,000

| Vehicle | Price Range | Base Drivetrain | EPA Fuel Rating (mpg) | Cargo Capacity | The Drive | The Ride | Design | Cargo/ Passenger Space | Overall Rating |
|---|---|---|---|---|---|---|---|---|---|
| Audi A4 | $29,150-$48,790 | 1.8L 4cyl 6M Inline 4 AWD | 21 city 29 hwy | 27.8 cu.ft. | 8.1 | 8.5 | 8.8 | 7.3 | 8.2 |
| Volvo V50 | $25,660-$28,910 | 2.4L 5cyl 5A Inline 5 FWD | 22 city 30 hwy | 14.7 cu.ft. | 7.6 | 8.3 | 8.6 | 7.0 | 8.0 |
| Saab 9-2X | $22,990-$26,950 | 2.0L 4cyl Turbo 5M AWD | N/A | 27.9 cu.ft. | 8.6 | 8.5 | 7.4 | 6.8 | 7.9 |
| BMW 3 Series | $31,200-$32,950 | 2.5L 6cyl 5M Inline 6 RWD | 20 city 29 hwy | 27.3 cu.ft. | 8.9 | 7.0 | 8.4 | 4.8 | 7.6 |
| Lexus IS 300 | $30,805 | 3L 6cyl 5A Inline 6 RWD | 18 city 24 hwy | 21.8 cu.ft. | 8.6 | 7.0 | 8.0 | 4.3 | 7.4 |
| Volvo XC70 | $34,810 | 2.5L 5cyl 5A Inline 5 AWD | 19 city 24 hwy | 37.5 cu.ft. | 6.8 | 7.5 | 8.0 | 6.8 | 7.3 |
| Volvo V70 | $28,760-$36,010 | 2.4L 5cyl 5M Inline 5 FWD | 22 city 30 hwy | 37.5 cu.ft. | 7.0 | 6.5 | 7.9 | 6.8 | 7.2 |
| Mercedes-Benz C-Class | $34,150-$35,350 | 2.6L 6cyl 5A V6 RWD | N/A | 25.2 cu.ft. | 7.5 | 7.3 | 6.5 | 6.8 | 7.0 |
| Saab 9-5 | $32,550-$40,750 | 2.3L 4cyl 5M Inline 4 FWD | 21 city 29 hwy | 31.4 cu.ft. | 6.3 | 7.5 | 7.0 | 6.8 | 6.7 |

# Wagon Under $35,000

| Vehicle | Price Range | Base Drivetrain | EPA Fuel Rating (mpg) | Cargo Capacity | The Drive | The Ride | Design | Cargo/ Passenger Space | Overall Rating |
|---|---|---|---|---|---|---|---|---|---|
| **Mercury Sable** | $25,130 | 3.0L 6cyl 4A V6 FWD | 19 city 26 hwy | 38.8 cu.ft. | 4.4 | 5.8 | 5.3 | 7.5 | **5.5** |

| Vehicle | Price Range | Base Drivetrain | EPA Fuel Rating (mpg) | Cargo Capacity | The Drive | The Ride | Design | Cargo/ Passenger Space | Overall Rating |
|---------|-------------|-----------------|----------------------|----------------|-----------|----------|--------|-----------------------|----------------|
| **Mercedes-Benz E-Class** | $50,750- $60,500  #1 Editors' Rating | 3.2L 6cyl 5A V6 RWD | 20 city 28 hwy | 24.4 cu.ft. | 8.6 | 9.5 | 8.8 | 6.8 | **8.4** |
| **Audi allroad quattro** | $40,250- $47,250 | 2.7L 6cyl 5A V6 AWD | N/A | 36.4 cu.ft. | 7.5 | 8.5 | 8.6 | 7.3 | **7.9** |
| **Jaguar X-Type** | $36,330 | 3.0L 6cyl 5A V6 AWD | N/A | 16 cu.ft. | 6.6 | 6.8 | 7.0 | 4.8 | **6.4** |

## Top 10 Things to Consider Before Buying

**Size/Market Segment:** Coupes and two-door hatchbacks are typically based on a corresponding four-door sedan. The majority of coupes currently on the market are either compact or midsize, while most hatchbacks are compacts.

**Price:** Economy two-doors start as low as $10K while some exotic coupes can run in excess of $100K. Lower-priced coupes and hatchbacks tend to cost slightly less than their four-door counterparts, while premium coupes are often several hundred dollars more than their sedan counterparts.

**Operating Costs:** Between their low prices and great mileage, economy coupes and hatchbacks promise exceptionally low operational costs. Midrange and luxury coupes generally offer mileage on par with their sedan counterparts, but some insurance companies consider them sportier than sedans so premiums are sometimes higher.

**Engine/Fuel Economy:** Economy coupes and hatchbacks generally use ultraefficient four-cylinder engines that can return as much as 30-40 mpg, but they can make for sluggish acceleration. Most midsize coupes use larger six-cylinder engines that deliver more exciting performance but reduced fuel economy. Luxury coupes often employ high-powered six- or eight-cylinder engines that provide thrilling performance but below-average gas mileage.

**Safety:** Lower-priced coupes and hatchbacks now offer side airbags on many models, but their small size does make them vulnerable to larger vehicles in the event of a crash. Midsize two-doors often employ the same sophisticated systems found in their family sedan counterparts, so overall protection is generally very good. Luxury coupes usually come standard with the latest in safety technology, such as side curtain airbags and stability control systems.

**Luxury and Convenience Features:** Economy coupes typically offer basic amenities like air conditioning, an AM/FM stereo and power windows and locks. Midlevel two-doors often come in uplevel trims only, so amenities like leather, CD stereos and power everything are common. Luxury coupes come loaded with everything from heated and cooled seats to navigation systems.

**Passenger Capacity/Interior Space:** Although coupes have backseats, they typically offer very limited passenger room. Economy two-doors often have bench seats in the rear, while some midlevel and luxury coupes are designed to accommodate two passengers only.

**Transmission Types: Manual vs. Automatic:** Lower-cost coupes often provide a choice between a manual or automatic transmission, while most midlevel and luxury coupes offer automatics only. Manual transmissions typically provide better performance and mileage, while automatics make stop-and-go driving less cumbersome.

**Cargo Capacity:** Most coupes provide as much cargo space as their sedan counterparts. Two-door hatchbacks offer additional cargo room in most cases compared to traditional trunks, as well as easier access to items stowed in back.

**Body Style:** Coupe or Hatchback—Like most sedans, a coupe typically has a standard trunk. Two-door hatchbacks provide more additional room by extending the roofline to the rear of the vehicle and using a rear hatch that opens much wider than most trunk lids.

## Coupes/Hatchbacks Under $15,000

**Market Leaders:** For buyers seeking a small, affordable coupe or two-door hatchback, our top recommendations are the Honda Civic and Ford Focus. The Civic is the clear leader in this group, as Honda's lineup of coupes offers a range of refined and fuel-efficient four-cylinder engines; balanced ride and handling characteristics; roomy interiors with excellent ergonomics and high-grade materials; excellent crash test scores; and a longstanding reputation for quality and reliability. Ford's Focus ZX3 hatchback is also a solid choice in this segment, though neither build quality nor reliability is up to the level of the Civic. Nevertheless, the Focus is a well-engineered vehicle that proves to be as entertaining to drive as it is comfortable. Moreover, the cabin quarters offer roomy front and rear seating, user-friendly controls and plenty of cargo space. Several manufacturers now offer performance versions of their small coupes and hatchbacks that are intended for driving enthusiasts on a budget (though bear in mind that these cars break the $15,000 barrier). Saturn's Ion Red Line coupe promises to offer plenty of bang for the buck for 2005, thanks to a supercharged 200-horsepower engine. Honda's Civic Si hatchback isn't as sporty as other Civics that have worn the "Si" badge, but for those seeking a spacious and reliable hatchback with a little extra power under the hood (160 hp), it's not a bad choice.

**Others to Consider:** Other players in this segment include Saturn's Ion coupe, which in standard (non-Red Line) form lags far behind competitors in cabin design and build and materials quality. If you're willing to step down a half size, the picture gets a little brighter. The two-door Hyundai Accent is a solid entry-level economy car with a decent equipment list and generous warranty coverage. The two-door Toyota Echo upholds the tradition of Toyota quality and reliability, but poor packaging forces buyers to spend a bundle on options just to cover the basics.

## Coupes/Hatchbacks Under $25,000

**Market Leaders:** Buyers will find both compact and midsize coupes and hatchbacks in this price range. Some are easygoing and some are sporty, so it's best to determine your priorities before purchasing one.

We'd zero in on sporting models like the Acura RSX, Ford Mustang, Mini Cooper and the Volkswagen GTI, as well as more relaxed cars like the VW New Beetle and Golf. Ford's venerable pony car has finally been completely redesigned from the ground up for the first time in a quarter-century, and it was worth the wait. A tight new platform, powerful engine options (including a standard 200-horse V6 and optional 300-horse V8) and retro good looks that drip with '60s style all make the new 'Stang a definite winner. A performance version of VW's Golf, the two-door GTI hatchback, has always been a good bet for enthusiasts seeking a fun-to-drive car that doesn't sacrifice an ounce of weekday comfort, and the German automaker has also introduced a high-performance Subaru-fighter called the R32, which offers a 237-horsepower VR6 engine, standard all-wheel drive and upgraded running gear. The RSX and Cooper also remain strong choices, as the Acura offers a great deal of performance, along with day-to-day livability, a generous standard features list and tight build quality. The Cooper ranges from pleasant-to-drive in base form to seriously entertaining in Cooper S trim. For less demanding drivers, the Beetle offers many of the GTI's attributes in a more stylish package, while the Golf offers greater practicality, thanks to its more spacious interior. A high-mileage diesel engine is available on both of the VWs.

If you're looking for the best midsize coupe in this price range, your decision basically comes down to the Honda Accord and the Toyota Camry Solara. Both offer a smooth, quiet ride; a choice between a healthy four-cylinder engine and a potent V6; and a stylish interior with high-quality materials. Beyond that, the Accord gives enthusiast-types the option of getting a manual transmission with the V6, while the Camry Solara offers a sport suspension for crisper handling.

**Others to Consider:** Toyota's younger, hipper Scion brand has introduced a sport coupe for 2005, called the tC. Powered by a smooth and tractable four-cylinder borrowed from the Camry and featuring well-tuned suspension tuning and high-performance-looking alloy wheels, the sporty tC should be an instant hit with those who desire Toyota reliability with a bit more style and spunk thrown in to keep things interesting. Attractive to behold, Hyundai's Tiburon isn't particularly fun to drive, but an available V6, a well-finished interior, a long list of standard features and affordable pricing offset this. Mitsubishi's Eclipse is similar in personality, but a dull interior and higher pricing make it less desirable than the Hyundai in our book. If you're looking for something a bit larger, the Dodge Stratus and Chrysler Sebring are decent choices. They're heavily based on the Eclipse, so driving characteristics and cockpit quarters are similar, but better packaging makes it easier to get basic safety features. Chevrolet's Monte Carlo is larger still, and until this year there was little reason to consider this coupe, which suffered for its mushy suspension and cheap interior. For 2005, however, a supercharged V6 engine and a tightened suspension add a little spark to its existence.

## Coupes Under $35,000

**Market Leaders:** At the front of this class is a longtime favorite, BMW's stellar 3 Series, and its most direct competitor, Infiniti's G35 Coupe. With rear-wheel drive, 280 flexible horsepower, communicative steering and a well-balanced chassis, the G35 offers virtually everything that makes the 3 Series so enticing, at a price thousands of dollars less. Still, the 3 remains a great choice, with a comfortable cockpit, timeless styling and that uncanny symbiosis between car and driver that even the G35 can't quite match. You won't go wrong even if you have to dig a little deeper into your piggy bank. Mazda's RX-8 is unique in this segment for a couple of big reasons; rotary engine power and an extra pair of doors. The rotary gives the RX-8 incredibly smooth power delivery that makes running through gears with the short-throw shifter as much fun as flicking the athletic Mazda through a series of S-curves. The RX-8's rear-opening rear doors allow easy access to the surprisingly accommodating rear quarters, where two adults can ride in comfort. Nissan's 350Z has also received a fair share of accolades, and rightfully so. A no-nonsense sports car, the Z has all the essentials an enthusiast wants—a powerful engine (287 horses worth) and brakes, taut suspension and responsive steering. Of course, the 350Z only seats two (which might account for some of its appeal) and the cabin trim is rather austere, so those seeking a similar driving experience with room for four and more luxury will be better served by its aforementioned cousin, the Infiniti G35.

**Others to Consider:** If the idea of Mercedes-Benz style and safety along with the convenience of a hatchback body style appeals to you, then the Mercedes C-Class "coupes" warrant your interest. Available with either supercharged four (C230 Kompressor) or V6 power, these unorthodox Benzes come with plenty of features such as standard stability control and dual-zone air conditioning. Audi's TT has been around a few years now, but this low-slung, high-style "2+2" still provides a pleasant, if not overtly sporting driving experience and features leather seating and xenon headlamps on its generous standard features list. Pontiac has resurrected the GTO, and those lamenting the departure of the Firebird/Camaro twins should be more than happy with this 400-hp, six-speed, rear-drive muscle coupe.

## Coupes Under $45,000

**Market Leaders:** Coupes constitute a narrow sliver of the market and when it comes to the luxury segment there are only two significant choices: the Chevrolet Corvette and the Mercedes-Benz CLK-Class. Available in coupe and convertible form, the new "C6" (so called because it is the sixth generation of the car) Corvette offers world-class performance in addition to its dramatic styling and legendary name. The standard coupes and convertibles are powered by a new 400-horsepower, 6.0-liter V8 hooked to either a four-speed automatic or six-speed manual transmission. Thanks to revised suspension and new bodylines that reduce overhang, America's sports car has finally come into its own as a world-class performance machine. As incredible as the various Corvette models perform, however, they still maintain a reasonably comfortable disposition in everyday driving making them legitimate daily drivers. The Corvette's biggest shortcoming is its interior, which is all new and better than ever, but still lacking the kind of high-end luxury you would expect from a car in this price range. Buyers looking for a more polished experience might be better suited to the CLK-Class of coupes from Mercedes-Benz. Like the Corvette, the CLK is available in coupe, convertible and high-performance guise courtesy of AMG. Redesigned just last year, the CLK features a sleek shape, luxurious interior and all the latest in technological gadgetry. Base CLK320 coupes and convertibles get a 215-hp V6 while the V8-powered CLK500 models offer a more robust 302 hp; both engines are mated to five-speed automatic transmissions. The high-performance AMG-tuned CLK55 boasts 362 hp from its supercharged V8 as well as a sport-tuned suspension and enhanced bodywork. All CLKs have lavishly appointed interiors, ample passenger room and fully automatic tops on convertible versions. The interior control layout is still a bit busy for our tastes, but the overall design is aesthetically pleasing and functional. If you're looking for a luxurious coupe that won't give you bouts of claustrophobia, the CLK is the two-door of choice.

## Coupes Over $45,000

**Market Leaders:** Thanks to the public's affinity for practicality over style, the market for luxury coupes has dwindled to the point of near extinction. The handful that have survived, however, represent some of the most stylish and desirable vehicles on the market today. At the top of our wish list sits the Mercedes CL-Class. Comprised of the standard CL500, V12-powered CL600 and AMG-tuned CL55 and CL65, these heavy-hitters deliver style, performance and luxury in a manner so refined you'll never grow tired of getting behind the wheel. Whether you're content with the 302 horsepower of the standard CL500 or you go all out for the CL65 with its twin-turbo V12, the CL is a swift, refined package with few faults. As powerful as they are, however, these coupes are perfectly content to glide around town in near silence, ensconcing their drivers in luxurious cabins trimmed in the softest leathers and finest wood trim. These furnishings are supplemented by all the latest features found on the top-line S-Class, including DVD navigation and driver-selectable ride control settings. For buyers who seek equal parts performance and luxury, the CL-Class delivers copious amounts of both.

BMW's 6 Series is another shapely luxury coupe worth considering. Regardless of whether you like the dramatic styling, its performance doesn't leave much room for complaints. The standard 4.4-liter V8 engine delivers 325 hp that can propel the big coupe to 60 mph in less than 6 seconds, and with three different transmissions to choose from you're bound to find a setup that suits your driving style. Like the new-for-2004 5 Series upon which it's based, the 645i features a vast array of electronic controls to maintain optimal stability and safety. BMW's Active Roll Stabilization nearly eliminates body sway during hard cornering and an optional Active Steering system can vary the steering ratio to deliver precise road feel in twisty canyons and minimal effort in parking lots. Other notable options include active headlights that turn with the curve of the road, a head-up display that projects vehicle information onto the windshield and active cruise control that automatically maintains a preset distance from the cars in front of you.

**Others to consider:** For drivers who prefer a more involved driving experience full of growling engines and do-it-yourself gearboxes, you need look no further than the latest generation of the legendary Porsche 911. Freshly redesigned for 2005 with a more traditional look reminiscent of the much-loved 993-series, the new 911 has been split into two distinct models, the 325-hp Carrera and the 355-hp Carrera S. Regardless of which model you choose, rest assured that it will have more power than you know what to do with and handling to match. The 911's interior is nowhere near as opulent as its Mercedes-badged competitors, but if you're worried about wood trim and how many cupholders there are the 911 may not be the car for you.

If electronic gadgetry isn't your thing, a ride in Jaguar's XK coupe might be more to your liking. Although it's getting on in years, the XK's timeless exterior design and finely trimmed interior make it worthy of consideration. The high-performance XKR model adds a supercharged V8 to the mix for those who desire top performance, but even the standard model provides plenty of on-demand power and tightly controlled handling.

| Vehicle | Price Range | Base Drivetrain | EPA Fuel Rating (mpg) | Cargo/ Trunk Capacity | The Drive | The Ride | Design | Cargo/ Passenger Space | Overall Rating |
|---|---|---|---|---|---|---|---|---|---|
| **Honda Civic** | $13,560-$19,470 | 1.7L 4cyl 5M Inline 4 FWD | 32 city 38 hwy | 13 cu.ft. | 7.9 | 9.3 | 7.9 | 7.5 | **8.0** |
| **Ford Focus** | $13,230-$17,130 | 2.0L 4cyl 5M Inline 4 FWD | N/A | 18 cu.ft. | 7.6 | 7.5 | 7.6 | 8.0 | **7.7** |
| **Hyundai Accent** | $9,999-$11,399 | 1.6L 4cyl 5M Inline 4 FWD | 29 city 33 hwy | 17 cu.ft. | 5.8 | 7.8 | 8.4 | 7.0 | **7.1** |
| **Toyota ECHO** | $10,355-$11,155 | 1.5L 4cyl 5M Inline 4 FWD | 35 city 43 hwy | 14 cu.ft. | 6.8 | 7.8 | 6.9 | 6.8 | **7.0** |
| **Saturn ION** | $11,995-$18,145 | 2.2L 4cyl 4A Inline 4 FWD | 24 city 32 hwy | 14.7 cu.ft. | 6.0 | 4.8 | 5.1 | 6.3 | **5.5** |
| **Chevrolet Cavalier** | $10,325-$17,510 | 2.2L 4cyl 5M Inline 4 FWD | N/A | 13 cu.ft. | 5.4 | 4.3 | 5.3 | 4.8 | **5.0** |
| **Pontiac Sunfire** | $10,895-$15,085 | 2.2L 4cyl 5M Inline 4 FWD | 26 city 37 hwy | 12 cu.ft. | 5.3 | 4.3 | 5.3 | 4.8 | **4.9** |
| **Chevrolet Cobalt** | $13,625-$21,430 | 2.2L 4cyl 5M Inline 4 FWD | N/A | 14 cu.ft. | N/A | N/A | N/A | N/A | **N/A** |

# Coupe Under $25,000

| Vehicle | Price Range | Base Drivetrain | EPA Fuel Rating (mpg) | Cargo/ Trunk Capacity | The Drive | The Ride | Design | Cargo/ Passenger Space | Overall Rating |
|---|---|---|---|---|---|---|---|---|---|
| **Scion tC** #1 Editors' Rating | $15,950-$16,750 | 2.4L 4cyl 5M Inline 4 FWD | 22 city 29 hwy | 13 cu.ft. | 8.4 | 8.8 | 8.3 | 8.3 | **8.4** |
| **Toyota Camry Solara** #1 Editors' Rating | $19,220-$26,095 | 2.4L 4cyl 5M Inline 4 FWD | 23 city 33 hwy | 14 cu.ft. | 8.0 | 8.5 | 9.3 | 7.8 | **8.4** |
| **Ford Mustang** | $18,785-$25,705 | 4L 6cyl 5M V6 RWD | 19 city 28 hwy | 12 cu.ft. | 8.5 | 7.8 | 8.6 | 6.8 | **8.2** |
| **Honda Accord** | $19,775-$28,800 | 2.4L 4cyl 5M Inline 4 FWD | 26 city 34 hwy | 13 cu.ft. | 7.8 | 8.8 | 7.9 | 8.5 | **8.1** |
| **Acura RSX** | $20,175-$23,570 | 2L 4cyl 5M Inline 4 FWD | 27 city 34 hwy | 16 cu.ft. | 9.0 | 7.5 | 7.4 | 7.8 | **8.0** |
| **Volkswagen GTI** | $19,510-$22,330 | 1.8L 4cyl 5M Inline 4 FWD | 24 city 31 hwy | 18 cu.ft. | 7.9 | 8.3 | 7.8 | 8.0 | **7.9** |
| **Hyundai Tiburon** | N/A | 2.0L 4cyl 5M FWD | 20-23 city 26-29 hwy | 14.7 cu.ft. | 7.6 | 7.5 | 8.6 | 6.8 | **7.8** |
| **MINI Cooper** | $16,449-$19,899 | 1.6L 4cyl 5M Inline 4 FWD | N/A | 5 cu.ft. | 8.6 | 7.0 | 8.3 | 6.0 | **7.8** |
| **Toyota Celica** | $17,670-$23,035 | 1.8L 4cyl 5M Inline 4 FWD | 27 city 33 hwy | 17 cu.ft. | 8.3 | 7.0 | 7.1 | 7.0 | **7.4** |

| Vehicle | Price Range | Base Drivetrain | EPA Fuel Rating (mpg) | Cargo/ Trunk Capacity | The Drive | The Ride | Design | Cargo/ Passenger Space | Overall Rating |
|---|---|---|---|---|---|---|---|---|---|
| Chevrolet Monte Carlo | $22,150-$28,225 | 3.4L 6cyl 4A V6 FWD | N/A | 16 cu.ft. | 7.5 | 7.5 | 6.6 | 7.3 | 7.2 |
| Pontiac Grand Am | $22,365-$23,615 | 3.4L 6cyl 4A V6 FWD | N/A | 15 cu.ft. | 7.4 | 7.0 | 7.1 | 7.0 | 7.2 |
| Chrysler Sebring | $22,145-$24,520 | 2.4L 4cyl 4A Inline 4 FWD | 21 city 28 hwy | 16 cu.ft. | 6.9 | 7.8 | 6.6 | 7.0 | 7.0 |
| Volkswagen Golf | $15,830-$20,655 | 2.0L 4cyl 5M Inline 4 FWD | 24 city 31 hwy | 18 cu.ft. | 7.3 | 7.3 | 7.8 | 5.3 | 7.0 |
| Volkswagen New Beetle | $16,570-$26,525 | 2.0L 4cyl 5M FWD | 21-36 city 29-42hwy | 27 cu.ft. | 6.9 | 7.0 | 7.6 | 6.3 | 7.0 |
| Mitsubishi Eclipse | $19,449-$25,849 | 2.4L 4cyl 5M Inline 4 FWD | 23 city 31 hwy | 17 cu.ft. | 6.5 | 6.0 | 7.0 | 6.0 | 6.5 |
| Honda Insight | N/A | 1.0L 3cyl Gas/Elec Hybrid 5M FWD | 57 city 56 hwy | 16 cu.ft. | 6.5 | 6.3 | 8.0 | 3.8 | 6.5 |
| Dodge Stratus | $20,905-$23,695 | 2.4L 4cyl 5M Inline 4 FWD | 24 city 32 hwy | 16 cu.ft. | 5.5 | 7.3 | 5.9 | 7.0 | 6.1 |

# Coupe Under $35,000

| Vehicle | Price Range | Base Drivetrain | EPA Fuel Rating (mpg) | Cargo/ Trunk Capacity | The Drive | The Ride | Design | Cargo/ Passenger Space | Overall Rating |
|---|---|---|---|---|---|---|---|---|---|
| BMW 3 Series | $31,700-$37,300 | 2.5L 6cyl 5M Inline 6 RWD | 20 city 29 hwy | 10 cu.ft. | 9.3 | 7.8 | 8.6 | 6.3 | 8.3 |
| Mazda RX-8 | $25,375-$26,875 | 1.3L cyl 4A Rotary RWD | 18 city 24 hwy | 8 cu.ft. | 8.9 | 8.3 | 8.1 | 6.8 | 8.2 |
| Infiniti G35 | $32,990 | 3.5L 6cyl 5M RWD | 18 city 26 hwy | 7.8 cu.ft. | 8.6 | 8.0 | 7.4 | 8.0 | 8.0 |
| Chrysler Crossfire | $29,045-$34,820 | 3.2L 6cyl 6M V6 RWD | 17 city 25 hwy | 8 cu.ft. | 8.3 | 8.8 | 7.6 | 6.0 | 7.8 |
| Nissan 350Z | $26,500-$35,150 | 3.5L 6cyl 6M V6 RWD | 20 city 26 hwy | 7 cu.ft. | 8.9 | 7.3 | 8.0 | 5.5 | 7.8 |
| Pontiac GTO | N/A | 6.0L 8cyl 4A RWD | N/A | 13 cu.ft. | 7.6 | 8.5 | 8.1 | 7.0 | 7.8 |
| Audi TT | $33,500-$40,150 | 1.8L 4cyl 6A Inline 4 FWD | 21 city 29 hwy | 14 cu.ft. | 7.1 | 6.3 | 8.5 | 6.3 | 7.3 |
| Mercedes-Benz C-Class | $25,850-$28,250 | 1.8L 4cyl 6M Inline 4 RWD | N/A | 10 cu.ft. | 7.5 | 7.3 | 6.5 | 6.8 | 7.0 |

| Vehicle | Price Range | Base Drivetrain | EPA Fuel Rating (mpg) | Cargo/ Trunk Capacity | The Drive | The Ride | Design | Cargo/ Passenger Space | Overall Rating |
|---|---|---|---|---|---|---|---|---|---|
| **Chevrolet Corvette** | $43,445 #1 Editors' Rating | 6.0L 8cyl 6M V8 RWD | N/A | 22 cu. ft. | 9.4 | 8.8 | 8.4 | 8.0 | **8.8** |

# Coupe Over $45,000

| Vehicle | Price Range | Base Drivetrain | EPA Fuel Rating (mpg) | Cargo/ Trunk Capacity | The Drive | The Ride | Design | Cargo/ Passenger Space | Overall Rating |
|---|---|---|---|---|---|---|---|---|---|
| Porsche 911 | $69,300-$118,700 | N/A | N/A | N/A | 8.6 | 8.0 | 9.0 | 8.3 | 8.6 |
| Mercedes-Benz CL-Class | $93,900-$127,900 | 5.0L 8cyl 7A V8 RWD | 16 city 24 hwy | 12 cu.ft. | 8.9 | 9.0 | 8.1 | 6.5 | 8.2 |
| BMW 6 Series | $69,900 | 4.4L 8cyl 6M V8 RWD | 17 city 25 hwy | 13 cu.ft. | 8.8 | 7.5 | 8.5 | 7.0 | 8.1 |
| Acura NSX | $89,000 | 3.0L 6cyl 4A V6 RWD | 17 city 24 hwy | 5 cu.ft. | 8.4 | 8.8 | 7.6 | 7.5 | 7.8 |
| Mercedes-Benz CLK-Class | $45,250-$53,750 | 3.2L 6cyl 5A V6 RWD | 20 city 26 hwy | 10 cu.ft. | 8.1 | 8.8 | 8.5 | 5.3 | 7.8 |
| Jaguar XK-Series | $69,830-$81,330 | 4.2L 8cyl 6A V8 RWD | 18 city 26 hwy | 12 cu.ft. | 7.8 | 6.8 | 7.6 | 6.8 | 7.4 |

# Top 10 Things to Consider Before Buying

**Size/Market Segment:** Convertibles range in size from two-seat roadsters to larger four-seat luxury models. The majority of convertibles on the market are luxury-brand vehicles, although there are still several affordable drop tops on the market.

**Price:** The cheapest convertible runs in the low-$20,000s while the most expensive luxury models can run well over $100,000. There are several convertibles that cost less than $35,000, but the most populated segment resides in the $35,000-$80,000 price range.

**Engine/Fuel Economy:** Most midsize models use four- and six-cylinder engines, while more expensive luxury-branded convertibles generally use V6 or V8 engines. Four- and six-cylinder models can get good mileage in the mid-20-mpg range, but most eight-cylinder drop tops turn in less than 20 mpg.

**Safety:** Newer convertibles generally offer some kind of roll bar that will pop up to protect passengers in the event of a rollover accident. Side airbags that deploy from the seats are also becoming popular in higher-end models.

**Luxury Features/Convenience:** A couple of the more inexpensive convertibles are sparsely appointed, but most drop tops provide a long list of standard amenities. Upper-level luxury models often feature the latest in electronic gadgetry and amenities.

**Passenger Capacity/Interior Space:** "Roadster" generally identifies a convertible as a two-seater only, while others have small rear seats to seat a total of four. A few models offer legitimate room for four adults but the majority have only enough room for small children in back.

**Cargo Space:** Most convertibles have limited trunk space when the top is folded down. With the top in place, however, most models offer as much cargo capacity as their coupe counterparts.

**Top Operation:** Manual vs. Automatic—Less expensive models generally use less complicated top mechanisms that require you to unlatch and/or snap a buckle or two to get them open and closed. Most models, however, feature fully automatic tops that raise and lower at the touch of a button. A few models offer retractable hardtops and are thus well suited to year-round use.

**Top-Down Driving:** Many new convertibles now provide windscreens that are placed behind the front seats that help keep turbulence down to a minimum while driving with the top down.

**Operating Costs:** Convertibles generally don't cost any more to operate than their coupe or sedan siblings. In the past, owners often had to replace soft tops, but with the advent of glass rear windows and more durable top construction methods, today's convertible tops last much longer.

## Convertibles Under $25,000

**Market Leaders:** Although one might assume that the pickings are slim in this category, there are actually a fair number of rag tops that clear the $25K limbo bar. And the choices range from genuine sports cars to a spacious (for a convertible) four-seat cruiser.

A fixture on lists like this since its debut in 1990, Mazda's evergreen Miata has the basic recipe for fun on four wheels down to a T: an easy-to-drop top, ultraresponsive steering, a stiff chassis and a cozy but functional cockpit. Factor in timeless styling and an eager and dependable in-line four and we doubt few could argue against this perennial favorite. Similar in spirit (pseudo British retro styling), the new Mini Convertible sports a low center of gravity and BMW-engineered suspension that gives it great handling. And like the Miata, the Mini possesses steering that is terrifically accurate, with great feedback and road feel and a peppy, if not overpowering four with similar output.

**Others to Consider:** Those with nostalgic leanings have another rag top to consider—the VW New Beetle Cabriolet. Although it took VW five years to offer the convertible version, New Bug fans should consider the time well spent; the top is a breeze to drop, is well insulated and retains the proper "stacked" look of the old Beetle. There are two four-cylinder engines available; a 115-horsepower 2.0-liter and a turbocharged, 150-horse 1.8. Unless you're going with a manual transmission, we suggest opting for the turbo as performance is marginal at best with the automatic gearbox (even though it now has *six* speeds).

In a similar vein, Chrysler has finally taken a scalpel to its popular little PT Cruiser and created a two-door convertible version. Offering a spacious four-person cabin, a smooth ride and sporty suspension coupled with unique looks, the PT Convertible is a unique option in the drop-top marketplace. Several engines are available, ranging from the base 150-hp, 2.4-liter four all the way up to the turbocharged 220-hp version of the same motor available in the GT. Manual and automatic transmissions are available, and a bevy of available airbags makes the PT a safe choice as well.

## Convertibles Under $35,000

**Market Leaders:** Four unlikely combatants make up the top dogs in this price bracket. Hard-core driving enthusiasts will want to give serious consideration to Honda's S2000, which wrings 240 horsepower out of its 2.2-liter inline four without requiring turbo- or supercharging. A bump in displacement last year gave the S2000's high-strung four-cylinder more torque down low, meaning the car is quicker around town without requiring excessively high engine speeds. Puttering from work to home, the 2.2-liter engine is far friendlier than the 2.0-liter and yet retains most of its eagerness to leap for the redline. Suspension tweaks were added along with the larger engine to maintain its razor-sharp responses while being a bit more forgiving. Should the tail start to come around, it's a more gradual action (and hence easier to catch) compared to the previous model. If serious torque is what you're looking for, you can't go wrong with the new Nissan 350Z roadster. This drop top will thrill you whether blasting down an on-ramp or carving up a twisty two-lane. The cockpit is comfortable with more room and amenities than you'll find in the S2000. Some of the materials used to construct it could be better, but for the price, it's hard to beat the 350Z. There's no denying the fact that BMW's new styling direction has cooled some enthusiasts' hearts toward the roundel. And so it is with the Z4, but whether you like the Z4's looks or not, the little roadster has a way of winning folks over once they get behind the wheel. Even if you only get the 2.5-liter version (versus the more potent 3.0), that small inline six packs a surprisingly strong punch. True to BMW tradition, the Z4's handling is tight and the steering is spot on. The union of man and machine is so seamless that it feels as if the car is reading your mind, and the lack of body shake over the bumps is impressive for a rag top. Yet another strong contender in this category is the Chrysler Crossfire. With its unique styling, German engineering and choice of standard or high-powered SRT trim, this drop top is hard to overlook. Although not quite as sporting as the other vehicles in this category, it still possesses a high enough "fun to drive" quotient to make it worth considering if you're looking for a roadster in this class.

**Others to Consider:** For those seeking a relaxed top-down experience and somewhat lower monthly payments, Toyota's redesigned Camry Solara convertible is an excellent choice. With its sleek new body and a luxurious interior, this is one of the best-dressed four-seat convertibles on the market. And thanks to a significant increase in rigidity, an available sport suspension and a standard smooth-running 3.3-liter V6, this Solara will have no difficulty keeping up even when the roads turn twisty. If you're on a tighter budget and/or need a little more room in the backseat, the Chrysler Sebring convertible is a smart choice. Neither acceleration nor handling is anything special, but if all you want to do is cruise down the coast, the Sebring should be fully adequate. The Chrysler's interior design and materials aren't up to the level of the Solara's, but your out-the-door price is apt to be much lower.

Although the Mitsubishi Eclipse Spyder is mechanically similar to the Sebring, on the whole, we find it a bit less enjoyable. For one thing, it's a smaller car with a smaller backseat, which makes it less usable for family types. For another, poor packaging forces you to spring for the high-line GTS model to get basic safety features like antilock brakes, traction control and side airbags. The one advantage the Eclipse holds over the Sebring is its more powerful 3.0-liter V6 engine, which gives it considerably more punch. As with Chrysler's drop top, handling is soft and nonathletic, which strikes us as ironic in light of the Eclipse's extroverted styling.

## Convertibles Under $45,000

**Market Leaders:** There is a surprising amount of diversity in this segment, and you're apt to find a winner no matter which way you're leaning. If something sporty but practical is what you need, then the BMW 3 Series should more than fill the bill. With performance that doesn't give much, if anything, away to two-seaters that cost twice as much, room for four and exemplary cockpit accommodations, it's an easy rag top to live with. Offering less all-out agility than the BMW but an equally solid feel and more luxury in the cabin, the Audi A4 also offers the advantage of available all-wheel drive, making it a year-round drop top even in inclement parts of the country. The new S4 version of the Audi adds a more spirited V8 engine and six-speed transmission to the mix, making it a taut and exciting ride perfect for daily commutes or spirited romps on the autobahn. Saab's 9-3 convertible splits the difference between the Germans, being sportier than the A4 yet not as athletic as the BMW. With competent handling, an expanding trunk that offers best-in-class capacity and attractive styling, the 9-3 deserves strong consideration in this class.

For more dedicated performance, enthusiasts willing to sacrifice a little space and comfort in the name of speed, the razor-sharp Lotus Elise has finally made its way to American shores. Known for decades as a purveyor of world-class sports cars, the engineers and designers at Lotus have managed to meld incredibly taut suspension and sinewy styling into one sharp little package. Power comes from a 190-hp Toyota-sourced four-cylinder, so reliability shouldn't be a problem. Luxury options are few and far between on the spartan 1,975-pound roadster, but cushy opulence isn't what this little beast was designed for.

Also residing in the two-seat sports roadster field is the talented but costly Porsche Boxster. An entertaining ride that provides midengine handling along with a lovely engine and exhaust soundtrack, the Boxster is Porsche's only entry in the convertible field until the new 911 drop top arrives in 2006. Due for a redesign next year, the Mercedes-Benz SLK is still worthy of a place on your "to drive" list. Although it's more grand tourer than sports car, this two-seater does have something over the more nimble Boxster—a retractable hardtop. The SLK's trick folding metal top provides the security and serenity of a coupe along with the open-air experience of a rag top. We're willing to bet that the current Benz roadster will hold onto its appeal and value for many years to come. Those planning to do some long-distance cruising should also take a look at the Audi TT. A potent new 250-hp, 3.2-liter V6; a soothing ride; and an artsy, industrial-themed cockpit that uses only top-grade materials are a few of the TT's strengths. Another is the availability of all-wheel drive. If carefree days on coastal highways and year-round use are in your forecast, a TT could be a nice addition to your garage.

**Others to Consider:** Although it may be getting long in the tooth, the Volvo C70 still has its charms, namely a roomy cabin, incredibly comfortable seats and Volvo's stellar safety factor. Due for replacement in the next year or so, the C70 can be had with either high- or low-pressure turbo power, the former offering more thrills with a stick and the latter being better suited for those who want an automatic.

Reaping the benefits of its Mercedes-Benz corporate ties, Chrysler's Crossfire convertible is the first true Mercedes-Chrysler collaborative effort, featuring 39-percent Mercedes-Benz technology. That figure alone should catch established import buyers' attention, along with the fact that the Crossfire is based on its corporate benefactor—the SLK roadster. Nimble handling and unique styling make the sporty German/American convertible an interesting option, although questionable interior materials and build quality means it isn't quite on the same plane as its cousin from across the pond.

## Convertibles Over $45,000

**Market Leaders:** In this category, practicality takes a backseat (if there is one) to performance and style. Yet the top choices are still cars that could be used as daily drivers, provided cargo space is not a chief concern. The Mercedes-Benz SL-Class and the BMW 6 Series provide the best of both worlds—the full wind-in-your-hair and sun-on-your face experience of a traditional ragtop with the comfort and security of a Teutonic luxury car when the top is raised.

We have to give the edge to the Benz due to its potential to combine world-class performance with the ability to coddle its passengers during the daily commuter grind. Along with the SL500, which is no slouch with its 302-horsepower V8, the SL stable includes a pair of near-500-hp road burners (the supercharged V8 SL55 AMG and the twin-turbo V12 SL600) that can rocket an SL to 60 mph in around 4.5 seconds. This is performance more likely associated with high-strung Ferraris and Lamborghinis, not Mercedes' classy and comfortable SL. In addition to the stunning performance, the SL has a semiactive suspension that provides a supple ride quality that tightens up when it should (such as when winging through canyon roads), a surprisingly spacious trunk and a veritable alphabet soup's worth of safety systems.

BMW's fresh 6 Series offers a larger, more comfortable choice for motoring enthusiasts who enjoy the precise and nimble feel of a BMW ragtop but find the 3 Series a bit too compact.

Powered by an incredibly smooth and powerful 4.4-liter V8 that can be shifted by your choice of six-speed transmissions (including a manual, automatic and SMG), the 6 Series is as fast as a sports car but comfortable enough to reside in touring car territory as well. A sport package adds active suspension management, larger alloy wheels with more aggressive tires and firmer suspension tuning for those who prefer curvy roads over the straight and narrow. While the styling can elicit love-it or hate-it responses, there's no arguing with this car's mechanical pedigree and plush interior.

Another worthy option in this category is Cadillac's new XLR, which like the Benz, will drop its metal roof from sight quickly at the push of a button. With 320 horses galloping out of its Northstar V8, the XLR should have enough thrust to satisfy most folks. Based on the Corvette platform, the XLR boasts a finely tuned suspension that, like the Benz, provides an optimum balance of ride comfort and handling prowess. Topping off the topless XLR is a leather- and wood-trimmed cabin that proves that GM can get it right in this critical area if it puts its mind (and money) on it.

**Others to Consider:** If the retractable hardtop idea strikes your fancy but you place luxury over sportiness and wouldn't mind saving $13 to $23 grand over our top picks, the Lexus SC 430 is a strong choice. Although capable for a softly tuned car, the SC feels isolated compared to the athletic feel of the SL or 6 Series. A butter-smooth powertrain and whisper-quiet operation characterize the Lexus' mechanical personality. Other SC 430 strong points include the cabin; few carmakers can equal the luxury of the SC's interior with its highly polished wood, sumptuous leather and top-notch audio system.

Similar in philosophy are the Jaguar XK8/XKR ragtops—fast grand tourers that are more at home covering gently curving coastal two-laners at a rapid clip than dissecting winding canyon roads. If you want to share the al fresco motoring experience with more than one adult, the Mercedes-Benz CLK500 Cabriolet offers the closest thing to a four-place SL500, as it boasts similar styling inside and out, fine performance and a real backseat, not a leather-upholstered package shelf.

# Convertible Under $25,000

| Vehicle | Price Range | Base Drivetrain | EPA Fuel Rating (mpg) | Cargo/ Trunk Capacity | The Drive | The Ride | Design | Cargo/ Passenger Space | Overall Rating |
|---|---|---|---|---|---|---|---|---|---|
| **Mazda MX-5 Miata** #1 Editors' Rating | $22,098- $24,903 | 1.8L 4cyl 5M Inline 4 RWD | 23 city 29 hwy | 5 cu. ft. | 8.8 | 8.0 | 8.1 | 4.8 | **7.8** |
| **MINI Cooper** | $20,950- $24,400 | 1.6L 4cyl 5M Inline 4 FWD | N/A | 6 cu. ft. | 8.5 | 6.3 | 7.6 | 5.3 | **7.3** |
| **Chrysler PT Cruiser** | $19,405- $28,380 | 2.4L 4cyl 5M Inline 4 FWD | N/A | 7 cu. ft. | 6.6 | 6.0 | 7.8 | 8.3 | **7.2** |
| **Volkswagen New Beetle Cabriolet** | $21,865- $27,100 | 2.0L 4cyl 5M FWD | 21-36 city 29-42hwy | 27 cu. ft. | 6.9 | 7.0 | 7.6 | 6.3 | **7.0** |
| **Mitsubishi Eclipse Spyder** | $24,899- $30,699 | 2.4L 4cyl 5M Inline 4 FWD | N/A | 7 cu. ft. | 6.5 | 7.0 | 7.0 | 6.0 | **6.6** |
| **Toyota MR2 Spyder** | $24,895 - $26,145 | 1.8L 4cyl 5M Inline 4 RWD | 26 city 32 hwy | 2 cu. ft. | 7.6 | 5.8 | 5.9 | 2.5 | **6.0** |

| Vehicle | Price Range | Base Drivetrain | EPA Fuel Rating (mpg) | Cargo/ Trunk Capacity | The Drive | The Ride | Design | Cargo/ Passenger Space | Overall Rating |
|---|---|---|---|---|---|---|---|---|---|
| **Honda S2000** '1 Editors' Rating | $32,950 | 2.2L 4cyl 6M Inline 4 RWD | 20 city 25 hwy | 5 cu.ft. | 8.9 | 8.3 | 8.8 | 6.0 | **8.2** |
| **Toyota Camry Solara** | $26,380- $29,650 | 3.3L 6cyl 5A V6 FWD | 20 city 29 hwy | 12 cu.ft. | 7.5 | 8.5 | 8.5 | 7.8 | **8.0** |
| **BMW Z4** | $34,300- $41,300 | 2.5L 6cyl 5M Inline 6 RWD | 20 city 28 hwy | N/A | 9.1 | 8.0 | 7.8 | 4.8 | **7.8** |
| **Chrysler Crossfire** | $34,085- $39,120 | 3.2L 6cyl 6M V6 RWD | 17 city 25 hwy | 7 cu.ft. | 8.3 | 8.8 | 7.6 | 6.0 | **7.8** |
| **Nissan 350Z** | $34,150- $37,550 | 3.5L 6cyl 6M V6 RWD | 20 city 26 hwy | 7 cu.ft. | 8.9 | 7.3 | 8.0 | 5.5 | **7.8** |
| **Chrysler Sebring** | $25,410- $31,020 | 2.4L 4cyl 4A Inline 4 FWD | 22 city 30 hwy | 11 cu.ft. | 6.9 | 7.8 | 6.6 | 7.0 | **7.0** |

# Convertible Under $45,000

| Vehicle | Price Range | Base Drivetrain | EPA Fuel Rating (mpg) | Cargo/ Trunk Capacity | The Drive | The Ride | Design | Cargo/ Passenger Space | Overall Rating |
|---|---|---|---|---|---|---|---|---|---|
| BMW 3 Series | $39,000-$44,600 '1 Editors' Rating | 2.5L 6cyl 5M Inline 6 RWD | 19 city 26 hwy | N/A | 9.3 | 7.8 | 8.6 | 6.3 | 8.3 |
| Audi A4/S4 | $35,750-$55,150 | 1.8L 4cyl CVT Inline 4 FWD | 23 city 30 hwy | 10 cu.ft. | 8.1 | 8.5 | 8.8 | 7.3 | 8.2 |
| Porsche Boxster | $43,800-$53,100 | 2.7L 6cyl 5M RWD | 17-18 city 26 hwy | 9 cu.ft. | 8.6 | 7.8 | 7.3 | 8.5 | 8.0 |
| Saab 9-3 | $37,100-$42,600 | 2.0L 4cyl 5M Inline 4 FWD | 23 city 34 hwy | 12 cu.ft. | 7.3 | 8.3 | 7.5 | 7.8 | 7.5 |
| Audi TT | $35,500-$43,150 | 1.8L 4cyl 6A Inline 4 FWD | 20 city 29 hwy | 8 cu.ft. | 7.1 | 6.3 | 8.5 | 6.3 | 7.3 |
| Volvo C70 | N/A | 2.4L 5cyl Turbo 5A FWD | 18 city 25-27 hwy | 8 cu.ft. | 6.8 | 8.0 | 7.5 | 7.3 | 7.3 |
| Ford Thunderbird | $37,460-$38,505 | 3.9L 8cyl 5A V8 RWD | 17 city 23 hwy | 9 cu.ft. | 7.8 | 8.3 | 6.0 | 5.8 | 6.9 |

| Vehicle | Price Range | Base Drivetrain | EPA Fuel Rating (mpg) | Cargo/ Trunk Capacity | The Drive | The Ride | Design | Cargo/ Passenger Space | Overall Rating |
|---|---|---|---|---|---|---|---|---|---|
| Chevrolet Corvette | $51,445 #1 Editors' Rating | 6.0L 8cyl 6M V8 RWD | N/A | 10 cu.ft. | 9.4 | 8.8 | 8.4 | 8.0 | 8.8 |
| Mercedes-Benz SL-Class | $89,900-$127,500 | 5.0L 8cyl 7A V8 RWD | 16 city 23 hwy | 10 cu.ft. | 8.9 | 9.3 | 8.5 | 7.0 | 8.5 |
| BMW 6 Series | $76,900 | 4.4L 8cyl 6M V8 RWD | 15 city 23 hwy | 12 cu.ft. | 8.8 | 7.5 | 8.5 | 7.0 | 8.1 |
| Cadillac XLR | $75,835 | 4.6L 8cyl 5A V8 RWD | N/A | 12 cu.ft. | 8.5 | 8.3 | 8.1 | 6.8 | 8.0 |
| Lexus SC 430 | $63,175 | 4.3L 8cyl 5A V8 RWD | 18 city 23 hwy | 9 cu.ft. | 7.6 | 7.8 | 8.8 | 7.8 | 8.0 |
| Mercedes-Benz CLK-Class | $52,700-$61,200 | 3.2L 6cyl 5A V6 RWD | 20 city 26 hwy | 9 cu.ft. | 8.1 | 8.8 | 8.5 | 5.3 | 7.8 |
| Mercedes-Benz SLK-Class | $45,500 | 3.5L 6cyl 6M V6 RWD | 18 city 25 hwy | 10 cu.ft. | 8.4 | 8.8 | 7.4 | 6.8 | 7.8 |
| Dodge Viper | $81,495 | 8.3L 10cyl 6M V10 RWD | N/A | 8 cu.ft. | 8.8 | 6.3 | 8.1 | 4.8 | 7.5 |
| Jaguar XK-Series | $74,830-$86,330 | 4.2L 8cyl 6A V8 RWD | 18 city 26 hwy | 11 cu.ft. | 7.8 | 6.8 | 7.6 | 6.8 | 7.4 |

# Top 10 Things to Consider Before Buying

**Size/Market Segment:** Sport-utility vehicles are generally classified into three groups: mini/compact, midsize and full-size. As you move up in size you also move up in engine power, towing ability, passenger room and price.

**Price:** Compact SUVs are the most affordable with prices for base models starting at less than $20,000. Mid- and full-size sport-utes vary greatly, with base models starting in the mid-$20Ks and going all the way up to the mid-$40Ks or higher for top-of-the-line luxury models.

**Engine/Fuel Economy:** Compact SUVs offer both four- and six-cylinder engines, while midsize sport-utes typically come standard with six-cylinder engines with V8s as options. All full-size SUVs use V8 engines. The most economical four-cylinder compact SUVs can achieve mileage figures in the mid-to-upper 20s, while most six-cylinder sport-utes average in the upper teens. Full-size vehicles generally get between 12 and 20 mpg.

**Safety:** Midsize and full-size SUVs generally have the latest, most extensive safety systems available. These include side curtain airbags, rollover protection systems and electronic stability control. Most compact sport-utes offer side airbags as an option, but none offer stability control and/or rollover protection systems.

**Luxury Features/Convenience:** Most compact sport-utes offer basic amenities along with simple upgrades like CD changers and leather. Midsize SUVs typically come packed with convenience features while offering additional luxury amenities as options. The full-size category offers the widest array of luxury sport-utilities, although several models also come in less opulent versions for more rugged use.

**Passenger Capacity/Interior Space:** All but a few SUVs are designed to carry at least five passengers. The rear seats in most compact SUVs are tight for three adults, but most midsize and full-size sport-utes offer comfortable second-row accommodations. Many mid- and full-size sport-utes now offer the option of adding a third-row seat for additional passenger capacity.

**Cargo capacity:** All sport-utes allow you to fold or remove the rear seats for more cargo capacity (many SUVs with third-row seats allow you to fold them into the floor). Compact sport-utes offer up to 65 cubic feet of capacity, while midsize 'utes can expand to as much as 100 cubic feet. Full-size SUVs offer cargo areas in excess of 100 cubic feet.

**Car-based vs. Truck-based:** Car-based SUVs generally provide sharper handling, a more comfortable ride and, in some cases, more interior room. Truck-based sport-utes are able to tow more weight, are more capable off-road and are generally sturdier all around due to their truck-derived hardware.

**2WD/4WD/AWD:** Two-wheel drive means that only the front or rear wheels provide power to the vehicle. Four-wheel-drive vehicles allow the driver to select between two- and four-wheel drive, and provide low-range gearing for off-roading. All-wheel-drive vehicles automatically distribute power in varying degrees to the wheels with the most traction.

**Operating Costs:** Since compact SUVs are generally smaller, lighter and have less complex four-wheel-drive systems, their maintenance and fuel costs are generally lower. With higher sticker prices and larger engines, midsize and full-size sport-utes generally get poor mileage and are more expensive to insure.

# SUVs Under $25,000

**Market Leaders:** This relatively new segment has experienced explosive growth over the last several years resulting in a wide range of vehicles to choose from. Designed to offer solid on-road handling and moderate off-road capability, most SUVs in this price range have room for five and decent cargo room. One of the newest vehicles in this class is also one of the most well thought out. Featuring innovative ideas like a sliding rear seat, an integrated cargo tray that doubles as a picnic table and even optional heated leather seats, the Chevrolet Equinox has taken the small SUV class to a totally new level. A 3.4-liter V6 provides plenty of power, and optional all-wheel drive lends surefooted capability in less-than-ideal conditions. The Ford Escape (and its Mazda twin, the Tribute) is another good choice, offering strong V6 power, a comfortable ride and tough suspension worthy of the occasional off-road excursion. Like many vehicles in this class, four-wheel-drive Escapes feature a drive system that automatically engages the rear wheels when traction is lost up front thereby making it a dependable all-weather companion. Ford has also come out with a new hybrid version of the Escape for 2005 that allows SUV buyers to literally have their cake and eat it too, thanks to a gas-electric drivetrain that offers plentiful power, a smooth ride and outstanding fuel economy that tops everything else in its class. For those who like the Escape's carlike ride and nimble handling but desire a little more luxury, Mercury offers its own version called the Mariner, which presents opulent options such as heated leather and suede seats, wood interior trim and a powerful Mach stereo. Another top choice is the recently introduced Kia Sorento. With a standard V6, roomy interior, dual-range gearing and a 100,000-mile drivetrain warranty, the Sorento promises a lot of utility for a very reasonable price. On a similar note, the new Hyundai Tucson has the same warranty along with features such as standard 16-inch alloy wheels, a fold-flat rear seat and a nimble size that make it a worthwhile option to consider. Buyers looking for more economical power plants and a more nimble feel might prefer the Toyota RAV4 or Honda CR-V utilities instead. Both offer smooth yet frugal four-cylinder engines along with quick steering and carlike handling that make them excellent commuter vehicles as well as weekend family haulers. Honda also offers the Element, a boxy, youth-oriented vehicle that shares the CR-V's mechanical elements but adds greater interior space and reverse-opening rear doors. Shoppers on a tight budget might do well to consider the all-new-for-'05 Kia Sportage, which should give its Japanese competitors a run for their money thanks to its standard 100,000-mile warranty, six standard airbags, unique interior trim and a powerful optional V6 engine. Lastly, the Subaru Forester doesn't look like a typical SUV, but with full-time all-wheel drive, respectable ground clearance and nearly as much interior room as its competitors, it has all the necessary ingredients to compete in this category.

**Others to consider:** Although most compact SUVs are designed for light-duty off-roading only, there are still a few that can tackle tougher trails. The Jeep Wrangler is your classic soft-top off-roadster. It has two doors, a bouncy ride and primitive interior ergonomics, but when it comes to rock crawling, especially in top-level Rubicon trim, it has no peer. The Wrangler Unlimited is essentially a stretched version of the classic Jeep, and an extra eight inches behind the doors transforms the primitive sport-ute into a fairly functional vehicle with a usable backseat. The significantly more modern four-door Liberty offers all the latest amenities and a plush interior along with excellent off-road ability and rugged styling. If you can do without off-road ability but need lots of room inside, the Hyundai Santa Fe and Saturn Vue are capable candidates. Both offer some of the highest cargo capacities in the class along with strong V6 engines and comfortable rides. Mitsubishi's Outlander is a strong choice if you're looking for unique styling inside and out. It offers a refined ride, nimble handling, comfortable seating and, thanks to a power increase for 2004, respectable acceleration. Pontiac's Aztek is a possibility for those who need extra space, but its awkward styling may not sit well with many buyers. Rounding out the category is the Suzuki XL-7. Although the XL-7 offers the advantage of three rows of seating in a compact SUV body, in all other respects, it's years behind the competition and doesn't warrant much consideration.

## SUVs under $35,000

**Market Leaders:** This is one of the most heavily populated categories in the industry and therefore offers the widest array of choices for the potential buyer. There are two general types of vehicles in this category: car-based SUVs that are biased toward on-road handling and comfort, and the more rugged truck-based vehicles that offer increased towing capacity and true off-road ability. The top truck-based SUVs are the Dodge Durango, Ford Explorer, Toyota 4Runner, Nissan Pathfinder and Jeep Grand Cherokee. All are similar in size, power and features and can tackle moderate terrain with ease. The Ford Explorer is an excellent all-around vehicle, as it provides solid handling, automatic four-wheel drive and a simple yet functional interior. It's not necessarily the biggest, fastest or most stylish, but when it comes to everyday family duty, you're not likely going to need much more than a well-equipped Explorer. Dodge's Durango straddles the line between midsize and full-size SUVs. Besides providing roomy quarters for seven, it offers a refined on-road demeanor and a diverse engine lineup that includes a 335-hp, 5.7-liter Hemi V8 for families with big towing jobs. Toyota's 4Runner lives up to its reputation as a tough, off-road-ready utility vehicle, while at the same time offering all the latest in modern conveniences. With electronic traction, stability and hill descent control, this is the SUV you want for tackling rough trails or snow-covered hills. Nissan's new Pathfinder uses a similar array of advanced off-road equipment to keep it nimble in the rough stuff while its powerful V6 assures plenty of power on the highway. However, if you plan on traveling far off the beaten path, the all-new Jeep Grand Cherokee would be your best bet. Capable of attacking treacherous trails while still maintaining civil manners on the street, the new Jeep features a refined interior and relatively plush surroundings perfect for commuter duty as well as hard-core options such as an available Hemi V8, locking low-range four-wheel drive and electronic traction control specifically designed for tackling off-road obstacles.

When it comes to car-based SUVs, there are several family-friendly vehicles to choose from along with a couple sporty European entries. The top contenders in the class include the Honda Pilot, Mitsubishi Endeavor and Toyota Highlander. With seating for up to eight, a strong V6, automatic all-wheel drive and a highly functional interior, the Pilot makes a great all-around family vehicle. Toyota's Highlander delivers a refined, carlike driving experience along with a sizable backseat, decent cargo room and excellent build quality; you can also get an optional third-row seat. Mitsubishi's new Endeavor packs a powerful V6 and a roomy cabin into a stylish outer shell that won't get lost in a crowd. If you don't need space for a big family, the BMW X3 and Land Rover Freelander provide the all-weather capability and high seating position of traditional SUVs along with excellent on-road handling characteristics.

**Other to consider:** Another car-based SUV to consider is the Nissan Murano. It offers sleek styling, a powerful V6 engine, comfortable interior and excellent handling; a poorly calibrated continuously variable transmission (CVT) is the only thing that keeps the Murano from being a top pick. Buick's Rendezvous also fits into this category, as it offers the traction of all-wheel drive along with a compliant ride, large cabin and numerous family-friendly features. Both the Chevrolet TrailBlazer and GMC Envoy are available in standard and long-wheelbase versions with the latter offering the most passenger and cargo room in the class as well as optional V8 power. Yet another variation is the Envoy XUV which is basically a long-wheelbase Envoy with a utility bed enclosed by a power-sliding roof. The Isuzu Ascender is also worth considering, as it is simply a rebadged version of the long-wheelbase TrailBlazer albeit with a longer warranty. All GM midsize SUVs get a strong standard six-cylinder engine, but overly soft suspensions deliver a less-controlled ride than the competition.

# SUVs Under $45,000

**Market Leaders:** This segment includes some of the most popular SUVs on the market and for good reason. With expansive cabins that seat up to nine, ample cargo capacities and the ability to tow and haul as much as most full-size pickups, the super-size family vehicles in this price bracket are some of the most versatile sport-utes on the market. Additionally, as sport-utility vehicles continue to push upscale, this category has expanded to include a lengthy list of luxury candidates, most of them midsize in dimensions.

Among the luxury vehicles, two of the top contenders are the Volkswagen Touareg and the Cadillac SRX. The Touareg may be Volkswagen's first SUV but it's competitive right out of the gate thanks to a sharp interior design, capable suspension and impressive handling dynamics. It offers six- and eight-cylinder gasoline engines, as well as a cutting-edge V10 TDI turbodiesel that pumps out an incredible 310 horsepower and 553 pound-feet of torque. Adjustable air suspension with a locking low-range offers true off-road ability, and the leather- and wood-lined cabin looks and feels first-class throughout. With no third-row seating and limited cargo room, the Touareg isn't the most practical SUV in this class, but in nearly every other respect it's an impressive vehicle. With seating for seven, an available 320-hp V8 and nimble carlike handling, the Cadillac SRX excels at providing functionality and performance in one complete package. Add in unique features like a nearly full-length sunroof, OnStar communications system, top-notch DVD entertainment center and a power-folding third-row seat, and it's easy to see why this new Cadillac presents an intriguing alternative to the dominant imports. Also worthy of a second look are the Infiniti FX35 and FX45. Both offer dynamic styling and handling to match, as they drive more like sport sedans than sport-utility vehicles. There's not much in the way of cargo space and its off-road capability is limited, but it's a thrill behind the wheel and comfortable for four. Other top contenders in this class include the Volvo XC90, Acura MDX and Lexus RX 330. The Volvo XC90 also offers three rows of seating, a substantial features list and, of course, Volvo's long-standing reputation for safety. Its standard turbocharged engine can't match the Cadillac's in terms of pure power, but a new V8 option should be more than enough to keep it competitive. Much the same could be said about Acura's MDX, as it offers a sizable interior that's loaded with features along with an ease about town that makes it a pleasant daily driver. For those willing to give up utility in the name of luxury, the Lexus RX 330 won't disappoint. It's not quite as athletic as the others, nor does it offer third-row seating, but when it comes to providing a plush ride and a luxurious interior, the RX 330 is hard to beat.

In the full-size SUV crowd, the top contenders are the Toyota Sequoia and the Chevrolet Tahoe/GMC Yukon twins. The Sequoia's strengths are its easy-to-drive character, well-appointed cabin and smooth, refined drivetrain. It's more nimble around town than its size might suggest, yet there are still three rows of seats and plenty of cargo space when needed. If you have a medium-size family and your trips don't often involve towing heavy toys, the Sequoia is a solid choice. The Chevy Tahoe (or its GMC Yukon twin) offers equivalent passenger and cargo room along with an optional 5.3-liter V8 that provides plenty of muscle for towing duty. The cabin is well laid out, if not a little heavy on the plastic, and its ride and handling are well suited for daily driving. For those who need a little extra when it comes to size and capability, the slightly larger Chevrolet Suburban and its GMC twin, the Yukon XL, add even more cabin space and get the larger V8 as standard equipment. These bigger sport-utes are also available in heavy-duty three-quarter-ton versions that offer options like four-wheel steering and high-torque engines that give them additional stability and power for towing heavy loads.

**Others to consider:** Its very existence may be sacrilegious to some, but the Porsche Cayenne is a surprisingly adept SUV that's impressive in almost any environment. On the street, it possesses the kind of sharp, precise handling you would expect from a Porsche, and the standard V6 model just barely lets it sneak in under the wire of this price category. Of course the top-of-the-line twin-turbo V8 adds thrilling performance that few sport-utes can match, and all-wheel drive helps put all that power to the pavement. Taken off-road, its dual-range gearing and compliant suspension allow it to tackle tougher terrain than you might think. While the Cayenne's interior accom-modations aren't geared toward maximum utility, there's enough room for four and a moderate amount of cargo. It's not an SUV for everyone, but for those who really want the Porsche of SUVs, the Cayenne lives up to its billing. For those seeking luxury and utility along with solid off-road ability, Land Rover has an exciting new offering that should help propel the British marque to the front of the pack. After two decades of production, the Discovery has been replaced with the all-new LR3, which boasts features like a 300-hp Jaguar-sourced V8, stadium-style seating that offers stellar views and unparalleled legroom in all three rows, a panoramic glass roof and an optional surround-sound stereo. A cutting-edge new suspension design that utilizes variable ride height and computer-controlled traction and stability assist should make trekking across jungle trails and traffic-clogged highways equally effortless, and the plush interior is exactly what one would expect from a Land Rover.

The Ford Expedition is another strong entrant in this category, as it features a manageable size, nicely appointed interior and smooth ride thanks to a fully independent suspension. Items like standard fold-flat third-row seats and optional side curtain airbags for the first two rows make it a safe and functional family vehicle. The Expedition's only major drawback is its overtaxed engine that fails to deliver much punch when passing or merging. No such problem exists with the other notable entrant in this category, as its burly V8 gives it acceleration on par with many sport sedans. We're talking about Nissan's new Pathfinder Armada, and in addition to its impres-sive power plant, the Armada also serves up a spacious interior, optional DVD navigation and extroverted styling that no other SUV in this segment can match. If you're looking for a vehicle that's a little bit different yet still provides all the latest features, the Pathfinder Armada is worth a look. Finally, there's Ford's extra-large Excursion sport-ute. This brute manages to provide even more passenger and cargo room than the Suburban, along with an optional diesel engine for heavy-duty towing tasks. It's not anywhere near as refined as the competition, but if you need maximum passenger and towing capacity, the Excursion provides more than enough of both.

Other luxury entrants include BMW's X5, which is light on utility but big on performance. A slight freshening for 2004 added a more powerful engine, a new all-wheel-drive system and slightly revised styling. With minimal cargo capacity, it's not the best family vehicle, but for those who want a tall vehicle that still drives like a sedan, the X5 has few peers. Lincoln's Aviator is another strong performer, thanks to a powerful V8 power plant and a well-sorted suspension. Although its over-the-road manners can't quite match the X5's, the Aviator offers a more complete overall package, as it also includes three rows of seats and a plush, fully-equipped interior. Mercedes' M-Class sport-ute is yet another solid all-around performer in this class, but with a full redesign on the way for the 2006 model year, buying this year's lame duck model is only recommended for bargain seekers.

## SUVs Over $45,000

**Market Leaders:** This was a virtually nonexistent group just a few years ago, but continued growth in the luxury SUV segment has generated several new contenders, particularly in the midsize category. As competent as the new competitors are, however, the dominant player in this field just so happens to be the oldest. The venerable Range Rover from the off-road specialists at Land Rover is a top-of-the-line sport-utility that delivers on its rugged heritage while at the same time offering all the latest amenities in a well-trimmed interior. Fully redesigned in 2003, the Range Rover sports a BMW V8 engine and a sophisticated height-adjustable air suspension. This combination provides above-average abilities both on- and off-road with plenty of power for any situation. Interior space is still at a premium, but a much improved cabin design gives it the kind of upscale look and feel you would expect from a vehicle in this price range. An equally capable vehicle is available in the form of the Lexus LX 470. Unremarkable in speed or style, the LX impresses with a level of refinement not usually found in an SUV. Its elegant interior is covered in the finest leather and wood trim and like most Lexus vehicles its build quality is first-rate. Like the Range Rover, the Lexus shines both on and off the pavement, although its smallish V8 isn't always up to the task of getting it up to speed in a hurry. Interior space is also at a premium, but unless you use the third-row seats on a regular basis you're not likely to notice. If you're looking for a luxurious SUV that leans toward the subtle side of the spectrum, the LX 470 won't disappoint.

If you're looking for a full-size luxury ride, GM offers a pair of 'utes with larger-than-life personalities, while Infiniti brings a new player to the segment. In GM's stable, you'll find the Cadillac Escalade, which packs the most powerful engine in the class and all the latest features into an in-your-face body style that leaves no question as to what class it belongs in. It doesn't pretend to be a true off-road vehicle but if asked it performs admirably in rough terrain. Behind the bold façade hides a well-rounded, easy-to-drive luxury vehicle that coddles its passengers with soft leather seats and the sounds of a high-powered Bose audio system. There's plenty of room for five passengers and some cargo, but if that's not enough, there's a long-wheelbase ESV version with even more space inside. There's nothing subtle about the Escalade, but there's not much wrong with it either. On the other side of the coin is the Hummer H2, a downsized version of the original H1. It shares its big brother's looks but packs modern mechanicals underneath for added civility on the street. It's still a bear in traffic and a pain to park, but out in the wild there are few vehicles that can match its abilities. The interior is geared toward functionality more so than luxury and cargo space is limited, but it's comfortable enough for four. If you're willing to make a few compromises and you don't need all the trappings of a true luxury sport-ute, the H2 is a unique vehicle unmatched by anything else in the category. Infiniti's QX56, an upscale version of Nissan's Pathfinder Armada, is a formidable challenger for the Escalade. With up to 390 lb-ft of torque churned out of its powerful V8, the QX56 now leads the group in towing capacity and an ideal choice for well-to-do families with a boat to tow. Inside, the Infiniti offers plenty of room for seven or eight passengers to spread out, along with a full load of amenities, including a standard power liftgate and DVD-based navigation system and options like adaptive cruise control and a DVD entertainment system.

**Others to consider:** A luxury sport-ute that's able to effectively bridge the gap between on-road luxury and off-road capability is the GX 470 from Lexus. Slightly smaller than the top-of-the-line LX 470, the GX shares the same drivetrain and offers a similarly impressive repertoire of skills both on the road and off. The lavish interior is as comfortable as it is functional and with three rows of seating it can carry seven in a pinch. Among the two other full-size candidates is another former military vehicle. The Mercedes G500 and performance-tuned G55 sport boxy styling and serious off-road prowess, along with an interior stuffed full of S-Class trimmings. Compared to more modern vehicles, they're crude on the street and interior ergonomics are poor, but when it comes to originality only the H2 can match the G-Class. Those looking for a more traditional luxury sport-utility might also check out the Lincoln Navigator. Much like the Escalade in price and purpose, the Navigator provides ample power, upscale styling and a plush interior for buyers more interested in around-town comfort than backcountry capability. It doesn't feel as quick on its feet as the Escalade, but for more relaxed efforts it handles itself well.

| Vehicle | Price Range | Base Drivetrain | EPA Fuel Rating (mpg) | Cargo Capacity | The Drive | The Ride | Design | Cargo/ Passenger Space | Overall Rating |
|---|---|---|---|---|---|---|---|---|---|
| Kia Sorento | $18,995-$25,500 '1 Editors' Rating | 3.5L 6cyl 5M V6 RWD | 16 city 19 hwy | 66 cu.ft. | 8.6 | 8.3 | 8.8 | 8.8 | 8.6 |
| Honda CR-V | $19,995-$25,050 | 2.4L 4cyl 5A Inline 4 FWD | 23 city 29 hwy | 72 cu.ft. | 7.6 | 8.3 | 8.9 | 8.8 | 8.3 |
| Chevrolet Equinox | $21,095-$24,435 | 3.4L 6cyl 5A V6 FWD | N/A | 69 cu.ft. | 7.8 | 9.0 | 8.1 | 8.3 | 8.2 |
| Honda Element | N/A | 2.4L 4cyl 5M FWD | 21-22 city 24-26 hwy | 75 cu.ft. | 8.1 | 7.8 | 8.4 | 8.0 | 8.1 |
| Subaru Forester | $21,295-$28,195 | 2.5L 4cyl 4A Horizontally Opposed AWD | 21 city 26 hwy | 64 cu.ft. | 8.1 | 7.8 | 8.3 | 7.5 | 8.0 |
| Ford Escape | $19,265-$28,005 | 2.3L 4cyl 5M Inline 4 FWD | 24 city 29 hwy | 66 cu.ft. | 8.1 | 8.0 | 7.4 | 8.0 | 7.8 |
| Mazda Tribute | $19,630-$24,390 | 2.3L 4cyl 5M Inline 4 FWD | 24 city 29 hwy | 67 cu.ft. | 8.3 | 7.5 | 7.5 | 8.0 | 7.8 |
| Mercury Mariner | $21,405-$26,405 | 2.3L 4cyl 4A Inline 4 FWD | 22 city 26 hwy | 66 cu.ft. | 8.1 | 7.5 | 7.6 | 7.8 | 7.8 |
| Jeep Liberty | $19,265-$25,110 | 2.4L 4cyl 6M Inline 4 RWD | 20 city 24 hwy | 69 cu.ft. | 7.8 | 8.3 | 7.8 | 7.3 | 7.7 |

# SUV Under $25,000

| Vehicle | Price Range | Base Drivetrain | EPA Fuel Rating (mpg) | Cargo Capacity | The Drive | The Ride | Design | Cargo/ Passenger Space | Overall Rating |
|---|---|---|---|---|---|---|---|---|---|
| **Mitsubishi Outlander** | $17,799-$25,179 | 2.4L 4cyl 5M Inline 4 FWD | N/A | 60 cu. ft. | 7.0 | 8.0 | 8.3 | 7.5 | **7.6** |
| **Toyota Highlander** | $24,080-$31,380 | 2.4L 4cyl 4A Inline 4 FWD | 22 city 27 hwy | 81 cu. ft. | 8.0 | 7.3 | 7.1 | 8.3 | **7.6** |
| **Toyota RAV4** | $18,550-$21,000 | 2.4L 4cyl 5M Inline 4 FWD | 24 city 30 hwy | 68 cu. ft. | 7.5 | 7.0 | 8.0 | 7.0 | **7.4** |
| **Hyundai Santa Fe** | $21,499-$25,499 | 2.4L 4cyl 5M FWD | 16-20 city 21-27 hwy | 78 cu. ft. | 7.6 | 7.3 | 6.6 | 7.8 | **7.3** |
| **Hyundai Tucson** | $17,499-$22,749 | 2.0L 4cyl 5M Inline 4 FWD | 22 city 27 hwy | 66 cu. ft. | 7.3 | 7.5 | 7.0 | 7.5 | **7.3** |
| **Suzuki XL-7** | $20,399-$27,799 | 2.7L 6cyl 5M V6 RWD | 17 city 22 hwy | 75 cu. ft. | 7.9 | 7.8 | 6.9 | 6.3 | **7.3** |
| **Suzuki Grand Vitara** | $18,399-$22,599 | 2.5L 6cyl 5M V6 RWD | 19 city 22 hwy | 50 cu. ft. | 6.0 | 7.5 | 8.0 | 6.8 | **7.0** |
| **Jeep Wrangler** | $17,900-$29,040 | 2.4L 4cyl 6M Inline 4 4WD | 18 city 20 hwy | 47 cu. ft. | 7.0 | 6.0 | 7.8 | 6.0 | **6.9** |
| **Pontiac Aztek** | $21,375-$24,290 | 3.4L 6cyl 4A V6 FWD | N/A | 94 cu. ft. | 6.4 | 8.0 | 6.5 | 7.8 | **6.8** |

| Vehicle | Price Range | Base Drivetrain | EPA Fuel Rating (mpg) | Cargo Capacity | The Drive | The Ride | Design | Cargo/ Passenger Space | Overall Rating |
|---|---|---|---|---|---|---|---|---|---|
| Saturn VUE | $17,630- $24,890 | 2.2L 4cyl 5M Inline 4 FWD | 24 city 29 hwy | 64 cu.ft. | 6.6 | 6.0 | 7.0 | 6.5 | 6.6 |
| Chevrolet Blazer | $21,165- $26,435 | 4.3L 6cyl 5M V6 RWD | 15 city 21 hwy | 61 cu.ft. | 5.1 | 5.8 | 5.0 | 6.5 | 5.4 |

# SUV Under $35,000

| Vehicle | Price Range | Base Drivetrain | EPA Fuel Rating (mpg) | Cargo Capacity | The Drive | The Ride | Design | Cargo/ Passenger Space | Overall Rating |
|---|---|---|---|---|---|---|---|---|---|
| Toyota 4Runner | $27,495-$37,495 '1 Editors' Rating | 4.0L 6cyl 5A V6 RWD | 18 city 21 hwy | N/A | 8.4 | 8.8 | 8.1 | 9.5 | **8.5** |
| Honda Pilot | $27,350-$34,120 | 3.5L 6cyl 5A V6 AWD | 17 city 22 hwy | 90 cu.ft. | 7.9 | 9.0 | 8.0 | 8.8 | **8.3** |
| Toyota Sequoia | $32,470-$44,960 | 4.7L 8cyl 5A V8 RWD | 14 city 18 hwy | 128 cu.ft. | 8.6 | 8.8 | 7.9 | 8.3 | **8.3** |
| BMW X3 | $30,300-$36,300 | 2.5L 6cyl 6M AWD | 16-18 city 23-24 hwy | 71 cu.ft. | 9.0 | 8.5 | 7.5 | 7.3 | **8.1** |
| Dodge Durango | $26,735-$35,590 | 3.7L 6cyl 4A V6 RWD | 15 city 21 hwy | 102 cu.ft. | 8.4 | 8.3 | 7.6 | 8.3 | **8.1** |
| Jeep Grand Cherokee | $26,130-$34,045 | 3.7L 6cyl 5A V6 RWD | 16 city 21 hwy | 67 cu.ft. | 8.5 | 8.0 | 7.8 | 8.0 | **8.1** |
| Nissan Murano | $26,850-$30,900 | 3.5L 6cyl CVT FWD | 20 city 24-25 hwy | 82 cu.ft. | 7.9 | 8.5 | 8.1 | 8.3 | **8.1** |
| Mitsubishi Endeavor | $25,399-$33,199 | 3.8L 6cyl 4A V6 FWD | N/A | 76 cu.ft. | 7.9 | 8.0 | 7.9 | 8.0 | **8.0** |
| Mercury Mountaineer | $29,685-$38,530 | 4.0L 6cyl 5A V6 RWD | 16 city 21 hwy | 81 cu.ft. | 7.8 | 8.3 | 7.4 | 9.0 | **7.9** |

| Vehicle | Price Range | Base Drivetrain | EPA Fuel Rating (mpg) | Cargo Capacity | The Drive | The Ride | Design | Cargo/ Passenger Space | Overall Rating |
|---|---|---|---|---|---|---|---|---|---|
| Nissan Armada | $33,600-$41,500 | 5.6L 8cyl 5A V8 RWD | 13 city 19 hwy | 97 cu.ft. | 8.4 | 7.8 | 7.6 | 7.8 | 7.9 |
| Volvo XC70 | $34,810 | 2.5L 5cyl 5A Inline 5 AWD | 19 city 24 hwy | 71 cu.ft. | 7.8 | 8.5 | 8.3 | 6.8 | 7.9 |
| Ford Expedition | $31,395-$43,860 | 5.4L 8cyl 4A V8 4WD | N/A | 111 cu.ft. | 7.8 | 7.8 | 7.3 | 9.0 | 7.8 |
| Ford Explorer | $26,770-$37,530 | 4.0L 6cyl 5A V6 RWD | N/A | 86 cu.ft. | 7.8 | 8.3 | 7.1 | 9.0 | 7.8 |
| Volvo XC90 | $34,840-$41,015 | 2.5L 5cyl 5A Inline 5 FWD | 18 city 24 hwy | 92 cu.ft. | 7.8 | 8.5 | 8.3 | 6.8 | 7.8 |
| Nissan Pathfinder | $24,650-$34,750 | 4L 6cyl 5A V6 RWD | 16 city 23 hwy | 79 cu.ft. | 7.6 | 7.0 | 7.3 | 7.8 | 7.4 |
| Land Rover Freelander | $26,830 | 2.5L 6cyl 5A V6 AWD | 18 city 21 hwy | 47 cu.ft. | 7.5 | 6.8 | 7.3 | 7.8 | 7.2 |
| Buick Rendezvous | $26,585-$39,220 | 3.4L 6cyl 4A V6 FWD | N/A | 109 cu.ft. | 6.0 | 7.0 | 6.9 | 8.5 | 6.8 |
| Isuzu Ascender | N/A | 4.2L 6cyl 4A RWD | 14-16 city 18-21 hwy | 80 cu.ft. | 6.0 | 7.3 | 6.9 | 6.8 | 6.6 |

# SUV Under $35,000

| Vehicle | Price Range | Base Drivetrain | EPA Fuel Rating (mpg) | Cargo Capacity | The Drive | The Ride | Design | Cargo/ Passenger Space | Overall Rating |
|---------|-------------|-----------------|-----------------------|----------------|-----------|----------|--------|------------------------|----------------|
| Chevrolet TrailBlazer/TrailBlazer EXT | $27,520-$34,220 | 4.2L 6cyl 4A Inline 6 RWD | N/A | 80 cu.ft. | 6.5 | 6.3 | 6.3 | 7.0 | 6.4 |
| GMC Envoy, Envoy XL, Envoy XUV | $29,750-$37,840 | 4.2L 6cyl 4A Inline 6 RWD | N/A | 80 cu.ft. | 5.8 | 6.5 | 6.4 | 7.5 | 6.4 |
| Mitubishi Montero | $35,799 | 3.8L 6cyl 5A 4WD | 15 city 19 hwy | 92 cu.ft. | 5.6 | 5.8 | 7.0 | 7.0 | 6.3 |
| Infiniti FX35 | $34,750-$36,250 | 3.5L 6cyl 5A V6 RWD | 17 city 23 hwy | 65 cu.ft. | N/A | N/A | N/A | N/A | N/A |

For the latest full vehicle reports, visit www.edmunds.com/bginfopak

| Vehicle | Price Range | Base Drivetrain | EPA Fuel Rating (mpg) | Cargo Capacity | The Drive | The Ride | Design | Cargo/ Passenger Space | Overall Rating |
|---|---|---|---|---|---|---|---|---|---|
| Land Rover LR3 | $44,330-$49,330 '1 Editors' Rating | 4.4L 8cyl 6A V8 4WD | 14 city 18 hwy | 90 cu. ft. | 8.4 | 8.8 | 8.5 | 9.0 | 8.6 |
| Lexus RX 330 | $35,775-$37,175 | 3.3L 6cyl 5A V6 FWD | 20 city 26 hwy | 85 cu. ft. | 8.0 | 8.5 | 8.6 | 8.3 | 8.3 |
| Cadillac SRX | $38,340-$52,035 | 3.6L 6cyl 5A V6 RWD | N/A | 70 cu. ft. | 8.0 | 8.8 | 7.9 | 8.3 | 8.1 |
| Acura MDX | $36,700-$43,775 | 3.5L 6cyl 5A V6 AWD | 17 city 23 hwy | 82 cu. ft. | 8.6 | 9.0 | 7.0 | 8.0 | 8.0 |
| BMW X5 | $41,700-$70,100 | 3.0L 6cyl 6M Inline 6 AWD | 15 city 21 hwy | N/A | 8.8 | 8.5 | 7.6 | 7.5 | 8.0 |
| Volkswagen Touareg | $37,140-$58,490 | 3.2L 6cyl 6A V6 AWD | 15 city 20 hwy | 71 cu. ft. | 8.0 | 7.0 | 7.8 | 7.5 | 7.6 |
| Chevrolet Suburban | $37,850-$47,550 | 5.3L 8cyl 4A V8 RWD | N/A | 132 cu. ft. | 7.5 | 8.0 | 6.6 | 8.0 | 7.4 |
| Lincoln Aviator | $40,615-$43,565 | 4.6L 8cyl 5A V8 RWD | 13 city 19 hwy | 78 cu. ft. | 6.8 | 7.5 | 7.8 | 8.0 | 7.4 |
| GMC Yukon/Chevrolet Tahoe | $35,460-$49,860 | 4.8L 8cyl 4A V8 RWD | N/A | 105 cu. ft. | 7.5 | 7.8 | 6.6 | 8.0 | 7.3 |

# SUV Under $45,000

| Vehicle | Price Range | Base Drivetrain | EPA Fuel Rating (mpg) | Cargo Capacity | The Drive | The Ride | Design | Cargo/ Passenger Space | Overall Rating |
|---|---|---|---|---|---|---|---|---|---|
| GMC Yukon XL | $38,510-$51,510 | 5.3L 8cyl 4A V8 RWD | 15 city 20 hwy | 132 cu. ft. | 7.5 | 7.8 | 6.6 | 8.0 | 7.3 |
| Mercedes-Benz M-Class | $37,950-$46,400 | 3.7L 6cyl 5A V6 AWD | 15 city 18 hwy | 81 cu. ft. | 6.9 | 7.0 | 7.6 | 6.8 | 7.0 |
| Buick Rainier | $35,080-$36,905 | 4.2L 6cyl 4A Inline 6 RWD | N/A | 80 cu. ft. | 6.1 | 7.0 | 7.0 | 6.8 | 6.6 |
| Ford Excursion | $37,165-$50,420 | 5.4L 8cyl 4A V8 RWD | N/A | 146 cu. ft. | 6.6 | 6.8 | 6.1 | 6.0 | 6.4 |

| Vehicle | Price Range | Base Drivetrain | EPA Fuel Rating (mpg) | Cargo Capacity | The Drive | The Ride | Design | Cargo/ Passenger Space | Overall Rating |
|---|---|---|---|---|---|---|---|---|---|
| Lexus LX 470 | $64,775 **#1** Editors' Rating | 4.7L 8cyl 5A V8 4WD | 13 city 17 hwy | 90 cu. ft. | 9.1 | 9.0 | 8.9 | 8.0 | **8.8** |
| Toyota Land Cruiser | $55,025 | 4.7L 8cyl 5A V8 4WD | 13 city 17 hwy | 91 cu. ft. | 8.6 | 9.0 | 8.8 | 8.8 | **8.7** |
| Land Rover Range Rover | $73,085 | 4.4L 8cyl 5A V8 4WD | 12 city 16 hwy | 62 cu. ft. | 8.4 | 8.0 | 8.4 | 7.0 | **8.0** |
| Lexus GX 470 | N/A | 4.7L 8cyl 5A 4WD | 15 city 18 hwy | 78 cu. ft. | 8.1 | 8.8 | 8.0 | 7.0 | **8.0** |
| Cadillac Escalade | $52,865- $55,765 | 5.3L 8cyl 4A V8 RWD | N/A | 105 cu. ft. | 8.0 | 8.8 | 7.5 | 7.5 | **7.9** |
| Cadillac Escalade ESV | $58,165- $69,535 | 6.0L 8cyl 4A V8 AWD | N/A | 132 cu. ft. | 8.1 | 8.8 | 7.4 | 7.5 | **7.9** |
| Lincoln Navigator | $49,790- $56,440 | 5.4L 8cyl 6A V8 RWD | N/A | 105 cu. ft. | 7.5 | 8.5 | 7.5 | 8.8 | **7.9** |
| Infiniti FX45 | $45,250 | 4.5L 8cyl 5A V8 AWD | 15 city 19 hwy | 65 cu. ft. | 7.5 | 7.5 | 7.6 | 6.5 | **7.4** |
| HUMMER H2/H2 SUT | $51,150- $55,945 | 6.0L 8cyl 4A V8 4WD | N/A | 87 cu. ft. | 6.4 | 7.5 | 7.0 | 6.0 | **6.6** |

# SUV Over $45,000

| Vehicle | Price Range | Base Drivetrain | EPA Fuel Rating (mpg) | Cargo Capacity | The Drive | The Ride | Design | Cargo/ Passenger Space | Overall Rating |
|---|---|---|---|---|---|---|---|---|---|
| **Mercedes-Benz G-Class** | $77,700 | 5.0L 8cyl 5A V8 4WD | 13 city 14 hwy | 80 cu. ft. | 7.3 | 5.0 | 6.1 | 5.5 | **6.2** |

# Top 10 Things to Consider Before Buying

**Size/Market Segment:** Most trucks fall into either the compact or full-size category, although there are a few models designated as midsize.

**Price :** Base model compact trucks are some of the cheapest vehicles on the market, but premium models can cost into the mid- to upper-$20Ks. Full-size trucks range from the low-$20,000s to the low-$40,000s.

**Engine/Fuel Economy:** Compact trucks offer four-, five- and six-cylinder engines that deliver respectable mileage. Full-size trucks offer six-cylinder engines on base models, but most trucks use V8 or even V10 engines that return marginal fuel economy numbers at best. Most full-size trucks also offer diesel engines that provide plenty of towing power and better mileage.

**Safety:** Most trucks offer basic safety equipment like front airbags and seatbelts for all passengers. Some newer full-size trucks offer more advanced systems like side curtain airbags and electronic stability control.

**Drivetrain:** Almost all trucks offer both manual and automatic transmissions, as well as two- and four-wheel drive. Many vehicles also offer traction-aiding devices like limited-slip/locking differentials and electronic traction control.

**Passenger Capacity/Interior Space:** There are three basic body styles for trucks: regular cab, extended cab and crew cab. Regular cabs have two doors and seat between two and three comfortably. Compact extended cabs add mostly extra storage space, while full-size versions can seat three additional passengers. Rear clamshell doors make it easier to get people and cargo in and out of the back of extended cabs. Crew cabs have four full-size doors and seat between five and six passengers comfortably.

**Versatility of Interior Seating:** Most trucks with extended or crew cabs offer the ability to either fold the entire rear seat up or at least one half or the other. Some newer full-size trucks also allow you to fold the front-passenger seat flat to provide a handy tablelike surface.

**Towing Ability:** Compact trucks can tow between 3,000 and 7,000 pounds, depending on how they're equipped. Full-size trucks can tow as much as 12,000 pounds with certain engines and suspension configurations, although most range between 8,000- and 10,000-pound capacities.

**Bed Capacity:** Most compact truck beds are 6 1/2 feet long, although a few models offer longer beds. Almost all full-size trucks offer long and short beds that range between 6 1/2 and 8 feet long depending on the brand and/or cab configuration.

**Operating Costs:** Compact trucks are generally very fuel-efficient and cheaper to insure because of their low buy-in cost. Adding four-wheel drive to any truck will further add to annual operating costs as well.

## Compact Trucks

**Market leaders:** Originally designed as economical alternatives to gas-guzzling full-size trucks, today's compact pickups offer a wide variety of sizes, features and prices. Almost every model can be found in regular, extended and crew cab body styles with four- or six- and even eight-cylinder engines. Most extended cabs offer smaller rear doors for easier access to the space behind the seats while crew cab models have full-size rear doors. After years of only minor changes in the class, Dodge, Nissan and Toyota all redesigned their compact trucks for 2005. The Dodge Dakota has the most spacious cabins, strongest engine lineup and highest maximum tow ratings. Combine these attributes with its well-sorted suspension and nicely weighted steering and it's easy to see why the Dakota is a great compromise between full-size capability and compact drivability. The base engine is a 3.7-liter V6 with 210 horsepower, but if you're willing to put up with the reduced gas mileage, the optional 230-hp, 4.7-liter V8 and new higher-performance 250-horse, 4.7 H.O. both deliver strong performance. The platform is all new for 2005, and a refined ride and optional all-wheel drive make the Dakota a stellar performer both on and off the beaten path. Another top contender is the Toyota Tacoma. With 18 different body styles, it offers something for everybody. Its range of high-tech engines includes an efficient 2.7-liter four-cylinder or a powerful 245-hp, 4.0-liter V6. Well-trimmed interiors, serious off-road hardware and several segment exclusive features are just a few more reasons why the Tacoma is worth a look. Nissan's newly invigorated Frontier doesn't offer quite as many body styles, but it does offer a class-leading V6 with its 265-hp, 4.0-liter V6. Like the Tacoma, the Frontier also offers a long list of unique options like a spray-in bedliner, adjustable bed tie-downs and several advanced off-road systems. Tough styling similar to Nissan's full-size Titan pickup also gives the Frontier an added dose of attitude for those looking for something a little different.

**Others to consider:** There are only two other significant players in this market beyond the top contenders. Although Chevrolet also calls the Colorado a midsize, it's slightly smaller than the Dakota and doesn't offer the kind of capability found in the Dodge, Nissan or Toyota pickups. What it does provide is a roomy cabin with side airbags and a choice of either a four- or five-cylinder engine. If you're not planning on doing any significant towing or hauling with your truck, the Colorado is worth looking into. Another notable truck in this class is the Ford Ranger and its Mazda twin. With its vast array of trim levels, body styles and engine options, the Ranger offers a little bit of something for everybody. Unfortunately, both of these trucks are decades-old and they deliver a choppy ride and a very average-looking interior. In the crossover department, there's the Ford Explorer Sport Trac and the Subaru Baja. Both are based on the sport-utility vehicles (the Explorer and Outback wagon, respectively) but have open utility beds instead of enclosed cargo areas. They make viable alternatives to pickups if all you need is a little extra space for weekend chores.

## Large Trucks

**Market Leaders:** The full-size pickup market is broken down into two segments: light-duty trucks that are versatile enough for everyday use, and heavy-duty trucks that are designed for worksite use or towing large loads. Trucks that are designated as "half-tons" are generally light-duty trucks while "three-quarter-ton" and "one-ton" trucks fall under the heavy-duty banner. Both segments are dominated by the offerings from Dodge, Ford and General Motors. The half-ton F-150 is the single most popular model as it offers one of the best compromises between everyday drivability and pickup practicality. A full redesign for the 2004 model year added an improved optional engine, a more carlike interior and significant improvements in ride and handling. It comes in five different trim levels ranging from the bare-bones XL to the leather-lined Lariat. It boasts the latest features and the most refined demeanor making it one of the front-runners in the category. The three-quarter-ton F-250 and one-ton F-350 models (otherwise known as the F-Super Duty) are still based on an older design, but continual improvements over the years have kept them competitive. The optional Powerstroke diesel engine gives the F-Super Duty trucks some of the highest towing and hauling ratings of any pickup truck on the market. A serious challenge to the dominance of the Big Three was launched by Nissan last year in the form of the Titan full-size pickup. It is the first full-size truck built by a foreign manufacturer that is designed to compete head-on with the dominant players from the Big Three. It matches up with the competition in virtually every dimension and capacity while offering one of the most powerful standard engines in the class. Offered as a half-ton only, the Titan comes in either extended- or crew cab body styles and boasts several segment exclusive features like a spray-in bedliner, push-button locking differential and DVD navigation. Up until the mid-'90s, Dodge's Ram truck barely registered in this segment but with two major redesigns since then it has become a more direct competitor to Ford and GM. Known for its "big rig" looks, the half-ton Ram 1500 features a spacious interior, precise steering and an optional 5.7-liter Hemi V8, the most powerful engine available in the half-ton segment. The heavy-duty Rams are well regarded for their optional Cummings turbodiesel engines that offer some of the highest towing and hauling ratings in the segment.

When it comes to sales figures, the closest competitors to Ford's F-150 are the Chevrolet Silverado/GMC Sierra twins. Other than exterior appearance, these two trucks are virtually identical. GM's lineup stacks up favorably with the F-Series trucks as it offers equally powerful drivetrains and similar features and body styles. Dull, cheaply constructed interiors have always been the biggest knock on GM's lineup, but recent upgrades have improved the build and materials quality. Like the Fords, GM's heavy-duty trucks offer optional diesel- and high-capacity V8 power for serious towing and hauling. Chevrolet's lineup also includes the Avalanche, a crew cab truck that can be converted to a long-bed pickup in just a few minutes. If you can't decide between a truck or an SUV, the Avalanche (and its upscale cousin, the Cadillac Escalade EXT) is a useful alternative.

**Others to Consider:** Nissan isn't the only foreign company to build big trucks, as Toyota also offers a large pickup known as the Tundra. While slightly smaller in stature than the Titan, the Tundra is geared toward those who are willing to trade off ultimate capability for added refinement. A V8 engine is available, but with only 282 horsepower it's not quite as powerful as the competition's comparable V8s. With solid Toyota build quality and enough size to tackle most small jobs, the Tundra is an excellent alternative for buyers with less demanding needs.

# Compact Truck

| Vehicle | Price Range | Base Drivetrain | EPA Fuel Rating (mpg) | Maximum Payload | The Drive | The Ride | Design | Cargo/ Passenger Space | Overall Rating |
|---|---|---|---|---|---|---|---|---|---|
| **Dodge Dakota** #1 Editors' Rating | $19,374-$28,679 | 3.7L 6cyl 6M V6 RWD | 16 city 22 hwy | 1730 lbs. | 8.9 | 8.8 | 8.3 | 9.3 | **8.7** |
| **Toyota Tacoma** | $13,415-$25,250 | 2.7L 4cyl 5M Inline 4 RWD | 21 city 27 hwy | 1410 lbs. | 7.9 | 8.0 | 7.6 | 7.5 | **7.8** |
| **Chevrolet SSR** | $42,430 | 6.0L 8cyl 4A V8 RWD | N/A | N/A | 8.0 | 7.5 | 8.1 | 6.0 | **7.6** |
| **Subaru Baja** | $22,195-$27,095 | 2.5L 4cyl 5M Horizontally Opposed AWD | N/A | 950 lbs. | 7.6 | 7.8 | 7.8 | 7.5 | **7.6** |
| **Ford Explorer Sport Trac** | $23,820-$31,090 | 4.0L 6cyl 5A V6 RWD | 16 city 21 hwy | 1525 lbs. | 7.1 | 8.3 | 7.0 | 6.8 | **7.1** |
| **Chevrolet Colorado** | $15,695-$28,330 | 2.8L 4cyl 5M Inline 4 RWD | N/A | 1733 lbs. | 7.1 | 6.3 | 6.8 | 7.5 | **6.9** |
| **GMC Canyon** | $16,025-$28,135 | 2.8L 4cyl 5M Inline 4 RWD | N/A | 1733 lbs. | 7.1 | 6.3 | 6.8 | 7.5 | **6.9** |
| **Mazda B-Series Truck** | $15,315-$26,145 | 2.3L 4cyl 5M Inline 4 RWD | 24 city 29 hwy | 1260 lbs. | 4.8 | 5.8 | 5.9 | 7.5 | **5.8** |
| **Ford Ranger** | $14,365-$26,025 | 2.3L 4cyl 5M Inline 4 RWD | 24 city 29 hwy | 1260 lbs. | 4.4 | 5.8 | 5.3 | 7.5 | **5.5** |

| Vehicle | Price Range | Base Drivetrain | EPA Fuel Rating (mpg) | Maximum Payload | The Drive | The Ride | Design | Cargo/ Passenger Space | Overall Rating |
|---|---|---|---|---|---|---|---|---|---|
| Nissan Frontier | N/A | N/A | N/A | N/A | N/A | N/A | N/A | N/A | N/A |

# Large Truck

| Vehicle | Price Range | Base Drivetrain | EPA Fuel Rating (mpg) | Maximum Payload | The Drive | The Ride | Design | Cargo/ Passenger Space | Overall Rating |
|---|---|---|---|---|---|---|---|---|---|
| Dodge Ram Pickup | $20,180- $40,920 '1 Editors' Rating | 5.7L 8cyl 5M V8 RWD | N/A | 1830 lbs. | 8.4 | 8.5 | 8.5 | 8.5 | **8.4** |
| Nissan Titan | $22,650- $35,100 | 5.6L 8cyl 5A V8 RWD | 14 city 19 hwy | 1640 lbs. | 8.4 | 7.8 | 8.1 | 9.0 | **8.3** |
| Ford F-150 | $19,800- $36,065 | 4.2L 6cyl 5M V6 RWD | N/A | 1830 lbs. | 8.1 | 8.3 | 7.9 | 8.0 | **8.0** |
| Chevrolet Silverado | $18,635- $41,040 | 4.3L 6cyl 5M V6 RWD | N/A | 1875 lbs. | 8.0 | 8.3 | 7.8 | 8.0 | **7.9** |
| GMC Sierra | $18,635- $41,500 | 6.0L 8cyl 5M V8 RWD | N/A | 4023 lbs. | 8.1 | 8.3 | 7.5 | 8.0 | **7.9** |
| Cadillac Escalade EXT | $53,045 | 6.0L 8cyl 4A V8 AWD | N/A | 1121 lbs. | 7.9 | 8.8 | 7.4 | 7.5 | **7.8** |
| Ford F-250 Super Duty | $22,570- $36,780 | 5.4L 8cyl 6M V8 RWD | N/A | 3000 lbs. | 7.6 | 8.5 | 7.6 | 8.0 | **7.8** |
| Ford F-350 Super Duty | $23,315- $38,645 | 5.4L 8cyl 6M V8 RWD | N/A | 4300 lbs. | 7.6 | 8.5 | 7.6 | 8.0 | **7.8** |
| Chevrolet Avalanche | $33,320- $42,195 | 5.3L 8cyl 4A V8 RWD | 14 city 18 hwy | 1363 lbs. | 6.9 | 9.3 | 6.5 | 8.8 | **7.4** |

| Vehicle | Price Range | Base Drivetrain | EPA Fuel Rating (mpg) | Maximum Payload | The Drive | The Ride | Design | Cargo/ Passenger Space | Overall Rating |
|---|---|---|---|---|---|---|---|---|---|
| Toyota Tundra | $15,955-$33,075 | 4.0L 6cyl 6M V6 RWD | 18 city 22 hwy | 1565 lbs. | 6.9 | 7.3 | 7.8 | 7.5 | 7.3 |

## Top 10 Things to Consider Before Buying

**Size/Market Segment:** Minivans come in two sizes -- regular (perfect for smaller families) and large (more space and amenities for larger broods). Full-size vans are larger and less maneuverable; they're for very large families and contractors.

**Price:** Plan to spend $20-25K for a minivan with basic features up to about $40,000 for one that's equipped like a luxury car. Full-size vans start in the mid-$20Ks and top off in the mid-$30Ks.

**Engine/Fuel Economy:** V6 power is the standard among minivans. Expect adequate to brisk acceleration and over 20 mpg on the highway. Full-size vans carry heavy loads, so they generally require larger V6, V8 or even V10 engines.

**Safety:** Minivans are some of the safest vehicles on the road, though shoppers should look at crash test scores and availability of features like side airbags. Full-size vans offer basic safety equipment only.

**Family-friendly Features:** Key items to look for in a minivan include power-sliding doors, rear air conditioning, an entertainment system, ample in-cabin storage and so on. Full-size vans offer a few luxuries but are low on conveniences.

**Versatility of Interior Seating:** Plenty of vans allow you to remove the rear seats, but family buyers should zero in on minivans with easily reconfigurable second-row seats and third-row seats that fold into the floor. Some minivans offer fold-flat seating in both the second and third rows. A few offer a second-row bench seat option for larger families.

**Passenger Capacity/Interior Space:** Minivans can seat seven or eight in comfort and are designed to allow parents to move about easily to tend to young children. Full-size vans are cavernous; they seat at least seven and up to 15 passengers.

**Cargo Capacity:** Minivans can hold more cargo than most SUVs, though bigger families will prefer the added luggage space of the larger models. For those with lots of heavy stuff to haul, nothing beats a full-size van.

**Do You Need All-Wheel Drive?** Some minivans and full-size vans offer all-wheel-drive systems—worth considering if you live in a particularly cold, snowy climate. Keep in mind that AWD vans get lower gas mileage.

**Operating Costs:** While SUVs may seem like the more stylish choice for family transportation, minivans are definitely the more financially savvy choice: They cost less to buy, insure and maintain. They seat more people comfortably in their roomier cabins. And they use a lot less gas. Full-size vans are truck-based; fuel costs are high, but time-tested components keep repair bills down.

# Minivans

**Market Leaders:** The minivan segment has been largely the domain of a few select manufacturers over the past decade, but the release of several all-new vans in the past year has increased the number of viable options considerably. The list of top-rated vans includes the Honda Odyssey, Nissan Quest, Toyota Sienna and the Dodge Caravan/Chrysler Town & Country twins. All of these vans offer strong V6 power plants, numerous family-friendly features and plenty of space to stretch out. The top-selling and freshly redesigned Odyssey remains a favorite thanks to carlike handling, a simple but functional interior and loads of passenger and cargo space. The competition has caught on to the usefulness of its fold-away third-row seat, but the Odyssey remains a top contender by virtue of its all-around competence and quality. The Toyota Sienna was completely redone last year and now equals the Honda in both size and functionality. Unique features like roll-down rear windows and a split-folding third-row seat give it a fresh take in the functionality area, but the Sienna is still a shade behind the Odyssey when it comes to overall handling dynamics. If you're looking for a high-quality van that offers nearly every feature imaginable, you can't go wrong with the Sienna. Nissan's all-new Quest attempts to inject a little fun into the category with a less traditional exterior design and a few unique design elements. The dashboard controls are clustered toward the center for an unobstructed view of the road while optional Skyview overhead windows bathe the rear of the van in plenty of natural sunlight. The third-row seat folds flat, of course, and the standard 240-horsepower engine provides plenty of power no matter how full you fill it. Chrysler's vans still lead the pack when it comes to overall driving dynamics as both the Caravan and the Town & Country feature excellent road feel and quiet cabins. Like the competition, Chrysler's vans offer features like DVD entertainment systems, reconfigurable seats and multizone climate control, but less powerful V6 engines keep them from dethroning the import vans.

**Others to consider:** GM revamped its entire minivan lineup for 2005 with the introduction of the Buick Terraza, Chevrolet Uplander, Pontiac Montana SV6 and Saturn Relay. All these vans are based on the same platform as last year's vans, but heavily revised interiors give them an all-new look and added features. A mediocre 200-hp engine leaves them trailing the frontrunners, but those who don't find any of the top-rated vans appealing shouldn't dismiss these well-thought-out vans. Ford introduced its Freestar van last year and as you might expect, the Freestar has all the latest features and a spacious cabin loaded with plenty of cupholders and storage space. It also features first- and second-row side curtain airbags along with available stability control and parking sensors for maximum safety. Its large displacement V6 provides plenty of torque for heavy loads, but it also uses more gas than most other vans so take that into consideration when assessing your particular needs. If it's value you're looking for in a minivan, you would be hard-pressed to find a better buy than the Kia Sedona. It has nearly as much room as the top nameplates, a nicely trimmed interior and a standard V6. Factor in Kia's 10-year drivetrain warranty and a price that's thousands less than the competition and it's easy to see why the Sedona is a popular choice for minivan buyers on a budget. Mazda's MPV minivan is a slightly smaller entry that gives up some size in return for a more nimble overall feel. It has functional features like roll-down rear windows, a disappearing third-row seat and cupholders galore that make it a great alternative for those who don't need eight-passenger capacity.

# Minivan

| Vehicle | Price Range | Base Drivetrain | EPA Fuel Rating (mpg) | Cargo Capacity | The Drive | The Ride | Design | Cargo/ Passenger Space | Overall Rating |
|---|---|---|---|---|---|---|---|---|---|
| **Honda Odyssey** | $24,995-$38,295 | 3.5L 6cyl 5A V6 FWD | 19 city 25 hwy | 147 cu.ft. | 9.1 | 9.0 | 8.4 | 9.0 | **8.9** |
| **Toyota Sienna** | $23,225-$37,495 | 3.3L 6cyl 5A V6 FWD | 19 city 26 hwy | 149 cu.ft. | 8.3 | 8.5 | 8.9 | 9.8 | **8.8** |
| **Chrysler Town and Country** | $24,960-$35,315 | 3.3L 6cyl 4A V6 FWD | 19 city 26 hwy | 168 cu.ft. | 8.4 | 9.3 | 7.9 | 9.5 | **8.5** |
| **Dodge Caravan/Grand Caravan** | $18,330-$26,505 | 2.4L 4cyl 4A Inline 4 FWD | 21 city 27 hwy | 147 cu.ft. | 8.0 | 9.3 | 7.8 | 9.5 | **8.3** |
| **Kia Sedona** | $20,200-$22,600 | 3.5L 6cyl 5A V6 FWD | 16 city 22 hwy | 128 cu.ft. | 7.9 | 8.0 | 7.5 | 9.0 | **8.0** |
| **Nissan Quest** | $23,350-$32,250 | 3.5L 6cyl 4A V6 FWD | 19 city 26 hwy | 149 cu.ft. | 8.8 | 8.5 | 7.0 | 8.3 | **8.0** |
| **Mazda MPV** | $22,940-$28,505 | 3L 6cyl 5A V6 FWD | 18 city 25 hwy | 127 cu.ft. | 8.0 | 6.8 | 7.9 | 7.0 | **7.6** |
| **Buick Terraza** | $28,110-$33,855 | 3.5L 6cyl 4A V6 FWD | N/A | 137 cu.ft. | 6.6 | 7.3 | 6.8 | 7.8 | **7.0** |
| **Chevrolet Uplander** | $23,635-$31,385 | 3.5L 6cyl 4A V6 FWD | N/A | 137 cu.ft. | 6.6 | 7.3 | 6.8 | 7.8 | **7.0** |

Honda Odyssey: '1 Editors' Rating

| Vehicle | Price Range | Base Drivetrain | EPA Fuel Rating (mpg) | Cargo Capacity | The Drive | The Ride | Design | Cargo/ Passenger Space | Overall Rating |
|---------|-------------|-----------------|-----------------------|----------------|-----------|----------|--------|------------------------|----------------|
| Pontiac Montana/Montana SV6 | $24,520-$30,210 | 3.5L 6cyl 4A V6 FWD | N/A | 137 cu.ft. | 6.6 | 7.3 | 6.9 | 7.8 | 7.0 |
| Saturn Relay | $23,770-$29,855 | N/A | N/A | N/A | 6.6 | 7.3 | 6.6 | 7.8 | 6.9 |
| Chevrolet Astro | $24,300-$31,445 | 4.3L 6cyl 4A V6 RWD | N/A | 170 cu.ft. | 6.4 | 7.0 | 6.5 | 7.3 | 6.6 |
| Chevrolet Venture | $23,365-$30,760 | 3.4L 6cyl 4A V6 FWD | N/A | 141 cu.ft. | 6.4 | 7.3 | 6.3 | 7.3 | 6.6 |
| Ford Freestar | $21,610-$32,710 | 3.9L 6cyl 4A V6 FWD | N/A | 137 cu.ft. | 6.1 | 7.3 | 6.8 | 6.8 | 6.5 |
| Mercury Monterey | $29,010-$34,910 | 4.2L 6cyl 4A V6 FWD | 16 city 22 hwy | 134 cu.ft. | 6.1 | 7.3 | 6.8 | 6.8 | 6.5 |

## Top 10 Cars With the Best Residual Value for 2005

Want to buy a car that really holds its value? If resale value is important to you, these are the cars likely to depreciate the least during the ownership period. Below we show the percentage of its original value that each vehicle is likely to retain after five years with an annual mileage of 15,000. Keep in mind that the residual value percentages are based on the national True Market Value® (TMV) price, plus typical options and destination charge.

1.  Mercedes-Benz CLK-Class, 55.2%

2.  Mini Cooper, 55%

3.  Ford GT, 52%

4.  Mercedes-Benz CLK55 AMG, 50%
    Toyota Camry Solara, 50%

5.  Lexus SC 430, 49.8%

6.  Lexus ES 330, 48.8%

7.  Chevrolet Corvette, 48.5%

8.  Audi S4, 48%

9.  Nissan Altima, 47.6%

10. Mercedes-Benz C55 AMG, 47.5%

## Top 10 Trucks With the Best Residual Value for 2005

Want to buy a vehicle that really holds its value? If resale value is important to you, these are the models among all trucks, SUVs and minivans sold this year that are likely to depreciate the least during the ownership period. Below is the percentage of its original value that each vehicle is likely to retain after five years with an annual mileage of 15,000. Keep in mind that the residual value percentages are based on the national True Market Value® (TMV) price, plus typical options and destination charge.

1. **Toyota Sequoia, 51.4%**

2. **Toyota 4Runner, 50.7%**

3. **Toyota Highlander, 50.1%**

4. **Toyota Tundra, 49.1%**

5. **Toyota Land Cruiser, 49%**

6. **Ford F-350 Super Duty, 47.9%**

7. **Ford F-250 Super Duty, 47.7%**

8. **Ford F-150, 47.5%**

9. **Chevrolet Silverado 1500HD, 47.4%**

10. **GMC Sierra 1500HD, 46.9%**

## Top 10 Most Fuel-Efficient Cars for 2005

We've compiled a list of the 10 most fuel-efficient cars currently sold in the U.S. based on the Environmental Protection Agency's (EPA) miles-per-gallon ratings for city and highway travel. In order to arrive at a final hierarchy, we used the EPA's combined fuel economy formula: 55 percent of city mpg rating plus 45 percent of highway mpg rating. The rating for each vehicle below is expressed in mpg as a city/highway ratio. All ratings apply to base models equipped with a manual transmission, except where indicated otherwise with an asterisk. Also, we only allowed a given model to appear once on the list, except in the case of the Honda Civic because it's available in both gas-electric hybrid and regular gasoline versions.

1.  **Honda Insight — 61/66**

2.  **Toyota Prius — 60/51***

3.  **Honda Civic Hybrid — 45/51**

4.  **Volkswagen Golf TDI — 38/46**
    **Volkswagen Jetta TDI — 38/46**
    **Volkswagen New Beetle TDI — 38/46**

5.  **Honda Civic HX — 36/44**

6.  **Toyota Echo — 35/42**

7.  **Toyota Corolla — 32/41**

8.  **Scion xA — 32/37**

9.  **Honda Accord Hybrid — 30/37***
    **Pontiac Vibe — 30/36**
    **Toyota Matrix — 30/36**
    **Scion xB — 31/35***

10. **Dodge Neon — 29/36**
    **Toyota Celica GT — 29/36***

## Top 10 Most Fuel-Efficient Trucks for 2005

In the past, new truck shoppers were more concerned with power, cargo capacity and off-road ability than fuel economy. Now that gas prices are hitting all-time highs, however, fuel-efficiency has become an important issue for buyers, even those who need a vehicle capable of hauling more than just a bag of groceries. With this in mind, we've compiled a list of the top 10 most fuel-efficient pickups and SUVs sold in the U.S. today, based on the Environmental Protection Agency's (EPA) miles-per-gallon ratings for city and highway travel. The only hybrid vehicle to make the list is the new Ford Escape, which offers stellar economy for such a versatile vehicle. Later in 2005, a hybrid version of Toyota's Highlander will also arrive — likely as a 2006 model. Our hierarchy is based on the EPA's formula for combined fuel economy: 55 percent of city mpg rating plus 45 percent of highway mpg rating. The rating for each vehicle below is expressed in mpg as a city/highway ratio. With exceptions for the Dodge Magnum, Ford Escape Hybrid, Honda CR-V, Jeep Liberty Diesel, Subaru Baja and Toyota Highlander, all ratings apply to base models equipped with a manual transmission — and for pickups, a regular cab/standard bed configuration. Likewise, all ratings apply to 2WD models, with the exceptions being all the Subarus and the Jeep Liberty Diesel. You'll notice that some decidedly carlike vehicles made the list this year, such as Chrysler's PT Cruiser and the Dodge Magnum, and that's because the EPA classifies them as SUVs — even though they're basically station wagons.

1. **Ford Escape Hybrid — 36/31**

2. **Toyota RAV4 — 24/30**

3. **Ford Ranger — 24/29**
   **Mazda B2300 — 24/29**
   **Ford Escape — 24/29**
   **Mazda Tribute — 24/29**

4. **Subaru Forester — 23/30**

5. **Honda CR-V — 23/29**
   **Saturn Vue — 23/29**

6. **Chrysler PT Cruiser — 22/29**

7. **Subaru Outback Wagon — 23/28**

8. **Mitsubishi Outlander — 22/28**

9. **Subaru Baja — 21/28**
   **Dodge Magnum — 21/28**

10. **Hyundai Tucson — 22/27**
    **Jeep Liberty Diesel — 22/27**
    **Toyota Highlander — 22/27**

# Top 10 Tips for Improving Your Fuel Economy

Filling up is a fact of every driver's life, but for some drivers it is a necessary evil. If you are one of those people who gulps every time you have to fill up your vehicle, there's good news: there are some simple things you can do to improve your fuel economy no matter what type of vehicle you drive.

Monitoring your average fuel economy regularly is a good idea, too. (Some vehicles have a handy computer that computes this for you.) If you notice a significant change, then something has changed with your vehicle.

Here are 10 things you can do today to get better gas mileage right away.

### 1. Follow the Recommended Maintenance

A vehicle that is well maintained means it will operate with greater efficiency. This not only improves your overall vehicle performance, but it will improve your fuel economy as well. Fouled spark plugs, a dirty air filter or clogged fuel filter will all affect your fuel economy. According to the U.S. Department of Energy (DOE), replacing a clogged air filter can increase your mileage by 10 percent, while replacing an oxygen sensor could result in an improvement as high as 40 percent. Proper maintenance also means using the right octane gas and the recommended grade of motor oil. Using the recommended types for your vehicle will give you optimum fuel economy — and can save you money as well. Check your owner's manual for your vehicle's recommendations and have maintenance performed regularly by a dealer or reputable mechanic.

### 2. Keep Your Tires Properly Inflated

Underinflated tires require more energy to roll, which translates into more frequent fill-ups. You can improve your fuel economy by about 3.3 percent if you keep your tires inflated properly, according to the DOE. The psi number noted on the sidewall of your tires is the maximum pressure of the tire and is not the proper inflation level for your car. Your vehicle manufacturer will list the recommended tire pressure in your owner's manual or a sticker on the doorjamb of the driver-side door. Buy a tire-pressure gauge and check your tires monthly, adding air as necessary.

### 3. Take a Load Off

Heavier vehicles require more energy to move, so carrying around excess weight will also affect your mileage. Empty out your trunk (or even your backseat) of unnecessary items. An extra 100 pounds in the trunk will reduce your fuel economy by 1 to 2 percent in the typical vehicle. If you have a roof rack or roof carrier, install it on your vehicle only when absolutely necessary. Not only does the carrier add extra weight, but it also increases the aerodynamic drag on the vehicle, which further contributes to a loss of fuel economy.

### 4. Don't Drive Aggressively

We're not talking road rage here, but the type of driving many people do when they are in a rush. Mashing the accelerator pedal from a stoplight, braking hard and speeding all contribute to a decrease in fuel economy. Give yourself extra time to get to your destination and think "steady and smooth" as you drive. On surface streets, driving at the speed limit will give you mostly green lights, which improves your gas mileage as well as reduces the wear on your brakes. On the highway, the DOE says that every 5 mph you drive over 65 mph represents a 7-percent decrease in fuel economy.

## 5. Use the Highest Gear Possible

Cars are designed to start in the lowest gear possible because that's where they have the most power, but that power translates to an increase in fuel consumption. To improve your fuel economy, drive in the highest gear possible when you are cruising at a steady speed, such as on the highway. If your vehicle has an automatic transmission with a "sport" mode, it's most likely that this is a computer program designed to shift later (and therefore keep you in a lower gear longer). While this gives you greater performance, driving in "sport" mode will also decrease your fuel economy.

## 6. Use Cruise Control—Selectively

Using cruise control can improve your gas mileage by helping you maintain a steady speed, but only if you are driving on mostly flat roads. If you are driving in hilly terrain, using cruise control typically causes your vehicle to speed up faster (to maintain the preset speed) than it would if you were operating the accelerator yourself. Before you push that cruise control button, think about the terrain ahead.

## 7. Think Clean

Keeping your car washed and waxed improves aerodynamics and therefore affects fuel economy. Engineer Tom Wagner, Jr. reported to Stretcher.com (as in stretching your dollars) a 7-percent improvement in fuel economy, from 15 to 16 mpg, during a 1,600-mile road trip.

## 8. Avoid Excessive Idling

When a car is idling, it is using fuel, yet not going anywhere. This translates to 0 mpg. When you leave your car running while you are waiting in line at the drive-thru, or as you wait outside your kids' school, you are wasting fuel. It is more efficient to turn the engine off while you wait and then restart the car. If that's not practical (like in the line at McDonald's), then park the car and go inside instead.

## 9. Think Before You Vent(ilate)

Running your air conditioner does cause your vehicle to consume more fuel, but driving with your windows rolled down can be even worse due to the increase of drag on the vehicle. If you are driving slowly, such as around town or in city traffic, then you are better off leaving your windows open, if at all possible. For highway driving, roll up the windows and turn the air conditioning on.

## 10. Combine Your Errands

A little planning can make a big difference in fuel economy. When your engine is cold, it uses more fuel than when it is warm. Combining errands can improve your gas mileage because your engine will be warm for more of the trip. It might also mean you travel less total miles. According to the DOE, several short trips all begun with a cold start can use twice as much fuel as a single, longer trip that covers the same distance.

## NHTSA Testing

In 1994, the National Highway Traffic Safety Administration (NHTSA—www.nhtsa.dot.gov) changed the way it rates frontal crash-test performances of the cars and trucks they run into a fixed barrier at 35 mph. Instead of the confusing numerical scale that had been in place for years, NHTSA decided to make the data more user-friendly for interested consumers by converting to a five-star rating system. To make these scores even easier to browse quickly, we have converted the 5-star system into a rating system that uses the following terms:

> 5 stars = Excellent
> 4 stars = Good
> 3 stars = Average
> 2 stars = Poor
> 1 star = Very Poor

In 1997, NHTSA began testing side-impact protection as well as frontal-impact protection. For side-impact testing, NHTSA runs a deformable barrier into the side of a car twice, once at the front passenger's level and once at the rear passenger's level. As with frontal-impact testing, the side-impact test is conducted at 5 mph above the federal standard, which means the deformable barrier hits the car at 38 mph. It should be noted that NHTSA only tests a vehicle with side airbags and/or side curtain airbags if they come as standard equipment across all trim levels.

In 2001, NHTSA began evaluating vehicles for rollover potential in a single-vehicle accident. Initially, the agency used a simple mathematical calculation based on a vehicle's track width and the distance from the ground to its center of gravity to determine its "top-heaviness" (known as the Static Stability Factor)—a reliable predictor of the vehicle's likelihood to roll over when tripped by a curb or shallow ditch, according to NHTSA. Starting in 2004, NHTSA began conducting a dynamic test that comes closer to approximating real-world driving conditions. In this test, the stability control system is left activated if more than 50 percent of a test model's sales had that option. A remote-controlled steering system then simulates what a person might do while trying to avoid a high-speed collision—suddenly turning sharply in one direction, then the other (often called a "fishhook"). Test instruments measure if the vehicle's tires lift off the pavement. If they lift off at least two inches, the vehicle is considered to have tipped up, the first stage of rolling over. Note that this type of rollover is considered an "untripped" rollover since the vehicle's tires made no contact with a curb or ditch. Because most rollovers are "tripped," though, the Static Stability Factor is weighted far more heavily than the dynamic test. Ratings are conveyed in the familiar five-star format.

## IIHS Testing

The Insurance Institute for Highway Safety (IIHS — www.hwysafety.org) began conducting frontal offset crash tests in 1995. The offset test is conducted at 40 mph, and vehicles crash into a fixed barrier just like in the NHTSA testing, but only half of the front of the vehicle contacts the barrier. The IIHS claims this test, at this speed, more accurately reflects the most deadly real-world crash situations. Offset crash tests do not conform to the scale listed above. Instead, the IIHS rates a vehicle good, acceptable, marginal or poor. There are currently no federally mandated offset crash standards that automakers must meet by law.

Like NHTSA, the IIHS also conducts side-impact tests in which a deformable barrier is run into the side of the car, in this case at 31 mph. Whereas NHTSA's test simulates what happens when another car strikes a vehicle from the side, the IIHS uses a barrier that weighs 3,300 pounds and has a front end shaped like that of a pickup truck or SUV. The Institute says that its test takes into account the large number of light trucks currently on the road and the increased head injury risks they present in side-impact collisions. Additionally, the dummies inside each test vehicle approximate a small adult woman (one seated in the driver seat and one seated in the rear), because crash data indicates that women are more likely to suffer head injuries in this type of accident. The IIHS only tests a vehicle with side airbags and/or side curtain airbags if they are standard equipment; a manufacturer may request a retest of a vehicle with optional airbags if it agrees to reimburse the cost of the vehicle. The rating system is the same as that used for the frontal offset test.

The IIHS also conducts bumper-bashing tests. They run cars and trucks into barriers at 5 mph to see how much damage results, in terms of dollars. Front ends are smacked into flat and angled barriers, and then they back vehicles into poles and angled barriers. Each vehicle is crashed four times; the lower the total cost for repair after all four tests, the better the vehicle scores. Federal law requires bumpers on passenger cars that can withstand an impact at 2.5 mph. Light trucks are not required to meet bumper-strength standards.

| | NHTSA | | | | | IIHS | |
|---|---|---|---|---|---|---|---|
| | Frontal Crash Driver | Frontal Crash Passenger | Side Crash Front Occupant | Side Crash Rear Occupant | Rollover Resistance | Bumper Bash | Offset |
| **Acura** | | | | | | | |
| MDX | Not Tested | Not Tested | Excellent | Excellent | Not Tested | Not Tested | Not Tested |
| NSX | Not Tested | Not Tested | Not Tested | Not Tested | Not Tested | Not Tested | Not Tested |
| RL | Not Tested | Not Tested | Not Tested | Not Tested | Not Tested | Not Tested | Not Tested |
| RSX | Excellent | Excellent | Good | Not Tested | Good | Not Tested | Not Tested |
| TL | Excellent | Excellent | Not Tested | Not Tested | Not Tested | Marginal | Good |
| TSX | Not Tested | Not Tested | Not Tested | Not Tested | Not Tested | Not Tested | Not Tested |
| **Audi** | | | | | | | |
| A4 | Good | Good | Excellent | Good | Good | Good | Good |
| A6 | Not Tested | Not Tested | Not Tested | Not Tested | Not Tested | Not Tested | Not Tested |
| A8 | Not Tested | Not Tested | Not Tested | Not Tested | Not Tested | Not Tested | Not Tested |
| allroad quattro | Not Tested | Not Tested | Not Tested | Not Tested | Not Tested | Not Tested | Not Tested |
| S4 | Good | Good | Excellent | Good | Not Tested | Not Tested | Not Tested |
| TT | Not Tested | Not Tested | Excellent | Not Tested | Excellent | Not Tested | Not Tested |
| **BMW** | | | | | | | |
| 3 Series | Good | Excellent | Average | Excellent | Good | Marginal | Good |
| 5 Series | Not Tested | Not Tested | Not Tested | Not Tested | Not Tested | Not Tested | Not Tested |
| 6 Series | Not Tested | Not Tested | Not Tested | Not Tested | Not Tested | Not Tested | Not Tested |
| 7 Series | Not Tested | Not Tested | Not Tested | Not Tested | Not Tested | Not Tested | Not Tested |
| M3 | Not Tested | Not Tested | Not Tested | Not Tested | Not Tested | Not Tested | Not Tested |
| X3 | Not Tested | Not Tested | Not Tested | Not Tested | Not Tested | Not Tested | Not Tested |
| X5 | Excellent | Excellent | Good | Excellent | Average | Acceptable | Good |
| Z4 | Good | Good | Average | Not Tested | Excellent | Not Tested | Not Tested |
| **Buick** | | | | | | | |
| Century | Good | Average | Average | Average | Not Tested | Acceptable | Acceptable |
| LaCrosse | Not Tested | Not Tested | Not Tested | Not Tested | Not Tested | Not Tested | Not Tested |
| LeSabre | Good | Excellent | Good | Good | Excellent | Marginal | Good |
| Park Avenue | Good | Good | Good | Good | Not Tested | Acceptable | Good |
| Rainier | Average | Average | Not Tested | Not Tested | Not Tested | Acceptable | Marginal |
| Rendezvous | Average | Average | Excellent | Excellent | Average | Poor | Acceptable |
| Terraza | Not Tested | Not Tested | Not Tested | Not Tested | Not Tested | Not Tested | Not Tested |
| **Cadillac** | | | | | | | |
| CTS | Good | Good | Good | Excellent | Not Tested | Poor | Good |
| CTS-V | Not Tested | Not Tested | Not Tested | Not Tested | Not Tested | Not Tested | Not Tested |
| DeVille | Very Poor | Average | Good | Good | Not Tested | Not Tested | Not Tested |

# Crash Test Scores

| | NHTSA | | | | | IIHS | |
|---|---|---|---|---|---|---|---|
| | Frontal Crash Driver | Frontal Crash Passenger | Side Crash Front Occupant | Side Crash Rear Occupant | Rollover Resistance | Bumper Bash | Offset |
| **Cadillac (cont'd)** | | | | | | | |
| Escalade | Good | Good | Not Tested | Not Tested | Not Tested | Not Tested | Not Tested |
| Escalade ESV | Good | Average | Not Tested | Not Tested | Average | Not Tested | Not Tested |
| Escalade EXT | Average | Good | Not Tested | Not Tested | Not Tested | Not Tested | Not Tested |
| SRX | Not Tested | Not Tested | Not Tested | Not Tested | Not Tested | Poor | Good |
| STS | Not Tested | Not Tested | Not Tested | Not Tested | Not Tested | Not Tested | Not Tested |
| XLR | Not Tested | Not Tested | Not Tested | Not Tested | Not Tested | Not Tested | Not Tested |
| **Chevrolet** | | | | | | | |
| Astro | Not Tested | Not Tested | Not Tested | Not Tested | Not Tested | Not Tested | Not Tested |
| Avalanche | Not Tested | Not Tested | Not Tested | Not Tested | Not Tested | Not Tested | Not Tested |
| Aveo | Not Tested | Not Tested | Not Tested | Not Tested | Not Tested | Not Tested | Not Tested |
| Blazer | Average | Good | Excellent | Excellent | Poor | Not Tested | Not Tested |
| Cavalier | Good | Good | Very Poor | Average | Good | Acceptable | Poor |
| Cobalt | Not Tested | Not Tested | Not Tested | Not Tested | Not Tested | Not Tested | Not Tested |
| Colorado | Good | Good | Good | Excellent | Not Tested | Not Tested | Not Tested |
| Corvette | Not Tested | Not Tested | Not Tested | Not Tested | Not Tested | Not Tested | Not Tested |
| Equinox | Excellent | Excellent | Excellent | Excellent | Not Tested | Not Tested | Not Tested |
| Express | Not Tested | Not Tested | Not Tested | Not Tested | Not Tested | Not Tested | Not Tested |
| Impala | Excellent | Excellent | Good | Good | Good | Marginal | Good |
| Malibu | Not Tested | Not Tested | Not Tested | Not Tested | Not Tested | Poor | Not Tested |
| Malibu Maxx | Not Tested | Not Tested | Not Tested | Not Tested | Not Tested | Not Tested | Not Tested |
| Monte Carlo | Excellent | Excellent | Average | Good | Good | Not Tested | Not Tested |
| Silverado 1500 | Not Tested | Not Tested | Not Tested | Not Tested | Not Tested | Not Tested | Not Tested |
| Silverado 1500 SS | Not Tested | Not Tested | Not Tested | Not Tested | Not Tested | Not Tested | Not Tested |
| Silverado 1500HD | Not Tested | Not Tested | Not Tested | Not Tested | Not Tested | Not Tested | Not Tested |
| Silverado 2500HD | Not Tested | Not Tested | Not Tested | Not Tested | Not Tested | Not Tested | Not Tested |
| Silverado 3500 | Not Tested | Not Tested | Not Tested | Not Tested | Not Tested | Not Tested | Not Tested |
| SSR | Not Tested | Not Tested | Not Tested | Not Tested | Not Tested | Not Tested | Not Tested |
| Suburban | Good | Average | Not Tested | Not Tested | Average | Not Tested | Not Tested |
| Tahoe | Average | Good | Not Tested | Not Tested | Average | Not Tested | Not Tested |
| TrailBlazer | Average | Average | Excellent | Excellent | Good | Acceptable | Marginal |
| TrailBlazer EXT | Not Tested | Not Tested | Not Tested | Not Tested | Not Tested | Not Tested | Not Tested |
| Uplander | Not Tested | Not Tested | Not Tested | Not Tested | Not Tested | Not Tested | Not Tested |
| Venture | Good | Good | Excellent | Good | Average | Poor | Poor |

# Crash Test Scores

| | NHTSA | | | | | IIHS | |
| --- | --- | --- | --- | --- | --- | --- | --- |
| | Frontal Crash Driver | Frontal Crash Passenger | Side Crash Front Occupant | Side Crash Rear Occupant | Rollover Resistance | Bumper Bash | Offset |
| **Chrysler** | | | | | | | |
| 300 | Not Tested | Not Tested | Not Tested | Not Tested | Not Tested | Not Tested | Not Tested |
| 300C SRT-8 | Not Tested | Not Tested | Not Tested | Not Tested | Not Tested | Not Tested | Not Tested |
| Crossfire | Not Tested | Not Tested | Not Tested | Not Tested | Not Tested | Not Tested | Not Tested |
| Crossfire SRT-6 | Not Tested | Not Tested | Not Tested | Not Tested | Not Tested | Not Tested | Not Tested |
| Pacifica | Not Tested | Not Tested | Not Tested | Not Tested | Not Tested | Not Tested | Not Tested |
| PT Cruiser | Good | Good | Good | Excellent | Good | Not Tested | Not Tested |
| Sebring | Excellent | Excellent | Average | Average | Excellent | Marginal | Acceptable |
| Town & Country | Good | Good | Excellent | Excellent | Average | Poor | Acceptable |
| **Dodge** | | | | | | | |
| Caravan | Good | Good | Good | Excellent | Average | Poor | Acceptable |
| Dakota | Not Tested | Not Tested | Not Tested | Not Tested | Not Tested | Not Tested | Not Tested |
| Durango | Excellent | Excellent | Not Tested | Not Tested | Not Tested | Not Tested | Not Tested |
| Grand Caravan | Good | Good | Excellent | Excellent | Not Tested | Poor | Acceptable |
| Magnum | Not Tested | Not Tested | Not Tested | Not Tested | Not Tested | Not Tested | Not Tested |
| Neon | Good | Good | Average | Average | Good | Acceptable | Marginal |
| Neon SRT-4 | Good | Good | Average | Average | Good | Acceptable | Marginal |
| Ram Pickup 1500 | Good | Excellent | Not Tested | Not Tested | Average | Marginal | Good |
| Ram Pickup 1500 SRT-10 | Not Tested | Not Tested | Not Tested | Not Tested | Not Tested | Not Tested | Not Tested |
| Ram Pickup 2500 | Not Tested | Not Tested | Not Tested | Not Tested | Not Tested | Not Tested | Not Tested |
| Ram Pickup 3500 | Not Tested | Not Tested | Not Tested | Not Tested | Not Tested | Not Tested | Not Tested |
| Stratus | Excellent | Excellent | Average | Average | Excellent | Marginal | Acceptable |
| Viper | Not Tested | Not Tested | Not Tested | Not Tested | Not Tested | Not Tested | Not Tested |
| **Ford** | | | | | | | |
| Crown Victoria | Excellent | Excellent | Good | Excellent | Excellent | Poor | Good |
| Econoline Wagon | Good | Good | Not Tested | Not Tested | Poor | Not Tested | Not Tested |
| Escape | Good | Good | Excellent | Excellent | Not Tested | Not Tested | Not Tested |
| Excursion | Not Tested | Not Tested | Not Tested | Not Tested | Not Tested | Not Tested | Not Tested |
| Expedition | Excellent | Excellent | Not Tested | Not Tested | Not Tested | Not Tested | Not Tested |
| Explorer | Good | Excellent | Excellent | Excellent | Average | Poor | Good |
| Explorer Sport Trac | Not Tested | Not Tested | Not Tested | Not Tested | Poor | Not Tested | Not Tested |
| F-150 | Excellent | Excellent | Not Tested | Not Tested | Not Tested | Poor | Good |
| F-250 Super Duty | Not Tested | Not Tested | Not Tested | Not Tested | Not Tested | Not Tested | Not Tested |
| F-350 Super Duty | Not Tested | Not Tested | Not Tested | Not Tested | Not Tested | Not Tested | Not Tested |
| Five Hundred | Not Tested | Not Tested | Not Tested | Not Tested | Not Tested | Not Tested | Not Tested |

# Crash Test Scores

| | NHTSA | | | | | IIHS | |
| --- | --- | --- | --- | --- | --- | --- | --- |
| | Frontal Crash Driver | Frontal Crash Passenger | Side Crash Front Occupant | Side Crash Rear Occupant | Rollover Resistance | Bumper Bash | Offset |
| **Ford (cont'd)** | | | | | | | |
| Focus | Not Tested | Not Tested | Not Tested | Not Tested | Not Tested | Not Tested | Not Tested |
| Freestar | Excellent | Excellent | Good | Excellent | Not Tested | Marginal | Good |
| Freestyle | Not Tested | Not Tested | Not Tested | Not Tested | Not Tested | Not Tested | Not Tested |
| GT | Not Tested | Not Tested | Not Tested | Not Tested | Not Tested | Not Tested | Not Tested |
| Mustang | Not Tested | Not Tested | Not Tested | Not Tested | Not Tested | Not Tested | Not Tested |
| Ranger | Good | Good | Excellent | Not Tested | Average | Marginal | Acceptable |
| Taurus | Good | Excellent | Average | Average | Not Tested | Acceptable | Good |
| Thunderbird | Good | Excellent | Excellent | Not Tested | Excellent | Not Tested | Not Tested |
| **GMC** | | | | | | | |
| Canyon | Good | Good | Good | Excellent | Not Tested | Not Tested | Not Tested |
| Envoy | Average | Average | Excellent | Excellent | Good | Acceptable | Marginal |
| Envoy XL | Average | Average | Excellent | Excellent | Good | Acceptable | Marginal |
| Envoy XUV | Average | Average | Not Tested | Not Tested | Not Tested | Not Tested | Not Tested |
| Safari | Average | Good | Not Tested | Not Tested | Average | Poor | Poor |
| Savana | Not Tested | Not Tested | Not Tested | Not Tested | Not Tested | Not Tested | Not Tested |
| Sierra 1500 | Good | Average | Not Tested | Not Tested | Good | Poor | Marginal |
| Sierra 1500HD | Not Tested | Not Tested | Not Tested | Not Tested | Not Tested | Not Tested | Not Tested |
| Sierra 2500HD | Not Tested | Not Tested | Not Tested | Not Tested | Not Tested | Not Tested | Not Tested |
| Sierra 3500 | Not Tested | Not Tested | Not Tested | Not Tested | Not Tested | Not Tested | Not Tested |
| Yukon | Average | Good | Not Tested | Not Tested | Average | Not Tested | Not Tested |
| Yukon XL | Good | Average | Not Tested | Not Tested | Average | Not Tested | Not Tested |
| **Honda** | | | | | | | |
| Accord | Excellent | Excellent | Good | Excellent | Good | Acceptable | Good |
| Civic | Excellent | Excellent | Good | Good | Good | Acceptable | Good |
| CR-V | Excellent | Excellent | Excellent | Excellent | Not Tested | Not Tested | Not Tested |
| Element | Not Tested | Not Tested | Not Tested | Not Tested | Not Tested | Not Tested | Not Tested |
| Insight | Good | Good | Good | Not Tested | Good | Not Tested | Not Tested |
| Odyssey | Not Tested | Not Tested | Not Tested | Not Tested | Not Tested | Not Tested | Not Tested |
| Pilot | Excellent | Excellent | Excellent | Excellent | Good | Acceptable | Good |
| S2000 | Good | Good | Excellent | Not Tested | Excellent | Not Tested | Not Tested |
| **HUMMER** | | | | | | | |
| H1 | Not Tested | Not Tested | Not Tested | Not Tested | Not Tested | Not Tested | Not Tested |
| H2 | Not Tested | Not Tested | Not Tested | Not Tested | Not Tested | Not Tested | Not Tested |
| H2 SUT | Not Tested | Not Tested | Not Tested | Not Tested | Not Tested | Not Tested | Not Tested |

# Crash Test Scores

| | NHTSA | | | | | IIHS | |
| --- | --- | --- | --- | --- | --- | --- | --- |
| | Frontal Crash Driver | Frontal Crash Passenger | Side Crash Front Occupant | Side Crash Rear Occupant | Rollover Resistance | Bumper Bash | Offset |
| **Hyundai** | | | | | | | |
| Accent | Good | Good | Excellent | Good | Good | Not Tested | Not Tested |
| Elantra | Excellent | Good | Excellent | Good | Not Tested | Good | Poor |
| Santa Fe | Excellent | Good | Excellent | Not Tested | Average | Poor | Good |
| Sonata | Good | Good | Good | Good | Excellent | Marginal | Acceptable |
| Tiburon | Excellent | Good | Good | Not Tested | Not Tested | Not Tested | Not Tested |
| Tucson | Not Tested | Not Tested | Not Tested | Not Tested | Not Tested | Not Tested | Not Tested |
| XG350 | Excellent | Excellent | Good | Good | Not Tested | Poor | Good |
| **Infiniti** | | | | | | | |
| FX35 | Excellent | Excellent | Excellent | Excellent | Not Tested | Poor | Good |
| FX45 | Excellent | Excellent | Excellent | Excellent | Not Tested | Poor | Good |
| G35 | Not Tested | Not Tested | Not Tested | Not Tested | Not Tested | Not Tested | Not Tested |
| Q45 | Not Tested | Not Tested | Not Tested | Not Tested | Not Tested | Poor | Good |
| QX56 | Not Tested | Not Tested | Not Tested | Not Tested | Not Tested | Not Tested | Not Tested |
| **Isuzu** | | | | | | | |
| Ascender | Average | Average | Excellent | Excellent | Good | Not Tested | Not Tested |
| **Jaguar** | | | | | | | |
| S-Type | Not Tested | Not Tested | Good | Excellent | Excellent | Not Tested | Not Tested |
| S-Type R | Not Tested | Not Tested | Not Tested | Not Tested | Not Tested | Not Tested | Not Tested |
| X-Type | Not Tested | Not Tested | Not Tested | Not Tested | Not Tested | Not Tested | Not Tested |
| XJ-Series | Not Tested | Not Tested | Not Tested | Not Tested | Not Tested | Not Tested | Not Tested |
| XK-Series | Not Tested | Not Tested | Not Tested | Not Tested | Not Tested | Not Tested | Not Tested |
| XKR | Not Tested | Not Tested | Not Tested | Not Tested | Not Tested | Not Tested | Not Tested |
| **Jeep** | | | | | | | |
| Grand Cherokee | Not Tested | Not Tested | Not Tested | Not Tested | Not Tested | Not Tested | Not Tested |
| Liberty | Excellent | Good | Excellent | Excellent | Average | Poor | Marginal |
| Wrangler | Not Tested | Not Tested | Not Tested | Not Tested | Not Tested | Not Tested | Not Tested |
| **Kia** | | | | | | | |
| Amanti | Not Tested | Not Tested | Not Tested | Not Tested | Not Tested | Not Tested | Not Tested |
| Optima | Good | Good | Good | Good | Excellent | Marginal | Acceptable |
| Rio | Good | Good | Poor | Poor | Good | Not Tested | Not Tested |
| Sedona | Excellent | Excellent | Excellent | Excellent | Good | Poor | Acceptable |
| Sorento | Good | Good | Excellent | Excellent | Average | Poor | Acceptable |
| Spectra | Good | Good | Average | Average | Good | Marginal | Poor |
| Sportage | Not Tested | Not Tested | Not Tested | Not Tested | Not Tested | Not Tested | Not Tested |

# Crash Test Scores

| | NHTSA | | | | | IIHS | |
|---|---|---|---|---|---|---|---|
| | Frontal Crash Driver | Frontal Crash Passenger | Side Crash Front Occupant | Side Crash Rear Occupant | Rollover Resistance | Bumper Bash | Offset |
| **Land Rover** | | | | | | | |
| Freelander | Not Tested | Not Tested | Not Tested | Not Tested | Not Tested | Poor | Acceptable |
| LR3 | Not Tested | Not Tested | Not Tested | Not Tested | Not Tested | Not Tested | Not Tested |
| Range Rover | Not Tested | Not Tested | Not Tested | Not Tested | Not Tested | Not Tested | Not Tested |
| **Lexus** | | | | | | | |
| ES 330 | Excellent | Excellent | Excellent | Good | Not Tested | Not Tested | Not Tested |
| GS 300 | Not Tested | Not Tested | Not Tested | Not Tested | Not Tested | Marginal | Good |
| GS 430 | Not Tested | Not Tested | Not Tested | Not Tested | Not Tested | Marginal | Good |
| GX 470 | Not Tested | Not Tested | Not Tested | Not Tested | Not Tested | Poor | Good |
| IS 300 | Not Tested | Not Tested | Excellent | Excellent | Excellent | Poor | Good |
| LS 430 | Not Tested | Not Tested | Not Tested | Not Tested | Not Tested | Marginal | Good |
| LX 470 | Not Tested | Not Tested | Not Tested | Not Tested | Not Tested | Not Tested | Not Tested |
| RX 330 | Excellent | Good | Excellent | Excellent | Not Tested | Marginal | Good |
| SC 430 | Not Tested | Not Tested | Not Tested | Not Tested | Not Tested | Not Tested | Not Tested |
| **Lincoln** | | | | | | | |
| Aviator | Good | Excellent | Not Tested | Not Tested | Average | Poor | Good |
| LS | Excellent | Good | Good | Excellent | Not Tested | Marginal | Good |
| Navigator | Excellent | Excellent | Not Tested | Not Tested | Not Tested | Not Tested | Not Tested |
| Town Car | Excellent | Excellent | Excellent | Excellent | Excellent | Poor | Good |
| **Mazda** | | | | | | | |
| B-Series Truck | Good | Good | Excellent | Not Tested | Average | Marginal | Acceptable |
| MAZDA3 | Good | Good | Average | Average | Not Tested | Not Tested | Not Tested |
| MAZDA6 | Excellent | Excellent | Average | Good | Excellent | Acceptable | Good |
| MAZDASPEED MX-5 Miata | Not Tested | Not Tested | Not Tested | Not Tested | Not Tested | Not Tested | Not Tested |
| MPV | Not Tested | Not Tested | Not Tested | Not Tested | Not Tested | Poor | Acceptable |
| MX-5 Miata | Good | Excellent | Average | Not Tested | Excellent | Not Tested | Not Tested |
| RX-8 | Not Tested | Not Tested | Good | Good | Not Tested | Not Tested | Not Tested |
| Tribute | Good | Good | Excellent | Excellent | Not Tested | Not Tested | Not Tested |
| **Mercedes-Benz** | | | | | | | |
| C-Class | Not Tested | Not Tested | Not Tested | Not Tested | Not Tested | Not Tested | Not Tested |
| C55 AMG | Not Tested | Not Tested | Not Tested | Not Tested | Not Tested | Not Tested | Not Tested |
| CL-Class | Not Tested | Not Tested | Not Tested | Not Tested | Not Tested | Not Tested | Not Tested |
| CL55 AMG | Not Tested | Not Tested | Not Tested | Not Tested | Not Tested | Not Tested | Not Tested |
| CL65 AMG | Not Tested | Not Tested | Not Tested | Not Tested | Not Tested | Not Tested | Not Tested |
| CLK-Class | Not Tested | Not Tested | Not Tested | Not Tested | Not Tested | Not Tested | Not Tested |

| | NHTSA | | | | | IIHS | |
| --- | --- | --- | --- | --- | --- | --- | --- |
| | Frontal Crash Driver | Frontal Crash Passenger | Side Crash Front Occupant | Side Crash Rear Occupant | Rollover Resistance | Bumper Bash | Offset |
| **Mercedes-Benz (cont'd)** | | | | | | | |
| CLK55 AMG | Not Tested | Not Tested | Not Tested | Not Tested | Not Tested | Not Tested | Not Tested |
| E-Class | Good | Good | Excellent | Excellent | Excellent | Not Tested | Not Tested |
| E55 AMG | Not Tested | Not Tested | Not Tested | Not Tested | Not Tested | Not Tested | Not Tested |
| G-Class | Not Tested | Not Tested | Not Tested | Not Tested | Not Tested | Not Tested | Not Tested |
| G55 AMG | Not Tested | Not Tested | Not Tested | Not Tested | Not Tested | Not Tested | Not Tested |
| M-Class | Not Tested | Not Tested | Not Tested | Not Tested | Average | Marginal | Good |
| S-Class | Not Tested | Not Tested | Not Tested | Not Tested | Not Tested | Not Tested | Not Tested |
| S55 AMG | Not Tested | Not Tested | Not Tested | Not Tested | Not Tested | Not Tested | Not Tested |
| SL-Class | Not Tested | Not Tested | Not Tested | Not Tested | Not Tested | Not Tested | Not Tested |
| SL55 AMG | Not Tested | Not Tested | Not Tested | Not Tested | Not Tested | Not Tested | Not Tested |
| SL65 AMG | Not Tested | Not Tested | Not Tested | Not Tested | Not Tested | Not Tested | Not Tested |
| SLK-Class | Not Tested | Not Tested | Not Tested | Not Tested | Not Tested | Not Tested | Not Tested |
| SLK55 AMG | Not Tested | Not Tested | Not Tested | Not Tested | Not Tested | Not Tested | Not Tested |
| **Mercury** | | | | | | | |
| Grand Marquis | Excellent | Excellent | Good | Excellent | Excellent | Poor | Good |
| Mariner | Not Tested | Not Tested | Not Tested | Not Tested | Not Tested | Not Tested | Not Tested |
| Montego | Not Tested | Not Tested | Not Tested | Not Tested | Not Tested | Not Tested | Not Tested |
| Monterey | Excellent | Excellent | Good | Excellent | Not Tested | Not Tested | Not Tested |
| Mountaineer | Good | Excellent | Excellent | Excellent | Average | Poor | Good |
| Sable | Good | Excellent | Average | Average | Not Tested | Acceptable | Good |
| **MINI** | | | | | | | |
| Cooper | Not Tested | Not Tested | Not Tested | Not Tested | Not Tested | Not Tested | Not Tested |
| **Mitsubishi** | | | | | | | |
| Eclipse | Good | Good | Average | Not Tested | Excellent | Not Tested | Not Tested |
| Eclipse Spyder | Not Tested | Not Tested | Not Tested | Not Tested | Not Tested | Not Tested | Not Tested |
| Endeavor | Not Tested | Not Tested | Not Tested | Not Tested | Not Tested | Not Tested | Not Tested |
| Galant | Excellent | Excellent | Not Tested | Not Tested | Not Tested | Acceptable | Good |
| Lancer | Good | Good | Poor | Good | Good | Marginal | Good |
| Lancer Evolution | Not Tested | Not Tested | Not Tested | Not Tested | Not Tested | Not Tested | Not Tested |
| Montero | Not Tested | Not Tested | Not Tested | Not Tested | Not Tested | Poor | Acceptable |
| Outlander | Good | Good | Excellent | Good | Average | Poor | Good |
| **Nissan** | | | | | | | |
| 350Z | Excellent | Good | Excellent | Not Tested | Excellent | Not Tested | Not Tested |
| Altima | Not Tested | Not Tested | Not Tested | Not Tested | Not Tested | Not Tested | Good |

# Crash Test Scores

| | NHTSA | | | | | IIHS | |
| --- | --- | --- | --- | --- | --- | --- | --- |
| | Frontal Crash Driver | Frontal Crash Passenger | Side Crash Front Occupant | Side Crash Rear Occupant | Rollover Resistance | Bumper Bash | Offset |
| **Nissan (cont'd)** | | | | | | | |
| Armada | Not Tested | Not Tested | Not Tested | Not Tested | Not Tested | Not Tested | Not Tested |
| Frontier | Not Tested | Not Tested | Not Tested | Not Tested | Not Tested | Not Tested | Not Tested |
| Maxima | Excellent | Good | Good | Good | Not Tested | Marginal | Good |
| Murano | Good | Good | Excellent | Good | Good | Marginal | Good |
| Pathfinder | Not Tested | Not Tested | Not Tested | Not Tested | Not Tested | Not Tested | Not Tested |
| Quest | Excellent | Excellent | Excellent | Excellent | Good | Poor | Good |
| Sentra | Good | Good | Poor | Not Tested | Good | Acceptable | Acceptable |
| Titan | Not Tested | Not Tested | Not Tested | Not Tested | Not Tested | Not Tested | Not Tested |
| Xterra | Not Tested | Not Tested | Not Tested | Not Tested | Not Tested | Not Tested | Not Tested |
| **Pontiac** | | | | | | | |
| Aztek | Average | Good | Not Tested | Not Tested | Not Tested | Marginal | Marginal |
| Bonneville | Good | Excellent | Good | Good | Not Tested | Marginal | Good |
| G6 | Not Tested | Not Tested | Not Tested | Not Tested | Not Tested | Not Tested | Not Tested |
| Grand Am | Good | Excellent | Very Poor | Good | Good | Marginal | Poor |
| Grand Prix | Average | Good | Average | Average | Not Tested | Not Tested | Not Tested |
| GTO | Not Tested | Not Tested | Not Tested | Not Tested | Not Tested | Not Tested | Not Tested |
| Montana | Good | Good | Excellent | Good | Average | Poor | Poor |
| Montana SV6 | Not Tested | Not Tested | Not Tested | Not Tested | Not Tested | Not Tested | Not Tested |
| Sunfire | Good | Good | Very Poor | Poor | Good | Acceptable | Poor |
| Vibe | Excellent | Excellent | Not Tested | Not Tested | Not Tested | Not Tested | Not Tested |
| **Porsche** | | | | | | | |
| 911 | Not Tested | Not Tested | Not Tested | Not Tested | Not Tested | Not Tested | Not Tested |
| Boxster | Not Tested | Not Tested | Not Tested | Not Tested | Not Tested | Not Tested | Not Tested |
| Cayenne | Not Tested | Not Tested | Not Tested | Not Tested | Not Tested | Not Tested | Not Tested |
| **Saab** | | | | | | | |
| 9-2X | Not Tested | Not Tested | Not Tested | Not Tested | Not Tested | Not Tested | Not Tested |
| 9-3 | Not Tested | Not Tested | Not Tested | Not Tested | Not Tested | Marginal | Good |
| 9-5 | Excellent | Excellent | Excellent | Good | Good | Poor | Good |
| 9-7X | Not Tested | Not Tested | Not Tested | Not Tested | Not Tested | Not Tested | Not Tested |
| **Saturn** | | | | | | | |
| ION | Excellent | Excellent | Not Tested | Average | Good | Not Tested | Not Tested |
| ION Red Line | Not Tested | Not Tested | Not Tested | Not Tested | Not Tested | Not Tested | Not Tested |
| Relay | Not Tested | Not Tested | Not Tested | Not Tested | Not Tested | Not Tested | Not Tested |

# Crash Test Scores

| | NHTSA | | | | | IIHS | |
|---|---|---|---|---|---|---|---|
| | Frontal Crash Driver | Frontal Crash Passenger | Side Crash Front Occupant | Side Crash Rear Occupant | Rollover Resistance | Bumper Bash | Offset |
| **Saturn (cont'd)** | | | | | | | |
| VUE | Excellent | Excellent | Excellent | Excellent | Not Tested | Poor | Good |
| VUE Red Line | Not Tested | Not Tested | Not Tested | Not Tested | Not Tested | Not Tested | Not Tested |
| **Scion** | | | | | | | |
| tC | Not Tested | Not Tested | Not Tested | Not Tested | Not Tested | Not Tested | Not Tested |
| xA | Not Tested | Not Tested | Not Tested | Not Tested | Not Tested | Not Tested | Not Tested |
| xB | Not Tested | Not Tested | Not Tested | Not Tested | Not Tested | Not Tested | Not Tested |
| **Subaru** | | | | | | | |
| Baja | Not Tested | Not Tested | Not Tested | Not Tested | Not Tested | Not Tested | Not Tested |
| Forester | Excellent | Excellent | Excellent | Excellent | Average | Good | Good |
| Impreza | Not Tested | Not Tested | Not Tested | Not Tested | Not Tested | Not Tested | Not Tested |
| Impreza WRX STi | Not Tested | Not Tested | Not Tested | Not Tested | Not Tested | Not Tested | Not Tested |
| Legacy | Not Tested | Not Tested | Not Tested | Not Tested | Not Tested | Not Tested | Not Tested |
| Outback | Not Tested | Not Tested | Not Tested | Not Tested | Not Tested | Not Tested | Not Tested |
| **Suzuki** | | | | | | | |
| Aerio | Good | Average | Excellent | Good | Not Tested | Poor | Good |
| Forenza | Good | Good | Average | Average | Not Tested | Not Tested | Not Tested |
| Grand Vitara | Good | Good | Excellent | Excellent | Average | Poor | Good |
| Reno | Not Tested | Not Tested | Not Tested | Not Tested | Not Tested | Not Tested | Not Tested |
| Verona | Not Tested | Not Tested | Not Tested | Not Tested | Not Tested | Marginal | Acceptable |
| XL-7 | Not Tested | Not Tested | Not Tested | Not Tested | Not Tested | Poor | Good |
| **Toyota** | | | | | | | |
| 4Runner | Good | Good | Excellent | Excellent | Average | Poor | Good |
| Camry | Good | Good | Good | Good | Not Tested | Acceptable | Good |
| Camry Solara | Excellent | Excellent | Not Tested | Not Tested | Not Tested | Not Tested | Not Tested |
| Celica | Good | Good | Average | Not Tested | Excellent | Not Tested | Not Tested |
| Corolla | Excellent | Excellent | Good | Good | Good | Good | Good |
| ECHO | Good | Good | Average | Good | Good | Not Tested | Not Tested |
| Highlander | Excellent | Excellent | Excellent | Excellent | Not Tested | Marginal | Good |
| Land Cruiser | Not Tested | Not Tested | Not Tested | Not Tested | Not Tested | Not Tested | Not Tested |
| Matrix | Excellent | Excellent | Not Tested | Not Tested | Good | Not Tested | Not Tested |
| MR2 Spyder | Not Tested | Not Tested | Not Tested | Not Tested | Not Tested | Not Tested | Not Tested |
| Prius | Excellent | Good | Good | Good | Not Tested | Not Tested | Not Tested |
| RAV4 | Good | Good | Excellent | Excellent | Not Tested | Poor | Not Tested |
| Sequoia | Excellent | Excellent | Not Tested | Not Tested | Average | Not Tested | Not Tested |

# Crash Test Scores

| | NHTSA | | | | | IIHS | |
|---|---|---|---|---|---|---|---|
| | Frontal Crash Driver | Frontal Crash Passenger | Side Crash Front Occupant | Side Crash Rear Occupant | Rollover Resistance | Bumper Bash | Offset |
| **Toyota (cont'd)** | | | | | | | |
| Sienna | Excellent | Excellent | Excellent | Excellent | Not Tested | Marginal | Good |
| Tacoma | Not Tested | Not Tested | Not Tested | Not Tested | Not Tested | Not Tested | Not Tested |
| Tundra | Good | Good | Excellent | Not Tested | Average | Poor | Good |
| **Volkswagen** | | | | | | | |
| Golf | Excellent | Excellent | Not Tested | Not Tested | Not Tested | Good | Good |
| GTI | Not Tested | Not Tested | Not Tested | Not Tested | Not Tested | Not Tested | Not Tested |
| Jetta | Excellent | Excellent | Good | Good | Good | Good | Good |
| New Beetle | Good | Good | Excellent | Average | Good | Good | Good |
| Passat | Excellent | Excellent | Good | Good | Good | Good | Good |
| Phaeton | Not Tested | Not Tested | Not Tested | Not Tested | Not Tested | Not Tested | Not Tested |
| Touareg | Not Tested | Not Tested | Excellent | Excellent | Not Tested | Not Tested | Not Tested |
| **Volvo** | | | | | | | |
| S40 | Good | Excellent | Excellent | Excellent | Not Tested | Not Tested | Good |
| S60 | Good | Good | Excellent | Excellent | Excellent | Poor | Good |
| S60 R | Good | Good | Excellent | Excellent | Excellent | Not Tested | Not Tested |
| S80 | Excellent | Excellent | Excellent | Excellent | Excellent | Poor | Good |
| V50 | Not Tested | Not Tested | Not Tested | Not Tested | Not Tested | Not Tested | Not Tested |
| V70 | Not Tested | Not Tested | Not Tested | Not Tested | Not Tested | Not Tested | Not Tested |
| V70 R | Not Tested | Not Tested | Not Tested | Not Tested | Not Tested | Not Tested | Not Tested |
| XC70 | Not Tested | Not Tested | Not Tested | Not Tested | Not Tested | Not Tested | Not Tested |
| XC90 | Excellent | Good | Excellent | Excellent | Good | Poor | Good |

All new vehicles sold in America come with at least three warranties, and many include roadside assistance. Described below are the major types of warranties and assistance provided to consumers.

### Basic:

Your basic warranty covers everything except items subject to wear and tear, such as oil filters, wiper blades, and the like. Tires and batteries often have their own warranty coverage, which will be outlined in your owner's manual or in separate documentation. Emissions equipment is required by the federal government to be covered by a manufacturer warranty for up to eight years or 80,000 miles.

### Drivetrain:

Drivetrain coverage takes care of most of the parts that make the car move, like the engine, transmission, axles and driveshaft. Like the basic warranty, parts subject to wear and tear like hoses and belts are not covered. However, most of the internal parts of the engine, such as the pistons and bearings, which are subject to wear and tear, are covered by the drivetrain warranty. See your owner's manual or local dealer for specific coverage.

### Rust or Corrosion:

This warranty protects you from rust-through problems with the sheetmetal. Surface rust doesn't count. The rust must make a hole to be covered. Keep your car washed and waxed, and rust shouldn't be a problem.

### Roadside Assistance:

Most manufacturers provide a service that will rescue you if your car leaves you stranded, even if it's your fault. Lock yourself out of the car? Somebody will come and open it up. Run out of gas? Somebody will deliver some fuel. Flat tire? Somebody will change it for you. See your owner's manual for details, or ask the dealer about specifics.

On the next page, you'll find a chart listing manufacturer warranties and customer service telephone numbers.

# Manufacturer Warranties

| Make | Basic | Drivetrain | Rust | Roadside Assistance | Customer Service # |
|------|-------|------------|------|---------------------|--------------------|
| Acura | 4/50,000 | 4/50,000 | 5/Unlimited | 4/50,000 | 1-800-382-2238 |
| Audi | 4/50,000 | 4/50,000 | 12/Unlimited | 4/Unlimited | 1-800-999-1009 |
| BMW | 4/50,000 | 4/50,000 | 12/Unlimited | 4/50,000 | 1-800-831-1117 |
| Buick | 3/36,000 | 3/36,000 | 6/100,000 | 3/36,000 | 1-800-521-7300 |
| Cadillac | 4/50,000 | 4/50,000 | 6/100,000 | 4/50,000 | 1-800-458-8006 |
| Chevrolet | 3/36,000 | 5/60,000* | 6/100,000* | 3/36,000 | 1-800-222-1020 |
| Chrysler | 3/36,000 | 7/70,000 | 5/100,000 | 3/36,000 | 1-800-992-1997 |
| Dodge | 3/36,000 | 7/70,000 | 5/100,000 | 3/36,000 | 1-800-992-1997 |
| Ford | 3/36,000 | 5/100,000* | 5/Unlimited | 3/36,000 | 1-800-392-3673 |
| GMC | 3/36,000 | 3/36,000 | 6/100,000 | 3/36,000 | 1-800-462-8782 |
| HUMMER | 3/36,000 | 3/36,000 | 6/100,000 | 3/36,000 | 1-800-732-5493 |
| Honda | 3/36,000 | 3/36,000 | 5/Unlimited | None Available | 1-310-783-2000 |
| Hyundai | 5/60,000 | 10/100,000 | 5/100,000 | 5/Unlimited | 1-800-633-5151 |
| Infiniti | 4/60,000 | 6/70,000 | 7/Unlimited | 4/60,000 | 1-800-662-6200 |
| Isuzu | 3/50,000 | 7/75,000 | 6/100,000 | 7/75,000 | 1-800-255-6727 |
| Jaguar | 4/50,000 | 4/50,000 | 6/Unlimited | 4/50,000 | 1-201-818-8500 |
| Jeep | 3/36,000 | 7/70,000 | 5/100,000 | 3/36,000 | 1-800-992-1997 |
| Kia | 5/60,000 | 10/100,000 | 5/100,000 | 5/Unlimited | 1-800-333-4542 |
| Land Rover | 4/50,000 | 4/50,000 | 6/Unlimited | 4/50,000 | 1-800-637-6837 |
| Lexus | 4/50,000 | 6/70,000 | 6/Unlimited | 4/Unlimited | 1-800-255-3987 |
| Lincoln | 4/50,000 | 4/50,000 | 5/Unlimited | 4/50,000 | 1-800-392-3673 |
| Lotus | 3/36,000 | 3/36,000 | None Available | None Available | 1-770-822-4566 |
| MINI | 4/50,000 | 4/50,000 | 6/Unlimited | 4/50,000 | 1-866-275-6464 |
| Mazda | 4/50,000 | 4/50,000* | 5/Unlimited | 4/50,000 | 1-800-222-5500 |
| Mercedes-Benz | 4/50,000 | 4/50,000 | 4/50,000 | Unlimited | 1-800-222-0100 |
| Mercury | 3/36,000 | 3/36,000 | 5/Unlimited | 3/36,000 | 1-800-392-3673 |
| Mitsubishi | 5/60,000 | 10/100,000 | 7/100,000 | 3/36,000 | 1-800-222-0037 |
| Nissan | 3/36,000 | 5/60,000 | 5/Unlimited | 3/36,000 | 1-800-647-7261 |
| Pontiac | 3/36,000 | 3/36,000 | 6/100,000 | 3/36,000 | 1-800-762-2737 |
| Porsche | 4/50,000 | 4/50,000 | 10/Unlimited | 4/50,000 | 1-800-767-7243 |
| Saab | 4/50,000 | 4/50,000 | 10/Unlimited* | 4/50,000 | 1-800-955-9007 |
| Saturn | 3/36,000 | 3/36,000 | 6/100,000 | 3/36,000 | 1-800-553-6000 |
| Scion | 3/36,000 | 5/60,000 | 5/Unlimited | None Available | 1-866-707-2466 |
| Subaru | 3/36,000 | 5/60,000 | 5/Unlimited | 3/36,000 | 1-800-782-2783 |
| Suzuki | 3/36,000 | 7/100,000 | 3/36,000 | 3/36,000 | 1-800-934-0934 |
| Toyota | 3/36,000 | 5/60,000 | 5/Unlimited | 3/36,000 | 1-800-331-4331 |
| Volkswagen | 4/50,000 | 5/60,000 | 12/Unlimited | 4/50,000 | 1-800-428-4304 |
| Volvo | 4/50,000 | 4/50,000 | 8/Unlimited | 4/Unlimited | 1-800-458-1552 |

All data sourced directly from manufacturer customer service assistance telephone operators. All data in years/miles. *On select models.

**By John Pearley Huffman**

For a car enthusiast, knowing the history of the Ford Mustang is as basic as knowing the laws of thermodynamics are to a physicist, knowing Hebrew is to a rabbi or knowing when the bacon is done to a cook at Denny's. The Mustang is a pillar of American automotive lore, and the car that brought sporting dash and styling at a price almost anyone could afford.

The Mustang has never been an exotic car. Even the rarest, most powerful Mustangs ever built (such as the '69 Boss 429) were assembled with haphazard care by a UAW workforce facing a quick-moving, continuous production line with parts that were shared in common with six-cylinder Falcons, four-door Fairlanes and stripped Galaxies. Handcrafting and taking the time to do something extra special has never been part of Mustang production.

But that hasn't kept the Mustang from capturing the hearts of drivers for nearly 40 years. As ordinary a car as the Mustang has always been, it has always been extraordinarily attractive.

## First Generation (1964 1/2-1966)

1964 1/2 Mustang coupe

Ford's Mustang was conceived in full knowledge that in the mid-'60s the biggest population bubble in history was coming of age in America. Baby boomers would rule the '60s and there was little reason to think they wanted cars that were anything like their parents' cars. The production Mustang was shown to the public for the first time inside the Ford Pavilion at the New York World's Fair on April 17, 1964—two months and nine days after the Beatles first came to New York to appear on *The Ed Sullivan Show*. It went on sale at Ford dealers that same day.

The 1964 1/2 production Mustang followed two Mustang concept cars. The Mustang I shown in 1962 was a midengine two-seater powered by a V4. The Mustang II show car first displayed at the United States Grand Prix in Watkins Glen, N.Y., during October 1963, was a front-engine, four-seater foreshadowing the production machine that went on sale six months later. Compared to those two, the production machine was dowdy. Compared to every other American car then in production, except the Corvette, the Mustang was gorgeously sleek.

To make the Mustang affordable it needed to share much of its engineering with an existing Ford product. That product was the smallest Ford of the time, the compact Falcon. In fact, the first Mustangs were built in the same Dearborn, Mich., plant as the Falcon.

Initially offered as either a notchback coupe or convertible, the Mustang's unibody structure was laid over a 108-inch wheelbase and stretched out 181.6 inches from bumper to bumper. While it shared its front double-wishbone/coil spring and leaf spring rear suspension as well as its overall length with the Falcon, the proportions of the Mustang were different. Its cockpit was pushed further back on the chassis, resulting in a longer hood and shorter rear deck design, and both its roof and cowl were lower. It's with those proportions — detailed with such iconic touches as the running horse in the grille, the side scallops along the flanks and the taillights divided into three sections — the Mustang became a car people were instantly passionate about.

Engine choices started with the utterly lame 170-cubic-inch (2.8-liter) OHV straight six that made just 101 horsepower; then proceeded through a 200-cubic-inch (3.3-liter) OHV straight six rated at a flaccid 116 horsepower; a 260-cubic-inch (4.3-liter) OHV V8 breathing through a two-barrel carburetor and making 164 horsepower; a 210-horsepower two-barrel-equipped 289-cubic-inch (4.7-liter) V8; a four-barrel 289 making 220 horsepower; and, at the top, the famous "K-code" high-compression, solid-lifter, four-barrel 289 pumping out a lusty 271 horsepower. K-code-equipped cars got a special badge on their front fenders indicating that not only did the engine displace 289 cubic inches, but that it was also the "High Performance" version.

A three-speed manual transmission was standard with every engine except the 271-horse 289, which was available only with the four-speed manual that was optional on other models. The Cruise-O-Matic three-speed automatic transmission was also offered.

Nothing could stop the 1964 1/2 Mustang (especially not its four-wheel drum brakes) and with Ford furiously adding production capacity for the "pony car" at plants around the country, the company sold an amazing 126,538 of them during that abbreviated 1964 model year — 97,705 coupes and 28,833 convertibles. The V8s outsold Mustangs equipped with the six by nearly three to one.

The three most significant additions to the Mustang for 1965 were the neat 2+2 fastback body, the optional GT equipment and trim package and optional power front disc brakes. Gone forever was the 260 V8 that few buyers were choosing anyhow.

Even Ford was shocked at America's appetite for the Mustang during '65. It sold an astounding 409,260 coupes, 77,079 2+2 fastbacks and 73,112 convertibles that year. That's a total of 559,451 Mustangs for the '65 model year.

With that many Mustangs in the nation's automotive bloodstream, it was natural that many of them would be raced. But in order to go road racing head to head against Chevrolet's Corvette, Ford needed a two-seater. And rules said that Ford had to make at least 100 of them by January 1965. That's where Carroll Shelby came in.

Shelby, a Texan and longtime racer, saw the potential to slay Corvettes with the Mustang and took 100 of the first 2+2s equipped with the K-code engine built at Ford's San Jose, Calif., plant down to Los Angeles for modification into "GT 350" models. Tossing the rear seats aside, Shelby added such performance items as oversize front disc brakes, a fiberglass hood and a lowered suspension with oversize tires on 15-inch wheels. Shelby's legendary series of modified Mustangs would be built through 1970 in various forms and are today considered some of the most desirable Mustangs ever built. It's impossible to ignore the Shelby Mustangs (which carried Shelby VIN numbers) when recounting Mustang history, but space considerations prevent further discussion of them in this article.

The easiest way to tell the 1966 Mustang from the '65 is the later car's lack of horizontal or vertical dividing bars in the grille — the running horse logo seems to float unsupported in the '66's slatted grille. Other changes were limited to color variations, a revised instrument cluster and a few trim tweaks. Incredibly, the '66 was even more popular than the '65 and Ford sold 607,568 of them — 499,751 coupes, 35,698 2+2s and 72,119 convertibles. That's still the most Mustangs ever sold during a single model year.

How do you follow total sales of 1,288,557 Mustangs over just two-and-a-half years? Carefully.

## Second Generation (1967-1968)

By 1967, the Mustang had something it hadn't had before: competition. Chevrolet was now making the Camaro, Pontiac the Firebird, and Plymouth had redesigned the Barracuda into a more serious machine. Even within Ford, Mercury was now selling the Cougar.

1968 Mustang GT fastback

Ford's response to that competition was a new, slightly larger Mustang with an all-new body over what was pretty much the same chassis. The wheelbase was still 108 inches, but total length was up two inches to 183.6 inches and every styling feature was just a little bit exaggerated — the grille opening was bigger, the side scallops deeper, the taillights were now larger and concave instead of modest and convex, the 2+2 fastback's roof now extended all the way back to the trunk lid's trailing edge and the convertible's rear window was now a two-piece item made of real glass instead of instantly hazing plastic. A hood with dual recesses was optional.

The standard power plant was now the 200-cubic-inch six making 120 horsepower with a 250-cubic-inch (4.1-liter) 155-horsepower six and the 200-, 225- and 271-horsepower K-code 289 V8s optional. New on the menu was a 390-cubic-inch (6.4-liter) "big-block" V8 breathing through a Holley four-barrel carburetor making 315 horsepower. Accommodating that wider engine meant that the front suspension's track needed to be widened by 2.5 inches for clearance.

With its wider track, the '67 Mustang was a more stable car than the '66. The seats were more comfortable, and the instrumentation was easier to read. It was, generally speaking, a better car in every way that counted. Ford sold 356,271 coupes, 71,042 2+2s and 44,808 convertibles during '67 despite the new competition. Of those, only 472 cars were equipped with the 271-horsepower 289, while around 28,800 had the 390 under their hoods.

Federally mandated side marker lights and a revised grille distinguished the 1968 Mustang from the '67 on the outside, while a slew of new engines set it apart mechanically. A low-performance 195-horsepower 289 V8 was still an option, but the other 289s were gone in favor of two new 302-cubic-inch (4.9-liter) versions of the small block V8. The two-barrel 302 made 220 horsepower, while the four-barrel-equipped version put out 230 horsepower.

More glamorous than the revised small V8s were new 427- and 428-cubic-inch (both convert to about 7.0 liters) versions of the big-block V8. The more radical 427, which had a slightly higher-compression ratio and wilder cam, was rated at 390 horsepower, while the more civilized 428 knocked out 335 horsepower. Both the 427 and 428 were very rare options. Those big engines hinted at what was in store for the Mustang over the next few years.

## Third Generation (1969-1970)

The Mustang got larger once again for 1969 even though the wheelbase remained 108 inches. The new body for 1969 featured four headlights, a sharp nose with a simpler grille that dispensed with the famed running horse centerpiece and a revision of the fake side scoops on the coupe and convertible. The fastback had large nonfunctional scoops dug high into its rear fenders. Unlike the '67, the '69 design clearly broke from established Mustang styling themes.

But under the sheet metal the Mustang still carried that Falcon-sourced front suspension and the solid rear axle was still perched on leaf springs.

The range of powertrain options grew once again for '69 and those led to the development of exciting new models. Base power still came from the 200-cubic-inch straight six, the 250 six was back again as an option. But the 289 V8s were gone for good with a two-barrel, 220-horsepower 302 now serving as the least intimidating V8 available. Beyond the 302 was a new 351-cubic-inch (5.8-liter) V8 which made 250 horsepower when gasping in air through a two-barrel carb and 290 horsepower with a higher-compression ratio and four-barrel carburetion. The

1969 Mustang fastback

390 was back making 320 horsepower and two 428s were offered, with the "Cobra Jet" version making 335 horsepower and the "Super Cobra Jet" pounding out 360.

For those who wanted a luxurious Mustang, Ford offered the '69 coupe as a "Grande" model. For those who wanted a performance image, the company came up with a "Mach 1" version of the 2+2 fastback available only with the 351, 390 or 428 engines.

The two most intriguing '69 Mustangs came in the middle of the model run. Both were named "Boss" and both were built for racing.

The Boss 302 Mustang arose because Ford needed a car to go up against the successful Camaro Z28 in the SCCA Trans Am road racing series. So Ford came up with the Boss 302, which benefited from an optimized suspension, a neat Larry Shinoda-designed body package (which included a flat-black hood, rear window louvers and a rear deck spoiler) and a high-compression, deep-breathing 302 V8 making a wicked 290 horsepower. Ford would sell 1,628 of these near-racers and they'd prove effective weapons on the racetrack as well.

The Boss 429 was built only to homologate Ford's spectacular 429-cubic-inch (7.0-liter) hemi-headed V8 for NASCAR stock car competition. The 429 was ludicrously underrated at 375 horsepower (500 horsepower was more like it), and there's no explanation as to why the company insisted on shoehorning the big engine into the Mustang (the front suspension had to be virtually redesigned) instead of putting it in the roomier bay of the Torino, which was the car Ford actually ran in NASCAR. Only 859 Boss 429 fastbacks were built during the '69 model year and they all had large functional scoops on their hoods.

Those Boss 429s were but a drop in the 1969 Mustang sales bucket. In all, Ford sold 299,824 Mustangs that year, including 72,458 Mach 1s and 14,746 convertibles.

Ford went back to just two headlights for the 1970 Mustang, replacing the outboard lights with attractive scoops that fed nothing at all. Other changes included the elimination of the phony side scoops from all models. Also, the 351 V8s now came from Ford's Cleveland plant and were of a slightly different design from the previous 351s that had been built at the Windsor, Ontario, facility.

During the '70 model year, sales dropped to 190,727 Mustangs including 6,318 Boss 302s, 499 Boss 429s and just 7,673 convertibles.

# Fourth Generation (1971-1973)

1972 Mustang coupe

Flat-featured and flabby, the 1971 Mustang was hardly beloved upon its introduction and has never really gained a place in enthusiasts' hearts. The wheelbase stretched to 109 inches and the car grew all the way to 187.5 inches long overall, and that was enough to kill the light, airy look and feel that had made the Mustang so engaging.

Still running on the Falcon-derived chassis, the '71 Mustang had engines ranging from the 250-cubic-inch six rated at 145 horsepower, through a plebeian 302 making 210 horsepower, two 351s at 240 and 285 horsepower and new Cobra Jet and Super Cobra Jet 429s pounding out 370 and 375 horsepower, respectively. Gone from the scene were both the Boss 302 and Boss 429 and in their place was a new Boss 351 with a (you guessed it) 351 V8 aboard that whacked out 330 horsepower.

Whether it was due to this new car's so-so appearance or the age of the Mustang concept is not known, but only 149,678 '71 Mustangs were produced. That's 41,049 less units than '70 and less than a quarter of the number sold during the 1966 model year.

While the 1972 Mustang was mostly carryover from '71, a change to net horsepower ratings and lower compression ratios (to reduce emissions) knocked the ratings of the 250-cube six to 98 horsepower, the lackluster 302 to 140 horsepower, and the three 351s offered to 163, 248 and 266 horsepower. Gone were both 429s, as well as the Boss 351. Sales slumped to just 111,015.

Power ratings dropped even further during the 1973 model year as emissions regulations began strangling output. The six now made a totally inadequate 88 horsepower, the 302 just 135 ponies, and the two remaining 351s (a two-barrel of Windsor design and a two-barrel Cleveland) just over 150 horsepower each.

Even though 1973 sales picked up to 134,867 cars, it was obviously time for Ford to rethink the Mustang.

## Fifth Generation (1974-1978)

1975 Mustang Cobra fastback

Everyone hates the Mustang II. It was too small, underpowered, handled poorly, terribly put together, ill-proportioned, chintzy in its details and altogether subpar. It also sold ridiculously well.

By the early '70s it was obvious to Ford that the pony car market the Mustang had established was changing. Emissions regulations made the high-compression, high-horsepower V8s unsustainable, and baby boomers were increasingly turning to smaller imported cars. Making the Mustang a smaller, more fuel-efficient car seemed like a good idea.

Tossing aside the Falcon components that had underpinned the Mustang from Day One, Ford plopped the 1974 Mustang II (Ford put the "II" there to indicate the extent of the car's change from the oversize '73) atop the basic structure and suspension of its subcompact Pinto. The Pinto was smaller than the Falcon, but otherwise similar. It was still a unibody design, the front suspension was still a double wishbone design and the rear suspension still bolted its solid rear axle to a pair of leaf springs. If there were any steps forward in technology with the Pinto chassis, it was that it had a rack-and-pinion steering gear rather than the Falcon's recirculating ball, and front disc brakes were standard.

The Mustang II rode on a miniscule 96.2-inch wheelbase and stretched out just 175 inches long total. That's 12.8 inches less in wheelbase and 12.5 inches less in overall length than the '73 Mustang. That's also 11.8 inches less in wheelbase and 6.6 inches less in overall length than the original Mustang. And it weighed in about 400 pounds lighter than the '73 version as well.

Despite the smaller size, the Mustang II actually revived traditional Mustang styling cues like the scalloped sides while retaining others like the three-piece taillights and the running horse in the grille. Available as either a notchback coupe or a fastback hatchback, the Mustang II's pricing ranged from $3,134 for a base coupe to $3,674 for a Mach 1 hatchback.

Lighter weight with the same power means more speed. But the Mustang II's reduced mass came along with less power. In fact, the '74 Mustang II was the first Mustang ever to be offered with a four-cylinder engine and without a V8.

The base engine was a single-overhead cam four displacing 2.3 liters (that's 140 cubic inches, and from here on out Ford expressed all Mustang engine sizes metrically) and rated at a truly pathetic 88 horsepower. The only optional engine was the German-built "Cologne" 2.8-liter

OHV V6 making an underwhelming 105 horsepower. In stock form, the first Mustang II was underpowered, period. Two transmissions were available, a standard four-speed manual or a three-speed automatic.

In addition to a base notchback and base fastback, a "Ghia" notchback and Mach 1 fastback were offered during '74. Ordering the Mach 1 mandated inclusion of the V6 in the package. The Ghia included a vinyl top and fancy interior trim.

Coming to the market while memories of the OPEC fuel embargo of 1973 were still fresh in buyers' minds, the more economical Mustang II sold a stunning 385,993 units during its inaugural year. As much as the Mustang II is despised today, Ford appreciated its success back then.

A V8 returned to the Mustang lineup for 1975. The 5.0-liter (302 in Amerispeak) V8 had only a two-barrel carburetor through which to breathe, and had to exhale through a catalytic converter; both conspired to limit output to an anemic 122 horsepower. Further, the automatic transmission was the only transmission available behind the V8. The addition of the catalytic converter also tempered the output of the standard four to just 83 horsepower and of the V6 to just 97 horsepower.

The model lineup for '75 was supplemented with a new "MPG" coupe aimed at budget shoppers, but the market's initial enthusiasm for the Mustang II was already waning and production dropped to 188,586 — that's just 49 percent of the number made during '74.

Returning essentially unchanged for 1976, the Mustang II was stagnant during the year. All the variations from '75 returned with a new "Stallion" appearance package available on the fastback. But the most notorious addition was the Cobra II package that added a big rear spoiler, a fake hood scoop and blue stripes across white paint to a V8-powered fastback. The Cobra II wasn't any faster than other similarly powered Mustang IIs, but it sure looked radical and Farrah Fawcett-Majors' character, Jill Munroe, drove one on the huge TV hit series Charlie's Angels. Also in '76, the now 134-horsepower V8 was available with a four-speed manual transmission, output of the standard four swelled to a heady 92 horsepower and the V6's rating went to 102 horsepower.

Maybe it was bicentennial-induced hysteria, but Mustang II sales came in at a surprisingly stable 187,567 units — a mere 1,019 less than in '75.

Except for some minor trim changes and the expansion of colors available on the Cobra II, the 1977 Mustang II was visually identical to the '76. New to the options list were T-top removable glass roof panels and simulated wire wheel covers. Power from the four and V6 dropped again to 89 and 93 horsepower, respectively. Production dropped about 18 percent to 153,117 cars.

For 1978 the Mustang II got some revised trim and the radical-looking (but mildly performing) "King Cobra" version debuted. The King Cobra wasn't much more than a Cobra II with revised graphics and the hood scoop turned around backward, but it was visually about as nutty a Mustang as has ever been built. Mysteriously, production climbed to 192,410 units.

Thankfully, it was time for Ford to put the Mustang II out of its (and our) misery.

## Sixth Generation (1979-1993)

Any car that stays in production through 15 model years has to be counted as a success. But when the all-new 1979 Mustang (no "II" and no "III") was introduced, few would have predicted

1986 Mustang coupe

such a long life for it. Or that it would inspire a passionate following of amazing breadth. Or that it would be used as a cop car.

Tossing aside the wimpy Pinto parts, the 1979 Mustang was built atop the shortened chassis of the Ford Fairmont "Fox" body that had been introduced for '78. While the Fox platform was still a unibody structure, it shared little else with previous Mustangs. The new front suspension was a modified MacPherson strut system that mounted a spring separate from the strut itself, while a new link and coil spring rear suspension held up the back of the car. This basic suspension system would remain in use on Mustangs through at least the 2003 model year.

Available as either a coupe or fastback hatchback, the new Mustang rode on a 100.4-inch wheelbase and was 179.1 inches long. That's a bit more than four inches longer in both dimensions over the Mustang II, but still shorter than the original Mustang's 108-inch wheelbase and 181.6-inch overall length. However, the '79 Mustang was significantly roomier inside than any previous Mustang thanks to a more upright-oriented cockpit and flatter doors that allowed more shoulder and hiproom.

The new Mustang's styling was angular and handsome, but hardly related to previous Mustangs. There was no running horse in the shovel nose grille which was flanked by four square headlights, the sides were devoid of the signature side scallop and the taillights were divided into six segments instead of three. With slightly different blistered fenders, a flatter grille and different taillights, Mercury sold the same car as the Capri. The '79 Mustang was at its best wearing the optional 390mm three-spoke "TRX" wheels and tires, but there was little about it that was intrinsically Mustanglike.

All three engines from the '78 Mustang II carried over to the '79 Mustang. The 2.3-liter SOHC was rated at 88 horsepower, the 2.8-liter Cologne V6 at 109 horsepower and the 4.9-liter (but called a 5.0-liter by Ford) V8 made 140 horsepower. They were joined by a turbocharged version of the four also making 140 horsepower but saddled with epic boost lag and hideously bad reliability. Late in the model year, the old 200-cubic-inch (3.3-liter) OHV straight six reappeared making 94 horsepower. Four-speed manual transmissions were standard behind all engines with a three-speed automatic optional.

The most desirable of all '79 Mustangs would turn out to be the 6,000 Indy pace car replica fastbacks, which featured a unique hood scoop, unique front air dam, unique rear spoiler, black and silver paint with orange graphics and an interior blessed with genuine Recaro front seats. The pace car was available with either turbo four or V8 power and included the TRX wheel and tire package.

With the Ghia trim back on the coupe and a "Cobra" package available on the hatchback (which had a fake hood scoop but no spoilers), the '79 Mustang was a hit. A healthy 369,936 Mustangs were built that model year.

In a very real way the 1980 Mustangs were worse than the '79s. While visually they changed very little (a few aerodynamic tweaks were made, including a subtle lip spoiler on the coupe's trunk lid), under the hood things got ugly. Gone from the line were both the 2.8-liter V6 and the 5.0-liter V8. The only six available was now the wheezy 3.3-liter straight six, while the sole V8 was a new version of Ford's small-block displacing 255 cubic inches (4.2 liters) and gasping out just 119 horsepower. It was the smallest — and the worst — V8 ever offered in a Mustang. By default the turbo four was the most powerful engine in the '80 Mustang inventory. Too bad it was a grenade waiting to detonate.

All the spoilers and scoops used on the '79 pace car were now part of the '80 Cobra package, which also included a tasteless oversize cobra hood decal. In what was the worst year ever for Mustang engine performance, Ford sold 271,322 examples of the breed.

A five-speed manual transmission finally came to the Mustang in 1981 as an option behind the regular and turbocharged fours. Also, making a return appearance on the options list was a T-top roof. Otherwise the '81 was much the same car as the '80, and sales slipped dramatically to 182,552 cars.

Big news came for 1982 in the form of a new "High Output" (HO) version of the 5.0-liter V8 making a healthy (for the time) 157 horsepower with two-barrel carburetion in a revived Mustang GT hatchback. Backed by a four-speed manual transmission and wearing many of the '79 pace car's body pieces, the '82 Mustang GT wasn't quite a return to the glory days of high-performance, but it was a step in the right direction.

The rest of the Mustang lineup was set up in three progressively more luxurious series: L, GL and GLX. The turbo four was gone (temporarily), but the base four, iron lump straight six and inexcusable 4.2-liter V8 all carried forward through '82. The most unusual model Mustang, however, wasn't sold to the public at all, but a "Special Service Package" notchback coupe equipped with the Mustang GT's 157-horsepower V8 and four-speed transmission that was used by the California Highway Patrol as a pursuit vehicle. The CHP bought 400 of the SSP Mustangs in '82 and they, along with numerous other state and local law enforcement agencies, would continue buying them right through 1993 when Ford ended production.

A new grille with Ford's Blue Oval logo at its center came along with the 1983 Mustang. But the grille was the least of the changes that year, as the Mustang convertible returned in the form of a conversion performed by ASC, Inc. on coupe bodies. The convertible was offered in GLX and GT trim and featured a real glass rear window, power operation and rear-quarter windows that rolled down. The convertible was instantly popular.

The drivetrain lineup was also revised for '83 with the straight six and 4.2-liter V8 being eliminated and quickly forgotten. A revised version of the turbocharged 2.3-liter SOHC four returned to the lineup, this time with electronic fuel injection that did a wonderful job of tempering turbo lag and increasing engine longevity. But its 142-horsepower output didn't seem all that impressive, especially since the 5.0-liter HO V8 now sported a four-barrel carburetor and was rated at 175 horsepower. And the V8 was now available with the excellent Borg-Warner T5 five-speed manual transmission.

The normally aspirated 2.3-liter SOHC four was still around for buyers too timid for anything else, but the six-cylinder option was the new "Essex" 3.8-liter V6 making 112 horsepower.

Despite all the improvements, the '83 Mustang was hardly a barn burner in the sales race. A total of 120,873 Mustangs were sold that model year, including 23,438 convertibles.

Much of the 1984 Mustang line was carried over from '83, but there were some significant changes and an unexpected new model in the line. True dual exhausts came to the 5.0 HO V8 that boosted output up to a healthy 205 horsepower in the Mustang GT. And a fuel-injected version of the HO V8 was offered with the automatic transmission (now with a fourth overdrive gear). The turbo four was back for one last year, now rated at 145 horsepower in the Mustang GT.

There were also revisions to suspension tuning, and at midyear Ford offered a "GT-350" 20th anniversary package for convertibles and hatchbacks. But the big surprise came in the form of the technologically sophisticated SVO Mustang.

With its own unique appearance (single square headlamps in a grille-free front end, plus a unique dual-plane rear spoiler), the SVO was powered by an intercooled version of the turbocharged 2.3-liter four rated at an impressive 175 horsepower. Wearing big 16-inch wheels on five-lug hubs, with four-wheel disc brakes aboard for better stopping, the lavishly equipped SVO was quick, agile and expensive with a base price of $15,596. However, no matter how interesting it was on a technical level, it wasn't as quick as the V8-powered Mustang GT and never sold in large numbers.

Another new grille design came along for the 1985 model year featuring a single large slit between the two pairs of headlights. The GT was treated to a new set of 15-inch cast-aluminum wheels shod with P225/60VR15 Goodyear Eagle "Gatorback" tires, and thanks to a serpentine single belt accessory drive system and revised roller cam, the 5.0 HO engine was now making a full 210 horsepower in four-barrel carbureted form. The fuel-injected HO hooked to the four-speed automatic now made 180 horsepower. The SVO continued forward, but the turbocharged four was gone from the Mustang GT options list.

Fuel injection became the only induction system on the 1986 5.0 HO, and output was 200 horsepower with both the five-speed manual and four-speed automatic in Mustang GTs. The SVO Mustang's turbo four was recalibrated and its output was also 200 horsepower.

With Mercury's Capri out of production after the 1986 model year, Ford simplified Mustang production in 1987 by eliminating the V6 engine option, killing the high-priced SVO, and paring down the trim levels to just LX and GT — the coupe in LX only with the hatchback and convertible available in both trims. The front end and taillights were redesigned once again with the GT getting its own grilleless face, flush single headlamps, specific taillights, rear spoiler, urethane side skirts and turbine wheels. But many found the low-key skirtless LX to be the real performance value, as it was offered with all the GT's performance options, but without the look-at-me exterior pieces. Both the LX and GT also got a new interior including an improved dashboard that grouped the instrumentation in a pod in front of the driver.

Carburetors were finally a thing of the past for Mustangs as even the 2.3-liter, SOHC four-cylinder engine now sported fuel injection and made 90 horsepower. The 5.0-liter HO was also revised and now made a robust 225 horsepower regardless of transmission. At this point in its development, the "5.0 Mustang" had reached its full flower and would remain mechanically unchanged through 1993. In fact, the 1988 and 1989 Mustangs were virtually unchanged from 1987.

There was a good chance the Mustang would be killed before the 1990 model year, as Ford contemplated re-engineering the car to accept a driver-side airbag. But Ford decided to spend the money and installed the airbag for 1990, eliminating the tilt steering column in the process.

A new five-spoke, 16-inch wheel was offered on both LX and GT 5.0-liter Mustangs for 1991. The car carried over into 1992 with only a few not-very-special "limited edition" models to goose sales by offering special wheels and paint.

While the basic Mustang LX and Mustang GT were unchanged for 1993 (the 5.0-liter engine's output was revised to 205 horsepower — probably for marketing reasons with the redesigned Mustang coming for '94), a new special-edition Mustang did appear in the form of the SVT Cobra. A parts bin mix of 1983 Mustang taillights, the front air dam from the GT, a new grille with the running horse emblem on it and 17-inch wheels scavenged from a delayed Thunderbird project, the SVT Cobra was nonetheless surprisingly attractive. The 5.0-liter in the Cobra was modified slightly to make 235 horsepower while the improved suspension, bigger wheels and tires and four-wheel disc brakes all expanded the other parameters of performance. Only 4,993 of the Cobras were built during the 1993 model year. Another 107 track-ready versions of the Cobra, known as the "Cobra R," were also built without such luxuries as a radio or backseat.

Even after 15 years in production, Ford still sold 114,228 Fox-based Mustangs during the '93 model year. Obviously the Fox-bodied Mustang was totally exhausted. Or was it?

## Seventh Generation (1994-1998)

By the early '90s, Ford knew it needed to keep the Mustang around no matter what — that wasn't something the company was so convinced of a decade earlier. Kill the Mustang and it would kill the one car the whole world associated with Ford. But a new Mustang would still have to be affordable, and the only way to control costs would be to build it atop the existing Fox chassis.

1996 Mustang GT

What appeared for 1994 was a Mustang clearly influenced by the styling themes of Mustangs past. There was the galloping horse in the grille, the side scallop reappeared and the taillights were split into three segments (albeit horizontally instead of vertically). Inside, the cockpit featured a twin-pod dashboard that recalled the dashes used between '64 1/2 and '73. Only two body styles were now offered, a two-door coupe with a semifastback roof and a convertible.

The Fox platform was thoroughly reinforced for the '94 Mustang, but the basic modified MacPherson strut front and coil sprung solid rear axle returned intact. Four-wheel disc brakes were now used throughout the line with ABS optional.

The biggest beneficiary of the new structure was the drop top; this was the first Mustang convertible since the '73 that was actually conceived as a convertible and not a conversion. The new convertible's structure was significantly stiffer and the car handled better than the outgoing '93.

Engine choices were also pared down to two for '94. Base Mustangs (no more LX, just Mustang) got a fuel-injected development of the 3.8-liter Essex V6 rated at 145 horsepower. The Mustang GT got a revised version of the 5.0-liter V8 with a flatter intake manifold that was rated at 215 horsepower. The disappointingly low-output rating of the V8 made many suspect that the '93 5.0's down-rating to 205 horsepower was done in a relatively shallow attempt to mitigate any outcry resulting from the squashed intake's stealing power from the '94 5.0-liter. Both engines could be mated to either five-speed manual or four-speed automatic transmissions.

Available with either 16-inch or 17-inch wheels and tires, the '94 Mustang GT proved to be a better handling, more secure driving car than ever before. But it wasn't really any more sophisticated than the '93. Most tests of the time found the 5.0-liter V8's performance to be soft in comparison to the 5.0-liter used in the '93 Mustang.

For the third time in its history, the Mustang was chosen to pace the Indianapolis 500. Instead of conjuring up some sort of special edition for the Speedway, Ford assigned its Special Vehicle Team (SVT) the task of building another Cobra version of the Mustang. The result was a slightly modified GT wearing 17-inch wheels and, thanks to a set of Ford's "GT40" cylinder heads and a different intake, a 5.0-liter V8 making 240 horsepower. Cobras were distinguished by their own uniquely blistered hood, rear spoiler and front fascia with round foglamps and snake logos on their fenders and in their grilles. While the Cobra used to pace the 500 was a convertible, the Cobra coupe was more common. Fully 5,009 Cobra coupes were sold along with just 1,000 convertibles during '94.

The new Mustang was a hit, but hardly overwhelming. Selling into a market vastly more fragmented than it was in 1965, Ford sold 123,198 Mustangs during '94. Not bad at all considering that the car didn't go on sale until January of 1994.

Why change something that was working? The 1995 Mustangs were virtually identical to the '94s. The only change to the model lineup was the introduction of a "GTS" model that essentially put the Mustang GT's drivetrain into a plain Mustang shell. Sales rose to 190,994 units that year, including 48,264 convertibles and another 5,006 SVT Cobras (1,003 of which were drop tops).

The big change for 1996 was the abandonment of the 5.0-liter V8 in favor of Ford's 4.6-liter, SOHC V8 in the GT. Rated at the same 215 horsepower as the outgoing 5.0, the 4.6 opened a new chapter in Mustang history as the good old small-block Ford V8 was left behind after serving in the Mustang for 31 of the previous 32 model years. In addition, the 3.8-liter V6 was rerated to 150 horsepower. Transmission choices remained the five-speed manual or four-speed automatic.

A special run of 250 Cobra R models were also produced for '95 powered by a 5.8-liter version of the Ford small-block V8 making 300 horsepower. The lack of a rear seat, radio or air conditioning didn't keep enthusiasts from snapping them up instantly.

Bowing to enthusiasts' demand, all Mustangs got new taillights for '96 that were divided vertically into three segments as tradition dictated. Otherwise, except for revised front fender badges on the GT announcing the 4.6 engine, styling was unchanged.

Also new for '96 was a heavily revised version of the SVT Cobra that now featured an all-aluminum, DOHC, 32-valve version of the 4.6-liter engine. To accommodate the tall engine, the hood sported a new bulge but otherwise the car looked quite similar to the '95. But with a full 305 horsepower available, it performed much better. This was, after all, the most powerful V8 in a Mustang since the Boss 351 back in '71. Cobra production expanded to 7,496 coupes and 2,510 convertibles during '96.

Some new upholstery, a new security system and new colors came for 1997, but that's about it. Ford built 108,344 Mustangs that model year, with 6,961 of them being Cobra coupes and 3,088 Cobra convertibles. Except for redesigned five-spoke wheels on the Cobra, revisions to the 4.6-liter V8 that increased output to 225 horsepower and the usual juggling of colors and trim, the 1998 Mustang carried over from '97. Inexplicably, sales increased to a healthy 175,522 total units that year, including 5,174 Cobra coupes and 3,480 Cobra convertibles. By the way, what is a "Mustang Cobra" anyhow? Is it a reptile? A horse? Or is it some cruel, misbegotten hybrid of the two?

## Eighth Generation (1999-2004)

New sharply creased fenders and revised front and rear fascias appeared on the 1999 Mustang while the windshield and roofs carried forward unchanged. An appreciated touch with the new styling was the "corral" around the galloping horse in the Mustang's grille. In fact, most of the interior and chassis was also unchanged, so it might be best to think of this as less a true eighth-generation Mustang than as an aesthetic development of the seventh. All 1999 Mustangs also got special 35th anniversary badges on their front fenders.

2003 Mustang convertible

Significant revisions to both the base Mustang's 3.8-liter V6 and the GT's 4.6-liter V8 seriously increased their horsepower ratings for '99. The V6 was now pumping out an impressive 190 horsepower and the V8 a stout 260. Transmission choices remained either the five-speed manual or four-speed automatic.

Intended to be the pride of the Mustang fleet for '99 was the seriously revised Cobra. The big news here was the first independent rear suspension ever offered under a Mustang; basically a trailing arm system incorporating lightweight aluminum control arms, that rode in its own cradle, which bolted in place of the solid rear axle still used on other Mustangs. The rear suspension worked well, but the revised 4.6-liter, DOHC, 32-valve V8 would wind up an embarrassment to Ford. Originally rated at 320 horsepower (up from 305 in previous-year Cobras), many owners were distressed to discover that their engines were often making less than 300 horsepower. Fueled by Internet bulletin board postings was a class-action suit by Cobra owners demanding refunds or new engines, Ford desperately trying to satisfy them and the suspension of Cobra production during the 2000 model year. While 8,095 Cobras escaped Ford during '99, only 454 made it out during 2000.

Except for new fender badges and the usual minor tweaks, the Mustang carried over for 2000. A limited run of 300 "Cobra R" models were produced this year powered by a 5.4-liter, iron-block version of the DOHC, 32-valve engine rated at a massive 385 horsepower. Stripped of such niceties as air conditioning and a backseat, and carrying a $55,845 price, the Cobra R sold out in no time at all. For the first time since 1989, Ford sold more than 200,000 Mustangs — a total of 215,393 found homes in 2000.

The Cobra returned for 2001, but the big news that year was the special "Bullitt" edition Mustang GT coupe designed to evoke memories of the '68 Mustang driven by Steve McQueen in the 1968 film of that name. The Bullitt, based on the regular GT, featured a lowered suspension, new five-spoke wheels evocative of the classic Torq-Thrust design and such neat exterior details as a fuel-filler door designed to look like that of an aircraft's. The interior was also redecorated with special graphics on the instrumentation and special upholstery, both reminiscent of the 1968 GT, as well as aluminum-finished pedals and an aluminum ball shift knob. A larger throttle body and other revisions to the engine pushed output to 265 horsepower.

Available in blue, black or, like the movie car, dark green, the Bullitt was an immediate hit and all 5,000 sold out quickly.

The gorgeous wheels from the Bullitt made it onto the regular Mustang options list for 2002, but the car was otherwise unchanged. The big news came for 2003 with a reborn, radically more powerful Cobra and a new limited-edition Mach 1 model.

The new Cobra uses a supercharged version of the 4.6-liter, DOHC, 32-valve V8 making a stupefying 390 horsepower. With that grunt traveling through a six-speed manual transmission, the latest Cobra is the quickest and fastest Mustang ever built by Ford.

Meanwhile, the new Mach 1 is almost mechanically identical to the 1998 Cobra in specification and uses a normally aspirated version of the 4.6-liter, DOHC engine now rated (again) at 305 horsepower, a solid rear axle and five-speed manual transmission. But it's the eye candy, which includes a flat black painted hood, 17-inch versions of the Magnum 500 wheels from the '60s and, most prominently, the return of the "Shaker" hood scoop, that make it such a special machine.

To celebrate the Mustang's 40th birthday, Ford stuck a 40th anniversary badge on each 2004 Mustang. An optional anniversary package could also be ordered that included Crimson paint, Beige stripes, Beige wheels and monogrammed floor mats. Knowing that an all-new Mustang was set to debut for 2005, other changes were minimal at best.

2005 Mustang

## Ninth Generation (2005-Present)

Shown as a concept at the 2003 North American International Auto Show, the 2005 Mustang finally ditched the antiquated Fox platform in favor of the DEW98 platform already used for the Thunderbird and Lincoln LS. Like the Thunderbird, the designers managed to pay homage to a classic style without having the end result looking like a caricature of the original. The canted nose with its big grille and round headlights recalls the '67 to '69 Mustangs, while the side sculpting, fastback roofline and taillights recall those ponies of the 1965 vintage. Even the triangular side windows are reminiscent of what Carol Shelby did when he made the 1965 Mustang "2 + 2" (a.k.a. the Fastback) into his Shelby GT 350.

The Mustang's interior is also reminiscent of the Mustang's glory days. A dual-hooded dash with (optional) aluminum accent panels pays homage to the 1967-'68 Mustang, as do the big speedo and tach, circular air vents and plump, round steering wheel hub. Changeable backlighting illuminates the nostalgic instruments; at the press of a button one can select from white, blue, green and orange hues. The "sitting on an ottoman" seating position and gorilla's-reach gearshifter location of the previous generation were exorcised for 2005. With the new car, one sits more in, rather than on the seats, and although the previous manual gearshifter was bolted directly to the gearbox, this year's is a remote-linkage setup that puts the stick within easy reach.

In the GT, no less than 300 horses and 315 lb-ft of torque are found behind the running pony in the grille. The 4.6-liter, all-aluminum V8 sports three valves per cylinder along with variable valve timing. Even the V6 has more muscle as specs for the six-shooter now stand at 200 hp and 235 lb-ft. Buyers of the GT have five gears at their disposal, whether they go with the automatic or manual gearbox. The V6 car comes with a choice of a five-speed manual or four-speed automatic. The newest pony also handles more crisply, thanks to the new suspension that features lighter-weight components (which allow the suspension to react quicker to changes in the road surface), repositioned and lighter coil springs, a stouter rear axle with more effective control arms and bigger brakes.

Initially, the latest Mustang will only be available as a coupe in either base or GT form, though it's only a matter of time before a convertible and any number of special models, such as the Cobra and Mach 1, return to the stable.

**By editors at Edmunds.com**

Toyota's pickup trucks have a worldwide reputation for quality and toughness. Forget the high school boys bouncing around in Tacomas over here, the Toyota Hi-Lux is the third world's favorite beast of burden. In parts of the globe so remote they barely qualify as being on the globe, Toyota trucks cross rugged trails overloaded with farm equipment, goods, soldiers, mining gear…anything and everything. There probably isn't a vehicle on Earth more abused than the Toyota pickup.

Toyota began building its first truck, the G1, back in 1935 just three months after the company made its first car, the A1. The G1 was basically a one-and-a-half-ton stake bed truck powered by the same Type A engine used in the A1 and production AA cars. It was intended, as virtually all trucks were back then, as a commercial vehicle. Toyota would make just 379 of the G1s. But that was enough for Toyota Motor Corporation's founder Kiichiro Toyoda to earn a certification for his nascent enterprise as a company under Japan's Automotive Manufacturing Industries Law.

The first pickup in Toyota's compact line would come after World War II in 1947 with the introduction of the Toyopet Model SB powered by a 995cc four making a scant 27 hp. With Japan still recovering from the war, the tiny SB was a perfect implement for farmers and newly established businesses. But it would have been a joke in a prosperous post-war America.

The SB would be refined and developed through the 1950s and even sold as a taxicab with a unique four-door body placed over the truck chassis. But none of these vehicles were anywhere near ready for U.S. consumption.

The Stout changed that in 1964.

## The Stout: 1964-1967

While the 1964 Stout was the first Toyota pickup sold in America, the dent it made in the market was almost imperceptible. Close to the size of the current Dodge Dakota, the Stout was a pretty homely beast with a windshield that looked like it was off a 1960 Chevy pickup, a cab that looked like it was swiped from International Harvester and a nose that put the turn signals high on the fenders where they could do the most aesthetic damage.

1967 Toyota Stout

But the big problem for the Stout was that it only had Toyota's 1.9-liter, OHV four making somewhere around 85 hp. So not only was it ugly, but it was slow, too. Beyond that, the cab could only have been more spartan if it was without seats. Through the four years it was sold in the U.S., changes were virtually nonexistent.

Despite the Stout's obvious inadequacies, it earned a reputation for reliability in the U.S. And that would carry over to the truck that would truly establish Toyota in America's pickup market.

## First-Generation Hi-Lux: 1969-1972

Though the 1969 Hi-Lux was initially powered by the same "3RC" 1.9-liter engine as the old Stout, it had the advantage of being a smaller truck with a more supple chassis and more comfortable cabin. That was enough to establish it in the market. And it was available in any form you liked as long as that was a two-wheel-drive machine with a standard cab and a short bed.

1971 Toyota Hi-Lux

There was nothing revolutionary about the Hi-Lux's engineering. The front suspension consisted of A-arms and coil springs, while the solid rear axle rode on a pair of semi-elliptical leaf springs. Not only was that typical of all truck engineering back then, it's still how virtually all trucks are made today.

By 21st-century standards, the Hi-Lux's interior was sparse with a bench seat covered in the toughest plastic imaginable spreading out from door to door. Compared to the Stout, though — and to a lot of full-size American trucks back then — it was neatly detailed with easily read instrumentation and easily reached ventilation and audio controls. And the four-speed manual transmission shifted with elegance and ease compared to the brutal transmissions used in domestic trucks.

It still wasn't a pretty truck, though. The styling was more contemporary, but the turn signals were now bolted to the top of the fenders as if they were an afterthought, and the bottom edge of the bed didn't even come close to aligning with the bottom edge of the cab. It wasn't ugly like the Stout, but it sure was boring.

The 1970 Hi-Lux got a new 1.8-liter, SOHC engine ("8RC" within Toyota) that was both more powerful (about 97 hp) and much more refined than the previous year's engine, but the rest of the truck was very much a carryover. Sales were growing, so Toyota didn't bother changing the truck for 1971.

At the start of the 1972 model year the Hi-Lux was blessed with yet another new engine as the 2.0-liter, SOHC, 18RC found a home in the truck. Its 108 hp was the most yet in a Toyota pickup. But the pickup around it would change at midyear.

## Second-Generation Hi-Lux: 1973-1974

A straightforward update of the Hi-Lux came on line midway through the 1972 model year (but marketed as a 1973) with revised styling that finally put the turn signals inside the front grille where they always belonged. The interior was updated as well with many elements seemingly lifted straight from the car lines to produce a more comfortable environment.

The big news for 1973 was literally big as a new "Long Bed" model appeared with a 7.5-foot bed that could haul many items that only a full-size truck could swallow before. It was so successful that Toyota did virtually nothing to update the truck for 1974.

1975 Toyota Hi-Lux

## Third-Generation Hi-Lux/Compact Truck: 1975-1978

With emissions requirements threatening to strangle down the 18RC, that engine grew to 2.2 liters to create the "20R" for 1975. The 20R (and its successor, the 22R) was the bedrock upon which the Toyota truck legend has been built. There are Toyota trucks out there with 20Rs under their hoods that have gone hundreds of thousands of miles with oil the consistency of oatmeal in their crankcases. These are the engines that would keep running even when their maintenance was entrusted to teenagers. The only way the 20R and 22R could have been more reliable is if they had no moving parts.

But the 20R wasn't the only change for '75, however. The cab was now larger in virtually every important internal dimension, and the styling and comfort became even more carlike. And for the first time a five-speed manual transmission was offered, which let the engine run slower at high cruising speeds, making it much better at commuting on American freeways. The basic chassis setup, however, carried forward pretty much unchanged.

The major change for 1976 was the deletion of the Hi-Lux name from the American version of the compact truck. The rest of the world could still get a Hi-Lux, but over here it was simply known as the "truck" or the "compact truck."

There were practically no significant changes to the truck-with-no-name for either 1977 or 1978.

## Fourth-Generation Truck: 1979-1983

1983 Toyota pickup

The 1979 Toyota truck was all new and again more carlike. But it was a more significant leap forward than ever before with four-wheel drive becoming available for the first time and the debut of a sport truck version known as the SR5.

"The Toyota SR5 is a quantum jump improvement over anything in the [Toyota truck's] past, for several excellent reasons," the *Motor Trend* editors wrote. "The most obvious is the SR5's new ride and handling feel which can be traced directly to the new torsion bar front suspension. It lends a much smoother ride than conventional coils did and helps the Toyota corner better than it ever could have with the old suspension. The torsion bar rates are softer than those of the old coil springs, and the original equipment Dunlop SP4 radials tend to accentuate the softness even more." Considering how brutal small truck suspensions had been until then, the new Toyota was a revolution.

Still, despite its bucket seats, tape stripes, chrome-ringed steel wheels and five-speed manual (or optional three-speed automatic) transmission, the SR5 wasn't particularly fast. After all, the 20R engine used in all Toyota compact trucks still made a slight 90 hp and a four-speed manual was standard in other Toyota trucks. *Motor Trend* measured its SR5 test truck accelerating from zero to 60 mph in a leisurely 12.4 seconds and completing the quarter-mile in 18.8 seconds at just 70.8 mph. Scarier was the 17 feet it took it to stop from 60 mph with the rear end sloshing ignobly from side to side.

With a solid front axle on leaf springs (much like the rear suspension) and a high-in-the-air stance, the new Toyota 4x4 pickup was an instant status symbol in high school parking lots across the country. "Toyota's new 4x4 is visually the most impressive," wrote the *Popular Science* editors in a comparison test with the barely remembered Subaru Brat and Chevy LUV four-wheel-drive pickups. "Its body stands high off the ground and it towers over the others on massive tires that give it the appearance of a swamp buggy.... Of prime importance are two protective skid plates (one under the transfer case and the other under the fuel tank) that were specially designed to let this truck shine in off-road driving.

"For all of its ruggedness, the Toyota (like LUV and Brat) is highly civilized inside the cab. The seat is a bench type that will hold three adults in an emergency, but furnishes comfortable space for two. The seat back folds forward with the release of a lever on either side, revealing a small, handy storage area hidden from outside view. An AM/FM stereo radio, plush carpeting and a sliding rear window add to the passenger-carlike comfort....

"Not everything about these vehicles is outstanding. Their acceleration is adequate, but no more. Toyota's 0-to-60-mph time averaged only 17.4 seconds, well over the 15-second benchmark we consider excellent on our test track. LUV and Brat were slower still at 19.0 and 19.6 seconds, respectively."

Still, the Toyota 4x4 had significant advantages over its competition, the *Motor Trend* editors concluded in their test. "The Chevy 4x4 LUV is an excellent road truck with above average off-road capability. The Toyota is basically a rugged off-road machine with adequate highway performance plus a choice of cargo bed and wheelbase lengths and several options — including power steering, tilt steering wheel and an instrument package — not available on the LUV."

Both the SR5 and 4x4 trucks were big hits, so Toyota didn't mess with the compact truck lineup for 1980.

Engines were the big news for 1981 as the 20R grew to 2.4 liters to become the 22R and a diesel engine was offered for the first time — and then only on an SR5 with the long bed.

*Car and Driver* found the diesel to have some virtues. "The 2.2-liter, L-series diesel utilizes an overhead camshaft and a Bosch-Nippondenso fuel-injection system," the magazine reported. "It operates at a 21.5-to-1 compression ratio, developing a reasonable 62 hp at 4,200 rpm and 93 pound-feet of torque at 2,400 rpm. The five-speed overdrive manual transmission is geared short on the low end to obtain maximum pull from the torquey diesel engine. A governor limits revs to 4,900 per minute. Basically you shift like crazy to 30 mph, then cruise in relative peace.

"Toyota's advances in diesel technology have eliminated, or at least minimized, many of the objections most of us have against diesels. For one thing, the harsh clacketing sound of most diesel engines has been virtually eliminated in the SR5 by a fabric-reinforced-rubber timing belt and increased sound insulation....

"One of the high points of the diesel is, of course, its 31 mpg (EPA city) rating which is lower than both VW's and Datsun's diesel trucks' rating but still better than the SR5 gas engine by 7 mpg. But before the diesel option will pay for itself, you have to put on at least 40,000 miles."

The fourth-generation Toyota pickup would play itself out through 1982 and 1983 essentially unchanged while selling exceedingly well.

## Fifth Generation: 1984-1988

1984 Toyota SR5 4WD

For the first time the Toyota pickup was available as an extended cab truck in the form of the new Xtracab for 1984 (regular cab trucks continued through the fifth generation as well). The Xtracab's additional length produced a more spacious environment, while the revamped interior was, once again, even more carlike than before. In fact, the whole truck was tuned more for comfort than ever before with some road tests actually commenting that the ride was too cushy. The 2.4-liter 22R four-cylinder, the transmissions and most of the suspension bits carried over intact to the new trucks that were covered in new, more angular sheet metal.

But not everyone was thrilled with the fifth-generation truck. "The Toyota has the best acceleration and fuel economy in the group," *Consumer Reports* wrote in a comparison of 1985 base model compact pickups. "But its ride and handling were abominable, even by small truck standards. And the design of its front bumper invites major frame damage in a low-speed crash." With a base price of just $5,998 (and an as-tested price of $6,838 for CR) however, Toyota's truck sure was inexpensive.

But the base truck wasn't really the news for '85, as electronic fuel injection was now an option on the 22R (to create the "22RE"), bringing with it a power boost and an available four-speed automatic transmission. Beyond that, there were new turbocharged versions of both the 22R and the diesel.

Known inside Toyota as the "22RTE," the turbocharged version of 22R was impressive in its day. "The boosted engine is currently offered on only one model," reported *Car and Driver*, "the long-cockpit Xtracab with two-wheel drive and only with an automatic transmission. Whether application will be broadened later is uncertain, as Toyota's future appears to lie in the more-cylinders, more-valves path." But 135 hp was a generous amount of power for a mid-'80s small pickup and the magazine found it gratifying. "The result is enough fresh power to revise your notions of mini-truck performance completely. Really, it's a new world. Sixty mph comes up from zero in just over 10 seconds," the publication wrote. "On a two-lane road, you can now safely pass in places that are out of the question for a normal mini. Eighty and even 90 mph appear very easily. The turbo truck will even hold 80 mph going uphill on part throttle. And it's real: if traffic drops the needle to, say, 45, a bootful of gas once you're by will soon show you 80 mph again — still going uphill. And in this case the siren sounds are more often than not from under the hood."

The turbocharged engine proved a relatively popular option, but the early-'80s heyday of the diesel was already fading as economic recovery and less expensive gasoline made it less attractive.

In fact, 1986 would be the last year for the diesel Toyota pickup in the United States. But it was the fans of the 4x4 pickup who went through the most wrenching change that year, as Toyota abandoned the solid front axle of previous models and adopted a new torsion bar independent front suspension. In compensation to the hard-core 4x4 nuts out there, Toyota now offered automatic locking front hubs and an electronically controlled transfer case integrated into the four-speed automatic transmission. Still, some enthusiasts have never forgiven Toyota for abandoning the solid front axle.

Virtually nothing changed about the 1987 Toyota pickups. But the turbo truck was gone from the 1988 lineup as Toyota replaced it with the new "3VZE" 3.0-liter SOHC V6 engine rated at 150 horsepower. It was not only a more powerful, easier-going engine than the old turbo four, but it also indicated where the future of Toyota trucks lay. And that future came up the very next year.

## Sixth Generation: 1989-1995

With more rounded sheet metal than before and, yet again, even more carlike ride and handling, the sixth-generation Toyota pickup logically followed the same well-established line of evolution as its predecessors. While short-bed trucks kept the 103-inch wheelbase of previous Toyota pickups, the long-bed versions now put a vast 122 inches between their front and rear axles. The 22RE 2.4-liter four's intake was modified slightly for the base trucks but was otherwise familiar and the optional engine remained the 3.0-liter, SOHC, 150-hp V6 introduced for 1988.

1989 Toyota SR5 Xtracab V6 4WD

In naming the Toyota Xtracab SR5 V6 its 1989 Truck of the Year, *Motor Trend* wrote that "…without the extra burden of the hardware necessary to drive the front wheels, the 2WD truck kicks up its heels with the unbound abandon of a ballet dancer. A liquid clutch and five-speed manual shifter changed the gears with delightful precision. To support the fury available under your right foot is a complete rack of readable analog instruments nestled in an instrument binnacle whose view is unimpeded." So maybe MT's writing was hyperbolic, but the '89 Toyota pickup was a definite improvement.

There were essentially no changes to the 1990 pickup. While the 1991 version was virtually identical to it, production began to shift from Japan to the shared GM-Toyota NUMMI plant in Fremont, Calif. By 1992, more than half the production for the U.S. was coming from NUMMI and virtually all of the U.S.-sold trucks came from that plant during the 1993 model year (even though the year was fruitless product development-wise). All the Toyota pickups sold in the U.S. during the 1994 model year were made in California, but the year was not without at least one product change — the addition of a third brake light atop the trailing edge of the cab.

By the middle of the 1995 model year, it was obviously time for a change in the Toyota truck world. And Toyota couldn't even wait until the next model year to make that change.

## Seventh-Generation Tacoma: 1995 1/2-2004

2002 Toyota Tacoma Xtracab

With production of its trucks for America now firmly planted in America, Toyota decided that its seventh-generation pickup could be tweaked to the specific demands of this specific market. And while it was at it, it could give it an American name, too: Tacoma.

By the way, the Hi-Lux name was (and is) still being used on Toyota pickups sold in the rest of the world.

While previous Toyota pickups had evolved slowly and methodically, the Tacoma not only featured new sheet metal, but a new frame, a fresh suspension and the choice of three new, more powerful engines. The Tacoma was truly all new.

The Tacoma still rode on a full frame and a solid rear axle supported by leaf springs, but the front suspension was redesigned with Toyota ditching the previously used torsion bars on 4x4s in favor of coil springs on both 4x2s and 4x4s. Naturally, the result was an even smoother ride, while suspension travel on the 4x4s grew from 5.9 to 7.7 inches. Of course, the cabs (regular and Xtracab) were roomier and better trimmed, and both bed lengths returned.

The old 22RE was finally dead, as base Tacoma regular cab and Xtracab 4x2s now came with a new 2.4-liter, DOHC, 16-valve four making 142 hp standard, while the 4x4s now came with a 2.7-liter version of the same engine knocking out 150 hp under their hoods. The optional V6 was a new 3.4-liter, DOHC, 24-valve unit making an impressive 190 hp. Combine that with even better five-speed manual and four-speed automatic transmissions, and these weren't just the most powerful Toyota pickups ever, but the quietest and most refined. They were an immediate hit.

Since there was only a half-year of sales behind the new Tacoma, it's no surprise that the 1996 Tacoma was very much a carryover. But a slightly revised grille with better integrated headlights came on board for 1997.

A passenger-side front airbag to go with the one already in the steering wheel was added for 1998 (a year ahead of the federally mandated time). At midyear, however, Toyota joined the growing market for 4x2 trucks that look like 4x4s with the introduction of the PreRunner Xtracab. Insurance rates, maintenance and fuel consumption costs for four-wheel-drive trucks can be prohibitive (particularly for younger drivers), so offering a 4x2 with the 4x4's suspension and oversize tires makes a good compromise for those more interested in looking good rather than actually bounding across sand dunes.

The PreRunner option spread to regular cab models for 1999, and all Tacomas equipped with antilock brakes were also equipped with daytime running lights. With the PreRunner package a certified hit, Toyota pushed the style envelope even further during 2000 with the introduction of a Tacoma StepSide model incorporating a bed with distinct fender blisters.

With the Tacoma now more than five years old, it underwent a mild restyling and a major increase in model count for 2001. All Tacomas now used a new trapezoidal grille somewhat reminiscent of that on a 1953 Buick with a wide mouth containing thick bars. The interior was also redesigned with a new dash that included rotary ventilation controls in place of the archaic sliders that had been used previously, new door trim and upholstery and a new four-spoke steering wheel. Beyond that, the mainstream SR5 and upmarket Limited models now had white-faced gauges with orange illumination.

But for that year it was the introduction of two new models that garnered the most attention: the Double Cab and S-Runner. The Double Cab was a four-door (crew cab) version similar to those Toyota had been selling in other markets around the world for decades, but never before in America. Appearing after Nissan's Frontier and Dodge's Dakota four-doors and at just about the same time that GM was introducing four-door versions of the GMC Sonoma and Chevy S-10, the Double Cab was hardly innovative. But it was a very versatile truck.

Riding on the same 121.9-inch wheelbase as the Tacoma Xtracab, the Double Cab's lengthier cab required that the bed length shrink 13.0 inches to 61.5 inches. And in every major interior dimension it clearly beat the Nissan competition, even though it was behind the larger Dodge. The Double Cab came as a two-wheel drive with either the 2.7-liter four or 3.4-liter V6 in its nose, or as a four-wheel drive powered by the V6 in SR5 or Limited trim levels.

The S-Runner was a sport truck geared for those more interested in street-bound handling than bounding over rocks — or just looking like they were. Available as a 4x2 Xtracab with either the regular or StepSide bed and with the V6 for power, the S-Runner hunkered down on a one-inch-lower suspension on Bridgestone Potenza P235/55R16 all-season radials on 16-inch alloy wheels. Monochromatically finished in either Black Sand Pearl or Radiant Red paint, it also got a tuned exhaust with a flashy chrome tip.

The 2001 Tacoma Double Cab was impressive enough to finish second in Edmunds.com's comparison of compact crew cabs, just behind the Dakota. "Perhaps the Tacoma's most endearing trait was its nimble nature," we wrote then. "On-road and off, the Toyota was never caught flat-footed. The V6's broad power band and the alert automatic gearbox were always ready to squirt the Tacoma away from a light or briskly down a fire road."

The Tacoma made it into 2002 unchanged, but that was enough for it for us to name it as the "Most Wanted" small pickup that year. It finished out its life in 2003 and 2004 virtually unchanged and fully successful — but never really stylish. That would come next.

## Eighth-Generation Tacoma: 2005-Present

As this is written, the new Tacoma is still a few months away. But we already know that it's bigger than ever, more powerful than ever and, Toyota promises, better handling and more capable than ever.

The 2005 Tacoma will be available in 18 different flavors; from a regular cab 4x2 stripper with a short bed and the 2.7-liter four to a Double Cab 4x4 with a new long bed and Toyota's latest 4.0-liter, DOHC, 24-valve, VVT-i V6 knocking out 245 hp. Wheelbases range from a relatively

2005 Toyota Tacoma X-Runner Xtracab

long 109.4 to a very, very long 140.9 inches, with both the front and rear tracks almost four inches wider than before. In fact, at 221.3 inches, the longest new Tacoma is three inches longer than an Access Cab version of the company's "full-size" Tundra pickup.

All three body styles return with the Xtracab morphing into an Access Cab with a set of rear-hinged smaller doors providing better access to the rear compartment. The S-Runner is gone, having been superseded by a new X-Runner model that features a six-speed manual transmission behind the 4.0-liter V6, a lowered suspension and massive 255/45R18 Bridgestone Potenza tires on, naturally, 18-inch diameter wheels. Other Tacomas can be had with a five-speed automatic, but the X-Runner is six-speed only.

The new Tacoma is aggressive in its styling in a way no previous Toyota truck has been, and with newfound power under the hood and Toyota's long-standing reputation for steadfast reliability, it should continue to be a popular truck choice for years to come.

The only thing worse than paying too much for a car or truck is finding out that a vehicle far more suited to your needs hit the market just after you signed on the dotted line. With this in mind, we have developed this Future Vehicles section, wherein we give you as much information as we can dig up on the all-new or totally redesigned models scheduled to hit showrooms beginning in 2005 and beyond. Buyers looking forward to purchasing a new vehicle between now and 2006 can map out their options and narrow their choices with far more confidence after reviewing the information presented in this section.

## Aston Martin AMV8

**What Edmunds.com Says:** A stunning coupe that could make Porsche's 911 look downright dull in comparison.

**What We Know:** Previewed last year in the AMV8 Vantage concept, the production version will wear either the DB8 label or simply lose a couple letters and debut as the V8 Vantage. Smaller than the DB9 and Vanquish models, the AMV8 will slot into the lineup as the entry-level Aston up against the likes of Porsche's 911 and other low six-figure sports cars. Henrik Fisker, formerly of BMW, penned the impressive concept with the intent of including plenty of traditional Aston styling cues while still offering a fresh overall look. Although we find it too close in design to the Vanquish to be called completely original, the AMV8 is a stunning car with few faults.

According to Aston Martin, the interior draws its influence from expensive sports watches and high-end home entertainment systems. A combination of anodized aluminum trim and custom-tailored leather gave the concept a truly opulent interior that would do any Aston model proud let alone the entry level version. When it goes into production, customers will have a nearly infinite choice of interior colors and upholstery options to make their AMV8 unique.

Power is likely to come from an all-new 4.3-liter V8 developed specifically for Aston Martin, but a version of Jaguar's 3.5-liter V8 may find its way into base models to get them in at a more competitive price. Either engine will be mounted in front but set back as far as possible to give the car perfect 50 to 50 weight distribution. Shorter than a 911, the AMV8 has a longer wheelbase and wider stance so handling should be on par with the world's best coupes.

## Audi A3

**What Edmunds.com Says:** Audi could redefine the premium compact segment with this slick-looking hatchback.

**What We Know:** After years of speculation, Audi has officially announced that it will sell a four-door version of its A3 hatchback in the U.S. starting this year. While European models will use a full range of power plants, the U.S.-spec version will be powered by a 2.0-liter turbocharged four-cylinder engine that develops an even 200 horsepower. Coupled with a six-speed manual transmission, Audi claims that the four-door A3 will hit 60 mph in just 7.1 seconds and have a top speed of 130 mph. Audi will also offer its Direct Shift Gearbox (DSG) for those who desire

the convenience of an automatic. A sport suspension package will be offered along with wheel and tire combinations that range from 16 to 18 inches in diameter. The four-door A3 made its official debut at the Paris auto show last September with U.S. sales beginning in May of 2005.

### Audi Q7

**What Edmunds.com Says:** This vehicle could prove to be the ultimate blend of utility and performance in the world of luxury SUVs.

**What We Know:** It was announced at last year's Paris auto show that Audi will, indeed, introduce a sport-utility dubbed the Q7. This large SUV is based on the Pike's Peak quattro concept which appeared in Detroit in 2003, although it will share its platform with the Volkswagen Touareg as well as the Porsche Cayenne. The Q7 will feature five doors and seven seats, divided up among three rows of seating. Power will come from the company's 4.2-liter V8. The Q7 will be positioned in Audi's lineup between the A6 and A8. Expect pricing to be in the $60,000 range.

### Bentley Continental GT

**What Edmunds.com Says:** If it looks anything like the coupe, this sedan should be an equally popular addition to the Bentley lineup.

**What We Know:** Bentley will expend its mid-level range this year with the addition of a sedan based on the Continental GT coupe. It will carry all the same hardware as the two-door while attempting to maintain a similarly attractive shape. It's expected to debut at this year's Geneva Motor Show with sales starting later this year.

### BMW 1 Series

**What Edmunds.com Says:** Using its luxury brand image to sell affordable cars could prove itself a tenuous plan of attack, but there's little doubt that the car will be an entertaining drive.

**What We Know:** BMW will attempt to bring its Bavarian magic to the masses with an all-new entry-level 1-Series. Although numerous body styles are scheduled for production, a traditional four-door sedan is the only one that has a chance to land at U.S. dealerships. And unlike its European counterparts, the U.S. model is likely to use six-cylinder power plants only. BMW officials have decided that hatchbacks and four-cylinder engines simply don't cut it in the American market when it comes to luxury branded cars.

### Cadillac STS-V

**What Edmunds.com Says:** Already a sharp handling sedan, the V-Series treatment should make the STS a true sport sedan.

**What We Know:** Cadillac has made it clear that it intends to give the V-Series treatment to more than just the CTS, so it wasn't much of a surprise when heavily modified prototypes of the STS were photographed making the rounds at Germany's Nurburgring test track. Power is expected to come from a supercharged version of Cadillac's 4.6-liter Northstar V8 putting the STS-V in the 400-500-horsepower range. And don't be surprised if it shows up with a six-speed manual transmission either as Cadillac fully intends for this car to be a true competitor to BMW's M5 super sedan.

## Cadillac XLR-V

**What Edmunds.com Says:** With the right engine and a little suspension tuning this could be a formidable foe to Mercedes' SL55.

**What We Know:** With the CTS-V already burning up the streets with its Corvette-sourced V8, Cadillac has turned its attention to the XLR for V-Series treatment. Instead of an LS6 V8, however, the XLR-V is expected to get a supercharged version of its standard 4.6-liter Northstar V8. A full complement of performance enhancements such as larger wheels and tires, recalibrated suspension and stronger brakes should round out the package giving Cadillac a serious performance entry in the luxury convertible segment.

## Chevrolet HHR

**What Edmunds.com Says:** Now that PT mania has died down, GM's version could have trouble drumming up interest with its lookalike wagon.

**What We Know:** Chevrolet has officially announced that it will build a new sport wagon dubbed the HHR. With styling cues borrowed from the SSR sport truck and a few vintage Chevrolet vehicles, the HHR is hoping to attract customers looking for a retro vehicle with modern conveniences. Think Chevrolet version of the PT Cruiser and that pretty much sums it up. It will be built on the same Delta platform used for Chevrolet's Cobalt sedan so expect various combinations of Ecotec engines and both automatic and manual transmissions. Production begins this summer.

## Dodge Charger

**What Edmunds.com Says:** Dodge puts up its "dukes" with the new Charger

**What We Know:** Uncle Jesse needn't worry any longer, for Chrysler has decided to resurrect this legendary vehicle. Out of production for some years, the Charger is set for a return this year. Based on the LX platform, which it will share with the Magnum, this modern version of the famous muscle car will feature rear-wheel-drive with a standard 3.5-liter V-6. Despite the similarities in its undercarriage with the Magnum, the Charger features completely different sheet metal than its wagon cousin. Thankfully, Dodge has remembered the drag-racing roots of this vehicle and plans on producing an R/T version complete with a 5.7-liter Hemi V-8.

## Ferrari F430

**What Edmunds.com Says:** It would be hard to improve on the Modena's shape, but more power should help it out in the performance department.

**What We Know:** The F430 was introduced in Paris last September as a replacement for the 360. As the first in a series of eight-cylinder vehicles which Ferrari is planning, the F430 expands upon the company's aluminum work that started with the vehicle's previously-mentioned predecessor. Exclusive features include an electronic differential, as well as steering wheel-mounted vehicle dynamics controls. The lightweight, V-8 powertrain produces a mammoth 490-horsepower and can reach a top speed above 196 miles-per-hour. The transmission has been tweaked in such a way so that drivers can reportedly shift gears in one-hundred fifty milliseconds. Braking is provided for by carbon-ceramic discs.

### Ford Fusion

**What Edmunds.com Says:** Ford needs a homerun with this Taurus replacement to get it back on the map of mainstream car buyers.

**What We Know:** The Fusion is aimed directly at midsize sedan stars such as Honda Accord, Toyota Camry and Nissan Altima. An all-aluminum 2.3-liter four-cylinder engine will be standard with an optional 3.0-liter V6 available. Both power plants will drive the front wheels and there will be a choice of manual, automatic or continuously variable transmissions. The Fusion will also be offered with a hybrid power plant. It's the same system that will power the Escape Hybrid -- a 2.3-liter four-cylinder engine mated to a 65 kilowatt electric motor and a 28 kW generator to charge a 300-volt nickel-metal-hydride battery -- which has impressive initial fuel consumption figures of 35 to 40 mpg in city driving.

### Honda Fit

**What Edmunds.com Says:** Honda is going to need more than just a low price to compete against Scion's distinctively-styled products.

**What We Know:** Honda has unofficially announced that it will begin selling a smaller, less expensive model below the current Civic. Designed to go head-to-head with the likes of the Scion xA and other sub-$15,000 compacts, Honda's new model is likely to be a version of the Fit hatchback currently sold in Japan.

### Honda SUT

**What Edmunds.com Says:** It may not be much of a real truck, but Honda's first shot at the pickup market should appeal to those looking for drivability and utility in one vehicle.

**What We Know:** Shown as a concept at the 2004 Detroit Auto Show, this half truck-half SUV combination will go on sale this year. As Honda's first shot at a pickup, its success would be crucial to Honda's future in the truck business. Built on the same platform that underpins the Pilot, the SUT will likely use the same V6 power plant and VTM four-wheel-drive system.

### HUMMER H3

**What Edmunds.com Says:** It certainly looks the part of a Hummer, but with meager power under the hood it remains to be seen whether it will be able to back it up.

**What We Know:** The Hummer lineup is set to expand once again this summer with the introduction of the all-new midsize H3 SUV. Built on a modified version of the platform used for GM's compact trucks, the H3 will use the same 220-horsepower, 3.5-liter, inline five-cylinder engine hooked to either a four-speed automatic or a five-speed manual transmission. Although it's significantly smaller than the H2, the H3 will offer all the off-road prowess of its bigger brothers. Specific options include ultralow rock-crawling gears, 33-inch tires, skid plates and an electronically locking rear differential. As tough as it is on the outside, the H3's interior looks the part of an upscale SUV with chrome accents and a clean design that's functional and comfortable. A wide variety of trim levels and options variations will allow you to order the H3 as a bare-bones off-roader or loaded family cruiser. Expect to see it on sale in late spring or early summer with prices in the $30,000-$40,000 range.

## Jaguar XK-Series

**What Edmunds.com Says:** Already a stunner in the looks department, a lighter and stiffer XK should have no trouble maintaining its allure.

**What We Know:** With the successful launch of the all-aluminum XJ sedan, Jaguar is now focusing its efforts on an aluminum-bodied XK coupe to be built in the same factory. Engine choices will mimic the current model, but with less weight to carry around and a significantly stiffer chassis, performance should be much improved.

## Jeep Commander

**What Edmunds.com Says:** With styling borrowed straight from the Rescue concept vehicle, the Commander should find plenty of willing customers.

**What We Know:** Although Jeep got plenty of attention for the Rescue concept vehicle that debuted in Detroit last year, no one figured anything like it would ever see a showroom floor. Recent information suggests otherwise, however, as the prototypes bear the same kind of boxy, over the top styling as the concept. Built on the same platform as the new Grand Cherokee, the Commander will be slightly larger and incorporate a third row of seats. Hemi power will be part of the package along with plenty of built in off road ability.

## Kia Sedona

**What Edmunds.com Says:** Lighter and more luxurious, the next-generation Sedona is bound to out-class its predecessor.

**What We Know:** Originally introduced in 2002, this Kia minivan will be reintroduced in 2006 with an all-new platform, which could shrink the vehicle's weight by as much as three hundred pounds. The sheet metal used in construction is also brand-new. A sister Hyunai model will be produced alongside the Sedona, marking the first occasion in which the two brands have shared a platform. Retaining its front-wheel-drive, the Sedona will also be offered with both short and long wheelbases. It is believed that the Hyundai variant will only be produced with the long wheelbase. It has also been speculated that the Sedona will receive a considerable upgrade in interior features without an appreciable increase in the price tag.

## Land Rover Range Rover Sport

**What Edmunds.com Says:** It may stray from Land Rover's heritage a bit, but with the right looks and performance there's no doubt that it could prove popular.

**What We Know:** As its name implies, the Range Rover Sport will not be an all-conquering off-road warrior like the flagship model. Instead, the Sport looks as though it will focus on the area where most drivers spend their time anyway -- the pavement. Although it draws styling cues from the Range Rover, the hardware underneath will most likely come from the revamped Discovery that's being readied for launch next year. Look for the supercharged version of Jaguar's AJ-V8 under the hood to give this performance-oriented sport-ute the kind of power it needs to fend off the X5's and FX45's of the world.

## Lexus IS-300

**What Edmunds.com Says:** Bolder styling and more body styles should make this successor to the IS 300 a more competitive product.

**What We Know:** Although the Lexus IS 300 has always been considered a strong first effort in the heavily populated entry-level luxury sport sedan category, it never materialized as a strong seller. Lexus is hoping to turn that slump around with a fully redesigned model that will be offered in sedan, coupe and convertible body styles. A preview of what's to come was shown at the New York auto show in the form of the LF- C concept. Expect to see the production vehicle retain much of the concept's distinctive styling as Lexus attempts to inject more design excitement into its entry-level car.

## Lincoln Zephyr

**What Edmunds.com Says:** This car needs a new name and a more powerful engine if it expects to make any impression in the ultracompetitive entry-level luxury sport sedan segment.

**What We Know:** Designed to compete in the entry-level luxury sedan market against the likes of BMW's 3 Series and the Infiniti G35, the Zephyr will be Lincoln's smallest and sportiest sedan when it goes on sale late this year. Given the segment's much younger demographics, Lincoln figured it needed a fresh, new look that wouldn't get dragged down with the baggage of its ancestors. Its wide stance, rakish lines and oversized wheels and tires are a big departure from most Lincoln sedans but the Zephyr still wears a few signature design cues like a waterfall grille and some strategically placed Lincoln stars.

The Zephyr also departs from Lincoln tradition with a powertrain that consists of front-wheel drive, a six-speed automatic transmission and a 3.0-liter V6. The fully independent suspension will be tuned to provide plenty of Lincoln luxury while at the same time keeping the Zephyr nimble enough to back up its sporty looks. An all-wheel-drive model will be added to the lineup shortly after the initial sedan's debut.

Its bright interior blends satin chrome, leather and wood to create an upscale atmosphere that's a little more expressive than most sedans in the segment. The wide, symmetrical dashboard recalls Lincolns of the past but the unmistakable waterfall center stack and THX sound system are modern touches that you won't find in any Town Car.

## Mazda Miata

**What Edmunds.com Says:** Mazda plans to add a new spark to its famously zippy convertible

**What We Know:** After 15 years of design continuity, Mazda plans to completely revise its popular convertible for the 2006 model year. It's believed that the new Miata will share sheet metal, and perhaps even its platform with the RX-8. The traditional soft top could even be replaced by a power-folding metal hardtop, adding to the belief that the 2006 Miata could end up being a heftier car than any of its lithe predecessors. The revised model will probably be powered by Mazda's 2.3-liter inline four-cylinder. The company is also likely to offer a MazdaSpeed version.

## Mercedes-Benz R-Class

**What Edmunds.com Says:** There's no hotter market than luxury crossovers right now and this new model from Mercedes stands to capitalize on the trend.

**What We Know:** This larger station wagon is based on the Grand Sports Tourer Vision R concept. The R-Class will be built in Vance, Ala. A long-wheelbase version will be produced for the U.S. market, alongside a short-wheelbase equivalent, which will be exported to Europe. Eventually, Mercedes is expected to sell the short-wheelbase version in the U.S. with its larger sibling. Annual production will fall around 50,000 units, about half of which will be intended for domestic consumption. The R-Class will be priced similarly to the E-Class.

## Mercedes-Benz S-Class

**What Edmunds.com Says:** Intense competition in the ultraluxury segment makes this redesign more important than ever before.

**What We Know:** Mercedes is hard at work revamping its flagship sedan in the face of stiff competition from Audi, BMW and Maserati. With its reputation taking a beating in recent reliability studies, Mercedes knows that this new sedan has to be perfect. Expect to see slightly larger dimensions with styling cues similar to the current version. The engine lineup will be roughly similar as well, with a range of V8s and V12s powering the lineup. As you would expect, the interior will boast all the latest features including a fully revamped Command system, a multipanel glass roof similar to the Maybach and Bluetooth phone connectivity. Production is expected to begin in the fall of 2005.

## Mitsubishi Eclipse

**What Edmunds.com Says:** New, futuristic lines, more power and a new platform should help this revamped Eclipse recapture some of the customers it lost due to the tepid performance of the current model.

**What We Know:** Mitsubishi's next vehicle off the Project America platform will be an all-new Eclipse coupe. A concept shown at last year's North American International Auto Show is a close approximation of the production model with its uniquely styled hatchback and distinctive lines reminiscent of the second-generation Eclipse. Like the Galant, the Eclipse is likely to feature both four- and six-cylinder power plants and a 10-year/100,000-mile warranty.

## Pontiac Solstice

**What Edmunds.com Says:** Easily one of the most anticipated new production cars from GM, the Solstice looks as though it will have all the style and the performance promised by the concept.

**What We Know:** First shown as a concept in 2002, the production version was revealed for the first time at the 2004 North American International Auto Show. Varying very little from the concept, the production model sports appealing looks inside and out. The Solstice rides on an all-new rear-wheel-drive chassis that promises exceptional performance. Power will come from a 170-hp, 2.4-liter engine running through a five-speed manual transmission. Eighteen-inch wheels and four-wheel disc brakes will come standard when the car goes on sale in the fall of 2005.

## Pontiac Torrent

**What Edmunds.com Says:** Pontiac ramps up the Torrent as a possible Aztek replacement

**What We Know:** The Pontiac Torrent will be one of a number of GM or GM-affiliated mid-size SUVs produced on the Theta platform in the next few years. Most likely to appear as a 2006 model, the Torrent will replace the poor-selling Aztek. It is likely that the Torrent will be constructed in Cambridge, Ontario, alongside the Chevrolet Equinox and a yet-unnamed Suzuki equivalent. In addition to the two latter vehicles, the Torrent will also share its platform with the Saturn Vue. The Torrent could share the Chinese-built, Shanghai-GM 185-horsepower, 3.4-liter V-6 engine of the Equinox.

## smart formore

**What Edmunds.com Says:** This quirky brand could do well in the U.S. with its off-beat, but functional designs.

**What We Know:** This new brand from DaimlerChrysler has been on sale in Europe for years but will finally attempt to make inroads into the U.S. market in 2006. Although its current European offerings are mostly two-seaters, the formore will be a four-seater with dimensions similar to a compact SUV. Few details have been released about the formore, but expect to see plenty of interest in this new SUV as its on-sale date approaches.

## Volkswagen Golf

**What Edmunds.com Says:** A new look and a larger interior should make this new Golf more popular than ever before.

**What We Know:** Volkswagen has already introduced the Golf in Europe and it looks to be yet another solid entry in this long line of popular hatchbacks. The new design is longer, wider and taller than the previous version resulting in more rear leg- and headroom as well as additional cargo capacity. Both two- and four-door versions are offered in three trim levels. U.S.-spec engine information has not yet been announced, but European versions use a mix of direct injection diesel and gas-powered units. A six-speed automatic is offered along with VW's Direct Shift Gearbox that blends elements of both automatic and manual transmissions. An all-new multilink suspension underpins the rear while struts are used up front. A unique electromechanical steering system is also new. The U.S. won't see the GTI until November of 2005 with standard Golf models following in early 2006.

## Volvo C50

**What Edmunds.com Says:** With the right look, this new convertible could go a long way toward improving Volvo's dowdy image.

**What We Know:** The C50 is the long overdue replacement for the current C70. Unlike the soft-top C70, however, the C50 is expected to show up sporting a retractable hardtop similar to Mercedes' SLK roadster.

# Edmunds.com Used Cars & Trucks Buyer's Guide

**2004 Annual**
**by the Editors at Edmunds.com**

**2005 Annual Edition available May 2005**

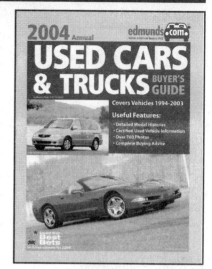

## The essential used car-buying resource in a comprehensive and user-friendly format.

For more than 39 years, millions of consumers have turned to Edmunds' buyer's guides for their shopping needs. This format makes it easy for consumers to get the advice and information they need to make a wise purchase on their next used vehicle. Readers benefit from features such as:

- Recommendations for the Best Bets in the used car market
- Detailed histories on popular models
- Certified Used Vehicle Information
- Hundreds of photographs
- Glossary of Used Car Buying Terms

In addition to these features, vehicle shoppers can benefit from the best they've come to expect from the Edmunds name:

- True Market Value pricing for trade-in, private party and dealer retail
- Highlighted yearly model changes
- In-depth advice on buying and selling a used car

**"A brand name car buyers trust."** —*The Wall Street Journal*

A trusted automotive resource since 1966, Santa Monica, California-based Edmunds.com is now the Internet's pioneer and leader in providing free third-party automotive information, tools and services for consumers. Edmunds.com empowers, educates and engages readers by providing them with straightforward information on all aspects of buying, selling and owning a vehicle.

# Edmunds.com
# Strategies for Smart Car Buyers

### By the Editors at Edmunds.com and Philip Reed

### Revised edition available February 2005

Strategies that guide consumers through the process of buying or leasing new and used cars, including all-new material to help consumers avoid the latest sales traps.

This book outlines proven buying scenarios, clearly explaining the consumer's course of action in simple terms. The complex and sometimes frightening process of car buying is demystified in a comprehensive guide that covers:

- How to choose the right car

- Getting a used car bargain

- Avoiding the pitfalls of leasing

- The acclaimed investigative series, "Confessions of a Car Salesman"

- Financing section detailing crucial contract dos and don'ts

- Commentary throughout text from undercover car salesman Chandler Phillips

- Edmunds' latest consumer tool: "Smart Car Buyer"

- Bonus section: "Verbal Self Defense" avoiding sales language pitches and traps

- New section: "Safely Navigating eBay Auctions"

**"A brand name car buyers trust." —*The Wall Street Journal***

A trusted automotive resource since 1966, Santa Monica, California-based Edmunds.com is now the Internet's pioneer and leader in providing free third-party automotive information, tools and services for consumers. Edmunds.com empowers, educates and engages readers by providing them with straightforward information on all aspects of buying, selling and owning a vehicle.

Please cut out or copy this page to order subscriptions to Edmunds.com Buyer's Guides.

All prices are in United States dollars.

| 2005 New Cars & Trucks Buyer's Guide<br>1 issue per year | Pay Only<br>(includes Shipping &<br>Handling) | Quantity |
|---|---|---|
| United States | $13.70 | |
| Canada | $14.70 | |
| International | $16.70 | |

| 2005 Used Cars & Trucks Buyer's Guide<br>1 issue per year | Pay Only<br>(includes Shipping &<br>Handling) | Quantity |
|---|---|---|
| United States | $13.70 | |
| Canada | $14.70 | |
| International | $16.70 | |

Make check or money order payable to:

**Edmunds.com, Inc.**
**PO Box 338**
**Shrub Oaks NY 10588**
**USA**

For more information or to order by phone, call (914) 962-6297. Please pay through an American bank or with American currency.
Rates subject to change without notice.

Name _____

Company/Library _____

Address _____

City _____ State/Province _____

ZIP/Postal Code _____ Country _____

Telephone _____

Credit Card # _____ Exp. Date _____

Cardholder Name _____

Signature _____